C0 BPQ 222

OXFORD MEDIEVAL TEXTS

THE LETTERS OF PETER OF CELLE

THE LETTERS OF PETER OF CELLE

EDITED BY
JULIAN HASELDINE

CLARENDON PRESS · OXFORD

OXFORD
UNIVERSITY PRESS

Great Clarendon Street, Oxford OX2 6DP

Oxford University Press is a department of the University of Oxford.
It furthers the University's objective of excellence in research, scholarship,
and education by publishing worldwide in

Oxford New York
Athens Auckland Bangkok Bogotá Buenos Aires Cape Town
Chennai Dar es Salaam Delhi Florence Hong Kong Istanbul Karachi
Kolkata Kuala Lumpur Madrid Melbourne Mexico City Mumbai Nairobi
Paris São Paulo Shanghai Singapore Taipei Tokyo Toronto Warsaw

and associated companies in Berlin Ibadan

Oxford is a registered trade mark of Oxford University Press
in the UK and certain other countries

Published in the United States
by Oxford University Press Inc., New York

First published 2001

British Library Cataloguing in Publication Data
Data available

Library of Congress Cataloging in Publication Data
Peter, of Celle, Bishop of Chartres, ca. 1115–1183.
[Correspondence, English]
The letters of Peter of Celle/edited by J. P. Haseldine.
p. cm.—(Oxford medieval texts)
Includes bibliographical references and index.
1. Peter, of Celle, Bisop of Chartres, ca. 1115–1183. I. Haseldine, Jullian.
II. Title. III. Series.
BX4705.P43477 A4 2001 282'.092–dc-21 [B] 00–057123
ISBN 0-19-820445-0

1 3 5 7 9 10 8 6 4 2

Typeset by Joshua Associates Ltd., Oxford
Printed in Great Britain
on acid-free paper by
T. J. International Ltd. Padstow, Cornwall

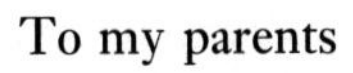

To my parents

PREFACE

In the course of preparing this edition I have benefited from the help, advice, and expert knowledge of a great many people, whose generosity it is a pleasure to acknowledge. The work has also brought me into contact with a number of people whose wisdom and friendship I would otherwise not have known. My thanks are due, first and foremost, to Christopher Brooke for his untiring assistance and advice at every stage of this project. As the supervisor of the Ph.D. thesis out of which this work arose, he has been an inspiration from the very beginning, and over the subsequent years his many and detailed comments on every aspect of this work have greatly improved the whole. For his guidance, scholarship, and generosity I am deeply grateful. I am also very grateful to Martin Brett who has been a tremendous help and a source of illumination on many points from the beginning of the project, as well as an excellent host on my frequent returns to Cambridge. I am extremely grateful to Barrie Hall and to Annabel Ritchie who were kind enough to read the whole of the text and translation in the later stages. Their rigorous critique has made a very large number of improvements throughout and opened my eyes to many aspects of a text I thought I already knew well.

Over the years many people have helped me with information, advice, and suggestions on many points. Michael Winterbottom was kind enough to comment on a number of the more difficult passages in the text. Anne Duggan has answered my many questions and offered much valuable help, particularly on the letters relating to Thomas Becket. Neil Wright has pointed out a number of classical allusions and quotations in the text which I would otherwise have missed and has also kindly helped me with a number of difficult passages. Teresa Webber's generous and expert help was invaluable in my examination of the Oxford manuscript. Ludwig Falkenstein has provided me with much useful information relating to the dating of some of the letters and some of the appendices, and has generously shown me the results of work still at press as I write. I am also very grateful to François Dolbeau, Frank Barlow, P. Gérard de Martel, Lena Wahlgren-Smith, John McLoughlin, Brian Patrick McGuire,

Falko Neininger, Lynn K. Barker, Debby Banham, and James Clark for their assistance on particular points of detail and to Greti Dinkova-Bruun for checking the text of the letter in MS Vatican Reg. Lat. 179. Finally I would like to thank Michael Lapidge, Timothy Reuter, and Barbara Harvey for their patience, advice, and encouragement during the preparation of the book for press, for any shortcomings in which I alone am responsible.

My thanks are due to the librarians of St John's College, Oxford, of Corpus Christi College, Cambridge, and of the Bibliothèques Municipales of Dijon, Douai, Metz, Reims, and Valenciennes, and to the Hill Monastic Manuscript Library, Minnesota. I would also like to thank the staff of the CNRS–IRHT, Paris, for their helpful guidance in the early stages of the project, and Anne-Marie Legras of the CNRS–IRHT, Orléans, for providing me with copies of the relevant folios of MS Reims 1602.

I began this project with a Crosse Studentship from the University of Cambridge, and with postdoctoral research awards from the Lightfoot Fund (Faculty of History, University of Cambridge), and the Jebb Fund (University of Cambridge). I should like to express my gratitude for this important assistance at the outset. I am grateful to Gonville and Caius College, Cambridge, for providing funds to purchase microfilms and for other research expenses; to Lincoln College, Oxford, for providing funds to travel to libraries and archives, and a convivial environment in which to continue the work; and to my colleagues, more recently, at the Universities of Sheffield and Hull, and particularly to David Luscombe for his support and advice over the years.

I owe a particular debt of gratitude to Henry Mayr-Harting, who first introduced me to the study of the Middle Ages, to Peter of Celle, and to Christopher Brooke, and so must take some credit for the origins of this book.

Finally, I would like to thank my parents for offering me both constant encouragement in my work and a welcome refuge from it when necessary. To them this book is dedicated.

JULIAN HASELDINE

CONTENTS

ABBREVIATIONS xi

INTRODUCTION xix

I Peter of Celle xix
1. The Correspondence xix
2. Life xxviii
3. Other Writings xxxiii

II The Textual Tradition of the Letters xxxiv
1. Texts based on a Sender's Archive xxxv
2. Texts based on Recipients' Archives xlviii
3. Letters preserved in Other Collections li
4. Printed Editions liv

III This Edition lvi

SIGLA OF MANUSCRIPTS CITED lix

TEXT AND TRANSLATION 1

The Early Letters (nos. 1-74) 3
The Late Letters (nos. 75-183) 337

APPENDICES 693

1. The Disputed Election at Saint-Méen-de-Gaël 695
2. The Dispute over the Cemetery of La-Celle-sous-Chantemerle 696
3. Peter of Celle's Appeal on behalf of Matilda of Fontevrault 699
4. The Disputes at Montier-en-Der 700
5. Eskil of Lund and the establishment of the Carthusians in Denmark (and the date of letter no. 12) 703
6. Simon of Chézy-l'Abbaye, Clairvaux, and the date of letter no. 39 705
7. Peter of Celle and Nicholas of Clairvaux's debate on the nature of the body, the soul, and God 706

8. The Sequence of surviving correspondence between Peter of Celle and John of Salisbury 712
9. Bishop Fulk and the mission to Estonia 719
10. The Disputes over the priory of Meerssen 721
11. Saint-Remi-de-Provence 725
12. Peter of Celle and the building works at Saint-Remi 726
13. Peter of Celle and Nicholas of St Albans' debate on the feast of the Conception of the Blessed Virgin Mary 727
14. The Case of the novices from Grandmont who had transferred to the Cistercians 730

CONCORDANCE 732

ADDENDUM 737

INDEXES 739

1. Dates of Letters 739
2. Quotations and Allusions 741
   A Biblical Quotations and Allusions 741
   B. Quotations and Allusions from Other Sources 760
3. Recipients of Letters 764
4. General Index 766

ABBREVIATIONS

Aniel, *Maisons de Chartreux*	J.-P. Aniel, *Les Maisons de Chartreux des origines à la chartreuse de Pavie*, Bibliothèque de la Société française d'archéologie, xvi (Geneva, 1983)
Arbois de Jubainville, *Abbayes cisterciennes*	H. d'Arbois de Jubainville, *Études sur l'état intérieur des abbayes cisterciennes et principalement de Clairvaux au XIIe et au XIIIe siècle* (Paris, 1858)
Arbois de Jubainville, *Comtes de Champagne*	H. d'Arbois de Jubainville, *Histoire des ducs et des comtes de Champagne*, 6 vols. (Paris, 1859–66)
Art de vérifier les dates	*L'Art de vérifier les dates des faits historiques, des chartes, des chroniques et autres anciens monuments, depuis la naissance de Notre-Seigneur*, 3 vols. (3rd edn., Paris, 1783–7)
Barlow, 'John of Salisbury'	F. Barlow, 'John of Salisbury and his brothers', *Journal of Ecclesiastical History*, xlvi (1995), 95–109
Barlow, *Thomas Becket*	F. Barlow, *Thomas Becket* (London, 1986)
Benton, *Culture*	J. F. Benton, *Culture, Power and Personality in Medieval France*, ed. T. N. Bisson (London, 1991)
Bernard de Clairvaux	*Bernard de Clairvaux*, Commission d'histoire de l'ordre de Cîteaux, iii, pref. T. Merton (Paris, 1953)
Bernard et Bruel	*Recueil des chartes de l'abbaye de Cluny*, ed. A. Bernard and A. Bruel, 6 vols. (Paris, 1876–1903)
Blaise, *Dictionnaire*	A. Blaise, *Dictionnaire latin-français des auteurs chrétiens* (Turnhout, 1954)
Blaise, *Lexicon*	A. Blaise, *Lexicon Latinitatis Medii Aevi*, *CCCM* (Turnhout, 1975)
Bur, *Champagne*	M. Bur, *La Formation du comté de Champagne v.950–v.1150* (Nancy, 1977)
Burn, *Nicene Creed*	A. E. Burn, *The Nicene Creed*, Oxford Church Text Books (London, 1913)

Cat. gén.	*Catalogue général des manuscrits des bibliothèques publiques de France. Départements*, octavo ser., 51 vols. (Paris, 1886–1956)
Cat. gén. in 4°	*Catalogue général des manuscrits des bibliothèques publiques des départements*, quarto ser., 7 vols. (Paris, 1849–85)
CCCM	*Corpus Christianorum Continuatio Medievalis* (Turnhout, 1966–)
CCSL	*Corpus Christianorum Series Latina* (Turnhout, 1954–)
Constable, *Letter Collections*	G. Constable, *Letters and Letter Collections*, Typologie des sources du moyen âge occidental, xvii (Turnhout, 1976)
Cott.	L. H. Cottineau, *Répertoire topo-bibliographique des abbayes et prieurés*, 3 vols. (Mâcon, 1935–70)
Councils and Synods	*Councils and Synods with other Documents relating to the English Church, I. A.D. 871–1204*, ed. D. Whitelock, M. Brett, and C. N. L. Brooke, 2 vols. (Oxford, 1981)
CSEL	*Corpus Scriptorum Ecclesiasticorum Latinorum* (Vienna and Prague, 1866–)
DD	*Diplomatarium Danicum*, ed. C. A. Christensen, H. Nielsen, N. Skyum-Nielsen, L. Weibull *et al.*, 4 parts in 28 vols. to date (Copenhagen, 1938–)
de Martel, 'Mabillon'	G. de Martel, 'Mabillon et la préface aux oeuvres de Pierre de Celle', *Revue Mabillon*, lviii (1974), 245–69
de Martel, *Petri Cellensis*	G. de Martel (ed.), *Petri Cellensis; Commentaria in Ruth, Tractatus de Tabernaculo*, *CCCM* liv (Turnhout, 1983)
de Martel, *Pierre de Celle*	G. de Martel (ed.), *Pierre de Celle: L'école du cloître*, Sources Chrétiennes, ccxl (Paris, 1977)
de Martel, 'Pierre de Celle à Reims'	G. de Martel, 'Pierre de Celle à Reims', *Mémoires de la Société d'agriculture, commerce, sciences et arts du département de la Marne*, lxxxiv (1974), 71–105
de Martel, 'Recherches'	G. de Martel, 'Recherches sur les manuscrits des sermons de Pierre de Celle', *Scriptorium*, xxxiii (1979), 3–16

de Martel, 'Une notice'	G. de Martel, 'Une notice inédite sur Pierre de Celle', *Mémoires de la Société d'agriculture, commerce, sciences et arts du département de la Marne*, xcvii (1982), 77–88
Depoin	J. Depoin ed., *Recueil de chartes et documents de Saint-Martin-des-Champs*, 5 vols., Archives de la France monastique xiii, xvi, xviii, xx, xxi (Ligugé–Paris, 1912–21)
Diceto	*Radulfi de Diceto Decani Lundoniensis, Opera Historica*, ed. W. Stubbs, Rerum Britannicarum Medii Aevi Scriptores, Rolls Series, 2 vols. (London, 1876)
DML	R. E. Latham, D. R. Howlett *et al.*, *Dictionary of Medieval Latin from British Sources* (Oxford, 1975–)
DP	J. N. D. Kelly, *The Oxford Dictionary of Popes* (Oxford, 1986)
DS	*Dictionnaire de spiritualité*, ed. M. Viller *et al.*, 14 vols. to date (Paris, 1937–)
Duggan, *Textual History*	A. Duggan, *Thomas Becket: A Textual History of his Letters* (Oxford, 1980)
Dunbabin, *France in the Making*	J. Dunbabin, *France in the Making 843–1180* (Oxford, 1985)
EEA	*English Episcopal Acta* (London, 1980–)
Falkenstein, 'Alexandre III et Henri de France'	L. Falkenstein, 'Alexandre III et Henri de France', *L'Église de France et la papauté, X^e^–XIIIe siècle/ Die französische Kirche und das Papsttum, 10.–13. Jahrhundert*, Actes du XXVIe colloque historique franco-allemand, ed. R. Grosse (Bonn, 1993), 103–76
Fasti	J. Le Neve, *Fasti Ecclesiae Anglicanae 1066–1300*, ed. D. E. Greenway (London, 1968–)
Gams	P. B. Gams, *Series episcoporum ecclesiae catholicae* (Regensburg, 1873)
Ganzer, *Entwicklung*	K. Ganzer, *Die Entwicklung des auswärtigen Kardinalats im hohen Mittelalter*, Bibliothek des Deutschen Historischen Instituts in Rom, xxvi (Tübingen, 1963)
GC	*Gallia Christiana*, 16 vols. (Paris, 1715–1865)
Glorieux, 'Candidats'	P. Glorieux, 'Candidats à la pourpre en 1178', *Mélanges de science religieuse*, xi (1954), 5–30
GM	J.-F. Lemarignier and F. Poirier-Coutansais,

	Gallia Monastica, i vol. to date, *Les Abbayes bénédictines du diocèse de Reims* (Paris, 1974)
Godefroy, 'Saint-Ayoul'	J. Godefroy, 'L'Histoire du prieuré Saint-Ayoul de Provins et le récit des miracles du saint', 3 parts, *Revue Mabillon*, xxvii (1937), 94–107 and xxviii (1938), 29–48 and 84–98
Grotefend	H. Grotefend, *Taschenbuch der Zeitrechnung des deutschen Mittelalters und der Neuzeit* (Hanover, 1982, 1st edn. 1898)
Handbook	*Handbook of British Chronology*, ed. E. B. Fryde, D. E. Greenway, S. Porter and I. Roy, 3rd edn. (London, 1986)
Haseldine, 'Friendship and rivalry'	J. P. Haseldine, 'Friendship and rivalry: the role of *amicitia* in twelfth-century monastic relations', *Journal of Ecclesiastical History*, xliv (1993), 390–414
Haseldine, 'Letters of Abbot Peter'	J. P. Haseldine, 'A study of the letters of Abbot Peter of La-Celle (*c.*1115–1183)', Ph.D. thesis (Cambridge, 1992)
Haseldine, 'Literary memorial'	J. P. Haseldine, 'The creation of a literary memorial: the letter collection of Peter of Celle', *Sacris Erudiri*, xxxvii (1997), 333–79
Heads	*The Heads of Religious Houses, England and Wales, 940–1216*, ed. D. Knowles, C. N. L. Brooke and V. C. M. London (Cambridge, 1972)
HLF	*Histoire littéraire de la France* (Paris, 1733–1949)
Hutchison, *Grandmont*	C. Hutchison, *The Hermit Monks of Grandmont*, Cistercian Studies, cxviii (Kalamazoo, 1989)
Janssen, *Die päpstlichen Legaten*	W. Janssen, *Die päpstlichen Legaten in Frankreich vom Schisma Anaklets II. bis zum Tode Coelestins III. (1130–1198)*, Kölner Historische Abhandlungen, vi (Cologne, 1961)
Janvier	*Petri Abbatis Cellensis primum, deinde S. Remigii apud Remos ac demum Episcopi Carnotensis, Opera Omnia*, ed. A. Janvier (Paris, 1671)
JL	P. Jaffé, *Regesta Pontificum Romanorum ab condita Ecclesia ad annum MCXCVIII*, 2 vols., 2nd edn. S. Loewenfeld *et al.* (Leipzig, 1885–8)

J.S. Epp.	*The Letters of John of Salisbury*, ed. W. J. Millor, H. E. Butler, and C. N. L. Brooke, 2 vols. (i: Edinburgh, NMT, 1955, reissued Oxford, OMT, 1986; ii: Oxford, OMT, 1979)
Kelly, *Athanasian Creed*	J. N. D. Kelly, *The Athanasian Creed* (London, 1964)
Kelly, *Creeds*	J. N. D. Kelly, *Early Christian Creeds* (London, 1950; 3rd edn. 1972)
Lalore, *Cartulaires*	C. Lalore, *Collection des principaux cartulaires du diocèse de Troyes*, 7 vols. (Paris, 1875–90)
Latham	R. E. Latham, *Revised Medieval Latin Word-List from British and Irish Sources* (Oxford, 1st edn., 1965; repr. with supplement 1980)
Laurent, *Cartulaires de Molesme*	J. Laurent, *Cartulaires de l'abbaye de Molesme, ancien diocèse de Langres, 916–1250*, 2 vols. (Paris, 1907–11)
Leclercq, 'Nouvelles'	J. Leclercq, 'Nouvelles lettres de Pierre de Celle', *Studia Anselmiana*, xliii (1958), 160–79
Le Couteulx	C. Le Couteulx, *Annales Ordinis Cartusiensis, 1084–1424* (Montreuil-sur-Mer, 1887–91)
Lexikon des Mittelalters	*Lexikon des Mittelalters*, 9 vols. (Munich and Zurich, 1980–1999)
Meinert, *Papsturkunden in Frankreich*	H. Meinert, *Papsturkunden in Frankreich, n.s.*, i: *Champagne und Lothringen*, Abhandlungen der Gesellschaft der Wissenschaften zu Göttingen, philologisch-historische Klasse, 3rd. ser., iii, and *Anhang: Urkunden und Regesten*, 3rd ser., iv (Berlin, 1932, 1933) [page nos. run through both vols.]
MGH	*Monumenta Germaniae Historica*
Mon. Belge	U. Berlière *et al.*, *Monasticon Belge*, 7 vols. in 19 to date (Abbaye de Maredsous, 1890–)
Morice, *Bretagne*	P. H. Morice, *Histoire ecclésiastique et civile de Bretagne*, 2 vols. (Paris, 1750–6, facsimile Farnborough, 1968)
Morice, *Mémoires*	P. H. Morice, *Mémoires pour servir de preuves à l'histoire ecclésiastique et civile de Bretagne*, 3 vols. (Paris, 1742–6, facsimile Farnborough, 1968)
Newman, *Seigneurs de Nesle*	W. M. Newman, *Les Seigneurs de Nesle en Picardie*, 2 vols. (Paris, 1971)

Niermeyer	J. F. Niermeyer, *Mediae Latinitatis Lexicon Minus* (Leiden, 1976)
Obits Sens	*Obituaires de la province de Sens*, ed. A. Longnon and A. Molinier, 4 vols. (Paris, 1902–23)
Orbis	*Orbis Latinus, Lexikon lateinischer geographischer Namen des Mittelalters und der Neuzeit*, ed. J. G. T. Graesse, F. Benedict and H. Plechl, 3 vols. (Brunswick, 1972)
Pacaut, *Élections*	M. Pacaut, *Louis VII et les élections épiscopales dans le royaume de France* (Paris, 1957)
Pacaut, *Ordre de Cluny*	M. Pacaut, *L'Ordre de Cluny* (Paris, 1986)
Papsturkunden	see references under individual eds. (Meinert, Ramackers)
PL	*Patrologiae Cursus Completus, series Latina*, ed. J.-P. Migne, 221 vols. (Paris, 1844–64)
Prache, *Saint-Remi*	A. Prache, *Saint-Remi de Reims, l'oeuvre de Pierre de Celle et sa place dans l'architecture gothique*, Bibliothèque de la Société Française d'Archéologie, viii (Geneva, 1978)
P. Ven. Epp.	*The Letters of Peter the Venerable*, ed. G. Constable, 2 vols. (Cambridge, Mass., 1967)
Ramackers, *Papsturkunden in Frankreich* v	J. Ramackers, *Papsturkunden in Frankreich n.s.*, v: *Touraine, Anjou, Maine und Bretagne*, Abhandlungen der Akademie der Wissenschaften in Göttingen, philologisch-historische Klasse, 3rd. ser., xxxv (Göttingen, 1956)
Ramackers, *Papsturkunden in Frankreich* vi	J. Ramackers, *Papsturkunden in Frankreich, n.s.*, vi: *Orleannais*, Abhandlungen der Akademie der Wissenschaften in Göttingen, philologisch-historische Klasse, 3rd. ser., xli (Göttingen, 1958)
Ramackers, *Papsturkunden in den Niederlanden*	J. Ramackers, *Papsturkunden in den Niederlanden (Belgien, Luxembourg, Holland und Französisch-Flandern)*, Abhandlungen der Gesellschaft der Wissenschaften zu Göttingen, philologisch-historische Klasse, 3rd. ser., viii (*Archivberichte*), and ix (*Urkunden*) (Berlin, 1933, 1934) [page nos. run through both vols.]
RHF	*Recueil des historiens des Gaules et de la*

	France, ed. M. Bouquet and M.-J. Brial, new ed. and cont. L. Delisle, 24 vols. (Paris, 1869–1904, facsimile Farnborough, 1967–8)
S. Bernardi Op.	*Sancti Bernardi Opera*, ed. J. Leclercq, C. H. Talbot, and H. Rochais, 8 vols. (Rome, 1957–77)
SEECO v	*Series Episcoporum Ecclesiae Catholicae Occidentalis ab initio usque ad annum MCXCVIII*, ed. S. Weinfurter and O. Engels, 5th ser., *Germania*, i. *archiepiscopatus Coloniensis* (Stuttgart, 1982)
SEECO vi	*Series Episcoporum Ecclesiae Catholicae Occidentalis ab initio usque ad annum MCXCVIII*, ed. H. Kluger, 6th ser., *Britannia, Scotia et Hibernia, Scandinavia*, ii. *archiepiscopatus Lundensis* (Stuttgart, 1992)
Sirmond	*Petri Abbatis Cellensis qui post deinde S. Remigij Remensis Abbas, et Episcopus fuit Carnotensis, Epistolarum libri IX. Item Alexandri III. Papae ad Petrum eundem et alios Epistolae LVI*, ed. J. Sirmond (Paris, 1613)
Talbot, 'Nicholas of St Albans'	C. H. Talbot, 'Nicholas of St Albans and St Bernard', *Revue Bénédictine*, lxiv (1954), 83–117
Torigni, ed. Delisle	*Chronique de Robert de Torigni*, ed. L. Delisle, Société de l'histoire de Normandie, 2 vols. (Rouen, 1872)
Varin, *Arch. admin.*	P. Varin, *Archives administratives de la ville de Reims*, 4 vols., Collection de documents inédits sur l'histoire de France, 1st ser., Histoire politique (Paris, 1839–53)
Varin, *Arch. lég.*	P. Varin, *Archives législatives de la ville de Reims*, 4 vols., Collection de documents inédits sur l'histoire de France, 1st ser., Histoire politique (Paris, 1840–53)
VCH	*Victoria History of the Counties of England*
Walther	H. Walther, *Proverbia Sententiaeque Latinitatis Medii Aevi: Lateinisches Sprichwörter und Sentenzen des Mittelalters in alphabetischer Anordnung*, 5 vols. (Göttingen, 1963–7)
Walther and Schmidt	H. Walther and P. G. Schmidt, *Proverbia Sententiaeque Latinitatis Medii ac recentioris Aevi: Lateinisches Sprichwörter und Sentenzen*

	des Mittelalters und der frühen Neuzeit in alphabetischer Anordnung, n.s., 3 vols. (Göttingen, 1982–6)
Zenker, *Kardinalkollegium*	B. Zenker, *Die Mitglieder des Kardinalkollegiums von 1130 bis 1159*, Diss. (Würzburg, 1964)

Other abbreviations used in the apparatus:

d'Achery	see Introduction, II. 2. i
Leclercq	emendations adopted from Leclercq, 'Nouvelles' (other conjectural emendations not my own are credited in the apparatus)
Picard	early printed edn. of the letters of Nicholas of Clairvaux (see Introduction, II. 3)
Sirmond	see list of abbreviations of printed works

INTRODUCTION

I. PETER OF CELLE

I. THE CORRESPONDENCE

Varietas was a guiding principle for the writers and compilers involved in the creation of the great epistolary collections of the eleventh and twelfth centuries, as it had been for their predecessors since antiquity. Diversity, style, and careful selection set the serious work of literature, the letter collection, apart from any mere assemblage of missives. This literary activity eclipsed simple preservation to such an extent that the vast majority of letters from this period survive not in archives or as individual survivals in the form in which they were delivered but as integral parts of larger works of literature, crafted and revised for posterity. Those letters or passages which demonstrated the writer's style or spiritual qualities, letters of exhortation or admonition, of friendship or consolation, have frequently stood a better chance of survival than those containing specific details of events or items of routine business. Consequently disappointing to historians seeking to mine them for data, these productions are now coming to be appreciated for the insights they offer into the culture and values of some of the most influential thinkers and leaders of the time. The renaissance of the twelfth century was one of the great periods of European letter-writing and also of letter-collecting. Peter of Celle's collection is a fine representative of that mature tradition. Rhetorically crafted, richly allusive, yet vibrant with a passionate concern for the values of the monastic order, its individual contents encompass the whole variety of themes and forms of the genre: spiritual exhortation, friendship, religious edification, allusive banter and trenchant criticism, local monastic business and high politics, from the briefest of notes to lengthy epistolary treatises. As evidence of the individual communications which lie behind them, the surviving versions of the separate letters are very valuable. Approached together, as a collection, a literary memorial to posterity, they offer deeper insights into the writer, his readers, and the culture in which they were formed, transmitted, and appreciated.[1]

[1] On letter-writing and letter-collecting, the principle of *varietas*, the important

Peter of Celle has enjoyed the perhaps unusual distinction of being admired in the twentieth century both for his piety and for his charm. The most famous remark made about him remains Beryl Smalley's that 'to receive a letter of spiritual direction from him conferred a certificate of piety'.[2] At the same time his lifelong friendship with John of Salisbury has granted him elevation by association to the ranks of the humanists.[3] Indeed Peter has sometimes seemed a writer more celebrated in his choice of correspondents than for what he has to say. Peter the Venerable, Thomas Becket, St Bernard, Heloise, the royal brothers Louis VII and Archbishop Henry of Reims, Count Henry the Liberal of Champagne, even Gerard Pucelle and Henry of Blois are all here. Yet often they have only incidental parts. The collection preserves as many letters to the semi-eremitical Carthusians of Mont-Dieu in the Ardennes as to all of these great names together. Addressed collectively, these monks are not the only recipients of Peter's letters whose separate identities surface, if at all, only occasionally or by chance. Yet Peter valued their friendship as highly as any.

Modern critics, it is true, have recognized in both St Anselm and Aelred of Rievaulx a similarly attractive combination of devotion and charm. Like Peter each drew powerful inspiration from the monastic ideal. Much of the modern debate has focused on their personal or spiritual anguish and struggles and their erudite articulation of their beliefs. With Peter of Celle one has the impression of encountering a more balanced character who, if he did question his vocation or have doubts about his place in the world,[4] has left few echoes of this in his

distinction between letter-writing and letter-collecting, and the principles of selection involved in the literary compilation of collections, and on the scholarly appreciation of the value of approaching letters as integral parts of collections, see Constable's comments and detailed review of the literature in *P. Ven. Epp.* ii. 1–12, and Constable, *Letter Collections*. See also Haseldine, 'Literary memorial', pp. 333–8, 373–9. There are important exceptions to this style of collection, notably the Becket letters.

[2] B. Smalley, *The Becket Conflict and the Schools* (Oxford, 1973), p. 113.

[3] Thus Christopher Brooke commented that the friendship between Peter and John 'reveal[s] a deeper charm in John than we might otherwise suspect and in Peter a fuller appreciation of humanism and secular learning' (*J.S. Epp.* i. p. li). Frank Barlow called them 'two choice souls and exquisite scholars' (Barlow, *Thomas Becket*, p. 274).

[4] Let alone his 'sexuality'—this is an aspect of the modern debate which risks paying too little attention to the context and genre of the relevant sources and imposing modern priorities and concepts on them; see the balanced discussions in R. W. Southern, *Saint Anselm: A Portrait in a Landscape* (Cambridge, 1990), pp. 148–53, and B. P. McGuire, *Friendship and Community: The Monastic Experience 350–1250* (Kalamazoo, 1988), pp. xliii–l. Both discuss the well-known work which sparked off much of the recent debate on this theme, J. Boswell, *Christianity, Social Tolerance and Homosexuality* (Chicago, 1980).

writings, yet whose evident renown as a spiritual director shows that he was very far from being a self-satisfied or complacent figure of authority. Peter's spirituality, which he may not have articulated with the same degree of philosophical introspection or classical erudition as these great figures, not infrequently found expression in more homely images of eating and drinking, of the cloister and the refectory, even of trading and the market place. This seems to reflect a certain reassuring air of stability which may in part account for his reputation as a friend and spiritual guide and for the modern judgement of his character.[5]

Friendship indeed is the key to much of Peter of Celle's epistolary activity. The bonds of friendship which he cultivated and maintained with members of the different monastic orders are the foundation of his influence. His success as a mediator in disputes between monastic orders (which must have added weight to his literary pronouncements on monastic life), the influence which he brought to bear to promote Carthusian expansion, even his ability to motivate active support for Thomas Becket in France, were all based on a network of friendships embracing both the new orders and traditional monasteries.[6] Over his career he built up a circle of friends in northern France and southern England which included Cistercians, Carthusians, Grandmontines, and Augustinian canons, as well as members of many great Benedictine houses such as Cluny, Molesme, and Fontevrault. Peter's

[5] The many letters of edification, exhortation, friendship, or consolation in his collection, a number of which seem to have been responses to requests for such material, testify to this side of Peter's reputation. For a detailed appreciation of his spirituality, see J. Leclercq, *La Spiritualité de Pierre de Celle* (Paris, 1946).

[6] On Peter's career see I. 2 below. On two notable occasions he acted to resolve disputes involving the Cistercians (in one case where another Benedictine house was involved), and he was evidently regarded by them as a trusted ally. See Haseldine, 'Friendship and Rivalry', pp. 406–8 on the cases of Chézy-l'Abbaye and of the Grandmontine monks who had transferred to Pontigny (see also letters 161 and 162 and appendix 14 below). For other examples of Peter's peacemaking and his assisting members of other orders, see e.g. letters 34, 35, 59, 82, 83, 101, 114, 145. For his attitude to monastic diversity in principle see also his treatise *De disciplina claustrali* (*PL* ccii. 1101–46), trans. H. Feiss, *Peter of Celle, Selected Works* (Kalamazoo, 1987), pp. 63–130. On his support for Carthusian expansion, see letter no. 35, n. 1, and appendix 5. His support for Thomas Becket is the subject of an article I hope to publish in the future. Note Lynn K. Barker's comment on Peter's role in the Becket affair, that 'it is difficult . . . to say anything about what role Peter may have played in these years of exile, but the view that he was no more than a hotelkeeper is probably exaggerated' (L. K. Barker, 'Ecclesiology in the twelfth century church in the Letters of Peter of Celle', M.A. thesis (University of North Carolina, Chapel Hill, 1978), p. 81). This is certainly right, if not indeed something of an understatement; Peter may have played a very positive role.

voice, rich with biblical allusion, is resonant with the sentiments and convictions of the monastic world. His involvement in the recurrent preoccupations and the occasional crises of those monasteries in whose affairs he took an interest, as much as his responses to the spiritual concerns and motivations of individual, ordinary monks, reveal an important side to the life of a politically influential abbot. The brilliant and well-defined character of John of Salisbury is still central, but he shares his place in Peter's circle with many little-known abbots, unidentified monks, and priests, and whole communities addressed collectively. And while Peter can at times sound dismissive, even critical, of John's problems, he agonized about John's brother Richard when he was evidently hesitating over his decision to enter the cloister, a vocation which Peter badly wanted him to embrace.[7]

Peter's letters do offer many examples of irony and sarcasm very much to modern tastes. His open-minded view of the monastic orders and their rivalries appeals to the pluralistic and liberal culture of the modern age. Yet one cannot escape the conclusion that the overriding concern here is for the proprieties and health of the monastic vocation and its role in the world. Peter may appear eclectic both in his writings on monastic life and in his active support for other orders, but there is nothing here so peripheral as freedom of lifestyle choice. His aim is ever to promote the monastic order, viewed as a single great enterprise, and it is precisely in criticizing the collective failings of monastic communities that Peter is most cutting.[8] It is this context which makes those occasional pieces of information which the letters preserve about the great events of the day such a rich source. Community life is so integral a part of the experience of pre-modern Europe—and not only for monks—that to appreciate its formative impact on more readily accessible areas of life such as politics and on personalities challenges the imagination. Its importance as an avenue of study can only increase and this in turn may add to our appreciation of the great monastic letter collections.[9]

[7] See esp. letters 163 and 171.

[8] For Peter's views on monastic diversity, see Haseldine, 'Friendship and rivalry'. For his criticisms of monastic failings, see e.g. letters 24 and 150 (Cluny) and 156 (Molesme).

[9] Recognition of the importance of the study of community in cultural as well as political history has been one of the more notable developments in recent years, and will surely continue to enrich our understanding of the past. While this is too complex a subject to be broached here, within medieval studies it has been steadily increasing its scope since Susan Reynolds's seminal and now long-established *Kingdoms and Communities in Western Europe 900–1300* (Oxford, 1984).

Peter of Celle has not been admired recently as a stylist. His highly wrought, often enigmatic prose lacks the fluency of a John of Salisbury or the urgency of a St Bernard. His is not a readily accessible manner. At the same time he may have been overlooked in this respect partly because of his overwhelmingly biblical choice of allusions. No amount of footnoting can capture the extent to which the Vulgate moulds and informs Peter's thoughts and expression; to attempt to disentangle it would risk reducing to a string of references what is a complex and subtle response to the central text of the Latin West. In places Peter adapts and applies Vulgate texts with an arresting boldness.[10] Elsewhere strings of quotations and allusions run together and rise in a crescendo of biblical vocabulary to create a sort of scriptural compendium on the theme or subject-matter at hand. At the same time his fusing of Lucan and Genesis in one sentence in a letter to his close friend Berneredus of Saint-Crépin is a fine example of his range of expression.[11] And while Peter was by no means a humanist of John of Salisbury's stature, their different styles did not stand in the way of a lifelong friendship.

Peter was an open-minded, generous-spirited but adamant defender of the monastic order, an established figure who was apparently at ease in the company of the great and secure in his political contacts yet eager to communicate with ordinary monks whose reputation for devotion he had come to hear of. He was diligent in his abbatial obligations, seeing the spiritual state of the monks and the material stability of the community as an inseparable whole.[12] At the same time his interests in Denmark and further afield, and in the Carthusian order, demonstrate an outward-looking and imaginative use of his influence. Since the popular (and indeed academic) stereotype of the 'renaissance man' first appeared, the invention of new renaissances has filled the 'middle' ages and enriched our appreciation of its culture. Perhaps this educated, well-connected abbot, in touch with some of the geniuses of his age, cultivating literary friendships with erudite humanists and spiritual monks,

[10] Indeed Peter's borrowings from the Vulgate and elsewhere often invert the sense of a text or stretch it beyond what its original context would allow. See e.g. his application or manipulation of biblical texts in letters 49 (see n. 18), 52 (see n. 51), 58 (see n. 17), 82 (see n. 6) and 99 (see n. 25). Naturally I do not imply that his use of the Vulgate was at all unusual; rather that Peter has not been singled out as atypical.

[11] Letter no. 131, n. 3.

[12] On these views, see e.g. letter no. 138. On Peter's successful administration of his own communities, see below pp. xxxii–xxxiii.

always in his powerfully biblical voice, driven always by the ideal of his monastic vocation, would be a suitable candidate, if such a creation were desirable, for 'twelfth-century renaissance man'. But if Peter is a figure of the twelfth-century renaissance, he lived closer to the centre of what has recently been called the 'reformation' of the twelfth century. Montier-la-Celle, the venerable Benedictine foundation of which he was abbot from *c.*1145 to 1162, lay just outside Troyes, the principal city of the counts of Champagne. At Saint-Remi, where he ruled from 1162 to 1181, he was close to the centre of one of the greatest ecclesiastical powers in the kingdom. Before his election to the see of Chartres, where he ended his life as bishop (1181–3), Peter does not seem to have travelled far from Champagne. But this was one of the regions at the heart of the revolution in religious life.[13] Peter's positions gave him considerable influence both within and beyond religious circles; his inclusive vision of the monastic order, upheld in theory and practice, was a noteworthy contribution to the course and tenor of that revolution.

The vision of fruitful religious diversity presented and defended in his treatise *De disciplina claustrali* is reflected in the range of Peter's monastic friendships and contacts.[14] Clairvaux had a special place in his circle. Almost the earliest evidence we have for Peter is of the crucial support which members of that community offered him at the outset of his first abbacy when he encountered resistance to his rule from some monks of Montier-la-Celle.[15] His principal contact here

[13] The term 'reformation' has been applied to this period by Brenda Bolton and Giles Constable: B. Bolton, *The Medieval Reformation* (London, 1983), esp. pp. 11–15 on the use of the term; G. Constable, *The Reformation of the Twelfth Century* (Cambridge, 1996), esp. pp. 3–5 on the use of the term. On the importance of the province of Reims in the religious developments of the time, see also *Libellus de diversis ordinibus et professionibus qui sunt in aecclesia* ed. G. Constable and B. Smith (OMT, 1972), p. xviii. On Peter's life, see below, s. 2. On the cultural life of the court of Champagne, see J. F. Benton, 'The Court of Champagne as a literary center', *Speculum*, xxxvi (1961), 551–91 and A. Putter, 'Knights and clerics at the court of Champagne', in *Medieval Knighthood V*, Papers from the Sixth Strawberry Hill Conference 1994, ed. S. Church and R. Harvey (Woodbridge, 1995), pp. 243–66. There is no evidence to suggest that Peter travelled far afield. The letters offer only negative evidence, in the form of his excuses for not travelling, e.g. to Canterbury (letters nos. 109, 174) and Rome (letter no. 80).

[14] Peter's circle is reconstructed at length in Haseldine, 'Letters of Abbot Peter', pp. 33–92. Particular relationships are detailed in the notes and appendices in this volume; some brief complementary comments on some of the main features and characters follow below. See also Haseldine, 'Friendship and rivalry', and id., 'Understanding the language of *amicitia*. The friendship circle of Peter of Celle (*c.*1115–1183)', *Journal of Medieval History*, xx (1994), 237–60.

[15] See Haseldine, 'Friendship and rivalry', p. 404, and the letter of the prior of

seems to have been Nicholas, St Bernard's secretary, but Peter addressed letters to many other individual monks of Clairvaux. His relations with St Bernard himself are hard to determine. Bernard evidently trusted Peter and on at least one occasion asked him to act on his behalf in a serious dispute. After Bernard's death Peter declared himself to have been an 'alumnus' of the great man. The relationship was probably one of distant respect on Peter's part—an interesting contrast with his cautious and respectful but nevertheless critical letter to Peter the Venerable. It is notable that Clairvaux is the provenance of many of the extant texts of Peter's treatises and sermons.[16]

To the Carthusians Peter was both a close friend and an active supporter of the expansion of their order. Among the early letters those of spiritual friendship addressed to the community of Mont-Dieu in the Ardennes are among the richest of their type in the collection. At least one monk of Peter's own community transferred to the Carthusians with his blessing, if also with his regrets for the loss. This was a time when the transfer of monks between orders was frequently a cause of bitter controversy. Peter's attitude here is a telling complement both to his mediation in the disputes of others, as a respected and influential Benedictine speaking up for the new orders, and to his theoretical writings on the subject. While it is surely wrong to speak of a monastic crisis at this time of unparalleled expansion, these conflicts did bring to the fore important questions about the nature of the monastic vocation and order and its future. The words and actions of an abbot of Peter's standing went beyond local dispute resolution and represent an

Clairvaux to Bishop Henry of Troyes at *PL* ccii. 476, no. li (and on this letter see also below, letter no. 46, n. 1).

[16] On Nicholas of Clairvaux, see letter no. 49, n. 1 and appendix 7; on Peter's other friends at Clairvaux, see letters 45, n. 1, 46, n. 1 and 48, n. 1; see also G. Wellstein, 'Die freundschaftlichen Beziehungen des Benediktiners Petrus Cellensis zu den Cisterziensern (1150–1183)', *Cisterzienser Chronik*, xxxviii (1926), 213–18. Peter describes himself as an alumnus of St Bernard in letter no. 147, addressed to the general chapter at Cîteaux; on Bernard's requesting Peter's assistance, see Haseldine, 'Friendship and rivalry', pp. 406–8, and *S. Bernardi Op.* viii. 211, letter no. 293; Peter's letter to Peter the Venerable is no. 24; on the provenance of MSS of Peter's works other than the letters see the summary at Haseldine, 'Letters of Abbot Peter', pp. 27–8, citing de Martel, 'Recherches'; de Martel, *Petri Cellensis*; A. Vernet, *La Bibliothèque de l'abbaye de Clairvaux du XIIème au XVIIIème siècle* (Paris, 1979), and *Cat. gén. in 4°*, ii. pp. 126–7, 459–60, 648. (In addition, Oxford, Bodleian Library MS Bodley 543 contains a copy of *De conscientia* of English provenance.) Of twelve MSS, four are from Clairvaux; these include the two biggest collections, MS Troyes BM 253 and MS Lisbon Alc. 232.

influential contribution to one of the great questions of monastic life of the time.[17]

Mont-Dieu was also evidently a favourite retreat of Peter's and some of his letters were written there. At the same time the Carthusian priors Simon of Mont-Dieu and Engelbert of Val-Saint-Pierre were part of a close circle which included the Benedictine abbot Berneredus of Saint-Crépin-le-Grand, Soissons, and John of Salisbury. Access to this inner circle via John of Salisbury provided Thomas Becket valuable support in his years of exile, and through it Peter seems to have been able to cultivate influential links at the papal Curia. When Berneredus became a cardinal, Peter took a direct interest in the succession at Saint-Crépin and the later affairs of his friend's old community. John of Salisbury was able to act for Peter's interests in England and in Rome, and it was Peter to whom people naturally turned when they encountered difficulties in their dealings with John after he had become bishop of Chartres. In these and many other ways a friendship circle crossing the boundaries of order and kingdom provides the key to the workings of political and community life at many levels.[18]

With both Clairvaux and Mont-Dieu the long spiritual and philosophical letters of the early period are not continued in the later letters, but there is evidence of continued contact. Eskil of Lund, who with Peter had attempted to establish the Carthusians in Denmark, retired to Clairvaux. Again while Peter's contact with Cluny, at least in so far as it is reflected in the letters, was never as frequent as it had been in the abbacy of Hugh de Fraisans (nor, it must be said, so

[17] On his support for the expansion of the Carthusian order, see letter no. 35, n. 1, letter no. 12, and appendix 5. His letters to Mont-Dieu are nos. 52–60 (see also no. 142). On the transfer of a monk to Mont-Dieu, see letter no. 58. On his attitude to *transitus* and on the notion of monastic crisis, see Haseldine, 'Friendship and rivalry'; on the frequent and inappropriate use of the term 'crisis' by many commentators, see also Constable, *The Reformation of the Twelfth Century*, pp. 1–2.

[18] The letters written at Mont-Dieu are nos. 28, 41, and 48 (see also letter no. 115 on a proposed meeting there). On this friendship circle, see e.g. letter no. 171 and n. 9. On the involvement of the Carthusian priors in the Becket affair, see e.g. Barlow, *Thomas Becket*, pp. 167, 179. On Engelbert and Peter's connections in the Curia, see letter no. 83, n. 1. On Peter's involvement with Saint-Crépin, see letters 135 and 145. On John of Salisbury acting in Peter's interests in England (and Rome), see letters 65 and 67–9 and appendix 8. On John of Salisbury's troubles at Chartres, see letter no. 176. On the value of friendship circles for reconstructing monastic relations, see G. Constable, 'Cluny, Cîteaux, La Chartreuse. San Bernardo e la diversità delle forme di vita religiosa nel XII secolo', *Studi su S. Bernardo di Chiaravalle* (Rome, 1975), pp. 93–114, and Haseldine, 'Friendship and rivalry'.

fraught), it would not be true to say that the move to Saint-Remi brought with it too much pressure to allow the time to cultivate either congenial or strategic friendships—links which were anyway too important to be regarded as personal indulgences for spare moments. The late letters are full of approaches to new contacts and overtures of friendship to newly elected abbots, while Richard of Salisbury only enters the picture as a fully developed character in the later period.[19]

Records of prayer associations survive from Saint-Remi, including those contracted during Peter's abbacy. Indeed the manuscript, evidently a chapter book, which also includes *obits*, saints' days, *acta*, charters, and a copy of the Rule, may be in origin the same book whose loss and rediscovery is the subject of a trivial miracle reported by Peter in letter no. 142. In many ways these records highlight the caution with which a selective letter collection needs to be treated as an indication of the full range of contact and activity of the head of a community. Only four of the many individuals and communities with whom Peter entered into prayer associations were also recipients of letters. To what extent this might represent chance overlap between two selective sources rather than a harder distinction between communal links and the abbot's own friendship circle cannot be determined from this isolated example. It nevertheless adds an extra dimension to our picture of Peter's world, and the prayer association entered into with the community of Mont-Dieu must surely be the result of Peter's own desire to sustain this close contact of his early years and to strengthen its existing ties with Saint-Remi.[20]

[19] On later contact with Clairvaux, see letters 99, 100 (cf. also letter no. 147) and 161–2, and with Mont-Dieu, letters 115, n. 14, and 142. On Richard of Salisbury, see letter no. 163, n. 1. The character of the later collection is certainly different but at least part of the reason for this must be the different degree of selection and editing apparently applied to each collection at Saint-Remi (see below II. 1).

[20] The MS is Reims B. M. 346; see Haseldine, 'Letters of Abbot Peter', pp. 90–2; *Cat. gén.* xxxviii. pp. 428–40; C. H. Talbot, 'Odo of Saint-Remy, a friend of Peter the Venerable', in *Petrus Venerabilis 1156–1956*, ed. G. Constable and J. Kritzeck, *Studia Anselmiana*, xl (1956), 21–37, at pp. 21–2; and L. Falkenstein, 'Le Calendrier des commémorations fixes pour les communautés associés à l'abbaye de Saint-Remi au cours du XIIè siècle', in J. L. Lemaitre (ed.), *L'Église et la mémoire des morts dans la France médiévale. Communications présentées à la Table ronde du C. N. R. S. le 14 juin 1982*, Études augustiniennes (Paris, 1986), pp. 23–9. The four names which also occur in the letters are the communities of Mont-Dieu and of Saint-Gilles, Peter of Pavia and Eskil of Lund. A number of other associations relate to monasteries with some connection to Peter, although not in every case a close one, including the community of Montiéramy (Nicholas of Clairvaux's first house), Nicholas de Roye of Cluny, Abbot Guy of Saint-Nicaise, Reims, Abbot Ebbo of Montier-en-Der, and John of Verneuil and Peter of Melun, both of Saint-Martin-des-Champs. The association with Eskil of Lund, fol. 188r, granted when he presided at the chapter of Saint-Remi, is ed. in

By contrast with this complex network of monastic contacts, the letters tell us tantalizingly little of Peter's relations with bishops, and less about those with lay rulers. It would be fascinating to know more of what lay behind Peter's acknowledgement of the special favour shown him by Henry of France, the king's brother (and a former Cistercian), then bishop of Beauvais, especially as Henry's election to the archbishopric of Reims was closely followed by Peter's to Saint-Remi. At Troyes Peter was close to the court of Henry the Liberal, count of Champagne (and Louis VII's son-in-law). The move to Saint-Remi made him the neighbour of the greatest Capetian power in the region. Peter acted as archiepiscopal vicar in Henry of France's absence from the city on at least one occasion. Henry's successor at Reims, William aux Blanches Mains, Henry the Liberal's brother, was evidently sufficiently sympathetic to Peter's circle (and influential with the king) to engineer John of Salisbury's election to Chartres and so earn Peter's praise. The power balance between the Capetians and the counts of Champagne was one of the more significant issues in determining the future shape of the kingdom; Peter co-operated closely with leading members of both families but his precise role in the politics of these years is not something on which the letter collection will shed much light.[21]

2. LIFE

The greater part of Peter's adult life was dedicated to governing two of the most important Benedictine foundations in the region, Montier-la-Celle, near Troyes, from which he took his name, from

DD i. 2. 227–8, no. 149. A detailed study of this MS is required before any firm conclusions can be drawn about its relevance to Peter's circle.

[21] On Henry of France, see letter no. 21. On Peter's role in Reims, see letter no. 181, n. 1; cf. de Martel, 'Pierre de Celle à Reims', pp. 74–5. Peter dedicated his treatise *De disciplina claustrali* to Henry the Liberal (see *PL*, ccii. 1098); on his relations with the count, see also J. F. Benton, 'The Court of Champagne as a literary center', *Speculum*, xxxvi (1961), 551–91. On William aux Blanches Mains and John of Salisbury's election, see letter no. 102. On the relations between Louis VII and Henry the Liberal, which combined close co-operation and distinct tensions, see e.g. Dunbabin, *France in the Making*, pp. 312–18, and T. Evergates, 'Louis VII and the Counts of Champagne', in M. Gervers (ed.), *The Second Crusade and the Cistercians* (New York, 1992), pp. 109–17. Much of this lies outside the scope of the present edn., which is necessarily limited to those events and characters which appear in the letters. Ludwig Falkenstein's forthcoming work on the collection of 56 papal letters (see p. 720), including lists of refs. to Peter as judge delegate, will add considerably to our understanding of Peter's role in the region.

1145 or before to probably 1162,[22] and Saint-Remi, Reims, from 1162 to 1181. He became bishop of Chartres in 1181 and died in 1183. The basic dates for Peter of Celle's life and career were established by Christopher Brooke;[23] some further evidence can be added here.

i. Birth and family background

The date usually given for Peter of Celle's birth, *c.*1115, seems to have been originally based on Mabillon's conjecture that Peter was under 30 in 1144.[24] All we can say for sure is that Peter was abbot of Montier-la-Celle by 1145 and died in 1183, so *c.*1115 or earlier would not be an unreasonable supposition for his birth date.

Peter evidently came from a noble Champenois family, possibly that of Aunoy-les-Minimes, from modern Seine et Marne. He may be the Petrus de Alnaio or Alneto of some local charters.[25] He was also related to Agnes de Baudement, the third wife of Robert of Dreux (Louis VII's brother), although the nature of the relationship is not known. Before her marriage to Robert, Agnes was countess of Bar-sur-Seine through her first husband, Count Milo (d. 1151).[26] John of

[22] Montier-la-Celle, founded by St Frodobert in the mid-seventh century, also known as Cella Trecensis, Cella Bobini, and Insula Germanica; dedication, St Peter; see *Lexikon des Mittelalters* vi. 807–8; Cott. ii. 1952–3 and *Orbis*.

[23] See *J.S. Epp* i, pp. ix–x, n. 1, citing the following (as noted below): R. L. Poole, *Studies in Chronology and History*, ed. A. L. Poole (Oxford, 1934); Depoin; Lalore, *Cartulaires*; *GC*; *Torigni*, ed. Delisle; E. de Lépinois and L. Merlet, *Cartulaire de Notre-Dame de Chartres d'après les cartulaires et les titres originaux*, 3 vols. (Chartres, 1862–5); *Obits Sens*. On Peter of Celle generally note the extensive bibliography in de Martel, *Petri Cellensis*, pp. xxx–xxxvii.

[24] Cf. *DS* xii. 2, 1525; J. Leclercq, *La Spiritualité de Pierre de Celle (1115–1183)* (Paris, 1946), p. 9, n. 2. Mabillon's conjecture is in his introduction to Janvier, but the relevant sections are reprinted in *PL* ccii. 399C and 402B; on Mabillon's introduction see below II. 4.

[25] The evidence is presented in J. Godefroy, 'La Maison d'Aunoy-les-Minimes, souche de Pierre de Celle', *Revue Mabillon*, xli (1951), 33–5. An 1155 charter of Le Paraclet (Lalore, *Cartulaires*, ii, pp. 75–6, no. 56) concerning a dispute with the monks of Saint-Pierre of Troyes (i.e. Montier-la-Celle, cf. Cott. ii. 1952, and *Orbis*), refers to the abbot Peter, and the witnesses include 'Petrus de Tornella' and 'Engenoldus, frater abbatis'. Apparently the only other local contemporary references are to an Engenoul 'de Alneto' (d'Aunoy). Separately, two other charters from the region refer to an 'Abbas uero ecclesie Trecensis sancti Petri de Alneto nomine [blanc] ad quam ecclesiam specialiter spectat illa ecclesia Sancti Aygulfi' [undated, but 1145 x 1150], and to a Peter 'abbas sancti Petri de Alnaio' [1147] in a Troyes context. Assuming a confusion between the name of the abbot and the abbey (there is no such church in Troyes, and Saint-Ayoul was certainly a dependency of Montier-la-Celle) this would seem to be a reference to Peter before he had assumed the style 'Cellensis', but see Godefroy, 'La Maison d'Aunoy-les-Minimes, souche de Pierre de Celle', for full refs. and further connections.

[26] Agnes de Baudement was the daughter of Guy de Braine and granddaughter of Andrew de Baudement (seneschal of Champagne) and Agnes de Braine. See A. W. Lewis,

Salisbury, in a letter to Thomas Becket written in 1165, refers to the wife of Count Robert as a relative of his friend the abbot, presumably meaning Peter of Celle.[27] She may be the character referred to by Peter in letter no. 128 as 'domina(e) et cognata(e) nostra(e)'. Another female relative of Peter's occurs in the correspondence, a niece (or close relative) Hadvide whose marriage to one Pierre de la Tournelle was contested sometime in the 1150s, but again the precise nature of the relationship is uncertain.[28] Peter's parents were named Hadvuide and Léthéric and he had at least two brothers, Engenoul and Gaucher.[29] Finally Peter refers to two relatives (*cognati*) in letter no. 178: Hugh, a canon of Reims, and G., an archdeacon of Chartres.[30]

ii. Early life

All that is known for certain of Peter's life before he became abbot of Montier-la-Celle is that he was for some time in his youth a monk of Saint-Martin-des-Champs.[31] *GC* notes that it is unclear whether he was professed in a Cluniac house, suggesting that he may have spent

'Fourteen charters of Robert I of Dreux (1152–1188)', *Traditio*, xli (1985), 145–79, at p. 158 and nn. 50, 51. Lewis corrects earlier confusions over her identity: she is not Agnes de Braine, daughter of Guy de Dampierre, as given in *Art de vérifier les dates*, ii. 670–1 and Poole, *Studies in Chronology and History*, p. 265. On Agnes de Baudement and Robert of Dreux, see also letter no. 78, n. 1. See also Godefroy, 'La Maison d'Aunoy-les-Minimes, souche de Pierre de Celle', who identifies her as Agnes de Baudement but says that she was the daughter of Andrew de Baudement; and Prache, *Saint-Remi*, pp. 30–1, for a full discussion and references, including discussion of a possibly more distant relationship to the Dampierre family.

[27] *J. S. Epp.* ii. 32, letter no. 144; 'comitem Robertum, cuius uxor, abbatis mei cognata . . .'.

[28] On Hadvide, Pierre de la Tournelle, and the marriage case, see letter no. 10, n. 1. This is presumably the same Pierre de la Tournelle who witnessed the 1155 charter of Le Paraclet noted by Godefroy (see above, n. 25). Godefroy assumes that he came from the Provins region, but his interests were evidently relatively widespread.

[29] See Prache, *Saint-Remi*, pp. 30–1, for a full discussion of the evidence for Peter's family, which will not be replicated here. Cf. also de Martel, 'Une notice', p. 81 and n. 20, citing an edition of the relevant entry in the *Monasticon Benedictinum*, a collection of notes towards a history of the order compiled in the 17th and 18th cents., formerly at Saint-Germain-des-Prés, now Paris BN MSS Lat. 12658–12704 (material on Saint-Remi appears in BN MSS Lat. 12693 and 12694 and also BN fr. 8339), and Godefroy (cf. above at n. 25).

[30] See letter no. 178, n. 6. (The wording is imprecise, and he may just conceivably be a relative of John of Salisbury.)

[31] He refers to this in letters 146, 150, and possibly 31. A Peter, monk of Saint-Martin, occurs in 1133–4 and Mar. 1144, and a Peter, subprior, in 1141–3 and 1144 (Depoin, ii. 13, 148, 125, 145–6; cf. also pp. 1–2, 18–19, 101–4, 108–9, for priors of two dependent houses called Peter who occur in the 1120s and 1130s), but the name Peter is too common for these references to prove anything.

his early years in Montier-la-Celle.[32] Letter no. 183 suggests an early period in Montier-la-Celle.

iii. Montier-la-Celle, Saint-Remi, and Chartres

Peter was abbot of Montier-la-Celle by 1145 and remained there until 1161 × 2 (probably 1162), when he became abbot of Saint-Remi, Reims. He was at Saint-Remi until 1181 (until March at least), when he became bishop of Chartres. He died on 19 February 1183.

Peter's predecessor at Montier-la-Celle, Walter (Gualterius), occurs in 1139.[33] Peter was abbot by 1145.[34] He was still at Montier-la-Celle in 1161[35] and first occurs as abbot of Saint-Remi in 1162 (*GC*, which may have had access to evidence no longer surviving, puts the move in 1162).[36] He most probably became bishop of Chartres in 1181, as attested in the cartulary of the cathedral and noted in *GC*[37] (his predecessor, John of Salisbury, had died on 25 October 1180[38]). This is corroborated by Meinert, *Papsturkunden in Frankreich*, which shows that he was still at Saint-Remi on 15 March 1181 (and still addressed as abbot, not bishop-elect, in a papal letter) and had been replaced by 5 May, either 1182 or 1183.[39]

[32] *GC* xii. 543E, but no specific evidence is cited.

[33] Lalore, *Cartulaires*, vi. 204–6, no. 194, dated 5 Apr. 1139; ibid. pp. 256–7, no. 217, dated 1139. Lalore states the dates as given in the dating clauses of the documents without accounting for the beginning of the year being reckoned from the Lady Day after Christmas (which it almost certainly would have been in this region at this time), so some of his dates between 1 Jan. and 25 Mar. (and possibly those with no month given) would be a year early. On the beginning of the year in France see letter no. 60, n. 1.

[34] Lalore, *Cartulaires*, vi. 41–2, no. 34; see also Arbois de Jubainville, *Comtes de Champagne*, iii. 430–1. Other dates sometimes still cited are: 1148 (cf. *GC* xii. 543) and *c.*1150 (cf. *GC* viii. 1150). There is no positive evidence for his succession before 1145.

[35] Lalore, *Cartulaires*, vi. 32–4, no. 26.

[36] He witnesses as such a charter dated 1162 in the cartulary of Saint-Thierry, Reims (Reims B. M. MS 1602, fos. 71^v–72^r). Benton, *Culture*, p. 10, n. 22, notes this charter but does not say in what capacity Peter signed. I am grateful to Anne-Marie Legras of the Institut de Recherche et d'Histoire des Textes (CNRS, Orléans), for supplying me with a copy of the document. This makes more likely the date 1162 given by *GC* ix. 234 without any source stated. Brooke provisionally accepted this date, while narrowing the range of certainty to 1161 x 3, noting the occurrence of a successor in 1163 (*J.S. Epp.* i, p. ix, n. 1, citing Lalore, *Cartulaires*, vi. 32–4, no. 26, and p. 6, no. 3). But this may not in fact have been Peter's immediate successor (see letter no. 131, n. 1). So 1161 x 2 seems certain, 1162 probable.

[37] E. de Lépinois and L. Merlet, *Cartulaire de Notre-Dame de Chartres d'après les cartulaires et les titres originaux*, 3 vols. (Chartres, 1862–5), i, p. xxxviii. *GC* viii. 1150 states 1181 noting that he first occurs Oct. 1181. Torigni gives 1182, 'but the chronology is mostly a year out at this point' (*J.S. Epp.* i, p. ix, n. 1; cf. *GC* ibid.): *Torigni*, ed. Delisle, ii. 103.

[38] *J.S. Epp. ii.* p. xlvii, n. 2.

[39] Meinert, *Papsturkunden in Frankreich*, pp. 338–9, no. 188 (15 Mar. 1181—the dates

Two documents now edited in Ramackers, *Papsturkunden in Frankreich* vi, show that Peter was still alive on 17 January 1183 and dead by 11 December 1183.[40] The date of Peter's death is given as 19 February in the necrology of the cathedral of Chartres and in that of Saint-Jean-en-Vallée. Other obituary lists give 20 February (which seems to have been the date of his burial) and other neighbouring dates.[41] On Peter's successor as bishop of Chartres, *GC* gives Reginald, occurs 1182, and another claimant Philip who occurs as *electus* for 1182.[42] However if the beginning of the year is taken as Lady Day, Peter's death would be given as 1182 and would fall in 1183 by our reckoning (a factor which Ramackers takes into account but *GC*'s sources presumably do not), and so if we assume that the election took place soon after Peter's death (i.e. before Lady Day), there is no contradiction here. Peter was buried at the abbey of Josaphat.[43]

Peter's abbacy has been remembered as the high point of a golden age for Montier-la-Celle. The community maintained an active

given by Meinert are modern style, i.e. correcting for the different beginning of the year), addressed to Peter 'abbati monasterii sancti Remigii' (and not as bishop-elect); also Ramackers, *Papsturkunden in den Nierderlanden*, no. 232 and JL 14376. See also Meinert, *Papsturkunden in Frankreich*, p. 356, no. 213 (5 May 1182–3), addressed to Peter's successor. The *Monasticon Benedictinum* has a ref. to a successor in 1181–2 (Prache, *Saint-Remi*, p. 33, n. 58).

40 Ramackers, *Papsturkunden in Frankreich* vi. 240–1, no. 178 (also noted in *GC* viii. 1150 and *Torigni*, ed. Delisle, ii. p. 118, n. 5), and Ramackers, *Papsturkunden in Frankreich* vi. 246–7, no. 184. J. B. Souchet, *Histoire du diocèse et de la ville de Chartres*, 2 vols. (Chartres, 1866–8), ii. 514, concludes that Peter was at Chartres from 24 Oct. 1180 until 19 Feb. 1182 'comptant à la Gauloise' (and so 1183); the date of Peter's succession to Chartres given by Souchet is simply that of the death of John of Salisbury, his predecessor at Chartres, and is refuted by the evidence of Meinert noted above (in any case, John d. 25 Oct., see *J.S. Epp.* ii, p. xlvii and n. 2). Various alternative years must be rejected for lack of evidence, but are sometimes still cited: 1182, 1187, and 1192 are rejected in *DS* xii. 2, p. 1526, correcting 1182 given in de Martel, *Pierre de Celle*, p. 18, n. 3, and id., 'Une notice', p. 77, n. 1. *GC* viii. 1150 rejects the account given 'in quodam Carnotensium episcoporum indice' that Peter was consecrated in 1180 and d. 1187, on the grounds that it does not fit with other evidence, nor with the evidence of Peter's successor (see below).

41 See *Obits Sens*, ii. 42–3, nécrologie de l'église de Chartres; p. 227, Saint-Jean-en-Vallée; p. 244, abbaye de Josaphat, 'depos.' 20 Feb.; p. 183, Saint-Père-en-Vallée, dioc. Chartres, 20 Feb.; p. 272, prieuré de Darron, 'depositio' 20 Feb.; and see also pp. 345, 350 and iv. 321. The cathedral *obit* is likely, though not certain, to be the most reliable. Janvier gives 21 Feb., citing 'Kalendarium Ecclesiae Carnotensis' (*PL* ccii. 404: but the dates *xi kal. Mart.* and *ix kal. Mart.* are easily confused). Note that Gams's implication that Peter resigned in 1182 and d. 20 Feb. 1187 (Gams, p. 526) must be wrong. The Josaphat necrology is also cited in *GC* viii. 1150, where it is noted that the incorrect year given here ('Hic obit anno M. CLXXXVII') is in fact in a later hand.

42 *GC* viii. 1152.

43 *Obits Sens*, ii. 244.

school and scriptorium, and its prosperity was enhanced by Henry the Liberal's grant of jurisdictional rights over Provins, where the dependency of Saint-Ayoul lay, during the fair.[44] Peter maintained his interest in Montier-la-Celle after his move to Reims, intervening to urge the deposition of an evidently disastrous successor, Drogo.[45] At Saint-Remi Peter continued the rebuilding of the abbey church. Some of its most impressive features, including the influential early-Gothic chevet, were constructed during his abbacy.[46] The letters also provide evidence of some of Peter's protracted activities in defence of the rights of the abbey's dependencies.[47]

In 1178 he was proposed as a candidate for the cardinalate by the papal legate Peter of Pavia.[48] At Chartres, according to the entry in the cathedral obituary, Peter was responsible for the completion and restoration of the city walls, for the improvement of the terms of the labour obligations of the bishop's men, and of some other local customs including those restricting the wine trade, and for the reparation of roads, and many other good works.[49]

3. OTHER WRITINGS

Most of Peter of Celle's other surviving writings appear, along with the rearranged copy of Sirmond's edition of the letters, in *PL* ccii. 405–636.[50] They comprise ninety-six sermons,[51] four treatises (*De*

[44] See *Lexikon des Mittelalters* vi. 807–8. I am grateful to Falko Neininger for providing me with a copy of the exhibition catalogue *Montier-la-Celle, abbaye bénédictine milieu du VIIe siècle—1792: exposition 28 octobre–1er décembre 1984* (Troyes, 1984), which lists further evidence—see esp. pp. 7–8: 'L'âge d'or: Pierre de la Celle'. See also A. Roserot, *Dictionnaire historique de la Champagne méridionale*, xiii (Langres, 1944), pp. 946–51, and de Martel, 'Une notice', p. 85.

[45] See letter no. 131 and n. 1, and letter no. 155.

[46] See appendix 12.

[47] See e.g. appendix 10 (Meerssen), letter no. 111, n. 1 (Lapley). See also appendix 11. Fuller discussions (with detailed references) of Peter's activities at Saint-Remi appear in de Martel, 'Pierre de Celle à Reims' and Prache, *Saint-Remi*, pp. 36–7. Notes in the present work are necessarily limited to names and events which occur in the letters. See also *GM* i.

[48] Glorieux, 'Candidats', pp. 20–1. The letter is *PL* cc. 1370–2.

[49] *Obits Sens*, ii. 42–3; see also E. de Lépinois, *Histoire de Chartres*, 2 vols. (Chartres, 1854), pp. 111–13.

[50] With the exception of the commentaries on Ruth. See the following notes for more recent editions of individual works. All are discussed in *DS* xii. 2, 1525–32. An anonymous poem 'Eructavit . . .' (based on Ps. 44), prob. wr. 1180 × 1187, has been ascribed to Peter of Celle on circumstantial and stylistic grounds by Bouvier, who assumed Peter to have lived until 1187 (H. Bouvier, *Histoire de l'église et de l'ancien archidiocèse de Sens*, 3 vols. (Paris, 1906–11), ii. 134–5, 465–9). There is no foundation for this ascription. On the poem, see Benton, *Culture*, pp. 18, 34–6.

[51] On these, see de Martel, 'Recherches', and his forthcoming edition in *CCCM*.

conscientia, *De puritate anime*, *De afflictione et lectione*, and *De disciplina claustrali*)[52] and five commentaries, two each on Ruth and the Tabernacle of Moses and *De panibus*, on references to bread in the Bible.[53]

II. THE TEXTUAL TRADITION OF THE LETTERS

Peter of Celle's letters were originally preserved in two distinct collections. The first comprised early letters, mostly written while he was abbot of Montier-la-Celle, and the second later letters, mostly written when he was abbot of Saint-Remi.[54] Both collections were brought together in one manuscript at Saint-Remi. That manuscript, now lost, was the sole basis for the early printed edition (Sirmond) which now represents the biggest single extant selection of the letters.[55] Sirmond is the only witness for most of the late letters while for the early letters there are two substantial supporting manuscript witnesses, both quite early. Each contains fewer letters than Sirmond, but one also preserves unique material. Their contents and organization suggest transmission not directly from the lost manuscript which Sirmond edited but from a common antecedent which was made up at and circulated from Saint-Remi.[56] The letters in this common antecedent were then, at a later stage, reorganized

[52] *De conscientia*, *De puritate anime*, and *De afflictione et lectione* are edited in J. Leclercq, *La Spiritualité de Pierre de Celle* (Paris, 1946), and *De disciplina claustrali* in G. de Martel ed., *Pierre de Celle, L'école du cloître*, Sources Chrétiennes, ccxl (Paris, 1977). *De conscientia* is often catalogued as 'Epistola ad Alcherum' [Alcher of Clairvaux], but is not part of the letter collection, having a separate transmission.

[53] See de Martel, *Petri Cellensis*. *De panibus* has no modern edition besides *PL*.

[54] There were some exceptions, as explained below, where letters have apparently been included in the 'wrong' collection, but that there were two collections is clear. See also Haseldine, 'Literary memorial', for a briefer overview of the textual transmission and a more extended discussion of the contents, principles of selection, and process of compilation of Peter's collections. What follows emends some of the details in that article.

[55] *Petri Abbatis Cellensis qui post deinde S. Remigij Remensis Abbas, et Episcopus fuit Carnotensis, Epistolarum libri IX. Item Alexandri III. Papae ad Petrum eundem et alios Epistolae LVI*, ed. J. Sirmond (Paris, 1613); hereafter: Sirmond.

[56] The overlap in their contents and similarities of organization make it certain that they do derive from the same archive and not from recipients' archives, as explained below, pp. xlv–xlviii. This is common. Most of the large letter collections we have derive from archives close to the author, see e.g. A. Morey and C. N. L. Brooke, *Gilbert Foliot and his Letters* (Cambridge, 1965), pp. 23–31, and *The Letters and Charters of Gilbert Foliot*, ed. A. Morey and C. N. L. Brooke (Cambridge, 1967), p. 8. But note also the unusually heavy dependence of St Anselm's collection on retrieved copies: see Southern, *Saint Anselm*, p. 466.

and further revised before being transcribed into the lost manuscript along with the later letters. Thus Sirmond would seem to be a faithful edition of the text closest to the author's latest version,[57] while the extant manuscripts represent an earlier transmission from a common antecedent for the early letters. In addition there exist a small number of individual letters and pairs which derive from recipients' archives or were included in other letter collections.

The extant texts of the letters of Peter of Celle can thus be divided into three categories: those based on a sender's archive (the overwhelming majority), those based on recipients' copies, and individual letters which owe their transmission to inclusion in or close association with other letter collections. A total of 177 letters survive in the first category, to which a further seven from the other two categories can be added.[58]

1. TEXTS BASED ON A SENDER'S ARCHIVE

The largest single group of letters based on a sender's archive (170 letters) is Sirmond. The two extant manuscripts in this category are Oxford St John's College 126 (O) and Valenciennes B. M. 482 (Val).

The lost Saint-Remi manuscript behind Sirmond will be referred to as R. The two collections which this incorporated will be referred to as Rc (early letters, mostly written at Montier-la-Celle) and Rr (later letters, mostly written at Saint-Remi). There are a few exceptions to this basic division: the first collection includes four letters written at Saint-Remi, and the second three letters written at Montier-la-Celle.[59] There are no letters which can be shown conclusively to have been written when Peter was bishop of Chartres. It is indeed unlikely that any in these Reims collections were; it was not uncommon for authors of this period to produce separate letter collections for their periods of tenure of different offices.[60]

[57] While we cannot tell the extent of Sirmond's possible emendations, he did not change the order of the letters (see below, p. xxxvi).

[58] Four of which were included by Migne in *PL* ccii (see below, s. 4). It is of course always possible that further strays, not integral to Peter's collection, will come to light.

[59] These are, respectively, R nos. 10, 13, 14, and 65 (in this edition, nos. 92, 94, 93, and 170) and R nos. 79, 80, and 81 (in this edition, nos. 60, 35, and 59). This is not hard to account for (on these and no. 169, see below, pp. xlv–xlvi, xlviii).

[60] See Haseldine, 'Literary memorial', pp. 336–7, on the relation between letter collections and the tenure of particular offices. In two letters Peter identified himself as bishop-elect of Chartres (nos. 147 and 160).

There are two strong reasons for regarding these sections as discrete, originally separate, bodies of material. Firstly, Rc is systematically arranged according to the rank of the recipients of the letters while Rr has no apparent organizing principle behind it.[61] Secondly, the smaller collections in O and Val overlap only with Rc, suggesting that this part of the collection enjoyed a separate circulation independently of the material which went into Rr.[62]

i. The lost Saint-Remi manuscript (R)

Sirmond represents an apparently faithful rendering of the version of the text whose provenance and history makes it certain to be the closest to the author's latest version.[63] Analysis of the original state of the collection in R is possible because Sirmond preserved the order of the letters as he found them.[64] Sirmond gave no further details of his manuscript source. However, Janvier, who incorporated Sirmond's

[61] Rc begins with letters to the pope and progresses through archbishops and bishops to monks and clerks. There are a few anomalies but the plan is clear. Rr has no such order nor any other discernible plan of compilation. There is a preponderance of early letters towards the beginning and of late letters towards the end but no consistent chronological order. There is no evidence either of a thematic arrangement, as e.g. in the letters of Lanfranc: see *The Letters of Lanfranc Archbishop of Canterbury*, ed. H. Clover and M. Gibson (OMT, 1979), pp. 13–15. Most of the reorganization which Migne undertook for the *PL* edition occurs in this part of the collection where, following Brial's suggestion (*HLF* xiv. 241), he reordered the letters by rank of recipient thus bringing them into conformity with Rc.

[62] NB the late letters in these MSS are those which were included in Rc.

[63] Letter collections present a particular problem for modern editors: they provide evidence both for a set of missives (the letters) and for a literary work (the collection). The contents of letter collections were subject to selection and revision, often for literary rather than archival ends. Thus the attempt to recover the lost original missive (e.g. by comparison with recipients' copies or by giving preference to earlier versions) can be at odds with the attempt to edit the literary collection in which the latest authorial version should logically be given priority (as with works deemed 'literary' by modern criteria, such as would be normal practice with treatises, which in this respect are often treated more like modern novels). In any case, earlier versions can still be drafted with a collection in mind. Indeed this problem demonstrates something of the artificiality of the modern concept of the definitive edition, and with modern genre classifications: see Haseldine, 'Literary memorial', pp. 358–60, 373–9.

[64] He renumbered them and divided them into nine books but without changing their order. He also noted the original numbers of the letters (an unbroken sequence from 1 to 169) in the margins, explaining: 'Epistolas omnes in libros IX partiti sumus. In antiquo enim exemplari nulla erat librorum distinctio: sed una omnium epistolarum series, quam perpetui ad earum initia numeri ostendunt' (there are no page numbers in the notes section of Sirmond; this statement appears at the beginning of the notes to book I, immediately after the words 'liber primus'). It is of course impossible to determine Sirmond's practice exactly, but the evidence of the other MSS does not suggest heavy intervention. NB Sirmond III.4 (= R. 46) is in fact two letters, giving the total of 170 above.

edition into his *Opera Omnia* of Peter of Celle, stated that Sirmond's source was a Saint-Remi manuscript.[65]

Other evidence corroborates this identification of Sirmond's source with a lost Saint-Remi manuscript. A 1697 catalogue of the library of Saint-Remi, made by Dom Guillaume Robin of Saint-Germain-des-Prés, records: 'Petri Cellensis abb. sermones.' and 'Petri Cellensis epistulae'.[66] The most likely explanation for the loss is that the manuscript was destroyed in the fire of 1774 which destroyed a large part of the library of Saint-Remi.[67] Secondly, Sirmond appended to his edition a collection of fifty-six letters of Alexander III, addressed to or concerning Peter of Celle, probably dating mostly from the years 1171–3.[68] This collection is unique to Sirmond and has been identified as a product of Peter's own archive.[69] We cannot know whether Sirmond found them in the same manuscript as the letters

[65] *Petri Abbatis Cellensis primum, deinde S. Remigii apud Remos ac demum Episcopi Carnotensis, Opera Omnia*, ed. A. Janvier (Paris, 1671), hereafter: Janvier. 'Thesaurus est refossus in agro tuo, hoc est in metropolis tuae monasterio Remigiano: ubi hactenus magna ex parte latuerat. Inde Jacobus Sirmondus Petri nostri epistolas, nos sermones ejus eruimus, ut Petrum tandem redivivum seu integrum tibi offeramus', Janvier (there are no page nos. in this part of Janvier; the quotation appears on the first page of the dedication, before the preface). The work is dedicated to Charles-Maurice Le Tellier, archbishop of Reims 1671–1710 (*GC* ix. 162–4). The dedication is reprinted in *PL* ccii. 397–8.

[66] Paris B. N. MS Lat. 13070, fos. 4–21 (an abridgement of a catalogue made by the same Dom Robin in 1686–7, now lost), at fo. 13. It also indicates that the MSS were 13th cent., although this, if verifiable, would represent only the transcription of the collection into the codex which Sirmond used rather than its original compilation. I am very grateful to Professor François Dolbeau of the École Pratique des Hautes Études, Paris, for answering my queries. See F. Dolbeau, 'Un catalogue fragmentaire des manuscrits de Saint-Remi de Reims au XIIIe siècle', *Recherches Augustiniennes* xxiii (1988), 213–43, at pp. 218–20.

[67] See de Martel, 'Recherches', pp. 11–12, for a discussion of the destruction of manuscripts (including those containing sermons of Peter of Celle) in this fire.

[68] It is possible that these letters, many of which are delegations of legal cases, are connected with the period when Peter was acting for Archbishop Henry of Reims during the latter's absence from the city. See de Martel, 'Pierre de Celle à Reims', pp. 74–5. See also L. Weibull, 'Påven Alexander III.s septemberbrev till Norden', *Scandia*, xiii (1940), 90–8, discussing those letters which concern Scandinavia. JL puts most of the letters between 1170 and 1172, with none earlier than 1169 and none later than 1173, but on what grounds is uncertain. Peter's co-addressee in many of the letters is Fulk, dean of Reims, who occurs between 1167/8 and 1175 (*GC* ix. 172; S. Chodorow and C. Duggan (eds.), *Decretales Ineditae Saeculi xii*, Monumenta Iuris Canonici ser. B, iv (Vatican, 1982), pp. 19–20). On the problem of dating Henry's probable journeys to Rome, see letter no. 110, n. 1, and no. 181, n. 1. (See also n. 21 above and p. 720.)

[69] See L. Falkenstein, 'Die beiden Versionen der Littera Alexanders III. JL 12116, (1171–1172) Sept. 9', *Proceedings of the Ninth International Conference of Medieval Canon Law, Munich 13–18 July 1992*, ed. P. Landau and J. Müller (Vatican, 1997), pp. 185–255.

but the close association of two texts each independently associated with Saint-Remi further strengthens the evidence for Saint-Remi as the provenance of R.

It has occasionally been suggested that Sirmond found the manuscript at Mont-Dieu, the Carthusian house with which Peter had strong links in his lifetime.[70] Le Couteulx states : 'Ejus quoque Epistolarum codex e Montis Dei bibliotheca erutus a R. P. Jacobo Sirmondo vulgatus est notisque illustratus, cum eleganti ad Montis Dei monachos in gratiam dati codicis dedicatoria Epistola.'[71] *DS* quotes Brial on the possible reasons for Sirmond's dedication of his letters to Mont-Dieu: 'apparement parce que Sirmond avait trouvé chez eux le ms.'[72] Sirmond himself in fact gives no such reason. He did dedicate his edition to Mont-Dieu, but makes no mention in his dedication of any manuscript. He gives among his reasons the touching thought that as Peter of Celle had visited Mont-Dieu in his lifetime so he should, in the form of his letters, go there in death, and also in effect that through the edition the monks might come to know of Peter's high opinion of their predecessors.[73] Further, and in addition to the positive evidence for a Saint-Remi manuscript already considered, Simone Collin-Roset's study of the manuscripts of Mont-Dieu shows no evidence for survival of Peter's letters here.[74] This survey does record two items from Ganneron's catalogue of the library of Mont-Dieu relating to Peter of Celle: 'Liber Petri abbatis Cellensis de laude heremiticae vitae', and 'Epistola Petri abbat. Cellensis (qui fuit postea abbas S. Remigii) ad Stephanum heremitam Montis Dei, prius suum monachum'.[75] These entries, however, must

[70] On Mont-Dieu, see letter no. 52, n. 1.

[71] Le Couteulx, ii. 286; cf. also ii. 147–8.

[72] *DS* xii.2, p. 1526 (cf. Brial in *HLF* xiv. 241); he is closer to the mark when he adds: 'ou peut-être pour leur rappeler que Pierre de Celle fut leur ami et qu'ils étaient redevables de leur établissement aux religieux de Saint-Remi.'

[73] 'Hinc ergo me, ut vobis, RR. Patres, hospitii gratiam his potissimum epistolis redderem, causa non una permovit. Primum quidem, ut earum auctorem vel hac ratione compotem voti facerem, ut qui ad Montem Dei libenter itare solitus est dum vixit, eo nunc etiam qua potest sui parte revertatur. Tum vos deinde in majorum vestrorum, quam ob oculos ponet, imagine, praesentia felicitatis vestrae bona, qui iisdem vestigiis inceditis, agnoscatis.' From Sirmond's dedicatory letter, reprinted in Janvier and now at *PL* ccii. 403–4. He would hardly have used the word *agnoscatis* if they already had the letters (i.e. in manuscript form).

[74] S. Collin-Roset, 'Les Manuscrits de l'ancienne chartreuse du Mont-Dieu (Ardennes)', *Bibliothèque de l'École des Chartes*, cxxxii (1974), 5–73. This cannot be absolutely conclusive as the library of Mont-Dieu was evidently subject to considerable disruption and depletion even before the Revolution. Nevertheless it affords no reason to think that the letters survived there.

[75] Ibid. p. 8.

refer to William of Saint-Thierry's *Golden Letter*, which had been misattributed to Peter of Celle, and possibly indicate the dedicatory letter and the epistolary treatise itself separately.[76]

ii. MS Oxford St John's College 126 (O)

An early thirteenth-century manuscript from the Augustinian priory of Southwick, O contains the largest extant collection of Peter's letters in manuscript form: sixty-three, of which fifty-six also occur in Rc. Of the remaining seven, six have been edited by Leclercq.[77] All of the letters in this manuscript were published as the letters of 'Walter of Dervy' by C. Messiter in 1850.[78] The letters were first recognized for what they are in 1955 by Heinrich Hohenleutner.[79]

The manuscript has six sections, each on self-contained groups of quires: letters of Arnulf of Lisieux (fos. 1^{r}–70^{v}), sermons of Arnulf of Lisieux (fos. 71^{r}–78^{v}), a *florilegium* based on letters of John of Salisbury and others concerning Thomas Becket (fos. 79^{r}–91^{v}), the Peter of Celle letters (fos. 92^{r}–144^{v}), a fragment of Ivo of Chartres' *Libellus de conuenientia Veteris ac Noui Testamenti* (fos. 145^{r}–150^{v}), and an incomplete copy of Jerome's *De interpretatione Hebraicorum nominum* (fos. 151^{r}–173^{r}). It is possible that most of these sections have different origins and may originally have been separate booklets.[80]

[76] This misattribution was corrected by Mabillon in his introduction to Janvier (now *PL* ccii. 399–402), although his correction has not always been noted since. On the misattribution, see J. Déchanet (ed.), *Guillaume de Saint-Thierry. Lettre aux frères du Mont-Dieu (Lettre d'or)*, Sources Chrétiennes, ccxxiii (Paris, 1975), pp. 22–3 and n. 28. On this reference specifically, see G. de Martel (ed.), *Pierre de Celle. L'École du cloître*, Sources Chrétiennes,ccxl (Paris, 1977), pp. 23–4.

[77] Leclercq, 'Nouvelles', excluding letter O 29.NB R 46 = O 34 and 35: see concordance.

[78] *Epistolae Walteri abbatis Dervensis*, ed. C. Messiter, Caxton Society, xx (London, 1850, repr. New York, 1967). On the unreliability of Messiter's edition, see Leclercq, 'Nouvelles', p. 165, n. 21. On his misattribution, see below pp. xl–xli. Messiter himself ventured the bizarre statement (op. cit., p. 1): 'It would appear from the style of these letters (which in many places are extremely difficult to understand) that their author belonged to a very strict and ascetic class of monks.' More oddly yet, the house to whose abbot he misattributed them, Montier-en-Der (Dervy), was Benedictine.

[79] H. Hohenleutner, 'Die Briefsammlung des sogenannten Walter von Dervy (Montier-en-Der) in der Oxforder Handschrift St. John's College, Mrs 126', *Historisches Jahrbuch*, lxxiv (1955), 673–80.

[80] I am indebted to Dr Teresa Webber for taking the time to examine this manuscript and to answer my questions, and particularly for her analysis of the rubrication and annotation upon which the following comments and notes are based.

There is a sequence of quire numbers running through the two Arnulf sections and apparently continuing in the Peter of Celle section, omitting the John of Salisbury *florilegium* (which is also on a rougher parchment than the other sections, has a quire missing, and ends on a catchword). However there is also an older sequence of quire

However, both the rubrication and the style of some of the annotation running through the manuscript indicate that at least the first four sections, and perhaps all, were put together at an early date, possibly in the early thirteenth century.[81] Thus while each section is written in a different hand (although the two Arnulf of Lisieux sections *may* be in the same hand),[82] one rubricator seems to have worked through all the sections supplementing the scribal rubrics. These common rubrics are in a rough, scratchy hand of the thirteenth century, not neatly composed in the spaces, in the same pale red ink as the *ex libris* inscription.[83] The evidence of annotation is less clear but suggests an early association between the first four sections: there is a repertoire of *notae* including chirograms, the letter A and *nota* monograms in the Peter of Celle section, and this same uncommon combination of *notae*, apparently in a different hand, also appears in the first three sections.[84]

At an early stage the letters of Peter of Celle in this manuscript were misattributed. In most cases the *salutatio* formulae, otherwise identical or very close to those in Sirmond, have 'G.', 'frater G.' or 'G. sacerdos Christi', or variations on this in place of Peter of Celle's

numbers in the Peter of Celle section starting from i. It thus appears that this was once separate, and the fact that the Arnulf sections end on x and the Peter section begins on xi in the later numeration may be mere coincidence. In any case, the other evidence is for each of the sections having a separate provenance.

[81] For further description see H. O. Coxe, *Catalogus Codicum MSS qui in Collegiis Aulisque Oxoniensibus hodie adservantur,* 2 vols. (Oxford, 1852), ii. 37, and Haseldine, 'Letters of Abbot Peter', pp. 281–5. See also *The Letters of Arnulf of Lisieux*, ed. F. Barlow, Camden 3rd ser., lxi (London, 1939), pp. lxvi–lxxxvi; and on the *florilegium* see *J.S. Epp.* ii, pp. li, lviii, and Duggan, *Textual History*, pp. 86, 95–8.

[82] Letters of Arnulf, perhaps a northern French hand, late 12th–early 13th cent.; sermons of Arnulf, 13th cent., but possibly same hand as above; John of Salisbury *florilegium*, possibly French hand, late 12th–early 13th cent.; letters of Peter of Celle, possibly English hand, but origin indeterminate (the style of capitals and rising ascenders suggest a scribe accustomed to writing charters), late 12th–early 13th cent.; Ivo of Chartres, possibly English hand, late 12th–early 13th cent.; Jerome, English hand, early 13th cent. (as identified by Dr Webber).

[83] The common rubricator first appears at fo. 42, in the Arnulf letters, and fills the gaps left by the scribe-rubricator in this and the Arnulf sermons section. In the John of Salisbury *florilegium* the scribe has written the long introductory rubric (also in red ink) but the common rubricator supplies most if not all of the rest of the rubrics. In the Peter of Celle section the common rubricator supplies what rubrics there are but leaves gaps which were never filled. There are no rubrics in the Ivo section. In the Jerome section most rubrics are by the scribe, some possibly by the common rubricator. The *ex libris*, however, which is in this section (fos. 151^v–152^r), is in a hand not dissimilar to that of the common rubricator.

[84] It is also possible that the annotation in the Peter of Celle section is the older and that in the first three sections is imitating it. The annotation in the Peter of Celle section is in a fluent cursive hand, or possibly two hands, of the 13th cent.

name or initial. In the first part of the collection, up to and including letter 26 (fo. 110^{v}), the initial 'G' is written over an erasure. After that point it is written directly into the text. The misattribution must therefore have occurred during the process of copying from an exemplar which, in all probability, had the correct initial.[85] It is impossible now to determine how or why the confusion arose. It was obviously this which led to the later misattribution to Walter (Gualterius) of Dervy (Montier-en-Der). One of Peter's letters, O 60 (fo. 139^{v}),[86] is written in the name of a G. of Montier-en-Der, and *GC* records a Gualterius as abbot in this period.[87] This, however, cannot explain satisfactorily the original scribe's confusion: the scribe was evidently working in England in the late twelfth or early thirteenth century and is unlikely to have been thinking of a French abbot of the 1160s who is not known to have written anything, especially as he is not directly named in O.[88] It is hard to see why a

[85] Analysis of the erasures under ultra-violet light at the Bodleian Library, Oxford, showed that nothing discernible remains of the original text beneath. Exemplars based on senders' copies may often have had abbreviated notes in place of the full salutation which the version sent to a recipient would require. Note the comment in R. W. Southern, 'The Letters of John of Salisbury' [review of *J.S. Epp.* i], *English Historical Review*, lxxii (1957), 495–7, at p. 496: 'one good reason for thinking that the two manuscripts [of John of Salisbury's early letters] are based on rough drafts is that they almost invariably omit the address and Valete clause. Instead of an address there is generally a heading taken probably from a note, possibly a much abbreviated note, on the draft.' To add to the confusion, letters O 47 and O 48, to monks of Montier-la-Celle, have 'P.' and O 48 has the rubric 'Abbas Cellensis conuentui suo hortatoria', yet O 46, also to Montier-la-Celle, has 'G.', while 'P.' also appears at O nos. 51, 55, and 56.

[86] Letter no. 6 in this edition.

[87] *GC* ix. 919. Gualterius first occurs in 1161 (although his predecessor last occurs in 1150) and last occurs in 1166. Even if the letters were not known to be Peter's, there are enough familiar names among the recipients for the period to be obvious (even without the palaeographical evidence). Letters written in the names of others were not uncommon.

[88] Indeed while Sirmond (R) has 'G.' in this one letter, O has 'frater G.' for the same letter, a styling which O employs throughout: i.e. the scribe in O has adopted a different styling altogether rather than merely substituting an initial. Also it is in Sirmond (R) not in O where this letter stands first. Had it done so in O this might have explained the confusion. The reference to Montier-en-Der comes only in the body of the text. The rubric in O, at the beginning of the collection, reads 'Epistole ad quasdam personas Gallie destinate' (fo. 92^{r}). Whatever the origin of the 'G.', the connection with 'Walter of Dervy' was made subsequently. A list of contents on the verso of the second of the two unnumbered folios at the beginning of the manuscript in a modern hand (possibly 19th-cent.) describes the Peter collection as 'Epistolae Guidone'. A 19th-cent. list on the front flyleaf reads: 'p. 92– 63 letters of William abbas Dervensis. (a small monastery Moutier-en-Der in France). All apparently are unpublished.' Coxe followed this misattribution in the catalogue to the Oxford College libraries: Coxe, *Catalogus Codicum MSS*, ii. 37.

scribe should have followed the salutation in one letter in preference to that in the majority.

Another possible source of the confusion is Guy of Southwick, who was prior of the house which owned the manuscript and was directly connected with at least one of the other sections of it. He is named in the prologue to the John of Salisbury *florilegium* as the compiler.[89] If the scribe took the letters to be Guy's also (e.g. perhaps because they had been in his possession), this would imply a later copying after Guy's death when he was no longer present to correct the misattribution. However, while the rubricator and possibly the annotator may have seen the other sections, we cannot know whether the scribe did. Nevertheless a possible connection between Peter of Celle and Guy of Southwick which could have given rise to later confusion is not hard to find. Guy was a friend of John of Salisbury who in turn was one of Peter of Celle's closest friends. (John's brother Richard, also close to Peter, was a canon of Guy's old house, Merton.[90]) Guy has also been suggested as the person responsible for the collection of letters of Arnulf of Lisieux in the same manuscript.[91] Thus the confusion may have arisen after Guy's death from his known involvement with or acquisition of the different sections which went into O. While this is inconclusive, taken together with other evidence it may also connect John of Salisbury with the transmission of Peter's letters. Letter O 29 (no. 69 in this edition), unique to O, is addressed to John. It is very brief and concerns a Thomas of La Celle, who had been in England and about whom John had cause to write to Peter.[92] If a copy was kept by Peter it did not find its way into Rc, probably being deemed too brief for publication and of little general interest.[93] Furthermore, this

[89] Prior Guy of Southwick first occurs 1185 or 1187, last occurs 1206 (*Heads*, p. 184), and prob. occurs as 'G.' 1177 x 82 (*EEA* viii, no. 163). The prologue to the *florilegium* is at O fo. 79^{r}: 'Incipit compendiosa defloratio ex libro epistolarum magistri Iohannis Saresberiensis, qui postmodum fuit episcopus Carnotensis, super causa beati Thome martyris, a Guidone priore Suwicense diligenter excerpta.' The full prologue is quoted in Duggan, *Textual History*, p. 85, n. 6, and the collection itself discussed ibid. pp. 95–8.

[90] On Richard of Salisbury, see letter no. 163, n. 1. Guy describes himself in the prologue to the *florilegium* as a canon of Merton at the time he helped John of Salisbury compile a collection of letters; see Duggan, *Textual History*, pp. 86 n. 6, 97.

[91] *The Letters of Arnulf of Lisieux*, ed. F. Barlow, Camden 3rd ser. lxi (London, 1939), pp. lxxxv–lxxxvi, and see especially (with reference to a group of forty letters unique to this MS) p. lxxxvi: 'One is tempted to think that Guy published the unique collection of Arnulf letters.' However, as the different sections in O appear to have different provenances the link is not a strong one.

[92] On this episode, see appendix 8.

[93] A parallel can be seen with the letters in MS Di where of the two letters which are

letter stands apart from the others addressed to John in O (O nos. 17–23) and so may be a separate addition to the collection.[94] It may be that this is a copy of a letter which John of Salisbury had received from Peter and which he put with the collection of materials which was eventually to find its way to England, that is to say it only survived because the recipient was also in possession of a collection of the early letters. John of Salisbury is thus the common link between Guy of Southwick and Peter of Celle, and may also be connected with the version of Peter's early letters which came to England. It must remain mere speculation, but it is possible that John of Salisbury took the early letters to England, perhaps on his return from exile in 1170, and gave them to Guy at Merton (where they worked on the *florilegium*, and where John's brother Richard was a canon), and that Guy later took them, along with other pieces, to Southwick where, after his death, they were found. Indeed John may have sent a collection of his letters to Peter in 1161 or 1162,[95] so it is not improbable that Peter reciprocated. It is yet more intriguing to note that the only known connection between Peter of Celle and Saint-Amand, the provenance of the only other extant manuscript based on a sender's archive (Val), was again John of Salisbury.[96] It would be attractive to think of John bringing the common antecedent to O and Val through Saint-Amand on his return from exile before taking it to Merton, but in the absence of conclusive evidence an attractive theory is all that it can be.

iii. MS Valenciennes B.M. 482 (Val)

A twelfth-century manuscript, provenance Saint-Amand, containing letter collections, Val has nineteen letters of Peter of Celle, all of which also occur in Sirmond and all but two in O. The contents are a small selection of letters of Fulbert of Chartres (fos. 1^r–8^r), a large Ivo

found in this recipient's archive only the more general occurs in R while the more specific letter preserved by the recipient may have been considered too detailed and local in its subject-matter to be included in the large Saint-Remi collection aimed at a wider readership. (It is this longer letter, however, which is preserved in two Alcobaça MSS: see below, s. II.2 i). Likewise O 29 is the sort of letter one might expect to be excluded from the later, more polished stage of a letter collection (see Haseldine, 'Literary memorial', pp. 360–8).

[94] On the significance of letters to the same recipient being grouped together, see below, s. II. 1 iv.

[95] See appendix 8.

[96] The only known contact being Peter's letter to Hugh of Saint-Amand asking him to intercede for John with the king, which forms part of John's collection and may have been drafted by him (see *J.S. Epp.* ii. 28–31, letter no. 143, reproduced in this edn. as no. 136).

of Chartres collection (fos. 9^{r} 70^{r} and 96^{v}–109^{r}), a section of letters relating to the Alexandrine schism, including letters from the collection of Philip of l'Aumône (fos. 70^{r}–96^{v}, i.e. interposed in the Ivo of Chartres letters), the letters of Peter of Celle (fos. 109^{r}–131^{r}) and a small group of letters concerning the crusades (fos. 131^{r}–144^{r}). The letters of Fulbert were clearly originally separate; the quire is a different size from the rest of the manuscript. The collections of Ivo of Chartres and Philip of l'Aumône and the letters relating to the schism may all be part of the same enterprise. The small Peter of Celle collection has apparently been added by a nearly contemporary copyist (late twelfth-century) and the letters concerning the crusades added in the thirteenth century.[97]

This is a very small selection of Peter's letters. If, as the evidence of organization and contents suggests, they were derived ultimately from a precursor common also to Rc and O, then they probably represent a deliberate selection from a much larger body of material rather than chance accumulation (as might be the case with an attempt to gather recipients' copies). The selection favours letters whose content is more spiritual and edifying rather than concerned with specific details of events or monastic business. The principles of selection would thus appear to be literary rather than archival. Letter Val 8 for example, to Alan of Auxerre, concerning the marriage of Peter's niece,[98] is a discussion of the potential conflict between justice and friendship. None of the other letters pertaining to this same case appear here. Again, the one letter here to Nicholas of Clairvaux (Val 18[99]) treats of friendship, whereas the majority, including the longest, in R to Nicholas concern a lengthy and detailed theological debate. Other letters in this small collection could almost be considered as models of their type. Letter Val 19 to John of Salisbury begins, 'Queris, frater, a me scripta exhortationis . . . Queris . . . consolationem', and goes on to offer an exhortation on the nature of divine consolation and propitiation.[100] Val 13, to John of Saint-Malo,

[97] For further description, see *Cat. gén.* xxv. 391–3, item 482; J. Mangeart, *Catalogue descriptif et raisonné des manuscrits de la bibliothèque de Valenciennes* (Paris, 1860), pp. 436–41, item 442 (*sic*, the MS was subsequently renumbered). See also *The Letters and Poems of Fulbert of Chartres* ed. F. Behrends (OMT, 1976), p. lxi, and J. Leclercq (ed.), *Yves de Chartres, corréspondence* 1, Les classiques de l'histoire de France au moyen âge, xxii (Paris, 1949). On the letters relating to the Alexandrine schism and those from the collection of Philip of l'Aumône, see T. A. Reuter, 'The papal schism, the empire and the west, 1159–1169', D. Phil. thesis (Oxford, 1975), appendix A.

[98] No. 23 in this edn.

[99] No. 49 in this edn.

[100] No. 64 in this edn.

is a letter of consolation on the death of St Bernard.[101] The selection also reflects the quantity of Peter's correspondence with certain recipients whom he clearly regarded as close friends. There are three letters each to Mont-Dieu and to John of Saint-Malo out of a total selection of only nineteen. These are also among the best represented recipients of letters in the larger collections, and Peter's letters to them generally are concerned more than most with friendship and spirituality. While the larger selections reflect the variety typical of letter collections, the selective focus here on spirituality and friendship may reflect something of Peter's particular renown.[102]

iv. The relationship between R, O, and Val

It has been established on the evidence of internal organization and apparent circulation that R comprised two discrete collections, which I have called Rc and Rr—and so while a tiny number of letters appear in the 'wrong' collection (early letters among the late and vice versa), there is no repetition of contents. Rc, being the more systematically organized (as noted above), may represent a collection put together by Peter of Celle himself shortly after he left Montier-la-Celle which was intended to form as complete a collection as possible for that part of his life. In all likelihood Rr, given the lack of evidence for any circulation and its apparently disordered state, is taken from a Saint-Remi archive which neither Peter nor his scribes had the opportunity to edit and organize in the same way as Rc.

While Rr has only minimal overlap with the other sources, the evidence of contents, collation, and to a lesser extent dating clearly indicates a common antecedent from which Rc, O, and Val derive independently of one another. O contains unique material, Val contains material not in O, and all three have unique textual variants. The likely dates of compilation of each of these versions, based on internal evidence of the datable letters, does not challenge this picture of the textual relationships. In its final state Rc cannot have been complete before 1167.[103] Since it contains four late letters (and only four, out of a

[101] No. 17 in this edn.

[102] Interestingly, the only piece of marginalia is a *nota* in the form of a hand indicating the line, 'Iam ergo amico loquar ut amico', in letter Val 16 (fo. 127^r; no. 30 in this edn.).

[103] Three letters in Rc, nos. R 10, R 13, and R 14, name Saint-Remi in the salutation (nos. 92, 94, and 93 in this edn.). R 10 post-dates 1164, R 13 cannot have been written before 1167, and R 14 is dated summer 1167. A fourth letter, R 65 (no. 170 in this edn.), has no place-name in the salutation but was written in 1164 (this date revises that given in Haseldine, 'Literary memorial', p. 351, but this does not affect the overall picture of the

total of sixty-eight), it is likely to have been formed at Reims soon after Peter's translation, with a few materials added over the years possibly as late as 1167 or later.[104] Thus between the amassing of the early letters and their final transcription into R, while a few items seem to have been added or accidentally included, the majority of Peter's new letters would most probably have been kept separately, in an archive which was to become Rr. Val and O include only one late letter each. Val has a copy of R 10 (written 1164 x 1170)[105] and O a copy of R 65 (written 1164, before November).[106] No other letters in either MS are firmly datable to after 1162, although a number are undatable. Thus at some point after 1164 a version or versions of early letters containing mostly letters written before 1162 left Saint-Remi, or circulated and returned, and selections from this were copied into Val and O. Later a version which was still at, or had returned to, Saint-Remi was turned into Rc. This preserved further letters, but it seems that some that had reached O were excluded or lost from the corpus before the production of Rc.[107] It is possible that some of the better readings which occur in Sirmond reflect further work on the common antecedent after O and Val were taken from it, in preparation for what became Rc.[108]

The internal organization of the letters in the extant texts provides some evidence for the form of the common antecedent. Rc is arranged according to the rank of the recipients. In O, while the collection is not so arranged, letters to each recipient are generally grouped together. In some cases the sequences within these groups are the same as those in R,[109] while in other cases they

textual history). I have also included R67 among the later letters (as no. 169), but its date is too uncertain for it to bear on these arguments

[104] It is not possible to tell whether or to what extent Peter was directly involved in this, but some sort of collaboration between him and his clerks seems a natural supposition.

[105] Val 7, and no. 92 in this edn.

[106] O 19, and no. 170 in this edn.

[107] Alternatively, they could have been sent out with the materials which formed the basis of O and never recovered.

[108] But, as noted, we cannot know the extent of Sirmond's emendation. This modifies slightly the statement in Haseldine, 'Literary memorial', p. 352, but not significantly. There is no reason to say that the collection behind O was definitely earlier than that behind Val on the basis of contents. The two are most probably nearly contemporary if not copied directly from the same exemplar. All we can say is that the late letter in Val could have been written much later than the one in O.

[109] There are five groups in this category, of which two are pairs only: O 7–10 = R 28–31 (letters to Peter the Venerable and Hugh of Cluny, but all given as letters to Peter the Venerable in O); O 12–13 = R 21–2 (letters to Theobald of Paris and Alan of Auxerre, but concerning the same case); O 31–6 = R 43–7 (letters to the monks of Mont-Dieu); O 40–1 = R 41–2 (letters to the monks of Chézy l'Abbaye); and O 44–5 = R 57–8 (letters to Nicholas of Clairvaux).

are different.[110] There are a few strays such as a letter to John of Salisbury at O 29 and a letter to Nicholas of Clairvaux at O 63 set apart from the others to the same recipients but, in all, forty of the letters in O form part of such a group and only twenty-three (including all seven of those unique to O) appear not to. Val has two such groups. The sequences of letters in these groups are identical across all three texts but in both cases what we have in Val is only a part of a larger group.[111] Similar evidence for the organization of letter collections before their transcription into extant manuscripts has been observed in a number of other cases from this period. In their early stages letter collections seem to have been preserved in a loose form rather than in single bound codices, i.e. as small groups of letters each on separate leaves or bifolia, and each containing letters to one recipient or on one topic or theme. In the collections as they were copied the letters within each group (which could be arranged chronologically but often were not) would remain together but the groups themselves were often in a different order. The appearance of parts of groups and internal rearrangements within groups could have arisen when a single group spread over more than one loose sheet and was subsequently split up. Thus while wholly different principles of arrangement might indicate radical reorganization of bound material, this shifting of groups suggests the handling of loose material organized in this way. Evidence for such a process has been found in the cases of Fulbert of Chartres, Lanfranc and John of Salisbury, and most recently and concretely, Adam Marsh.[112] The common antecedent to Rc, O, and Val most

[110] There are five groups in this category, in two of which O omits some of the letters which appear in R: O 1–6 = R 15, 20, 16, 17, 19, and 18 (letters to John of Saint-Malo); O 14–16 = R 8, 9, and 11 (letters to Hugh of Sens, omitting R 10 to Thomas Becket); O 17–23 = R 61, 64, 65, 59, 62, 60, and 66 (letters to John of Salisbury); O 25–7 = R 55, 54, and 53 (letters to various monks of Clairvaux); and O 57–61 = R 2, 7, 3, 1, and 5, omitting R 4 and 6 (letters to Roland Bandinelli, both as cardinal and as Pope Alexander III).

[111] Val 1–3 = R 43–5 = O 31–3 (letters to the monks of Mont-Dieu), and Val. 13–15 = R 16–18 = O 3, 4, and 6 (letters to John of Saint Malo).

[112] See *The Letters and Poems of Fulbert of Chartres*, ed. and trans. F. Behrends (Oxford, OMT, 1976), pp. l–lx, and *The Letters of Lanfranc Archbishop of Canterbury*, ed. H. Clover and M. Gibson (Oxford, OMT, 1979), pp. 13–15. Behrends concluded of Fulbert's letters that 'the underlying collection was not a bound codex, but consisted of small gatherings and separate leaves which could be rearranged' (Behrends, *op. cit.*, p. li). The same point was made about the John of Salisbury letters by Southern in his review of *J.S. Epp.* i (*English Historical Review*, lxxii (1957), 495–6), and incorporated into the 2nd edn. (see *J.S. Epp.* i, 2nd. edn., 1986, pp. 297–8). These loose folios do not survive physically; their existence is deduced from the state of the surviving evidence, but in the case of Adam Marsh there is more concrete evidence of a similar process: see C. H. Lawrence, 'The

probably comprised such loosely bound groups on separate leaves and bifolia.

Taking all of this evidence together, it seems that between the transmission to O and Val and the final transcription into Rc some letters of this common antecedent were overlooked, lost, or deliberately excluded, some material was added, and a systematic reorganization of the groups by rank of recipient was undertaken. We can assume therefore two separate bodies of material behind the extant texts: a common antecedent of the versions of the early letters (α) and, separately, the collection of materials which later became Rr (β). The fact that α and β have the same provenance and were almost certainly loosely bound easily accounts for the few cases where individual letters have apparently crossed over between the two collections. Table 1 represents the transmission of the letters as it can be constructed from this evidence.

TABLE 1

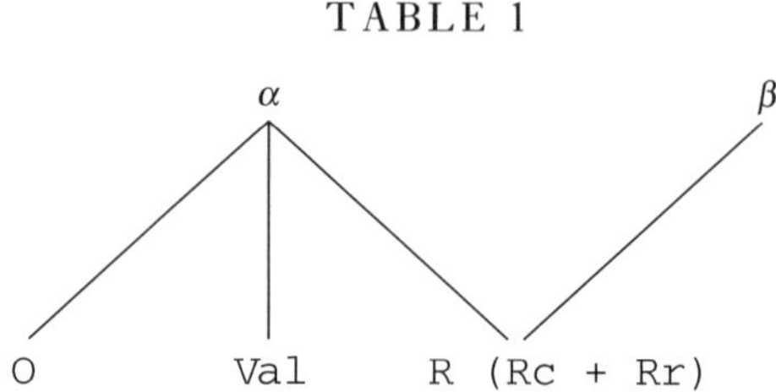

2. TEXTS BASED ON RECIPIENTS' ARCHIVES

There are five known letters preserved in texts based on recipients' archives, of which three are not found in the sender's archive. These are the two letters in MS Di, of which one occurs separately in Sirmond-R based on a sender's copy, and the other in two Alcobaça MSS; the letter to Gossuin of Anchin with a reply in MSS M. and Do; and two letters to Erlembald of Stavelot transcribed in 1909 from a now lost MS associated with Stavelot (of these, one occurs separately in Sirmond-R based on a sender's copy).

letters of Adam Marsh and the Franciscan school at Oxford', *Journal of Ecclesiastical History*, xlii (1991), 218–38, esp. pp. 220–1.

i. The letters to the Grandmontine novices

MS Di is a late twelfth-century manuscript, provenance Cîteaux, containing works of St Bernard (letters and the *De diligendo Deo*), to which a small collection of four letters has been added later.[113] This small collection comprises two letters of Peter of Celle (nos. 161 and 162 in this edition), one by Stephen of Tournai, and one by a 'G.' of 'sancto V.' (probably Abbot Guarinus of Saint-Victor).[114] Three of these (the two by Peter and the one by 'G.') appear in d'Achery's *Spicilegium*, in the same order as in Di. One of the two letters by Peter (no. 162 in this edition) occurs along with the letter of Stephen of Tournai in MSS A1 and A2. In A1 these are a later (? after 1200) addition to a twelfth-century MS. A2 is fourteenth-century. The two texts differ in only one place, while they differ considerably from both Di and d'Achery. Of the two letters by Peter, only one (no. 161 in this edition) also occurs in Sirmond-R.[115] Thus three clearly different recipients' versions exist: Di has all four letters, d'Achery both of Peter's plus that of 'G.' and the A1–A2 version only one of Peter's plus Stephen of Tournai's, and all three versions exhibit considerable variations.

All four letters concern a group of Grandmontine novices who had transferred to the Cistercian house of Pontigny and who had enquired about the legitimacy of their move. Their case was brought before the papal legate Peter of Pavia by a monk of Pontigny, Robert Galardon, probably in 1181.[116] All three writers advised the monks to remain

[113] See *Cat. gén.* v. 55. There are also some sermons on parchment used in the (later) binding.

[114] See appendix 14.

[115] J. L. d'Achery, *Veterum aliquot scriptorum qui in Galliae Bibliothecis maxime Benedictinorum latuerant Spicilegium*, 13 vols. (Paris, 1657–77), ii. 447–51, nos. 28–9; and in the re-edition, J. L. d'Achery, nova ed. S. Baluze, E. Martène and L.-F.-J. de la Barre, *Spicilegium sive collectio veterum aliquot Scriptorum qui in Galliae Bibliothecis delituerant*, 3 vols. (Paris, 1723), pp. 544–5. The letter by the 'G.' of 'sancto V.' (inc. 'Iuxta consequentiam eorum') does not appear among the letters associated with Saint-Victor in *PL* cxcvi, nor is it recorded in G. Teske, *Die Briefsammlungen des 12. Jahrhunderts in St. Viktor/Paris* (Bonn, 1993). D'Achery gives as his source 'Ex MS Nicolai Camuzat Canon. Trec. [Troyes]'. His text differs considerably from that in Di, suggesting that it may have been based on a different, lost MS. For the one letter they have in common Sirmond (based on R, from the sender's archive) is closer to Di than is d'Achery, but Di alone has a salutation, suggesting a sent copy. On MSS A1 and A2 see T. L. Amos, *The Fundo Alcobaça of the Biblioteca Nacional, Lisbon*, ii *Manuscripts 151-301* (Collegeville, Minnesota, 1989). In A1 Peter's letter is at fos. 79^r to 81^r, and in A2 fos. 128^v to 130^r.

[116] See appendix 14, and Haseldine, 'Friendship and rivalry', p. 408.

with the Cistercians. The polemical intention of this tiny collection is clear: a Cistercian has gathered together letters written on a specific case by non-Cistercians which praise his order and advise those who have transferred to it to remain.[117] Of Peter's letters it is the shorter of the two, giving a brief statement of his position on the question of changing orders, which also survives separately in Sirmond-R. The longer letter, which is divided into three sections each dealing with the individual case of one of the monks, was evidently not included in R. It is possible that no sender's copy was kept for the main collection because it was considered that so specific a set of messages would be of little interest to a wider audience, especially since the point of principle at issue was dealt with in the shorter letter.

ii. The Anchin and Stavelot Letters

MSS M and Do each contain copies of an exchange of letters between Peter and the abbots Gossuin and Alexander of Anchin. Peter wrote to Gossuin to console him in his illness but the letter (no. 137 in this edition) apparently arrived after his death. The second letter is the reply of Gossuin's successor, Alexander. M is a twelfth-century manuscript, provenance Saint-Sauveur d'Anchin, containing hagiography, to which copies of these letters have been added. Its provenance makes it certain that the letter is based on the recipient's copy. Do is a sixteenth-century collection of material relating to the history of the abbey of Anchin with particular attention to Abbot Gossuin. It was compiled by, or belonged to, François de Bar, Grand Prior of Anchin 1575–1606, who wrote a history of the abbey.[118] Provenance, date, and collation show that the version in Do is a copy of that in M.[119]

Copies of two letters addressed to Erlembald of Stavelot were printed in J. Halkin and C.-G. Roland, *Recueil des chartes de l'abbaye de Stavelot-Malmedy*, vol. 1 (Brussels, 1909), pp. 509–11, from a now lost MS then owned by a M. Crahay of Liège. The MS was

[117] Stephen of Tournai was an Augustinian canon, as was the author of the last letter, if it is indeed by the abbot or a monk of Saint-Victor.

[118] See E. A. Escallier, *L'Abbaye d'Anchin 1079–1742* (Lille, 1852), pp. 305–7, 328–30, 477.

[119] These letters are edited in Leclercq, 'Nouvelles', pp. 160–79. MS M also contains Eadmer's life and miracles of St Dunstan and Fulbert's life of St Aichadrus (see *Bibliotheca Hagiographica Latina*, 2 vols. (Brussels, 1898–1901), i. nos. 182, 2346–7), and an antiphon and hymn; see also *Cat. gén.* xlviii. 398, item 1168. In MS Do the letter from Alexander is cut short at 'sine consolatione dereliquit'; see also *Cat. gén. in 4°*, vi. 548–51.

thirteenth-century, provenance Stavelot, containing various texts relating to the abbey (see ibid. pp. xlviii–xlix). In Halkin and Roland the letters are nos. 270 (a version of letter no. 118), and 271, a unique letter, inc. *Cum multo gaudio* (no. 119). They are given respectively as Crahay MS fos. 23^{v} and 94.

3. LETTERS PRESERVED IN OTHER COLLECTIONS

Six letters owe their transmission to their inclusion in or close association with other letter collections. Of these, only three were also preserved, separately, in the sender's archive (nos. 27, 50, and 51).

'Stilum cohibere . . .' (letter no. 75 in this edition), to Pope Alexander III in support of Thomas Becket, survives as part of the Becket collections. Migne added it to the *PL* edition from Giles's edition of the Becket letters. All of the relevant manuscripts are discussed by Anne Duggan.[120] 'Amicorum fidem articulus . . .' (letter no. 136 in this edition), to Hugh of Saint-Amand on behalf of John of Salisbury, is part of the later letters of John of Salisbury. Migne added it to the *PL* edition from Giles's edition of John of Salisbury's letters.[121] 'Mandastis michi palefridum . . .' (letter no. 180 in this edition), to Louis VII, comes from one of the Saint-Victor letter collections. Migne added it to the *PL* edition from Duchesne's *Historiae Francorum Scriptores*.[122]

'Inspector conscientiarum Deus . . .' (letter no. 27 in this edition), to Matilda of Fontevrault, appears in more than ten Austrian and German manuscripts having been transmitted along with the letters of, and in some cases misattributed to, St Bernard. These are

[120] These are, using Duggan's sigla, AlanT (A), AlanT (B), AlanT (C), Bodl. B, Lamb, and Vat (see list of sigla below; where modern eds. or studies exist of MSS in this category, the same sigla are used in this edn.). I am grateful to Anne Duggan for her help with the MSS for this letter; I follow her in taking AlanT (A) as the base text. On these MSS, see Duggan, *Textual History*, pp. 9–15, 47–53, 66–84, 98–145, 236–64. The letter is also *PL* ccii. 532–3, no. LXXXV; J. A. Giles (ed.), *Epistolae Sancti Thomae Cantuariensis*, Patres Ecclesiae Anglicanae, 2 vols. (Oxford, 1845), ii. 172–3, letter no. 336.

[121] *J.S. Epp.* ii. 28–31, letter no. 143, which is reproduced here by permission of Oxford University Press. The text is based on MS Q (using Brooke's sigla; see list of sigla below). The letter also appears in British Library Additional 11506 and Cotton Vitellius E. xvii: see *J.S. Epp.* ii, pp. xlvii–xlix, lxxx. The letter is also *PL* ccii. 591–2, no. CXLVII; J. A. Giles (ed.), *Joannis Saresberiensis postea Episcopi Carnotensis Opera Omnia*, 5 vols., Patres Ecclesiae Anglicanae (Oxford, 1848), i. 192, letter no. 156.

[122] See Teske, *Briefsammlungen*, p. 382, MS F item 316 (see also list of sigla below). The letter is also *PL* ccii. 636, no. CLXXVII; A. Duchesne, *Historiae Francorum Scriptores*, 5 vols. (Paris, 1636–49) iv. 678; *RHF* xvi. 170.

obviously not significant for the sender's collection, and there may well be further copies. I will publish separately on this complex transmission. For present purposes, variations from a sample have been recorded. These are MSS Admont 446 (Ad1), Admont 451 (Ad2), Graz 1287 (G), Zwettl 187 (Z), Vienna Nationalbibliothek 1255 (Vi), and Vienna, Schottenkloster 28 (VS).[123] Three of these, Ad1, Ad2, and G., all twelfth-century, misattribute the letter to St Bernard, while the other three, Z, Vi, and VS (twelfth, fourteenth, and fifteenth centuries respectively), attribute it correctly. The letter also occurs in Sirmond, and so in R, and in O and Val, and so a separate sender's copy must have been kept.[124] Ad1 contains only a fragment of 'Inspector . . .', at fo. 110^{v}, and no other letters. Ad2 has 'Inspector . . .' at fos. 1^{r}–2^{v}; otherwise it contains only works of Bernard, including letters. G is also a collection made up exclusively of the works of St Bernard, with 'Inspector . . .' appearing as a separate item at fos. 178^{r}–180^{r}; it contains no other letters.[125] Z contains works by Hegesippus and Jerome to which a thirteenth-century copy of 'Inspector . . .' has been added at fo. 160^{r}–160^{v}. Vi has 'Inspector . . .' at fos. 40^{r}–41^{v}; it includes works of Bernard *et al.*, but no other letters.[126] VS has 'Inspector . . .' at fos. 215^{r}–216^{v}, separately from the collection of Bernard's letters which is also included.[127]

Finally two letters from Peter of Celle to Nicholas of Clairvaux (nos. 50 and 51 in this edition) also occur in the printed editions of Nicholas of Clairvaux's collection, where they are numbered 51 and

[123] Information on these manuscripts provided by the Hill Monastic Manuscript Library, Collegeville, Minnesota. My sigla. This letter, while associated with and in some cases misattributed to St Bernard, always appears as a separate inclusion and is nowhere incorporated into Bernard's letter collection; it is not in *S. Bernardi Op.*

[124] In such cases, agreements between one or more sender's texts and one or more recipient's texts might point to the reading of the archetype, i.e. the sent letter. There are, however, no significant instances of this here, and in any case (apart from the expansion of the abbreviated addressee's name and one case of the inversion of a pair of words), no instance of two sender's texts agreeing with recipient's texts.

[125] See also A. Kern, *Handschriftenverzeichnisse österreichischer Bibliotheken, Steiermark b.2, Die Handschriften der Universitätsbibliothek Graz* (Vienna, 1956), pp. 280–1.

[126] See also Academia Caesarea Vindobonensis (eds.), *Tabulae Codicum Manu Scriptorum in Bibliotheca Palatina Vindobonensi Asservatorum*, 7 vols. (Vienna, 1864–75), i. 209.

[127] See also P. A. Hübl (ed.), *Catalogus Codicum Manu Scriptorum qui in Bibliotheca Monasterii B. M. V. ad Scotos Vindobonae servantur* (Vienna, 1899), pp. 17–19. Other copies of the letter are: Munich, Bayerisches Staatsbibliothek MSS 15911 (s.xii, prov. Salzburg, letter ascribed to Bernard) and 28195 (s.xiii in., fos. 47^{r}–48^{v}); Augsburg, *Staats- und Stadtbibliothek* MS 79 (s.xv mid., fol. 162^{r}); Erlangen-Nürnberg, *Universitätsbibliothek* MS 224 (s.xiii in.) and Vorau, *Stiftsbibliothek* MS 33—in every case associated with Bernard texts.

53.[128] These are the only two of all the letters exchanged between Peter and Nicholas which occur separately in both collections. Nicholas of Clairvaux's collection survives in an early printed edition and partially in two MSS.[129] Berlin MS Phillipps 1719 contains letters 2–42 of this collection, and Paris B.N. MS Lat. 3012, which is damaged at the beginning and end, letters 28–49 (missing the beginning of no. 28 and the end of no. 49). Thus neither of the letters which overlap with the Peter of Celle collection occur in extant MSS of Nicholas's collection. The printed edition, by Jean Picard, appeared in la Bigne's *Magna Bibliotheca*.[130] There are considerable variations between the versions of the two letters preserved by Picard and by Sirmond. Sirmond is closer to O (suggesting not surprisingly that Picard preserves recipient's copies of Peter's letters) and gives generally better readings, but given the state of the texts we cannot know the extent of editorial emendation in either case.[131]

[128] In both the *PL* edn. of Peter's letters and in Nicholas's collection (see below) the letters appear in the same sequence (and both also occur in O, as nos. 44 and 63). In Sirmond-R they are in the reverse order. *PL*'s sequence makes sense (see also letter no. 50, n. 1 and appendix 7). A third letter from Peter to Nicholas (no. 49 in this edn.) does not occur in Nicholas's collection. The letters from Nicholas to Peter which are printed in *PL* ccii formed no part of Peter's collection. *PL* merges the letters exchanged between the two, printing them in Peter's collection and providing only cross-references in Nicholas's collection (*PL* cxcvi. 1593–1654). Where the two collections overlap *PL* uses Sirmond's text (but does note one major variant, the alternative ending to letter no. 50, which is not in Sirmond); otherwise its texts of Nicholas's letters reproduce Picard (see below).

[129] I am grateful to Lena Wahlgren-Smith of Southampton for information on the manuscripts of the letter collection of Nicholas of Clairvaux. Her edition of the letters is in progress, and an article on the textual tradition is forthcoming. In the meantime, see Benton, *Culture*, pp. 7–9, 47 n. 5, 79 n. 5, 123.

[130] M. de la Bigne *et al.* (eds.), *Magna Bibliotheca Veterum Patrum et Antiquorum Scriptorum Ecclesiasticorum*, 15 vols. (Cologne, 1618–22), t. xii. I, pp. 645–77. It was reprinted in the expanded M. de la Bigne *et al.* and P. Despont (eds.), *Maxima Bibliotheca Veterum Patrum et Antiquorum Scriptorum Ecclesiasticorum*, 27 vols. (Lyons, 1677), xxi. 517–53, and reprinted with additions in *PL* cxcvi. 1593–1654. It was not part of la Bigne's original *Sacra Bibliotheca Sanctorum Patrum*, 8 vols. in 2 (Paris, 1575) and appendix vol. (Paris, 1579), the basis for the two later, larger collections which bear his name. Of the two letters in question, no. 50 (Picard no. 51) is la Bigne 1618, pp. 672–3, and la Bigne 1677, pp. 547–8; no. 51 (Picard no. 53) is la Bigne 1618, pp. 675–6 and la Bigne 1677, pp. 551–2.

[131] It might be possible to assume that agreement between either of the sender's copies (O or Sirmond) and Picard would point to the reading of a common archetype, i.e. the sent letter. However, leaving aside minor errors which could easily have arisen independently, the case is complicated by the fact that Sirmond knew Picard's text (as his own notes make clear), and in neither case do we have the MSS they worked from. Furthermore, while any reading in Sirmond could represent his intervention, it could equally reflect the lost MS R, and so a Saint-Remi text closer to the latest authorial version, which, in the context of a letter collection, would not in principle be preferable to what might or might not be the reading of a sent letter (on this point see also s. III below). Given the degree of uncertainty,

4. PRINTED EDITIONS

The first printed edition of Peter's letters, Sirmond, appeared in 1613 and again in 1696 and included the fifty-six letters of Alexander III to Peter and others.[132] It was reprinted in Janvier along with Peter's sermons and four treatises (*De panibus, De tabernaculo, De conscientia*, and *De disciplina claustrali*), again with the fifty-six letters of Alexander III.[133] *PL* reprints Janvier and so, as far as the letters are concerned, Sirmond, but with minor additions and considerable rearrangement.[134] The additions comprise four letters written by Peter[135] and eight addressed to him. These eight are all taken from the collection of Nicholas of Clairvaux.[136] The main rearrangement of contents in *PL* involved bringing the late letters into conformity with the early by arranging them by rank of recipient.

Of the seven letters unique to MS O, six were edited by Leclercq, along with the two letters in MSS M and Do.[137] All other printed copies of the letters of Peter of Celle are taken from Sirmond.[138] Of these, the earliest was la Bigne's *Magna Bibliotheca*, which included the whole text and the fifty-six letters of Alexander III and some of Peter's other works (*De panibus*, the two commentaries on the Tabernacle, and *De conscientia*).[139] In the expanded 1677 version of

it seems preferable, in the context of Peter of Celle's collection, to give the readings from the sender's side of the transmission and to record all variants.

[132] The first edn. is Sirmond; the later printing appears in *Jacobi Sirmondi Opera Varia*, 5 vols. (Paris, 1696; 2nd edn. Venice, 1728), iii. 659–850. On the fifty-six letters of Alexander III, see above II. 1. i.

[133] On Janvier see de Martel, 'Mabillon', p. 245.

[134] *PL* ccii. 405–636.

[135] Nos. 75, 136, 162, and 180 in this edn. (see II. 3 above).

[136] See above, II. 3. In *PL* ccii they are numbered XLIX–LII, LX, LXII–LXIII, and LXV, and in *PL* cxcvi (Nicholas's collection) the same letters are numbered XX, XXII, XXIV–XXV, XXVIII, XLVIII–XLIX, and LII (but here they are not printed, but cross-references are given to *PL* ccii).

[137] Leclercq, 'Nouvelles'; note also Messiter's edn. of O (see above, II. 1. ii) and Leclercq's comment on its unreliability at 'Nouvelles', p. 165 and n. 21.

[138] Most are listed in A. Potthast, *Bibliotheca Historica Medii Aevi: Wegweiser durch die Geschichtswerke des europäischen Mittelalters bis 1500*, 2 vols. (Berlin, 1896), ii. 912. The database *In Principio* (Brepols) gives some references, which are likewise ultimately from Sirmond. In addition, a few *acta* and judge-delegate decisions in Peter's name or joint name are included in the *Papsturkunden* series but do not form part of the letter collection: see Meinert, *Papsturkunden in Frankreich*, p. 295 (no. 113); D. Lohrmann, *Papsturkunden in Frankreich*, n.s. vii. *Nördliche Ile-de-France und Vermandois*, Abhandlungen der Akademie der Wissenschaften in Göttingen (Göttingen, 1976), p. 399 (no. 130), p. 437 (no. 156), p. 517 (no. 225).

[139] M. de la Bigne *et al.* (eds.), *Magna Bibliotheca Veterum Patrum et Antiquorum*

the same collection the Peter of Celle texts printed in the Cologne edition are replaced by a copy of Janvier. This makes no difference as far as the letters are concerned as both Janvier and the *Magna Bibliotheca* had reprinted Sirmond. The fifty-six letters of Alexander III are omitted.[140]

Janvier includes a preface written by Mabillon which was the object of some controversy at the time of publication. The preface as it was eventually published in Janvier's edition included a simple account of the different stages of Peter's career and a brief paragraph on each of his works. Mabillon's original version had a further seventeen sections discussing Peter's opinions and spiritual life illustrated largely with quotations from the letters. This included, for example, paragraphs headed 'Pietas', 'Amicitia', 'Sinceritas', etc. The fifteenth section concerned Peter's zeal for upholding the discipline of the Benedictine Order. Headed 'Zelus pro Ordine', it begins: 'Praecipue tamen zelum suum contra observationum monasticarum violatores exacuit exercuitque. Status monastici miserabilem statum luget, tum in libri 7 epistola 14 . . . tum in epistola 18. . . . Quae epistolae adeo vehementes sunt et justae indignationis plenae, adeo elegantes et graves, ut quid ex illis eligam, dubias pendeam.'[141] At the time of writing the preface Mabillon was already in dispute with the Maurists Dom Mège and Dom Bastide over the

Scriptorum Ecclesiasticorum, 15 vols. (Cologne, 1618–22), t. 12. II, pp. 544–634 (letters of Alexander III at pp. 634–92). This is an expansion of M. de la Bigne's original *Sacra Bibliotheca Sanctorum Patrum*, 8 vols. in 2 (Paris, 1575), and appendix vol. (Paris, 1579), which contained nothing of Peter of Celle. The Cologne edition can be confusing to reference as it comprises fourteen tomes distributed unevenly across fourteen volumes. The tome nos. correspond to the century of the works contained, while the vols. are of roughly equal length, thus vol. 1 comprises tomes 1–3 (works written in the 1st to 3rd cents. AD), vol. 2, t. 4 etc., while some centuries spill over into two vols. The sequence is as follows, giving tome nos., each vol. separated by semi-colons: 1–3; 4; 5. I; 5. II; 5. III; 6. I; 6. II; 7–8; 9. I; 9. II; 10–11; 12. I; 12. II; 13–14 (a 15th vol. was produced in 1622 comprising various additions to the collection, and not 15th-cent. works). Thus Peter of Celle's letters are t. 12. II, which is vol. 13.

[140] M. de la Bigne *et al.* and P. Despont (eds.), *Maxima Bibliotheca Veterum Patrum et Antiquorum Scriptorum Ecclesiasticorum*, 27 vols. (Lyons, 1677), xxiii. 636–907, letters at pp. 824–907. In the earlier *Magna Bibliotheca* the other works of Peter were taken from an edn. of Le Fevre de la Boderie (see the ref. at J. A. Fabricius, *Bibliotheca Ecclesiastica*, 6 vols. [Hamburg, 1718; facsimile Farnborough, 1967], vi. 64), but this has no bearing on the letters.

[141] From the edition of the original preface in de Martel, 'Mabillon', p. 262. Quotations from the letters follow. The numbers given are those of Sirmond's edition (nos. 156 and 90 in this edn.), addressed, respectively, to the community of Molesme and to Peter of Pavia.

Acta Sanctorum O. S. B. from which he had omitted a number of saints traditionally accepted by the order. Taking the opportunity to further their dispute with Mabillon, his opponents complained that this particular section needlessly exposed their internal weaknesses at a time when the order needed to display its unity, and could only give ammunition to their enemies. Mabillon's response, which he explained in a letter to Dom Claude Martin, was to declare that if he were not allowed to write freely and give the truth as he saw it, he would publish nothing but the bare details of Peter's life and works. This is what now stands in Janvier and *PL*.[142]

III. THIS EDITION

Sirmond represents R, the version of the text closest to the latest authorial recension, but O, Val, and R all stand equally in the stemma as far as it can be reconstructed, so better readings from O and Val have been adopted where appropriate and all variants recorded.[143] While O and Val seem to have been taken from earlier recensions of the common archetype, they are earlier recensions of a sender's collection and cannot be assumed in principle to be closer to the individual missives actually sent, which are technically a lost source.[144] For letters based on recipients' archives or other collec-

[142] The whole affair is related in de Martel, 'Mabillon', which includes an edition of the unpublished sections of the preface, based on Paris B. N. MS Lat. 12694, fos. 31^r–42^v. Mabillon's letter to Martin, along with an explanation of the *Acta Sanctorum O. S. B.* controversy, can be found in L. Delisle, 'Dom Jean Mabillon, sa probité d'historien', *Mélanges et documents publiés à l'occasion du 2e centenaire de la mort de Mabillon*, *Archives de la France Monastique*, v (1908), 91–104. The preface in the form in which it appeared in Janvier is reprinted in *PL* ccii. 399–402.

[143] While there is no way of knowing the nature of his intervention, Sirmond is still the only witness to the latest authorial recension of the collection (and the only witness for most of the later letters). In all likelihood fewer hands intervened between the compilation of R at Saint-Remi and Sirmond's transcription of it than in the untraceable processes of copying and rearrangement which led to the eventual production of the extant MSS. This edition does not record excerptions and selections derived from Sirmond.

[144] See above II. 1. iv. While earlier recensions of the collection *may* be closer to the versions of the letters sent, they are not in any way an archive of sent letters and to prefer them on the principle of recreating lost correspondence rather than collected letters would be to make false assumptions about the nature of the text. To attempt the re-creation of a non-existent source from a different type of text is a valid historical enterprise but one of a different nature from editing a surviving text (see also Haseldine, 'Literary memorial', pp. 358–60, 373–9, but NB the table at p. 377 [table 3] is misprinted, all the lines running diagonally downwards from left to right having been omitted by the printers. There should be three of these as follows: one running from the words 'letters sent' to the box

tions, see above II. 2–3 and the apparatus. Conjectural emendations not my own are acknowledged in the apparatus. Where the apparatus indicates no other source or origin for a reading, the reading is editorial conjecture. Angle brackets indicate editorial insertion.

The salutations are from Sirmond and concur with those in Val as far as identification of recipients is concerned. The problems with the salutations in O are discussed above, at II. 1. ii. Identifications of individual recipients are discussed in the notes. The headings are my own, and based on these identifications.

Orthography is based on the most common usages in MS O, the longest extant MS.[145] The text has been punctuated on modern principles according to OMT practice, and some of the longest letters have been divided into paragraphs for ease of reading.

The order of the letters is a medieval not a modern one, and reflects the basic principle of organization evident behind Rc, i.e. by rank of recipient. Anomalies have been corrected and the same order applied to the late letters. Letters not in Sirmond-R have been incorporated into this order, not reduced to addenda. (However, it is important to note that these are not part of the sender's collection, and are included in the order purely for convenience. They are marked * in the headings.) This order is evidently the one envisaged by the author (or by those at Saint-Remi responsible for organizing the collection), and is closely related to that adopted in the extant MSS. It thus most closely reflects the author's intention for the appearance of the collection. A chronological arrangement (which is not found in the MSS) would be vague as many letters are not closely datable. Within groups of letters to the same recipient, a chronological order has been adopted for convenience where possible.[146]

Biblical quotations are from the Douai-Reims translation, according to OMT practice. Verbatim quotation from the Vulgate is indicated by quotation marks. In the far more frequent cases where

'recipients' archives'; the second from the box 'early letters' to the words 'copied into lost ms'; and the third from the box 'late letters' also to the words 'copied into lost ms').

145 MS O is not consistent, and with rarer words where there is no clear majority practice, or with those almost always found in abbreviated form, I have adopted the more familiar forms, or those consistent with practice in similar words in the same text.

146 See above II. 1. iv. To keep the exact order of Sirmond–R would mean reducing other letters (most importantly those unique to O but still based on a sender's archive) to addenda. Applying this order to the late letters, where no other principle of organization is apparent, has the advantage of consistency. The few letters to lay recipients mostly fall outside Rc, O, and Val, with the exception of one to the count of Troyes, which is included among those to the abbots in Rc. They are kept separate here.

Peter adapts, alludes to or deliberately echoes the Vulgate text, or where a chosen term seems to signal a reference, Douai-Reims language and vocabulary have been incorporated into the translation where appropriate. Where I have quoted from or adapted a printed translation of a quotation this is recorded in the notes; otherwise translations of quotations or near quotations are my own. The aim of the translation has been to provide as close a guide to the Latin as the sense in English will bear rather than to impose an imagined modern English version of twelfth-century epistolary style.[147] The annotation refers to quotations, near quotations, and those allusions or less direct references where the sense depends to some extent on knowledge of the text alluded to, or where the choice of a particular term in context seems to carry a specific meaning. The intention is to identify the most direct borrowings and to aid understanding of the sense of passages where the meaning depends on the allusion.[148] This volume brings together all the known letters of Peter of Celle for the first time, and is the first attempt at a complete edition in nearly 400 years. It will, I hope, prove a help in further research into this complex and fascinating character.

[147] Quotations and allusions are at times adapted to contexts where their original meaning is deliberately changed for effect; at others a precise word or phrase is selected to signal a very specific meaning, and here the Douai-Reims vocabulary, while often archaic, can serve to alert a modern reader to such a reference. It is also too easy to assume a greater standardization of the Vulgate text than was the case, but the use of inverted commas here does have the advantage of similarly replicating for modern readers something of the experience of the medieval reader, by calling attention to very familiar quotations and allusions. More generally, English of the later 20th cent. is not a rhetorical idiom—indeed it is the language of a culture which regards rhetoric less as an art form or educational cornerstone (as it had been regarded for centuries) than as a species of deception. Neither an archaic English rhetoric nor a casual or naturalistic modern prose would reflect Peter's tone and style.

[148] To record every allusion, especially the biblical ones, in an author who, in common with many of his contemporaries, had so appropriated the language of the Vulgate, would necessitate a full-scale commentary running in places to more than a footnote on each line and hampering the flow of the text. A complex pastiche of biblical imagery and vocabulary was simply integral to the style of the genre; I have not noted every echo of common biblical and other imagery and piece of vocabulary, but have tried to identify as many as possible of the more direct and significant allusions.

SIGLA OF MANUSCRIPTS CITED

A1	Lisbon, Biblioteca Nacional, Codices Alcobacences MS LXXVIII/154
A2	Lisbon, Biblioteca Nacional, Codices Alcobacences MS XXVIII/180
Ad1	Admont, Stiftsbibliothek MS 446
Ad2	Admont, Stiftsbibliothek MS 451
AlanT (A)	London, British Library MS Cotton Claudius B. ii
AlanT (B)	Vatican MS Latin 1220
AlanT (C)	Cambridge, Corpus Christi College MS 295
Bodl.B	Oxford, Bodleian MS Bodley 937
Di	Dijon, Bibliothèque Municipale MS 189
Do	Douai, Bibliothèque Municipale MS 827
G	Graz, Universitätsbibliothek MS 1287
Lamb	London, Lambeth Palace MS 136
M	Metz, Bibliothèque Municipale MS 1168
O	Oxford, St John's College MS 126
Q	Paris, Bibliothèque Nationale MS Latin 8562
R	the lost Saint-Remi MS; see Introduction, II. 1. i
Val	Valenciennes, Bibliothèque Municipale MS 482
Vat	Vatican MS Latin 6024
Vat Reg	Vatican MS Reg. Lat. 179
Vi	Vienna, Nationalbibliothek MS 1255
VS	Vienna, Schottenkloster MS 28
Z	Zwettl, Zisterzienserstift MS 187

TEXT AND TRANSLATION

BOOK ONE
THE EARLY LETTERS
(nos. 1–74)

I

To Pope Eugenius III[1]

15 Feb. 1145 × 1147

Domino et patri Dei gratia summo pontifici Eugenio humilis conuentus sancti Meuenni, humilem cum omni subiectione salutem.

Ad sinum uestre pietatis qui debita humilitate recurrit, non solum materne lenitatis blandimenta sed et paterne sollicitudinis solet inuenire indubia tutamina. In manu namque uestra est post Deum pax omnium simul ecclesiarum et nostra. Vestram itaque, pater piissime, rogamus adesse beneuolentiam paupercule ecclesie nostre, et ne longiori tempestate conuellatur, diuinitus indulta auctoritate uentis et mari silentium placeat uobis maturius imperare.[2] Vt itaque uehementius et celerius uestra erga nos moueatur clementia, nostra breuiter noua et antiqua intimamus pericula. Religionis disciplina et feruor monachici ordinis, tam nostra quam abbatis negligentia, olim in ecclesia nostra in unum intepuerat. Zelo itaque zelatus pro domo Dei Israhel,[3] sanctissime memorie Lucius predecessor uester mandauit humilitati nostre, et uenerabili episcopo nostro Iohanni,[4] studiosius ordinem reformare, disciplinam renouare, et insolitam tumultuationem resecare. Eius itaque nos tam precepto quam grata exhortatione ad obediendum inclinati, ut uerum fateamur, ad radicem arboris securim extendimus;[5] et abbatem negligentem excidi uoluimus ut uigilantiorem reciperemus.[6] Sic, domine et uenerande pater, fuerat nisi totius malignitatis repertor Satanas rursus aduersaretur[7] et nisi domini archiepiscopi Turonensis facies et sententia iusta circa hoc negotium peruerse mutaretur.[8] Namque electionem nostram prius laudauit et uestra auctoritate confirmauit, quorumdam uero malignantium postea ductus, ne dicamus seductus, machinationibus, nulla rationabili existente causa, aggrauauit erga

1 *Sirmond I. 6*]

1 [1] Written in the name of the community of Saint-Méen-de-Gaël (Brittany) concerning a disputed election. On this case and the date of this letter, see appendix 1.

[2] Cf. Matt. 8: 24–7; Mark 4: 37–40; Luke 8: 23–5.

[3] Cf. 3 Kgs. (1 Kgs.) 19: 10, 14.

[4] Bishop John of Saint-Malo, 1144–1 Nov. 1163 (see letter no. 14, n. 1).

I

To Pope Eugenius III[1]

15 Feb. 1145 × 1147

To their lord and father Eugenius, by the grace of God supreme pontiff, the humble community of Saint-Méen, humble greetings with all obedience.

He who runs back to the bosom of your mercy with due humility is accustomed to find not only the comforts of motherly tenderness but also the sure defences of fatherly concern. For the peace of all the churches at once, ours included, is in your hands after God's. We ask therefore, most loving father, that your good offices protect our poor little church, and, lest it be tossed about by a protracted storm, may it please you to command with all speed by divinely granted authority that the wind and the sea be calm.[2] And so that your mercy may be moved more powerfully and more quickly on our behalf, we briefly confide our trials, present and past. Long since, both through our own neglect and the abbot's, religious discipline and the fervour of the monastic order in our church had cooled together. Fired therefore with zeal for the house of the God of Israel,[3] your predecessor Lucius, of most blessed memory, ordered us in our humility, and our venerable bishop John,[4] to reform the order more assiduously, to renew discipline and to put a stop to the unwonted disorder. We therefore, inclined to obedience both by his command and by his welcome exhortation, if truth be told, aimed the axe at the root of the tree;[5] and we wanted the negligent abbot driven out so that we might receive one more vigilant.[6] So, lord and venerable father, would it have been had not Satan, the instigator of all evil, stood up again to be an adversary,[7] and had not the just attitude and judgement of the lord archbishop of Tours on this affair been perversely changed.[8] For at first he approved our election and confirmed it by your authority, but later, led on, not to say led astray, by the contrivances of certain evil people, though there was no reasonable cause, he made heavy his

[5] Cf. Matt. 3: 10; Luke 3: 9.
[6] i.e. the abbots Henry and Robert respectively (see appendix 1).
[7] Cf. Zech. 3: 1.
[8] Archbishop Hugh of Tours, 1133–47 (see appendix 1).

nos et pastorem nostrum consilium suum, uolens et consulens illi gregem dimittere sibi commissum.[9] Grauamen itaque iniuste sibi imminens abbas dum attendit, uestram recte audientiam appellauit. Post hanc autem appellationem, quidam de familia archiepiscopi et de mensa eius insecuti et persecuti sunt abbatem nostrum ita ut unum de monachis, unum de clericis suis cum equis et quibusdam caperent et turpiter tractarent. Eapropter uestram efflagitamus, pater et pastor uniuersalis ecclesie, gratiam ut oculo pietatis nostram attendatis miseriam et causam nostram sinatis, immo precipiatis tractari non in archiepiscopi curia sed in qua ex equo nostra audiatur et eius iustitia, seu iniustitia. Excuset autem abbatem nostrum quod nequaquam uobis se presentauerit tam illata iniuria quam corporis grauis infirmitas.

2

? To Pope Alexander III[1]

? July 1153 × 1162 (poss. end of July 1160 × 1162)

[a]Domino suo et patri A. summo pontifici frater Petrus humilis abbas Cellensis, debitam subiectionem filii et deuotionem.[a]

Cui preter sinus paternos alia non suppetunt refugia, instantius eadem requirit in necessitate suffragia. Ad uos, pater sanctissime, a multis que circumdant nos tribulationibus[2] [b]et principum nostrorum[b] oppressionibus merito confugimus, cuius studio et sollicitudini regendam ecclesiam suam in mundi fluctuationibus commisit Christus. Iam enim perimus nisi respexerit naufragia[c] nostra benignus Deus.[3] Iustitia, ratio, ueritas, lex et equitas de die in diem a [d]finibus nostris[d] exterminantur et earum memoria absque modo et misericordia extinguitur. [e]Super his itaque et pro his respiciat in nos

2 *O fo. 139^r^, Sirmond I. 2*]

[a–a] Domino suo et patri Alexandro . . . deuotionem *Sirmond;* Domino et patri karissimo A. uniuersalis ecclesie summo pontifici filius suus frater G. suus semper debitam subiectionem filii cum deuotione *O* [b–b] *om. O* [c] *om. O* [d–d] nostris finibus *Sirmond* [e–e] Proinde respiciat, quesumus, super nos misericordia uestra, ut uiuere possit anima nostra. Vale. *Sirmond*

[9] Cf. *Regula S. Benedicti*, c. ii.

2 [1] In Sirmond this letter is addressed to Alexander III (7 Sept. 1159–30 Aug. 1181). However other letters in the collection similarly addressed cannot have been written during

counsel against us and against our pastor, wishing and advising him to let go the flock committed to him.[9] The abbot therefore, while he awaited the heavy blow unjustly hanging over him, rightly appealed to your jurisdiction. After this appeal, however, certain members of the archbishop's household and of his company pursued and harried our abbot to the point of seizing and treating shamefully one of his monks and one of his clerics, along with their horses and certain chattels. On this account, father and pastor of the universal Church, we earnestly entreat Your Grace to look upon our affliction with the eye of mercy and to grant our case, nay, to order that it be dealt with not in the archbishop's court but in one where both our justice and his justice, or rather injustice, may be heard on an equal footing. May both the injury inflicted on him and his grave bodily infirmity excuse our abbot for not presenting himself in person before you.

2

? To Pope Alexander III[1]

? July 1153 × 1162 (poss. end of July 1160 × 1162)

To his lord and father A., supreme pontiff, brother Peter, humble abbot of Montier-la-Celle, the obedience and devotion owed by a son.

He to whom other refuges are not available save the paternal bosom seeks out that support the more urgently in times of pressing need. To you, most holy father, to whose devotion and care Christ committed the task of directing His Church amid the fluctuations of the world, we rightly flee from the many troubles which surround us[2] and from the oppressions of our princes. For now we perish unless God look with a kindly eye upon our shipwreck.[3] Justice, reason, truth, law and equity are day by day driven out of our land, and the memory of them is extinguished without measure or mercy. Concerning these things therefore and because of these things let

Alexander's pontificate (see letters 3 and 5 below). This suggests that the name Alexander in Sirmond is the expansion of an abbreviation which could refer equally to Popes Anastasius IV (12 July 1153–3 Dec. 1154) or Hadrian IV (4 Dec. 1154–1 Sept. 1159). If the letter was addressed to Alexander, then this would presumably have been after his recognition in France at the end of July 1160 (see letter no. 22, n. 1). Eugenius III is not impossible, but *HLF*'s argument (xiv, p. 243) that letters 2–6 were all to him is based only on their order in R and so without real foundation (and in any case almost certainly impossible for no. 4).

[2] Cf. Ps. 31 (32): 7.

[3] Possibly alluding to Matt. 8: 25; Mark 4: 38; Luke 8: 24.

misericordia uestra et prouideat ut uiuere possit anima nostra.[4] Fratres isti fidelissimi relatores sunt nostrarum necessitatum. Hos benigne suscipiatis et in suis petitionibus clementer exaudiatis. Valeat sanctitas uestra.[e]

3

To Pope Anastasius IV or Pope Hadrian IV[1]

late 1153 × 1155/6

Domino et patri karissimo A.[a] uniuersalis ecclesie summo pontifici filius suus Petrus Cellensis indignus abbas, cum omni dilectione obedientiam ⟨et⟩[b] uoluntariam subiectionem.

De multa bonitate uestra plurimum confidens, etiam pro negotiis aliorum uobis aliquando scripsi. Nunc uero in propriis uestrum, pater sanctissime, cogor expetere pium auxilium. Est autem huiusmodi pro necessitatibus ecclesie nostre negotium: habemus prioratum apud Cantumerulam in cuius cemeterio ius sepeliendi omnes qui de castello[2] sunt, et de quibusdam aliis uillis, hactenus dignoscuntur habuisse. Constat etenim[c] antiquitus non fuisse cemeterium in castello dum ibi essent canonici seculares. Cum autem successissent regulares ab antecessore nostro impetratum est, interuenientibus comite Theobaldo et Hatone episcopo Trecensi,[3] quatinus ibi fieret cemeterium tantummodo ad sepulturam canonicorum et conuersorum suorum.[4] Abbas autem cum canonicis suis contra pactum ueniens, illos etiam qui tam iure quam pacto in cemeterio nostro sepeliri debuissent sepeliuit. Cum de his utrinque altercatum in curia

3 *Sirmond I. 4*]
[a] Alexandro *Sirmond* [b] *suppl. Hall* [c] etiam *Sirmond*

[4] Cf. Ps. 68 (69): 33.

3 [1] The addressee could be either Pope Anastasius IV (July 12 1153–3 Dec. 1154) or Pope Hadrian IV (4 Dec. 1154–1 Sept. 1159); on this case see appendix 2.

[2] See Niermeyer, *castellum*; for *castellum* meaning town, and the interchangeable use of *castrum* and *castellum* for fortified town and castle; see also J. F. Verbruggen, 'Note sur le sens des mots *castrum*, *castellum*, et quelques autres expressions qui désignent des fortifications', *Revue belge de philologie et d'histoire*, xxviii (1950), 147–55 (cf. also letter no. 132, and n. 2). The priory at (*apud*) Chantmerle (La Celle-sous-Chantmerle) is not inside the town.

your mercy look upon us and ensure that our soul can live.[4] These brothers are most trustworthy bearers of our pressing business. May you receive them kindly and hear them indulgently in their petitions. May Your Holiness fare well.

3

To Pope Anastasius IV or Pope Hadrian IV[1]

late 1153 × 1155/6

To his dearest lord and father A., supreme pontiff of the universal Church, his son Peter, unworthy abbot of Montier-la-Celle, obedience and willing subjection with all love.

Trusting completely in your great benevolence, I have written to you on occasion concerning even the affairs of others. Now however, most holy father, I am forced to seek your kindly aid in my own affairs. The matter bearing on the urgent needs of our church is of this kind: we have a priory at Chantemerle and in its cemetery all who come from the town,[2] and those from certain other townships, are known until now to have had the right to be buried. For the fact is that in former times there was no cemetery in the town while the canons there were secular. When, however, the regulars had succeeded it was requested by our predecessor, and granted, with the intervention of Count Theobald and Bishop Hato of Troyes,[3] that there should be a cemetery there solely for the burial of the canons and their lay brothers.[4] The abbot, however, acting with his canons against the agreement, has buried even those who by right as much as by the agreement ought to have been buried in our cemetery. When both sides had debated these matters in the court at Troyes and the

[3] Count Theobald II of Champagne and IV of Blois, count of Champagne 1125–10 Jan. 1152 (Arbois de Jubainville, *Comtes de Champagne*, ii. 267, 275–6, 398, and see *Lexikon des Mittelalters* viii. 519–20 and the genealogies in Dunbabin, *France in the Making*, p. 390 and Bur, *Champagne*, p. 308). Bishop Hato of Troyes, 1122–1145/6 (*P. Ven. Epp.* ii. 97–8). The original grant of a cemetery to the canons must thus have been 1125 × 1145/6 (see appendix 2). The count at the time of the present letter must have been Henry the Liberal (1152–81, see letter no. 71, n. 1). Peter's predecessors at Montier-la-Celle were Ralph (occurs between 1104 and 1117) and Walter (occurs between 1132 and 1139); on both, see *GC* xii. 543.

[4] But see G. Constable, *The Reformation of the Twelfth Century* (Cambridge, 1996), pp. 77–9, on the changing use of the term *conuersus* in this period.

Trecensi et ad iudicium uentum esset appellauit abbas.[5] Pro huiusmodi, pater dulcissime, benignitatem uestram obsecramus, supplicantes ut et nuntium nostrum benigne suscipiatis et petitiones nostras efficaciter exaudiatis.

4

To Pope Anastasius IV or Pope Hadrian IV[1]

1154 × 1156

[a]Venerando patri et domino Dei gratia uniuersalis ecclesie summo pontifici frater Petrus Celle sancti Petri Trecensis humilis abbas,[a] quicquid potest.

Qui nostram humilitatem alicuius momenti apud sublimitatem uestram reputant, utinam spei sue fructum in effectu precum suarum inueniant. Hinc enim et uestra benignior apparebit dignatio, et nostra confortabitur de uobis gloriatio, et amicorum pro impetratis gratiosior erit exultatio. Amici nostri, immo ueritatis[2] et honestatis, sunt isti: R. archidiaconus et magister H.[3] qui pro prepositura Suessionensis ecclesie [b]domino Guillelmo[b] concedenda pietatem et prouidentiam uestram adeunt.[4] Guillelmus uero iste quam de magno

4 *O fos. 139*^{v}*–140*^{r}*, Sirmond I. 5*]
[a–a] Eidem idem *O* [b–b] domino G. *O;* D. Guillelmo *Sirmond*

[5] Presumably the episcopal court, given the nature of the case. The bishop would have been Henry, *c.*1145–*c.*1169 (see *GC* xii. 500–1; Pacaut, *Élections*, p. 141 n. 3).

4 [1] An appeal for the appointment of William aux Blanches Mains (see n. 4 below) to the provostship of Soissons. William is said to have been provost of Soissons in the 1150s (*GC* ix. 384, which gives no dates, but his predecessor left the post in 1152, and a successor occurs from 1156). This letter must have been written after 1154 since it refers to William's brother, Theobald V of Blois, as seneschal to Louis VII, 'dapifer regis' (see Arbois de Jubainville, *Comtes de Champagne*, iii. 96–9). The problem was almost certainly William's age. In 1151 Bernard of Clairvaux had written to William's father, Count Theobald II of Champagne and IV of Blois (1125–52, see letter no. 3, n. 3), warning that the boy was too young to receive ecclesiastical preferments (see *S. Bernardi Op.* viii, pp. 181–2, no. 271). He nevertheless held a number of preferments when young (*GC* viii. 1145). If indeed he received the provostship he can only have held it briefly. In 1165 he required a papal dispensation to assume the see of Chartres because he was neither of canonical age nor in major orders (see Pacaut, *Élections*, p. 50).

[2] Cf. Cicero, *De officiis*, i. 19. 63.

[3] Archdeacon R. is most probably Ralph (occurs 1139 × 1154), who also occurs as provost himself 1156 × 1157 (Newman, *Seigneurs de Nesle*, i. 110 and 115, n. 12; see also *GC* ix. 384, which gives his death as Dec. 1157). He would seem to have helped William to

matter had come to judgement the abbot appealed.[5] Therefore, dearest father, we beg your indulgence, asking that you receive our messenger kindly and that you hear our petitions to good effect.

4

To Pope Anastasius IV or Pope Hadrian IV[1]

1154 × 1156

To his venerable father and lord, by the grace of God supreme pontiff of the universal Church, brother Peter, humble abbot of La Celle de Saint-Pierre, Troyes, all that he is able to do.

I would that those who reckon that our humility is of some account with Your Sublimity may find the fruit of their hope in the effect of their prayers. For from this your condescension will appear more benign and our glorying in you will be strengthened, and the rejoicing of our friends will be the more delightful for what has been attained. Our friends, nay the friends of truth[2] and honesty, are these: archdeacon R. and master H.,[3] who approach your piety and providence to ask that the provostship of the church of Soissons be given to Lord William.[4] I would explain from how great, or rather how good, a

the post as indicated in the present letter, only to have secured it for himself shortly after. Ralph himself was succeeded as provost, evidently quite promptly, by another archdeacon of Soissons, Nivelon, who occurs as provost 1158 × 1170 (Newman, *Seigneurs de Nesle*, i. 110 and 115 n. 10), so William's provostship cannot really be fitted in after Ralph's death. Another possibility for Archdeacon R. is Roger de Porte Chacre, who succeeded to the same archdeaconry as Ralph, and occurs 1157 × 1172 (Newman, *Seigneurs de Nesle*, i. 110 and 116 n. 16). It is possible that either Ralph or Roger was archdeacon between 1154 and 1156. Master H. is unidentified, but may be linked to John of Salisbury (see n. 10 below).

[4] William aux Blanches Mains, brother of Count Henry the Liberal of Champagne, bishop-elect of Chartres 1165–7, consecrated 22 Dec. 1167 and appointed archbishop of Sens in spring 1168; held both sees until 1176; el. archbishop of Reims 13 Nov. 1175 × 25 Mar. 1176, probably occupied the see from 1176 (25 April x 8 Aug.) and was certainly enthroned by 16 Sept. 1176; simultaneously Cardinal Priest of S. Sabina from Mar. 1179; d. 7/9 Sept. 1202 (for his dates at Chartres and Sens see *J. S Epp.* ii. 567 n. 28; for his dates at Reims see Newman, *Seigneurs de Nesle*, i. 117, and see also letter no. 102, n. 1; for a detailed account of his activities and movements after 1179 and of his relations with the papacy, and for the date of his death, see Ganzer, *Entwicklung*, 125–9; see also *GC* viii. 1144–6 [Chartres], xii. 50–3 [Sens] and ix. 95–101 [Reims], *Lexikon des Mittelalters*, ix. 158–9, and Pacaut, *Élections*, 50, 87). William's contribution to learning is discussed in J. R. Williams, 'William of the White Hands and Men of Letters', in C. H. Taylor (ed.), *Anniversary Essays in Medieval History by students of Charles Homer Haskins* (Boston, 1929), pp. 365–87, which relies for dates mainly on J. Mathorez, *Guillaume aux Blanches Mains* (Chartres, 1912).

genere, immo quam de bono, sit uel cuius filius fuerit exprimerem nisi uirtutes et probitatem patris eius in omni genere uirtutum adhuc in curia Romana spirare sperassem. Certe quod optabilius est nec ramusculus ipse a radicis pinguedine paterne[c] degenerat. Talem itaque suscitare in ecclesia Dei cum omnino expediat, quia multi insurgunt aduersus eum[d] dicentes, 'Non est salus ipsi in Deo eius,'[5] non respuat[e] dextera[f] Dei et beati[g] Petri et uestra, quia faciet 'fructum iuxta genus suum'[6] quod omni obsequio et obedientia semper obtemperauit[h] preceptis curie Romane et summorum pontificum. Habet autem et duo brachia preclara et fortissima quibus poterit releuare incuruantem et debellare[i] refrenantem,[7] quibusque umbraculum Dei protegat 'a turbine et a pluuia'.[8] [j]Comes Henricus et comes siue dapifer regis Theobaldus,[j] hi fratres eius sunt[9] et erunt ei in omni [k]auxilio et consilio.[k] Valete. Magister H., uir apud nos probate honestatis, magistrum Io.[l] clericum nostrum[m] et amicum nostrum docuit et multa bona ei fecit.[10] Hunc uobis attentissime commendamus.

5

? To Pope Hadrian IV[1]

4 Dec. 1154 × 21 May 1155

Domino et patri karissimo A.[a] summo pontifici frater [b]Petrus Cellensium fratrum minus idoneus abbas,[b] se ipsum cum deuotione.

Vbi cause postulande [c]perorare per se sufficit[c] prerogatiua, solet rogantis etiam minus idonea recipi persona, supplet namque dignitas

[c] *om. O* [d] eam, *O, Simond* [e] respuit *O* [f] clementia *O* [g] B. *Sirmond* [h] obtemperauerit *Sirmond* [i] rebellare *Sirmond* [j–j] Comes H. et comes T. *O* [k–k] consilio et auxilio *O* [l] I. *Sirmond* [m] uestrum *O*

5 *O fo. 139*[r–v], *Sirmond I. 3*]
[a] Alexandro *Sirmond* [b–b] G. humilis Christi sacerdos *O* [c–c] per se sufficit perorare *O*

[5] Cf. Ps. 3 (3): 2–3. i.e. the opposition to him proves his worthiness (he is likened to David); the *eam* must be intruded from Ps. 3 (3): 3: 'multi dicunt animae meae: non est salus . . .'—but here the object must be masculine.

[6] Gen. 1: 11; given the context and William's age, the subject of what follows must be *genus*, i.e. his ancestors and family.

[7] Cf. Isa. 9: 14; 19: 15.

[8] Isa. 4: 6 (*umbraculum* appears in various contexts in Isaiah, cf. also Isa. 1: 8; 25: 4).

[9] Count Henry the Liberal of Champagne (1152–81, see letter no. 71, n. 1) and Count

lineage this William is and whose son he is, save that I would hope that his father's virtues and reputation for every kind of virtue were still alive in the Roman Curia. And, what is certainly more desirable, this little branch does not fall short of the richness of the paternal root. Since therefore it is altogether expedient that such a one be elevated in the Church of God, for many rise up against him saying, 'There is no salvation for him in his God,'[5] let not the right hand of God, of St Peter and of you reject him, for he shall yield 'fruit after his kind,'[6] who have always obeyed the injunctions of the Roman Curia and of the supreme pontiffs with all compliance and obedience. Moreover he also has two arms, magnificent and most powerful, with which he will be able to raise up him that bends down and to defeat him that holds back[7] and with which he may protect the covert of God 'from the whirlwind and from rain'.[8] Count Henry and Count Theobald the king's steward, these are his brothers and shall be a help and a counsel to him in all things.[9] Farewell. Master H., a man of proven worth among us, taught master Jo., our cleric and our friend, and did many good things for him.[10] We most eagerly commend him to you.

5

? To Pope Hadrian IV[1]

4 Dec. 1154 × 21 May 1155

To his dearest lord and father A., supreme pontiff, brother Peter, least worthy abbot of the brothers of Montier-la-Celle, himself with devotion.

Where the special claim of the case to be put is enough to carry the matter by itself, even the least worthy person making the request is

Theobald V, le Bon, of Blois (1152–91, *Art de vérifier les dates* ii. 618–21; *Dictionnaire de biographie française* vi. 686). See the genealogies in Dunbabin, *France in the Making*, p. 390, and Bur, *Champagne*, p. 308.

[10] Master H. is unidentified; 'Io.' is possibly a reference to John of Salisbury. Elsewhere Peter refers to John as 'quondam clericus noster' (letter no. 97) and addresses him as 'suo clerico' (letters 65 and 170) and 'magistro suo' (letter no. 70)—see also *J. S. Epp.* i, p. xvii—but of course this is far from certain, and Io. may not even be a contraction of Iohannes.

5 [1] The addressee was most probably Pope Hadrian IV, but Anastasius IV is possible. The abbess of Fontevrault is Matilda of Anjou (1149, after Apr.–21 May 1155) and the bishop of Poitiers Calot (1155–1157/8) or possibly his predecessor Gilbert de la Porrée (1141/2–26 Nov. 1154). On the date of this letter, these identifications, and this dispute, see appendix 3.

petitionis insufficientiam[d] postulantis. Predecessorum uestrorum priuilegiis et beneficiis abbatiam Fontis Ebraldi sublimatam et communitam ubique diuulgatum et notum est in partibus nostris. Episcopus autem Pictauensis, cum rigare debuisset et fauere plantationi dextere Dei[2] et uestre, nititur libertatem huius ecclesie diminuere et contra priuilegium consuetum abbatissam cogit professionem sibi et obedientiam promittere quam sibi sedes Petri retinuit. Gloriam itaque uestram alteri non detis,[3] sed omni remoto mediatore, propria benedictione et protectione et abbatissam et abbatiam ut dignum est foueatis.

6

? To Pope Alexander III[1]

? end of July 1160 × 21 Sept. 1161 (or later)

[a]Domino suo Alexandro Dei gratia summo pontifici, G.[a]

In grauissimis questionibus sicut olim ad Moysen sic nunc, pater uenerande, ab omni ecclesia Dei recurritur ad beati Petri et uestram sedem. Tam enim communiter communis imponitur uobis 'sollicitudo omnium ecclesiarum'[2] quam singulariter et specialiter Petro [b]dictum uidetur,[b] 'Et tu conuersus confirma fratres tuos.'[3] Vt tamen compendium de prolixo negotio [c]in auribus uestris[c] faciam, ecclesia nostra Deruensis [d]immo uestra[d] de manu potentis G. non liberabitur nisi per manum omnipotentis Dei, nisi in arcu uestro et brachio extento.[4] Clamat itaque[e] de angustia et afflictione sua ad uos quia salus eius in manu Dei et uestra est. Non enim[f] respicit ad adiutorium hominum,[5] quorum uana spes, promissio cassa, nulla confidentia; uobis autem sine dubio et sermo potens ad liberandum et uirtus sufficiens ad redimendum. In umbra itaque uestra aut est ei uiuendum aut sub umbra mortis,[6] uidelicet G., deficiendum. 'Dic

[d] insufficiantiam *O* [*sic*]

6 *O fo. 139*^{v}, *Sirmond I. 1*]
[a–a] Domino suo A. Dei gratia summo pontifici frater G. semper suus *O* [b–b] uidetur dictum *Sirmond* [c–c] uobis *Sirmond* [d–d] *om. Sirmond* [e] utique *O* [f] enim tam *O*

[2] Alluding to Isa. 61: 3. [3] Cf. Isa. 42: 8; 48: 11.

accustomed to be received, for the worthiness of the petition makes up for the inadequacy of the petitioner. It is common knowledge everywhere in our region that the abbey of Fontevrault is sustained and fortified by the privileges and benefices of your predecessors. Yet the bishop of Poitiers, when he ought to have watered and tended the plantation of God's right hand[2] and yours, strives to diminish the liberty of this church and, contrary to the accustomed privilege, is forcing the abbess to offer to him the profession and the obedience which the see of Peter has reserved to itself. So do not give up your glory to another;[3] rather with every intermediary removed, support both the abbess and the abbey, as is right, with your own blessing and protection.

6

? To Pope Alexander III[1]

? end of July 1160 × 21 Sept. 1161 (or later)

To his lord Alexander, by the grace of God supreme pontiff, G.

In the most serious cases, venerable father, the whole Church of God has recourse to the see of the blessed Peter, which is now yours, as it once had to Moses. For the general 'solicitude for all the churches'[2] is as generally your responsibility as it is seen to be said particularly and specially to Peter, 'And thou being converted, confirm thy brethren.'[3] To present for your ears, however, a summary of a long drawn out affair, our church, indeed your church, of Montier-en-Der shall not be freed from the hand of the powerful G. except by the hand of the all-powerful God, except by your bow and stretched-out arm.[4] She cries out to you therefore from her distress and her anguish, for her salvation lies in the hand of God and in your hand. For she does not look to the succour of men,[5] of whom the hope is empty, the promise void, the trust worthless; but without doubt you have the voice with power to set free and the strength sufficient to redeem. Thus she must either live in your shadow or wane beneath the shadow of death,[6] that is of G. 'Say the word,' holy

6 [1] Evidently written in the name of the Abbot Gautier (or Walter) of Montier-en-Der; on the date and the circumstances of this letter, and the G. against whom Peter is complaining, see appendix 4.

[2] 2 Cor. 11: 28.

[3] Cf. Luke 22: 32.

[4] Cf. Deut. 5: 15; 7: 19; 9: 29, and many other refs.

[5] Cf. Ecclus. 51: 10.

[6] Cf. Job 3: 5; 10: 22; 24: 17, and many other refs.

uerbo', sancte pater, 'et sanabitur' ecclesia uestra.[g] [7] Ecce languore desperatissimo iam diu egrotat. Appone malagma, ut cuius est filia, ex se languida, sit per te deuotissima ancilla et redempta. In ore huius nuntii nostri posuimus et que dicat et que faciat. Rem ut est latius ipse exponet,[h] siue quomodo iustitiam in presentia episcopi Cathalaunensis subterfugerit, siue quomodo apud Remensem archiepiscopum [i]sola causa frustratorie[i] dilationis appellauerit,[8] siue quomodo interposita fide in dominum Henricum[j] Trecensem comitem compromiserit[k] et postea resilire temptauerit.[9] Capite uulpem que demolitur uineam nostram.[10] Petitio nostra hec est, ut sub tali tenore ad archiepiscopum Senonensem[11] remittatur causa quod uel compromisso[l] suo stare cogatur aut possessio seu inuestitura nobis restituatur, quam ecclesiam nostram aliquando habuisse probare poterimus.

7

To Cardinal Roland Bandinelli, papal chancellor[1]

May 1153 × 1154

[a]Domino et patri karissimo Rolando cancellario sancte Romane ecclesie frater Petrus indignus abbas Trecensis monasterii,[a] id modicum quod est et quod potest.

Nullis meritorum suffragiis subnixus sed sola bonitate uestra confisus, nostris uestram adesse dignationem petitionibus deposco. Artius siquidem uerbum promissionis uestre, per nuntios nostros

[g] *om. O* [h] exponit *O, with superscript corr.* -e [i–i] sola frustratione causa *Sirmond* [j] H. *O* [k] cum promiserit *O* [l] cum promisso *O*

7 *O fo. 139*[r], *Sirmond I. 7*]
[a–a] Domino patri karissimo R. cancellario sancte Romane ecclesie frater G. suus semper et ubique totum *O*

[7] Cf. Matt. 8: 8; Luke 7: 7.
[8] Cf. Gratian, *Dec.* ii. 2. 6, xiv (Friedberg i. 470; *PL* clxxxvii. 622-3).
[9] If the date is secure, then the bishop of Châlons-sur-Marne must be Boson, 1153–25 Mar. 1162 (*GC* ix. 882), and the archbishop of Reims, Samson, 1140–21 Sept. 1161 (*GC* ix. 84–8), but see appendix 4 on the dating. Lord Henry of Troyes is Count Henry the Liberal of Champagne (1152–81; see letter no. 71, n. 1). *Compromiserit* (and not *promiserit*) indicates a mutual promise to abide by the decision of an arbiter, see e.g. Niermeyer, *compromittere* 2.; *DML compromittere* 2.
[10] Cf. S. of S. 2: 15.
[11] Presumably Archbishop Hugh of Sens (1142–68, see letter no. 8, n. 1).

father, and your church 'shall be healed'.[7] See how for a long time now she grows sick with a most desperate affliction. Apply the ointment so that she, sick on her own account, may become, through you whose daughter she is, the most devout and redeemed handmaiden. We have told this our messenger both what he should say and what he should do. He will expound the facts of the matter as it is at greater length, both how G. evaded justice in the presence of the bishop of Châlons-sur-Marne, and how he appealed to the archbishop of Reims solely for the sake of mischievous delay,[8] and how he made a promise, with his pledge given before Lord Henry the count of Troyes and afterwards attempted to go back on it.[9] Catch the fox which is tearing down our vineyard.[10] This is our petition, that the case be referred to the archbishop of Sens[11] in such a manner that either G. is forced to stand by his promise or else possession or investiture is restored to us, for we shall be able to prove that our church formerly held it.

7

To Cardinal Roland Bandinelli, papal chancellor[1]

May 1153 × 1154

To his dearest lord and father Roland, chancellor of the holy Roman Church, brother Peter, unworthy abbot of the monastery of Troyes, that little which he is and which he is able to do.

Propped up by no support of my own merits but confiding only in your goodness, I earnestly beg Your Honour to attend to our petitions. Taking to heart more closely the word of your promise,

7 [1] Roland Bandinelli, papal chancellor, first occurs as such 4 May 1153, el. Pope (as Alexander III), 7 Sept. 1159 (*JL* ii. 21, 90, 103; Zenker, *Kardinalkollegium*, pp. 85–8; *DP*, 176–7). The letter is a request for help in a case concerning the priory of Saint-Flavit-de-Villemaur (dioc. Troyes, Cott. ii. 3389), a dependency of Montier-la-Celle (see also letter no. 71). No details are given in this letter but the priory was restored to Montier-la-Celle by Bishop Henry of Troyes in 1154, after its prebends and benefices had evidently been seized by secular canons (presumably those referred to in the present letter): Lalore, *Cartulaires*, vi. 261–3, no. 221; also *GC* xii. 544A and Instrumenta 269C–270B; see also the bull of Roland as Alexander III to Montier-la-Celle, Lalore, *Cartulaires*, vi. 221–5, no. 199, dated 8 March 1164, which includes Saint-Flavit-de-Villemaur among the possessions of Montier-la-Celle. This would place the present letter between Roland's appointment as chancellor and 1154, although presumably the case was at the Curia when this letter was written, and some time would have elapsed between its delegation to Henry of Troyes and his settlement. On Bishop Henry of Troyes, *c*.1145–*c*.1169, see letter no. 3, n. 5. The salutation echoes 1 Cor. 15: 10.

acceptum, in corde reponens, tanquam michi [b]obligatam ipsorum[b] iure personam uestram teneo ut itaque in causa de ecclesia [c]de Villa[c] Mauri contra iniustitiam canonicorum pro nobis[d] ualenter assistatis. Non remordeat uos conscientia uestra quia iusta est causa nostra. Valete. Parisiensis episcopus[2] exponet uobis tenorem facti.

8

To Archbishop Hugh of Sens[1]

*c.*1145 × 1162

[a]Venerabili domino et patri karissimo Hugoni Senonensi archiepiscopo frater Petrus Cellensis humilis abbas,[a] se ipsum cum deuotione.

Vinee Christi deuastatores uuas, sicut[b] eius ouilis oues 'lupi rapaces'[2] toto ore[c] deuorant,[3] pede conculcant,[4] manu dilaniant, et uestra, benignissime pater, uigilantia obuiare dissimulat? Quare non attenditis quid pro officio, quid pro sponsione, quid pro dilectione, summi pastoris ouibus magnus pastor debetis? Certe defensionem, certe instructionem, certe sollicitudinem. Sed qualem uel quantam? Sine dubio quantam Christus, qualem Petrus. Christus enim diligit 'usque ad mortem';[5] pascit Petrus secundum triplicem pastionem.[6] Verbis namque[d] exemplis et miraculis pauit animas fideles Petrus. Non omnino cuilibet pastori impossibile est pabulum diuini uerbi ouibus sue cure apponere, exempla bona demonstrare, sed graue ualde est miracula antiquorum resuscitare. Quod si supra homines huius temporis sit patrare[e] miraculum, sufficit nobis fidele propugnaculum. Vobis siquidem in Petro dictum est, 'Pasce agnos meos',[7] sana scilicet doctrina. Vobis rursum dictum est, 'Confirma fratres tuos',[8]

[b–b] obligatum ipso *O* [c–c] uille *O* [d] uobis *O*

8 *O fo. 104*[r], *Sirmond I. 8*]
[a–a] Idem H. Senocensi archiepiscopo *O* [b] *corr. Hall;* siue *O, Sirmond* [c] die *Sirmond* [d] namque et *O* [e] prestare *O*

[2] Bishop Theobald of Paris (1144–8 Jan. 1159, see letter no. 13, n. 1).

8 [1] Hugh de Toucy, archbishop of Sens 1142 (Jan. or Feb., and certainly before June)–28 March 1168; *GC* xii. 47–50; Pacaut, *Élections*, p. 98, n. 2 and p. 99; *Obits Sens*, i. 6. The letter cannot be dated more closely than Peter's abbacy of Montier-la-Celle as it contains no concrete details about the case to which it refers. [2] Matt. 7: 15.
[3] Cf. Isa. 9: 12 (Douai-Reims: 'they shall devour Israel with open mouth').

received through our messengers, I hold your person as it were bound to me by their oath, accordingly to stand up forcefully for us in the case of the church of Villemaur against the injustice of the canons. Let your conscience not vex you, for our cause is just. Farewell. The bishop of Paris[2] will explain to you the course of the affair.

8

To Archbishop Hugh of Sens[1]

*c.*1145 × 1162

To his venerable lord and dearest father Hugh, archbishop of Sens, brother Peter, humble abbot of Montier-la-Celle, himself with devotion.

The destroyers of Christ's vine, just as the 'ravening wolves'[2] with mouths agape devour[3] the sheep of His fold, are treading the grapes underfoot,[4] ripping them apart with their hands, and yet do you in your vigilance, most benign father, decline to prevent them? Why do you as a great shepherd not consider what you owe out of duty, out of obligation, out of love, to the sheep of the greatest shepherd? Surely you owe them protection, instruction and concern. But in what manner and to what degree? Without doubt to the same degree as Christ, in the same manner as Peter. For Christ loves 'even unto death';[5] Peter feeds the flock according to the triple pasturing.[6] For Peter has nourished the faithful souls with words, deeds and miracles. It is not totally beyond the bounds of possibility for any pastor to serve up the food of the divine word to the sheep in his care and to set good examples but it is exceedingly difficult to revive the miracles of the ancients. Yet if it is beyond the men of these times to perform wonders a faithful bulwark is enough for us. Indeed in Peter is this said to you: 'Feed my lambs,'[7] that is with sound teaching. Again it is said to you: 'Confirm thy brethren,'[8] that is by good example. You no

[4] Cf. Judg. 9: 27.

[5] Matt. 26: 38; Mark 14: 34; Acts 22: 4; Phil. 2: 8, 27, 30; Rev. 2: 10; 12: 11.

[6] i.e. in the ways which follow, but also an allusion to Christ's triple repetition of the command to Peter, 'Pasce agnos\oues meos', cited below; cf. John 21: 15–17.

[7] John 21: 15, 16, i.e. the words addressed to Peter are addressed to all pastors (not uncommon, cf. e.g. Augustine, *Serm. de script.* cxlvii. 2, *de sanct.* ccxcvi. 3–4 (*PL* xxxviii. 798, 1354); Bede, *Hom. euang.* i. 6. 210–17 (*CCSL* cxxii. 42).

[8] Luke 22: 32.

bono utique exemplo. Nichilominus 'claues regni celorum'[9] tenetis ut hedos excludatis et agnos admittatis.[10] Interim in agro mundi, dum agnus et hedus simul habitant, hedus iniustior extollitur,[f] agnus innocentior opprimitur. 'Dum' enim 'superbit impius incenditur pauper.'[11] Quamobrem Sara,[g] id est patientia ecclesie, aduersus Abraham, id est pastores suos, conqueritur quod Ismahel ⟨filius⟩ secundum carnem ludat cum Ysaac promissionis[h] filio, cuius querimonie diuinum iungitur mandatum, 'Eice', inquiens, 'ancillam et filium eius'.[12] Vtinam, amantissime pater, Ismahel nostrum iuxta [i]domini pape preceptum[i] eiecissetis. Fiat tamen non mea sed uestra uoluntas.[13] Sacrarium nempe secretorum uestrorum impudens perscrutator non attingam, sed humilis supplicator. Fortassis longa [j]temporis dispendia[j] resarciet plena et perfecta iustitia. [k]Si ad diem illam datam probationes uel testes ducere mecum debeam, si placet, remandate. Valete.[k]

9

To Archbishop Hugh of Sens[1]

*c.*1145 × 1162

[a]Karissimo domino et patri Hugoni Senonensi archiepiscopo frater Petrus humilis abbas Cellensis,[a] 'spiritum gratie et precum'.[2]

Si patientiam monemur pro contumeliis rependere,[3] quid pro gratia nisi gratiam[4] tum lege nature tum precepto ipsius gratie debemus reddere? Et si inimicos iubemur amare,[5] amicis quid habemus facere? Credo tanquam ipsam[b] animam nostram suscipere. Certa uero perfecti[c] amoris hec est testificatio si [d]amicorum utilitati[d] omnis postponatur occasio. [e]Sic, sic magister M.[6] non obliuiosus factus beneficiorum uestrorum, ne uobis materia scandali fieret et

[f] extollitur et *O*   [g] rebecca *O, with a marginal note:* sara.   [h] promotionis *O*
[i–i] mandatum domini pape *O*   [j–j] tempora *O*   [k–k] *om. O*

9 *O fo. 104*[v], *Sirmond I. 11*]
[a–a] Eidem idem *O*   [b] *om. O*   [c] profecti *O*   [d–d] utilitati amicorum *O*
[e–e] *om. O*

[9] Matt. 16: 19.   [10] Cf. Matt. 25: 32–3.
[11] Ps. 9 (10): 23 (2).
[12] Cf. Gen. 21: 9–12 and Gal. 4: 22–31 (esp. 23: 'sed qui [Ismael] de ancilla secundum

less hold 'the keys of the kingdom of heaven'[9] that you may shut out the kids and admit the lambs.[10] In the meantime, in the field of the world, while the lamb and the kid abide together, the more unjust kid is raised up and the more innocent lamb is oppressed. For 'whilst the wicked man is proud the poor is set on fire'.[11] For this reason Sarah, that is the endurance of the Church, complains against Abraham, that is her pastors, that Ismael ⟨the son⟩ according to the flesh plays with Isaac the son of the promise—and she to whose complaint is joined the divine command, says, 'Cast out the bondwoman and her son'.[12] If only, most loving father, you had cast out our Ismael according to the command of the lord pope. But yet not my will but thine be done.[13] For I would surely not aspire to be the shameless examiner of the shrine of your secret heart, but a humble suppliant. Perhaps full and perfect justice will mend long-standing injuries. If I ought, on that appointed day, to bring with me proofs or witnesses, if it pleases you, send word. Farewell.

9

To Archbishop Hugh of Sens[1]

c.1145 × 1162

To his dearest lord and father Hugh, archbishop of Sens, brother Peter, humble abbot of Montier-la-Celle, 'the spirit of grace and of prayers'.[2]

If we are admonished to repay abuses with patience,[3] what ought we to give back in return for grace but grace,[4] according alike to the law of nature and to the precept of grace itself? And if we are commanded to love enemies,[5] how must we behave towards friends? We must, as I believe, receive them as our very own soul. Truly this is a certain witness of perfect love, if every other commitment is put aside for the sake of the service of friends. Thus, thus indeed master M.[6] has not grown forgetful of your bounty but, so that he should not become a cause of scandal for you, and Your Highness feel the full

carnem natus est', and 28: 'nos autem fratres secundum Isaac promissionis filii sumus'). The command is spoken by Sarah and endorsed by God.

[13] Cf. Luke 22: 42, cf. also Matt. 26: 39; Mark 14: 36.

9 [1] Dated as letter no. 8. [2] Zech. 12: 10.
[3] Alluding to Matt. 5: 39; Luke 6: 29. [4] Cf. John 1: 16.
[5] Cf. Matt. 5: 44; Luke 6: 27. [6] Unidentified.

iram regis uestra sublimitas persentiret, tulit in se periculum inimicitiarum et ab honore interim, donec iniquitas transiret[7] aduersarii, gratia uestri cessauit.[e] Foueat itaque pietas [f]quem sic inuenit non ingratum alumnum experientia uestra,[f] et contemperet malitiam molestiarum, quia spem habet in protectione alarum uestrarum.[8] [g]Tenerius namque, immo secretius, dicitur diligi cui nichil carius fuit pace benefactoris sui.[g] Facite ipsi pacem qui nec [h]paci sue[h] pepercit propter uestram pacem.

10

To Archbishop Hugh of Sens[1]

? 30 Nov. 1152 (or earlier) × 1157, prob. not later than Aug.

[a]Venerabili domino et patri Hugoni Senonensi archiepiscopo frater Petrus humilis abbas Cellensis,[a] se ipsum cum deuotione.

Si patienter dominus meus seruo suo ubi pena debetur plagas amicales admoueret et ubi iustitia debetur premium rependeret, tam facile confiterer culpam quam secure sperarem ueniam. Prius tamen quam pelagus formidabilis censure ingrediar, an accusem an deplorem sortem qua huc delatus serenitatem uestram siue merito siue immerito obnubilatam in me audio,[2] satis anxie delibero. Quomodo enim non accusare uel potius execrari[b] casum illum debeo per quem tantum casum sentio? Pereat omnis casus[3] a quo amicitie infertur occasus. Sit solitarius nec laude dignus qui uenas interrumpens dilectionis inimicitiarum conglomerat uirus. Rursus

[f–f] magistrum N. quem non inuenit ingratum experientia uestra *O* [g–g] *om. O*
[h–h] sue paci *O*

10 *O fos. 104v–105r, Sirmond I. 9*]
[a–a] Eidem idem *O* [b] execrare *O*

[7] Cf. Ps. 56 (57): 2. [8] Cf. Ps. 16 (17): 8; 35 (36): 8; 56 (57): 2; also 62 (63): 8.

10 [1] Hugh de Toucy, archbishop of Sens 1142–68 (see letter no. 8, n. 1). A defence of the legitimacy of the marriage of Peter's niece (or female relative at least), Hadvide, to Pierre de la Tournelle, most likely the minor seigneur from the Nesle in Picardy, who was advocate of Pronastre, Faverolles and Mesvillers, and occurs between 1153 and 1171/2; his wife, Hadvide, occurs in 1158 and *c.*1172 (see Newman, *Seigneurs de Nesle,* i. 199–200, with genealogy). The marriage case had apparently been concluded by the second half of 1157 when Peter wrote to John of Salisbury telling him that it was over (letter no. 67). Pierre de

force of the king's anger, he has taken upon himself the peril of enmities and for your sake has withdrawn from the honour for a while, until the iniquity of the adversary has passed away.[7] So let mercy nourish him whom you know from experience is not an ungrateful disciple, and temper the evil of his troubles, since he puts his hope in the protection of your wings.[8] For he is said to be more tenderly, nay more intimately, beloved to whom nothing was dearer than the peace of his benefactor. Grant peace to him who for the sake of your peace did not spare his own.

10

To Archbishop Hugh of Sens[1]

? 30 Nov. 1152 (or earlier) × 1157, prob. not later than Aug.

To his venerable lord and father Hugh, archbishop of Sens, brother Peter, humble abbot of Montier-la-Celle, himself with devotion.

If my lord in his forbearance would deal out friendly blows to his servant where punishment is due, and where justice is due repay him with a reward, I would just as easily confess a wrong as I would safely hope for pardon. Before, however, I enter the sea of terrible judgement, I am debating with some anxiety whether I ought to denounce or to grieve for that mischance by which I who am come hither learn that your serenity is rightly or wrongly overcast against me.[2] For how should I not denounce, or rather curse, that fate through which I suffer so great a calamity? May every fall[3] which causes the downfall of friendship perish. Let him stand alone, unworthy of praise, who opening up the veins of love pours in the poison of enmities. On the other hand perhaps that fate should rather

la Tournelle is named in the present letter, a niece in letter no. 23, and 'Hadvide our niece' in letter no. 67; all three letters refer to a marriage case and the other two also to Peter's kinship with the female party, so presumably all refer to this same case. If so, then the involvement of Bishop Alan of Auxerre (30 Nov. 1152–1167, see letter no. 23, n. 1) suggests that the present letter may not have been written before 30 Nov. 1152. These two letters cannot be put in sequence with any certainty. They would seem, however, to be approximately contemporary with each other. Even if the case itself arose as early as 1152, it was probably some time after the original marriage, since two sons, Robert and Rogue, occur in a charter of 1158 (see Newman, *Seigneurs de Nesle*, i. 200).

[2] With a word play on *obnubilatam* and *serenitatem*, which also has the sense of clear weather.

[3] A word play with *occasus*; *casus* can also mean 'legal case' (Niermeyer, *casus* 2; cf. *DML*, 3. *casus* 5; Blaise *Dictionnaire*, *casus* 3), and the subject of the letter is a legal case.

deploranda forte potius[c] est sors illa que cogit utrinque[d] in precipitium ut scilicet [e]pruinam fugiens incidat 'arcum ereum'.[e] [4] Iuxta illud Amos: 'Dies', inquit, 'Domini tenebre et non lux. Quomodo si fugiat uir a facie leonis et occurrat ei ursus, et ingrediatur domum et innitatur manu sua super parietem, et mordeat eum coluber.'[5] Ecce amici et domini offendo maiestatem si stetero pro [f]Petro de Tornella.[f] [6] Ecce iterum frater dissipantis opera sua appellor[7] si quod bona fide, [g]titulo iusto[g] et more ecclesiastico a me factum est dissimulauero. Hinc ciuile ius, [h]inde ius[h] naturale de me conqueritur. [i]Sed quid? Ciuilia, nunquam naturalia, corrumpunt. Dicitur ergo michi, immo non michi sed de me dicitur: 'Heccine est Cellensis religio? Heccine est ueritas? Heccine est fama? Ecce quomodo adulterium immo incestum fouet, ecce quomodo carnem suam diligit, canones et euangelium contempnit, ecce quomodo iniquitati patrocinatur.' Non a uobis sed a uestris, karissime pater, ista aduersum nos dicuntur.[i] Vicem quidem [j]reddere possem in multis[j] sed infrenat linguam meam sanctissime reuerentie uestre auctoritas, et conscientie mee professionisque non rumpenda integritas. Victoriosissimo enim triumpho tripudiat aduersarius si de castris patientie [k]et humilitatis ad cuneum me prouocat impatientie et falsitatis.[k] Tunc certe solummodo me superatum estimo cum irritatione quacunque terminos religionis transgredior. Audiant igitur, audiant obtrectatores mei: carnem quidem meam diligo sed post spiritum; carnem diligo sed secundum Apostolum; carnem diligo sed non supra modum. 'Carnem tuam', ait scriptura, 'ne despexeris.'[8] Beatus quoque Gregorius dicit: 'Sunt quidam qui diligunt, sed per affectum[l] cognationis et carnis, quibus sacra eloquia non contradicunt.'[9] Et Apostolus: 'Nemo unquam carnem suam odio habuit.'[10] [m]'Nos', inquiunt emuli mei, 'diligendam carnem concedimus sed non contra iustitiam; aduersatur autem prorsus iustitie adulterium siue incestus.' Nichil uerius. Sed ego incestum ignoro; matrimonium legitime factum agnosco. Conuocaui namque seniores quos, coniunctim et separatim, publice et priuatim, diligentissime examinaui, nec impedimentum coniugii aduertere ex uerbis eorum potui. Testes

[c] *om. O* [d] utrumque *Sirmond* [e–e] uel pruinam fugiens incurrat uel arcum ereum *Sirmond* [f–f] N. *O* [g–g] iusto titulo *O* [h–h] hinc *O* [i–i] *om. O* [j–j] mentiendo et certe uera dicendo reddere possem *Sirmond* [k–k] non uiolentam uictoriam sed innocentem reportauerit patientiam *O* [l] affectionem *O* [m–m] *om. O*

[4] Cf. Job 6: 16; 20: 24.
[5] Amos 5: 18–19.
[6] Pierre de la Tournelle, see n. 1 above.
[7] Cf. Prov. 18: 9.

be lamented which drives one to the precipice either way so that for sure fleeing the hoary frost one falls upon 'a bow of brass'.[4] As Amos said: 'The day of the Lord is darkness and not light. As if a man should flee from the face of a lion and a bear should meet him, or enter into the house and lean with his hand upon the wall and a serpent should bite him.'[5] So it is that I shall offend the honour of a friend and a lord if I stand up for Pierre de la Tournelle.[6] But then again I am called the brother of him that wasteth his own works[7] if I conceal that which was done by me in good faith, with a just reason and according to ecclesiastical custom. On the one side civil law lays charges against me, on the other side natural law. But on what grounds? Civil precepts, never natural ones, corrupt. Thus it is said to me, or rather not to me but about me: 'Is this the way the religious life goes on at Montier-la-Celle? Is this its true path? Does this accord with its reputation? See how he promotes adultery, nay incest, see how he loves his own flesh, how he spurns the canons and the Gospel, see how he protects wickedness.' These things are spoken against us not by you, dearest father, but by your people. I could respond to many of these things but the authority of your most holy reverence restrains my tongue, and the integrity of my conscience and of my profession must not be destroyed. For the enemy dances in most victorious triumph if he calls me forth from the fortress of patience and humility to the troop of impatience and falsehood. Only then, to be sure, do I reckon myself overcome, when, under whatever provocation, I transgress the bounds of the religious life. Let them hear then, let my detractors hear: I love my flesh indeed, but second to the spirit; I love the flesh, but in the manner of the Apostle; I love the flesh, but not beyond measure. Scripture says: 'Despise not thy own flesh.'[8] St Gregory also says: 'There are those who love, but through affection for kindred and for flesh, which Scripture does not forbid.'[9] And the Apostle says: 'No man ever hated his own flesh.'[10] My opponents say: 'We too admit love of the flesh, but not when it goes against justice; but adultery or incest is absolutely contrary to justice.' Nothing is more true. But I know of no incest; I see a marriage lawfully contracted. For I summoned the elders and, together and individually, in public and in private, I questioned them most carefully, and I was not able to discover from what they said any bar to the marriage. Furthermore, of those witnesses who

[8] Isa. 58: 7. [9] Cf. Gregory, *Hom. .xl. in Evang.* ii. 27. 1 (*PL* lxxvi. 1205).
[10] Cf. Eph. 5: 29.

quoque qui nunc proferuntur, alter est minus idoneus propter apparens odium alter propter causam reticendam usque ad suum locum.[m] [11] Non itaque euangelii seu canonum contemptor iniquitatem patrocinandam suscepi, qui de lege Domini iota unum aut unum[n] apicem pro temporis opportunitate uolens non preteriui.[12]

11

To Archbishop Theobald of Canterbury[1]

1157, after July/Aug.

Domino et patri karissimo Theobaldo[a] Cantuariensi archiepiscopo et apostolice sedis legato frater [b]Petrus Cellensis[b] qualiscunque minister, se ipsum.

'Facti sumus sicut consolati'[2] in consolatione sanctitatis uestre tam affectuosa, tam pia, tam plena dulcedine et caritate. Reddat uobis Spiritus Paraclitus consolationem suam quia [c]respicere uoluistis misericorditer[c] desolationem nostram. Suscitauit siquidem corda nostra, etsi non emortua iam tamen elanguida,[d] susceptio litterarum uestrarum. Dominis et amicis nostris hanc uestram dignationem et consolationem ostendimus, et in spe uiua ex consilio eorum martyrem[e] nostrum peregrinari ad uos destinauimus. Excipite illum et quia uix in terra sua 'habet ubi caput reclinet'[3] interim sub umbraculo uestro militet et stipendia ad nos condigna reportet. Confidimus equidem in bonitate Dei et in liberalitate[f] animi uestri, quam iam pregustauimus,

[n] *om. O*

11 *O fos.* 124[v]–125[r], *Val fos.* 119[v]–120[r], *Sirmond I.* 12]
[a] T. *O;* Thome *Val, Sirmond* [b–b] G. *O* [c–c] respicere misericorditer uoluistis *O*; misericorditer respicere uoluistis *Val* [d] prelanguida *O* [e] fratrem *Sirmond* [f] libertate *Val*

[11] Or possibly meaning the place or seat of judgement: *locus* can indicate a law court (see Niermeyer, *locus* 12, re. recourse to a law court; cf. *DML locus* 6 b; Blaise, *Lexicon*, *locus* 6); i.e. when it comes to be judged on its own account—the implication may be that, while not directly related to the present case, it yet impugns the character of the witness.

[12] Cf. Matt. 5: 18; cf. also Luke 16: 17.

11 [1] This letter must concern the appeal for the priory of Saint-Ayoul-de-Provins which suffered a fire in 1157 (prob. July/Aug., and not before April; see appendix 8). Peter is sending the martyr (i.e. relics, as referred to elsewhere in the letters—see appendix 8—and not a brother, as Sirmond reads) 'on pilgrimage' to raise funds for the rebuilding. John of

have now been produced, one is unfit on account of his evident hatred, the other for a reason which should be kept silent until its proper place.[11] I have not therefore, like one who despises the Gospel or the canons, upheld the defence of wickedness, I who have not willingly, for the sake of the expediency of the moment, set aside one jot or one tittle of the law of God.[12]

II

To Archbishop Theobald of Canterbury[1]

1157, after July/Aug.

To his dearest lord and father Theobald, archbishop of Canterbury and papal legate, brother Peter, minister such as he is of Montier-la-Celle, himself.

'We have become like men comforted'[2] in the comfort of your holiness, so affectionate, so kindly, so full of sweetness and love. May the Holy Spirit the Comforter grant you His comfort because you were willing to look mercifully upon our desolation. The receipt of your letter indeed lifted up our hearts which though not dead were yet now failing. I have shown this your condescension and comfort to our lords and friends, and in lively hope, on their advice, I have determined to send our martyr on a pilgrimage to you. Receive him and, since he has scarcely any place in his own land 'where to lay his head',[3] let him in the meantime serve under your banner and bring back to us worthy rewards. We trust indeed, in God's bounty and in the generosity of your soul, of which we have already had a foretaste,

Salisbury refers, in his letter no. 32 (*J. S. Epp.* i. 54, Jul.–Aug. 1157, addressed to Peter), to Theobald promising his help with the appeal, and there may have been a letter, now lost, accompanying John's no. 32, to which Peter is referring here. Compare also letter no. 18 where similar language and the same quotation from Matt./Luke is used in the same connection. The recipient must be Archbishop Theobald of Canterbury, el. 24 Dec. 1138, consecrated 8 Jan. 1139, d. 18 Apr. 1161 (*Fasti*, ii. 4), who was papal legate from probably early 1150 until the death of Pope Hadrian IV (1 Sept. 1159: it is unlikely that the appointment was renewed between the English recognition of Alexander III in 1160 and the death of Theobald in 1161–see C. R. Cheney, 'On the Acta of Theobald and Thomas, archbishops of Canterbury', *Journal of the Society of Archivists*, vi (1981), 467–81, at p. 468 and n. 6. However, if this letter can be securely dated by the reference to the Saint-Ayoul fire, then the dates of Theobald's legatine office, even if Peter was aware of its lapse in 1159, have no bearing here). The name Thomas, which appears in the salutation in MS Val and in Sirmond, cannot be right. A rubric in MS O gives Theobald as the addressee.

[2] Ps. 125 (126): 1.

[3] Matt. 8: 20; Luke 9: 58.

quia quamuis in baculo suo transeat mare uestrum,[4] tamen sit rediturus in turmis multarum benedictionum. Discretioni[g] sanctitatis uestre fratres nostros et nuntios disponendos committimus. Dominum quoque et confratrem in omni oratione et beneficio omnium nostrorum[h] uos annumeramus. Valete.

12

To Archbishop Eskil of Lund[1]

late 1157 or early 1158 × autumn 1161, (poss. late).

Domino et patri suo karissimo [a]Eskilo Lundensi archiepiscopo frater Petrus Cellensis abbas,[a] omne bonum a Domino Deo.

[b]De superhabundanti[b] bonorum celestium gratia eatenus tam uultus quam manus uestre resudant ut nisi uerecundia his temporibus ab humana regione se subduxisset suffunderentur maximo rubore noti et amici uestri in benedictionum uestrarum largitione. Equidem malim dicere in dando uos pluere quam seminare. Nam qui seminat primum in spe percipiendi fructus seminat, deinde non fundit sed spargit, postremo non nisi culte terre semen suum credit. Horum nichil imitatur pluuia, sed se ipsam, ut sic dicam, perdit in terre uisceribus ut postea resurgens cum maxima frugum prole afferat fructum tricesimum, sexagesimum et centesimum.[2] Aliud rursum caritatis indicium in pluuia reperio quia sine delectu rigat fecunda et infecunda, fertilem agrum et sterilem, granum electum et germen reprobum. Estne uirtutis an uitii, hec bonitatis et beneficiorum prodigalitas? Sed hoc Dei, nec aliud [c]in eo inuenitur[c] uitium nisi quod benignus ad ingratum, largus ad auarum, pius ad impium existit. Ista sua uitia comparant mansuetissimo innumera conuitia. Aliquando moti sunt pedes nostri mitissimi Dauid quia eruperat

[g] Discretione *Sirmond* [h] uestrorum *Sirmond*

12 *O fos.* *123*^{v}–*124*^{v}, *Sirmond I. 23*]
[a–a] E. Lugd. archiepiscopo frater G. Christi sacerdos *O* [b–b] Desuper mundanti *O*
[c–c] inuenitur in eo *O*

[4] Cf. Gen. 32: 10.

12 [1] Eskil of Lund, bishop of Roskilde from 1134 (soon after June 25); became archbishop of Lund between 18 Sept. 1137 and 9/31 Aug. 1138; resigned in spring

that, although he is crossing your sea by his own means,[4] he may however return amid throngs of many blessings. We entrust the arrangements concerning our brethren and messengers to your holiness's discretion. We also count you as lord and brother in every prayer and blessing of our whole community. Farewell.

12

To Archbishop Eskil of Lund[1]

late 1157 or early 1158 × autumn 1161 (poss. late)

To his dearest lord and father Eskil, archbishop of Lund, brother Peter, abbot of Montier-la-Celle, every blessing from the Lord God.

Both your features and your hands exude the superabundant grace of heavenly blessings so far that, had modesty not withdrawn from the province of men in these times, your acquaintances and friends would be suffused with the deepest embarrassment at the generosity of your favours. Indeed I would prefer to say that in giving you rain rather than sow. For the sower first sows in the hope of gathering harvest, then he does not pour out the seed but scatters it, finally he entrusts his seed only to cultivated land. Rain is not at all like this, but loses itself, so to speak, in the bowels of the earth so that afterwards, rising again with the greatest burden of fruit, it brings forth produce thirty, sixty, and one hundredfold.[2] Again I perceive in rain another token of love, that it waters without distinction the fruitful and the unfruitful, the fertile field and the sterile, the chosen seed and the rejected shoot. Is it a mark of virtue or of vice, this prodigality of blessings and favours? But this is of God, and no other vice is found in Him but that He is kind to the ungrateful, generous to the greedy, and merciful to the wicked. These His faults earn the most merciful God numerous rebukes. Once the feet of our most gentle David were moved because the rain of the most merciful God had burst upon the

1177 to become a monk of Clairvaux; d. Sept. 6/7, 1181 (*SEECO* vi. ii. 86–7 and 20–8). Lund, now in Sweden, was the primatial see of Denmark at this time. On the circumstances and date of this letter, see appendix 5. Eskil and Peter may have been acquainted from their early years (see letter no. 99, n. 1). The opening echoes 1 Tim. 1: 14.

[2] Cf. Matt. 13: 8, 23; Mark 4: 8, 20; cf. also Luke 8: 8 (the rain imagery here is not from the parable of the sower—he may have in mind Ecclus. 35: 26, but there are many biblical refs. to God as raingiver). What follows echoes Matt. 5: 45 and Luke 6: 35.

pluuia mansuetissimi Dei super malos et iniustos, ita ut diceret, 'Sine causa iustificaui cor meum et laui inter innocentes manus meas.'[3] Exciderat a mente quod in libro Sapientie dicitur: 'Tu autem Deus noster suauis et uerus es et sapiens, patiens[d] et in misericordia disponens omnia. Etenim si peccauerimus tui sumus, scientes magnitudinem tuam, et si non peccauerimus scimus quoniam apud te sumus computati.'[4] Ecce cuius imitator reprehenditur qui de bonitate siue largitate redarguitur. Annon Ecclesiastes in contione sua proprio decreto et sententia hoc 'malum' estimat 'sub sole', ut 'cui dedit Deus diuitias et substantiam et honorem' non habeat in eis potestatem, sed extraneus illas rapiat?[5] Ad quid hec uobis uerborum congeries? Vt ignis perpetuus de sancto altari cordis uestri non deficiat sed hac congerie magis ac magis conualescat donec holocaustum uestrum pingue[6] in nebula in qua habitat Deus[7] suscipiatur, et a cineribus omnium superfluitatum facies altaris eiusdem expietur. Ostiolum per quod aditus ad sancta sanctorum patet de lignis est oliuarum[8] quia procul dubio iuxta sacre fidei tenorem non ei negabitur sanctorum ingressus qui ab operibus misericordie non fuerit alienus. Suppresso pudore in auribus domini mei id persuaserim, non mea tamen presumptione sed alterius persuasione.[e] Nequaquam tamen difficilis ad persuadendum extiti, faciei uestre, sermonis et totius gestus insignia penes me retinens, nec me in humilitate similem reperisse de filiis hominum coniciens. Non [f]igitur ei[f] scribere uereor quem nisi malis et superbis uerendum non reor. Et de his hactenus. Ceterum culpari non debet seruus de contemptu mandati cuius mens et uoluntas nulla negligentia reuocatur ab impletione uoluntatis domini. Ex uestra dignatione in mandato ab anno preterito accepi quatinus Carthusienses fratres expeterem et de maturando negotio uestro eos commonefacerem. Erat autem negotium, sicut scitis, quatinus ad uos mitteretur frater Rogerius ad locum ordini illorum in partibus uestris perquirendum et preparandum.[9] Disposuerat namque in animo uestro plena et perfecta caritatis effusio, noua seminaria de omni genere sacrorum ordinum seminare

[d] *om. O* [e] suasione *O* [f-f] ei igitur *O*

[3] Ps. 72 (73): 13; cf also 25 (26): 6; the preceding echoes Matt. 5: 45.

[4] Cf. Wisd. 15: 1–2.

[5] Cf. Eccles. 6: 1–2, i.e. that hoarding and covetousness are vain.

[6] Cf. Lev. 6: 13; Ps. 19 (20): 4.

[7] Cf. 3 Kgs. (1 Kgs.) 8: 12.

[8] Cf. 3 Kgs. (1 Kgs.) 6: 31.

[9] Possibly the same Roger as in letter no. 59, who came from Mont-Dieu (according to

wicked and the unjust, so that he said, 'Then have I in vain justified my heart and washed my hands among the innocent.'[3] He had forgotten what is stated in the book of Wisdom: 'But thou, our God, art gracious and true and wise, patient and ordering all things in mercy. For if we sin we are thine, knowing thy greatness, and if we sin not we know that we are counted with thee.'[4] See who he, who is being rebuked, is imitating when he is charged with kindness or generosity. Does not Ecclesiastes in his discourse, by his own decree and judgement, reckon this 'an evil under the sun', that he 'to whom God hath given riches and substance and honour' should not have power over them, but a stranger should seize them?[5] What is the point of this heap of words in your case? It is that the perpetual fire may not fail in the holy altar of your heart, but through this heap may grow ever stronger until your fatty burnt offering[6] be received in the cloud in which God dwells[7] and the surface of that same altar be cleansed of the ashes of all superfluities. The little door through which entry to the holy of holies lies is made of olive-wood,[8] for without doubt, according to the tenet of the sacred faith, entrance to the holy place shall not be denied to him who was not a stranger to the works of mercy. It is not through my own presumption however that, suppressing modesty, I would urge that upon my lord's attention, but owing to the persuasion of another. I was nevertheless by no means difficult to persuade, for the impressions of your face, of your words and of your whole demeanour were ever before me, nor could I imagine finding your equal in humility among the sons of men. I am not therefore afraid to write to him whom I do not believe should be feared except by the wicked and the proud. But enough of these matters. As for the rest, the servant ought not to be accused of defying a command when, with no negligence on his part, his mind and will are diverted from fulfilling his lord's wish. I received an order last year from your honour to seek out the Carthusian brothers and remind them about the expedition of your business. The business was, as you know, that Brother Roger should be sent to you to seek out and prepare a site for their order in your region.[9] For the full and perfect outpouring of love had planted it in your mind that new seminaries from every kind of holy order should sow the province

Le Couteulx, ii. 230–2), but no. 59 was written 1159 × 1162, when Roger would presumably have been in Denmark. Le Couteulx suggests that letter no. 59 was written earlier than the present letter, but there is an overlap in their possible outline dates which neither excludes nor proves this sequence. If the identification of Roger with the Roger of no. 59 is correct, it could indicate a *terminus a quo* for the present letter of 1159+.

prouinciam uobis a Deo commissam ut exinde fructus qui permanent in eternum[10] susciperetis et manipulos iustitie de laboribus eorum ad eterna tabernacula reportaretis. Iam non solum in herbam sed et[g] in spicas Cisterciensis siue Clariuallis ordo ibi multiplicatione fratrum[h] excreuit, nichilominus et religio Premonstratensis.[11] Quia igitur gustauit et uidit prudentia uestra quod bona sit negotiatio ista, ad ulteriora manum porrexistis et de illo ordine qui quasi cherubin siue seraphin, [i]in medietate[i] residenti agno qui habet oculos septem et cornua septem, in throno gratie, accedunt, gazas uestras exornare uoluistis.[12] Ecce 'factum est ut imperastis'.[13] Adquieuit sanctus Cartusiensium fratrum conuentus iustis petitionibus uestris. Equidem res impetratu[j] difficilis, sed quis uobis negaret quod forte Spiritus sanctus in sancto templo suo suggerebat? Certe nec illi nec nos diffidimus seruum suum fidelissimum et amicum Domini nos[k] possidere, cuius famam et [l]opera tam[l] preclarissima reclamat mundus. Quod cepistis [m]tam sancte, tam auide,[m] tamque quodammodo intemperanter pre desiderio anime, sic effectui mancipate ut 'melior sit finis orationis quam principium'.[14] Valete.[n]

13

To Bishop Theobald of Paris[1]

*c.*1145 × 8 Jan. 1159

[a]Domino et patri suo karissimo Theobaldo[a] Parisiensi episcopo frater [b]Petrus Cellensis humillimus,[b] salutem.

Qui transuadari non potest fluuius occursantium causarum tam ab executione[c] mandati uestri me inhibet quam ab impletione desiderii

[g] *om. Sirmond* [h] *om. O* [i–i] *corr. Hall;* in mediate *O*; immediate *Sirmond* [j] impetrata *Sirmond* [k] *corr. Hall;* uos *O, Sirmond* [l–l] operatam *O* [m–m] tam auide et tam sancte *O* [n] *om. O*

13 *O fo. 103*[r–v]*, Sirmond I. 21*]
[a–a] Domino suo et patri karissimo T. *O* [b–b] G. humilis *O* [c] excusatione *O*

[10] Possibly alluding to John 4: 36 and 6: 27; *eterna tabernacula* below recalls Luke 16: 9, but the context here is different.

[11] On the establishment of the Cistercians in Denmark, see also B. P. McGuire, *The Cistercians in Denmark*, Cistercian Studies, xxxv (Kalamazoo, 1982); ch. 2 deals with the early period, 1144–77, and on Eskil's role see pp. 63–74. On Eskil and the Premonstratensians, see ibid. pp. 68, 73. On the imagery, cf. Mark 4: 28.

committed to you by God so that you might reap thereafter the fruits which last for all time,[10] and carry the sheaves of justice born of their labours to the everlasting storehouses. Already the order of Cîteaux, or Clairvaux, has there grown not only into stalks but even into ears through the multiplication of the brethren, and no less so that of Prémontré.[11] Since therefore your prudence has tasted and seen that this business is going well you have stretched out your hand further and have wished to embellish your treasures from that order which, like the cherubim or the seraphim at the throne of grace, approaches the Lamb sitting in their midst who has seven eyes and seven horns.[12] See, 'it is done as thou hast commanded'.[13] The blessed chapter of the Chartreuse has assented to your just requests. It is indeed a difficult task to accomplish, but who would deny you what perhaps the Holy Spirit was urging in His holy temple? Certainly neither they nor we doubt that we have in you His most faithful servant and a friend of the Lord, whose exceptional reputation and deeds the world proclaims. What you have begun with such piety and such zeal and as it were with such a lavish hand, following your soul's desire, bring it to completion in such a way that the end of the speech be better than the beginning.[14] Farewell.

13

To Bishop Theobald of Paris[1]

*c.*1145 × 8 Jan. 1159

To his dearest lord and father Theobald, bishop of Paris, the most humble brother Peter of Montier-la-Celle, greetings.

That river of opposing troubles which cannot be crossed holds me back as much from the execution of your command as from the

[12] Cf. Prov. 31: 18–19; Rev. 5: 6, 11. [13] Luke 14: 22 (Vulgate reads *imperasti*).
[14] Cf. Isa. 26: 8 and Eccles. 7: 9.

13 [1] Bishop Theobald of Paris, 1144–8 Jan. 1159 (*GC* vii. 65–7; Gams, p. 596–but see Depoin, ii. 268, n. 394, showing that Theobald d. 8 Jan. 1159). Theobald was prior of Saint-Martin-des-Champs, first occurs 1136 (*GC* vii. 521–2; *Obits Sens*, i. 422), which might have been while Peter was there (see Introduction, p. xxx). He continued to administer the house during the first year of his tenure at Paris (see Depoin, ii. 142 and n. 237). The *terminus post quem* for this letter is the beginning of Peter's abbacy. Theobald's only other known connection with Peter is his involvement in the case of Saint-Flavit-de-Villemaur (see letter no. 7). The count is presumably the count of Champagne, and so either Theobald II (1125–52, see letter no. 3, n. 3) or Henry the Liberal (1152–81, see letter no. 71, n. 1). The reference to the count's anger here may

nostri.[d] Sermones enim de aduentu Redemptoris ut componerem uobis in mandato acceperam, sed malitie sollicitudinis sue[e] etiam raritatem lucis dies presens adiunxit. Breues enim sunt dies isti ad lucendum, grandes et graues ad occupandum, ita ut non 'sufficiat diei malitia sua'.[2] Nouit prudentia uestra non concurrere quietem[f] contemplationis et distentionem mentis per occupationes seculi. Coangustatum est pallium; utrumque operire[3] immo utrumque operari, non ualet. Quamuis enim in fronte duos quis habeat oculos, tamen ab uno eos officio disiungere non ualet ut altero celum altero contueatur terram; quantominus unam rationis et ingenii aciem simul ad tam diuersa porrigere poterit ut eadem mente celestium misterialiter et terrenorum causas discutiat? Sic domine, sic pater karissime, [g]nisi saltem[g] clausero, ne dicam[h] eruero, oculum qui me scandalizat[4]—scandalum enim est mundus querentibus Dominum—'reuelata facie gloriam Domini'[5] siue faciem Moysi splendidam[6] non contemplabor. Quale uero aut quam credibile est eius testimonium qui nec uisa nec audita loquitur? Immo refellendus et repellendus tanquam sompnia narrans qui, cecus et manu temptans sicut talpa, non de scripturarum contemplatione asserit que dicit sed[i] ydola cogitationum et phantasmatum suorum in templo Dei audet statuere. 'Non est', inquit propheta, 'ydolum in Israhel',[7] quia qui in lege Domini die ac nocte meditatur[8] et legis uestigia stricto pede obseruat non diuinationes cordis sed mentem legis quando scribit interpretatur. Hec ad excusandam non meam inertiam sed oppressam miseriam prelibauerim. De his que circa me sunt, credere N.[j] debetis.[9] Ipse uobis[k] narrabit de commotione ire comitis quam nobis suscitauit latro[l] ille, potius Barrabas[10] quam abbas, [m]siue de aliis. Tres sermones de aduentu Domini et unum de natiuitate orditus sum uobis. Valete.[m]

[d] uestri *O* [e] continue *O* [f] quiete *O* [g–g] saltem nisi *Sirmond* [h] dicam si *Sirmond* [i] si *O* [j] magistro *Sirmond* [k] uero *Sirmond* [l] latini *or* latinus *O* [m–m] *om. O*

suggest a connection with Count Henry's displeasure implied in letter no. 71, and which might thus give *c.*1152 × 1154/5 as a possible rough date for the present letter. However this is inconclusive and the unnamed abbot also mentioned in the present letter cannot be securely identified. Peter left a number of sermons on both the Advent (*PL* ccii. 637–54, nos. 1–6) and the Nativity (ibid. 654–74, nos. 7–12).

fulfilment of my own desire. Certainly I had received an order to compose some sermons for you on the Advent of the Redeemer, but this present day has added even lack of daylight to the malice of its affliction. For these days are short of light, great and heavy with business, so that not 'sufficient for the day is the evil thereof'.[2] You know in your wisdom that the silence of contemplation and the distraction of the mind with the occupations of the world do not go together. The cloak is narrow, it cannot cover both,[3] rather it cannot serve both. For although a man has two eyes in his head, yet he is not able to disengage them from one object so that he may look at the sky with one and with the other at the earth; how much less shall he be able to direct one glance of reason and intellect towards such different things at the same time so that, with the same mind, he can discern the things of the heavens transcendently and also those of the earth? Thus lord, thus dearest father, unless at the very least I close, not to say pluck out, the eye which offends me[4]—for the world is a cause of offence to those who seek the Lord—I shall not look upon 'the glory of the Lord with open face'[5] or upon the shining visage of Moses.[6] Of what kind indeed, or how credible, is the witness of one who speaks of things which he has neither seen nor heard? Rather is he to be refuted and rejected like one relating dreams who, blind and feeling his way with his hand like a mole, does not make his statements from consideration of Scripture but dares to set up the idols of his own thoughts and imaginings in the temple of God. The prophet says, 'There is no idol in Israel,'[7] since he who meditates on the law of God day and night[8] and walks closely in the footprints of the law expounds, when he writes, not the divinations of the heart but the intention of the law. This I have set forth not to excuse my idleness but to give you a taste of my crushing misery. Concerning these matters which surround me, you must believe N.[9] He will tell you about the incitement of the count's anger which that thief, a Barabbas[10] rather than an abbot, has stirred up against us, or of other matters. I have begun for you three sermons on the Advent of the Lord and one on the Nativity. Farewell.

[2] Matt. 6: 34 (Vulgate reads *sufficit*).
[3] Cf. Isa. 28: 20.
[4] Cf. Matt. 5: 29; 18: 9; Mark 9: 46.
[5] 2 Cor. 3: 18.
[6] Cf. Exod. 34: 29–35; Moses descending from Sinai; cf. also 2 Cor. 3: 7, 13.
[7] Cf. Num. 23: 21: 'Non est idolum in Iacob nec uidetur simulacrum in Israhel.'
[8] Cf. Ps. 1 (1): 2.
[9] Presumably the bearer of the letter; the 'N.' in MS O may be a cipher.
[10] Cf. Matt. 27: 16; Mark 15: 7; Luke 23: 18; John 18: 40.

14
To Bishop John of Saint-Malo[1]

*c.*1145 × 1162

[a]Domino et patri karissimo Iohanni episcopo Sancti Maclouii frater Petrus Cellensis humilis abbas, salutem.[a]

Nullius ponderis esse [b]in uera dilectione pomposa et uacua uerba nouit[b] qui caritatis medullam uel semel degustauit. Vanum certe et abiciende simulationis reputo [c]replicare cotidie elementa amoris[c] ex quo fideliter et firmiter [d]inheserit radicibus cordis.[d] Metuentis quoque aut diffidentis est semel natos amores sermonibus uelle renouare quasi uetustas temporis soleat ueros affectus antiquare. Non est imaginis Dei ab inceptis deficere. Non est uirtutis uacillare, non est solii glorie Dei in diuersum se uertere. Annon anima ad imaginem Dei?[2] Annon caritas uirtus Dei? Annon pura conscientia thronus Dei et sedes diuine maiestatis? Vt ergo Filius, qui est imago Patris,[3] que creauit semel semper gubernat et regit, utque uirtus Altissimi que operatur confirmat et perficit, ac denique incommutabiliter manet incommutabilis Dei sessio eternitatis, sic radicata caritas et fundata[4] 'de corde puro et conscientia bona et fide non ficta'[5] ignorat occasum, corruptionem abhominatur, [e]mortem in eternum non gustat.[e][6] Hec interno coagulo suo coniunxit nostros adinuicem affectus. Hec inter nos mediatrix unico amore dulciter,[f] fortiter et sapienter animas nostras conglutinauit. Hec in me uestrum tenaciter amorem effudit[g]

14 *O fo.* 93[r–v], *Val fos.* 125[v]–126[r], *Sirmond I.* 17]

[a–a] Eidem idem *O;* Domino et patri karissimo I. episcopo S. Maclovii, frater P. Cellensis humilis abbas salutem *Val* [b–b] nouit in uera dilectione uerba uacua et pomposa *O* [c–c] amoris elementa cotidie replicare *O* [d–d] radicibus cordis inheserit *O* [e–e] mortem non gustauit in eternum *O* [f] adinuicem dulciter et *O* [g] effundit *O*

14 [1] Bishop John of Saint-Malo, 1144–1 Feb. 1163: *GC* xiv. 1001–2; Morice, *Bretagne*, ii, pp. xlv–xlvi; F. Duine, *Catalogue des sources hagiographiques pour l'histoire de Bretagne jusqu'à la fin du XII[e] siècle* (Paris, 1922), pp. 13–14. John was an Augustinian canon of Bourgmoyen, Blois (Cott. i. 398–9), before 1134, then first abbot of the Augustinian house of Sainte-Croix-de-Guingamp after its re-establishment in 1134 (dioc. Tréguier, Cott. i. 1362; *GC* xiv. 1137). When the sees of Saint-Malo and Tréguier became vacant within eight days of one another in 1144, John was elected to both and chose Saint-Malo. He moved the see from the old city of Alet to the Isle d'Aaron (or Isle de Saint-Malo), occasioning a dispute with the monks of Marmoutiers to whom the island belonged. He prevailed with the help of Bernard of Clairvaux and Archbishop Henry of Reims, but there

14

To Bishop John of Saint-Malo[1]

*c.*1145 × 1162

To his dearest lord and father John, bishop of Saint-Malo, brother Peter, humble abbot of Montier-la-Celle, greetings.

He who has even once tasted the essence of love knows that pompous and empty words are of no consequence in true affection. I think it is surely vain, and deriving from a pretence which must be rejected, to repeat every day the elements of love, out of which it has adhered faithfully and firmly to the roots of the heart. Moreover the wish to renew with words loves that have once been born, as if it were usual for the passage of time to cause affection to fade, is the sign of a man both fearful and distrusting. It is not in the nature of the image of God to fail in an undertaking. It is not in the nature of virtue to waver, nor of the throne of the glory of God to turn to face another way. Is the soul not made in the image of God?[2] Is love not the virtue of God? Is a pure conscience not the throne of God and the seat of the divine majesty? Therefore just as the Son, who is the image of the Father,[3] always rules and reigns over that which He once created, and as the might of the Most High strengthens and perfects that which He enacts, and finally as the court of the God of unchangeable eternity endures unchanging, so love, rooted and founded[4] in 'a pure heart and a good conscience and an unfeigned faith,'[5] knows not disaster, spurns decay, tastes not eternal death.[6] This love by its own internal bonding has joined together our loves mutually. This mediator between us has bound together our souls delightfully, powerfully, and wisely with one love. It poured out your love into

are no echoes of this affair in Peter's correspondence with John. The origins of his acquaintance with Peter are not known. John become known to posterity as Saint Jean de la Grille because of the iron grill around his tomb; Pacaut doubts, for lack of evidence, *GC*'s ascription to him of the surname 'de Châtillon' (Pacaut, *Élections*, p. 126). Duine, *Catalogue*., lists sources relating to John. This letter, as letters 15 and 16, can be dated no more closely than Peter's abbacy of Montier-la-Celle.

[2] Not an uncommon formulation, cf. e.g. Ambrose, *Exameron*, vi. 7. 43 (*CSEL* xxxii/1. 234; *PL* xiv. 274). The following formulations are not evidently common, but cf. e.g. Jerome, *Ep.* cxxxii. 15, 'uirtus est caritas' (*CSEL* lvi/1. 236; *PL* xxii. 1144, where it is no. cxxxi—from Augustine).

[3] Cf. 2 Cor. 4: 4.

[4] Cf. Eph. 3: 17.

[5] 1 Tim. 1: 5.

[6] Cf. John 8: 52.

et ad uos non dissimiliter me ipsum totum diffundendo contulit. Ad unicum itaque et specialem amicum, singulari spe et unica rogo, accedat uestra sanctitas. Non diffidat suum esse cuius ueraciter affirmat se esse. Nisi autem iusta occasione inuenta ad nos ueneritis, satis de integritate amoris nostri diminuetis. Valete.[h]

15

To Bishop John of Saint-Malo[1]

*c.*1145 × 1162

[a]Domino et patri suo karissimo Iohanni Dei gratia episcopo Sancti Maclouii frater Petrus humilis abbas Cellensis,[a] quicquid est et potest.

Valet dominus meus? Viuitne? Vt credo, aut est alteratus [b]episcopus Sancti Maclouii[b] aut alter a meo est substitutus. Si alter est, mirari sed non dolere desino tacuisse qui loqui non poterat. Nam surrexit nouus rex qui non nouerat Ioseph.[2] Si alteratus, nollem [c]tantam fuisse[c] alterationem que pene accedit[d] usque ad alienationem. Alienum ab amico equidem est posse dissimulare eque et simulare. Non simulat amicus propter[e] ueritatem, non dissimulat propter[f] respirantem ardorem.[g] [h]Non simulat quia sine adulatione, non dissimulat quia, efficacissime nature existens, sepulcrum reputat latibulum et non apparere existimat non esse. Non simulat quia nescit, non dissimulat quia non potest. Hoc ignorat, illud non potest.[h] Quid enim non nouit sapientia? Quid non potest caritas? Quodcunque est scire nouit sapientia, quodcunque est posse potest caritas. Non est scire scire adulari, non est[i] posse posse obliuisci. O amice et domine karissime, obliuioni an negligentie uestre obiciam quod abstinuistis tam a uisitatione quam a salutatione amicorum uestrorum ultra tempus et modum? Estne obliuio? Si est, digna est morte, digna exilio, que [j]diadema tulit[j] de capite episcopi, que de pectore [k]rationale

[h] *om. O;* Vale *Val*

15 *O fos.* 93^{v}–94^{v}, *Sirmond I. 19*]
[a–a] Eidem idem *O* [b–b] N. *O* [c–c] fuisse tantam *O* [d] accidit *O* [e] sed propter *O* [f] *corr. Hall;* sed propter *O, Sirmond* [g] addorem *O* [h–h] *om. O* [i] *om. Sirmond* [j–j] tulit diadema *O* [k–k] sustulit rationale *O*

me firmly and joined me wholly to you by pouring out love in the same way. And so I ask with a singular and unique hope that your holiness come to visit a unique and special friend. Let him not doubt that the one who truly claims to be his is his. But if you do not come to us when you have found some good reason, you will destroy a good part of the integrity of our love. Farewell.

15

To Bishop John of Saint-Malo[1]

*c.*1145 × 1162

To his dearest lord and father John, by the grace of God bishop of Saint-Malo, brother Peter, humble abbot of Montier-la-Celle, all that he is and that he is able to do.

Is my lord well? Is he alive? As far as I can make it out, either the bishop of Saint-Malo has changed or another has been put in place of mine. If it is another, I cease to wonder, but not to grieve, that he who was not able to speak was silent. For there arose a new king that knew not Joseph.[2] If he has changed, I could wish that the alteration had not been so great, for it almost approaches alienation. It is indeed alien to the nature of a friend to be able equally to dissimulate and to simulate. For truth's sake a friend does not simulate; on account of his lively ardour he does not dissimulate. He does not simulate because he is not a flatterer; he does not dissimulate because, being of a most active nature, he reckons a hiding place to be a tomb and thinks that what does not show is not there. He does not simulate because he does not know how; he does not dissimulate because he cannot. This he does not know, that he cannot do. For what does wisdom not know? Of what is love not capable? Whatever knowledge is, wisdom knows; whatever ability is, love is able. It is not knowledge to know how to flatter; it is not ability to be able to forget. O dearest friend and lord, shall I charge it to your forgetfulness or to your negligence that you have kept from visiting, as well as from greeting, your friends for too long and beyond measure? Is it forgetfulness? If it is it is deserving of death, deserving of exile, for it has taken the

15 [1] Dated as letter no. 14. The end of this letter suggests that John had once visited Montier-la-Celle.

[2] Cf. Exod. 1: 8.

sustulit.[k] [3] Obliuio delet et quod precipuum est[l] in honore et quod fortissimum est in robore, id est sapientiam et memoriam. Rea ergo crimine tante[m] maiestatis capite plectatur et non memoretur ultra. Negligentia quid? Non sit dissimilis in pena que precessit in culpa. Talis etenim soboles tali de matre nascitur, ex negligentia scilicet obliuio. [n]Doleo, pater, excessum memorie uestre iam per biennium suspense, decessum quoque amicitie quatriduane multo tempore quasi sepulte.[n] [4] Nuntium saltem sue salutis, si uiuit, mittere debuit amicitia, cuius nature[o] est semper odisse absentiam et appetere [p]amicorum presentiam.[p] Forte occupata est:[5] sed non est grata que semper est occupata. Mansio est, immo possessio, non occupatio que iugiter retinet. Quis ergo ita[q] preoccupauit, quin immo possedit, amicitiam ne libertate, ne ingenuitate sua utens radios suos ad nos usque expanderet [r]ab annis prioribus? Suntne montes interiacentes? Estne mare interiacens?[r] Estne chaos magnum firmatum inter nos et uos 'ut hi qui uolunt hinc transire [s]ad uos[s] non possint, neque inde huc transmeare'?[6] Sed caritas omnem altitudinem exuperat, sed 'aque multe non possunt extinguere caritatem',[7] sed non 'est qui se abscondat a calore eius',[8] sed 'attingit [t]a fine[t] usque ad finem fortiter et disponit omnia suauiter'.[9] [u]In episcopo nostro, immo sancto et Dei famulo,[u] quis te, o dilectio, debilitauit? Quis obumbrauit? Quis hebetauit? Quis commutauit? In aliis quidem non ignoro superueniente iniquitate uirtutem tuam debilitari, obliuione lucem tuam obumbrari, negligentia acumen tuum hebetari et[v] totam substantiam posse odio commutari. Sed in sancto que iniquitas? In studioso que obliuio? In uiro forti que negligentia? In pleno caritate quod odium? Si quando enim tepescit, si quando flaccescit,[w] si quando hebescit in sancto caritas, ea que extrinsecus sunt accusanda non que intrinsecus. [x]Obstacula enim opposita[x] mentiuntur ueritatem supposite[y] lucis, caloris et aciei. Oppone gladio ancipiti [z]durissimum ferrum uel lapidem,[z] retrocedit uis impenetrabilis. Murum spissum oppone

[l] *om.* O [m] *om.* O [n–n] *om.* O [o] naturale O [p–p] presentiam amicorum O [q] *om.* O [r–r] *om.* O [s–s] *om.* Sirmond [t–t] *om.* Sirmond [u–u] In tam sancto dei famulo O [v] *om.* Sirmond [w] flauescit O [x–x] Opposita enim obstacula O [y] superposite *Sirmond* [z–z] ferrum uel lapidem durissimum O

[3] Cf. 2 Kgs. (2 Sam.) 1: 10.

[4] Perhaps meaning that their friendship was literally based on some encounter which lasted only four days (see also n. 1 above); 'cottidiane' is possible, but there may be a lost allusion here, and four days is a period of time mentioned by Peter more than once in the letters (cf. letters 156, n. 3 and 176 n. 1).

[5] *occupata* here implies both preoccupation with daily affairs and being taken possession

diadem from the bishop's head and removed the pectoral from his chest.[3] Forgetfulness wipes out both what is outstanding in honour and what is most vigorous in strength, that is, wisdom and memory. Charged therefore with such high treason let it be punished by death and remembered no more. What of negligence? Let that which has preceded in guilt be not dissimilar in punishment. For such progeny is born of such a mother, that is forgetfulness is born of negligence. I grieve, father, for the loss of your memory, now lapsed for two years, and also for the death of a four-day friendship, as good as buried for a long time now.[4] Friendship, in whose nature it is always to hate absence and to strive after the presence of friends, ought at least to have sent news of its health, if it lives. Perhaps it is occupied;[5] but that which is always occupied is not pleasing. It is dwelling, even possession, not occupation, which holds on to a thing constantly. Who therefore has so preoccupied, rather possessed, friendship that it cannot use its liberty and freedom to spread out its rays as far as us from previous years? Are there mountains lying between us? Is there a sea lying between us? Is there a great chaos fixed between us and you 'so that they who would pass from hence to you cannot, nor from thence come hither'?[6] Yet love exceeds all heights, yet 'many waters cannot quench charity,'[7] yet 'there is no one that can hide himself from its heat,'[8] yet it 'reacheth from end to end mightily and ordereth all things sweetly'.[9] In the case of our bishop, a holy man, say I, and a servant of God, who has discouraged you, o friendship? Who has made you overcast? Who has dimmed you? Who has changed you? In the case of others indeed I am not unaware that your virtue can be weakened by overpowering wickedness, your light be darkened by forgetfulness, your keenness dulled by negligence, and the whole substance be changed by hatred. But what wickedness is there in a holy man? What forgetfulness in the conscientious? What negligence in an upright man? What hatred in one filled with love? For if love ever cools, if it ever flags, if it is ever dulled in the holy man, external causes are to be blamed, not internal. For obstacles put in the way obscure the true nature of the light, the warmth and the keen vision hidden beneath. Set the hardest iron or stone against the two-edged sword and the unconquerable force recedes. Set a thick barrier against

of, in which sense it is contrasted with true possession or dwelling (which allows friendship the freedom to reach out), whereas (returning to the earlier meaning) (pre-)occupation possesses friendship in such a way as to stifle it.

[6] Cf. Luke 16: 26.

[7] Cf. S. of S. 8: 7.

[8] Cf. Ps. 18 (19): 7, where the subject is God.

[9] Cf. Wisd. 8: 1, where the subject is wisdom.

igni, tardius calefacit. Candele accense superpone[a] modium, in luce non gaudebit.[10] Non est proinde putandum non lucere candelam, non ardere ignem, non secare gladium, sed contrariis obstaculis imputandum. Sic sanctorum uirtutes a radice sua non euanescunt sed plerumque propter sabbatum Iudeorum conticescunt. Aromata enim sua interim et[b] in secreto distillant et repensant ut cum dies opportunitatis illuxerit, diluculo in effectum desiderati operis prorumpant. Eque tamen repensatur et desiderium ardens in otii quiete et opus feruens in actione. Acceptat namque Deus opus propter affectum non affectum propter opus. Magnus, immo longus nobis est iste dies sabbati cuius ferias non[c] feriales uel solennes sed ferales et olentes reputamus. Negligentia siquidem male olet, diligentia semper bene redolet. Iners Iudaizantium pigritia non diligit sabbatum quia sanctum sed quia otiosum. Iesus[d] uero stabat in die magno festiuitatis et clamabat, 'Si quis sitit, ueniat ad me et bibat.'[11] [e]Magnus dies festiuitatis uere magnum habet clamorem caritatis.[12] Iam non taceat[e] caritas uestra, iamiam loquatur, immo ueniat, et immo accurrat. Desiderat uos anima mea, desiderant uos amici uestri.[f] Ostendite faciem uestram, [g]sonet uox uestra in auribus nostris.[g] [13] [h]Episcopos diuites multos habemus, pauperem episcopum querimus qui non habeat 'ubi caput reclinet'.[14] Adhuc penes nos reclinatorium non aureum[15] sed luteum in quo aliquando quieuistis habemus. Et de his hactenus.[h]

[a] suppone *Sirmond* [b] *om. O* [c] uel *O* [d] Iohannes *O* [e–e] Vere magnus est dies festiuitatis. Magnum habet clamorem *Sirmond* [f] nostri *O* [g–g] sonet uox in auribus *Sirmond* [h–h] *om. O*

the fire and it burns more slowly. Place a bushel over a lit candle and it will not shine out.[10] You must not conclude from this that the candle does not shine, that the flame does not burn, that the sword does not cut, but rather the effect is to be attributed to the intervening obstacles. Thus the virtues of the holy do not vanish from their root but very often fall silent on the Sabbath of the Jews. For in the meantime and in secret they distil and weigh in the balance their odours so that when the day of opportunity lights up the dawn they may burst forth at daybreak to accomplish the desired work. But desire glowing in the silence of leisure and a deed burning in action are reckoned equally. For God accepts the deed on account of the desire, not the desire on account of the deed. This Sabbath day is heavy and even long for us who reckon its festivals not holy or solemn but funereal and rank. Idleness indeed has a bad odour, diligence always has a good odour. The indolent sloth of the Judaizers does not love the Sabbath because it is holy but because it is an idle day. Jesus indeed was standing up on the great day of the festival and shouting, 'If any man thirst, let him come to me and drink.'[11] Truly there is a great cry of love on the great day of the festival.[12] Do not let your love be silent now, let it speak now, nay, let it come, let it even hurry to us. My soul desires you, your friends long for you. Show your face to us, let your voice sound in our ears.[13] We have many rich bishops, we seek a poor bishop who has not 'where to lay his head'.[14] We still have in our possession a seat not of gold[15] but of clay, in which you once rested. But enough of these matters.

[10] Cf. Matt. 5: 15; Mark 4: 21; Luke 8: 16; 11: 33.
[11] Cf. John 7: 37.
[12] Cf. John 7: 37.
[13] Cf. S. of S. 2: 14.
[14] Cf. Matt. 8: 20; Luke 9: 58.
[15] Cf. S. of S. 3: 10.

16

To Bishop John of Saint-Malo[1]

*c.*1145 × 1162

[a]Domino suo et patri karissimo Iohanni episcopo Sancti Maclouii frater Petrus Cellensis qualiscunque minister,[a] salutem que est in Christo Iesu.

'Spes que differtur affligit animam.'[2] Verus amor impatientia[b] sui desiderii quandoque non irascitur commendabiliter superari. Nichil enim pene aliud est in uita hominum quod quadam[c] arte mitigari non possit. Spes itaque aduentus uestri nuntiati quanto uberius amicum[d] letificauit tanto amplius ex mora dilationis hactenus affligit. Estuat siquidem animus in reuolutione fortuitorum casuum, nunc hoc nunc illud reformidans [e]contrarium subito[e] accidisse. Quid plura? Cogitatio preterit[f] et cogitatio aduenit, morarum uero dubitatio nec ad punctum ab[g] animo recedit. Alia inquit, 'iamiam uenit,' alia, 'forte non ualet.' Ista incommoda temporis replicat, illa intolerabile negotiorum pondus anxia suspirat. Ecce quanta caligo, quanta suspicionum tumultuatio. Vbi ueritas? [h]Cuiusnam supradictarum cogitationum uerior sententia?[h] An forsan[i] error est, ubi latet quod uerum est, et non sententia? Sed 'adhuc sub iudice lis est'.[3] Ex multis enim ambiguitatibus aut uix aut nunquam certum aliquid sine doctoris demonstratione elicitur. Renunciate ergo[j] amicis diuine circa uos[k] miserationis operam ut, omnimode soluto dubitationis uinculo, indubitanter aut uiam sinistram compassionis aut dexteram apprehendamus congratulationis. Satis enim iniuriose deturpatur nobilis animus si se non preparat mutuis obuiare beneficiis saltem equis passibus.[4] Turpe etiam estimo non omnimodo cauere superari beneficio. Vnicum quid et singulare natura, siue creator nature, tanquam speciale priuilegium imagini sue hoc impressit quatinus

16 *O fo.* 92[r–v], *Sirmond I.* 20]
[a–a] Eidem idem *O* [b] inpatientiam *O;* in patientia *Sirmond* [c] qualibet *O* [d] animum *O* [e–e] subito contrarium *O* [f] *om. O* [g] *om. Sirmond* [h–h] *om. O* [i] forsitan *O* [j] igitur *O* [k] nos *O*

16 [1] Dated as letter no. 14. [2] Prov. 13: 12.
[3] Horace, *Ars Poet.* 78.

16

To Bishop John of Saint-Malo[1]

*c.*1145 × 1162

To his dearest lord and father John, bishop of Saint-Malo, brother Peter, servant such as he is of Montier-la-Celle, greetings in Christ Jesus.

'Hope that is deferred afflicteth the soul.'[2] True love is sometimes not angry to be commendably overcome by impatience for its desires. For there is scarcely anything else in the life of men that cannot be alleviated by some means. The more immensely therefore the hope of your announced arrival cheered your friend the more deeply it troubles him still owing to the delay of postponement. Indeed the mind rages in the whirlpool of unpredictable calamities, fearing that now this, now another untoward event has suddenly occurred. What more can I say? A thought passes away and a thought comes, and indeed doubt about delays does not leave the mind even for a second. This thought says, 'Now indeed he is coming,' the other, 'Perhaps he is unwell.' This one mulls over the inconveniences of the season, the other, troubled, sighs over the unbearable weight of business. See how much darkness there is here, how much confusion of suspicions. Where is the truth? Which of these thoughts gives the truer judgement? Or perhaps it is an error, where the truth lies hidden, and not a judgement? But 'the case is still being tried'.[3] For out of many ambiguities hardly ever or never is anything certain ascertained without the elucidation of a master. Proclaim therefore to friends the work of divine compassion about you so that, with the bond of every kind of doubt loosed, we may take clearly either the left-hand road of compassion or the right-hand road of felicitation. For the noble mind is most harmfully corrupted if it does not prepare itself to meet mutual kindnesses at least with matching steps.[4] Moreover I reckon it corrupt not to guard in every way against being outdone in kindness. Nature or the Creator of nature has stamped something unique and singular as this special privilege on His image so that it may more

[4] Cf. Virgil, *Aen.* ii. 724, 'non passibus aequis'. Peter seems here to be changing the subject from concern about whether or not John will visit to thanking him for a gift.

commodius et prestantius haberet stricta equitatis ratione, 'dare quam accipere'.[5] Hanc uobis formam nec rubigo exilii, nec [l]paupertatis tinea[l] excussit.[6] Ex hac prodiit quod magna pro paruis, pro uilibus cariora, magnifice rependistis,[m] quin immo solenne donum absque precedentis comparatione obsequii misistis. Species quidem doni carius estimanda sed affectio donatoris potius incomparabiliter est compensanda. Quicquid namque aliud datur, in comparatione sublimis animi uilipenditur. Valete.[n]

17

To Bishop John of Saint-Malo[1]

after 20 Aug. 1153

[a]Domino et patri karissimo Iohanni episcopo Sancti Maclouii frater Petrus Cellensis indignus abbas,[a] cum Apostolo 'in labore et erumpna'.[2]

Etiam in amaritudinibus nostris[b] congratulatur anima mea; quanto magis in consideratione [c]gloriose remunerationis?[c] Reminiscor siquidem quia iusti 'in paucis uexati, in multis bene disponentur',[3] et quia reddet Deus mercedem laborum sanctorum suorum,[4] atque ideo non [d]uana est[d] expectatio ubi tam certa, tam grata, tam larga speratur remuneratio. Certa propter ueritatem promittentis, grata propter consummationem desideriorum recipientis, larga propter exuberantiam bonorum celestium in communicatione diuinitatis. Hec reposita est in sinu nostro,[5] hec inter ubera commoratur,[6] hac quelibet insipida condiuntur et gustui nostro commodissime aptantur.[e] O anime mee dulcedo, quid putatis Dominum [f]non attendere miserias[f] compeditorum suorum, non librare in statera eternorum iudiciorum penas filiorum? 'Nonne', inquit, 'hec condita sunt apud me et signata in thesauris meis?'[7] Miror uos scripsisse destitutum [g]patrocinio sanctis-

[l–l] tinea paupertatis *O*   [m] rependitis *O*   [n] *om. O*

17 *O fos.* 92^{v}–93^{r}, *Val fo.* 125^{r-v}, *Sirmond I. 16*]
[a–a] Eidem idem feliciter sollicitari *O;* Domino et patri karissimo, I. episcopo sancti Maclovii frater P. Cellensis indignus abbas *Val*   [b] uestris *O, Val*
[c–c] remunerationis gloriose *O*   [d–d] est uana *O*   [e] adaptantur *O*
[f–f] miserias non attendere *Val*   [g–g] patris nostri sanctissimi Bernardi solatio *O*

[5] Acts 20: 35. The form, below, is the image (i.e. man, made in the image of God)

suitably and distinctively hold in strict proportion of equity to the precept, 'better to give than to receive'.[5] Neither the rust of exile nor the moth[6] of poverty has stripped you of this form. It has followed from this that you have splendidly repaid great for little, dear for cheap, nay more, you have sent the customary gift without comparing the preceding service. The nature of the gift is to be valued highly but the affection of the giver is rather to be weighed as beyond compare. For whatever else is given is held in low esteem in comparison to an exalted mind. Farewell.

17

To Bishop John of Saint-Malo[1]

after 20 Aug. 1153

To his dearest lord and father John, bishop of Saint-Malo, brother Peter, unworthy abbot of Montier-la-Celle, with the Apostle 'in labour and painfulness'.[2]

Even in the midst of our bitter sufferings my soul rejoices; how much more so in the contemplation of a glorious reward? I recall indeed that the just, 'afflicted in few things, shall be well rewarded in many,'[3] and that God shall render the wages of the labours of His saints,[4] and so it is not futile to hope for so certain, so pleasing, and so great a reward. Certain because of the truthful nature of the one making the promise, pleasing because of the fulfilment of the desires of the recipient, great because of the superabundance of heavenly blessings in communion with the Godhead. This hope is laid up in our bosom[5] and abides between the breasts;[6] in this hope all manner of bland things are spiced and adapted most favourably to our taste. O delight of my soul, how can you think that the Lord does not attend to the sufferings of His prisoners nor weigh the punishments of His sons on the scales of the eternal judgements? He says: 'Are not these things stored up with me and sealed up in my treasures?'[7] I am

stamped with the special privilege, i.e. so that he will not fail to live up to the maxim, 'better to give than to receive'.

[6] Cf. Matt. 6: 19.

17 [1] John of Saint-Malo (see letter no. 14, n. 1). Written after the death of St Bernard, 20 Aug. 1153.

[2] 2 Cor. 11: 27. [3] Wisd. 3: 5. [4] Cf. Wisd. 10: 17.

[5] Cf. Job 19: 27. [6] Cf. S. of S. 1: 12. [7] Deut. 32: 34.

simi patris nostri Bernardi[g] cum sancta eius anima nexibus expedita mortalitatis non caritatis, corruptionis non affectionis,[h] necessitatis non uoluntatis, liberius [i]aures nunc[i] appellet piissimi conditoris pro necessitatibus populi sui. Non michi contingat de gratia ipsius diffidere, de orationibus eius desperare. Nimio uobiscum loquendi tentus desiderio uix finem facio. Quem enim sine fine diligo nunquam satis ei scribere, nunquam satis loqui ualeo. [j]Conuentus noster uester est populus, noster populus uester est,[8] anima mea uestra est. Vtinam uiderem uos antequam transiretis ad montes illos, ubi tot sunt, sicut audiuimus, pericula. Valete.[j]

18

To Bishop John of Saint-Malo[1]

1157, not before April (poss. not before July/Aug.)

[a]Domino et patri suo karissimo Iohanni episcopo Sancti Maclouii frater Petrus humilis abbas Cellensis,[a] quicquid est et potest.

Miramur plurimum tanto nos tempore insalutatos a uestra paternitate quasi neglectos fuisse. Non credimus ex negligentia sed forte ex ineuitabili occupationum uestrarum pondere sic oppressum siluisse. Clamamus tandem post uos.[b 2] Volumus enim suscitare compassionem in uobis passionibus nostris.[c] Neque enim superbe est ab[d] amicis celandum forte subrepens infortunium, nec contumaciter aut [e]inuerecunde petendum[e] necessarium suffragium. [f]Precauendum utrumque, sed maxime alterum.[f] Vitium utrumque, sed [g]alterum patienti[g] grauius, alterum roganti ignobilius. Malum namque absconditum

[h] afflictionis *Sirmond* [i–i] nunc aures *Val* [j–j] *om. O*

18 *O fo. 94*^{v}, *Val fo. 126*$^{r-v}$, *Sirmond I. 18*]
[a–a] Eidem idem *O;* Domino et patri karissimo I. episcopo Sancti Maclouii, frater P. humilis abbas Cellensis *Val* [b] nos *O* [c] uestris *O* [d] *om. O* [e–e] inuerecundie petentum *O* [f–f] *om. O* [g–g] patienti alterum *Val*

[8] Cf. Ruth 1: 16 (but such formulations are common in letters).

18 [1] John of Saint-Malo (see letter no. 14, n. 1). The fire at the priory of Saint-Ayoul-de-Provins (Cott. ii. 2368, a dependent priory of Montier-la-Celle; also St Aigulf), to

surprised that you have written that you are deprived of the protection of our most holy father Bernard since his holy soul, freed from the bonds of mortality not those of love, from those of decay not those of affection, from those of need not those of will, now entreats the ears of the most holy Creator more freely for the needs of his people. Let it not fall to me to distrust his grace or despair of his intercessions. Held by too great a desire to go on speaking with you, I can scarcely end this letter. For I am never able to write enough or to speak enough to him whom I love without limit. Our community is your people, our people are yours,[8] my soul is yours. I wish that I were able to see you before you cross over to those mountains where, as we have heard, there are so many dangers. Farewell.

18

To Bishop John of Saint-Malo[1]

1157, not before April (poss. not before July/Aug.)

To his dearest lord and father John, bishop of Saint-Malo, brother Peter, humble abbot of Montier-la-Celle, all that he is and that he is able to do.

We are most amazed that for so long a time we have been without a greeting from, almost neglected by, you, father. We do not believe that you have been silent through negligence, but it may be because you are so overwhelmed by the unavoidable burden of your responsibilities. At length we are crying out after you.[2] For we wish to stir up in you compassion for our sufferings. For neither is misfortune which steals suddenly upon one to be proudly hidden from friends, nor is necessary help to be demanded obstinately or shamelessly. Both must be guarded against, but especially the latter. Both are faults, but the one is more burdensome to the sufferer while the other is more ignoble for the petitioner. For a hidden evil goads more fiercely, while one flagrantly

which this letter refers, had happened by July or Aug. 1157, and cannot have happened, it seems, before April (see appendix 8). The present letter must post-date the fire, but unlike letter no. 68, which also refers to it, need not pre-date John of Salisbury's letter no. 32 (which gives the *terminus ad quem* for letter no. 68). The tone suggests that the fire is a recent event—Peter seems to assume that it will be news to John—and that the fund-raising journey with the relics is planned but not necessarily begun (see n. 6, below).

[2] Cf. Matt. 15: 23.

urget acrius, indecenter propalatum[h] nocet apertius. Exoritur aliud a nobilitate nature, aliud a necessitatis propagine. Semper enim natura suis [i]contenta est[i] limitibus, necessitas uero nullis reprimitur legibus. [j]De uentre igitur necessitatis primogenita [k]importunitas exorta,[k] cum sit molestissima quia 'manus eius contra omnes et manus omnium contra eam',[3] amicorum nunquam fores cum tedio pulsare, nunquam aures debet aggrauare. Quamobrem propensata deliberatione apud me ipsum decerno potius quantiscunque malorum confodi iaculis quam quieta carorum silentia interrumpere congestis clamoribus et lacrimis. Suggerere tamen eis quorum fides certa, amicitia indubitata est, non recuso tam dolores nostros[l] quam necessitates ut et satisfaciam proprie conscientie propter compendiosam insinuationem et non ledam amicum propter contemperatam inordinationem.[m] Vtrumque siquidem suggerens operatur, et necessitatem non tacet et amicitie leges retinet. Nam[j] amicum uel non habet [n]uel habere se non credit[n] qui fortunam suam quamcunque dubitat aperire aut instat tanquam ab inuito aliquid extorquere. Amicus nempe tam omnium consiliorum debet[o] esse conscius quam coadiutor in omnibus uoluntarius. Nolo igitur aures uestras implere uastissimis querimoniis quia stultum[p] est uerbis uelle explicare ubi uidetur res fidem dictorum excedere.[4] Hec iccirco diximus quia nobilis beati Aigulfi ecclesia cum omnibus appendiciis suis prorsus ita combusta est ut nichil preter libros et sanctorum reliquias ab incendio seruaretur. Preterea et domos quamplures in cineres[q] redegit ut sic appareat in oculis nostris tanquam gallina depilata nec pennas habens quibus pullos suos protegat nec cibos quibus alat. Non [r]aliquid aliud[r] exigimus a uobis nisi compassionem, orationem et consilium. Necesse est autem qui 'non habet ubi caput reclinet',[5] Aigulfum, peregrinari apud amicos et uicinos et rogare quod solebat rogatus et etiam non rogatus prebere.[6] Si uenerit ad partes uestras, suscipite illum tanquam illum. Nostis enim quis sit et[s] quo honore dignus sit. [t]Ad episcopum Carnotensem super hoc scribite[7] et ad alios quibus uisum fuerit. Valete.[t]

[h] prolatum *Sirmond* [i–i] est contenta *Sirmond* [j–j] *om. O* [k–k] exorta inportunitas *Val* [l] meos *Val* [m] moderationem *Val* [n–n] uel se habere non credit *O;* uel non credit se habere *Val* [o] dicitur *Sirmond* [p] stultissimum *O* [q] cinerem *O* [r–r] aliud aliquid *Val* [s] uel *Val* [t–t] *om. O*

[3] Cf. Gen. 16: 12.

[4] *fides* can carry the connotation of giving legal surety or a pledge on oath; words are not simply inadequate to carry the meaning here, but disqualified from so doing as incapable. See Niermeyer, *fides* 6, 7; cf. *DML*, 1. *fides* 6.

bandied about causes harm more openly. The one arises from the nobility of human nature, the other from the growth of necessity. For nature is always content with her own bounds, while necessity is restrained by no laws. Importunity, therefore, risen as the first-born from the womb of need, since it is most troublesome because 'its hand will be against all men and all men's hands against it,'[3] ought never to beat irksomely on the door of friends nor to assault their ears. For this reason, having considered the matter in my own mind, I am resolved to be pierced by any number of darts of misfortunes rather than to disturb the still silence of beloved ones with a mountain of cries and tears. I do not refuse, however, to confide to those whose faith is certain and whose friendship is beyond doubt both our miseries and our urgent needs so that at the same time I might satisfy my own conscience by making a brief report and not hurt a friend by making little of a calamity. Indeed both ends are served by confiding, neither keeping silent about troubles nor breaking the laws of friendship. For he who hesitates to make plain his fate, whatever it is, or presses as to extort something from one unwilling to give it, either has no friend or does not believe that he has one. For a friend ought to be both a confidant in all deliberations and equally a willing assistant in all things. I do not wish therefore to fill your ears with prodigious complaints, because it is foolish to wish to explain in words when the matter is seen to go beyond the power of speech to convey.[4] We have said this for this reason, that the noble church of Saint-Ayoul, along with all its appurtenances, has been so utterly burnt out that nothing was saved from the fire except books and the relics of saints. In addition, the fire reduced so many buildings to ashes that the church appears to our eyes like a plucked hen, having neither feathers to protect its chicks nor food to feed them. We demand nothing else of you except compassion, prayer, and counsel. But it is essential that Ayoul, who 'hath not where to lay his head,'[5] should go on a pilgrimage around friends and neighbours and ask for that which he was accustomed to offer, asked or even unasked.[6] If he should come to your region, receive him as he is. For you know who he is and of what honour he is worthy. Write to the bishop of Chartres about this,[7] and to others whom you think fit. Farewell.

[5] Matt. 8: 20; Luke 9: 58.

[6] i.e. they plan to travel with the relics of the saint to request donations towards the cost of rebuilding the priory.

[7] The bishop of Chartres at this time was Robert III, a Breton (first occurs 18 Oct. 1156, d. 23 Sept. 1164; *GC* viii. 1143–4).

19

To Bishop John of Saint-Malo and an unidentified other[1]

*c.*1145 × 1162 (poss. *c.*1161)

Domino suo karissimo et precordiali Iohanni[a] episcopo Sancti Maclouii [b]et Mag⟨no⟩ presbytero,[b] id quod est et potest.

Caritas patiens,[2] quod mirum dictu est, pene ad impatientiam me impellit. Vidi nuntium uestrum litteris uacuum. Quid hoc est? Estne tanta penes uos cartarum raritas[c] an sic uestra abbreuiata est caritas?[3] Que tam importuni silentii causa? Que ratio tam mute et silentis dilectionis? Estne, [d]inquam, in Britannia[d] consecutiuum ut ubi[e] sterilitas panis, sequatur et defectio cordis? Et panis quidem[f] inopiam audiebam,[g] sed famem ex hoc uirtutum succedere non credideram. Certe farina et lechitus olei apud Sareptenam ex quo Helias noster [h]dominus Maclouiensis[h] de his gustauit[i] non defecit.[4] Certe non defluit amor noster sed influit atque[j] effluit. Et episcopum[k] quidem excusat instantia laborum, sollicitudo ecclesiarum, compassio afflictorum, reconciliatio dissidentium? Clericum[l] quid uetat scribere, quid impedit [m]amicales litteras[m] componere? Desidia? Sed hanc studium excludit. Insipientia? Sed est ei [n]litterarum peritia multa.[n] Ignorantia nuntii uenientis? Sed michi[o] nudam salutationem detulit.[p] Festinatio properantis? Sed plura sigilla pluribus attulit.[5] Restat igitur[q] condempnanda in amicis negligentia. Quia igitur oleum non misistis, aculeum sumitis, et ideo pungi meruistis quia ungere[r] noluistis. Valete.[s] Si ualetis bene est nobis.

19 *O fo. 92*[r], *Sirmond I. 15*]
[a] J. *O* [b–b] suus Christi sacerdos *O* [c] caritas *Sirmond* [d–d] apud uos *O* [e] ubi est *O* [f] quidam *O* [g] audieram *O* [h–h] N. *O* [i] degustauit *O* [j] et *O* [k] alterum *O* [l] Alterum *O* [m–m] litteras amicales *O* [n–n] multa literatura *O* [o] hic *O* [p] attulit *O* [q] itaque *O* [r] ungi *O* [s] *om.* *O*

19 [1] John of Saint-Malo (see letter no. 14, n. 1). It is unclear whether *Mag⟨no⟩ presbytero* indicates a co-recipient, a priest or elder possibly called Magnus, or is a familiar or joking reference to John himself (he may be the *clericum* below) (but cf. also letter no. 183). The reference to famine in Brittany may be to that of 1161 (Morice, *Bretagne*, i. 105). The salutation echoes 1 Cor. 15: 10.

19

To Bishop John of Saint-Malo and an unidentified other[1]

*c.*1145 × 1162 (poss. *c.*1161)

To his dearest and beloved lord John, bishop of Saint-Malo, and to Mag⟨nus⟩, priest, what he is and what he is able to do.

Patient love,[2] amazing as it is to say it, is driving me almost to impatience. I saw your messenger without a letter. What is this? Is there so great a scarcity of writing materials in your part of the world, or is your love so abridged?[3] What is the cause of so uncivil a silence? What is the explanation for such mute and silent love? Does it follow in Brittany, I ask you, that when there is a shortage of bread there then follows a failing of the heart? For I have indeed been hearing about a scarcity of bread yet I had not believed that a famine of the virtues would follow from this. Surely the meal and the cruse of oil at the house of Sareptha from which our Elijah, the bishop of Saint-Malo, has tasted of these things have not wasted.[4] Certainly our love has not drained away but has filled up and overflowed. And does pressure of work or concern for his churches or caring for the afflicted or the settlement of disputes indeed excuse a bishop? What prevents a cleric from writing, what stops him from composing friendly letters? Idleness? But exertion drives this out. Inability? But he has great skill in writing. Ignorance of the arrival of a messenger? But he brought me a bare greeting. The speed of his departure? But he has brought here many sealed notes to many people.[5] There remains therefore negligence, to be condemned in the case of friends. Since therefore you have not sent oil you are receiving a stinging rebuke, and you deserve to be stung because you refused to apply a balm. Farewell. It is well with us if you fare well.

[2] Cf. 1 Cor. 13: 4. [3] Cf. Micah 2: 7. [4] Cf. 3 Kgs. (1 Kgs.) 17: 14, 16.

[5] i.e. John cannot claim either to have been unaware of the messenger's arrival, as he has used him to carry a simple (presumably not written) greeting, or to have been caught out by his rapid departure, as he has had time to compose other messages and give them to the same messenger.

20

To Bishop Baldwin of Noyon[1]

1148 × 1162

Domino et patri karissimo Balduino Dei gratia Nouiomensi episcopo frater Petrus abbas Cellensis, non auferre sal federis Dei sui ab omni sacrificio.[2]

Scriptum est: 'Honor regis iudicium diligit.'[3] Angeli autem Dei in celo sicut sunt ministri diuine uoluntatis ut 'fiat sicut in celo et in terra';[4] sic equissimi moderatores sunt diuini honoris ut utrumque pedem regis sui, misericordie scilicet et iustitie, sic uestiant cum digno honore ne altero neglecto uocetur palatium eorum 'domus discalceati'.[5] Iam pene in terra nostra conqueritur iustitia aduersus misericordiam dum agrum iustitie nemo uelit excolere neque 'pondus diei et estus' pro conuentione denarii diurni portare.[6] Confluunt autem glomeratim 'uiri diuitiarum'[7] et deliciarum ad amena prata misericordie, et non uere, abscondentes manum sub ascella[8] et folia ficus sue turpitudini consuentes,[9] et consulentes, dicentesque, 'Pax, pax', et non est pax.[10] Hec, domine et pater karissime, non ex supercilio Phariseorum sed suauitate litterarum uestrarum dulciter commonitus rescripserim uobis. Valete.

20 *Sirmond I. 25*]

20 [1] Baldwin II, de Boulogne, bishop of Noyon 1148–2/4 May 1167: *GC* ix. 1002–3; E. Lefèvre-Pontalis, 'Histoire de la cathédrale de Noyon', *Bibliothèque de l'École de Chartes*, lx (1899), 457–90, at p. 474, gives d. 4 May; previously abbot of Sainte-Eloi-Fontaine, Aug., dioc. Noyon, *c*.1130–*c*.1139 (*GC* ix. 1126), and abbot of Châtillon-sur-Seine, Augustinian, dioc. Langres, occurs 1145 × 1147, predecessor occurs 1138 (*GC* iv. 772). The *terminus ad quem* for this letter is the end of Peter's abbacy of Montier-la-Celle.

20

To Bishop Baldwin of Noyon[1]

1148 × 1162

To his dearest lord and father Baldwin, by the grace of God bishop of Noyon, brother Peter, abbot of Montier-la-Celle, not to take away the salt of the covenant of his God from any sacrifice.[2]

It is written: 'The king's honour loveth judgement.'[3] Moreover the angels of God in heaven are as ministers of the divine will so that it 'may be done on earth as it is in heaven';[4] thus they are the most just moderators of the divine honour that they may adorn each foot of their king, that of mercy and that of justice, with suitable honour lest if either be neglected their palace be called 'the house of the unshod'.[5] Now it has almost come about in our land that justice rails against mercy since no one wishes to tend the field of justice nor to bear 'the burden of the day and the heats' for the agreed penny a day.[6] But the 'men of riches'[7] and pleasures come together in hordes to the pleasant fields of mercy, yet not sincerely but hiding their hands under their armpits[8] and sewing together fig-leaves in their shame[9] and deliberating and saying, 'Peace, peace,' and there is no peace.[10] Let me have sent this reply to you, dearest lord and father, not out of the arrogance of the Pharisees but charmingly prompted by the elegance of your letter. Farewell.

[2] Cf. Lev. 2: 13.
[3] Ps. 98 (99): 4.
[4] Cf. Matt. 6: 10.
[5] Cf. Deut. 25: 10.
[6] Cf. Matt. 20: 2, 12.
[7] Ps. 75 (76): 6.
[8] Cf. Prov. 19: 24; 26: 15, 'the slothful hideth his hand under his armpit'.
[9] Cf. Gen. 3: 7.
[10] Cf. Ezek. 13: 10.

21

To Henry of France, bishop of Beauvais[1]

? Mar. 1151 × Jan. 1162

[a]Domino et patri suo karissimo Henrico Dei gratia episcopo Beluacensi frater ⟨Petrus⟩ Cellensis abbas,[a] salutem.

Plus satis egena est beneficiorum recordatio cuius titulus non[b] inscribitur, saltem uerbo tenus gratiarum actio.[2] Proinde 'stilo ferreo in ungue adamantino'[3] profunde memorie mandaui manipulos [c]liberalitatis uestre[c] ut nulla[d] capitis uertigine uacillare, nullo temporalis reuolutionis diluuio absorberi, nulla denique obliuionis rubigine ualeant obfuscari. Clarum, nouum et recens penes me retineo semper beneficium acceptum. Quo animo gratiosus cum acciperem ferebar[e] in dati et dantis deuotionem, eo [f]in illa[f] senescentis glorie defecatione mutato, robustius preparor[g] ad obsequium, uerius eliquesco in amorem benefactoris totum animi balsamum. Superaccessit dono uestro uultus hylaris, animus gratus, modus honestus, et manus quidem larga in beneficium totam se expandit, sed uoluntas in circumstantiis doni se supermensurauit. Quid enim fuit conuocare diocesaneos, abbates et priores? Quid iterum indicii amoris expressit tam benigna persone et negotii nostri commendatio? Quis non est admiratus tam despectam personam a fratre regis sic honorari, ab

21 *O fo. 113*[r–v], *Sirmond I. 24*]
[a–a] Domino Beluacensi frater G. suus semper *O* [b] *om. O* [c–c] libertatis nostre *O* [d] nullo *O* [e] inclinabar *O* [f–f] nulla *O* [g] propero *O*

21 [1] Henry of France, bishop of Beauvais (el. autumn 1149, cons. 1150), later archbishop of Reims (el. 14 Jan. 1162, rec. *pallium* after 30 April 1162, d. 13 Nov. 1175), brother of Louis VII. In his early years he held multiple benefices, which he gave up to enter Clairvaux in 1146 or 1147. On his early life and the date of his election to Beauvais, see the discussion and full references in *P. Ven. Epp.* ii. 195–6; on his other dates see Falkenstein, 'Alexandre III et Henri de France', pp. 104, 110; *J. S. Epp.* ii. 6 n. 13; *GC* ix. 723–31 [Beauvais], ix. 88–94 [Reims] (see also *Annales S. Dionysii Remenses*, ed. G. Waitz, MGH Scriptores xiii. 83, which also gives el. 19 Kal. Feb. 1161, i.e. 14 Jan. 1162 for his el. to Reims); on his death see also letter no. 102, n. 1. On his relations with Louis VII and Robert of Dreux, see Newman, *Seigneurs de Nesle*, i. 225–7, 246. For a detailed account, with extensive references, of much of Henry's activity in Reims and his relations with Alexander III, see Falkenstein, 'Alexandre III et Henri de France', and on his letters, esp. pp. 104–5. See also *Lexikon des Mittellaters*, iv. 2134–5.

The present letter thanks Henry for favour shown and gifts offered to Peter. *GC* ix. 729

21

To Henry of France, bishop of Beauvais[1]

? Mar. 1151 × Jan. 1162

To his dearest lord and father Henry, by the grace of God bishop of Beauvais, brother ⟨Peter⟩, abbot of Montier-la-Celle, greetings.

Most necessary is the recollection of benefits whose claim is not written down, or at least a verbal vote of thanks.[2] Thus 'with a pen of iron, with the point of a diamond'[3] I have committed the sheaves of your generous acts to the depths of memory so that they cannot be shaken by any whirling of the mind, nor engulfed by any flood of changing circumstances, nor lastly blackened by any rust of oblivion. I carry in my mind always, clear, new, and fresh, the favour I have received. The mind with which I was drawn to devotion for the gift and the giver when I gratefully received it has now been transformed by the well-known refining of ageing glory, and I am prepared more sturdily for the duty, I distil more truly all the perfume of the heart in love for the benefactor. Your cheerful expression, your gracious spirit, your honest manner has more than added to your gift, and while your generous hand opened itself wholly to confer the benefit, your good will in the circumstances in which the gift was given meted itself out beyond measure. For what was it to call together the diocesan bishops, the abbots, and the priors? Again, what proof of love did such a generous commendation of our person and business display? Who was not amazed that such an insignificant person was so honoured by the

suggests that it refers to events after the resolution of Henry's dispute with the local aristocracy and the king, when he regained full control of his see and dispensed a good deal of patronage. After his election Henry had refused to pay the *beneficia denariorum*, customary dues paid by previous bishops to the lords of the diocese for their protection. This brought him into conflict with Louis VII, who threatened to deprive him of the temporalities of the see. Henry met the pope in Jan. or Feb. 1151 and received confirmation of his rights and possessions in a letter of 7 Mar. 1151 (JL ii, no. 9456; *GC* x. Instr. 259; *PL* clxxx. 1458). On this dispute, see Falkenstein, 'Alexandre III et Henri de France', p. 107 and n. 12, and *The Historia Pontificalis of John of Salisbury*, ed. M. Chibnall (OMT, 1986), pp. 69–70 and n. 3. If the patronage referred to here is connected with the end of the dispute, then a date sometime after March 1151 is possible for this letter, but it could be much later as the imagery suggests. (*GC*'s dates are innaccurate on the dispute, as it puts the crucial letters of Bernard of Clairvaux in 1153 instead of 1150/51–see *S. Bernardi Op.* viii, nos. 278, 305 and 307, pp. 190, 222 and 226–7.)

[2] Cf. Latham, *verb/um *-otenus.*

[3] Jer. 17: 1.

episcopo Beluacensi sic amplecti, a tanto homine tantillum monachum sic nominari? Non sustinui que de me supra me[h] efferebantur, pre ruboris uerecundia; immo pro ueritatis conscientia, que admonebat me non esse illum de quo talia dicebantur, fugi, recessi, sed non longe, quia maiora pati cogebar instanti necessitate. Necessitate reuera pallium erubescentie [i]illo tempore[i] reieci cum amicorum fores ut acciperem intraui. Certe accepi a multis multa, sed a nullo tanta quanta a domino meo. Vicit notos, uicit alios amicos, uicit omnes uicinos et summa doni et modus donandi. Non sum locutus sed, quia ueni, optime recessi locatus. Non enim beneficium rogando sed ueniendo [j]consecutus sum.[j] Preuenit spondens lingua [k]rogantis linguam.[k] Pepercit regia nobilitas teneritudini frontis cito se in ruborem uerecundie conspergentis.[4] Hec omnia beneficia tua, domine, 'signata' sunt 'in thesauris meis'.[5] Quid ergo retribuam domino meo pro omnibus his que michi tribuit?[6] Me ipsum sine dubio, non contra legem me liberum in seruitutem distrahendo sed seruum amicitie tue in libertatem uindicando. Potius enim libertate ista gaudeo, si seruus tuus sum munere amicali, quam libertate qua sim[l] alienus ab officio seruiendi tibi. Valete.[m]

[h] *om. Sirmond* [i–i] *om. Sirmond* [j–j] *om. O* [k–k] linguam rogantis *O*
[l] sum *Sirmond* [m] *om. O*

king's brother, was embraced in such a way by the bishop of Beauvais, that such a paltry monk was so singled out by so great a man? I could not endure what was being proclaimed about me beyond my worth, because of humble embarrassment; nay, because of my awareness of the truth, which was reminding me that I was not the one about whom such things were being said, I fled, I withdrew, but not far, because I was compelled by pressing necessity to put up with even more. Indeed it was out of necessity that I cast off the cloak of embarrassment at that moment when I entered the doors of friends to make my acceptance. Certainly I have received much from many, but from none so much as from my lord. Both the magnificence of the gift and the manner of the giving have surpassed my familiar friends and others and all my neighbours. I did not speak up but, because I came, I left excellently set up. For I did not obtain the benefit by asking but simply by being present. The voice making the offer preceded the voice of the petitioner. Regal noblesse spared the modesty of the face being instantly suffused with humble embarrassment.[4] All these your favours, lord, are 'sealed up in my treasures'.[5] What therefore shall I render to my lord for all these things that he has granted to me?[6] Myself for sure, not distraining myself, a free man, into servitude contrary to the law but vindicating myself, a slave, into the freedom of your friendship. For I rejoice rather in this freedom, if I am your slave with a friendly obligation, than in that freedom by which I would be estranged from the duty of serving you. Farewell.

[4] *regia*: Henry was the king's brother.

[5] Deut. 32: 34.

[6] Cf. Ps. 115 (116): 12.

22

To Henry of France, bishop of Beauvais[1]

July 1160 (or Sept. 1159 × July 1160)

Domino et patri karissimo Henrico Dei gratia Beluacensi episcopo frater Petrus Cellensis abbas, zelo zelari pro domo Dei Israhel.[2]

Hactenus in palestra prelium ignaue uires non deposcebat egregias. Satis fidum erat equitare sine lorica, sine lancea, sine gladio. Sed nunc qui habet gladium tollat similiter et loricam. Ecce tempus, ecce dies, ecce causa, ubi fortissimi Israhel gladio accingi debent super femur, potentissime.[3] Nam ecce Philistiim qui secundum carnem in baculo arundineo ambulant,[4] de foueis occulte malignitatis erumpentes, castra innumerabilia, castra fortia, castra fulgurantia posuerunt. Octauianus princeps est militie ne dicam malitie huius, qui sine Deo, ut dicitur, pro Deo uult regnare.[5] Ecce ipse non uelum templi[6] sed tunicam Christi,[7] non saccum mortalitatis sed soccum maiestatis in Christo et ecclesia, iterum rescindere nititur. Hoc abhominabilius reputat unitas catholice fidei quam perfossionem lateris,[8] pedum confixionem et manuum Christi. De perfossione namque redemptio, de confixione comparata est nostra liberatio. Sed quid de scissione, de diuisione, de schismate, nisi anathematis uibratio, animarum dampnatio, morum deprauatio? Ecce 'aqua contradictionis ubi iurgati sunt filii Israhel'.[9] Tu uero, domine mi, quid? Sta cum Iosue, immo cum Iesu euaginato gladio dic omni

22 *Sirmond I. 26*]

22 [1] Henry of France, bishop of Beauvais 1149–Jan. 1162 (see letter no. 21, n. 1). This letter urges support for Pope Alexander III (el. 7 Sept. 1159, consecrated 20 Sept.) against the anti-pope Victor IV (el. 7 Sept. 1159, consecrated Oct. 4; *DP*, pp. 176–7). It may have been sent to Henry in his capacity as host of the Council of Beauvais (July 1160), at which Henry II of England and Louis VII of France were to declare their allegiances in the schism (see *Councils and Synods* i. 2, pp. 835–7), but Reuter suggests that since it does not mention the Emperor Frederick it may have been written before the news of the Council of Pavia (Feb. 1160) had reached the west (see T. A. Reuter, 'The papal schism, the empire and the west, 1159–1169', D. Phil. thesis (Oxford, 1975), p. 33 and n. 3., and see pp. 32–5 for the political and diplomatic context). Henry of France himself was a staunch supporter of Alexander III, so the aim of the present letter was certainly not simply to persuade him of the case for supporting Alexander, but was rather a public declaration of sympathy. On Henry's attitudes in the schism see Falkenstein, 'Alexandre III et Henri de France', pp. 108–15 (with extensive references)—which states that by late 1159 'Henri de France était évidamment devenu . . . le principal partisan des Alexandrins en France' (at p. 109).

22

To Henry of France, bishop of Beauvais[1]

July 1160 (or Sept. 1159 × July 1160)

To his dearest lord and father Henry, by the grace of God bishop of Beauvais, brother Peter, abbot of Montier-la-Celle, to be zealous with zeal for the house of the God of Israel.[2]

So far in the arena the struggle, being tame, has not called for outstanding powers. It was safe enough to ride without breastplate, without lance, without sword. But now let him who has a sword also put on a breastplate likewise. Behold the time, behold the day, behold the cause in which the strongest men of Israel must gird the sword upon the thigh, o thou most mighty.[3] For see how the Philistines, who walk in the flesh, leaning on a staff of a reed,[4] bursting forth from pits of hidden evil, have set up camps without number, mighty camps, resplendent camps. Octavian is the leader of this infantry, or rather of this infamy, who, godless as the saying goes, would reign in God's place.[5] See, he is trying to tear anew not the curtain of the temple[6] but Christ's tunic,[7] not the sackcloth of mortality but the sandal of majesty in Christ and the Church. The unity of the Catholic faith regards this as more abominable than the piercing of Christ's side[8] and the nailing of His feet and hands. For our redemption was won through this piercing, our delivery through this nailing. But what comes from splitting, from division, from schism, except the hurling of anathema, the damnation of souls, and the corruption of morals? Behold 'the water of contradiction, where the children of Israel strove with words'.[9] But what of you, my lord? Stand with Joshua, nay, drawing your sword with Jesus say to all who pass by,

[2] Cf. 3 Kgs. (1 Kgs.) 19: 10, 14. [3] Cf. Ps. 44 (45): 4; cf. also Exod. 32: 27.

[4] Combining 2 Cor. 10: 2–3 (v. 3: 'in carne enim ambulantes, non secundum carnem militamus') with the staff of a reed of 4 Kgs. (2 Kgs.) 18: 21; Isa. 36: 6; Ezek. 29: 6.

[5] i.e. the anti-pope Victor IV, Cardinal Octavian of Monticelli (el. 7 Sept. 1159, consecrated 4 Oct. 1159, d. 20 Apr. 1164; *DP*, pp. 177–8, and see n. 1 above); *Octauianus* suppl. by Sirmond—lacuna in R (*PL* ccii. 423, n. 28). There is also a possible echo of Bede, *In Sam. proph. allegorica expos.* ii. 10. 17–19 (*CSEL* cxix. 90; *PL* xci. 564).

[6] Cf. Matt. 27: 51; Mark 15: 38; Luke 23: 45.

[7] Cf. John 19: 23–4, i.e. he is like the Roman soldiers at the crucifixion, and not like Christ. On *saccum mortalitatis* cf. Augustine, *Enarr. in Ps.* xxix. ii. 21 (*CCSL* xxxviii. 185); Peter Lombard, *Comm. in Ps.* xxix (*PL* cxci. 297)–Ps. 29 (30): 12.

[8] Cf. John 19: 34. [9] Num. 20: 13, which continues ' . . . contra Dominum'.

transeunti, 'Noster es an aduersariorum?'[10] Habes Alexandrum, immo Petrum, aut potius Christum, qui habet ministros Petrum et Alexandrum.[11] Quis timere poterit cum Alexandro potentissimo, quis uacillare cum Petro supra petram fundato,[12] quis non superare[a] cum Christo cui data est 'omnis potestas in celo et in terra'?[13] Noui in te regiam animositatem, noui contra inflexam iniustitiam inflexibilem ceruicem, noui ardorem zeli. Age ergo pro dignitate officii, pro sublimitate natiui sanguinis, pro religione ordinis,[14] pro debito Christiane professionis, quod debes et potes. Multum enim debes; nichilominus et plurimum potes. Satis dictum est sapienti.[15] Sanum et incolumem te custodiat manus dextera[b] Dei. Vale.

23

To Bishop Alan of Auxerre[1]

30 Nov. 1152 × 1157, prob. not later than Aug.

[a]Domino et patri suo karissimo Alano Autissiodorensi episcopo, frater Petrus indignus abbas Cellensis, salutem.[a]

Verum est quia caro et sanguis regnum Dei non possidebunt.[2] Scio nec de ignorantia excusor. Ambigo tamen, uirtus pietatis in una eademque causa cum affectu carnis concurrens, utrum equiponderet[b] uel preponderet ad meritum. Sine merito namque est sola carnis affectio, aliquando tamen cum exuberat oneratur merito, sed utique malo. Sequela[c] denique cum fuerit pietatis honoratur[d] merito, sed bono. Vbi autem preuia, tunc in ambiguum replicatur sententia.

[a] superabit *Sirmond* [b] dextere *Sirmond*

23 *O fos.* 103^v–104^r, *Val fo.* 121^{r-v}, *Sirmond I. 22*]

[a–a] Idem A. autisiodorensi episcopo *O;* Domino et patri suo karissimo A. Authisiodorensi episcopo frater P. indignus abbas Cellensis salutem *Val* [b] eque ponderet *Sirmond* [c] Sequax *Sirmond* [d] honeratur *O;* oneratur *Val*

[10] Josh. 5: 13 (words spoken by Joshua to the angel holding the drawn sword).

[11] i.e. Pope Alexander III and St Peter.

[12] Cf. Matt. 16: 18; cf. also Matt. 7: 24–5; Luke 6: 48.

[13] Matt. 28: 18.

[14] *Sanguinis* and *ordinis*: Henry was the king's brother and had been a Cistercian monk (see letter no. 21, n. 1).

[15] Cf. Terence, *Phormio*, iii. 3. 541 (8), 'dictum sapienti sat est'.

'Art thou one of ours or of our adversaries?'[10] You have Alexander, or rather Peter, or more truly Christ, who has as His attendants Peter and Alexander.[11] Who can tremble at the side of all-powerful Alexander? Who can waver at the side of Peter founded on a rock?[12] Who can not prevail at the side of Christ to whom is given 'all power in heaven and in earth'?[13] I know in you regal courage, I know a neck unbending against perverse injustice, I know the fire of zeal. For the sake therefore of the dignity of your office, of the excellence of your bloodline, of the sanctity of your order,[14] and of the obligation of the Christian profession, do what you ought and can do. For you ought to do much; equally you can do very much. A word is enough to the wise.[15] May the right hand of God keep you healthy and safe. Farewell.

23

To Bishop Alan of Auxerre[1]

30 Nov. 1152 × 1157, prob. not later than Aug.

To his dearest lord and father Alan, bishop of Auxerre, brother Peter, unworthy abbot of Montier-la-Celle, greetings.

It is true that flesh and blood shall not possess the kingdom of God.[2] This I know, nor am I excused out of ignorance. I am uncertain, however, whether the virtue of mercy going hand in hand with the affection of the flesh in one and the same case should be given equal weight or whether it should have more weight in counting towards merit. For affection of the flesh alone is without merit, yet when from time to time it overflows it is loaded with desert, but that bad. Then when it has followed upon mercy it is lauded with desert, but in this case good. But where it goes first, then it is judged equivocally.

23 [1] This letter concerns the same case as no. 10, to Hugh of Sens. An appeal to a bishop would normally precede one to a metropolitan but the present letter suggests that the archbishop is already involved and none of the characters concerned have any obvious relation to the dioc. of Auxerre. This letter and no. 10 cannot therefore be put in sequence with any certainty, but would seem to be approximately contemporary. Alan of Auxerre, the author of the *Vita Secunda* of St Bernard, was el. bishop of Auxerre 30 Nov. 1152, and retired 1167 (*GC* xii. 293–5; Pacaut, *Élections*, pp. 45 and n. 3, 55, 65, 85–6 and n. 4; C. B. Bouchard, *Spirituality and Administration: the Role of the Bishop in Twelfth-Century Auxerre* (Cambridge, Mass., 1979), pp. 69–81. He d. 11 Oct., year unknown (*Obits Sens*, iii. 265, but the eds. mistakenly give 1167). See also *Dictionnaire de biographie française* i. 1070–1.

[2] Cf. 1 Cor. 15: 50.

Semitas cordis mei ad plenum inuestigare obstante uarietatum caligine nequeo, quantominus apprehendere? Sic astans turba phantasmatum [e]cordis mei audit[e] in interioribus, sic refert foris sensibus rem ut est exquirentibus. Ad quid hec quasi parabola, uel potius enigma, ut his qui foris sunt, et de his [f]que intus sunt iudicant,[f][3] satisfaciam, [g]neptis nostre[h] causam non affectu solo carnis me fouere, sed in spiritu uere pietatis et iustitie?[4] Absit a sensu meo, immo a uestro, propter carnalem supradicte neptis copulam, meam eternis condempnare ignibus animam! Quod procul dubio facerem si matrimonium illegitimum defenderem.[g] O domine et semper pater, quando autem uolueritis amice karissime, qua ascendit spiritus ille infidelitatis ad sanctam anime religiose sedem ut fidem duobus inhonestissime uite et fame haberetis et de amici expressa uobis ueritate[i] hesitaretis? Que spes amicitie in me potuit subsistere cum michi non crederetis[j] et contra me testes falsissimos reciperetis? [k]Plane contra ueritatem, quam retinere me iam in aure persuaseram, eorum recepistis uerbum, certe qui pro uino uenderent iustum et pro buccella uenderent si haberent primogenita?[5] Sic lesistis amicum? Sed dicitis: 'Non est amicus qui obstitit in uia ueritatis.' Plane inquam: 'Ita est ut dicitis.' Sed ubi est ueritas? In numero? Plures enim fuerunt. In ebriosis et impudicis? Tales siquidem sunt in conductis gratia, pretio et timore. Ita esse etsi modo non affirmo, saltem presumptione maxima in hoc credere attrahor. Pessimus inimicus et aduersarius est nepti et marito eius auunculus qui equitaturis[6] suis et sumptibus forte illum deduxit. Archiepiscopus abbati ut canonicos mitteret scripsit;[7] rebelles et inobedientes sero precedenti abbati ad tempus reconciliauit, donec fieret iniquitas. Estne hic ueritas, uel saltem species ueritatis? Fitne tediosa uobis hec nostra relatio? Certe ut saluo gratie uestre residuo dicam, tediosius in sententiam processistis. Dilationem cur negastis? Que lex, quis canon hoc docuit ut uel una dilatio in hoc articulo negaretur? Ne dicatis quod eam habuerim

[e–e] cordi meo audit a conscientia *O*; cordi meo audit *Val* [f–f] iudicant que intus sunt *O* [g–g] *om.* *O* [h] mee *Val* [i] ueritatis *O* [j] crederitis *O* [k–k] *om.* *O*

[3] Cf. 1 Cor. 5: 12–13.

[4] The marriage of Hadvide to Pierre de la Tournelle; see letter no. 10, n. 1.

[5] Cf. Gen. 25: 29–34; Prov. 28: 21.

[6] See *DML*, *equitatura* 4 (note the different sense at letter no. 36, see n. 8; cf. Niermeyer, *equitatura* 7). Presumably here the implication is, 'by force/armed force'. The uncle is unidentified: Newman's genealogy (see letter no. 10, n. 1) begins with Pierre de la Tournelle.

I cannot search out fully the byways of my heart with the darkness of indecision blocking the way; how much the less then can I comprehend them? Thus the attendant crowd of phantasms of my heart listens in the inner self and sets forth the matter as it is outwards to the senses which are seeking it out. What is the meaning of this parable, so to speak, or rather enigma, which says that I should apologize to those who are without and who are judging those things which are within[3] for supporting the cause of our niece not out of affection for the flesh alone but in a spirit of true mercy and justice?[4] Far be it from my intention, as from yours, that on account of the carnal bond of this same niece my soul be condemned to the eternal flames! This I would be bringing about without doubt if I were defending an illegal marriage. O my lord, always my father and, when you will it so, dearest friend, how did that spirit of faithlessness rise up to the holy seat of the religious soul to cause you to give credence to two men of most dishonest life and reputation and to hesitate over the truth told to you by a friend? What hope of friendship towards me could remain when you would not believe me and were admitting utterly false witnesses against me? Have you accepted, clearly contrary to the truth (which, as I had already persuaded you face to face, lies with me), the word of those who would surely sell justice for wine, and their birthright, if they had any, for a morsel of bread?[5] Can you have wounded a friend in this way? But you say: 'He is not a friend who stood in the way of truth.' Clearly I say: 'It is as you say.' But where lies the truth? In numbers? For they were more. With drunkards and shameless people? Such persons belong among those hired by favour, by money, and by fear. Even though I do not now affirm that it is so, at least I am drawn to believe this by a strong supposition. The worst enemy and adversary of the niece and her husband is the uncle who as it happened brought him to trial by means of his horsemen[6] and his riches. The archbishop wrote to the abbot that he should send canons;[7] he reconciled the rebels and the disobedient ones to the lately preceding abbot for a time, until the injustice was done. Is this not the truth, or at least the semblance of truth? Does our account grow irksome to you? Certainly, so I would say, saving what remains of your grace, you have proceeded most irksomely to your judgement. Why did you refuse an adjournment? What law, what canon, taught this, that even one adjournment be refused on this point? Do not say

[7] The archbishop is Hugh of Sens, 1142–68 (see letter no. 8, n. 1, and letter no. 10); the abbot is unidentified.

quia ante a uobis nec petii nec impetraui. Prolati namque in iudicio uestro, ita ut supputatio matrimonii fieret, nunquam fuerant.[k] Excessistis domine, excessistis. Presumptuosus [l]nimirum in hoc[l] uideor quod sic ad unguem episcopum abbas, dominum seruus, de uiis suis redarguere, immo ab eo ei[m] illatas iniurias referre, presumo. Non facerem hoc nisi auroram resurgentis[n] amicitie per concessam et recognitam in litteris uestris culpam aspicerem.[o] Nunquam petenti uenia deneganda,[p] nunquam penitenti culpa[q] imputanda. Satis est. 'Mittite gladium in uaginam.'[8] Valete.[r]

24

To Peter the Venerable[1]

*c.*1145 × 1156

[a]Domino et patri suo karissimo Petro Dei gratia uenerabili Cluniacensium abbati, frater Petrus humilis Cellensis abbas,[a] se ipsum.

Igniculum scintillantis in me spiritus uestri cineres nostri tenaciter euaporant et carbones seraphin[2] nunquam extinguendos assidua meditatione renouant. Tetigistis fateor in me non labia oris sed uenas cordis.[3] Aculeus siquidem collocutionis inter nos habite nostras interiores medullas perforauit ac in consideratione sui omnia anime interiora coegit. Reuera sermo ille efficax fuit ad torpentis anime excitationem, ad uite huius momentanee inspectionem, ad regularis professionis obseruationem, ad angelice puritatis emulationem, ad summe et ineffabilis trinitatis expeditam contemplationem. Viuus

[l–l] in hoc nimirum *Val* [m] michi *O* [n] insurgentis *Val* [o] recognoscerem *Val* [p] de neganda *Val* [q] culpa est *O* [r] *om. O*

24 *O fos.* 95[r]–98[r], *Val fos.* 115[r]–119[r], *Sirmond II.* 1]
[a–a] Domino suo et patri karissimo P. Dei gratia Cluniacensium abbati, frater G *O*; Domino et patri suo karissimo Petro Dei gratia uenerabili Cluniacensium abbati frater Petrus humilis Cellensium abbas *Val*

[8] Cf. John 18: 11.

24 [1] Peter the Venerable, abbot of Cluny 22 Aug. 1122–Christmas 1156 (*P. Ven. Epp.* ii. 257–69). The letter can be dated no more closely than the beginning of Peter of Celle's abbacy and the death of Peter the Venerable. Constable suggests (*P. Ven. Epp.* ii. 206) that

that I had that, because previously I neither demanded nor received it from you. For witnesses had never been brought forward in your court so that an assessment of the marriage might be made. You have gone too far, lord, you have gone too far. I appear too presumptuous in this matter since as an abbot I presume thus to contradict a bishop, as a servant to contradict his master about his way of acting, down to the last detail; indeed I even presume to refer back to him the injuries inflicted by him. I should not do this unless I saw the dawn of resurgent friendship through the fault being conceded and acknowledged in your letter. Pardon should never be denied to him who seeks it, sin never charged to the penitent. Enough. 'Put up the sword into the scabbard.'[8] Farewell.

24

To Peter the Venerable[1]

*c.*1145 × 1156

To his dearest lord and father Peter, by the grace of God venerable abbot of Cluny, brother Peter, humble abbot of Montier-la-Celle, himself.

Our ashes tenaciously breathe out a tiny flame of your spirit sparkling within me and fire up anew with zealous meditation the coals of the seraphim[2] which are never to be extinguished. I confess you have touched in me not the lips of my mouth but the veins of my heart.[3] Indeed the sharp point of the dialogue held between us has pierced my inner heart and has concentrated all the inner parts of the soul in contemplation of it. Truly that discourse was effective in stirring up a sluggish soul and in encouraging scrutiny of this brief life, observation of the religious life we have professed, emulation of angelic purity, and unhindered contemplation of the supreme and ineffable Trinity. It is a living discourse because it considers the true

this letter, with its criticisms of meat-eating at Cluny (see n. 43 below), prompted Peter the Venerable's letter no. 161 (which itself cannot be dated more closely than the present letter). Peter may have known Peter the Venerable's defences of Cluniac practice; on these and their context, see D. Knowles, *Cistercians and Cluniacs: The Controversy between St Bernard and Peter the Venerable* (Oxford, 1955). Peter's point, which comes towards the end of the letter, is diplomatically tempered with heavy self-criticism.

[2] Cf. Isa. 6: 6 (this must be the allusion intended given the ref. below).

[3] Cf. Isa. 6: 6–7.

quia de uera uita, purus quia de puritate summa, uerus quia de ueritate eterna. Non parcit malis sed placet bonis; remordet uitia, uirtutes suadet. Adducit in lucem obscura; tanquam speculum perlucidum uultus prospicientium renuntiat. Fateor in huius contuitu rugas meas inspexi et quod in interiori homine pulchrum prius estimaueram deforme repperi. In lucerna ista accensa domum euerti[4] et in peculio multo minus quam computaueram accepi. Marcidum inueni quod floridum credidi. Et quid plura? Fetores niduli mei uix fero quia ibi 'reptilia quorum non est numerus'[5] aspicio. Vrticarum ibi punctiones, spinarum compunctiones, ueprium complicationes, et tam paliuri sollicitudinum[6] quam cardui afflictionum[b] non parcentes exustiones. Quid namque peccatum, quid pena peccati, nisi stimuli mortis,[7] animam cruentantes, lacerantes et dilaniantes? Misera miseriis suis depascitur anima; 'mors', inquit psalmista, 'depascet eos'.[8] Vnde[c] Ysaias, 'dilatauit', inquit, 'infernus animam suam absque ullo termino quia non habuit populus scientiam'.[9] Nimium nimiumque [d]certe se infernus[d] dilatat cum etiam quosdam in corpore uiuentes gehennalibus conscientiis iamiam excruciat. Sed usque ad ostium, seu hostiam crucis, et non ultra, cruciatus isti pertingunt. Cetus namque iste qui etiam Ionam deuorat[10] omnia rapit, uniuersa deuastat, in gutture et uentre[e] malitie sue quicquid extra archam inuenerit includit. At quam felicius et quam iocundius anima capientem se caperet,[11] deuorantem[f] se absorberet, persequentem se triumpharet? Draco enim sic illuderetur, sic denique mors interficeretur, sic anima liberaretur. Vtinam sic se uindicaret anima mea[g] de aduersario suo, immo utinam infernales sic absorberet [h]in presenti miserias[h] ut nullas in crastinum futuri iudicii dimitteret penarum reliquias! Vtinam, inquam, reliquias saluationis que 'diem festum agent'[12] potius expectaret anima mea quam reliquias fecis que subsidunt in calice qui est 'in manu Domini, uini meri plenus mixto'![13] Reliquias prandiorum tuorum, Domine

[b] affectionum *O, Val, Sirmond* [c] et *O* [d–d] se certe infernus *O;* certe infernus se *Val* [e] uentee *O* [f] deuorentem *O* [g] *om. Val, Sirmond* [h–h] miserias inpresenti *O*

[4] Cf. Luke 15: 8 (Peter always has *euerto* here where the Vulgate has *euerro*).

[5] Ps. 103 (104): 25. [6] Cf. Isa. 34: 13. [7] Cf. 1 Cor. 15: 56.

[8] Ps. 48 (49): 15. [9] Cf. Isa. 5: 14; Isa. 5: 13.

[10] Cf. Jonah 2. In this passage a number of images are run together: the opening of the abyss, which is compared to the whale's mouth in this sentence, is punned with the offering of Christ on the cross which closes off Hell to the penitent (*ostium*, 'door', but here

life; it is pure because it considers the highest purity; it is true because it considers eternal truth. It does not spare the wicked but pleases the good; it rebukes vices and encourages virtues. It brings those things which are hidden out into the light; like a very clear mirror it reflects the faces of the onlookers. I confess that, looking hard into this mirror, I have seen my wrinkles, and that which I had first reckoned to be beautiful in the inner man I found to be ugly. With that candle lit I turned out the house,[4] and I found that I had far less to my name than I had reckoned. That which I thought was blooming I found to be withered. What more besides? I can scarcely tolerate the stenches of my little nest because I see there 'creeping things without number'.[5] There are the stings of nettles, the pricks of thorns, the thickets of thorn-bushes and the merciless scourgings of the torments of the thorn[6] and of the afflictions of the thistle. For what is sin, what is the penalty of sin, if not the stings of death,[7] mutilating, lacerating, and tearing apart the soul? The miserable soul is consumed by its miseries; 'death', says the Psalmist, 'shall feed upon them'.[8] Hence Isaiah says: 'Hell hath enlarged her soul without any bounds, because the people had not knowledge'.[9] Assuredly hell enlarges itself too much, far too much, when even now it torments some who are still alive with premonitions of the abyss. But these torments reach only as far as the opening, that is the offering of the cross, and no further. For this whale which also swallows Jonah[10] seizes everything, lays waste everything and shuts up in the throat and stomach of its wickedness whatever it finds outside the ark. But how much more happily and more joyfully would the soul make captive the one that was taking it prisoner,[11] swallow the one that was devouring it, triumph over the one that was pursuing it? For thus would the dragon be mocked and thus would death be slain and the soul set free. If only my soul might so deliver itself from its enemy, if only indeed it might now, in the present, so swallow up the hellish miseries as to put off no remainders of punishment to the morrow of future judgement! If only, I say, my soul was able to look forward to the remainders of salvation which 'shall keep the holiday'[12] rather than the remainders of the dregs which settle in the cup which is 'in the hand of the Lord, of strong wine full of mixture'![13] I long for the remainders of your feasts, Lord

'opening' to convey the word play, and *hostiam*—there may also be a distant echo of Lev. 17: 5).

[11] Cf. Isa. 14: 2.

[12] Cf. Ps. 75 (76): 11.

[13] Cf. Ps. 74 (75): 9; i.e. that which sinners shall drink.

Iesu, suspiro. Venter meus absque spiraculo[14] en totum se expandit et de micis siue[i] reliquiis tuis repleri appetit. [j]Quero etiam uinum, quero et uestimentum.[j] Opto quoque a sanguine peccati sanguine tuo mundari,[15] opto lineis[16] tuis, [k]Iesu, uestiri,[k] quibus in sacris uisceribus uirgineis insignitus ad offerendas [l]preces et munera pro nobis[l] processisti. Hanc sacrosanctam oblationem[m] in sancto cene conuiuio exuisti, in cruce conscidisti, in resurrectione innouatam resumpsisti, in ascensione uultibus paternis in propitiationem nostram representasti. Laua me a sordibus,[17] sana a doloribus, mundator filiorum[n] Leui, reparator filiorum Dei. Quod si manum iam glorificatam clementissime ad tam ulcerosa officia inclinare propter defluentes egroti assiduas reumatizationes refugis, habes aliam [o]inferiorem manum[o] sed bene doctam, sed satis [p]piam, sed multum[p] gratiosam, sed similem nobis passibilem, cui si dederis, immo si iusseris, facile faciles[q] curationes animarum nobis propinabit. Cluniacensem tuum loquor, cui dedisti in corde sapientiam, in ore facundiam, in sermone gratiam, in uultu auctoritatem, in operatione uirtutem, in intellectu subtilitatem. Dedisti ei et[r] licentiam ut secundum cor tuum operetur, et laborantium officinas ingressus manibus tuis confectam medicinam pro cuiusque[s] ualetudine dispenset fideliter et nummum[t] gratie pro gratia[18] opere dispensationis reportet.

Grauaris quidem, domine [u]karissime et pater,[u] in hac administratione tante multitudinis tam spatiosis discursibus[v] ut modo ad [w]celorum fines[w] curribus igneis[19] amore auido conscendas,[x] modo ad terre inferiora et partes ultimas sollicitudine populi proni in culturam 'uituli comedentis fenum'[20] resilias; modo tam procul, modo tam prope, modo supra nubes, modo iuxta uel[y] etiam infra ciues,[21] modo supra spiritum, modo infra te ipsum cogaris te leuare et deponere. Laboras sed[z] si non amas, laboras sed si fructum non uideas, laboras sed si finem non speras, laboras sed si retributionem non consideras. Et de fine quidem scriptum est quia, 'ecce finis uenit, uenit finis'.[22]

[i] siue de *O* [j–j] *om. O* [k–k] uestiri Iesu *Val* [l–l] pro nobis preces et munera *O* [m] *om. Val, Sirmond* [n] a filiorum *O* [o–o] manum inferiorem quidem *O* [p–p] *om. Sirmond* [q] *om. Val, Sirmond* [r] *om. O* [s] cuiuscumque *Val* [t] mummum [*sic*] *O;* minimum *Sirmond* [u–u] et pater karissime *O* [v] decursibus *Sirmond* [w–w] fines celorum *O, Val* [x] contendas *Val, Sirmond* [y] Goel *Sirmond* [z] *om. Val, Sirmond*

[14] Cf. Job 32: 19. [15] Cf. Rev. 1: 5. [16] i.e. the garment of the flesh.
[17] Cf. Ps. 50 (51): 4. [18] Cf. John 1: 16.
[19] Cf. 4 Kgs. (2 Kgs.) 2: 11; Ecclus. 48: 9.
[20] Ps. 105 (106): 20; i.e. the Israelites, here meaning the widespread Cluniac houses.

Jesus. My belly which is without vent[14] expands itself to the limit and hungers to be filled with your crumbs or remainders. I seek wine as well, and clothing. I wish also to be cleansed from the blood of sin by your blood,[15] I wish to be clad in your garment,[16] Jesus, decked with which in the holy Virgin's womb you came forth to offer prayers and dues on our behalf. You threw off this sacrosanct offering at the holy banquet, you tore it to pieces on the cross, you took it up again renewed at the resurrection, you presented it again at the ascension to the paternal countenance for our atonement. Cleanse me from filthiness,[17] heal me from illness, cleanser of the sons of Levi, restorer of the sons of God. But if you decline most mercifully to turn the hand which is now glorified to such ulcerous duties on account of the unending flow of diseased pus, you have another hand, lesser but well skilled, sufficiently merciful, most gracious, capable of suffering like us, which, if you permit, nay command it, will readily furnish us with ready remedies for souls. I mean your Cluniac, to whom you have given wisdom in the heart, eloquence in speech, grace in discourse, authority in expression, virtue in deeds, and keenness in understanding. You have also given him freedom to toil according to the wishes of your heart, and, having entered the workshops, to dispense faithfully the medicine prepared by your hands for the health of everyone and to earn the payment of grace for the grace[18] of the action performed.

You are burdened indeed, dearest lord and father, in this administration of such a multitude with such widespread journeyings that now you ascend in fiery chariots[19] with ardent love to the outer limit of the heavens, now you retreat to the furthest lands and the most remote regions in your care for the people who are dedicated to the nurture 'of the calf that eateth grass';[20] now very far, now near at hand, now above the clouds, now next to or even beneath the citizens,[21] now higher than the spirit, now beneath yourself, you are forced to raise yourself up and to lower yourself down. You labour even if you do not love, you labour even if you do not see the fruit, you labour even if you do not hope for the end, you labour even if you do not consider the reward. And indeed concerning the end it is written: 'Behold, the end is come, the end is come.'[22] And so the time

[21] The reading in Sirmond, 'Goel', may be an allusion to Gaal (cf. Judg. 9: 26–41), destroyed with his citizens. For Goel, cf. e.g. Jerome, *Lib. int. Heb. nom.* (*CCSL* lxxii. 75), but the relevance here is unclear.

[22] Cf. Ezek. 7: 2.

Denique appensum est in statera laboris tempus et inuentum est minus habens quam retributionis denarius.[23] Non in dies et annos producitur labor quia in modico, et in[a] breui fiet[b] laborum retributio. Iterum de fructu uidendum est quia fructus tuus fructus sublimis est,[c] fructus lucis, fructus benedictionum Domini, fructus innumerabilis. Dinumera stellas celi, dinumera[d] arenam maris, et dinumerare poteris fructum horti Domini, scilicet ecclesie[e] Cluniacensis. Quid dicam de dilectione? Annon amas, pater amantissime, dilectum ex dilecto,[24] uulneratum caritate in ligno? Noui, noui ego, nouit et angelus tuus dilectionem tuam flammescentem in Deum fortiter, recalescentem in proximum non mediocriter. Denique pius et largus remunerator non solum operum sed et affectionum ante faciem tuam, Christus Iesus, accinctus plena manu precurrit, in latere claro uultu concurrit, et[f] post tergum extento brachio[25] succurrit. Precurrit ut preuius, concurrit ut socius, succurrit ut medicus. Precurrit ut imiteris, concurrit ne lasseris, succurrit ne labaris.[g] Precurrit predestinatione, concurrit uocatione, succurrit iustificatione. Iacob in[h] utero matris preuium habuit, cum 'non ex operibus sed ex uocante dictum est, "Iacob dilexi, Esau autem odio habui"'.[26] Angelica quoque natura in confirmatione sue stabilitatis concurrentem gratiam habuit. Saulo nichilominus[i] in languore sue infidelitatis nonne gratia [j]de celo[j] succurrit?[27] Post hunc currens non deficies, cum isto uadens ad omnia sufficies, huic toto totus innixus omnia te posse non desperes. 'Omnia', inquit Apostolus, 'possum in eo qui me confortat.'[28] [k]Pennis quidem paterne necnon et materne generationis reuolat iste Filius Dei et preuolat ad sinus paternos, sed tamen gressum retardat, sustinens lassos.[k] Itineris quoque duriora et asperiora sibi[l] non ignarus sed benignus secernit. Non enim 'est dolor sicut dolor' eius,[29] et nobis planiores semitas, lapides de uia tollens, proponit.[30] Vnde ait, [m]'Pacem relinquo uobis, pacem meam do uobis',[m] [31] quasi, 'guerre uestre et debiti penalis discrimina persolui et pacis integre remedia indulsi.' Partem, inquam,[n] suam [o]meliorem

[a] *om.* *O, Val* [b] erit *O* [c] *om.* *O* [d] *om.* *O* [e] *om.* *O* [f] quia *Val* [g] labores *Sirmond* [h] cum in *O* [i] *om. Val, Sirmond* [j–j] *om. Val* [k–k] *om. O* [l] sibi Christo *O* [m–m] Pacem meam do uobis, pacem relinquo uobis *Val, Sirmond* [n] itaque *Val* [o–o] non molliorem sed meliorem *O*

[23] Cf. Matt. 20: 1–16. [24] Cf. S. of S. 5: 9.
[25] Cf. Deut. 5: 15; 7: 19; 9: 29; and many other refs.
[26] Cf. Rom. 9: 12–13.

spent working is weighed in the balance and is found to merit less than the penny reward.[23] The work is not drawn out for days or years because the toil is but little and its reward will come soon. Again concerning the fruit, it is to be seen that your fruit is sublime fruit, the fruit of light, the fruit of God's blessings, countless fruit. Count the stars in the sky, count the sand of the sea, and you will be able to count the fruit of the garden of the Lord, that is of the church of Cluny. What shall I say about love? Do you, most loving father, not indeed love the beloved of the beloved,[24] the one wounded by love on the cross? I know, I know and your angel knows, of your love, burning powerfully for God, growing warm again for your neighbour in no small way. In sum, the merciful and bountiful rewarder not only of deeds but also of affections, Jesus Christ, girt up runs ahead before your face with a full hand, runs at your side with a shining countenance, and runs behind you with his stretched-out arm.[25] He runs ahead as a guide, he runs at your side as a companion, he runs behind as a healer. He runs ahead that you may emulate, he runs at your side lest you tire, he runs behind lest you fall. He runs ahead in prefigurement, he runs at your side in vocation, he runs behind in justification. Jacob in his mother's womb had this guide ahead of him, since 'not of works but of him that calleth, it was said, "Jacob I have loved, but Esau I have hated"'.[26] The angelic nature likewise had grace running beside it in confirmation of its stability. Did not heavenly grace run behind Saul none the less in the weakness of his faithlessness?[27] Running after this guide you will not falter, advancing with him you will be equal to everything, relying completely on this complete support you should not despair of your ability to achieve everything. 'I can do all things in him who strengtheneth me,' says the Apostle.[28] This the Son of God indeed flies back on the wings engendered of the Father, and also of the mother, and flies on to the paternal bosom, but yet He slows His step, supporting the weary. He also takes upon Himself, not unwittingly but mercifully, the harsher and tougher parts of the journey. For there is 'no sorrow like to' His 'sorrow,'[29] and He lays out smooth paths for us, taking up stones from the road.[30] Whence He says, 'Peace I leave with you, my peace I give unto you,'[31] as if to say, 'I have resolved the crises of your struggle and of the debt of punishment and have granted remedies of perfect peace.' He has, I say,

[27] Presumably an allusion to Acts 9: 3–7. [28] Phil. 4: 13.
[29] Cf. Lam. 1: 12. [30] Cf. Jer. 50: 26. [31] John 14: 27.

non molliorem[o] fecit, quia simul molliorem et meliorem in mundo, ubi pressuram promittit,[32] neminem posse habere docuit. Volo quidem [p]ego meliorem,[p] sed ex gratia; eligo sepe molliorem, sed ex humanitatis natura. Non sic uero, non sic legit Deus. Diuisit enim aliter. Seorsum sed sursum posuit meliorem, [q]seorsum sed dorsum molliorem.[q] Homines autem tanquam molliores, infirmiores, seu inferiores, adhuc limum[33] plasmationis pre oculis habentes, molliora et dulciora, non meliora et duriora, appetunt. Optioni siquidem[r] nostre relinquitur utrum accipiamus meliora sed[s] duriora an[t] molliora sed deteriora. Video[u] autem humanitatem meam frequenter et diu in hoc discrimine uacillare. Modo enim[v] temptat et attrectat durum propositum quia melius, modo relabitur ad molle quia delectabilius. In istius contractu placet emptio sed displicet condicio, in alterius contractu[w] facilis condicio sed uilis emptio.

O anceps, o dubia negotiatio! Superflua carnis equidem delectatio non usquequaque est omni homini odiosa sed multum[x] quesita, multum[y] appetita, multumque a multis amplexata. Sed quousque? Modica est, transitoria est; etiam cum [z]uidetur esse,[z] non est. Se ipsam consumit, se ipsam destruit, in se crudeliter seuit. Acerbius tamen dampnum quod naturam ledit quam quod se ipsum[a] interimit. Intrat [b]in aliquem[b] huiusmodi delectatio et natura fugit.[c] Rerum omnium domina ancillam istam uelut pestem refugit, uelut mortem euitat, uelut infernum cauet. Nunquam enim aut raro in una sede morantur, uix aut nunquam simul[d] operantur. Semper namque alia est operatio necessitatis, que et nature, alia superflue delectationis. Verbi gratia, cum sepelitur aliquis uino, cibo usque ad nausiam ingurgitatur, eneruatur luxuria, nonne hinc[e] luget natura, nonne egrotat, nonne grauiter laborat? Citius procul dubio [f]deserit hunc[f] flos etatis, et morbi siue mortis intempestiue accersiuntur nuntii. Hec tamen opera carnis esse siue superflue delectationis quis ignorat? Natura uero his gaudet abstinere et, ut ait Seneca, paucis contenta est.[34] Et ratione quidem ista regitur, illa uero abusione. Illa in ueritate ambulat, monstri uero huius facies blanda ut decipiat, sed

[p–p] meliorem ego *O* [q–q] *om. Sirmond* [r] quidem *O* [s] et sed *O* [t] an uero *O* [u] Videro *Val* [v] *om. Val* [w] confractu *Val* [x] multis *Val* [y] multis *O* [z–z] esse uidetur *Val, Sirmond* [a] *corr. Hall;* ipsam *O, Val, Sirmond* [b–b] *om. Val, Sirmond* [c] refugit *O* [d] *om. Sirmond* [e] *om. Val* [f–f] hunc deserio *Val*

[32] Cf. John 16: 33 ('Partem . . . meliorem' echoes Luke 10: 42).
[33] Cf. Gen. 2: 7.

made His the better part, not the easier, for He has taught that no one can have at the same time the easier and the better in this world where He promises distress.[32] I myself indeed wish to take the better way, but owing to divine grace; I frequently choose the easier, but owing to human nature. Truly indeed God does not choose this way. For He apportioned things otherwise. He placed the better on one side, but above, the easier on another, but below. But men, being feebler, weaker and lower, having the slime[33] of creation still before their eyes, seek out the softer and sweeter ways, not the better and harder. It is left indeed to our free will whether to take up the better but harder way or the easier but poorer. But I see my human nature wavering frequently and protractedly in this critical dilemma. For at one moment it strives and gropes towards the hard resolution because it is the better, the next it relapses to the easy choice because it is more agreeable. In the first deal the purchase is pleasing but the terms are not, in the second the terms are easy but the purchase worthless.

O uncertain, o doubtful business! Excessive delight of the flesh indeed is not everywhere hateful to every man but is much sought after, much desired, and much embraced by many. But to what end? It is trifling, it is transient; even when it appears to be, it is not. It devours itself, it undermines itself, it rages savagely against itself. This offence however is more bitter because it harms nature than because it undermines itself. Delight of this sort enters into someone and nature flees. The mistress of all things flees from this handmaiden as from a pestilence, shuns her like death and is wary of her as of hell. For never or rarely do they linger in one seat, and hardly or never do they work together. For in every case the process of necessity, and likewise that of nature, is one thing, while that of excessive delight is another. For example, when someone is drowned in wine, gorged with food to the point of sickness, debilitated by excess, does not nature weep for this, does she not grow sick because of this, does she not suffer terribly because of this? Certainly the bloom of life deserts that person more rapidly and the messengers of disease or of death are unseasonably summoned. Yet who does not know that this is the work of the flesh, or rather of excessive delight? But nature is glad to abstain from these things and, as Seneca says, is content with few things.[34] It is by reason indeed that the one, nature, is guided, but the other, excess, is guided by misuse. The former walks in truth but the

[34] Cf. Boethius, *De cons. philos.* ii. prose v. 16: 'Paucis enim minimisque natura contenta est,' (*CCSL* xciv. 27).

in posterioribus circumfert aculeum scorpionis ut perimat. Mentum simplicium apprehendit[35] sed inguina ferit. Cohors et tribunus[36] synagoge peccantium huius[37] principatum sibi assumit in caput et regem et respuit super mulam regis uerum Salomonem.[38] O peccatum! O iniquitas! 'Pater mi, pater mi, currus Israhel et auriga eius',[39] non sileat saltem [g]in ore uestro[g] spiritus iusti Nathan, non sinat fieri tantum nefas in Israhel Dei. Sceptrum namque regni superflua carnis delectatione obtinente, que pax super Israhel?[40] Immo que iura non subuertuntur, que leges non obliterantur, que ratio non exulatur, que uirtus non confunditur, que boni species non suffocatur, quod genus erroris non 'extollitur supra omne quod dicitur Dominus aut quod colitur'?[41] Hec [h]radix est[h] peccati, totius honestatis tinea, fouea uitiorum, puteus demonum, uorago animarum. Recludite, obsecro, recludite feram istam pessimam que deuorat Ioseph nostrum[42] uel potius filios Iacob et Ioseph. Certe nimium efferatur[i] et rupto propositi ac religionis repagulo usque ad sancta sanctorum Cluniacensis ordinis imperii sui fines propagare conatur. Vbi enim sine licentia [j]carnes comeduntur,[j] nonne Ade preuaricatio renouatur,[43] nonne uoti et sancte institutionis paradisus uiolatur? Nonne legitur quia 'Inebriabo sagittas meas sanguine et gladius meus deuorabit carnes'?[44] Sanctitatis opprobrium, religionis abhominatio est, non quidem carnes edere, sed cum sanguine inobedientie. Vnde a sanguine et[k] suffocatis iubet lex abstinere.[45] A suffocatis non abstinet qui furtim edere non timet. Periculo namque prelatorum fiunt transgressiones commissorum. Vasorum custodes sacrorum puniuntur cum negligentia sua de templo Domini asportantur et usque ad manus concubinarum regis Babilonis humiliantur.[46] Sapientiorem me non doceo, sanctiorem non instruo, feruentiorem non excito, studiosiorem non prouoco, sed timores meos manifesto, sed dolores aperio, sed consilium quero, sed euadendi semitam interrogo. Audio

[g–g] more uestro *Sirmond* [h–h] est radix *O* [i] effertur *O* [j–j] comeduntur carnes *Sirmond* [k] et a *Val*

[35] Cf. 1 Kgs. (1 Sam.) 17: 35.
[36] Cf. John 18: 12.
[37] Cf. Ecclus. 16: 7; 21: 10.
[38] Cf. 3 Kgs. (1 Kgs.) 1: 33, 38, 44 (also Christ, the true Solomon, entering Jerusalem).
[39] 4 Kgs. (2 Kgs.) 2: 12; 13: 14.
[40] Cf. Ps. 124 (125): 5; 127 (128): 6; the ref. to Nathan here is presumably to his words in 2 Kgs. (2 Sam.) 12: 1–14.
[41] Cf. 2 Thess. 2: 4 (Vulgate has 'Deus' not 'dominus').

face of the latter monster is pleasant so that it may deceive, yet it carries in its rear quarters a scorpion's sting so that it may destroy. It seizes the throat[35] of the simple but strikes at the groin. The band and the tribune[36] of this congregation of sinners[37] usurps the sovereignty, as head and king, and despises the true Solomon on the king's mule.[38] O sin! O wickedness! 'O my father, my father, the chariot of Israel and the guider thereof,'[39] at least let the spirit of the righteous Nathan not be silent on your lips, let it not permit so great an evil to be done in God's Israel. For if the sceptre of the king is held by excessive worldly delight, what peace can there be upon Israel?[40] Nay, what rights are not overturned, what laws are not effaced, what reason is not cast out, what virtue is not confounded, what kind of good is not stifled, what type of wrongdoing is not 'lifted up above all that is called Lord or that is worshipped'?[41] This is the root of sin, the worm that gnaws at all integrity, the snare of vices, the pit of demons, the abyss that devours souls. Lock up, I beg you, lock up that evil beast which is devouring our Joseph,[42] or rather the sons of Jacob and Joseph. Truly it is grown too fierce and, having burst the bond of the profession of a religious, is trying to extend the bounds of its rule even as far as the holy of holies of the Cluniac order. For where meat is eaten without licence, is not the transgression of Adam renewed,[43] is not the paradise of the vow and of the holy ordinance violated? Is it not written: 'I will make my arrows drunk with blood and my sword shall devour flesh'?[44] It is a reproach to sanctity, an abomination of the religious life, not indeed to eat meat, but to do so with the blood of disobedience. Thus the law orders us to abstain from blood and from strangled animals.[45] He is not abstaining from strangled animals who is not afraid to eat them secretly. For to the peril of the leaders arise the transgressions of those set under them. The guardians of the sacred vessels are punished when through their negligence those vessels are carried away from the temple of God and are abused at the hands of the very concubines of the king of Babylon.[46] I do not presume to teach one who is wiser than I, to instruct one who is more devout, to stir up one who is more zealous, to challenge one who is more eager, but I am making my fears plain, laying bare my sorrows,

[42] Cf. Gen. 37: 20, 33 (Joseph of course was not so devoured). The sons of Jacob and Joseph means all those favoured of God, i.e. the faithful.

[43] This criticism of meat-eating at Cluny is the point to which Peter has been building (see n. 1 above); on the transgression of Adam, cf. Rom. 5: 14.

[44] Deut. 32: 42.

[45] Cf. Lev. 3: 17; Acts 15: 20, 29; 21: 25.

[46] Cf. Dan. 5: 2–3, 23; cf. also 4 Kgs. (2 Kgs.) 25: 13–21.

principes populi suspensos in patibulis[l] et affixos contra solem propter peccata populi,[47] et sompno uacare ualeo? Dicentem Iacob ad Laban in summo articulo iudicii[m] lego: 'Oues tue et capre steriles non fuerunt, arietes gregis tui non comedi, nec captum a bestia ostendi tibi. Ego dampnum[n] omne restituebam; quicquid furto peribat a me exigebas. Die noctuque estu urebar et gelu, fugiebatque sompnus ab oculis meis. Sic per uiginti annos [o]in domo tua seruiui tibi.'[o] [48] Hec, inquam, lego et [p]non inconsolabiliter inertiam meam[p] lugeo? Vbi namque[q] oues cure mee, ubi capre non[r] steriles? Qui enim a pueritia sua in claustris regulariter eruditi sunt et tunicam uite atque[s] conuersationis sue immaculatam seruauerunt, oues Domini sunt. Qui de seculo fetorem luxurie fugientes penitentie habitum sumunt [t]et seruant,[t] capre Domini nichilominus sunt. Sed ubi Iacob, ubi denique[u] abbas, tam sedulus exhortator, tam feruidus redarguitor, tam cautus prouisor, tam beneuolus persuasor, tam contra rabiem luporum potens, tam contra morborum pestilentiam sapiens, tam ad aeris intemperiem[v] patiens, tam ad latronum insidias prudens, tam fidelis in commisso, tam uigil in euitando dampno, tam perseuerans in incepto seruitio? Dampna Domini mei uideo sed quomodo resarciam ignoro. Esset quidem iusta recompensatio si numero numerum equarem, si pretium par pari pretio restituerem. Nunc uero cum non sit michi nisi una anima, si[w] perierint per culpam meam tres aut quattuor quid faciam? Anne triplicatam uel[x] quadruplicatam penam persoluam? Quod si quoquo modo penam istam pati possem, centuplicatam forte[y] qua patientia sustinerem? Ista attendens miror me non mirari, expauesco me non expauescere. Certe non est sompnus[z] simplex; sopor est[a] aut letargia que[b] me tenet. Obsecro mittite antidotum.

[l] patibulo *O, Val* [m] indicii *Val* [n] dampnum tibi *O* [o–o] seruiui tibi in domo tua *Val* [p–p] inconsolabiliter inertiam meam non *Val* [q] nam *O* [r] *om. Val* [s] ac *O* [t–t] *om. Val, Sirmond* [u] *om. Val, Sirmond* [v] intemperantiam *O, Val* [w] nisi *O* [x] aut *O* [y] *om. Val* [z] *om. O* [a] *om. Sirmond, Val* [b] est que *Sirmond*

seeking counsel, asking after the path of escape. Can I listen to the princes of the people, the princes who are hanging in gibbets and placed out facing the sun on account of the sins of the people,[47] and still have peace to sleep? I read the words of Jacob speaking to Laban, in the final part of the dispute: 'Thy ewes and goats were not barren, the rams of thy flock I did not eat, neither did I shew thee that which the beast had torn. I made good all the damage; whatsoever was lost by theft, thou didst exact it of me. Day and night was I parched with heat and with frost, and sleep departed from my eyes. And in this manner have I served thee in thy house twenty years.'[48] Can I, I ask you, read this and not lament my idleness inconsolably? For where are the sheep in my care, where are the fertile goats? For those who have been educated in the cloister from their childhood according to the Rule and have kept pure the cloak of their life and conversation are the sheep of the Lord. Those who, fleeing the stench of decadence in the world, take up and keep on the garb of penitence are no less the goats of the Lord. But where is Jacob, where then is the abbot, at once the zealous encourager, the keen corrector, the careful provider, the kindly persuader, powerful against the savagery of wolves, wise in the face of the pestilence of diseases, enduring of the inclemency of the skies, perceptive of the tricks of thieves, faithful in his commission, vigilant in avoiding harm, persevering in the service he has undertaken? I see the wounds of my Lord but I do not know how to heal them. It would indeed be just recompense if I matched number with number, if I paid equal price for equal price. Now, however, since I have only one soul, what should I do if through my fault three or four should perish? Should I pay a three- or a four-fold penalty? But if somehow I were able to bear that penalty, by what capacity for endurance should I withstand perhaps a hundredfold multiplication? Awaiting this, I wonder that I do not wonder, I fear that I am not afraid. Surely it is no ordinary sleep but a stupor or lethargy which holds me. I beg you, send the remedy.

[47] Cf. Num. 25: 4.

[48] Gen. 31: 38–41 (Vulgate has *reddebam* not *restituebam* and *fugiebat* not *fugiebatque*).

25

? To Heloise[1]

*c.*1145 × 1162

Domine sue seruus suus, spiritum rectum.

Quod Filius hominis non uenerit pacem mittere in terram sed gladium,[2] et quod Spiritus sanctus super principes nostros in igne descenderit,[3] quodque [a]Ysaac ignem[a] pene et ligna discipline nostre portauerit,[4] scienti refero. Hec etiam fortassis ratio quare[b] Iacob in benedictione filiorum ⟨ad⟩[c] Ioseph manus transuersauerit,[5] quatinus singulorum non natiuitatis ordo aut priuilegia sed meritorum et morum attendantur officia. Virtute namque discretionis seruata et misericordia in sua triumphat patria et iustitia congrue disponit totius regni gubernacula. Cum itaque palatium ingredimur misericordie, flores et fructus decerpimus olive. Cum ad tribunal iustitie assistimus, palmam reportamus et de pomis [d]solis et lune[d] [6] satiamur. †Hec in regine nostre uestimento delectabilis uarietas[7] ad[e] tollenda fastigia[f] filiorum [g]hominum Dei immutabilis mutabilitas et eterna alteritas.† [8] Idem namque iustus et misericors Deus non uarietate proprie substantie dicitur, sed mutabilitate culpe nostre uel penitentie talis uel talis nominatur.[g] Iohannes in[h] aqua tantum baptizat nec uulnus originalis peccati sanat; Christus Iesus in spiritu iudicii et spiritu ardoris, et celum reserat.[9] 'Omnia', inquit Apostolus, 'mundantur in

25 *O fo. 140^{r-v}, Sirmond II. 11*]
[a–a] ignem Isaac *O* [b] quare est *O* [c] *Hall* [d–d] lune et solis *Sirmond* [e] et ad *Sirmond* [f] fastidia *O* [g–g] non solum hominum sed et Dei immutabilis immutabilitas et eterna eternitas *Sirmond* [h] quoque in *O*

25 [1] Heloise, abbess of Le Paraclet 1129–16 May 1163/4: E. McLeod, *Héloïse* (London, 1938, 1971), pp. 116, 225 and n. 219; *GC* xii. 572–4. Sirmond puts this together with letter no. 27 (as nos. II. 10 and II. 11–see concordances), and gives Matilda of Fontevrault as recipient of both (and *PL* follows this). *O* sets the two apart (25 = *O*62, 27 = *O*11), and has the rubric 'Abbatisse de paraclito que pro fugitiuo rogabat' for this letter. While *O*'s rubrics and salutations are generally confused, the reference to the prior of Saint-Ayoul, which was in Provins and thus very close to Le Paraclet, does support the identification of Heloise as the more likely recipient. On Saint-Ayoul, see appendix 8. The priors of Saint-Ayoul in this period were Eudes, occurs 1138, Milon, occurs 1145, Simon, 1148–1154/5 (see also letter no. 59, n. 1), Joscelin, 1155–9, and Nivelon, occurs 1163: Godefroy, 'Saint-Ayoul', ii. 30–5 (but he follows *PL* in giving Matilda as the recipient of this letter). The dates are those of Peter's abbacy of Montier-la-Celle. (Salutation echoes Ps. 50 (51): 12.)

[2] Cf. Matt. 10: 34. [3] Cf. Acts 2: 3.

25

? To Heloise[1]

*c.*1145 × 1162

To his lady, her servant, a proper spirit.

I remind one who knows it well that the Son of man came not to send peace upon the earth but the sword,[2] and that the Holy Spirit descended upon our leaders in fire,[3] and that Isaac bore the fire of our punishment and the rods of our instruction.[4] This too is perhaps the reason why Jacob, conferring blessings on his sons, turned his hands to Joseph,[5] to the end that not the status or the privileges of birth of individuals but rather their dutiful actions arising from their merits and conduct be considered. For when the virtue of discernment is preserved mercy triumphs in its own land and justice harmoniously sets the government of the whole kingdom in order. And so when we enter the palace of mercy we pluck the flowers and the fruit of the olive. When we stand before the tribunal of justice we receive the palm and are filled with the fruits brought forth by the sun and the moon.[6] †This variety in the dress of our queen[7] is agreeable for removing the pride of the sons of men; God's immutable mutability and eternal otherness.†[8] For the same just and merciful God is thus described, not by the variableness of His own substance but by the mutability of our guilt or penitence, to be such or such. John baptizes only in water and he does not heal the wound of original sin; Christ Jesus baptizes in the spirit of justice and in the spirit of ardour and opens up the heavens.[9] 'All things', says the Apostle, 'are cleansed

[4] Cf. Gen. 22: 6. Isaac signifies Christ sacrificed for our sins, cf. e.g. *Glossa ad loc.*: 'Abraham ergo Deum Patrem significat, Isaac Christum . . . Et sicut Isaac ligna portabat, quibus imponendus erat, sic Christus crucem, in quo figendus erat' (*PL* cxiii. 139).

[5] Cf. Gen. 49: 1–28, esp. 22–6.

[6] Cf. Deut. 33: 14.

[7] Cf. Ps. 44 (45): 10, 14–15.

[8] 'Dei . . . alteritas' is difficult to accommodate syntactically, and the passage is corrupt. The point of the whole passage is that mercy based on consideration for individual circumstances should prevail over unbending justice even if this seems inconsistent; God's justice itself is apparently variable, from a mortal perspective, but is in fact unchanging in its apparent changeableness, and so there is nothing to fear if mere human justice appear changeable. Peter is excusing his leniency towards the prior of Saint-Ayoul, whose case he is going on to discuss.

[9] Cf. Matt. 3; Mark 1: 1–11; Luke 3: 1–22; John 1: 6–36; Acts 1: 5; 11: 16.

sanguine, et non fit remissio nisi in sanguine.'[10] Neque[i] itaque 'uestimentum mixtum sanguine sit in combustionem'[11] propter peccati transgressionem. Christus septies contra uelum sanctuarii proprio digito suum aspersit [j]ad emundationem criminum nostrorum sanguinem.[j][12] Hoc nos docuit unus magister noster qui in celis est, hoc legislator in figura monuit, 'non auferes', inquiens, 'sal federis Dei[k] tui in omni sacrificio.'[13] Satis dictum est sapienti.[14] Priorem illum sancti Aigulfi excuso quia quod facere potuit et debuit fecit.[15] Si aliud uel aliter fecisset offensam nostram incurreret. Vale.[l] Proderit tamen peccanti precedente penitentia oratio uestra et sancti conuentus uestri. [m]Iterum uale.[m]

26

To the prior of Montier-la-Celle[1]

*c.*1145 × 1162

Priori suo suus abbas.[a]

Res humane qualiter in mente diuina pensentur conspectibus hominum in hac uolubilitate mundanorum absconditur. Solummodo angelica puritas his prout datur admiscetur archanis, ac de profundo misteriorum edocta quibus dignum uidetur reuelare sufficit. Interim temeritas nostra sic in se ipsa obscurata confunditur ut nec remota sensibus aliquatinus apprehendat nec saltem uicina cognitione perfecta contingat. Digna hec ultio in presumptorem ut et de preteritis arguatur et a futuris coherceatur. Timore huius periculi, mi dulcissime, admonitus, de presentibus quidem angor, et tamen futurorum presentiens caliginem uias incognitas reformido. Gratia uero diuini

[i] ne *O* [j–j] sanguinem ad emundationem criminum nostrorum *O* [k] *om. O*
[l] ualete *O* [m–m] *om. O*

26 *O fo. 114[r–v], Val fos. 123[v]–124[v], Sirmond II. 12*]
[a] G. *O*

[10] Cf. Heb. 9: 22. [11] Cf. Isa. 9: 5.
[12] Cf. Lev. 4: 6, 17, prefiguring the rending of the veil of the temple at the crucifixion (Matt. 27: 51; Mark 15: 38; Luke 23: 45); cf. also *Glossa ad* Lev. 4: 6 (*PL* cxiii. 306).
[13] Cf. Lev. 2: 13.
[14] Cf. Terence, *Phormio*, iii. 3. 541 (8), 'dictum sapienti sat est'. [15] See n. 1 above.

26 [1] The addressee may be the prior of Montier-la-Celle, but could be the prior of one of its dependencies. There is no evidence to connect the letter with any particular absence

with blood, and without blood there is no remission.'[10] Nor thus let 'the garment fouled with blood be burnt'[11] on account of the transgression of sin. Seven times Christ sprinkled His blood against the veil of the sanctuary with His own finger for the cleansing of our sins.[12] Our one teacher who is in heaven taught us this; the lawgiver cautioned us about this in an allegory, saying, 'Neither shalt thou take away the salt of the covenant of thy God from any sacrifice.'[13] A word is enough to the wise.[14] I am excusing that prior of Saint-Ayoul because he did what he could and what he ought to have done.[15] If he had done other or otherwise he would incur our displeasure. Farewell. Your prayer and that of your holy community will, however, be effectual for the sinner following on his repentance. Farewell again.

26

To the prior of Montier-la-Celle[1]

*c.*1145 × 1162

To his prior, his abbot.

The manner in which human affairs are weighed in the divine mind escapes the perception of men, caught up in the instability of earthly things. Angelic purity alone, according as it is granted, has access to these secrets and, instructed in the depth of mysteries, is sufficient to reveal them to those to whom it is judged fitting to do so. Meanwhile our rash understanding, blinded in itself, is so confused that it neither grasps at all those things which are remote from the senses nor even has a complete understanding of those which are near at hand. It is a fitting judgement on a presumptuous person that he is both censured for the past and constrained by future events. Having been cautioned by fear of this danger, my dearest one, although I am indeed suffering under the present circumstances, yet having a presentiment of the darkness of future things I am in dread of the unknown roads ahead. But with the grace of divine aid, if it is at hand,

of Peter's from Montier-la-Celle. Little is known of his travels, which were probably not extensive. This letter appears to refer to a dispute between the prior and some of the monks, to which Peter may be alluding in the metaphor of the relationship between heart and body. Godefroy, 'Saint-Ayoul', ii. 35, suggests that the recipient is Prior Joscelin of Saint-Ayoul (1155–9), but Montier-la-Celle had many dependencies. The priors of Montier-la-Celle itself in this period are not known, but a Prior Peter occurs 1152 (Lalore, *Cartulaires*, vi. 54–5, no. 46).

auxilii, si affuerit, nec profunda pelagi pertimesco nec etiam queque intemptata arripere diffido. Etsi enim parum roborata trepidet[b] affectio, poterit sine dubio consolidari insuperabili superni luminis patrocinio. O Iesu! Cui uanum fuit ad te confugere[c]? Cui male cessit te et 'inter uepres herentem cornibus'[2] querere? Te quidem nec pietas deserit nec omnipotentia atque ob id tuis nec pium ferre recusas suffragium [d]nec de impotentia pretendis suffugium.[d] Sua potius perit quicunque periclitatur diffidentia quam tua inclementia. Nostro si dignaris obsequio mentem nostram compunge tactu interno et in funiculis amoris tui reduc a seculo et deduc in heremo. Tumultus non quiescat donec tanquam spumam ad littoris quieta nos eiciat. Fiat, fiat super nos misericordia tua, Domine.[3] Non conuertatur amaritudo potionis[e] nisi omnia expurgauerit superflui humoris. Honoris ambitio, carnis delectatio, amicorum confabulatio, consanguineorum uisitatio, subiectorum prelatio, maioris potestatis ostentatio, ut quid? Nonne his anima compeditur ne ad superna euadat? Nonne his complicatur ne uirtutum pennis celestia petat? [f]Et horum quidem finis erit,[f] sed sine fine pena durabit. Alterum horum fieri necesse est, aut uincere hec aut ab his uinci, aut superare aut subdi, aut fugere aut includi. Sanius est igitur nudum enatare quam uestitum submergi, solum effugere quam cum multis periclitari. Quid, cor humanum, expauescis? Quid refugis? Fructus solitudinis non est quidem mollis est tamen fortis, non est pinguis est tamen dulcis, est durus sed in cortice, est acerbus sed in superficie, est noui saporis sed inchoantibus, est conterens dentes sed non consuescentibus. O cor humanum, cur times renouari? Cur abhorres reparari? Velis nolis hinc abire compelleris, uelis nolis sine mora emigrabis. O cor excors, cur non curris ad Dominum cordis? Cur omnia colligis et te ipsum non colis? Dignitate precellis, potestate excedis, auctoritate quicquid creatum sub celo est euincis.[g] Nobilitatis tue progenies quanti sit, ob ignobilem conuersationem non attendunt qui post corpus suum te ponunt;[4] exemplar tue formationis non meminerunt qui inter corpus et spiritum que sit

[b] tepidet *O* [c] fugere *Val* [d–d] *om. Sirmond* [e] passionis *Sirmond*
[f–f] Et homini quidem finis finis erit *O* [g] uincis *O*

[2] Gen. 22: 13; i.e. like the kid which saved Isaac by being sacrificed in his place.
[3] Cf. Ps. 32 (33): 22.
[4] Cf. Ezek. 23: 35.

I am not terrified by the depths of the sea nor do I hesitate to seize even things untried. For even if an insufficiently strong affection should waver it will without doubt be able to be strengthened by the unquenchable protection of the celestial light. O Jesus! For whom was it fruitless to fly to you? For whom did it turn out ill to seek you even 'amongst the briars sticking fast by the horns'?[2] You indeed neither mercy nor omnipotence deserts and for this reason you neither refuse to bring kindly help to your own nor do you offer a refuge from a position of weakness. Whoever is endangered perishes rather through his own faithlessness than through your lack of mercy. If you deem our service worthy, goad our mind with an inward touch and lead it from the world with the cords of your love, and guide it in the wilderness. Let the storm not grow calm until it throws us like foam on to the tranquillity of the shore. Let thy mercy, O Lord, be upon us.[3] Let not the bitterness of the draught be transformed unless all of the excess fluid has been expelled. To what end are ambition for honour, worldly delight, the society of friends, visiting of relatives, the promotion of dependants, the display of greater power? Is the soul not shackled by these things so that it cannot ascend to the heights? Is it not entangled with them so that it cannot seek out the heavens on the wings of virtue? And of these things indeed there will be an end, but the punishment will endure without end. It is necessary that one or other of these things should happen, that we should either defeat or be defeated by them, overcome or be subdued, flee or be trapped. It is healthier therefore to swim away naked than to be drowned fully clothed, to flee alone than to be imperilled with many others. What are you afraid of, you human heart? What are you running from? The fruit of solitude is certainly not soft but it is firm, it is not fleshy but it is sweet, it is tough but only on the outside, it is bitter but only on the surface, it has a new flavour but only for the inexperienced, it is tooth-grinding but not to those accustomed to it. O human heart, why are you afraid to be renewed? Why do you shrink from being restored? Willing or unwilling you will be forced to take your leave from here, willing or unwilling you will depart without delay. O senseless heart, why do you not rush to the Lord of the heart? Why do you procure all these things and not provide for your own self? You excel in worth, exceed in power, and surpass in authority whatever is created beneath the heavens. Those who turn their back on you[4] do not, through their ignoble manner of life, consider how worthy is the progeny of your nobility; those who do not reflect on the difference between body and spirit have forgotten the

differentia non animaduertunt. Natales tuos relege et de quam spectabili[h] [i]sis genere[i] recole. Generi tuo maculam seruitutis noli irrogare quia seruitus tibi, non a te, debetur. Etenim tu in loco sublimi sedere, ceteri[j] uero tibi debent assistere. Tuum est mandare, ceterorum ad mandatum uenire uel[k] pro contemptu uindictam excipere. Tuum est iniungere, subiectorum sine discrimine iniuncta effectui mancipare. Soli Deo si dignum prestiteris obsequium, tuum ad omnia ualebit imperium. Hoc interim confabulatorium omittam et tempus et locum constituam quo narrationes, rationes et[l] allegationes utrinque liberius audiam. Valete.

27

To Matilda of Fontevrault[1]

1149, after April × 21 May 1155

Venerabili abbatisse Fontisebraldi Matildi,[a] [b]frater Petrus Cellensis abbas,[b] suus in Christo amicus, gratiam et gloriam sponsi eterni.

Inspector conscientiarum Deus et testis nouit quibus dignationem uestram precordiis exceperim, quam incomprehensibiliter [c]ad confederationem[d] mutui amoris exultauerim, quamque[e] incomparabiliter[c] omni auro familiaritatem uestram pretulerim. Vnica siquidem et pura me uobis prius conciliauit gratia, tum[f] deinde ampliandi[g] amoris multiplex superuenit causa. Vbi enim nulla[h] operum preludia, nulla precedunt officiorum blandimenta, unde amorem dixerim procedere nisi ex[i] gratia? Hec enim operatur motibus propriis et spontaneis in [j]corde hominum sine[j] penitentia, cum multa reuerentia, et absque inuidorum calumpnia. Hec aufert suspicionem, confert affectionem, defert honorem, refert pudorem. Hac interueniente[k] soluuntur malignantium[l] susurria, consolidatur bonorum[m] concordia et prorsus adimuntur insidiantium machinamenta.[n] Hec spirituum coagulum

[h] expectabili *O, Val* [i–i] genere sis *Val* [j] cetera *O, Val* [k] et *Sirmond* [l] *om. O*

27 *O fos. 101*[v]*–103*[r], *Val fos. 122*[r]*–123*[v], *Sirmond II. 10*, *Ad1* (*fragment only, ends at: 'Si enim sanctius . . .'*) *fo. 110*[v], *Ad2 fos. 1*[r]*–2*[v], *G fos. 178*[r]*–180*[r], *Z fo. 160*[r–v], *Vi fos. 40*[r]*–41*[v], *VS fos. 215*[r]*–216*[r]]

[a] M. *O. Val, Ad1, Ad2, Z, Vi, VS* [b–b] frater G. Christi sacerdos indignus *O;* frater Petrus Cellensium abbas *Val;* B. Clareuallensis abbas *Ad1;* B. Clarevallis abbas *Ad2;* P. Cellis abbas *Z, Vi;* frater P. Cellis abbas *VS* [c–c] *om. Z*

pattern on which you are moulded. Consider your origin again and recall of what admirable descent you are. Do not inflict the shame of servitude on your kin, for servitude is owed to you not by you. For you must sit in the highest place, but the rest must wait upon you. It is your place to give the order, theirs to attend the summons or be punished for contempt. Your role is to demand, that of your subjects to carry out whatever is demanded without question. If you display a worthy obedience to the only God, your command will avail in all things. Meanwhile let me cease this chattering and appoint a time and a place in which I shall have more leisure to hear what stories, arguments, and allegations there are on both sides. Farewell.

27

To Matilda of Fontevrault[1]

1149, after April × 21 May 1155

To the venerable abbess of Fontevrault, Matilda, brother Peter, abbot of Montier-la-Celle, her friend in Christ, the grace and glory of the eternal bridegroom.

God the examiner and witness of consciences knows with what emotions I received your worthiness, how immeasurably I rejoiced at the alliance of mutual love, and how incomparably high I set your friendship above all gold. Indeed a singular and pure grace first united me with you, but then followed many reasons for enhancing love. For where no preparatory services, no flattering courtesies precede it, where can I say love comes from except from grace? For this works by its own spontaneous motions in the heart of men, without remorse, with much reverence, and free from the calumny of the envious. It removes suspicion, bestows affection, brings honour, and restores modesty. By its intervention the whispers of the malicious are dissolved, the harmony of the good strengthened, and the stratagems of the cunning utterly undone. This, the bond of

[d] considerationem *O, Ad1* [e] quam *Vi* [f] tunc *Val;* tamen *Ad1, Ad2, Z, Vi, VS* [g] ampliandam *Ad1* [h] nulla causa *Ad1* [i] a *Ad1, Ad2, Z, Vi, VS* [j-j] cordibus hominum sepe *VS* [k] interuentione *Ad1* [l] malignantiant *Ad1* [m] honorum *O* [n] malignamenta *O*

27 [1] Matilda of Anjou, abbess of Fontevrault 1149 (after April)–21 May 1155 (see appendix 3, and also n. 16 below). The dates are those of Matilda's abbacy.

ac[o] indissolubile bithumen animarum diuersitates morum ad unam consonantiam reducit et meritorum inequalitates [p]ad equalitatis[p] contemperantiam proportionaliter[q] recolligit. O gratia gratiosa! Sine te omnia mala, tecum omnia bona. Sine te, inquam,[r] inanis uniuersa creatura[s] et a te repletur angelica cum humana natura.[t] Tu reformas deformia, lapsa reparas, confirmas debilia, clausa reseras, congregas dispersa et obscura illuminas. Tuum est quod sum,[u] quod uiuo, quod sapio, quod sanctorum uestigiis [v]deuotus procumbo;[v] tuum inquam, tuum est quod te in templo sancti[w] tui nominis, quod in sanctuario tue glorificationis uidere et adorare te[x] merui. Si enim sanctius adoraris in animabus sanctis quam in templis lapideis et manufactis,[2] quanto magis in sacris uisceribus uirgineis? Nichil [y]enim est[y] tibi his[z] carius, acceptabilius nichil, cum ethere nitidius, firmamento reluceant iocundius, celoque sublimius. Vbinam tale quid inter homines reperies? Credo in illa [a]tua Fontisebraldi[a] abbatissa[b] que nobilitate carnis nemini secunda, spiritus generositate in multis[c] celeberrima, castitate precipua, humilitate conspicua, liberalitate[d] profusa, feruore religionis est decenter succensa. Reprimo stilum ne assentatoris sustineam periculum. Parcius enim laudare amicos, amplius amare debemus, seuerius quoque [e]mala eorum[e] corrigere quam male sana palpando contrectare. Condempnatur uero[f] non minus desidie qui uano timore gloriam Dei reticet[g] quam inuidie quem[h] alterius fortuna contorquet. Solem etiam de mundo tollere[3] non immanioris estimo[i] sceleris quam dotem nature et gratie a creatore in creatura[j] collatam obumbrare silentio malignitatis. Virtutum namque predicatio Dei est glorificatio; nec tutum est cuiquam se nescire [k]quod habet habere,[k] cum dampnum exinde[l] citius possit euenire. 'Nos', inquit Apostolus,[m] 'non[n] spiritum huius mundi accepimus, sed[o] Spiritum qui ex Deo est, ut sciamus que a Deo[p] donata sunt nobis.'[4] In filiis huius seculi hec comprobatur prudentia si res familiaris frequenti supputatione creuerit multiplicata. Itidem celestium[q] negotiator mercedum cotidiana emolumenta assidua ratiocinatione debet compensare et

[o] hac *VS* [p–p] *om. Z* [q] proportionabiliter *Vi* [r] inquit *VS* [s] natura *G* [t] creatura *Sirmond, Ad1, G* [u] suum *Vi* (*obscured and partly scored through*) [v–v] procumbo deuotus *Ad1, Ad2, Z, Vi, VS* [w] sancto *VS* [x] *illegible ins. VS* [y–y] est enim *Z, Vi, VS* [z] *om. Z* [a–a] fontis tua ebraldi *O* [b] abbatisse *Z, Vi, VS* [c] multis uel *VS* [d] libertate *Vi* [e–e] errores eorum *Ad2, Z, Vi;* eorum errores *VS* [f] *om. Ad2, Z, Vi* [g] non reticet *O* [h] quam *O* [i] extimo *Val;* existimo *VS* [j] creaturam *Val, Z, Vi, VS* [k–k] habere quod habet *O* [l] inde *Ad2, Vi, VS; om. Z* [m] *om. Z* [n] non per *VS* [o] sed per *VS* [p] Deo data uel *Ad2, VS* [q] celestium idoneus *Ad2, Z, Vi, VS*

spirits and indissoluble pitch of souls, draws differences in characters back into a single harmony and restores the inequalities of the deserving proportionately to a proper degree of equality. O gracious grace! Without you all is bad, with you all is good. Without you, I say, the whole of creation is empty and by you angelic as well as human nature is replenished. You re-form the deformed, restore the fallen, strengthen the weakened, open up again the sealed places, bring together the dispersed, and light up the hidden places. It is because of you that I exist, that I live, that I have sense, that I prostrate myself devotedly at the feet of the saints; because of you, I say, I have earned the right to see and to worship you in the temple of your holy name, in the sanctuary of your glorification. For if you are worshipped more reverently in pure souls than in temples of stone made by hands,[2] how much more so in the bodies of holy virgins? For nothing is dearer to you than these, nothing more acceptable, since they shine out more brightly than the upper air, more joyfully than the sky, higher than the heavens. Yet where will you find such a thing among mankind? In her, so I believe, your abbess of Fontevrault, who is second to none in nobility of birth, most renowned far and wide for her greatness of spirit, outstanding in chastity, distinguished in humility, lavish in generosity, fittingly inflamed with religious ardour. I restrain my pen in case I run the risk of becoming a flatterer. For we ought to praise friends more sparingly and love them more deeply, we ought, moreover, to correct their wrongs more severely rather than wrongly to treat their virtues with flattery. But there is condemnation no less for the sloth of him who through vain fear keeps silent about the glory of God, than for the envy of him who is tormented by the good fortune of another. Moreover I believe that even to remove the sun from the world[3] is no greater act of wickedness than to conceal by spiteful silence the endowment of nature and grace settled by the Creator on the creation. For to praise virtues is to glorify God; nor is it safe for anyone not to know that he has what he has, since harm can arise the more quickly because of this. 'We', says the Apostle, 'have received not the spirit of this world, but the Spirit that is of God, that we may know the things that are given us from God.'[4] Among the children of this world it is acknowledged as wisdom if the fortunes of a family, on a frequent reckoning, shall have increased many times over. Likewise the dealer in heavenly payments must balance profits

[2] Cf. Acts 17: 24.
[3] Cf. Cicero, *De amicitia*, xiii. 47.
[4] Cf. 1 Cor. 2: 12.

que[r] minus ad thesaurum sufficiunt omni instantia perquirere. Vnde psalmista: 'Notum fac michi, Domine, finem[s] meum et numerum dierum meorum quis est, ut sciam quid desit michi.'[5] Quomodo namque potest scire is[t] quod sibi deest cui non constat quod adest? Itaque requirat sarcinulas, marsupia excutiat, pecuniam appendat in statera, cogitet sumptus, dragmas computet, [u]domumque euertat[u] [6] ut sciat quid desit sibi. Si desunt 'agri primitiarum',[7] fertilis uidelicet caritas supernarum uirtutum, si 'paradisus malorum punicorum',[8] scilicet plenitudo bonorum operum, si 'fons hortorum',[9] hoc[v] est uena[w] sanctarum deuotionum, si 'reclinatorium aureum',[10] quod est requies[x] omnium affectionum, festinet, discurrat,[y] transmigret per nundinas, per marina discrimina et per regiones remotas, quia[z] ubi non sufficiunt propria succurrunt aliena. Preterea et puella querat lanam et linum[11] ut [a]ex uno[a] calidam ex altero[b] [c]faciat candidam tunicam.[c] Martha calida utatur,[d] [e]Maria candida.[e] Hec enim actioni, illa contemplationi aptatur; hec orat, illa laborat; sedet ista, [f]sudat illa;[f] hec quiescit, illa currit; exit ista, [g]illa intrat;[g] [h]ista inchoat, illa consummat.[h] [12] Felix anima cuius promptuarium talia resudat[i] unguenta, cuius dolium [j]talia refundit[j] libamina, cuius uirgultum[k] eiusmodi stillat balsama, cuiusque horreum simillima continet aromata. Felicem dixerim et locum ubi tales comparantur species, ubi gemme ueneunt incomparabiles, ubi exiguo pretio res adquiruntur ualde desiderabiles. [l]Vidi, uidi[l] in foro speculum non alteri[m] quam filie[n] regis congruum. Vidi monile[o] non alterius quam intacte uirginis collo appendendum. Hoc speculum castitatis est, uirtutis et humilitatis, que[p] terra nostra in publicis contractibus hactenus [q]habere non[q] consueuit. Res siquidem [r]pretii est[r] inestimabilis, raro inueniens uenditorem, rarius emptorem. In eius certe comparatione celestes exhauriuntur thesauri, negotiatores requiruntur ditissimi[s] et diuinissimi, comparatores quoque liberalissimi. Celeste siquidem[t] commercium superceleste desiderat pretium. Quid nempe[u] uirginitate

[r] eque *Z* [s] *om. Vi* [t] his *Val* [u–u] domum euertat *O, Z;* domumque euerrat *G* [v] hec *Ad2* [w] fons *VS* [x] plena requies *Ad2, Z, Vi;* plena *VS* [y] transcurret *VS* [z] *om. O* [a–a] altero *Ad2, Z, Vi, VS* [b] alio *Val* [c–c] candidam faciat tunicam *Ad2* [d] utitur *O;* utebatur *VS* [e–e] candida Maria *O, Ad2, Z, Vi* [f–f] illa sudat *O, Val, Ad2, Z, Vi, VS* [g–g] intrat illa *O, Ad2, Z, Vi, VS* [h–h] inchoat ista, consummat illa *Ad2, Z, Vi, VS* [i] refundit *Z;* refudit *VS* [j–j] refundit talia *Z;* similia refundit *VS* [k] uirtutum *VS* [l–l] uidi *Ad2, Z, Vi, VS* [m] alterius *Z, Vi, VS* [n] filia *O* [o] monilem *Z* [p] quod *Z, Vi* [q–q] *om. Z;* non *Vi* [r–r] est pretii *O* [s] altissimi *Ad2, Z, Vi, VS* [t] quidem *Z* [u] namque *VS*

daily with acute reckoning and inquire with all urgency which things are wanting to the treasury. Hence the Psalmist says: 'O Lord, make me know my end and what is the number of my days, that I may know what is wanting to me.'[5] For how can he who is not certain what he has know what he is lacking? And so let him search again through pockets, shake out purses, weigh cash on the scales, ponder over expenses, count coins, and turn out the house[6] so that he may know what he lacks. If the 'fields of first fruits',[7] that is to say the fertile love of heavenly virtues, are lacking, or 'the paradise of the pomegranates',[8] that is the abundance of good works, or 'the fountain of gardens',[9] that is the vein of holy devotions, or 'the seat of gold',[10] that is the resting place of all affections, let him hurry, let him hasten back and forth, let him travel through fairs, across dangerous seas and through distant regions, because where his own resources are not sufficient those of others succour him. Furthermore, let the maiden look for both wool and flax[11] so that from one she may make a warm cloak and from the other a pure white one. Let Martha use the warm one, Mary the white. For one is suited to action, the other to contemplation; this one prays, that one works; this one sits, the other sweats; this one is calm, the other runs about; this one goes out, the other enters; this one makes a beginning, the other brings it to completion.[12] Happy the soul whose store room exudes such perfumes, whose vessel pours out such libations, whose bush distils balms of such a kind and whose storehouse contains spices of like quality. Happy also should I call the place where such riches are brought together, where incomparable gems are sold, where for a small price exceedingly desirable objects are acquired. I have seen, I have seen in the market place a mirror suitable for none other than the daughter of a king. I have seen a necklace fit to hang around the neck of none other than a pure virgin. This is the mirror of chastity, of virtue and of humility, which qualities our world has not so far been accustomed to have any use for in public transactions. Indeed this is an item of inestimable value, rarely finding a seller, more rarely still a buyer. Certainly in acquiring it the heavenly treasuries are emptied, the most affluent and reverent traders are called for and also the most generous purchasers. To be sure, celestial trade commands a super-

5 Ps. 38 (39): 5.
6 Cf. Luke 15: 8 (cf. letter no. 24, n. 4).
7 2 Kgs. (2 Sam.) 1: 21.
8 S. of S. 4: 13.
9 S. of S. 4: 15.
10 S. of S. 3: 10.
11 Cf. Prov. 31: 13; here the virtuous woman is married (Matilda had been betrothed), and in the next verse she is like 'the merchants' ship', hence Peter's change of metaphor.
12 Alluding to Luke 10: 38–42.

celestius? Humilitate quid excelsius? In diademate Salomonis prefulget altera, in thesauris regiis pretiosior est altera. Ex utraque tamen omnium artifex sapientia[13] monile composuit et uenale proposuit. 'Qui potest', inquit,[v] 'capere capiat.'[14] Ad hoc manus adolescentularum satis ambitiose quasi temptantes emere[w] circumuolitabant, sed audito pretio statim[x] omnes resiliebant. Ad extremum pene [y]iam desperato[y] negotio, uirguncula quedam Andegauensis comitis[z] filia surrexit, manum ad fortia misit,[15] et noua commutatione pro rege Anglorum regem commutauit angelorum.[16] Hec gloriosa dicta sunt [a]de te, karissima domina.[a] Indulge autem michi quod sermone diffusiore[b] te plus iusto detinuerim[c] et credas ex habundantia amoris copiam protulisse sermonis. Ora ergo pro nobis. De componendis autem quibusdam [d]sententiolis sermonis tui[d] non sum oblitus, sed tam[e] cito implere non potui pluribus impeditus. Vale.[f]

28

To Abbot Hardouin of Larrivour[1]

1152/5 × 1162

Domino et amico suo karissimo H⟨arduino⟩ abbati de Ripatorio frater Petrus[a] semper suus, salutem que perficitur in Monte Dei.[2]

De statu suo amico scribere soluere est debitum, et creditor si a debitore debitum receperit debitor liberabitur. Si amplius donum est

[v] *om. O* [w] emere est *Z* [x] *om. Ad2, Z, Vi, VS* [y–y] desperato iam *Ad2, Z, Vi, VS* [z] comites *O* [a–a] domina karissima *Val;* karissima domina *Z* [b] diffusiori *O, Ad2, Vi, VS* [c] tenuerim *O* [d–d] sententiis sermonis tui *Ad2, Z, Vi;* tui sermonis sententiis quod *VS* [e] tamen *Z;* iam *VS* [f] *om. O, Ad2, Z, Vi, VS*

28 *O fos. 134r–135v*]
[a] G. *O*

[13] Cf. Wisd. 7: 21. [14] Matt. 19: 12. [15] Cf. Prov. 31: 19.
[16] Matilda, the daughter of Fulk V of Anjou (1109–29, king of Jerusalem from 1131, d. 1143) and Erembourg of Maine, was betrothed in 1119, as a child, to William Atheling (son of Henry I of England), who died the next year in the White Ship (see e.g. Dunbabin, *France in the Making*, pp. 333–5 and the genealogy at p. 389). Peter's statement that she exchanged the king of the English for the king of the angels (i.e. religious life) thus stretches the facts somewhat: her betrothed was the heir to the throne, and she took the veil some time after his death, entering Fontevrault in 1122 and taking the veil in 1128

celestial price. For what indeed is more celestial than virginity? What is more exalted than humility? One shines out above all else in Solomon's crown, the other is more highly valued in the king's treasury. From both however, wisdom, the fashioner of all things,[13] made a necklace and laid it out for sale. 'He that can take it', he says, 'let him take it.'[14] For this the hands of young girls, in all eagerness as if intending to buy, were flocking about, but when they heard the price all of them instantly leapt back. Finally when the sale was almost despaired of, a certain young girl, the daughter of the count of Anjou, came forward, put out her hand to strong things,[15] and in an unparalleled transformation exchanged the king of the English for the king of the angels.[16] These glorious things are being said of you, dearest lady. Forgive me for having detained you longer than was fair with a long-winded discourse, and trust that the prolixity of the speech arose from an abundance of love. Pray therefore for us. I have not, however, forgotten about putting together some little ideas for your homily, but I was not able to finish so quickly, having been held up by many things. Farewell.

28

To Abbot Hardouin of Larrivour[1]

1152/5 × 1162

To his dearest lord and friend Hardouin, abbot of Larrivour, brother Peter, his own always, a greeting perfected on the Mount of God.[2]

To write to a friend about one's own condition is to pay a debt, and if the creditor receives the debt from the debtor the debtor shall be

(J.-M. Bienvenu, 'Aliénor d'Aquitaine et Fontevraud', *Cahiers de civilisation médiévale*, xxix (1986), 15–36, at pp. 18–19). The reference above to the daughter of a king alludes to her father's later kingship of Jerusalem (14 Sept. 1131–10 Nov. 1143: H. E. Mayer, *The Crusades*, trans. J. Gillingham (Oxford, 1972), pp. 86, 94).

28 [1] Hardouin, abbot of Larrivour ?*c*.1152–89/92. He first occurs 1155, but was the successor to Alan of Auxerre who was el. bishop of Auxerre in Nov. 1152 (see letter no. 23, n. 1), and so may himself have been el. to the abbacy earlier than 1155. Hardouin last occurs 1189 but his successor first occurs 1192: *GC* xii. 598, but see also A. Roserot, 'Les Abbayes du département de l'Aube, additions et corrections à la Gallia Christiana', 3 parts, *Bulletin historique et philologique du Comité des Travaux Historiques*, pt. i (1887), pp. 288–305, pt. ii (1890), pp. 150–80, pt. iii (1899), pp. 78–91, at ii. 158, 170, showing that Hardouin first occurs 1155, not 1157. On Larrivour, Cistercian, dioc. Troyes, see Cott. i. 149.

[2] Cf. Exod. 3: 1, but here meaning Mont-Dieu, the Carthusian monastery in the Ardennes at which Peter was a frequent guest and whose semi-eremitical life-style he is about to describe. Peter's visits to Mont-Dieu cannot be dated (see also letter no. 52, n. 1).

iam datoris non creditoris debitum. Debet itaque pro beneficio huiusmodi gratiarum actionem non pro solutione debiti liberationem. Non dispari forma debitorem quidem me uestrum fateor, pro amicitia que circa amici statum semper sollicita est, quomodo me habeam uobis insinuare. Sed cum et aliud supererogauero, et debitum et donum uos recepisse[b] sciatis. Manu igitur larga et quod debeo soluam et quod non debeo superimpendam. Cum enim non meum tantum sed et eorum cum quibus sum uobis descripsero statum, de lucro super adiecto amicum tenebo obnoxium. Forte 'usque ad tertium celum'[3] non Paulum Tharsensem sed Petrum Cellensem raptum ut sinu pleno reuelationum et archanorum rediens uel sero descendat[4] prestolamini. Iam saccum uestrum benedictionibus implendum resoluitis,[5] iam de cumulatis gratiarum adoribus[c] partem bonam deposcitis. Dicis: 'A nundinis tam copiosis tamque supereffluentibus uacuus nunquam est amicus.' Vtinam iocando serium sed et uerum loquamini. Sed aliter est, amice karissime. Prouerbium est: qui stultus pergit ad forum stultus redit.[6] Sic est, confiteor infirmitatem meam. Pauper et stultus ueni, sed non ad pauperes et stultos, nisi 'pauperes spiritu'[7] et stultos propter Christum.[8] Sapientes enim sunt sapientia que desursum est, primum quidem pudica, deinde pacifica, suadibilis, ad omne opus bonum consentiens,[9] diuites quoque in bonis operibus,[10] in scientia, in ueritate, puritate, pace, humilitate et huiusmodi. Reuera merces suas statuerunt in nundinis, uendentes que apud illos sunt et ementes que de longinqua regione necessaria usibus futuris et presentibus ad bene uiuendum reperiunt. Hoc in negotiationibus eorum pro miraculo teneo quod de superfluis suis supplere uolunt non solum que ad necessitatem sed etiam que ad uoluptatem profutura sunt. Superflua uero omnia illa reputant sine quibus uiuere utcunque possunt. Certe ista non proiciunt in uentum humane adulationis sed quanto carius possunt Deo et angelis pro eterna retributione uendunt. Videres singulos tanquam formicas impigras ad speluncam suam ab oratorio, tanquam de agro, manipulos iustitie[11] referre, spicas orationum, fasciculos mirre, id est congeriem passionis Christi dilecti sui inter ubera[12] in principali cordis sui collocantes. Et reuera mirram redolent quia carnem suam

[b] recipisse *O* [c] adoriis *O*

[3] Cf. 2 Cor. 12: 2. [4] Possibly an echo of 2 Cor. 12: 4. [5] Cf. Gen. 43: 21–3.
[6] Cf. Walther, iv. no. 24805: 'Qui stultus exit, stultus reuertitur.'
[7] Matt. 5: 3. [8] Cf. 1 Cor. 4: 10. [9] Cf. Jas. 3: 17.
[10] Cf. 1 Tim. 6: 18. [11] Cf. Lev. 23: 10. [12] Cf. S. of S. 1: 12.

freed. If more, it is now a gift from the giver, not the creditor's due. He ought therefore to offer thanks for a kindness of this sort rather than an acquittal for the payment of a debt. In a similar way it is as your debtor that I, for the sake of the friendship which is always concerned for the condition of a friend, confess that I am confiding to you how I am. But when I have also paid something else in addition you should know that you have received both the debt and a gift. With a generous hand therefore I shall both pay what I owe and add on top what I do not owe. For when I have described to you not only my own condition but also that of those with whom I am staying, I shall hold a friend indebted for the extra sum added on top. Perhaps you are now expecting to hear that not Paul of Tarsus but Peter of Celle has been snatched up 'even to the third heaven'[3] so that, returning with his heart full of revelations and secrets, he may descend, though belatedly.[4] Now you open your sack to be filled with blessings[5] and demand the good part of the abundant grains of grace. 'A friend', you say 'never comes empty away from fairs so well-supplied and overflowing.' If only you were speaking seriously and truly when jesting so. But it is not so, dearest friend. There is a proverb: he who goes out to the market place a fool returns a fool.[6] Such is the case; I confess my weakness. Poor and foolish I came, but not to paupers and fools, unless to 'the poor in spirit'[7] and to the fools for Christ's sake.[8] For they are wise in the wisdom that is from above, first indeed chaste, then peaceable, easy to be persuaded, consenting to every good work,[9] rich also in good works,[10] knowledge, truth, purity, peace, humility, and all things of this kind. Truly they have laid out their goods in the fairs, selling what they have and buying what they find, things from distant regions essential for living well both in the future and the present. This I think wondrous in their dealings, that by disposing of their surplus they seek to furnish not only those things which will be of avail in need but even those which will be of avail in spiritual delight. As surplus they count all those things without which they can manage somehow to live. Certainly they do not fling these wares away to the wind of human adulation, but as dearly as they can, sell them to God and the angels for an eternal repayment. You may see individuals like busy ants bringing back to their nest from the church, as if from the fields, sheaves of righteousness,[11] ears of prayers, bundles of myrrh, that is gathering together in the chief part of their heart the harvest of the passion of their beloved Christ who is between the breasts.[12] Indeed they give

crucifigunt,[13] et hanc non diffusam uel dispersam sed colligatam et constrictam, quo scilicet odor ipsius densior reddatur et uehementior. Tali odore respersi intrant in tabernacula sua quasi turtures solitudinum et columbe gementes ad fenestras suas.[14] Est in cella eorum fenestra orientalis,[15] est et australis, est occidentalis, est et septentrionalis. Orientalis est fides que illustrat summo diluculo mentis intentionem in ciuitate Domini, 'in matutino' per confessionem interficiens 'omnes peccatores terre',[16] id est fragilitatis humane. Australis ⟨est⟩ feruor dilectionis que fenestram aperit australem circa horam tertiam uel sextam, quando et Christus in cruce 'omnia opera nostra operatus est nobis',[17] et Spiritus sanctus promissum Filii soluit apostolis.[18] Occidentalis est timor lapsuum et subreptionis culparum, que fenestram aperit ad uergentem et occiduum solem, quando Adam inuentus est nudus et eiectus de paradiso.[19] Septentrionalis est timor iudicii, que fenestram aperit septentrionalem ad medie noctis profundas tenebras, de qua fenestra trepidi[d] et a uero lumine illuminati[e] implorant ne quis obdormiat in mortem,[20] quando primogenita Egyptiorum occisa sunt et filii Israhel ad sacrificandum exire compulsi sunt.[21] Iccirco tunc de strato quasi Egypto sompniorum et phantasmatum surgunt et egrediuntur 'uiam trium dierum',[22] in fide trinitatis ituri et Deo 'uitulos labiorum',[23] oculorum, pedum, cantando, plorando, uel uigilando et stando, immolaturi. Vere namque hi sunt stantes in atriis Ierusalem.[24] Vix enim infirmus in choro sedet, sanus rarissime; et quia cepi de choro dicere, quid in nocte, quid in die faciant[f] quando conueniunt dicere uolo. Raro enim conueniunt in die nisi ad missas in omnibus Dominicis, in quadragesima tota singulis diebus, in precipuis solennitatibus, et quando presens adest defuncti corpus. Quacunque autem occasione uel quandocunque ibi conueniunt, uideres[g] eos plane astare 'Dominatori uniuerse terre',[25] uultus tam fixus, oculus tam depressus, gestus tam mortificatus, homo exterior totus diuinis intentus. Quid interior? 'Nescio, Deus

[d] tepidi *O* [e] *corr. Hall;* illuminari *O* [f] faciunt *O* [g] *corr. Leclercq;* uidens *O*

[13] Cf. Gal. 5: 24.

[14] Cf. Isa. 60: 8; Ps. 101 (102): 7; cf. also Lev. 1: 14; 5: 7, 11; 12: 6, 8; 14: 22, 30; 15: 14, 29; Num. 6: 10.

[15] Possibly a distant allusion to 4 Kgs. (2 Kgs.) 13: 17.

[16] Cf. Ps. 100 (101): 8.

[17] Cf. Isa. 26: 12; (Christ died at the ninth hour after darkness had fallen at the sixth: cf. Matt. 27: 45–50; Mark 15: 33–7; Luke 23: 44–6).

off the fragrance of myrrh because they crucify their flesh;[13] nor is this spread out and scattered around, but tied and bound together, clearly so that its fragrance is given out more richly and more powerfully. Sprinkled with such a fragrance they enter their tabernacles like turtle doves of the wilderness and like doves sighing at their windows.[14] There is in their cell an east window[15] and a south window, a west window and a north window. To the east is the faith which lights up at dawn the striving of the mind towards the city of the Lord, putting to death 'in the morning', through confession, 'all the wicked of the land,'[16] that is of human frailty. To the south is the fire of love which throws open the south-facing window around the third hour or the sixth, when Christ on the cross 'wrought all our works for us'[17] and the Holy Spirit fulfilled the promise of the Son to the apostles.[18] To the west is the fear of falling away and of the stealthy approach of sins which opens the window on the waning and setting sun when Adam was found naked and thrown out of paradise.[19] To the north is the fear of judgement which opens the northern window on to the deep shadows of midnight, and from this window, trembling and illumined by the true light, they pray that no one should sleep in death,[20] when the first-born of the Egyptians were killed and the children of Israel were forced to go out to perform the sacrifice.[21] Then they arise therefore from the couch as though from the Egypt of dreams and visions and go out on the 'three days' journey',[22] ready to go forward in the faith of the Trinity and to sacrifice to God 'the calves of' their 'lips',[23] eyes and feet, by singing, weeping, or watching and standing. For truly these are the ones who stand in the courts of Jerusalem.[24] Hardly ever does one of them who is ill sit down in the choir, and the healthy scarcely at all; and since I have begun to speak of the choir, I want to tell you what they do, by night and by day, when they gather together. For they rarely come together in the daytime except for masses every Sunday and every day during Lent, on the holiest festivals, and whenever the body of a dead brother is laid out. But for whatever occasion or whensoever they gather together there, you would see them standing simply 'before the Lord of the whole earth,'[25] the face so immovable, the eye so cast down, the bearing so humbled, the external man wholly concentrated

[18] Cf. Acts 1: 8; 2: 1–5, 15.
[19] Cf. Gen. 3: 7–24.
[20] Cf. Ps. 12 (13): 4.
[21] Cf. Exod. 12: 29–32.
[22] Cf. Exod. 3: 18; 5: 3; 8: 27.
[23] Hos. 14: 3.
[24] Cf. Ps. 121 (122): 2.
[25] Cf. Zech. 4: 14.

scit.'[26] Cum[h] per fenestras suas aliquando prospiciunt,[i] perfusus nescio quibus stillicidiis humectatus apparet. Audires pectora eorum tanquam gigantes gemere sub aquis.[27] Neque enim aridi sunt licet lignum aridum sit corpus eorum;[28] et miror cum uirtus in corpore pene defecerit unde tantus gemitus in pectore, cum fluuius humorum naturalium rigore abstinentie exhaustus sit unde tantus impetus lacrimarum. Dico cui rei michi uideantur comparandi in missa, sed prius quid faciant dicam.

Post Sanctus, quasi claudat ostia ut gratuito siue in abscondito ad altare Dei immolent hostiam iubilationis, capita intra capitia recondunt, similitudinem mortis Iesu representantes ut, sicut ille in sepulcro tribus diebus et tribus noctibus humanis aspectibus se celauit,[29] sic isti usque ad finem misse lucem huius solis non uideant. Tunc quasi dolia musto nouo plena collisione quadam non se capientis spiritus spumas ad litus oris, oculorum et narium excutiunt, si quas Egyptiorum reliquias repererint demersuri.[30] 'Oculi' eorum in monasterio comparantur 'piscine in Esebon',[31] in celo aquile, in claustro columbe, in refectorio talpe. Manus confixe in signa otiosa non soluuntur, pedes iter sabbati habent[32] a cella in oratorium, ab oratorio in cellam, compedem suum laxantes. Aures surde. Quid enim audirent? Cantus tantum[j] auium in cella, in ecclesia laudem diuinam exaudiunt integre. 'Os habent et non loquuntur.'[33] Quid multa? Simulacra sunt carnea et animata. O si uideres quomodo pelles suas desiccent in sole ieiuniorum, abstinentie et mortificationis quatinus cordas uel corda psalterio nouo et cithare, quibus dicitur, 'Exurge psalterium et cithara',[34] ad opus pasche preparent. Patientiam, industriam, extensionem—quid dicam?—mirationi haberes, tum[k] etiam supra hominem reputares. Certe corde ille non reddunt auribus nostris multam exclamationem sed Dei credo auditui reddunt placidam modulationem. Sicut milites armati ad congressum faciendum in hostes gradatim et communiter tendunt, sic isti contra

[h] *corr. Hall;* tamen *O* [i] *corr. Hall;* prospiciens *O* [j] *corr. Hall;* tamen *O*
[k] cum *O*

[26] 2 Cor. 12: 2, 3. [27] Cf. Job 26: 5.

[28] Cf. Ezek. 17: 24: '. . . I the Lord . . . have dried up the green tree and have caused the dry tree to flourish.' Physical dryness in this letter signifies ascetic austerity (see below), which produces spiritual moistness or fecundity.

[29] Cf. Matt. 12: 40.

[30] With the overtone of 'submerge'; cf. Exod. 14: 31.

[31] Cf. S. of S. 7: 4.

[32] Cf. Acts 1: 12; cf. also *Regula S. Benedicti* c. vii: 'Et custodiens se omni hora a

on the divine offices. What of the interior man? 'I know not, God knows.'[26] When they look out of their windows at any time, a mist, distilled by I know not what rains, appears. You would hear their hearts groaning like giants under the waters.[27] Neither are they dried up, although their body be a dry tree;[28] and I wonder whence comes such a lamentation of the heart, since strength has almost given out in the body; whence comes such a flow of tears, since the river of natural moisture has dried up through the rigour of abstinence. I am telling you what, as it seems to me, they should be compared to during the mass, but first let me say what they do.

After the Sanctus, as if it closed the doors so that they may offer the sacrifice of jubilation at the altar of God without distraction and in private, they hide their heads within their hoods, thus representing the likeness of Christ in death so that, just as He hid Himself from human sight in the tomb for three days and three nights,[29] they may not see the light of this sun until the end of the mass. Then they shake out like wine-jars full of new must in a kind of collision the foaming waters of the overflowing spirit on to the shores of the mouth, eyes, and nose, to overwhelm any remnants of the Egyptians they find.[30] Their eyes in the monastery are like 'the fish pool in Esebon',[31] in the sky like the eagle, in the cloister like the dove, in the refectory like the mole. Their hands, fixed, are not released for useless gestures, their feet do not exceed a sabbath day's journey[32] from their cell to the church, from the church to the cell, loosening their fetter. Their ears are deaf. For what should they hear? They hear only the songs of birds in the cell and, purely, holy praise in the church. 'They have mouths and speak not.'[33] Need I say more? They are statues made of flesh and living. O if you could see how they dry out their skins in the sun of fasts, abstinence and mortification so that for the Easter office they may prepare their strings, that is to say their hearts, for a new psaltery and harp, to which it is said, 'Arise psaltery and harp'.[34] You would be amazed—how can I put it?—at their patience, their diligence, their exertion, and then you would even consider them superhuman. Certainly those strings do not impart a very loud blast to our ears but rather, I believe, a peaceful harmony to the hearing of God. As armed soldiers march out to fight their enemies in good

peccatis et uitiis, id est cogitationum, linguae, oculorum, manuum, pedum uel uoluntatis propriae.'

[33] Cf. Ps. 113 (114): 13 (5). The Carthusians, the most eremitical of the orders, spend more time in solitude (as Peter notes above) and silence than other monks.

[34] Ps. 56 (57): 9; 107 (108): 3

spiritales nequitias in omni genere actionum castra mouent aut simul in hostem irruentes aut insultum in aliquem factum simul et compassionem suscipientes. Nox in cellis consolationem huius luminis non habet, sed 'nox illuminatio mea in deliciis meis'[35] resonat cella ipsa. Multe ibi delicie solis occasu prestantur quia tunc occurrit illud psalmographi: 'Deum exquisiui manibus meis nocte contra eum, et non sum deceptus',[36] et cetera que in psalmo sequuntur. Delicie ciliciorum que dormientium latera pungunt ne dormientes obdormiant,[37] delicie lectorum ad similitudinem Iacob in lapidum duritiam conuersorum,[38] delicie uirgarum mutuarum ad confodienda carnis et sanguinis coria desiccata, delicie deliciarum lucem sibi adesse in tenebris,[39] que rationem illustrat, mentem letificat, ad se ipsam animam conuertit.[l] Quid amplius? Non extinguitur in nocte lucerna eorum.[40] Deinde nec cultus eorum, nec in pretio, nec in numero, nec in mensura incircumcisus, nature suffragiis tantum intendens et fines curiositatis prorsus non tangens. Victus qualis? Pene in culpam cadit non superfluitatis sed parcitatis. Nimium est parcus, ne dicam auarus, uentris appetitum non excitans sua oblectatione nec satis compescens sua quantitate. Nabuzardan princeps coquorum[41] nec nominatur inter eos nisi quod quisque sibi Nabuzardan ignorans delicias ollam Helie supponit.[42] Quid multa? Paulo amplius supra homines nostri temporis institutio uite, nec habet in ea uiuere nisi qui mundo mortuus uiuit Deo. Que parua et indifferentia sunt quodammodo bonis et malis enumeraui, mortificationem uidelicet extrinsecus apparentem, sed crede sub sagis cilicinis, sub 'pellibus arietum rubricatis',[43] archam sanctificationis contegi, ubi manna dulcedinis quam abscondit Deus timentibus se,[44] de qua dicitur: Dabo tibi manna absconditum.[45] Ibi etiam altare holocaustorum,[46] ibi altare incensi,[47] sed etiam sancta sanctorum nouit sanctus sanctorum. Ad sancta enim sanctorum non accedo sed sancta secularia[48] uideo. Non diffido autem ueritatem secretorum quorum euidentia signa representant opera manifesta sanctorum. Queris quid inter hec faciam? Certe appendo in statera

[l] conuertat *O*

[35] Cf. Ps. 138 (139): 11. [36] Ps. 76 (77): 3. [37] Cf. Acts 7: 59.
[38] Cf. Gen. 28: 18. [39] Possibly alluding to John 1: 5. [40] Cf. Prov. 31: 18.
[41] He is commander of the army in 4 Kgs. (2 Kgs.) 25: 8, 11, 20; Jer. 39: 13; 41: 10; 43: 6; 52: 12, 15, 16, but *princeps coquorum* sec. LXX.
[42] Cf. 4 Kgs. (2 Kgs.) 4: 38–41; Elisha had boiled up wild herbs and other bitter fare to relieve the famine.
[43] Cf. Exod. 26: 7; 36: 19. [44] Cf. Ps. 30 (31): 20.

order and formation, so these ones march forth against spiritual foes in all types of engagement, either charging the enemy at once or receiving at once an attack made against any one of them as a common suffering. At night in the cells there is not the consolation of this light, but the cell itself re-echoes with the words, 'night shall be my light in my pleasures'.[35] In that place many delights are brought out by the setting of the sun because then that of which the Psalmist spoke occurs: 'I sought God with my hands lifted up to Him in the night, and I was not deceived,'[36] and the rest which follows in the psalm. There there are delights of the hair shirts which rasp the skin of those sleeping so that sleeping they do not fall into the sleep of death,[37] there delights of beds in the likeness of Jacob's, converted to the hardness of stone,[38] there delights of the rods used mutually for piercing the dry skins of flesh and blood, there delight of delights is that they have a light in the darkness[39] which enlightens reason, cheers the mind, and turns the soul back to itself. What else? Their lamp is not put out in the night.[40] Then their dress is uncircumcised neither in cost nor quantity nor degree, only intended for supporting life and in no way bordering on refinement. What is the nature of their sustenance? It almost falls into the fault not of excess but of paucity. It is excessively small, or should I say miserly, neither exciting the appetite of the belly by being delectable nor satisfying it by its amount. Nabuzardan, chief of the cooks,[41] is not even mentioned among them unless one of them, taking no account of the pleasures of Nabuzardan, gives himself instead the pot of Elisha.[42] Why say more? More than a little above the men of our times is their way of life, and no man can live according to it unless, dead to the world, he is alive in God. I have listed those things which are trifling and, so to speak, indifferent for good and evil, that is the self-denial which is manifest on the outside; but you must believe that beneath the curtains of goat's hair, beneath 'the rams' skins dyed red',[43] there is concealed the ark of sanctification where is the manna of sweetness which God hides for them that fear him,[44] of which it is said: I will give you hidden manna.[45] There also the holy of holies recognizes the altar of sacrifices,[46] the altar of incense,[47] even the holy of holies. I do not approach the holy of holies, but I see worldly sanctuaries.[48] I do not doubt, however, the truth of the mysteries, sure signs of which the manifest works of the saints represent. Do you ask what I am doing in

[45] Cf. Rev. 2: 17 (cf. also Exod. 16).
[46] Cf. Exod. 35: 16; 38: 1, and many other refs.
[47] Cf. Luke 1: 11.
[48] Cf. Heb. 9: 1 (*sancta sanctorum*: Exod. 30: 29 etc.; Heb. 9: 3).

eorum tam iusta[49] officium et opus meum, et inequalia reperio. Recurrit sursum dignitas officii, iacet in imo deorsum opus, leue quidem per meritum sed graue per excessum. Officio uicarius Christi, opere seruus corporis, officio medicus animarum, opere corruptor morum, officio sanctus, opere peccator, officio sanctum Augustinum, opere malum seruum retinens, a quo 'et quod habet auferetur ab eo'.[50]

29

To Abbot Robert or Abbot Ralph of Boulancourt[1]

*c.*1152 × 1162

Roberto[a] abbati de Bullencurte frater [b]Petrus Cellensis abbas,[b] salutem.

Infra robur animi tui, que a[c] me prodire possunt[d] consolationes residere non ignoro. Commendabilis illa solum fortitudo est que fatigata robustior, oppressa liberior consurgit. Leuat namque fortune importunas [e]sine molestia sarcinas,[e] portat sine pondere, deponit sine lassitudine. Accrescit forte cumulus ponderis sed et uirtutis. Iacet enim uirtus sine palestra. Vbi deest lucta, uirtus uidetur quasi discincta. Mollis et tenera est cum in lectulo prosperitatis extenuatur. Sumit uero suum habitum, immo se ipsam, cum obuiauerit quod euincendum sit. Exerta concurrit ubi de uictoria palmam reperit. Prouocata melior, lacessita recentior, subito deprehensa et[f] moderatior et cautior efficitur. Non turbatur repentino incursu, non

29 *O fo. 137*[r–v], *Val fos. 121*[v]*–122*[r], *Sirmond II. 9*]

[a] Radulfo *O* [b–b] G. semper suus *O;* P. Cellensis abbas *Val* [c] ad *Val* [d] possit *O* [e–e] sarcinas sine molestia *O* [f] *om. O*

[49] Cf. Job 31: 6. [50] Matt. 13: 12; Luke 19: 26; cf. Mark 4: 25.

29 [1] To either Abbot Robert or Abbot Ralph of Boulancourt. *GC* xii. 605–6 gives no dates for Robert, whose predecessor last occurs 1152, and for Ralph gives: occurs 1155 × 1160, successor occurs 1168, but C. Lalore, 'Cartulaire de l'abbaye de Boulancourt', *Mémoires de la société académique d'agriculture, des sciences, arts et belles-lettres du département de l'Aube*, xxxiii (1869), 101–92, revises *GC* to give the following sequence, with more abbots, including two Ralphs: Ralph, late 1152 × 1153, Gerard, 1153 × 1155, Ralph, 7 Mar. 1155 × 1160, Robert, no dates (but gives 1148–62 in parenthesis, the dates Peter of Celle was believed to have been at Montier-la-Celle, see Introduction, p. xxxi), and Odelinus, occurs *c.*1168. If this is the same abbot of Boulancourt who visited John of

this place? For sure I am weighing my duty and my achievement in their balance, which is so just,[49] and I find them unequal. The worthiness of my duty rises up in the scales, the achievement lies at the very lowest point, for while it is certainly light in merit yet it is heavy in failings. By my office I am Christ's vicar, by my actions a slave of the body; by my office I am a healer of souls, by my actions a corruptor of morals; by my office I am holy, by my actions a sinner, in my office recalling St Augustine but in my actions the bad servant from whom 'even that which he hath shall be taken from him'.[50]

29

To Abbot Robert or Abbot Ralph of Boulancourt[1]

*c.*1152 × 1162

To abbot Robert [or Ralph] of Boulancourt, brother Peter, abbot of Montier-la-Celle, greetings.

I know that the consolations which can come forth from me reside beneath the strength of your soul. That strength alone is commendable which rises up more powerfully when exhausted and more freely when oppressed. For it takes up the troublesome burdens of fate without difficulty, bears them without feeling the weight, and sets them down without fatigue. The magnitude of the burden perhaps increases, but so does that of virtue. For virtue not exercised lies idle. Where there is no struggle, virtue is seen as if ungirded. It is soft and tender when it is weakened in the bed of prosperity. But it assumes its true form, nay itself, when it meets whatever has to be overcome. Stripped, it engages when it perceives the palm of victory. When provoked it is made better, when wounded fresher, and when taken by surprise more moderate and cautious. It is not perturbed by a

Salisbury's brother Richard, mentioned but not named in John's letter no. 19 to Peter (*J. S. Epp.* i. 32) which was written in autumn 1156, then it would be Ralph, who was abbot by that time. The MSS witnesses are inconclusive: O has Ralph, while Val, which has equal authority from the stemma, has Robert. *GC*, following Sirmond, gives Robert as recipient, but Sirmond may be expanding an abbreviation in the lost Reims MS. The letter's praise of virtue in adversity *may* be an oblique reference to the recent reform of the house and its transfer to the Cistercian order. This took place between 1150 and 1152 (presumably during the abbacy of Thierry, who occurs in 1152, Robert's predecessor) when the abbey was given to Bishop Henry of Troyes who gave it, in 1152, to Bernard of Clairvaux and the Cistercian Order (Cott. i. 453; Lalore, 'Cartulaire de l'abbaye de Boulancourt', pp. 115–17; *GC* xii, Instr. col. 268, no. 31).

frangitur hostium coaceruato exercitu. Non senescit debilitate sed consenescit maturitate. Deserit quem in se non conuerterit. Vtitur siquidem hec aliter isto,[g] aliter illo homine. Aut enim se tibi contemperat aut [h]te sibi[h] informando comparat. Nec est minor si minus in alio, nec amplior si amplius in alio. Proficere dicitur cum ex ea proficitur. Hec a corporea natura diuersum sortitur, et quod est ab origine et quod efficit in homine. Origo eius a creatore, sed ad utilitatem creature. Quid enim [i]est uirtus hec[i] de qua loquimur nisi uapor et emanatio uirtutis Dei?[2] Vaporatur subdita Deo anima uitali tam calore quam odore quatinus calore iustificetur, odore glorificetur. O glorie odor! O calor uite! Tam nemo sine altero bene uiuit quam nemo sine altero beate; beati ex alio angeli, ex alio homines boni. Sic autem angeli beati, ut et boni, quia nec beati essent nisi boni fuissent, sicut odor semper cum calore. Nam sine calore nichil olet. Calet tamen aliquid quod non olet, sicut et bonus quandoque inuenitur qui necdum beatus est. Est uero arra beatitudinis bonitas, quam qui non deserit, eius consecutiuo carere non poterit. Vale.[j]

[g] isto et *O* [h–h] se sibi *O*; se tibi *Sirmond* [i–i] hec uirtus est *Val* [j] *om. O*

sudden attack nor smashed by the massed army of enemies. It does not age with debility but ages together with maturity. It forsakes whomever it has not turned to itself. Indeed it makes use of one person in one way, another in a different way. For it either moulds itself to you or joins you to itself by shaping you. Neither is it less if it does this less in one person nor more if it does this more in another. It is said to advance when advancement is made from it. It receives different allotments from bodily nature, both that which exists from birth and that which it effects in the man. It is born of the Creator but exists for the benefit of the created. For what is this virtue of which we are speaking other than the vapour and emanation of the virtue of God?[2] The soul subject to God is suffused with both vital heat and fragrance so that it is justified by the heat and glorified by the fragrance. O fragrance of glory! O heat of life! No one lives well without the one any more than he lives happily without the other; the angels are blessed from one, men are good from the other. For the angels are blessed just as they are also good, because they would not be blessed unless they were good, just as the fragrance always exists with the heat. For without heat nothing gives off fragrance. There is heat, however, in something which has no fragrance, as a good man is sometimes found who is not yet blessed. But goodness is the pledge of blessedness and he who does not desert goodness cannot lack its consequence. Farewell.

[2] Cf. Wisd. 7: 25.

30

To the abbot of Molesme[1]

1156, not before Sept.

Venerabili [a]domino et patri A. Molismensium abbati frater Petrus humilis abbas Cellensis,[a] salutem.

In omni possessione precellit amicorum possessio. Potest enim parari sed comparari non potest amicus. Nam quod incomparabile est comparari quomodo potest? Annon uero incomparabile est quod nondum habitum emi non potest, perditum eque redimi non ualet? Talem amicum frequenter quero nec inuenio etiam in grege amicorum. Egregium, non de grege gregalem, desidero amicum. Numero gaudeant amicorum qui unum nesciunt habere amicum. Vt enim ait Seneca, plura habeant hospitia, raras amicitias.[2] Non aliter amicis utuntur quidam quam hospitiis. Si nocturnum bene se prebuerit hospitium, mane laudant et abeuntes commutant, et quot dies erunt peregrinationis tot numerabuntur releuationes itineris. Ad tempus occurrit hospitium, nec sui causa petitur sed tantum ut fessi releuentur. Non ita perfunctorie amicus forte occurrens recipiendus, sed cum labore querendus, cum deliberatione admittendus, cum studio retinendus, cum omni uigilantia lesus reconciliandus, cum instantia forte elapsus prosequendus et reuocandus. Non possideas amicum tanquam predium. Nam infructuosum respuis aut alienas a te predium, lucrosum studiosius colis et ad possidendum auidiorem intendis animum. Ita qui in[b] amico requirit non animum sed aurum, non fidem sed faciem, non mores sed uestes, non naturam sed fortunam, causa proprie utilitatis non naturalis bonitatis amicum querit. Repentina quoque non omnimodo approbanda est amicitia,

30 *O fos.* 126^r–127^v, *Val fos.* 126^v–128^r, *Sirmond II. 7*]
[a–a] molismensium abbati frater G. *O;* domino et patri A. Molismensium abbati frater Petrus humilis Cellensium abbas *Val* [b] *om. O*

30 [1] The recipient is evidently Abbot Villain de Choiseul, 1156–63 (predecessor d. 19 Sept. 1156), and the initial A. a cipher (no abbot of Molesme had this initial during the period when Peter was abbot of Montier-la-Celle). It was written on the occasion of his el. One other el., that of Villain's predecessor Stephen I (who first occurs 1148, not before Sept., and d. 19 Sept. 1156) falls within the possible dates, and he is associated with Peter of Celle in three charters, but the recipient of the present letter is said to be the ex-prior, and so must be Villain (who occurs as prior 1152, 1153). Villain, who had previously been

30

To the abbot of Molesme[1]

1156, not before Sept.

To his venerable lord and father A., abbot of Molesme, brother Peter, humble abbot of Montier-la-Celle, greetings.

Among all possessions the possession of friends is the most excellent. For a friend can be obtained but cannot be purchased. For how can that which is beyond price be purchased? And is that not beyond price which, not yet possessed, cannot be bought, and equally if lost cannot be redeemed? I often search for such a friend and do not find one even amid a flock of friends. I desire a friend who surpasses, is not just one of, the masses. Let them rejoice in the number of their friends who do not know what it is to have one friend. For as Seneca says, they have many acquaintances but few friendships.[2] Some treat friends no differently from acquaintances. If the night's hospitality has been well furnished they praise it in the morning and, leaving, move on to the next, and however many days they travel, as many refreshing breaks in the journey will be counted. Acquaintance appears for the moment, nor is it sought for its own sake but only so that the tired may be relieved. A friend appearing by chance should not be received in such a careless way but should be sought out with effort, admitted with deliberation, retained with assiduity, reconciled with all attentiveness when offended, followed after and recalled with perseverance if by chance lost touch with. You should not possess a friend like an estate. For you cast off or alienate from yourself an unprofitable estate, while you cultivate a lucrative one more ardently and direct your thoughts more eagerly to possessing it. Thus he who requires in a friend not a soul but gold, not faith but face, not conduct but appearance, not character but fortune, seeks a friend for the sake of his own advantage not for the sake of natural goodness. Furthermore, hasty friendship should by no means be approved, but rather that which germinates in acquaintance, grows in

prior of Varennes, was deposed from Molesme in 1163 and retired to Varennes, where he was still living in 1170 (on these abbots, see Laurent, *Cartulaires de Molesme*, i. 164–5, 187, and *GC* iv. 734).

[2] Cf. Seneca, *Ad Lucil. ep. mor.* ii. 2.

sed que germinat cognitione, crescit familiaritate, frondescit con suetudine, germinascit[c] cordis amplitudine, fructificat perfecta identitate. Hic arbor fici plantanda et circumfodienda est[3] ut[d] dulcedinis fructum in agro amicorum afferat. Hic triplici filo contorquendus est dilectionis funiculus ne facile rumpatur.[4] Funiculum hunc torquebo ut potero cum ad me per obsequium, per recompensationem, per uicissitudinem[5] forte torquendus occurrerit. Verso enim iam[e] pollice,[6] de amicitia scribendo filum contorqueo.[f] Si placet pactum coagulande societatis, prefigantur termini arcentes presumptionem odiose preuaricationis. Liceat tamen metas transire sine reprehensione proficientem, sed impune non liceat deficientem. Illa namque bona est [g]transgressio cum ultra estimationem amare accelerauerit inchoata dilectio. Illa inquam bona est[g] non transgressio sed progressio, cum iustam[h] mensuram impleuerit amicorum adinuicem fidei promissio. Semper in amicitia [i]minus pollicendum,[i] amplius prestandum. Iam ergo[j] amico loquar ut amico. Amice karissime, gratie sue Deus addidit nouam gratiam cum te de priore abbatem, de oue fecit pastorem. Recole statum, reminiscere meritum, attende donatorem et datum. Donum Dei Deo resignes non homini. Tanquam de summo Dei uertice coronam auellit qui quod a Deo datum est ab homine recognoscit. Ydololatria[k] est Deo debitam homini rependere gratiam. Noui quorumdam blanda lenocinia, noui uanitates et insanias falsas. Quidam sic, si molestum fuerit claustrum, dicit: 'Ego nocte et die ad Deum manus, ut hanc tibi potestatem concederet, expandi,[7] et singultibus continuis donec id efficeretur aures diuinas pulsaui.' Alius autem sic: 'Ego ille prolocutor, ego persuasor, ego aliorum monitor, uniuersorum animos ad te inclinaui, et modo quod uolo impudenter negas?' Alius 'Te Deum laudamus' recinit; alius nominationem a se uel concessionem factam improbe meminit. Sic plures sunt tui abbates quam quorum tu sis abbas. Non ita, domine et amice karissime, fiat ut quod ab Vno habes, a multis te habere credas. Non monachus qui orauit abbatem constituit [l]sed Deus qui concessit,[l] non qui uoce nominauit sed qui cordibus intimauit. Non ista scribens ad

[c] geminascit *O, Val;* germascit *Sirmond* [d] uel *Val* [e] *om. Sirmond* [f] retorqueo *Val* [g–g] *om. O;* transgressio . . . Illa quam bona est *Sirmond* [h] iustum *O* [i–i] pollicendum minus *Val* [j] igitur *O* [k] Ydolatria *O, Val* [l–l] *om. Val*

[3] Cf. Luke 13: 6–9.

[4] Cf. Eccles. 4: 12.

[5] 'reward', cf. Niermeyer, *vicissitudo*; Blaise, *Lexicon*, *vicissitudo*.

[6] Cf. Juvenal, *Sat.* iii. 36, although Peter implies a very different meaning in context.

[7] Cf. 1 Esd. (Ezra) 9: 5; Ps. 87 (88): 10; 142 (143): 6.

familiarity, puts out leaves in habituation, sends forth shoots in fullness of heart, and bears fruit in perfect unity. Here a fig-tree is to be planted and dug about[3] so that it may bring forth the fruit of sweetness in the field of friends. Here a slender cord of love is to be plaited from a triple thread so that it may not be broken easily.[4] I shall wind this cord as far as I am able since it came to me by chance to be plaited through service, recompense, and reward.[5] For with thumb now turned down,[6] by writing about friendship I wind the thread. If a pact of joint fellowship is acceptable, let limits be fixed which keep away the presumption of tiresome prevarication. However, let it be permitted when going forwards to cross the boundary marks without reprimand, but not to do so with impunity when going backwards. For the former is a good transgression, since an affection begun will have been speeded on towards love beyond expectation. That, I say, is a good progression not a transgression, when the friends' promise of mutual faith has filled its just measure. In friendship there should always be less promised and more performed. Now therefore let me speak to a friend as a friend. Dearest friend, God added new grace to His grace when He made you an abbot from a prior, a shepherd from a sheep. Reflect upon your status, recall what has been earned, pay heed to the giver and to what has been given. You should attribute a gift of God to God, not to man. He who acknowledges that which is given by God as if it came from man in effect tears off the crown from the top of the head of God. It is idolatry to return to man thanks owed to God. I know the smooth flatteries of certain people, I know their deceptions and false delusions. If the cloister is troublesome, one man speaks thus: 'Day and night I stretched out my hands to God[7] that He should give this power to you, and I accosted the divine ears with unbroken sobs until it was effected.' Another speaks thus: 'I the advocate, I the pleader, I the adviser of the others, I have inclined the minds of all towards you, and now do you shamelessly deny me what I want?' Another sings again: 'Te Deum laudamus'; another recalls a nomination he has made or a concession given improperly. Thus you have more abbots than those over whom you are abbot. Forbid, dearest lord and friend, that you should believe that what you have from One you have from many. It is not the monk who has prayed who has made the abbot, but God who has granted it, not he who spoke the name out loud, but He who imparted it to the hearts. In writing this I am not pushing you to ingratitude so that you be

ingratitudinem prouoco ut immemor sis beneficii, non in arrogantiam extollo ut non respicias[m] deuotionem congregationis te sibi prefici rogantis, hoc enim [n]non esset amicum[n] instruere sed destruere, non ueraciter bona suadere sed nequiter uitio nequissimo subdere. Ad quid ergo ista prestruxi? Vt uana loquentes compescas, ut statum dignitatis et officii tui importunitate aliquorum non minuas, ut solum Deum auctorem huius[o] tue sublimationis[p] recognoscas, et ad eius gloriam et honorem omnia facias. Obnoxium te habeat congregatio pro deuotione sua, sed cum auctoritate tua; monachus te propitium inueniat pro deprecatione sua, sed cum integritate tua. Sis beneuolus sed et rectus, sis pius sed et discretus, sis compatiens infirmitati sed impatiens mali, sis bonis consentiens sed inordinatis non parcens, sis humilis sed non deiectus, sis largus sed non prodigus, sis prouidus sed non auarus. Sis in templo Domini basis argentea[8] per patientiam, sis columpna marmorea[9] per inflexibilem iustitiam, sis capitellum habens sculpturam liliorum[10] per contemplationem assiduam. Sis archa testamenti[11] per habundantem gratiam, sis uirga Aaron[12] per disciplinam, sis mensa Domini[13] per doctrinam, sis candelabrum de auro mundissimo[14] per bonam famam, sis propitiatorium[15] per misericordiam, sis tabule testamenti[16] per ueteris et noue legis scientiam, sis cortina[17] per caritatem, sis saga cilicina[18] per humilitatem, sis templum Domini per continentiam et castitatem. Non habitet iuxta te malignus, non audias uocem sanguinis,[19] non sermonem susurrii. Fortissimi in Israhel et doctissimi ad bella, id est honestissimi et probatissimi monachi, lectulum tuum ambiant propter timores nocturnos.[20] Male suspicionis homines non tibi cohabitent, non coambulent, nisi forte raro ut[q] secretius corrigas et benignius[r] corripias. Aliquando enim sic emendantur mali dum pietate reuocantur pastoris. Que namque cum aliis, uel saltem post alias oues, non recurrit ad ouile, si ex infirmitate portanda, si ex malignitate cogenda est.[21] Ad te confugientes[s] per humilitatem inueniant matrem, a te

[m] respuas *O* [n–n] esset amicum non *Val* [o] *om.* *Val* [p] sublimitationis *Sirmond* [q] et *Sirmond* [r] benignus *O* [s] fugientes *Val*

[8] Cf. Exod. 26: 19, 21, 32; 36: 24, 25, 30, 36.

[9] Cf. S. of S. 5: 15.

[10] Cf. 3 Kgs. (1 Kgs.) 7: 22.

[11] Cf. Exod. 25: 10–22, and many other refs., and Heb. 9: 4.

[12] Cf. Exod. 7: 9–12; 8: 17, 19–20, and many other refs, and Heb. 9: 4.

[13] Cf. Exod. 25: 23; 1 Cor. 10: 21.

[14] Cf. Exod. 25: 31; 37: 17; Lev. 24: 4; Num. 8: 4.

[15] Cf. Exod 25: 17–22, and many other refs.

[16] Cf. Exod. 31: 18; 32: 15–19, and many other refs, and Heb. 9: 4.

forgetful of favours, I am not raising you to arrogance so that you do not consider the devotion of the community asking that you be set over them, for this would be not to instruct but to injure a friend, not to persuade him truthfully of good things but scurrilously to undermine him with the most wicked vice. Why then have I set these things down? So that you may restrain those speaking empty words, so that you may not lessen the standing of your dignity and your office by the importunities of others, so that you may acknowledge God alone as the author of this your elevation and do all things to His glory and honour. Let your community hold you bound to it because of its devotion, but under your authority; let the monk find you well-disposed because of his prayers, but as befits your integrity. You should be benevolent yet upright, merciful yet judicious, patient with weakness but impatient of evil, sympathetic to the good but not sparing of the insubordinate, humble but not abject, generous but not extravagant, prudent but not miserly. You should be a silver pedestal in the temple of the Lord[8] through patience, you should be a marble column[9] through unbending justice, you should be a capital with sculpted lilies[10] through keen meditation. You should be the ark of the testament[11] through plentiful grace, the rod of Aaron[12] through discipline, the table of the Lord[13] through teaching, the candlestick of finest gold[14] through good reputation, the propitiatory[15] through mercy, the tablets of the testament[16] through knowledge of the old and new law, a curtain[17] through love, curtains of goat's hair[18] through humility, the temple of the Lord through self control and chastity. Let not the wicked one live beside you; hear not the voice of blood[19] or the whispered speech. Let the most valiant in Israel and the most expert in war, that is the most honest and most tested monks, surround your bed because of fears in the night.[20] Let men of evil reputation neither live with you nor walk with you, except perhaps occasionally that you may correct them discreetly and reproach them gently. For thus sometimes the wicked are amended when recalled by the mercy of the pastor. For that sheep which does not run back to the fold along with the others, or even behind the other sheep, has to be carried if the reason is infirmity, or driven if the reason is perversity.[21] When they flee to

[17] Cf. Exod. 26: 1–6; 35: 17, and many other refs.

[18] Cf. Exod. 26: 7–13; 36: 14–18.

[19] Cf. Gen. 4: 10.

[20] Cf. S. of S. 3: 7–8.

[21] Alluding to Matt. 18: 12–13; Luke 15: 4–6.

resilientes per contumaciam sentiant seuerum patrem. Non sis preceps in iudicio, non mutus in consilio, non uerbosus in conuiuio, non arrogans in publico, non detrahens in secreto, non auarus in proprio, non prodigus in alieno, non contumeliosus in capitulo, non negligens in monasterio, non effusus[t] in refectorio; frequens in oratione, discretus in confessione, assiduus in lectione, profusus in lacrimarum effusione, largus in pauperum miseratione, ardens in contemplatione, affabilis in hospitum susceptione. Pauca et uera sint eloquia oris tui.[u] Procul a te simulatio, dolus nunquam in corde, fraus nunquam in ore[v] tuo. Pre oculis timor diuinus, pre manibus beatus Benedictus. Extra Deum nichil agas, extra Benedictum nichil precipias. Vale.

31

To Abbot Hugh of Cluny[1]

late 1157 (or 1158, but earlier than letter no. 32)

[a]Domino et patri suo karissimo Hugoni Dei gratia Cluniacensi abbati frater Petrus humilis Cellensis abbas,[a] se ipsum cum deuotione.

Serenior post nubila dies succedit, dulcedo crescit ex amaritudine precedenti, ruina statum amplius commendat. Sic in auditu commotionis magne que in Cluniacensi electione facta est non parum concussa sunt uiscera nostra sed rursum in concordia letatur[b] anima nostra. Ab occasu[c] enim sancti patris nostri, predecessoris uestri, eatenus tanquam parturiens erat donec reciperet uirum alium qui consolaretur eam ab operibus suis.[2] In dolore suspirabat,[d] sed ecce 'iam non meminit pressure propter gaudium', quia et libertatem recepit et unum de filiis uteri sui[3] cum principibus populi sui

[t] refusus *Val* [u] tuis *O* [v] cordo *O* [*sic*]

31 *O fo. 98*$^{r-v}$, *Sirmond II. 2*]
[a–a] Eidem idem *O* [b] letata est *Sirmond* [c] occasione *O* [d] suspirat *O*

31 [1] Hugh de Fraisans, abbot of Cluny 1157–1161/3. Hugh was el. late 1157, either Nov. or as early as Sept., consecrated late 1157 or more likely 1158, and deposed 1161, April or soon after. After his deposition he continued to enjoy imperial favour and to be recognized as abbot of Cluny within the empire until his submission to Alexander III at Venice, 1 Aug. 1177. Despite the deposition, he may only have departed Cluny as late as 1163 (but he possibly occurs within the bounds of the empire as early as 26 Sept. 1162); his

you humbly let them find a mother, when they recoil from you stubbornly let them experience a strict father. Be not hasty in judgement, not silent in counsel, not talkative at table, not boastful in public, not disparaging in private, not miserly of your own, not prodigal of another's, not abusive in chapter, not negligent in the monastery, not unrestrained in the refectory; you should be regular in prayer, judicious in confession, assiduous in reading, profuse in pouring out tears, generous in mercy for the poor, zealous in meditation, courteous in the reception of guests. May the words of your mouth be few and true. Avoid pretence, let there never be deception in your heart nor deceit on your lips. May fear of God be before your eyes and holy Benedict always to your hand. Do nothing without God, order nothing without Benedict. Farewell.

31

To Abbot Hugh of Cluny[1]

late 1157 (or 1158, but earlier than letter no. 32)

To his dearest lord and father Hugh, by the grace of God abbot of Cluny, brother Peter, humble abbot of Montier-la-Celle, himself with devotion.

The light of day follows more brightly after clouds, sweetness rises out of preceding bitterness, disaster casts a better light on good order. Thus, hearing about the great turmoil which arose in the election at Cluny, our inwards were deeply stirred, but our soul is gladdened again by the peace. For, since the death of our holy father your predecessor, Cluny was as it were in travail until the time when she should receive another man who would comfort her from her works.[2] She was sighing in anguish, but see now, she does not remember the oppression on account of the joy, for she has received her liberty and has set one of the sons of her womb[3] up with the leaders of her

successor Stephen was el. possibly as early as 1161, and was in control of Cluny by 19 May 1163. After his submission, Hugh may have entered Vaux-sur-Poligny; he d. 15 March, year unknown. The complex evidence for these events is fully analysed in G. Constable, 'The abbots and anti-abbot of Cluny during the papal schism of 1159', *Revue Bénédictine*, xciv (1984), 370–400; on the dates cited here, see esp. pp. 382, 392–3. The present letter was written soon after Hugh's election, and presumably earlier than letter no. 32 (as explained at letter no. 32, n. 1).

[2] Cf. Gen. 5: 29.

[3] Cf. John 16: 21; Job 19: 17; Isa. 49: 15.

collocauit. 'Filii alieni[e] mentiti sunt' ei 'et claudicauerunt a semitis suis'[4] quia non ex ore Domini sed ex[f] propria usurpatione et consilio Achitophel regnare attemptabant.[5] Odiosa nimirum presumptio Cluniacensem tam castam matronam prostituere, tam religiosam publicare, tam honestam deuenustare. Reprimenda temeritas matrimonii leges tam petulanter infringere ut non uoluntas nobilissime puelle queratur sed uiolentia inferatur, torus[g] immaculatus[6] non cum reuerentia poscatur sed impudice exigatur. Prorsus inaudita miseria si hac necessitate materfamilias addicatur ut non tanquam libera 'cui uult nubat,[h] tantum[i] in Domino',[7] sed cui respuit nolens succumbat famulari,[j] immo concubinatus, obsequio. Vbi est: 'Non uos me elegistis sed ego elegi uos'?[8] Vbi est: 'Non sumat quisquam sibi honorem sed qui uocatur a Deo tanquam Aaron'?[9] Annon ista libera est, liberam habens electionem in libertate spiritus, cuius et ancilla et sponsa est; ancilla utique ex deuotione, sponsa ex caritate? Vbi, inquam, reuerentia sponsi, sponse gloria, quam Iohannes Baptista reformidat, Moyses uelat, Rebecca operit pallio, cherubin glorie obumbrant,[10] et quam caro et sanguis si contingat[k] ut fumus euanescit? 'Caro', inquit Apostolus, 'et sanguis regnum Dei [l]possidere non possunt.'[l] [11] Iccirco Moyses soluit calciamentum de pedibus suis ne si forte in terra sancta curis carnis impeditus consisteret faciem in rubo radiantis Dei offenderet.[12] Non estimo leue dispendium 'flammeum gladium atque uersatilem'[13] nuda manu accipere,[m] uel cecis obtutibus fornacem iracundie inconsulte transsilire. Culmen huius honoris, uel potius oneris, tam est pendulum ad casum quam debile ad flatum. Vrit sollicitudine, pungit timore, urget inquietudine. Fortuna si utrinque et undique uersata discutiatur, plus meroris et minus letitie refert. Iugiter siquidem ratiocinatio supputanda, tam accepti muneris quam soluendi debiti; hinc equitas iudicis, illinc difficultas iniuncte administrationis pensanda. Venia etiam speranda,

[e] enim alieni *O* [f] *om.* *O* [g] chorus *O* [h] *om.* *O* [i] tamen *Sirmond* [j] familiari *O* [k] contingit *Sirmond* [l–l] non possidebunt *Sirmond* [m] arripere *O*

[4] Cf. Ps. 17 (18): 46.
[5] Cf. 2 Kgs. (2 Sam.) 15: 31, 34; 16: 23; 17: 7, 14, 21, 23.
[6] Heb. 13: 14. [7] 1 Cor. 7: 39.
[8] John 15: 16. [9] Cf. Heb. 5: 4.
[10] Cluny, the chaste lady, is now likened to the Church in general, the bride of Christ, and to the tabernacle (veiled in e.g. Exod. 26 etc.) and the propitiatory with cherubim set over it (e.g. Exod. 25: 17–22.; Heb. 9: 5). Rebecca veils herself with a cloak on seeing Isaac in Gen. 24: 65, signifying the Church before Christ—cf. e.g. pseudo-Bede, *In Pent.*, Gen. c. xxiv (*PL* xci. 246); Gregory, *Mor. in Iob*, i. 15. 21 (*CCSL* cxliii. 34–5; *PL* lxxv. 536).

people. 'The children that are strangers have lied to' her 'and have halted from their paths'[4] because they were trying to rule not by the word of the Lord but from their own usurpation and by the counsel of Achitophel.[5] Truly it was a most detestable presumption to prostitute so chaste a lady as Cluny, to expose one so devout, to disfigure one so honest. It is a temerity which must be restrained to break the laws of marriage so impudently as when the will of the noblest maiden is not sought but violence is brought to bear, and an undefiled bed[6] is not requested with reverence but shamelessly exacted. It is an absolutely unheard of misery if the lady of the house be handed over under such compulsion that she may not, like a free woman, marry whom she wishes, only in the Lord,[7] but must rather submit unwillingly to him whom she despises in servile obedience, or rather the obedience of a concubine. Where is: 'You have not chosen me but I have chosen you'?[8] Where is: 'Neither let any man take the honour to himself but he that is called by God as Aaron was'?[9] Is not she the free woman who has a free choice in the freedom of the Holy Spirit, of whom she is both handmaiden and bride; a handmaiden, that is to say, out of devotion, a bride out of love? Where, I ask, is the reverence of the groom, the glory of the bride, of which John the Baptist stands in awe, which Moses veils, which Rebecca covers with a cloak, which the glories of the cherubim overshadow,[10] and which, if flesh and blood come into contact with it, vanishes like smoke? 'Flesh and blood', says the Apostle, 'cannot possess the kingdom of God.'[11] Therefore Moses put off the shoes from his feet lest, if by chance he should stand on holy ground burdened with earthly concerns, he might offend the face of God shining in the bush.[12] I do not consider it a trifling sacrifice to take up with a bare hand the 'flaming sword turning every way'[13] or heedlessly to leap blindfold over the furnace of anger. The summit of this honour, or rather burden, is as poised to collapse as it is feeble in the face of the wind. It burns with worry, it stings with fear, it presses hard with concern. If it is shattered by changed fortune from both sides and from all sides at once, it gives rise to more sorrow and less joy. Indeed the calculation must be made constantly of gifts received on the one hand and of debts to be paid on the other; on one side the fairness of the judge must be considered, on the other the difficulty of the task of administration which is enjoined. One must also hope for indulgence, so long as culpable negligence does not stand in the way. The time must be

[11] 1 Cor. 15: 50. [12] Cf. Exod. 3: 2–5. [13] Gen. 3: 24.

si non obstiterit punienda negligentia. Tempus numerandum, usura replicanda, fructus computandi, et summa totius dispensationis colligenda. Si minus inuentum fuerit, danda ante articulum supremum pecunia ad mensam, renouandus ad nummularios uirtutum siue fidei cursus. Gratia pro grauitate discriminis imploranda, arbitrium pro posse impendendum,[n] legatio excusatoria pro impossibili mittenda. Ex equo enim si ad pugnam congrediatur, nulla proportione ad Dominum homo miser et inualidus subsistet. Pondus terre, celi infinita spatia, diffusiones aeris et maris profusiones intra pugilli angustias facilius coartabis quam Deo celi paria respondere possis. O [o]abbas Cluniacensis,[o] attende 'quia fecit tibi magna qui potens est, et sanctum nomen eius'.[14] Fecit tibi Deus ut Deus, ut pius, ut bonus. Exaltauit humilem, deposuit potentem.[15] Ecce itaque oculus monachorum factus es, speculum et exemplar[p] huius ordinis. 'Si oculus tuus [q]fuerit simplex,[q] totum corpus' monachorum, quod est congregatio Cluniacensis, 'lucidum erit, si autem nequam fuerit, etiam corpus tenebrosum erit. Vide ergo ne lumen quod in te est tenebre sint',[16] ut sic loquar. Facit audere quod uestibulum familiaritatis tue aliquando penetraui, et religionis tue[r] sancta deuotio.[17] [s]Sed de his hactenus. Ceterum, more nostro obediens amantissimo et pie recordationis uiro, domino Petro abbati, fideiussi cum abbate Arremarensi pro eo multam pecuniam aduersus Hulduinum de Vendopera.[18] Priores quatuor proinde secundario ut regressum ad eos haberemus accepimus fideiussores. Hi sunt . . .[s] [text breaks off here]

[n] implorandum *O* [o–o] N. *O* [p] exemplum *O* [q–q] simplex fuerit *Sirmond* [r] *om. O* [s–s] *om. O*

[14] Cf. Luke 1: 49.

[15] Cf. Luke 1: 52.

[16] Luke 11: 34–5 (Vulgate has *corpus tuum* not *corpus*).

[17] A possible reference to Peter's early years in the Cluniac house of Saint-Martin-des-Champs (see Introduction, p. xxx).

[18] Hilduin of Vendeuvre, of the minor aristocracy of the Aube. He may be the same

reckoned, the interest reconsidered, the profits calculated, and the balance of the whole transaction drawn up. If it shall be found to be in deficit, a sum must be laid on the table before the final moment and the path to the money-lenders of virtue or of faith retrod. Grace must be implored in proportion to the amount of the difference, the adjudged amount must be laid out to the best of one's ability, an embassy bearing excuses must be sent out to account for that which cannot be paid. For if indeed he were to confront Him in a fight on equal terms, the wretched and weak man could in no measure stand up to the Lord. You could more easily hold the weight of the earth, the infinite spaces of the sky, the breadths of the air and the depths of the sea in your clenched fist than you could respond on equal terms to the God of heaven. O abbot of Cluny, consider this, 'because He that is mighty hath done great things to you, and holy is His name'.[14] God has done to you as befits God, the holy, the good. He has exalted the humble, He has put down the mighty.[15] And so behold, you have been made the eye of the monks, the mirror and example of this order. 'If thy eye be single, the whole body' of monks, that is the congregation of Cluny, 'will be lightsome, but if it be evil, the body also will be darksome. Take heed therefore that the light which is in thee be not darkness,'[16] if I may speak out so. The fact that I have once already entered the forecourt of your familiarity, and the holy devotion of your religious way of life, make me bold.[17] But enough of these matters. Regarding the rest, obeying in our usual way the most loving man of holy memory, Lord Abbot Peter, I, along with the abbot of Montiéramy, gave security for a large sum of money against Hilduin of Vendeuvre.[18] We have accepted four priors as back-up guarantors so that we can have recourse to them. These are . . . [text breaks off here]

Hilduin of Vendeuvre who occurs in 1121, in a charter along with a Roscelin of Vendeuvre (see Bur, *Champagne*, p. 260, and Lalore, *Cartulaires*, vii. 38–41, no. 23, which gives 31 Aug. 1121 × 25 Sept. 1122). Vendeuvre was a small lordship in the Aube whose seigneurs evidently came under the sway of the counts of Champagne early in the twelfth century (see Bur, *Champagne*, pp. 260, 397, and Arbois de Jubainville, *Comtes de Champagne*, iii. 27, 144; see also Lalore, *Cartulaires*, vii. 87). The abbot of Montiéramy in 1157/8 would have been Guy III, first occurs 1137, d. 1163 (*GC* xii. 554–5).

32

To Abbot Hugh of Cluny[1]

? late 1157

[a]Domino et patri suo karissimo Hugoni uenerabili Cluniacensi abbati P⟨etrus⟩ humilis abbas Cellensis, cum omni deuotione.[a]

Vna eademque hora, denique et ore uno, saporis dulcedinem a medullis epistole uestre accepi[b] et reciproco munere manum ad scribendum deflexi. Semper namque nescio quid plus dulcedinis habet res presumpta primo uoluntatis appetitu quam post desiderii tempus. Nolui igitur opportunitatem tanquam recalefaciendam in horas differre; unde fueram quasi monitus ipsa tante maiestatis dignatione. Et primum quidem moram dampnosam sed bene compensatam hac satisfactione remitto. Deinde negligens inueniri apud uos in huius officii munere precaueo. Cartam et carte scripturam satis eleganter compositam suscipiens,[c] [d]semel non[d] aspicio sed diligentiam hominis etiam in paruissimis rebus non pretereundam in memetipsum cum admiratione replico. Exemplum[e] est certe compositionis intime refiguratus quandoque[f] habitus in exteriori homine, et uini bonitas calicis accrescit idoneitate. Suggessit ipsa sue faciei uenustate quod et exhibuit in lectione, magnum quid in absconditis suis repositum apportare. De paradiso, de Egypto, et de quibuscunque locis scripturarum tam pretiosas merces et margaritas plenis marsupiis [g]ex se[g] refudit carta uestra, quod ad ipsam coartata sit intelligentie nostre archa. Sed quid mirum si dominus abbas Cluniacensis de thesauris suis tot et tanta proferat, quot et quanta Cellensis uix efferre ualeat? Nonne sic a quodam dictum legimus: Ex te [h]non poteris

32 *O fos.* 99^r–101^v, *Sirmond II. 4*]

[a–a] Eidem idem seipsum cum deuotione *O* [b] accepti *O* [c] suspiciens *O* [d–d] non semel *O* [e] Exempli *O* [f] quando *O* [g–g] sese *O* [h–h] prebere non poteris *O*

32 [1] Hugh de Fraisans, abbot of Cluny (see letter no. 31, n. 1). Hugh is referred to in this letter as a new abbot but it seems to be later than letter no. 31 which is apparently Peter's first reaction to Hugh's el. Henry of Blois, who is mentioned at the end of this letter, was at Cluny from late 1155 until *c.*1157. Henry, formerly a monk of Cluny, was bishop of Winchester 1129–8 Aug. 1171 (*EEA* viii, pp. xxxv–xlix); on his movements in these years, see *EEA* viii, pp. xlvii–xlviii: he fled to Cluny in late 1155, returning sometime in 1157 (but on the evidence of the present letter, probably late in 1157, as explained below), but was anyway definitely in England by autumn 1158; he visited Cluny again in

32

To Abbot Hugh of Cluny[1]

? late 1157

To his dearest lord and father Hugh, venerable abbot of Cluny, Peter, humble abbot of Montier-la-Celle, with all devotion.

In one and the same hour, and then with one voice, I received the sweetness of the taste from the pith of your letter and by a reciprocal duty turned my hand to writing. For a thing anticipated always has a certain something more of sweetness at the first onset of the inclination than after a period of wishing for it. I did not want therefore to put off the opportunity for hours so that it would have had to be, so to say, reheated; I was, as it were, deterred from that course by the very fact of being honoured by one so great. In the first place I am remitting an injurious delay, but one well compensated for by this repayment. Then I am guarding against being found negligent by you in the duty of this service. Taking up the letter and the text of the letter so elegantly composed, I am not looking over it just once, but am repeating to myself with admiration the carefully chosen words of the man, which should not be passed over even in the smallest details. The outward appearance of a man, at some time refashioned, is assuredly an image of his inner make-up, just as the goodness of the wine is enhanced by a fitting cup. It has suggested by the beauty of its appearance that which it has also demonstrated in the text, that it brings something great laid up in its hiding places. Your letter has poured forth from itself such precious goods and pearls from full purses, about Paradise, about Egypt, and about all possible passages of the Scriptures, that the treasure chest of our understanding is too small for it. But what wonder is it if the lord abbot of Cluny brings forth so many and such great things from his treasury that he of Montier-la-Celle is scarce able to carry them away? Do we not read this, which someone said: And you will not be able on your

1161. The present letter seems to assume that Henry is at Cluny, although this would suggest that at the time of writing Hugh was el. but not yet blessed, or that his blessing was late 1157 rather than 1158 (but on these dates, see letter no. 31, n. 1); in any case, if the two coincided then Henry of Blois cannot have left Cluny before Sept., or possibly even Nov., 1157. On Henry of Blois and Cluny, see also L. Voss, *Heinrich von Blois, Bischoff von Winchester (1129–71)*, Historische Studien, ccx (Berlin, 1932), pp. 108–21.

prebere[h] ascensores equorum quos ego dabo tibi.[2] Ambulant uobiscum innumerabiles forte sicut monachi sic et sententie. Certe sic est, negari non potest. Res in euidenti est.[i] Quis sic ad manum, sic ad nutum cogere tantum exercitum philosophicorum exemplorum tam cito potuit? O uena diues! Beatus qui uigilat ad postes ostii tui.[3] Mane panibus, uespere carnibus satiari[j] poterit.[4] Pulsaui et aperuistis.[5] Vnum locutus sum, quod dixisse me non penitet. Vna siquidem et modica punctione tetigi uos, quin immo tetigi aceruum Mercurii,[5A] siue nouarum frugum, sed non modica estimatione excepi thesaurum multarum sententiarum. Quid? Mensuram bonam et confertam et coagitatam et supereffluentem remisistis in sinum nostrum.[6] Proinde exulto ad dignationem uestram, stupeo ad eloquentiam, curro sicut ceruus sitiens ad fontes[k] [7] historiarum, ad profunditatem sententiarum, ad suauitatem exhortationum. Interea duo proponitis sumpta a nomine uno, quod est Petrus, fortitudinem scilicet et agnitionem. De utraque exemplificatis non auare. Honesto deinde modo qualis esse debeam instruitis cum[l] talem esse dicitis qualem fieri uultis. Modus hic suadibilis ad docendum. Naturale siquidem est anime rationali uoluntario motu occurrere de se bene opinanti et humeros inclinare indubitate affectioni. Pronum [m]quoque sibi[m] redhibet animum ad obediendum qui prius amicitie fidem fecerit et de probitate persuaserit. Crederem uobis si michi conscius in contrarium non essem; [n]utinam sicut sentit in uobis caritas sic in me michi responderet ueritas, immo[n] utinam sicut a caritate uestra profertur sic a uobis in ueritate perficeretur.[o] Sed ut uerum fatear, † rara in nobis nominis nostri[p] interpretata ueritas.[8] † Vnus enim est, et secundum non habet, cui dicitur, 'Secundum nomen tuum, ita et laus tua in fines terre'.[9] Quod[q] hoc nomen? Iesus. Que ista laus? Saluabit[r] Dominus 'populum suum a peccatis eorum'.[10] Reuera hic Iesus in cuius manu salus nostra est. Hic [s]'nomen' habet[s] quod est 'super omne nomen'.[11] Hic denique uirtutem nomine suo non inferiorem [t]implet, quin immo[t]

[i] *om. Sirmond* [j] edere *Sirmond* [k] fontem *O* [l] et *Sirmond* [m–m] sibi quoque *O* [n–n] *om. Sirmond* [o] proficeretur *O* [p] uestri *Sirmond* [q] Quid *O* [r] Saluauit *O* [s–s] habet nomen *O* [t–t] quin potius numero *O*

[2] Cf. Isa. 36: 8. [3] Cf. Prov. 8: 34. [4] Cf. Exod. 16: 12.
[5] Cf. Matt. 7: 7–8; Luke 11: 9–10. [5A] Cf. Prov. 26: 8.
[6] Cf. Luke 6: 38. [7] Cf. Ps. 41 (42): 2.
[8] The sense would seem to be Peter modestly denying that he possesses the attributes associated with the interpretation of the name Peter; but the text is evidently corrupt (*interpretati* is possible for *interpretata*). From the foregoing, Hugh has written to Peter

part to find riders for the horses which I will give you.[2] Perhaps just as countless monks walk with you so also do countless precepts. Certainly it is so, it cannot be denied. The matter is clear. Who could marshal so great an army of philosophical examples so quickly at his signal and at his will? O rich vein! Blessed is he that watches at the posts of your doors.[3] He will be able to have his fill of loaves in the morning, of meats in the evening.[4] I have knocked and you have opened.[5] I have mentioned one matter, and I do not regret having spoken of this. Indeed I have touched you with one, and that a modest, point, nay rather I have touched the heap of Mercury,[5A] or of new harvest, but I have received in return a treasury of many thoughts of no small value. What do I mean? You have returned to our bosom a good measure, pressed down, shaken together and running over.[6] Thus I rejoice at your worthiness, I am amazed at your eloquence, I run like the thirsty deer to the fountains[7] of knowledge, to the deep well of thoughts, to the sweetness of exhortations. Meanwhile, you set forth two qualities taken from one name, that is Peter, namely strength and knowledge. You demonstrate each generously. Then you teach me in a worthy manner how I ought to be when you say I am as you wish me to become. This is a persuasive method of teaching. It is indeed natural for a rational mind to go to meet of its own free will one that thinks well of it and to bow the shoulders to undoubted affection. He who has first formed a bond of friendship and convinced his friend of his sincerity also receives for himself in return a mind eager to obey. I would believe you if I did not in my heart know the contrary; if only as love feels in you, so in me might the truth answer to me, or rather, if only just as it is put forward by your love so it might be accomplished by you in truth. But to tell the truth, † [there is] in me scant truth in [your] interpretation of my name.†[8] For there is One, and He has no second, to whom it is said, 'According to thy name, so also is thy praise unto the ends of the earth'.[9] What is this name? Jesus. What is that praise? The Lord shall save 'His people from their sins'.[10] Truly this is Jesus in whose hand our salvation lies. He has 'a name which is above all names'.[11] In short he embodies a virtue which is not beneath his name, nay rather surpassing it in time

praising him by ascribing to him qualities derived from the interpretation of his name. Peter responds with humility that Hugh has said he (Peter) has qualities which in reality he can only wish him to have, adding that he could wish that Hugh's praises might be borne out in reality. So such an interpretation of the present sentence would seem natural.

[9] Cf. Ps. 47 (48): 11. [10] Cf. Matt. 1: 21. [11] Cf. Phil. 2: 9.

et tempore et pondere excellentiorem. Parum dixi, 'tempore', melius enim dicerem, 'eternitate'. Virtus hec ab eterno, nomen hoc ab euo. Virtus sine tempore, nomen ex tempore. In pondere nichilominus omnia uirtus diuinitatis operatur, ipsum quoque nomen Iesu. O pondus nominis Iesu! Quis appendere, quis dinumerare, quis estimare ualeat hoc nomen in pondere? Nunquam sine pondere nominandus est Iesus, pondere utique sanctuarii, quia 'nemo potest dicere Dominus Iesus, nisi in Spiritu sancto'.[12] Et in lege Moysi sic dicitur: 'Non assumes nomen Dei tui in uanum.'[13] Paulus Apostolus ne[u] in uanum curreret ut potuit in uinculis et in catenis per passiones cotidianas hoc nomen semper apposuit et appendit.[v] Hoc enim est quod ait: 'Non sunt condigne passiones huius temporis'[w] etc.,[14] et alibi[x] de eodem pondere: 'Stigmata', inquit, 'Iesu porto in corpore meo.'[15] Alibi dicit: 'Dedit ei Pater nomen, quod est super omne nomen' etc.[16] Preponderat hoc nomen quodcunque creature nomen est.

Hoc compendiose dixerim ut solum designarem qui[y] scilicet nomen habet et uirtutem. Rursus inflecto[z] intuitum ad epistolam que 'sicut turris edificata est cum propugnaculis; mille clipei pendent ex ea, omnis armatura fortium'.[17] Ad quid tantus apparatus? Opinor uoluistis in me aut terrere sensus hebetes maiestate sensuum, numerositate exemplorum, perplexione rationum[a] subtilium, aut inertem prouocare emulatione studiorum, aut mestum consolari pulchritudine sermonum, aut indoctum edificare persuasione adhortationum, aut satisfacere importunitati[b] mee habundantiori gurgite auctoritatum. Sed quodcunque horum attenderitis,[c] optabile et ualde carum habeo quod occupationibus uestris cesseritis[d] et, sicut Rebecca, hydriam de scapulis lassitudini nostre[e] inclinaueritis.[18] Refluentes quippe procellarum reuolutiones quibus interdum ascenditur usque ad celum et descenditur usque ad abyssum,[19] quis uel ad modicum credat abesse abbati nouo Cluniacensi? Quis 'de abyssis terre'[20] uel post tertium diem[21] non miretur emergere? Quis non compatiatur gementi sub aquis?[22] Scribere quomodo ualet quem degrandinat

[u] non *O* [v] *corr. Hall;* apprehendit *O, Sirmond* [w] *om. Sirmond*
[x] alias *O;* alius *Sirmond* [y] *corr. Hall;* quis *O, Sirmond* [z] reflecto *O*
[a] ratiocinationum *O* [b] opportunitati *Sirmond* [c] attenditis *Sirmond*
[d] succensetis *Sirmond* [e] uestre *O*

[12] 1 Cor. 12: 3. [13] Cf. Exod. 20: 7.
[14] Rom. 8: 18; the text continues '. . . ad futuram gloriam que reuelabitur in nobis'.
[15] Cf. Gal. 6: 17. [16] Cf. Phil. 2: 9. [17] Cf. S. of S. 4: 4.
[18] Cf. Gen. 24: 46. [19] Cf. Ps. 106 (107): 26. [20] Ps. 70 (71): 20.

and in authority. I have put it too low, saying 'in time', I should better say 'in eternity'. This virtue exists from eternity, this name from time. This virtue is without time, the name is of time. In authority, no less, the virtue of divinity accomplishes all things, as does the very name of Jesus. O authority of the name of Jesus! Who could weigh, who could reckon, who could estimate the authority of that name? Jesus should never be named without that authority, without the authority particularly of the sanctuary, because 'no man can say "the Lord Jesus" but by the Holy Ghost'.[12] Also it is thus stated in the law of Moses: 'Thou shalt not take the name of thy God in vain.'[13] The Apostle Paul, so that he should not run in vain, as far as he was able, in fetters and in chains, through daily sufferings, set this name always beside himself and weighed it. For this is what he says: 'The sufferings of this time are not worthy' etc.,[14] and elsewhere on the subject of the same authority he says: 'I bear the marks of Jesus in my body.'[15] Elsewhere he says: 'The Father hath given Him a name, which is above all names' etc.[16] This name outweighs the name of any created being.

Let me say this briefly, only to point out who it is who has the name and the virtue. I turn again to look at the letter which 'is built like the tower with bulwarks; a thousand bucklers hang upon it, all the armour of valiant men'.[17] What is the purpose of such a great array? I believe that you wished either to frighten my dull perceptions by the greatness of your perceptions, by the multitude of examples, by the intricacy of subtle reasonings, or to stir my lethargy with a desire to emulate your studies, or to console my misery with the beauty of your discourses, or to edify my ignorance with the persuasion of your encouragements, or to answer my questions with a more abundant stream of authorities. But whichever of these you intended, I consider it valuable and extremely kind that you have given up time from your occupations and, like Rebecca, let down the pitcher from your shoulders for our weariness.[18] Who would believe, even for a moment, that the turning tides of stormy weather by which one is at times raised up to the heavens, at times lowered down to the depths[19] do not beset the new abbot of Cluny? Who would not be astonished at one arising 'from the depths of the earth'[20] even after the third day?[21] Who would not feel compassion for one groaning under the waters?[22] How can he find the strength to write whom the

[21] Cf. Matt. 20: 19; Mark 9: 30; 10: 34; Luke 9: 22; 18: 33; 24: 7, 46; 1 Cor. 15: 4.
[22] Cf. Job 26: 5.

sollicitudo continua et nunquam quieta? Sed ubi obstaculum egrius, ibi necesse est se expediat ingenium egregius. Procul dubio animi elegantis est cure [f]secularis oneribus[f] indignari et per medias interpellantium acies ad lectionum amenissima prata et solitudinem liberam uelut solitarius onager[23] euolare. Contra hanc uim a pretore nullum proponitur interdictum. Hec uis probabilior quam desidiosa patientia. Vis, inquam, hec non improbabilis si rumpantur noui funes[24] contexti et concatenati[g] nexibus causarum tanquam a profundo maris emergentium. Est et aliud consilium ut ubi non sunt uires ad uim faciendam adsit ingenium ad laudabile[h] furtum committendum, de quo tamen non nascatur actio furti. In euangelio enim commendatur mulier que tangens Iesum uirtutem a fimbria uestimenti eius furto subripuisse commemoratur.[25] Furtum prorsus commendabile si te ipsum tibi[i] ipsi et Deo tuo ab incursu concursantium subduxeris. 'Aque' enim 'furtiue dulciores sunt et panis absconditus suauior.'[26] Valde saporabilis lectio quam non[j] interpellata sorbet anime intentio. Studium, lectio et oratio turbam non amat.[k] Impediuntur plerumque peregrino superuentu quia uix patitur [l]se partiri cum aduueniente inquietudine nobilis[l] anime consolatio. Forte onera grauia et importabilia que nec digitis tangere possum humeris uestris impono.[27] Quo[m] enim modo dominus meus Cluniacensis poterit hec[n] unquam uel experiri? Immo uiuere quomodo poterit si hec non fecerit? Si post omnes se[o] habiturus est, quando se habebit? Rursum si eum non habuerint[p] qui sine eo uiuere non debent, quanta pestis et iniquitas. Expedit potius ut unus moriatur homo quam tota gens pereat. Sed rursum, quid prodest si totum mundum lucretur 'se autem ipsum perdat et detrimentum sui faciat'?[28] Ecce, ut attenditis, res in arto posita est. Neque ad dexteram pro se, neque ad sinistram pro aliis excedendum est. Quid igitur? Medium eligat, et si non potest omnem diem, saltem diem inter diem habeat. Habeant eum alii, sed[q] ipse habeat se ipsum, sed et alii. Non diuidat infantem uiuum ut decreuit[r] Solomon; habeat eum uel mater, uel non mater, immo semper habeat mater.[29] Non sibi uiuat tantum, non aliis tantum, sed

[f-f] secularibus hominibus *O* [g] cathenati *O* [h] *om. Sirmond* [i] uel *O* [j] *om. Sirmond* [k] amant *O* [l-l] non se partiri aduenienti nobili *Sirmond* [m] quoniam *O* [n] *om. O* [o] om. *Sirmond* [p] habuerit *O* [q] sed et *O*

[23] Cf. Hos. 8: 9. [24] Cf. Judg. 15: 13–14; 16: 11–12.
[25] Cf. Matt. 9: 20–22; Mark 5: 25–34; Luke 8: 43–8. [26] Prov. 9: 17.
[27] Cf. Matt. 23: 4; Luke 11: 46. [28] Luke 9: 25; cf. Matt. 16: 26; Mark 8: 36.
[29] Cf. 3 Kgs. (1 Kgs.) 3: 16–28 (the whole passage echoes St Bernard, *De consideratione*, i. 5. 6.).

storm pelts with constant worry and never leaves in peace? But where there is a more difficult obstacle, there the rarer spirit must needs extricate itself. Without doubt it is characteristic of the discriminating mind to disdain the burdens of worldly preoccupation and to fly forth through the throngs of hinderers to the sweetest meadows of reading and to the freedom of solitude, like a wild ass alone.[23] No prohibition is set against this determination by the chief magistrate. This determination is more commendable than slothful endurance. This determination, I say, is not objectionable if the new cords,[24] woven together and linked up with knots of cares, rising as it were from the depths of the sea, are broken. There is also an alternative plan, so that where the strength capable of acting with determination is lacking, the wit is there to carry out a praiseworthy theft, from which however a charge of theft should not arise. For in the Gospel the woman is commended who, touching Jesus, is recorded as having stolen the virtue from the hem of His garment by theft.[25] Theft is certainly commendable if you steal yourself from the press of people around you for yourself and for your God. For 'stolen waters are sweeter and hidden bread is more pleasant'.[26] That reading can be best appreciated which the uninterrupted concentration of the mind absorbs. Study, reading and prayer do not like a crowd. They are often disturbed by the arrival of a stranger because the consolation of the noble soul is scarce able to share itself with the advent of distraction. Perhaps I am placing on your shoulders the heavy and unbearable burdens which I cannot even touch with my fingers.[27] For how will my lord of Cluny ever be able even to experience these things? Nay, how will he be able to live if he does not do them? If he is to have himself only after everyone else, when will he have himself? Yet how great a pestilence and evil it will be if those who ought not to live without him do not have him. It is better for one man to die rather than for the whole race to perish. But again, what does it profit a man if he gain the whole world 'and lose himself and cast away himself'?[28] See, as you consider it, the problem is critical. There is no escape either on the right, for his own benefit, or on the left, for the benefit of others. What then? Let him choose the middle way, and if he cannot have every day, at least let him have occasional days to himself. Let others have him, but let him, as well as others, have himself. Let him not divide the living child, as Solomon decreed; let either the mother or the one who is not the mother have him, or rather let the mother have him in every case.[29] Let him not live

sibi et aliis[s] ne ipse pereat, [t]sed aliis et sibi[t] ne oues sine pastore succumbant. Et de his hactenus.

Preterea non[u] indignetur dominus meus si dixero quod sentio. Dicam, sed cum licentia dicam. Quid? Quia deest semper aliquid [v]culture Dei.[v] Hoc forte apud uos[w] prouerbium est, sed faciam uerbum de prouerbio. Laqueum debiti quadam perplexione ratiocinando[x] differtis ita scribendo in epistola: 'Si redditum est, non debemus super hoc inquietari; si propter reddendum questio aliqua uentilatur, debet iudiciario ordine diffiniri, et partium allegatione et iudicis sententia terminari.' Bone domine, bene docuit uos[y] magister noster[z] [30] proponere, utinam sic bene soluere—soluere, dico, debitum non syllogismum. Videritis non extensa disputatione sed compendiosa relatione, uel[a] potius ratione, inter quos questio hec uersari debeat,[b] cui competat actio, et aduersus quem detur. Principalis profecto debitor et suus creditor ad inuicem habent actiones, alius directam, alius utilem.[31] Sed quid ad fideiussorem? Semper liberandus fideiussor proposita actione pignoraticia a principali debitore contra creditorem, soluto prius duntaxat debito ad restituendum pignus et ad liberandum fideiussorem. Hoc fecit dominus Wintoniensis, sed non effecit, nam creditorem conuenit sed nobis pignus non restituit. Iccirco dixi quod curta [c]est res[c] donec restitutum sit nobis quod tenetur pro uobis. Est et aliud notandum[d] in epistola uestra, quia suspensiue et indefinite dixistis quid agendum esset, sed non quando; neque diem, neque horam posuistis, forte quia non est nostrum scire tempora que in potestate sua habet dominus[e] Wintoniensis.[32] Scio, domine mi, scio quia in multiloquio non deest peccatum. Ignoscite si quid egressum est de labiis nostris quod minus rectum appareat in oculis uestris. Vt uero[f] hoc auderem uos occasionem dedistis. Valete.[g]

[r] decreuerit *O* [s] aliis. Non aliis tantum *O* [t–t] Non sibi tantum *O* [u] non id *Sirmond* [v–v] curre rei *O* [w] nos *O* [x] ratiocinandum *O* [y] nos *O* [z] uester *O* [a] et *Sirmond* [b] dicitur *Sirmond* [c–c] res est *O* [d] notatum *Sirmond* [e] *om. Sirmond* [f] tamen *O* [g] *om. O*

[30] Unidentified, but the reference may indicate a long acquaintance with Hugh.

[31] 'in equity', i.e. a case for which there is no express legal principle, or an action decided on principle and not on a legal technicality. On Henry of Blois, see n. 1 above. It

entirely for himself nor entirely for others, but for himself and others lest he perish, but also for others and himself lest the sheep without a shepherd succumb. But enough of these matters.

Furthermore, may my lord not be angry at this if I speak my mind. I shall speak, but let me speak with your permission. How so? Because something is always lacking in the worship of God. This may be a proverb in your region, but I shall say a word about the proverb. You are postponing the noose of debt by reasoning with some degree of confusion, by writing thus in your letter: 'If it is repaid, we ought not to be concerned about this; if some question is aired regarding the repayment, it ought to be settled by judicial process and brought to an end through the testimony of the parties and by the decision of the judge.' My good lord, our master[30] taught you well how to propose a problem, if only he had taught you equally well how to solve one—to resolve, I say, a debt not a syllogism. You should have seen, not by prolonged discussion but by a brief report, or rather reasoning, between whom this case ought to be contested, to whom the action is due, and against whom it is brought. The principal debtor, certainly, and his creditor have actions against one another, one straightforward, the other in equity.[31] But what about the guarantor? The guarantor should always be freed by an action brought on account of a pledge by the principal debtor against the creditor, with the debt first forgiven to this extent, that the pledge is restored and the guarantor freed. This the lord bishop of Winchester did, but he did not put it into effect, for he summoned the creditor but did not restore the pledge to us. For this reason I have said that the case is defective until that which is held on your account be returned to us. There is also another thing worth noting in your letter, that you have said hesitantly and vaguely what ought to be done, but not when; you have appointed neither the day nor the hour, perhaps because it is not for us to know the times which the lord bishop of Winchester has in his own power.[32] I know, my lord, I know that in speaking out too far error is not absent. Pardon me if something has come from my lips which might in your eyes appear less than proper. Yet truly you have given me cause to venture it. Farewell.

appears from this letter and no. 33 that Peter had given a pledge to a creditor of Hugh's but that Hugh had initiated a counter-action against his creditor and recovered the pledge, evidently through the intervention, or by the judgement, of Henry of Blois. This however has not been repaid to Peter.

[32] Cf. Acts 1: 7.

33
To Abbot Hugh of Cluny[1]

late 1157 × Sept. 1159

[a]Domino suo et patri karissimo Hugoni abbati Cluniacensi frater Petrus Cellensis, salutem.[a]

Iustitia nostra superhabundare debet iustitie scribarum et phariseorum et[b] non subiacere. Miror iustitiam hanc quis nouus legislator, uel unde, attulerit[c] ut non restituatur a principali debitore pignus fideiussori[d] a creditore[e] detentum. Miror et nouam benignitatem uestram que nec semel respondere uoluit iam secundo uocanti. Durius hoc silentio quam dampno permoueor. Ad dampnum enim leuius ferendum[f] cooperatur patientia cum illud noueris resarciendum amici [g]bona et noua[g] gratia. Silentium uero post beneficium mortui beneficii representat sepulcrum. Malum[h] tanquam abortiuum amici primogenitum facere, cum potius semper obsequii memoria uigere debeat et uiuere apud amicos. Et dampnum et[i] dampni hactenus patientiam prestabam; sed amicis, sed dominis, sed ueracibus monachis, qui et si me ipsum uellent inuadiare possent, sed quid dicam? Plane minus dicam ne forte et cum pecunia amicos perdam. [j]Dicam prorsus, dicam. Quicunque forte hoc audieritis, quod Cellensis simplicitas sic elisa, ne dicam elusa, sit ab amicis suis karissimis, pro quibus et se et omnia sua ponebat, nolite annuntiare in Geth, neque in compitis Ascalonis.[2] Hoc potius etsi non uerius dicatur: 'Abbas uetera non nouit debita. Iam[k] cum audierit et creditoribus satisfaciet et fideiussores liberabit et gratiam amicis equa lance

33 *O fo. 99^r, Sirmond II. 3*]
[a–a] Eidem idem *O* [b] *om. O* [c] attulit *Sirmond* [d] fideiussoris *O* [e] debitore *Sirmond* [f] perferendum *O* [g–g] noua et bona *O* [h] Malum est *O* [i] *om. O* [j–j] *om. O* [k] *corr. Hall;* Nam *Sirmond*

33 [1] Hugh de Fraisans, abbot of Cluny (see letter no. 31, n. 1). Neither this nor any of the other letters to Hugh mention the papal schism which broke out in Sept. 1159; there is no evidence that Peter maintained his contact with Hugh after the latter's deposition. Hugh was excommunicated by Alexander III, who instructed Henry of France, in a letter of 7 Apr. 1161, to depose him without appeal—see G. Constable, 'The abbots and anti-abbot of Cluny during the papal schism of 1159', *Revue Bénédictine*, xciv (1984), 370–400, at pp. 388–9. Given Peter's sympathies in the schism it is unlikely that he was writing to Hugh after Sept. 1159 anyway, although Hugh was casting around for support between his deposition in 1161 and final departure from Cluny in 1163; see A. Morey and C. N. L.

33

To Abbot Hugh of Cluny[1]

late 1157 × Sept. 1159

To his dearest lord and father Hugh, abbot of Cluny, brother Peter of Montier-la-Celle, greetings.

Our justice ought to surpass that of the scribes and the Pharisees and not be subject to it. I wonder what new lawgiver can have brought in this justice, and from where, that the pledge which has been held by the creditor be not restored by the principal debtor to the guarantor. I wonder also at your new-found benevolence that would not even once reply to one calling now for the second time. I am struck by this silence harder than by the wrong you have done me. For patience contributes to making a loss easier to bear when one knows that the loss can be mended by the good and new grace of a friend. But silence after good favour represents the tomb of deceased kindness. It is as bad as making the first-born child of a friend miscarry, when the memory of the duty should rather thrive always and live on among friends. So far I have guaranteed the debt and shown patience in my loss; but to friends, to lords, to true monks, who if they wanted to could make a pledge even of me—what should I say? Clearly I should say less, lest by chance I should lose friends as well as money. But I shall speak out directly, I shall. You, whoever you are, who perhaps have heard that the simplicity of him of Montier-la-Celle has been so knocked, or should I say mocked, by his dearest friends, for whom he was pledging both himself and all of his own, tell it not in Gath, nor in the streets of Ascalon.[2] Let this rather be said, although it is not more true: 'The abbot knew of no old debt. Now he has heard of it he will at once satisfy the creditors, free the guarantors and repay grace to friends in equal measure.' Farewell.

Brooke, *Gilbert Foliot and his Letters* (Cambridge, 1965), pp. 3–4 and n. 3. On the dispute treated in the present letter, see letter no. 32 and n. 31. Again Peter complains that the pledge which he had given, having been recovered by Hugh, has not been returned to him. While the same situation is described, the phrases '... iam secundo uocanti' and '... calami nostri ualde fatigati' would seem to indicate that this letter is the later of the two. Also, there is no mention here of Henry of Blois, who left Cluny in 1157 (see letter no. 32, n. 1), but this is inconclusive.

[2] Cf. 2 Kgs. (2 Sam.) 1: 20.

rependet.[y] Valete. Ecce calami nostri ualde fatigati pro labore suo mercedem reposcunt, bibere in calice post estum et hiemem.

34

To Abbot Hugh of Cluny[1]

late 1157 × Sept. 1159

Domino et patri karissimo Hugoni Cluniacensi abbati frater Petrus Cellensis abbas, salutem.

Pro amicis nostris, immo pro amicis iustitie, amico nostro, ueritatis immo amico,[2] nunquam refelleremus scribere. Etenim illa amicitia in diuersis amicorum causis debet interuenire que, non plus iusto uergens se in fauorem alterius, equitatis rectitudine pensat negotium, non fauoris aut odii iniqua inflexione. Quanquam igitur uobis et excellentem prerogatiuam dilectionis debeam et honoris, huic tamen abbati Sancti Laurentii Leodiensis[3] nouo confederatus amicitie pacto, propter Christum quem in ipsum suscepi, me ipsum nichilominus concedo. Cum igitur utrinque Christus in causa sit, utrumque ad debitum honorem rependendum medius ipse commoneo, uos quidem ut quanto magnus dignitate, prelatione et nomine estis, tanto habundantiori humilitate illum suscipiatis, illum ut secundum excellentiam maiestatis uestre cogitet qualiter summam in summo uiro humilitatem excipiat, et obuiis, ut dicitur, brachiis deuexam bonitatem sustentet; uos ut honestatem persone et iustitiam quam habet ad uos equa libratione appendatis, et persone honorem, cause iudicium reddatis. Vidi personam et amaui, audiui causam et approbaui. In persona prudentiam, religionem, litteraturam, simplicitatem notaui, in causa retentionem pacis, malitie exterminationem, simultatis repressionem et iustitie tenorem animaduerti. Qui de tam longe querit pacem, nonne amat quod querit? Qui tempore tanto et tali a sancta fratrum suorum congregatione peregrinatur, quibus putas stimulis affectionum remordetur, ut

34 *Sirmond II. 5*]

34 [1] Dated as letter no. 33. [2] Cf. Cicero, *De officiis*, i. 19. 63.
[3] The abbot of Saint-Laurence, Liège, at this time would have been either Wazelin de Fexhe (occurs from 1150, d. 14 June, ?1158), or Wautier (occurs from ?1157, certainly 1159, d. 25 July 1160, or more likely 1161): *Mon. Belge*, ii.1, pp. 38–40, which suggests

See how our pens, much worn, seek payment for their labour—to drink from the cup after the heat and the cold.

34

To Abbot Hugh of Cluny[1]

late 1157 × Sept. 1159

To his dearest lord and father Hugh, abbot of Cluny, brother Peter, abbot of Montier-la-Celle, greetings.

We would never refuse to write on behalf of our friends, nay the friends of justice, to our friend, nay the friend of truth.[2] For that friendship ought to intervene in the various affairs of friends, which, not inclining in favour of either side more than is just, weighs the matter with the rectitude of equity, not with the unequal bias of favour or hatred. Therefore although I owe to you the highest prerogative both of love and of honour, yet to this abbot of Saint-Laurence, Liège,[3] bound by a new pact of friendship for the sake of Christ whom I received in him, I yield myself none the less. Since therefore Christ is on both sides of the issue, I myself as mediator urge each of you to repay the honour due: I urge you indeed, by as much as you are great in worth, in position, and in name, to receive him with so much the more abundant humility; him I urge, according to the excellence of your majesty, to consider how he should respond to the greatest humility in the greatest man, and how he should with arms extended, as they say, bear your condescending goodness; and I urge you to weigh on equal scales the honesty of the character and the case which he has brought before you, and to give honour to the character and judgement in the case. I have seen his character, and I loved it; I have heard his case, and I have approved it. In his character I remarked prudence, devotion, erudition, and simplicity; in the case I observed the maintenance of peace, the driving out of malice, the suppression of dissension and holding fast to justice. Does not he who seeks peace for such a long time love what he seeks? He who wanders for so long and at such a time from the blessed company of his brethren, by what stings of affection do you suppose he is tormented,

Wautier as the recipient, but gives no reasons or evidence beyond the present letter (see also *GC* iii. 987). He was evidently at Montier-la-Celle when this letter was written.

uacce ille, reclusis uitulis, mugientes,[4] uincens[a] sanctitate propositi usitatum et consuetum affectum carnalitatis? Sed gratias Deo quia illorum dampnum quibus abfuit, et suus dolor recalcitrans qui abfuit, nobis in lucrum uersum est quibus affuit. Moueant itaque et commoueant pia uiscera uestra que auditis, et intendite uiro bono, uiro pacifico, uiro honesto, immo uestris monachis et fratribus, quibus ualde credimus utile si pacem tenuerint, inhonestum et inutile si a pace resilierint. Valete.

35

To Prior Basil of La Grande Chartreuse and the general chapter of the Carthusian order[1]

? *c.*1160 or earlier

Dominis et patribus karissimis Basilio priori Carthusiensium cum ceteris prioribus et sancto conuentui frater Petrus abbas Cellensis, consilium et auxilium ueritatis et pacis.

Refusione uberiore irrigatur 'hortus' Dei ille 'conclusus, fons signatus',[2] quotiens in unum conueniunt fistule et canales benigni spiritus Dei,[3] non ad calices Babilonicos absorbendos[4] sed ad feces Iacob expurgandas[5] et uentres steriles fecundandos. Spiritus Dei a quatuor uentis celi[6] singulos uestrum de loco suo euocauit ut unum corpus plenum gratia et ueritate efficeremini. Vos enim qui priores estis et curam aliorum suscepistis, quasi uene in corpore Carthusiensis

[a] uincentes *Sirmond*

35 *Sirmond V. 12*]

[4] Cf. 1 Kgs. (1 Sam.) 6: 7, 10, 12, i.e. which drew the ark back to Bethsames.

35 [1] Basil, prior of La Grande Chartreuse, el. ? 1151, cert. by 1155, resigned *c.*1173/4 (*J. S. Epp.* ii. 556–7, n. 8; Le Couteulx, ii. 123–4, 371–3; *GC* xvi. 275). The letter refers to the plan of Count Henry the Liberal of Champagne (1152–81, see letter no. 71, n. 1) to found a charterhouse on his lands, and to his request that the priors of Mont-Dieu and of Val-Saint-Pierre be sent to choose a site. This took place *c.*1160 (Le Couteulx, ii. 217–20, but Le Couteulx cites only Peter of Celle's letters as evidence, and this dating may be based on the assumption that the prior of Mont-Dieu here is Simon, 1159–*c.*1184, the addressee of letter no. 59, in which the renewal of the mission is mentioned; this is not necessarily so, and an earlier date may be possible). The plan evidently failed, the Carthusians found no suitable site on this occasion (see letter no. 59), and ultimately the project came to nothing (but Godefroy, 'Saint-Ayoul', ii. 33 says that a similar plan was

like those cows, with their calves shut up, lowing,[4] overcoming by the holiness of the resolution the usual and accustomed affection of the flesh? But thanks be to God that the suffering of those who miss him, and his pain in separation from them, are turned to advantage for us who enjoy his presence. Therefore may your merciful heart be moved and stirred by what you hear and give heed to a good man, a peaceful man, a worthy man, and to your own monks and brothers, to whom we believe it most advantageous if they hold fast to peace, and shameful and useless if they depart from it. Farewell.

35

To Prior Basil of La Grande Chartreuse and the general chapter of the Carthusian order[1]

? *c.*1160 or earlier

To his dearest lords and fathers, Prior Basil of La Grande Chartreuse along with the other priors, and the blessed assembly, brother Peter, abbot of Montier-la-Celle, the counsel and the aid of truth and peace.

That 'garden' of God 'enclosed', that 'fountain sealed up'[2] is watered by a more abundant outpouring as often as the water pipes and channels of the kindly Spirit of God converge in one place,[3] not to fill the cups of Babylon[4] but to purge the dregs of Jacob[5] and to make the barren wombs fruitful. The Spirit of God has called forth each of you from his own place from the four winds of heaven[6] so that you will become one body full of grace and truth. For you who are priors and have taken on the care of others are like the veins in the

realized in Troyes in 1315). The letter is addressed to all the priors of the order and was presumably sent at the time of the order's general chapter. The first of these took place *c.*1141 and they were annual from 1155: see B. Bligny, *Recueil des plus anciens actes de la Grande-Chartreuse (1086–1196)* (Grenoble, 1958), pp. xix–xx, 53–64. The salutation and final sentence seem to be echoing an oath of fealty.

[2] S. of S. 4: 12.

[3] i.e. the general chapter of the order (see n. 1), when the priors converge on the mother house.

[4] Possibly alluding to Jer. 51: 7.

[5] Possibly alluding to Isa. 49: 6: 'et dixit parum est ut sis mihi seruus ad suscitandas tribus Iacob et feces Israhel conuertendas'.

[6] Cf. Matt. 24: 31 (' . . . and [the angels] shall gather together [God's] elect from the four winds'); Mark 13: 27; (the phrase 'four winds *of heaven*' occurs only in very different contexts; cf. Dan. 7: 2; 8: 8; 11: 4; Zech. 2: 6; 6: 5).

ordinis estis. Tam itaque unanimiter regimini uestro inuigilare omnes et tam temperanter a subiectis uestris mandata et consuetudines ordinis exigere debetis, quanta caritate in humano corpore uene omnes sibi sociantur et salubrem uegetationem omnibus membris equa distributione sanguinis largiuntur. Eadem siquidem cautela fugere debet nimiam exilitatem et subtilitatem uena, qua immoderatam grossitudinem et repletionem. Nimia namque repletio, nisi cito euacuetur, acutam facit et longam egritudinem gignit, rursum nimia exinanitio uires detrahit et bona ualetudine destituit. Domini et patres karissimi, ostium uestri ordinis et uisione rara et interrogatione assidua iam triui, et si consilium alterius Iethro admittitis, non usquequaque dispensationes que de corde caritatis procedunt anathematizabitis.[7] Quam enim friuolum et inconstans est sine ratione et auctoritate meliorum mutare decreta et statuta seniorum, tam pertinax est et extra regulam temperantie, que est mater uirtutum, uelle temporibus et moribus hominum negare que deceant et expediant. Ignoscite quod uocem, funestam quidem quantum ad sonum sed ueram quantum ad sensum, in uestro sancto conuentu de latibulo meo ausus sum proferre; et de his hactenus. Ceterum salutat uos dominus Henricus comes Trecensis et uniuersitati uestre mandat cum omni supplicatione ut sue petitioni adquiescatis; et nobis hoc iniunxit ut ad uos unum de nostris mitteremus per quem uoluntas et desiderium cordis uobis innotesceret. Quod autem non proprio sigillo scripsit uobis, occupationis maxime fuit de suis et regiis negotiis. Est autem petitio ut ei concedatis locum preparare ordini uestro sumptibus suis, iuxta morem uestrum, in terra sua, ubi uisum fuerit his quibus hoc negotium iniunxeritis. Petit etiam ut priori de Monte Dei et priori de Valle Sancti Petri iniungatis hanc curam.[8] A multis enim temporibus hoc ipsum cepit et orationibus uestris adiutus cupit perficere. Ex parte etiam nostra hoc ipsum humiliter et deuote petimus quia Deo iuuante auxilium et consilium non ficte huic operi subministrabimus.

[7] Cf. Exod. 18: 14–27; Jethro counselled Moses to delegate his authority of judgement in lesser matters to others. This may refer to some proposed reform, but neither Le Couteulx nor Bligny (*op. cit.*) record anything which fits this context. This allusion to visits here almost certainly refers to Mont-Dieu, not to La Grande Chartreuse itself.

body of the Carthusian order. You ought all therefore to watch over your rule as harmoniously, and to enforce the injunctions and customs of the order on those subject to you as moderately as, in the human body, all the veins are united by love and bestow healthy vitality on all the limbs by the even distribution of blood. Indeed with the same caution a vein must avoid both excessive thinness and emaciation and also immoderate thickening and fullness. For excessive fullness, unless it be drained off quickly, causes acute fever and produces chronic sickness, while too much letting drains the strength and undermines good health. Dearest lords and fathers, I have now worn down the threshold of your order both with occasional visits and with constant enquiry, and if you accept the counsel of another Jethro you will not totally condemn dispensations which proceed from the heart of love.[7] For as it is frivolous and inconstant to alter the decrees of better men and the statutes of elders without reason and authority, so it is obstinate and beyond the rule of moderation, which is the mother of the virtues, to wish to deny things which are fitting and advantageous for the times and the natures of men. Pardon me that I have dared in your blessed assembly to bring forth from my hiding place this voice, gloomy indeed in its tone but truthful in its meaning; but enough of these matters. Regarding other affairs, the Lord Henry, count of Troyes, sends greetings and charges your entire assembly with every supplication to accede to his request; and he has enjoined this on us that we should send to you one of our number through whom the will and desire of his heart may be known to you. That he did not write to you under his own seal was chiefly occasioned by his involvement in his own affairs and those of the king. Now his request is that you should allow him to prepare a house for your order at his expense, according to your custom, on his land, wherever it seems good to those to whom you charge this project. He also asks that you entrust this matter to the prior of Mont-Dieu and the prior of Val-Saint-Pierre.[8] He began this particular business a long time ago and he wishes to complete it aided by your prayers. For our part also we look for this humbly and devoutly, for with God's aid we shall furnish genuine help and counsel for this work.

[8] Count Henry the Liberal of Champagne (1152–81; see letter no. 71, n. 1); prior of Mont-Dieu, either Gervase (1150–9; Le Couteulx, ii. 113–14, 192) or Simon (1159–*c.*1184; see letter no. 59, n. 1.); prior of Val-Saint-Pierre, Engelbert (1140–1173/9; see letter no. 115, n. 1).

36

To Abbot Hugh of Preuilly[1]

*c.*1160

Amico suo karissimo H⟨ugoni⟩ abbati Pruliaci frater Petrus[a] Cellensis abbas, accipere de spiritu Moysi.

Amicorum monita eo affectuosius suscipiuntur quo ambitiosius animorum compago adinuicem consolidatur. Nescit mutui [b]nostri amoris[b] coagulum qui familiariter non est admissus ad secreta ipsarum medullarum. Ab ipsis igitur medullis uerbum amice consolationis mutuans, eque usque ad tui cordis secretiora rogo ut admittatur, et uice mei fungatur officio dilectionis et suppleat dispendia solite confabulationis. Quid est, domine, immo[c] frater et amice, nondum enim dominum redoles, quid est? De statione quietissimi portus ad marina discrimina transtulerunt te[d] amici tui, aut, ut uerius fatear, ad molam te posuit benignissima manus Dei tui. Quid igitur facies? Plane 'tolle molam et mole farinam'[2] de qua subcinericium facias in conuersione peccatorum ut conuertantur a uiis suis pessimis et uiuant, similaceum nichilominus in exhortatione bonorum ne peccent et non[e] recordentur iustitie eorum que[f] fecerant. Reuera, karissime, ad molam positus es, qua 'in spiritu uehementi conteras'[3] alios in malis et ipse conteraris in afflictionibus. Sed attende diligenter, quia mola, orbiculari motu nunquam et nusquam excedens, orbem persequendo superficiem grani suppositi extenuat in minutissime[g] farine speciem unde conficiatur panis in escam hominum. Sic nempe omnis labor et uexatio tua, que tibi dabit intellectum, equitatis rotunditate circumuoluatur ut ne quid nimis[4] facias uel feruentius agendo quam toleret complexio tua siue infirmitas tibi commissorum, uel remissius quam expediat ordini et officio tuo, siue

36 *Val fos. 128ʳ–129ʳ, Sirmond II. 8*]

[a] P. *Val* [b–b] amoris uestri *Sirmond* [c] Immo domine *Val* [d] *om. Sirmond* [e] ne *Val* [f] quas *Val, Sirmond* [g] minutissimam *Val*

36 [1] Hugh, abbot of Preuilly 1160–83 (*GC* xii. 216: Hugh ordained 1160, successor ordained 1183; Preuilly, Cistercian, dioc. Sens). The occasion of the letter was evidently Hugh's election to the abbacy, and Peter offers advice on the responsibilities and duties of the position. Peter's insistence that Hugh 'take a millstone and grind meal', and his statement 'nondum enim dominum redoles' suggest that at this stage Hugh was still

36

To Abbot Hugh of Preuilly[1]

*c.*1160

To his dearest friend Hugh, abbot of Preuilly, brother Peter, abbot of Montier-la-Celle, to receive of the spirit of Moses.

The admonitions of friends are received the more affectionately the more closely the mutual juncture of souls is consolidated. He who is not admitted intimately to the secret recesses of the very heart does not know the bond of our mutual love. Borrowing therefore a word of friendly consolation from the very heart, I ask equally that it be admitted to the deeper recesses of your heart and in my stead discharge the obligation of my love and make good the loss of accustomed conversation. What is this, lord, or rather brother and friend—for you do not yet have the fragrance of a lord—what is this? Your friends have carried you out from the security of the most tranquil port to the dangers of the sea, or rather, to put it more truthfully, the kindliest hand of your God has placed you on the millstone. What therefore will you do? Plainly 'take a millstone and grind meal'[2] from which you may make hearth-cakes in the conversion of sinners so that they may be turned from their evil ways and live, and equally you may make white bread in the exhortation of the good lest they sin and fail to consider the justice of what they did. Truly, my dearest one, you have been set to the millstone on which 'with a vehement wind you may break in pieces'[3] others in their wicked deeds and be broken yourself in afflictions. But listen carefully, for the millstone, never at any point deviating from its circular motion, following its circle, grinds down the surface of the grain beneath it into the form of the finest flour, from which bread is made which people can eat. Thus to be sure all your exertion and trouble, which will furnish you with understanding, should revolve with an even roundness so that you do nothing to excess[4] either by acting more zealously than your constitution or the infirmity of those entrusted to you can bear, or by acting more indulgently than

expressing reluctance to take up the abbacy, but Peter addresses him as abbot, and it may simply be that he has not yet been installed or blessed. The salutation echoes Num. 11: 25.

[2] Isa. 47: 2. [3] Cf. Ps. 47 (48): 8. [4] Cf. Terence, *Andria*, i. 1. 61 (34).

quam permittat regula et regularis consuetudo. Rotundo itaque perge cursu in omni negotio tuo, modestiam[h] seruans in his que ipse geris et in his que aliis ingeris. Appende mores temporis cum hominum moribus et uersa 'ex hoc in hoc', 'quia calix in manu Domini plenus mixto'; nondum eliquata est natura, nondum defecata, nondum fex corporee grauedinis exinanita.[5] 'Corpus quod corrumpitur aggrauat animam.'[6] Parcendum itaque interim corpori, nec danda licentia anime ut suis excurrens appetitibus in ipso itinere tardum et lassum reiciat corpus. 'Spiritus enim promptus est, caro autem infirma.'[7] Iugale suum ferre debet anima, non interficere. Moueat se quidem semper spiritus ad meliora, sed egrotantem equitaturam[8] suam calcaribus cruentis supra modum non uexet ne forte cede lacerata obeat et sanguinem eius de manu immoderati spiritus [i]Dominus requirat.[i] 'Nemo unquam carnem suam odio habuit, sed fouet eam, sicut et Christus ecclesiam.'[9] Procedat et precedat anima carnem, sed stationem faciat quo saltem sero mansionem possit assequi subsequens caro. Morandum tamen, non remanendum est propter carnem. Non erit molesta mora si sit modesta. Quousque respiret caro subsistendum, non quousque expiret. Sciat se caro uti itinerariis recreationibus non mansionariis delectationibus. Si de itinere grauatur, festinet ad mansionem. Erit enim illi mansio et grata pro requie et certa pro eternitate. Huc applicuit nos orbicularis motus.[10] Vale.[j]

[h] modestiam tuam *Val* [i–i] requirat Dominus *Val* [j] *om. Sirmond*

[5] Cf. Ps. 74 (75): 9.
[6] Cf. Wisd. 9: 15.
[7] Cf. Matt. 26: 41; Mark 14: 38.

befits your rank and duty or than the Rule and custom of the order permits. Pursue therefore a well-rounded course in all your dealings, preserving moderation in those which you bear yourself and in those which you lay upon others. Weigh the customs of the time with the customs of the people and turn 'from this to that', 'for in the hand of the Lord there is a cup full of mixture'; nature is not yet cleansed nor yet purified, the dregs of bodily sickness are not yet emptied.[5] 'The corruptible body is a load upon the soul.'[6] In the meantime, then, the body should be spared and licence should not be given to the soul to run ahead by its own desires and, on its journey, to cast aside the sluggish and tired body. For 'the spirit is willing but the flesh is weak.'[7] The soul must bear up the one to which it is yoked, not kill it. Let the spirit indeed always direct itself towards better things but not torment its sick mount[8] too far with cruel spurs lest by chance it should die, lacerated by rending, and the Lord should demand its blood from the hand of the immoderate spirit. 'No man ever hated his own flesh, but cherisheth it, as also Christ doth the Church.'[9] The soul should lead the flesh and go before it, but should allow for a rest so that the flesh, following behind, can reach the abode, albeit belatedly. It must, however, only tarry, not stay, on account of the flesh. The delay will not be troublesome so long as it be moderate. The flesh should pause until it be revived, not until it expire. The flesh should know that it is enjoying refreshment on the journey, not the pleasures of abode. If it is burdened by the journey, let it hurry to the final abode. For it shall have an abode which is both agreeable for repose and sure for eternity. And so here we have come around full circle.[10] Farewell.

[8] See Niermeyer, *equitatura* 4, 5; *DML*, *equitatura* 3 (note the different sense at letter no. 23, see n. 6). What follows alludes to Ezek. 3: 18, 20; 33: 6, 8.

[9] Cf. Eph. 5: 29.

[10] i.e. the argument has come around 'full circle' to another invocation of peace and security, but by implication describing a better state than that from which Hugh has been taken; at the same time the image of the turning millstone is again evoked.

37

To Prior Thomas of Molesme[1]

1160, or earlier × 1162

Frater [a]Petrus Cellensis abbas T⟨home⟩[a] priori Molismensi, salutem.

Sacratissime passionis et resurrectionis Dominice solennnes ferie, dies cum suis horis, membra cum suis officiis non immerito hactenus uindicauerunt.[b] Quid enim digitis meis cum calamo scribere in die quo[c] distenditur in cruce dilectus ex dilecto[2] qui factus est sponse sue 'fasciculus mirre'?[3] 'Manus' Domini 'tornatiles, auree, plene hyacinthis,'[4] clauis perforantur, et manus mea[d] ad aliud quam ad [e]mirram distillandam[e] probatissimam[5] occupabitur? In uno oculorum et in uno crine colli sponse uulneratum est[f] cor eius,[6] et cor meum inania et superuacua meditabitur?[g] Potius resignet dies hec in affectu Christiani affectum morientis Christi, compassionem in membris, mortificationem in concupiscentiis, expiationem a uitiis, conformationem in officiis caritatis. Ecce cur non responderim epistole tue die sequenti postquam eam accepi. Accepi namque eam cum de uituli saginati pelle detrahenda et de agno assando iam ageretur[7]—et manus ac pedes iunioris filii Rebecca parabat superuestire 'uestibus Esau ualde bonis',[8] [h]id est[h] sacramentis ecclesiasticis. Iesus uestimenta[9] sordida non propter peccati contaminationem sed propter mortalitatis contaminatam[i] conditionem deponebat et sacram manuum ac pedum ablutionem non carnis depositione sordium sed conscientie bone interrogatione in Deum[10] intitulabat. Iam ex odore unguenti a peccatrice, sed penitente, in caput uel pedes Saluatoris effusi

37 *O fos.* 127^v–129^r, *Sirmond II. 13*]
[a–a] G. Christi seruus *O* [b] uindicarunt *O* [c] qua *O* [d] meas *Sirmond* [e–e] distillandam mirram *Sirmond* [f] *om. Sirmond* [g] medicabitur *O* [h–h] ut *O* [i] *om. O*

37 [1] Thomas de Chacenay, prior of Molesme, occurs 1160/1, predecessor occurs 1153, successor occurs 1164; later abbot of Molesme 1171/2, deposed 1175, restored by *c.*1177 (briefly), possibly prior of Saint-Quentin-de-Troyes 1177–9. On his life, see Laurent, *Cartulaires de Molesme*, i. 168–9, 187; also *GC* iv. 734, which Laurent amends. While Thomas's precise dates as prior are unknown, the present letter must predate Peter's move to Saint-Remi. Sirmond assumed the recipient to be Theobald of Molesme (later abbot of Molesme, as successor to Thomas, 1166–Jan. 1171), but Theobald was prior of Cluny not Molesme (see letter no. 138, n. 1, and Laurent, *Cartulaires de Molesme*, i. 169 n. 2).

37

To Prior Thomas of Molesme[1]

1160, or earlier × 1162

Brother Peter, abbot of Montier-la-Celle, to Thomas, prior of Molesme, greetings.

The solemn festivals of the most sacred passion and resurrection of the Lord have until now rightly laid claim to my days with their offices and to my limbs with their duties. For what have my fingers to do with writing with a pen on the day on which the beloved of the beloved[2] who was made 'a bundle of myrrh' to His bride[3] is stretched out on the cross? The 'hands' of the Lord 'which are turned and as of gold, full of hyacinths,'[4] are pierced with nails, and shall my hand be taken up with anything other than dripping choicest myrrh?[5] His heart was wounded with one of the eyes and with one hair of the neck of the bride,[6] and shall my heart meditate on vain and useless things? Let this day rather reveal, in the love of a Christian, the love of the dying Christ, fellow suffering in the body, mortification of desires, expiation for sins, and strict adherence to the duties of love. So you can see why I did not reply to your letter the day after I received it. For I received it when we were already occupied with skinning the fatted calf and roasting the lamb,[7] and Rebecca was preparing to clothe the hands and feet of the youngest son with 'the very good garments of Esau',[8] that is the sacraments of the Church. Jesus was putting off fouled garments[9] not on account of the contamination of sin but on account of the contaminated state of mortality, and was establishing a blessed cleansing of hands and feet not by the putting away of the filth of the flesh but by the examination of a good conscience towards God.[10] Now the house was filled with the odour of the ointment poured on the head or feet of the saviour by the

[2] Cf. S. of S. 5: 9.
[3] Cf. S. of S. 1: 12.
[4] S. of S. 5: 14.
[5] Cf. S. of S. 5: 5.
[6] Cf. S. of S. 4: 9.
[7] Cf. Luke 15: 23, 27, 30; Exod. 12: 8–9.
[8] Cf. Gen. 27: 1–29, esp. 15: Jacob, following Rebecca's advice, obtained Isaac's blessing in place of Esau. Jacob signifies the Church, Christ and the New Testament superseding the Old, Rebecca the Holy Spirit (cf. e.g. *Glossa*, *PL* cxiii. 149–51).
[9] i.e. his earthly body.
[10] Cf. 1 Pet. 3: 21.

implebatur domus;[11] iam conuiuium pinguium, conuiuium medullatorum[12] apponebatur, uinum meracissimum crateris[j] infundebatur. O bone amice, quis tunc[k] scriberet, immo quis non biberet? 'Comedite amici et bibite et inebriamini karissimi'[13] continuabatur, et de morticinis pellibus atramento liniendis cogitaretur? Ecce quare [l]statim non[l] respondi cum libentius illis pulmentis intenderem quam de responsione uestra cogitarem. Quid de Sabbato dicam? Quid, inquam, dicam, nisi quia[m] Sabbatum est? Sabbatum reuera sed delicatum, sed sanctum, sed gloriosum. Non licet igitur 'digitum extendere et loqui quod non prodest'.[14] Deinde die sequenti, resurgente et cum spoliis multis Domino redeunte, aliquid de preda pretiosissima ueniens in occursum deposco. Rursum[n] intueor triumphum, excipio renascentia sidera; post solis ortum et auroram nascentem in thesauris meis[15] consigno ut [o]hec spes[o] reposita in sinu meo[16] doceat quod 'flebile principium melior fortuna' sequeretur.[17] In [p]his diebus[p] nemo alius scripsit, nisi tantum Pilatus, quin immo destructum est 'quod aduersum nos erat cyrographum'.[18] Post hec uero tandem, cum 'exiuit homo ad opus suum et ad operationem suam usque ad uesperam',[19] recogitaui seriem[q] sompniorum atque sermonum epistole tue et extrahens eam de tenebris[r] ad lucem deprehendi non esse meam. Vbi enim mea que de me in principio narrat super id quod uidit aut audiuit ex me, in medio fingit me dixisse uel fecisse quod non est uerum, in fine comparat me[s] illi qui sine peccato est?[t] Non sibi conuenit imago epistole tue, bone frater et amice. Primum uinum ponis, deinde acetum supponis, ad ultimum mixturam mirre et aloes[20] apponis. Non reicio[u] usquequaque laudem michi propinatam, amplectens dicentis beneuolentiam non dicti conscientiam. Languor enim ille fortissimus, quo sub sole uniuersa uanitas hominum laborat,[21] et me cum aliis corripuit[v] quatinus suaues illas aurium modificationes necdum propulsare didicerim. Naturale est hoc[w] uitium et, ut ait Seneca, naturalia corporis aut animi uitia leniri arte possunt, deleri non possunt.[22] Hoc animi scabies est, sed differenter occupat; inuadit quandoque

[j] crateribus *O* [k] *om. Sirmond* [l–l] non statim *O* [m] quod *O* [n] Cursum *O* [o–o] spes hec *O* [p–p] diebus his *O* [q] *om. O* [r] *corr. Hall;* tenebrosis *O, Sirmond* [s] *corr. Hall;* se *O, Sirmond* [t] non est *Sirmond* [u] proicio *O* [v] corrumpit *O* [w] *om. O*

[11] Cf. John 12: 3; also Matt. 26: 7; Mark 14: 3; Luke 7: 37–8.
[12] Cf. Isa. 25: 6. [13] S. of S. 5: 1. [14] Isa. 58: 9.
[15] Cf. Deut. 32: 34. [16] Cf. Job 19: 27. [17] Cf. Ovid, *Metam.* vii. 518.

sinner now penitent,[11] now a feast of fat things, a feast of things full of marrow,[12] was being appointed and the purest wine was filling the cups. My good friend, who then could write, nay who then could not drink? 'Eat, o friends, and drink and be inebriated, my dearly beloved'[13] was the refrain, and could covering dead skins with ink be thought of? See why I did not reply at once when I was concentrating on these delicacies more joyfully than I was thinking of your reply. What shall I say of the Sabbath? What, I ask, shall I say, except that it is the Sabbath? The Sabbath indeed, but delightful, blessed, and glorious. It is not permitted therefore 'to stretch out the finger and to speak that which profiteth not'.[14] Then on the next day, the Lord rising again and returning with many spoils, I, coming to meet Him, demand something from the most precious booty. Again I contemplate the victory, I catch up the rising stars, afterwards I seal up the rising of the sun and the new dawn in my treasures[15] so that this hope laid up in my bosom[16] may show that 'better fortune should follow the unhappy beginning'.[17] In these days no one else wrote, save only Pilate, but rather 'the handwriting that was against us'[18] was destroyed. Finally indeed after this, when 'man went forth to his work and to his labour until the evening,'[19] I thought over again the series of imaginings and opinions in your letter and, taking it out from the darkness into the light, I discovered that it was not about me. For how could it refer to me, which at the beginning says things about me beyond what it saw or heard from me, in the middle makes me say or do what is not true, and at the end compares me to Him who is without sin? The imagery of your letter is not consistent, good brother and friend. First you put out wine, then you substitute vinegar, and finally you add a mixture of myrrh and aloes.[20] I do not altogether reject praise which is offered to me, embracing the kindness of the speaker, not the wisdom of what is said. For that most powerful weakness with which the entire vanity of men struggles under the sun[21] has also seized me, like others, so much so that I have not learnt yet to ward off those melodies sweet to the ears. This vice is a natural one and, as Seneca says, natural vices of the body or the soul can be alleviated by art but not eliminated.[22] This is the ulcer of the soul, but it takes hold in different ways, sometimes

[18] Cf. Col. 2: 14, but linked here to Pilate writing the inscription on the cross in John 19: 19.

[19] Cf. Ps. 103 (104): 23 (Vulgate has *exibit*).

[20] Cf. S. of S. 4: 14.

[21] Cf. Ps. 38 (39): 6; Eccles. 1: 3, 14.

[22] Possibly an allusion to Seneca, *Ad Lucil. ep. mor.* xi. 1.

inferiora, quandoque superiora, quandoque totum simul, et superiora et inferiora. Superius est in animo quod ad rationem pertinet, inferius quod ad sensualitatem, totum quod ad destinationem siue[x] deliberationem. Fallaci igitur suppositione, dum alias animus forte ad quedam maiora et meliora occupatur, subintrat inanis glorie amor et foliis ficus turpitudinem suam obumbrans[23] in latibulo anguli sedet ut cum domina sua ratio absens fuerit uiro, id est naturali appetitui, sese misceat, et ex tali concubitu Ammonite et Moabite qui non intrant in ecclesiam Dei usque ad tertiam [y]et quartam generationem[y] procreantur.[24] Quod enim ab initio conceptionis et generationis uitiosum erit, ad innocentie gloriam quomodo intrabit? Nunquam igitur opus uane glorie numerabitur in remuneratione uere[z] glorie. Ideo Abrahe dicitur, 'Eice ancillam et filium eius, non enim erit heres filius ancille cum filio libere.'[25] Deinde, quod periculosius est, ascendit sursum hec scabies et tangit ipsum uerticem sanctum anime ubi est imago et similitudo Dei.[25A] Querit suam non Dei gloriam; abutitur uoluntate diuina[a] tam generationis quam regenerationis. Non nominat filium suum, id est opus, Iohannem sed Zachariam.[26] Hec [b]iam non[b] celat et[c] non uelat sed reuelat turpitudinem suam, et iuxta sapientissimum, contra animam suam Adonias petit Abisac Sunamitem[27] que regi Dauid solebat obsequia prestantissima et incentiua castissima prebere.[28] 'Vnum est', inquit Salomon, 'ac si regnum petat.'[29] Adonias cupidissimus regni est ratio infecta amore priuati boni. Ambit iste Abisac sibi assumere cum tota ratio absorbetur a uoragine cenodoxie, sed occiditur quia a Deo separatur. Hoc malum sub sole est.[30] Adhuc amplius malum est cum tota hominis intentio et operatio ad hanc iniquitatem et negationem contra Deum se incuruat. A laqueo sic contorto triplici funiculo[31] caue tibi, o amice, quia malum est oblatis honoribus[d] delectari, peius negatos appetere, pessimum pro sublatis in iram prosilire. An erat meum abbatiam illam[e] dare cui uellem, subtrahere cui uellem? Et quis

[x] seu *O* [y–y] generationem et quartam *O* [z] eterne *O* [a] diuine *O*, *Sirmond* [b–b] non iam *O* [c] *om.* *O* [d] hominibus *O* [e] *om.* *O*

[23] Cf. Gen. 3: 7.

[24] Cf. Deut. 23: 3: 'Ammanites et Moabites etiam post decimam generationem non intrabunt ecclesiam Dei in eternum'; for the phrase 'unto the third and fourth generation' cf. Exod. 20: 5; Num. 14: 18; Deut. 5: 9.

[25] Cf. Gal. 4: 30; Gen. 21: 10. [25A] Cf. Gen. 1: 26.

[26] Cf. Luke 1: 59–63, i.e. it disobeys the divine will; in Luke John the Baptist *was* named John and not Zacharias.

[27] Cf. 3 Kgs. (1 Kgs.) 2: 17–23.

attacking the lower parts, sometimes the higher, sometimes all together at the same time, both higher and lower. The higher part is in the mind, and pertains to reason, the lower is that which pertains to the senses, the whole is that which pertains to purpose or deliberation. By a deceitful substitution therefore, while the mind is perhaps otherwise occupied with something greater and better, love of worthless glory enters by stealth and with fig-leaves covering its shame[23] sits hidden in the corner so that when its mistress, reason, is absent it may attach itself to the man, that is to the natural appetite, and from such a union are begotten the Ammonite and the Moabite who do not enter into the Church of God even to the third and fourth generation.[24] For how shall that which will be wicked from the very moment of its conception and begetting enter the glory of innocence? Never therefore shall the work of empty glory be counted towards the reward of true glory. Therefore it is said to Abraham, 'Cast out the bondwoman and her son, for the son of the bondwoman shall not be heir with the son of the free woman.'[25] Then, and this is more dangerous, this ulcer ascends on high and touches the holy summit itself of the soul, where lies the image and likeness of God.[25A] It seeks its own glory, not God's; it abuses the divine will as much in birth as in rebirth. It does not call its son, that is its work, John, but Zacharias.[26] Now it neither conceals nor veils but unveils its shamefulness, and according to the most wise, Adonias against his own life sought Abisag the Sunamitess[27] who used to offer King David most excellent services and most chaste pleasures.[28] 'It is the same', said Solomon, 'as if he should ask for the kingdom.'[29] Adonias, most covetous of the kingdom, is reason infected with love of private good. He strives to join Abisag to himself, since all reason is devoured by the whirlpool of vanity, but he is killed because he is set apart from God. This is an evil under the sun.[30] It is an even greater evil when the whole purpose and labour of a man bends itself against God to this iniquity and denial. Guard yourself, o friend, against a snare wound thus from a threefold cord,[31] for it is wicked to be enticed by honours which are offered, worse to seek out those which are forbidden, worst of all to burst forth in anger on account of those which are withheld. Was it my business to give that abbey to whom I wished, to take it from whom I wished? And who am I, and what am

[28] Cf. 3 Kgs. (1 Kgs.) 1: 3–4.
[29] Cf. 3 Kgs. (1 Kgs.) 2: 22: 'postula ei et regnum.'
[30] Cf. Eccles. 4: 3; 6: 1; 10: 5.
[31] Cf. Eccles. 4: 12.

ego, et quid ego, precipue comparatione tanta,[f] archiepiscopi scilicet Lugdunensis, episcoporum quoque Lingonensis et Augustudunensis, abbatum etiam Molismensis et[g] sancti Iohannis Quintiacensis, quid ego nisi 'puluis et cinis'?[32] Celum et terram cum istis testes inuoco nisi forte euanuit [h]a sensibus tuis[h] quod de persona tua nil inhonestum, nil criminosum in eorum auribus deposuerim. Reuera non statim adquieui, [i]'abiit' autem extemplo sermo 'in regionem longinquam'[33] et simul cepit et desiit.[i] Nominatus est iste [j]abbas sed[j] non dissimulaui dicere quod audieram uel uideram. Reticui tamen quod ignorabam. Nominatus est et[k] Petrus de Viuariis[34]—heu michi!—pro quo contra amicos et episcopos et clericos et familiares alia uice fortissime steteram et constantissime, nunc quoque ut potui steti. Quia[l] non potui[m] ut esset abbas, uertit ad me cum quibusdam suorum terga et non faciem.[35] Hoc anno multa horum similia non per uisum sed per sensum et experimentum passus sum. Amici quondam mei a longe steterunt et iam non ambulant mecum.[36] Quid itaque faciam? Non[n] ibo? Sed inobediens ero. Non ibo? Sed superbus apparebo. Tacebo? Sed conscientiam timeo. Tacebo? Sed pecuniam Domini abscondo. Tacebo? Sed callidus uel stultus reputabor.[o] Vtrique parti[p] placebo? Sed hoc erit simulatio, sed hoc erit impossibile. Quid igitur? Dirige, Domine Deus meus, in conspectu tuo uiam meam.[37] Quid inquam? Da sermonem rectum et bene sonantem in os meum. Hucusque satis. Nam parietem litterarum fodere, ne dicam impugnare, parco. Rimas tantum et quasdam[q] scissuras per circuitum obambulans designo, sed et resigno. Nam quod fractum est, si quid tamen fractum est, malo resarcire quam noua dampna facere. Fiat pax.

[f] tanti *O* [g] *om. Sirmond* [h–h] ascensibus meis *O;* a sensibus meis *Sirmond* [i–i] et abiit sermo in regionem longinquam *Sirmond* [j–j] *om. Sirmond* [k] *om. Sirmond* [l] Tamen quia *O* [m] obtinui *O* [n] Vocatus ne *O* [o] reputor *Sirmond* [p] *om. O* [q] quosdam *O*

[32] Cf. Gen. 18: 27. The archbishop of Lyons was Heraclius de Montboissier, el. 1153, d. 1163 (*GC* iv. 121–5; *P. Ven. Epp.* ii. 241–2); the bishop of Langres, Godfrey, 1138/9–1161/3, or possibly his successor Walter, 1163 or earlier–1179 (*GC* iv. 575–8); the bishop of Autun, Henry, 1148–70/1 (*GC* iv. 394–6); the abbot of Molesme, Villain de Choiseul, 1156–63 (see letter no. 30, n. 1); the abbot of Quincy (Cistercian, dioc. Langres), Hugh, occurs 1153 × ? 1163; predecessor last occurs 1146 (*GC* iv. 830).

I, especially in so great a comparison, namely with the archbishop of Lyons, the bishops also of Langres and Autun, the abbots too of Molesme and of Saint-Jean of Quincy; what am I but 'dust and ashes'?[32] I call upon heaven and earth as witnesses, along with these, in case by any chance it has escaped your memory that I have confided to their ears nothing dishonourable, nothing slanderous about your character. Indeed I did not acquiesce at once, but the speech 'went' forthwith 'into a far country'[33] and began and failed all at once. That abbot was named, but I did not keep secret what I had heard or seen. I kept silent, however, about that of which I knew nothing. Pierre de Viviers[34] was also named—alas for me!—for whom I had stood up on another occasion against friends and bishops and clerics and intimate acquaintances most vigorously and constantly, and now too I have stood up for him as far as I was able. Since I could not make him abbot, he, along with certain of his people, turned his back to me and not his face.[35] This year I have suffered many similar things, not face to face but by feeling and experiencing them. Those once my friends have stood far off and now no longer walk with me.[36] So what should I do? Shall I not go? But then I shall be disobedient. Shall I not go? But I shall appear proud. Shall I remain silent? But I fear my conscience. Shall I remain silent? But then I hide the treasure of the Lord. Shall I remain silent? But I shall be thought either sly or stupid. Shall I please both sides? But that will be a pretence, and impossible. What then? Direct, O Lord my God, my way in thy sight.[37] What should I say? Put into my mouth words which are right and well-sounding. This is enough for now. For I desist from undermining, not to say attacking, the wall of your letter. As I walk around the circuit I observe chinks and some cracks, but I too close them up. For I prefer to patch what is broken, if anything indeed is broken, badly than to cause new damage. Let there be peace.

[33] Luke 19: 12.

[34] Pierre de Viviers, otherwise unknown. Thomas had evidently requested that Peter support him for an abbacy, in which he was unsuccessful. The contested election must have been in the diocese of Langres: Molesme and Quincy are both in the diocese of Langres, which itself is in the province of Lyons.

[35] Cf. Jer. 2: 27; 32: 33.

[36] Cf. Ps. 37 (38): 12; John 6: 67.

[37] Cf. Ps. 5 (5): 9.

38

To the community of Chézy-l'Abbaye[1]

*c.*1145 × ? 1157

Frater [a]P⟨etrus⟩ Cellensis abbas[a] dilectis fratribus, filiis[b] et amicis Caziacensibus, sapientiam scribere in tempore odii.[c] [2]

Preter solitum nec non et uotum meum, in uirga non in spiritu mansuetudinis scribere uobis proposui,[3] qui paterna precordia aculeis litterarum uestrarum absque misericordia perfodere non timuistis. Mouet me et commouet plurimum pia senectus in patre, miseranda compassio in fratris abiectione, seua[d] et intemperata oratio in paginarum serie. Dissimulare,[e] nec tam manifesta redarguere, pars eiusdem criminis uidetur esse. Quis enim iste impetus? Que ista ebrietas? Quod suffugium mentis et sensuum fratrem abdicare, patri contradicere, ius [f]monastici ordinis[f] sic perturbare? Dura et dira, fratres mei, emulatio uestra,[g] morte tristior, inferno inferior, saxo durior, amarior absintio, felle acetosior. Quid enim? Pietas negatur, necatur misericordia, honor paternus conuiciatur, insimulatur amor fraternus, societas repellitur, regula uiolatur. O irreligiosa religio! O ficta sanctitas! O inuidiosa caritas! Siccine, fratres mei karissimi, siccine Christum didicistis? Nonne Deus noster Deus pacis est et non dissensionis?[4] O stulta uecordia illorum qui pacem[h] dicunt si fratrem non receperint, mortem si uiderint, prosperitatem si socium exterminauerint, deuotionem si opus deuotionis condempnauerint. Hec in te pestis, Ioseph, grassatur,[i] hoc in tuum caput infortunium sine culpa refunditur. Vendere enim te fratres uolunt quem uidere nolunt.[5] Paterne gratie ⟨te⟩ impedimentum sibi credunt quia patri gratiosum sentiunt. Sic sic fratrum ingratitudinem mercatur gratitudo patris. 'Si

38 *O fo.* 125^{r-v}, *Sirmond II.* 14]
[a–a] G. Christi presbyter *O* [b] *om. O* [c] otii *O, Sirmond* [d] seria *Sirmond* [e] Dissimilare *O* [f–f] ordinis monastici *O* [g] nostra *O* [h] *corr. Hall;* pacem suam *Sirmond;* parem suam *O* [i] crassatur *O*

38 [1] Chézy-l'Abbaye (Benedictine, dioc. Soissons, Cott. i. 767). Written in support of 'Tes.' (unidentified; a rubric in MS *O* gives 'Tezelinum'), evidently a favourite of the abbot whose position and influence has incited the opposition of other members of the community—hence the comparison with Joseph. The details of the abbots of Chézy in this period are vague: Peter occurs 1108 × 1112; Simon first occurs 1134, retired 1157 (on the evidence of letter no. 39, and not 1156 as stated in *GC*, as explained in appendix 6), d.

38

To the community of Chézy-l'Abbaye[1]

*c.*1145 × ? 1157

Brother Peter, abbot of Montier-la-Celle, to his beloved brothers, sons and friends of Chézy-l'Abbaye, words of wisdom in a time of hatred.[2]

Contrary to my usual custom and no less to my vow, in chastisement, not in a spirit of clemency,[3] I have determined to write to you who have not feared to pierce the paternal heart mercilessly with the barbs of your letter. The devout old age in the father, pitiable compassion in the rejection of the brother, the savage and intemperate harangue in this series of pages, moves and disturbs me exceedingly. To dissemble and not to refute things so palpable appears to be a part of the same wrongdoing. For what is this attack? What drunkenness is this? What flight of the mind and senses is it to disown a brother, to speak out against a father, to throw into disorder in this way the justice of the monastic order? Your harsh and horrible envy, my brothers, is more saddening than death, lower than the pit, harder than rock, more bitter than wormwood, more sour than bile. What then comes of this? Piety is denied, mercy murdered, paternal honour is abused, fraternal love is falsely accused, fellowship is rejected, the Rule violated. O disorderly order! O false blessedness! O invidious love! Is this the way, my dearest brothers, is this the way you have learned Christ? Is not our God a God of peace and not of dissension?[4] O stupid folly of those who call it peace not to receive a brother, death to see him, prosperity to drive out a companion, devotion to condemn the work of devotion. This pestilence rages against you, Joseph, this misfortune is poured out over your guiltless head. For your brothers wish to sell you whom they do not want to see.[5] They believe that you are an obstacle to them in the way of paternal grace because they understand that you are in their father's favour. Just so, just so the goodwill of the father buys the ill-will of

27 July 1163 at Clairvaux; Helias d. 6 June 1171 (on all of these, see *GC* ix. 431). Although the present letter concerns a different matter from letter no. 39, the reference here to the old age of the abbot (as well as the general sense of crisis) suggest that the letter was probably written during Simon's abbacy.

[2] Cf. Eccles. 3: 8.

[3] Cf. 1 Cor. 4: 21..

[4] Cf. Eph. 4: 20; 1 Cor. 14: 33.

[5] Cf. Gen. 37: 18–28.

defuerit', inquiunt, 'amatus filius, ad nos resiliet paternus affectus. Dum Ioseph uisibus sistitur patris, rarior ad nos deflectitur dulcedo paternitatis. Tollamus fratrem et habebimus patrem.' Quam iustius et iocundius faceretis si uobis filialem deuotionem inuisceraretis. Hoc nempe affectum multiplicaret non deuastaret. Boni fratres et amici karissimi, currebatis bene; quis uos fascinauit[6] sic patri scribere, sic fratrem proscribere? Quid enim Tes. mali fecit? Quid [j]tam atrocis iniurie dignum perpetrauit? Quod[j] tam immanissimum suum facinus ut sic contra legem sine lege uestro iudicio non rediret? Vbi sunt misericordie uestre[k] antique quibus ueniam criminosis indulsistis, quibus sceleratis commissa facinora remisistis? O quanto impurioris,[l] quantoque indignioris uite pluribus et locum misericordie impetrastis et gratiam immeritam prorogastis? Vbi fornicationes T., ubi inordinate comestiones, ubi ignominiose operationes, ubi innominande confusiones? Opera lucis non tenebrarum opera T., opera diei non noctis,[7] opera predicanda non preiudicanda. O liuor! O inuidia! Quo ausu ingressa es sanctuarium Dei, cubile Altissimi, thronum regis eterni? Qua tyrannica presumptione sanctorum precordia rupisti et irrupisti, quin immo et dirupisti? Ecce pondere tuo[m] gemitum et clamorem ualidum de corde amicorum[n] pressisti. Vnde namque ustio illa cordis, unde angustie mentis, nisi te succendente, nisi te constringente? Prorsus usque ad internecionem [o]omnia comburis,[o] et ex hoc paupertas et angustia cordis. Non, fratres, non aduersum me ira siue commotio uestra exardescat. Nequaquam enim[p] tacere uobis debui insipientiam uestram. Adquiescite tamen consiliis meis, et quod inconsulte factum est, consulto corrigere ne differatis. Quam citius ergo poteritis ad pedes domini abbatis simul procumbatis satisfacientes pro erratu non leui, neque surgatis nisi benedictionem ab ore paterno reportaueritis. Michi quoque, si in aliquo excesserim, obsecro indulgeatis. Diligo enim uos, Deus scit. Valete.

[j–j] *om.* *O* [k] nostre *O* [l] impuriores *O* [m] *om.* *Sirmond*
[n] amicorum meorum *O* [o–o] anime combureris *Sirmond* [p] *om.* *O*

[6] Cf. Gal. 5: 7; 3: 1; *proscribere*, below, lit. 'proscribe', but here, with the word play on *scribere*, probably suggests 'write against', referring to the written allegation which is mentioned earlier.

[7] Echoing Rom. 13: 12; 1 Thess. 5: 5.

the brothers. 'If the beloved son is not here', they say, 'paternal affection will spring back to us. While Joseph is set before the father's eyes, the sweetness of fatherly feeling is turned the more rarely to us. Let us carry off the brother and we shall have the father.' How much more justly and joyously would you act if you were to implant filial devotion in your hearts. This would certainly multiply affection not lay it waste. Good brothers and dearest friends, you did run well; who bewitched[6] you to make you write in this way to the father, to make you write in this way against a brother? For what evil did Tes. commit? What did he perpetrate worthy of so cruel an injustice? What action of his was so excessively monstrous that in this way, contrary to the law, without the law, by your judgement, he should not return? Where are your old feelings of compassion by which you granted mercy to the guilty, by which you forgave crimes committed by the wicked? O how much more impure and how much more unworthy were the lives of many for whom you have procured a place of mercy and to whom you have extended undeserved favour? Where are T.'s fornications, where are his excessive gluttonies, where are his ignominious machinations, where are his unnameable disruptions? The works of light not of darkness are the works of T., the works of day not of night,[7] works to be praised not prejudged. O malice! O envy! With what boldness did you enter the sanctuary of God, the chamber of the Most High, the throne of the eternal king? With what tyrannical presumption have you broken and broken into, nay even broken into pieces, the hearts of the blessed? See, by your weight you have squeezed a groan and a mighty cry from the heart of friends. For where does that burning of the heart come from, where that straitening of the mind, except from your kindling, from your constraint? You are burning up all things to utter destruction, and from this comes the poverty and straitening of the heart. Do not, brothers, do not let your anger or your agitation flare up against me. For by no means ought I to say nothing to you about your folly. Acquiesce, however, in my counsel and make haste to correct advisedly what was done inadvisedly. As quickly as you can therefore you should prostrate yourselves together at the feet of the lord abbot, making amends for what is no trivial error, nor should you rise until you have obtained a blessing from the paternal mouth. I beg that you pardon me also if I have gone too far in any way. For I love you, as God knows. Farewell.

39

To the community of Chézy-l'Abbaye[1]

? 1157

Fratribus, filiis et amicis suis karissimis Caziacensibus frater [a]Petrus humilis abbas Cellensis,[a] salutem.

Non leuitas aut leuis necessitas ut loquar suadet, patris languorem, matris desolationem, fratrumque attendens commotionem.[2] Verum est, uerum est, fratres karissimi, illud euangelicum: 'Percutiam pastorem et dispergentur oues gregis.'[3] Quid autem horum grauius, percussio pastoris an dispersio gregis? Equidem diuisum sine dubio alterum satis graue, simul uero utrumque pene dampnum intolerabile. Immorabor igitur plangendo patris passionem an consequar reuocando fratrum exterminationem? Sed ut uerum fatear, utrumque si utrumque contigerit lugebo, sed alterum affectuosius, alterum ambitiosius. Nam patri uberius lacrimas profundam laboranti in defectu nature, fratribus emittam intensius redargutionum sagittas propter excessum culpe. Morbis namque[b] nature compassionem, corruptioni animarum debemus reprehensionem. Condolendum non imputandum est seni quod[c] egreditur mundum, imputandum uel potius amputandum in Christiano si [d]rumpere temptet[d] dilectionis uinculum. Re integra, fratres karissimi, nondum imminentia lucrosius euitantur pericula si affuerit oculus[e] prouidentie et manus uigilantis cautele. Casus fortium terere[f] debet fortunam pauperum. 'Nam tua res agitur paries dum proximus ardet.'[4] Quantumlibet potentissima, [g]quantumlibet opulentissima[g] regna in breui contentionum molestia succrescente[h] corruunt. Mundi ipsius machina stare non poterit si [i]elementorum contemperantia se[i] conturbauerit. In proximo Cluniacensis ecclesia antiquitate senior, religione feruentior, rerum habundantia plenior, multitudine numerosior, quid fecit? Scandalum

39 *O fos. 125*^{v}*–126*^{r}*, Sirmond II. 15*]
[a–a] G. Christi sacerdos *O* [b] nempe *O* [c] si *O* [d–d] erumpere temptat *O* [e] et oculus *O* [f] *corr. Ritchie;* terrere *O, Sirmond* [g–g] *om. O* [h] succensente *Sirmond* [i–i] se elementorum incontemperantia *Sirmond*

39 [1] Chézy-l'Abbaye (see letter no. 38, n. 1). This letter may refer to a threatened succession dispute occasioned by the imminent departure of Abbot Simon for Clairvaux, but on this, and the date of this letter, see appendix 6.

[2] i.e. abbot, monastery, and monks.

39

To the community of Chezy-l'Abbaye[1]

? 1157

To his dearest brothers, sons and friends of Chézy-l'Abbaye, brother Peter, humble abbot of Montier-la-Celle, greetings.

It is not levity or a light necessity which urges me to speak when I consider the weakness of the father, the desolation of the mother, and the agitation of the brothers.[2] It is true, it is true, dearest brothers, as it says in the Gospel: 'I will strike the shepherd, and the sheep of the flock shall be dispersed.'[3] Yet which is the more serious of these, the striking of the shepherd or the dispersal of the flock? Indeed without doubt one separately is serious enough but both at the same time is an almost insupportable loss. Shall I linger therefore, bewailing the suffering of the father, or shall I follow, recalling the banishment of the brothers? But to confess the truth, I shall bewail both if both take place, but the one with deeper feeling, the other with a more energetic response. For I would pour forth tears more abundantly for the father travailing in the failing of nature, I would let fly the arrows of reproofs more fiercely against the brothers on account of excess of guilt. For we ought to show compassion for the sicknesses of nature, censure for the corruption of souls. One ought to offer condolence towards an old man, not blame, because he is leaving the world; one should blame, or rather amputate, in a Christian any attempt to break the chain of love. When the position is secure, dearest brothers, dangers not yet imminent are more profitably avoided if the eye of providence and the hand of sure vigilance are present. The fall of the strong must damage the fortune of the poor. 'For it is your own safety that is at stake when your neighbour's wall is in flames.'[4] The most powerful kingdoms whatsoever, and the richest, fall together in a moment when the mischief of quarrelling rises up from below. The fabric of the very world will not be able to stand if the blending of the elements convulse itself. What did the church of Cluny, senior in age, more zealous in religious life, fuller in abundance of possessions, more numerous in its multitude, recently perpetrate? A stumbling

[3] Matt. 26: 31; cf. also Mark 14: 27, referring to Zech. 13: 7.

[4] Horace *Ep.* i. 18. 84 (reading *dum* for *cum*); trans. cf. Loeb edn. (H. R. Fairclough).

paruulis, piis mestitiam, religiosis uerecundiam, amicis pudoris iacturam, uniuerse ecclesie uelamen opprobrii.[5] Vbi enim ambitur honor secularis sub tegumento religionis, quando ab eodem arcebitur crudus animus in maturitate dilectionis? Si ita fauus mellis acescit quid absinthii amaritudo, quid aceti faciet acredo? Prouerbium est: suauiter corrigitur qui exemplo aliorum emendatur. Maneant[j] igitur in uobis unitas, pax et concordia ut id ipsum dicatis omnes et non sint in uobis schismata. Quandiu patrem uestrum, immo nostrum, uobiscum retinere poteritis, alium ne cogitetis. At ubi ineuitabili cogente necessitate aliter disponendum fuerit,[6] Spiritus Paraclitus inuocandus, cetus sanctorum conuocandus, et uir bonus, religiosus, discretus, litteratus, pius et in sancta religione enutritus, qui patris uestri[k] imitator sit, omnimodo inuestigandus. Valete.

40

To the community of Montier-la-Celle[1]

*c.*1145 × 1162

Fratribus [a]et filiis[a] dilectissimis frater [b]Petrus humilis eorum dictus abbas,[b] spiritum dilectionis et pacis.

Quam unica et singulari erga omnium et singulorum uestrorum salutem affectione et sollicitudine tenear, unicus ille spiritus nouit qui 'scrutatur etiam profunda Dei'.[2] Non ignorat hoc ipsa quoque anima mea, quam utinam sicut est intueretur oculus mentis uestre, et sine dubio compateretur doloribus suis.[c] Presumo etiam in conscientiis quorumdam manifestos nos esse[3] quibus idem suadet puritas sua et ueritas mea. Nullis uos circumuenire adulationibus, nullis allicere fomentationum fallaciis, fratres karissimi, uolo, sed ut pax uestra firma sit ad Deum et me non estimetis a cordibus uestris alienum hec scribo. Ceterum, si quis aliter sapit, desipit. Itaque resipiscat animam

[j] Maneat *O*   [k] nostri *O*

40 *O fo. 131*[r]*, Sirmond III. 7*]
[a–a] in Christo *O*   [b–b] G. Christi sacerdos *O*   [c] meis *O*

[5] See appendix 6.   [6] i.e. when he dies, and not before.

block for the little ones, sorrow to the devout, shame for the professed religious, loss of propriety before friends, a veil of opprobrium to the whole Church.[5] For where the honour of the world is sought beneath the cover of religion, when will the fledgling soul be guarded from that very thing in the maturity of love? If the honeycomb has so turned sour, what will the bitterness of wormwood or the sharpness of vinegar do? There is a proverb: He who is improved by the example of others is gently corrected. Therefore let unity, peace, and concord remain among you so that you may all speak in accord and there be no be divisions among you. For so long as you can keep your, nay our, father with you, do not consider another. But when it has been disposed otherwise by unavoidable pressing necessity,[6] let the Holy Spirit the Paraclete be invoked, the assembly of the holy convoked, and a good man of religious life, discreet, learned, kind, and nourished in the holy religious life, who should be an imitator of your father, be sought out by all possible means. Farewell.

40

To the community of Montier-la-Celle[1]

*c.*1145 × 1162

To his most beloved brothers and sons, brother Peter, called their humble abbot, the spirit of love and peace.

That unique spirit which 'searcheth even the deep things of God'[2] knows by how unique and singular an affection and concern I am gripped regarding the well-being of each and every one of you. My soul itself is also not ignorant of this, and oh that the eye of your mind could see it as it is, then it would doubtless share its sufferings. I even presume that we are manifest in the consciences of certain ones[3] whom their purity and my truthfulness persuade of the same. I wish, dearest brothers, to surround you with no flatteries, to entice you with no deceptions of alluring concoctions, but I write this that your peace may be firm before God and that you should not reckon me alienated from your hearts. Moreover, if anyone thinks differently he is being foolish. And so let him who seeks to disturb your peace and

40 [1] Presumably addressed to Montier-la-Celle, as it is among the early letters (see Introduction, pp. xxxiv, xxxv, xlv–xlvi, xlviii).

[2] Cf. 1 Cor. 2: 10.

[3] Cf. 2 Cor. 5: 11.

suam ledere, immo dampnare, qui pacem uestram et meam querit perturbare. Non designo aliquem uel impropero cuiquam stultitiam suam. Sufficit enim accusatio proprie conscientie, et ad tormentum pro malis et ad premium pro meritis bonis. Prorsus nemo ex hoc inter uos conturbetur quia inanis nunquam erit penitentia duntaxat si fuerit uera. Filio uirginis castas mentes preparate, Filio Altissimi humiles animas exhibete, angelo sanctitatis habitacula cordium uestrorum emundate. Valete.

41

To the prior and community of Montier-la-Celle[1]

*c.*1145 × 1162

Karissimis filiis et fratribus suis priori cum ceteris Cellensis monasterii monachis frater P⟨etrus⟩ abbas suus, salutem et in Christo ueram dilectionem.

Quibus lingua et uoce presens persuadere soleo morum honestatem, ordinis obseruationem, hospitum susceptionem, dilectionis integritatem, in diuinis laudibus iubilationem, obedientiam in inuicem, et certam[a] euangelii et regule beati Benedicti preceptorum adimpletionem, absens nunc corpore non spiritu,[2] scripto uestre fraternitati eadem replico, et uisceribus uestris mandare tanto studiosius exopto, quanto remotus a uobis introitum et exitum uestrum[3] uidere non ualeo. Prorsus, fratres mei karissimi et amantissimi, non est elongata a uobis anima mea. Inter uos, intra uos, 'uespere, mane et meridie'[4] ingreditur oculus anime mee ut uideat quos tanquam se ipsum diligit,[5] sanctas animas, puras conscientias, orationes deuotas, suspiria celum penetrantia, lacrimas thronum agni[6] petentes. Quare ergo egressus sum? Coram Deo in Christo Iesu, 'testimonium michi perhibente conscientia mea',[7] fateor non me mores uestri sed moles seculi expulerunt, quas misera illa anima mea pre tedio iam ferre non ualens dormitat, et gemens incolatum

41 *O fo. 131*$^{r-v}$]
[a] *corr. Hall;* cetera *O*

41 [1] Written at Mont-Dieu (see n. 10 below; on Mont-Dieu, see letter no. 52, n. 1). Neither the number nor the dates of Peter's visits to Mont-Dieu are known.
[2] Cf. 1 Cor. 5: 3; Col. 2: 5.

mine come to his senses and see that he is harming his soul, nay damning it. I am not pointing to anyone or reproaching anyone for his foolishness. For the indictment of his own conscience is enough, both as a scourge for wicked deeds and as a reward for good deeds. Let no one at all among you be disturbed by this because repentance will never be vain so long as it be genuine. Prepare chaste minds for the Son of the Virgin, show humble souls to the Son of the Most High, cleanse the dwellings of your hearts for the angel of holiness. Farewell.

41

To the prior and community of Montier-la-Celle[1]

*c.*1145 × 1162

To his dearest sons and brothers, the prior along with the rest of the monks of the monastery of Montier-la-Celle, brother Peter, their abbot, greetings and true love in Christ.

To those whom I am accustomed, when I am present, to urge by word of mouth to probity of conduct, to observance of the rules of the order, to the welcoming of guests, to wholeness of love, to rejoicing in divine praises, to courtesy to one another, and to the sure fulfilment of the precepts of the Gospel and of the Rule of St Benedict, now that I am absent in body but not in spirit,[2] to your fraternity I repeat the same things in writing, and I desire to commit them to your hearts so much more keenly, as being far from you I am not able to see your coming in and your going out.[3] Certainly, my dearest and most loving brothers, my soul is not withdrawn from you. The eye of my soul enters among you, within you, 'evening, morning, and at noon',[4] so that it may see those it loves like itself,[5] holy souls, pure consciences, devout prayers, sighs reaching to heaven, tears entreating the throne of the Lamb.[6] Why then have I gone out? Before God in Christ Jesus, 'my conscience bearing me witness',[7] I confess that it was not your mode of living but the burdens of the world which drove me out, which because of weariness that wretched soul of mine cannot now

[3] Cf. Ps. 120 (121): 8; (also 1 Kgs. (1 Sam.) 29: 6).
[4] Cf. Ps. 54 (55): 18.
[5] Cf. Lev. 19: 18; Matt. 19: 19; 22: 39; Mark 12: 31, 33; Luke 10: 27; Jas. 2: 8.
[6] Cf. Rev. 7: 9, 17; 22: 1, 3.
[7] Rom. 9: 1.

suum prolongari[8] miserabiliter proclamat: 'Quis me liberabit de corpore mortis huius',[9] immo de onere oppressionis huius? Ecce, boni filii et amici, ingredior pro uobis ad solitudinem non Synai sed Montis Dei[10] si forte manus graues ad propitiatorium extollere possim, si forte Amalech deuincere,[11] si forte fimbriam miserationum Dei apprehendere,[12] et 'in ictu oculi'[13] in toto tempore isto contingat michi. Iuuate me, quia non michi soli laboro sed uobis omnibus, et utinam sicut affectu sic effectu omnes uos inueniam mecum 'in uisceribus Iesu Christi'.[14] Laborate instantius 'in ieiunio et fletu et planctu'[15] ut cum rediero palmas in manibus uestris[16] tam letus aspiciam quam desideratus uenero. Vere enim me desideratis si in pace et sanctitate proficitis. De me autem nulla uobis suboriatur suspicio quasi deserturus sim uos. Mors tantum me separabit a uobis, et modo, credite michi, retorto capite ad pennulas,[17] non die, non nocte, recedit a uobis anima mea, sed modo oratorium, modo claustrum, modo capitulum, modo refectorium, modo dormitorium, modo cetera officia circuibo, et ad inordinationem quidem molestabor, ad bonam uero conuersationem hylaris et gaudens congratulabor. Ecce, singulos singillatim manu propria saluto, omnes simul toto corde et ore saluto semper. De noua illa propositorum[18] institutione iterum commoneo ut non sit uobis molestum. Illis in communi mando, et auctoritate qua possum precipio, ut simul in bona pace et concordia maneant et negotia uestra bene procurent. Valete et orate pro me.

[8] Cf. Ps. 119 (120): 5.

[9] Rom. 7: 24.

[10] Cf. Exod. 19: 1; the Mount of God (cf. Exod. 3: 1, etc.) is here the charterhouse of Mont-Dieu, where Peter is writing.

[11] Cf. Exod. 17: 8–13.

[12] Cf. Matt. 9: 20; 14: 36; Mark 6: 56; Luke 8: 44.

[13] 1 Cor. 15: 52.

[14] Cf. Phil. 1: 8.

[15] Cf. Joel 2: 12.

[16] Cf. Rev. 7: 9 (given the context he cannot be thinking of Christ's entry to Jerusalem).

bear but sleeps, and groaning that its sojourn is to be prolonged,[8] cries out wretchedly: 'Who shall deliver me from the body of this death,'[9] nay from the burden of this oppression? See, good sons and friends, I enter on your account the wilderness not of Sinai but of the Mount of God[10] in the hope that I might be able to stretch out heavy hands to the propitiatory, to defeat Amalech,[11] to grasp the hem of the mercies of God,[12] and that it may fall to me 'in the twinkling of an eye'[13] in all this time. Help me, for I am not labouring for myself alone but for all of you, and would that I might find all of you together with me in effect as you are in affection 'in the bowels of Jesus Christ'.[14] Labour more earnestly 'in fasting and in weeping and in mourning'[15] so that when I return I may behold palms in your hands[16] with as much joy as you long for my coming. For you are truly longing for me if you are advancing in peace and holiness. But concerning me let no suspicion arise in you that I am about to abandon you. Only death will separate me from you, and now, believe me, with its head twisted back to the little pinions,[17] my soul withdraws from you neither by day nor by night, but I will go now around the oratory, now the cloister, now the chapter house, now the refectory, now the dormitory, now other parts of the monastery, and while I will be troubled by any irregularity, I will cheerfully and joyfully join in thanksgiving at good living. See, I greet each of you individually by my own hand; I greet all of you together always with my whole heart and voice. Concerning that new arrangement of the priors,[18] I impress upon you again that it should not be a burden to you. I am ordering them jointly, and directing them by what authority I can, to remain together in good peace and concord and to advance your affairs well. Farewell and pray for me.

[17] Cf. Lev. 1: 15; 5: 8; he seems to mean that his soul (the bird) is hopping about at Montier-la-Celle while Peter himself is absent, but the allusion to Lev. recalls the bird killed for the sacrifice ('[sacerdos] retorquebit caput eius ad pinnulas ita ut collo hereat et non penitus abrumpatur . . .'—5: 8).

[18] If *propositus* (prior) is correct (and not e.g. *propositor* [servant], which is unlikely given the qualified statement 'auctoritate qua possum'), this must refer to some administrative office other than that of the main prior. Leclercq, 'Nouvelles', p. 166 n. 24 (reading *praepositorum*) suggests that these are lay advocates (and the tone of the last sentence certainly suggests non-members of the community, but MS *O* reads *propositorum*).

42

To brother A. and the community of Montier-la-Celle[1]

*c.*1145 × 1162

Frater P⟨etrus⟩ karissimo in Christo fratri A. et eiusdem ecclesie uniuerso conuentui, semper quod bonum est imitari.[2]

Vobis otia et negotia mea debeo, quibus astringor dilectione, sollicitudine, sed et defensione in magna iudicii Dei discussione.[3] Vos itaque in otio celle,[4] de celesti beatorum spirituum otio non otioso, et pro officio iniuncto et pro negotio suscepto, commonere bona spe mercedis in tempore suo[5] metende aggredior. Fratres mei dilectissimi, regnum Dei pacatissimum pacificos recipit filios, clarissimum castos, amenissimum iocundos, uernans floribus plenos uirtutibus, irrigatum fluminibus inebriatos compunctionibus, latum longum et immensum dilatatos in caritate, patientia extensos, perseuerantia longanimes, in spe uel proposito usque ad finem uite. Reuiuiscat igitur spiritus uester, karissimi, contemplatione et expectatione tantorum bonorum quia omnia ista filiorum Dei sunt. Vos autem filii Dei estis[6] si habitat in uobis spiritus Christi.[7] Qui enim habet spiritum Christi, hic ex Deo est et Deus in eo est. Humiliaui, fratres, stilum[8] ad eam que ab omnibus simplicibus capi possit materiam, uulgariter scribens ad intelligentiam omnium quatinus me modo scripto audiant et capiant qui presenti sermone non possunt. Vadit et uenit ad uos et a uobis cotidianis, immo assiduis, recursibus animus meus, de uobis cogitans, pro uobis orans, uos et que circa uos fuerint[a] pre nimia sollicitudine nescio uere aut ficte sompnians. Non enim sompnia obseruanda sunt. Affinitate tamen nescio qua sompniis quandoque admiscentur quedam inter ueritatem et falsitatem media que etsi non exprimant ipsam ueritatem, simulacrum tamen ueritatis

42 *O fos. 131ᵛ–134ʳ*]
[a] fuerit *O*

---

42 [1] Montier-la-Celle is not named (except in the rubric of MS *O*), but Peter is clearly addressing his own community (although from where is not clear). A. is unidentified (and may be a cipher); Leclercq's suggestion that it might be an Arnulf who occurs as *praepositus* 1169 × 1180, as *sacrista* 1176, and as *monachus* 1182 × 1190 cannot be shown (even if these are one person) and seems late (see Leclercq, 'Nouvelles', p. 166 n. 25, citing Lalore, *Cartulaires*, vi. 54, 36, 61).

[2] Cf. 3 John 11.

42

To brother A. and the community of Montier-la-Celle[1]

*c.*1145 × 1162

Brother Peter, to his dearest brother in Christ A. and the whole community of the same church, to follow always that which is good.[2]

I owe to you my leisure and my labours, you to whom I am bound by love, by concern, but also by defence in the great trial[3] of God's court. Accordingly, in the leisure of the cell,[4] which is not leisurely in the way of the celestial leisure of blessed spirits but enjoined by office and undertaken as business, I move to admonish you in good hope of the reward to be reaped in His time.[5] My dearest brothers, the most peaceful kingdom of God receives peaceable sons, the brightest kingdom pure sons, the most delightful kingdom joyful sons; blooming with flowers it receives sons who are full of virtues, watered with rivers it receives sons drunk with the stings of remorse, broad, long, and huge it receives sons broadened in love, extended in patience, long-suffering in perseverance, in hope and resolution even unto the end of life. Therefore let your spirit be revived, dearest ones, in contemplation and expectation of such great good things because all these things belong to the sons of God. And you are sons of God[6] if the spirit of Christ dwells in you.[7] For he who has the spirit of Christ, he is from God and God is in him. Brothers, I have lowered my pen[8] to that subject-matter which can be understood by all the simple ones, writing plainly for the understanding of all so that they who cannot do so by speaking face to face may hear and grasp my meaning now in writing. My mind goes to you and returns from you by daily, nay continual, comings and goings, thinking about you, praying for you, dreaming about you and your circumstances, truly or falsely I do not know, owing to excessive worry. For dreams must not be heeded. However, by what affinity I do not know, sometimes certain things half way between truth and falsity are mixed up in dreams which, although they may not express truth itself, yet are

[3] Cf. *DML* 2 *discussio* 2a: judicial proceedings, trial; here meaning that Peter must guide them to Heaven defending them at the last judgement.

[4] With a word play on Montier-la-Celle.

[5] Cf. Ecclus. 51: 38.

[6] Cf. Rom. 8: 14.

[7] Cf. Rom. 8: 9.

quarumdam imaginationum coloribus non nunquam refigurare solent. Sicut enim plerumque inter uigilantes euenit ut et mendaces quandoque uera dicant et uaniloqui seria—'ridentem' enim 'dicere uerum quid uetat?'[9]—sic [b]in caligine[b] phantasticorum sompniorum naturali quadam cerebri fumigatione expressiuas subinde formas rerum que fiunt in abscondito uel future sunt aliquo modo nescio quo spiritus presagax conicit. Hec iccirco premiserim ut uos certificem non solum de his que a me uigilante fiunt, satis utique gratia Dei iuuante prospere, sed et de his que dormientem tangunt.

Quadam nocte uidebar adesse uobis in monasterio presens cum quibusdam fratribus et, quantum de sompnio dici potest, conuentus forte in choro, altareque maius paratum quasi ad missam, et super pallas altaris, nescio quo casu, corpus Domini de pyxide elapsum iacebat. Cum ergo quesitum reperiretur, inuentum est a muribus et muscis corrosum et infectum stercoribus muscarum, et de rotunditate hostie aliquid detractum. Hoc euigilans sompnio ualde permotus sum, timens ne minus quam decet honestas conscientias ad inuiolabile et cum tremore nominandum, multo magis sumendum, Dominici corporis misterium aliqui ministrantium deferrent. Mures enim et muscas quam indecens sit hec sancta misteria contingere, lippis etiam et tonsoribus patet.[10] Multo sine dubio periculosius mens mala ad hoc uiuificum misterium accedit, que sola inter creaturas alias sortem sub sole[11] habentes aut pro bonis remunerabitur aut pro malis operibus eternaliter condempnabitur. Non, inquam, accedere aliter decet nisi prius deuotione in aspersione sanguinis eiusdem agni[12] ab omni macula criminalis peccati fuerit mens emundata, nisi fuerit confessione lota, nisi oratione detersa, nisi sole abstinentie desiccata, nisi ueste caritatis induta, nisi amictu castitatis ornata, nisi gratie inunctione perfusa. Vas enim tam mundum, linteum tam purum, stratum tam honestum, in pascha suo, immo et nostro, non aspernatur neque corpus, neque spiritus Christi. Vas equidem calix est, linteum corporale, stratum patena; uas aureum uel argenteum ad minus, sicut etiam apud cellistas nostros instituimus, debet esse. Similiter

[b–b] *corr. Winterbottom;* caligo *O*

[8] i.e. he has adopted a simpler style.

[9] Horace, *Sat.* i. 1. 24–5; trans. P. M. Brown, *Horace Satires I* (Warminster, 1993).

[10] Cf. Horace, *Sat.* i. 7. 3; i.e. everyone.

[11] Cf. e.g. Eccles. 1: 3, 10, 13, 14; 2: 3, 11, 17, etc.

[12] Cf. 1 Pet. 1: 2; on *criminalis* see *DML*, *criminalis* 2: (of offence) culpable, grave (esp. with ref. to mortal sin).

accustomed on occasion to refashion a simulacrum of truth with the colours of certain fancies. For just as it happens commonly among the wakeful that liars sometimes utter the truth and prattlers serious things—for 'what is there to stop anyone telling the truth with a laugh?'[9]—likewise in the obscurity of fantastic dreams, by a certain natural emission of the brain, a presaging spirit somehow or other divines from time to time shapes that indicate things that are done in secret or destined to come about. Let me therefore have begun with these things so as to inform you not only of what I am doing while I am awake, profitably enough, at least with the aid of God's grace, but also about those things which affect me when I am asleep.

On a certain night I seemed to be present with you in the monastery with certain of the brothers, and, so far as one can speak in this way about a dream, the community by chance was in the choir and the high altar was prepared as if for the mass, and on the altar cloths, by I know not what accident, the body of the Lord was lying where it had fallen out of the pyx. When therefore it had been sought out and was found again, it was discovered to have been nibbled by mice and flies and polluted with fly droppings, and from the round shape of the host a piece had been taken away. On waking, I was powerfully disturbed by this dream, fearing that some of the celebrants might have been bringing to the inviolable mystery of the body of the Lord, which ought to be named, and much more to be taken, with awe, consciences that were less pure than is fitting. For it is obvious to the blear-eyed and the barbers[10] how unworthy mice and flies are to touch this holy mystery. Without doubt, a bad mind approaches this life-giving mystery with much more peril because, alone among other creatures having a destiny under the sun,[11] it will either be rewarded for its good actions or eternally condemned for its evil actions. It is not, I say, proper to approach unless the mind has first been cleansed of every stain of mortal sin by devotion in the sprinkling of the blood of the same Lamb,[12] unless it has been washed by confession, wiped clean by prayer, dried out by the sun of abstinence, clothed with the attire of love, adorned with the cloak of chastity, and sprinkled with the unction of grace. For at His supper, nay ours also, neither the body nor the spirit of Christ disdains the vessel so clean, the linen so pure, the covering so worthy. The vessel indeed is the chalice, the linen the corporal, the covering the paten; the vessel ought to be golden, or at least silver, as indeed we have established among our monks. Likewise the corporal ought

corporale[c] linteum, lineum albissimum, mundissimum, splendidissimum et iuste plicatum. Si senex uel negligens est sacrista uester, corripiatur ab omnibus, iudicetur ab omnibus, quia salus[d] omnium in his periclitatur. Commune autem dampnum communi studio resarciendum est. 'Viscera mea in Domino',[13] fratres dulcissimi, 'qui habet aurem audiat'[14] et me a uisibilibus ad inuisibilia oculos leuare intelligat. Quasi enim scalam itineribus eternitatis posui quibus pede infixo a corpore ad animam prius ascendatis, deinde ad corpus Christi ex quo anima uiuit, post ad animam mediatoris Dei et hominum hominis Iesu Christi,[15] tandem ad dexteram Patris, ubi sedens interpellat pro nobis. Sed quomodo fient hec? Bene et ordinate si corporis primitiua elementa et posteriores reliquias in statera iuste † animandum si omnis † compensaueritis.[16] Sunt autem primitie eius semina, ut ait scriptura, immunda maris et femine. Vnde Iob: 'Quis potest facere mundum de immundo conceptum semine?'[17] Que uero reliquie? Cadauer utique exangue, putredo, uermis, cinis, puluis. Vnde psalmista: 'Mane', id est in iuuentute, 'floreat et transeat, uespre', id est in senectute, 'decidat' in morte, 'induret' in insensibilitate, 'arescat' in puluere.[18] Talis est materia corporis nostri. Inde ergo humilietur et conglutinetur in terra uenter noster.[19] De anima uero quid dicam? Natura anime angelis comparatur, sed reclusione corporali compedita gemit in laqueo isto, euolare cupiens ad fratres et ad Patrem Deum, et benigna quidem expectat patienter ut possit corpus suum ita purificare quatinus corpori Iesu ualeat conformare. Eius natura immortalis immortaliter, aut beate aut infeliciter, facit sine fine eam uiuere. Hoc de anima nostra que uiuit in corpore. De corpore Iesu quid dicam cum scriptura dicat: 'Generationem eius quis enarrabit?'[20] Dicam tamen de illo aliquid etsi non ut est uel quod est nequaquam tamen quod non est. Dicam, inquam, quod fides mea sentit, sic corde credens sicut ore proferens.

Corpus Iesu quod de Virgine sumptum est, ut ita dixerim,[21] de purioribus et principalioribus guttis nature humane eliquatum, fidei

[c] patena *O* [d] *corr. Leclercq;* solus *O*

[13] Cf. Philem. 20.

[14] Rev. 2: 7, 11, 17, 29; 3: 6, 13, 22; 13: 9 (but many similar phrases in the Gospels, e.g. Matt. 11: 15).

[15] Cf. 1 Tim. 2: 5 (the image of a ladder in the context of a dream also recalls Jacob's ladder: cf. Gen. 28: 12).

[16] i.e. the first seeds from which we are born, and the final dust and ashes to which the body returns. The words 'animandum si omnis' do not seem to fit the sense, and the sentence may be corrupt. [17] Job 14: 4. [18] Cf. Ps. 89 (90): 6.

to be linen, of whitest, purest, and brightest linen and properly folded. If your sacrist is old or negligent, let him be rebuked by all, judged by all, because the salvation of all is endangered by these things. And a communal wound must be mended by communal endeavour. 'My bowels in the lord,'[13] dearest brothers, 'he that hath an ear, let him hear',[14] and let him understand that I have raised my eyes from the visible to the invisible. For it is as if I have set up a ladder for the journeys of eternity, by setting your foot on which you may first ascend from the body to the soul, then to the body of Christ from which the soul derives life, after that to the soul of the mediator of God and men, the man Jesus Christ,[15] and at last to the right hand of the Father, where, sitting, He intercedes for us. But how shall these things come about? Well and in an orderly manner if you weigh justly in the balance the first elements of the body and last remains.[16] But its beginnings are, as Scripture says, unclean seeds of male and female. Whence Job: 'Who can make him clean that is conceived of unclean seed?'[17] Indeed what are the remains? A bloodless corpse, assuredly, putridity, worm, ash, dust. Whence the Psalmist: 'In the morning', that is in youth, 'he shall flourish and pass away, in the evening', that is in old age, 'he shall fall' in death, 'grow dry' in insensibility, 'wither' in dust.[18] Such is the material of our body. Because of this, let our belly accordingly be humbled and cleaved to the earth.[19] But what shall I say about the soul? The nature of the soul is comparable to the angels but, shackled by being shut up in the body, it groans in this trap, desiring to fly away to its brothers and to God the Father, and gracious indeed patiently waits to be able so to purify its body that it may be able to conform it to the body of Jesus. Its immortal nature causes it to live immortally, either happily or unhappily without end. But enough about our soul, which lives in the body. What shall I say about the body of Jesus, since Scripture says: 'Who shall declare his generation?'[20] Let me, however, say something about it, even if not as it is, or what it is, by no means however what it is not. I shall declare, I say, what my faith perceives, uttering with my mouth what I believe in my heart.

The body of Jesus, which was incarnate of the Virgin, being refined, so to say,[21] from purer and more elemental drops of human nature, was conceived in the maiden womb by coagulation

[19] Cf. Ps. 43 (44): 25.

[20] Isa. 53: 8; cf. Acts 8: 33.

[21] *ut ita dixerim* seems out of place, as it cannot apply to what precedes it; it must apply to what follows.

uirginalis coagulatione et Spiritus sancti obumbratione in utero puellari conceptum est, et in Virgine quidem eatenus originali obnoxium culpe quatinus nondum Verbo unicum fuit. Nam in Iesu iam assumptum nunquam in hora nec ab hora conceptionis peccato extitit subditum. Nunquam enim simul fuit caro Iesu et caro peccati; hoc corpus gestatorium, immo reclinatorium, diuinitatis fuit. In eo enim habitauit diuinitas non sicut in aliis omnibus creaturis substantialiter et potentialiter uel sicut in quibusdam per gratiam singulariter sed in eo solo solummodo semper singulariter et personaliter. Nec fuit reclinatorium hoc diuisum uel diuisibile ab ea Filii diuinitate que in eo indiuisibiliter quieuit, quia in cruce in morte in sepulcro unita cum eo inseparabiliter permansit. Hoc tabernaculum Dei est ubi habitauit in hominibus homo Deus, hoc a morte resurrexit, hoc celos ascendit, hoc ad dexteram Patris sedet,[22] hoc, hoc corpus, fratres karissimi, in mensa altaris conficitur, contractatur, sumitur tam ab indignis quam a dignis sacerdotibus. Nec a malo minus, nec a bono maius aliquid aliis exinde ministratur, sed sibi melius, sed sibi peius ministrat quantum ad susceptionem, non quantum ad consecrationem, minister dignus uel indignus. Hoc de corpore Iesu cui configurabitur illud nostrum uermiculosum corpus 'in die uirtutis, in splendoribus sanctorum',[23] si tamen in passionibus et in morte eius complantatum 'similitudini mortis eius'[24] fuerit repertum. Etiam in hoc 'spes mea, portio mea in terra uiuentium'.[25] Anima Iesu, te adoro, te laudo, te glorifico, quia tu portas ereas et uectes ferreos confregisti,[26] tu uiam in inferno fecisti qua regressus pateret ad superos. Sanguis Iesu in quo tu eras (omnis enim anima in sanguine est)[26A] tecum fusus, per te et in te uera diuinitate habitante, in te saluauit, redemit, iustificauit nos. Tu uita uiuens, tu uita uiuificans, uiuifica animas nostras. 'Si' enim 'non' proposuero te 'in principio letitie mee', 'adhereat lingua mea faucibus meis'.[27] Quid ultra te? Diuinitas utique. Sed tamen in unitate persone immediata sunt anima et diuinitas Iesu. Nam animam Iesu sine diuinitate non habebis, nec diuinitatem ab anima separare poteris. Amplius adhuc, anima mea in animam Iesu rapitur, illi quodammodo cumulatius dedicans labores nostre restaurationis. Que enim, ut dicendi compendium faciam, de tribus in Iesu unitis substantiis, id est diuinitate anima et carne,

[22] Cf. Kelly, *Athanasian Creed*, p. 20, vv. 38–9; Kelly, *Creeds*, pp. 297–8; Burn, *Nicene Creed*, pp. 112–13. [23] Cf. Ps. 109 (110): 3. [24] Cf. Rom. 6: 5.
[25] Ps. 141 (142): 6. [26] Cf. Ps. 106 (107): 16; Isa. 45: 2.
[26A] Cf. Paschasius Radbertus, *Lib. de corp. et sang. domini* xi. 3 (*PL* cxx. 1309), echoing Lev. 17: 14. [27] Cf. Ps. 136 (137): 6.

of virginal faith and overshadowing of the Holy Spirit, and in the Virgin indeed was subject to original sin to the extent that it was not yet at one with the Word. For once assumed in Jesus, it was never subject to sin, neither in the hour nor from the hour of conception. For it was never simultaneously the flesh of Jesus and the flesh of sin; this body was the litter, nay the seat of divinity. For divinity lived in it not as in all other creatures substantially and potentially or as in certain ones through grace singularly, but in it alone only and always singularly and personally. Nor was this seat divided or divisible from that divinity of the Son which rested indivisibly in it, because that endured inseparably united with it on the cross, in death and in the tomb. This is the tabernacle of God where God the man lived among men; this rose again from death, this ascended into the heavens, this sits at the right hand of the Father,[22] this, this body, dearest brothers, is prepared on the table of the altar, is touched, is taken up by unworthy and worthy priests alike. Nor is anything less of it administered to others by the bad, nor anything more by the good; but the worthy or unworthy celebrant administers it in a better or worse way to himself only in so far as receiving it is concerned, but not in so far as consecration is concerned. This I say about the body of Jesus, with which this our worm-ridden body shall be assimilated 'in the day of strength, in the brightness of the saints,'[23] if, that is, in its sufferings and death it shall be found 'planted together in the likeness of His death'.[24] Even in this is 'my hope, my portion in the land of the living'.[25] Soul of Jesus, I adore you, I praise you, I glorify you, because you have burst gates of brass and iron bars;[26] you made a road in hell by which the way back to the world above has been opened. The blood of Jesus, in which you were existing (for every soul exists in blood),[26A] poured out with you, through you, and in you, with true divinity indwelling, has saved, redeemed, and justified us in you. You who are the living life, you who are the life-giving life, give life to our souls. For 'if I do not make' you 'the beginning of my joy,' 'let my tongue cleave to my jaws'.[27] What is beyond you? Divinity, certainly. But still the soul and the divinity of Jesus are unmediated in the unity of the person. For you will not have the soul of Jesus without the divinity, nor can you separate the divinity from the soul. Still more, my soul is drawn towards the soul of Jesus, dedicating to it in some way more abundantly the labours of our renewal. For to sum up briefly what I have said, which of the three substances united in Jesus, that is divinity, soul, and flesh, felt the pains of the flesh more harshly

durius pro nobis dolores carnis sensit? Caro? Sed sine anima non sentit. Diuinitas? Sed absit ut passibilis sit. Ergo anima, que sentit per se et carnem sentire facit, totum sentit quod caro et amplius quam caro. Vnde: 'Tristis est anima mea usque ad mortem.'[28] Ipsa, inquam, est que miserendi, que redimendi, que reconciliandi, que saluandi affectus tanquam propriam Saluatoris pecuniam de suo marsupio protulit. Caro enim sic erat pauper ut non haberet uel ubi caput reclinaret.[29] Diuinitas affectuum marsupium non nouit. Non enim proprie affectus habere dicitur Deus cum nullus sine passione quadam cadat in [e]aliquem affectum.[e] Anima uero ipsa proprie affectus sustinere dicitur. Omnes itaque in Iesu affectus secundum animam fuerunt. Vnde et de quibusdam dicitur: 'Non est anima mea ad populum istum'[30]—quod absit a populo nostro. Itaque anima Iesu, spongiosis quibusdam affectuum tota referta cauernis, pie refluxit ad cicatricum nostrorum uulnera medicinalia que a manu diuinitatis sumpserat antidota atque compassionis affectione prelambens[f] apostematum putrefactam saniem, uere languores nostros sanauit et dolores nostros portauit,[31] immo potauit et absorbuit. Quid igitur retribuam tibi, anima Dei, pro his que retribuisti nobis?[32] Quid? Animam pro anima? Tua sit anima mea. 'In manus tuas commendo spiritum meum',[33] animam meam et congregationem meam. Hec de anima Iesu que in sacramento altaris in corpore Iesu sine dubio adest. Hec, quia cubicularia trinitatis est, ad cubiculum, intra cubiculum deducat animas nostras. Ibi cubantem, immo manentem, ostendat nobis Patrem in Filio, Filium in Patre, Spiritum sanctum procedentem ab utroque.[34] Caste igitur, quiete, mansuete, uerecunde et modeste stantes ibi secretum illud importunitate nulla interpellemus.[g] 'Potens' enim est et, forte 'crapulatus a uino'[35] glorie, usque mane non euigilabit ut aperiat archana illa seruis suis. Satis autem deliciarum et glorie in foribus et atriis uenientibus peregrinis defixit. Sunt autem fores et atria[h] ista celestia sacramenta que animam interim, donec potiora et noua superueniant, habundanter sed et delectabiliter pascunt. In hoc igitur atrio anima calice aureo utatur ad bibendum, patena argentea ad comedendum, [i]linteo lineo[i] ad dormiendum,

[e–e] *corr. Leclercq;* aliquam affectus *O* [f] *corr. Winterbottom;* prolambens *O* [g] *corr. Winterbottom;* interpellens *O* [h] *corr. Winterbottom;* foris *O* [i–i] *corr. Leclercq;* linteum lineum *O*

[28] Matt. 26: 38; Mark 14: 34. [29] Cf. Matt. 8: 20; Luke 9: 58.
[30] Jer. 15: 1. [31] Cf. Isa. 53: 4.
[32] Cf. Ps. 115 (116): 12 (what follows, cf. Exod. 21: 23; Deut. 19: 21, but not in this context). [33] Luke 23: 46; cf. Ps. 30 (31): 6.

on our account? The flesh? But without the soul it does not feel. The divinity? But forbid that that could be capable of suffering. It is the soul therefore, which feels through itself and makes the flesh feel, which feels all that the flesh feels and more than the flesh. Whence: 'My soul is sorrowful even unto death.'[28] It is this itself, I say, which produced from its own purse the affections for pitying, redeeming, reconciling, and saving, as if it were the Saviour's own coin. For the flesh was so poor that it had not even where to lay its head.[29] Divinity does not know the purse of affections. For God is not properly said to have affections, since nothing may be subject to any affection without some suffering. But the soul itself is properly said to feel affections. And so all affections existed in Jesus in relation to the soul. Hence also it is said about certain persons: 'My soul is not towards this people'[30]—I pray that this be not said of our people. And so the soul of Jesus, wholly filled with certain porous cavities of affections, mercifully poured back on the wounds of our scars medicinal antidotes which it had taken up from the hand of divinity and, bathing the putrefied bloody issue of the ulcers with the affection of compassion, surely it has cleansed our infirmities and taken away, nay taken down and swallowed, our sorrows.[31] What therefore shall I render to you, soul of God, for these things which you have rendered to us?[32] What? A soul for a soul? Let my soul be yours. 'Into thy hands I commend my spirit,'[33] my soul, and my community. These things concern the soul of Jesus, which without doubt is present in the sacrament of the altar in the body of Jesus. Let this, because it is the attendant of the Trinity, lead our souls to the chamber and into the chamber. To us let it show reclining there, waiting there, the Father in the Son, the Son in the Father, the Holy Spirit proceeding from both.[34] Standing there therefore chastely, quietly, calmly, modestly, and moderately, let us disturb that mystery by no importunity. For He is 'mighty', and, being powerfully 'surfeited with wine'[35] of glory, He will not wake until morning to disclose those mysteries to His servants. But He has set a sufficiency of delights and glory firmly in the doorways and courtyards for arriving pilgrims. And these doorways and courtyards are the heavenly sacraments which feed the soul in the meantime abundantly but also delightfully until more powerful and new ones supersede them. Therefore in this courtyard let the soul indulge in drinking from a golden cup, eating

[34] Cf. Kelly, *Athanasian Creed*, p. 19, v. 23; Kelly, *Creeds*, pp. 297–8; Burn, *Nicene Creed*, pp. 112–13.

[35] Cf. Ps. 77 (78): 65.

patiens in calice, diligens in patena, casta in linteo. Ecce, o anima, Christus rex concupiscens decorem tuum[36] in deliciis istis ad amplexus tuos immo sinus tuos inter ubera tua[37] tibi uniendus, illa hora sacrificii sumendi, de sanctis suis sedibus accurrit, in altari, non quidem sedes illas euacuans et deserens sed de ualle plorationis te maiestate indicibili eleuans ut sedeas cum principibus populi sui,[38] ut pullos desideriorum ponas sub altare Dei donec miluus iniquitatis transeat. Non te ergo aggraues, anima, non recuses currus Dei ascendere,[39] non tergiuerseris quasi existimans nondum te posse uidere quod Deus uelit ostendere. Immo intra et uide situm et dispositionem ciuitatis cuius platee sternuntur auro mundo, ubi uitreis canalibus, immo cristallinis, id est inspiratione inuisibili, aque uiue de trono ad singulas sanctarum conscientiarum tanquam cellas in plenitudine gratiarum profluunt siue ad bibendum propter delectationem, siue ad lauandum propter munditiam, siue ad irrigandum propter fecunditatem. Meliora et maiora his uidebis, o anima, illa hora eucharistie si cor mundum habueris, si non intraueris in abyssum malitie. Quid tunc phantasmata uanitatis audite uel uise, clamoris scilicet de capitulo, generalis uel pitantie[40] de refectorio, sompnii de dormitorio, signi[41] uel risus de claustro, speciei male blandimentis uiri uel femine de foro? Quid enim ad te? Immo quid ad hostiam immolationis hec? Reuera muscarum superflua sunt, immunda sunt stercora murium hec et similia. Grauiora[j] autem, que nec nominentur inter uos,[42] comparantur potius uenenosis effluxionibus serpentium quam his minutiis muscarum. Fiat autem cor uestrum et corpus immaculatum[43] tam ab his quam ab illis. Sed noui uos, quia et me ipsum noui eadem circumdatum infirmitate,[44] noui, inquam, uos ad hec cordis instabilitatem obicere et quibus nodis constringi possit ne pereffluat interrogare. Bene, respondeo et michi et uobis. Iuuenculus siue uitulus lasciuus est cor humanum, uentilans cornibus uentum cum uacat pre nimia crassitudine, leuitate, uacatione et uanitate.[k] Certe si castratus, si loris astrictus glebas a mane

[j] grauoria *O* [k] *corr. Hall;* sanitate *O*

[36] Cf. Ps. 44 (45): 12. [37] Cf. S. of S. 1: 12.
[38] Cf. 1 Kgs. (1 Sam.) 2: 8 and Ps. 83 (84): 7; 112 (113): 8. [39] Ps. 67 (68): 18.
[40] The generals were the two dishes prescribed by the Rule, and the pittance a third and often additional one: cf. B. Harvey, *Living and Dying in England 1100–1540* (Oxford, 1993), pp. 10–11 and nn. 10–11. The city, above, recalls Rev. 21–2.
[41] Monastic sign language used during periods, or in places, of silence; cf. W. Jarecki, *Signa loquendi*, Saecula Spiritualia 4 (Baden-Baden, 1981).
[42] Cf. Eph. 5: 3. [43] Cf. Ps. 118 (119): 80. [44] Cf. Heb. 5: 2.

from a silver paten, sleeping on a linen cloth; patient in the cup, loving in the paten, chaste on the cloth. Behold, o soul, Christ the king greatly desiring your beauty[36] hastens forth from His holy abodes to these delights, to your embraces, or rather to your bosom, to be united with you between your breasts[37] at that hour of receiving the sacrifice on the altar, not indeed deserting those dwellings and leaving them empty but elevating you by indescribable majesty from the valley of tears that you may sit with the princes of His people,[38] that you may place the chicks of desires beneath the altar of God until the kite of iniquity pass. Do not then, o soul, burden yourself, do not refuse to mount the chariots of God,[39] do not turn back as if reckoning you are not yet able to see what God may wish to show you. Rather enter and see the site and arrangement of the city whose broad streets are paved with fine gold, where living waters flow forth in fullness of blessings through glass, or rather crystalline, channels, that is by invisible inspiration, from the throne to each of the cells, as it were, of holy consciences, whether for drinking for the sake of pleasure, or for washing for the sake of cleanliness, or for irrigation for the sake of fertility. Better and greater things than these will you see, o soul, in that hour of the Eucharist if you have kept a pure heart, if you have not entered into the abyss of evil-doing. What then of the apparitions of vanity heard or seen, that is of clamour from the chapter, of the general or the pittance[40] from the refectory, of sleep from the dormitory, of sign language[41] or laughter from the cloister, of the sight of unseemly dalliance of men and women outside the cloister? For what are they to you? Or rather, what are these things to the host of the sacrifice? Truly these are the traces of flies, they are the filthy droppings of mice and such like. But the graver things, which should not be named among you,[42] are comparable rather to the venomous fluxes of serpents than to these trifles of flies. But let your heart and body be undefiled[43] by these as much as by those others. But I know you, because I also know myself to be compassed by the same infirmity,[44] I know, I say, that you can only put up against these things instability of the heart, and you are inquiring by what knots it can be constrained so that it does not slip through. Very well, I reply both for myself and for you. The human heart is a wanton bullock or calf, raising the wind with its horns when it is idle, owing to excessive fatness, levity, idleness, and empty-headedness. Certainly if it is castrated, if bound in a harness it has been breaking sods of

usque ad uesperum sub stimulo confregerit, humiliabit ceruicem erectam, temperabit motum lasciuum, fenum manducabit non uentum uentilabit. Credite michi, cor[l] uestrum, si caro afflicta fuerit et disciplinis assueta, mansuescet indomitum, quiescet uagum, et stabit in loco suo pacatum. Ligetur itaque in uinculis quibus hostia nostra Iesus ligatus est, nam ligatus est et ductus est ad Annam primum.[45] Noui tamen etiam cum ligauero cor meum quod si pedem operis non mouerit tamen collum cogitationis circumagitare non cessabit.[46] Quid ergo faciam? Certe torquem auream imponam collo eius[47] ut extra illam non efferat caput et intra quantulumcunque libuerit circumducat. Describam itaque formam crucis et omnes circumstantias eius, ubi Christus Iesus 'cum lanternis et facibus'[m] [48] tanquam latro ducitur, ubi a Iuda uenditur, ubi uestimentis suis nudatur, ubi per ciuitatem ab alio ad alium deridendus et iudicandus circumducitur, ubi spuitur, ubi colaphizatur, ubi facies uelatur, ubi flagellatur, ubi de pluribus inquisitus pauca respondet, ubi suspenditur, ubi aceto cibatur, ubi lancea latus aperitur, ubi clauis configitur, ubi spinis coronatur, ubi latro absoluitur, ubi matri uicarium Iohannem substituit sibi, ubi clamat et expirat.[49] Quid ibi Maria mater Iesu? Quid Iohannes? Quid Maria Magdalena? Quid Petrus? Nonne tunc rupti sunt fontes et cataracte celi[50] in flumine, immo 'in diluuio aquarum multarum'?[51] Hac descriptione in murenula siue torque aurea impressa et collo cordis [n]imposita, ineat[n] cor quocunque impetus duxerit.[o] [52] Non enim infra hunc circulum errare poterit. Ecce quod habeat cor uestrum meditari a principio misse usque ad finem.

[l] si cor *O* [m] fascibus *O* [n–n] *corr. Hall;* impositam eat *O* [o] duxerit eum *O*

[45] Cf. John 18: 13.
[46] Even if it does not drive him to good deeds, it still restrains wicked thoughts.
[47] Cf. Prov. 1: 9: 'ut addatur gratia capiti tuo et torques collo tuo' (cf. also Gen. 41: 42).

earth from morning until evening under the goad, it will lower its high neck, temper its wanton impulse, chew hay not raise the wind. Believe me, your heart, if your flesh be afflicted and accustomed to chastisement, will grow tame where it was wild, will grow quiet where it was errant, and will stand pacified in its place. And so let it be bound in those chains with which our sacrificial victim Jesus was bound, for he was bound and led away to Annas first.[45] However, I know also that when I bind my heart, if it does not spur the foot to action yet it shall not cease to twist about the neck of thought.[46] What then shall I do? Certainly I shall place a chain of gold about its neck[47] so that it cannot lift up its head outside it, and within this it can turn it around as much as it likes. And so I shall trace the form of the cross and all its stations, where Christ Jesus is led like a thief 'with lanterns and torches',[48] where He is sold by Judas, where He is stripped of his garments, where He is led around the city from one to another to be mocked and judged, where He is spat upon, where He is beaten about the ears, where His face is covered, where He is scourged, where, asked about many things, He responds with few words, where He is hung, where He is fed with vinegar, where His side is opened by the lance, where He is pierced with nails, where He is crowned with thorns, where the thief is absolved, where He gives John to his mother as a substitute for Himself, where He cries out and dies.[49] What did Mary mother of Jesus there? What did John? What did Mary Magdalene? What did Peter? Were not then the fountains and the flood gates of heaven broken open[50] in a flow, or rather 'in a flood of many waters'?[51] With this description engraved in the necklace or chain of gold and set on the neck of the heart, let the heart advance wherever the impulse shall lead.[52] For it shall not be able to err beneath this circlet. See what your heart has to reflect upon from the beginning of the mass right through to the end.

[48] John 18: 3.
[49] The Stations of the Cross, with some elaboration.
[50] Cf. Gen. 7: 11; 8: 2.
[51] Ps. 31 (32): 6.
[52] Alluding to Ezek. 1: 12; 10: 22.

43

To the community of Grandmont[1]

*c.*1145 × 1162

Karissimis patribus et dominis suis de Grandi Monte frater [a]Petrus Trecensis abbas,[2] fideles orationes.[a]

Scio quia 'in consilio iustorum et congregatione, magna opera Domini'.[3] [b]Iccirco, fratres karissimi,[b] longe licet a uobis remotus, tamen anime mee intentionem et supplicationem in presenti conuentu[4] transfero quatinus portiunculam cuiuslibet celestis benedictionis referat unde consoletur et longo tempore confortetur. Credo enim si uel unam oratiunculam angeli illi uestri, qui faciem[c] Patris semper uident in celis, ad ipsum Patrem luminum[5] et ad thronum gratie[d] Filii eius ab ore et corde uestro pro me detulerint, quod faciet fructum sursum et germen ponet in terra deorsum. Hinc uero fructus uite et spes misericordie egeno et pauperi erit. Manus igitur illas uestras puras ab omni sanguine et crimine, et oculos columbinos, ad fenestras celi[6] per quas ad propitiatorium et ad sancta sanctorum intrare soletis leuate, nec aliquo modo deponatis donec uos exaudierit qui desiderium pauperum exaudit Dominus.[7] Vester sum, sed tunc dignius et affectuosius. Valete.

43 *O fo. 123*^{v}, *Sirmond III. 8*]
[a–a] G. Christi sacerdos orationes fideles *O* [b–b] Ideo patres sanctissimi *O* [c] faciam *O* [d] glorie *O*

43 [1] Grandmont, dioc. Limoges: Cott. i. 1326–8; see also C. Hutchison, *The Hermit Monks of Grandmont*, Cistercian Studies, cxviii (Kalamazoo, 1989), with extensive bibliography. The prior of Grandmont at this time was Stephen of Liciac (1139–63; Hutchison, *Hermit Monks*, pp. 54–64).

43

To the community of Grandmont[1]

*c.*1145 × 1162

To his dearest fathers and lords of Grandmont, brother Peter, abbot of Troyes,[2] faithful prayers.

I know that 'in the counsel of the just, and in the congregation, great are the works of the Lord'.[3] And so, dearest brothers, although I am far removed from you yet I am bringing the attention and the supplication of my soul before the chapter[4] so that it may bring back a tiny portion of some heavenly blessing by which it may be consoled and comforted for a long time. For I believe that if those angels of yours, who always look on the face of the Father in the heavens, should offer only one little prayer from your mouth and heart for me to the very Father of lights[5] and to the throne of grace of His Son, then that will bear fruit above and will set the seed in the earth below. From here will come the fruit of life and the hope of mercy for a needy and poor man. Lift up therefore those hands of yours, free from all blood and crime, and your doves' eyes, to the windows of heaven[6] through which you are accustomed to approach the propitiatory and the holy of holies, and do not by any means lower them until the Lord, who hears the desire of the poor,[7] hears you. I am yours, but then I shall be so more worthily and affectionately. Farewell.

[2] An unusual styling (Montier-la-Celle was, of course, just outside Troyes). It could indicate that the letter is early, written before Peter was very widely known as 'Cellensis', but it is used in letter no. 73 which is 1155 or later.

[3] Ps. 110 (111): 1–2.

[4] Possibly a reference to the general chapter of the order. This was evidently held on the feast of Saint John the Baptist (24 June), as indicated by letter no. 149; see also J. Becquet, *Scriptores Ordinis Grandimontensis*, *CCCM* viii (Turnhout, 1968), p. 504.

[5] Cf. Jas. 1: 17.

[6] Cf. S. of S. 1: 14; 4: 1; Isa. 60: 8.

[7] Cf. Ps. 9 (10): 38 (17).

44

To P., monk of Norwich[1]

*c.*1145 × 1162

Frater [a]Petrus abbas indignus Cellensis monasterii[a] P. monacho Noruicensi, spiritum salutis.

Vt ignotus ignoto scriberem[b] T. uester, immo noster, [c]rogauit et impetrauit.[c] Iniustum namque esset si in re tam honesta pater filium confunderet.[2] Quia igitur uite, scientie et professionis probate, profunde nec ignote estis, pallio uerecundie uultum abscondo et uocem uix tremulam emitto. Audite itaque, si placet, ueritatem non uanitatem, pietatem non falsitatem, admonitionem non adulationem. Scio quia unius uiri filii sumus, unius ordinis[d] regula informamur, in domo una unum[e] ab uno requirimus.[3] Quapropter si trahimur trahamus, si uocamur inuitemus, si currimus currere moneamus. 'Qui audit dicat: Veni.'[4] Ceterum si sequi noluerint, liberi a coniuratione qua coniurati sumus, inter innocentes manus nostras lauabimus[5] et sic ab introitu glorie Dei epulabimur. Hec ideo dixerim quia in nostra, credo quod et in uestra, patria non[f] monachi, ut pace illorum dicam, sed ex monachis super numerum multiplicati,[6] nomini sancto quod inuocatum est super eos[7] contumeliam faciunt dum turpiter uiuunt, dum uentris, gule et luxurie desideriis se exponunt, dum corpus suum, quod dici nefas est et negatio contra Deum, contumeliis afficiunt. Nomen itaque Dei per eos blasphematur inter gentes.[8] Vtinam Finees resurgeret! Vtinam[g] Helias zelo zelatus[9] pro domo Israhel recumbentes in ydolio[10] igne celesti consumeret. Vtinam[h] saltem Ieremias captiuitatem filie Syon triplici luctu, scilicet[i] orationis predicationis et exempli, doceret moneret

44 *O fos. 136*[v]*–137*[r]*, Sirmond IV. 13*]

[a–a] G. rector scolarum Siluanecterii *O* [b] scribere *O* [c–c] impetrauit et rogauit *Sirmond* [d] *om. Sirmond* [e] uestrum *O* [f] ut *O* [g] uter *O* [h] uter *O*

---

44 [1] Recipient unidentified. It appears that T., a monk of Montier-la-Celle and nephew of this P., has told Peter that he fears his uncle falling under the influence of lax and worldly monks. Peter is diplomatic, avoiding direct censure, while exhorting P. to play his part in maintaining monastic standards.

[2] i.e. as his father in religion, Peter should not refuse T.'s request.

[3] i.e. both are the sons of St Benedict and live by his Rule.

44

To P., monk of Norwich[1]

*c.*1145 × 1162

Brother Peter, unworthy abbot of the monastery of Montier-la-Celle, to P., monk of Norwich, the spirit of salvation.

That I should write as a stranger to a stranger was asked for and obtained by your T., nay ours. For it would be unjust if in a matter so honourable the father were to confound the son.[2] Because therefore you are of a life, wisdom, and profession which are proven, deep, and not unknown, I am hiding my face with a cloak of shame and scarcely letting out a trembling voice. Hear then, if it please you, truth not vanity, piety not falsity, admonition not adulation. I know that we are sons of one man, that we are shaped by the rule of one order, that in one house we seek one thing from one.[3] For this reason, if we are drawn we should draw, if we are called we should invite, if we are running we should admonish to run. 'He that heareth, let him say: Come.'[4] But if they do not want to follow, we being free from the sworn association by which we were bound together will wash our hands among the innocent,[5] and so from the coming in of the glory of God we shall feast. I say this because in our country, as also I believe in yours, those who are not monks, if I may say so with respect to them, but are multiplied above number[6] among monks, bring scandal to the holy name which is invoked upon them[7] while they live filthily, while they deliver themselves to the desires of the belly, of the palate, and of extravagance, while they afflict with abuses their body, which is conduct shocking to be mentioned and a denial of God. And so the name of God through them is blasphemed among the gentiles.[8] If only Phineas were to rise again. If only Elijah, fired with zeal[9] for the house of Israel, were to consume with heavenly fire those sitting at meat in the idol's temple.[10] If only at the least Jeremiah were to teach about, warn of, and lament the captivity of the daughter of Zion with the triple lamentation, that is to say, of prayer, preaching, and

[4] Rev. 22: 17. [5] Cf. Ps. 25 (26): 6; 72 (73): 13. [6] Cf. Ps. 39 (40): 6.
[7] Cf. Ecclus. 36: 14. [8] Cf. Rom. 2: 24.
[9] Cf. 3 Kgs. (1 Kgs.) 19: 10, 14 (and for Phineas, see Num. 25: 7–8, 11).
[10] Cf. 1 Cor. 8: 10.

defleret. Verus nempe[j] Pharao qui omnia dissipat [k]et cum Deo non congregat,[k] lapides sanctuarii per platearum compita disseminat,[11] uasa templi Domini in delubris suis iuxta Dagon asportat,[12] Filium Virginis cum filio Veneris collocat, et in phialis et ciphis cum concubinis suis usque ad mane potare non cessat,[13] usquequo, Domine, non est qui pennam moueat et gannire audeat.[14] Medium silentium tenent[l] omnia.[15] Moyses non extendit manus ad celos, graues enim sunt et plene sanguine. Ideo uincitur Israhel et uincit Amalech.[16] Quatuor fabri cornibus suis uentilant uniuersum Iudam et Israhel,[17] dum 'residuum eruce comedit locusta, et residuum locuste bruchus, et residuum bruchi rubigo'.[18] Hec sunt tertia et quarta generatio in quibus Dominus reddit peccata patrum in filiis.[19] Prima scilicet[m] generatio est suggestio carnis, secunda primus pulsus cogitationis, tertia deliberatio uel perpetratio operis, quarta gloriatio[n] sceleris. Felix qui his cornibus non uentilatur. Si qua itaque in uobis est misericordie scintilla, si qua uiscera pietatis, si quis ros benignitatis, compungimini. Lacrime procul dubio iste nequaquam inutiles erunt. Aut enim illis proderunt et conuertentur[o] aut ad uos redient et in sinum uestrum reuertentur. Vt redeant itaque a[p] uia sua mala, monendo[q] transite de porta ad portam gladio potenter accinctus.[20] Nemini parcat,[r] sed 'dispereat[s] de terra memoria[t] eorum' qui ad cor redire distulerint,[u] qui iniquitatem que in manu eorum est non abstulerint.[21] Hec ad uos tanquam ad amicum iustitie, zelatorem domus Dei, odio habentem eos qui contradicunt sermonibus Sancti.[v] [22] Ad eos uero[w] quibus nichil dulce est[x] preter uinum et pretium, nichil amarum preter claustrum et silentium, nichil amandum preter carnem et mundum, nichil exosum preter Dei uerbum et spiritum, nubes Dei choruscant, tonitrua celi fulgurant, uentus uehemens et

[i] silicet *O* [j] namque *O* [k–k] *om. O* [l] teneret *O* [m] *om. O* [n] regulatio *O* [o] conueruentur *O* [p] de *O* [q] molenda *O* [r] pareat *O* [s] disperdat *O*, *Sirmond* [t] memoriam *Sirmond* [u] distulerunt *O* [v] sanctis *O* [w] *om. O* [x] *om. Sirmond*

[11] Cf. Lam. 4: 1: 'dispersi sunt lapides sanctuarii in capite omnium platearum.'

[12] Cf. 1 Kgs. (1 Sam.) 5: 2, but possibly also alluding to 4 Kgs. (2 Kgs.) 24: 13–15, which would fit with the ref. to Dan. below.

[13] Cf. Dan. 5: 2–3, 23.

[14] Cf. Isa. 10: 14.

[15] From antiphon for Sunday after Christmas ('Dum medium silentium tenerent omnia . . .'); cf. Wisd. 18: 14 (cf. letter no. 127 n. 5, but also no. 172 n. 2).

[16] Cf. Exod. 17: 8–13, where of course Amalech is defeated (but Peter is speculating on the outcome of those he is denouncing continuing in their ways).

[17] Cf. Zech. 1: 20–1.

[18] Cf. Joel 1: 4.

example. To be sure, a true Pharaoh, who scatters all and does not gather together with God, strews the stones of the sanctuary through the crossroads of the streets,[11] carries away the vessels of the temple of the Lord to his shrines next to Dagon,[12] places the Son of the Virgin alongside the son of Venus, and does not cease drinking in vials and goblets with his concubines right through until morning,[13] as long, o Lord, as there is none to move the wing and to dare to make the least noise.[14] All things keep an interval of silence.[15] Moses does not stretch his hands to the heavens, for they are heavy and full of blood. Therefore Israel is defeated and Amalech conquers.[16] Four smiths scatter with their horns the whole of Judah and Israel,[17] while 'that which the palmer-worm hath left the locust hath eaten, and that which the locust hath left the bruchus hath eaten, and that which the bruchus hath left the mildew hath eaten'.[18] These are the third and fourth generation, in whom the Lord renders the sins of the fathers upon the children.[19] Understand that the first generation is the intimation of the flesh, the second the first impulse of thinking, the third the deliberation or performance of actions, the fourth glorying in wickedness. He is fortunate who is not scattered with these horns. And so if there is any spark of mercy in you, any bowels of compassion, any dew of benevolence, be stung with conscience. Without doubt these tears will in no way be useless. For either they will profit those persons and they will be converted, or the tears will return to you and come back to your bosom. And so that those persons may turn back from their evil way, pass with admonition from gate to gate powerfully girt with a sword.[20] Let it spare no one but 'let the memory of them perish from the earth' who have put off returning to the heart, who have not put aside the wickedness which is in their hand.[21] This I say to you, a friend of justice, a zealot for the house of God, hating those who contradict the words of the Holy One.[22] But for them to whom nothing is sweet apart from wine and profit, nothing bitter apart from the cloister and silence, nothing lovable apart from the flesh and the world, nothing hateful apart from the Word of God and the Spirit, the clouds of God are shining, the thunders of heaven flashing, the furious wind and enveloping fire

[19] Cf. Exod. 20: 5; 34: 7; Num. 14: 18; Deut. 5: 9.

[20] Cf. Exod. 32: 27 (the slaying of the idolaters): 'ponat uir gladium super femur suum, ite et redite de porta usque ad portam per medium castrorum et occidat unusquisque fratrem et amicum et proximum suum.'

[21] Ps. 108 (109): 15; and cf. Isa. 46: 8; Job 11: 14.

[22] Cf. Job 6: 10.

ignis inuoluens[y] [23] accelerant. [z]O insensati,[z] quis poterit [a]habitare ex uobis[a] cum igne deuorante aut cum ardoribus sempiternis?[24] Nonne[b] ibi recipietis uenenum pro uino, supplicium pro pretio? Seris et uectibus ferreis porta inferni conseretur uobis qui claustro noluistis[c] includi, et[d] clamor quoque et continuus luctus, qui non siluistis a facie Domini.[25] Caro quam curiose nutristis, sollicite fouistis, studiose lactastis, regnum Dei non possidebit.[26] Mundus, cui mundi creatorem postposuistis, in quo immunde sorduistis, cuius fallaci pulchritudine oblectati patrie celestis obliti estis, non eruet uos de manu inimici. Verbum Dei tunc uos uerberabit non liberabit, accusabit non excusabit, dampnabit non saluabit. Quid uobis cum spiritu Dei cuius contumeliis non parcitis, cuius templum uiolatis, quem contristare[e] non reformidatis?[f] Ni fallor, quod in eum peccastis 'non remittetur' uobis 'neque in hoc seculo neque in futuro'.[27] Sed de his hactenus. Vos autem qui apertos habetis oculos, in uiam istorum ne abieritis,[g] actibus eorum ne assentiatis, neque consiliis eorum[h] adquiescatis. Vt prolixus nimium essem nepos uester[i] coegit, qui iterum atque iterum rogando stilum resumere[j] monuit. Vtinam uirtus uestra amplior sit quam fama. Vtinam uos uidere, cognoscere, et dextras societatis uobiscum habere merear. Vtinam saltem, si non datur ultra, uel unam precem pro peccatis meis pio iudici per manum sancti angeli offeratis. Valete.

[y] inuolutus *Sirmond* [z–z] Omni sensati *O* [a–a] ex uobis habitare *O* [b] Non *O* [c] uoluistis *O* [d] *om.* *O* [e] contristari *O* [f] formidatis *O* [g] habieritis *O* [h] *om.* *O* [i] noster *O* [j] sumere *O*

hastening.[23] O senseless ones, which of you shall be able to dwell with devouring fire or with everlasting burnings?[24] Will you not receive there poison in place of wine, punishment in place of profit? The gate of hell will be sealed with bars and bolts of iron for you who refused to be enclosed in the cloister, and there will be a cry also and continual grief for you who kept not silent before the face of the Lord.[25] The flesh which you have nourished with care, cherished with concern, suckled eagerly, shall not possess the kingdom of God.[26] The world, behind which you have set the Creator of the world, in which you have wallowed filthily, diverted by whose deceptive beauty you have forgotten the heavenly homeland, will not pluck you from the hand of the enemy. The Word of God will then lash you not liberate you, will accuse you not excuse you, will damn you not save you. What have you to do with the Spirit of God, whom you do not spare your insults, whose temple you violate, whom you do not dread to sadden? Unless I am mistaken, 'it shall not be forgiven' you, 'neither in this world nor in the world to come,'[27] that you have sinned against Him. But enough of these matters. But you who have your eyes open, turn not aside on to their road, nor approve their actions, nor acquiesce in their counsels. Your nephew has forced me to be too prolix, admonishing me with repeated requests to take up the pen again. I would that your virtue were greater than your repute. I would that I were deserving of seeing you, knowing you and holding the hand of fellowship with you. I would at least, if more is not granted, that you would offer even one prayer for my sins to the righteous judge, through the hand of the holy angel. Farewell.

[23] Cf. Exod. 40: 33; Ezek. 1: 4.
[24] Cf. Gal. 3: 1; Isa. 33: 14.
[25] Cf. Hab. 2: 20.
[26] Cf. 1 Cor. 15: 50.
[27] Cf. Matt. 12: 32.

45

To subprior H., Thomas and Ascelinus of Clairvaux[1]

*c.*1145 × 1162

Suis karissimis [a]amicis H. suppriori, Thome et Ascelino[a] Clareuallensibus frater [b]Petrus humilis abbas Cellensis,[b] 'gratiam pro gratia'.[2]

Quibus gratiosiori affectu dulcius copulamur eisdem non immerito meliora et dulciora scribimus. Vt enim dignior animus quam corpus sic animi potiora sunt bona quam corporis; fidelis uero sui ipsius interpres est animus. Itaque et nos potius que ad animum pertinent colimus quam que ad corpus. Nam si de affectu non secundum affectum scribis, utique mentiris. Igitur affectus cum de se loquitur, se et non alium loquatur. Est enim hypocritarum aliena tanquam sua, sua tanquam aliena dicere. Nichilominus et simulatorum est neque simpliciter diligere neque ueraciter ad amicos loqui uel scribere. Quamobrem in Christo et in conscientia uera pronuntio quod erga me sinceriorem et puriorem habeatis affectum, ut credo, quam ego ipse. Nam quo purgatior est in uobis oculus[c] mentis eo perspicacior est etiam in amicis diligendis, et quo expeditior ad clare uidendum eo liberior ac iustior de omni causa decernendum. Solummodo siquidem corporum nebula obstat ne se uicissim meus et uester spiritus sublatis impedimentis clare uideat.[d] Attamen ut in corpore mortali immortalia corda et ad se per amorem accedere et sese per mutua desideria possunt contingere, sic unica et speciali dilectione, cotidiano recursu a suis commeant regionibus, quatinus datur, ad se salutandos et osculandos affectus nostri. Quotiens enim uos recogito totiens pedibus animi uos adeo. Itaque, fratres karissimi et desideratissimi, uestras consolationes et sitienter suscepi et ardenter perlegi et uelociter compleui. Et attendite etiam in hoc quam bene cohereant, quam perfecte sibi consentiant, conscientie nostre. Quando enim scribebat dictante animo digitus uester, iam[e] cogitabat animus

45 *O fos. 112ʳ–113ʳ, Sirmond III. 11*]
[a–a] H. suppriori T. et As. *O* [b–b] G. humilis Christi sacerdos *O* [c] oculis *O* [d] uideant *O* [e] *om. Sirmond*

45 [1] H., subprior: Arbois de Jubainville, *Abbayes cisterciennes*, p. 196, gives no subprior with this initial in the twelfth century; *Bernard de Clairvaux*, p. 242, suggests 'Hugh', which may be a confusion with the Hugh who appears later as prior (1156–68; see letter

45

To subprior H., Thomas, and Ascelinus of Clairvaux[1]

*c.*1145 × 1162

To his dearest friends H., subprior, Thomas, and Ascelinus of Clairvaux, brother Peter, humble abbot of Montier-la-Celle, 'grace for grace'.[2]

To those to whom we are joined more sweetly in more gracious affection we write, not undeservedly, better and sweeter things. For as the soul is worthier than the body so the gifts of the soul are preferable to those of the body; but truly the soul is a faithful interpreter of itself. So again we cherish those things which pertain to the soul rather than those which pertain to the body. For if you write about affection without being moved by affection you are simply lying. Therefore when affection speaks about itself it should express itself and nothing else. For it is hypocritical to talk of the qualities of another as if they are your own, and of your own as if they belong to another. Equally it is deceitful neither to love simply nor to speak or write truthfully to friends. For which reason I declare in Christ and in true conscience that you have a more sincere and pure affection towards me, so I believe, than I have myself. For the more purified the eye of your mind is so the more acute it is also in loving friends, and the less impeded it is from seeing clearly so the more free and just it is in deciding in all cases. Indeed only the mist of bodies stands in the way and prevents my spirit and yours from seeing each other clearly with all obstacles removed. However, as immortal hearts in a mortal body are able both to approach one another through love and to touch one another through mutual desires, so with a unique and special love our affections pass back and forth between their regions, returning daily, as far as it is granted, to greet and kiss one another. For I approach you on the feet of my soul whenever I recall you to mind. So then, dearest and most longed-for brothers, I received your consolations thirstily, read through them eagerly and

no. 48, n. 1), and in any case there is no conclusive evidence for this identification. It is possible that this H. is the Henry named in the alternative ending to letter no. 50, but this can not be certain. Thomas and Ascelinus are unidentified.

[2] John 1: 16.

noster, et quod scripserat[f] digitus, hoc elegerat animus.[3] Plane priusquam audirem obediui, antequam consilium daretur adquieui. Tanta dilectionis uelocitas ut audire non expectet quod facere debet. Ledi namque se estimat nisi amicorum uoluntates precurrat. De merito suo plurimum sibi preripi gemit nisi etiam motum uoluntatis uigilanter preoccupauerit. Tunc leta, tunc gratulabunda, cum precesserit ueniendo et quodammodo excesserit maiora faciendo. O excessus caritatis![g] O excedens caritas! Sola in omni genere uirtutum excedendo non excedis, ascendendo non corruis, descendendo ascendis. Ad modum proprium cohibetur humilitas, terminos suos habet castitas, ad malum non laxamus obedientie habenas, ad fines suos nec extra[h] extenditur largitas, ad fines mendacii non accedit ueritas. Sic denique et alie uirtutes cursus [i]suos tantum[i] excurrere sed non transcurrere debent. Constituti sunt eis termini qui preteriri non poterunt. At caritas usque ad celum, immo et supra celum, ueluti cui lex non est posita, conscendit, usque ad infernum et etiam in inferno ipso aliquando descendit.[4] Amicos amplectitur nec ab inimicis arcetur. Cum se extendit non leditur, cum se superextendit non rumpitur. Semper crescit, nunquam senescit. Anni eius non deficiunt[5] sed perficiunt. Quo enim uetustior, immo diuturnior, neque enim ueterascit, eo carior[j] et clarior, 'sicut uinum Libani'.[6] Semper nouatur, semper confortatur, semper cumulatur. Vires semper accrescunt, splendores faciei eius nunquam deflorescunt.[7] O uirtutum uirtus, semper in me sic excedas ut nunquam decedas. Non sinis decedere in quo dignaris iustos excessus creare. Sic nouit Apostolus mente excedere[8] et celum tertium penetrare,[9] sic propheta 'in excessu mentis'[10] supra hominem de Deo sentire. Pre stupore Petrus in consideratione glorificate maiestatis sic excesserat cum dicebat, 'Faciamus hic tria tabernacula, tibi unum, Moysi unum, et Helie unum.'[11] Secundo etiam et tertio sic excessit, uel quando Christum non sustinens mori, dicit, 'Absit a te, Domine',[12] uel quando abscidit

[f] scribebat *O* [g] caritas *Sirmond* [h] ultra *O* [i–i] tantum suos *Sirmond*
[j] *om. Sirmond*

[3] The image is of dictation to a scribe (perhaps the most common method of composition), applied here to the mind as if it were dictating to the hand. The point here is that owing to the union of minds and souls in friendship, his mind knew what the mind was dictating even as the hand was writing it.
[4] Cf. Ps. 138 (139): 8; also possibly an allusion to the harrowing of hell.
[5] Cf. Ps. 101 (102): 28. [6] Hos. 14: 8.
[7] The whole passage echoes 1 Cor. 13, but with no specific quotation.
[8] Cf. 2 Cor. 5: 13. [9] Cf. 2 Cor. 12: 2.
[10] Cf. Ps. 30 (31): 23; 67 (68): 28; Acts 10: 10; 11: 5.

finished them speedily. And see even in this how well our consciousnesses cleave together, how perfectly they accord together. For when your hand was writing at the dictation of your mind, our mind was already contemplating, and what the hand had written the mind had picked up.[3] Clearly I obeyed before I heard, I acquiesced before the advice was given. Such is the speed of love that it does not wait to hear what it ought to do. For it reckons itself wounded unless it anticipates the wishes of friends. It laments that a great part of its merit is snatched away from it prematurely if it does not seize in advance, vigilantly, upon even the motion of the will. Then it is joyful, then it is thankful, when in coming it goes ahead, and in doing greater things it goes further, in a manner of speaking. O excess of love! O surpassing love! You alone of all the virtues do not exceed in exceeding, do not fall in ascending, but even ascend in descending. Humility is confined to its proper degree, chastity has its limits, we do not loose the reins of obedience more than is good, generosity is extended to its bounds and not beyond, truthfulness does not approach the bounds of mendacity. So then, in short, other virtues also ought to run forth only along their own courses but not to run beyond them. Limits are set for them which cannot be passed. But love ascends even to heaven, nay beyond, as to that over which no law is set, and descends as far as hell, and even sometimes into hell itself.[4] It embraces friends and is not kept from enemies. When it stretches itself out it is not harmed, when it overstretches itself it is not torn. It always grows yet never grows old. Its years do not fail[5] but fulfil. For the older, nay the more lasting it is—for it does not grow old—the dearer and brighter it is, 'as the wine of Libanus'.[6] It is always renewed, always strengthened, always increased. Its powers always increase, the splendours of its countenance never wither.[7] O virtue of virtues, may you always so exceed in me that you never expire. You do not permit to expire that in which you deign to create just excesses. Thus the Apostle knows how to exceed in the mind[8] and to penetrate the third heaven;[9] thus the prophet knows how 'in excess of mind'[10] to go beyond man's scope in perception concerning God. Peter had so exceeded on account of his astonishment when, contemplating the glorified majesty, he said, 'Let us make here three tabernacles, one for thee, one for Moses, and one for Elias.'[11] He so exceeded a second time also and a third, as when, unable to bear Christ's dying, he said, 'Lord, be it far from thee,'[12] or when he

[11] Cf. Matt. 17: 4; Mark 9: 4; Luke 9: 33.
[12] Matt. 16: 22.

auriculam serui,[13] uel etiam in captura piscium cum dicit, 'Exi a me, Domine, quia homo peccator sum.'[14] O quotiens sponsa ad sponsum excurrit aut, ut uerius dicam, se ipsam et omne quod creatum est pro[k] amore sponsi excedit. Quandocunque enim uel de sponso uel ad sponsum loquitur, per excessum transuolare dicitur.[l] Hos saltus siue excessus non nouit nisi qui experientia didicit. Quapropter de his michi parcius loquendum, uobis idoneum est; latius et largius agendum potius quam disserendum. Valete. Quam citius potero ueniam ad uos.

46

To R. of Clairvaux[1]

*c.*1145 × 1162

Suo R. Clareuallis suus [a]Petrus Cellensis.[a]

Solet nimia festinatio etiam semicruda quasi iam bene cocta pre nimio appetitu insumere et tanquam famis necessitatem interdum temperare. Instas et ostium amici uelut[b] necessitate hospitis superuenientis inquietare non cessas.[2] Credo potius ex crassitudine anime [c]quam ex[c] necessaria paupertate id te actitare, ut neque importunitatibus tuis occupationes mee satisfaciant neque uoluntati tue solennes iste ferie silentium imponant.[3] Quid igitur? Experior nunc quod in Ysaia iam ante legeram: 'Venerunt filii usque ad partum' et tempus siue uirtus pariendi non est.[4] Estuo siquidem noui amici nouam et primam promissionem adimplere sed contradicentium irruptiones uix ualeo mitigare. Quis itaque, a quo, uel quid petas michi consideranti offert ratio copiosam fortunam petitoris,[d] pauperem [e]inopiam postulati,[e] difficultatem petitionis. Quis [f]enim est petitor[f] nisi qui ambulat

[k] pre *O* [l] uidetur *O*

46 *O fos.* 110^v–112^r, *Sirmond III.* 12]
[a–a] G. *O* [b] *om.* *O* [c–c] uel ex non *Sirmond* [d] petitoriis *O* [e–e] postulanti *O* [f–f] saltat *Sirmond*

[13] Cf. John 18: 10; Matt. 26: 51; Mark 14: 47; Luke 22: 50. [14] Cf. Luke 5: 8.

46 [1] R. is unidentified. One possibility is Rainier of Thérouanne, prior of Clairvaux, possibly from 1146, whose successor occurs 1152: see *P. Ven. Epp.* 320 n. 21, which also discusses his connection with Nicholas of Clairvaux (this evidence would also suggest

cut off the ear of the servant,[13] or even when, engaged in catching fish, he said, 'Depart from me, o Lord, for I am a sinful man.'[14] O how often does the bride run out to greet the bridegroom or, as I should say more truthfully, exceed herself and all that is created, for love of the bridegroom. For whenever she speaks either of the bridegroom or to the bridegroom she is said to take wing through excess. No one knows these leaps or excesses except one who has learned by experience. For this reason it is appropriate for me to speak about them more sparingly, and for you; they are to be acted upon more widely and more abundantly rather than discussed. Farewell. I shall come to you as speedily as I can.

46

To R. of Clairvaux[1]

*c.*1145 × 1162

To his R. of Clairvaux, his own Peter of Montier-la-Celle.

Excessive haste, because of an excessive appetite, generally swallows up even that which is half-cooked as if it were already well-done, and as it were tempers the exigency of hunger for the time being. You press hard and do not cease to bang at a friend's door as though with the urgency of a guest arriving.[2] I believe that you keep doing this rather on account of a richness of the soul than of pressing poverty, so that the fact that I am busy cannot assuage your importunities, nor can that solemn feast impose silence on your will.[3] What then? I am experiencing now what I had read before in Isaiah: 'The children are come to the birth' and there is not time or strength to bring forth.[4] I am burning indeed to fulfil the new and first promise to a new friend, but I am scarce able to mitigate the intrusions of those things which stand in my way. So as I consider who you are who are seeking, and from whom and what you are seeking, reason shows to me the abundant fortune of the petitioner, the scant poverty of the one being petitioned, and the difficulty of the petition. For who is the petitioner

Rainier rather than Rualen as the prior in whose name Nicholas wrote to Peter in the letter included among Peter's collection at *PL* ccii. 476, letter no. LI (see Introduction, p. xxv)). However, the R. in the present letter is given no title. Another possibility is the Robert mentioned in the alternative ending to letter no. 50, but there is no conclusive evidence for either of these.

[2] Cf. Luke 11: 5–8.

[3] Possibly Lent.

[4] Cf. Isa. 37: 3; cf. also 4 Kgs. (2 Kgs.) 19: 3.

'in medio lapidum ignitorum',[5] nisi qui cedrorum medullam[6] consueuit lambere et preclara sententiarum stipendia de castris philosophorum reportare? A quo nisi ab eo qui inter sentes, ne dicam sententias, delicias[7] reputat dormire? [g]A quo[g] nisi ab eo qui neque ungulam findit meliorum dictorum distinctione neque ruminat[8] si qua contigerit audire uel legere? Quis a quo nisi doctus ab indocto, nisi plenus a uacuo, nisi uidens a ceco? Non leue et simplex fateor impedimentum sustineo ne intrem in sanctuarium Dei ut de manu cherubin carbones consolatorios tibi accipiam.[9] Obstat hinc flammeus gladius atque uersatilis[10] sollicitudinum usque ad medullam anime penetrantium, illinc caterua Philistinorum puteos meos[11] terra mortuorum replentium. Preter hec, tanta[h] certe confusio concurrentium ad me fit cum incipio scribere ut pene syllabe singule noua cogantur habere principia.[12] Ecce monachus confitetur, ecce alius diffitetur, ecce miles saltat,[i] ecce clericus salutat, ecce famulus inquietat, ecce nuntius coruum frequentius quam columbam resonat.[13] Mi dilecte, quam[j] interim cor humanum congregare poterit sanctarum scripturarum[k] meditationem, quod componere commonitorium? Sed forte hec ipsa non monendo monent, inquietando suadent quietem, in diuersum decerpendo uerum id ipsum querere admonent. Sic enim esuriens panem quero, aquam sitiens, algens ignem, caligans lucem, deficiens refectionem.[14] Verum tu aliud habens melius et uerius commonitorium rursus aliud mendicaris potius ex uoluntate quam ex necessitate. Exemplo credo apostolorum id facis qui cum Iesum haberent Patrem nichilominus uidere cupiebant. 'Domine', inquiunt, 'ostende nobis Patrem et sufficit nobis.'[15] Nondum nouerant quia cui Filius non sufficit nec Patrem habere poterit. Plena etenim Filii cognitio uniuerse rationalis creature est plenissima recreatio. O quam preclara[l] Clareuallensium commonitoria. Quid enim lacrime huius nisi compunctionis sunt incentiuum?[m] Quid alterius continue orationes nisi superne contemplationis adiumentum? Huius humilitas

[g–g] *om.* *Sirmond* [h] *om.* *O* [i] fabulationes narrat *O* [j] quid *O* [k] scripturarum quid *O* [l] iocunda *O* [m] incitamentum *O*

[5] Ezek. 28: 14. [6] Cf. Ezek. 17: 3, 22.
[7] Cf. Job 30: 7. [8] Cf. Lev. 11: 3 etc.; Deut. 14: 6 etc.
[9] Cf. Isa. 6: 6–7, where a seraph touches Isaiah's mouth with a 'live coal' (*calculus*).
[10] Cf. Gen. 3: 24.
[11] Cf. Gen. 26: 14–15, 18; for *terra mortuorum*, which ususally means the land of the dead, cf. e.g. Hrabanus Maurus, *Comm. in Ezek.* vi. c. 13 (*PL* cx. 654).
[12] i.e. he is disturbed so frequently that he can only proceed one syllable at a time between interruptions (*syllaba* suggests dictation to a scribe).

if not the one who walks 'in the midst of the stones of fire',[5] if not the one who is accustomed to lick the marrow of the cedars[6] and to bring back splendid tributes of ideas from the camp of the philosophers? From whom is he seeking, if not from him who reckons sleeping among briars, or should I say ideas, a delight?[7] From whom, if not from him who neither divides the hoof with the discrimination of better words nor chews over[8] anything he has chanced to hear or read? Who is seeking, and from whom, if not the learned from the ignorant, the full from the empty, the sighted from the blind? I confess that I endure no light or simple impediment to entering the sanctuary of God so as to receive for you the consoling coals from the hands of the cherubim.[9] The flaming sword turning every way[10] of cares piercing even to the marrow of the soul, stands in the way on this side; on the other stands the troop of Philistines filling my wells[11] with the earth of the dead. Besides these, there is certainly such a confusion of things rushing upon me all together when I begin to write that I am forced to start again with each syllable.[12] See, a monk makes his confession, see, another disavows, see, a soldier dances, see, a cleric offers a greeting, see, a servant worries, see, a messenger re-echoes the raven more often than the dove.[13] My beloved, how in the midst of this will the human heart be able to focus its meditation of holy Scriptures? What sort of admonition will it be able to compose? But by chance these things themselves do give a warning by not warning, by causing a disturbance they encourage peace, by plucking the truth apart they admonish one to seek truth itself. For thus hungry I seek bread, thirsty I seek water, cold I seek fire, in darkness I seek light, fainting I seek refreshment.[14] But you, having one better and truer admonition, beg for yet another, out of desire rather than necessity. I believe you are doing this after the example of the apostles who, although they had Jesus, nevertheless desired to see the Father. 'Lord', they say, 'show us the Father and it is enough for us.'[15] They had not yet learnt that he for whom the Son is not enough will not be able to have the Father either. Indeed, full knowledge of the Son is the fullest re-creation for every rational creature. Oh how outstanding are the admonitions of the monks of Clairvaux! For what are the tears of this one if not an incentive to remorse? What are the continual prayers of that other if not an aid to the highest contemplation? This monk's humility confounds the pride

[13] Cf. Gen. 8: 6–11; Noah sent the raven which did not return, then the dove which brought back the olive branch. [14] Cf. Ps. 106 (107): 5; Matt. 25: 35–45.

[15] John 14: 8 (words spoken by Philip alone).

superbiam confundit apostate angeli et hominis, obedientia illius pendentis in cruce Christi emulatur obedientiam. Iste Iacob assimilatur in laboribus, simplicitas Ioseph hunc exornat, zelus ordinis in isto Moysen reddit. O Dauid mansuetudo![16] O feruor Helie! O Danielis abstinentia! O castitas Samuhelis et, quod maius est, o Christi caritas! O Marie uirginitas! 'Castra Dei sunt hec.'[17] Quid uidebis in Sunamite tua, in coccinea tua, 'nisi choros castrorum'?[18] Chorum alium uideo[n] procedentem aduersus phalangas uitiorum innumerabilium dum iste non querens[o] que sua sunt[19] spiritum auaritie strangulat, iste mundi gloriam calcans [p]principem superbie[p] suffocat, iste carnem macerans luxurie caput detruncat, et cuicunque obuiauerit quisque de aduersariis sine misericordia fortiter in ore gladii enecat.[20] Pluunt denique instanter post terga hostium sagitte; uibrant hastas, frameam effundunt et siue leones siue unicornes cum omni bestia saltus exterminant.[21] 'Non est [q]deficiens neque laborans in eis.'[q] [22] In dextro cornu iterum considero alium 'in equis albis'[23] chorum certantem non iam pro uictoria sed ad coaceruanda pretiosiora spolia,[r] et[s] iam pregustat alius mercedem laborum[t] suorum, alius 'gratiam labiorum'[24] consequitur, alius de ligno 'quod est in medio paradisi',[25] superextensus in ulteriora uelaminis[26] per obliuionem terrenorum et contemplationem celestium, edit. Isti sunt qui stolas suas dealbauerunt in sanguine agni[27] resistendo usque ad sanguinem uitiis et pertingendo usque ad patientiam agni immaculati.[u] Hi docent te arcum et sagittam, hi 'sanguinem uue et mori'[28] propinant. 'Arcum prauum'[29] isti non intendunt sed spiritali subtilitate etiam capillum[30] minime cogitationis in arcu proprie reprehensionis citissime feriunt. Prorsus conuersi[v] sunt in die[w] belli quia neque in incerto currunt[31] neque segniter uiuunt. Ad hoc te mitto commonitorium. Omnia enim eorum commonent, siue consessus siue incessus, siue sermo siue silentium, siue ieiunium siue prandium.

[n] uidero *Sirmond* [o] querit *O* [p–p] superbie principem *O* [q–q] in eis deficiens neque laborans *Sirmond* [r] emolumenta *O* [s] cum *O* [t] labiorum *O* [u] immolati *O*, *but either reading is possible* [v] reuersi *O* [w] diem *O*

---

[16] Cf. Ps. 131 (132): 1. [17] Gen. 32: 2.

[18] Cf. S. of S. 7: 1; also S. of S. 4: 3: 'sicut uitta coccinea labia tua'; Sunamitess, cf. 3 Kgs. (1 Kgs.) 1: 3 or 4 Kgs. (2 Kgs.) 4; but here a likely corruption of *Sulamite*.

[19] Cf. 1 Cor. 13: 5. [20] Cf. Ecclus. 28: 22.

[21] Unicorns are usually good, and a symbol of Christ: see F. Bond, *Wood Carving in English Churches, I, Misericords* (London, 1910), pp. 49–53, and M. D. Anderson, *Animal Carvings in English Churches* (Cambridge, 1938), pp. 73–4; there are distant echoes of Ps. 56 (57): 5 throughout this passage. [22] Isa. 5: 27 (Vulgate has *eo* for *eis*).

of the apostate angel and man; that monk's obedience emulates the obedience of Christ hanging on the cross. This monk is like Jacob in his labours; the simplicity of Joseph adorns this one; the zeal for the order in this monk brings back Moses. Oh the meekness of David![16] Oh the fervour of Elijah! Oh the abstinence of Daniel! Oh the chastity of Samuel and, what is greater, oh the love of Christ! Oh the virginity of Mary! 'These are the camps of God.'[17] What will you see in your Sunamitess, in your scarlet one, 'but the companies of camps'?[18] I see another company advancing against the ranks of innumerable vices while he who seeks not his own[19] strangles the spirit of avarice, he who disdains the glory of the world stifles the prince of pride, he who mortifies his body cuts off the head of lechery, and whoever meets any of his adversaries boldly and mercilessly destroys them with the edge of the sword.[20] Then arrows instantly rain down on the backs of the enemies; they shake their spears, they brandish the sword and they drive out lions as well as unicorns along with all the beasts of the forest.[21] 'There is none that shall faint nor labour among them.'[22] Again on the right flank I am watching intently another company 'on white horses'[23] fighting not now for victory but to amass the more precious spoils; and now one of them has a foretaste of the reward of his labours, another pursues the 'grace of the lips',[24] another eats from the tree 'which is in the midst of paradise,'[25] stretched out beyond the veil[26] through forgetfulness of earthly things and contemplation of the heavenly. These are they who have made their robes white in the blood of the Lamb[27] by resisting vices even unto blood and by attaining even to the suffering of the immaculate Lamb. These teach you the bow and arrow, these give you to drink 'the blood of grapes and mulberries'.[28] These do not draw the 'crooked bow'[29] but strike most swiftly, with spiritual penetration, even a hair[30] of the least thought with the bow of proper reproof. They were converted directly on the day of the battle because they neither run an uncertain course[31] nor live slothfully. I direct you to this admonition. For all they do serves as admonition, both their sitting together and their entering in, both their

[23] Rev. 19: 14; also a reference to the colour of the Cistercian habit.

[24] Prov. 22: 11.

[25] Cf. Gen. 3: 3, but the context here suggests a good action, so he must have in mind Rev. 2: 7.

[26] The veil, which is Christ's flesh; cf. Heb. 10: 20.

[27] Cf. Rev. 7: 14; also another possible reference to the colour of the Cistercian habit.

[28] 1 Macc. 6: 34.

[29] Ps. 77 (78): 57.

[30] Cf. Judg. 20: 16; they could hit even a hair.

[31] Cf. 1 Cor. 9: 26.

Ecce 'mille clipei pendent'[32] non solum ad te commonendum sed etiam ad muniendum; et 'tibi post hec, fili mi, ultra quid faciam?'[33] Habes quoque et alium Paraclitum,[34] tanquam aliud commonitorium, quod prope est in ore et in corde tuo, unctionem spiritus qui[x] te docet de omnibus. Habes sapientiam que non 'inuenitur in terra suauiter uiuentium',[35] quam filii Agar non inueniunt,[36] de qua philosophorum abyssus loquitur, 'Non[y] est mecum'.[37] Liga eam in corde tuo iugiter per amorem, describe eam[z] in tempore otii tripliciter, cogitando, loquendo, operando. Discurre scripturarum amenissimos campos; lege tanquam apis et reconde in alueolo[38] memorie suauissimi odoris flores, castitatis lilium, oliuam caritatis, patientie rosam, uuas spiritalium charismatum. Considera diligenter que apponuntur quia quedam ad consolationem, quedam ad correctionem[a] sunt, alia ad sanitatem, alia ad satietatem, alia ad suauitatem. Spes premii promissi merentem consolatur, corrigit comminatio eterni supplicii, medicamine penitentie sanantur omnes languores, presentis iustificationis exultatio famelicum iustitie satiat, adueniens gratia uirgam timoris amouet et sua infusione animam letificat. O Iesu, conuiuatoribus[b] tuis quis sapor in faucibus, quis odor in naribus, quis splendor pre oculis, que auditus modulatio, que cordis iubilatio? Nichil infra uotum supra omnia habundant, immo superhabundant, gaudia. Explicat et extendit se uoluntas ad uolendum, uel etiam ad uolandum, sed non sufficit. Supercurrit oleum quia uasa deficiunt. Hic, hic manus dantis largior et accipientis rarior. Sola hec ministrorum indignatio quia pauci sunt quibus fiat celestium ferculorum distributio. 'Longos fac funiculos tuos', extende pelles tuas, ne parcas,[39] quia dilataberis ad orientem diuine contemplationis, ad occidentem humane per Christum reparationis, ad septentrionem demoniace deiectionis et ad austrum gloriose ascensionis.[40] Vale, nec sine recompensatione [c]nostram paupertatem[c] uelis accipere. Karissimum nostrum suppriorem[41] ex toto corde et ex tota anima et ex tota uirtute saluto,[42] et ceteros amicos nostros.

[x] que *Sirmond* [y] nec *O* [z] illam *Sirmond* [a] correptionem *Sirmond*
[b] comminatoribus *Sirmond* [c–c] paupertatem nostram *O*

[32] S. of S. 4: 4; Clairvaux itself provides a better spiritual admonition, by the example of its life, than anything Peter can write.
[33] Gen. 27: 37. [34] John 14: 16.
[35] Job 28: 13. [36] Cf. Baruch 3: 23.
[37] Cf. Job 28: 14: 'The depth saith: It is not in me, and the sea saith: It is not with me.'
[38] A rare term, but see *DML*, *alueolus* c. [39] Cf. Isa. 54: 2.
[40] Cf. Gen. 28: 14; the subject here is the Cistercian order.

speech and their silence, both their fast and their feast. See 'a thousand bucklers hang'[32] not only to admonish you but also to protect you; 'and after this, what shall I do more for thee, my son?'[33] You have another Paraclete[34] also, like another admonition, which is close by in your mouth and in your heart, that is the anointing of the Spirit which teaches you about all things. You have the wisdom which is not 'found in the land of them that live in delights,'[35] which the children of Hagar do not find,[36] of which the depth of the philosophers says, 'It is not with me'.[37] Bind that wisdom in your heart constantly through love; when you have the leisure copy it in three ways, in thought, in word, and in deed. Run through the most delightful fields of the Scriptures; gather like the bee and store away in the hive[38] of memory the flowers of the sweetest fragrance, the lily of chastity, the olive of love, the rose of suffering, the grapes of spiritual gifts. Consider carefully those things which are gathered, for some are for consolation, some for correction, some are conducive to health, others for satisfying hunger, others for your delight. The hope of the promised reward consoles the deserving, the threat of eternal punishment corrects, all languors are healed by the medicine of penitence, the rejoicing of the justification at hand satisfies the hunger for justice, grace approaching removes the rod of fear and gladdens the soul with its infusion. O Jesus, what savour do those who share your feast have in their throats, what odour in their nostrils, what brightness before their eyes, what melody in their ears, what jubilation in their hearts? Joys no less than wished for abound beyond all wishes, are indeed superabundant. The will stretches out and extends itself to wishing, even to flying, but it is not enough. The oil runs over because the containers are insufficient. Here, here the hand of the giver is too abundant and that of the recipient too small. This is the only resentment of the servants, that they to whom the distribution of the celestial dishes is to be made are few. 'Lengthen thy cords', stretch out your skins, spare not,[39] for you will be spread abroad to the east of divine contemplation, to the west of human renewal through Christ, to the north of the dethronement of the devil, and to the south of glorious ascension.[40] Farewell, and may you not wish to receive our poor offering without repayment. I send greetings to our dearest subprior[41] with my whole heart and with my whole soul and with my whole strength,[42] and to our other friends.

[41] The subprior mentioned here *may* be the H. of letter no. 45 (see no. 45, n. 1).
[42] Cf. Deut. 6: 5; Matt. 22: 37; Mark 12: 30, 33; Luke 10: 27.

47

To R. of Clairvaux[1]

*c.*1145 × 1162

[a]Petrus Cellensis R. suo Clareuallensi.[a]

Excusationis mee[b] proemium siue uelamentum rusticitati mee superinducerem si clerico scolari non monacho Clareuallensi, si[c] spumanti in secularibus non sudanti in regularibus, si denique Sirenarum oblectamenta captanti non aspera queque per desertum sectanti scriberem. Nunc autem quia id solum quod honestum est bonum esse non dubito, omne uero uerum honestum, si uerum dixero, ab honesto non recedens[d] confusionem non timeo. Scio itaque manum te ad fortia misisse[2] et satis perplexum antiquo sophiste[e 3] sophisma fecisse. Crede michi, frendens et rugiens[4] querit soluere quod nequit ex ratione refellere. Callidus est et in arte peruerse calliditatis potenter callens[5] utpote cui, ab incomprehensibilitate retro labentium temporum, annus, mensis, dies, hora uel breuissimum momentum non est elapsum absque huiusmodi conflictationibus. Quoties uicit et uictus est, deiecit et deiectus est, obruit et obrutus est! Non est ei pudor, timor procul abest, spes euertendi semper adest. Fulminat timens, attrectat tremens,[f] recedit sperans, accedit dubitans. O astutia, simplicitatis inimica, malignitatis filia, unica totius religionis tinea,[6] patrem nostrum a paradiso exclusisti, in exilio detrusisti, in morte conclusisti,[7] nos beatitudine spolias, miseriis cumulas, a Deo separas. Quid tibi et nobis? Cepisti et decepisti sed non recepisti. Qui enim fecit ipse reficiendo[g] recepit. Seductor igitur, karissime, cauendus est, et laqueo suo[8] capiendus, et gladio suo detruncandus. Sicut[h] fecit nobis sic faciamus illi. Si malum

47 *O fos. 109ᵛ–110ᵛ, Val fos. 124ᵛ–125ʳ, Sirmond III. 13*]
[a–a] P. clerico suo [. . .] Clarevallensi *O* [b] *om. O* [c] sed *Val* [d] discedens *Val* [e] sophismate *Sirmond* [f] tumens *O, Val* [g] recipiendo *O* [h] sic *Sirmond*

47 [1] R. of Clairvaux, see letter no. 46, n. 1. [2] Cf. Prov. 31: 19.
[3] i.e. the devil, who is the subject of the letter henceforth, and is also the raging lion of 1 Pet. 5: 8 (see n. 4 below), and the subtle serpent of Gen. 3: 1 (see nn. 5 and 8 below).
[4] Cf. 1 Pet. 5: 8 ('your adversary the devil, as a roaring lion . . .'); also Isa. 5: 29, and many other refs.
[5] Cf. Gen. 3: 1. [6] Cf. Matt. 6: 19.

47

To R. of Clairvaux[1]

*c.*1145 × 1162

Peter of Montier-la-Celle to his own R. of Clairvaux.

I would draw over my rusticity a veil, in the form of a preface, of my apology if I were writing to a clerk in the schools and not to a monk of Clairvaux, to one boiling amidst worldly concerns and not to one toiling amidst those of the regular life, finally to one striving for the delights of the Sirens and not to one pursuing all manner of harsh things through the desert. But as it is, because I do not doubt that that alone is good which is honourable, in truth that every truth is honourable, if I speak truly, not retreating from honour, I am not afraid of being confounded. Thus I know that you have put out your hand to strong things[2] and have made a sophism convoluted enough for the old sophist.[3] Believe me, gnashing his teeth and roaring[4] he seeks to unravel that which he cannot refute from reason. He is subtle and powerfully skilled in the art of wicked cunning[5] since for him, thanks to the unfathomable nature of times slipping past, not a year, not a month, not a day, not an hour, or even the briefest moment has elapsed without conflicts of this sort. How often has he won and lost, knocked down and been knocked down, overwhelmed and been overwhelmed! He has no shame, fear is far from him, hope of overturning things is ever present. Fearing he rages, shivering he gropes forward, hoping he withdraws, doubting he advances. O subtlety, enemy of simplicity, daughter of malice, the single moth in the fabric of the whole religious life,[6] you shut our father out of paradise, you drove him into exile and enclosed him in death,[7] you despoil us of blessedness, load us with miseries, and separate us from God. What have you and we to do with each other? You have seized and deceived, but you did not receive. For He who made received by remaking. The seducer therefore, my dearest one, must be guarded against and seized with his own snare[8] and beheaded with his own sword. As he did to us so let us do to him. If it is wicked to be a

[7] Ref. to Adam; cf. Gen. 3 (where the serpent is *callidior*). The next sentence echoes Matt. 8: 29; Mark 1: 24; Luke 4: 39. [8] Cf. 2 Tim. 2: 26.

est esse homicidam, sed non diabolicidam, caput ergo eius contere,[9] caudam apprehende,[10] corpus medium scinde,[11] et sic 'uespere et mane et meridie' narrabis in confessione, annuntiabis in satisfactione, exaudieris in oratione.[12] Sophista iste male proponit, peius assumit, pessime concludit. Suggerendo praua proponit, ad delectationem trahendo assumit, in consensum deiciendo concludit. Si itaque suggestionem prudenter preuidens scuto sacre[i] institutionis propuleris, delectationem fortiter memoria passionis Christi excusseris, consensum constanter timore et amore Dei negaueris, tendiculas eius tanquam fila aranearum abrumpens, 'coronaberis de capite Amana, de uertice Sanir et Hermon'.[13] Vale.[j]

48

To Prior H., G. the cellarer, H. his nephew, and T. the infirmarer of Clairvaux[1]

? 1156 × 1162

Karissimis suis H. priori Clar⟨euallensi⟩, G. cellarario, H. nepoti eius et T. infirmario, frater Petrus,[a] caput, medium et caudam holocausti matutini[2] offerre in odorem suauitatis.[3]

Cum Ysaac[b] uel Abraham ad Montem Dei ascendi, sed asinus cum pueris carnalium sensuum in conuallibus me expectat.[4] Cum hostiam iubilationis immolauero, iterum rediturus sum. Sed 'ubi est uictima holocausti?'[5] An de grege omnium bonorum meorum dignum aliquid inueniam sacrificiis tuis, Deus cordis mei? Totum maculosum, totum uario colore respersum quod apud Laban seruitute dura et graui hactenus merui.[6] Vbi enim cordis puritas, ubi oris ueritas, ubi operis

[i] sacrare *O* [j] *om. O, Sirmond*

48 *O fo. 109*[r–v]]
[a] G. sacerdos *O* [b] *corr. Leclercq;* Ysaia *O*

[9] Cf. Ecclus. 36: 12.
[10] Cf. Exod. 4: 4, although the connection here is the serpent, not evil.
[11] Cf. Dan. 13: 55. [12] Cf. Ps. 54 (55): 18. [13] S. of S. 4: 8.

48 [1] The only prior with this initial known during Peter's lifetime is Hugh (1156–68, subsequently abbot of Longpont: Arbois de Jubainville, *Abbayes cisterciennes*, p. 188). The other characters are unidentified. Three cellarers with the initial G. are recorded for the period pre-1156 to 1174 (Arbois de Jubainville, *Abbayes cisterciennes*, pp. 228–30). This

murderer but not so to be a slayer of the devil, then crush his head,[9] seize his tail,[10] cut his body in two;[11] and so 'evening and morning and at noon' you will speak it in confession, declare it in your penance, be heard in your prayer.[12] This sophist states a bad first premiss, states a worse minor premiss, and draws the worst conclusion. He begins by suggesting base things, continues by seducing one to delight, and concludes by overthrowing one into agreement. If then, anticipating wisely, you repel the suggestion with the shield of the holy ordinances, if you bravely drive out delight with the memory of Christ's passion, if you steadfastly refuse agreement in the fear and love of God, tearing his little snares like cobwebs, 'thou shalt be crowned from the top of Amana, from the top of Sanir and Hermon'.[13] Farewell.

48

To Prior H., G. the cellarer, H. his nephew, and T. the infirmarer of Clairvaux[1]

? 1156 × 1162

To his dearest H., prior of Clairvaux, G. the cellarer, H. his nephew, and T. the infirmarer, brother Peter, to offer the head, the middle part, and the tail of the morning sacrifice[2] for an odour of sweetness.[3]

I have ascended with Isaac and with Abraham to the Mount of God, but the ass along with the young men of carnal senses awaits me in the valleys.[4] When I have burnt the sacrifice of jubilation I will return again. But 'where is the victim for the holocaust?'[5] Shall I find among the flock of all my goods something worthy for your sacrifices, Lord of my heart? Spotted, speckled with divers colours, is all that I have hitherto earned by harsh and heavy servitude in Laban's house.[6]

letter was written at Mont-Dieu (see n. 4 below; on Mont-Dieu see letter no. 52, n. 1; the number and dates of Peter's visits to Mont-Dieu are not known).

[2] Cf. Lev. 9: 17.

[3] Cf. Num. 28: 27; 29: 2, 8, 13, 36.

[4] Cf. Gen. 22: 3–5; the Mountain of God (cf. Exod. 3: 1, etc.) is here the charterhouse of Mont-Dieu where Peter is writing (see below).

[5] Gen. 22: 7, the words of Isaac.

[6] Cf. Gen. 30: 32–3, 35, 39. Peter's rewards for his time spent at Mont-Dieu (or possibly in the religious life) are, like the sheep and goats which Jacob took in payment for his work for Laban, only spotted and speckled (in Gen. however this does not have the negative connotation which Peter gives it, and which he strengthens with the reference to Lev. and Mal. below—see n. 8) and so he has, returning to the image of Abraham, no suitable sacrifice to offer.

simplicitas de toto tempore conuersationis mee? Simulatio in religionis ostentatione, in ore dolus, negligentia in obseruatione regule, circa commissa torpens sollicitudo, ad extranea negotia uigilantia indecens; mordax aliorum reprehensor, propriorum largus dissimulator. Ecce gregis mei animalia que non sufficiunt, immo nec offeruntur, ad holocaustum.[7] Maledictus enim qui offert Domino claudum, debile uel cecum, habens in grege suo masculum.[8] Recordor huius auctoritatis cum ad labores seculi promptos et infatigabiles conuolare quosdam 'a custodia matutina usque ad noctem'[9] intueor, ad susurrium uero 'aure lenis'[10] psalmorum et lectionum sic obdormire, sicut Adam in paradiso, ut de eis tollatur costa uirtutis et fabricetur mulier fragilitatis.[11] Bases enim et plante non subsistunt donec compleatur euangelium in choro, que totam litem finierunt inflexibiles in foro.[12] Oculi grauati sunt in primo psalmo,[13] qui continuauerant in fabulis et ludicris usque ad galli cantum tempus diurnum cum nocturno. De his propheta: 'Ephraim uitula docta diligere[c] trituram';[14] 'quorum primus' uel certe unus 'ego sum'.[15] Certe ad opera carnis robustior sum, debilior uero ad ea que neque in carne sunt neque de carne studia. Hanc confessionem in conspectu Dei et uestrum effundo ut sciatis quare uenerim ad Montem Dei, ut scilicet fetum meliorem Rachel pariat michi quam hactenus Lia conceperit, Rachel enim continuo murmure quod eam despicerem et nunquam copularer ei aures meas implebat.[16] Vel una igitur nocte indulta temptabo si de uentre eius Ioseph aspectu decorum[17] seu Beniamin filium dextere[18] generare possim; et Ioseph quidem propter famam bonam, Beniamin uero propter conscientiam. In aspectu enim fama, in abdito conscientia. Fama ad sacrificium, conscientia pertinet ad holocaustum. Fama est aries qui cornibus heret inter uepres[19] malorum hominum, 'inter quos', Apostolus inquit, 'lucetis sicut luminaria in mundo'.[20] Conscientia est Ysaac unigenitus Abrahe[21] in quo benedicentur qui benedicuntur a Domino.[22] Amen. Huius

[c] *Vulgate rest. by Leclercq;* dilige *O*

[7] Cf. Isa. 40: 16.
[8] Cf. Lev. 22: 22; Mal. 1: 8.
[9] Ps. 129 (130): 6.
[10] Job 4: 16
[11] Cf. Gen. 2: 21–2; cf. Augustine, *Serm. suppos.* cclxxxix. 1 (*PL* xxxix. 2292); Ivo *Dec.* viii. c. 210; *Panormia* vii. c. 13 (*PL* clxi. 627, 1282).
[12] i.e., the monks are too tired from conducting public business to follow the mass standing, even as far as the Gospel. 'Bases . . . et plante' alludes to Acts 3: 7.
[13] i.e. they fall asleep as soon as the office has begun.
[14] Hos. 10: 11.
[15] 1 Tim. 1: 15.
[16] Cf. Gen. 30: 1.
[17] Cf. Gen. 39: 6; cf. also Gen. 30: 22–4.
[18] Cf. Gen. 35: 18.

For where is the purity of heart, where is the truth of the mouth, where is the simplicity of the work from the whole time of my sojourn? Rather there is pretence in the show of the religious life, deceit in the mouth, negligence in the observation of the Rule, slackening concern for those tasks undertaken, unseemly vigilance towards outside affairs, there a bitter critic of the faults of others, a generous neglecter of his own. See the beasts of my flock which are not sufficient, nor even are they offered, for a burnt offering.[7] For cursed is he who offers to the Lord the lame, the infirm, or the blind when he has healthy animals in his flock.[8] I recall this authority when I observe some men flocking together ready for the labours of the world and indefatigable 'from the morning watch even until night,'[9] yet falling asleep at the whispering of the 'gentle wind'[10] of the psalms and the readings, just like Adam in paradise, so that the rib of manly strength is taken from them and the woman of fragility fashioned.[11] For the feet and soles which stood unwearying throughout a whole case in the courtroom cannot stand up even until the Gospel is finished in the choir.[12] Those eyes which had joined day to night in stories and games right up to cock crow are weighed down during the first psalm.[13] Of these the prophet says, 'Ephraim is a heifer taught to love to tread out corn'[14]—these 'of whom I am the chief,'[15] or certainly one. Certainly I am sturdier in the works of the flesh but weaker in those endeavours which are neither in the flesh nor of the flesh. I am pouring out this confession in the sight of God and of you that you may understand why I have come to Mont-Dieu, plainly so that a better child should be born to me of Rachel than Leah has conceived so far, for Rachel was filling my ears with a continuous murmuring that I was despising her and never lying with her.[16] So I shall try, with just one night granted, to beget from her womb, if I am able, Joseph comely to behold[17] or Benjamin the son of the right hand[18]—Joseph indeed on account of good repute but Benjamin for conscience's sake. For reputation is in the appearance, conscience in that which is secret. Reputation pertains to sacrifice, conscience to burnt offering. Reputation is the ram which is sticking fast by the horns among the briars[19] of wicked men, 'among whom', the Apostle says, 'you shine as lights in the world'.[20] Conscience is Isaac, the only begotten of Abraham,[21] in whom they shall be blessed who are blessed by the Lord.[22] Amen. The Apostle in speaking demonstrates the

[19] Cf. Gen. 22: 13, i.e. which was sacrificed in place of Isaac.
[20] Phil. 2: 15. [21] Cf. Gen. 22: 2. [22] Alluding to Gen. 22: 17–18.

caput, medium et caudam ostendit Apostolus dicens: 'De corde', inquit, 'puro et conscientia bona et fide non ficta.'[23] Orate pro seruo uestro. Salutate dominum abbatem.[24]

49

To Nicholas of Clairvaux[1]

1146 × 1152

Nicolao suo Petrus[a] suus.

Mirabili conditas sapore litteras auiditati mee componitis[b] quotiens scribitis. Vt enim ueraci amico ueraciter loquar, illud pene [c]proprie proprium[c] apud me habent: 'Qui edunt me adhuc esurient et qui bibunt me adhuc sitient.'[2] Ipse autem etsi imperitus [d]sum stilo[d] rescribendi non tamen scientia redamandi. Scio quem amare debeam, quare et quantum et quandiu. Quem nisi seruum Dei, nisi qui diligit iustitiam et odio habet iniquitatem,[3] nisi denique qui 'in Deo manet et Deus in eo'?[4] Quare nisi quia conseruus et[e] frater est, nisi pro quo Christus passus est? Quantum nisi quantum me Filius Dei, quantum me ipsum, quantum manus oculum?[5] Quandiu nisi 'usque ad mortem',[6] nisi usque in seculum seculi, nisi usque in eternum et ultra? Generaliter sic afficiuntur qui non que sua sunt querunt sed que Iesu Christi,[7] qui pleni caritate et dilectione in cubilibus et in hortis aromatum in meridie cubant et pascunt.[8] Isti sunt tui, immo mei Clareuallenses. Hi sunt qui non sicut ille

49 *O fos. 130ʳ–131ʳ, Val fo. 129ʳ⁻ᵛ, Sirmond IV. 3*]
[a] G. *O* [b] opponitis *O* [c–c] proprium proprie *Val* [d–d] stilo sum *Val* [e] est *O, Val*

[23] 1 Tim. 1: 5; also recalling the salutation.

[24] On the abbots of Clairvaux after Bernard, see P. Piétresson de Saint-Aubin, 'Le Livre des sépultures: chronique inédite des abbés de Clairvaux (1114–1678)', *Revue Mabillon*, xix (1929), 303–23 (discussing the dates, including Roserot's corrections to *GC*—see letter no, 28, n. 1), which gives for this period: Robert of Bruges, 1153, after Aug.–29 April 1157; Fastrud, 1157–61; and Geoffrey, 1161–5 (i.e. Geoffrey of Auxerre, on whom see *J. S. Epp.* ii. 178–9, n. 36 and refs., and 557–8, n. 10, which gives 1162–5).

49 [1] Nicholas of Clairvaux, educated at Montiéramy (Benedictine, dioc. Troyes), acted in his youth as chaplain to Bishop Hato of Troyes, entered Clairvaux in 1146, where he acted as secretary to St Bernard until his expulsion in 1152 for misuse of Bernard's seal and forgery of letters; he was back in Montiéramy by 1158, and became prior of Saint-Jean-en-Châtel (a dependency of Montiéramy in Troyes) from 1160; d. 1175/8: see *P. Ven. Epp.* ii. 316–30. Constable here revises the conventional dating for Nicholas's entry to and

head, the middle part, and the tail of this: 'From a pure heart', he says, 'and a good conscience and an unfeigned faith.'[23] Pray for your servant. Greetings to the lord abbot.[24]

49

To Nicholas of Clairvaux[1]

1146 × 1152

To his own Nicholas, his own Peter.

Each time you write you compose for my appetite letters spiced with marvellous flavour. To speak truly to a true friend, people almost properly hold this of me, that 'they that eat me shall yet hunger and they that drink me shall yet thirst'.[2] Yet even if I myself am unskilled in the manner of writing back, yet I am not so in the science of loving back. I know whom I ought to love, why, how much and for how long. Whom except the servant of God, except him who loves justice and hates iniquity,[3] except, in short, he that 'abideth in God and God in him'?[4] Why except because he is a fellow servant and a brother, except because Christ suffered for him? How much except as much as the Son of God loves me, as much as I love myself, as much as the hand loves the eye?[5] For how long except 'even unto death',[6] except even for ever and ever, except even to eternity and beyond? In general they are so affected who seek not things of their own but the things of Jesus Christ,[7] who full of affection and love lie down in the middle of the day and feed in the beds and in the garden of aromatic spices.[8] These are your, nay my, brothers of Clairvaux. These are they who do not follow Jesus from afar off, like the one who

expulsion from Clairvaux (1146 not 1145, and 1152 not 1151 respectively; ibid., p. 320, n. 21, and pp. 326–7), and gives extensive bibliographical references for Nicholas (now see also Benton, *Culture*, pp. 7–9). On the confusion between this Nicholas and the English monk Nicholas of St Albans, who exchanged letters with Peter of Celle on the question of the Immaculate Conception of the Virgin Mary (letters 157–60)—an identification refuted by Mabillon, but subsequently revived—see C. H. Talbot, 'Nicholas of St Albans and Saint Bernard', *Revue Bénédictine*, lxiv (1954), 83–117, at pp. 83–7. The present letter is evidently a response to a question about Jerome in a lost letter.

[2] Ecclus. 24: 29.

[3] Cf. Ps. 44 (45): 8; Heb. 1: 9.

[4] 1 John 4: 16; cf. John 6: 57.

[5] Possibly an echo of 1 Cor. 12: 21, 'and the eye cannot say to the hand: I need not thy help . . .'.

[6] Matt. 26: 38; Mark 14: 34; Acts 22: 4; Phil. 2: 8, 27, 30; Rev. 2: 10; 12: 11.

[7] Cf. Phil. 2: 21.

[8] Cf. S. of S. 1: 6; 4: 16.

negaturus Iesum a longe sequuntur,[9] non sicut alii appropinquantes stant, uel ab eo recedentes post Sathanam redeunt, sed sindone reiecta nudi post nudum ambulant,[10] agni uestigiis inherentes, ad celum transuolant et, donec ad sedentem in throno accedant et regi opera sua dicant, 'super montes aromatum'[11] transsilire properant. Hi sunt cerui montium, capree camporum, hinnuli siluarum.[12] Denique ipsi sunt 'lilium conuallium',[13] cedri Libani,[14] oliue uberes in domo Dei.[15] 'Pulchre sunt gene'[16] eorum absque eo quod intrinsecus latet. Amplior uirtus quam fama, flamma non tanta quantus ardor, laus eorum confortata est, nec possum ad eam.[17] 'Vere et tu ex illis es nam et loquela tua' et opera 'manifestum te faciunt.'[18] Si[f] ergo, ut predixi, mutua dilectione adinuicem specialiter afficimur, et quis et quare et quantum et quandiu firmiter conseruabimus. Pene tanquam oculis captus non attendens quis et cui scribam. Qua enim fronte insipientiam meam, turpitudinem meam, tarditatem meam non abscondo, non operio, non celo? Et si 'oculis insipientium'[19] illudo, capree et lyncis[g] oculos sic quoque decipere posse presumo? Sed ne decipiaris, plus in me aliquid quam audis sensus et ingenii suspicans, prorsus [h]aperio paupertatis mee inopiam.[h] Nempe quia 'fodere non ualeo, mendicare' non 'erubesco'.[20] Aperi igitur[i] manum, resera os, ut parturiat sapientiam.[20A] Quero autem quid sit quod ait Hieronymus in epistola ad Rufinum, exponens iudicium Salomonis super questione duarum meretricum:[21] '"Tertia die postquam ego peperi, peperit et hec".[22] Si consideres', inquit, 'Pilatum lauantem manus atque dicentem, "Mundus ego sum a sanguine iusti huius",[23] si centurionem ante patibulum confitentem, "Vere hic erat Filius Dei,"[24] si eos qui ante passionem per Philippum Dominum uidere desiderant,[25]

[f] Sic *O, Val* [g] *corr. Winterbottom;* linceis *O, Val;* lyncei *Sirmond* [h–h] paupertatis mee inopiam aperio *O* [i] ergo *Val*

[9] i.e. St Peter at the court of the high priest, after Christ's arrest; cf. Matt. 26: 58; Mark 14: 54; Luke 22: 54; John 18: 15.

[10] A commonplace for following Christ (see e.g. *P. Ven. Epp.* ii. 108–9); 'sindone reiecta', cf. Mark 14: 51–2. Cf. letter no. 179 and n. 16.

[11] S. of S. 8: 14.

[12] Cf. S. of S. 2: 7; 3: 5; 8: 14; *hinnulus*, young mule, and *hinnuleus*, young stag, but Peter's *hinnuli* is evidently an abbreviated reference to *hinulo ceruorum* (S. of S. 2: 9, 17; 8: 14) and so here a young stag or hart; *cerui montium* is poss. alluding to Ps. 103 (104): 18.

[13] S. of S. 2: 1.

[14] Cf. Judg. 9: 15; 3 Kgs. (1 Kgs.) 4: 33; 5: 6; 4 Kgs. (2 Kgs.) 14: 9, and many other refs.

[15] Cf. Ps. 51 (52): 10.

[16] S. of S. 1: 9; cf. also S. of S. 6: 6: 'Thy cheeks are as the bark of pomegranate, beside what is hidden within thee.'

[17] Cf. Ps. 138 (139): 6.

[18] Cf. Matt. 26: 73; words addressed to Peter when he denied Christ. Here, as

was about to deny Him,[9] who do not like others approach and stop, nor falling away from Him turn back to Satan, but who with the linen cloth cast off walk naked after the naked One,[10] following closely the footprints of the Lamb, who ascend to heaven, who hasten to leap 'upon the mountains of aromatical spices'[11] until they reach the One sitting on the throne and declare their works to the king. These are the harts of the mountains, the roes of the fields, the young harts of the woods.[12] In fine, they are 'the lily of the valleys',[13] the cedars of Lebanon,[14] the plentiful olive trees in the house of God.[15] Their 'cheeks are beautiful',[16] besides what lies beneath. Their virtue is greater than their repute, their flame less than their heat, their praise is strong, nor can I reach to it.[17] 'Surely thou also art one of them, for even thy speech' and deeds 'do discover thee.'[18] If therefore, as I said before, we are particularly affected with mutual love for one another, we shall firmly hold on to the who and why and how much and for how long. Almost like one who has lost his sight, I am not paying attention to who I am and to whom I am writing. For by what impudence am I not hiding, covering up, or concealing my folly, my foulness, or my sloth? And if I mock 'the sight of the unwise'[19] can I presume to be able to deceive in the same way the eyes of the roe and the lynx? But in case you be deceived, believing there to be something more in the way of perception and genius in me than you can hear, I shall demonstrate directly the privation of my poverty. Indeed, it is because 'I am not able to dig' that 'I am' not 'ashamed to beg'.[20] Therefore open the hand, unseal the mouth, so that it may bring forth wisdom.[20A] But I ask what it is that Jerome says in the letter to Rufinus, expounding the judgement of Solomon on the question of the two harlots:[21] '"The third day, after that I was delivered, she also was delivered."[22] If you consider', he says, 'Pilate washing his hands and saying, "I am innocent of the blood of this just man,"[23] or the centurion before the gibbet confessing, "Indeed this was the Son of God,"[24] or those who desire through Philip to see the Lord before the passion,[25] you will not doubt that the Church first gave birth, and

elsewhere, Peter alters the contextual meaning of the passage he is quoting: no denial is in question, the point being simply that Nicholas is as worthy as the others.

[19] Wisd. 3: 2.

[20] Cf. Luke 16: 3, Peter alters the meaning by adding *non* before *erubesco*.

[20A] Cf. Prov. 10: 31.

[21] i.e. Jerome, *Ep.* lxxiv (see nn. 27 and 28 below); cf. 3 Kgs. (1 Kgs.) 3: 16–28.

[22] 3 Kgs. (1 Kgs.) 3: 18.

[23] Cf. Matt. 27: 24.

[24] Cf. Matt. 27: 54; Mark 15: 39.

[25] Cf. John 14: 8.

haud ambiges[j] primam peperisse ecclesiam, et postea natum populum Iudeorum pro quo Dominus precabatur: "Pater, ignosce illis", etc.[26],[27] De centurione et de his qui Dominum uidere querunt, quod ecclesie filii sint non tam durum michi uidetur, sed de Pilato prorsus incredibile estimo.[k] Sequitur in eadem epistola: 'Nulla', inquit, 'dubitatio est quin cuncta que dicuntur non Salomoni mortuo sed Christi[l] conueniant maiestati. Simulat ignorantiam et humanos pro dispensatione [m]carnis mentitur[m] affectus, etc.'[28] Si Dominus noster Iesus Christus quicquid humane nature est preter peccatum assumpsit, et humanos affectus non fallaciter sed ueraciter habuit, quomodo ergo mentitur humanos affectus?

50

To Nicholas of Clairvaux[1]

1146 × 1152 (or ? × 1149)

[a]Suo suus.[a]

'Bestia' que 'tetigerit montem lapidabitur'.[2] Cacumina, dilectissime,[b] litterarum tuarum in tantam nubium densitatem subleuata sese recipiunt quod [c]uix conatibus difficillimis[c] acumen luminum meorum quoquomodo admittant. Nunc enim uolas et peruolas[d] in sublimitate cedrorum, nunc nidificas in altissimis[e] cauernis maceriarum,[3] nunc ambulas 'super pennas uentorum',[4] nunc denique curris et discurris incomprehensibiliter[f] 'super montes aromatum'.[5] Siue[g] inuenias semitam per quam ambulauerit homo siue non inuenias non multum curas. Nec mirum, nam tuus[h] ille [i]ceteris familiarior[i]

[j] ambige *O, Val, Sirmond; Jerome has* ambiges [k] extimo *Val* [l] Christo *Val* [m–m] mentitur carnis *Val*

50 *O fos. 129ʳ–130ʳ, Sirmond IV. 2, Picard 51; cf. Introduction p. liii and n. 131.*]
[a–a] *om. Picard* [b] dulcissime *Picard* [c–c] conatibus difficillimis uix *O* [d] preuolas *O, Picard* [e] altis et abditis *Picard* [f] incomprehensibiliter et *Picard* [g] si *O* [h] tuis *Sirmond* [i–i] familiarium familliarissimus *Picard* (*with note: peruerse in exscripto* familiarum)

[26] Cf. Luke 23: 34: 'Pater dimitte illis, non enim sciunt quid faciunt.'
[27] Cf. Jerome, *Ep.* lxxiv. 4 (*CSEL* lv. 26; *PL* xxii. 683–4).
[28] Cf. Jerome, *Ep.* lxxiv. 5 (*CSEL* lv. 27; *PL* xxii. 684).

50 [1] This letter is a reply to Nicholas of Clairvaux's letter 'Nuper cum aquilonaris . . .'. It is part of an exchange of letters on aspects of Neoplatonic philosophy between Nicholas and Peter both sides of which survive (on these letters, which have separate numbers in *PL* cxcvi and ccii, see Introduction, pp. lii–liv; on the dates, see letter no. 49, n. 1 and below

only afterwards was born that Jewish people for whom the Lord prayed, "Father, forgive them" etc.[26].'[27] Concerning the centurion, and those who seek to see the Lord, it does not seem so hard to me that they may be sons of the Church; but as for Pilate, I think this is absolutely incredible. This follows in the same letter: 'There is', he says, 'no doubt that everything which is spoken applies not to the dead Solomon but to the majesty of Christ. He pretends ignorance and feigns human affections on account of the dispensation of the flesh, etc.'[28] If our lord Jesus Christ took on all aspects of human nature except sin, and had human affections not fallaciously but genuinely, how therefore does he feign human affections?

50

To Nicholas of Clairvaux[1]

1146 × 1152 (or ? × 1149)

To his own from his own.

The 'beast' which 'shall touch the mount shall be stoned'.[2] The heights, my dearest one, of your letters recede, raised up into such a density of clouds that they scarcely admit by any means, even with the most strenuous efforts, the gaze of my eyes. For now you fly and soar high among the cedars, now you nest in the loftiest hollows of the walls,[3] now you walk 'upon the wings of the winds,'[4] now finally you run and roam about illimitably 'upon the mountains of aromatical spices'.[5] You do not much care whether or not you find a path along which some man has walked. Nor is this any wonder, for your friend Seneca, better known to you than the rest, divides human natures into

n. 25; on the philosophical issues discussed, see appendix 7). The sequence is 1: Nicholas to Peter, 'Nuper cum aquilonaris . . .' (*PL* ccii. 491–5, letter no. LXIII); 2: the present letter; 3: Nicholas to Peter, 'Anxietatem michi generat . . .' (*PL* ccii. 498–505, letter no. lxv), 4: Peter to Nicholas, 'Vt perniciosum optimis . . .' (letter no. 51 below). Only Peter's side of the correspondence is ed. here as only these letters formed part of his own collection. The exchange may fall late in the possible period, as Nicholas refers in the first letter in this sequence to renewing a correspondence (*PL* ccii. 491). This may be a reference to a lapse of time between letter no. 49 and these letters, or a reference to an earlier correspondence (although this would be before Peter was abbot of Montier-la-Celle and before Nicholas entered Clairvaux, and no such letters survive from Peter, while only a few of Nicholas's predate his entry to Clairvaux).

[2] Cf. Heb. 12: 20.

[3] Cf. S. of S. 2: 14.

[4] Ps. 17 (18): 11; 103 (104): 3; cf. also 2 Kgs. (2 Sam.) 22: 11.

[5] Cf. S. of S. 8: 14.

Seneca hominum ingenia per tria diuidit[j] genera. Primum [k]ponit ut tuum[k] uias sibi [l]aperire et queque remota[l] ui propria penetrare. Secunde sortis ingenium[m] non adeo ingenuum[n] quod preire[o] nescit, sequi tamen non intumescit. Infelicioris tertium fortune dicit[p] quod nisi coactum, manu tractum,[q] currui impositum, ab inertia sua minime concalescit et exilit.[r] Huic me [s]larga manu[s] natura,[t] [u]primum et etiam secundum michi inuidens ingenium,[u] quam astrictissime ni fallor[v] obligauit, et funiculo sue dimensionis in hereditatem [w]preclaram confirmauit[w] [6] [x]sigilloque communiuit[x]–[y]o dolor![y] Tibi quidem oculo nequam nequaquam[z] inuideo, attamen michi condoleo quia quanto sors tua mee uicina relucet splendidior tanto ipsa[a] sublucet obscurior. Dum ergo repagula ori induxisti, dum oculis dormitationem indulsisti,[b] dum manum ad pharetram non adduxisti,[c] magna maiorum celeritate uerborum effabar, perspicacitate ingenii non[d] adequabar, locupletem [e]scientia scripturarum me[e] arbitrabar. At [f]ubi fulgurare[f] cepisti tonitrua sententiarum, uibrare iacula argumentorum, pluere monita dulcium exhortationum,[g] [h]tardior lingua, sensu pauperior, stilo rusticior inuentus sum.[h] Video igitur [i]paupertatem meam,[i] mirantem non migrantem in habundantiam tuam, suspicientem non suscipientem scientiam tuam; confortata est [j]et non[j] possum ad eam.[7] Quanta enim putas profunditate, caligine, obscuritate recondatur:[k] 'Corpus est uiuens, anima uiua, Deus uita'?[8] Demum[l] 'abyssus abyssum inuocat'.[9] 'Viuens', inquis,[m] 'ex uanitate,[n] uiuum ex simplicitate, uita ex unitate'.[10] Hic, hic tenebre, hic umbra ex nube, nubilosus aer in meridie. Sed que culpa solis si non illuminor priuatus[o] oculis? [p]O dignum, fortasse inquis,[p] risu hominem qui diem noctem,[q] umbram lucem, tenebras autumat solem. Neque, inquam, solem, neque diem, neque lucem, sed plane palpabilem offendo[r]

[j] diuisit *Sirmond* [k–k] ut tuum ponit *Picard* [l–l] adcomperiret quemcunque *O;* adaperire queque *Picard* [m] *om. O* [n] *om. O* [o] aperire *Picard* [p] asserit *Picard* [q] tactum *O* [r] conualescit *Picard* [s–s] *om. Picard* [t] natura obligauit *O* [u–u] *om. Picard* [v] fallor larga manu *Picard* [w–w] confirmauit preclaram *O* [x–x] proprioque sigillo communiuit hec primum etiam secundum michi inuidens *Picard* [y–y] *om. O* [z] *om. Picard* [a] mea ipsa *Picard* [b] induxisti *Picard* [c] conduxisti *Picard* [d] nulli *Picard* [e–e] me scientia scripturarum *O* [f–f] uero ubi figurate *O* [g] exhortationum seminare *O* [h–h] inuentus sum lingua tardior, sensu pauperior, stilo rusticior *Picard* [i–i] meam paupertatem *O* [j–j] nec *O, Picard* [k] reconditum inuoluatur *Picard* [l] Deinde *O, Picard* [m] inquit *O, Picard* [n] unitate *Sirmond* [o] obductis *O, Picard* [p–p] fortasse ais, o dignum *Picard* [q] mortem *Picard* [r] *om. O, Picard*

[6] i.e. a line for dividing up inheritances of land; cf. e.g. Ps. 77 (78): 54. The passage paraphrases Seneca, *Ad Lucil. ep. mor.* lii. 3–4.

three types. The first he posits to be like yours, opening up paths for itself and penetrating to all manner of distant things by its own power. The second type of character is not so noble, for it does not know how to lead, yet is not too haughty to follow. He calls the third a nature of less happy fortune, for unless it is compelled, dragged by the hand or put into the chariot, it does not at all grow warm and leap out of its inertia. Nature, unless I am deceived, has with a generous hand bound me as tightly as possible to this last, begrudging me the first and even the second type of character, and has, with its measuring line, confirmed me in a magnificent inheritance[6] and secured it with a seal—oh misery! Certainly I do not by any means envy you with a mean eye, but I still pity myself because the more brightly your fortune, the neighbour of mine, shines out, so the more dimly this one glimmers. So as long as you closed the bolts on your mouth, as long as you allowed your eyes to sleep, as long as you did not lay your hand on the quiver, I spoke with great fluency and greater words, I was not equalled for natural perceptiveness, I was reckoning myself rich in the knowledge of the Scriptures. But when you began to illuminate the thunder of opinions with flashes of lightning, to hurl the spears of arguments, to rain down the warnings of sweet exhortations, I was found to be slower of speech, poorer in understanding, coarser in style. I see therefore my poverty engrossed by, not encroaching upon, your wealth, looking up, but not latching on, to your knowledge; it is strong and I cannot reach to it.[7] For how great a depth, a darkness, an obscurity, do you reckon it is hidden in: 'The body is living, the soul is alive, God is life'?[8] Then 'deep calleth on deep'.[9] 'Living', you say, 'derives from vanity, being alive from simplicity, life from unity.'[10] Here indeed is darkness, here is the shadow of a cloud, an overcast sky in the middle of the day. But what fault is it of the sun if I am not enlightened when I am deprived of my eyes? Oh what a man deserving of ridicule, you may say, who asserts that day is night, shade is light, darkness is the sun. I tell you, I am striking neither at the sun nor at the day nor at the light but clearly at

[7] Cf. Lam. 3: 1; Ps. 138 (139): 6.

[8] Nicholas of Clairvaux, letter no. LXIII, in the numbering system of *PL* ccii, at col. 493B; Nicholas is quoting Claudianus Mamertus, *De statu anime* iii. 6. 2: 'Corpus est uiuens, anima uiua, Deus est uita' (*CSEL* xi. 162–4; *PL* liii. 766).

[9] Ps. 41 (42): 8.

[10] Cf. Nicholas of Clairvaux, letter no. LXIII, in the numbering system of *PL* ccii., at col. 493B. Here and below Peter substitutes *uiuum* (which in this context thus seems to mean: a state of being alive) for Nicholas's *uiua* when it is used independently of *anima*. This is Nicholas's own extrapolation from Claudianus Mamertus (see appendix 7). Here and at the end of letter no. 51 Peter accuses him of adding to Claudianus Mamertus, and of citing Claudianus as an authority for his own (Nicholas's) views.

obscuritatem. Cum enim corpus ab anima, animam a Deo, Deum uitam habere a semetipso[11] irrefragabiliter credatur, nonne etsi rusticius tamen[s] [t]uerius diceretur corpus uiuificatum ab anima,[t] animam uiuificatam a Deo, et uiuificantem corpus Deum omnia uiuentia[u] uiuificantem, [v]in se et[v] ex se uiuum et uiuentem? Sed rursum quid[w] est 'corpus uiuens ex uanitate'? 'Corpus', inquit Apostolus, 'mortuum est propter peccatum.'[12] Quod ergo Apostolus mortuum uocat propter peccatum tu uiuens dicis ex uanitate? Annon uanitas peccatum? An idem simplici [x]sensu intellectum[x] operatur mortem et uitam? Odit Deus obseruantes uanitatem.[13] Dilectio autem Dei uiuificat, odium mortificat. Non [y]ergo est[y] aliquid uiuens ex uanitate, sed ex ueritate. Quod[z] factum est in illo, [a]id est[a] Verbo ueritatis, uita erat.[13A] In se et ex[b] se profecto creatura nulla terrestris uel supercelestis uita[c] est, cum[d] tamen in illo uniuersa siue uiuens[e] siue uita carens[f] uitam suam habeat.[g] Addis:[h] 'Viuum', id est animam, 'ex simplicitate, uita', id est Deum, 'ex unitate'.[14] Istis non sic 'in spiritu uehementi'[15] offendor, sed nec penitus assentio.[i] Nam anima, ex unitate [j]immortali et indissolubili,[j] sicut et Deus suo singulari et alio[k] modo immortalis est et indissolubilis, ex nichilo creata esse creditur; iccirco namque 'ad imaginem et similitudinem' suam creauit [l]eam Deus.[l] [16] Per hoc etiam, quod[m] per omnes particulas corporis tota simul adest, [n]nec minor in minoribus nec in maioribus maior[n] sed tamen, ut Augustinus testatur, in aliis intensius, in aliis remissius effectus suos exercet, cum in singulis particulis corporis essentialiter sit,[17] unitati magis quam simplicitati obnoxia perpenditur.[o] [p]Omnis enim res simpliciter simplex, una et unum est,[p] non autem si una, statim et simplex.[q] Vnde [r]dicitur Deus[r] simplex non ob aliud, teste Isidoro, nisi 'quia non est aliud [s]ipse et[s] aliud quod[t] in ipso est'.[18]

[s] tamen et *O* [t–t] ueracius dicetur corpus ab anima uiuificatum *Picard* [u] sensibilia *Picard* [v–v] et in se *Picard* [w] quod *Picard* [x–x] sensus intellectu *O* [y–y] est ergo *Picard* [z] Quod enim *Picard* [a–a] uel *Picard* [b] per *O* [c] uita aut uiua *Picard* [d] *om.* *O* [e] uiuentia *Picard* [f] carentia *Picard* [g] habeant *Picard* [h] Adde *Picard* [i] assentior *Picard* [j–j] immortalis et indissolubilis *Picard* [k] proprio *Picard* [l–l] Deus eam *Picard* [m] que *Picard* [n–n] nec maior in maioribus nec minor in minoribus *Picard* [o] penditur *Picard* [p–p] *om.* *Picard* [q] Si qua enim simplex res est, refugit et respuit omnem prorsus admixtionem, omne consortium. Res uero una, duo simul uel plura conuenientia aliquando in sese recipiendo conuertit ut unum sint. *ins.* *Picard* [r–r] et Deus dicitur *Picard* [s–s] et ipse *Picard* [t] quam *Picard*

[11] Cf. Claudianus Mamertus, *De statu anime*, iii. 6. 2 (the passage following that which Nicholas has quoted): '. . . ita scilicet ut anima que in se uiua est, corpori uita sit; ut sic corpus sine anima non uiuat, sicuti ipsa sine Deo' (*CSEL* xi. 162–4; *PL* liii. 766). What follows may echo Augustine, *Serm. de script.* clxxx. 7 (*PL* xxxviii. 976).

palpable obscurity. For since it is held irrefutably that the body has life from the soul, the soul from God, and God from Himself,[11] could it not be said, albeit more simplistically but yet more truthfully, that the body is given life by the soul, the soul by God, and that God, giving life to the body, is giving life to all living things, alive and living in Himself and from Himself? But again, what is 'the body living from vanity'? 'The body', says the Apostle, 'is dead because of sin.'[12] Do you say therefore that that which the Apostle calls dead because of sin is living from vanity? Is not vanity a sin? Can the same thing, understood in its simple sense, produce death and life? God hates them that regard vanity.[13] Yet the love of God gives life, hatred of Him brings death. There is therefore nothing living from vanity, but from truth. That which was made in Him, that is in the Word of truth, was life.[13A] Certainly no creature on earth or above heaven is life in itself and from itself, whereas every creature, whether living or lacking life, has its life in Him. You add: 'Being alive', that is the soul, 'from simplicity; life', that is God, 'from unity.'[14] By these things I am not so much struck as 'with a vehement wind',[15] but nor do I wholly assent. For the soul is held to be created from nothing, out of immortal and indissoluble unity, as also God in His own unique and different way is immortal and indissoluble, because it was for that reason that God created it in His own 'image and likeness'.[16] For this reason too—that it is wholly present at once throughout all parts of the body, neither less in the lesser parts nor greater in the greater, but yet, as Augustine testifies, works its effects more intensely in some parts, more languidly in others, while being present in essence in each part of the body[17]—it is considered to be subject to unity rather than to simplicity. For every thing that is simply simple is one and one thing, but if something is one, it is not also at once thereby simple. Hence God is called simple for no other reason, according to Isidore, than 'that Himself is not one thing and what is in Himself another'.[18] In truth, two or more things joining together at

[12] Cf. Rom. 8: 10. [13] Cf. Ps. 30 (31): 7. [13A] Cf. John 1: 4.

[14] Cf. Nicholas of Clairvaux, letter no. LXIII, in the numbering system of *PL* ccii., at col. 493B: 'Corpus denique est uiuens, anima est uiua, Deus uita; uiuens ex uanitate, uiua ex simplicitate, uita ex unitate.' i.e. Peter is inserting Nicholas's own connections from the first part of this sentence into his quotation of the second (cf. above nn. 8 and 10).

[15] Ps. 47 (48): 8. [16] Cf. Gen. 1: 26.

[17] Cf. Augustine, *Ep.* clxvi. c. 2. 4 (*CSEL* xliv. 550–3; *PL* xxxiii. 722). Peter reverses Nicholas's proposition: the soul, not God, is characterized by unity, God by simplicity (see also appendix 7).

[18] Isidore, *Etym.* vii. 1. 26 (W. M. Lindsay ed., 2 vols. [Oxford, 1911], ii: vii. I. 26; *PL* lxxxii. 262) and *Sent.* i. 2. 6 (*PL* lxxxiii. 540) [both reading *aliud est* for *est aliud*]. The reverse formulation below may be a derivation from this by Peter.

[u]Rem uero unam conuenientia duo simul uel plura aliquando faciunt, ut unum corpus constans ex quatuor elementis.[u] Anima[v] itaque quamuis diuersarum compactionem partium in sui confectionem non recipiat [w]sicut denique incomprehensibilis est pro sui immensitate, sic etiam diuisibilis pro sui simplicitate.[w] Quia tamen aliud ipsa et aliud in ipsa est, secundum auctoritatem prelatam, potius ex[x] unitate quam ex simplicitate conuenit[y] ei esse. Hac etiam eadem[z] rationis demonstratione Deus ex simplicitate dicitur[a] magis proprie, cum pene nichil aut prorsus nichil de eo dicatur nisi improprie.[b] Quid enim est[c] quod dicitur, 'Deus ex unitate uel ex simplicitate', nisi 'Deus ex Deo, Pater[d] scilicet a semetipso,[e] Filius a Patre, Spiritus sanctus a Patre et Filio'?[19] An desipit[f] ita quispiam ut participatione simplicitatis simplicem, participatione unitatis unum, participatione bonitatis bonum existimet[g] Deum, sicut sapiens participatione sapientie efficitur homo, et cetera huiusmodi? Quicquid[h] in Deo est Deus est; sapientia in Deo est et Deus sapientia est; potentia in Deo est et Deus potentia[i] est; bonitas in Deo est et Deus bonitas est. Non magis ergo Deus ex unitate quam ex simplicitate.

Iam extorsissem digitis stilum et ori meo imperassem[j] tempestiuum silentium si non decreuissem expirare hic[k] quicquid de amico remordet animum. Durius siquidem pungitur cor meum dum[l] uspiam pingitur Filius medius inter Patrem et Spiritum. Prorsus ydolum abhominationis[20] conflaret qui sculptile quodlibet sic sculperet uel depingeret. Consubstantialitas enim, [m]coeternitas, coequalitas[m] unius trinitatis et trine unitatis, Patris ac[n] Filii ac[o] Spiritus sancti, non recipit prius ac posterius, maius et[p] minus, inferius et superius, sed totus Pater in toto Filio, totus Filius in toto Patre, totus Spiritus sanctus singillatim et communiter in unoquoque et in utroque simul.[21] Hec sancta et semper cum tremore nominanda trinitas ubique tota per essentiam et potentiam non per gratiam diffusa, non[q] spatiosa magnitudine quemadmodum lux uisibilis uel aliud[r] uisibile, sed sicut sapientia in homine. Vides enim duos homines, unum paruum et alium magnum corpore, in [s]sapientie tamen participatione[s] equales[t]

[u–u] Rem uero unam conuenientia duo simul uel plura aliquando faciunt, ut unum corpus ex iiii[r] constans elementis *O; om. Picard* [v] animam *Picard* [w–w] *om. Sirmond;* et *Picard* [x] *om. Sirmond* [y] congruit *O* [z] *om. Picard* [a] diceretur *O;* dicetur *Picard* [b] ipse *Picard* [c] *om. O* [d] Patre *Picard* [e] se ipso *O, Picard* [f] descipiat *O* [g] estimet *O* [h] quid *O* [i] ipsa potentia *Picard* [j] parassem *Picard* [k] his *O* [l] dummodo *Picard* [m–m] coeternitas et coequalitas *O;* coequalitas coeternitas *Picard* [n] et *O, Picard* [o] et *O, Picard* [p] ac *O* [q] nisi *Picard* [r] aliud quodlibet *Picard* [s–s] unius sapientie participatione pares et *Picard* [t] pares *O*

the same time sometimes do make one thing, like one body composed of four elements. Thus the soul, although it does not admit the conjuncture of diverse elements to make it, just as it is certainly illimitable in respect of its greatness, so also it is divisible in respect of its simplicity. Since, however, itself is one thing and another thing is in it, according to the best authority, its being comes to it from unity rather than from simplicity. By this same demonstration of reason also, God is more properly said to exist from simplicity, although almost nothing, or absolutely nothing, is said about Him except improperly. For what does it mean to say 'God from unity or from simplicity', except 'God from God, that is to say the Father from Himself, the Son from the Father, the Holy Spirit from the Father and the Son'?[19] Is anyone so foolish that he would reckon God to be simple through participation in simplicity, one through participation in unity, good through participation in goodness, in the same way that man is made wise by participation in wisdom, and other qualities of this sort? Whatever is in God is God; wisdom is in God and God is wisdom; power is in God and God is power; goodness is in God and God is goodness. God is therefore no more from unity than from simplicity.

Now I would have wrenched the pen from my fingers and commanded my mouth to keep a timely silence had I not determined at this point to speak freely about every thing coming from a friend which vexes the soul. Indeed my heart is sorely afflicted when the Son is depicted anywhere as an intermediary between the Father and the Holy Spirit. Were anyone to sculpt or paint such an image he would immediately produce an idol of abomination.[20] For the consubstantiality, the co-eternity, the co-equality of the one Trinity and the threefold Unity, of the Father, and of the Son, and of the Holy Spirit, does not admit first and last, greater and lesser, inferior and superior, but rather the whole Father in the whole Son, the whole Son in the whole Father, the whole Holy Spirit, singly and jointly, in each one and in both at once.[21] This Holy Trinity, always to be named in trembling, is everywhere whole in its essence and power, not diffused in grace, not spacious in magnitude, like the visible light or any other visible thing, but like wisdom in man. For you see two men, one physically small and the other large, to be however equals in

[19] Cf. Kelly, *Athanasian Creed*, p. 19, vv. 22–3; also Kelly, *Creeds*, pp. 297–8 and Burn, *Nicene Creed*, pp. 112–13.

[20] Cf. Ezek. 16: 36.

[21] Cf. the Athanasian Creed (see n. 19 above).

esse. Sic diuina essentia uniformis et uniusmodi est et in maximis et in minimis. Sicut denique incomprehensibilis est pro sui immensitate sic etiam[u] indiuisibilis pro[v] sui simplicitate. 'Intelligamus', inquit Augustinus,[w] 'Deum quantum possumus sine qualitate bonum, sine quantitate magnum, sine indigentia creatorem, sine situ presentem, sine loco ubique totum, sine tempore sempiternum, [x]sine commutatione mutabilia facientem, nichil patientem.'[x] [22] Iuras, credo, sic te nec aliter credere uel credidisse. Protestor et ipse in fide mea, si lingua [y]quia in udo[y] est errauit, corde[z] sic tenuisse. [a]Simplex enim res refugit et respuit omnem adiunctionem, omne consortium.[a] Ne diu tamen a cogitationibus conturberis,[b] reuoluens ubi hoc dixeris, in sermone de sancto Victore scribis:[c] '. . . ubique autem est in medio. Nam et[d] in illa deitatis essentia est[e] medius Filius inter Patrem et Spiritum.'[23] Meminisse debes nunc[f] quia mediator Vnius non est, Deus autem unus[g] est, Pater et Filius et Spiritus sanctus. Quod si creatum, non increatum, Spiritum, [h]ideo quia[h] 'sanctum' non subiunxisti, intelligendum aliquis estimat, regulam Hieronymi de significatione huius nominis penitus ignorat: 'Vbi', inquit, '"Spiritus" sine adiunctione aliqua in scripturis ponitur, "Spiritus sanctus" recte intelligitur.'[24] Si autem intellector iam dictus de creato spiritu dictum prorsus contenderit[i] nec minor abusio quam de increato superius ostensum est remanebit.[j] Qui enim, pugillo concludens omnia, extra et intra, infra et supra est,[k] qua ratione medius dicatur qui[l] comprehendat nemo est. [m]Clamitas totum me effudisse spiritum meum. Quidni? Cum tibi effundo non effundo sed infundo.[m] [25]

[u] et *Picard* [v] est pro *O* [w] Augustinus contra Arrium *Sirmond* [x–x] *om. O*; sine commutatione multa facientem *Picard* [y–y] que in mundo *Picard* [z] cor *Picard* [a–a] Simplex enim res refugit et respuit omnem prorsus admixtione, omne consortium *O; om. Picard* [b] turberis *O;* perturberis *Picard* [c] sic scribis *Picard* [d] *om. O* [e] *om. Picard* [f] non *Picard* [g] unius *O* [h–h] ideoque *Picard* [i] contenderet *O* [j] remaneret *O* [k] *om. Picard* [l] et qui *O* [m–m] Clamitas, totum me effudisse spiritum meum. Quid enim? Cum tibi effundo, non effundo, sed infundo *O;* in carnis quoque assumptionem Filius inter Patrem et Spiritum nullo modo medius, sed inter hominem et Deum dicatur et credatur. Vnde et mediator dicitur. Sed de his hactenus. Audio nempe te intra fauces clamitantem et infringentem. Vt quid hec effusio uerborum et temporum? Prorsus effudi tibi animam meam, dimidium anime mee. Vale. Priorem dominum meum Henricum, Ascelinum, Guillelmum, Robertum, Hugonem scriptorem tuum, et Thomam et ceteros amicos nominatim saluta, ignosce michi *Picard*

[22] Cf. Augustine, *De trinitate*, v. i. 2 (*CCSL* l. 207; *PL* xlii. 912).

[23] Nicholas of Clairvaux, sermon on St Victor's day. The sermon was misattributed to Peter Damian, and appears in Peter Damian, *Sermones*, xliii (*PL* cxliv. 505); it is, however,

participation in wisdom. So the divine essence is uniform and of one manner in the greatest and in the smallest. Finally, as it is beyond comprehension on account of its vastness, so also it is indivisible on account of its simplicity. 'Let us understand God', says Augustine, 'in so far as we are able, as good without quality, great without size, the Creator without need, present without location, whole everywhere without place, eternal without time, changeless, making the changeable, suffering nothing.'[22] You swear, I believe, that you neither hold nor ever have held any other belief. Yet I too assert on my faith that I have held this in my heart even if my tongue has erred because it is slippery. For a simple thing avoids and rejects all addition, all consortium. To save you being troubled for a long time by ruminations, wondering where you have said this, you write in the sermon about Saint Victor: ' . . . in every case He is in the middle. For also in that essence of deity, the Son is the mediator between the Father and the Spirit.'[23] You ought now to recall that there is no mediator in the One, but God is one, Father and Son and Holy Spirit. But if somebody thinks the Spirit should be understood as created, not uncreated, because you have not added the word 'Holy', he is deeply ignorant of the ruling of Jerome on the meaning of this name: 'Where', he says, '"Spirit" is written without any addition in the Scriptures, "Holy Spirit" is rightly understood.'[24] But if this one who is understanding so, whom I have spoken of, disputes flatly what was said about the created spirit, no less an abuse will remain than that which has been shown above concerning the uncreated. For there is no one who understands by what reasoning He is said to be in the middle who, enclosing all things in His clenched hand, is without and within, below and above. You cry out that I have poured out my whole spirit. Why not? When I pour it out for you I am not pouring out but pouring in.[25]

attributed to Nicholas here, and the attribution noted in *PL* cxcvi. 1589, where Nicholas's other works appear. J. Lucchesi (ed.), *Sancti Petri Damiani Sermones*, *CCCM* lvii, omits this sermon.

[24] Cf. Jerome, *In Abacuc* i. 2. 19/20 (*CCSL* lxxvi. A. 616; *PL* xxv. 1306).

[25] The list of characters preserved in the Picard text is presumably a Clairvaux list. Arbois de Jubainville, *Abbayes cisterciennes*, has no prior Henry during Peter's lifetime. However, if the punctuation were changed, it could read: 'Priorem, dominum meum Henricum . . .' ('the prior [and] my lord Henry'). This could be a reference to Henry of France still at Clairvaux, which would put the letter before 1149 (see letter no. 21, n. 1), but this can not be certain, nor strictly would it affect the dating of other letters to Nicholas. Alternatively he could be the H. of letter no. 45. Ascelinus and Thomas are unidentified, but cf. also letter no. 45. Robert could be the R. of letters 46 and 47, but there is nothing to demonstrate this.

51
To Nicholas of Clairvaux[1]

1146 × 1152

Suo suus.

Vt perniciosum optimis telum inuidiam nostra[a] proscribat[b] epistola,[c] communis exorat caritas.[d] Satis namque superque [e]quod michi[e] scripsisti dulce, utile[f] et honestum fuit. Quid enim dulcius amore? Quid utilius diuinarum et humanarum rerum[2] subtili et compendiosa descriptione? [g]Quid honestius morum salubri informatione?[g] His nostrum torpens ingenium excitasti, causam non causandi de secularibus parumper prebuisti ac otiose sollicitudinis uela [h]relaxasti. Sic irrigant, inebriant et tranquillant scripta tua,[i] dulcissime, animam meam. Sterilitati denique ubertate, tumultuositati libera pausatione, occupationum insolentie renuntians ad remotiora secessione, Nicholai mei hoc[j] agi contestor scriptitatione. Deficiente ergo spiritu, manu trepidante, repugnante ingenio, grandiora presumo, pretempto[k] fortiora, uix explicabilia arripio. Vtrinque[l] enim spiritu uehementi[m] [3] ex quatuor uentis conglobato, cuius spei robore floris teneritudo non euanescat, pulchritudo non deficiat, uiror non emarcescat? Infidum est irato obuiare leoni, stultum[n] nichilominus emissam non declinare sagittam. 'Omnis armatura fortium'[4] tuis militat castris itaque congredi timeo. Nam cum propria satis armatura triumphare posses[o] quorumcunque[p] etiam potentissimorum arma mutasti ut superuinceres. Solo clipeorum aureorum fulgore deicior. Exclamo tamen: 'Pone non tua.' Nam plurimum intererit utrum maiestate [q]irrefragabili auctoritatis[q] philosophorum an propriarum rationum et sententiarum conspicuitate castra [r]nostra poteris[r] debellare. Tibi an illis

51 *O fos.* 140[v]–143[v], *Sirmond IV.* 1, *Picard* 53; *cf. Introduction, p.* liii, *and n.* 131.]
[a] uestra *O;* a suis finibus nostram *Picard* [b] proscribit *O* [c] epistolam *Picard* [d] *om. Picard* [e–e] quod *O;* michi quod *Picard* [f] michi *Picard* [g–g] Ista procul dubio continent epistole tue principia, media et ultima *Picard* [h] protensa *ins. Picard* [i] uestra *O* [j] hec *Picard* [k] pertento *Picard, with marginal note:* Alias pretento. [l] utrumque *O;* utcumque *Picard* [m] uehementia *Picard* [n] stultum est *O* [o] posset *Picard* [p] quorum que *O* [q–q] et irrefragabile auctoritate *O;* irrefragabile auctoritate *Picard* [r–r] uestra potius *Picard*

51 [1] On the date see letter no. 49, n. 1, and on the context, letter no. 50, n. 1 and appendix 7; this is a response to Nicholas of Clairvaux's letter 'Anxietatem michi generat . . .'.

51

To Nicholas of Clairvaux[1]

1146 × 1152

To his own from his own.

Common charity requires that our letter proscribe ill will, that dart baneful to the best of men. For that which you wrote to me was more than sufficiently sweet, profitable, and honourable. For what is sweeter than love? What is more profitable than a fine and succinct discussion of things divine and human?[2] What is more honourable than a salutary informing of dispositions? With these you have stirred up our sluggish mind, you have afforded a reason for not reasoning about secular concerns for a little while, and you have slackened the sails of futile concern. Thus, sweetest one, your words water, inebriate and pacify my soul. In fine, renouncing barrenness in favour of plenty, tumult in favour of an untrammelled respite, pressure of business in favour of retreat to higher things, I bear witness that this is caused by the frequent writing of my Nicholas. Therefore with a failing spirit, a trembling hand and a reluctant mind, I take on greater things, I attempt harder things, I grasp at things scarcely explicable. For pressed in on all sides by a vehement wind[3] from the four winds, what strength is there in the hope that the tenderness of the flower may not die away, its beauty not wane, its verdure not wither? It is unsafe to stand in the way of an angry lion, no less stupid not to turn aside from a discharged arrow. 'All the armour of valiant men'[4] serves your camp, and so I am afraid to engage. For while you could triumph well enough with your own armour, you have borrowed the arms of whatever others there might be, even of the most powerful, so that you might prevail. I am overcome by the brightness of the golden shields alone. I cry out, however: 'Lay down the arms that are not yours.' For it will make a great difference whether you will be able to overthrow our camp by the irrefutable might of the authority of the philosophers or by the distinction of your own reasons and opinions. It will be clear at once

[2] Cf. Cicero, *De amicitia*, vi. 20.
[3] Cf. Ps. 47 (48): 8 (on the image of four winds, see e.g. letter no. 35, n. 6).
[4] S. of S. 4: 4.

deputetur uictoria cum sine discriminis examinatione illorum uestigiis [s]procumbam uolens,[s] contra te autem[t] arma, sed [u]pacis, feram,[u] statim elucescet. Quid enim? Vera sint [v]falsa sint[v] philosophorum inattingibilia acumina cum ingeniorum nostrorum uis sola queritur quid nostra interest? Prorsus eorum cedo auctoritati. Non sic uero,[w] non[x] sic suffugiet[y] pupillam oculi mei quod egressum fuerit de labiis tuis. Iure suo priuari se[z] amicitia aliter conquereretur nisi res amicorum equo libramine discuteretur. Decursis itaque et discussis uernantis eloquentie tue[a] sermonibus et sensibus, iterum iterumque[b] tua reuoluens et mea euoluere gestiens, timeo sub luce uideri. Quid ergo? Periculum experiar? Sed non in filia.[5] Loquar? Sed utinam non inania. Reprehendam? Sed amici superflua. Laudabo? Sed philosophorum ingenia. Hinc tamen non progrediar nisi prius data manu initum [c]fuerit pactum prorsus[c] nequaquam irasci pro aliqua contumelia. Ingrediens itaque aggrediar non ueritatis domicilia subuertere sed amici, si qua est, et[d] propriam de preiacentibus uerborum diuersitatibus calumpniam arguere, et quibus potero auctoritatum[e] rationibus refellere.

Video autem in uestibulo et in fronte[6] epistole tue quod nimia formositate sui curiositatem oculorum meorum sic allicit ut uix eos [f]eicere et elicere[f] ualeam. Est enim quiddam cuius 'nomen super omne nomen',[7] cuius forma [g]formosior omni forma,[g] cuius statura et altitudo a fine superioris celi usque ad finem inferioris inferni.[8] Imago est inimitabiliter nata, non facta. Vnus est qui hanc de corde suo excogitauit et eructauit, non artifex huius sed omnium, huius autem[h] Pater. Huic conformari est reformari. Hanc loquentem et se exprimentem, aptis coloribus renitentem,[i] sceptro imperiali cuncta regentem, celicolas cum terrigenis in brachiis coniungentem inueni, adoraui et tenui. Decor eius inestimabilis, dulcedo insatiabilis, claritas inaccessibilis. Tam suaue [j]loqui de illa[j] quam admirabile amplecti illam. Ad hanc qui accedit aut uix aut nunquam recedit. Oculus non

[s–s] uolens procumbam *O, Picard* [t] an *O;* ante *Picard* [u–u] pacifera *Picard* [v–v] *om. Sirmond* [w] autem *Picard* [x] *om. O* [y] effugiet *Picard* [z] *om. Picard* [a] *om. Picard* [b] et iterum *Picard* [c–c] prorsus fuerit pactum *Picard* [d] *om. Sirmond* [e] auctoritatis *Picard* [f–f] elicere et eiicere ab isto intuitu ad penetralia interioris et ulterioris paradisi *Picard* [g–g] *om. O* [h] autem patet *O* [i] neruorum et uenarum uigore uigentem uultus uenustate ridentem *ins. Picard* [j–j] de illa loqui *Picard*

[5] i.e. it is too serious a matter to take a chance: cf. Terence, *Andria*, iii. 565–6 (33–4): 'Simo: "Qui scis ergo istuc, nisi periculum feceris?" | Chr: "At istuc periculum in filia fieri grauest."' (Loeb edn., J. Sargeaunt, trans.: 'Simo: "Well but how can you tell if you don't make the trial?" | Chr.: "But to make the trial in the case of a daughter is no light matter."')

whether the victory should be assigned to you or to them when I fall down willingly at their feet without questioning their argument but wield against you arms, but arms of peace. But what then? For of what benefit is it to us whether the unmatchable subtleties of the philosophers are true or false when the power of our minds alone is considered? I concede to their authority absolutely. Yet not so, not so will that which has come forth from your lips escape the pupil of my eye. Friendship would complain otherwise that it was deprived of its own right, if matters between friends were not discussed on an equal footing. Accordingly, having run through and analysed the words and opinions of your flourishing eloquence, repeatedly pondering yours and longing to unravel my own, I am afraid to show myself openly in the light. What then? Should I take a risk? But not where a daughter is concerned.[5] Should I speak? But I hope not empty words. Should I give a rebuke? But such things are unnecessary in a friend. Should I offer praise? But only to the minds of philosophers. However, I shall not go on from here unless an agreement be made first on a handshake not to be angry at all, henceforth, for any reproach. Entering the field therefore, I shall advance not to overturn the dwellings of truth but to prove to a friend his own fallacy, if it be so, from the foregoing inconsistencies, and to refute it with whatever arguments based on authorities I can.

But I see in the opening and first part[6] of your letter that which so entices the curiosity of my eyes by its excessive beauty that I am scarce able to disengage them and draw them away. For there is something of which the 'name is above all names,'[7] whose beauty is more beauteous than all beauty, whose stature and height reaches from the limit of the highest heaven to the bottom of the lowest hell.[8] This is an image inimitably born, not made. There is One who devised this and brought it forth from His heart, not the fashioner of this but of all things, but of this the Father. To be conformed with this is to be reformed. I have found, I have worshipped, and I have held to this image, speaking and expressing itself, resplendent with proper colours, ruling all things with imperial sceptre, uniting the heaven-dwellers with the earth-born in its arms. Its beauty is inestimable, its sweetness never sates, its splendour is unapproachable. It is as sweet to speak of as it is wonderful to embrace. He who approaches it scarcely or never draws back. The eye is not sated by seeing, nor the ear by

[6] Cf. *DML*, 2 *frons* 5a. He is comparing the opening of a letter to a beautiful face.
[7] Cf. Phil. 2: 9. [8] Cf. Ps. 138 (139): 8.

satiatur uisu nec auris auditu. 'Qui edunt me[k] adhuc esurient', etc.[9] Hec osculata est 'me[l] osculo oris sui'.[10] Hec digito manus sue tenens animam meam, uoce propria monuit[m] ne declinarem ab ea. Huiusmodi attractus et delinitus blanditiis,[n] an ulterius progrediendum sit hesito. Bonum enim est hic[o] esse.[11] Tandem uero innuente et annuente ut irem non discedens, redirem permanens, aliam uidi uisionem.[12] Rubus ardens in interiora deserti apparuit.[13] Suspensus intenta[p] cogitatione, 'Num',[q] inquam, 'sicut Moysi rubus ardebat et non consumebatur,[14] sic meus[r] iste reddit splendorem lucentem non calorem urentem?' Amici enim increpatio grata potius [s]correptio est[s] quam molesta exustio. [t]Est autem.[t] Vos uenator tam uerborum quam sensuum, et conclusum[u] retibus et percussum uenabulo credidistis. Hic enim[v] rubus ruborem ingerens, sed perfecte et solide caritatis robur nescienti. Oculus pupilli[w] pungeretur, uel etiam[x] compungeretur, si spina huiusmodi configeretur. Non uero contingat hoc oculo caritatis cuius solius est colligere immo producere rosam de spinis. Sic Iesus de spinis[y] passionis rosam protulit redemptionis. Annon eius imitatione et tu reddis bona pro malis,[15] qui mollia duris, dulcia amaris, uera retribuis uanis? Reuera tu simplex et domi habitans, ut dicis, in simplicitate cordis tui[16] scripsisti. Animaduerto igitur 'ad thronum gratie'[17] miro pennarum iuuamine te conuolasse, et ibi quia citra non repperisti, simpliciter simplicem Deum didicisse. Quero itaque anne simplicitatem tuam ab illo fonte reportaueris et [z]utrum tantum[z] transeundo quantum celicole manendo et stando exhauseris. Quod si fieri non potuit, constat non iniuriose inestimabiliter illorum tuam precellere simplicitatem, sicut et beatitudinem. Animam siquidem humanam naturaliter simplicem, angelorum uero naturam etiam[a] simpliciter simplicem, [b]celum quoque singulariter et ineffabiliter esse simplicem indubitabili fide[b] credo et confiteor. Quod ut euidentius appareat, uerba[c] nostra de simplicitate et[d] tua sub oculis compendiosa[e] adnotatione uolo colligere.

[k] *om. Sirmond, Picard* [l] caput meum *Picard* [m] *om. Sirmond* [n] blandius *Picard* [o] *om. Picard* [p] interdum attenta *Picard* [q] non *Picard* [r] mensis *O* [s–s] est correctio *Picard* [t–t] *om. Picard* [u] clausum *Picard* [v] *om. Picard* [w] pusilli *O, Picard* [x] *om. Picard* [y] spina *O, Sirmond, Picard* [z–z] utrum tamen *O;* utinam tantum *Picard* [a] et *Picard* [b–b] indubitabili fide *Sirmond;* indubitabiliter *Picard* [c] *om. Sirmond* [d] et nostra *O* [e] compendiosa hic *Picard*

[9] Ecclus. 24: 29: 'et qui bibunt me adhuc sitient'. [10] Cf. S. of S. 1: 1.

[11] Cf. Matt. 17: 4; Mark 9: 4; Luke 9: 33: Peter's words at the Transfiguration.

[12] The first of the two visions is of God's image, the second Nicholas's version (as

hearing. 'They that eat me shall yet hunger,' etc.[9] It has kissed 'me with the kiss of its mouth'.[10] This, holding my soul in the fingers of its hand, warned me with its own voice not to turn away from it. Led on and enticed by such allurements, I am hesitating as to whether I should go further. For it is good to be here.[11] But when finally it nodded and signed that I should go while not departing and return while standing still, I saw another vision.[12] There appeared a bush burning in the inner parts of the desert.[13] Deliberating in concentrated thought, 'Surely', I say, 'as Moses' bush burned and was not consumed,[14] does not mine offer a brilliant light rather than burning heat?' For the rebuke of a friend is a pleasing reproach rather than a grievous scorching. But it is so. You, the hunter of words as much as of meanings, have believed me both trapped in your snares and stuck by your spear. For this bush is one that brings shame, but only to one who does not know the power of perfect and solid love. The eye of the orphan would be stung or even goaded to remorse if it were pierced by a thorn of this type. But this could not happen to the eye of love, which alone has the ability to pluck, or rather to produce, a rose from thorns. Thus Jesus produced the rose of redemption from the thorns of the passion. Do you not also, in imitation of Him, return good things for evil,[15] you who return tender things for harsh, sweet things for bitter, true things for worthless? In truth, simple and living at home, as you say, you have written in the simplicity of your heart.[16] I observe therefore that you have flown up 'to the throne of grace'[17] with the wondrous help of wings, and there, because you did not find Him here below, you have learnt simply the simple God. And so I ask whether you have brought back your simplicity from that fountain, and whether you have drawn out as much in crossing over as the heaven-dwellers in remaining and standing there. But if that could not be, it is not unjustly established that their simplicity transcends yours inestimably, as also their blessedness. Indeed, I believe and confess with unshaken faith that the human soul is naturally simple, but that the nature of angels is even simply simple, and that heaven also is uniquely and ineffably simple. To make this clearer, I wish to gather together before your eyes, in a brief summary, our words and yours on the subject of simplicity.

conveyed by his subsequent arguments about the nature of God), which the image of the first vision allows Peter to see, but not to fall for. Both are reflected in Nicholas's letter.

[13] Cf. Exod. 3: 1–2. [14] Cf. Exod. 3: 2–3. [15] Echoing Rom. 12: 17.

[16] Cf. Gen. 20: 5; 3 Kgs. (1 Kgs.) 9: 4; Wisd. 1: 1; Acts 2: 46; Eph. 6: 5; Col. 3: 22.

[17] Heb. 4: 16; *didicisse* below, cf. Eph. 4: 20.

Dixi quia: Omnis res simpliciter simplex, una et unum est, non autem si[f] una, statim et simplex.[18] Simplex enim [g]respuit et refugit[g] omnem prorsus admixtionem.[19] Rem uero unam conuenientia duo simul uel plura aliquando faciunt, ut unum corpus constans ex quatuor elementis.[20] 'Ista', inquis, 'aut non intelligo aut uos minus [h]attenditis.' Malo me minus attendere[h] quam te non intelligere. Tamen parumper attende et de simplicitate si male sensi,[i] quia cepisti, iterum corrige. Interim ipse ut decet consignatam tuis exhibens reuerentiam sensibus et sermonibus, meos, etsi non uerba, sensus uallo ueritatis communiam fortius.[j] Omne igitur quod est, aut simplex aut compositum est.[21] Compositum autem aut substantiale aut[k] partiale: substantiale ueluti cum una substantia alii[l] substantie[m] iungitur, partiale cum unius substantie partes coniunguntur. Hoc autem compositum superiori[n] simplicius est. Illud uero ex toto et naturaliter dicitur simplum quod caret et substantiali et partiali compositione.[22] Anima itaque quia neque diuersarum substantiarum neque eiusdem substantie diuersarum partium in sese[o] suscipit coniunctionem, naturaliter est simplex. Non enim ex prius existente aliqua materia creata est ut respectu materiei sue composita dici possit, sicut in omni corpore[p] id quod factum est[q] respectu illius [r]de quo factum est compositum dicitur; respectu uero ⟨illius⟩[r] quod de eo factum est simplum;[22A] sed de nichilo facta catholice creditur. Angelica uero natura, quia hoc [s]habet amplius[s] quod nullis[t] subiacet [u]corruptionibus, quemadmodum anima ex coniunctione corporis,[u] liberius euolat ad secretissimos simplicitatis recessus. [v]'In hoc'[v] etiam fere 'omnes philosophi consentiunt quod[w] principium rerum est perfecta sapientia, lumen preclarum, substantia substantiarum, argumentum rerum uniuersarum.'[23] Id autem unum et simplex cuius simplicitas confert non aufert simplicitatem. Neque enim creature sue suam inuidet simplicitatem cui suam non negauit imaginem.[x] Eo igitur in arce vere et summe simplicitatis illocaliter locato rationalis

[f] et *Picard* [g–g] res refugit et respuit *Picard* [h–h] attenditis . . . intendere *O, Sirmond;* attendere *Picard* [i] sentio *Picard* [j] fortis *O* [k] est aut *Picard* [l] alteri *O* [m] *om. Picard* [n] superiore *Picard* [o] se *Picard* [p] opere *O;* tempore *Picard* [q] est dicitur *O, Sirmond* [r–r] *om. O, Sirmond* (*but necessary to the logic of the sentence*) [s–s] amplius habet *Picard* [t] nulli *Picard* [u–u] quemadmodum anima ex coniunctione corporis corruptionibus *Picard* [v–v] Inde *O* [w] et *O* [x] *Picard ends here*

[18] Letter no. 50, p. 208. [19] Cf. letter no. 50, p. 212.
[20] Letter no. 50, p. 210. (The four elements are earth, air, fire, water.)
[21] Cf. Gerbert of Aurillac, *De rationale et ratione uti*, vii (*PL* cxxxix. 162); Gilbert of La

I said that every thing that is simply simple is one and one thing, but if some thing is one, it is not also at once thereby simple.[18] For the simple rejects and avoids absolutely all admixture.[19] In truth, two or more things joining together at the same time sometimes do make one thing, like one body composed of four elements.[20] You say: 'Either I do not understand these matters or you pay less heed to them.' I would rather that I pay them less heed than that you not understand them. However, pay heed for a little while, and if I have misunderstood concerning simplicity, since you have grasped it, correct me again. Meanwhile I myself, showing a confirmed respect for your arguments and words as is proper, will more strongly fortify my arguments, if not my words, with a rampart of truth. Everything therefore which exists is either simple or compound.[21] But the compound is either substantial or partial: substantial, as when one substance is joined to another substance, partial when parts of one substance are joined together. This latter compound is simpler than the former. But only that which lacks both substantial and partial composition is said to be entirely and naturally simple.[22] And so the soul, because it sustains in itself the conjunction neither of different substances nor of different parts of the same substance, is naturally simple. For it is not created out of any pre-existing material, so that it can be called compound with regard to its matter, as, in every body, that which is made is said, in regard to that from which it is made, to be compound, but in regard to that which is made from it to be simple;[22A] but it is held, according to the Catholic faith, to be made out of nothing. Angelic nature however, because it has this in addition, that it is subject to no corruptions—as the soul is on account of union with the body—flies more freely up to the most secret retreats of simplicity. 'In this', moreover, almost 'all philosophers agree, that the origin of things is perfect wisdom, the splendid light, the substance of substances, the basis of everything.'[23] But that is one and simple whose simplicity confers, does not take away, simplicity. For He does not begrudge His simplicity to His creation, to whom He has not denied His image. The rational creation, therefore, participates in

Porrée, *Comm. in lib. de duabus nat.* (*PL* lxiv. 1380) (cf. also Isaac of Stella, *Sermo* xxi (Sources Chrétiennes, ccvii. 54; *PL* cxciv. 1759), possibly contemporary with this letter).

[22] Cf. Petrus Alfonsi, *Dialogi*, tit. i (*PL* clvii. 556): 'Omne corpus est compositum, omne autem compositum aut est substantiale aut partitiale: substantiale, ueluti cum una substantia alii iungitur; partitiale, cum unius substantie partes coniunguntur . . . Hoc autem compositum superiori simplicius est. Illud uero ex toto dicitur simplum, quod huius utriusque compositionis est expers.'

[22A] Cf. ibid.

[23] Cf. ibid. (*PL* clvii. 555).

participat creatura. Fiunt autem magis et minus simplicia magis et minus eo participantia. Ideo namque simplex, immo simplicitas simplicium, sicut Deus deorum in simplicitate iubet se querere,[24] cum simplicibus se dicit ambulare. Dat autem inuenire et habere si queratur quomodo iubet querere. Aliter querentibus, 'Queretis', inquit,[y] 'me et non inuenietis'.[25] Quia itaque nisi in simplicitate non inuenitur, simplicitate autem simplicem fieri non dubitatur, quicunque eum per simplicitatem inuenerit participatione eiusdem simplicitatis simplicior efficitur. Inequali autem proportione participantes inequaliter inueniuntur simplices. Ipsa autem simplicitas in se uera et summa est unitas. Sciendum uero quia, sicut aliud est participans, aliud participatum, sic etiam aliud simplex, aliud simplicitas. Nec habet lingua et ratio hominis, nescio si angeli, idem esse simplex et simplicitatem, sicut nec album et albedinem.

Noli, noli simplicitati[z] nostre, immo tue, risum insimulare. De Deo enim nichil[a] habes opponere cum quicquid ipse est legatur omnem sensum transcendere. Tamen quod bonus, quod pius, quod iustus, quod simplex dicitur, figuratiua locutione accipitur. Vt enim Plato ait, Deum inuenire difficile est, inuentum digne profari impossibile.[26] Nulla certe oratione, uel orationis parte, Deum potest aliquis describere uel definire.[b] Itaque de Deo nulla fiat oppositio quia ipse est omnium conclusio, nichilominus et exclusio. Ex eius stabili simplicitate sortitur ordinem, causas et formas, ut Boetius testatur, 'omnium generatio rerum, cunctusque mutabilium naturarum progressus, et quicquid aliquomodo mouetur'.[27] Eius natura 'in sue[c] simplicitatis arce composita' ⟨rebus⟩ regendis multiplicem modum[d] statuit.[28] Potius ergo bonitas ipse, et participatione eius creatura bona; potius pietas ipse, et consortio pietatis creatura pia; potius denique simplicitas, et possessione simplicitatis dicatur creatura simplex: eiusdem autem locutionis genere quo Deus iustus, et nos iustitia Dei[e] appellamur. Vide etiam utrum bona similitudine utatur Boetius

[y] *om.* *O* [z] simplicitate *O* [a] nil *O* [b] diffinire *O* [c] sua *Sirmond* [d] mouendum *O* [e] eius *O*

[24] Cf. Wisd. 1: 1. [25] John 7: 36.

[26] Cf. J. H. Waszink (ed.), *Timaeus a Calcidio translatus commentarioque instructus*, Plato Latinus, iv (London and Leiden, 1962), p. 21: 'Igitur opificem genitoremque uniuersitatis tam inuenire difficile quam inuentum impossibile digne profari.'

[27] Cf. Boethius, *De cons. philos.* iv. prose vi. 7 (*CCSL* xciv. 79). The translations of Boethius in this letter are reprinted by permission of the publishers and the Loeb Classical Library from *Boethius: The Theological Tractates, The Consolation of Philosophy*, translated by H. F. Stewart and E. K. Rand, revised by S. J. Tester, Cambridge, Mass.: Harvard University Press, 1918, revised 1973. This, the best known English translation, provides a

Him who is placed placelessly in the citadel of true and supreme simplicity. However they become more and less simple the more and less they participate in Him. And so therefore the simple One, nay the simplicity of the simple, like the God of gods, orders us to seek Him in simplicity[24] and says that He walks with the simple. But if He is sought in the way in which He orders us to seek, He imparts to us the way to find and to possess. To those who seek in another way, He says, 'You shall seek me and shall not find me'.[25] And so because He is not found except in simplicity, and because there is no doubt that one becomes simple through simplicity, whoever finds Him through simplicity is made more simple by participating in the same simplicity. Yet those participating in unequal proportions are found unequally simple. And that simplicity is the true and highest unity in itself. But it should be known that just as he who participates is one thing and that in which he participates another, so also the simple is one thing and simplicity another. Nor does man's tongue and reason hold—I do not know if an angel's do—that being simple and simplicity is the same thing, just as being white and whiteness are not.

Do not, I say, provoke mockery of our simplicity, nay of yours. For you can argue nothing about God since we read that whatsoever He is transcends all perception. However, that He is said to be good, loving, just, and simple is to be understood as figurative speech. For as Plato says, it is difficult to find God, impossible to speak of Him worthily when found.[26] Surely no one can describe or define God by any argument or part of speech. And so let there be no argument about God because He Himself is the conclusion of all things and no less the exclusion. 'The generation of all things, and the whole development of changeable natures, and whatever moves in any manner' is given its order, causes, and forms from His stable simplicity, as Boethius attests.[27] His nature 'firmly placed in the citadel of its own simplicity established the manifold manner in which all things behave'.[28] Rather therefore let Himself be called goodness, and creation good by participation in it; rather Himself love and creation loving by sharing in love; rather finally Himself simplicity and creation simple by possession of simplicity: and by that same type of speech by which God is called just, we too are called the justice of God. Consider also whether Boethius employs a good analogy to demonstrate not only

homogeneous rendering of the philosophical language. I have occasionally adapted the translations to fit Peter's use of Boethius' text.

[28] Cf. Boethius, *De cons. philos.* iv, prose vi. 8 (*CCSL* xciv. 79): '... multiplicem rebus regendis modum statuit.'

ad exprimendum non tantum simplicem aliquem fieri sed etiam simplicitatem ex strictissima connexione et societate simplicitatis. De prouidentia profecto et fato sic dicit: 'Prouidentia est ipsa illa diuina ratio in summo omnium principe constituta que cuncta disponit; fatum uero inherens rebus mobilibus dispositio, per quam prouidentia suis queque nectit ordinibus.'[29] Et post pauca: 'Manifestum est immobilem simplicemque gerendarum formam rerum esse prouidentiam, fatum uero eorum que diuina simplicitas gerenda disposuit mobilem nexum atque ordinem temporalem.'[30] Inducta itaque similitudine paulo post subdit: 'Nam ut orbium circa eundem cardinem sese uertentium[f] qui est intimus ad medietatis simplicitatem accedit ceterorumque extra locatorum ueluti[g] cardo quidam circa quem uersentur[h] existit; extimus uero maiore ambitu rotatus, quanto a puncti media indiuiduitate discedit tanto amplioribus spatiis explicatur; si quid uero illi se medio connectat[i] et societ, in simplicitatem cogitur diffundique ac diffluere cessat: simili ratione quod longius a prima mente discedit maioribus fati nexibus implicatur.'[31]

Medium quod ait, siue media indiuiduitas puncti,[32] intelligitur ueritas et simplicitas Dei. Quod enim huic amori consociatur, in simplicitatem cogitur. Diuine igitur superneque substantie quibus et iudicium perspicax et incorrupta uoluntas et efficax optatorum presto est potestas, quid est quare non inhereant illi summe et unice simplicitati? Coherent procul dubio et dotantur largiori simplicitatis priuilegio. An[j] ista recusas credere et paras contradicere? 'Nequaquam,' inquis, 'sed quod creatoris est, creature nolo attribuere.' Quare? Quia emularis Deum, sed non bona emulatione. Quantum enim desipit qui non a Deo collata munera propria usurpatione rapere presumit? Tantumdem a pietate resilit qui data negat, uel abscondit. 'Nos', inquit Apostolus, 'non spiritum huius mundi accepimus sed Spiritum qui ex Deo est ut sciamus que a Deo donata sunt nobis.'[33] Datum est enim omni corpori ut, sicut iam dictum est, compositione sit multiplex, anime ut, carens partibus, naturaliter sit simplex sed propter [k]limi[34] societatem[k] subiciatur uanitati que est multiplex.

[f] uertentem *O* [g] uelud *O* [h] uersantur *O* [i] coniectat *O*
[j] En *O* [k–k] finam felicitatem *O*

[29] Cf. ibid. 9 (*CCSL* xciv. 79). [30] Ibid. 13 (*CCSL* xciv. 80).
[31] Ibid. 15 (*CCSL* xciv. 80) [32] Cf. ibid.
[33] Cf. 1 Cor. 2: 12.
[34] Cf. Gen. 2: 7: 'the slime of the earth', from which man was created.

that someone becomes simple, but also that simplicity arises, from the closest connection and sharing in simplicity. About providence assuredly and fate he speaks thus: 'Providence is the divine reason itself, established in the highest ruler of all things, which disposes all things; but fate is a disposition inherent in movable things, through which providence binds all things together, each in its own proper ordering.'[29] And a little further on: 'It is clear that the unmoving and simple form of the way things are done is providence, and fate is the movable interlacing and temporal ordering of those things which the divine simplicity has disposed to be done.'[30] And having introduced the comparison he adds a little later: 'For just as, of a number of spheres turning about the same centre, the innermost one approaches the simplicity of middleness and is a sort of pivot for the rest which are placed outside it, about which they turn; but the outermost one, turning with a greater circumference, the further it is separated from the indivisibility of the central point the wider the spaces it spreads over; and if anything is joined or associated with that centre it is gathered into its simplicity and ceases to spread and diffuse itself: in a similar manner, that which is furthest separated from the principal mind is entangled in the tighter meshes of fate.'[31]

The middle of which he speaks, or rather the indivisibility of the central point,[32] is understood to be the truth and simplicity of God. For that which is joined to this love is impelled towards simplicity. How is it then that the divine and celestial substances, on which penetrating judgement, incorrupt will, and the effective power of prayers depend, do not inhere to that highest and unique simplicity? Doubtless they hold together and are endowed with the more abundant privilege of simplicity. Would you refuse to believe these things and prepare to contradict them? 'Not at all,' you say, 'but I do not wish to attribute to the creation that which pertains to the Creator.' How is this? For you emulate God, but not in a good way. For how foolish is he who presumes to seize by his own usurpation gifts not conferred by God? He leaps back as far from righteousness who denies that they were given, or conceals them. 'We', says the Apostle, 'have received not the spirit of this world but the Spirit that is of God, that we may know the things that are given us from God.'[33] For it has been given to every body, as we said just now, that it be manifold in composition, and to every soul that, lacking parts, it be naturally simple but on account of its union with slime[34] it be subject to vanity, which is manifold. Furthermore, it is

Supercelesti quoque indultum est creature[35] ut, ultra [l]sensum humanum[l] sed citra diuinum, et naturaliter et simpliciter sit simplex. Tu uero corpus multiplex asserens, animam quoque comparatione corporis non per se simplicem astruens, transuolas ad supercelestes et ex gratia non ex natura imitationem tantummodo simplicitatis indulges.[36] O nimium simplex! Forsitan enim angelus tuus hoc audiens irascitur et quod dona gratie et nature sue commutaueris indignatur. Nam ipse quidem nichil minores gratias agit creatori nature quam datori gratie. Gratia namque creatum, gratia beatificatum, gratia nouit se confirmatum. Ab eadem tamen gratia aliud in creatione, aliud meminit se accepisse in beatificatione siue in confirmatione. Quod accepit in creatione dona sunt nature, quod meruit in confirmatione dona uocantur gratie.[m] Igitur aut multiplex est angeli natura, quod soli conuenit corpori, aut simplex,[n] quod tantum spiritui. Quia autem nullum tertium est, simplex, ut estimo, concedas necesse est. Simplex itaque cum sit natura, et uicinitate, ut ostensum est, ipsius summe simplicitatis artius exprimatur et imprimatur in eo radius simplicitatis, non iam tantum simplex est sed simpliciter, ut opinor, simplex. Ministrando namque indefesse[o] assistit et adheret diuine simplicitati. Ipsa autem diuina simplicitas non naturaliter tantum, non simpliciter tantum, sed singulariter[p] et ineffabiliter simplex est. Iam credo satisfactum est[q] quare dixerim 'omnis res simpliciter simplex', uel quare[r] dicere potuerim.

Quod autem sequitur, 'una et unum,' est inculcatio uerborum.[s] Tamen, ut uel tenuiter sic distinguam, una profecto est quia, ut Seneca testatur, diuinorum una est natura et nichil est diuino diuinius, celesti celestius, et Boetius, quia eorum eadem est substantia quorum diuersus effectus non est.[37] Vnum iccirco, quia natura simplicium indissolubilis, diuersarum pluralitatem partium ad sui efficentiam non admittit. Quod enim ex diuersis partibus compositum est naturaliter solubile est. Omne autem simplex et incompositum unum est et caret partibus resolutionis. Quecunque igitur substantia tam simplex est et una prorsus non admiscetur, neque cum alia simplici et incorporea, neque cum multiplici et

[l–l] humanum sensum *O*   [m] *om. O*   [n] multiplex *O*   [o] *om. Sirmond*
[p] simpliciter *O*   [q] *om. O*   [r] quia *O*

[35] i.e. angels.

[36] Cf. Nicholas of Clairvaux, letter no. LXV, in the numbering system of *PL* ccii. at col. 502.

granted to the supercelestial creation[35] that, being beyond human perception but below the divine, it be simple both naturally and simply. But you, asserting that the body is manifold and arguing also that the soul is simple not in itself but in comparison with the body, flit on to the supercelestial beings and grant them a mere imitation of simplicity by grace not by nature.[36] O far too simple! Perchance your angel, hearing this, is growing angry, and is indignant that you have switched around the gifts of grace and of his nature. For he himself gives no less thanks to the Creator of nature than to the Giver of grace. For he knows that he was created, blessed and confirmed by grace. He recalls, however, that he received from the same grace one thing in being created, another in being blessed or confirmed. What he received in creation are the gifts of nature, what he earned in being confirmed are called the gifts of grace. Therefore either the nature of the angel is manifold, which applies to the body alone, or simple, which applies only to the spirit. Since there is no third alternative, you must concede, I believe, that it is simple. And so since the angel's nature is simple, and since the ray of simplicity is more straitly expressed and stamped on him, as has been shown, by proximity to the highest simplicity itself, he is now not only simple but, as I think, simply simple. For he is at hand tirelessly to serve and adheres to divine simplicity. And divine simplicity is not only naturally and simply, but uniquely and ineffably, simple. Now I believe I have satisfactorily shown why I said, and why I could say, 'every thing that is simply simple'.

Now that which follows, 'is one and one thing,' is a reinforcement of the words. However, to make even this slight distinction, it is assuredly one (*una*) because, as Seneca testifies, the nature of divine things is one (*una*), and nothing is more divine than the divine, more heavenly than the heavenly, and as Boethius also says, because those things have the same substance whose effect is not different.[37] The one (*unum*), because the nature of simple things is indissoluble, does not therefore admit to its effective power the plurality of different parts. For that which is composed of different parts is by nature soluble. But everything which is simple and not a compound is one (*unum*) and does not have parts which can be dissolved. Therefore whatever substance is simple in this way and single (*una*) is absolutely not mixed, neither with another simple and incorporeal substance nor with a multiple and corporeal

[37] Cf. Seneca, *Ad Lucil. ep. mor.* lxvi, 11–12; and cf. Boethius, *De cons. philos.* iii. prose xi. 9 (*CCSL* xciv. 57).

corporea. Nam ubicunque et quotienscunque substantie immiscentur necesse est ut in[t] se inuicem [u]commutentur et transformentur.[u] Rerum enim quarumlibet coniunctio nisi in sese transfundantur et a propria forma transformentur[v] copulatio uel[w] adiunctio uel aliquid huiusmodi, non autem admixtio uel commixtio, [x]dicitur proprie.[x] Vnde et Verbum assumptione carnis et indisiuncta unione caro factum, ne substantiarum transfusio, scilicet carnis in diuinitatem annihilatio uel diuinitatis in carnem substantialis exinanitio, ab hereticis persuaderentur, non commixtionem passum dicitur, et ne rursum alius Dei alius hominis Filius[y] crederetur, et una in duas personas diuideretur, illico sequitur, neque diuisionem. Si noua et ideo cassa me confingere[z] arbitraris, et uera et uetera statim si placet subiunctis rationibus comprobabis.

'Non', inquit Boetius, 'omnis in omnem rem uerti ac transmutari potest. Nam cum substantiarum alie sint corporee, alie incorporee, neque corporea in incorpoream, [a]neque incorporea[a] in eam que corpus est mutari potest, nec uero incorporea in se inuicem proprias formas mutant; sola enim mutari transformarique in se possunt que habent unius materie commune subiectum, neque hec omnia, sed ea que in se et facere et pati possunt. Idque probatur hoc modo: neque enim potest es in lapidem mutari, nec idem es in herbam; nec quodlibet aliud corpus in quodlibet aliud transfigurari potest nisi et eadem sit materia rerum in sese transeuntium et a se et facere et [b]pati possint,[b] ut cum uinum et aqua miscentur, utraque enim sunt talia que actum [c]et passionem sibi[c] communicent. Potest enim aque qualitas a uini qualitate aliquid pati. Atque iccirco, si multum quidem fuerit aque, uini uero paululum, non dicuntur immixta, sed alterum alterius qualitate corrumpitur. Si quis enim uinum fundat in mare, non mixtum est uinum mari, sed in mare corruptum, iccirco quod qualitas aque multitudine sui corporis nichil passa est a qualitate uini, sed potius in se ipsam uini qualitatem propria multitudine commutauit. Si uero sint mediocres, sibique equales, uel paulo inequales nature, que a se facere et pati possunt, ille miscentur, et mediocribus inter se qualitatibus temperantur. Atque

[s] uerborum est *O* [t] *om.* *O* [u–u] commutent et transforment *O* [v] transformantur *O* [w] et *O* [x–x] proprie dicitur *O* [y] *om.* *O* [z] fingere *O* [a–a] *om.* *O* [b–b] pati possit *O;* poti possint *Sirmond* [c–c] sibi et passionem *O*

one. For wherever and however often substances are mingled, they must needs be changed and transformed into one another. For the conjunction of any things, unless they are poured into one another and are transformed from their own form, is rightly said to be a coupling or conjunction or something of that sort, but not a mixture or mingling. Whence the Word made flesh by assumption of flesh and by indissoluble union is said not to have suffered mingling, lest a transformation of substances (that is to say, annulment of flesh into divinity, or substantial emptying out of divinity into flesh) be advocated by heretics; nor again, it follows from this, is it said to have suffered division, lest there be held to be one Son of God and another Son of man, and one person be divided into two. If you reckon that I am fabricating novelties and therefore vanities, you will assent at once, if it please you, to truths and ancient words, coupled with rational arguments.

'Not everything', says Boethius, 'can be changed and transformed into everything else. For since some substances are corporeal and others incorporeal, neither can a corporeal substance be changed into an incorporeal, nor can an incorporeal be changed into that substance which is body, nor yet incorporeals interchange their proper forms; for only those things can be interchanged and transformed which possess the common substrate of the same matter, nor can all of these so behave, but only those which can act upon and be acted on by each other. Now this is proved as follows: copper cannot be converted into stone nor indeed can the same copper be changed into grass, and no body can be transformed into any other body unless the things which pass into each other have a common matter and can act upon and be acted on by each other, as when wine and water are mingled, for both are of such a nature as to allow reciprocal action and influence. For the quality of water can be influenced in some degree by that of wine. And therefore if there be a great deal of water but very little wine, they are not said to be mingled, but the one is brought to nothing by the quality of the other. For if anyone pours wine into the sea the wine is not mingled with the sea but is brought to nothing by the sea simply because the quality of the water owing to its bulk has been in no way affected by the quality of the wine, but rather by its own bulk has changed the quality of the wine into water. But if the natures which are capable of reciprocal action and influence are in moderate proportion and equal or only slightly unequal, they are really mingled and form a mixture with the qualities which are in moderate relation to each other.

hec quidem in corporibus, neque omnibus sed tantum que a se, ut dictum est,[d] facere et pati possunt, communi atque eadem materia subiecta. Omne autem corpus quod in generatione atque corruptione subsistit communem uidetur habere materiam, sed non omne ab omni uel in omni uel facere aliquid uel pati potest. Corporea uero in[e] incorporea nulla ratione poterunt permutari quoniam nulla communi materia subiecta participant que susceptis qualitatibus in alterutrum permutetur. Omnis enim natura incorpore substantie nullo materie nititur fundamento, nullum uero corpus est cui non sit materia subiecta. Quod cum ita sit, cumque ne ea quidem que communem materiam naturaliter habent in se transeant nisi illis adsit potestas in se et a se faciendi ac patiendi, multo magis in se non permutantur[f] quibus non modo [g]communis materia[g] non est [h]sed cum[h] alia res materie[i] fundamento nititur ut corpus, alia omnino materia subiecta non egeat ut incorporeum. Non igitur fieri potest ut corpus in incorporalem speciem permutetur, nec uero fieri potest ut incorporalia in[j] sese commixtione aliqua permutentur. Quorum enim communis nulla materia est nec in se uerti ac permutari queunt. Nulla autem in incorporalibus[k] materia rebus. Non poterunt igitur in se inuicem admisceri uel permutari.'[38]

Iure igitur simplex res refugit omnem commixtionem quia nullam in quamlibet creaturam recipit commutationem. Item quod a nobis ponitur sumptum a nobis: [l]rem autem unam duo simul uel plura conuenientia aliquando in sese recipere[l] et conuertere ut unum sint. In exemplari quod manibus meis scripsi sic habetur: 'Rem uero unam conuenientia duo uel plura aliquando faciunt, ut corpus unum constans ex quatuor elementis.'[39] Hic nullius cauillationis locum aliquatenus animaduerto et ideo respondere parco. Itemque intulisse me scribis Deum magis proprie ex simplicitate quam unitate.[40] Miror calumpniam. Nonne enim statim subiunxi nichil de Deo proprie dici? Iam quia, mi dilectissime, dulcedo uiscerum meorum, lumen amicorum meorum, pro me satisfeci, epistole tue sententias quasdam digna inuectione corrigendas et lima correptionis explanandas[m] reperi.

[d] est et *O* [e] uel *O*, *Sirmond* [f] permutentur *O* [g–g] materia communis *O* [h–h] sicut *O* [i] *om.* *O* [j] *om.* *O* [k] corporalibus *O* [l–l] duo simul uel plura conuenientia aliquando in se concipere reuertere *O*

[38] Cf. Boethius, *Contra. Eut.* vi. 18–72 (H. F. Stewart, E. K. Rand and S. J. Tester eds, *Boethius. The Theological Tractates. The Consolation of Philosophy*, Loeb Classical Library, rev. edn. (Cambridge, Mass., 1973), pp. 109–13; on the trans, see n. 27 above).

[39] Letter no. 50, p. 210 (here omitting *simul*); also quoted above, see n. 20.

This indeed takes place in bodies but not in all bodies, but only in those, as has been said, which are capable of reciprocal action and influence, having the same common material substrate. For every body which subsists in conditions of birth and decay seems to possess a common matter, but every body is not capable of reciprocal action and influence on and by every other. But bodies will not be able in any way to be changed into incorporeals because they do not share in any common material substrate which might be changed into this or that thing by taking on its qualities. For the nature of no incorporeal substance rests upon a material basis, but there is no body that has not matter as a substrate. Since this is so, and since not even those things which naturally have a common matter pass over into each other, unless they have the power of acting on each other and being acted upon by each other, far more do those things not suffer interchange which not only have no common matter but are different since one of them, being body, rests on a basis of matter, while the other, being incorporeal, cannot possibly stand in need of a material substrate. It is therefore impossible for a body to be changed into an incorporeal species, nor is it ever possible for incorporeals to be changed into each other by some process of mingling. For things which have no common matter cannot be changed and converted one into another. But incorporeal things have no matter. They will never therefore be able to be mingled or changed about among themselves.'[38]

Justly therefore a simple thing avoids all mixture because it admits no alteration into any created matter. What we set down next is taken from our own words: that two or more things joining together at the same time sometimes receive one thing into themselves and change it so that they are one. In the copy which I wrote with my own hands it goes thus: 'In truth, two or more things joining together sometimes do make one thing, like one body composed of four elements.'[39] On this point I see no room anywhere for criticism, and so I forbear to reply. Again, you write that I have implied that God is more properly derived from simplicity than from unity.[40] I am amazed at this calumny. Did I not add immediately that nothing can be said of God properly? Now since, my dearest one, sweetness of my heart, light of my friends, I have given satisfaction for myself, I have found certain opinions in your letter which must be corrected with proper criticism and smoothed with the file of reproof.

[40] Nicholas of Clairvaux, letter no. LXV, in the numbering system of *PL* ccii. at col. 503.

Quid dicis, amor? Placetne quod loquor? Gratiamne tuam persequor? Quoduis iube, et faciam. Clauem oris mei custodi ne lesio prorumpat amici. Constringe fauces maxillarum ne profluant iocos Sirenarum. Aperi tamen aliquando labia ut excludam grauamina mea. Nicholaus enim tuus, immo noster, gratias superuacuas agit gratie,[41] ut asserit, mee, 'quia uerba', inquit, 'nostra uel ex parte recipitis,[n] receditis autem in omnibus a Claudiano'.[o] [42] Iudica, iudica[p] iudicium meum, amor, iuste. Quid enim? Pene neruorum et uenarum fila nimie inflationis protensione intensa rumpuntur. Protestando iurant et contestantur intellectus, ratio, et memoria, falsum contra se latum testimonium. Vix patientiam persuadeo. Amicus est, inquies, facetus, lepido iocorum sermone urbanus. Sine itaque et disceptatione inextricabilem laberintum rationibus suis intexentem, et nunc quidem qua egreditur introeuntem, nunc uero qua[q] ingreditur exeuntem, sustine; complicata eius explica, male explicata replica. O dulcissime, dormiebas quando epistolam nostram legebas? Forte eras occupatus et ideo non es culpandus. In hoc tamen inexcusabiliter culparis, quod gratiarum tuarum nimium prodigus, dum male locas perdis. Illas [r]enim meas[r] gratias ubi deprehendisti quibus ingratiose gratias agis? Sed quid miror te mirabili et inaudita nouitate gratiam que non est gratia asserere, cum mutandi et permutandi rerum et uerborum proprietates auctoritate iam pristina ceperis pollere? Quid non faciat Nicholaus qui[s] de nigro factus est albus?[43] Credo, ista ductus et edoctus auctoritate, uerba quoque et sensus uerborum presumis quandoque inuertere. Nigredinem tamen pristinam sompniasti ubi me a Claudiano[t] dissentire notasti. Nempe sermonibus adquieui et adquiesco tuis, in parte contradixi[u] et contradico. Vbi enim corpus uiuere, animam uiuam, Deum uitam esse negaui? Nusquam, crede michi, nusquam. Tantummodo enim assignationes proprietatum quas subiunxisti, 'uiuens', uidelicet, 'ex uanitate, uiuum

[m] explanandas partim contemplandas *Sirmond* [n] recepistis *O* [o] Claudio *O* [p] *om.* *O* [q] quo *O* [r–r] meas enim *Sirmond* [s] enim nisi *O* [t] Claudio *O* [u] contradixisti *Sirmond*

[41] Cf. John 1: 16, and Nicholas of Clairvaux, letter no. LXV, in the numbering system of *PL* ccii. at col. 501: 'Gratias enim gratie uestre, quia uerba uestra [*leg.* nostra] uel ex parte recipitis receditis autem in omnibus a Claudiano'. Here and below Peter picks up Nicholas's use of John 1: 16 ('gratiam pro gratia'), complaining that his thanks are misplaced as he has misunderstood Peter. The word play does not translate.

[42] Cf. ibid. (the *nostra* here must be right and the *uestra* in *PL*'s edn. of the original

What do you say, love? Does what I say please you? Do I not seek your favour? Command what you will and I shall do it. Guard the key of my mouth lest anything injurious to a friend should burst forth. Bind the opening of the jaws lest they pour forth the frivolities of the Sirens. Yet open my lips once so that I may shut out my grievances. For your Nicholas, nay ours, gives superfluous thanks for our favours,[41] as he terms them, 'because', he says, 'you accept our words at least in part, but differ in all respects from Claudianus Mamertus'.[42] Judge, love, judge my judgement justly. For what is this? The threads of nerves and veins are nearly bursting with the intense tension of excessive swelling. Understanding, reason, and memory declare and testify unanimously that false witness has been brought against them. I persuade them to be patient only with difficulty. The friend, you will say, is facetious, witty, with a charming speech full of pleasantries. Let it be so therefore, and put up with him as he weaves an inextricable labyrinth with disputation by his reasonings, now entering where he leaves but now leaving where he enters; unravel his complexities, fold again that which has been unfolded badly. O sweetest one, were you sleeping when you were reading our letter? Perhaps you were occupied and so you are not to blame. You are, however, inexcusably culpable in this, that being excessively lavish with your thanks you waste them when you bestow them badly. For where did you seize upon those favours of mine for which you give thanks most ungraciously? But what wonder is it that you, with wondrous and unheard-of novelty, call a favour that which is not a favour, since you have begun to be mighty in ancient authority, to change and transform the properties of things and words? What may Nicholas not do, who from being black was made white?[43] I believe that, led on and led forth by this authority, you presume sometimes to invert words and the senses of words. However, you dreamt your old blackness when you indicated that I dissented from Claudianus Mamertus. To be sure, I have assented and I do assent to your words; in part I have contradicted and I do contradict them. For where did I deny that the body is living, the soul alive, God life? Nowhere, believe me, nowhere. For I began to find fault only as regards the assignations of properties which you added, that is 'living derives from vanity, being alive from simplicity, life

wrong: see previous note). On their arguments over the interpretataion of Claudianus Mamertus' *De statu anime*, see letter no. 50 and appendix 7.

[43] Nicholas had transferred from the Benedictines to the Cistercians.

ex simplicitate, uitam ex unitate,'[44] aggressus sum reprehendere. Scd monachum illum qui cum amico in epistole tue principio[45] contendebat et reticens, has iam pre tedio emittere audio uoces. 'Vtilius', inquit amor, 'claustra oris continuissemus quam rescribendo tot exundantium impetus torrentum incurrissemus. Redundant enim torrentes uanitatis et distillant ab ore amici nostri sermones superflue garrulitatis. Totus profluit et pereffluit.[46] Silentia nostra confundit, consuetudinis nostre morem et ordinem conturbat et concutit, ad pomposa et superflua queque improbitate sua, si adquieuerimus, prouocat et attrahit.' Deinceps itaque[v] noli scribere.

52

To the community of Mont-Dieu[1]

*c.*1145 × 1162

Dominis et patribus suis de Monte Dei frater [a]Petrus Cellensis,[a] dulcedinem gratie quam repromisit Deus diligentibus se.

'Exultat spiritus meus in Deo salutari meo'[2] tum quia uidere et audire uos[b] uel semel merui tum quia familiaritatis gratiam, gratia superna largiente, inueni. Accedit huic[c] beatitudini mee dulce adinuicem commercium litterarum unde et amaritudinibus meis mitigatiuum paratur electuarium,[d] et inquietudini sopitiuum[e] medicamentum, et hebitudini non mediocre eruginamentum. Denique quotiens formam et uultum inspicio sermonum uestrorum, magna uirtute ueneniferos morsus euado rugientium curarum, inundationes contempero influentium occupationum, assultus reprimo internarum et ueternarum inimicitiarum. Placet sensus profunditas, dictorum

[v] itaque iam *O*

52 *O fos. 116^r–118^v, Val fos. 110^v–113^r, Sirmond III. 2*]
[a–a] G. *O* [b] nos *Val* [c] hinc *Sirmond* [d] lectuarium *O, Val* [e] sopotiuum *Val*

[44] Cf. letter no. 50, pp. 206, 208; i.e. Peter does not dissent from Claudianus Mamertus, but only from Nicholas's additions. Cf. Claudianus Mamertus, *De statu anime*, iii. 6. 2: 'Corpus est uiuens, anima uiua, Deus est uita' (*CSEL* xi. 162–4; *PL* liii. 766); the rest is Nicholas's extrapolation (Nicholas, letter LXIII, in the numbering system of *PL* ccii, at col. 493); see also appendix 7.

[45] A reference to the opening of Nicholas of Clairvaux's letter no. LXV, in the numbering system of *PL* ccii, at col. 498, where Nicholas describes his struggle between

from unity'.[44] But that monk in the first part of your letter[45] who was struggling with a friend in silence, I hear now letting forth these cries out of weariness. 'We would have more profitably drawn closed the lock of the mouth', says love, 'than have rushed against such a fury of overflowing torrents by responding. For torrents of vanity flow forth and speeches of excessive garrulousness pour from the mouth of our friend. The whole flows forth and drains away.[46] It confounds our peace, it disturbs and strikes at our habitual custom and order, it calls forth and draws towards all pompous and empty things by its mischievousness, if we let it.' And so please write no more.

52

To the community of Mont-Dieu[1]

*c.*1145 × 1162

To his lords and fathers of Mont-Dieu, brother Peter of Montier-la-Celle, the sweetness of grace which God has promised in return to those who love Him.

'My spirit rejoices in God my saviour'[2] both because I have deserved to see and to hear you at least once and again because I have found the grace of friendship bestowed by the celestial grace. To this my blessedness is added the sweet mutual exchange of letters, whence a soothing medicine is prepared for my bitter sorrows, a soporific drug for my disquiet, and a considerable polish for my dullness. Then, as often as I contemplate the form and aspect of your words, I evade by their great power the venomous bites of clamant cares, I temper the floods of preoccupations pouring in, I curb the assaults of internal and ancient enmities. Pleasing is the depth of

the duties of religion and those of friendship: 'Anxietatem michi generat et scribere et non scribere uobis; in altero leditur amicitia, in altero propria conscientia . . .' etc.

[46] Cf. the end of letter no. 50, where the image is the opposite.

52 [1] Mont-Dieu (Carthusian, dioc. Reims, nr. Signy in the Ardennes, Cott. ii. 1894, and see Aniel, *Maisons de Chartreux*, pp. 84–7) was evidently a favourite retreat of Peter's, but neither the number nor the dates of his visits can be determined. The house was founded in 1132 by Abbot Odo of Saint-Remi (see also C. H. Talbot, 'Odo of Saint-Remy: A friend of Peter the Venerable', in *Petrus Venerabilis 1156–1956*, ed. G. Constable and J. Kritzeck, *Studia Anselmiana*, xl (1956), 21–37, at pp. 31–2, which however gives 1137, the date of the earliest charter). Peter's confirmation of its rights is preserved in Le Couteulx, ii. 284–5.

[2] Cf. Luke 1: 47.

ueritas, morum informatio, errorum redargutio, amputatio uanitatum, condempnatio ambitionum. Plus medulle farine, minus corticis et furfuris habent. Facile ex his perpendi potest quid in se de se anima religiosa sentiat, quid supra se de creatore suo obstupescat, quid infra se de peregrinatione mundi et temptatione carnis pertimescat. Plane ad seipsam conuersa conturbatur, ad factorem suum suspensa dilatatur, ad corpus reuersa confunditur. Quid enim corpus nisi terra inanis?[3] Quid anima nisi abyssus impenetrabilis? Quid Deus nisi lux incomprehensibilis? Igitur ut caro sterilis et infecunda impregnetur, ieiuniis et uigiliis affligatur; ut anima tetra et tenebrosa clarificetur, pristinis uitiis et phantastica ignorantia exuatur. Caro abstinendo fiat paradisus deliciarum,[4] anima orando et contemplando efficiatur serenissimum celum. Custos et operator paradisi deputetur ratio, protector et inhabitator anime ipsius creator. Adhibeatur corpori diligens disciplina ne tanquam puer immaturus in perniciem sui immaniter[f] efferatur, cultura impendatur ne uelut ager neglectus mala prole urticarum inutiliter occupetur,[5] uomere et sarculo conscindatur[g] et bono semine impleatur. Nam huius nature est hoc corpus ut quo magis opprimitur eo amplius multiplicetur.[5A] Terra huius carnis, nisi aratro discipline conuulsa fuerit, quasi clausa uulua inutilis erit. At ubi fortiter concussa uel conscissa semen Domini exercituum[6] exceperit, germinare secundum genus suum[7] incipiet.[h] Denique secundo uulnerata tanquam gladio ancipiti,[8] amore uidelicet et timore, uberes fructus iustitie, largissimas aquas interne compunctionis, immo sanguinem et aquam in redemptionem [i]preuaricationum suarum[i] et emundationem originalium delictorum, in uitam eternam saliendo[9] profluit. Atteratur itaque contritione ualida ne insolescat et pro frumento bonorum operum 'spinas et tribulos'[10] desideriorum malignorum afferat. Fodiatur, immo confodiatur, lancea Saluatoris ne animam in sepulcro uitiorum defossam eternis addicat incendiis. Duobus funiculis Dauid admetiatur, uno ad mortificandum, uno[j] ad uiuificandum,[11] ut quod nature est conseruetur et quod uitii destruatur. Sic, sic quantumcunque lapidosa, fiet mollis et tenera,

[f] *om. Val, Sirmond* [g] scindatur *O* [h] incipit *O, Val* [i–i] suarum preuaricationum *O* [j] alio *O, Val*

[3] Cf. Gen. 1: 2. [4] Alluding to Ezek. 28: 13. [5] Cf. Prov. 24: 30–1.
[5A] Cf. Exod. 1: 12. [6] Cf. 1 Kgs. (1 Sam.) 1: 3, 11; 4: 4.
[7] Cf. Gen. 1: 11, 12, 24. [8] Cf. Judg. 3: 16; Ps. 149 (149): 6; Heb. 4: 12.
[9] The imagery here combines allusions to John 4: 14 and 19: 34; the water of life everlasting of Christ and the blood and water from Christ's side at the crucifixion.
[10] Gen. 3: 18; cf. Heb. 6: 8. [11] Cf. 2 Kgs. (2 Sam.) 8: 2.

understanding, the truth of the words, the informing of conduct, the refutation of errors, the cutting out of vanities, the condemnation of ambitions. They contain more of the finest flour, less of the husk and the chaff. From these one can easily weigh what the devout soul perceives in itself about itself, what it wonders at above itself concerning its Creator, what it fears below itself concerning the pilgrimage through the world and the temptation of the flesh. Clearly the soul turned in on itself is thrown into confusion, raised up to its maker it is enlarged, turned back to the body it is confounded. For what is the body if not empty earth?[3] What is the soul if not an impenetrable abyss? What is God if not light incomprehensible? Therefore, so that sterile and barren flesh be made fruitful, let it be afflicted with fasts and vigils; so that the foul and dark soul be made light, let it be stripped of its ancient vices and superstitious ignorance. Let the flesh become the paradise of pleasures[4] through abstinence, let the soul be made the calmest heaven through prayer and contemplation. Let reason be appointed guardian and labourer of paradise, let its Creator be the protector and inhabitant of the soul. Let careful discipline be applied to the body lest like an immature boy it be puffed up excessively to its own undoing; let it be subject to cultivation lest like a neglected field it be taken over wastefully by the base progeny of nettles;[5] let it be torn up by the ploughshare and the hoe and filled with good seed. For this body is of this nature, that the more it is oppressed the more fully it is increased.[5A] The earth of this flesh will be useless, just like a closed womb, unless it is turned over by the plough of discipline. But when, having been struck powerfully or torn open, it has received the seed of the Lord of hosts,[6] it will begin to bring forth according to its kind.[7] Then wounded twice as if with a two-edged sword,[8] that is by love and by fear, springing up into life everlasting, it pours forth the plentiful fruits of justice, the most abundant waters of inner compunction, nay the blood and water[9] for the redemption of its transgressions and the cleansing of its original sins. Let it be worn down then by powerful contrition lest it grow haughty and bring forth 'thorns and thistles'[10] of malicious desires in place of the fruit of good works. Let it be pierced, nay pierced through, by the Saviour's spear lest it sentence to eternal flames the soul, buried in the tomb of vices. Let David measure with two lines, one to put to death, one to save alive,[11] so that that which comes from nature may be conserved and that which comes from vice be destroyed. Thus, thus, however stony, it shall be made soft and

quantumcunque salsuginis plena, fiet dulcis et bona. Fiet, inquam, de benedictionibus celi frugifera, fiet quasi 'horti iuxta fluuios irrigui',[12] quasi 'areole consite a pigmentariis',[13] quasi mons coagulatus et pinguis,[14] tanquam uallis nemorosa,[15] uelut terra sancta et uberrima. De hac solummodo oritur ueritas, in hanc iustitia de celo prospicit, hanc inhabitat et inambulat[k] sanctitas. Ferrum de hac tollitur;[16] 'malleus uniuerse terre'[17] et securis suggestionis diabolice in hac[l] non auditur.[18] Hec terra benedictioni proxima est. Hec, inquam, accipit tanquam lac [m]diuinorum uberum[m] primam benedictionem in iustificatione, secundam in glorificatione. 'Omnis' igitur, [n]iuxta Apostolum, 'qui[n] lactis est particeps',[19] uelut ab uberibus materne gratie, exugat ab ista lac sanctificationis, ab illa consolationis. Hoc enim est quod ait Apostolus: 'Habetis fructum [o]uestrum in sanctificationem,[o] finem uero uitam eternam.'[20] Sic, sic uiuitur, et in talibus uita spiritus. Sic uiuunt paruuli tui, Domine Deus, ab ubere presentis uisitationis, sic ab ubere future expectationis. Hec duo 'sicut duo hinnuli capree gemelli'[21] quia ex habundantia diuine iam prelibate dulcedinis et ex indubitata[p] certitudine sequentis remunerationis, iam ad Deum, sicut ceruus, inequalitatem aduersitatum transcurrimus, iam 'super montes aromatum,'[22] mundarum orationum, pre alacritate transsilimus, exclamantes cum Apostolo quia 'non sunt condigne passiones huius temporis ad futuram[q] gloriam que reuelabitur in nobis'.[23] Cuiusmodi autem [r]lac, fratres,[r] esuriatis, hesito, quia ad humanos usus non simplex, sed aliud ouinum, aliud caprinum, aliud uaccinum a Deo creatum perpendo. Habet et humana infantia lac proprium, et etati sue congruum, mamillarum maternarum. Ex qualitate uero substantiali[s] uniuscuiusque lactis, cui magis persone uel etati[t] quodlibet horum competat [u]non est difficile[u] disserere. Est namque caprinum parum nutritiuum sed satis digestiuum, uaccinum multum nutritiuum sed durum ad digerendum, ouinum ex his medie contemperatum. Quamobrem ex alio serui, ex alio filii, itemque ex alio pascuntur domini. Qui domini, nisi qui dominantur in uniuersa Egypto carnis sue? Qui filii, nisi qui [v]de uentre nati sunt[v] gratie? Qui

[k] in ambulat *O* [l] *corr. Hall;* ea *O, Val, Sirmond* [m–m] diuinum uberum *O, Val*; diuini uberis *Sirmond* [n–n] qui iuxta Apostolum *Val* [o–o] in sanctificatione *Val* [p] indubitate *Sirmond* [q] *om. O* [r–r] fratres lac *O, Val* [s] uberali *Sirmond* [t] erati *Sirmond* [u–u] ut est difficile *O;* non est *Sirmond* [v–v] nati sunt de uentre *O*

[12] Num. 24: 6. [13] Cf. S. of S. 5: 13. [14] Cf. Ps. 67 (68): 16. [15] Cf. Num. 24: 6. [16] Cf. Job 28: 2. [17] Jer. 50: 23. [18] Possibly alluding to 3 Kgs. (1 Kgs.) 6: 7.

tender, however salty, it shall be made sweet and wholesome. It shall be made, I say, fruitful by the blessings of heaven, it shall be made like 'watered gardens near the rivers,'[12] like 'beds of spices set by the perfumers,'[13] like a curdled mountain, and fat,[14] like a woody valley,[15] like earth blessed and most bountiful. Truth rises out of this alone; on this, justice looks forth from heaven; in this, holiness lives and walks. Iron is extracted from this;[16] 'the hammer of the whole earth'[17] and the axe of devilish suggestion is not heard in it.[18] This earth is closest to blessing. This, I say, receives like milk from the divine breasts the first blessing in justification, the second in glorification. Therefore 'every one', according to the Apostle, 'that is a partaker of milk'[19] may suck, as if from the breasts of maternal grace, from this one the milk of sanctification from the other that of consolation. For this is what the Apostle says: 'You have your fruit unto sanctification, and the end life everlasting.'[20] Thus, thus is it lived, and in such things the life of the spirit. Thus your little ones live, Lord God, from the breast of the present visitation, thus from the breast of future hope. These two are 'like two young roes that are twins'[21] because, on account of the abundance of divine sweetness already tasted in advance and of the undoubted certainty of the reward to follow, now we run over the unevenness of adversities towards God, like a deer, now in our eagerness we leap 'upon the mountains of aromatical spices,'[22] of pure prayers, crying out with the Apostle that 'the sufferings of this time are not worthy to be compared with the glory to come that shall be revealed in us'.[23] But I am not sure, brothers, which type of milk you thirst for, since, as I reckon it, there is not simply one type created by God for human use, but one from sheep, another from goats, another from cows. Furthermore, the human child has its own milk, and one suited to its age, from its mother's breasts. But it is not difficult to determine from the substantial quality of each type of milk to which person or age any of them is better suited. For that of goats is scarcely nutritious but easily digestible, that of cows very nutritious but hard to digest, that of sheep midway between these. For this reason slaves are nourished from the one, sons from another and masters from another again. Who are the masters if not those who have dominion over the whole Egypt of their flesh? Who are the sons if not those who are born of the womb of grace? Who are the slaves if

[19] Heb. 5: 13, but given a rather different meaning here by the context.
[20] Rom. 6: 22; what follows echoes Isa. 38: 16.
[21] S. of S. 4: 5; 7: 3. [22] S. of S. 8: 14. [23] Rom. 8: 18.

serui, nisi quorum manus seruierunt in cophino[24] ueteris uite? Serui necessitate indigentie, filii suauitate indulgentie, domini deliciarum plenitudine lac edere solent. Vtinam michi peccatori indulgeatur lac uenie, uobis iam expiatis lac gratie, tandem expiatis lac glorie! O clarum lac! O suaue! O iocundum! Clarum quia per ueniam transferimur de regione tenebrarum ad lucem gaudiorum. Suaue quia per suauitatem gratie ab amaritudine temptationum ad dulcedinem deducimur immarcescibilium delectationum. Iocundum quia [w]per gloriam[w] a seculi tristitia euadimus ad eternum et incommutabile gaudium. O habundans iocunditas! O iocunda habundantia! 'In die' enim 'illa nutriet homo uaccam boum', ut ait Ysaias, 'et pre ubertate lactis comedet[x] butyrum.'[25] Que namque est uacca boum nisi anima consors nature et glorie celestium[y] spirituum quam homo Christus nutriet, non sicut nunc in umbra sacramenti obumbrata[z] ueritate, sed in declaratione ueritatis et in detectione reserati per clauem Dauid[26] misterii[a] de mensa corporis et de uino pretiosi sanguinis, de uestimentis glorie, et de lacte matris sue[b] gratie, quod pre ubertate misericordiarum uertitur in butyrum dulcedinum,[c] quia omni fluxibilitate et mortalitate de medio sublata, omnimoda commutatione, transformabitur 'a claritate in claritatem'[27] et sic in Deum? Tunc [d]enim erit 'Deus[d] omnia in omnibus'.[28]

Quid hoc butyro pinguius? Quid hoc melle dulcius? Hoc mel celeste est, non campestre, non denique siluestre. Iohannes in solitudine 'mel siluestre' edit satisfactionis,[29] Ionathas in procinctu belli campestre iustificationis,[30] puer Iesus in Virgine et de Virgine mel celeste integerrime[e] incorruptionis. Sufficit enim lucerne que lucet et ardet,[31] 'in campis silue'[32] penitentiam predicare[f] et quomodo[g] fugiat a uentura ira[33] populum edocere; iuueni qui in agone fideliter et uiriliter decertat, in uirge,[h] uidelicet iustitie, summitate futuram dulcedinem pregustare;[34] at uero Christo Iesu, qui lux est illuminans non illuminata, creatrix non creata, propter 'altitudinem

[w–w] *om. O* [x] comedat *O, Sirmond* [y] celestium et *O* [z] obumbrati *Sirmond* [a] mysterio *O, Val* [b] *om. Val, Sirmond* [c] beatitudinum *O, Val* [d–d] erit Deus *O;* enim erit *Sirmond* [e] *om. Sirmond* [f] *corr. Hall;* predicari *O, Val, Sirmond* [g] quando *Sirmond* [h] uirga *O*

[24] Cf. Ps. 80 (81): 7, referring to the delivery from Egypt and so developing the image above.

[25] Cf. Isa. 7: 21–2.

[26] Cf. Isa. 22: 22; Rev. 3: 7.

[27] 2 Cor. 3: 18.

[28] Cf. 1 Cor. 15: 28.

[29] Lit. 'of the woods' (or 'woodland'), but cf. Matt. 3: 4; Mark 1: 6.

[30] Cf. 1 Kgs. (1 Sam.) 14: 25–9, the honey in the 'forest' (*saltus*).

not those whose hands have served in the baskets[24] of the old life? Slaves are accustomed to consume milk out of the necessity of indigence, sons out of the pleasure of indulgence, masters out of the abundance of delicacies. Would that the milk of mercy could be granted to me a sinner, and the milk of grace to you already purified, and the milk of glory to those purified at the last. O clear milk! O sweet milk! O happy milk! Clear because through mercy we are brought over from the region of darkness to the light of rejoicings. Sweet because we are led by the sweetness of grace from the bitterness of temptations to the pleasure of unfading delights. Happy because we go forth through glory from the sadness of the world to eternal and unchangeable joy. O abundant happiness! O happy abundance! For 'in that day a man shall nourish a young cow', as Isaiah says, 'and for the abundance of milk he shall eat butter'.[25] For what is the young cow if not the soul, consort of the nature and the glory of the celestial spirits, which the man Christ shall nourish, not as now with truth hidden in the shadow of the sacrament, but in the proclamation of truth and in the uncovering of the mystery unlocked by the key of David,[26] the mystery of the meal of the body and the wine of the precious blood, of the vestments of glory and of the milk of the grace of its mother, the milk which on account of the abundance of mercies is turned into the butter of sweetness, because with all changeability and mortality removed from the midst, with every type of change, it will be transformed 'from glory to glory'[27] and thus to God? For then 'God' shall be 'all in all'.[28]

What is richer than this butter? What is sweeter than this honey? This honey is of heaven, not of the fields, nor again of the woods. John in the wilderness ate the 'wild honey' of satisfaction;[29] Jonathan girded for battle ate that of the field, of justification;[30] the boy Jesus ate the heavenly honey of complete incorruptibility, in the Virgin and of the Virgin. For it is enough for the lamp which shines and burns[31] to preach repentance 'in the fields of the wood'[32] and to teach the people how it should flee the wrath to come,[33] and it is enough for the youth who fights faithfully and powerfully in the struggle to have a foretaste of future sweetness on the end of the rod, that is of justice;[34] but for Christ Jesus, who is the light illuminating not illuminated, the Creator not the creation, on account of 'the depth of the riches of the

[31] i.e. John the Baptist, the lesser light than Jesus; cf. John 5: 35.
[32] Ps. 131 (132): 6.
[33] Cf. Matt. 3: 7; Luke 3: 7.
[34] Cf 1 Kgs. (1 Sam.) 14: 27, 43.

diuitiarum sapientie et scientie' thesauri absconditi,[35] parum est ut sit predicator nisi[i] sit et dator non solum uenie sed et gratie. Denique ut de maximis ad minora trahamus exemplum, cor cuiusque religiosi ad similitudinem baptiste Domini, a strepitu seculi quietum, in baptismo deuotionis emundatum, in mortificatione[j] carnis preparatum, in amore uerbi Dei confirmatum, in religione angelorum stabilitum, et si nondum celeste mel pleno ore et uentre eructat,[k] siluestre saltem pregustat. Aliter enim gratia sapit in patria, aliter in exilio; aliter rara, aliter larga; aliter continua, aliter interpolata; aliter in corpore mortali, aliter in immortali; aliter inuisibiliter data, aliter uisibiliter administrata. Calore igitur caritatis liquefacta et colatorio[36] discretionis eliquata, nichilominus et infusorio exquisite ueritatis infusa homini, gratia, asperitates faucium in confessione mitigat, stomachum receptiuum innumerabilium cogitationum mundificat, discretiuam cerebri rationem ad certam mensuram modificat, et uitalem uenam ad ueram immortalitatem cordi subministrat. Hic autem interim[l] nos cum turba tanquam in campestribus[37] ad gratiam suspiramus, ibi[m] uelut in monte[n] contemplationis glorificatam Iesu faciem suspicimus.[o] Hic expectamus ibi spectamus, hic petimus ibi accipimus, hic rogamus ibi erogamus, hic inopes ibi locupletes, hic pauperes ibi diuites, hic cum Iohanne in deserto[38] ibi cum Iesu in regno, hic in carcere Herodis[39] ibi in palatio eterne hereditatis. Hic ad reparationem gratia commodatur,[p] ibi ad refectionem prestatur, hic in mensura ibi supra mensuram, hic in utre ibi in uentre, hic in cortice sacramenti ibi in manifestatione summi et incircumscripti luminis. Ecce lac, immo butyrum, ecce mel, uel potius fauum mellis, offert seruus uester mense dominorum suorum. Ad quid iterum uobis[q] uas aque cum amfora uini?[40] O domini et amici karissimi, 'puteus altus est'[41] et lapis superpositus quem michi angelus nondum reuoluit,[42] Iacob nondum amouit,[43] et quomodo dicam, 'Bibe, domine, et camelis tuis potum tribuam'?[44] O ardens desiderium! Fossoria[45] habetis, 'uenas

[i] non *Sirmond* [j] mortificationem *Sirmond* [k] eructuat *O*, *Val* [l] *om. Val* [m] ubi *Val* [n] montem *O*, *Val* [o] suscipimus *O*, *Val* [p] commendatur *Val* [q] nobis *O*

[35] Cf. Rom. 11: 33 and Col. 2: 3.
[36] Cf. Niermeyer; *DML*; Blaise, *Dictionnaire*. [37] Alluding to Luke 6: 17.
[38] i.e. John the Baptist (cf. Matt. 3; Mark 1: 1–11; Luke 3: 1–22; John 1: 6–36).
[39] Cf. Matt. 14: 3; Mark 6: 17; Luke 3: 20.
[40] Possibly an allusion to the miracle of turning water into wine (John 2: 1–11), but in any case anticipates the refs. to wine at the end of the letter.
[41] John 4: 11.

wisdom and of the knowledge' of the hidden treasure,[35] it is too little that He be the proclaimer unless He is also the giver not only of mercy but also of grace. Finally then, to draw an example down from the greatest to lesser matters, the heart of each religious, in the likeness of the Baptist of the Lord, at peace from the tumult of the world, cleansed in the baptism of devotion, prepared in mortification of the flesh, strengthened in the love of the Word of God, made stable in the religious life of the angels, even if it does not yet pour forth heavenly honey from a full mouth and stomach, at least it has a foretaste of the honey of the woods. For grace has one savour in the homeland, another in exile, one when it is sparse, another when it is bountiful, one when it is continuous, another when it is interrupted, one in the mortal body, another in the immortal, one when it is given invisibly, another when it is administered visibly. The grace therefore made molten by the heat of love and strained by the filter[36] of discernment, and no less poured out into man through the funnel of choice truth, soothes sorenesses of the throat in confession, cleanses the stomach which is receptive of innumerable thoughts, moderates the discriminating reason of the brain to a sure measure, and furnishes to the heart the vital vein for true immortality. But here meanwhile we, with the throng, as if in the plains,[37] sigh for grace; there we look up at the glorified face of Jesus as if on the mountain of contemplation. Here we look out for it, there we look upon it, here we seek, there we receive, here we beg, there we bestow, here we are needy, there we are wealthy, here paupers, there rich men, here with John in the desert,[38] there with Jesus in the kingdom, here in Herod's prison,[39] there in the palace of the eternal inheritance. Here grace is lent for renewal, there it is offered for refreshment, here within measure, there beyond measure, here in a vessel, there in the belly, here in the husk of the sacrament, there in the manifestation of the highest and infinite light. See, your servant brings milk, nay butter, see he brings honey, or rather honeycomb, to his lords' table. To what end do you have a vessel of water when you have an amphora of wine?[40] O dearest lords and friends, 'the well is deep'[41] and a stone placed over it which the angel has not yet rolled back for me,[42] which Jacob has not yet removed,[43] and how shall I say, 'Drink, lord, and to thy camels I will give drink'?[44] O burning desire! You have spades,[45]

[42] Cf. Matt. 28: 2; Mark 16: 4; Luke 24: 2; John 20: 1.
[43] Cf. Gen. 29: 10.
[44] Cf. Gen. 24: 46.
[45] Or 'mattocks', 'hoes': *DML*; Niermeyer; Blaise, *Dictionnaire*.

aquarum uiuentium'[46] possidetis, puteos quos fodit Abraham et filii[r] eius, Ysaac et pueri eius, habetis,[47] et adhuc 'aquam de cisterna que est in Bethleem'[48] suspiratis? Equidem[s] hec aqua etsi bona ad bibendum sed difficilis ad inueniendum. Iter prolixum et obsessum, locus remotus et ignotus, uires pauce et rare, undique hostis et ensis, nox instans et pre foribus tenebre. Nisi itaque ad incomparabilem thesaurum obtinendum tanti labores non sunt insumendi. Quid dicam? Momento[t] tamen sui hec purissima gutta superat omnem[u] laborem quia sitim satiat, sordes lauat, estum temperat, humectat arida, dura emollit, sterilia fecundat. Ex hac lagenas oculorum suffusas in libamentis uestris[v] effunditis et cum hac altissimo Deo uota placabilia offertis. Hec ignem inextinguibilem extinguit. Hec rigorem iudicis ad pietatem inflectit. Hec 'cherubin, et flammeum gladium atque uersatilem'[49] ne ledant compescit. Hanc in uinum Saluator[w] conuertit,[50] et suo more potiora exhibet in benedictione quam in creatione. Procul dubio sunt nobis plures fortes ad bibendum uinum et ad miscendam ebrietatem; ad hoc[x] autem poculum quis idoneus? Verus Noe noster qui requiem nobis dedit ab operibus mortuis, hoc uino debriatus, turpitudinem humane infirmitatis in cruce denudauit et a medio filio,[51] qui neque calidus est neque frigidus,[52] irrisionem sustinuit. Ideo pauci procedunt ad emendum, pauciores ad possidendum, paucissimi ad bibendum, fere nemo ad ebriandum.[y] [z]Potens potator huius uini[z] fuit filius fabri.[53] Post hunc emigrauerunt ad 'uineas Engaddi' qui 'bibebant uinum libaminum'.[54] Quia igitur nunc non est 'relictus in Syon, et residuus in Ierusalem'[55] qui de manu Domini calicem uini meri suscipiat,[56] accedite uos qui estis de domo Dei [a]et de Monte Dei,[a] et 'bibite et inebriamini, karissimi'.[57] Valete.[b]

[r] filius *Val* [s] Et quidem *Val* [t] Memento *O* [u] *om. O* [v] nostris *O* [w] *om. Val, Sirmond* [x] hunc *O, Val* [y] debriandum *O* [z–z] Potator huius uini potens *O* [a–a] *om. O* [b] *om. O, Sirmond*

[46] Cf. Jer. 17: 13, but possibly also recalling again John 4: 11 (see above) and Gen. 26: 19 (see below).

[47] Cf. Gen. 26: 15–33. [48] Cf. 2 Kgs. (2 Sam.) 23: 15; 1 Chr. 11: 17.

[49] Gen. 3: 24. [50] Cf. John 2: 1–11.

[51] A bold image even for Peter, presumably meaning Jesus on the cross, as the true Noah, laying bare the shame of human weakness (on Noah's drunkenness and nakedness

you possess 'veins of living waters',[46] you have the wells which Abraham and his servants, Isaac and his servants, dug,[47] and do you still long for 'the water out of the cistern that is in Bethlehem'?[48] Indeed this water, while it is good to drink, is difficult to find. The route is long and blockaded, the place remote and unknown, your strength small and scattered, the enemy and the sword on every side, the night pressing in and darkness before the doors. Such great labours then are not to be undertaken except to obtain incomparable treasure. What should I say? This purest drop, however, by its own momentum, overcomes all labour because it satisfies thirst, washes filth away, tempers fever, moistens the dry, softens the hard, makes fruitful the sterile. From this drop you pour out the full flasks of the eyes in your libations and with this you offer acceptable vows to the highest God. This extinguishes the inextinguishable fire. This bends the inflexibility of the judge to mercy. This restrains the 'cherubims, and the flaming sword turning every way'[49] lest they inflict harm. This the Saviour turned into wine,[50] and according to His fashion He proves it more valuable by His blessing than in creation. Without doubt there are many among us strong to drink wine and to mingle in drunkenness, but who is suitable for this cup? Our true Noah, who gave us rest from dead works, drunk on this wine, laid bare the shame of human weakness on the cross, and suffered the mockery of His middle son,[51] who is neither hot nor cold.[52] And so few go forth to purchase, fewer to possess, very few to drink, and scarcely any to get drunk. The carpenter's son[53] was a mighty drinker of this wine. After Him, they who 'drank the wine of their drink-offerings' departed to 'the vineyards of Engaddi'.[54] Therefore, since there is now no one 'left in Zion, and no one remains in Jerusalem'[55] to take up the cup of strong wine from the hand of the Lord,[56] approach, you who are of the house of God and of the Mount of God, and 'drink and be inebriated, my dearly beloved'.[57] Farewell.

cf. Gen. 9: 21–5; cf. also 5: 29; Christ was given 'vinegar' on the cross). The imagery of the cup recalls Christ praying in Gethsemane (but cf. also the ref. to Ps. below).

[52] Cf. Rev. 3: 15–16.

[53] Cf. Matt. 13: 55; cf. also Mark 6: 3.

[54] S. of S. 1: 13 and Deut. 32: 38.

[55] Cf. Isa. 4: 3, 'every one that shall be left in Sion, and that shall remain in Jerusalem, shall be called holy'.

[56] Cf. Ps. 74 (75): 9.

[57] S. of S. 5: 1 (the Mount of God—cf. Exod. 3: 1, etc.—is here Mont-Dieu).

53

To the community of Mont-Dieu[1]

*c.*1155 × 1162

Suis de Monte Dei, suus [a]Petrus Cellensis,[a] a claritate transferri in claritatem.[2]

Venerunt filii usque ad partum, et tempus non est pariendi.[3] Manus ad rescribendum parabatur, animus ad dictandum, locus ad sedendum, et ecce, uentus occupationum nuntii uestri, uela occupans nauigii nostri, ad portum silentii retorsit. Quid enim? Nonne iocundius et uoluptuosius paulatim uinum bonum quod seruatis[b] usque adhuc[4] per tempus et tempora degustabitur quam uno haustu cum dampno optande suauitatis deglutitur? Etsi enim[c] in transitu desidero uos uidere, saltem nolo in transitu scribere. Gustaui et uidi quia bona est negotiatio uestra.[5] Nequaquam manus uestre in cophinis[d] seruiunt, nequaquam ciuitates Egypti 'in luto et latere'[6] construunt, sed queque pretiosa et speciosa requirunt, sed fusum[7] et colum ad nendum siue contexendum rationale et superhumerale et cetera summi pontificis insignia ornamenta apprehendunt.[8] Hinc est quod non de stupis synagoge peccatorum[9] grossiora uestimenta anime uestre delicate apponitis, neque contra legem ex lana linoque uestimento induimini,[10] sed abdicantes occulta dedecoris faciem lauatis, caput ungitis, et de uelleribus ouium uestrarum[11] uenientes ab aquilone[12] calefacitis, cum etiam de confessione uestre integerrime simplicitatis exempla sumuntur sancte religionis. Sic est, dilectissimi, sic est: accedit homo ad cor altum, et exaltabitur[e] Deus.[13] Annon in luna cum lumini solis appropinquat sic euenit ut eo a suo fulgore uideatur deficere quo fuerit effecta uicinior? Ceci domus non ideo pulchra quia deformitatem eius non uidet, non ideo sana quia ubi

53 *O fos. 120^r–121^r, Sirmond III. 4*[1]]
[a–a] G. *O* [b] seruastis O [c] enim uel *O* [d] cophino *O* [e] exaltatur *O*

53 [1] This and letter no. 54 are run together as one letter in Sirmond (which *PL* follows); there is no way to tell whether this error originates in the lost MS (R), or in Sirmond. In O they are separate letters (see concordances). Letter no. 54 is presumably the answer to the question mentioned at the end of this letter. The *terminus post quem* for both is the earliest possible date for Lombard's *Sent.* (I. C. Brady, *Magistri Petri Lombardi . . . Sententiae in IV libris distinctae*, 2 vols. + proleg. (Grottaferrata, 1971–81), i. 1, p. 126: 1155–8) and so is tentative. [2] Cf. 2 Cor. 3: 18.
[3] Cf. Isa. 37: 3 (Vulgate has *uirtus* for *tempus*); cf. also 4 Kgs. (2 Kgs.) 19: 3.

53
To the community of Mont-Dieu[1]

*c.*1155 × 1162

To his own of Mont-Dieu, their own Peter of Montier-la-Celle, to be translated from glory to glory.[2]

The children are come to the birth and there is not time to bring forth.[3] The hand was prepared for writing back, the mind for dictating, the place for sitting, and see, the wind of the affairs of your messenger, filling the sails of our ship, drove it back to the port of silence. What of this? Will not that good wine which you are still keeping even now[4] be savoured more joyfully and pleasurably little by little from time to time than when gulped down in one draught, with the loss of the desired sweetness? For even if I do desire to see you in passing, at least I do not wish to write in passing. I have tasted and seen that your merchandise is good.[5] Your hands by no means serve in baskets, by no means do they build the cities of Egypt 'in clay and brick',[6] rather they seek out whatever things are precious and splendid, rather they take hold of the spindle[7] and the distaff to spin or weave the rational and the ephod and the other distinguishing insignia of the high priest.[8] Hence it is that you do not set the coarser vestments made of the tow of the congregation of sinners[9] upon your delicate soul, nor, contrary to the law, are you clothed in a garment of wool and linen,[10] but abandoning the hidden things of shame you wash the face, you anoint the head, and you warm with the fleeces of your sheep[11] those coming from the north,[12] since they also derive examples of the holy way of life from the acknowledgement of your most irreproachable simplicity. So it is, my dearest ones, so it is: man comes to a deep heart and God shall be exalted.[13] Is it not so in the case of the moon that when it approaches the light of the sun it seems to decline from its own splendour the nearer it comes? The house of the blind man is not beautiful because he does not see its unsightliness; it

[4] Possibly an allusion to the miracle at Cana (i.e. keeping the best until last), cf. John 2: 10.
[5] Cf. Prov. 31: 18.
[6] Cf. Ps. 80 (81): 7; Judith 5: 10; cf. Exod. 1: 14.
[7] Cf. Prov. 31: 19.
[8] Cf. Exod. 25: 7; 28; 29: 5; 35: 9, 27; 39: 1–28.
[9] Cf. Ecclus. 21: 10: 'the congregation of sinners is like tow heaped together'.
[10] Cf. Deut. 22: 11.
[11] Cf. Job 31: 20.
[12] Cf. Jer. 13: 20, here simply meaning sinners.
[13] Cf. Ps. 63 (64): 7–8.

uentrem faciat non considerat. Cani, iuxta prophetam, in Ephraim effusi sunt, et ipse ignorauit.[14] Doletis fetorem Lazari,[15] truncum iam emortuum miramini reuirescere,[16] muros Ihericho non patimini consurgere,[17] facitis namque quod ait Naum propheta:[f] 'Aquam propter obsidionem hauri tibi, intra in[g] lutum et calca, et subigens tene laterem.'[18] Intelligitis obsidionem principis huius mundi; aqua de cisternis sicut nec de cellis deficit.[19] Lutum carnis ut fortius prematis et ualidius calcetis intratis si subigendo tenere laterem[h] memineritis.[20] Non itaque usque ad internecionem deseuiat mucro uester.[21] 'Tolle', ait Dominus, 'grabatum tuum et ambula,'[22] id est corpori indulgeas non seruias. Quam suauiter in impetu spiritus euehor dum uobis scribo tam egre fero dum in medio itineris subsistere cogor. Ad questionem respondere parco quia non perfunctorie eam tractare dispono. Valete.

54

To the community of Mont-Dieu[1]

*c.*1155 × 1162

Destitutus spe ulterius procedendi subsederam non uolens sed propter eum qui quasi media uia me deserebat. Interim flauit spiritus bonus,[2] et dum illius cassauit propositum nostrum compleuit desiderium. Moram procul dubio timebam et temporis siue portatoris importunitatem ad meam referri ignauiam satis pertinaciter deuitabam. Vt itaque meam insipientiam oculis amicorum et dominorum

[f] prophetam *Sirmond* [g] *om. O* [h] lapidem *O*

54 *O fos. 121ʳ–123ʳ, Sirmond III. 4²*]

[14] Cf. Hos. 7: 9.
[15] Cf. John 11: 39. Peter contrasts the Carthusians with lesser men, including by implication himself, but adds below a familiar caution against excessive asceticism.
[16] Cf. Job 14: 7–8. [17] Cf. Josh. 6: 26. [18] Cf. Nahum 3: 14.
[19] i.e. monks' cells. The devil ('the prince of this world', cf. John 12: 31; 14: 30; 16: 11) is here likened to Holofernes who tried to break the Israelite resistance by keeping the cisterns dry (cf. Judith 7, esp. 11).
[20] The *si* seems odd here, but in the context no criticism or qualified praise of the Carthusians can be intended. Peter's sense must be that their pressing and treading (which

is not clean because he does not consider where to relieve himself. Grey hairs, according to the prophet, were spread about upon Ephraim, and he was ignorant of it.[14] You pity the stench of Lazarus,[15] you marvel that the trunk which is already dead grows green again,[16] you do not permit the walls of Jericho to rise up,[17] for you do as the prophet Nahum says: 'Draw thee water for the siege, go into the clay and tread, and work it and make brick.'[18] You understand the siege of the prince of this world; water fails not from the cisterns as it fails not from the cells.[19] You enter the clay of the flesh to press it and tread it, the more strongly and the more powerfully if you remember to work it and make brick.[20] Therefore let not thy sword rage unto utter destruction.[21] The Lord says: 'Take up thy bed and walk,'[22] that is be kind to the body not a slave to it. As I am borne up sweetly in the impulse of the spirit while I am writing to you, so to the same degree do I find it disagreeable when I am forced to come to a halt in the middle of my journey. I forbear to respond to the question because I do not plan to treat it perfunctorily. Farewell.

54

To the community of Mont-Dieu[1]

*c.*1155 × 1162

Abandoned by hope of proceeding further I had sat down not willingly but on account of him who was, as it were, deserting me in the midst of my journey. In the meantime the good wind blew,[2] and while it destroyed his intention it fulfilled our desire. Without doubt, I was afraid of delay and I was trying with some persistence to avoid having the importunity of the time or of the bearer put down to my laziness. To set my folly straightforwardly on record then, before the

is not in doubt, as it would be if the passage were read as: 'You enter . . . to press . . . more strongly . . ., if you remember to work it . . .') is even stronger if they remember its ultimate purpose—i.e. asceticism should not be practised for its own sake but only in so far as it assists spiritual progress.

[21] Cf. 2 Kgs. (2 Sam.) 2: 26.

[22] Mark 2: 9; John 5: 8.

54 [1] Dated as letter no. 53; see also letter no. 53, n. 1, on the running together of letters 53 and 54 in Sirmond and *PL*. This letter is a response to questions about the definitions of *imago* and *similitudo* (presumably the questions mentioned at the end of letter no. 53; the two may have been sent together). The discussion relates mainly to Peter Lombard, *Sent.* ii. dist. xvi.

[2] Cf. Exod. 15: 10; Ps. 147 (147): 18.

meorum simpliciter prodam, non quod ex promptuario aridi pectoris sed quod de horreis Ioseph in saccis filiorum Iacob[3] mutuaui proponam. Apponam uero prius in mensa ista 'panes propositionis'[4] uestre ut cum his sumantur legumina decoctionis nostre. Quosdam uestrorum ita scribitis sentire de uerbis Apostoli, ubi[a] ait 'Renouamini spiritu mentis uestre',[5] et alibi 'Et si homo exterior[b] corrumpitur sed qui intus est renouatur de die in diem',[6] et de paradiso deliciarum in quo Adam positus est,[7] siue etiam de[c] hoc, quod homo 'ad imaginem et similitudinem' Dei conditus asseritur,[8] ut sub eodem sensu omnia ista accipiantur. Addunt etiam hec bona deliciosa bifarie debere accipi, scilicet secundum substantiale bonum et accidens, referentes ad essentialia dona imaginem, similitudinem uero ad ea que adesse et abesse possunt.[9] Priusquam his bonis coloribus et a doctis pictoribus imaginem sensuum istorum compositam in sacrario Dei statuam, quero de origine, de auctore et de uirtute, uel etiam utilitate eius. Vt enim religiosum sit quod adoratur in templo,[d] non noua, non ignota, non denique ficta debent esse numina. 'Israhel', ait propheta, 'si [e]audieris me,[e] non erit in te deus recens, neque adorabis deum alienum.'[10] Non minus abhominabile est simulacrum in ecclesia Dei uiui quam de sancta scriptura sensus peruersus in anima Christiani. Delectus tamen et hic habendus est. In his siquidem que ad sancte trinitatis uel incarnationis fidem seu sacramentorum ecclesie pertinent, errare periclitari est. De multiplici uero sensu scripturarum uel iudiciorum Dei que nunc plura fiunt quasi diuersa non tamen contraria, [f]a fide sentire non est[f] exorbitare.[11] Hic enim sonus est alarum animalium in Ezechiel se adinuicem percutientium,[12] quia sancte anime de thesauro sapientie et scientie Dei largiter accipiunt unde corpus ecclesie in augmentum corporis Christi diuersarum gratiarum compagine satis eleganter componunt. Itaque

[a] ut *O* [b] qui exterior est *O* [c] *om. Sirmond* [d] templis *O*
[e–e] me audieris *Sirmond* [f–f] sentire non est a fide *O*

---

[3] Cf. Gen. 42.

[4] Exod. 25: 30; 35: 13; 39: 35; 40: 21; Lev. 21: 8; 24: 5–8; Num. 8: 2, and many other refs. i.e. he will recapitulate their questions before giving his answers.

[5] Eph. 4: 23 (omitting *autem*).

[6] Cf. 2 Cor. 4: 16: 'sed licet is qui foris est noster homo corrumpitur, tamen is qui intus est renouatur de die in diem'.

[7] Cf. Gen. 2: 15. [8] Cf. Gen. 1: 26.

[9] Cf. Boethius, *Comm. in Porph.* iv. *de accidenti* (*CSEL* xlviii; *PL* lxiv. 133).

[10] Cf. Ps. 80 (81): 9–10; setting up the image in the sanctuary here means accepting their arguments.

eyes of my friends and lords, let me lay out what I have borrowed, not from the store-house of a barren heart but from the granaries of Joseph in the sacks of the sons of Jacob.[3] But let me set out first on this table the 'loaves' of your 'proposition'[4] so that the vegetables of our pottage may be consumed along with them. Regarding the words of the Apostle, where he says, 'Be renewed in the spirit of your mind,'[5] and elsewhere, 'And if the outward man is corrupted, yet the inward is renewed day by day,'[6] and regarding the paradise of delights in which Adam was set,[7] or even this, that man is asserted to be made 'to the image and likeness' of God,[8] you write that certain of you are of the opinion that all of these things are to be understood under the same sense. They also add that these delectable good things ought to be understood in two ways, that is to say according to the substantial good and the accidental, referring the image to essential gifts but the likeness to those which can be present and absent.[9] Before I set in the sanctuary of God the image of these senses, composed with these good colours and by skilled painters, I ask about their origin, their authority and their power, indeed even their usefulness. For if that which is adored in the temple is to be a proper object of worship, the divinities should be neither novel nor unknown nor, finally, false. 'O Israel,' says the prophet, 'if thou wilt hearken to me there shall be no new god in thee, neither shalt thou adore a strange god.'[10] An idol in the Church of the living God is no less abominable than a false understanding of holy Scripture in the mind of a Christian. Even here however a distinction should be made. In those things indeed which pertain to faith in the holy Trinity or the incarnation or the sacraments of the Church, to err is to be endangered. But to perceive in faith the manifold meanings of the Scriptures or the judgements of God, which are now become many, as if they are different yet not contradictory,[11] is not to go astray. For this is the sound of the wings of the living creatures in Ezekiel striking one against another,[12] because holy souls receive in abundance from the treasure chest of the wisdom and knowledge of God those things with which they construct the body of the Church with much discernment, by the conjunction of diverse graces, to augment the body of Christ. And so

[11] 'quasi diuersa non tamen contraria': on the importance of the concept of diversity within unity in 12th-cent. thought see J. de Ghellinck, *Le Mouvement théologique du XIIè siècle* (Bruges, 1948), pp. 472–99, 517–23, and, e.g., H. Silvestre, 'Diversi sed non adversi', *Recherches de théologie ancienne et médiévale*, xxxi (1964), 124–32, and Haseldine, 'Friendship and rivalry', pp. 390–1.

[12] Cf. Ezek. 3: 13.

frater ille suo bono quidem sensu domum sibi eburneam fabricauerit[13] et bicameratam siue tricameratam archam 'in diluuio aquarum multarum' preparauerit,[14] miror illum tamen tantum edificium paruis sumptibus extruxisse et cum illud fundamentis solidissimis apostolorum et prophetarum firmare, floribus[15] doctorum fulcire, malis martyrum stipare ut sapiens architectus debuisset, oblitus paxillos ereos[16] auctoritatum ueteris et funes argenteos[17] noui testamenti inserere, quasi clipeis denudauit parietem. Sed ut de proprietate huius nominis que occurrunt in instanti edisseram, sciendum est quod proprie imago relatiue dicitur ad aliud cuius similitudinem gerit, et ad quod representandum facta est, sicut imago Cesaris que ipsius similitudinem preferebat.[18] Improprie autem imago dicitur id ad quod aliud fit, sicut exemplum, quod sumitur,[g] proprie dicitur exemplum, exemplar a quo sumitur. Tamen abusiue aliquando alterum pro altero ponitur.[19] Secundum istam rationem proprie imago Patris dicitur Filius.[20] Iuxta alium uero modum quo unum nomen pro alio ponitur, dicitur homo imago Dei quia uidelicet imago Dei in eo est, sicut imago dicitur tabula et pictura, sed propter picturam que [h]in ea est[h] simul et tabula imago appellatur. Ita propter imaginem trinitatis etiam illud in quo est hec[i] imago imaginis nomine uocatur. Homo itaque imago et ad imaginem, Filius imago non ad imaginem.[21]

Volo denique, si placet, et in quo similitudo differat ab imagine, breui exemplo signare. Pono animam lapidem pretiosum et imaginem aliquam in eo expressam a qua similitudo secundum imaginem impressa ostendatur. Nonne [j]est aliud[j] imago exculpta et aliud similitudo ab imagine redempta? Sit igitur bonitas Dei causa huius similitudinis, quia cum beneuolentia sua, que Spiritui sancto attribuitur, Deus Deum hominem uel[k] post Deum facere uellet, et

[g] similiter *Sirmond* [h–h] est in ea *O* [i] *om. O* [j–j] aliud est *O* [k] *om. O*

[13] Cf. 3 Kgs. (1 Kgs.) 22: 39; Ps. 44 (45): 9. [14] Cf. Gen. 6: 14–22; Ps. 31 (32): 6.
[15] 'carved capitals', i.e. *flos* in the sense of ornament.
[16] Cf. Exod. 35: 18; 38: 20, and many other refs.
[17] Cf. Exod. 35: 18, and many other refs.; for pins and cords together, cf. Exod. 35: 18; 39: 40; Num. 3: 37; 4: 32.
[18] Cf. Peter Lombard, *Sent.* ii. dist. xvi. 3. 1 (Brady i. 2, p. 407); cf. also Matt. 22: 17–21; Mark 12: 14–17; Luke 20: 22–5.
[19] Cf. ibid., but the text is corrupt. *Sent.* reads 'Improprie autem imago dicitur id ad quod aliud fit, sicut exemplum proprie dicitur, quod sumitur ex aliquo; et exemplar, ex quo sumitur aliquid. Ponitur tamen aliquando abusiue alterum pro altero'. Peter is quoting, apparently selectively, from some, presumably early, version of the *Sent.* The aim here is to preserve his intended meaning not to superimpose the text of the modern edn. of the *Sent.*

that brother by his own good understanding may indeed have built his house of ivory[13] and prepared the two- or three-storied ark against the 'flood of many waters',[14] but yet I am amazed that he has built such a structure with few expenses, and whereas he ought, like a wise architect, to have strengthened it with the most solid foundations of the apostles and prophets, to have supported it with the carved capitals[15] of the learned, to have compounded it with the beams of the martyrs, he has forgotten to insert the bronze pins[16] of the authorities of the Old Testament and the silver cords[17] of the New Testament, and has, as it were, stripped the wall of shields. But to set out what occurs to me at present about the proper meaning of this noun, one should know that 'image' is properly used in relation to another thing whose likeness it bears and to represent which it is made, like the image of Caesar which bore his likeness.[18] But that thing is properly called an image to which another thing is fashioned, just as an *exemplum* (that which is taken up) is properly called an *exemplum*, and that from which it is taken, an *exemplar*. Sometimes however, by improper usage, one is substituted for the other.[19] According to this reasoning, the Son is properly said to be the image of the Father.[20] But following the other method, by which one noun is substituted for another, man is said to be the image of God because clearly the image of God is in him, just as 'imago' is used of 'tabula' and 'pictura', but, on account of the 'pictura' which is in it, the 'tabula' also is called at the same time 'imago'. Thus, on account of the image of the Trinity, even that within which this image resides is known by the name of 'imago'. Man is thus an image, and based on an image; the Son is an image, but not based on an image.[21]

Finally I wish, if it please you, to indicate also by a brief example in what way likeness differs from image. I postulate the soul as a precious stone and some image impressed in it from which a likeness appears imprinted in accordance with the image. Is not the engraved image one thing and the likeness redeemed by means of the image another? Let the goodness of God therefore be the cause of this likeness, for when by His benevolence, which is attributed to the Holy Spirit, God wished to make God man even after God, and by

[20] Cf. Peter Lombard, *Sent.* ii. dist. xvi. 3.2 (Brady i. 2, p. 407), with ref. to Augustine, *De trin.* vii. 6 (*CCSL* l. 266; *PL* xlii. 946).

[21] Cf. Peter Lombard, *Sent.* ii. dist. xvi. 3.6–4.1 (Brady i. 2, p. 407): 'sicut imago . . . nomine uocatur'. Cf. also Augustine, *De trin.* xv. 23 (*CCSL* lA. 520; *PL* xlii. 1090), but the source here is *Sent.*

naturaliter id fieri non posset (non enim naturaliter Deus est, nisi is, qui Deus natus est, non factus),[22] concessit ut saltem similitudinem Dei haberet. 'Que similitudo Dei ut sedem uel receptaculum haberet imago siue figura substantie Dei, que est Filius, anime hominis impressa est ut a suo sancto[l] Spiritu predictam similitudinem reciperet, quomodo pretioso lapidi foramen aperitur per quod gracilem auri uirgulam recipiat qua constringatur et teneatur.'[23] Ad imaginem itaque secundum naturales anime uirtutes, memoriam scilicet,[m] intelligentiam et dilectionem, ut optime dixit tractator uester, et ad similitudinem secundum innocentiam et iustitiam, que in mente rationali potius naturaliter quam accidentaliter insunt, conditus est homo.[24] Stupeo siquidem me audiuisse, quod nollem uel sompniasse, similitudinem Dei donum esse accidentale, quod[n] non accidentale sed ueraciter substantiale [o]immo supersubstantiale[o] [25] nouit qui Apostolum intelligit. 'Scimus', inquit, 'quia cum apparuerit similes ei erimus quia uidebimus eum sicuti est.'[26] Quid est 'similes erimus', nisi, 'similitudinem eius habebimus'? Quam enim similitudinem in creatione accepimus, eamdem in resurrectione prima, denique et in secunda, sed aliter, habituri sumus. Nam in creatione ita collata est quod amitti potuit cum etiam peccare potuit, uel potius deformari, sed in uera immortalitate cum nec mori nec peccare homo poterit de similitudine Dei eternaliter gaudebit. Quid igitur? Itane summa illa beatitudo et gloria seculorum accidentalis erit ut possit 'adesse et abesse preter [p]subiecti corruptionem'?[p] [27] Hoc enim accidentis est. Vbi es, homo? Nonne in mortalitate, uel potius in morte? Quare? Nonne quia amisisti Dei similitudinem? Quid enim Deus? Nonne uita?[28] Et que est similitudo uite nisi uita? Aut que dissimilitudo nisi mors? Mortem namque inuenit qui similitudinem Dei amiserit. Quod si ideo dicitur accidentale similitudo Dei quia auferri potuit, non uera est consequentia. Sic enim sequeretur quod accidentaliter uiueremus quia mori possumus. Nature siquidem accidentis est ut possit 'adesse et abesse preter subiecti corruptionem'. Quod

[l] *om. O* [m] similiter *O* [n] quod a Deo *O* [o–o] *om. O* [p–p] corruptionem subiecti *O*

[22] i.e. Christ; the first *Deum* may be wrong, unless it is a ref. to the incarnation not the creation. [23] Cf. Rupert of Deutz, *De diu. offic.* xi. 17 (*PL* clxx. 310).

[24] Possibly referring to a comment in the letter to which this is evidently a reply, referring to Peter Lombard, *Sent.* ii. *dist.* xvi. 4 (Brady i. 2, p. 408), but with some elaboration. [25] Cf. Matt. 6: 11.

[26] 1 John 3: 2 (Vulgate has *quoniam* for *quia* in both cases).

nature this could not be done (for God does not exist by nature, except Him who was born God, not made),[22] He granted that man should have at least the likeness of God. 'In order that this likeness of God should have a seat or resting place, the image or figure of the substance of God, which is the Son, was imprinted on the soul of man that it might receive from His Holy Spirit the aforesaid likeness, in the same manner as an aperture is opened up in a precious stone through which it may receive the slender rod of gold by which it is bound and held together.'[23] Man is made then in the image in so far as the natural powers of the soul, that is memory, intelligence, and love, are concerned, as your author puts it best, and in the likeness in so far as innocence and justice, which exist in the rational mind naturally rather than accidentally, are concerned.[24] I am stunned to have heard it said (something I would not wish even to have dreamt) that the likeness of God is an accidental gift—that very thing which he who understands the Apostle knows to be not accidental but truly substantial, indeed supersubstantial.[25] 'We know', he says, 'that when He shall appear we shall be like to Him, because we shall see Him as He is.'[26] What does it mean, 'we shall be like', except, 'we shall have His likeness'? For that likeness which we received in creation we are to have the same in the first resurrection and again, but in another manner, in the second. For in creation it was conferred in such a way that it could be lost, when it could indeed sin, or rather be deformed, but in true immortality, when man will be able neither to die nor to sin, he will rejoice in the likeness of God eternally. What then of this? Can it be that the highest blessedness and glory of the ages will be accidental, so that it can be 'present and absent irrespective of the corruption of the subject'?[27] For this is the property of accident. Where are you, o man? Are you not in mortality, or rather in death? How so? Is it not because you have lost the likeness of God? For what is God? Is He not life?[28] And what is the likeness of life if not life? Or what is the unlikeness, if not death? For he who has lost the likeness of God has found death. But if the likeness of God is said in this way to be accidental, because it could be taken away, the consequence is not true. For it would then follow that we were living accidentally because we can die. It is the nature of accident that it can be 'present and absent irrespective of the corruption of the subject'. But who of

[27] Boethius, *Comm. in Porph.* iv. *de accidenti* (*PL* lxiv. 133).

[28] Cf. here the debate in letters 50–1 over Claudianus Mamertus' *De statu anime*, iii. 6. 2: 'Corpus est uiuens, anima uiua, Deus est uita' (*CSEL* xi. 162–4; *PL* liii. 766).

quis sani cerebri uel cordis affirmare[q] audeat de uirtute, iustitia, bonitate et amore uirtutis in anima? Prorsus, ut ait Augustinus, ut uita corporis anima, sic anime uita Deus.[29] Vera quoque uirtus, uera bonitas, uera iustitia, immo ipsa ueritas est Deus. Sine his igitur si fuerit anima moritur. Et dicis esse accidentalia dona? Vertens iterum oculos et relegens apices uestros inueniensque non donum sed bonum accidens maiores phantasias admiror. Nonne enim similitudo Dei Deus est? Eque bonum Dei nunquid aliud a Deo est? Clamat Augustinus, 'Quicquid de Deo dicitur, Deus est, et nichil secundum accidens dici de Deo,'[30] et dicis secundum bonum accidens [r]similitudinem Dei dici.[r] At inquis: 'Quod dico similitudinem Dei donum esse accidens, non ad Deum dantem sed ad hominem accipientem respicio.' Michi uero uidetur satis ex superioribus probatum neutrum esse uerum. Hec sufficiant de similitudine.

Nunc reuertamur ad imaginem et audiamus quid nobis dicat imago uera. Sic enim loquitur: 'Qui me uidet, uidet et Patrem.'[31] In quibus uerbis desiderantibus faciem Patris uidere omnino simillimam et in nullo disparabilem imaginem semetipsum representans, desideria cordis eorum de bonis suis satiare uoluit. Rursus hec eadem imago renouare uolens imaginem suam in imagine sua, alias dicit, 'Sancti estote, quia[s] ego sanctus sum'.[32] Tanquam bonus pictor animarum Deus primam animam in primo homine cum omni benedictione spiritali, ad quam meliorem et formosiorem inuenit imaginem non [t]in iam[t] creatis sed in non creatis,[33] pingendo creauit et creando depinxit. Creauit, inquam, in anima imaginem suam, uel potius animam ad imaginem suam. Depinxit, iterum, in anima similitudinem suam, uel magis animam ad similitudinem suam.[34] Fumo autem iniquitatum et transgressionum suarum decoloratam et usque ad extremam deformitatem fedatam, auctor et amator suus [u]uoluit eam[u] reparare. Et quia eque idoneus pictor neque in celo angelus, neque in terra homo iustus, neque subtus terram aliquis spiritus inueniebatur, accessit imago ad imaginem, formosa ad deformem, iusta ad iniustam,[v] nobilis ad ignobilem, pia ad impiam, eterna ad transitoriam. Venit reparare quod perierat, uenit reficere quod defecerat. Hec imago Dei inuisibilis

[q] sentire *O* [r–r] dici similitudinem Dei *O* [s] quam *O* [t–t] unam *O*
[u–u] eam uoluit *O* [v] iniustum *Sirmond*

[29] Cf. Augustine, *Enarr. in Ps.* lxx. ss. ii. 3 (*CCSL* xxxix. 962; *PL* xxxvi. 893); *De libero arbitrio*, ii. 16. 41 (*CCSL* xxix. 265; *PL* xxxii. 1263), but neither are verbatim quotations and many similar occur in the *Serm. de script.* (*CCSL* xli; *PL* xxxviii, cols. 23–994).

[30] Cf. Augustine, *De trinitate*, v. 3–5 (*CCSL* l. 208–11; *PL* xlii. 912–14).

sound mind and judgement would dare to assert this about virtue, justice, goodness, and love of virtue in the soul? It is precisely, as Augustine says, that as the soul is the life of the body, so God is the life of the soul.[29] God is also true virtue, true goodness, true justice, nay, truth itself. Therefore the soul, if it is without these, dies. And do you say that these are accidental gifts? Looking back again and re-reading your words, and finding not 'gift' but 'good' to be an accident, I am astounded at these greater fancies. For is the likeness of God not God? Equally is the good of God anything other than God? Augustine cries out, 'Whatever is said of God, God is, and nothing is said of God in terms of accident,'[30] and you say the likeness of God is spoken of in terms of a good accident. But you say: 'In saying that the likeness of God is an accidental gift I am considering not God giving but man receiving.' But to me it seems sufficiently proven by what is said above that neither is true. Let these points suffice about likeness.

Now let us turn back to the image and hear what the true image says to us. For He speaks thus: 'He that seeth me seeth the Father also.'[31] In presenting Himself, as an image wholly alike and in no way dissimilar, with these words, to those desiring to see the face of the Father, He wished to satisfy the desires of their heart concerning His blessings. Again this same image, wishing to renew His image in its image, says elsewhere, 'Be holy because I am holy'.[32] God, like a good painter of souls, created by painting and depicted by creating the first soul in the first man with every spiritual blessing, in respect of which He found a better and more beautiful image not in that which was already created but in the uncreated.[33] He created, I say, His image in the soul, or rather the soul in His image. He painted, again, His likeness in the soul, or rather the soul in His likeness.[34] But when it was discoloured by the smoke of its iniquities and transgressions and defiled to the point of extreme deformity, its maker and lover wished to restore it. And since an equally suitable painter was not found, neither an angel in heaven nor a just man on earth nor any spirit beneath the earth, the image approached the image—the lovely the unlovely, the just the unjust, the noble the ignoble, the righteous the unrighteous, the eternal the transitory. He came to restore what had perished, He came to remake what had broken. This image of the invisible God is the Son

[31] Cf. John 14: 9 (words spoken by Christ).

[32] Cf. Lev. 11: 44; 19: 2; 1 Pet. 1: 16: Peter moves between Christ and God the Father in his references to *imago*; note the different sense of *imago* above.

[33] i.e. God took the model from Himself not from His creation.

[34] Here and in the previous sentence Peter is recalling again Gen. 1: 26: 'Faciamus hominem ad imaginem et similitudinem nostram.'

Filius est Altissimi. De Filio namque ait Apostolus, 'Qui est imago Dei inuisibilis'.[35] Sanius uero [w]nichil creditur,[w] nichil dicitur quam unam esse imaginem totius trinitatis, Patris uidelicet,[x] Filii et Spiritus sancti. Vnde Beda [y]super 'Faciamus[y] hominem ad imaginem et similitudinem nostram':[36] 'In eo [z]quod dicit[z] "faciamus", una operatio trium personarum ostenditur, in hoc uero quod dicit[a] "ad imaginem et similitudinem nostram", una et equalis substantia trium personarum monstratur. Ex persona enim Patris hoc dicitur ad Filium et Spiritum sanctum, non ut quidam putant angelis,[b] quia Dei et angelorum non est una et eadem similitudo uel imago.'[37] Proprie itaque Filius dicitur imago Patris, trinitatis essentia minus proprie, homo improprie.[38] Sic autem homo dicitur imago Dei quia similitudinem eius in se gerit, sicut imago Cesaris que similitudinem eius prefert.[39] Hucusque satis dilatauerim philacteria mea, et magnificauerim fimbrias.[40] Si qua tamen durius dixerim, obsecro indulgeatis. [c]Valete et orate pro me.[c]

55

To the community of Mont-Dieu[1]

*c.*1145 × 1162

Dominis suis de Monte Dei suus Cellensis,[a] portam atrii interioris penetrare.[2]

Etsi apices salutationum a uobis mea humilitas accipere non meretur, mereatur saltem munera orationum. Vtrumque quidem si fieri posset satis gratanter acciperem, alterum tamen ambitiosius deposco si ad utrumque non ualeo. Letificarent me littere si scriberetis,[b] sed iuuant orationes si [c]pro me eas[c] funditis. Insipientia mea indiget bonorum instructione, infirmitas anime mee deuota et assidua

[w–w] mimi [*sc.* mihi] credite *Sirmond* [x] scilicet *O* [y–y] superfaciamus *O* [z–z] qui dixit *O* [a] dixit *O* [b] angeli *O*, *Sirmond* [c–c] *om.* *O*

55 *O fo. 123[r], Sirmond III. 5*]
[a] G. *O* [b] scriberitis *O* [c–c] eas pro me *O*

[35] Col. 1: 15. [36] Gen. 1: 26.
[37] Peter Lombard, *Sent.* ii. dist. xvi. 2 (Brady, i. 2, p. 406); cf. Cf. Bede, *In Genesim* i. 1, 26 (*CCSL* cxviii. A, 25 lines 746–9 and 754–8).

of the Most High. For the Apostle says of the Son, 'He who is the image of the invisible God'.[35] But nothing is believed, nothing said more soundly than that there is one image of the whole Trinity, that is the Father, Son, and Holy Spirit. Whence Bede on 'Let us make man to our image and likeness':[36] 'When He says "let us make", one operation of three persons is indicated, but when He says "to our image and likeness," a single and equal substance of three persons is demonstrated. For this is said in the person of the Father to the Son and to the Holy Spirit not, as some think, to the angels, because God and angels do not have one and the same likeness or image.'[37] And so the Son is properly called the image of the Father, the essence of the Trinity less properly, man improperly.[38] But man is called the image of God in this sense, that he bears His likeness in him, in the same fashion as the image of Caesar, which displays his likeness.[39] Thus far let me have made my phylacteries broad enough and enlarged the fringes.[40] If, however, there be any things I have spoken at all harshly, I beg you to forgive me. Farewell and pray for me.

55

To the community of Mont-Dieu[1]

*c.*1145 × 1162

To his lords of Mont-Dieu, their own of Montier-la-Celle, to pass through the gate of the inner court.[2]

Although in my humility I do not deserve to receive a letter of greeting from you, may I at least merit the gifts of prayers. I would indeed accept both gratefully enough if it were possible, the latter however I beg the more keenly if I am not able to have both. Letters would delight me if you were to write them, but prayers help me if you pour them out for me. My folly needs the instruction of the good, the weakness of my soul needs devout and assiduous prayer. If only

[38] Cf. Peter Lombard, *Sent.* ii. dist. xvi. 3.2 and 3.1 (Brady i. 2, p. 407).
[39] Cf. ibid. 3.1 (Brady, i. 2, p. 407), cf. also Matt. 22: 17–21; Mark 12: 14–17; Luke 20: 22–5.
[40] Cf. Matt. 23: 5, i.e. he has spoken too much, and so made too much display, like the scribes and Pharisees.

55 [1] Dated as letter no. 52.
[2] Cf. Ezek. 40: 23; 44: 17; 45: 19; 46: 1 (of the Temple).

oratione. O utinam perspiceretis plagas anime mee misere et desolate in uastitate hostili. Certe si eam diligeretis, super eam lugeretis. O domini et patres karissimi, cur non liberatis animam quamuis miseram tamen uestram? Cur non eruitis de ore leonis iam semipastam? Cur non redimitis sub uinculo captiuitatis usquequaque humiliatam? Sufficiat uobis ad commouendos pietatis affectus recordatio antiquarum miseriarum a quibus redimit[d] uos qui passus est pro uobis. Vltra extenditur cumulus peccatorum meorum et nisi Dominus iuuerit, sanctissimis orationibus uestris interpellatus, iam inferno appropinquat.[e] Valete.[f]

56

To the prior and community of Mont-Dieu[1]

*c.*1145 × 1162

Karissimis dominis et fratribus de Monte Dei, priori cum ceteris sanctis, frater Petrus Cellensis indignus abbas, salutem.

Forte sicut pulli de nido non auolantes[2] paternas esuriunt escas, sic uos, filii karissimi, qui in nidulo uestro plumescitis, ut cum tempus uenerit in altum euoletis dignum faucibus et stomacho sanctitatis a me refundi expectatis. Sed quid coruus ad pullos gallinarum? Non enim eisdem aluntur cibis. Coruus pascitur cadaueribus putredinis, columba uescitur granis puris tritici electi. Noui, noui quibus apud uos per dimidium temporis alitus sum cibis.[3] Si dixero, 'Noui quibus modo usque ad nauseam onerer,' parum profecto dixerim cum sapientia uincat scientiam et plus sit tenorem saporis in ore retinere quam preterita ad animum reuocare. Anxior igitur in his et gemo et horum[a] gustu uehementer afficior. Nolo ruminatione reiterata refricare dolores preteritos, sufficiat enim diei malitia sua,[4] sufficiat gustui amaritudo sua amarissima.[5] Vos denique, fratres et filii karissimi, simplicitate ciborum contenti, sicut didicistis Christum,[6] sicut gus-

[d] redemit *O* [e] apppropinquant *O* [f] *om.* *O*

56 *Sirmond III. 6*]
[a] quorum *Sirmond*

56 [1] Dated as letter no. 52. On the priors for this period see letter no. 35, n. 8.
[2] Possibly alluding to Isa. 16: 2, but there the chicks are flying out of the nest.
[3] Cf. Rev. 12: 14 (cf. also Dan. 7: 25; 12: 7).

you were able to see the wounds of my soul, wretched and forsaken in a hostile desert. Certainly if you loved it you would weep over it. O dearest lords and fathers, why do you not free a soul which although wretched is yet yours? Why do you not pluck it, now half eaten, from the lion's mouth? Why do you not redeem it, continually humiliated beneath the chains of captivity? The recollection of ancient sufferings from which He who suffered for you redeems you should be enough to stir in you kindly sympathies. The mass of my sins is spread out further and, unless the Lord solicited by your most holy prayers aid me, it already approaches the pit. Farewell.

56

To the prior and community of Mont-Dieu[1]

*c.*1145 × 1162

To his dearest lords and brothers of Mont-Dieu, to the prior and the other holy brethren, brother Peter, unworthy abbot of Montier-la-Celle, greetings.

Perhaps just as chicks which do not fly out of the nest[2] hunger for the food provided by their parents, so you, dearest sons, who are fledglings in your nest, in order that when the time comes you may fly on high, are waiting for me to disgorge something worthy of the throat and stomach of the holy. But what use is the raven to the chicks of the hens? For they are not nourished by the same foods. The raven feeds on rotting corpses, the dove eats pure grains of choice wheat. I know, I know on which food I was nourished among you for half a time.[3] If I say, 'I know with which food I am now gorged even to the point of sickness,' I should surely say too little since wisdom is superior to knowledge and since it is a greater thing to retain a flavour in the mouth than to recall to mind things past. Therefore I am made anxious in these things and groan, and am also affected powerfully by the taste of them. I do not wish to scratch open again past wounds by repeated rumination, for sufficient for the day let the evil thereof be,[4] sufficient for the taste let the bitterness most bitter[5] thereof be. You then, dearest brothers and sons, content with the simplicity of the foods, just as you have learned Christ,[6] just as you have tasted and

[4] Cf. Matt. 6: 34. [5] Cf. Isa. 38: 17. [6] Cf. Eph. 4: 20.

tastis et uidistis quia bona est negotiatio uestra,[7] sic perseuerantes, non queratis aliam mensam, non aliam escam. Bonam enim mensam, bonam utique habetis et escam, qua uiuit anima uestra. Quid ipse dicere possum de mensa mea? Certe ex quo descendi de sancto monte Dei mei[8] aut rarissime aut nunquam data est michi mensa ut cum amicis meis epularer. Statim que in insidiis expectabant egressum meum sollicitudines rapuerunt et absorbuerunt me, continuo refluxu super caput meum redundantes. Satis immisericorditer uindicatum est in me si quid otii, si quid boni, in requie illa habuerunt caro mea et cor meum. Seuerius in me exarserunt 'et ne spiraculum quidem incedit per eas'.[b] [9] Apud uos, karissimi et desideratissimi, conqueror de me ipso contra me ipsum. Hec certe, immo multo peiora, merui qui de pena non emendor sed cum pena et culpam multiplico. Orate pro seruulo uestro qui uos omni die desiderat umbram uestram suspirans et faciem uidere sitiens. Valete.

57

To the prior and community of Mont-Dieu[1]

? *c.*1154, or earlier

Dominis et amicis suis, priori et ceteris fratribus de Monte Dei, frater [a]Petrus Cellensis,[a] brauio diurni denarii non fraudari.[2]

Suauissimi 'saporis' buccellas 'quasi panis oleati'[3] [b]auido ore[b] in mensa litterarum[c] uestrarum pregustans, iucunditatem spiritus cepi eructare[4] et iterum atque iterum pre desiderio spiritum bonum attrahere. In crassitudine quippe anime bene paste, in habundantia dulcedinis Dei scripsistis, et 'sicut adipe et pinguedine'[5] spiritalis letitie fauces meas replestis. Sermo namque[d] uester non est talis qui

[b] ea *Sirmond*

57 *O fos. 118^v–120^r*, *Val fos. 113^r–115^r*, *Sirmond III. 3*]
[a–a] G. suus semper *O* [b–b] ore auido *O* [c] *Val has lacuna after* litterarum *with erasure* [d] nempe *O, Val*

[7] Cf. Prov. 31: 18.
[8] Cf. Exod. 3: 1, etc.; Dan. 9: 20, but here meaning Mont-Dieu where (as is also made clear below) he has been on retreat and whose spiritual food is better than that which he now endures, and which (as he implies above) sickens him and blocks out the taste, if not the memory, of theirs. [9] Job 41: 7.

57 [1] If the Simon recommended at the end of this letter is the Simon who transferred from Montier-la-Celle to Mont-Dieu, then this letter may have been written in or before

seen that your dealings are good,[7] persevering thus, seek not another table nor other food. For you have a good table and assuredly good food by which your soul lives. What can I myself say about my own table? Certainly, from the time when I descended from the holy mountain of my God,[8] most rarely or never has a meal been set before me so that I could dine with my friends. Immediately those cares which were waiting in ambush for my departure seized and swallowed me up, pouring over my head with a continuous flow. If in that retreat my flesh and my heart had anything of leisure, anything of good, I have been punished with little enough mercy. They have blazed out against me more fiercely 'and not so much as any air can come between them'.[9] Before you, my dearest and most longed-for ones, I am complaining about myself, against myself. I, who am not corrected by punishment but even with punishment multiply the fault, have surely deserved these things, nay much worse. Pray for your little servant who desires you every day sighing for your shadow and thirsting to see your face. Farewell.

57

To the prior and community of Mont-Dieu[1]

? *c.*1154, or earlier

To his lords and friends, the prior and the other brothers of Mont-Dieu, brother Peter of Montier-la-Celle, not to be cheated of the reward of a penny a day.[2]

Having a foretaste with a keen appetite, at the table of your letter, of morsels of the sweetest 'taste of bread tempered with oil,'[3] I began to utter[4] the joy of the spirit, and again and again, even beyond what I had desired, to draw in the good spirit. For surely you have written in the richness of a soul well fed, in the abundance of the sweetness of God, and you have replenished my throat 'as with the marrow and fatness'[5] of spiritual joy. For your speech is not such as to display, with false forms superimposed, the outer appearance of devotion and

1154 (see letter no. 58, n. 1). He may or may not be the later Prior Simon of Mont-Dieu (see letter no. 59, n. 1). The prior would have been Gervase (1150–9, see letter no. 35, n. 8). On Mont-Dieu, see letter no. 52, n. 1. [2] Cf. Matt. 20: 2. [3] Cf. Num. 11: 8.
[4] Or 'belch forth' (the metaphor does not translate); for 'utter', cf. e.g. Ps. 44 (45): 2.
[5] Ps. 62 (63): 6.

adulterinis formis superinductis speciem pietatis representet et uirtutem abneget. Hoc enim illorum est qui 'in corde et corde' loquuntur[6] uel qui molliunt sermones suos super oleum cum ipsi sint iacula.[7] Non autem uerbum uestrum sic insulsum, sic infatuatum, sed sale salitum,[8] sed gratie plenitudine confortatum, uiscera replet sanctorum, uires reparat animarum, languores sanat egrotantium, fortitudinem conseruat sanorum. Preterea delicatorum sufficit gulositati et nausiantium medetur reiectioni. Pascit ut panis, ut uinum letificat, ut paradisus deliciarum[9] exuberat in omni suauitate, ut templum speciosissimum refulget in omni pulchritudine. Plane suadibilis ad commonendum, rectus ad componendum, efficax ad commouendum, potens ad corroborandum, dulcis ad demulcendum,[e] ardens ad inflammandum. Cum enim pure de puro uase purus effunditur sermo, quid ad emundandum aptius, quid ad informandum apertius, quid ad omne opus bonum utilius? Sane uerbum bonum de bono Dei uerbo frequenti meditatione decoctum,[10] exercitatione corporali et spiritali tanquam mola inferiori et superiori molitum, continua examinatione cogitationum accusantium aut etiam defendentium cribratum, [f]ossibus humilitatis[f] [11] confert medullam, [g]spiritui contrito medelam,[g] et anime esurienti adhibet satietatem bonam. Decoquitur uero panis iste aut in clibano profundi misterii incarnationis Christi aut in sartagine uiuifice crucis aut in craticula mortis et sepulcri, cum uita uestra,[h] locutio uestra, cogitatio uestra commoritur et concorporatur, uel consepelitur, Christo nouo genere uiuendi. Videte panem de clibano, 'memor esto Dominum Iesum resurrexisse a mortuis,[i] ex semine Dauid'.[12] Comedite panem de craticula; cum adhuc peccatores essemus Christus pro impiis mortuus est.[j] [13] De sartagine frixum apprehendite; cum iniquis deputatus est,[14] et 'uere languores nostros ipse tulit, et' infirmitates nostras 'ipse portauit'[15] 'in corpore[k] suo super [l]lignum'[16] crucis.[l] Panis iste triplex itinerantibus per desertum ad 'uiam trium dierum'[17] non deficit quia etiam tertium celum[18] petentibus seu penetrantibus fides incarnationis, passionis[m] et mortis, tanquam scala Iacob,[19] uehiculum existit. In introitu uero 'tabernaculi non manufacti, id est non huius creationis,'[20]

[e] emulcendum *Val* [f–f] humilitatis ossibus *Sirmond* [g–g] *om.* *O* [h] nostra *O* [i] *om.* *O* [j] *om.* *Sirmond* [k] cor *O* [l–l] crucis lignum *Val* [m] et passionis *Val*

[6] Cf. Ps. 11 (12): 3. [7] Cf. Ps. 54 (55): 22. [8] Cf. Ezek. 16: 4.
[9] Possibly alluding to Ezek. 28: 13. [10] See *DML*, *decoquere* 1.
[11] Cf. Ps. 50 (51): 10. [12] Cf. 2 Tim. 2: 8 (*consepelitur* above echoes Rom. 6: 4).

to renounce virtue. For this is a characteristic of those who speak 'with a double heart'[6] or who make their words smoother than oil when the same are darts.[7] But your word is not insipid like this, not tasteless like this but, salted with salt,[8] strengthened with fullness of grace, it replenishes the stomachs of the holy, it restores the strength of souls, it heals the weaknesses of the sick, it preserves the strength of the healthy. Besides this, it satisfies the gluttony of the voluptuaries and relieves the vomiting of the sick. It nourishes like bread, it delights like wine, it abounds in all sweetness like the paradise of pleasures,[9] it shines out in all beauty like the most splendid temple. It is clearly persuasive in admonition, straightforward in composition, effectual in inspiration, powerful in corroboration, sweet in mollification, ardent in excitation. For when a pure speech pours forth purely from a pure vessel, what is more suited for cleansing, what is more open for instruction, what is more useful for every good work? Truly a good word, baked[10] from the good word of God by frequent meditation, ground by bodily and spiritual exertion as if by the lower and upper millstone, sifted by the continuous examination of the thoughts of persons accusing or even defending, bestows marrow on the bones that have been humbled,[11] healing on a contrite spirit, and brings a good sufficiency to a hungry soul. But this bread is baked, either in the oven of the profound mystery of the incarnation of Christ or in the pan of the life-giving cross or on the grill of death and the tomb, when your life, your discourse, your thought dies with Christ and is embodied or entombed with Christ in a new kind of life. See the bread from the oven, 'be mindful that the Lord Jesus is risen again from the dead, of the seed of David'.[12] Eat the bread from the grill; when as yet we were sinners Christ died for the ungodly.[13] Take up from the pan that which is fried; with the wicked was he reckoned[14] and 'surely he hath borne our infirmities and carried' our weaknesses[15] 'in his body upon the tree'[16] of the cross. This threefold bread does not fail travellers on the 'three days' journey' through the desert[17] because even to those seeking or entering into the third heaven[18] the faith of the incarnation, passion, and death is a vehicle like Jacob's ladder.[19] But in the entrance of the 'tabernacle not made with hand, that is, not of this creation,'[20] which clearly God set

[13] Cf. Rom. 5: 6.
[14] Cf. Luke 22: 37.
[15] Isa. 53: 4 (but for 'infirmitates nostras' cf. Matt. 8: 17).
[16] 1 Pet. 2: 24.
[17] Cf. Exod. 3: 18; 5: 3; 8: 27, i.e. to the sacrifice.
[18] Cf. 2 Cor. 12: 2.
[19] Cf. Gen. 28: 12–15.
[20] Cf. Heb. 9: 11.

quod scilicet fixit[n] Deus et non homo, porrigitur panis 'de duabus decimis simile',[21] id est consolatio eterna pro legis et euangelii consummatione, nec non pro carnis perfecta incorruptione, et uera sanctitate anime. Hastam aut gladium ad quid petitis? Quem interficere uultis? Quem ferire? Vbi est uel quis est aduersarius uester? Nonne uos confugistis ad tutissima loca Engedi?[22] Nonne Christus est uobis petra refugii?[23] Nonne 'turris fortitudinis'?[24] Nonne 'omnis armatura fortium'?[25] Nonne inattingibile propugnaculum? Nonne 'gladii duo',[26] scutum, arcus et sagitta?[27] O fortissimi milites Christi,[28] hastam protensam habetis in orationibus continuis, gladium in mortificatione carnis, panem sanctum in spe eterne glorificationis. Hasta uestra non est auersa[o] in aduersitatibus mundi quia rectos facitis gressus ad celum; gladius non declinat in conflictu[p] desideriorum et impetu suggestionum quia ante[q] Dominum est omne[r] desiderium uestrum;[29] panis non inueteratur ex dilatione premiorum quia reuirescit caritas certa spe promissorum bonorum. In calore namque suo perdurat panis quia caritas non tepescit in cordibus uestris. Non hebetatur acies gladii quia non deferuescit rigor discipline ac sancti propositi. Hasta non infringitur quia oratio uestra acumine suo celum penetrans nullis obstaculis reuerberatur. O bellum grande et graue, in stationibus dissimile, in uiribus inequale, in armis incomparabile! O rector et moderator omnium, quam nisi [s]a te fieret[s] ridiculosa pugna uermis et gigantis, hominis et demonis, animalis terreni et aerii, uelocissimi et tardissimi, stultissimi et callidissimi, antiqui et moderni, mortalis et immortalis! Stat ille in superioribus, iacet iste in inferioribus. Pennas ille habet, iste nec pedes. Videt ille quem persequitur, iste sentit nec attendit a quo tam crudeliter uerberetur.[t] Mole carnis molestatur iste, bonitate creatoris ex creatione sua libero uolatu quolibet deuolitat ille. Vtitur hostis mundo isto ut decipiat, utitur homine aduersus hominem ut occidat, utitur eodem aduersus eundem ut absorbeat. Sensibus suis tanquam propriis armis triumphat et strangulat[u] captiuum cum spiritus in seruitutem non redigit mortale corpus suum. O pestis iniqua! O sors hominum misera! Non est tibi in te uirtus; non in arcu uirtutis tue neque in hasta liberi arbitrii tui saluat Dominus. Sic collisa inter

[n] fuit *O* [o] aduersa *Val* [p] confluctu *O* [q] autem *O* [r] omne est *Val* [s–s] fieret a te *Val* [t] uerberatur *O*, *Val* [u] transgulat *O*, *Sirmond*

[21] Lev. 23: 17. [22] Cf. 1 Kgs. (1 Sam.) 24: 1. [23] Cf. Ps. 103 (104): 18.
[24] Ps. 60 (61): 4. [25] S. of S. 4: 4. [26] Luke 22: 38.

up and not man, bread is offered 'of two tenths of flour',[21] that is eternal consolation, on account of the fulfilment of the law and of the Gospel, and also of the complete incorruption of the flesh, and of the true sanctity of the soul. To what end do you seek a spear or a sword? Whom do you wish to kill? Whom to strike down? Where or who is your adversary? Did you not flee to the stronghold of Engaddi?[22] Is Christ not your rock of refuge?[23] Is He not your 'tower of strength'?[24] Is He not 'all the armour of valiant men'?[25] Is He not the unassailable bulwark? Is He not the 'two swords',[26] the shield, the bow, and the arrow?[27] O bravest soldiers of Christ,[28] you have the spear outstretched in continuous prayers, the sword in the mortification of the flesh, holy bread in the hope of eternal glorification. Your spear is not turned aside among the adversities of the world, because you make a straight course for heaven; your sword is not turned aside in the conflict of desires and the assault of temptations, because all your desire is before the Lord;[29] your bread does not grow stale through the delaying of rewards, because love is refreshed by the certain hope of the promised good things. For the bread endures in its own heat because love is not tempered in your hearts. The blade of your sword is not blunted, because the rigour of discipline and holy purpose does not cool. The spear is not broken, because your prayer, penetrating the heavens by its own acuity, is repelled by no obstacles. O great and harsh battle, unlike in positions, unequal in strength, not comparable in arms! O ruler and moderator of all things, how laughable but for you would be the fight of the worm and the giant, man and demon, creature of the earth and of the air, fastest and slowest, most foolish and most skilled, ancient and modern, mortal and immortal! That one stands among the greatest, this one lies among the lowest. That one has wings, this one has not even feet. That one sees whom he pursues, this one feels but does not perceive the one by whom he is so cruelly beaten. This one is burdened by the burden of the flesh; by the goodness of the Creator, that one, from its creation, flies away where it pleases in free flight. The enemy uses this world to ensnare, he uses man against man to kill, he uses like against like to devour. He triumphs by his own senses as if with his own arms and strangles the prisoner when a spirit does not reduce its own body to slavery. O cruel curse! O wretched lot of men! In yourself you have no strength; the Lord saves not in the bow of your strength nor in the spear of

[27] Cf. 2 Esd. (Neh.) 4: 16; Jer. 50: 42.
[28] Cf. 2 Tim. 2: 3.
[29] Cf. Ps. 37 (38): 10.

scopulos, sic contracta[v] inter populos, habes tamen prelium cum filiis Enachim quibus comparata uideris quasi locusta,[30] habes capitale duellum cum principibus tenebrarum, uictori uel uicto proposita morte et uita. Non resurget, non qui ceciderit sed qui cesserit; non addet[w] [31] qui destituerit; non rursus accedet qui elapsus[x] fuerit. [y]Primo uictus primus homo, quia secundus uenit de celo, habuit in ceno subleuantem se,[y] [32] denuo autem[z] si succubuerit contumaciter,[a] non reparabitur quia alius deinceps non generabitur ex uirgine Dei Filius. Voluntarie enim peccantibus 'non relinquitur hostia pro peccatis'.[33] Instantius[b] itaque agendum [c]in presenti stadio[c] ne urgeamur redire cum inclusi in morte iterum non sinemur [d]tunicam oblitam repetere.[d] Tunicam enim penitentie qui neglexerit in corpore, opportunitatem nullam habebit post transitum uite. Ecce, domini [e]mei et amici[e] karissimi, statim ut uidi angelum uestrum cucurri ad armentum cum Abraham, uocaui Saram memorie, puerum[f] cordis, et miscui uobis farinam ut facerem[g] subcinericium.[34] Habetis itaque cilicium uestrum, habetis et subcinericium nostrum. Cooperantur hec duo ad extrahendam peccati rubiginem, ad delendam pruriginem, ad extergendam sorditiem. Iccirco sana et sancta potuit ueraciter exclamare conscientia, uasa puerorum munda esse.[35] O gemma pretiosissima et preclarissima, pro qua si dederit homo omnem substantiam domus sue,[36] tamen nichil estimatur in comparatione illius. Detineo sancta corda, mundos oculos, puras manus, plusquam debeam a pabulo uite, ab introitu glorie, a contemplatione faciei Iesu iam glorificate et deificate. Sed nunc iam remitto; et ut me[h] commemoratione pia[37] in humeris uestris perferatis ad thronum glorie deposco. Valete. Fratrem[i] Simonem 'lumen oculorum meorum',[38] partem uiscerum meorum, attentius uobis commendo.[39]

[v] confracta *O, Val* [w] *poss. corrupt or a confusion based on Ps.* 40 (41): 9. [x] lapsus *Sirmond* [y–y] Primo quidem uictus est primus homo, sed quia secundus Adam uenit de celo, habuit iacens instanter qui limo subleuantem se *O* [z] *om. Val, Sirmond* [a] *om. Val, Sirmond* [b] Instantibus *Val* [c–c] *om. Val, Sirmond* [d–d] oblitam repetere tunicam *Val* [e–e] et amici mei *O, Val* [f] et puerum *O* [g] facerem uobis *Val* [h] *om. Val* [i] *om. Val*

your free will. Crushed thus between the rocks, pressed thus in the throng, you have yet a battle with the sons of Enac, in comparison with whom you seem like a locust;[30] you have a fight to the death with the leaders of darkness, with death and life offered to the victor and the vanquished. It is not the one who falls but the one who yields who will not rise again; he who deserts will not rise again;[31] he who slips away will not advance again. Because a second came from heaven, the first man who was first defeated had someone raising him in the mire,[32] but should he disobediently succumb again he will not be restored because another Son of God will not be born hereafter from a virgin. For 'there is left no sacrifice for sins'[33] to those who sin out of free will. And so we must act the more urgently in the present contest lest we be forced to return when, closed up in death we shall not once more be permitted to seek again the lost tunic. For he who neglects the tunic of penitence in the body shall have no opportunity after he has passed out of this life. See, my dearest lords and friends, as soon as I saw your angel I ran to the herd with Abraham, I called to Sarah of memory and to the boy of the heart, and I mixed flour for you that I might make cakes upon the hearth.[34] And so you have your haircloth and you have our cakes of the hearth. These two work together to extirpate the shame of sin, to obliterate the itch, to expunge the filth. And so the whole and holy conscience was able to cry out truthfully that the vessels of the young men were clean.[35] O most precious and brightest jewel! If a man give in exchange for it the entire substance of his house,[36] yet that substance is reckoned as nothing in comparison with it. I am detaining the holy hearts, the untainted eyes, the pure hands, longer than I ought from the food of life, from the entry to glory, from contemplation of the face of Jesus now glorified and deified. But now finally I let go, and I beg that you carry me on your shoulders by devout commemoration[37] to the throne of glory. Farewell. I commend to you more fervently brother Simon, 'the light of my eyes',[38] a very part of my being.[39]

[30] Cf. Num. 13: 34, the 'monsters . . . of the giant-kind'. What follows alludes to Eph. 6: 12.

[31] Cf. Ps. 40 (41): 9—*addet* here seems to be an abbreviation of the Vulgate idiom 'addet ut resurgat' (Ps. iuxta Hebr.)—('rise again', Douai-Reims), and not a corruption of, e.g., *audet*, or some such.

[32] Cf. 1 Cor. 15: 47 (Christ and Adam).

[33] Cf. Heb. 10: 26.

[34] Cf. Gen. 18: 6–7 (subcinericios panes).

[35] Cf. 1 Kgs. (1 Sam.) 21: 5.

[36] Cf. S. of S. 8: 7.

[37] i.e. by intercessory prayers.

[38] Ps. 37 (38): 11.

[39] Simon; see n. 1 above.

58

To the prior and community of Mont-Dieu[1]

? *c.*1154 (or *c.*1145 × 1162)

Dominis suis et patribus, priori cum ceteris de Monte Dei, frater [a]Petrus Cellensis indignus abbas,[a] 'usque ad montem Dei, Oreb'.[2]

Aliud materia, aliud suadet scribere uestra reuerentia. Et materia quidem que est karissimi filii nostri translatio ad uos potius semper silere uel instantius flere quam scribere admonet, sanctitatis autem[b] uestre reuerentia sancta et digna exigit. Itaque non quelibet leuia et secularia sed fortia et celestia debet assumere qui uobis proponit scribere. Quid autem caritate fortius que 'fortis est ut mors'?[3] Quid celestius, que etiam celestium[c] omnem exuperat sensum?[4] Et de hac quidem, quantum ad nostrum se inclinare dignata est sensum:[d] 'Maiorem hac dilectionem nemo habet ut animam suam ponat quis pro amicis suis.'[5] Quanti igitur apud meam humilitatem uestra profecerit dilectio estimare poterit qui quod pro ea reposuerim pretium diligenter pensauerit.[6] Certe non aurum sed uirum secundum cor meum, certe non argentum sed quem habebam quasi[e] unigenitum, certe non lapides pretiosos sed lapidem quem [f]michi erexeram[f] in specialis amoris titulum[7] in hoc proposui[g] commercio. Scio, nec prorsus dubito, quod si omnem substantiam domus mee dederim pro sancto amore[8] uestro nichil tamen in comparatione[h] illius attulerim. De Monte namque Dei non amor mundi sed amor celi descendit, non carnalis amor qui tanquam nubes matutina

58 *O fos. 114*[v]*–116*[r]*, Val fos. 109*[v]*–110*[v]*, Sirmond III. 1*]

[a–a] G humilis Christi sacerdos *O* [b] enim *O* [c] *om. Sirmond* [d] sensum euangelium illud dicimus quia *O* [e] tanquam *O* [f–f] erexeram michi *O* [g] propositi *O* [h] operatione *O*

58 [1] This letter concerns the transfer of a monk of Montier-la-Celle to Mont-Dieu. This could refer to the Robert named in letters 59 and 60, or to Simon of Mont-Dieu (on whom see also letter no. 59, n. 1). The other monk of Montier-la-Celle believed to have transferred to Mont-Dieu, the Stephen named in letter no. 59, would have gone before Peter became abbot of Montier-la-Celle (see letter no. 59, n. 39, but this identification cannot be certain). On Robert we have no dates other than the fact that he was (if it is the same Robert) already at Mont-Dieu when letters 59 and 60 were written—when Simon was prior (1159–*c.*1184). Le Couteulx suggests that Robert transferred *c.*1154 and that Simon preceded him, proposing that the 'Joseph' here refers to Simon and the 'Benjamin' to Robert (Le Couteulx, ii. 144–7; but the monk Simon and the later Prior Simon may not

58

To the prior and community of Mont-Dieu[1]

? *c.*1154 (or *c.*1145 × 1162)

To his lords and fathers, the prior and the others of Mont-Dieu, brother Peter, unworthy abbot of Montier-la-Celle, 'unto the mount of God, Horeb'.[2]

The matter in hand urges me to write one thing, the reverence owed to you urges me to write another. Now the matter in hand, which is the transfer to you of our dearest son, urges me to remain ever silent, or to weep more vehemently, rather than to write, but holy and proper reverence for your holiness demands it. And so he who proposes to write to you must take up not any things trivial and worldly but those things which are strong and heavenly. But what is stronger than love, which 'is strong as death'?[3] What is more heavenly than love, which surpasses all understanding,[4] even that of the heavenly ones? And of love indeed, in so far as it has deigned to incline itself towards our understanding: 'Greater love than this no man hath, that a man lay down his life for his friends.'[5] He then who weighs up carefully what sum I have put down for it, shall be able to estimate how much your love has profited my humility.[6] Certainly I have offered in this trade not gold but a man after my own heart, certainly not silver but him whom I was regarding as my only begotten, certainly not precious stones but a stone which I had set up myself for a title[7] of particular love. I know, nor by any means do I doubt, that should I give all the substance of my house for your holy love[8] I should yet offer nothing in comparison with it. For from the Mount of God it is not the love of the world but the love of heaven which descends, not the love of the flesh, which passes away like a

be the same person). However, there is no conclusive evidence for the date of the transfer of Robert, or for the order in which Simon and Robert went, so a date as late as 1159 × 1162, when we know a Robert to have been at Mont-Dieu under Prior Simon, remains possible. (MS O has a rubric: 'Pro Simone cum iret ad montem dei', but this is presumably an inference from letter no. 57 which appears later in O.) The prior for most of this period was Gervase (1150–9, see letter no. 35, n. 8). On Mont-Dieu, see letter no. 52, n. 1.

2 3 Kgs. (1 Kgs.) 19: 8; cf. Exod. 3: 1.

3 Cf. S. of S. 8: 6.

4 Cf. Phil. 4: 7.

5 John 15: 13.

6 The sum being the monk given up, i.e. allowed to transfer.

7 Cf. Gen. 28: 22; 31: 45; 35: 14.

8 Cf. S. of S. 8: 7.

pertransit[9] sed eterna 'caritas' que 'nunquam excidit'.[10] Non enim recipit estimationem quod omnem excedit accidentium licitationem. Diuini siquidem amoris suauitatem sanctarum animarum pius redolet amor, et quid humana paupertas dignum recompensationis, non dicam ad supernum amorem sed saltem ad quamlibet sanctorum dignationem, in omni thesauro inopie copiose habundantis reperire poterit? Sane nil sanioris michi uidetur ad hoc consilii quam ut 'gratiam' rependat 'pro gratia',[11] ad illius imitationem qui potius ex habundanti quam ex indigenti non aliud [i]quam 'gratiam'[i] solet dare 'pro gratia'.[12] Itaque et ego gratie vestre gratias ago, non tamen uanas,[j] non uacuas, sed ultra facultatum mearum sufficientiam largas et diuites. Non enim de archa sed de conscientia, non de fundo marsupii sed de intimo cordis, non de supellectili domus sed de intimis uisceribus profero quod accipitis. Si enim aliter fieri posset, si aliud pretium quantumcunque magnum uestra sanctitas exposceret, si aliquam commutationem commercium illud[k] admitteret, o quam libenter darem, o cum quanta gratiarum actione numerarem! O Deus cordis mei, quanta anime mee '[l]usque ad mortem'[l] [13] in hoc partu angustia, quam importabilis; nisi tu mecum portaueris, in separatione ista affectionis semper duratura[m] erumpna. Iesu bone, indubitanter pro te aliquid me fecisse iam deinceps fateri non erubesco. Sed quid aliud facerem? Tuus est ille, tuus sum ego. Et utinam [n]sic tuus[n] ego sicut ille tuus. Et qua fronte tibi de tuo tuus contradicere presumam? Non resisto uoluntati tue contumaciter ut tu assistas desolationi mee misericorditer. 'Vide humilitatem meam[o] et laborem meum, et dimitte uniuersa delicta mea.'[14] Domine, Domine, nonne totam mitius a me tolleres animam quam partem dimidiam?[15] Placeat tibi saltem non deserere partem residuam quia tibi assumis precipuam. Vere nunc experior quod 'separare' ueneris 'hominem aduersus patrem suum'.[16] Vere hic gladius Salomonis 'uiuus et efficax et penetrabilior omni[p] gladio ancipiti, pertingens usque ad diuisionem anime et[q] spiritus'.[17] Quare propter te [r]et per

[i–i] quidem *Sirmond* [j] uacuas *Sirmond* [k] istud *O* [l–l] *om. Val* [m] duratur *Sirmond* [n–n] tuus sic *O* [o] *om. O* [p] o. *ins. O* [*the quotation is represented by initial letters, with an extra* o *at this point*] [q] ac *Val* [r–r] *om. Sirmond*

[9] Cf. Hos. 6: 4; 13: 3.

[10] 1 Cor. 13: 8; the Mount of God here is Mont-Dieu.

[11] John 1: 16.

[12] John 1: 16. The 'gratias' which Peter is giving (see next sentence) is the monk being transferred.

[13] Matt. 26: 38; Mark 14: 34; Acts 22: 4; Phil. 2: 8, 27, 30; Rev. 2: 10; 12: 11.

morning cloud,[9] but the eternal 'charity' which 'never falleth away'.[10] For that which exceeds all offers of inessentials does not admit of valuation. Devout love of holy souls is indeed redolent of the sweetness of divine love, and what shall human indigence be able to procure in all its treasure chest of copiously abundant poverty as worthy repayment, I should not say for the love of God but at least for any graciousness of his saints? Truly nothing seems to me to be of sounder counsel in this matter than that man in his poverty should repay 'grace for grace,'[11] in imitation of Him who, abundantly rather than with a miserly hand, is accustomed to give nothing but 'grace for grace'.[12] And so I also give thanks for your grace, not however worthless nor empty thanks, but great and rich beyond the sufficiency of my resources. For I produce what you receive not from a money-chest but from conscience, not from the bottom of my purse but from the depth of my heart, not from the resources of my household but from the depth of my being. For if it could be done otherwise, if you in your holiness were asking another price, however great, if that transaction admitted some change, o how gladly would I give it, o with how great a performance of thanks would I pay it out! O God of my heart, how great is the anguish of my soul 'even unto death'[13] in this begetting, how unbearable; unless you bear it with me, the distress in this severing of affection will last for ever. Good Jesus, I am not ashamed now to confess finally that without hesitation I have done something for you. But what else could I do? He is yours, I am yours. And I wish that I were yours in the way that he is yours. And by what impudence would I, being yours, presume to contradict you concerning your own? I am not resisting your will stubbornly, and so may you stand by my desolation mercifully. 'See my abjection and my labour, and forgive me all my sins.'[14] Lord, Lord, would it not be more merciful of you to take my whole soul from me than half of it?[15] May it please you at least not to abandon the remaining part because you are taking the chief part unto yourself. Truly now I find that you have come 'to set a man at variance against his father'.[16] Truly this is the sword of Solomon 'living and effectual and more piercing than any two-edged sword, reaching unto the division of the soul and the spirit'.[17] Why is the partition of souls, when bodies are present,

[14] Ps. 24 (25): 18.

[15] Cf. Horace, *Odes* i. 3 line 8.

[16] Matt. 10: 35.

[17] Cf. Heb. 4: 12; a ref. to the word of God, not the sword of Solomon, but with characteristic boldness in manipulating biblical quotations, Peter is alluding to Solomon's judgement here.

te[r] diuisa est maceries[18] animorum, presentia corporum—tu mediator, tu lapis angularis,[19] tu dispersos Israhel congregas,[s] tu Deus unus, ad te et in te utraque faciens unum—quare sic facis, uel si non facis, quare pateris ut caream baculo mee debilitatis, ut suam columpnam sua[t] deserat basis, ut sine Aaron non Moyses sed tuus miser cogatur sustinere questiones siue molestias huius talis ac[u] tante multitudinis? Pie Iesu, non sustineat pietas tua sine consolatione meam diutius fragilitatem conquassari, sine uisitatione fatigari. Quid est hoc? Vobis cepi scribere, uobis loqui, et sic in mediis sermonibus cum tanta mora meas miserias misericordissimi Dei conspectibus explicui certe ut uideatis, certe ut intelligatis quis sit dolor filium dextere amittere[v] et nec saltem sublato Ioseph Beniamin retinere,[20] quin immo ut 'Deum totius consolationis',[21] meis compatiendo meroribus, dulcius et obnixius pro me exoretis. Est enim [w]benignus piorum[w] exauditor, largus pro se aliquid facientibus remunerator. Orate itaque ut et istum quem quasi in uinculis Christi retinetis non amittam, et ut optando scripsistis pro Samuhele nostro prophetam non inferiorem recipiam.[22] Sic enim dote bona ditatus, consolationem aliquam uestris orationibus accipiens, potero expectare illam ueram et eternam pro qua desolationem suscipio temporalem et transitoriam. Valete.

[s] congregaris *O* [t] *om. Sirmond* [u] et *Sirmond* [v] admittere *Val*
[w–w] piorum benignus *Val*

[18] Cf. Gen. 38: 29: 'dixitque mulier, quare diuisa est propter te maceria.' By 'presentia corporum' Peter evidently means that the souls are parted while they are still alive, i.e. the monk is taken away from him before, not by, death. The passage is a mock complaint that the transfer is to Jesus's benefit and Peter's detriment.

divided for you[18] and through you—you who are the mediator, you the corner-stone,[19] you who gather the dispersed of Israel, you the one God, making both one with you and in you—why do you bring it about or, if you do not, why do you suffer that I should be deprived of the staff of my weakness, that the column should lack its pedestal, that, without Aaron, not Moses but your wretched one should be forced to bear trials or tribulations of this sort and in such great numbers? Merciful Jesus, may your mercy not suffer my fragility to be shaken any longer without consolation, to be wearied without your presence. What is the point of this? It was to you that I began to write and to speak, and in this way, in the midst of my discourse, I have unfolded my miseries at such length before the eyes of the most merciful God, assuredly so that you may see, that you may understand what pain it is to lose the son of the right hand, and with Joseph carried away not even to keep Benjamin,[20] nay more, so that you may pray on my behalf more kindly and more resolutely to 'the God of all comfort,'[21] feeling for my sorrows. For He is the benign hearer of the devout, the generous rewarder of those doing something for Him. Pray therefore both that I do not lose that one whom you are keeping as if in the bonds of Christ, and that, as you have written in hope, I may receive no less a prophet in place of our Samuel.[22] For thus enriched with a good dowry, receiving some consolation from your prayers, I shall be able to await that true and eternal consolation for which I am suffering temporal and transient desolation. Farewell.

[19] Cf. Eph. 2: 20.

[20] Cf. Gen. 35: 18 (Benjamin as the son of the right hand); Gen. 37 (Joseph taken away); on the possible significance of these references, see n. 1 above. He has now switched back from addressing Jesus to addressing the recipients directly.

[21] Cf. 2 Cor. 1: 3.

[22] i.e. unlike the Israelites who asked for and received a king not a prophet in Samuel's place, to the Lord's displeasure—1 Kgs. (1 Sam.) 8.

59

To Prior Simon and the community of Mont-Dieu[1]

1159 × 1162

Dominis et patribus suis de Monte Dei, Simoni priori cum ceteris fratribus, frater Petrus qualiscunque Cellensis abbas, uultus in propitiatorium[2] semper tenere.

Varius rerum cursus, seculorum uolubilitati irremediabiliter innexus, nichil stabile, nichil eternum sibi inesse euidenti ratione approbat. Currit, fluit, fugit, labitur et euanescit quicquid unquam habere potest mundanus usus. Precurrit defectus satietatem, preterfluit adeptio appetitum, effugit instantiam desiderii fumus glorie, elabitur utenti imago felicitatis, euanescit a uiuentibus uita, quia 'dum ordirer succidit me'.[3] Summa itaque dementia est currere post defectum, appetere non apprehensibile, instare fumo, uti imagine pro ueritate, uelle diu ea uita uiuere que, iuxta Gregorium, uite eterne comparata mors potius dicenda est quam uita.[4] Alias sine dubio cursum uestrum conuertistis, fratres et domini karissimi, alio appetitu uiuitis, alia instantia pretiosas margaritas in foro et nundinis ueteris et noui testamenti queritis,[5] alio usu, in carne preter carnem uiuendo, corpora uestra que sunt super terram[6] Christo concrucifigitis, alia conuersatione eterna et que non uidentur concupiscitis, 'que enim

59 *Sirmond V. 13*]

---

59 [1] Simon, prior of Mont-Dieu 1159–*c.*1184 (Le Couteulx, ii. 144–7, 192–3; iii. 9–11). He may be the monk of Montier-la-Celle who transferred to Mont-Dieu, possibly in or before 1154 (on this, see also letter no. 58, n. 1). Godefroy identifies this Simon with Prior Simon of Saint-Ayoul-de-Provins, 1148–54/5, and with Abbot Simon of Saint-Remi, 1182–98: Godefroy, 'Saint-Ayoul', ii. 30–3, and esp. p. 31, n. 8, which cites a charter of 1196 referring to Abbot Simon of Saint-Remi as having once been prior of Saint-Ayoul (the entry for Simon of Saint-Remi in *GC*, ix. 234, does not make this identification). However, the further identification of this figure (if indeed it is one figure) with Simon of Mont-Dieu is insecure, being based only on the recommendation by Peter of Celle of a Simon to the monks of Mont-Dieu (in letter no. 57; see also letter no. 58, n. 1)—i.e. taking this as proof that a monk of Peter's own community, here taken to include the dependency of Saint-Ayoul, was transferring to Mont-Dieu, and then assuming that this is the same Simon who later became prior of Mont-Dieu. A Prior Simon of Provins occurs in John of Salisbury's early correspondence, see *J. S. Epp.* i. 62, n. 9, and refs. On Simon of Mont-Dieu's activities in the Becket affair see *J. S. Epp.* ii, pp. xxxiv, xli.

This letter must have been written between Simon's election as prior and Peter of Celle's departure from Montier-la-Celle. By the time of writing the mission to select a site

59

To Prior Simon and the community of Mont-Dieu[1]

1159 × 1162

To his lords and fathers of Mont-Dieu, to Prior Simon and the other brothers, brother Peter, abbot of whatever sort of Montier-la-Celle, to fix your gaze always upon the place of expiation.[2]

The varying course of affairs, irretrievably entangled with the instability of worldly things, proves by manifest reason that there is in it nothing stable, nothing everlasting. Anything which worldly use can ever lay hold on runs, flows, flees, slips away, and vanishes. Lack outruns satisfaction, attainment flows beyond the reach of longing, the smoke of glory escapes the pursuit of desire, the image of happiness slips away from its possessor, life vanishes from the living, because 'while I was beginning he cut me off'.[3] It is therefore the height of madness to run after that which is lacking, to long for what cannot be grasped, to pursue smoke, to possess an image instead of the truth, to wish to live for a long time in that life which, according to Gregory, when compared to eternal life should be called death rather than life.[4] Doubtless, dearest brothers and lords, you have turned your course elsewhere, you live by a different longing, by a different type of pursuit you seek the precious pearls[5] in the forum and the market of the Old and New Testaments, by a different custom, living in the flesh without the flesh, you crucify with Christ your bodies which are upon the earth,[6] partaking in a different type of converse you long for those things which are eternal and which are not seen, 'for the things which are seen are temporal but the things

for a new Carthusian foundation on Henry the Liberal's lands had failed (? *c.*1160, see letter no. 35, n. 1). While this letter must thus post-date letter no. 35, there is no indication of how much time elapsed between letter no. 35, the failed mission, and this letter, although the amount of activity may suggest a later date within the given frame (but note also that, while Simon is the addressee of the present letter, there is no conclusive evidence that letter no. 35 was written when he was prior—see no. 35, n. 1). On Mont-Dieu, see letter no. 52, n. 1.

[2] Cf. Exod. 25: 17, 20, 22; 26: 34; 30: 6; 31: 7; 35: 12; 37: 6–9; 39: 34; Lev. 16: 2, 14; Num. 7: 89; Heb. 9: 5.

[3] Cf. Isa. 38: 12.

[4] Cf. Gregory, *Hom. .xl. in Evang.* ii. 37. 1 (*PL* lxxvi. 1275), 'ea uita' being 'temporalis uita'.

[5] Cf. Matt. 13: 45.

[6] Cf. Gen. 9: 17; Gal. 5: 24.

uidentur temporalia sunt, que autem non uidentur eterna'.[7] Ideo ad Montem Domini sicut passer[8] euolastis et nidificastis 'in foraminibus petre, in cauernis macerie',[9] ne procella aeriarum suggestionum uos inuolueret, ne diluuium carnalium titillationum absorberet, ne laqueus sollicitudinum secularium concluderet, ne aura humani fauoris '⟨in⟩ omnem uentum'[10] a facie terre dispergeret. Ecce locus iste est quem constituit Dominus Moysi, in quo uidit posteriora eius dum ante eum transiret.[11] Ni fallor, uir ille bonus qui Sunamiti mortuum puerum reddidit, cui illa cum uiro suo cenaculum preparauerat et lectum et mensam et candelabrum, per uos sepe transitum facit[12] contemplatus a uobis in cenaculo glorie, inuentus in lecto mundate conscientie, cibatus et potatus in sacramento eucharistie diuine, accensus per donum sapientie et intelligentie. 'Adiuro uos per capreas[a] ceruosque camporum'[13] ut cum transierit post tergum eius clametis pro pace uniuersalis ecclesie, pro his 'qui in sublimitate sunt',[14] pro comite nostro cuius cor tetigit Deus edificare uobis locum in quo secundum genus uestrum fructum faciatis,[15] pro me peccatore suo et uestro, pro omnibus nobis commissis. Transite cum illo et post illum ut manentem in perpetuas eternitates uel 'in ictu oculi',[16] uel media hora,[17] uel momento[18] conspiciatis donec transfiguremini 'a claritate in claritatem'.[19] Certe qui sequitur transeuntem uidebit stantem uel sedentem.[20] Fratres mei karissimi, 'si delibatio sancta ⟨est⟩ et massa',[21] si memoria eius uinum Libani,[22] quid presentia nisi inebriatio uberum,[23] nisi obliuio preteritorum et iubilatio interminabilis de plenitudine gaudiorum? Expectatio horum letitia; quid fruitio nisi letitia sempiterna? Ad instar grani sinapis[24] uisio tua, Iesu; modico sibilo aure tenuis[25] aures cordis percellis, et

[a] campos *Sirmond*

---

[7] 2 Cor. 4: 18.

[8] Cf. Ps. 10 (11): 2 (the 'Mountain of the Lord' is an allusion to Mont-Dieu).

[9] S. of S. 2: 14. The place (*locus*) which the Lord appointed for Moses in Exod. 33: 22, from which Peter quotes below, is also a 'cleft [or hole] of the rock' (S. of S. 2: 14, 'in foraminibus petre'; Exod. 33: 22, 'in foramine petre').

[10] Jer. 49: 32; Ezek. 5: 10, 12; 12: 14; 17: 21.

[11] Cf. Exod. 33: 22–3 (see n. 9 above).

[12] i.e. Elisha, cf. 4 Kgs. (2 Kgs.) 4: 8–10, 32–5 (v. 9: 'I perceive that this is a holy man of God, who often passeth by us'); below he speaks of Christ passing by.

[13] Cf. S. of S. 2: 7; 3: 5.

[14] 1 Tim. 2: 2.

[15] Cf. Gen. 1: 11. On Henry the Liberal of Champagne's plan to found a new charterhouse on his lands, see letter no. 35, n. 1.

[16] 1 Cor. 15: 52.

[17] Cf. Rev. 8: 1.

[18] Cf. 1 Cor. 15: 52.

[19] 2 Cor. 3: 18.

which are not seen are eternal'.[7] So you have flown to the Mountain of the Lord like a sparrow[8] and made a nest 'in the clefts of the rock, in the hollow places of the wall'[9] so that the storm of transitory promptings may not sweep you away, the flood of the titillations of the flesh may not swallow you up, the snare of the concerns of the world may not entrap you, the breath of human favour may not scatter you from the face of the earth 'into every wind'.[10] See, this is the place which the Lord appointed for Moses, in which he saw the back parts of Him while He was passing before him.[11] Unless I am deceived, that good man who restored the dead son to the Sunamitess, he for whom she with her husband had prepared a chamber and a bed and a table and a candlestick, often passes by you,[12] contemplated by you in the chamber of glory, discovered in the bed of pure conscience, given food and drink in the sacrament of the divine Eucharist, set alight by the gift of wisdom and understanding. 'I adjure you by the roes and the harts of the fields'[13] to call out after him when he passes by for the peace of the universal Church, for those 'that are in high station,'[14] for our count whose heart God has touched to build a house for you in which you may yield fruit after your kind,[15] for me, his poor sinner and yours, and for all of those committed to us. Pass by with him and follow after him so that you may see the One abiding through all eternity, either 'in the twinkling of an eye',[16] or for half an hour,[17] or in a moment,[18] until you be transformed 'from glory to glory'.[19] Certainly he who follows the one passing by shall see the One standing or sitting.[20] My dearest brothers, 'if the first fruit be holy, so is the lump also,'[21] if the memory of Him be the wine of Lebanon,[22] what have we now if not the drunkenness of the breasts,[23] forgetfulness of the past, and unending jubilation from the fullness of joy? The expectation of these things is a joy; what shall their enjoyment be if not boundless? Your appearance is like a mustard seed,[24] o Jesus; with a slight whistling of a gentle air[25] you strike the ears of the heart, and who shall be able to contemplate the hour of your passing? If I am asleep I can dream and I cannot see. If I am awake, detained by other occupations and concerns, I cannot detach myself so quickly. If I

[20] i.e. God; there are many references in Rev. to God sitting and standing.
[21] Rom. 11: 16, '. . . and if the root be holy, so are the branches'.
[22] Cf. Hos. 14: 8.
[23] Cf. Prov. 7: 18.
[24] Cf. Matt. 13: 31; 17: 19; Mark 4: 31; Luke 13: 19; 17: 6.
[25] Cf. 3 Kgs. (1 Kgs.) 19: 12.

quis poterit cogitare horam transitus tui? Si dormio sompniare possum et uidere non possum. Si uigilo detentus aliis occupationibus et curis, tam cito exoccupari nequeo. Si uigilo et uacauero tunc forte uenam susurrii eius[26] audio, sed nondum uideo. Quando ergo uidebo transeuntem? Si mundum cor sursum[27] habuero, si puras manus, si lotam faciem, si tota anima, tota uirtute[28] in omnibus solum Deum quesiero et me totum in ipsum conflauero ut non ego in me uiuam sed Christus uiuat in me,[29] qui factus est nobis a Deo sapientia et iustitia et sanctificatio et redemptio. De mendacio autem, uenia petita, me ipsum condempno apud uos. Nec enim solui quod promisi, uel semel in anno reuisere nidum illarum sanctarum uirtutum, Montem Dei, in quo plumescunt anime charismatibus gratiarum. Fefellit me tunc ignota futurorum facies et inuoluta plurimorum casuum series. De presenti affectu quo mens mea tota illa quadragesima impinguata eructabat mellis et butyri riuulos[30] pensabam sequentes annos. Sed eruca, locusta, bruchus et rubigo[31] deuorauerunt 'speciosa deserti',[32] expandentes retia cotidianarum sollicitudinum pedibus meis ut quod egressum est de labiis meis facerem irritum. Peccaui, quid aliud dicam? Si me excuso 'os meum condempnabit me'.[33] Magis autem meretur ueniam culpe humilis confessio erroris quam argumentosa extenuatio criminis. Verumtamen cum redditur ratio facti, rei ueritas non obfuscatur neque rei culpa si qua est dissimulatur. Distinguitur namque falsa excusatio et rationabilis satisfactio. Alterum culpam cumulat, alterum quatinus culpandus uel non culpandus sit qui arguitur declarat. Vterque etiam peccat, et qui mentitur in sui accusatione et qui dedignatur falsa obiecta uera relatione diluere. Reproba humilitas est plus quam in corde tuo sentias uane te deicere, detestanda presumptio famam suam negligere et suspicionis neuum non abolere. Vtroque genere, deuitans tam quod a uero deuiat quam quod presumptionem redoleat, et me non uenisse fateor et innumerabilibus detentum occupationibus attestor. Factum, immo non factum, agnosco; causam facti, siue non facti, uobis diiudicandam relinquo. Quid pluris sit, uel quodlibet alteri preiudicet, id est factum cause aut causa facto, definite. Cedo enim sententie uestre qua credo uos de facto secundum causam non de causa secundum facti

[26] Cf. Job 4: 12.
[27] A possible echo of 'sursum corda', in the mass.
[28] Cf. Mark 12: 30; cf. also Deut. 6: 5; Matt. 22: 37; Mark 12: 33; Luke 10: 27.
[29] Cf. Gal. 2: 20.
[30] Cf. Job 20: 17.
[31] Cf. Joel 1: 4; 2: 25.
[32] Cf. Joel 1: 19–20.
[33] Job 9: 20.

am awake and unoccupied, then perhaps I do hear the vein of its whisper[26] but do not yet see. When therefore shall I see Him passing? If I keep a clean heart on high,[27] pure hands, a cleansed face, if I seek God alone with my whole soul, with my whole strength[28] in all things and kindle myself entirely for Him so that I live not in myself but Christ live in me,[29] who was formed by God for us as wisdom and justice and sanctification and redemption. But having sought forgiveness I condemn myself before you of falsehood. For I have not fulfilled what I promised, to visit again at least once within the year the nest of those holy virtues, Mont-Dieu, in which souls are fledged with the gifts of grace. The unknown shape of future events, as well as the complicated series of very many occurrences, deceived me then. In the state of mind of that moment, in which my soul, fattened through the whole of Lent, was pouring out streams of honey and of butter,[30] I was weighing up the years ahead. But the palmer-worm, the locust, the bruchus, and the mildew[31] have devoured 'the beautiful places of the wilderness',[32] spreading snares of daily concerns beneath my feet so that I have made void what issued from my lips. I have sinned, what else can I say? If I make excuses for myself, 'my own mouth shall condemn me'.[33] But a humble confession of error merits forgiveness of a wrong more than does a plausibly argued extenuation of the offence. Nevertheless, when an account of the deed is given the truth of the matter is not hidden, nor is the fault in the matter, if such there is, dissembled. For a deceitful excuse is distinct from a rational explanation. The one compounds the guilt, the other clarifies how far the one who is accused is to be blamed or not blamed. Moreover each sins, both the one who lies in charging himself and the one who disdains to wash away false charges with a true account. It is spurious humility vainly to cast yourself down lower than you feel in your heart, it is a detestable presumption to neglect one's reputation and not to wipe out the blemish of suspicion. In both sorts, avoiding that which departs from truth as much as that which may smell of presumption, I both confess that I have not come and swear that I am detained by innumerable occupations. I admit the deed or rather the non-deed, I submit the reason for its being done or not done to your adjudication. State clearly which is more important or which you deem to prejudice the other, that is to say, the deed the cause or the cause the deed. For I yield to your judgement, by which I believe you determine a dispute judging the deed by the cause, not the cause by the nature of the deed. For more attention should be

qualitatem litem dirimere. Plus enim attendendum est quare aliquid fiat quam quid fiat. Informis namque est actus ille qui nullam habet causam quare fiat, deformis qui malam, bene formatus qui bonam. Vnde et bonus est omnis actus ille qui iustam habet causam, malus qui iniustam. Indifferens uero dicitur actus ille cuius causa parum concurrit uel ad iustificationem uel ad corruptionem. Augustinus de bona causa: 'Causa non pena martyrem facit.'[34] De mala, Dominus in euangelio: 'Si oculus tuus nequam est totum corpus tuum tenebrosum erit.'[35] Item in legibus de indifferenti: 'Voluntas et propositum distinguunt maleficium.'[36] Dicit Ambrosius, 'Affectus tuus operi tuo nomen imponit.'[37] Subtiliter tamen ratione quorumdam actuum pensata, nulla intentione, nulla affectione boni fieri possunt ut crucifigere Christum, ut adulterari, et similia. Vt ad propositum redeam et congrua structura coherere primordiis extrema faciam, uenire ad Montem Dei inter illa numero que si bono animo fiant remunerabilia sunt, si malo dampnabilia. Fur enim ille qui fratris illius leprosi pannos dum missa celebraretur abstulit premium bonum pro tali facinore non habebit. Recipiet uero mercedem qui pro sancto desiderio uidere castra Dei[38] apud uos properauerit. Satis est, si non plus satis sit. More enim meo tarde incipio sed et tarde finio. Comes Henricus reaccenso spiritu instat querere locum idoneum et asserit illum alium locum non se dimisisse nisi quia uos noluistis adquiescere.[39] Consulo ergo ut non graue sit iterum mittere aliquem de fratribus cum quo ipse uideam, uel per me uel nostros, locum, ut iam dictum est, aptum ordini uestro. Sine mora facite hoc. Singillatim et generaliter omnes uos saluto, quandoque uenturus ad uos, si Deus uoluerit, et forte cum redierit nuntius uester ad uos. Interim orate pro nobis. Robertulum nostrum saluto, Richardum, Stephanum, Rogerium, Nicolaum et iterum omnes simul.[40]

[34] Cf. Augustine, *Ep.* cciv. 4 (*CSEL* lvii. 319; *PL* xxxiii. 940); *Serm. de sanctis*, cclxxxv. 2 (*PL* xxxviii. 1293); cccxxvii. 1 (*PL* xxxviii. 1450); cccxxxi. 2. 2 (*PL* xxxviii. 1459); *Contra Cresc.* iii. 47. 51 (*CSEL* lii. 459; *PL* xliii. 524).

[35] Cf. Matt. 6: 23; cf. also Luke 11: 34.

[36] Cf. Peter Cantor, *Verb. Abbrev.* xii (*PL* ccv. 56).

[37] Cf. Ambrose, *De officiis min.* i. 30. 147 (M. Testard, *Saint Ambroise, les Devoirs* (Paris, 1984), i. 166; *PL* xvi, 71).

[38] Cf. Gen. 32: 2.

[39] On Henry the Liberal of Champagne's plan to found a charterhouse on his lands, see letter no. 35, n. 1.

[40] On Robert, see letter no. 58, n. 1, and no. 60, n. 36. Stephen may be another monk of Montier-la-Celle who had transferred from there to Mont-Dieu before Peter's time: he has

paid to the reason why a thing is done than to what is done. For a particular action is formless if it has no cause by which it is done, deformed if it has an evil cause, well-formed if it has a good cause. Hence also every such action is good which has a just cause and evil which has an unjust cause. But that action is said to be indifferent the cause of which does not tend towards either justification or corruption. Augustine said of a good cause, 'The cause not the punishment makes a martyr.'[34] Concerning an evil cause, the Lord said in the Gospel, 'If your eye is evil, your whole body shall be darksome.'[35] Again it is said in the laws, concerning indifferent causes, 'Will and intention define wickedness.'[36] Ambrose says, 'Your state of mind gives a name to your deed.'[37] However, when the reason for certain actions has been minutely weighed, by no intention, by no state of mind can actions such as crucifying Christ, being defiled, and the like, be made good. To return to my point, and to make the end cohere with the beginning in a harmonious structure, I count coming to Mont-Dieu among those things which, if they be done with a good spirit, deserve profit, if with a bad one, deserve loss. For that thief who stole the bread of that leprous brother while the mass was being celebrated shall not enjoy a good reward for such a crime. But he who hastens to you with holy desire to see the camps of God[38] will receive his due. This is enough, if not more than enough. For in my usual way I begin slowly and I finish slowly. Count Henry, his spirit kindled anew, is eager to seek out a suitable place, and declares that he abandoned that other place only because you did not want to agree to it.[39] I feel therefore that it would be no trouble to send one of the brothers again with whom I may myself see, either in person or through our brothers, a place, as we have discussed before, suitable for your order. Do this without delay. I greet you all individually and generally, intending to come to you at some time if God wills, and perhaps when your messenger returns to you. Meanwhile pray for us. I send greetings to our little Robert, to Richard, Stephen, Roger, Nicholas, and again to everyone together.[40]

been identified as the Stephen mentioned in the dedication to William of Saint-Thierry's *Golden Letter*, which would put his transfer before 1144, but this is not conclusive (see Le Couteulx, ii. 113, and J. Déchanet (ed.), *Guillaume de Saint-Thierry, Lettre aux frères du Mont-Dieu (Lettre d'Or)*, Sources Chrétiennes, ccxxiii (Paris, 1975), pp. 22, 26–the dating of the transfer is based on the dating of the *Golden Letter* to 1144). Richard and Nicholas are not identified. A Roger appears in letter no. 12, but if this is the same Roger the date is a problem as he should have been in Denmark during these years (see letter no. 12, n. 9).

60

To Prior Simon and the community of Mont-Dieu[1]

Easter 1161

Dominis suis de Monte Dei, Simoni priori et toti sancto conuentui, frater Petrus abbas Cellensis, sanctum pascha.

Cotidianum pascha celebrare non cessat anima uniuscuiusque uestrum dum quasi columba stat ad fenestras suas[2] et uocem de celo explorat, a Libano uocantem sponsam suam.[3] Extento prorsus et retorto collo ad caput uestrum quod in celis est, sine cessatione uitam istam umbrosam fastidientes, euolare 'super pennas uentorum'[4] contenditis, iam ibi uerum non annua repetitione sed continua stabilitate celebraturi pascha cum illo et in illo, qui 'pascha nostrum immolatus est Christus'.[5] Ita est. Sed adhuc ascenditur et descenditur per scalam Iacob[6] donec quod ex parte est euacuetur,[7] quod fiet quando uotum in habitum conuertetur et in Ierusalem hymnus Deo soluetur.[8] Interim, fratres, in umbraculis habitantes[9] et sub umbra illius quem desideratis sedentes, coquite, immo assate, carnes agni tota nocte, singuli in cella sua, et mane comedetis eas. Certe tota nocte debet cremari caro agni quia toto mortalitatis tempore, accensa caldaria conscientie, facies Saluatoris desideranda, et undis desideriorum fortiter bullientibus ne in die iudicii semicocta offeratur percoquenda. Habete uascula munda, iuxta namque et in oculis preterfluit aqua. Sed numquid uane? Sed numquid gratis? Plane supina et crassa negligentia imputanda est singulis nisi sint omnia munda, quibus et copia aquarum redundat et temporis opportunitas superest et amor incumbit totius munditie et ordinis consuetudo non

60 *Sirmond V. 11*]

60 [1] Simon, prior of Mont-Dieu 1159–*c.*1184 (see letter no. 59, n. 1). This letter was written at Easter 1161, the year mentioned in the text. Peter presumably reckoned the year from the Lady Day (25 March) after Christmas, the style prevalent in most of France in the 12th cent.: see R. L. Poole, 'The beginning of the year in the middle ages', *Proceedings of the British Academy*, x (1921), 113–37, at pp. 125–36; Grotefend, p. 13, and A. Giry, *Manuel de diplomatique*, nouv. ed., 2 vols. (Paris, 1925), i. 117 (Grotefend notes that both 25 March and Easter were used in the province of Reims, while Giry suggests that Champagne and Reims and the surrounding bishoprics were using Easter dating by the 12th cent.; Montier-la-Celle fell within Sens). On Mont-Dieu, see letter no. 52, n. 1.

[2] Cf. Isa. 60: 8.

[3] Cf. S. of S. 4: 8.

60

To Prior Simon and the community of Mont-Dieu[1]

Easter 1161

To his lords of Mont-Dieu, Prior Simon and the whole blessed community, brother Peter, abbot of Montier-la-Celle, a holy Easter.

The soul of each one of you does not cease to celebrate the daily paschal offering while it stands like a dove at its windows[2] and seeks out the voice from heaven calling his spouse from Lebanon.[3] With the neck fully extended and turned towards your head which is in heaven, never ceasing to despise this shadowed life, you strive to fly 'upon the wings of the winds'[4] now to celebrate there the true Easter not by an annual recurrence but with unbroken constancy, with Him and in Him who, 'Christ, our pasch, is sacrificed'.[5] So it is. But for now we go up and down by the ladder of Jacob[6] until such time as that which is in part is done away,[7] which will happen when the vow is turned into a way of living and the hymn is paid to God in Jerusalem.[8] Meanwhile, brothers, dwelling in bowers[9] and sitting beneath the shadow of Him whom you desire, cook, or rather roast, the flesh of the lamb all night long, each of you in his cell, and in the morning you will eat it. Certainly the flesh of the lamb should be heated all night long because with the cauldron of conscience fired the face of the Saviour is to be desired for the whole of mortal life, and it should be cooked through vigorously in the boiling waters of desire lest it be offered up half-cooked on the day of judgement. Keep your vessels clean, for water flows past nearby and within your sight. But is it in vain? But is it without reward? Clearly the indolent and gross negligence of individuals is to be blamed if all things are not pure when for these individuals an abundance of water flows, and suitable times exist in plenty, and love of complete cleanliness is incumbent, and the custom

[4] Cf. Ps. 17 (18): 11; 103 (104): 3; cf. also 2 Kgs. (2 Sam.) 22: 11; the preceding seems to echo Lev. 1: 15; 5: 8, but the connection is unclear.

[5] Cf. 1 Cor. 5: 7.

[6] Cf. Gen. 28: 12–15.

[7] Cf. 1 Cor. 13: 10, 'But when that which is perfect is come, that which is in part shall be done away.' The whole passage is contrasting the annual celebration of Easter on earth with the perpetual celebration in heaven.

[8] Cf. Ps. 64 (65): 2.

[9] Cf. Lev. 23: 42, i.e. the feast of tabernacles, the Passover observance, ('And you shall dwell in bowers seven days: every one that is of the race of Israel, shall dwell in tabernacles').

refragatur. Sic est, ego uidi, ego interfui, et utinam totiens et tam sedulo cor expurgassem quotiens et quam indesinenter manus et faciem die et nocte rigaui, non lacrimis sed aquis. Hoc autem feci ut hospes quia non ultra ostium sed in ostio tenui. Vos autem intra et ultra ostium promouistis pedem, non aduene sed domestici celle et celi effecti. Postquam uero uasa uacua ab ambitione emundaueritis confessione et scripturarum meditatione, implete aqua et ad ignem mittite et tanquam unguenta pretiosa bullire facite.[10] Subintrauerat bucce mee et stilo iam suggerebat improuida cogitatio scribere ut carnes agni sic decoquerentur, sed memor mandati legalis quo prohibetur ne aqua coquantur,[11] subicio non ut agni sed hedi carnes taliter coquantur. Simul enim et agnum et hedum tollere in pascha precipimur. Quid ergo? Agnus in ueru, uel in craticula crucis, hedus in aqua coquitur, ut si innocens fueris solo spiritus ardore in pascha adapteris, si uero fetore graui oppressus per ignem et aquam expieris. Hedus etiam est corpus quod corrumpitur et aggrauat animam, agnus qui in latitudine pascitur[12] benignus ille spiritus qui infestationibus carnis agitatus non cornu ferit sed oculo simplici liberatorem querit, dicens, 'Quis me liberabit de corpore mortis huius?'[13] In sanguine agni, id est in contritione cordis et spiritus contribulati,[14] liberaris de Egypto et de manu Pharaonis quia cor contritum et humiliatum Deus non spernit.[15] De sanguine hedi non lego misterium nisi quod tunica Ioseph tincta in sanguine hedi missa est ad patrem.[16] Ad Patrem spirituum si miseris in confessione flens et eiulans tunicam Ioseph litam in sanguine hedi, id est simplicitatis et castitatis amictum fucatum et fecatum corruptione libidinis et fraude diabolice circumuentionis, sanguis hedi in purpuram commutabit quia per penitentiam non solum indulgentia sed etiam gratia adipiscitur. Sed de his hactenus. Vnde namque michi ut tepidus feruentes, mundatos sordidus, iacens currentes, piger commoneam alacres? Deus scit me non presumptione sed amoris impatientia laxasse

[10] Cf. Job 41: 22 (although the image is applied oddly to this context).

[11] Cf. Exod. 12: 9; what follows is not obvious: the lamb and the kid are to be treated equally in Exod. 12: 5, but victims of peace offerings are boiled separately from the roasted sacrifices in 2 Chr. 35: 13 (of course the lamb is also Christ below); on 'per ignem et aquam', cf. Ps. 65 (66): 12.

[12] Cf. Hos. 4: 16. [13] Rom. 7: 24. [14] Cf. Ps. 50 (51): 19.

[15] Cf. Exod. 12; 14: 30 and Ps. 50 (51): 19. [16] Cf. Gen. 37: 31.

of the order does not stand in the way. So it is, I have seen it, I have been present, and if only I had purified my heart as often and as keenly as I have often and incessantly rinsed my hands and face day and night, not with tears but with water. But I have done this like a stranger because I have remained not inside the door but in the entrance way. You on the other hand have stepped forward within and beyond the doorway, not strangers but at home in the cell and in heaven. After the vessels are empty of ambition and you have cleansed them by confession and meditation on Scripture, fill them with water and set them on the fire and make them boil like precious ointments.[10] An improvident thought had stolen into my speech and was just now prompting my pen to write that the flesh of the lamb should be boiled so, but mindful of the legal mandate by which it is prohibited that it be cooked in water,[11] I correct myself and say instead that not the flesh of the lamb but that of the kid should be cooked in this way. For we are instructed to put both the lamb and the kid into the paschal offering at the same time. What then? The lamb is cooked on a spit, or on the grill of the cross, the kid in water; thus should you be guiltless you may be prepared by the heat of the spirit alone at the paschal sacrifice, but if oppressed by a great stench you may be expiated through fire and water. Moreover the kid is the body which is corrupted and oppresses the soul, while the lamb which is fed in a spacious place[12] is that kindly spirit which, provoked by the disturbances of the flesh, does not strike with the horn but looks for the liberator with a simple eye, saying, 'Who shall deliver me from the body of this death?'[13] In the blood of the lamb, that is in the contrition of the heart and an afflicted spirit,[14] you are freed from Egypt and from the hand of Pharaoh because a contrite and humbled heart God does not despise.[15] I do not read a mystery into the blood of the kid, unless it be that the coat of Joseph was sent to the father dipped in the blood of a kid.[16] If you, weeping and wailing in confession, send to the Father of souls Joseph's coat smeared in the blood of the kid, that is to say, the garment of simplicity and chastity discoloured and defiled by the corruption of lust and by the fraudulence of devilish deceits, the blood of the kid will change into purple because not only forgiveness but even grace is attained through penitence. But enough of these matters. For how does it come about that I being lukewarm should admonish those who are boiling hot, I being soiled admonish those who are clean, I lying prone admonish those who are running, I being idle admonish those who are vigorous? God knows that it was not

habenas, et cum non haberem quid dicerem, dicere tamen aliquid uellem, dixi quod innotesceret affectum etsi non idoneum esset facere fructum. Adhuc impetus me trahit et redire ad festum festorum cogit ut, quasi incipiens, spiritui indulgeam currere quousque lassetur et sponte petat stationem et metas silentii. Sub exemplo ergo cuiusdam pretiosi inuolucri,[17] in quo stupendum sit tam ipsum repositorium quam repositum, aliquid de pascha prosequar quasi quemdam pannum pretiosum et multicolorium de diuinis thesauris assumens. Moyses in illo quadragenario ieiunio, ubi a colloquio diuino cornutam faciem reportauit,[18] pascha illud in litteris suis prenominauit et, in illo sacro sanctas reliquias religans, annuo recursu ad publicum nostrum deuoluendum constituens diem certum prefixit. Siquidem hic pannus, id est pascha, in exteriori facie plurimum nitoris exhibet, sed ualde ampliora intrinsecus continet et cariora pignora. Rubet igitur purpureo colore propter passionem, rutilat hyacinthina specie propter resurrectionem,[19] subobscurus est propter sputorum et alaparum et flagellorum et ceterarum iniuriarum coaceruationem,[20] albet unica nube propter innocentie integritatem et peccati immunitatem. Ecce colores, colores cingentes pascha gloriosum et delicatum anime pallium quo melius amiciuntur pauperes semicincti quam diuites 'purpura et bysso' induti.[21] Reuoluere autem illas pretiosas margaritas que sigillantur in sigillo isto aureo et argenteo quis accedat nisi mundas habuerit manus, nisi oculos columbinos,[22] nisi labia purgata, nisi abluto toto homine interiori et exteriori sacro Iordanici fluminis baptismate? Quia ergo uobis sunt 'manus tornatiles'[23] per obedientiam, oculi clari per pudicitiam, labia stillantia mirram primam[24] per accusationem reatuum uestrorum et ad scurrilia eternam clausuram, applicate pannum paschalem et expandite thesaurum absconditum[25] ut exinde captiuus mutuet redemptionem, mortuus resurrectionem, peccator iustificationem, afflictus consolationem, religatus solutionem, anathematizatus absolutionem. Sanctificate ora uestra sanctis harum[a] osculis, oculos tangite his smaragdis,

[a] *corr. Hall;* horum *Sirmond*

[17] Possibly an allusion to Ezek. 27: 24, but in what follows the Easter festival is the garment which (like the covering) is as wondrous as the truth which it celebrates.

[18] Cf. Exod. 34: 28–30, 35; on the establishing of the holy days cf. Exod. 34 and Lev. 23.

[19] Cf. Exod. 25: 4; 26: 1, and many other refs. to purple and violet associated with the tabernacle. Red recalls the blood of the passion.

[20] i.e. inflicted on Christ, cf. Matt. 26: 67; Mark 14: 65; Luke 22: 63–4; John 18: 22; 19: 1.

through presumption but through the impatience of love that I loosed the reins, and when I did not have anything to say yet wished to say something, I said that which would make known affection even if it was not apt to bring forth fruit. That force still drags me along and compels me to return to the festival of festivals so that, as if I were just setting out, I allow the spirit to run until it is tired and seeks of its own accord a resting place and the boundaries of silence. Following the example therefore of a certain precious covering,[17] according to which the container itself should be as wondrous as the contents, I shall proceed on the theme of Easter as if putting on a certain precious and multicoloured garment from the holy treasury. Moses, in that forty-day fast, when he returned with a face horned from the divine converse,[18] first named that paschal festival in his writings and, binding the holy remnants in that sacrament, fixed a certain day, establishing that it be handed down in an annual renewal to our general benefit. Indeed this garment, that is the paschal festival, displays great splendour on the outside, but contains far fuller and dearer pledges within. Thus it glows red with a purple hue on account of the passion, turns red of a violet sort on account of the resurrection,[19] is clouded over on account of the accumulation of spittle, blows, scourgings, and other injuries,[20] and is white with a cloud unique on account of the integrity of innocence and immunity to sin. See the colours, the colours encircling the glorious paschal festival and the delicate cloak of the soul in which the half-clad poor are better dressed than the rich clothed 'in purple and fine linen'.[21] But who may come forward to examine those precious pearls set in the seal of gold and silver unless he has clean hands, eyes like doves',[22] purified lips, with the whole man cleansed inside and out by holy baptism in the river Jordan? Since therefore you have 'hands turned'[23] through obedience, eyes bright through modesty, lips dropping choice myrrh[24] through indictment of your wrongs and eternal closure against irreverence, put on the paschal garment and open up the hidden treasure[25] so that thereafter the captive may obtain redemption, the dead resurrection, the sinner justification, the afflicted consolation, the bound release and the anathematized absolution. Sanctify your mouths by reverently kissing these pearls, touch your eyes with these emeralds, make joyful each particular

[21] Cf. Luke 16: 19.
[22] Cf. S. of S. 1: 14; 4: 1.
[23] Cf. S. of S. 5: 14.
[24] Cf. S. of S. 5: 13.
[25] Cf. Deut. 33: 19.

singulos sensus exhilarate singulis benedictionibus. Sed que sunt pignora tam cara pro pretio, tam efficacia pro remedio, tam rara pro numero, tam sancta pro merito, tam perpetua pro euo, tam amabilia pro beneficio? Pignora, fratres mei, ista ore pudico et timore debito nominanda et amplectenda sunt caro et sanguis agni incontaminati, Iesu Christi ossa, nerui, medulla, cartilagines, corium,[b] et quecunque membra in corpore Iesu de sacris suis uisceribus edidit Virgo uirginum. Addamne clauos, lanceam, coronam spineam, sputa, irrisiones et illusionem, albam uestem, uestimentum purpureum, fel, acetum, mirram et aloes?[26] Quanto enim hec in se duriora et uiliora tanto in Saluatore nostro pretiosiora et appetibiliora facta sunt. Quis modo Christianorum si unum horum reperiret nisi super aurum et lapidem pretiosum multum uenerabilius coleret, ambitiosius seruaret et adoraret? Dignum est, iustum est. Si enim immundus erit tangens morticinum et captum a bestia,[27] id est Adam et Euam quorum alter captus est suasu uxoris, Eua morticinum facta est suggestione serpentis,[28] quomodo non iustus emundatur ab operibus mortuis qui uiuentem in secula seculorum contingit credendo, amando, colendo, adorando? Nam non sicut delictum ita et donum. Pluris enim donum quam delictum est. Sed quid[c] est hoc donum? Iesus Christus sanctus. Quid est, inquam, hoc donum? Natiuitas Iesu, passio Iesu, resurrectio Iesu, ascensio Iesu; 'quomodo non etiam omnia cum illo nobis donauit?'[29] Clamat Apostolus: 'Omnia', inquit, 'uestra sunt, siue mors, siue uita',[30] quia est mortuus propter peccata nostra[31] 'et resurrexit propter iustificationem nostram'.[32] Domini et fratres, detineo uos plus iusto ad quorum ianuam stat et pulsat Iesus[33] uolens suum pascha uobiscum recolere; et de reliquiis mense illius magne partem bonam reseruauit, quam adhuc recentem et calentem denuo de archa celi refert et profert uobis.[34] Ne uereamini ne caro antiquata sit et putrefacta uetustate nimia quia annus iam millesimus centesimus sexagesimus primus est. Nequaquam, fratres, nequaquam ascendat in cor uestrum hesitatio ista quia caro eius etiam dum esset corruptibilis non uidit corruptionem, multo uero minus facta incor-

[b] cutis corium *Sirmond* [c] *corr. Hall;* quod *Sirmond*

[26] The final stages of the Passion (see Matt. 27; Mark 15; Luke 23; John 19).

[27] Cf. Lev. 7: 24.

[28] Cf. Gen. 3: 1–6.

[29] Cf. Rom. 8: 32: 'He that spared not even His own Son, but delivered Him up for us all, how hath He not also, with Him, given us all things?' ('qui etiam Filio suo non pepercit, sed pro nobis omnibus tradidit illum, quomodo non etiam cum illo omnia nobis donabit').

[30] Cf. 1 Cor. 3: 21–2.

sense with each particular blessing. But what are the pledges so dear in price, so effective in remedy, so few in number, so blessed in merit, so enduring in time, so beloved for their benefits? These pledges, my brothers, which must be named with a pure mouth and embraced with due fear, are the flesh and blood of the undefiled lamb, the bones of Jesus Christ, His nerves, marrow, cartilages, skin, and whatever members the Virgin of virgins brought forth from her blessed womb in the body of Jesus. Should I add the nails, the spear, the crown of thorns, the spitting, the mocking and jeering, the white garment, the purple cloak, the gall, the vinegar, the myrrh and aloes?[26] For the more harsh and vile these things were in themselves so the more rich and desirable were they made in our Saviour. Who would now rank among Christians if, finding one of these, he did not cherish it much more reverently and safeguard and adore it much more zealously than gold and precious stones? It is fitting, it is just. For if he be unclean through touching one that has died of itself and one caught by a beast[27]—that is Adam and Eve, of whom the one was caught by the persuasion of his wife, while Eve was brought unto death by the suggestion of the serpent[28]—how, then, may he the just one, who touches the One living for ever and ever by believing, loving, cherishing, and adoring, not be cleansed from deathly works? For the offering is not like the transgression. The offering is greater than the transgression. But what is this offering? The blessed Jesus Christ. What, I ask, is this offering? The birth of Jesus, the passion of Jesus, the resurrection of Jesus, the ascension of Jesus; 'how hath He not also, with Him, given us all things?'[29] The Apostle cries out: 'All things', he says, 'are yours, whether it be death or life,'[30] because He died for our sins[31] 'and rose again for our justification'.[32] My lords and brothers, I am detaining unfairly you at whose door Jesus stands and knocks[33] wishing to celebrate again His Passover with you; and He has kept back the good part of the remnants of that great feast which once again He brings back to this place fresh and hot from the store of heaven and offers to you.[34] Do not be afraid that the flesh may be old and rotted with excessive age because it is now the year eleven hundred and sixty one. By no means, brothers, let that doubt rise in your heart, by no means, for His flesh even while it was prone to corruption did not see corruption, much less so when it was rendered

[31] Cf. 1 Cor. 15: 3. [32] Rom. 4: 25. [33] Cf. Rev. 3: 20.
[34] i.e. His body and blood, the bread and wine. (There may be an echo here of John 2: 10.)

ruptibilis et genere uiuendi et loco manendi. Recens est, calida est, sana est, uitalis est, regnum celorum dat quia possidet. Non est illa caro et sanguis de quo dicitur quia caro et sanguis regnum Dei non possidebunt.[35] Quo studiosius arcentur a dentibus et stomachis uestris carnes animalium que corrumpunt et corrumpuntur, eo dignius accedunt ad animas uestras sanctificandas carnes ille que sicut non moriuntur ita nec corruptionem inesse patiuntur ubicunque refectionem prestauerint. Has imperat religio, et quo religiosior sis, eo frequentius et, ut ita dicam, glutinosius comedere debes. Nondum quieuisset manus, uel animus, sed reprimit et modus dictorum et tempus alia faciendi. Orate pro nobis. Nouellum illum angelum uestrum A. salutate, et Robertulum nostrum.[36] Plurimum et multum singulos et singillatim et communiter saluto.

61

To A., a priest of Provins[1]

*c.*1145 × 1162

Frater [a]Petrus Cellensis abbas[a] uenerabili A. sacerdoti Sancti Petri Pruuinensis, salutem.

Non immerito illi presumo scribere quem non presumo non diligere. An impune non diligerem quem adprime honorandum utinam [b]uel simpliciter[b] suscepissem? Sed quid tantopere laudo quem uel rarissima uisione cognosco? Sed plus hunc fateor cognosco auditione quam uisione, plus fide quam confabulatione,[c] plus religione quam familiari cohabitatione. Audiui enim uiri huius[d] non elatam seculi pompam sed electam doctrine formam, non ebrietatem sed sobrietatem, non uanam pecuniarum sollicitudinem sed uariam scripturarum meditationem, non curiositatem formarum et

61 *O fos. 137^v–138^r, Sirmond III. 9*]
[a–a] G. Christi presbyter *O* [b–b] *om. O* [c] fabulatione *O* [d] *om. Sirmond*

[35] Cf. 1 Cor. 15: 50.

[36] A. is unidentified, and may be a cipher, but Le Couteulx suggests an Albert, who took his vows in 1160 (Le Couteulx, ii. 224). Robert may be the monk of Montier-la-Celle who transferred to Mont-Dieu at some time during Peter's abbacy of Montier-la-Celle (see letter no. 58, n. 1). He is mentioned again in letter no. 59.

incorruptible both by the manner of its living and the place of its abiding. It is fresh, it is hot, it is sound, it is life-giving, it bestows the kingdom of heaven because it possesses it. It is not that flesh and blood of which it is said that flesh and blood shall not possess the kingdom of God.[35] The more conscientiously the flesh of animals, which corrupts and is corrupted, is kept away from your teeth and stomach the more worthily there approaches, for the sanctification of your souls, that flesh which, as it does not die, so neither does it suffer corruption to be in it wherever it affords refreshment. Religious duty enjoins this flesh, and so that you may be the more dutiful, so the more frequently and, so to say, greedily you ought to eat it. My hand, or rather my mind, would not yet have fallen silent, but both the length of the letter and the time needed to do other things restrain it. Pray for us. Greet that new little angel of yours, A., and our little Robert.[36] I send you great and many greetings both individually and all together.

61

To A., a priest of Provins[1]

*c.*1145 × 1162

Brother Peter, abbot of Montier-la-Celle, to the venerable A., priest of Saint-Pierre, Provins, greetings.

It is not without cause that I presume to write to him whom I do not presume not to love. For could I with impunity not love the one whom I had accepted to be first, nay even simply, honoured? But why do I praise so greatly one whom I only know from the most fleeting sight? Yet I confess that I know him more from report than from sight, more from faith than conversation, more from his religious life than from living in the same community. For I have heard of this man not exalted pomp of the world but the choice quality of his learning, not drunkenness but sobriety, not vain concern for riches but varied meditation on Scripture, not the curiosity for the external forms of beauty that lights the torches of hell, but the cleansing of the

61 [1] A. is unidentified and may be a cipher. This is presumably one of many contacts in a town where Montier-la-Celle had two dependent priories, Saint-Ayoul (see appendix 8) and Sainte-Croix (Cott. ii. 2368–9).

pulchritudinum[e] faces[f] gehennales accendentem[g] sed emundationem deformitatum proprie conscientie iuxta diuini speculi illuminationem. Hec, bone iuuenis, de te ab aliis cum desiderio audiui, cum fide accepi, cum gaudio aliis enarraui. Nichil[h] itaque mirum si tali scribo quem talem describere non uereor ex relatu eorum quibus firmiter credo. Huius tamen ardentius cum auiditate faciem uiderem et uocem audirem quam mortuis apicibus [i]mortua uerba[i] ederem ut, cuius amor uiuit[j] in animo, eius presentia scintillaret in oculo. Ampliat[k] enim calorem latentem in remotis [l]admixta facula scintillantibus uenis.[l] Mutuo namque sese ita fouent [m]ut uterque ignis alium ad se trahendo confortet et confortetur, quatinus[m] interior eo magis ferueat quo exterior ei appropinquat, et exterior eo clarius luceat quo ei interior uehementius participat. Huius exempli similitudine,[n] quem amas absentem, incipis superamare presentem. Crescit enim in oculis amor; reuehitur meatu aurium cordi[o] diligentis uox dilecti expressa caractere dilectionis. Iam amor incipit esse cum gaudio, qui prius erat sine[p] gaudio aut cum tedio. Tedet enim non habere quem tendit semper amare. Sine gaudio quoque est qui eum non habet sine quo gaudere non potest. Apponitur igitur amori gaudium cum amicus cernit suum amicum. Valete.[q]

62

To G., a priest of Hastings[1]

*c.*1145 × 1162

Petrus abbas indignus Celle monasterii, G. sacerdoti Hastingiarum, spiritum salutis.

Non in presumptione spiritus mei[2] ad te transmarinum sacerdotem scribo, sed reiterata petitione R. quem tu quidem carne, ego uero spiritu per euangelium in Christo genui. Is siquidem quos habet impari generatione patres, pari desiderat affectione coniungere fratres. Et me certe iam fratrem tibi constituit nisi in oculis tuis mea fraternitas forte propter uestem peregrinam sorduerit. Vix tamen

[e] pulchritudinem *Sirmond* [f] fasces *O* [g] *corr. Winterbottom;* accendentes *O, Sirmond* [h] Nil *O* [i–i] uerba mortua *O* [j] uiget *O* [k] Applicat *Sirmond* [l–l] scintillantibus uenis admota et admixta facula *O* [m–m] fomenta amoris quatinus flamma *O* [n] similitudinem *O* [o] ad cor *O* [p] siue *Sirmond* [q] *om. O*

62 *Sirmond III. 10*]

deformities of one's own conscience by the illumination of the divine mirror. These things, good youth, I have heard about you from others with pleasure, I have accepted them with faith, I have told them to others with joy. And so it is no wonder if I write to such a one whom I am not afraid so to describe from the account of those in whom I firmly trust. I would however more ardently with eagerness see his face and hear his voice than utter dead words with dead letters, so that the presence of him, love of whom lives in the soul, might sparkle in the eye. For a torch thrust into glittering embers increases warmth hidden in the recesses. For they warm one another mutually so that each flame, by drawing the other to it, strengthens and is strengthened, with the result that the inner warms the more as the outer approaches it, and the outer shines the more clearly the more powerfully the inner partakes in it. By analogy with this example, he whom you love when absent you begin to love beyond measure when he is present. For love grows in the eyes; the voice of the beloved, expressed with the mark of love, is carried back by way of the ears to the heart of the lover. Now love which before was joyless, or rather weary, begins to be joyful. For it is wearisome not to have someone whom love always strives to love. Love is also joyless when it does not have one without whom it cannot rejoice. Therefore joy is added to love when a friend sees his friend. Farewell.

62

To G., a priest of Hastings[1]

*c.*1145 × 1162

Peter, unworthy abbot of the monastery of Montier-la-Celle, to G., priest of Hastings, the spirit of salvation.

Not in the presumption of my spirit[2] do I write to you, a priest beyond the sea, but at the repeated petition of R., whom you indeed begat in the flesh but I in the spirit through the Gospel in Christ. He indeed longs to join together as brothers in equal affection those whom he holds as fathers in unequal begetting. And surely he has now established me as your brother, unless my brotherhood grows foul in your eyes on account perhaps of a foreign dress. Scarcely,

62 [1] G. is unidentified; he was evidently the father of a monk of Montier-la-Celle, R.
[2] Cf. Eccles. 6: 9.

apud sensatos tanta habetur uestium diuersitas ut eorum exinde diuellatur identitas. Proinde nuda corda melius copulantur, affectius uniuntur, castius immiscentur. Cor namque iusti non induitur 'purpura et bysso'[3] sed sapientia et consilio, non pannis et serico sed uirtutibus et Deo. His enim secundum creationis naturam in principio amictus, stolas non erubescebat angelicas, nec ipsius increati candoris lucem reformidabat quandiu diuinitus insite imaginis lineamenta incorrupta mutuo aspectu resignabat.[4] At ubi huiuscemodi splendoribus nocturnis dispoliatus[a] insidiis pre confusione atrocioris incommodi foliis cepit circumtegi ficulneis,[5] uenit Christus ut reiceret[b] uestem cilicinam, saccum scinderet, et nudus nudis obtutibus paternis in carne nostra, immo sua, appareret. Filii itaque nudi Christi, nuda adinuicem corda pandamus ac stabili compagine in Christo ea compingamus.[6] Fluant ad Christum, refluant ad celum, confluant ad trinum et unum. 'O quam bonum et quam iocundum', frater, 'fratres habitare in unum.'[7] 'Vnum est necessarium.'[8] Quid uero multa? Non necessaria. Que ergo uanitas est filiorum hominum ut multa querant et non curent unum? Prius est unum quam multa, et facilius consequimur unum quam multa. Cum ergo sine uno non subsistimus, et in multis deficimus, in multa tamen insania unum postponimus et multa cupimus. Desipit qui ad unum uerum esse non tendit, sapit qui ad incommutabilem beatitudinem contendit. Reuera solus ille sapit qui unum solum sapit, solus ille desipit qui multa preter unum sapere cupit. Vnde ait Apostolus, 'non multum sapere sed sapere ad sobrietatem'.[9] Solent homines terre tue potius sapere ad ebrietatem quam ad sobrietatem. Vitium ignobile, et inter cetera uitia ignobilius, ebrietas. Vbi enim sensus ebrii? Vbi reuerentia in ebrio? Vbi dignitas? Immemor est preteriti, futuri ignarus, presentis nescius. Discretio confunditur, ratio hebetatur, sensus ligantur, mens ipsa sepelitur. Risui derisoribus exponit magis se ipsum ridens. Ex hac uiperea radice surgit, uel potius serpit, deuastans totius religionis anime uigorem luxuria. Denique tanquam ex magno gurgite

[a] dispoliatur *Sirmond* [b] reiteraret *Sirmond*

[3] Cf. Luke 16: 19.

[4] i.e. Adam before the fall, made in the image of God (Gen. 1: 26–7), but here, by extension, mankind.

[5] Cf. Gen. 3: 7. There may be an echo, in what follows, of Ps. 29 (30): 12, but this is fairly common biblical vocabulary.

[6] The whole passage recalls the commonplace, 'nudus sequi nudum Christum'.

[7] Cf. Ps. 132 (133): 1.

however, is so great a diversity of dress found among the wise that their common identity can be torn asunder thereby. Just so, naked hearts are better joined, more affectionately united, more chastely mingled. For the heart of the just is not clothed 'in purple and fine linen'[3] but in wisdom and counsel, not in silken garments but in virtues and in God. For dressed with these in the beginning, according to the nature of creation, he was not ashamed of the angelic robes, nor did he dread the light of uncreated radiance itself, so long as he was revealing, by a shared appearance, the incorrupt features of the divinely implanted image.[4] But when, despoiled of such splendours by nocturnal ambush, he began, because of the disaster of very harsh misfortune, to be covered with fig-leaves,[5] Christ came to reject the hairshirt, rend the sackcloth garment and appear naked before the naked paternal eyes in our flesh, or rather His. And so, as sons of the naked Christ, let us throw open to one another naked hearts and let us join them in Christ in a firm union.[6] Let them flow to Christ, flow back to heaven, flow together to the Three and One. 'O how good and how pleasant it is', brother, 'for brethren to dwell together in unity.'[7] 'One thing is necessary.'[8] But what of the many? These are not necessary. What vanity is it then on the part of the sons of men that they seek the many and take no care for the one? The one is prior to the many, and we follow the one more easily than the many. Even though, therefore, without the one we do not stand firm, and amidst the many we fail, yet still in great madness we put off the one and desire the many. Foolish is he who does not strive towards the one true being, wise is he who strains towards the immutable blessedness. Truly he alone is wise who savours only the one, he alone is foolish who desires to savour many besides the one. Whence the Apostle says, 'not to savour much but to savour unto sobriety'.[9] The men of your land are accustomed to savour unto drunkenness rather than to sobriety. Drunkenness is a base vice, and one of the baser among the other vices. For where is the sense of the drunkard? Where is the shame in a drunkard? Where is the dignity? He is forgetful of the past, unmindful of the future, and ignorant of the present. Discretion is confounded, reason is blunted, sense is bound up, the mind itself is entombed. Laughing, he exposes himself more to laughter by those

[8] Luke 10: 42; the contrast between 'unum' and 'multa' in what follows echoes that between 'unum' and 'plurima' in Luke 10: 41–2.

[9] Cf. Rom. 12: 3, 'non plus sapere quam oportet sapere, sed sapere ad sobrietatem' (Douai Reims translates 'to be wise', but Peter's imagery stretches the sense further).

perditionis prosiliunt non rara germina pestifere preuaricationis. Pes errat, labitur lingua, trepidat manus, labia tremunt, caligat uisus, auditus surdescit. Adde his intrinsecus furias debacchantes et miserum pectus miserabiliter lacerantes. O bone uir, nonne uidentur tibi hec principia mortis, fomenta ignis eterni, esca supplicii, illecebra dampnationis? Vt igitur morsum colubri euadas, fugienda est ebrietas. Muscipula uenantium capitur qui uel semel inebriatur. Lusus demonum est homo ebrius. Tanquam prostibulum uitiorum reputatur qui gule et uentris tyrannidi subiugatur. Mari commoto quid tempestuosius? Excusso fulgure quid formidabilius? Abysso quid profundius? Nullum tamen horum nequius quam homo ebrius. Desistendum est a ueneno, immo a uino quod hominem uertit in truncum. Diuinorum lectio librorum preceptis et exemplis ostendit quam turpiter natura ex hoc dehonestetur, quam crudeliter condempnetur, quam interminabiliter crucietur, quam immisericorditer a regno Dei excludatur. 'Neque ebriosi', ait Apostolus, 'regnum Dei possidebunt.'[10] Diutius impressi stilum si forte refellerem, uel saltem reprimerem, uitium. Interim collactaneam eius luxuriam eodem acumine potius pungamus quam pingamus.[11] Pinguius namque et ista pinguissima de pinguedine terre apud uos exuberat.[12] Vbi namque iuuenum et puellarum forma decentior, aspectus gratiosior, cibus habundantior, potus crassior, aer salubrior, terra fertilior, amenitas iocundior, prauus his eneruatur animus. Satius est namque ei frui cupiditatibus uanis quam eternis bonis. Colore adulterino deceptus, que intus latet falsitatem non attendit. Mendax mendaciter mulier de specie uana se iactat. Certe pulchritudo illa nec uera est nec sua. Si enim uera esset semper durasset. Vnde quod semel est uerum, semper est uerum. Si sua, non in foro emeret. Fallax gratia, et uana est pulchritudo. Abicienda est autem que fallit gratia, ambienda que liberat. Vmbratilis postponenda pulchritudo, utilis appetenda. Communi hactenus admonitione premissa, ut tue unice et singularis anime curam maximam habeas rogamus. Nemo enim de seculo egrediens animam suam ulterius commutat. Hic locus, hoc[c]

[c] hic *Sirmond*

[10] Cf. 1 Cor. 6: 10.

[11] The image recalls the two actions of the *stilus*, to puncture and to draw a picture. Here and in the previous sentence Peter seems also, with characteristic diplomacy, to be suggesting that these are general criticisms, and not directed personally at the recipient (a point which he stresses again below), although it is clear from the end of the letter that they are so directed.

[12] The word play on *pingo* and *pinguis* does not translate.

who mock. Sensuality rises, or rather snakes up, from this viperous root, laying waste the vigour of the whole religious discipline of the soul. Finally, as if from the great abyss of perdition, dense shoots of dangerous transgression spring up. The foot errs, the tongue stumbles, the hand trembles, the lips quaver, the vision darkens, the hearing fades. Add to these the furies raging within and wretchedly tearing the wretched heart. O good man, do not these things seem to you the beginnings of death, the kindlings of the eternal fire, the food of punishment, the allurements of damnation? To avoid the bite of the snake therefore you must flee from drunkenness. He who is drunk even once is caught by the hunters' trap. The drunken man is a plaything of demons. He who is subject to the tyranny of the throat and the belly is reckoned as it were a prostitute of vices. What is more turbulent than the sea stirred up? What is more terrifying than lightning let loose? What is deeper than the abyss? Yet none of these is more wicked than a drunken man. One must desist from venom, still more from wine which turns a man into a dolt. The study of holy books shows by precepts and examples how foully nature is disgraced by this, how cruelly condemned, how interminably crucified, how mercilessly excluded from the kingdom of God. 'And neither shall drunkards', says the Apostle, 'possess the kingdom of God.'[10] I would have pressed down the point of my pen for longer if perchance I were refuting or at least checking a fault. Let us meantime with the same point prick rather than paint[11] luxury which is its fellow-nursling. For more richly does this too, at its richest, spring up among you from the richness of the earth.[12] For where the forms of youths and girls are more comely, their appearance more agreeable, food more abundant, drink richer, the air healthier, the land more fertile, the delightfulness more pleasant, by these things the wicked mind is weakened. For it is more satisfying to it to enjoy empty desires than eternal goods. Deceived by false colour, it does not attend to the falsehood which lies within. The lying woman boasts mendaciously about her vain outer appearance. Certainly that beauty is neither true nor hers. For if it were true it would endure always. For what is true once is always true. If it were hers, she would not have bought it in the market-place. Her grace is false and the beauty vain. But that grace which deceives should be cast aside, that which liberates, sought for. Meretricious beauty should be left behind, the beneficial sought out. Having thus far first set down a general admonition, we now beg you to take the greatest care of your unique and particular soul. For no

tempus commutationis faciende; mores hic commutandi et corrigendi. Ceterum correptio non correctio in futuro dabitur; fiet comminatio non commutatio, nisi forte de pena in penam, de morte in mortem, de miseria in miseriam. Muta itaque uitam dum uiuis in hac uita ne si forte modo cum potes distuleris mutare, tunc uolens mutare cogaris tenere.

R.:[13] Timet sibi anima mea, timet et tibi. Pater meus es tu, et ego filius tuus. Et quia per te ingressus sum in uita corruptibili utinam per me peruenires ad disciplinam Dei. Non contingat me sine te gaudere, contingat autem te et me cum Christo regnare.[14] Vale.

63

To John of Salisbury[1]

1147 × 1162

[a]Frater Petrus magistro Iohanni.[a]

'Fauus distillans labia tua, mel et lac sub lingua tua.'[b][2] Vt [c]uidi litteras tuas[c] cor meum iubilo, os meum impletum[d] est risu.[3] Miscuisti siquidem iocos seriis, sed temperatos et sine detrimento dignationis et uerecundie. Sales tui sine dente sunt, ioci sine uilitate. Sic decurrit oratio tua tanquam illa que aliquando nubes capite tangit aliquando[e] uultum in terra demittit. Inuenit hec gratiam in oculis meis, mecum manebit et apud me tota nocte erit. Est namque uox tua dulcis in auribus meis et monitus tui satis amabiles in faucibus meis. Insurgit autem [f]sepe uentus contrarius,[f][4] imbrium turme quatiunt domum, et bruchus, locusta,[g] eruca et rubigo[5] hortuli mei areolas[6] deuastare

63 *O fo. 105*[r–v], *Sirmond IV. 6*]
[a–a] Idem magistro I. *O* [b] *om. Sirmond* [c–c] litteras tuas uidi *O* [d] repletum *O* [e] aliquando autem *Sirmond* [f–f] contrarius uentus sepe *O* [g] et locusta *O*

[13] This must be a postscript by R. himself, an unusual feature in a letter of this period.
[14] Cf. Rev. 22: 5.

63 [1] This letter could have been written at any time between John's return to England from Montier-la-Celle (1147, see *J. S. Epp.* i. [1986 edn.], pp. xviii–xix and Corrigenda, p. 298) and Peter's transfer to Saint-Remi (1162). This is a response to a letter but there is no evidence to connect it with certainty with any of John's extant letters. John of

one, after leaving the world, changes his soul again. This is the place, this the time for making changes; conduct must be changed and corrected here. For the rest, castigation, not correction, will be given in the future; there will be commination not transformation, except perhaps from punishment to punishment, from death to death, from misery to misery. And so change your life while you are alive in this life, lest if perchance you put off changing now when you can, you should then be forced, when you wish to change, to stay the same.

R.:[13] My soul fears for itself and also for you. You are my father and I am your son. And because I have entered corruptible life through you, I would that you might attain to the discipline of God through me. Let it not befall me that I rejoice without you, let it fall to our share, you and I, rather to rule with Christ.[14] Farewell.

63

To John of Salisbury[1]

1147 × 1162

Brother Peter to master John.

'Thy lips are as a dropping honeycomb, honey and milk are under thy tongue.'[2] When I saw your letter my heart was filled with rejoicing, my mouth with laughter.[3] You have indeed mixed jokes with serious matters, but moderate ones and without detriment to dignity and modesty. Your witticisms are not fanged, your jokes not cheap. Your speech runs along like that which one minute touches the clouds with its head, the next lowers its face to the earth. This finds favour in my eyes, it will stay with me and will be by me the whole night. For your voice is sweet in my ears and your admonitions are most lovely to my palate. But a contrary wind[4] often gets up, rainstorms shake the house, and the bruchus, the locust, the palmer-worm, and the mildew[5] try to lay waste the beds of my little garden.[6] But the angel of great counsel rises from the ship and

Salisbury's letter no. 112 (of uncertain date; *J. S. Epp.* i. 183–4 and see ibid., pp. xlvii–l) is possible, as a jesting letter, but there is nothing there which Peter's references to admonitions or his allusions to teaching seems to echo. On John's relations with Peter of Celle and the sequence of their datable letters, see appendix 8.

[2] Cf. S. of S. 4: 11.

[3] Cf. Job 8: 21; cf. also Ps. 125 (126): 2.

[4] Cf. Matt. 14: 24; Mark 6: 48.

[5] Cf. Joel 1: 4; 2: 25.

[6] Cf. S. of S. 5: 13; 6: 1.

temptant. Sed angelus magni consilii surgit de naui et facit tranquil litatem uentorum, serenitatem nimborum, exterminationem inutilium uermium. Cum enim 'Deus pro nobis, quis contra nos?'[7] Sunt certe mortis pericula, sunt in deserto serpentium uenena mortifera, sunt prorsus amaritudines aquarum,[8] sed serpens eneus,[9] sed uirga Moysi,[10] sed columpna nubis per diem et ignis per noctem,[11] amarum uertit in dulce, eripit a morte, liberatque a morsu. Sumus quasi 'nichil habentes et omnia possidentes',[12] 'quasi morientes et ecce uiuimus'.[13] Hec consolatio mea est[h] 'in loco peregrinationis mee',[14] quia nichil intulimus in hunc mundum sed nec quid auferre possumus,[15] quia uolucres celi non serunt neque metunt et tamen Pater celestis pascit illas.[i] [16] 'In baculo meo transiui Iordanem istum, et nunc cum duabus turmis regredior.'[17] Cum denique uia sit breuis, locus prope quo tendimus, quare tot onera humeris debilibus imponimus? Quare incassum multa portamus? Certe si Dominus Deus[j] fuerit mecum in uia ista qua ego ambulo, non deerit michi panis ad edendum et uestimentum ad induendum. His paucis natura contenta erit.[18] Tu autem, pars magna deliciarum mearum, in te opes mee, tu capitis mei reclinatorium aureum;[19] utinam corporum eadem semper mediante Christo propinquitas esset que[k] animorum. Nolo ut piger sis, non ualens [l]manum ad os[l] mittere,[20] id est, [m]bonum quod[m] doces facere. Deliciosus[21] enim et improbus monitor est qui in eo quod alium docet se ipsum non docet.

[h] *om. Sirmond* [i] illa *O, Sirmond* [j] *om. O* [k] que et *O* [l–l] ad os manum *O* [m–m] quod bonum *O*

[7] Rom. 8: 31.
[8] Cf. Exod. 15: 23.
[9] Cf. Num. 21: 8–9.
[10] Cf. Exod. 4: 2, and many other refs.
[11] Cf. Exod. 13: 21–2; Exod. 14: 24; Num. 14: 14; Deut. 1: 33.
[12] 2 Cor. 6: 10.
[13] 2 Cor. 6: 9.

effects calmness of the winds, tranquillity of the clouds, extermination of the useless worms. For when 'God is for us, who is against us?'[7] There are surely dangers of death, there are in the desert the deadly poisons of snakes, there are truly bitter waters,[8] but the brazen serpent,[9] the rod of Moses,[10] the pillar of cloud by day and of fire by night,[11] turn the bitter sweet, snatch us from death, and free us from the sting. We are 'as having nothing and possessing all things,'[12] 'as dying, and behold we live'.[13] This is my consolation 'in the place of my pilgrimage,'[14] that we brought nothing into this world but neither can we carry anything out,[15] that the birds of the air neither sow nor do they reap, and still the heavenly Father feeds them.[16] 'With my staff I passed over this Jordan, and now I return with two companies.'[17] And finally, since the road is short, the destination near, why do we impose so many burdens on weak shoulders? Why do we carry many things to no purpose? Certainly if the Lord God be with me on this road along which I am walking, I will not lack bread to eat and clothing to wear. Nature will be content with these few things.[18] But you, o great part of my delights, in you are my riches, you are the golden couch[19] for my head; if only the proximity of our bodies might, by the mediation of Christ, be always the same as that of our minds. I do not wish you to be idle, unable to put your hand to your mouth,[20] that is, to do the good which you teach. For it is a self-indulgent[21] and dishonest monitor who does not instruct himself in that which he teaches others.

[14] Ps. 118 (119): 54.

[15] Cf. 1 Tim. 6: 7.

[16] Cf. Matt. 6: 26, cf. also Luke 12: 24.

[17] Gen. 32: 10.

[18] Cf. Boethius, *De cons. philos.* ii, prose v. 16 (*CCSL* xciv. 27).

[19] Cf. S. of S. 3: 10.

[20] Evidently meaning something like, 'put your hand where your mouth is'—i.e. practise what you preach, but there may also be an allusion to Job 39: 34, used here to mean, be silent in order rather to act.

[21] Or 'fastidious': *DML*, *deliciosus* 2; cf. Niermeyer, *deliciosus* 2.

64

To John of Salisbury[1]

1147 × 1162 (poss. late 1156 × early 1157)

Petrus[a] Dei gratia Cellensis[b] monasterii dictus abbas Iohanni[c] amico suo, a Deo 'totius consolationis' consolari.[2]

Queris, frater, a me scripta exhortationis parum pensans torrentes nostre occupationis. Queris, inquam, consolationem quia sentis desolationem, postulas auxilium quia portas exilium, imploras remedium quia ploras discidium. Quis ergo ego sum qui tibi scribere possim[d] unde fouearis, unde conforteris, unde consoleris? Orare quidem pro te uix possum, perorare[e] nullo modo possum. Filius uero olei[f][3] qui conceptus [g]est de Spiritu sancto,[g][4] quem unxit Deus pre participibus suis, cuius nomen oleum[h] effusum,[5] Christus Iesus, uenit, ut ipse dicit, consolari lugentes Syon.[6] Vtinam secundum multitudinem dolorum tuorum consolationes eius letificent animam tuam.[i][7] 'In tribulatione', inquit,[j] 'sua mane consurgent ad me.'[8] Et tu Iesu quid? Quousque auertis faciem tuam? Quousque non profers manum de sinu?[9] Quousque nubem opponis ne transeat ad te oratio nostra? Tempus est miserendi. Conuertere, respice, et deprecabilis esto.[10] Da auxilium de tribulatione, erue ab oppressione, protege a temptatione.[11] Filii hominum cui [k]supplicare habent[k] nisi Filio hominis? Quem interpellare nisi mediatorem Dei et hominis? Vbi confugere nisi ad patibulum crucis? Hic, hic turtur pullos suos reponit,[12] uultur

64 *O fo. 138*[r–v], *Val fos. 129*[v]*–131*[r], *Sirmond IV. 8*]
[a] P. *O, Sirmond* [b] Celle *O, Val* [c] I. *O, Val* [d] possum *Sirmond* [e] perorare tibi *O* [f] Dei *O* [g–g] de Spiritu sancto est *O* [h] *om. Sirmond* [i] meam *O* [j] inquio *O* [k–k] habent supplicare *O*

64 [1] The reference to exile here may indicate John's anticipated exile at the time of his disgrace (late 1156–early 1157, see letter no. 66, n. 1) or may simply be a spiritual metaphor. It cannot be John's actual exile of 1164–70, since Peter was still at Montier-la-Celle when he wrote it (separation here may be a poetic metaphor for John's departure from Peter at Montier-la-Celle, and so ironically for his return to England in 1147, but the references here to evil and the scourge seem too strong for this). It is evidently a response to a request for a letter of comfort or consolation from John, but cannot be connected to any existing letter of John's. (John's letter no. 19 tells Peter of his imminent disgrace, but does not request a consolation as specifically as the present letter implies; it also announces John's intention to travel to France, of which no mention is made here. On John's letter no. 19 see *J. S. Epp.* i. 31–2.)

64

To John of Salisbury[1]

1147 × 1162 (poss. late 1156 × early 1157)

Peter, by the grace of God called abbot of the monastery of Montier-la-Celle, to his friend John, to be comforted by the God 'of all comfort'.[2]

You seek from me, brother, words of exhortation, weighing little the torrents of our affairs. You seek, I say, consolation because you feel desolation, you beg aid because you bear exile, you beseech me for a reparation because you bewail separation. Who then am I to be able to write to you in such a way that you may be encouraged, strengthened, comforted? Indeed, I can scarce pray for you; in no way can I achieve anything by my prayer. But the son of the oil[3] who was conceived from the Holy Spirit,[4] whom God anointed above his fellows, whose name is as oil poured out,[5] Christ Jesus, comes, as He Himself says, to comfort the mourners of Zion.[6] O that His consolations might gladden your soul according to the multitude of your sorrows.[7] 'In their affliction', He says, 'they will rise early to me.'[8] And you, Jesus, why? How long do you turn away your face? How long do you not bring out your hand from your bosom?[9] How long do you set a cloud in the way so that our prayer does not cross over to you? It is time for mercy. Turn round, look back, and be entreated.[10] Grant aid in tribulation, deliver from oppression, protect from temptation.[11] To whom can the sons of men make supplication except to the Son of man? To whom can they appeal except to the mediator of God and man? Where can they flee except to the gibbet of the cross? Here, here the turtle-dove lays her young ones,[12] the vulture lays down his boldness, the dove

[2] Cf. 2 Cor. 1: 3–4.

[3] Alluding to Heb. 1: 8–9. Isa 5: 1 is closer in form but cannot be the reference intended as it goes with *cornu* and refers to a hill by a usage unique to the OT (MS O's reading *Dei* is obviously plausible, but corruption from *olei* to *Dei* is the more likely).

[4] Apostles' Creed; cf. Kelly, *Creeds*, p. 369.

[5] Cf. Heb. 1: 9; cf. also Ps. 44 (45): 8; and S. of S. 1: 2.

[6] Cf. Ecclus. 48: 27; Isa. 61: 2–3.

[7] Cf. Ps. 93 (94): 19.

[8] Hos. 6: 1.

[9] Cf. Exod. 4: 6–7.

[10] Cf. Ps. 89 (90): 13.

[11] Echoing the Lord's Prayer, cf. Matt. 6: 13; Luke 11: 4.

[12] Cf. Ps. 83 (84): 4.

audaciam ponit, columba [l]gemitus promit.[l][13] Hic 'botrus cypri',[14] 'flos campi',[15] odor lilii, flumina paradisi,[16] 'porta celi',[17] salus mundi. Ecce portus, ubi potus uini mixti,[18] ubi cibus panis in ligno crucis decocti et[m] a Patre[n] signati. Vbinam tanta oculorum delectatio tantumque[o] aurium melos? Iuxta[p] figenda sunt castra, nec infra remanendum, nec ultra progrediendum. Hic compone mores, depone merores, appone tuos amores. Nusquam alibi propitiatio, non propitiator, neque 'cherubin glorie obumbrantia propitiatorium'.[19] Oblitusne es Abraham ad ilicem Mambre angelos uidisse,[20] sub arbore malo sponsum sponsam suscitasse,[21] omnem aquarum amaritudinem tactu ligni in dulcedinem Moysem conuertisse?[22] Omnibus itaque molestiis carnis, infestationibus antiqui hostis, machinationibus omnimode malignitatis, oppone clipeum crucis. Manus Domini que tetigit te recordare quia ipsa est que creauit te. Nunquid lutum dicit figulo suo, 'Quare fecisti sic?' Loquere potius in amaritudine anime tue et dic Deo, [q]"Noli me condempnare.'[23] Dic inquam Deo,[q] 'Misericordissime Domine et Pater misericordiarum, posito in labore hominum[24] da requiem angelorum, eiecto a facie terre[25] da ingressum superne patrie, consolatione destituto humana adsit diuina.' Vsque ad[r] sedentem in throno[26] uox hec euolabit si non [s]doloris impatientia[s] uel cordis insipientia illam retardauerit. Equidem, frater, dolores apprehenderunt te inter angustias. Quid mirum? 'Non est', inquit Iesus, 'dolor sicut dolor meus.'[27] Quare? 'Quia non peccaui et [t]penam peccati[t] tolero, quia non rapui et soluere exigor.[28] Immo non "est dolor sicut dolor meus" quia seruus emptus[29] contempnit pati que sustinet dominus eius. "Filii hominum, usquequo graui[u] corde?"[30] Nonne cum essem Dominus factus sum seruus? Cum essem impassibilis factus sum passibilis, mortalis cum essem immortalis?' Vt quid fenum recusat quod celum immo Dominus celorum portat? Ex hoc mundo Iesus transiuit et fenum manebit?[31]

[l–l] promit gemitus *O* [m] *om. Sirmond* [n] parte *O* [o] tantusque *O, Val* [p] Iusta *Val* [q–q] *om. Sirmond* [r] in *Val* [s–s] impatientia doloris *O* [t–t] peccati penam *O* [u] gratia *O*

---

[13] Cf. Isa. 59: 11. [14] S. of S. 1: 13. [15] S. of S. 2: 1.
[16] Cf. Gen. 2: 10–14. [17] Gen. 28: 17; cf. Ps. 77 (78): 23.
[18] Cf. Ps. 74 (75): 9. [19] Heb. 9: 5; cf. Exod. 25: 17–22.
[20] Cf. Gen. 18. [21] Cf. S. of S. 8: 5. [22] Cf. Exod. 15: 23–5.
[23] Cf. Isa. 45: 9; Job 10: 1–2. [24] Cf. 2 Cor. 1: 3; Gen. 3: 17.
[25] Cf. Gen. 4: 14. [26] Cf. Rev. 5: 13.
[27] Cf. Lam. 1: 12. [28] Cf. Ps. 68 (69): 5.
[29] Cf. Exod. 12: 44, also Gen. 17: 12, 27; Lev. 22: 11 (empticius), i.e. who shall be circumcised and admitted to the Passover feast along with the children of Israel (but here

sends forth her laments.[13] Here is 'a cluster of cypress',[14] 'the flower of the field',[15] the scent of the lily, the rivers of paradise,[16] 'the gate of heaven',[17] the salvation of the world. Behold the haven where is the drink of mixed wine[18] and the meal of bread baked on the wood of the cross and sealed by the Father. For where is there such delight to the eyes and such a melody to the ears? The camp is to be pitched close by, and one should neither remain within nor advance beyond. Here establish your life, lay down your sorrows, add to your loves. Nowhere else is there propitiation, nor a propitiator, nor 'the cherubims of glory overshadowing the propitiatory'.[19] Have you forgotten that Abraham saw angels at the oak of Mambre,[20] that the bridegroom raised up the bride under the apple tree,[21] that Moses turned all the bitterness of the waters to sweetness with the touch of his staff?[22] And so against all vexations of the flesh, persecutions of the ancient enemy, contrivances of every type of evil, set the shield of the cross. Remember that the hand of the Lord which has touched you is the very same which created you. Does the clay say to Him that fashioneth it, 'Why have you made it so?' Speak rather in the bitterness of your soul and say to God, 'Do not condemn me.'[23] Say to God, I tell you, 'Most merciful Lord and Father of mercies, grant the peace of the angels to one set in the labour of men,[24] grant entry to the celestial homeland to one cast out from the face of the earth,[25] to one destitute of human comfort, let the divine be at hand.' Even unto the One sitting on the throne[26] this cry will fly if the impatience of sorrow or the folly of the heart does not hold it back. Indeed, brother, sorrows have seized you in the midst of your perplexities. What wonder is it? 'For there is', Jesus says, 'no sorrow like to my sorrow.'[27] Why? 'Because I have not sinned and I bear the penalty for sin, because I have not plundered and I am forced to make repayment.[28] Indeed there is no "sorrow like to my sorrow" because the bought slave[29] scorns to undergo that which his master bears. "O ye sons of men, how long will you be dull of heart?"[30] Was I not made a slave although I am Lord? Was I not made capable of suffering although I am incapable of suffering, mortal although I am immortal?' Why does the grass reject what heaven, indeed the Lord of the heavens, bears? Jesus has passed out of this world, and shall the grass remain?[31] 'Heaven and earth shall' also

with the implication of inferiority: they are admitted, but are nevertheless not, metaphorically, true Israelites, and so unworthy to make satisfaction for their sin, which Christ must do in their place).

[30] Ps. 4 (4): 3.

[31] Cf. Isa. 40: 6–8 (esp. 7: 'uere fenum est populus'); 1 Pet. 1: 24; Jas. 1: 11.

'Celum' quoque 'et terra transibunt'[32] et cinis et puluis habitabunt? Propterea frater consoletur te 'flagellum inundans'[33] immo mundans. Hec, inquam, tibi sit consolatio ut affligens te[v] manus Dei[w] non parcat. Sic ad purum scoria tua excoquatur[x] ut anima tua tanquam[y] ex auro obrizo celeste uas celesti forma formetur. Filius fabri[34] sedet conflans et emundans argentum, et 'aliud quidem uas' [z]facit 'in honorem, aliud in contumeliam'.[z] [35] Vis uidere uas in honorem? 'Ad tertium celum' rapitur Paulus 'uas electionis'[36] ubi [a]ab ubertate domus Dei inebriatus[a] [37] exclamat, 'O Domine, "calix"[b] tuus "inebrians[c] quam preclarus est!" '[38] Sic inebriatus nec uerberibus cedit, nec flagellis, nec plagis, nec doloribus, nec etiam[d] mortibus.[39] Hic Ioseph ciphus est in quo augurari[e] solitus preterita, presentia et futura genti sue enuntiat.[40] Iohannes Euangelista nonne[f] regressus a cella uinaria[41] exfecatum[42] nobis uinum propinat, 'In principio', inquiens, 'erat Verbum'[43] etc? Ecce uas in honorem. Vasa quoque stulti pastoris[44] uasa sunt contumelie in quibus uini sapor in saporem uertitur aceti. Hec exufflantur a mensa regis quia inflantur scientia carnis. Hec, inquam, per superbiam inflantur, per inuidiam siccantur, per iram crepant, per accidiam[g] franguntur, per auaritiam disperguntur, per gulam inficiuntur, per luxuriam conculcantur, et in lutum rediguntur.[45] Vale.[h]

[v] *om. O* [w] domini *O, Val* [x] decoquatur *Val* [y] numquam *Sirmond* [z–z] in honorem aliud in contumeliam facit *Val* [a–a] inebriatus ab ubertate domus Dei *O* [b] poculus *O, Val* [c] inest *O* [d] *om. Val, Sirmond* [e] auguriari *O, Val* [f] in me *O* [g] acediam *Sirmond* [h] *om. O, Sirmond*

[32] Matt. 24: 35; Mark 13: 31; Luke 21: 33; cf. also Matt. 5: 18.
[33] Isa. 28: 15, 18. [34] Cf. Matt. 13: 55; cf. also Mark 6: 3; i.e. Jesus.
[35] Cf. Rom. 9: 21; 2 Tim. 2: 20.
[36] Cf. 2 Cor. 12: 2 and Acts 9: 15 ('uas electionis').

'pass'[32] and shall ashes and dust inhabit it? For this reason, brother, let the 'overflowing scourge',[33] nay the cleansing scourge, comfort you. Let this, I say, be to you a comfort, that the hand of God afflicting you spares not. Let your dross so be refined into pure metal that your soul may be fashioned with a heavenly form like a heavenly vase out of pure gold. The carpenter's son[34] sits smelting and purifying silver, and indeed he makes 'one vessel unto honour and another unto dishonour'.[35] Do you wish to see the vessel made unto honour? Paul 'the vessel of election' is caught up 'to the third heaven'[36] where, inebriated with the plenty of the house[37] of God, he shouts out, 'O Lord, your "chalice which inebriateth me, how goodly is it!"'[38] Thus inebriated he yields neither to stripes nor to scourges, nor to blows, nor to pains, nor even to death.[39] This is the cup of Joseph in which, being accustomed to prophesy, he declares the past, present, and future to his people.[40] Does John the Evangelist, having returned from the wine cellar,[41] not give us purified wine[42] to drink when he says, 'In the beginning was the Word'[43] etc.? Behold, this is the vessel made unto honour. Those vessels also of the foolish shepherd[44] are the vessels made unto dishonour in which the taste of the wine is turned into the taste of vinegar. These are blown away from the table of the king because they are blown up with carnal knowledge. These, I say, are blown up by pride and dried up by envy, they snap in anger, they are broken by sloth, scattered by avarice, corrupted by greed, crushed by sensuality, and brought to clay.[45] Farewell.

[37] Cf. Ps. 35 (36): 9.
[38] Ps. 22 (23): 5.
[39] Cf. 2 Cor. 11: 23.
[40] Cf. Gen. 44: 5.
[41] Cf. S. of S. 2: 4.
[42] Possibly a coinage; the context suggests a positive connotation, e.g. a synonym for *defecatum*—'cleansed of' rather than 'pressed from' the dregs.
[43] John 1: 1.
[44] Cf. Zech. 11: 15.; *aceti* following, cf. Matt. 27: 48; Mark 15: 36; Luke 23: 36; John 19: 29–30.
[45] Cf. Job 13: 12.

65

To John of Salisbury[1]

5 Dec. 1154 × Oct. 1155/6

Suo clerico suus abbas.[a]

Tibi an occupationibus tuis uisitationum tuarum raritatem imputare debeam non plane[b] discerno. Hoc unum perpendo, quod litterarum tuarum ad nos rarissima peruenit salutatio. Et fortassis fluctus marini hoc faciunt? Sed quas absorbuerunt? Ostende michi cartam caritatis deperisse et non me causabor oblitum fuisse. Rursus[c] quem mittas non habes? Et unde hec inopia nisi forte ex copia? Certe ante te currunt plures, post te innumerabiles. Dicis 'huic, Vade, et uadit, et alii, Veni, et uenit'.[2] Ignoras quo me requirere debeas? Plane 'in medio populi mei[d] habito',[3] non in secessu siluarum, non in uoragine terrarum.[4] Potesne te excusare et dicere, 'Domine, Babilonem non uidi, et lacum nescio'?[5] Sed hic, hic tu mecum frequenter sedisti, dormisti, fuisti; taceo quod aliquando pre multis aliis locis et terris dilexisti. His uerborum nexibus[e] alius quilibet irretitus et illaqueatus, cessante excusationum suarum ratione humiliter misericordiam peteret et patientiam imploraret. At tu cornu legum siue[f] dialecticarum argumentationum armatus, uelut fila aranee ista contempnis et alia exire [g]uia contendis.[g] 'Est', inquis, 'michi dominus, sunt et alii amici, quibus trahor uel necessitate obedire uel caritate prouidere.' Bene. Nonne prius et plus omnibus amaui? Nonne dextras societatis et ipse dedi? Equidem tibi [h]fecundiora lucra[h] apud alios reperisti, sed non fidem, sed non amorem. Plus quidem donare, non tamen plus possunt amare. Communicaui namque[i] tibi non solum substantiam sed et animam. Non est occultatum os meum a te, non consilium, non denique quantumlibet remotissimum archanum. Et 'tibi post hec, fili mi, ultra quid faciam?'[6] Addam, si [j]addi

65 *O fos. 105^{v}–106^{r}, Sirmond IV. 9*]

[a] G. *O* [b] plene *O* [c] Rursum *O* [d] mei ego *Sirmond* [e] retiaculis *O* [f] seu *O* [g–g] contendis uia *O* [h–h] lucra fecundiora *O* [i] quidem *O* [j–j] potest addi *O*

65 [1] On the date of this letter, see appendix 2. It is unlikely that this letter contains the rebuke to which John refers in his letter no. 31, as that concerned John changing his mind over his plans to travel to France, and also John's disgrace, neither of which figure in the present letter (see also appendix 8).

65

To John of Salisbury[1]

5 Dec. 1154 × Oct. 1155/6

To his clerk, his abbot.

I cannot discern clearly whether I should ascribe the infrequency of your visits to you or to your affairs. I take careful note of this one fact, that only very rarely does the greeting of your letters reach us. Is this then perhaps the fault of storms at sea? But what letters have they swallowed? Show me that a charter of love has perished and I will not plead that I have been forgotten. Again, do you not have anyone whom you could send? And whence does this paucity arise if not perchance from plenty? To be sure, many run ahead of you, countless numbers run behind you. You 'say to this, Go, and he goeth, and to another, Come, and he cometh'.[2] Do you not know where to seek me out? 'I dwell' openly 'in the midst of my own people,'[3] not in the solitude of the woods, not in a cave of the earth.[4] Can you excuse yourself and say, 'Lord, I never saw Babylon, nor do I know the den'?[5] But here, here you often sat, slept, and were present with me; I say nothing of the fact that you once loved it more than many other places and lands. Anyone else entangled and ensnared in these coils of words would have abandoned any ground for his excuses and humbly sought mercy and begged forbearance. But you, armed with the horn of laws, or of dialectical arguments, despise them as if they were spiders' webs and strive to go out by another road. 'I', you say, 'have a lord and other friends whom I am drawn either to obey out of necessity or to provide for out of love.' Very well. Did I not love you first, and more than all others? Did not I myself also give a pledge of friendship? Certainly you have found for yourself richer gains among others, but not faith, but not love. They can indeed give more but they cannot love more. For I have shared with you not only worldly goods but also my soul. My words are not hidden from you, nor my counsel, nor even the deepest secret whatsoever. 'And after this, what shall I do more for thee, my son?'[6] I would add more if anything can be

[2] Cf. Matt. 8: 9; Luke 7: 8.
[3] 4 Kgs. (2 Kgs.) 4: 13.
[4] Cf. Isa. 2: 19.
[5] Dan. 14: 34.
[6] Gen. 27: 37.

potest[j] ad animam. Quid, inquis, queris? 'Animam pro anima, oculum pro oculo, dentem pro dente',[7] non eruendum sed impendendum, non extrahendum sed conserendum.[k] Ad dominum papam appellatus sum[l] pro cemeterio Sancti Sereni de Cantumerula quod imminuere uel auferre nobis nititur canonicorum et abbatis nimis presumptuosa superbia, contra priuilegium Anastasii Pape quod tu ipse uidisti et partim fabricasti,[8] contra ius antiquissimum nostrum, et[m] Luce Euangeliste[9] coartaui terminum quem ipsi perduxerant in primam Dominicam aduentus Domini. Causa ista tua est; cogita tanquam tuam, uel de tua. Non uadam, sed mittam iuxta consilium tuum. Valete.

66

To John of Salisbury[1]

1156, after July and before autumn

Suo suus semper suus.

Stella quandoque de celo [a]ad ima uidetur,[a] sed oculis insipientium, defluere; coagulis tamen nature et diuini clauis mandati sic defixa, in eternum celo adheret ut [b]prius sicut[b] liber idem celum conuoluatur[c] quam stella ab ipso diuellatur. Sic sic, mi karissime, ex quo Deus in firmamento cordis nostri stellam amoris mutui impressit, etsi fefellit oculum ignorantis leges amicitie repentina scintillatio instabilis fortune, non tamen cessit aut decessit igniculus stelle. Vnde et tunc cum quasi ledebam, non quasi sed reuera diligebam, et cum auertebam oculum non auertebam[d] animum. Deo autem gratias

[k] conseruandum *Sirmond* [l] *om. Sirmond* [m] *om. Sirmond*

66 *O fos. 106^v–107^r, Sirmond IV. 4*]
[a–a] uidetur ad ima *O* [b–b] sicut prius *Sirmond* [c] conuolitatur *O*
[d] euertebam *O*

[7] Exod. 21: 23–4; Deut. 19: 21. Douai Reims translates 'Life for life', but Peter links the quotation to what precedes it in the letter, and also, as is clear from what follows, changes the meaning: what is torn out etc. in Exod. is here to be bestowed on the friend. There appears however to be a reference here to a lost letter of John which would give the context for this allusion.

[8] On the bull of Anastasius and John's role in this business, see appendix 2. On the precise meaning of *fabricasti* in this context see also *J. S. Epp.* i. 255.

[9] 18 Oct.

added to the soul. What do you say you are seeking? 'Soul for soul, eye for eye, tooth for tooth,'[7] not for tearing out but for bestowing, not for drawing out but for planting. An appeal has been made against me before the lord pope in the case of the cemetery of Saint-Serein-de-Chantemerle, which the excessively presumptuous arrogance of the canons and the abbot is struggling to encroach on or deprive us of altogether, contrary to the privilege of Pope Anastasius which you yourself saw and had a hand in producing,[8] contrary to our most ancient right, and I have brought forward to Luke the Evangelist's day[9] the term-day which they had put back to the first Sunday of Advent. This case is yours; think of it as yours, or your business. I shall not go myself but shall send according to your advice. Farewell.

66

To John of Salisbury[1]

1156, after July and before autumn

To his own from his own, always his own.

Sometimes a star appears to float down from the sky to the lowest regions, but only to the eyes of the foolish; in fact, fixed with the bonds of nature and the nails of the divine command, it cleaves for eternity to the sky in such a way that the very sky could sooner be rolled up like a scroll than the star be torn out of it. Thus, thus, my dearest one, ever since God impressed the star of mutual love in the firmament of our heart, even if the sudden twinkling of unstable fortune has deceived the eye of one ignorant of the laws of friendship, yet the spark of the star has not ceased or disappeared. Hence at that time when I was apparently causing harm, I was loving not apparently but really, and when I was averting my eye I was not averting my soul. But thanks be

66 [1] A warning to John of adverse rumours being spread about him at court. These evidently concerned his activities in Rome in the first half of 1156 and led to his disgrace at the English court in the autumn of that year. The present letter must have been sent before John's letter no. 19 to Peter (*J. S. Epp.* i. 31–2, dated autumn 1156), by which time the royal displeasure was manifest. It was presumably also sent shortly before John wrote his letter no. 27 to master Ernulf (*c.*Dec.–Jan. 1156–7; *J. S. Epp.* i. 44 and n. 2) which seems to describe the same situation and also associates John's loss of favour with activities in the papal Curia. John had evidently still been unaffected when he wrote his letter no. 13 (addressed to William Turbe, bishop of Norwich, *J. S. Epp.* i. 21–2), at some time before July 1156. On the disgrace, which seems to have been over by April 1157, see *J. S. Epp.* i, appendix ii, 257, and on the present letter, p. 257, n. 2.

quia in plenilunio suo reformata denuo quasi uiribus resumptis, radios primos,[e] solito splendidiores tanquam in inuidia prioris defectus, amplificato affectu remisit. Procul iam deinceps sit tam noctis tenebrosa interpolatio quam diei nubilosa caligo. Sed de his hactenus. Quia uero minus iacula feriunt que preuidentur,[2] mando et moneo ut caueas tibi 'a labiis iniquis et a lingua dolosa'.[3] Apud nos enim quedam de te disseminata sunt, quibus forte nisi clipeum caute prouisionis opposueris ledi in curia poteris. Summi nempe quidam uiri cuidam de curia qui apud nos est, ut ipse audiui, insusurrauerunt te de curia dixisse quedam inhonesta et te falsum legatum domini pape in his partibus gessisse. Que nescio utrum sint magis falsa quam maligna uel e conuerso. Sapiens es; esto tibi in his sapiens. Valete.

67

To John of Salisbury[1]

1157, after July/Aug., (and earlier than no. 68)

[a]Suo Iohanni suus Petrus abbas Cellensis,[a] bonum quod est super omne bonum.

Aliter fit frequenter in rerum euentu quam perpendat hominis prouidentia. Ea precipua[b] est in causis quare amatores ueritatis quandoque loquuntur etsi non contra ueritatem tamen extra orbem ueritatis. Vnde si huius rei in luce exprimatur continentia, nec mendaces dicendi sunt qui[c] contra ueritatem non loquuntur, nec proprie ueraces qui[d] aliud quam contingat opinantur. Itaque sicut precipitium falsitatis usquequaque deuitare uolo, sic ueritatis ripam etsi non contingo saltem affecto. Reducor proinde a falsitate uolens, a uero nolens, teneo autem medium, immo retineor a confinio huius et illius dolens quia semper quod est uel futurum est tam uellem amico[e] dicere quam scire. Scio equidem non imputandum alicui malum quod

[e] priores *O*

67 *O fos. 108ᵛ–109ʳ, Sirmond IV. 11*]
[a–a] Eidem idem *O* [b] precipue *O* [c] *corr. Hall;* quia *O, Sirmond* [d] quia *O* [e] amice *Sirmond*

[2] Cf. Gregory, *Hom. .xl. in Euang.* ii. 35. 1 (*PL* lxxvi. 1259). [3] Ps. 119 (120): 2.

to God because the star, made anew in its full moon with its powers as it were restored, has with magnified affection returned its first rays, more splendid than usual as though angry on account of the earlier eclipse. From now on may both the dark interval of the night and the cloudy fog of the day stay far away. But enough of these matters. But since the darts which are anticipated strike less,[2] I send word and warning that you should be on your guard against 'wicked lips and a deceitful tongue'.[3] For certain things have been spread about over here concerning you and unless you put in their way the shield of cautious foresight you may perhaps be harmed at court. Assuredly, certain men of the highest position whispered to a certain one from the court who is with us, as I myself heard, that you have said certain dishonourable things about the court and that you have played the false legate of the lord pope in these regions. I do not know whether these things are more mistaken than malicious or the other way around. You are wise; be wise for yourself in these matters. Farewell.

67

To John of Salisbury[1]

1157, after July/Aug., (and earlier than no. 68)

To his John, his Peter, abbot of Montier-la-Celle, the good which is above all good.

Things frequently turn out differently in the event from what the foresight of man may suppose. That is the especial reason why lovers of truth sometimes speak if not against the truth yet beyond the truth. For this reason, if the content of this matter is clearly expressed, they are not to be called liars who do not speak against the truth, neither properly called truth-tellers who hold other than what is contingent. And so, just as I wish always to avoid the precipice of falsehood, so, although I do not reach the shore of truth, at least I am striving for it. I am led accordingly away from falsehood willingly and away from truth unwillingly, but I am holding to the middle way, nay, I am held back from the border both of falsehood and of truth, grieving because I would wish always as much to tell my friend what is or what will be as to know it. I know indeed that one should not blame anyone for an

67 [1] A reply to John of Salisbury's letter no. 32 (Jul.–Aug. 1157; *JS Epp.* i. 52–4, and see p. 55, n. 3); on the context and date of this letter, see appendix 8.

patitur sed quod facit uel meretur. Similiter estimo asserendum in eo qui tantum ex insidiis fortune fallitur et nunquam ex proposito fallit, ut dignus sit compassione non condempnatione. Hec, amice karissime, premiserim quatinus noueris [f]me retentum[f] inuitum ab executione sponsionis qua[g] uel nuntios nostros[h] uel cineres beati Aigulfi mittere debui. Interuenerunt plurima que huic preualide obstiterunt. Vnum horum fuit quod W. uester, immo uere noster, a Roma per nos redire debuit, et iuxta suum consilium disponere negotium illud distuli. Non autem per nos uenit itaque mitto fratrem W. monachum nostrum ut iuxta exemplar quod ab ore tuo detulerit omnia faciamus.[2] Ad nutum enim tuum semper facturus sum, precipue in Anglia, quicquid dixeris. Neque enim uolo [i]tibi esse[i] honeri hoc genus negotii quod omni honesto uiro molestum esse non dubito. Cuiuscunque namque emolumenti lucra[3] reportaturi sint,[j] pro uilissimo stercore habiturus sum si uel ad modicum fides uel pudor faciei tue contra senserint. Mando igitur, immo adiuro amicitiam tuam sanctissimam, ne de statu [k]rectitudinis tue[k] propter me pedem moueas sed quod iustum et bonum in oculis tuis fuerit indubitanter remandes. Pace et patientia indissimili, iuxta uerba oris tui, alterum quodlibet accepturus sum, scilicet mittere uel non mittere predicatores.[4] De his hactenus. Ceterum, 'exultat spiritus meus in Deo salutari meo'[5] tam de suauissimo bono odore opinionis tue quam de [l]prosperitate tua.[l] Vnus es [m]omnium mortalium[m] cui pene [n]omnes inuiderent non immerito amici nostri[n] si quanta prerogatiua pre omnibus illis sedem tuam in principali nostro collocaueris attenderent. Inter tres priores tu princeps et ad te nescio si aliquis peruenire possit.[6] Magister W. et magister R. amicitiam quam ad te habent in negotio Hauwidis neptis nostre comprobauerunt.[7] Steterunt enim pro

[f–f] retentum me *O* [g] quia *O* [h] uestros *Sirmond* [i–i] esse tibi *O* [j] sunt *O* [k–k] tue rectitudinis *O* [l–l] prosperitatis tue *Sirmond* [m–m] mortalium omnium *O* [n–n] inuiderent omnes amici nostri non immerito *O;* omnes inuiderint non immerito amici nostri *Sirmond*

[2] On these characters, see appendix 8.

[3] i.e. gifts brought back from the appeal for rebuilding Saint-Ayoul.

[4] A puzzling use of the word; he seems to mean monks who can travel around declaring the virtues of St Ayoul, and his needs, i.e. fund-raisers (see also letter no. 68 and n. 10). Cf. Latham, *predicamentum*: '(?) preaching fee, collection at sermon, 13C'.

[5] Cf. Luke 1: 47.

[6] Cf. 2 Kgs. (2 Sam.) 23: 18–19, apparently used rhetorically here rather than as a reference to three specific individuals, and meaning that John has the first place in his affections.

[7] It is unlikely that the W. here is the same as the first W. above, who had been in

evil which he suffers but only for an evil which he occasions or merits. I think one should assert the same of him who is so deceived by the traps of fortune and never deliberately deceives, that he is worthy of compassion not of condemnation. Let this serve for the present, my dearest friend, so that you may know that I am unwillingly prevented from fulfilling the promise by which I ought to have sent either our messengers or the ashes of the blessed Ayoul. Very many things have intervened which have put very powerful obstacles in the way of this. One of these was the fact that your W., nay truly ours, ought to have returned from Rome by way of us, and I put off arranging that matter on his advice. But he did not pass our way and so I am sending brother W., our monk, so that we might do everything according to the plan which he will bring back from your lips.[2] For I shall always at your command do whatever you say, especially in England. For I do not wish you to be burdened with this type of business, which I do not doubt is troublesome to every honest man. For whatever profit and gain they may bring back,[3] I shall regard it as the vilest dung if, even to a small degree, your loyalty or your sense of propriety has any feeling against it. I charge you therefore, or rather I entreat your most holy friendship, not to move a foot on my account from your place of righteousness but without hesitation to enjoin in reply what is just and good in your eyes. I am ready, in peace and patience alike, to accept either alternative according to the words of your mouth, that is whether to send or not to send preachers.[4] But enough of these matters. For the rest, 'my spirit rejoices in God my Saviour'[5] as much from the sweetest good odour of your repute as from your good fortune. You are unique among mortals in being one whom almost all our friends would envy, not without cause, if they were to consider by how great a prerogative you have set up your seat ahead of all of them in our principal place. Among the three foremost you are the chief, and I do not know if anyone can approach you.[6] Master W. and master R. have proved the friendship which they have for you in the business of our niece Hadwide.[7] For they stood up

Rome. The marriage case to which Peter here refers was most likely concluded at the archiepiscopal court in Sens not the papal Curia (see letters 10 and 23, for which the reference in the present letter gives a *terminus ad quem*). The second W. above is called 'brother' (on him see appendix 8; possibly the same character as in John of Salisbury's letter no. 35). This must be a third W. The R. is unidentified, but could conceivably be John's brother Richard (evidently at Montier-la-Celle at some point, but not otherwise mentioned in Peter's early letters; on him see letter no. 163, n. 1). Their involvement in this case is offered as proof of their friendship for John, which may indicate that they were legal advocates recommended by John.

marito siue matrimonio eius ne scinderetur tam constanter in curia quam fideliter. Non eis modicas grates referas. Dominum archiepiscopum ex parte nostra saluta, et omnes amicos nostros [o]sancti B.[o] [8]

68

To John of Salisbury[1]

1157, after July/Aug. (and later than no. 67)

[a]Suo suus semper et unice suus.[a]

Ecce in cineribus beati Aigulfi[2] cum beato Iob lugens et dolens, debeone studere uerborum elimatis splendoribus, exquisitis faleris?[b] Quin immo iuxta uiscerum commotionem, lugubri, ut sic dicam, et fumoso sermone afflictum represento animum? Mi karissime, curro et discurro quasi uagus et profugus si forte dispersos cineres a quatuor uentis celi[3] recolligere possim. Hinc est quod non cineres sed fruges pretiosas etiam ubi non seminaui, uidelicet de Anglia, metere uolo.[4] Manipulos etenim[c] helemosinarum gentis illius ut metat beatus Aigulfus iniungo. Quid mea interest falcem extendere ubi nunquam uel arare potui uel seminare? Sed non usquequaque absurdum est[d] quod facere propono quia etsi terram illam non colui, te tamen quasi 'areolam aromatis'[5] pro tempore conseui bonis specieriis[e] cum mecum fuisti, cum tecum habitaui, cum te amaui, cum te retinere promerui. O bone Deus, quam feliciter prosperata est bona ista area, immo pinguissima oliua, quomodo sursum germinauit et radicem deorsum misit,[6] quomodo ramos suos expandit,[f] quomodo iamiam replentur famelici de fructu propaginum eius. Gustaui et uidi quia bona est pinguedo eius et fructus eius dulcis gutturi meo.[7] Non est conuersa in amaritudinem uitis aliene. Iam in umbra eius quam desideraueram

[o–o] *om. O*

68 *O fos. 107v–108v, Sirmond IV. 5*]
[a–a] Eidem idem *O* [b] facibus *Sirmond* [c] enim *O* [d] *om. O* [e] *corr. Hall;* speciebus *O, Sirmond* [f] extendit *Sirmond*

[8] Archbishop Theobald of Canterbury (24 Dec. 1138–18 Apr. 1161; see letter no. 11, n. 1), whose help in the appeal John promised in his letter no. 32. St B. is presumably a reference to St Benedict; Theobald was a Benedictine.

68 [1] Peter is finally sending the relics promised in letter no. 67 (the present letter cannot thus be the one to which John's no. 32 is a reply: on the sequence and dates, see appendix 8).

for her husband, or her marriage, so that it should not be annulled, with as much constancy in the court as fidelity. Please thank them heartily. Greet the lord archbishop on our behalf, and all our friends of St B.[8]

68

To John of Salisbury[1]

1157, after July/Aug. (and later than no. 67)

To his own, from his own, always and singularly his own.

Behold, weeping and lamenting with the blessed Job over the ashes of the blessed Ayoul,[2] ought I not to strive for the polished splendours of words, for exquisite verbal trappings? Nay, why do I not, in accordance with the turmoil of my deepest feelings, display an afflicted soul with a mournful and, as I might say, obscure speech? My dearest one, I run hither and thither like one wandering and a fugitive on the chance that I might be able to gather together again the ashes scattered by the four winds of heaven.[3] Hence it is that it is not ashes but precious fruits that I wish to reap, even where I have not sown,[4] that is from England. For I enjoin that the blessed Ayoul may reap handfuls of the alms of that people. What business is it of mine to stretch out the sickle where I was never able either to plough or to sow? But that which I propose to do is not completely absurd because, although I have not cultivated that land, I have planted you, like a 'bed of aromatical spices',[5] with good spices in return for the time when you were with me, when I lived with you, when I loved you, when I deserved to keep you. O good God, see how abundantly this goodly plot, or rather this richest of olive trees, has prospered, how it has germinated above ground and sent a root beneath,[6] how it has spread out its branches, how even now the famished are filled with the fruit of its stock. I have tasted and I have seen that its richness is good and its fruit is sweet to my throat.[7] It has not been turned to the bitterness of a foreign vine. Now I am sitting in its shade as I had desired, now its

[2] i.e. the fire at Saint-Ayoul; see appendix 8.

[3] Cf. Dan. 7: 2; 8: 8; 11: 4; Zech. 2: 6; 6: 5.

[4] Cf. Matt. 25: 24, 26; Luke 19: 21, 22 (here and below).

[5] S. of S. 6: 1; cf. 5: 13.

[6] Cf. 4 Kgs. (2 Kgs.) 19: 30.

[7] Cf. Ps. 33 (34): 9; Prov. 31: 18; what follows echoes Jer. 2: 21.

sedeo, iam umbracula eius 'ab estu', 'a turbine et a pluuia' me defendere sufficiunt.[8] Dies illa sit benedicta, hora nunquam pertranseat cum defectu temporis, qua Iohannem meum feci, qua talem et tantum amicum in filiis hominum apprehendi. Tibi Deus, custos anime mee, tibi commendo illum; tu ei uitam, tu bonam uitam, tu prosperitatem dones, tu inter brachia tua, tu 'sub umbra alarum tuarum'[9] semper illum conserues. Quid enim melius optari potest amico? Vt nichil aliud queram uel michi uel amicis meis isti quos nunc aspicio cineres monent. Retro paululum laquearia, trabes, postes et ligna robusta erant, qui modo puluis tenuissimus et cinis uilissimus est. O munde, aut res mundane, quid estis? Immo quam uane nos decipitis. Certe non estis quod esse uidemini. Certe [g]uidetur in uobis[g] pulchritudo aliqua, dulcedo et utilitas, sed ueritate requisita neque pulchritudo, neque dulcedo, neque utilitas uera est in uobis. Vera est, uera est de uobis sententia quia cum sit in uobis uanitas cor uanum facitis quod possidere poteritis. Sed de his hactenus. Vt ad rem accedamus, scito, amice, quia pretiosum martyrem Aigulfum in uase non uili, ecce, ad peregrinandum in egestate sua destinamus.[10] De manu mea in manum meam illum depono.[11] Quodcunque uolueritis, quodcunque disposueritis de nuntiis, ratum habeo. Generalem administrationem et curam in his amicitie tue assigno.

69

To John of Salisbury[1]

prob. late 1157, or later (poss. × Apr. 1161)

Vnico amico suo I⟨ohanni⟩ de Sar⟨esberia⟩ unicus suus ⟨Petrus⟩,[a] unicam et eternam salutem.

Munera tua frequentissima non magis sua refricatione animum nostrum in amorem tuum semel et semper accensum propensius

[g–g] in uobis uidetur *O*

69 *O fo. 113*[v]]
[a] G. *O*

[8] Cf. Isa. 4: 6; 25: 4.
[9] Ps. 16 (17): 8; cf. also Ps. 35 (36): 8; 56 (57): 2; 62 (63): 8.
[10] i.e. the monks are carrying the relics of the martyr round to raise funds for the repair of the priory; this letter evidently accompanied the reliquary.

bowers are sufficient to protect me 'from the heat,' 'from the whirlwind and from rain'.[8] Blessed be that day, may that hour never fade away with the lapse of time, in which I made John mine, in which I took hold of such and so great a friend among the sons of men. To you God, guardian of my soul, to you I commend him, may you grant him life, a good life, prosperity, may you preserve him always in your arms, 'under the shadow of thy wings'.[9] For what better could one wish for a friend? Those ashes which I now look upon warn me that I should seek nothing else either for myself or for my friends. A short time ago there were panelled ceilings, beams, posts, and sturdy timbers, and now they are finest dust and basest ash. O world, or worldly things, what are you? Nay, how vainly you deceive us. To be sure you are not what you seem to be. To be sure a certain beauty, sweetness, and usefulness are seen in you, but when truth is sought there is in you neither true beauty nor true sweetness nor true usefulness. It is true, it is true what is said of you, that since there is vanity in you you make vain the heart which you are able to take possession of. But enough of these matters. To come to the matter in hand, know, friend, that we are sending the precious martyr Ayoul on a pilgrimage in his need, in a costly vessel, as you see here.[10] I commit him from my hand into my hand.[11] Whatever you want, whatever you arrange concerning the messengers, I confirm. I assign the general administration and care of these matters to your friendship.

69

To John of Salisbury[1]

prob. late 1157, or later (poss. × Apr. 1161)

To his special friend John of Salisbury, his special Peter, special and eternal greetings.

Your most frequent gifts cause our soul, once and always kindled to your love, to burn more readily by their rekindling just as much as

[11] i.e. John is so close and reliable a friend that by committing the business to him it is as good as if it were under his own control.

69 [1] This brief note, unique to MS O, may be connected to a series of letters of John of Salisbury (letters nos. 33–5) which largely concern the activities of a number of Peter's monks in England (*J. S. Epp.* i. 55–65), but it presents a number of problems: see appendix 8.

ardere faciunt quam numero et pretio faciem meam confundunt. Cum enim nichil remittam et frequenter accipiam, uideor aut nichil habere aut minus amare. Sed quem sine pretio et supra omne pretium diligo, nouis rursum redimere munerum blandimentis supersedeo. Thomam nostrum quantacunque instantia poteris reuocare intende, doleo enim de lapsu eius.[2] Pro archiepiscopo oramus et orabimus.[3] Valete.

70

To John of Salisbury[1]

1161 × 1162

Magistro suo I⟨ohanni⟩ de Saresberia, suus [a]abbas Cellensis,[a] quicquid melius est in uita presenti siue futura.

More sitientis sub estu et prestolatione diu desiderati potus[b] iamiam supra modum fatigati, uasculum litterarum tuarum amanter suscipiens, ardenter relegens, frequenter resupinans et quasi noui gustus iteratione in dulcedinis habundantia ad fundum usque ebibo. Duplicatur immo triplicatur legentis affectus ubi materia, gratitudine dilecti animi et stili [c]iocunda lepiditate,[c] optatam narrationis seriem prefert.[d] Sensibus philosophicis que scribis condiuntur, rethoricis coloribus uestiuntur, decentissimis legum ornamentis decorantur, columpnis euangelicis fulciuntur et, quod ad amicos attinet, mellito sapore decentissime dulcorantur. Si lucrum quero sententiarum, si doctrinam, si uoluptatem, si uerborum iuncturam, si amoris ueritatem et dulcedinem, in litteris tuis hec omnia[e] habunde reperio. Nauis ibi ad natandum, hortus deliciarum ad deambulandum, mensa plena et parata ad conuiuandum, lectulus floridus[2] ad quiescendum, gymnasium ad philosophandum. Non est ydolum mendacii, non fallacie lenocinia, non denique adulationis profunda uorago. Non lasciuiose diffunditur ab exigua cordis uena uerbum promissiuum

70 *O fo.* 107[r–v], *Sirmond IV.* 7]
[a–a] G. sacerdos *O* [b] potius *O* [c–c] iocundam lepiditatem *O* [d] profert *Sirmond* [e] *om. O*

---

[2] On Thomas, see appendix 8.

[3] Evidently Theobald of Canterbury (24 Dec. 1138–18 Apr. 1161, see letter no. 11, n. 1), who fell seriously ill in 1155 and was thereafter never free from sickness for long (see *J. S. Epp.* i, p. xxxvii, and n. 2).

they make me blush by their number and their value. For when I send nothing in return and frequently receive, I appear either to have nothing or to love less. But I forbear to buy back again with new blandishments of gifts the one whom I love without price and beyond all price. Endeavour to recall our Thomas with as much urgency as you can, for I grieve over his lapse.[2] We are praying and will pray for the archbishop.[3] Farewell.

70

To John of Salisbury[1]

1161 × 1162

To his own master John of Salisbury, his own abbot of Montier-la-Celle, whatever is better in this life or the one to come.

Like one thirsting in the heat and already wearied beyond measure by long anticipation of the desired drink, taking up the vessel of your letters lovingly, re-reading them ardently, tipping it up frequently and by the repetition receiving almost a new flavour, in an abundance of sweetness I drain it right to the bottom. The affection of the reader is doubled, nay tripled, when the content, by the graciousness of a beloved soul and the pleasant charm of the style, manifests the perfect arrangement of the narrative. What you write is seasoned with philosophical perceptions, adorned with the colourings of rhetoric, embellished with the most seemly adornments of the laws, supported by the pillars of the Gospels and, in that which pertains to friends, sweetened most fittingly with the flavour of honey. If I seek wealth of opinions, or sound teaching, or pleasure, or literary composition, or the truth and sweetness of love, I find all these things abundantly in your letters. There is the ship for sailing in, there the garden of delights to wander in, there the table full and set for feasting, there the garlanded couch[2] for resting on, there the school for philosophizing. There is no idol of falsehood, there no enticements of deceit, there lastly no deep abyss of adulation. The pledged word is not scattered about wantonly from a narrow vein of the heart after the

70 [1] The dating of this letter depends on the interpretation of what Peter has received from John: a single letter or a copy of John's entire early collection. On this question, and the additional complication of the reference here to the translation of the relics of St Ayoul, see appendix 8.

[2] Cf. S. of S. 1: 15.

iuxta illos qui 'dicunt et non faciunt'.[3] Sed quid? Latior in corde, rarior in ore amor. Ardet sine[f] fumo, currit sine spuma, mouet alas sed silenter, petit ima sed tam sublimiter pro animi generositate quam fortiter pro integritate. Accendit[g] sed non incendit, nam calorem facit sed[h] non cinerem. Finem quidem nouit sed cum termino consummationis non consumptionis. Qualem loquor scribendo amorem talem in amicum cogito immo recognosco. Felix anima mea que talem peperit, uel saltem reperit, amicum. Domine Deus cordis mei, tuus erat Iohannes et michi eum dedisti.[4] Proinde tuus sum ego—dicam amicus? Vtinam uel seruus—certe seruus, sed emptitius.[5] Siquidem redemisti me dando pro me Filium tuum, profecto et emisti dando michi famulum tuum. Precipua hec inter cetera beneficia que etsi modo reticeo non tamen pretereo, non denego, non obliuiscor. Nam et ipsa consignata[i] in thesauris[6] memorie consepelio ad conuiuendum et ad[j] commoriendum.[7] Sine his enim nec uiuere ualeo nec mori uolo. Ad Iohannem meum accedo quem a manu gratie accepi tanquam gratiam a gratia, sed tamen non pro gratia.[8] Vacuum namque gratia inuenit me gratia, denique et plenum, sed culpa et pena. Iam penam extenuare, culpam uero euacuare cepit cum Iohannem in amicum subrogauit, qui nescientem instrueret, laborantem iuuaret, errantem corrigeret, pigrum excitaret, exulantem[k] foueret, dolentem releuaret. Quem respiciunt hec munera? Te [l]Domine Deus summe et[l] principaliter, te karissime amice secundario et multipliciter. Sub modio[9] humilitatis nostre aliquando latuisti,[m] iam lucerna ardens quidem conscientia sed non adeo lucens fama. Posuit autem te Dominus in lucem gentium[10] ut sis oculus ceco, pes claudo, lingua stulto, [n]manus manco, auris surdo,[n] ut secundum nomen tuum gratia in predictis suppleat quod natura minus poterat. Profecto licet doleat absentiam tuam tamen in his consolabitur anima mea, iura publica non ignorans preferenda priuatorum utilitatibus. Sic cepisti. Caudam appone in sacrificiis Dei tui.[11] Hoc iuxta capellam [o]scripsi Sancti Aigulfi[o]

[f] in *Sirmond* [g] Accedit *Sirmond* [h] *om.* *O* [i] consignata sunt *Sirmond* [j] *om.* *O* [k] exulentem *O* [l–l] Deus Domine et summe *O* [m] latuistis *O* [n–n] auris surdo manus manco *O* [o–o] sancti Aygulfi scripsi *O*

[3] Cf. Matt. 23: 3. [4] Cf. John 17: 6.
[5] Cf. Exod. 12: 44; also Gen. 17: 12, 27; Lev. 22: 11; bought slaves (or 'servants', Douai-Reims) are to be circumcised and admitted to the Passover meal along with the children of Israel. Not only is he a slave, but he is not even of the chosen by birth, thus reinforcing the profession of humility, and linking the image to what follows. [6] Cf. Deut. 32: 34.
[7] Cf. 2 Tim. 2: 11, also Rom. 6: 8: i.e. the two gifts are Christ, given to redeem, and John. Peter means to die with them and so live with them eternally. [8] Cf. John 1: 16.

fashion of those who 'say and do not'.[3] But what is there? A love more generous in the heart, more sparing in words. It burns without smoke, it flows without foaming, it moves its wings, but noiselessly, it seeks out the lowest places, but it does so as sublimely on account of its nobility of soul as it does powerfully on account of its integrity. It sets alight but does not burn up, for it produces heat but not ash. It knows the end indeed, but the limit is set by consummation not consumption. Such a love as I describe in writing, such do I contemplate, nay recognize, in a friend. Happy soul of mine which has given birth to, or in any event found, such a friend. O Lord, God of my heart, John was yours and to me you gave him.[4] Hence I am your—should I say friend? If only I could even be your slave—your slave certainly, but one bought.[5] For you have redeemed me by giving your Son for me; assuredly you have also bought me by giving your servant to me. These gifts are supreme among all others, and even if now I keep quiet about them, yet I do not disregard them, nor do I deny or forget them. For these also I bury, sealed in the treasure chests[6] of my memory, to live and die with me.[7] For without these I have neither the strength to live nor the wish to die. I approach my John whom I received from the hand of grace, as grace from grace but not for grace.[8] For grace found me empty of grace, then also full, but of guilt and torment. Now it has begun to diminish the torment and to empty out the guilt since it has set John in their place as a friend to instruct the ignorant one, to help one struggling, to correct one erring, to arouse the slothful one, to comfort the exile, and to relieve one grieving. To whom can these gifts be traced? To you, Lord God, above all and first of all; to you, dearest friend, secondly and in a multitude of ways. You once lay hidden beneath the bushel[9] of our humility, now you are a light burning indeed with conscience but not yet shining out with fame. But the Lord set you up to be a light of the gentiles[10] that you might be an eye for the blind, a foot for the lame, a tongue for the mute, a hand for the maimed, an ear for the deaf, so that according to your name grace should make up in these cases what nature could not. Assuredly, although my soul grieves for your absence, it will however be consoled by these things, not being ignorant that the people's rights should be preferred to the interests of private individuals. So you have begun. Add the rump to the sacrifices of your God.[11] I have written this

[9] Cf. Matt. 5: 15; Mark 4: 21; Luke 11: 33; presumably a reference to John's time at Montier-la-Celle (see *J. S. Epp.* i, pp. xvi–xvii).

[10] Cf. Acts 13: 47.

[11] Cf. Lev. 7: 3: 'rump' (Douai-Reims) or 'tail', here implying to complete what he has begun, with the overtone (from Lev.) of doing what is enjoined by God's law.

tibi,[12] opportunitate nuntii tui[p] nunquam fraudari uolens quin[q] aliquid rusticitatis nostre ad rusticandum mittam.[13] Cras in decentissimo tumulo, uidelicet capsa noua, reposituri sumus sacratissimum corpus domini tui beati Aigulfi cuius caput et corpus habemus. Vale.

71

To Henry the Liberal, count of Champagne[1]

1152 × 1154/5

Domino suo Henrico comiti palatino frater Petrus de Cella humilis abbas, bene regnare.

A collateralibus uestris a nobis quesitum est quid uobis daremus, et dies capiendi super hoc consilii prefinita. Primo itaque miror quid ego fecerim mali quod sic semper a me faciem uestram auertitis, quod uenire ad eam uel rogare aut nunquam aut rarissime possim, secundo utrum ab illa tenacissima uestra memoria exciderit quod nondum expletus sit cursus anni, quod LX libras tam uobis quam uestris persoluerim. Tertio non parum doleo quod nostra paupertas et debita propter presentis anni negotia, tum de itinere Romano, tum pro ecclesia de Villa Mauri, tum pro infirmaria fratrum quam fecimus, tum pro multis aliis, ad aures pietatis uestre non potuit peruenire.[2] Videat itaque benignitas uestra et condescendens necessitatibus nostris parcat, et his non addat grauamen sed leuamen. Valete.

[p] *om. O* [q] quod *Sirmond*

71 *Sirmond II. 6*]

[12] A reference to the imminent translation of the relics of St Ayoul follows. The rededication of the restored church of Saint-Ayoul took place on 30 Aug. 1159, but the translation of relics may have been later (see appendix 8).

[13] i.e. the letter being sent across country with the messenger, but possibly also alluding to Peter himself having travelled across country to Provins, to the priory of Saint-Ayoul; in any case, 'rustic' meaning 'course', 'crude' or 'unlettered' is a common metaphor.

71 [1] Count Henry the Liberal of Champagne, 10 Jan. 1152–16/17 Mar. 1181: see Arbois de Jubainville, *Comtes de Champagne*, iii. 28, 111; *J. S. Epp.* ii. 314–5, n. 1; *Lexikon des Mittelalters*, iv. 2068; *Dictionnaire de biographie française*, xvii. 943–4; Dunbabin, *France in the Making*, esp. pp. 315–18 and the genealogy at p. 390; J. F. Benton, 'The court of Champagne as a literary center', *Speculum*, xxxvi (1961), 551–91, at pp. 553–4. For his death, Arbois de Jubainville gives 17 Mar., Benton, 16 Mar., and *Obits Sens*, i. a range of dates, including 16 × 18 Mar. Benton's work on the charters of the court of Champagne 1152–97 was never published (see Bur, *Champagne*, p. 25). Henry was the son of Theobald

to you by the chapel of Saint-Ayoul,[12] not wanting to be cheated of the opportunity presented by your messenger of sending an example of our rustic speech on a rustic trip.[13] Tomorrow we will replace the holiest body of your lord the blessed Ayoul, whose head and body we have, in the most fitting shrine, that is to say, the new reliquary. Farewell.

71

To Henry the Liberal, count of Champagne[1]

1152 × 1154/5

To his lord Henry, count palatine, brother Peter, humble abbot of Montier-la-Celle, to rule well.

Your aides have enquired of us what we would give you, and the day for taking counsel on this matter is fixed. And so I wonder first what evil I have committed that you always turn your face away from me so that I am never, or only very rarely, able to approach it or to put a request, and secondly, whether it has escaped that most tenacious memory of yours that the course of the year is not yet complete and that I have paid back sixty pounds to you and to yours. Thirdly, I grieve not a little that word of our poverty and debts on account of the business of the present year, concerning the journey to Rome, then the church of Villemaur, then the infirmary for the brethren which we built, then many other things, was not able to reach your kindly ears.[2] And so may your benevolence see and, condescending, spare us in our pressing needs, and add to them not oppression but relief. Farewell.

II of Champagne and IV of Blois, and brother of Theobald V of Blois, and later married Marie de France, the daughter of Eleanor of Aquitaine and Louis VII (see letter no. 132, n. 3). The present letter must pre-date 1154 since it refers to litigation over the priory of Villemaur, which was settled by 1154 (see letter no. 7, n. 1), as being in progress, or at least as having still been so during the year running up to the writing of this letter (which could thus have been written sometime in 1155).

[2] Peter's list of troubles includes a journey to Rome, which may have been by a representative at his expense (there are no other references to Peter travelling to Rome, and at least one instance of his excusing himself from attending a council (letter no. 80)). The journey to the Curia (which was mostly in or near Rome in these years) may be connected with John of Salisbury's journey to the Curia of Anastasius IV, at which time he acted for Peter, obtaining a bull in Dec. 1153 (see letter no. 65 and n. 7, and appendix 2). This would fit with the dates for this letter but is not conclusive. Peter may have been at the Curia with John, or have contributed to John's travelling funds. On the Villemaur case, see letter no. 7. The construction of an infirmary at Montier-la-Celle is not independently dated.

72

To Thomas Becket[1]

Jan. 1155 × May 1162

Domino et amico suo karissimo Thome[a] cancellario regis Anglie frater Petrus[b] [c]humilis abbas Cellensis,[c] se et sua.

Quem fortuna non extollit prospera, magis pro humilitate quam pro sublimitate est admirandus. Gloria in[d] uobis cum prosperitate, ut accepi ab his qui uiderunt et nouerunt,[e] [2] ambitiosius quam contentiosius contendit, nec confunditur[f] aliquando superata, nec unquam insolescit de uictoria. Cedit gloria prosperitati sed gloriose, [g]cedit prosperitas glorie[g] sed prospere. Quelibet obtineat, humilitatem seu moderationem non amputat. Gloria accedit sed[h] non superba,[i] prosperitas uenit sed non effusa. Inde est quod de nube tante sublimitatis ad latibulum nostre paupertatis misistis quia uenire non potuistis. Rogastis[j] de familiaritate et amicitia. Quod rogastis[k] si admitteretis admirationi procul dubio habendum esset pro inequali rogantis et rogati fortuna. Que enim proportionalitatis habitudo inter abbatem Cellensem et cancellarium regis Anglie? Pene non est comparatio ubi non est existimationis adaptatio. Secundum post regem [l]in quattuor regnis[l] quis te ignorat?[3] Primum in miseriis fratrum nostrorum quis me non reputat? Dicam de compendio quia quantum de uobis excellentiora tantum[m] de me sentio et scio uiliora. Nullo igitur[n] modo ad ingressum amicitie manum porrigo, sed si uel de grege accidentalium amicorum[4] fuero, bene mecum fecisse dignationem uestram estimabo. Primitias autem[o] illas non mitto quia ampliorem gratiam facere propero. Non habebam sermones

72 *O fos. 138ᵛ–139ʳ, Val fo. 119ʳ⁻ᵛ, Sirmond I. 27*]
[a] T. *O* [b] P. *O* [c–c] seruus seruorum Dei, et *O*; cellensium abbas *Val* [d] *om. Val* [e] *om. O* [f] *corr. Hall;* confundit *O, Val, Sirmond* [g–g] *om. Val, Sirmond* [h] *om. O* [i] superbia *O* [j] Rogatis *O* [k] rogatis *O* [l–l] iiii^or regnorum *O* [m] tanto *O, Sirmond* [n] ergo *Val* [o] aut *Val*

72 [1] Thomas Becket is addressed as royal chancellor, an office to which he was appointed in Jan. 1155 and which he retained until his election to Canterbury in May 1162 (see Barlow, *Thomas Becket*, pp. 38, 42, 82–3; while, as Barlow points out, it is difficult to determine exactly when Becket gave up the office, it is inconceivable that Peter would have addressed him in this way after his election to Canterbury).

72

To Thomas Becket[1]

Jan. 1155 × May 1162

To his dearest lord and friend Thomas, chancellor of the king of England, brother Peter, humble abbot of Montier-la-Celle, himself and his own.

He whom prosperous fortune does not puff up is to be admired more for humility than for eminence. Glory, as I have heard from those who have seen and know,[2] contends in you with prosperity more for the honour than for contention, and it is never confounded when overcome nor ever arrogant in victory. Glory concedes to prosperity but gloriously, prosperity concedes to glory but prosperously. Whichever may prevail, it does not cut off humility or moderation. Glory advances but not proud glory, prosperity comes but not extravagant prosperity. So it is that you have sent from the cloud of such eminence to the poor refuge of our poverty because you were not able to come. You have asked about intimacy and friendship. If you were to allow that which you have asked for, this would beyond doubt be a cause for astonishment owing to the unequal fortune of the petitioner and the petitioned. For what semblance of parity is there between the abbot of Montier-la-Celle and the chancellor of the king of England? There is virtually no comparison where there is no congruity of reputation. Who does not know that you are second to the king in four kingdoms?[3] Who does not reckon me first in the lowly estate of our brethren? Let me say briefly that the more excellent the things I perceive and know about you, the more worthless are the things I perceive and know about myself. Therefore in no way am I extending my hand to enter into friendship, but if I shall be even among the flock of your casual friends[4] I shall reckon that your worthiness has treated me well. I am not indeed sending those first-fruits because I am hastening to offer a more ample favour. I did not

[2] Possibly a reference to John of Salisbury, among others, through whom Peter may have come to be in contact with Becket. [3] i.e. to Henry II.

[4] *DML*, *accidentalis* a., and Blaise, *Lexicon*, *accidentalis* 3, cite this letter for *accidentalium amicorum*. It seems to mean those friends who are not of the substance of but accidental to his friendship circle.

illos[p] magistri G.[5] sed quero, et statim scriptorem cum omni instantia huic operi ad opus uestrum designo. Valete.[q]

73

To Thomas Becket[1]

Jan. 1155 × May 1162

Domino et amico suo karissimo T⟨home⟩ cancellario regis Anglie frater P⟨etrus⟩ Trecensis, salutem.

Magnus animus hoc precipue precipuum inter nobilitatis sue insignia refert ne uel minimam saltem minimi delati obsequii patiatur obliuionem. Semel suscepisse beneficium eterna lege est esse obligatum. Non radit hoc decidens necessitas, non delet negligens incuria, non sepelit occupationum arena; etiam in morte uiuit uitalius uita, fortius morte, perennius temporalitate. Egrum est apud magnanimos non egregium si se obtulerit opportunitas beneficium amico non referre. Mora est non mature quod debeat soluisse, immo gratie dampnum non super soluisse. Non exhonerat quoque liberalitatem suam a debito gratie cum soluerit debitum quia debiti solutio non est gratie absolutio sed renouatio. Mens enim bona gratiam non minuit quam semel alicui aperuit. 'Fiet', inquit Dominus, 'in eo fons uite.'[2] Preterea lucro temporis gratulatur, prona ad usuram beneficii, cum sine mora prestat etiam quod et quando non meruerat creditor obsequii. Tempus namque obsequii gratanter accepto cum, occasione inuenta, concepta obsequia in effectu operis parturio. Grauidata enim mens quid nisi tempus expectat et optat pariendi? Nunquam parit

[p] *om. O* [q] *om. O;* Vale *Val*

73 *O fo. 136*$^{r-v}$]

[5] Possibly the sermons of Gebuin of Troyes. John of Salisbury had requested a *florilegium* including selections from Gebuin's work from Peter in 1157 (on this request and on Gebuin, see *J. S. Epp.* i. 51 and n. 7; see also *P. Ven. Epp.* ii. 144–5). It is very likely that Gebuin's work came to Thomas Becket's attention through John of Salisbury. On Becket's early years at Canterbury and in Archbishop Theobald's household, and his connections there with John of Salisbury in the late 1140s and early 1150s, see A. Saltman, *Theobald, Archbishop of Canterbury* (London, 1956), esp. pp. 166–9, and Barlow, *Thomas Becket*, pp. 28–40. Barlow agrees with the identification of the G. here with Gebuin (Barlow, *Thomas Becket*, p. 63); see also B. Smalley, *The Becket Conflict and the Schools*

have those sermons of master G.[5] but I am seeking them and I am appointing a scribe to this task at once, with all urgency, to work on your commission. Farewell.

73

To Thomas Becket[1]

Jan. 1155 × May 1162

To his dearest lord and friend Thomas, chancellor of the king of England, brother Peter of Troyes, greetings.

A great soul reckons this chiefly pre-eminent among the emblems of its nobility, that it should not suffer even the least forgetfulness of even the least service done to it. To have received a favour once is to be under obligation by a law which is eternal. Grinding necessity does not reduce it, negligent carelessness does not wipe it out, the arena of daily affairs does not bury it, even in death it lives, more lively than life, stronger than death, longer lasting than time. It is, among the magnanimous, debility, not nobility, not to give a gift in return to a friend if the opportunity presents itself. Not to have paid in good time what one owes is a postponement of gratitude, nay, not to have paid above what one owes is a failure of gratitude. Furthermore, when he pays the debt, this does not free his liberality from the debt of gratitude because the payment of a debt is not the absolution of gratitude but its renewal. For the good mind does not diminish the gratitude which it has once opened to anyone. 'It shall become in him', says the Lord, 'a fountain of life.'[2] Moreover, the good mind is grateful for a gain of time, being favourably inclined to pay interest for a favour, when without hesitation it guarantees even what and when the creditor of the service is not entitled to. For I gratefully accept time for my service when, the time being ripe, in completing my labour I give birth to the services conceived. For what does the mind in travail expect and desire except the time of delivery? For that

(Oxford, 1973), p. 114. Sirmond suggested Gilbert the Universal, whom he identified as the author included by Peter in a list of writers recommended to a monk of Saint-Bertin in letter no. 152 (see letter no. 152, n. 5).

73 [1] Dated as letter no. 72. This letter must be later than no. 72 (which is evidently responding to a first approach), but neither can be dated more closely than their common bounding dates. [2] Cf. Ps. 35 (36): 10; John 4: 14.

que nunquam grauidatur. Sterilis suffocans aborsum facit infra germinales uulue areas quodcunque semen susceperit. Ariditas, immo malignitas, ingratitudinis suffocat quod manus agricole de labore et horreis suis plantauerit. Vitio tamen ingratitudinis eatenus nemo redarguitur quousque uel neget debitum uel perpetret debito contrarium. Hactenus, karissime domine et amice, non me arbitreris inuectionem in nobilitatem et liberalitatem tuam facere, que omnes pene non tantum inferiores, non coequales, sed etiam superiores radio suo obnubilat. Certe et usque ad tuguriola nostra fragor ille expensarum et largitatum tuarum tinnitus suos remandat. Tantum autem his commune facere uolui occupationes tuas me obtemperasse in his que aliquando iubere uoluisti per litteras tuas, de sermonibus uidelicet conscribendis et archidiacono transmittendis.[3] Pre modicitate sua nullum fuit obsequium, sed pre affectu uolentis non nullum beneficium.[4] Effectu enim obsequia, affectu pensanda sunt beneficia. De his hactenus. Stephanus iste clericus quidem est comitis.[5]

74

Recipient unidentified

*c.*1145 × 1162

Suo suus, semper suus.

A retro longis temporibus pactum inter nos amicitie compactum durat eatenus in uigore suo semper nouum et firmum ut sint ei succedentium seculorum momenta singula, incrementa uirtutis non detrimenta senectutis. Basis namque supposita columpne amicitie nostre nec titubatione aliqua uacillat nec uetustate putrescit. Quare? Quia nec casualis est etiam repentine ortis affectionum euagationibus,

74 *O fos. 135^{v}–136^{r}*]

[3] The sermons are presumably those of Gebuin of Troyes mentioned at the end of letter no. 72. The archdeacon cannot be identified, and tone and context suggest that it is not a reference to Becket himself (who was archdeacon of Canterbury from late 1154 until sometime before 8 Mar. 1163: see Barlow, *Thomas Becket*, pp. 37–8, 82).

[4] The sense of *beneficium* here (in any case frequently a complex and loaded term in this period) is puzzling. The tone of the rest of the letter makes it unlikely that Peter is

mind which is never in travail never gives birth. The sterile mind, suffocating whatever seed it receives, aborts it within the fertile parts of the womb. The dryness, nay the malignity, of ingratitude suffocates what the hand of the farmer has planted by his labour and out of his granaries. However, no one is convicted of the crime of ingratitude until such time as he either denies the debt or acts contrary to the debt. Thus far, dearest lord and friend, do not think that I am making an attack on your nobility and generosity, which overshadow with their radiance almost all, not only inferiors, not only equals, but even superiors. Certainly that applause for your disbursements and largesse re-echoes even as far as our little hut. But with these words I wished only to make it generally known that I have attended to your affairs in those matters which it once pleased you to enjoin in your letters, that is concerning the sermons to be copied out and sent to the archdeacon.[3] The service was nothing, being a small thing in itself, but on account of the affection of the willing performer, it was no small honour.[4] For services should be weighed by effect, favours by affection. But enough of these matters. That Stephen is indeed a clerk of the count.[5]

74

Recipient unidentified

*c.*1145 × 1162

To his own from his own, always his own.

The compact of friendship contracted between us a long time ago endures to such a degree, always new and firm in its vigour, that the individual moments of the passing years are to it the increments of virtue not the detriments of old age. For the pedestal set beneath the column of our friendship neither wavers with any unsteadiness nor moulders with age. Why so? Because it is neither casual, even with suddenly arising vacillations of the affections, nor corruptible in

attempting to put Becket in his debt by claiming that he has offered him no small favour. Rather he is honoured to have been asked to perform the small service—i.e. it was no small honour to be asked..

[5] Unidentified; possibly a clerk of Count Henry the Liberal of Champagne (1152–81: see letter no. 71, n. 1).

nec corruptibilis, materiam habens in his que amicos fingunt non faciunt. Deus est materia nostri amoris, honestas intentio, utilitas in inuicem pia consolatio. Materia bona, intentio cara, utilitas necessaria. A materia nunquam recedendum, intentioni semper insistendum, utilitati assidue attendendum. Sine materia omnia sunt cassa, sine intentione erronea, sine utilitate superflua. Materie nobilitas etiam ignobilia ingenia fecundat. Rectitudo intentionis et caligantes illustrat. Fructus utilitatis etiam merces excitat. Materia gloriam, intentio lucem, utilitas subministret eternam iocunditatem. In hac materia, intentione et utilitate, libellum amoris nostri explicari desidero ut nichil preter materiam subintroducatur, nichil intentionem declinet, finalem utilitatem nichil excludat. Valete. Anulum aureum in quo est lapis smaragdinus in signum dilectionis mitto.

having its material substance in those things which fake rather than make friends. God is the substance of our love, honourableness the purpose, kindly mutual consolation the benefit. A good substance, a dear purpose, a necessary benefit. One should never withdraw from the substance, one should always pursue the purpose, one should strive constantly for the benefit. Without the substance all things are empty, without the purpose all things are aimless, without the benefit all things are superfluous. Nobility of substance makes even ignoble natures fruitful. Correctness of purpose enlightens even those in darkness. The reward of the benefit even bears fruit. Let the substance furnish glory, the purpose light, and the benefit eternal joy. In this substance, purpose, and benefit I desire the little book born of our love to come to an end such that nothing should be appended besides the substance, nothing deflect the purpose, nothing preclude the final benefit. Farewell. I am sending as a token of love a golden ring in which is set an emerald stone.

BOOK TWO
THE LATER LETTERS
(nos. 75–183)

75*

To Pope Alexander III[1]

mid-Nov.–Dec. 1167 (or poss. *c.*11 Dec. 1167)

Alexandro[a] pape Petrus abbas Sancti Remigii.

Stilum cohibere poterat apostolice contemplatio[b] maiestatis si non erigeret animum humanitatis respectus et prouocaret ausum paruulis Christi condescendere solita clementie uestre[c] gloriosa dignatio; inter quos audeo et ego, cum uix ante dominum meum, patrem fidelium, consolatorem depressorum et deprimentium iudicem [d]'sim puluis'[d] estimandus 'et cinis',[2] uerbum facere pro ecclesia Dei ad apostolatus uestri gloriam et honorem quem in exhibitione iustitie qua totus indiget mundus et operibus misericordie qua[e] sublimantur[f] oppressi et inopes reficiuntur[3] letus audio dilatari. His, pater, titulis sanctitas uestra promeruit ut eam in brachio potenti et patenti uirtute in tot periculis Dominus antecedat et ante uos et pro uobis gloriosos terre humiliet et prosternat.[4] Reuoluantur ab initio et introitus uester et uariorum processus euentuum et plane luce clarius erit quia non manus hominum sed Dominus fecit hec omnia: ille uero qui cepit in uobis miserationis sue magnalia et apostolatus uestri consolidabit tronum quia mundo palam est uos ambulare in semitis eius qui

75 *AlanT* (*A*) *fo.* 204^{r-v}, *AlanT* (*B*) *fo.* 166^{r}, *AlanT* (*C*) *fo.* 109^{r-v}, *Bodl.B fo.* 317^{r-v}, *Lamb p.* 172*a*-*b*, *Vat fo.* 89^{r-v}]

[a] Domino *Vat* [b] contemplatione *AlanT* (*B*) [c] nostre *AlanT* (*B*) [d-d] puluis sim *AlanT* (*C*), *Bodl.B*, *Lamb* [e] quibus *AlanT* (*C*) [f] subleuantur *AlanT* (*C*), *Bodl.B*, *Lamb*, *Vat*

75 [1] The rubrics in all of the MSS which contain it (it comes from the Becket collections) identify this as a letter from Peter of Celle to Alexander III. It evidently concerns the legation of Cardinals William of Pavia and Otto in 1167, in the Becket affair. Peter hints at Frederick Barbarossa's defeats in Italy—he had entered Rome 1 Aug., but by Sept. was a fugitive in the area of Pavia. It is possible that the present letter is contemporary with John of Salisbury's letter no. 219 (*c.* Sept.-Oct. 1167), which also raises suspicion of the legates whose arrival from Aquitaine was anticipated (*J. S. Epp.* ii. 370–9, cf. p. xxxv), but it is more probably contemporary with his letter no. 233 (*c.* Nov.–Dec. 1167; *J. S. Epp.* ii. 424–7). In *c.* Oct.–Nov. 1167 John of Salisbury had written his letter no. 226 (*J. S. Epp.* ii. 395–7, cf. p. xxxv), when the legates had arrived in the north, and was again cautiously hopeful. A flurry of diplomatic activity followed before the 18 Nov. meeting (cf. *J. S. Epp.* ii. xxxv–xxxvi). Peter's references here to the transgression of the legates, and to the French church groaning a second time, seem to put the present letter after this 18 Nov. meeting. In his letter no. 233 John of Salisbury refers to letters of complaint sent to the Pope from the French king and magnates, and describes the French

75*

To Pope Alexander III[1]

mid-Nov.–Dec. 1167 (or poss. *c.* 11 Dec. 1167)

To Pope Alexander, Peter, abbot of Saint-Remi.

Contemplation of the apostolic majesty might have restrained my pen did not a consideration of its human kindness encourage my mind, and did not the renowned dignity of your clemency, which is accustomed to condescend to Christ's little ones, provoke my daring; among them, although before my lord, the father of the faithful, the consoler of the oppressed, and judge of the oppressors I can scarcely be reckoned 'dust and ashes,'[2] even I venture to speak a word on behalf of the Church of God to the glory and honour of your apostolic office, which I am delighted to hear is spread far and wide by the manifestation of justice of which the whole world stands in need, and in the works of that mercy by which the oppressed are raised up and the destitute restored.[3] By these titles of honour, father, has your holiness merited this, that the Lord should precede it in so many dangers with a powerful arm and manifest strength and should humble and cast down the great ones of the earth before you and on your behalf.[4] Let both your accession and the chain of diverse events be considered again from the beginning and it will plainly be clearer than light that it is not the hand of men but the Lord who has performed all these things, He indeed who began mighty works of His mercy in you and will strengthen the throne of your apostolic office, because it is known to the world that you walk in the footsteps

reaction to the legates' mission ('Missum est ad dominum papam cum literis Christianissimi regis et optimatum Francorum. Cardinalium nomen uiluit apud Francos . . .'—*J. S. Epp.* ii. 424; cf. p. xxxvi). Peter's reference here to the prayers of the king, queen, bishops, and nobles may describe part of the same reaction. John of Salisbury also complained in letters of Nov. 1167 and later—see *J. S. Epp.* ii, p. xxxvi; and on the complaints arising from the failure of the Nov. meeting from all sides, see Barlow, *Thomas Becket*, p. 174 and n. 11. For accounts of the events of 1167, see Barlow, *Thomas Becket*, pp. 169–74 and *J. S. Epp.* ii. pp. xxxiii–xxxviii). Anne Duggan in her forthcoming edn. of the Becket correspondence (OMT) links both the present letter and the (lost) letter from the French king and magnates with Becket's letter no. 331 (no. 150 in the forthcoming edn.), *Miseriarum cumulus*, dated *c.*11 Dec. 1167.

[2] Gen. 18: 27.

[3] Cf. Isa. 1: 17; Jer. 22: 3; Ps. 81 (82): 3–4.

[4] Cf. Isa. 45: 2; also a reference to the failure of Frederick Barbarossa in Italy (see n. 1 above).

pauperem liberat a potente,[5] qui acceptionem reprobat personarum,[6] qui in iudicio respondebit unicuique secundum opera sua. Exultat in his que de uobis[g] audit deuotus filius uester Christianissimus rex Francorum; letatur ecclesia Gallicana cuius tristitia de uanitate quorumdam insultantium ueritati nuper est in gaudium commutata.[7] Nam in aduentu dominorum uestrorum[h] cardinalium didicit quod uenerabilis uiri pro libertate ecclesie laudabiliter decertantis Cantuariensis archiepiscopi fouetis causam, et mendaces esse conuincitis qui se ruinam innocentum et confusionem ecclesie gloriabantur a uobis impetrasse. Et plane saperent cardinales si starent in finibus uestris sed, quod iterum gemit ecclesia Gallicana, iam in hac parte dicuntur excessisse. Vnde paternitatem uestram toto corde prostratus imploro quatinus Christianissimi regis et regine et episcoporum et procerum Gallie preces pro domino Cantuariensi porrectas audiatis et deducatis in irritum quicquid contra iustitiam eius noueritis esse presumptum.

76

To Pope Alexander III[1]

1171/2, before Sept. (or earlier)

Alexandro pape Petrus abbas Sancti Remigii.

Que in euidenti et manifesto sunt uera, se ipsa loquuntur, se ipsa nullo adiuncto adminiculo testantur. Que autem remotione loci, euolutione temporis uel cuiuslibet implicatione caliginis profundum tenent ignorantie, cum rei publice poposcerit utilitas, sub luce uolunt uideri. Hinc est, pater sanctissime, quod lator presentium, in gremio nostre humilitatis coalescens,[2] habitum religionis a nobis in monasterio Cellensi suscepit, diuque ibi ubera uino

[g] nobis *Bodl.B, Lamb* [h] nostrorum *AlanT* (*C*), *Bodl.B, Lamb*

76 *Sirmond V. 19*]

[5] Cf. Ps. 71 (72): 12.
[6] Cf. 2 Chr. 19: 7; Ecclus. 20: 24; Rom. 2: 11; Eph. 6: 9; Col. 3: 25; Jas. 2: 1.
[7] Cf. Esther 9: 22; 13: 17; 16: 21; Jer. 31: 13.

of Him who delivers the poor from the mighty,[5] who condemns respect of persons,[6] and who will respond in judgement to each one according to his deeds. Your devout son, the most Christian king of the French, rejoices in these things which he hears about you; the French church, whose sorrow at the vanity of certain revilers of truth has recently been turned to joy,[7] is delighted. For at the arrival of your lords the cardinals she learnt that you support the cause of that venerable man the archbishop of Canterbury who strives in praiseworthy fashion for the freedom of the Church, and that you prove to be liars those who were boasting that they had won from you the ruin of the innocent and the confounding of the Church. And clearly the cardinals would be wise if they stood within the boundaries set by you, but, and this is something that the French church groans about a second time, they are now said to have transgressed in this. For which reason, prostrate, I beg with my whole heart that you in your fatherly concern hear the prayers of the most Christian king and queen, and of the bishops and nobles of France, offered for the lord archbishop of Canterbury, and that you bring to nought whatever you know to have been ventured in prejudice to his justice.

76

To Pope Alexander III[1]

1171/2, before Sept. (or earlier)

To Pope Alexander, Peter, abbot of Saint-Remi.

Those things which are plainly and manifestly true speak for themselves and bear witness for themselves with no additional support. But those things which, owing to remoteness of place or to the passage of time or to being shrouded in any darkness, cleave to the depths of ignorance, demand to be seen in the light when the public good urgently requires it. Hence it is, holiest father, that the bearer of this letter, growing up in the bosom of our humility,[2] received the religious habit from us in the monastery of Montier-la-Celle and, taking nourishment there for a long time at the breasts that

76 [1] Both this letter and no. 77 concern Fulk, missionary bishop to Estonia. On the context and date see appendix 9 and letter no. 96, n. 1.

[2] The bearer is Fulk (see appendix 9); *gremium* can also mean 'community' (see *DML*, *gremium*, 5), and Fulk, as mentioned below, took his vows at Montier-la-Celle.

meliora[3] sugens, in uirum episcopalem gratia Dei cooperante profecit, reuera opus et onus iniuncti officii amplectens, non aurum robur suum ponens nec obrizo dicens, 'Fiducia mea'.[4] Querit enim a sede apostolica mortem per mortem quia et in itinere quo pergit mortem minatur estas et imperialis potestas,[5] et quam exposcit si obtinuerit mortem importat, barbarorum infida societas. Habet itaque animam suam in manibus suis[6] offerens illam Deo per manum celestis clauicularii[7] et uestram. Excipite si placet hostiam sanctam, 'Deo placentem, rationabile obsequium',[8] et beatissimi apostolatus uestri auctoritate exponite ouem lupis si forte beata conuersatione non lupus comedat agnum sed agnus conuertat lupum. Quodlibet autem horum fiat, Deus glorificabitur, ministerium uestrum honorificabitur et anima fratris nullum detrimentum patietur. Presumo enim a preteritis que in eo enutriui, et multis didici argumentis, quod in commisso fidelis erit et a tramite fidei nullo incursu exorbitabit, potiusque dabit sanguinem quam imminuat fidem. Ait Apostolus, 'Spiritum nolite extinguere'[9] et lucernam iam in modio accensam amplioribus suffusoriis accendite,[10] quia hec est gloria et corona uestra, si granum frumenti per manum uestram in terram cadens multum fructum attulerit.[11]

[3] Cf. S. of S. 1: 1, also 4: 10. [4] Cf. Job 31: 24.

[5] During the Alexandrine schism (1159–77) travel through imperial territory was difficult for supporters of Alexander. Fulk was most probably carrying papal letters (see appendix 9) and Eskil, to whom he was travelling, had himself been held captive by an ally of Barbarossa when returning from Rome to Denmark in 1157/8.

[6] Cf. Judg. 12: 3; 1 Kgs. (1 Sam.) 19: 5; 28: 21; cf. also Job 13: 14; Ps. 118 (119): 109.

are better than wine,[3] has advanced with the aid of God's grace to be a man fit to be a bishop, truly embracing the labour and the load of the office imposed on him, not supposing gold to be his strength nor saying to fine gold, 'My confidence'.[4] For he seeks from the apostolic see death through death, both because in the journey by which he proceeds the summer heat threatens death, as also does the imperial power,[5] and because the faithless company of the barbarians which he is asking for, if he should obtain it, brings with it death. And so he holds his life in his own hands,[6] offering it to God through the hand of the keeper of the keys of heaven,[7] and your hand. Accept, if it please you, the holy sacrifice 'pleasing unto God, the reasonable service,'[8] and by the authority of your most blessed apostolic office expose the sheep to the wolves in the hope that, through a blessed conversion, the wolf shall not eat the lamb but the lamb convert the wolf. But whichever of these possibilities shall occur, God will be glorified, your ministry will be honoured, and the soul of the brother will suffer no detriment. For I believe from the past achievements which I have nourished in him, and I have learned from many proofs, that he will be faithful in the commission and will not deviate from the path of faith in the face of any assault, and that he will rather give his blood than do harm to his faith. The Apostle says, 'Extinguish not the spirit'[9] and light the candle now kindled under a bushel[10] with fuller pitchers of oil because this is your glory and crown, if the grain of wheat falling by your hand into the ground should bring forth much fruit.[11]

[7] Cf. Matt. 16: 19 (St Peter).

[8] Cf. Rom. 12: 1; there are echoes of Matt. 10: 16 and Rom. 11: 13 in what follows.

[9] 1 Thess. 5: 19.

[10] Cf. Matt. 5: 15; Mark 4: 21; Luke 8: 16; 11: 33.

[11] Cf. John 12: 24–5, 'unless the grain of wheat falling into the ground die, itself remaineth alone. But if it die, it bringeth forth much fruit. He that loveth his life shall lose it, and he that hateth his life in this world, keepeth it unto life eternal.'

77

To Pope Alexander III[1]

1171/2, before Sept. (or earlier, but later than letter no. 76)

Domino et patri Alexandro summo pontifici Petrus abbas Sancti Remigii, quicquid filius patri.

Nullis bona uoluntas a sancto Spiritu incitata cohercenda est habenis, nullis a proposito retardanda dissimulationibus. Sic enim iam totius nostre Christianitatis religio intepuit ut uix in toto grege Christiani populi aliqui inueniantur qui non malint sub ficu et oliua terreni honoris et delectationis delitescere quam procul odorari[a] bellum[2] et audacter occurrere in occursum cum filiis Beniamin et dimidia tribu Manasse[3] expediti armatis inimicis Christi. Ad uos itaque, pater sanctissime, qui estis in corpore ecclesie caput de quo oleum non deficit[4] et qui australe sufflatorium habetis, respicit desides excitare, excitatos uero ad 'meliora et uiciniora saluti'[5] iuuare et impellere. Nunquam ergo uobis molestum debet esse quod a uobis postulatur in auxilio propagande catholice fidei quia et Dei et Domini nostri Iesu Christi laus inde augmentatur, meritum uestrum cumulatur, salus infideli populo adquiritur. Proinde petitiones pauperis illius episcopi Fulconis,[6] qui hoc anno curiam uisitauit et modo nobiscum hospitatur, apud uestram sanctitatem commendamus, scientes et pensantes quia ubi nulla aut rara fidei supellectilia sunt, suffragio copiosiore indigetur. Indulgendum est ergo illi in multis qui omnibus indiget. Sic magister et Dominus noster,[b] cum discipulos suos mitteret ut noua predicarent, addidit eis ut mira quoque facerent.[7] Non a uobis hoc exigitur ut uirtus miraculorum tribuatur sed auctoritas uestra, cum ipso et in ipso operans ut facilius ei ab incredulis credatur. Nam et Moyses cum a Domino ad filios Israhel mitteretur, signum rogauit dari in quo sibi crederetur.[8] Priuilegia

77 *Sirmond VI. 6*]
[a] odorare *Sirmond* [b] uester *Sirmond*

77 [1] Dated as letter no. 76 (see appendix 9). [2] Cf. Job 39: 25.
[3] In Judg. 20 the children of Benjamin fought against the Israelites, but elsewhere the half tribe of Manasseh fought with the Israelites (cf. Josh. 1: 12; 4: 12, and many other refs.).
[4] Cf. Eccles. 9: 8. [5] Cf. Heb. 6: 9. [6] See appendix 9.

77

To Pope Alexander III[1]

1171/2, before Sept. (or earlier, but later than letter no. 76)

To his lord and father Alexander, supreme pontiff, Peter, abbot of Saint-Remi, whatever a son owes to a father.

A good intention inspired by the Holy Spirit should be restrained by no reins nor held back from its purpose by any dissemblings. For now the religious life of our whole Christian realm has cooled so that scarcely any can be found in the whole flock of the Christian people who would not rather hide beneath the fig and the olive of worldly honour and delights than smell the battle afar off[2] and boldly rush into the fight with the children of Benjamin and the half tribe of Manasseh,[3] lightly equipped against the fully armed enemies of Christ. And so to you, holiest father, who are the head of the body of the Church, from which the oil does not depart,[4] and who holds the bellows of the south wind, Christendom looks to stir up the idle and to aid and impel those who are stirred up to 'better things and nearer to salvation'.[5] What is asked of you in aiding the propagation of the Catholic faith ought never to be a burden to you because the glory both of God and of our Lord Jesus Christ is augmented thereby, your merit is piled high, and salvation is obtained for the faithless people. Hence we commend to Your Holiness the petitions of that poor bishop Fulk[6] who has visited the Curia this year and is now a guest with us, knowing and considering that where there are no, or few, furnishings of faith, there is the need of more abundant support. For he who lacks all things should be granted many things. Thus our master and Lord, when He sent out His disciples to preach the good news, granted it to them also to perform wonders.[7] You are not required to bestow the power of performing miracles but rather to bestow your authority, acting with him and in him so that he may be believed more readily by the unbelievers. For Moses also, when he was sent by God to the children of Israel, asked for a sign to be given by which he should be believed.[8] Those privileges therefore which

[7] Cf. Matt. 10: 8; Mark 3: 15; Luke 10: 9; cf. also John 13: 14.

[8] Cf. Exod. 4: 1–9; the rod which turned into a serpent (mentioned below) was the first of three signs bestowed on Moses.

ergo que a uobis petit, et pro uirga Moysi et pro miraculis discipulorum Christi suffragabuntur ei. Nemo enim Deo faciente contempnet auctoritatem uestram uel personam illius uestra auctoritate munitam. Valeat sanctitas uestra cui debeo quicquid sum et possum, a multis enim audio et in multis experior magnificentissimam gratiam uestram.

78

To Pope Alexander III[1]

? *c.*1177 (or 1176 × 1181)

Alexandro pape Petrus abbas sancti Remigii.

Sicut a paternitate domini nostri Remensis Willelmi in mandatis acceperamus de causa terminanda que uertitur inter episcopum Suessionensem et Comitem Robertum, Suessionis accessimus, et nobiscum abbates Sancti Crispini, Sancti Iohannis et Vallis Serene.[2] Ibi allegationibus utriusque partis auditis, ab episcopo productorum testium attestationes scriptas recepimus. Deinde aliam diem Remis utrique parti statuentes, iterum conuenimus et post multa, quia dominus rex super hoc negotio litteras suas episcopo direxerat, ex uoluntate et consensu eorum diffinire causam distulimus donec cognosceremus an dominus rex controuersiam illam inter eos pacificaret. Postea uero nulla interpellatione interueniente nec diem sibi dari episcopo a nobis postulante, interdicto excommunicationis[3] nobis

78 *Sirmond VIII. 10*]

78 [1] Concerning a case evidently delegated to Peter by William aux Blanches Mains, archbishop of Reims (1175/6–1202, see letter no. 4, n. 4): a dispute between Bishop Nivelon of Soissons (Nivelon de Quierzy, el. 1175, consecrated 9 Aug. 1176, d. 13 Sept. 1207; Newman, *Seigneurs de Nesle*, i. 160; *GC* ix. 362–6) and a Count Robert (see below). *GC* ix. 363, puts the dispute in *c.*1177, but *c.*1176 is given at *GC* ix. 398, in the entry for Berneredus of Saint-Crépin, who was also involved (see below, n. 2). There is no Count Robert of Soissons in this period; the counts of Soissons were Ivo II (1171–Aug. 1178), Conon (1178–80, before 20 Apr.) and Ralph (1180–1235): Newman, *Seigneurs de Nesle*, i. 59–65, and nn. 23–4. This is almost certainly Robert of Dreux (d. 1188), eldest lay brother of Louis VII, whose second wife, Agnes de Baudemont, presumably the countess mentioned here, was hereditary lady of Braine, close to Soissons (and possibly a relative of Peter of Celle). Robert m. Agnes in 1152, and this would explain his interest in the region. He was often called simply 'count', rather than 'count of Dreux' or 'of Braine', as these lordships were only accorded the status of counties under his successor, Robert II.

Fulk asks for from you will support him after the fashion both of the rod of Moses and of the miracles of Christ's disciples. For no one, with God acting, will despise your authority or the person of him who is fortified by your authority. May Your Holiness, to whom I owe whatever I am and whatever I have power to do, fare well, for I hear from many and I experience in many things your most magnificent grace.

78

To Pope Alexander III[1]

? *c.*1177 (or 1176 × 1181)

To Pope Alexander, Peter, abbot of Saint-Remi.

As we had been instructed by the orders of the fatherly authority of our lord of Reims, William, to conclude the case which is in progress between the bishop of Soissons and Count Robert, we arrived at Soissons, and the abbots of Saint-Crépin, Saint-Jean-des-Vignes, and Valsery were with us.[2] There, having heard the allegations of both sides, we received the written testimonies of the witnesses produced by the bishop. Then, fixing with both sides another day at Reims, we met again and, after much discussion, because the lord king had sent a letter to the bishop on this matter, we adjourned the case, by their will and consent, until we should know whether the lord king was settling the dispute between them. But thereafter, with no appeal lodged in the meantime, and without the bishop having requested from us a day to be appointed for him, the bishop without consulting us subjected the land of the

From *c.*1150 Robert was a close and loyal ally of his brothers Louis VII and Henry of France, which would explain the king's involvement in this case. On his titles and politics, see A. W. Lewis, 'Fourteen charters of Robert I of Dreux (1152–1188)', *Traditio*, xli (1985), 145–79, esp. pp. 147–50, 156–7; cf. also p. 158 and nn. 50–1 on Agnes, correcting earlier confusions over her identification (see Introduction, pp. xxix–xxx).

[2] If this is 1177, then the abbot of Saint-Crépin-le-Grand is Berneredus (*c.*1162/3–79, see letter no. 128, n. 1); the abbot of Valsery (Premont., dioc. Soissons) is Herbert I (occurs ?1167, cert. by 1176 × 1189; *GC* ix. 487), and the abbot of Saint-Jean-des-Vignes (the most likely identification of this name—Augustinian, nr. Soissons, Cott. ii. 3051), is either John I (occurs 1168 × 1172), Regnerus (no dates), or Hugh (occurs 1179 × 1181, d. by 1186; *GC* ix. 458).

[3] An unusual combination of interdict (which applies to areas, as is clearly meant here) and excommunication (which applies to persons), and which are normally distinguished, but cf. Blaise, *Dictionnaire*, *interdictus* 2, and Niermeyer, *interdictus* 4.

inconsultis terram prefati comitis episcopus subiecit. Proinde comitissa ex parte sua et comitis conquerens de hac iniuria ut terram suam absolueremus a nobis exegit. Consilio itaque sapientium habito, accepta cautione a parte comitis quod si nouum dampnum uel iniuriam episcopo fecisset plene resarciret, terram absoluimus. Hanc igitur huius rei ueritatem uobis mandamus et testamur.

79

To Pope Alexander III[1]

early 1178

Alexandro pape Petrus abbas Sancti Remigii.

Cum uniuersitas Christianitatis, pater sanctissime, uestro regatur moderamine, et cura uestre sollicitudinis ad plura distendatur quam sit stellarum numerus uel arene maris, satis mirum sit[a] si nunquam circumueniatur. Plures enim uenantur in curia uestra subreptione quam famulentur fideli deuotione. Excipio sinceritatem sanctorum cardinalium quorum fides satis nota est Deo et uobis. Aduenientium redarguo fallacem simulationem, precipue Teutonicorum, quorum insidias et nos experti sumus et uos uiuo carbone tactus[2] non ignoratis. Hi namque toto tempore schismatis, cum expositos nos et quasi sine defensore calumpniis et dampnis pluribus afficerent, nunquam tamen in guerra obtinuerunt quod modo in pace uestra et sancte Romane ecclesie nituntur ab ecclesia nostra auferre.[3] Dominum namque imperatorem frequenter sollicitauerunt ut de prebendis Marsne aliquas[b] subripere possent, quas olim a multis retro temporibus concessione Leodiensium episcoporum et tam priuilegio pie memorie predecessoris uestri Innocentii[4] quam uestro confirmatas habemus. Mandastis preposito nostro de Marsna quatinus cuidam clerico imperatoris prebendam que non est daret.[5] Petit igitur

79 *Sirmond VIII. 16*]
[a] est *Sirmond* [b] *corr. Brooke;* aliqua *Sirmond*

79 [1] On Meerssen, this dispute and the date of this letter, see appendix 10 (see also letters 86 and 94).

[2] Cf. Isa. 6: 6–7: '. . . unus de seraphin . . . in manu eius calculus quem forcipe tulerat de altari . . . tetigit os meum . . .'

[3] Meerssen was in imperial territory and now, with the end of the schism (Peace of

aforesaid count to the interdict of excommunication.[3] Thereupon the countess, complaining on her own behalf and that of the count concerning this injury, demanded of us that we release their land. And so having taken the counsel of the wise and having received a pledge on behalf of the count that if he should cause any new harm or injury to the bishop he would make full restoration, we released the land. Therefore we commit and testify to you this true account of this matter.

79

To Pope Alexander III[1]

early 1178

To Pope Alexander, Peter, abbot of Saint-Remi.

Since the whole of Christendom, holiest father, is subject to your direction, and the care of your solicitude is extended to more things than there are stars in the sky or grains of sand in the sea, it would be a great wonder if it were never circumvented. For in your Curia more hunt by deception than serve by faithful devotion. I do not impugn the sincerity of the holy cardinals, whose fidelity is well enough known to God and to you. I am rebuking the deceitful pretence of those coming from outside, especially Germans, whose plots we have experienced and which you who have been touched with a live coal[2] are also aware of. For these, during the whole time of the schism, when they were afflicting us who were exposed and virtually defenceless with many calumnies and injuries, still never obtained in war that which now in your peace and that of the holy Roman Church they are striving to take from our church.[3] For they solicited the lord emperor frequently that they might be able to steal some of the prebends of Meerssen which now and for a long time past by grant of the bishops of Liège and by the privilege of your predecessor Innocent of devout memory,[4] and by yours, we have held confirmed. You have ordered our provost of Meerssen to give to a certain clerk of the emperor a prebend which does not exist.[5] Therefore

Venice, 24 July, 1177; *DP*, p. 176) the Germans, presumably those in Cologne involved in this dispute, can take their case to the Curia.

[4] Innocent II (14 Feb. 1130–24 Sept. 1143); see appendix 10.

[5] Peter also refers in letter no. 86 to a prebend which 'nec prepositus dare possit, nec sit prebenda que dari possit'. Either there has been a confusion over the number of prebends or Peter is using dramatic language to make the point that the prebend in question is not in the provost's gift.

conuentus noster prostratus pedibus uestris reuocare mandatum et ulterius nullam recipere alicuius super hac re petitionem. Deuoti enim sunt filii uestri et exinde deuotiores efficientur.

80

To Pope Alexander III[1]

1178 (summer or later)

Domino pape Petrus abbas sancti Remigii.

Ad generale concilium, pater uenerande, cum ceteris Catholice ecclesie filiis citatus excusationem prefero, non friuolam de perfunctoriis euangelicis aliquam quibus ad cenam inuitati se excusando accusant,[2] sed manifestis documentis probabilem et ueram. Prompta siquidem est in me ad omnem obedientiam deuotio sed succumbit propter inualetudinem languida executio. Inest uoluntas sed impedit infirmitas; 'spiritus quidem promptus est, caro autem infirma.'[3] Apud igitur paternam clementiam et equissimam apostolice discretionis censuram etas annosa, longa uia, breuis uita, fessa membra sint nostre excusationis probabilia et necessaria argumenta. Mauult habere filium absentem uiuum quam secum semimortuum, uel certe extinctum. Percussus sum ut fenum quod iam exaruit,[4] 'quod hodie est, et cras' non 'in clibanum' sed in feretrum mittetur,[5] et quomodo tanquam 'plaustrum onustum feno'[6] prosequi potero ambulantes in equis et uolantes in pennis sanitatis et robuste etatis? Quid enim si presens essem nec interesse possem? Quid faceret facula fumigabunda[a] inter astra lucentia? Parcite ergo in hoc nunc sicut semper fecistis, nostras preces benigne suscipiendo et efficaciter implendo.

80 *Sirmond VIII. 12*]
[a] fumibunda *Sirmond*

80 [1] Excusing himself from attending the Third Lateran Council (5–19 Mar. 1179); possibly written soon after the invitations were sent out at various times from the summer of 1178 (see e.g. *Councils and Synods*, i. 2, pp. 1011–14; JL 13099; Ramackers, *Papsturkunden in Frankreich* v, pp. 361–3). This letter may have accompanied letter no. 81.

our community, prostrate at your feet, begs you to revoke the order and accept no further petition from anyone on this matter. For your children are faithful and on this account they will be rendered more faithful.

80

To Pope Alexander III[1]

1178 (summer or later)

To the lord pope, Peter, abbot of Saint-Remi.

Having been summoned to the general council, venerable father, along with the other sons of the Catholic Church, I proffer an excuse—not a frivolous one, like one of the perfunctory excuses in the Gospels with which those who were invited to the supper accuse themselves by making excuses,[2] but one which is, by clear proofs, demonstrable and true. There is in me indeed a willing devotion to every kind of obedience, but my weak performance sinks down on account of my infirmity. The will is present but weakness hampers it; 'the spirit indeed is willing but the flesh weak.'[3] Therefore let old age, a long journey, the brief span of life, and tired limbs be the demonstrable and necessary grounds of our excuse before the fatherly clemency and most equitable judgement of the apostolic wisdom, which would rather have an absent son alive than one present who is half dead, or expired for sure. I am smitten as grass which now has withered,[4] 'which is today, and tomorrow' shall not be cast 'into the oven' but into the bier,[5] and how, like 'a wain that is laden with hay,'[6] shall I be able to follow those travelling on horses and flying on the wings of health and of sturdy age? And what if I were present and not able to take part? What would a smoking faggot achieve amongst shining stars? Be merciful therefore now in this matter, as you have always been, receiving our prayers benignly and fulfilling them effectually.

[2] Cf. Luke 14: 16–24, esp. 18–20; Matt. 22: 2–10, esp. 5.
[3] Matt. 26: 41; Mark 14: 38.
[4] Cf. Ps. 101 (102): 5; cf. also Ps. 128 (129): 6.
[5] Cf. Matt. 6: 30; Luke 12: 28.
[6] Amos 2: 13.

81

To Pope Alexander III[1]

1179, before Mar. (or poss. as early as summer 1178)

Alexandro summo pontifici Petrus abbas Sancti Remigii.

Totius Christianitatis onus humeris apostolicis impositum non ignorat qui Christum principi apostolorum dixisse non dubitat, 'Tu es Petrus et super hanc petram edificabo ecclesiam meam'.[2] Necesse itaque est ut Aaron qui penetrauit celos[3] in sanguine suo,[4] pontifex a Deo Patre constitutus in eternum,[5] et Vr qui in igneis linguis super apostolos descendit,[6] tam manus quam humeros uestros auxilio suo subleuent et ne deficiant sustentent.[7] Iniquitas namque que sedet super talentum plumbi[8] geminatis quin potius iunctis alis ecclesiam Dei et uestram, Dei desponsatione, uestram procuratione, usquequaque opprimit tam in subditis quam in prelatis adeo ut iam possit dici, 'sicut populus sic sacerdos',[9] sicut oues sicut canes. Quid dicam, et quare dicam quod patet lippis et tonsoribus?[10] Nonne clamor tanti mali, ne dicam furor, usque ad nubes ascendit? Et quis uos dubitat ista scire cuius est non solum morbos discernere sed etiam queque morbosa secare aut sanare? Tamen, summe pastor, duo mala facit populus tuus.[11] Descende et inuenies uitulum conflatilem[12] lasciuientem 'in uaccis populorum'[13] et lingentem herbam usque ad radicem.[14] In altero notatur luxuria, in altero auaritia. Olim hec tenebrarum familia tenebant ualles, iamiam occupant montes. Olim fedabant templum Veneris sed iam polluunt atria Virginis quam Pater desponsauit Filio suo et Paulus tanquam uni uiro uirginem castam

81 *Sirmond VIII. 11*]

---

81 [1] This and letter no. 80 concern the Third Lateran Council, 5–19 March 1179, and may have been sent together (see letter no. 80, n. 1). The present letter is a general message of exhortation and admonition. If it did accompany letter no. 80, then it could be as early as summer 1178.

[2] Matt. 16: 18.

[3] Cf. Heb. 4: 14, where this is said of Jesus.

[4] Cf. Acts 20: 28; Heb. 13: 12 (applied to Jesus).

[5] Cf. Exod. 35: 19; Heb. 6: 20. This whole passage combines Exodus and Hebrews, and Aaron and Jesus.

[6] Cf. Acts 2: 3; on Hur signifying the Holy Spirit cf. e.g. Gregory, *Hom. .xl. in Evang.* ii. 33. 8 (*PL* lxxvi. 1244) and Bede, *In Luc.* ii. 6. 19 (*CCSL* cxx. 137; *PL* xcii. 401).

[7] Cf. Exod. 17: 10–12; Aaron and Hur held up Moses' hands to ensure the defeat of Amalech.

81

To Pope Alexander III[1]

1179, before Mar. (or poss. as early as summer 1178)

To Alexander the supreme pontiff, Peter, abbot of Saint-Remi.

He who does not doubt that Christ said to the chief of the apostles, 'Thou art Peter and upon this rock I will build my Church,'[2] is not unaware that the burden of the whole of Christendom is laid upon the apostolic shoulders. And so it is necessary that Aaron, who passed into the heavens[3] in his own blood,[4] having been appointed high priest by God the Father for ever,[5] and Hur, who descended in tongues of fire on the apostles,[6] lighten your hands and equally your shoulders by their support and stay them up lest they fail.[7] For wickedness, which sits on the talent of lead[8] with twinned, or rather conjoined, wings, everywhere oppresses God's Church and yours—God's by betrothal, yours by His commission—as much in the members of its flock as in its prelates, to such an extent that it can now be said, 'as with the people, so with the priest,'[9] as with the sheep, so with the dogs. What should I say, and why should I say that which is obvious to every blear-eyed man and barber?[10] Does the clamour, or should I say the fury, of such great evil not ascend even unto the clouds? And who doubts that you know these things, you whose business it is not only to diagnose sicknesses but also to cut off or to cure every diseased part? Yet, supreme pastor, your people is committing two evils.[11] Come down and you will find the molten calf[12] frisking wantonly 'with the kine of the people'[13] and grazing the grass down to the very roots with its tongue.[14] In one man lechery is notorious, in another avarice. Once this company of darkness used to keep to the valleys, now they occupy the mountains. Once they used to defile the temple of Venus but now they pollute the courts of the Virgin whom the Father betrothed to His Son, and whom Paul wishes

[8] Cf. Zech. 5: 7–8 (the reference to wings is odd, as the only joined wings in the Vulgate refer to a vision of glory, not evil—cf. Ezek. 1: 9, 'iunctaque erant pinne eorum').

[9] Isa. 24: 2.

[10] i.e. to everyone, cf. Horace, *Sat.* i. 7. 3 (trans., cf. Loeb, H. R. Fairclough).

[11] Cf. Jer. 2: 13.

[12] Cf. Exod. 32: 4, 7–8; Deut. 9: 16.

[13] Ps. 67 (68): 31.

[14] Cf. Num. 22: 4.

uult exhibere Christo.[15] Olim denique regnabant in Babilonia, nunc in Ierusalem. Ieremias lamentatur auaritiam sedere 'in capite omnium compitorum',[16] ubi concurrunt in dandis honoribus ecclesiasticis aut carnalis affinitas aut pecuniaria cupiditas. Dei quidem solius est ista amputare et tollere, uestrum autem securim ad radicem ponere[17] et pro posse 'in sententia uigilum'[18] statuam istam confringere et arborem succidere sollicitudine non pigra.[19] Quomodo autem fiat istud docebit uos qui 'incerta et occulta sapientie' sue manifestauit[20] Dauid puero suo, et omnia que audiuit a Patre suo nota fecit suis apostolis.[21] Lator quoque presentium fidelissimus uester et totius honestatis et bone fame uir insinuabit. Pungenda tamen est gladio ancipiti[22] luxuria que non solum thalamos pudicitie sed etiam terminos totius uerecundie transgreditur, quatinus etsi stimulus eius non confringitur saltem retundatur, etsi non sepelitur saltem recondatur. Auaritie duo cornua in ecclesiasticis traiectionibus prorsus anathematizentur, in secularibus rapinis ungule ipsius aut eradicentur aut execentur. Spiritus Domini, quia omnia continens replet orbem terrarum, ori et cordi uestro semper adsit, et precipue in hac secunda generali congregatione.[23]

[15] i.e. the Church, the bride of Christ.
[16] Lam. 2: 19.
[17] Cf. Matt. 3: 10; Luke 3: 9.
[18] Dan. 4: 14.
[19] Cf. Dan. 4: 11, 20

to present to Christ like a chaste virgin to a single husband.[15] Finally, they once used to rule in Babylon, now they rule in Jerusalem. Jeremiah laments that avarice sits 'at the top of all the streets,'[16] where either blood relationships or desire for money go hand in hand in the granting of ecclesiastical honours. God alone can cut away and remove these things, but it is your responsibility to lay the axe to the root[17] and, as far as possible, to break in pieces that statue, 'by the sentence of the watchers',[18] and to cut down the tree with zealous concern.[19] How that may be accomplished, He who made manifest to His son David 'the uncertain and hidden things of' His 'wisdom',[20] and made known to His apostles all things which He heard from His Father,[21] will teach you. Your most loyal servant, the bearer of this present letter, a man both of complete honesty and good reputation, will also make this known to you. Wantonness, however, which transgresses not only the marriage beds of modesty but even the boundaries of all shame, should be struck with the two-edged sword,[22] so that even if its spur is not shattered it should at least be blunted, and even if it is not buried in the tomb it should at least be hidden. Let the two horns of avarice engaged in ecclesiastical traffickings be anathematized utterly and let the hooves of avarice engaged in worldly pillage be either pulled out by the roots or cut out. May the spirit of the Lord be always present in your mouth and heart, and especially in this second general council, for encompassing all things it fills the whole world.[23]

[20] Cf. Ps. 50 (51): 8.
[21] Cf. John 15: 15.
[22] Cf. Judg. 3: 16; Ps. 149 (149): 6; Heb. 4: 12.
[23] Cf. Wisd. 1: 7; Lateran III was Alexander's second general council, after Tours 1163 (*Councils and Synods*, i. 2, pp. 845–7).

82

To Pope Alexander III[1]

late 1178 × Mar. 1179

Alexandro summo pontifici Petrus abbas Sancti Remigii.

Apostolice sedis oraculum nec sine reuerentia penetrandum est nec sine fiducia adeundum. Tibi itaque, pater uenerande, cui date sunt claues regni celorum,[2] non est data potestas sine indulgentia nec iustitia absque misericordia. Interpellet igitur et inclinet ad petitionem nostram auctoritatem tue potestatis sobria indulgentia, temperet eque rigorem iustitie pia misericordia. Intutum proinde est thronum magni regis qui est in seculum seculi[3] aliquatenus concutere, nec minus periculosum lectulum Salomonis, propter ambientes gladios uersatiles,[4] citra decubantis placitum qui dormit ut catulus leonis, excitare; sedentem et quiescentem ⟨ante⟩[a] Deum in sanctis quis audeat dubitare? De numero et sorte istorum,[5] teste sancta conuersatione, confratrem nostrum dilectissimum Clareuallensem abbatem fide oculata[b] cernimus et credimus. Forte electus est in episcopum Tolosane ciuitatis, ut autem uere religiosus, metiens se sibi et insufficientiam suam metuens, repudiato connubio mauult discalceari et sputa cuiuslibet improperii in faciem cum Iesu excipere[6] quam uitis, oliue et ficus assumpte professionis dulcedinem deserere. Nec in hoc usus est reprehensibili leuitate, cum hoc faciat ex legislatoris

82 *Sirmond VIII. 8*]
[a] *suppl. Ritchie* [b] *corr. Brooke;* occulta *Sirmond*

82 [1] Henry de Marcy, abbot of Clairvaux 1176–9, was elected to the see of Toulouse when it fell vacant some time after Aug. 1178. He appealed against having to take up the bishopric and Peter wrote this letter in support of his stance. The letter must fall between the vacancy at Toulouse (1178, not before Aug.) and Henry's appointment as cardinal bishop of Albano (14 Mar. 1179). He was recommended as a potential cardinal by Peter of Pavia in the same letter which also named Peter of Celle (see Glorieux, 'Candidats', pp. 21–2; see also letter no. 128, n. 1). For a full account of Henry's life, with extensive references, see Y. Congar, 'Henri de Marcy abbé de Clairvaux, cardinal-évêque d'Albano et légat pontifical', *Studia Anselmiana*, xliii (1958), 1–90 (see also *GC*, xiii. 18–19). Letter no. 88 to Albert of Morra is evidently a companion letter to this.

[2] Cf. Matt. 16: 19.

[3] Common biblical phrase.

[4] Apparently combining S. of S. 3: 7–8 ('en lectulum Salomonis sexaginta fortes ambiunt ex fortissimis Israel, omnes tenentes gladios et ad bella doctissimi') with an

82

To Pope Alexander III[1]

late 1178 × Mar. 1179

To Alexander the supreme pontiff, Peter, abbot of Saint-Remi.

The oracle of the apostolic see should neither be penetrated without reverence nor approached without trust. And so to you, venerable father, to whom are given the keys of the kingdom of heaven,[2] power is not given without leniency nor justice without mercy. Therefore let sober leniency intercede and incline the authority of your power to our petition and equally let kindly mercy temper the rigour of justice. Accordingly it is unsafe to shake in any way the throne of the great king who endures for ever and ever,[3] nor is it any less dangerous to disturb the bed of Solomon, on account of the surrounding swords turning every way,[4] without the agreement of the one lying down who sleeps like a lion cub; who would dare to doubt that he is seated and at peace among the saints before God? We discern and we believe, as an eye witness, that our brother the most beloved abbot of Clairvaux is, by the witness of his holy conduct, one of the number and lot of the saints.[5] It happens that he has been elected to the bishopric of the city of Toulouse, but as a true religious, measuring himself against himself and fearing his insufficiency, having repudiated the marriage he prefers to go unshod and to receive with Jesus the spittle of any reproach in his face[6] rather than to abandon the sweetness of the vine, the olive, and the fig of the profession which he has adopted. Nor has he acted in this matter with reprehensible levity since he does this on the authority of the

allusion to Gen. 3: 24 ('cherubin et flammeum gladium atque uersatilem ad custodiendam uiam ligni uitae'). What follows may echo Num. 24: 9; Deut. 33: 20.

[5] Cf. Wisd. 5: 5 ('. . . inter sanctos sors illorum est'); Acts 26: 18 ('ut accipiant . . . sortem inter sanctos . . .').

[6] Cf. Deut. 25: 5–10, on a brother's duty to marry his brother's widow ('if he answer: I will not take her to wife, the woman shall . . . take off his shoe from his foot, and spit in his face'); on Christ's suffering being spat at cf. Matt. 27: 30; Mark 15: 19. The point here is that Henry should rather be left in peace at Clairvaux and not disturbed (see the imagery above) by being forced to take up the bishopric, even if this means his being reproached for neglecting his duty and being spat at (the Old Testament sanction referred to), for while the spitting is a sign of reproach in the Old Testament, in the New Testament (which of course supersedes the Old) it means sharing Christ's sufferings.

auctoritate, Moysi utique qui 'grandis factus negauit se esse filium filie Pharaonis, magis eligens affligi cum populo Dei quam temporalis peccati habere iucunditatem, maiores diuitias estimans thesauro Egyptiorum improperium Christi. Aspiciebat enim in remunerationem.'[7] Reputat etiam quod in Lamentationibus legitur, quia 'mutatus est color optimus' postquam 'dispersi sunt lapides sanctuarii in capite platearum'.[8] Timet in se fieri eclipsim solis si de statione Hebreorum transierit in castris eorum 'quorum os locutum est uanitatem'[9] et quorum pedes currunt ad malum.[10] Citius enim inficit uenenum quam curet antidotum et fragilis natura difficilius reparatur cum facile frangatur. Concedat igitur apostolica licentia hominem istum in paradiso Clareuallensi operari cibum qui non perit[11] et in sudore uultus sui panem suum manducare[12] quia nec uult uetitum tangere[13] nec tunicam pelliceam assumere.[14] Fixit namque tentorium suum de pellibus Salomonis[15] iuxta 'puteum Viuentis et uidentis',[16] iuxta 'aceruum nouarum frugum',[17] iuxta denique propitiatorium, intra sanctuarii uelum,[18] 'subter alas cherubin',[19] sancti Benedicti et beati Bernardi. Supposuit quoque humerum arche federis Dei in qua est uirga crucis que floruit in apostolis, fronduit in regeneratis fidelium turbis et nuces protulit in martyribus, confessoribus atque uirginibus, in qua due tabule testamenti, una asperitatem legis continens, altera euangelii mansuetudinem et gratiam conferens. Ad ultimum manna est ibi absconditum promisse dulcedinis Dei quam abscondit timentibus se[20] et dabit diligentibus se. Habitat 'in medio lapidum ignitorum',[21] quorum contemplatione uisus acuitur, torpor excutitur, uitalia nutriuntur, morticina reiciuntur, religio perpetuatur. O quam dura, quam amara separatio religiosi affectus cui succedit[c] carnalis necessitudo, cui supponitur delectatio, cui ambitio substernitur. Quam infelix commutatio ubi 'pro suaui odore' recipitur 'fetor, pro crispanti crine caluitium, pro fascia pectorali cilicium'.[22] Nequaquam

[c] *corr. Hall;* cedit *Sirmond*

[7] Heb. 11: 24–6. [8] Cf. Lam. 4: 1 (Vulgate has *omnium platearum*).
[9] Ps. 143 (144): 8, 11. [10] Cf. Prov. 1: 16; Isa. 59: 7.
[11] Cf. John 6: 27. [12] Cf. Gen. 3: 19.
[13] Given the references to Adam and Eve here, this must mean the forbidden fruit of the tree of life (cf. Gen. 2: 17). The images are not entirely consistent, as eating bread in the sweat of the face was also, like wearing the garments of skins, a consequence of eating the fruit. [14] Cf. Gen. 3: 21. [15] Cf. S. of S. 1: 4.
[16] Gen. 16: 14; cf. Gen. 24: 62; 25: 11. [17] Ezek. 3: 15.
[18] Cf. Exod. 26: 33; 30: 6; 40: 3 and many other refs. cf. also Lev. 16: 2.
[19] 3 Kgs. (1 Kgs.) 8: 6; 2 Chr. 5: 7.

lawgiver, that is Moses, who 'when he was grown up, denied himself to be the son of Pharaoh's daughter, rather choosing to be afflicted with the people of God than to have the pleasure of sin for a time, esteeming the reproach of Christ greater riches than the treasure of the Egyptians. For he looked unto the reward.'[7] He considers also that which is written in Lamentations, that 'the finest colour is changed' after 'the stones of the sanctuary are scattered in the top of the streets'.[8] He fears an eclipse of the sun within himself if he should cross over from the post of the Hebrews to the camp of those 'whose mouth hath spoken vanity'[9] and whose feet run to evil.[10] For the poison infects more quickly than the antidote would cure and a fragile nature is restored with more difficulty since it is easily fractured. May apostolic license therefore allow this man to labour in the paradise of Clairvaux for the meat which does not perish[11] and to chew his bread in the sweat of his face[12] because he wishes neither to touch that which is forbidden[13] nor to take up the garment of skins.[14] For he has pitched his tent, made from the curtains of Solomon,[15] next to 'the well of Him that liveth and seeth',[16] next to 'the heap of new corn,'[17] next finally to the propitiatory, within the veil of the sanctuary,[18] 'under the wings of the cherubims,'[19] of St Benedict and of the blessed Bernard. He has also set his shoulder to the ark of the covenant of God, in which is the branch of the cross which flowered in the apostles, put out leaves in the regenerated crowds of the faithful, and brought forth nuts in the martyrs, confessors, and virgins; in which are the two tablets of the covenant, one containing the harshness of the law, the other conferring the clemency and grace of the Gospel. Finally, hidden away there is the manna of the promised sweetness of God which He has hidden for them that fear Him[20] and will give to them that love Him. He dwells 'in the midst of the stones of fire,'[21] by the contemplation of which the vision is sharpened, torpor is shaken off, the living parts are nourished, the deathly are cast off, and the religious life is perpetuated. Oh how harsh, how bitter is the severing of religious affection to which carnal necessity succeeds, for which carnal delight is substituted, over which carnal ambition is spread. Oh how unfortunate is the exchange in which 'instead of a sweet smell a stench' is received, 'instead of curled hair baldness, instead of a stomacher haircloth'.[22] By no means is this

[20] Cf. Ps. 30 (31): 20; Rev. 2: 17.
[21] Ezek. 28: 14.
[22] Cf. Isa. 3: 24.

est hec commutatio dextere excelsi. Non igitur audiat auris apostolica aduersus Mariam ad pedes Iesu sedentem, Martham conquerentem, que solicita est 'circa frequens ministerium',[23] nec gustauit 'poculum ex uino condito'[24] sancte contemplationis et in lege Dei assidue meditationis.

83

To Albert of Morra[1]

1172, poss. May or earlier

Domino Alberto cardinali et Romane sedis legato.

Nisi tanta distantia locorum et multiplex occupationum impedimentum nos retineret, dilectissimam nobis paternitatem uestram uisitare nullatenus tandiu postposuissemus. Est enim in pectore nostro multa de negotio uobis iniuncto et de fine eius sollicitudo quia honor Dei et ecclesie utilitas et fame uestre integritas atque totius curie Romane circumspectio[2] ex eo accipiet apud conscientiam omnium laudem et magnificentiam si secundum regulam equitatis et ueritatis sortitum fuerit effectum. Quatinus ergo res iam processerit, non sit uobis tediosum amicum uestrum certificare. Habetis autem idoneum, si placuerit, per quem fideliter remandare et secure potestis, priorem utique de Valle Sancti Petri,[3] karissimum filium uestrum quem in Christo genuistis et cuius[a] spiritum in omnibus uobis obnoxium reddidistis. Ad locum namque qui Vallis Dei appellatur

83 *Sirmond VI. 1*]
[a] eius *Sirmond*

[23] Cf. Luke 10: 39–40. [24] S. of S. 8: 2.

83 [1] Albert of Morra was cardinal deacon of S. Adriano 1155/6–8, cardinal priest of S. Lorenzo in Lucina from 1158, chancellor of the Roman Church from Feb. 1178, and Pope Gregory VIII 21 Oct.–17 Dec. 1187 (*J. S. Epp.* ii. 427, n. 1 and 754, n. 1; Zenker, *Kardinalkollegium*, pp. 125–9; JL ii. pp. 145–6; *DP*, pp. 182–3; *Councils and Synods*, ii/1. 943). He is here addressed as legate, and said to be in the vicinity of the charterhouse of Val-Dieu (dioc. Sées). The legation referred to must be that of 1171–3 which he undertook along with Theodwin of S. Vitale to Henry II, after the death of Becket, leading to the compromise of Avranches. Albert and Theodwin arrived in northern France towards the end of 1171, and met Henry II on a number of occasions during the second half of May 1172 (Gorron, 16th; Savigny, 17th; Avranches, 19th, and the larger more public assembly at Caen, 30th; Barlow, *Thomas Becket*, pp. 260–1). Peter seems to indicate that negotiations are in progress, which may put the present letter in or about May (i.e. certainly not after

an exchange belonging to the right hand of the Most High. Therefore may the apostolic ear not hear Martha, who is concerned 'about much serving'[23] and who has not tasted the 'cup of spiced wine'[24] of holy contemplation and of constant meditation on the law of God, complaining against Mary, sitting at the feet of Jesus.

83

To Albert of Morra[1]

1172, poss. May or earlier

To his lord Albert, cardinal and legate of the Roman see.

If the great distances involved and the manifold impediment of affairs did not detain us, we would by no means have postponed for so long visiting your fatherly presence which is most dear to us. For there is great concern in our heart about the business charged to you and its outcome, because the honour of God and the good of the Church as well as the integrity of your reputation and the prudence[2] of the whole Roman Curia will be praised and glorified in the conscience of all if its outcome is according to the rule of justice and of truth. Let it not therefore be tiresome to you to apprise your friend as to how far the matter has now proceeded. And you have a suitable person, if it pleases you, by whom you can send a reply faithfully and securely, that is to say the prior of Val-Saint-Pierre,[3] your dearest son whom you begot in Christ and whose spirit you have

May, when the outcome was known, but possibly earlier if Peter did not know how long Henry II had delayed in coming). This also corroborates the year given by Le Couteulx for the crisis at Val-Dieu (whose first prior, identified only as 'R.', had died within two years of the foundation), and so for this letter—i.e. 1172: Le Couteulx, ii. 366–8; see also letter no. 101, and on the foundation of Val-Dieu, by Count Rotrou of Perche, with the assistance of William aux Blanches Mains, see Le Couteulx ii. 327–30. Engelbert of Val-Saint-Pierre (1140–1173/9; see letter no. 115, n. 1) had gone to Val-Dieu to oversee the installation of one of his own monks, Ralph, as prior, and was still there at the time of writing of this letter (see also letter no. 101 to William aux Blanches Mains on behalf of Val-Dieu). It is not known how Peter first came into contact with Albert, a former canon regular at Laon and a professor of law at Bologna, but it may well have been through Engelbert. Val-Saint-Pierre is in the dioc. of Laon and Albert was evidently Engelbert's mentor or patron in some capacity: the phrase 'quem in Christo genuistis' (below, and see n. 3) implies some influence on his entry to religious life.

[2] Cf. *DML*, *circumspectio* b.

[3] Engelbert of Val-Saint-Pierre, see n. 1 above.

profectus ut ibi priorem substituat, non multum a uobis remotus; si ei mandaueritis uenire ad uos, tutis auribus instillare poteritis que de statu uestro grata uel ingrata uobis occurrunt. Et michi quidem uidetur, prefatum locum uestro auxilio et consilio multum indigere quia episcopus ad cuius diocesim pertinet manum benedictionis et auxilii differt apponere.[4] Neque enim cemeterium neque monasterii[5] sui consecrationem fratres qui ibi manent habere possunt. Vestra itaque interest quod de facili potestis, pauperes Christi in hoc iuuare ut in loco benedicto creatorem suum benedicant. In calce litterarum supponimus uobis commendare priorem qui ibi substitutus est, quem de fornace religionis et regularis subiectionis nouiter extractum, ad curam animarum regendam filius uester manum mittere coegit. Doctrina itaque et auxilio uestro instruite illum quia scitis quam difficilem rem arripit qui animas suscipit regendas.[6]

[4] Bishop Froger of Sées, 1157/8–84 (*GC* xi. 689–90). Froger did soon grant letters of confirmation to Val-Dieu (see Le Couteulx, ii. 330–2, who speculates that the problem may have arisen out of the rival loyalties of bishop and count to the French and English kings respectively; he gives no dates for the bishop's concession, but on the evidence of the present letter it cannot have been before May 1172). In 1181 he consecrated the monastic church (*GC* xi. 690).

made beholden to you in all things. For having gone out to that place which is called Val-Dieu in order to appoint a new prior there, he is not very far away from you; if you order him to come to you, you will be able to pour out into safe ears what is happening to you as far as your situation is concerned, be it agreeable or disagreeable. And indeed it seems to me that that aforementioned house stands in great need of your help and counsel because the bishop to whose diocese it pertains is putting off applying the hand of blessing and aid.[4] For the brothers who live there are able to obtain neither a cemetery nor the consecration of their monastery.[5] And so it is for you to do that which you can easily do, to help the poor of Christ in this matter so that they may bless their Creator in a blessed house. At the foot of this letter we add our commendation to you of the new prior who has been appointed, whom, newly drawn forth from the crucible of religious discipline and subjection to the Rule, your son forced to set his hand to directing the cure of souls. And so prepare him with your instruction and aid because you know what a difficult task is grasped by one who takes on the direction of souls.[6]

[5] Presumably meaning the monastic church.

[6] Cf. *Regula S. Benedicti* c. ii.The new prior is Ralph (see above n. 1), whom Engelbert of Val-Saint-Pierre has promoted to prior, as Peter seems to be suggesting here, only shortly after his completion of the novitiate.

84

? To Albert of Morra[1]

1162 × 1181 (? *c.*1172)

Vni cardinalium.

Vna sua Christus amplissima et generalissima regula omnes tam precedentium quam subsequentium catholicorum patrum sanctissimas sanctiones compendiose includit, dicens de dilectione Dei et proximi, 'In his duobus tota lex pendet et prophete.'[2] Reuocanda igitur sunt omnia que fiunt in ecclesia Dei ad hanc ornatissimam regulam quia quicquid ab ea discordat a spiritu pacis et caritatis non manat. Inde est, pater uenerande, quod dispensationes quarumdam institutionum non indigne admittuntur pro maiori et meliori recompensatione. Volumus igitur uobis notificare quanta mala et quanta hominum strages in terra nostra ex guerris quorumdam nobilium hominum, uidelicet comitis Vuischardi de Ruzeio et comitis Recensis atque Hugonis de Petriponte,[3] diebus nostris et antecessorum nostrorum acciderunt. Homines innumerabiles tam occisi quam capti et redempti sunt et nouissima dampna sustinuerunt. Religiose domus depredate sunt et multa alia mala prouenerunt. Interuentu tandem bonorum et sapientum et religiosorum, matrimonia inter se contrahere

84 *Sirmond VI. 3*]

84 [1] The cardinal may be Albert of Morra (as suggested by the eds of *PL* and *RHF*; on Albert see letter no. 83, n. 1). The letter is also reprinted in *RHF* xvi. 712, no. XX (part of a small selection of Peter's letters taken from Sirmond), where it is dated 1172/3 by association with another reference to troubles in the region, Peter of Celle's concession to Archbishop Henry of Reims of the possessions of Saint-Remi in Sept-Saulx and Marmery, both near Reims, giving as his reason the state of war and disruption prevalent in the countryside, and especially on the road to Châlons-sur-Marne (*RHF* xvi. 195, no. CLXXV, and *GC* x. Instr. col. 47–8, no. XLVII, where it is dated 1172). The state of affairs described in the present letter accords more with that attested in this document than with the accounts of the troubles in Reims in 1167 (with which it has sometimes been associated), an uprising directed against Archbishop Henry (see letter no. 93). (See also Varin, *Arch. admin.* i. 377, which cites *RHF*.) Henry of Reims had previously been in conflict with Count Henry the Liberal of Champagne and others over his activities in this area. In 1169–70 he had had a fortress at Champigny (or Sampigny) destroyed and a new one built at Sept-Saulx. This came to form part of his wider dispute with the count in 1171–2 (see also letter no. 132). However, the ref. to *antecessorum nostrorum* here seems to connect this letter to a longer-running dispute (and to a marriage which cannot be identified), so the connection to *c.*1172 is not secure. On these other events in Reims, see

84

? To Albert of Morra[1]

1162 × 1181 (? *c*.1172)

To one of the cardinals.

Christ in His one widest and most comprehensive rule embraces succinctly all the holiest ordinances of the Catholic fathers, preceding and succeeding, when He says of the love of God and of one's neighbour, 'On these two dependeth the whole law and the prophets.'[2] Therefore all things which are done in the Church of God should be referred to this most eminent rule because whatever is out of harmony with this does not flow from the spirit of peace and love. And so it is, venerable father, that dispensations from certain points of law are admitted without impropriety in return for a greater and better recompense. We wish therefore to let you know how many evils and how many massacres of men have occurred in our land, in our times and those of our predecessors, owing to the wars of certain noblemen, that is of Count Robert Guiscard of Roucy and the count of Rethel, and also of Hugh of Pierrepont.[3] Innumerable men have either been killed, or captured and ransomed, and have sustained extremes of loss. Religious houses have been plundered and many other evils have arisen. At last, by the intervention of the good and the wise and those of the religious life, they have arranged to contract

Falkenstein, 'Alexandre III et Henri de France', p. 143, and L. Falkenstein, 'Pontificalis Maturitas vel Modestia Sacerdotalis? Alexander III. und Heinrich von Frankreich in den Jahres 1170–1172', *Archivum Historiae Pontificiae*, xxii (1984), 31–88, at pp. 56–62, which do not connect this letter to 1172.

The heading reads more like a rubric than a salutation, but Sirmond does not distinguish it typographically from the other headings and so it is not known how it appeared in R. (Similar headings occur in letters 96, 97, 109, 111, 115, 116, 122, 124, 127, 141, 142, 157, 163, 174 and 182; *PL* reprints them in the same style as its own interpolated rubrics, but this confusion does not reflect Sirmond, of which *PL* is a copy with some minor alterations.)

[2] Cf. Matt. 22: 40: 'in his duobus mandatis uniuersa lex pendet et prophete'.

[3] Count Robert Guiscard of Roucy, *c*.1160–*c*.1180: *Art de vérifier les dates*, ii. 740; J. M. J. L. de Mas Latrie, *Trésor de chronologie, d'histoire et de géographie pour l'étude et l'emploi des documents du Moyen-Âge*, vi (Paris, 1889), 1670. Count Manasses III of Rethel, *c*.1158–*c*.1200: *Art de vérifier les dates*, ii. 632; Mas Latrie, *op. cit.*, col. 1670; *RHF* xvi. 712, note 'd'. Hugh of Pierrepont, unidentified. On other relations between the counts of Roucy and of Rethel with Saint-Remi, see de Martel, 'Une notice', pp. 81, 87, and Prache, *Saint-Remi*, pp. 36, 41, and refs. therein.

disposuerunt ut saltem isto nexu confederati inter se pacem tenerent et haberent.[4] Penset itaque uestra discretio ut si quid de gradu consanguinitatis obstat, pro bono pacis et pro tantorum malorum recompensatione, quecunque fieri potest a domino papa non recusetur dispensatio. Valete.

85

To Albert of Morra[1]

Feb. 1178 × 1181 (most likely early)

Alberto cancellario Petrus abbas Sancti Remigii.

Archa Dei Israhel, archa sanctificationis, archa federis[2] quondam ex precepto legislatoris 'circumtecta[a] ex omni parte auro'[3] antiquorum patrum sanctitate et doctrina, quam etiam 'cherubin glorie obumbrantia propitiatorium'[4] desuper tegebant, nunc in presentiarum abusione et negligentia filiorum Heli[5] uestimentis glorie sue spoliata, atque infecundis salicibus operta,[6] et relicta iuxta Ysaiam 'sicut tugurium in cucumerario' et 'umbraculum in uinea',[7] recordatur 'dierum adolescentie' sue[8] et plorans atque in maxillis suis lacrimas reponens[9] dicit, 'Reuertar ad uirum meum priorem quia michi melius erat tunc magis quam nunc.'[10] Boues calcitrantes,[11] uidelicet doctores a semitis iustitie per sua desideria aberrantes, declinant eam cum deberent glorificare Deum et portare in corpore suo. Verus itaque dolor illos tangit qui diligunt illam non sermone et lingua sed opere et ueritate.[12] Non ignoramus uos unum esse et specialem amicum siue filium uniuersalis sancte ecclesie cuius typum et figuram illa archa tenuit. Ad luctum itaque et compassionem materne angustie siue

85 *Sirmond VIII. 13*]
[a] circumtexta *Sirmond*

[4] Possibly here alluding to the marriage vows, but not an uncommon phrase in charters.

85 [1] Written to Albert of Morra most likely, but not necessarily, soon after his appointment as papal chancellor in Feb. 1178 (see letter no. 83, n. 1). The final sentence may be a reference to the Third Lateran Council (Mar. 1179; see letter no. 80, n. 1).

[2] Cf. 2 Kgs. (2 Sam.) 11: 11; Ps. 131 (132): 8; Josh. 3: 11. The ark here is the Church, as is clear from what follows below. It is more commonly linked to Noah's ark, but cf. e.g. Bede, *De tab.* i. 5. 610–11 (*CCSL* cxix A. 20; *PL* xci. 406); *Glossa ad* Exod. 25 (*PL* cxiii. 267).

[3] Heb. 9: 4; cf. Exod. 25: 11 (the lawgiver is Moses).

[4] Heb. 9: 5; cf. Exod. 25: 17–22.

[5] Cf. 1 Kgs. (1 Sam.) 2: 12–14.

marriages among themselves so that, allied by this bond at least, they might have and hold[4] peace among themselves. And so may you in your discretion weigh the matter up so that, if there is any obstacle concerning degree of consanguinity, then for the good of peace and for the recompense of so many evils, whatever dispensation can be made by the lord pope should not be refused. Farewell.

85

To Albert of Morra[1]

Feb. 1178 × 1181 (most likely early)

To Albert, chancellor, Peter, abbot of Saint-Remi.

The ark of the God of Israel, the ark of sanctification, the ark of the covenant,[2] was once, according to the precept of the lawgiver, 'covered about on every part with gold'[3] with the sanctity and teaching of the ancient fathers, and also 'the cherubims of glory overshadowing the propitiatory'[4] were covering her from above. Now in this present day, through the abuse and neglect of the children of Heli,[5] stripped of the vestments of her glory and concealed by the infertile willows[6] and left, as Isaiah says, 'as a lodge in a garden of cucumbers' and as 'a covert in a vineyard',[7] she remembers 'the days of' her 'youth'[8] and, weeping and letting tears fall on her cheeks again,[9] says, 'I will return to my first husband because it was better with me then than now.'[10] Oxen given to kicking,[11] that is to say teachers wandering from the paths of justice through their own desires, turn away from her when they ought to glorify God and to carry Him in their body. True misery, then, touches those who love her not in speech and words but in deed and truth.[12] We are not unaware that you are a singular and special friend, or son, of the universal holy Church, whose type and figure that ark contained. In respect of grief and compassion for the mother's anguish or desolation

[6] Vestments of glory, cf. Isa. 52: 1; the willows here and the remembering of youth and weeping below (and see nn. 8 and 9) also recall Ps. 136 (137), with a possible echo of Exod. 2: 3.

[7] Cf. Isa. 1: 8.

[8] Cf. Ezek. 16: 22, 43.

[9] Cf. Lam. 1: 2.

[10] Cf. Hos. 2: 7.

[11] Cf. 2 Kgs. (2 Sam.) 6: 6, i.e. which caused Oza to take hold of the ark, for which he was struck down. On what follows, not an uncommon idea but not evidently a close quotation, cf. e.g. Gratian, *Dec.* ii. 2. 7, xxvii (Friedberg i. 490; *PL* clxxxvii. 647).

[12] Cf. 1 John 3: 18.

desolationis, uos aduocamus ut quicquid affectualis deuotio exigit maternis impendatis doloribus. Secundum enim locum post dominum papam a Deo in his corrigendis tenetis; sed cauete ne in uacuum gratiam Dei acceperitis.[13] Qui enim spiritum uestrum et sanctam conuersationem ante multis retro temporibus uiderunt et cognouerunt de meliorando statu ecclesie spem optimam conceperunt cum factum cancellarium audierunt. Nisi uero ubique essent notoria et uobis notissima de his latius scriberemus. Tamen ne clausis labiis potius singultiamus quam loquamur declarat carta quod non silet uita: dilatat infernus animam suam absque ullo termino[14] dum immaniter grassatur tam in oues quam in pastores. Qui enim preuii constituti sunt ad celum malo exemplo suos sequaces trahunt in infernum. Non de omnibus dico, nouit enim Dominus qui sunt eius.[15] Quo autem mercede meliori digni sunt boni eo amplius increpatione et correptione indigent mali. Ysaias, Ieremias, Ezechiel sua prophetia nostra deprehenderunt tempora, contra pastores namque et peruersos rectores nuda sed et uera retorserunt iacula, auaritiam eorum, luxuriam, gulam, rapinam et omnem iniustitiam non in angulis sed in plateis declamantes.[16] Ingrediatur itaque in ossibus et medullis uestris et impleat spiritum et os uestrum spiritus illorum zelotypus, conterens montes et petras, et efficax 'usque ad diuisionem anime et spiritus'.[17] Gladius uester deuoret carnes inebriatus in celo[18] quatinus emendatos remittatis nobis pastores nostros et omnibus serpentinis exuuiis spoliatos.

[13] Cf. 2 Cor. 6: 1.
[14] Cf. Isa. 5: 14.
[15] Cf. John 10: 14; 2 Tim. 2: 19.

therefore, we call upon you to bestow on the mother's afflictions whatever affectionate devotion demands. For you hold from God the second place after the lord pope for mending these afflictions; but take care that you have not received the grace of God in vain.[13] For those who have before seen and know your spirit and holy manner of life for a long time past have conceived the highest hope of the improvement of the state of the Church now that they have heard that you have been made chancellor. Indeed if these things were not common knowledge everywhere and very well-known to you, we would write more on the subject. However, so as not to sob with sealed lips rather than speak out, my letter declares what life does not hold secret: hell enlarges her soul without any bounds[14] while she rages fiercely as much against the sheep as against the shepherds. For those who are appointed leaders on the way to heaven by a bad example draw their followers down to hell. I am not referring to all of them, for the Lord knows who are His own.[15] But the better the reward the good are worthy of, the more the wicked need rebuke and reproach. Isaiah, Jeremiah, and Ezechiel by their prophecy apprehended our times, for they turned naked, but also true, darts against pastors and wicked leaders, denouncing their greed, wantonness, gluttony, rapine, and every injustice not in corners but in the streets.[16] May their zealous spirit, then, enter into your bones and heart and fill your spirit and mouth, grinding down mountains and rocks, and effectual 'unto the division of the soul and the spirit'.[17] Let your sword inebriated in heaven devour flesh[18] so that you may send back to us our pastors corrected and despoiled of all the trappings of the serpent.

[16] Cf. Jer. 23: 1–3; Ezek. 34 (*pastores*); cf. e.g. Isa. 57: 17 (*auaritia*); Isa. 3: 14 (*rapina*); also a possible echo of Prov. 1: 20, but this is common biblical vocabulary.

[17] Cf. Heb. 4: 12.

[18] Cf. Deut. 32: 42; Isa. 34: 5–6; Jer. 46: 10.

86

To Albert of Morra[1]

1178, after June

Alberto cancellario Petrus abbas Sancti Remigii.

Quotiens naufragia patimur, totiens ad portum festinamus. Portum autem tutissimi refugii in littore uestre amicitie iamdudum fiximus. Molestiarum quidem uentos frequenter contrarios sentimus sed portum uestrum usque ad grauiorem non infestamus tempestatem, leuiora enim discrimina aut patientia tolerat aut uirtus fortiter superat; cum autem nubes magna et ignis inuoluens[2] nauiculam nostram inuadit statim aut est periclitandum aut cito enauigandum. Hoc anno dominus papa uestro interuentu priuilegium suum ecclesie nostre indulsit in quo specialiter expressit canonias seu prebendas de Marsna, et quas in usus proprios iam a multis retro temporibus retinemus tenendas in perpetuum confirmauit.[3] Que etenim quondam fuerunt canonicorum prebende, a longissimis retro temporibus donatione episcoporum Leodiensium et confirmatione Pape Innocentii, in proprietatem transierunt et possessionem monasterii nostri. Nuper uero dominus papa rem, ut credimus, ignorans iam secundo scripsit preposito nostro de Marsna ut daret prebendam cuidam clerico imperatoris, cum nec prepositus dare possit nec sit prebenda que dari possit. Insinuate ergo domino nostro ne uelit panem filiorum tollere et dare canibus[4] qui non cessant aduersum nos latrare et bona nostra auferre. Alias enim dicere compellimur, 'Ecce in pace amaritudo nostra amarissima',[5] nam per imperatorem tempore schismatis instantissime id efficere plures conati sunt sed minime preualuerunt.

86 *Sirmond VIII. 15*]

---

86 [1] On Albert of Morra, see letter no. 83, n. 1; on the Meerssen dispute and the date of this letter, see appendix 10 (see also letters 79 and 94). [2] Cf. Ezek. 1:4.
[3] See appendix 10. [4] Cf. Matt. 15: 26; Mark 7: 27.

86

To Albert of Morra[1]

1178, after June

To Albert, chancellor, Peter, abbot of Saint-Remi.

Whenever we suffer shipwrecks we hurry into port. But we docked firmly long ago in the port of safest refuge on the shore of your friendship. We do indeed frequently feel the opposing winds of troubles but we do not disturb your port until a severer storm arises, for either endurance bears or strength powerfully overcomes less serious hazards; but when a great cloud and enveloping lightning[2] assails our little ship we must choose instantly between risking danger or sailing quickly away. This year the lord Pope, at your intervention, granted his privilege to our church, in which he explicitly mentioned the canonries or prebends of Meerssen and confirmed that those which we have retained for a long time now for our own use are to be held in perpetuity.[3] For the prebends, which once belonged to the canons, passed over, a very long time ago, by the donation of the bishops of Liège and with the confirmation of Pope Innocent, into the ownership and possession of our monastery. But recently the lord pope, not, as we believe, being informed about this matter, has now written a second time to our provost of Meerssen ordering him to give a prebend to a certain clerk of the emperor, when neither can the provost give this nor is there a prebend which can be given. Recommend to our lord therefore that he should not wish to take the bread of the children and give it to the dogs[4] who bark at us incessantly and carry away our possessions. For otherwise we are compelled to say, 'Behold, in peace is our bitterness most bitter,'[5] since in the time of schism many tried most urgently to accomplish this through the emperor but prevailed not at all.

[5] Isa. 38: 17 (Vulgate has *mea* not *nostra*). What Peter managed to retain during the schism, when Meerssen fell under the influence of the supporters of the anti-popes, he now risks losing through the actions of the legitimate pope (see appendix 10).

87

To Albert of Morra[1]

summer 1178 × early 1179

Alberto R⟨omane⟩ E⟨cclesie⟩ cancellario Petrus abbas Sancti Remigii.

En auctoritatis apostolice gallina grauida[a] et fetosa congregat pullos suos obedientia et subiectione sub alas benigne protectionis et discrete consultationis.[2] Quid fotura? Quid paritura?[3] Quod scribatur in generatione altera ut populus qui creabitur laudet Dominum.[4] Ecce Iacob 'senex et plenus dierum'[5] qui diu luctatus est cum angelo schismatico,[6] expectans salutare Dei conuocat filios ad benedictionem.[7] Nunquid taciturus quid Ruben fecerit, quod cubile patris ascenderit et stratum eius maculauerit,[8] quid 'Simeon et Leui, uasa iniquitatis bellantia';[9] non predicturus aut constituturus quid facere habeat posteritas futura?[10] Grandis equidem apparatus Romani concilii grandes portendit secuturas nuptias Filii Regis Iesu Christi. Ministeriales et officiales huius sancti concilii cum ceteris, immo pre ceteris, cardinalibus non ignoro uos a Deo predestinatos, quorum fidem, religionem, constantiam et equitatem in multis iam expertus est sponsus ecclesie unicus Dominus noster. Adhuc habet opus ut obsequium uestrum sit rationabile et acceptabile[11] in hoc concilio, ut accincti gladio utrinque acuto super femur, potentissime,[12] putridas amputetis carnes et insanas superstitiones que fiunt cotidie in orbe Christiano. Ramosa siquidem et siluosa cotidie pullulat apud nos malitia, securis autem euangelice discipline, fabro dormiente et negligente, pene ubique iacet retunsa. Rarus est qui eam, uel hebetatam, apponat ad radicem arboris.[13] Vt exprimam quod sentio,

87 *Sirmond VIII. 14*]
[a] *corr. Brooke;* grandosa *Sirmond*

---

87 [1] The reference to a great council after years of schism must be the Third Lateran Council (5–19 Mar. 1179); this letter could have been written any time between the issue of the invitations (summer 1178 or later) and the council itself (see letter no. 80, n. 1; on Albert of Morra, see no. 83, n. 1) allowing time for travelling.
[2] Cf. Matt. 23: 37. [3] Meaning the outcome of the Council.
[4] Cf. Ps. 101 (102): 19.
[5] Gen. 35: 29 (applied to Isaac); the reference here is to Alexander III.
[6] Cf. Gen. 32: 24. [7] Cf. Gen. 49: 1, 18. [8] Cf. Gen. 49: 4.
[9] Cf. Gen. 49: 5. [10] Cf. Gen. 49.

87

To Albert of Morra[1]

summer 1178 × early 1179

To Albert, chancellor of the Roman Church, Peter, abbot of Saint-Remi.

Behold, the pregnant and prolific mother hen of apostolic authority gathers her chicks in obedience and submission under the wings of benign protection and discerning deliberation.[2] What is she about to foster? What is she about to hatch?[3] That which should be written unto another generation, that the people that shall be created should praise the Lord.[4] See how Jacob 'being old and full of days,'[5] who wrestled for a long time with the angel of schism,[6] waiting for God's deliverance, calls his sons together for a blessing.[7] Will he pass over in silence what Ruben has done, that he went up to his father's bed and defiled his couch,[8] what 'Simeon and Levi, vessels of iniquity waging war,'[9] did; will he not foretell or establish what future posterity must do?[10] Indeed the great preparation of the Roman council foreshadows the great forthcoming nuptials of the Son of the King, Jesus Christ. I am not unaware that you were predestined by God to be minister and official of this holy council along with, or rather ahead of, the other cardinals, you whose faith, religious life, constancy, and fairness the bridegroom of the Church, our only Lord, has already experienced in many things. He still requires that your service be reasonable and acceptable[11] in this council, that with the double-edged sword girt upon the thigh, o thou most mighty,[12] you cut out the putrid flesh and the mad superstitions which arise daily in the Christian world. Indeed many-branched and thickly planted evils sprout forth daily in our midst, but with the woodcutter asleep and neglectful the axe of evangelical teaching lies blunt almost everywhere. Scarcely a man can be found to lay it, even blunted, to the root of the tree.[13] Let me

[11] Echoing the canon of the Mass: 'Quam oblationem tu Deus in omnibus quaesumus benedictam adscriptam ratam rationabilem acceptabilemque facere digneris . . .'; see e.g. B. Botte (ed.), *Le Canon de la messe romaine, édition critique* (Louvain, 1935), pp. 36–8, s. viii (but cf. also Rom. 12: 1).

[12] Cf. Ps. 44 (45): 4; cf. also Exod. 32: 27, a ref. picked up again below; cf. the double-edged sword of Rev. 1: 16; 2: 12; 19: 15.

[13] Cf. Matt. 3: 10; Luke 3: 9.

quam irrisoria subsannatio, quam laboriosa et lacrimosa, ne dicam tediosa, peregrinatio, quamque dampnosa expensarum iactura et bona bonorum consumptio, si cassa et sine fructu benedictionis redierit tam solennis magnorum uirorum et religiosarum personarum congregatio. Cauete ne dicatur, 'Parturient montes, nascetur ridiculus mus.'[14] Inueniat igitur uos Iesus amicos ueritatis ut a 'porta usque ad portam' transeuntes, uituli conflatilis cultoribus non parcatis.[15] Commendo uobis presentium latores, karissimos amicos et filios nostros abbates Sancti Petri de Montibus et Omnium Sanctorum de Insula et Sancte Marie Virtuensis,[16] ut de gratia quam habemus in uobis, gratiam inueniant in oculis uestris. Quam citius poteritis cum gratia domini pape et uestra nobis eos remittite.

88

To Albert of Morra[1]

late 1178 × Mar. 1179

Domino Alberto cancellario Petrus abbas Sancti Remigii.

Pro aliis rogare cogimur, qui pro nobis uix exorare sufficimus. Nec tamen in postulatione hesitamus quam commendat iustitia postulationis, conscientia postulantis et pietas postulati. Iustitia est suum ius unicuique seruare,[2] conscientia bona est dilecto domino pro conseruo fideli humiliter supplicare, pietas paterna est propositum etiam inflexibile anxiato filio benigne remittere. Scimus, domine amantissime, potestati apostolice subesse quod mandare uoluerit, et dicere 'huic, Vade, et uadit, et alio, Veni, et uenit, et seruo, Fac hoc, et facit'.[3] Sed iungatur currus potestatis et pietatis, sublimitatis et mansuetudinis, ut media sternatur caritas propter filias Ierusalem.[4] Certe, ut credo, aut nullas filias in terris habet ecclesia que est mater

88 *Sirmond VIII. 9*]

[14] Horace, *Ars Poet.* 139.

[15] Cf. Exod. 32, esp. 27; cf. also Cicero, *De officiis* i. 19. 63.

[16] The most likely identifications are Saint-Pierre-aux-Monts (Benedictine, Châlons-sur-Marne, Cott. i. 675); Toussaints en l'Ile (Augustinian, Châlons-sur-Marne, Cott. i. 676); and Notre-Dame-de-Vertus (Augustinian, dioc. Châlons-sur-Marne, Cott. ii. 3349). The abbots were Thomas of Saint-Pierre-aux-Monts (el. 1166, last occurs 1187, *GC* ix. 929), Roger of Toussaints-en-l'Ile (occurs 1174 × 1189, *GC* ix. 948) and William of Notre-Dame-de-Vertus (occurs 1173, resigned by 1183, *GC* ix. 955).

88 [1] Albert of Morra was chancellor from Feb. 1178 (see letter no. 83, n. 1). This letter

express what I feel: how scornful a mockery it would be, how painful and tearful, not to say tiresome, a pilgrimage, and how damnable a waste of money and how fine a squandering of resources, if so solemn a gathering of great men and religious dignitaries were to return empty and without the fruit of a blessing. Take care lest it be said, 'The mountains will labour, there will be born a ridiculous mouse.'[14] May Jesus then find you to be friends of truth so that, passing 'from gate to gate', you do not spare the worshippers of the molten calf.[15] I commend to you the bearers of this letter, our dearest friends and brothers the abbots of Saint-Pierre-aux-Monts, of Toussaints-en-l'Île, and of Notre-Dame-de-Vertus,[16] that by virtue of the favour which we enjoy with you they may find favour in your eyes. Send them back to us as quickly as you can, with the favour of the lord pope and your own.

88

To Albert of Morra[1]

late 1178 × Mar. 1179

To his lord Albert, chancellor, Peter, abbot of Saint-Remi.

We are compelled to make a request on behalf of others, we who are scarcely worthy to beg on our own behalf. And yet still we do not hesitate in making a demand which the justice of the demand, the conscience of the one making the demand, and the kindness of the one of whom it is demanded, commends. It is justice to preserve for each his right;[2] it is good conscience to supplicate humbly the beloved lord on behalf of a faithful fellow servant; it is fatherly kindness benignly to relax for the anxious son even an inflexible precept. We know, most loving lord, that it is in the apostolic power to order what it wants, and to say 'to this, Go, and he goeth, and to another, Come, and he cometh, and to a servant, Do this, and he doeth it'.[3] But let the chariot of power and pity, of sublimity and clemency, be yoked so that love may be strewn in the midst for the daughters of Jerusalem.[4] Certainly, so I believe, either the Church which is our mother has no

must be another appeal on behalf of Henry de Marcy, who wished to decline the bishopric of Toulouse, and is possibly a companion letter to no. 82 (and so dated as no. 82).

[2] Cf. Justinian *Inst.* i. 1. 1. [3] Matt. 8: 9; Luke 7: 8 (Vulgate has *servo meo*).

[4] Cf. S. of S. 3: 10. In the first part of the sentence, he means that the pairs of qualities should each be joined together, but two chariots cannot be yoked together (as e.g. reading *iungantur currus*).

nostra, aut in Clareuallensi cenobio cotidie parturit et maternis uberibus alit matrissantes filias.[5] Siquidem Iesu Christi de Virgine nati, in mundo religiose conuersati, in cruce sub Pontio Pilato affixi,[6] uera uestigia uestri Clareuallenses sequuntur, caste uiuendo, Patri spiritali in omnibus obediendo, carnem suam 'cum uitiis et concupiscentiis' cotidie crucifigendo.[7] Si Deus pro his, quis contra illos?[8] Ecce pulli isti, sub alis galline[9] que se contra miluos spiritalis nequitie opponit, lambunt sanguinem[10] Dominice passionis et dormiunt sub umbra iuniperi,[11] labores suos consolantes dilectione protectoris sui. Quanti itaque periculi sit excitare quiescentes sub hac ficu et uinea,[12] non carnali sed spiritali dulcedine, discernat discretissima moderatio apostolica, et non auferat ab eis desiderabile oculorum suorum.[13] Annon sunt alii preter istum? Immo super numerum multiplicati sunt qui dicunt, 'Ecce ego, mitte me',[14] cum iste dicat, 'A, a, Domine Deus nescio loqui, quia puer sum.'[15] Forte dicitis: 'Quid ad te de Clareuallensibus, cum Samaritani non coutantur Iudeis et nigra Ethiopisse facies et uestis differat ab illa ueste et facie que apparuit apostolis in transfiguratione Domini?'[16] Ad quod ego: 'Ex multarum facierum personis regina que assistit a dextris Filii in uestitu deaurato, circumdata uarietate,[17] cantat in psalterio decachordo[18] ante sedentem in throno gratie unde procedunt diuersa charismata gratiarum cum sit tamen unus atque idem spiritus, idem Dominus.'[19]

[5] i.e. if the monks of Clairvaux are not true Christians then no one is.
[6] Cf. Kelly, *Creeds*, p. 369; Burn, *Nicene Creed*, pp. 112–13.
[7] Cf. Gal. 5: 24.
[8] Cf. Rom. 8: 31.
[9] Cf. Matt. 23: 37.
[10] Cf. Job 39: 30, where the young of the eagle suck up blood (the association of images and references is, as elsewhere, not straightforward).
[11] Cf. 3 Kgs. (1 Kgs.) 19: 5; what follows echoes Gen. 5: 29.
[12] Common biblical vocabulary. For the image of rousing those at rest applied to Henry, cf. letter no. 82 and n. 4.

daughters on the earth or she gives birth daily in the monastery of Clairvaux and nourishes with maternal breasts daughters who take after their mother.[5] Indeed your monks of Clairvaux follow in the true footsteps of Jesus Christ who was born of the Virgin, lived in a religious manner in the world, and was fastened to the cross under Pontius Pilate,[6] by living chastely, by obeying the spiritual Father in all things, by crucifying their flesh every day 'with the vices and concupiscences'.[7] If God is for these, who is against them?[8] See how these chicks, beneath the wings of the hen[9] who sets herself against the kites of spiritual wickedness, suck up the blood[10] of the Lord's passion and sleep under the shade of the juniper,[11] lightening their labours with the love of their protector. Let then the most discerning apostolic guidance perceive how dangerous it is to rouse up those resting in spiritual not carnal sweetness beneath this fig and vine,[12] and take not the desire of their eyes from them.[13] Are there not others besides this man? Rather are they multiplied beyond number who say, 'Lo, here am I, send me,'[14] when this man says, 'Ah, ah, Lord God, I cannot speak, for I am a child.'[15] Perhaps you are saying: 'What have you to do with the monks of Clairvaux when the Samaritans do not associate with the Jews and the black face and attire of the Ethiopian woman differs from that attire and face which appeared to the apostles in the transfiguration of the Lord?'[16] To which I reply: 'Formed out of persons of many diverse qualities, the queen who stands on the right hand of the Son in gilded clothing, surrounded with variety,[17] sings on the ten-stringed psaltery[18] before the One sitting on the throne of grace, whence proceed divers spiritual gifts of graces, although there yet is one and the same spirit, the same Lord.'[19]

[13] Cf. Ezek. 24: 16, 21.
[14] Cf. Isa. 6: 8.
[15] Cf. Jer. 1: 6; i.e. there are others willing to take on what Henry is refusing.
[16] i.e. what has a Benedictine (black monk) to do with the affairs of the Cistercians (white monks; Christ's garments appeared white at the transfiguration—cf. Matt. 17: 2; Mark 9: 2; Luke 9: 29); Samaritans and Jews, cf. John 4: 9.
[17] Cf. Ps. 44 (45): 10.
[18] Cf. Ps. 32 (33): 2; 91 (92): 4; 143 (144): 9.
[19] Cf. 1 Cor. 12: 4–5, here meaning that the monastic orders are different but united (on this aspect of Peter's thought, see Haseldine, 'Friendship and rivalry').

89

To Peter of Pavia[1]

late 1174 × Dec. 1176 (poss. late 1176)

Petro cardinali Sancti Chrysogoni Petrus abbas Sancti Remigii.

Amplexus uestre familiaritatis michi gratissimos oro non senescere sed cum ligno uite[2] dies eternos tenere. Res siquidem est familiaris amicitia, cotidianis refricanda salutationibus, immo irriganda mutuis collocutionibus, et forte renouanda munerum compensationibus. Placuit dignationi uestre me annumerare in amicorum uestrorum collegio,[3] sine merito quidem meo sed non sine uestro. Meritum namque equitatis est si summus se inclinat ad infimum, magnus ad paruum, ualens ad infirmum. Me uermem, me putredinem, me iamiam ad non esse tendentem reputo; uos cum senatoribus celi thronum iustitie honorantem suspicio et angelos cum Apostolo iudicantem non dubito.[4] An irrisorium est et non uerum quod dico? Plane scripture auctoritate id assero, nam 'labia sacerdotis custodiunt scientiam, quia angelus Domini exercituum est'.[5] Amicabilia sunt, exhortatoria sunt, ne dominus et amicus obliuiscatur casum grauiorem de excelso quam de imo. Certe sollicitudo amicalis frequenter tangit me inquirere de omni statu uestro, tam de interiori quam de exteriori, et gratias ago Deo meo quia non nisi bona nuntiantur, non nisi honesta, non nisi ordini et officio uestro congrua. Oro ut qui cepit ipse perficiat.[6] Magister Crispinus[7] de uobis me

89 *Sirmond VII. 16*]

89 [1] Peter of Pavia, Augustinian, former abbot of Saint-André, Chartres, was bishop el. of Meaux 1171–3, cardinal priest of S. Grisogono from 1173 (first occurs 14 Oct.), cardinal bishop of Tusculum from 2 or 3 May 1179, last occurs 14 July 1182, d. 1 Aug. 1182. There is some evidence that he was postulated for the archbishopric of Bourges in 1180 × 1181, but he died as cardinal bishop of Tusculum. He held two legations, the first as cardinal priest of S. Grisogono, May 1174–late 1178, in France, and the second, as cardinal bishop of Tusculum, 1181–Feb. 1182, in Germany and from the end of April 1181 in France. On Peter, see Ganzer, *Entwicklung*, pp. 123–5; H. Delehaye, 'Pierre de Pavie, légat du Pape Alexandre III en France', *Revue des questions historiques*, xlix (1891), 5–61, and on the legations pp. 23–57; JL ii. 145, 431. For a detailed itinerary of the legations, see Janssen, *Die päpstlichen Legaten*, pp. 92–108, 119–22; on his bishopric of Meaux, see also letter no. 102, n. 8. In the present letter and no. 90 Peter of Celle recommends a master Crispin, travelling to the schools at Paris, who wished to be ordained by the legate (whom he has evidently met at least once). This presumably dates from Peter of Pavia's first legation (he is addressed as cardinal of S. Grisogono): he was in Paris at the turn of 1174/5 and again in early 1176; by late autumn 1176

89

To Peter of Pavia[1]

late 1174 × Dec. 1176 (poss. late 1176)

To Peter, cardinal of S. Grisogono, Peter, abbot of Saint-Remi.

I pray that the embraces of your friendship, which are most pleasing to me, do not grow old but will, with the tree of life,[2] have eternal days. For friendship is indeed a familiar thing, to be refreshed by daily greetings, nay watered by mutual conversation, and perhaps to be renewed with reciprocation of gifts. It pleased your worthiness to number me among the college of your friends,[3] without indeed any merit on my part, but not without merit on yours. For it is a merit of fairness if the highest bends down to the lowest, the great to the small, the strong to the weak. I reckon myself a worm, a putrid object, already heading for non-existence; I look up at you who with the senators of heaven honour the throne of justice, and I do not doubt that you with the Apostle are judging the angels.[4] Is what I say laughable and untrue? Plainly I am making this assertion with the authority of Scripture, for 'the lips of the priest keep knowledge, because he is the angel of the Lord of hosts'.[5] They are lips of friendship, of exhortation, so that my lord and friend should not forget that a fall from on high is harder than one from the bottom. Friendly concern, to be sure, frequently moves me to inquire about your whole state, interior as well as exterior, and I give thanks to my God because nothing but good is reported, nothing but what is honourable, nothing but what is fitting to your order and office. I pray that He who has begun this good work may Himself perfect it.[6] Master Crispin[7] has gladdened my heart on your account, reporting

he was in Burgundy whence he travelled to Champagne, and was in Paris again by Dec. 1176; from mid-1177 he was mainly in Toulouse and the south (see Janssen, *Die päpstlichen Legaten*, pp. 95–100). Crispin could have hoped to intercept him at any time between late 1174 and Dec. 1176. Peter's valediction at the end of the present letter might indicate that the letter was written after the legate's visit to Champagne, and so in late 1176 (see also Janssen, *Die päpstlichen Legaten*, pp. 99–100, who puts a strange interpretation on letters 91 and 92). (It is unlikely that this is the same Crispin as in letters 97 and 98.)

[2] Cf. Gen. 2: 9; Rev. 22: 2, and many other refs.

[3] It is not known when they first met; on Peter of Pavia's later visit to Saint-Remi, in 1181, see letter no. 91, n. 3. [4] Cf. 1 Cor. 6: 3. [5] Cf. Mal. 2: 7.

[6] Cf. Phil. 1: 6: 'qui coepit in uobis opus bonum perficiet usque in diem Christi Iesu.'

[7] See n. 1 above.

letificauit, referens unde gauderem et Deo gratias agerem. Clericus et amicus noster est; eque desiderat esse et uester. Ecce Parisius ad scolas uadit sed et ubique nomen uestrum super se inuocari postulat. Vtile equidem est tanto homini qui tanta omnium sollicitudine pene continue uexatur quod sui corporis necessaria et salubria postponens ad intemperiem corporalem sepe delabitur. Rogo pro ipso et cum ipso quatinus gratiam non qualem qualem inueniat in oculis uestris, sed bonam, sed confertam, sed coagitatam[a] et supereffluentem.[8] Dico autem gratiam non pecuniam. Hec enim iuxta Apostolum operanti reddatur secundum meritum.[9] Pre ceteris hoc unum ad presens postulat ut de manu uestra primitias clericatus, id est coronam, accipiat. Hoc etenim signo accepto, magis se obligatum erga obsequium uestrum non immerito deinceps arbitrabitur, et uos tanquam plante uestre bonum iure prouidebitis. Credo per Dei gratiam quod alter de altero gaudebit et Deo cooperante fructum salutis faciet. Diu siquidem laboraui et monitis induxi ut iugum in area Domini traheret et glebas post ipsum confringeret.[10] Vale, et de reditu uestro cum potueritis nos certificate.

90

To Peter of Pavia[1]

late 1174 × Dec. 1176 (poss. late 1176)

Petro cardinali Sancti Chrysogoni Petrus abbas Sancti Remigii.

Raro meus sum, cuius ergo? forte Apollo? forte Pauli? forte Cephe?[2] Vtinam! Nam bonam habent mensam, mansuetam et fructuosam disciplinam, donatiuum denique precipuum et perpetuum. Diuersorum autem subsellia et iniquam tyrannidem frequenter experior, utique Roboam qui cedit scorpionibus,[3] Pharaonis qui affligit 'in luto et latere',[4] Nabuchodonosor qui potat urinam

[a] superagitatam *Sirmond*

90 *Sirmond VII. 18*]

[8] Cf. Luke 6: 38.

[9] Apparently alluding to Rom. 2: 6 or 1 Cor. 3: 8; cf. also Ps. 61 (62): 13; Matt. 16: 27; Rev. 2: 23.

[10] Alluding to Lam. 3: 27 and Job 39: 10.

such things as made me rejoice and give thanks to God. He is our clerk and friend; he wishes to be yours equally. See, he goes to the schools in Paris, but also everywhere he asks that your name be invoked upon him. It is useful indeed to such a man who is troubled almost continuously by so much worry about everything that he disregards those things which are necessary and healthy for his body and often lapses into bodily disorder. I ask for him and with him that he may find in your eyes a grace which is not indifferent but good and pressed down and shaken together and running over.[8] But I say grace, not money. For let it, as the Apostle says, be rendered to the doer according to desert.[9] He asks this one thing at present above all else, that he may receive the first-fruits of the clerical office, that is the tonsure, from your hand. For having received this sign he will rightly thereafter consider himself bound the more to your service, and you will justly do good, as to your own scion. I believe that through the grace of God each will rejoice in the other and with God's help will produce the fruit of salvation. I have toiled indeed for a long time and I have led him by admonitions to draw the yoke in the field of the Lord and to break up the sods after him.[10] Farewell, and inform us of your return when you are able.

90

To Peter of Pavia[1]

late 1174 × Dec. 1176 (poss. late 1176)

To Peter, cardinal of S. Grisogono, Peter, abbot of Saint-Remi.

I am seldom my own man; whose then am I? Perhaps Apollos'? Perhaps Paul's? Perhaps Cephas'?[2] If only I were! For they have a good table, gentle and fruitful discipline and lastly pre-eminent and perennial largesse. I on the other hand frequently experience the courts of enemies and unjust tyranny, that is to say of Roboam who beats with scorpions,[3] of Pharaoh who casts down 'in clay and brick,'[4] of Nebuchadnezzar who drinks the urine of his cattle which he had

90 [1] Dated as letter no. 89. This letter may be the later of the two, as no. 89 seems to be acknowledging admission to the legate's friendship circle and contains a fuller recommendation of Crispin, but this is not certain and as they seem to assume the same point in Crispin's relations with Peter of Pavia the sequence cannot be known for certain.

[2] Cf. 1 Cor. 1: 12. [3] Cf. 3 Kgs. (1 Kgs.): 12: 11, 14; 2 Chr. 10: 11, 14.

[4] Judith 5: 10; cf. Exod. 1: 14; Pharaoh forced the Israelites to labour 'in clay and brick'.

pecudum suorum quos sub iugo carnis, uentris et gule incscaucrat.[5] Denique in captiuitate mea et uniuersa uanitate sub sole[6] concaptiuam habeo puellam, nobilissimis ortam natalibus, uidelicet pudicitiam. Huius me iniuriosa dampnatio illorum 'quorum carnes sunt ut carnes asinorum'[7] non minus aggrauat quam propria miseria. Volui siquidem cum illa fedus amicitie inire ab ineunte etate propter decorem suum et genus illustrissimum, nec non et pacatissimum atque honestissimum contubernium. Cum itaque chaos siue cohors spurcissimorum hominum tanquam porci pretiosissimam margaritam de celo lapsam pedibus suis conculcent, que pax ossibus meis, que requies anime mee?[8] Clamo, 'Nolite, nolite,' sed non est uox neque sensus.[9] Quin immo apponunt 'iniquitatem super iniquitatem'[10] ut cum pudicitia obruant religionem. Huic[a] nulla parcentes miseratione oculos eruunt, conuertendo ad uanitates et insanias falsas; nasum precidunt, discretionis temperantiam euertentes; aures obstruunt, obedientiam non tenentes; labia concidunt, turpiloquio et scurrilitatibus assuescentes; linguam decapulant,[11] uerum[b] redarguentes et mendacium semper loquentes; manus ligant, helemosinam non dantes, sanguini et auaritie insistentes, pedes in neruo ponentes, Christum in carcere non uisitantes. Quid amplius? Neruos detrahunt religioni effeminati qui sanctorum patrum abstinentiam, uigilias, psalmodiam, silentium, regularem disciplinam, claustralem remotionem a secularibus negotiis dissipant et uilipendunt. Forte dicitis: 'Quid ad me?' Certe uestra interest et certe officii uestri est, certe debito tenemini pro posse uestro districta censura his occurrere iniuriis, his aurem benignam accommodare clamoribus, has dirimere questiones et, amputatis Dagon brachiis et capite,[12] archam Dei restituere Bethsamitis.[13] An habetis iudicare causas pecuniarias et non diuinas? Quis uos misit? Ad quid uos destinauit Dominus Deus per uicarium suum dominum apostolicum? Ad quid? Vt solueretis asinam, id est religionem alligatam, et pullum cum ea, id est pudicitiam. 'Dicite', inquit, 'quia Dominus his opus habet.'[14] Sedet enim super utrumque qui sedet super cherubin.[15] Non negligatis Dominicum preceptum, immo non extinguatis in uobis spiritum

[a] *sic PL;* hinc *Sirmond* [b] *corr. Hall;* malum *Sirmond*

[5] Cf. Dan. 4: Nebuchadnezzar as the tree which fed the beasts, then fell among them; on the imagery, cf. 4 Kgs. (2 Kgs.) 3: 27; Isa. 36: 12.

[6] Cf. Eccles. 4: 7, with a possible echo of Ps. 38 (39): 6.

[7] Ezek. 23: 20.

[8] Cf. Matt. 7: 6; Ps 37 (38): 4.

[9] Cf. 4 Kgs. (2 Kgs.) 4: 31.

[10] Cf. Ps. 68 (69): 28.

[11] Evidently a coinage, but presumably by analogy with *capulo* (see *DML*; Niermeyer).

satiated beneath the yoke of the flesh, of the belly, and of the gullet.[5] Finally, in my captivity and universal vanity under the sun,[6] I have a young maiden as fellow captive, sprung from the noblest stock, namely chaste modesty. The unjust condemnation of her by those 'whose flesh is as the flesh of asses'[7] is no less a burden to me than my own misery. Indeed I wished to enter with her the pact of friendship from my earliest years on account of her beauty and most illustrious birth, and also her most tranquil and honourable companionship. And so since chaos, or rather the cohort of the basest men, tramples underfoot like swine the most precious pearl fallen from heaven, what peace do my bones have, what rest does my soul have?[8] I call out, 'Hold off, hold off,' but there is neither voice nor sense.[9] They rather add 'iniquity upon iniquity'[10] so that they strike down the religious life along with chaste modesty. Showing no mercy to her, they tear out her eyes and turn to worthless things and spurious follies; they cut off her nose and overturn the moderation of discernment; they block up her ears and do not maintain obedience; they cut off her lips and grow accustomed to obscenity and scurrilities; they cut out[11] her tongue and reprove truth and always speak falsehood; they bind her hands and do not give alms, pursuing bloodshed and greed, putting her feet in the fetter and not visiting Christ in prison. What more? Those weaklings, who overthrow and hold cheap the abstinence of the holy fathers, vigils, psalmody, silence, regular discipline, and claustral seclusion from worldly affairs, draw out the sinews of the religious life. Perhaps you are saying: 'What is this to me?' Certainly it concerns you, and certainly it pertains to your office; certainly you are bound by your duty to oppose these injustices to the best of your ability with strict censure, to lend a benign ear to these clamours, to settle these questions and, having cut off the arms and head of Dagon,[12] to restore the ark of God to the Bethsamites.[13] For have you to judge financial cases and not religious? Who has sent you? To what has the Lord God appointed you through His vicar the apostolic lord? For what? That you should loose the ass, that is religion bound, and with her the colt, that is chaste modesty. 'Say ye', He tells them, 'that the Lord hath need of them.'[14] For He sits upon both who sits upon the cherubims.[15] Do not neglect the precept of the Lord, or rather do

[12] Cf. 1 Kgs. (1 Sam.) 5: 4.

[13] Cf. 1 Kgs. (1 Sam.) 6.

[14] Cf. Matt. 21: 2–3; Mark 11: 2–3; Luke 19: 30–1.

[15] God sits upon the cherubim in 1 Kgs. (1 Sam.) 4: 4; 4 Kgs. (2 Kgs.) 19: 15; 1 Chr. 13: 6; Ps. 79 (80): 2; Ps. 98 (99): 1; Isa. 37: 16; Dan. 3: 55 etc.

Moysi de quo dictum est, 'Auferam de spiritu tuo et dabo septuaginta senioribus',[16] de quibus et cum quibus unum uos constituit gratia sua Deus. Quis autem est spiritus Moysi? Spiritus iniquitatem non sustinens, spiritus occidens iniuriam facientem et uindicans patientem, spiritus defendens septem puellas filias Iethro sacerdotis Madiam,[17] spiritus principem Egypti decem plagis feriens[18] et tandem in mare demergens.[19] Diu detineo uos quia non possum ore proprio saltem scripto. Dulce namque michi 'super mel et fauum'[20] uos alloqui et uobiscum fauellare.[21] Huius tamen causa et materia est magister Crispinus, clericus noster, immo et uester,[22] nam populus meus populus tuus,[23] amice et domine karissime. Commendo itaque uobis eum tanquam uiscera mea quia uidi honestam conuersationem eius et procliuem ad 'meliora et uiciniora saluti'.[24] Noui uos, quia talium familiaritatem non respuistis.[c] Habeat itaque uos dominum et signo clericatus[25] a uobis suscepto patronum et auctorem huius ordinis habeat.

91

To Peter of Pavia[1]

? summer 1180

Tusculano episcopo Petrus abbas Sancti Remigii.

Ignis diuinus non minus est perpetuus quam in hostiis Deo dicatis sanctificandis sanctus. Hinc est quod in altari ubi tam holocausta quam sacrificia cotidie ad expiationem peccatorum Deo immolantur iugis et perpetuus ardet. Quid autem hoc est nisi quod Apostolus ait: 'Caritas nunquam excidit'?[2] Nam pura a simulatione, munda a seculari ambitione corda, Christi acceptabilia sunt altaria, siue templa. Forcipe igitur litterarum uestrarum suscepi in aureo thuribulo bonorum uerborum sacras euaporationes iamdudum succense

[c] *sic PL;* respuitis *Sirmond*

91 *Sirmond IX. 6*]

[16] Cf. Num. 11: 16–17, 24–5.
[17] Cf. Exod. 2: 16–17.
[18] Cf. Exod. 7–12.
[19] Cf. Exod 14: 23–31.
[20] Cf. Ps. 18 (19): 11; Ecclus. 24: 27.
[21] But with a pun on *fauum* (*fauillare*).

not extinguish within yourself the spirit of Moses of which it is said, 'I will take of thy spirit and will give to the seventy ancients',[16] of whom and with whom God by His grace made you one. But what is the spirit of Moses? The spirit not upholding iniquity, the spirit striking down the wrongdoer and vindicating the sufferer, the spirit defending the seven maidens, daughters of Jethro the priest of Madian,[17] the spirit smiting the prince of Egypt with ten plagues[18] and finally submerging him in the sea.[19] I am detaining you for a long time because if I cannot do this with my own mouth at least I can do so with the written word. For it is sweeter to me 'than honey and the honeycomb'[20] to speak to you and to chat with you.[21] The reason and occasion of this letter, however, is master Crispin, our clerk, nay yours also,[22] for my people are your people,[23] dearest friend and lord. And so I commend him to you as my own heart because I have seen his honest manner of life and his inclination to 'better things and nearer to salvation'.[24] I know that you have not rejected the friendship of such people. Let him then have you as a lord, and having received the clerical sign[25] from you, let him have you as patron and author of this status.

91

To Peter of Pavia[1]

? summer 1180

To the bishop of Tusculum, Peter, abbot of Saint-Remi.

The divine fire is no less perpetual than it is sacred in sanctifying the hosts consecrated to God. Hence it is that it burns continual and perpetual on the altar where burnt offerings as well as sacrifices are offered daily for the expiation of sinners. But what is this if not what the Apostle says: 'Charity never falleth away'?[2] For hearts which are free from deceit and cleansed of worldly ambition are acceptable altars or temples of Christ. Therefore I have taken up, with the tongs of your letter, in the golden censer of good words, the sacred emanations of the furnace long since fired by our sight of one another

[22] On Crispin, see letter no. 89, n. 1. [23] Cf. Ruth 1: 16.
[24] Cf. Heb. 6: 9. [25] i.e. the tonsure.

91 [1] Written on the death of Berneredus of Saint-Crépin, poss. summer 1180 (1181 is poss. but unlikely: see letter no. 128, n. 1); on Peter of Pavia, see letter no. 89, n. 1.
[2] 1 Cor. 13: 8; for the perpetual fire, cf. Lev. 6: 12–13.

fornacis ex mutua inter nos uisione et allocutione.[3] Deo gratias quia non inueni aquam crassam imminute dilectionis sed ipsum ignem,[4] non fumantem sed flammantem in penetralibus tanti domini et amici. Putabam illum suffocatum cineribus tantarum sollicitudinum et uarietate succedentium occupationum. Preterea causam et questionem grauissimam aduersum uos habebam si iustum habuissem iudicem. A quo enim primordia cognitionis et dilectionis cum abbate Sanctorum Crispini et Crispiniani pie memorie habuistis nisi a nobis?[5] Quare ergo de nostro bono opere nos lapidastis? Annon lapidastis quem tot amaritudinibus et afflictionibus de eius absentia concussistis? Annon ⟨uelut⟩ Iacob furtum Laban de filiabus suis fecistis?[6] Forte furtum non negatis sed pium appellatis. Sed si furtum quomodo pium? Si pium quomodo furtum? Probo autem furtum, nam furtum est contrectatio rei aliene inuito domino.[7] Romam certe ad concilium non iuisset nisi illum misissem. Preter spem et preter uoluntatem meam illum retinuistis et fratrem et parem uobis fecistis. Hoc tamen nec illi nec nobis placuit. Mallet cellam Montis Dei incolere, ut frequenter michi scripsit, quam episcopalem cathedram tenere. Quid igitur? Deus qui omnia conclusit[8] et meas querimonias preuenit, faciendo quod facere pie et misericorditer consueuit. Preuenit illum benedictionibus suis, et quem olim amicum et fratrem in terris habebamus, nunc dominum et sanctum in celis ueneramur. Miracula enim que facit Deus testimonia credibilia sunt sancte conuersationis eius.[9] Itaque digitum superpono ori meo.[10]

[3] Cf. Num. 16: 46 (putting fire in a censer) and 1 Chr. 28: 17; Heb. 9: 4; Rev. 8: 3 (golden censer). On the reference here to their earlier meeting, it is likely that Peter of Pavia met Peter of Celle on his first mission to France—the legate was in Champagne in late 1176 (see letter no. 89, n. 1) and the legation was preceded by a letter of Alexander III recommending Peter of Pavia to Archbishop Henry of Reims (JL ii. 12370; *PL* cc. 987), who was close to Peter of Celle both geographically and, it would seem, politically (on Henry, see letter no. 21, n. 1; see also letter no. 22). Peter of Pavia also visited Saint-Remi in May 1181 and was accorded confraternity with the community. See Janssen, *Die päpstlichen Legaten*, pp. 93, 122.

[4] Cf. 2 Macc. 1: 20.

and our conversation together.[3] Thanks be to God that I have not found the thick water of diminished love but the fire itself,[4] not smouldering but flaming in the inner chambers of so great a lord and friend. I was supposing that it had been stifled by the ashes of such great worries and by the variety of successive affairs. Furthermore I would have had a most serious case and complaint against you if I had had a just judge. For from whom did you have the beginnings of acquaintance with and love for the abbot of Saint-Crépin of devout memory if not from us?[5] Why then have you stoned us for our good deed? For have you not stoned the one whom you have struck with so many bitternesses and afflictions on account of that abbot's absence? Have you not like Jacob stolen away the daughters of Laban?[6] Perhaps you do not deny the theft but call it worthy. But if it is a theft, how is it worthy? If worthy, how is it a theft? But I judge it a theft, for a theft is the appropriation of another's possession against the will of the owner.[7] It is certain that he would not have gone to the council in Rome unless I had sent him. Against my hope and against my will you kept him there and made him your brother and equal. This, however, pleased neither him nor us. He would have preferred to dwell in a cell at Mont-Dieu, as he told me in his letters frequently, rather than to hold an episcopal throne. What then? God who has concluded all[8] also anticipated my complaints by doing what He is accustomed to do kindly and mercifully. For He went before him with His blessings, and he whom we once had as a friend and brother on earth we now venerate as a lord and saint in heaven. For the miracles which God performs are credible witnesses of his holy manner of life.[9] And so I lay my finger on my mouth.[10]

[5] Berneredus, see n. 1 above, and letter no. 128, n. 1. Peter's 'accusation' is that Peter of Pavia had 'stolen' Berneredus and taken him to the Curia. On the legate's role in Berneredus' el. to the cardinalate see Glorieux, 'Candidats', pp. 21–2; this happened after he had accompanied Peter of Pavia to the Third Lateran Council, hence the reference to the Council below. Crispin and Crispinian are the two patron saints of Saint-Crépin (also called Saint-Crépin-le-Grand). What follows echoes John 10: 32.

[6] Cf. Gen. 31.

[7] Cf. Justinian, *Inst.* iv. 1. 1, 6.

[8] Cf. Rom. 11: 32.

[9] On miracles at Berneredus' tomb, in the Lateran, see also the letter of P., canon of Saint-Ruf, in E. Martène and U. Durand (eds.), *Thesaurus Novus Anecdotorum*, 5 vols. (Paris, 1717), i. 625–6.

[10] Cf. Job 21: 5; 29: 9.

92

To Thomas Becket[1]

1164 × 1170 (poss. 1169, Aug.–Nov.)

Domino et patri karissimo Thome uenerabili Cantuariensi archiepiscopo frater Petrus abbas Sancti Remigii, ex toto corde deuotissimam salutem.

Sollicito reuoluens[a] animo quam potius materiam assumam cum uobis scribere uolo uix occurrit, non deficiente[b] quid dicatur sed reuerentia eius comprimente manum cui dicatur. Nichil enim dignum uestri animi fortitudine dicere possum, nichil addere constantissime tolerantie uestre, nichil denique docere omnia a longe prospicientem atque fines rerum et causarum futurarum plenissime demetientem[c] [d]animum. Feni[d] atque palearum aceruum ut quid anteponerem presepio cui adheret bos 'adipe et pinguedine'[2] opulentissima [e]satiatus et saginatus?[e] Equidem hoc unum[f] michi ad ministerium aliquod impendendum in obsequio uestro non indigne reseruatum reperio, si muscas abigere possem uestram sanctitatem oblatratione inuidiosa pungere[g] uolentes, uel saltem interpretatione peruersa denigrare sinceritatem fidei uestre insistentes. Plane 'musce' iste 'morientes'[3] que in Egypto habundant et Pharaonem regem Egypti tanquam uirum muscarum circumdant, Deo opitulante non 'perdent suauitatem unguenti'.[4] Seruabitur namque in diem sepulture Iesu,[5] et predicabitur in generatione et generationem quod archiepiscopus Cantuariensis murum se opponens pro domo Israhel[6] uestigia sanctorum antiquorum imitatur dum Christum in cruce nudum pendentem nudus sequitur. Quomodo ergo cum Abraham potero abigere easdem muscas contaminare uolentes illibatum Domini

92 *Val fos. 120ʳ–121ʳ, Sirmond I. 10*]
[a] reuolens *Val* [b] deficiendo *Sirmond* [c] dimetientem *Sirmond* [d–d] *om. Sirmond* [e–e] saginatus et satiatus *Val* [f] *corr. Duggan;* unde *Val; om. Sirmond* [g] pongere *Val*

92 [1] Thomas Becket, archbishop of Canterbury el. 23 May 1162, consecrated 3 June, papal legate for England from 24 Apr. 1166, d. 29 Dec. 1170 (*Fasti* ii. 4; Barlow, *Thomas Becket*, pp. 70–2, 247; C. R. Cheney, 'On the acta of Theobald and Thomas, archbishops of Canterbury', *Journal of the Society of Archivists*, vi (1981), 467–81, at p. 468 and n. 7). The letter was written to the archbishop during his exile (Nov. 1163–Dec. 1170; Barlow, *Thomas Becket*, pp. 116, 224). The reference to his refusal to abandon his material claims

92

To Thomas Becket[1]

1164 × 1170 (poss. 1169, Aug.–Nov.)

To his dearest lord and father Thomas, venerable archbishop of Canterbury, brother Peter, abbot of Saint-Remi, the most devoted greeting from his whole heart.

As I turn over in an anxious mind what matter by preference I should take up when I wish to write to you, scarcely anything occurs, not for lack of a topic but because reverence for the addressee restrains my hand. For I can say nothing worthy of the fortitude of your mind, add nothing to your most constant endurance, and lastly teach nothing to the mind which foresees all things from afar and most fully measures the consequences of events and matters yet to come. Why should I place a heap of hay and chaff before the stable to which clings the ox full and fattened with the richest 'marrow and fatness'?[2] I find indeed this one thing not unworthily reserved for me, for discharging some function in your service, that I might be able to drive off the flies which are trying to sting your holiness with invidious railing, or are at least persisting in defaming the sincerity of your faith with a perverse interpretation. Clearly these 'dying flies'[3] which abound in Egypt and surround Pharaoh the king of Egypt as if he were a man of flies will not, with God's help, 'spoil the sweetness of the ointment'.[4] For this will be kept against the day of Jesus' burial,[5] and it will be proclaimed from generation to generation that the archbishop of Canterbury, setting himself up as a wall for the house of Israel,[6] follows in the footsteps of the ancient saints while he follows naked the naked Christ hanging on the cross. How then shall I be able, with Abraham, to drive off those same flies which are trying

against the king may link this letter to the legatine mission of Vivian and Gratian in Aug.–Nov. 1169.

[2] Cf. Ps. 62 (63): 6; cf. also Ps. 147 (147): 14; Luke 15: 23; presumably also an allusion to the ox associated with Christ's nativity in popular belief, a traditoin derived from Isa. 1: 3 and pseudo-Matthew (*Corpus Christianorum Series Apocryphorum* ix. 431).

[3] Eccles. 10: 1.

[4] Cf. Eccles. 10: 1; cf. also Exod. 8: 21–4.

[5] Cf. John 12: 7.

[6] Cf. Ezek. 13: 5. (On 'Christum . . . nudum . . . nudus sequitur', see e.g. *P. Ven. Epp.* ii. 108–9.)

sacrificium,[7] nisi facto[h] uentilabro de authenticis scripturis quo[i] uel feriantur uel saltem effugentur? Dicunt enim: 'Non debet archiepiscopus tam instanter sua repetere a rege Anglie ut dimittat reconciliationis pacem pro amissa pecunia.' Falluntur specie[j] ueri uel adulatione falsi. Qui specie[k] ueri decipiuntur instruendi sunt, qui adulatione falsi repellendi. Simplicitas enim reuocanda est, malitia prorsus abicienda. Certe[l] pensandum est in omni tam contractu quam actu quid propter quid faciendum uel quid[m] dimittendum sit. Pensanda etiam sunt tempora et diuersi status temporum secundum quos mutantur merita causarum. Nam in primitiua ecclesia sola patientia locum habuit, ut auferenti tunicam dimitteret et pallium.[8] Alius enim erat et alibi, id est extra ecclesiam, qui persequebatur, alius et alibi, id est intra ecclesiam, qui patiebatur. Modo uero iam adulta ecclesia non licet filiis ecclesie quod aliquando licuit inimicis.[9] Decet enim matrem corrigere filium sicut decuit pupillam[n] tolerare aduersarium. Distinctus namque sapphiris legitur uenter sponsi[10] et,[o] quemadmodum ante passionem suam [p]Iesus dixerat,[p] 'Qui non renuntiauerit omnibus que possidet non potest meus esse discipulus'[11] et similia, in passione dicit apostolis, 'Qui non habet gladium uendat tunicam et emat.'[12] Verba quidem bona, uerba consolatoria non immerito exigeret[q] causa iusta in oculis Dei, in oculis autem insipientium dubia et infirma, nisi uirtus patientie omnem transcenderet consolationem et plus gauderetis de patientia[r] quam malleus feriens proficeret de percussione. 'Ferrum ferro acuitur',[13] et de malitia regis Anglie uirtus uestra inuincibilis clarius illustratur. Quo fortius premit [s]torcular oliuam[s] [14] eo profusius oleum producit. 'Candelabrum ductile de auro' purissimo[15] non facit Beseleel in tabernaculo Domini nisi productis laminis contritione lime et mallei. Nondum 'contritus est malleus uniuerse terre';[16] adhuc

[h] sancto *Sirmond* [i] quod *Val* [j] spe *Sirmond* [k] spe *Sirmond*
[l] Ceterum *Sirmond* [m] *om.* *Sirmond* [n] pupillo *Val* [o] ut *Val*
[p–p] dixerat Ihesus *Val* [q] exigent *Val* [r] consolatione *Val, Sirmond*
[s–s] oliuam torcular *Val*

[7] Cf. Gen. 15: 11, Abraham protecting his sacrifice from fowls. 'Illibatum . . . sacrificium' echoes the canon of the Mass; cf. e.g. B. Botte (ed.), *Le Canon de la messe romaine, édition critique* (Louvain, 1935), p. 32, s. iii.

[8] Cf. Matt. 5: 40; Luke 6: 29.

[9] i.e. passive martyrdom was an acceptable response to pagan rulers, but there is a duty to resist the actions of Christian kings against the Church.

[10] Cf. S. of S. 5: 14. [11] Cf. Luke 14: 33.

[12] Cf. Luke 22: 36: 'sed nunc qui habet sacculum tollat similiter et peram, et qui non habet uendat tunicam suam et emat gladium'.

to contaminate the unviolated sacrifice of the Lord,[7] except with a fan fashioned from the genuine Scriptures, by which they may be struck, or at least put to flight? For they say: 'The Archbishop ought not to claim back his own from the king of England so earnestly as to forgo the peace of reconciliation for the sake of lost wealth.' They are deceived by a semblance of the truth or by the blandishments of falsehood. Those who are ensnared by a semblance of truth should be instructed; those who are ensnared by the blandishments of falsehood, repulsed. For honesty should be recalled, malice cast away utterly. Certainly one must consider in every contract as in every act what should be done or what forgone for the sake of what. The times also and the varying conditions of the times should be considered, according to which the merits of cases are changed. For in the early Church endurance alone had a place so that one surrendered the cloak also to him who was taking away the coat.[8] For there was one in one place, that is outside the Church, who was persecuting, and another in another place, that is within the Church, who was suffering. But now that the Church has grown up, that which was once permitted to her enemies is not permitted to the sons of the Church.[9] For it is proper for a mother to correct a son just as it was proper for the young girl to endure the enemy. For we read that the belly of the groom is set with sapphires,[10] and also, just as Jesus had said before His passion, 'He who does not renounce all that he possesses cannot be my disciple'[11] and similar things, so during the passion He says to the apostles, 'He who has not a sword, let him sell his coat and buy one.'[12] A cause which is just in God's eyes but doubtful and weak in the eyes of the foolish would indeed draw forth not undeservedly good words, words of consolation, did not the strength of endurance transcend all consolation and did you not rejoice more in endurance than the striking hammer profits by its blow. 'Iron sharpeneth iron',[13] and your invincible strength is more clearly manifested by the malice of the king of England. The more powerfully the press squeezes the olive,[14] the more profusely it produces oil. Beseleel does not make 'a candlestick of beaten work of' the purest 'gold'[15] in the tabernacle of the Lord except with sheets which he has drawn out by crushing with the file and the hammer. For 'the hammer of the whole earth is' not yet 'destroyed';[16] it is still

[13] Prov. 27: 17.

[14] Cf. Joel 3: 13.

[15] Cf. Exod. 25: 31; 37: 17; also Num. 8: 4 (Vulgate has *mundissimo*); Beseleel, cf. Exod. 36: 1; 38: 21–2.

[16] Cf. Jer. 50: 23, the hammer here being presumably Henry II.

necessarius ut suppleat que desunt passioni Christi in corpore uestro.[17] Sed quem moneo? Quem exhortor? Cui calcaria adhibeo? Sine dubio qui freno indiget, qui paratus est plus ambulare quam uia extendatur, qui etiam metas[t] uelociter transcurrere nullis retardatur periculis. 'Procul' enim 'odoratur bellum';[18] exilium reputat patriam, quia 'omne solum forti patria est'.[19] Sine labore laborat, sine fame esurit, sine dolore patitur, sine amaritudine felle et absinthio cibatur.[20] Vir est in milibus unus;[21] cum 'gigantes gemunt sub aquis'[22] ipse ridet et irridet fortunam cum inuersione rote sue.[23] Vale.

93

To Henry of France, archbishop of Reims[1]

summer 1167

Venerabili domino et patri karissimo Henrico Remensium archiepiscopo frater Petrus humilis abbas Sancti Remigii, se ipsum deuotissime.

Cum semper presentia uestra nobis et toti prouincie Remensi necessaria sit, quia nunc solite[a] increuerunt et intumescunt tribulationes que circumdederunt nos, omnino postulantes rogamus ne moram faciatis redire ad nos.[2] In absentia enim uestra cornua sibi assumunt[3] inimici uestri et nostri adeo ut non sit pax ingredienti uel

[t] metens *Val*

93 *Sirmond I. 14*]
[a] solito *Sirmond*

[17] Cf. Col. 1: 24. [18] Job 39: 25.
[19] Ovid, *Fasti*, i. 493 (trans. Loeb, J. G. Frazer). [20] Cf. Jer. 23: 15.
[21] Cf. Ovid, *Ex Ponto*, ii. 3. 11–12: 'nec facile invenias multis in milibus unum, | virtutem pretium qui putet esse sui.' Cf. also Eccles. 7: 29.
[22] Job 26: 5.
[23] On wheel of fortune imagery, see e.g. A. Murray, *Reason and Society in the Middle Ages* (Oxford, 1978), pp. 98–101.

93 [1] The letter seems to refer to the uprising in Reims of 1167, which John of Salisbury describes (in his letter no. 223, of *c.* Oct. 1167) as having raged almost all summer (*J. S. Epp.* ii. 384–7). There were in fact two disputes in Reims at this time, which presumably became conflated as disorder spread. The first was between Archbishop Henry and his chapter over capitular rights and the second involved a rising of the townspeople. John of Salisbury's letter no. 223 says that the rising is over but that the archbishop is still in dispute with his clergy (*J. S. Epp.* ii. 386–7), while his letter no. 225 (also dated *c.* Oct.

necessary for making up those things which are lacking of the passion of Christ in your body.[17] But whom am I advising? Whom am I exhorting? To whom am I applying the spurs? Without any doubt to him who needs the rein, to him who is prepared to walk further than the road extends, to him too who is restrained by no dangers from running swiftly past the winning posts. For 'he smelleth the battle afar off';[18] he considers exile to be his homeland, because 'every land is to the brave his country'.[19] He toils without toil, starves without hunger, suffers without pain and is fed on gall and wormwood without tasting the bitterness.[20] He is one man in a thousand;[21] when 'the giants groan under the waters'[22] he laughs and ridicules Fortune and the turning of her wheel.[23] Farewell.

93

To Henry of France, archbishop of Reims[1]

summer 1167

To his venerable lord and dearest father Henry, archbishop of Reims, brother Peter, humble abbot of Saint-Remi, himself most devotedly.

Although your presence is always necessary to us and to the whole province of Reims, now because the usual troubles surrounding us have increased and swell up, we beg with all urgency that you do not delay returning to us.[2] For in your absence your enemies and ours take horns unto themselves[3] to such a degree that there is no peace for

1167, *J. S. Epp.* ii. 388–95, see esp. pp. 394–5) refers to a peaceful conclusion to the rebellion. On the uprising, see *J. S. Epp.* ii. 384, n. 1, and Falkenstein, 'Alexandre III et Henri de France', pp. 124–8, 151 and n. 164. While John of Salisbury clearly indicates the involvement of the clergy in the rising (*J. S. Epp. ii.* 384–5), Falkenstein distinguishes between the two disputes and their causes (but shows from independent evidence that the capitular dispute did coincide with the rising). On the present letter, see also *RHF* xvi. 184. This letter cannot refer to the troubles of *c.*1172 (see letter no. 84, n. 1), which were not directed against the archbishop, and the situation described also seems different from that revealed in letter no. 132 (probably 1171/2), which seems to refer to the dispute between the archbishop and Count Henry the Liberal of Troyes, and which in any case does not indicate the level of crisis suggested in the present letter. (On Archbishop Henry, see letter no. 21, n. 1.)

[2] It is not certain where Archbishop Henry was when this letter was written, but it is likely that he had not withdrawn far. There is no evidence that he had gone to Rome as suggested in *RHF* xvi. 710–11, which tries to link this letter with letters 110–a letter written in time of peace!—and 181. This reasoning is followed by others (including Varin, *Arch. admin.* i. 347), but dismissed by Falkenstein, 'Alexandre III et Henri de Reims', p. 126, n. 77.

[3] Cf. Amos 6: 14.

egredienti.[4] Indifferenter ingrediuntur rapere, uastare et deuorare omnia in quibus manus inicere possunt. Monacho, clerico, laico, pauperi, uidue, nullique conditionis miserie parcunt. Placeat igitur, pater amantissime, sollicitudini uestre inclinare animam necessitatibus et angustiis terre uestre que clamant ad uos et post uos.

94

To Archbishop Philip of Cologne[1]

Sept. 1167 × 1181 (poss. before July 1177)

Domino suo et patri karissimo Philippo Coloniensi archiepiscopo frater Petrus humilis abbas Sancti Remigii, salutem cum omni deuotione.

Frequenter cum beato Remigio patrono nostro uestre sublimitati humiles porreximus preces, si quo modo animum sine culpa nostra ut credimus hactenus implacatum nobis ad misericordiam faciendam flectere possemus. Denique iterum atque iterum, quanta humilitatis supplicatione potest, tota congregatio nostra appellat, si qua sunt in uobis 'uiscera misericordie'[2] ne adhuc extenta in flagello nostro perseueret manus uestra. De clementia namque Dei indultum est ut potestatem habeatis et bene facere et male nobis si uultis. Nolite obliuisci quia limites quos Dominus dominationi uestre posuit certi et finiti sunt in predestinatione Dei. Vtimini ergo potestate uobis concessa semper ad bonum, nunquam ad malum, nam indubitanter utriusque sequitur retributio eterna. Pro Iesu itaque amore et per Christum Iesum contestamur uos quatinus misereamini pauperum compeditorum quibus nec ingredi nec egredi licet nisi sub manu et cum licentia pastoris.[3] Boues sunt triturantes,[4] nocte et die pro peccatis suis et totius mundi Dominum deprecantes. Ne obturetis ora eorum subtrahendo alimoniam a predecessoribus fideliter pro

94 *Sirmond I. 13*]

---

[4] Cf. Deut. 28: 6.

94 [1] Archbishop Philip of Cologne, 1167, after 21 Sept.–13 Aug. 1191, previously dean of Cologne, 1156–67, and provost and archdeacon of Liège, 1165–67 (*SEECO* v. 1, pp. 38–

anyone coming in or going out.[4] They come in indiscriminately to plunder, lay waste, and devour everything which they can lay their hands on. Monk, clerk, layman, pauper, widow, they spare none, however wretched their condition. Therefore, most loving father, may it please your solicitude to incline your mind to the urgent needs and perils of your land, which cry out to you and after you.

94

To Archbishop Philip of Cologne[1]

Sept. 1167 × 1181 (poss. before July 1177)

To his dearest lord and father Philip, archbishop of Cologne, brother Peter, humble abbot of Saint-Remi, greetings with all devotion.

Frequently have we with our patron the blessed Remigius stretched out humble prayers to your sublimity in the hope that we might be able by some means to incline to mercy the mind thus far implacable towards us through no fault of our own, so we believe. In short our whole community calls upon you again and again, with as great a supplication of humility as possible, in the hope that there are in you some 'bowels of mercy'[2] so that your hand, up to now stretched out to lash us, should not persevere. For the power has been granted to you from the clemency of God to do both good and evil to us if you wish. Do not forget that the limits which the Lord has set to your dominion are fixed and defined in the predestination of God. Therefore use the power conceded to you always for good, never for evil, for without doubt eternal repayment follows for either. And so for the love of Jesus and through Christ Jesus we adjure you to take pity on the poor men who are shackled, who are permitted neither to enter nor to depart except under the hand and with the permission of the pastor.[3] They are the oxen treading out the corn,[4] supplicating the Lord night and day for their sins and for those of the whole world. Do not stop up their mouths by pulling away from under them the food bestowed on them faithfully by your predecessors for the remission of their

40). On the Meerssen dispute and the date of this letter, see appendix 10 (see also letters 79 and 86).

[2] Luke 1: 78; Col. 3: 12.

[3] i.e. monks.

[4] Cf. 1 Cor. 9: 9; 1 Tim. 5: 18; Deut. 25: 4.

remissione peccatorum suorum eis concessam.[a] [5] Certe non erit fame et glorie uestre augmentum nec cumulus diuitiarum nisi tantummodo peccatorum. Respondemus itaque pro prebendis de Marna, de quibus mandastis ut de manu nostra eximendo quibuslibet personis eas daremus, quod nullatenus in seculum seculi id facturi sumus. Prouoluti etiam genibus uestris,[6] ne id ulterius a nobis exigatis exoramus. Valete.

95

To Archbishop Eskil of Lund[1]

late 1167 × Oct. 1173, or autumn 1176 × spring 1177

Domino suo et amico karissimo Eskilo Lundensi archiepiscopo frater Petrus humilis abbas Sancti Remigii, salutem et deuotionis obsequium.

Suauissimus odor miserationum uestrarum non solum presentes recreat afflatu delectabili, sed etiam absentes et remotos attrahit ad se, spe nimirum tam dulci quam inconfusibili. Quis enim uestra expetiuit suffragia et inconsolatus recessit? Quis ad ostium uestrum pulsauit et non aperuistis ei?[2] Quis de manu uestra benedictionem petens, tanquam de thesauris opulentissimis copiosam non retulit? Inter ceteros itaque et de ceteris unus est T. presentium lator quem tot pericula itineris, tot difficultates ad uos perueniendi non exterruerunt nec retinuerunt, compellente et instigante illum tantum laborem insumere fama que de uobis ubique terrarum diffunditur.[3] Non equidem rerum inopia, non abiectio et uilitas inter suos, euomuit illum in terram uestram, cum et canonicus Sancti Timothei sit et frater Hilduini uicedomini et canonici Sancte Marie Remensis.[4] Rogamus igitur ne frustretur spe sua, ne quando apud se penitens

[a] *sic PL;* concessa *Sirmond*

95 *Sirmond V.5*]

[5] This may be a reference to the involvement of Arnold II of Cologne in the 1152 settlement at Meerssen (see appendix 10 and n. 15). The principal evidence for the settlement comes from the imperial *acta* and subsequent papal confirmations, but the combination of this reference with that in Wibald of Stavelot's letter to Arnold may suggest Arnold's direct involvement. The image picks up the references to 1 Cor., 1 Tim, and Deut. above, and is closest to 1 Cor. 9: 9, '. . . non alligabis os boui trituranti . . .'.

[6] Lit. 'knees', implying supplication.

sins.[5] Certainly there will be no increase of your reputation and glory nor an accumulation of riches but only of sins. And so regarding the prebends of Meerssen, in respect of which you ordered that, delivering them out of our own hands, we should give them to any persons you will, we respond that we shall in no wise do so, now or ever. We entreat you also, prostrate at your feet,[6] that you demand this of us no more. Farewell.

95

To Archbishop Eskil of Lund[1]

late 1167 × Oct. 1173, or autumn 1176 × spring 1177

To his dearest lord and friend Eskil, archbishop of Lund, brother Peter, humble abbot of Saint-Remi, greetings and devoted service.

The sweetest odour of your mercies not only revives those who are present with a delightful breath but even draws unto itself those who are absent and far away, with a hope which is certainly as agreeable as it is pure. For who has sought out your support and come away unconsoled? Who has knocked at your door and you have not opened to him?[2] Who, seeking a blessing from your hand, did not carry away an abundant one as if from the richest treasure chests? And so among the others and one of the others is T., the bearer of this letter, whom the many dangers of the journey and the many difficulties in reaching you neither frightened off nor held back, driven forward and urged on to undertake such a labour by your reputation which is spread about in every land.[3] It was not want of material goods nor rejection and contempt among his own people which drove him out to your land, since he is both a canon of Saint-Timothée and the brother of Hilduin, a *vicedominus* and canon of Sainte-Marie-de-Reims.[4] We ask therefore that he not be frustrated in his hope lest some day

95 [1] The dates are those periods when Peter's abbacy of Saint-Remi coincided with Eskil's presence in Denmark (on Eskil, see letter no. 12, n. 1, and appendix 5).

[2] Cf. Matt. 7: 7, 8; Luke 11: 9–10; cf. also Luke 12: 36.

[3] Cf. 2 Macc. 8: 7.

[4] T. is otherwise unidentified; his brother Hilduin is presumably a canon of the cathedral (Notre-Dame de Reims; for a similar styling, see letter no. 115 and n. 15); for *uicedominus* there is no exact English term (French 'vidâme'; see Niermeyer, *vicedominus* 2,3; Latham, *vice/-dominus*: '*vidâme*, deputy'). Cf. Prache, *Saint-Remi*, p. 36.

et dolore cordis intrinsecus tactus[5] dicat, 'Periit opera et impensa.' Ego cum toto conuentu beati Remigii uester sum,[6] et pro uobis orationem fundimus ad Deum ut sanctissima anima uestra thesauros quos in celo posuit per manus pauperum in exitu suo reperiat, et bonis domus Dei repleta cum sanctis angelis eterna letitia congaudeat. Valete.

96

To Archbishop Eskil of Lund[1]

after Sept. 1171, or 1172 × 1173, before Oct.

Lundensi archiepiscopo.

Eternas et antiquas uenas misericordiarum et benedictionum suarum, profusa in omni largitate diuina gratia his temporibus, licet caritas multorum refrigescat,[2] nondum exclusit. Quamuis enim reconditos et latentes[a] sinus gratie in mentibus multorum fidelium Deus in ecclesia sua adhuc retineat, uos precipue tanquam lucernam super candelabrum positam[3] oleo multiplici perfudit, unde multe areole ecclesiarum, episcoporum, pauperum, uiduarum tam suauiter quam habundanter irrigantur. A multis siquidem retro temporibus non in uacuum siue gratiam siue pecuniam Dei excepistis ligando illam in sudario[4] uel intra[b] domesticos parietes[5] recludendo. Quis enim ad uos accedens uestram non sensit benedictionem? Quis quantumlibet tepens, audiens uel uidens conuersationem uestram, manum egenis expositam, ostium uiatoribus patens, iudicium et iustitiam equa lance causam non personam discernens,[6] omnemque

96 *Sirmond VI. 15*]
[a] *corr. Winterbottom;* labentes *Sirmond* [b] infra *Sirmond*

[5] Cf. Gen. 6: 6.
[6] He was a *confrater* of Saint-Remi and is included in the list in MS Reims BM 346, fo. 188[v] (see Introduction, p. xxvii), and part of which is edited in *DD* i.2, pp. 277–8, no. 149. What follows echoes Matt. 19: 21

96 [1] A recommendation of Fulk, missionary bishop of Estonia (see letter no. 76, n. 1, and appendix 9). The mission to Estonia and Finland was funded by Eskil of Lund and supported by Peter (*DD* i. 3, pp. 31–2). After some delay (see letter no. 181) Fulk is now finally making the journey north, in all likelihood bearing this letter. The present letter probably post-dates the papal letters of 7 × 17 Sept. 1171 or 1172, addressed to leading figures in Scandinavia and including a recommendation of Fulk, which he most probably

regretting within himself and touched inwardly with sorrow of heart,[5] he even says, 'The labour and the expense has come to nothing.' I am yours, along with the whole community of the blessed Remigius,[6] and we pour forth a prayer to God for you that your holiest soul may find again at its going out the treasures which it has laid up in heaven through the hands of the poor, and that, replenished with the good things of the house of God, it may rejoice with the holy angels in eternal delight. Farewell.

96

To Archbishop Eskil of Lund[1]

after Sept. 1171, or 1172 × 1173, before Oct.

To the archbishop of Lund.

Although the love of many grows cold,[2] the divine grace which is poured forth with all generosity in these times has not yet shut off the eternal and ancient veins of its mercies and blessings. For while God in His Church still preserves the secret and hidden folds of grace in the minds of the many faithful, He has filled you in particular with a far greater measure of unction, like a lamp set up on a lamp-stand,[3] whereby the many gardens of churches, of bishops, of the poor, and of widows are watered as sweetly as they are abundantly. Indeed for a very long time now you have received the grace and the riches of God without vainly binding it in a napkin[4] or hiding it in the wall of the house.[5] For who approaching you has not known your blessing? Who, however lukewarm, on hearing of or seeing your manner of life, your hand held open to the poor, your door open to travellers, your judgement and justice distinguishing the cause[6] and not the person

would also have carried with him (see appendix 9). It is unlikely to have been written later than Oct. 1173, by which time Eskil was in France, where he stayed until autumn 1176 (on Eskil of Lund, see letter no. 12, n. 1, and appendix 5). On the heading, see letter no. 84, n. 1.

[2] Cf. Matt. 24: 12.

[3] Cf. Num. 8: 3; cf. also Matt. 5: 15; Mark 4: 21; Luke 8: 16; 11: 33. Douai-Reims has 'candlestick', but Peter is clearly thinking of an oil-lamp (however, he goes on to mix his metaphor with one of water).

[4] Cf. Luke 19: 20.

[5] Cf. Sulpicius Severus, *Vita S. Martini*, preface (Sources Chrétiennes 133, p. 249; *PL* xx. 159).

[6] Cf. Ps. 42 (43): 1.

reliquam actionum et sermonum uestrorum regionem perlustrans, non calefactus, non melioratus, non bene instructus abiit? Deo gratias qui iuxta consuetudinem suam 'gratiam pro gratia'[7] superhabundare facit in uobis ut 'melior sit finis orationis quam principium'[8] et ut 'exitus matutini et uespere' delectabiles[9] fiant. Adhuc enim stillant manus uestre aromata[10] Dei que de thuribulis sanctorum per manus angelorum in incensum suauitatis naribus sedentis super thronum gratie referantur quatinus in eterna tabernacula uos recipiant[11] qui, de bonitate et beneficiis uestris in terris sustentati, per gratiarum actionem in celo iam sunt recepti uel adhuc recipiendi. Pauper iste episcopus dominus Fulco[12] quem per euangelium in Christo ego genui monachum et uos episcopum, de magnificentissima liberalitate uestra Deo gratias nobiscum refert exponens quod sustentamentum uite et peregrinationis sue uos habet et semper habiturum confidit. Scitis, domine pater, quam duram prouinciam[13] sortitus sit et quod animam suam in manibus suis posuerit potius mortem semper expectans quam longam uitam. Scitis etiam quia qui prophetam in nomine prophete recipit mercedem prophete recipiet.[b] [14] Vnde remittimus eum ad uos et commendamus eum Deo et uobis. Retinuimus eum siquidem malo tempore, remittimus autem bono et congruo ut uisitet messem utrum matura sit ad metendum an immatura ad laborandum. Manum siquidem misit ad aratrum,[15] ope uestra et opere, ad Christianitatem dilatandam et horrea Dei fertiliori segete implenda. Vestrum enim, uestrum est quicquid incrementi prouenerit ex labore ipsius quia et de uestro uiuit tanquam operarius Dei et uester, et ad gloriam uestram respicit atque coronam quodcunque Christo adquirere potuerit. Non igitur obturandum est 'os boui trituranti',[16] neque palea subtrahenda.[17]

[b] recipit *Sirmond*

[7] John 1: 16; and cf. Rom. 5: 20; Eph. 1: 7–8; 1 Tim. 1: 14.
[8] Cf. Eccles. 7: 9.
[9] Cf. Ps. 64 (65): 9.
[10] Cf. S. of S. 5: 5.
[11] Cf. Rev. 4: 9; 5: 1; Heb. 4: 16; and Luke 16: 9.
[12] See n. 1 above and appendix 9.

with an even scale, and who surveying all the remaining extent of your deeds and words, has not gone away warmed, improved, and well-instructed? Thanks be to God who according to his custom causes 'grace' to abound exceedingly 'for grace'[7] in you so that 'better is the end of a speech than the beginning'[8] and so that 'the outgoings of the morning and of the evening' are made delightful.[9] For your hands still drip the aromatic spices[10] of God which are borne back from the censers of the saints through the hands of the angels as incense of sweetness for the nostrils of the One sitting on the throne of grace so that those who, sustained by your goodness and favours on earth, have already by act of grace been received or are still to be received in heaven, may receive you into everlasting dwellings.[11] This poor bishop the lord Fulk[12] whom I begot as a monk in Christ through the Gospel and you begot as a bishop returns thanks to God with us for your most magnificent generosity explaining that he has you as the support of his life and his pilgrimage and that he trusts he will always have you thus. You know, lord father, how harsh a province[13] he has been assigned and that he has put his life in his hands always expecting death rather than a long life. You know also that he that receives a prophet in the name of a prophet shall receive the reward of a prophet.[14] Hence we are sending him back to you, and we commend him to God and to you. We have kept him back at a bad time indeed, but we are sending him back at a good and suitable time, that he may inspect the harvest, whether it be ripe for reaping or unripe and for working. He has indeed put his hand to the plough,[15] with your help and support, to extend the bounds of Christianity and fill the granaries of God with a more fertile crop. For whatever increase shall come forth from his labour is yours, yours indeed both because he lives from your resources like a worker for God and for you and because whatever he may be able to acquire for Christ concerns your glory and crown. Therefore 'the mouth of the ox that treadeth out the corn'[16] should not be stopped up, nor his straw taken from him.[17]

[13] Cf. Terence, *Phormio*, i. 2.72–3 (22–3); on what follows, cf. Judg. 12: 3; 1 Kgs. (1 Sam.) 19: 5; 28: 21; Job 13: 14; Ps. 118 (119): 109.

[14] Cf. Matt. 10: 41.

[15] Cf. Luke 9: 62.

[16] 1 Cor. 9: 9; 1 Tim. 5: 18; and cf. Deut. 25: 4.

[17] Possibly an echo of oxen eating straw in Isa. 11: 7; 65: 25.

97

To Archbishop Eskil of Lund[1]

1176, poss. autumn or later

E⟨skilo⟩ Londensi archiepiscopo.

Vacillans fluctuatione inter spem et deliberationem, ultra se intra metas patientie non potuit continere uerus amicitie affectus. Suadebat spes cotidie diligentissimum et dilectissimum dominum et amicum statum suum renuntiaturum. Vrgebat deliberatio nil immorandum ad querendam certitudinem de incertitudine aduersi casus qui dicebatur oppressisse tantum dominum. In his itaque procellis usque ad lassitudinem animo laborante et diutius pensante quid inde potius esset eligendum, communicato consilio cum dilecto filio uestro abbate Sanctorum Crispini et Crispiniani,[2] festinaui mittere ad uos nuntium nostrum ut sciremus quomodo temptauerit uos et probauerit Dominus tam in mari quam in terra. Nam parumper laxauit frena leonis rugientis[3] que tenet in manu sua, sed nec rupit nec soluit. Siquidem si Deus soluisset aut diabolus rupisset, aqua nimia uos absorbuisset. Ad torporem itaque, si quis in uobis aut in uestris erat, excitandum iuste passus est dare fremitum; ad ostendendum erga uos filialem affectum, pie reclusit ora leonum[4] et maris ferocem tumultum. Non dormiuit Dei iustitia, nec se elongauit diuina clementia. Impugnari ⟨uos⟩[a] uoluit diabolus, sed sola peccata purgauit Dominus; fidem puram, deuotionem sanctissimam obfuscare uoluit princeps tenebrarum, sed 'Deus' qui 'lux est, et tenebre in eo non sunt ulle',[5] de camino clariorem extraxit et aurum suum pretiosius reddidit.[6] Si superest dilectus noster Crispinus, attentissime illum uobis commendamus, et filium Iohannis Burgensis nostri et omnes quos uobiscum duxistis.[7]

97 *Sirmond VII. 6*]
[a] *suppl. Ritchie*

97 [1] The letter refers to the translation of William aux Blanches Mains to the see of Reims (el. 13 Nov. 1175 × 25 Mar. 1176, probably occupied the see 25 Apr. x 8 Aug. 1176, and certainly enthroned by 16 Sept. 1176, see letter no. 4, n. 4 and letter no. 102, n. 1) and to the promotion of John of Salisbury to Chartres (notified of el. 22 July 1176, consecrated 8 Aug.: see letter no. 102, n. 1). The main theme is a shipwreck involving Eskil as well as a Crispin and a John '*Burgensis*' (see below and n. 7). Eskil travelled from France to Denmark in autumn 1176 (see appendix 5), so both pieces of news seem a little old, and

97

To Archbishop Eskil of Lund[1]

1176, poss. autumn or later

To Eskil, archbishop of Lund.

Wavering unsteadily between hope and deliberation, the true affection of friendship could contain itself no longer within the bounds of patience. Hope was daily persuading me that the most loving and beloved lord and friend was about to send word of his state. Deliberation was urging that I make no delay in seeking certainty about the uncertainty surrounding the calamity which was said to have crushed so great a lord. With my mind then toiling in these storms to the point of exhaustion, and weighing up for a long time which of these courses I should rather choose, having taken the advice of your beloved son the abbot of Saint-Crépin,[2] I hastened to send our messenger to you so that we might know how the Lord has tested and proved you both at sea and on land. For He loosed for a short while the reins of the roaring lion[3] which He holds in His hand, but He neither broke nor untied them. For if God had untied them or the devil had broken them, a mighty flood would have engulfed you. And so to stir up the torpor, if there was any in you or in yours, He justly permitted it to roar; to demonstrate towards you the affection due to a son He mercifully closed again the mouths of the lions[4] and the fierce tumult of the sea. The justice of God did not sleep, nor did divine mercy withdraw itself. The devil wanted you to be assailed, but the Lord purged sins alone; the prince of darkness wanted to darken the pure faith and the most holy devotion, but 'God', who 'is light, and in Him there is no darkness,'[5] drew it out of the furnace the brighter and rendered His own gold more richly.[6] If our beloved Crispin survives, we commend him to you most assiduously, and also the son of our John

it is odd that Eskil would not know these things if he had been in France. This may suggest that the date of his journey may need revising (as also may our knowledge of Crispin's movements—see letter no. 98, n. 1). On the heading, see letter no. 84, n. 1.

[2] Berneredus; see letter no. 128, n. 1; he is mentioned again at the end of the letter.

[3] The devil; cf. 1 Pet. 5: 8.

[4] Cf. Dan. 6: 22; Heb. 11: 33.

[5] 1 John 1: 5.

[6] Possibly alluding to Prov. 17: 3 or Eclus. 2:5.

Dilectissimus uester abbas Sanctorum Crispini et Crispiniani salutat uos. De his que apud nos fiunt suggero domino meo quia satis prospera sunt. Senonensis archiepiscopus factus est Remensis; magister Iohannes Saresberiensis, quondam clericus noster, factus est episcopus Carnotensis. Conuentus noster semper orat pro uobis. Iohannes Burgensis multum salutat uos.

98

To Archbishop Eskil of Lund[1]

late 1176 × spring 1177, (prob. spring 1177)

Londensi archiepiscopo Petrus abbas Sancti Remigii.

Imago uestre dilectionis impressa et expressa 'stilo ferreo in ungue adamantino'[2] cordis nostri uiget et in eo uigere non cessabit. Radicem namque misit deorsum quam irrigare non cessat iugis et cotidiana recordatio benignitatis uestre ad amicum, ne dicam ad seruum uestrum. Totum enim me occupat gratia et amicitia, excluso et expulso timore tanquam mercenario. Inde est, pater reuerentissime, quod in oblatione primitiarum mearum Domino uiuo et uero, uestri quoque memoriam eius propitiationi pro posse cotidie represento. Rediit ad nos magister Crispinus marina potione non parum amaricatus,[3] uestro tamen beneficio aliquantulum recreatus. Inter cetera retulit nobis duram historiam naufragii uestri in qua elatione seuissima mare aduersum uos intumuit, uentus immoderatus nauem ferocissime repercussit, tempestas paulo minus absorbuit. Recordor Petrum in fluctibus ambulantem et uentum ualidum contra illum uenientem,[4] Paulum tertio naufragantem,[5] Ionam absorptum a bellua que tamen illum retinere non potuit.[6] Domine Iesu, ubi eras? Manum auxilii quare tunc subtrahebas nisi forte ut de

98 *Sirmond VII. 13*]

[7] Iohannis Burgensis is unidentified, possibly 'of Bourg', which could apply to a number of places: Bourg, Haute-Marne, nr. Langres, is the closest to Peter's normal sphere of contact and activity, and so a possibility ('of Bourges' would be 'Bituricensis'). Crispin and John's son were travelling with Eskil and suffered shipwreck together. Crispin survived and returned to tell the tale (see letter no. 98). It is unlikely that this is the same Crispin who is the subject of letters 89 and 90.

98 [1] Master Crispin, who had travelled north with Eskil and been involved in the shipwreck of autumn 1176 (see letter no. 97, n. 1 on possible problems with this dating),

Burgensis and all whom you led away with you.[7] Your dearest abbot of Saint-Crépin sends you greetings. As for matters here, I can advise my lord that they are favourable enough. The archbishop of Sens has been made archbishop of Reims; master John of Salisbury, once our clerk, has been made bishop of Chartres. Our community prays for you always. John *Burgensis* sends you many greetings.

98

To Archbishop Eskil of Lund[1]

late 1176 × spring 1177, (prob. spring 1177)

To the archbishop of Lund, Peter, abbot of Saint-Remi.

The image of your love, impressed and engraved 'with a pen of iron, with the point of a diamond,'[2] flourishes in our heart and will not cease to flourish in it. For it sent down a root which the continual and daily recollection of your kindness to your friend, not to say servant, waters without ceasing. For gratitude and friendship occupy me entirely having shut out and expelled fear like a mercenary. Hence it is, most reverend father, that in offering my first-fruits to the living and true Lord I am also presenting before His mercy every day as far as possible my remembrance of you. Master Crispin has returned to us much embittered by drinking sea water[3] yet somewhat restored by your blessing. Among other things, he reported to us the harsh tale of your shipwreck in which the sea rose up against you with a most violent swell, the unrestrained wind knocked the ship about most ferociously, and the storm all but devoured it. I recall Peter walking on the waves and the strong wind coming against him,[4] Paul shipwrecked for the third time,[5] and Jonah swallowed by the whale, which however could not retain him.[6] Lord Jesus, where were you? Why were you withholding the hand of aid at that moment, unless

has now returned. A spring rather than a winter return journey may be more likely, but in any case the present letter must have been written by spring 1177, before Eskil retired to Clairvaux (on Eskil of Lund, see letter no. 12, n. 1, and appendix 5).

[2] Jer. 17: 1, and *cordis* following echoes the same verse. What follows echoes 4 Kgs. (2 Kgs.) 19: 30.

[3] On the shipwreck, see also letter no. 97. The word play with *portionem/potionem* below is not translatable.

[4] Cf. Matt. 14: 29–30. [5] Cf. 2 Cor. 11: 25. [6] Cf. Jonah 2.

reliquiis calicis tui, quem cum in passione gustasses bibere noluisti, ministri tui et sequaces de eodem mixto portionem siue potionem que sibi contingebat ad recuperandam sanitatem immo hereditatem ⟨biberent⟩[a]?[7]

99

To Archbishop Eskil of Lund[1]

Spring 1177 × 1181 (poss. early)

Londensi archiepiscopo Petrus abbas Sancti Remigii.

De duobus oculis meis, alterum ad me retineo alterum frequenter ad uos, pater et domine karissime, retorqueo. Qui meus michi remanet, quid in me uidet? Certe plura quibus condolet, quibus illacrimatur, quibus usque ad nimiam suffusionem[2] turbatur, certe 'reptilia quorum non est numerus',[3] certe gentem illam nefariam quam Ezechiel uidit depictam in pariete domus quam iubente Domino effoderat,[4] ad ultimum quedam ineffabilia non profunditate misterii sed enormitate corrupti animi. Sed quando ista cernit oculus? Quando incuruatur ad suas feces reuoluendas, quando lucernam accendit et euertit domum querens dragmam perditam,[5] quando scissuras in muris Ierusalem et ruinas respicit[6] si forte cum Zorobabel et Esdra reparare licitum sit.[7] Occurrunt uestigia eruce, locuste, bruchi, rubiginis que deuorauerunt uniuersa 'speciosa deserti',[8] pilosi,[9] onocentauri,[10] ulule,[11] simie, et omnis generis phantasmatum grandis silua. Si quando autem idem oculus sursum palpebras erexerit

[a] *suppl. PL, om. Sirmond* (*text breaks off here*)

99 *Sirmond VII. 17*]

[7] Cf. Matt. 27: 34, but also Christ's prayer before the Passion, 'transeat a me calix iste' (Matt. 26: 39, cf. Mark 14: 35, Luke 22: 42 for variations): his followers by sharing in his sufferings and death gain salvation. *Hereditatem* meaning 'salvation' echoes many passages in the NT, e.g. Acts 20: 32; Gal. 3: 29; Heb. 1: 14 and many other refs.

99 [1] This and letter no. 100 were written to Eskil of Lund after his retirement to Clairvaux (spring 1177; on Eskil see letter no. 12, n. 1, and appendix 5). The address to Eskil as archbishop, contrasted with the 'quondam archiepiscopo' in letter no. 100, suggests that the present letter is the earlier of the two, and was probably written soon after his retirement. The *terminus ad quem* is the end of Peter's abbacy of Saint-Remi. Peter seems to suggest in this letter that his friendship with Eskil goes back to their youth.

perhaps so that from the dregs of your cup, which you were unwilling to drink when you had tasted it in the passion, your servants and followers ⟨might drink⟩ the portion or potion of the same mixture which fell to them for the restoration of health, nay of inheritance?[7]

99

To Archbishop Eskil of Lund[1]

Spring 1177 × 1181 (poss. early)

To the archbishop of Lund, Peter, abbot of Saint-Remi.

Of my two eyes, one I keep on myself, the other I turn back frequently on you, dearest father and lord. That which remains on me, what does it see in me? Certainly many things for which it suffers greatly, for which it weeps, for which it is distressed even to the point of extreme soreness,[2] certainly 'creeping things without number,'[3] certainly that nefarious people whom Ezekiel saw painted on the wall of the house which at the Lord's command he had dug out,[4] and finally certain things unutterable not on account of the profundity of the mystery but of the wickedness of the corrupt soul. But when does the eye perceive these things? When it is bent on picking over its dregs, when it lights a candle and turns out the house seeking the lost groat,[5] when it looks upon the breaches and the ruins in the walls of Jerusalem[6] in case by chance it may, with Zorobabel and Ezra, be permitted to restore them.[7] There appear traces of the palmer-worm, the locust, the bruchus, and the mildew which have devoured all of 'the beautiful places of the wilderness,'[8] and of the satyr,[9] the ass-centaur,[10] the screech-owl,[11] and the ape, and a great throng of every kind of phantom. But if ever the same eye raises its brows upwards

[2] *suffusio (oculorum)*, often cataracts etc., but also redness in e.g. Prov. 23: 29, in which sense, although in a different context, it is used here.

[3] Ps. 103 (104): 25.

[4] Cf. Ezek. 8: 8–10 (also another ref. to *reptilia*).

[5] Cf. Luke 15: 8–9 (cf. letter no. 24, n. 4).

[6] Cf. Isa. 22: 9–10.

[7] Cf. the restoration of Jerusalem after the Babylonian captivity, as described in 1 Esd. (Ezra) and 2 Esd. (Neh.).

[8] Cf. Joel 1:4, 19–20; 2: 25.

[9] Cf. Isa. 13: 21; 34: 14 (Douai-Reims trans. 'hairy ones').

[10] Cf. Isa. 34: 14 (Douai-Reims trans. 'monsters').

[11] Isa. 13: 22 (Douai-Reims trans. 'owls').

et celum aspexerit, uidet 'Dominum innixum scalc'[12] uocantem et expectantem male soporatum, et dicentem, 'Surge qui dormis et exurge a mortuis',[13] et 'Lazare ueni foras',[14] et 'Adolescens tibi dico surge',[15] et 'Puella surge'.[16] Porrigit quoque manum Petro naufraganti,[17] occurrit in uia Saulo spiranti minas et cedes in discipulos Domini;[18] prodigo filio reuertenti, stolam, anulum et calceamenta restituit, conuiuium et uitulum immolat;[19] et misericordiarum suarum siluam condensam[20] fugientibus et ereptis de laqueis ferreis[21] ad sese refouendos[a] offert. Huiusmodi collyrio releuatur turbatus de se ipso ad se ipsum oculus. Iam illum conuenio oculum qui de uobis amicabiliter sollicitus lustrat[22] uias uestras[b] et studia ab adolescentia. Dic michi, bone ocule, de amico nostro quod occurrit, quod sentis, quod intelligis. 'Non sine multa fatigatione', inquit, 'gesta eius recolo quia aliquando uidi illum supra nubes ambulantem et usque in densissimam altitudinem euolantem. Quis gloriam illam, quis potestatem, quis dominationem, quis rerum omnium opulentiam, quis erogationes et donationes tam largas, tam innumeras enarrare sufficiat? Quis enauigationes, quis marina pericula, quis insidias magnorum latronum dicat? Tandem Lucifer ille qui mane oriebatur, qui inter astra Dei solium glorie et archiepiscopatus tenuerat, non sicut fulgur de celo cecidit[23] sed sicut Filius hominis "semet ipsum exinaniuit, formam" pauperis assumpsit,[24] principis mundi exuuias reiecit,[25] ut si Laban Iacob insecutus fuerit, ydola sua apud illum non inueniat, et cum Domino, saltem cum beato Martino, dicat, "Nichil in me reperies, inimice."[26] Ecce sic humiliatus in Claraualle "spicas" recolligit "post terga metentium",[27] non glorians de labore sed se humilians de impossibilitate. Voluntate quidem currit et caritate cum prioribus et iuuenibus, sed etate et infirmitate sortem habet cum nouissimis ut sit nouissimus uocatione, primus remuneratione,[28] quia apud patrem familias, cuius uniuerse uie misericordia et ueritas, non

[a] refouendum *Sirmond* [b] nostras *Sirmond*

[12] Gen. 28: 13 (Jacob of course was not 'wrongly' sleeping—see the ref. to Eph. below for this; cf. also Smaragdus, *Comm. in Reg. S. Ben.* (*PL* cii. 703)).

[13] Eph. 5: 14. [14] John 11: 43.

[15] Luke 7: 14. [16] Luke 8: 54, cf. Mark 5: 41, cf. also Acts 9: 40.

[17] Possibly alluding to Matt. 14: 29–31, but recalling Eskil's shipwreck (see letter no. 97); or to Christ calming the storm, Matt. 8: 18 etc., but not a shipwreck.

[18] Cf. Acts 9: 1, 3. [19] Cf. Luke 15: 27, 30. [20] Cf. Ps. 28 (29): 9.

[21] Cf. Ps. 24 (25): 15 (what follows poss. alluding to Rev. 3: 18).

[22] 'surveys', cf. e.g. Eccles. 7: 26. In what follows the eye is speaking.

[23] Cf. Isa. 14: 12–15; Luke 10: 18 (with a poss. allusion to 1 Kgs. (1 Sam.) 2: 8).

[24] Cf. Phil. 2: 7.

and looks at the sky it sees 'the Lord leaning upon the ladder,'[12] calling and waiting for the one wrongly sleeping, and saying, 'Rise thou that sleepest and arise from the dead,'[13] and 'Lazarus come forth,'[14] and 'Young man, I say to thee, arise,'[15] and 'Maid, arise.'[16] He also reaches out His hand to Peter shipwrecked;[17] He appeared on the road to Saul who was breathing out threats and slaughter against the disciples of the Lord;[18] to the prodigal son returning He restored the robe, the ring, and the shoes, and He offers up a banquet and the calf,[19] and He offers the thick wood[20] of His mercies to those fleeing and snatched out of iron snares,[21] that they might revive themselves. With an eye-salve of this sort the eye which is distressed about itself is restored to itself. Now I meet that eye which, being concerned about you in a friendly way, surveys[22] your paths and your occupations since the time of your youth. Tell me, good eye, about our friend, what is happening, what you perceive, what you understand. 'I cannot', it says, 'recall his deeds without great exhaustion because once I saw him walking above the clouds and flying even unto the most impenetrable height. Who would be adequate to tell of his glory, his power, his dominion, his wealth in all things, his alms-giving and his gifts so bountiful and so innumerable? Who could speak of his voyages, the dangers at sea, the ambushes of mighty robbers? In the end that Lucifer who rose in the morning, who had held the throne of glory and of the archiepiscopate among the stars of God, did not fall like lightning from heaven[23] but like the Son of man "emptied himself," took on the form of a poor man,[24] rejected the spoils of the prince of the world,[25] so that if Laban should follow Jacob he will not find his idols with him and Jacob may say with the Lord, or at least with the blessed Martin, "You will find nothing on me, enemy."[26] See how in humility at Clairvaux he gleans again "the ears of corn after the reapers,"[27] not boasting of his labour but humbling himself in the impossible task. In will and charity he runs with the first and the youthful but in age and infirmity has his lot with the last so that he is the last to be called but the first in his reward,[28] because with the head of the house, all of whose ways are mercy and

[25] Cf. John 12: 31; 14: 30; 16: 11, i.e. Eskil was glorious in his episcopate, like Lucifer when he was the greatest of the angels, but turned out not to fall in the end, going to Clairvaux and not to hell, and so being more like Christ than the devil.

[26] Jacob fleeing Laban did not know that Rachel had stolen Laban's idols (cf. Gen. 31: 17–35); cf. Sulpicius Severus, *Ep.* iii. 16 (Sources Chrétiennes 133, p. 342; *PL* xx. 183): 'nihil in me, funeste, reperies.'

[27] Cf. Ruth 2: 3.

[28] Cf. Matt. 19: 30; 20: 16; Mark 10: 31; Luke 13: 30.

est potior remuneratione qui prior tempore, sed prior denarii acceptione qui posterior labore et tempore.[29] Annon ita est? Plane hoc probat Veritas qui prius latronem de cruce transtulit in paradisum quam principem apostolorum Petrum, cui tamen dederat claues regni celorum.[30] Pietatis est parum de meritis presumentem suscipere, securum uero, si necesse sit, differre, et citius trepidantem a timore excutere quam iam subarratum admittere.' Ecce, pater amantissime, ut credo, non me fefellit oculus meus. Hec enim eadem preter illum multi alii de te michi dixerunt. Sit itaque pax cum spiritu tuo, sit anima tua cum Deo meo.[31] Sit 'melior finis orationis quam principium'[32] quia omnis laus in fine canitur. Totus sum uester.

100

To Archbishop Eskil of Lund[1]

Spring 1177 × 1181

Eskilo Londensi quondam archiepiscopo Petrus abbas Sancti Remigii.

Frequens corporis molestia hortatur cogitare de patria ubi nulla est tristitia. Quanto enim ista infelicior quam patimur tanto illa felicior quam speramus. Vtinam iam littus eius attingeremus! Vtinam fluctus istius euaderemus! Circumferimur, periclitamur, naufragia experimur, et exire dissimulamus. Quis non optat portum ne incurrat naufragium? Quis non precidit herentis in salo nauicule funem ne sentiat tempestatem? Quis negligit patriam et amat exilium? Quis fugit Patrem et sequitur hostem? Gaudeo quia iam tenetis portum et sedetis ad portam sancte ciuitatis cuius participatio in id ipsum.[2] Vacillat quidem adhuc nauicula nostra sed spero et expecto solatium uestrum, cuius per integram amicitiam possideo totum animum. 'Adiuro uos, si inueneritis dilectum', immo si ueneritis ad eius

100 *Sirmond VIII. 1*]

[29] Cf. Matt. 20: 1–16.

[30] Cf. Luke 23: 43 (the thief on the cross); Matt. 16: 19 (the keys of heaven); Truth is Christ here, hence *qui*.

[31] *meo* reads oddly; it is either wrong or an allusion to Isa. 61: 10.

[32] Cf. Eccles. 7: 9. What follows may be a liturgical allusion (cf. also letter no. 114 and n. 2).

truth, he is not preferred in payment who is first in time, but he is first to receive the penny who is last in labour and time.[29] Is this not so? Truth proves this clearly, who sent the thief on the cross up to paradise before Peter the first of the apostles, to whom however He had given the keys of the kingdom of heaven.[30] It is righteousness to raise up one presuming little in his own merits but to put off if necessary one confident in them, and more promptly to shake out of his fear one trembling than to admit one already guaranteed.' See, most loving father, my eye has not, I believe, deceived me. For many others besides it have told me these same things about you. And so may peace be with your spirit and may your soul be with my God.[31] Let 'the end of the speech be better than the beginning,'[32] because all praise is sung at the end. I am wholly yours.

100

To Archbishop Eskil of Lund[1]

Spring 1177 × 1181

To Eskil of Lund, one-time archbishop, Peter, abbot of Saint-Remi.

Frequent physical affliction urges one to contemplate the homeland where there is no sadness. For the more unfortunate is this which we suffer, so much the happier is that which we hope for. If only we were already approaching its shore! If only we were escaping the turbulence of this one! We are being tossed about, we are imperilled, we are suffering shipwrecks, and we dissemble our departure. Who does not long for the port lest he suffer shipwreck? Who does not cut free the rope of the little boat anchored in the sea lest he endure the storm? Who is indifferent to his homeland and loves exile? Who flees from the Father and follows the enemy? I rejoice because you have now reached port and are sitting at the gate of the holy city which is at unity in itself.[2] Our little boat is indeed still tossing about but I am hoping for and awaiting solace from you whose whole soul I possess by virtue of a perfect friendship. 'I adjure you, if you find the beloved', nay if you come to his chamber, 'that

100 [1] After Eskil's retirement, and dated as letter no. 99 above. On the actual shipwreck, see letters 97 and 98.

[2] Cf. Ps. 121 (122): 3.

cubiculum, '⟨ut⟩ nuntietis ei quia amore langueo.'[3] Credite michi, si uenirem ad porticum Salomonis,[4] ne dicam ad sanctuarium Saluatoris, loquerer pro amico, postularem pro domino meo, pronuntiarem in auribus Domini Sabaoth[5] et que michi et que per me pauperibus fecistis. Appellarem pium, compellarem iustum, dicens: '"Memor esto uerbi tui seruo tuo",[6] est enim uerbum tuum: quod uni ex minimis meis fecistis, michi fecistis.[7] Ecce substantia domini mei Londensis quondam archiepiscopi nunc pauperis Clareuallensis per manus pauperum tuorum apud te est. Repende ergo ei uicem et da ei substantiam tuam qui tibi dedit suam, tamen quam tu dederas, quam a te acceperat.' Amantissime pater, non dormit neque dormitat in recordatione uestra cor meum.[8] Clamat, pulsat, statque ad fores uestras,[a] 'Quando', inquiens, 'uidebo quem desiderat anima mea, quando ueniam et uidebo illum?'[9] Via longa est, pedes uix mouentur, renes congelantur, et quomodo longe positus amicus uidebitur? Querendum est ergo remedium ubi primum deest solatium. Pergere nequeo, scribere saltem ualeo. Cernere non potest oculus, alloquatur stilus. Currat in membranis littera quia in membris suis retardatur corporalis presentia. Referat carta quod non potest lingua. Suppleat imago mortua quod non ualet uiua et uera. Syllabe fortunam nostram nuntient quia eloquia oris nequeunt. Desidero uos uidere.[10] Pax Christi et gratia Dei uobiscum semper. Saluto capellanos et priorem, dominum Gaucherium et dominum Autissiodorensem episcopum, et Philippum et omnes amicos nostros.[11] Valete.

[a] nostras *Sirmond*

[3] Cf. S. of S. 5: 8.
[4] Cf. John 10: 23; Acts 3: 11; 5: 12.
[5] Cf. Jer. 11: 20; Rom. 9: 29; Jas. 5: 4.
[6] Ps. 118 (119): 49.
[7] Cf. Matt. 25: 40.
[8] Cf. Ps 120 (121): 4; refs. to *substantia*, above, may be alluisons to Ps. 38 (39): 6 and 2 Chr. 1: 12.
[9] Cf. S. of S. 3: 1–4; also echoing Luke 13: 25.
[10] Cf. Rom. 1: 11.
[11] The priors of Clairvaux known for this period are Gerard (occurs 1176, succeeded by

you tell him that I languish with love.'[3] Believe me, if I came to Solomon's porch,[4] not to say to the sanctuary of the Saviour, I should speak on behalf of a friend, make requests on behalf of my lord, announce to the ears of the Lord of Sabaoth[5] what you have done for me and what you have done through me for the poor. I should appeal to the righteous One, address the just One, saying: '"Be thou mindful of thy word to thy servant,"[6] for your word is: That which you did to one of my least ones, you did it to me.[7] Behold the substance of my lord, once archbishop of Lund, now a poor man of Clairvaux, is now with you through the hands of your poor ones. Repay him then in turn and give your substance to him who gave you his, albeit what you had given, what he had received from you.' Most loving father, in constant recollection of you my heart neither sleeps nor slumbers.[8] It cries out, knocks, and stands at your doorway asking, 'When shall I see the one whom my soul desires, when shall I come and see him?'[9] The road is long, the feet scarce move, the marrow is frozen, and how will a friend far away be seen? A remedy then must be sought when the best solace is lacking. I cannot go but at least I have the strength to write. The eye cannot see so let the pen speak. Let the letter run on membranes since bodily presence is held back within its own members. Let the parchment report back what the tongue cannot. Let the dead image make up for what the living and true one lacks the strength to do. Let syllables give word of our circumstances because utterance from the mouth cannot. I long to see you.[10] May the peace of Christ and the grace of God be always with you. I send greeting to the chaplains and the prior, to lord Gaucher and to the lord bishop of Auxerre, and to Philip and all our friends.[11] Farewell.

1179), John (d. 1179), Garnier de Rochefort (became abbot of Auberise 1180), Roger (left 1181, occurs later as abbot of Trois-Fontaines), and Gerard again: see Arbois de Jubainville, *Abbayes cisterciennes*, pp. 188–92. The bishop of Auxerre at the time was William I, de Toucy, 2 July 1167–27 Feb. 1181 (*GC* xii. 295–6), but this is more likely to be a reference to Alan of Auxerre (albeit a late one), who retired to Clairvaux; see letter no. 23, n. 1.) The other figures are unidentified.

101

To William aux Blanches Mains[1]

1172, not before May

Archiepiscopo Senonensi Petrus abbas Sancti Remigii.

Opus manuum uestrarum, locum utique qui dicitur Vallis Dei, non tradatis obliuioni, quia nouella plantatio cito deficit siue arescit nisi frequenti irrigatione ei succurratur et fomento multiplici foueatur. Ad suam patriam, ut credimus, euolauit spiritus filii uestri fratris R.[2] quem sicut paternis gremiis dum in carne esset continuistis, sic iustum est ut orationibus et benedictionibus uestris usque ad thronum gratie conducatis. Quia ergo sublato pane de mensa Domini, in Sabbato nouum substituendum non ignoratis, eamdem dilectionem et protectionem oramus impendi bono et religioso iuueni quem amicus et filius uester karissimus ibi ex uoluntate fratrum preposuit, prior de Valle Sancti Petri.[3] Vt scitis, domus ista domus orationis uocatur.[4] Necesse est ergo ut sine dilatione auxilio uestro consecretur quatinus ueraciter et non fallaciter locus ille sanctus uocetur. Quicquid enim ibi religionis, orationis, sanctificationis, mortificationis et aliarum sanctarum obseruationum serui Dei inibi conseruando celeste premium promeruerint, in sinu uestro reuertetur et ad caput uestrum defluet,[5] quia 'qui recipit prophetam in nomine prophete mercedem prophete accipiet'.[6] Non ergo pigeat uos cepisse expendere in usus pauperum aliquid de substantia uestra quia uos recepturi sunt 'in eterna tabernacula'.[7]

101 *Sirmond VI. 2*]

101 [1] William aux Blanches Mains, archbishop of Sens 1168–76 (see letter no. 4, n. 4). Peter asks William to give his support to the charterhouse of Val-Dieu after the death of its first prior ('R', see letter no. 83, n. 1), and to Engelbert of Val-Saint-Pierre (see letter no. 115, n. 1), temporarily overseeing the affairs of the house and the appointment of a new prior. This letter must have been written around the same time as letter no. 83, as the prior is installed and the problem of the bishop's licence or letters not yet resolved—i.e. the same state of affairs as that described in letter no. 83. Le Couteulx puts these events and

101

To William aux Blanches Mains[1]

1172, not before May

To the archbishop of Sens, Peter, abbot of Saint-Remi.

Do not consign to oblivion the work of your hands, namely that place which is called Val-Dieu, for a new plantation quickly fails or dries up unless it be succoured by frequent irrigation and fostered with many kinds of nourishment. The spirit of your son brother R.[2] has flown, so we believe, to its homeland, and as you held him in paternal embraces while he was here in the flesh so it is just that you should conduct him even to the throne of grace with your prayers and blessings. Since therefore you are not unaware that when the bread has been taken from the table of the Lord new should be put in its place on the Sabbath, we beg that that same love and protection be applied to the good and religious young man whom your dearest friend and son the prior of Val-Saint-Pierre has set in charge there, according to the wish of the brothers.[3] As you know, this house is called a house of prayer.[4] It is therefore necessary that with your help it be consecrated without delay so that that place may truly and not falsely be called holy. For whatever of the religious life, of prayer, of sanctification, of mortification and of other holy observances the servants of God shall have conserved in that place to earn a heavenly reward, it will return to your bosom and will flow over your head,[5] for 'he that receiveth a prophet in the name of a prophet shall receive the reward of a prophet'.[6] May it not then irk you that you have undertaken to spend something of your substance to the benefit of poor men, for they will receive you 'into everlasting dwellings'.[7]

this letter in 1172 (Le Couteulx, ii. 366–8), and this is corroborated by other evidence pertaining to letter no. 83 (see letter no. 83, n. 1 and n. 4).

[2] The first prior of Val-Dieu; see letter no. 83, n. 1.

[3] i.e. that as the consecrated bread is constantly replaced on the altar, so the succession of priors in Val-Dieu must be maintained unbroken.

[4] Cf. Isa. 56: 7; Matt. 21: 13; Mark 11: 17.

[5] Combining allusions to Luke 6: 38 and Ps. 132 (133): 2.

[6] Matt. 10: 41.

[7] Cf. Luke 16: 9.

102

To William aux Blanches Mains[1]

July × Sept. 1176, probably early

Vnico et unice reuerendo patri et domino Willelmo Dei gratia Senonensi immo Remensi archiepiscopo frater Petrus humilis abbas Sancti Remigii, salutem et promptum cum omni deuotione obsequium.

In insigni electione Carnotensi de magistro Iohanne stellam matutinam[2] produxit Deus de thesauris suis. Affuit, affuit huic predestinationis Dei partui uigilantissima sagacitas domini mei,[3] et manum obstetricantem supposuit ne aborsum pateretur incommutabilis Dei preelectio. Deus, tibi laus, tibi gratiarum actio; archiepiscope, tibi merces, tibi eterna remuneratio. Hoc opus de raritate admirabile, de singularitate incomparabile, de puritate commendabile, de bonitate speciali omnibus imitabile. Quando et ubi simile factum est in regno Francie ut remotis omnibus simonie speciebus, nullis munerum suffragiis incumbentibus, nullis clientum uellicationibus pruritum aurium excitantibus, solus Dei honor et populi salus in episcopali electione quereretur?[a] Certe hoc in rationali et superhumerali tuo,[4] pater amantissime, 'stilo ferreo, ungue adamantino'[5] scribetur quod in uicariis Petri eligendis nulla te mouet humana gratia, nullus fauor, nullus carnalis affectus,[6] nulla pecunie auaritia. Trecensem episcopum, uirum qui ministerium suum honorificat, elegisti et consecrasti.[7] Meldensi ecclesie tres uiros honorificentissimos, dominum scilicet cardinalem, magistrum Petrum et Simonem

102 *Sirmond VII. 8*]
[a] queretur *Sirmond*

102 [1] William aux Blanches Mains, archbishop of Reims 1176–1202, previously bishop of Chartres and archbishop of Sens in plurality (see letter no. 4, n. 4). Peter congratulates William for his part in the el. of John of Salisbury to Chartres. William was evidently the prime mover in the el. John was notified of his el. 22 July 1176 and consecrated 8 Aug. (see *J. S. Epp.* ii, pp. xlvi–xlvii and Diceto, i. 410–12). William is here addressed as archbishop of Sens 'immo' Reims, indicating that the process of translation may not have been complete. He certainly continued to act as archbishop of Sens after his el. to Reims. William was el. to Reims 13 Nov. 1175 × 25 March 1176, seems to have occupied the see some time between 25 Apr. and 8 Aug. 1176, and was certainly enthroned by 16 Sept. 1176

102

To William aux Blanches Mains[1]

July × Sept. 1176, probably early

To his singular and singularly venerable father and lord William, by the grace of God archbishop of Sens, or rather of Reims, brother Peter, humble abbot of Saint-Remi, greetings and ready service with all devotion.

In the admirable election of master John to the see of Chartres God has produced the morning star[2] out of his treasuries. Present there, assisting at this bringing forth of the predestination of God, was the most vigilant wisdom of my lord,[3] and he provided the supporting hand of a midwife lest the preferred choice of the unchangeable God should be aborted. To you, God, be praise, to you thanks; to you, archbishop, a reward, to you eternal repayment. This work is admirable in its rarity, incomparable in its unique nature, commendable in its purity, and an example to all in its particular goodness. When and where was the like done in the kingdom of France, that, all semblance of simony being removed, no inducements of gifts being added to the scales, with no canvassings of clients making the ears itch, only the honour of God and the salvation of the people was sought in an episcopal election? Surely, most loving father, this will be written on your rational and ephod[4] 'with a pen of iron, with the point of a diamond,'[5] that in the election of vicars of Peter no human favour influences you, no partiality, no affection of the flesh,[6] no greed for money. You chose and consecrated the bishop of Troyes, a man who does honour to his office.[7] You appointed three most honourable men in turn to the church of Meaux, that is the lord

(Newman, *Seigneurs de Nesle*, p. 117). At the time of writing of the present letter it seems John of Salisbury was already el. to Chartres and William awaiting enthronement at Reims. The present letter also corroborates the conclusion that Henry of France, William's predecessor as archbishop of Reims, must have died in Nov. 1175, not Nov. 1176 as sometimes given, since he was clearly off the scene by the time of John of Salisbury's el. to Chartres, which is dated independently (on Henry of France, see letter no. 21, n. 1).

[2] Ecclus. 50: 6.

[3] i.e. William himself.

[4] Cf. Exod. 28; 29: 5; 39: 2–19.

[5] Cf. Jer. 17: 1.

[6] i.e. nepotism.

[7] Bishop Matthew of Troyes, 1169–80 (*GC* xii. 501–2).

archidiaconum, uicissim assignasti,[8] sed nunc superlatiue hominem de alia gente, amore Dei tantummodo ductus, in ecclesia Carnotensi substituisti.[9] Vbicunque hoc euangelium predicabitur dicetur quod sis amicus sponsi[10] cum tam uerax sis et fidelis non iam in querenda uxore Ysaac sed inueniendo 'Ioseph uirum Marie'.[11] Vere Maria ueneratur in Carnotensi ecclesia.[12] Vere uir iste Iohannes pretioso sanguine beati Thome pontificis et martyris intinctus,[13] lege diuina ad plenum instructus, bonis moribus et piis actibus ornatus, apostolico ad Timotheum catalogo uirtutum bene depictus,[14] ad Dei honorem et ad uestram perpetuam laudem columpna factus est in ecclesia Dei. Reuiruit in uobis antiquus apostolice ordinationis ramusculus cum pro patribus filii ungebantur immo pro panibus omni Sabbato calidi cum thure substituebantur panes.[15]

103

To Archbishop Richard of Canterbury[1]

July 1176 × 1181

R⟨ichardo⟩ Cantuariensi archiepiscopo Petrus Sancti Remigii.

Maximum argumentum est honestatis et religionis ad se uocare et iuxta se statuere alumnos et cultores bone conuersationis. Probata

103 *Sirmond VII. 21*]

---

[8] The three bishops of Meaux present some problems. The lord cardinal is evidently Peter of Pavia, bishop elect 1171–3, who became cardinal bishop of S. Grisogono in 1173 and was ordered by Alexander III on 8 Sept. 1175 to vacate the see (*PL* cc. 1033, no. MCLXXXVIII; see also letter no. 89, n. 1; *GC* viii. 1616–17, and Pacaut, *Élections*, pp. 46, 106). Archdeacon Simon must be the bishop who first occurs 1177, and d. 7 May 1194 (*GC* viii. 1617–18, but the reference to him in the present letter shows that he must have been el. by July 1176). This leaves little room for 'master Peter': *GC* records a Peter II between Peter of Pavia and Simon, who occurs in 1175 (*GC* viii. 1617), but notes that the evidence is confused, repeating the same date of vacating the see for both Peters ('sedes vacabat die Dominica post octavas Pentecostes [i.e. 6 June], ex tabulario Jotrensi'). If this is a resignation, it probably refers to Peter of Pavia, finally resigning the see almost a year after the pope's order. If Simon were el. by July 1176, this would leave less than a month for Peter II, who may thus be an erroneous addition. It is possible that the present letter originally referred to two bishops, master Peter the cardinal and Simon (and so punctuated: 'domnum . . . cardinalem magistrum Petrum et Simonem archidiaconum'), and that the *tres* is a later, and mistaken, emendation.

[9] i.e. he is English.

[10] Cf. Matt. 26: 13; Mark 14: 9, and John 3: 29.

cardinal, master Peter, and archdeacon Simon,[8] but now, surpassing all this, you have put in place in the church of Chartres, led solely by the love of God, a man of another people.[9] Wheresoever this Gospel shall be preached it will be said that you are the friend of the bridegroom[10] since you are so true and faithful not now in searching for a wife for Isaac but in finding 'Joseph the husband of Mary'.[11] Truly Mary is venerated in the church of Chartres.[12] Truly this man John, dipped in the precious blood of the blessed bishop and martyr Thomas,[13] fully learned in divine law, adorned with good conduct and kindly deeds, well described by the list of virtues addressed by the Apostle to Timothy,[14] has been set up as a pillar in the Church of God to the honour of God and to your everlasting praise. The old branch of apostolic consecration grew green again in you when sons were anointed in place of their fathers, nay hot loaves with frankincense were put forth instead of loaves on every Sabbath.[15]

103

To Archbishop Richard of Canterbury[1]

July 1176 × 1181

To Richard, archbishop of Canterbury, Peter of Saint-Remi.

It is the greatest proof of honesty and of a religious life to summon to oneself and to place by one's side nurslings and cultivators of good

[11] Matt. 1: 16; on finding a wife for Isaac (Rebecca), cf. Gen. 24. John's election is superior to the earlier elections to Meaux as the NT is superior to the OT.

[12] A reference to the dedication of the cathedral, and to its possession of one of the major Marian relics, the Sancta Camisia.

[13] A reference to John of Salisbury's involvement with Thomas Becket, and possibly to his presence at the murder.

[14] Cf. 1 Tim. 3: 1–7, a long list of the virtues required of a bishop.

[15] Cf. 1 Kgs. (1 Sam.) 21: 6.

103 [1] Richard of Dover, archbishop of Canterbury, el. 3 June 1173, consecrated 7 Apr. 1174, papal legate for the province of Canterbury 9 Apr. 1174–30 Aug. 1181, d. 16 Feb. 1184 (*Fasti*, ii. 4–5). Recommendation of master G., whom Richard has summoned to Canterbury. The present letter refers to John of Salisbury as bishop of Chartres, and so must fall between July 1176 (see letter no. 102, n. 1) and Peter's departure from Saint-Remi. The subject of the letter cannot be master Gerard Pucelle, whom Peter had evidently supported previously (see letter no. 179), for he was established at Canterbury and serving as principal clerk to Archbishop Richard from *c.*1174 (see letter no. 179, n. 1). The G. of this letter was probably a monk of Canterbury (as the present letter suggests; see below and n. 2), like Richard himself (*Fasti*, ii. 4). This G. also spent a long time with

namque uirtus consimili gaudet reclinatorio, uires cotidianis resumens incrementis non solum de natiuo germine sed et de uterina propagine.[2] Inde est, pater sancte, quod ad commendationem non modicam uestri nominis magistrum G. aduocatis et mundanis destitutum copiis in spe bona sub alis uestris, ut audiuimus, nidificare compellitis. Nouimus eum non transitoria aut aduenticia familiaritate sed longa et diuturna uicinitate ac beneficiorum nostrorum communicatione. Vtinam suffecisset ei nostra paupertas, nec amouisset illum a nobis tam patrie amicitia quam uestre largitatis fiducia. Raros ei similes penes nos habemus quos sic ornet doctrina quam uita. Dignus est latere sacerdotali qui sua non inquinat uestimenta, qui secularia lenocinia postponit pro uera philosophia. Cum granis siquidem philosophie etiam quisquilias retinet, amans sententias, nec uerba respuens, legens codices et corrigens mores. Excipite pauperem et facite diuitem. Imitetur manus uestra mundi fabricatorem qui in creatione terram, prius inanem et informem, fecundauit tam multipliciter et formauit tam mirabiliter ut fetus sint innumerabiles, forme incomparabiles. Sanctissime memorie predecessor uester, archiepiscopus Theobaldus, de gremio et sinu nostro magistrum Iohannem Carnotensem episcopum, inopem et pauperem suscepit, sed Deo iuuante usque ad 'nomen magnorum qui sunt in terra'[3] fomentis suis prouexit. Mortuus quidem est ille archiepiscopus corpore sed adhuc uiuit in propagine, et durat in illo adhuc suauissimum memoriale. Sicut successistis ei et sancto Thome in episcopatum sic in isto magistro G. succedat amplissimum uestrum beneficium.[4] Valeant ei preces nostre quia etsi ignoti sumus uobis facie, non tamen, si opportunitas se preberet, obsequio et interim bona uoluntate.

Peter, and is probably the same G. referred to in letter no. 143 as 'clericum nostrum'. The *acta* of Richard have more than one signatory with the initial G., so this is inconclusive (see *EEA* ii, p. xxix, and the index in *EEA* iii).

[2] Literally, offspring of the same mother; this could mean his own protégés and his fellows, but it also appears to indicate that G. is a fellow son (monk) of Canterbury. The

conduct. For proven virtue rejoices in a similar couch, recovering its force by daily increases not only from its own seed but also from its closest kin.[2] Hence it is, holy father, and it is no mean commendation of your name, that you are summoning master G. and, so we hear, directing him, destitute of worldly riches, to build a nest in good hope beneath your wings. We know him not by a passing or casual acquaintance but by long and lasting contact and by the sharing of our blessings. If only our poverty had been sufficient for him, and the friendship of his homeland along with the assurance of your generosity had not taken him away from us. We have among us few like him whom learning so adorns as much as life. He who does not defile his own vestments, who puts off worldly allurements for the sake of true philosophy, is worthy of the priestly fellowship. Indeed, along with the seeds of philosophy, he even holds on to the sweepings, loving opinions, not rejecting words, reading texts and correcting his conduct. Receive him poor and make him rich. May your hand imitate the maker of the world who in the creation made the land, at first empty and unformed, fruitful so multifariously and fashioned it so wondrously that the offspring are innumerable and the forms incomparable. Your predecessor of holiest memory, Archbishop Theobald, took up from our lap and bosom master John, bishop of Chartres, when he was needy and poor, but with God's help promoted him by his nourishment even unto 'the name of the great ones that are on the earth'.[3] That archbishop is indeed dead in the body but he still lives in his offspring, and in John his most delightful memorial still endures. As you have succeeded Theobald and St Thomas in the episcopate, so also in the case of this master G. may your most abundant bounty succeed theirs.[4] May our prayers for him be strong because, although we are unknown to you personally, yet we would not be so, should the opportunity arise, through our service, and in the meantime through our goodwill.

point of the proverb is that the virtuous benefit from supporting their own fellows or protégés as opposed to strangers.

[3] 2 Kgs. (2 Sam.): 7: 9; on the significance of this passage in reconstructing John of Salisbury's life, see *J. S. Epp.* i, pp. xviii–xix.

[4] i.e. follow their example in patronizing the deserving.

104
To Archbishop Absalon of Lund[1]

Feb. 1178 × 1181

Archiepiscopo Lundensi Petrus abbas Sancti Remigii.

Spiracula uirtutum et odoramenta suauia sunt et perpetua nam nec longeuitate ueterascunt nec longinquitate odorem suum minuunt. Ecce uestra Dacia remota est a nostra Francia; distant enim et moribus hominum et consuetudinibus siue situ terrarum. Sed uirtus, siue hic siue illic, nec uultum mutat nec habitum nec fructum nec usum.[2] Species illi una et in Dacia et in Francia. Quorsum hec? Quid ad materiam presentem attinet de insolubili et immobili uigore et decore uirtutis scribere cum sufficit grates referre uobis pro beneficiis fratri et amico nostro Fulconi episcopo collatis, et quod obsequium suum tantus dominus tam indigno monacho litteris suis porrexit?[3] Sed peccatum reputo falsa dicere, nichilominus et uera tacere. Sicut enim improbus incenditur aut inflatur si falso laudetur, sic preditus naturali et gratuita bonitate humiliatur et fortius ad meliora accenditur cum ad se et ante se relatione non adulatoria sed uera reuocatur. Timet enim ne non sit uel minus sit quam dicitur. A multis retro annis, pater karissime, de uestra nobilitate et industria plura audiuimus, et quod feruentissimo zelo que Dei sunt in uobis et in aliis augmentare studeatis. Tenui fama hoc didiceram, sed cumulum ueritatis et certitudinis adiecit karissimus noster et uester Fulco episcopus. Finees utinam tam apud uos quam apud nos resurgeret[4] et filii Mathatie antiqua pro lege Dei bella renouarent[5] et sibi usque ad animas[6] non parcerent. Feruentis illius spiritus

104 *Sirmond VIII. 19*]

104 [1] Absalon, archbishop of Lund *c.*21 Feb. 1178–21 Mar. 1201; previously bishop of Roskilde from 1158, after 18 Apr., resigned 1192; held Roskilde and Lund in plurality 1178–92; *SEECO* vi, pp. 28–33, 89–93. The address is simply to the archbishop, but this is evidently not Eskil; see below n. 8. The *terminus ad quem* of this letter is the end of Peter's abbacy of Saint-Remi.

[2] Alluding to *usufructum* ('usufruct'), i.e. its rights, which are everywhere the same.

[3] On Fulk, the missionary bishop to Estonia, see appendix 9. He has evidently received some sort of favour from Absalon, or secured his position with the incoming archbishop. He may be in France with Peter at the time of writing (he is here given as the source of news about Absalon), but in any case in letter no. 105 he is definitely described as being

104

To Archbishop Absalon of Lund[1]

Feb. 1178 × 1181

To the archbishop of Lund, Peter, abbot of Saint-Remi.

The breaths and the perfumes of the virtues are sweet and everlasting for they neither grow old with longevity nor lessen their odour over long distances. See, your Denmark is far removed from our France, for they are set apart both in the manners and customs of the men and in geographical location. But virtue, be it here or there, changes neither its countenance nor its dress, neither its enjoyment nor its use.[2] Its form is one and the same both in Denmark and in France. Where is this leading? What relevance has it to the matter in hand to write about the indissoluble and immovable strength and beauty of virtue when it is enough to return our thanks to you for the favours conferred on our brother and friend the bishop Fulk and for the fact that so great a lord has extended his indulgence to so unworthy a monk by his letters?[3] But I reckon it a sin to speak falsehood and no less so to keep quiet about truths. For just as a wicked man is either inflamed or inflated if he is falsely praised, so one endowed with natural and spontaneous goodness is humbled and more powerfully incited to better things when he is recalled to himself and set before himself by a report that is true not flattering. For he fears lest he be not, or be less than, what he is said to be. For many years now, dearest father, we have heard many things about your nobility and industry, and that with most fervent zeal you are eager to increase in yourself and in others the things that are of God. I had learnt of this by way of a slight rumour, but our, and your, dearest bishop Fulk added on top of this a whole accumulation of truth and certainty. If only Phineas would rise up again among you and among us,[4] and the sons of Mathathias renew the ancient battles for the law of God[5] and not spare themselves even unto death.[6] May

with Peter, and so presumably at least visited France at some point in 1178 × 1181 (on his earlier movements, see appendix 9).

[4] Cf. Num. 25: 7–8, 11.

[5] Cf. 1 Macc. 2 (with a ref. to Phineas at v. 26).

[6] Cf. Ps. 68 (69): 2; Jer. 4: 10; Jonah 2: 6.

stillicidium in uobis infundat Spiritus sanctus. Satis dictum sit sapienti.[7] Pro his que aguntur in partibus uestris erga nepotes et amicos predecessoris uestri, utinam ea michi esset apud uos gratia et amicitia que apud illum est,[8] et sicut illi honore sic dilectione succedatis. Valete.

105

To Archbishop Absalon of Lund[1]

Feb. 1178 × 1181

Archiepiscopo Londensi Petrus abbas S⟨ancti⟩ Remigii.

Gratias diuine agimus gratie de bono odore gratissime fame uestre cuius tam copiosa redundat affluentia ut celos ascendat et terras etiam finitimas suauiter respergat. Larga Dei manus de oleo celestis promptuarii mensuram bonam et confertam et coagitatam et supereffluentem dedit in sinum, immo in caput, uestrum.[2] De hoc itaque oleo et lampas proprie conscientie decenter ornatur et lucerne totius prouincie uestre sufficienter suffunduntur. Scio et pro certo habeo quod nisi fundamentum subesset bone conscientie non sic dilataretur et continuaretur uapor tam lucide et preclare fame. Germen antiquum predecessoris uestri non sub una nocte aruit sicut cucurbita Ione;[3] 'requieuit spiritus Helie super Heliseum',[4] utique Esquilii super Absalonem. Rigauit quod ipse plantauit; nec sufficit rigare nisi adieceritis et noua plantare. Deus itaque incrementum dabit,[5] nec erit utriusque uestrum labor inanis ubi superaddit gratiam manus superni remuneratoris.[6] Nunquam enim Deus fraudat operarium

105 *Sirmond VIII. 20*]

---

[7] Cf. Terence, *Phormio*, iii. 3. 541 (8): 'dictum sapienti sat est.'

[8] Present tense because Eskil, his predecessor, is still alive, in retirement at Clairvaux. That the recipient is Absalon is clear from the following letter (no. 105), where he is named. *DD* i.3, 123, links the reference to Eskil's relations and friends here to Karl and Knud Karlsen, who fled to Sweden and attacked Halland in spring 1178; Karl was killed and Knud imprisoned (cf. SEECO vi. 26–7). Whatever the situation, Peter wishes to ensure that his bond with Absalon should not be weakened by the Danish situation, but rather should be as it was with Eskil.

105 [1] Dated as letter no. 104, but possibly the later of the two: Fulk is now definitely back in France, and Peter states that he is writing a second time. It is however conceivable that this is the earlier letter, and that no. 104 was taken by Fulk to Denmark, possibly

the Holy Spirit pour over you the shower of that fervent spirit. Let a word be enough to the wise.[7] Regarding those things which are being done in your lands in respect of the nephews and friends of your predecessor, I would that you extend to me the same grace and friendship as he does,[8] and as you are his successor in honour so may you be in love. Farewell.

105

To Archbishop Absalon of Lund[1]

Feb. 1178 × 1181

To the archbishop of Lund, Peter, abbot of Saint-Remi.

We give thanks to the divine grace for the good odour of your most gracious reputation, the affluence of which overflows so copiously that it ascends to the skies and sweetly sprinkles even neighbouring lands. The generous hand of God gave of the oil of the heavenly store room good measure and pressed down and shaken together and running over, into your bosom, nay over your head.[2] And so from this oil the torch of your own conscience is suitably provided and the lamps of your whole province are sufficiently suffused. I know and am sure that unless there were a foundation of good conscience the vapour of so bright and outstanding a reputation would not be diffused so widely and would not persist. The old shoot of your predecessor did not wither in one night like the gourd of Jonah;[3] 'the spirit of Elias hath rested upon Eliseus,'[4] that is that of Eskil upon Absalon. He watered what he himself planted; nor is it enough to water unless you also add new plants. And so God will give the increase,[5] and the labour of neither of you shall be in vain where the hand of the celestial rewarder[6] adds grace also. For God never cheats

along with other requests—i.e. that Peter requested favour for Fulk from the new archbishop in the present letter (and so the reference below to another letter—see below and n. 10–would be to a yet earlier, now lost, letter), and in letter no. 104 he thanked him for the favour shown.

[2] Cf. Luke 6: 38, with an allusion to Ps. 132 (133): 2 (cf. letter no. 101, n. 5) and possibly also to Eccles. 9: 8.

[3] Cf. Jonah 4: 6–10, where it is an ivy (*hedera*) not a gourd.

[4] 4 Kgs. (2 Kgs.) 2: 15 (Douai-Reims has Elias for Elijah and Eliseus for Elisha); cf. Ecclus. 48: 13.

[5] Cf. 1 Cor. 3: 6.

[6] Cf. Heb. 11: 6.

suum digna mercede.[7] Vtique et pie iuuat laborantem et iuste remunerat operatorem, unde et suum est opus nichilominus et suum munus. Nequaquam igitur mentitur opus oliue[8] ubi cooperatur donum gratie. Non cesset itaque operatio ubi restat certissima remuneratio. Denique, pater amantissime, carbones uiuos[9] et consolatorios instantissime animo uestro suggerat non solum spes futurorum sed etiam ipsa prelibatio qua iam nunc memoria uestri traditur et commendatur orationibus fidelium et sanctorum uirorum. Interim ne miremini[a] quod ego ignotus et terra remotus iam secundo scribo uobis. Habetis amicos iuxta nos[b] et notos: Fulconem quondam monachum nostrum, nunc episcopum, qui multis persuasionibus pulsat me et compellit uobis scribere,[10] [c]presentium quoque latorem[c] qui uos usque ad angelos Dei extollit.

106

To Richard Peche, bishop of Coventry[1]

1162 × *c.*1173

Episcopo Cestrensi Petrus abbas Sancti Remigii.

Vestri officii est, pater karissime, calamum quassatum non conterere[2] et religionem impulsam uero aut falso rumore non penitus euertere sed sustentare et releuare. Nichil namque in hominibus cuiuscunque professionis adeo sanctum et perfectum, quandiu in eodem statu nullus reperitur, ut nulla impostura seu scissura interueniat. Vt enim ait Gregorius, 'Vera religio compassionem habet, non indignationem.'[3] Vnde et Iesus inclinans se scribebat in terra: 'Si quis sine peccato est uestrum, prior in adulteram lapidem mittat.'[4]

[a] miramini *Sirmond* [b] uos *Sirmond* [c–c] *corr. Hall;* Presentium quoque lator *Sirmond*

106 *Sirmond VII. 10*]

[7] Cf. Luke 10: 7; 1 Tim. 5: 18. [8] Cf. Hab. 3: 17.
[9] Cf. Prov. 25: 21–2; Rom. 12: 20; *carbones uiuos*, cf. Tobias 8: 2.
[10] On Fulk, see appendix 9 and letter no. 104, n. 3. He is evidently now in France, and may be seeking letters of recommendation to take to Denmark (but see n. 1 above).

106 [1] Richard Peche, bishop of Coventry (or Chester), 1160–82, resigned and d. 6 × 7 Oct. 1182 (*EEA* xvi. 109). The title 'of Chester' was still in use after the move to Coventry

His worker of a fitting wage.[7] That is to say, He both righteously helps the labourer and justly rewards the worker, whence His is the work and His no less the reward. The labour of the olive tree therefore by no means fails[8] where the gift of grace works alongside. And so let the work not cease where the surest repayment awaits. Moreover, most loving father, may not only the hope of future things but even this foretaste, by virtue of which now already your memory is being passed down and commended to the prayers of the faithful and of holy men, furnish your soul most powerfully with living and comforting coals.[9] Meanwhile do not wonder how it is that I, unknown and from a distant land, am now writing to you a second time. You have friends and acquaintances with us: Fulk, once a monk of ours, now a bishop, who urges and compels me with many persuasive words to write to you,[10] and also the bearer of this letter who exalts you to the angels of God.

106

To Richard Peche, bishop of Coventry[1]

1162 × *c.*1173

To the bishop of Chester, Peter, abbot of Saint-Remi.

It pertains to your office, dearest father, not to break the bruised reed[2] and not to overturn completely the religious community which has been struck by rumour, true or false, but rather to support it and raise it up again. For nothing among men of whatever order is so holy and perfect, for so long as no man is found in the same condition, that no imposture or schism may occur. For as Gregory says, 'True religion has compassion not indignation.'[3] Whence also Jesus, bowing Himself down, wrote on the ground: 'If any one is without sin among you, let him first cast a stone at the adulteress.'[4] Finally He absolved the guilt

(confirmed in 1102), but Richard Peche used 'of Coventry' exclusively in own *acta* (*EEA* xvi. p. xliii). This letter presumably refers to the crisis at Lapley, a dependent priory of Saint-Remi in the dioc. of Coventry, which resulted in the deposition of the prior. This occurred 1162 × *c.*1173 (see letter no. 111, n. 1).

[2] Cf. Isa. 42: 3.

[3] Cf. Gregory, *Hom. .xl. in Evang.* ii. 34. 2 (*PL* lxxvi. 1246): '. . . uera iustitia compassionem habet, falsa iustitia dedignationem.' The point of the above being that since all men are, by virtue of their imperfections, inconstant, compassion is needed (on the above, cf. Job. 14: 2).

[4] Cf. John 8: 6–8.

Tandem reatum soluit et ream absoluit non fauendo iniquitati sed commissa delendo et non committenda precipiendo. Venerande pater et domine, non excusamus peccata nostra siue illorum qui in opprobrium sui ordinis faciunt ea que non conueniunt. Secretius tamen, non mitius, arguendos decerno illos quorum uita spectaculum debet esse mundo et angelis et hominibus, si 'offenderint in lapidem offensionis',[5] non suo sed sancti ordinis merito. Cum enim causa distinguat inter personam et regulam, salua regula tangatur persona ne nomen Christi blasphemetur inter gentes.[6] Hactenus monachi solent iudicari in capitulo non in consilio, inter monachos non inter presbyteros, ab abbate non ab archidiacono, corporali non pecuniaria pena. Scitis, ut credo, quia si notificasset nobis paternitas uestra aut sedulitas archidiaconi enormitates monachorum nostrorum, nec oculos nec aures clauderemus, sed iuxta antiquorum patrum consuetudinem regulariter male acta corrigeremus. Amouemus igitur tam priorem illum quam fratrem suum a prioratu illo et subrogamus bonos ut credimus fratres quos uestre paternitati attentius commendamus quatinus sub alis uestre protectionis miluorum rapacitatem non timeant et cum Dei adiutorio, uestro fulti auxilio, ruinam, si qua est, in domo illa reparent.

107

To the bishop of Avignon[1]

? *c.*1167 × 1181

Auinionensi episcopo Petrus abbas Sancti Remigii.

Virtutis propago ramos gratie sue semper pullulans, in ecclesia Christi beneficio suo rigat nouellas sicut antiquas paradisi plantationes quando in decessu religiosi prelati bonus nichilominus et

107 *Sirmond VIII. 2*]

[5] Cf. Rom. 9: 32–3; cf. also Isa. 8: 14; 1 Pet. 2: 8; *Secretius* may echo *Reg. S. Ben.* c. xxiii, but the context is different. [6] Cf. Rom. 2: 24.

107 [1] Greeting to a newly appointed bishop, reminding him of his predecessor's defence of the rights of Saint-Remi in his diocese. Saint-Remi's only interest in the dioc. of Avignon was the dependent priory of Saint-Remi-de-Provence, with the church of Saint-

and acquitted the accused not by conferring favour on wickedness but by wiping out those things which had been committed and teaching that such things should not be committed. Venerable father and lord, we are not excusing our sins or the sins of those who to the disgrace of their order perpetrate those things which are not fitting. I deem, however, that those whose life ought to be an example to the world, to angels and to men alike, should be reproved more privately, not more mildly, if they have 'stumbled at the stumbling stone,'[5] not for their own sake but for that of the holy order. For, since a case may distinguish between the person and the Rule, let the person be dealt with and the Rule preserved lest the name of Christ be 'blasphemed among the gentiles'.[6] Hitherto monks are accustomed to be judged in the chapter not in the council chamber, among monks not among priests, by an abbot not by an archdeacon, with corporal not pecuniary punishment. You know, so I believe, that had your fatherly person or the sedulousness of the archdeacon made known to us the irregularities of our monks, we would have shut neither our eyes nor our ears but would, after the custom of the ancient fathers, have corrected wrong-doing according to the Rule. We are therefore removing that prior and likewise his brother from that priory and putting in their place, so we believe, good brothers whom we commend very earnestly to your fatherly care, so that beneath the wings of your protection they should not fear the rapacity of the kites, and with God's aid and supported by your help they may repair the ruin, if such it is, in that house.

107

To the bishop of Avignon[1]

? *c.*1167 × 1181

To the bishop of Avignon, Peter, abbot of Saint-Remi.

The shoot of virtue, ever sending forth branches of its grace, waters with its bounty the new-set plants in the Church of Christ just as it did the ancient plantings of paradise when, on the death of a prelate of religious life, one no less good and worthy is put in his

Martin (see *GM* i. 57, 78, and Cott. ii. 2865). It seems that the occasion for the present letter is the appointment of a new prior of Saint-Remi-de-Provence, but the reference to the replacement of prelates and to the bishop's predecessor suggests that the bishop was also recently el. On the possible identification of the recipient, the date of this letter and the background to Saint-Remi's interests in the area, see appendix 11.

honestus substituitur. Sic ignis in altari perpetuatur,[2] sic in Sabbato 'panes propositionis' renouantur,[3] sic pro patribus filii ecclesie nascuntur, sic denique uectes in archa semper circumferenda infiguntur.[4] Predecessoris uestri gratiam, ut decet, firmiter teneamus, qui tanquam pius pastor et pater fratres nostros et quod in episcopatu uestro habemus[5] dum uixit seruauit et pro posse ab infestatione defendit. Oramus ut spiritus eius duplex fiat in uobis quatinus nec farina regiminis nec oleum mansuetudinis in lecytho deficiat.[6] Habetis fidelem in celo remuneratorem beatum Remigium cuius oues sumus, et si necesse et opportunum fuerit, tam de lacte quam de lanis nostris ad usum uestrum mutuare poteritis. Mittimus itaque iuuenem istum etate, sed moribus ut experti sumus maturum, ad partes uestras, cui tradidimus et committimus prioratum nostrum cum his que ad nos pertinent in Prouincia.[7] Vt ergo sub alis uestris ipsum excipiatis et foueatis rogamus et obsecramus.

108

To Bishop Bartholomew of Exeter[1]

after 29 Sept. 1169

Domino et patri suo karissimo B⟨artolomeo⟩ Dei gratia episcopo Excestriensi frater Petrus Sancti Remigii dictus abbas, salutem deuotissimam.

Sententia dubia questionibus uentilata clarescit, species aromatica pistillorum tunsione fragrascit, ecclesia oppressione malorum crescit.

108 *Sirmond V. 4*]

[2] Cf. Lev. 6: 12.

[3] Cf. Exod. 25: 30 ('et pones super mensam panes propositionis in conspectu meo semper'); Lev. 24: 5–8.

[4] Cf. Exod. 25: 13–15, and many other refs.

[5] Saint-Remi-de-Provence and the church of Saint-Martin; see appendix 11.

[6] Cf. 3 Kgs. (1 Kgs.) 17: 14, 16.

[7] The priors of Saint-Remi-de-Provence are not known for this period. Letter no. 127 mentions a Stephen being sent to run the house under his brother, 'B.', but the present letter is not necessarily referring to the same characters and it is uncertain what position Stephen was to hold.

108 [1] Bishop Bartholomew of Exeter (el. early 1161, consecrated after 18 Apr. 1161,

place. Thus the fire on the altar is kept alive,[2] thus 'the loaves of proposition' are renewed on the Sabbath,[3] thus in place of the fathers sons are born for the Church, thus, finally, the bars are fastened into the ark which is always to be carried about.[4] May we retain securely, as is proper, the favour we enjoyed from your predecessor, who like a kindly pastor and father protected, while he lived, our brothers and that which we hold in your diocese[5] and preserved them as far as possible from harm. We pray that his spirit may be replicated in you so that neither the meal of authority nor the oil of clemency in the cruse should waste.[6] You have a faithful rewarder in heaven, the blessed Remigius, whose sheep we are and, should it be necessary and opportune, you will be able to borrow for your use both of our milk and of our wool. We are sending to your region this young man then, young in years but mature in conduct as we know from experience, to whom we have given and commit our priory along with those things which pertain to us in Provence.[7] We ask and pray therefore that you receive and cherish him beneath your wings.

108

To Bishop Bartholomew of Exeter[1]

after 29 Sept. 1169

To his dearest lord and father Bartholomew, by the grace of God bishop of Exeter, brother Peter, called abbot of Saint-Remi, most devoted greetings.

An obscure opinion becomes clear when winnowed with questions; an aromatic spice grows fragrant with the beating of the pestles; the Church thrives on the oppression of the wicked. The strength of the

d. 15 Dec. 1184; *Handbook*, p. 246; see also *EEA* xi, pp. xxxix–xli). On Bartholomew's life, see also A. Morey, *Bartholomew of Exeter, Bishop and Canonist* (Cambridge, 1937), which puts the present letter in the period immediately after Henry II's failed attempt to force the English bishops to side unequivocally with him against the pope and Becket, in 1169, and Bartholomew's subsequent declaration of his readiness to obey the mandates of the pope and Becket, and his withdrawal to a religious house (which must have been after 29 Sept. 1169). On these events, see Morey, *Bartholomew of Exeter*, p. 29. Bartholomew did not need to avail himself of Peter's offer, in this letter, of a comfortable refuge in exile, and continued to walk his political tightrope, being involved with both sides until the end of the Becket affair. On Bartholomew and the Becket affair generally, see Morey, *Bartholomew of Exeter*, pp. 15–30, and the index references in Barlow, *Thomas Becket*; on his links with John of Salisbury, see *J. S. Epp.* ii, pp. xxi, xxviii–xxx, xli–xlii.

Virtus quoque bonorum, aduersariorum infestatione lacessita, flore uernat et fructu. Equus ille qui 'procul odoratur bellum' ad uocem buccine dicit, 'uah,'[2] eoque amplius feruet in certamine quo acrius concitatur fuso undique clamore. Quas enim uires collectas tempore pacis dissimulabat, fenore multiplicato exsoluit cum expostulauerit necessitas ut tanquam de grano sinapis uirtutem mireris si speciem simpliciter minutissimi grani intuearis.[3] Tunc igitur uirtus se expandit propagine multa cum malis reluctantibus fuerit prouocata, nec ad plenum fides discernitur nisi telo infidelitatis fortiter impetatur. Iustus denique qui ut leo confidens absque terrore est, quando gloriatur nisi quando experimentum sui ex aliquo discrimine capit ut tunc se aliquid posse cognouerit cum locum uirtutis oblato labore inuenerit? Gloriosos faciunt martyres nostros causa cum pena et pena cum causa.[4] Diu est quod in terra uestra latuit, immo consopita iacuit, fidei uirtus, ubi plures ad se euocabat poculum confectionis quam euangelium apostolice predicationis. Vnde igitur sic effloruit et refloruit moderna in uobis religio ut apostolicos spiritus ebiberitis et tota fiducia in medium prosilientes dicatis, 'Melius est Deo obedire quam hominibus'?[5] Certe musto non sicera pleni sunt[6] qui concepto robore 'pellem pro pelle et cuncta que' habent dant pro animabus suis.[7] De his hactenus. Ceterum si magna illa bellua euomuerit uos de terra uestra, est apud nos domus noua uobis parata cum omni sumptu, sine auro et argento, ubi et copiam librorum et studendi otium pro libitu inuenietis. Valete.

[2] Cf. Job 39: 25.

[3] Cf. Matt. 13: 31; 17: 19; Mark 4: 31; Luke 13: 19; 17: 6.

[4] Both the persecution and the reason for it together constitute martyrdom; this may refer to the doubts over Becket's status as a martyr on the grounds that he was defending the material rights of Canterbury rather than the faith (for Peter's views on this, see also letter no. 171).

good also, assailed by the persecution of enemies, blooms with flower and fruit. That horse who 'smelleth the battle afar off' says at the voice of the trumpet, 'ha, ha,'[2] and rages the more in the battle the more vehemently he is stirred up by the clamour streaming on all sides. For this concentrated strength, which he concealed in time of peace, he let loose with interest multiplied when necessity demanded it so that you would have been astonished at the strength as of a mustard seed if you were to consider simply the outer appearance of the smallest seed.[3] It is then, when it has been challenged by wicked opponents, that strength expands itself with much proliferation, nor is faith perceived to the full unless it be powerfully assailed by the spear of faithlessness. And finally the just man who is bold and fearless like a lion, when does he glory if not when he snatches from some danger proof of himself so that he knows he is capable of something just at the moment when, confronted by hardship, he finds in it an opportunity to display strength? It is the cause combined with the penalty and the penalty combined with the cause that makes our martyrs glorious.[4] For long the strength of faith lay hidden, or rather lay sleeping, in your land where the cup of confection was summoning more people to itself than was the Gospel of apostolic preaching. Whence therefore has the present religious observance in you so flourished and flourished again that you have drunk deep of the inspiration of the apostles and, leaping forth into the midst with all fidelity, say, 'It is better to obey God than men'?[5] Certainly they are full of new wine not strong drink[6] who take on strength and give 'skin for skin and all that' they have for their souls.[7] But enough of these matters. As for the rest, if that great beast should vomit you out of your land, there is here with us a house newly prepared for you with every provision, without gold or silver, where you will find for your pleasure both a store of books and leisure for study. Farewell.

[5] Cf. Acts 5: 29.

[6] Combining allusions to Acts 2: 13 and Luke 1: 15. The disciples who received the Holy Spirit at Pentecost were said by others to be full of new wine; John the Baptist, in Luke, will not drink wine or strong drink.

[7] Cf. Job 2: 4.

109

To Bishop Bartholomew of Exeter[1]

after Feb. 1173 (or poss. earlier)

Episcopo Exoniensi.

Luctus noster in gaudium uertitur[2] cum de terris amicus noster ad celum leuetur.[a] Spem quidem bonam de ipso, si diu inter nos uiueret, conceperamus, sed iam optimam in celo repositam habemus. Episcope Exoniensis, quid et de quo loquamur nostis. Non dubito partes uestras plenissime interpositas ubi tantum perpetratum est nefas. Remanserunt huius aquile que ad astra euolauit pulli lambentes sanguinem eius[3] et sese cotidie inebriantes felle et absinthio.[4] Sit eis tamen solatium spes futurorum, euidentia miraculorum et patientia presentium malorum. 'Quis dabit michi pennas sicut columbe' ut euolem[5] et uisitem tumbam pretiosi martyris sancti Thome? Credite michi, confidenter ueniam impetraturus de peccatis meis adirem locum illum de quo sanctissima eius anima per proprium sanguinem assumpta est ad consortium sanctorum omnium.[b] Vos ergo uices nostras supplete et pro nobis orate, atque dulcissimos illos amicos nostros et uestros benigne fouete.[6]

109 *Sirmond V. 16*]
[a] leuatur *Sirmond* [b] meorum *Sirmond*

109 [1] On Bartholomew of Exeter, see letter no. 108, n. 1. This letter seems to be a reaction to Becket's canonization (21 Feb. 1173, Barlow, *Thomas Becket*, p. 269); Becket is referred to as 'sanctus' as well as martyr (although Peter made it clear in letter no. 171 that he did not consider formal papal recognition crucial in determining Becket's status as a martyr). The reference to 'those sweetest friends of ours' is most likely to John of Salisbury and his brother Richard. Peter seems to assume that they are together: John was frequently at Exeter until his el. to Chartres in July 1176, which would give a *terminus ad quem* for the letter (on his movements in the years 1170–6, and his connections with both Canterbury and Exeter, see Barlow, 'John of Salisbury', pp. 103–8; on this and his el. to Chartres, see also *J. S. Epp.* ii, p. xlvi and n. 2, and letter no. 102, n. 1); Richard, however, was at Merton priory by spring 1172 at the latest (he returned to Exeter at the end of 1170, but disappears from view, appearing at Merton in late 1171 or early 1172–see Barlow, 'John of Salisbury', pp. 103–4, and letter no. 171, n. 1; on Richard generally, see letter no. 163, n. 1 and Barlow, 'John of Salisbury', pp. 100–8). However, Barlow takes Peter's request that

109

To Bishop Bartholomew of Exeter[1]

after Feb. 1173 (or poss. earlier)

To the bishop of Exeter.

Our mourning is turned to joy,[2] for our friend is raised up from earth unto heaven. We had conceived a great hope of him, if he should have survived among us for long, but now we have the best of hopes laid up in heaven. O bishop of Exeter, you know of what and of whom we are speaking. I have no doubt that your good influence was brought to intervene to the full where so great a crime was perpetrated. The chicks of this eagle who has flown up to the stars have remained sucking up his blood[3] and daily intoxicating themselves with gall and wormwood.[4] Yet may the hope of future things, the proof of miracles, and the capacity to endure evils in the present be a solace to them. 'Who will give me wings like a dove' that I may fly[5] and visit the tomb of the precious martyr St Thomas? Believe me, I would go confidently to procure pardon for my sins to that place whence his holiest soul was taken up to the company of all the saints through his own blood. Take our place then yourself and pray for us and cherish those sweetest friends of ours and yours benevolently.[6]

Bartholomew take his place at Becket's tomb (as also a similar request in letter no. 174 to John of Salisbury) to be a reference to the reconciliation of the defiled Canterbury Cathedral (ceremony held 21 Dec. 1171, Barlow, *Thomas Becket*, p. 264; on the interpretation of these references, see Barlow, 'John of Salisbury', p. 106), which would put it some time before 21 Dec. 1171. This would explain the apparent assumption here that Richard is with John, and thus not yet at Merton (see also letter no. 171, n. 1, and letter no. 174, n. 1, on this), but this is not conclusive, and does not fit with the reference to Becket's sanctity. The tone of the letter makes it sound as if Becket is very recently martyred, but this is not supported by the context whichever dating is preferred and possibly rather reflects the fact that this is Peter's first contact with Bartholomew since the murder. There is no evidence to suggest that Peter ever did visit England. On the heading, see letter no. 84, n. 1.

[2] Cf. Esther 9: 22; 13: 17; 16: 21; Jer. 31: 13.

[3] Cf. Job 39: 30.

[4] Cf. Jer. 23: 15.

[5] Cf. Ps. 54 (55): 7.

[6] Most likely John of Salisbury and his brother Richard (see n. 1 above).

110

To John de Breteuil, chancellor to Archbishop Henry of Reims, and Rainald, cantor of Compiègne[1]

prob. early 1171

Magistro Iohanni cancellario et R. cantori Compendiensi.

Tam sedula dilectissimi domini mei archiepiscopi in pectore meo uiget memoria ut non solum uigilans sed etiam dormiens frequentissima uisione et allocutione fruar de absente quod modo non possum de presente. Nulla falsitas in sua et nostra dilectione quia benignissimum et dilectum semper habeo illum patronum. Tam de ipso itaque quam de uobis et omnibus sociis uestris habetur apud nos continua et indefessa oratio. De statu autem nostro et terre uobis remando quia in pace sunt quecunque ad dominum nostrum pertinent. Vndecunque enim bene agitur circa negotia eius, et nepotes sani sunt. Dominus quoque Galerannus strenue agit, et dominus Thomas sacerdos et magister Radulfus nec non et archidiaconus et omnes amici uestri.[2] Vnum solum est quod nobis deest, presentia uestra, et domini nostri, quam rogamus ut saluo eius honore maturetis citius nobis et patrie restitui. Omnes socios uestros et amicos salutate, precipue abbates Belliloci et Sancti Petri de Montibus.[3]

110 *Sirmond VI. 7*]

110 [1] This letter, addressed to two members of the household of Archbishop Henry of Reims (1162–75, see letter no. 21, n. 1), probably coincides with a journey to Rome of early 1171. Henry may have travelled to Rome in person during his dispute with Bishop Barthélemy of Beauvais, where he obtained a favourable judgement dated 4 March 1171. Furthermore, there is evidence that the abbot of Saint-Pierre-aux-Monts de Châlons, one of the characters to whom Peter sends greetings in the present letter, was in Rome, possibly in 1171–2. On these connections, see Falkenstein, 'Alexandre III et Henri de France', p. 137 and nn. 110, 111. This may be the same journey of Archbishop Henry as referred to in letter no. 181, but this connection is not without problems (see no. 181, n. 1).

The chancellor is John de Breteuil, first occurs as such 1168. The R. is Rainald, cantor of Saint-Corneille de Compiègne, one-time canon of Reims and, from 1174, bishop of Noyon. In 1175, after the death of Henry of Reims, John de Breteuil became dean of the cathedral chapter of Noyon. On John, see Falkenstein, 'Alexandre III et Henri de France', p. 126, n. 77 and pp. 139–43 (cf. also *GC* ix. 1033). On Rainald, see Falkenstein, 'Alexandre III et Henri de France', p. 142 and n. 129 (*GC* ix. 1004, gives him as bishop of Noyon, first occurs 1175, d. 1188).

RHF xvi. 710, no. 13, note 'c', suggests that the references to Henry's absence here and

110

To John de Breteuil, chancellor to Archbishop Henry of Reims, and Rainald, cantor of Compiègne[1]

prob. early 1171

To Master John, chancellor, and R., cantor of Compiègne.

So constant a memory of my dearest lord the archbishop flourishes in my breast that not only waking but also sleeping I delight in the most frequent sight of and conversation with him in his absence, which I cannot now enjoy in his presence. There is no falsity in his love and ours because I hold him always to be a most benevolent and beloved patron. And so for him, as for you and all your companions, we maintain continuous and indefatigable prayer. But I report to you regarding our state and that of our land that whatsoever things pertain to our lord are at peace. For in every respect things are proceeding well concerning his business, and his nephews are well. Lord Waleran is also in good health, and lord Thomas the priest, and master Ralph, and the archdeacon no less, and all your friends.[2] We lack this one thing alone, your presence, and that of our lord, which we beg you to hasten to restore to us and to the homeland, saving his honour. Greet all your companions and friends, especially the abbots of Beaulieu and Saint-Pierre-aux-Monts.[3]

in letter no. 181 are connected to the conflict of 1167 (which is followed by Varin, *Arch. admin.* i. 346; on the 1167 conflict see letter no. 93, n. 1). In addition to the evidence above for 1171, Falkenstein also points out that there is no evidence that Henry went to Rome during this dispute, and that John de Breteuil occurs as chancellor only from 1168 (Falkenstein, 'Alexandre III et Henri de France', p. 126 n. 77). One could also add that Peter of Celle here speaks of peace, a stark contrast in tone to letter no. 93, and that there is further evidence to date letter no. 181 to 1171 × 1173, even if it and the present letter refer to different journeys (see letter no. 93, n. 2 and letter no. 181, n. 1).

[2] The *nepotes* may be Philip and Henry of Dreux; Waleran was a canon of Reims, Thomas the later *cantor*, and Ralph, Ralph of Sarre; the archdeacon is most likely Boso: on these identifications, see the *addendum* at p. 737.

[3] Saint-Pierre-aux-Monts (Benedictine, Châlons-sur-Marne); the abbot would be Thomas, el. 1166, last occurs 1187 (*GC* ix. 929). There are many Beaulieus and variations on the name (Cott. i. 294–303), but the most likely is the dependency of Arrouaise, founded 1137 or a little earlier: see L. Milis, *L'Ordre des chanoines reguliers d'Arrouaise*, 2 vols. (Bruges, 1969), i. 149.

111

To Ralph of Bedford, prior of Worcester[1]

1162 × *c.*1173

Priori Wigornensi.

Rerum et temporum uarietas que nos ubique et undique circumuallat non sinit nos stabili gradu in eodem stare, aliquando quidem nostro, aliquando alterius uitio. Nam cum in eodem proposito uolentes stare pedem figimus frequenter irruit et occupat propositum stabilitatis nostre decursus et incursus instabilitatis aliene. Inde est, karissime amice, quod contra propositum et uoluntatem cordis uestri fratrem P. priorem de Lappelee cogimur amouere. Totiens siquidem rumores malos de prioratu illo accipimus quotiens transmarinos de illis partibus hospites suscipimus. Claustrales et ministeriales uno impetu concitati clamant perire domum, prioratum ad nichilum redigi et in summa iam paupertate detineri. Quid ultra? Nullum ibi monachum esse, solum priorem semiuiuum palpitare. Mittimus itaque a latere nostro fratrem Absalonem cuius industriam in multis experti sumus et cuius studio si ei gratia Dei affuerit ruinas illas reparandas et in melius commutandas speramus. Commendamus ergo illum uobis ut consilio et auxilio uestro fultus, ad honorem Dei et anime sue salutem ac ecclesie nostre utilitatem ualeat commissa sibi strenue adimplere. Valete.

111 *Sirmond VI. 21*]

---

111 [1] Ralph of Bedford, prior of Worcester, 1146, after 26 Jan.–1189, probably 23 July (*Fasti* ii. 103; *Heads*, p. 83). The crisis at Lapley leading to the deposition of prior P. and his replacement by Absalon must fall between Peter's becoming abbot of Saint-Remi and John of Salisbury's letter no. 310, which indicates that Absalon has been in place for some (unspecified) time (*J. S. Epp.* ii. 754–61, no. 310, dated ? *c.*1173). The other letters dealing with the crisis are nos. 106, 112, and 113. Letter no. 113 is clearly the latest in the sequence, as by this time Peter is commending the new monks who are in place. Letter

111

To Ralph of Bedford, prior of Worcester[1]

1162 × *c.*1173

To the prior of Worcester.

The changing nature of things and of times, which blockades us at all times and on all sides, does not permit us to stand in the same place with a firm footing, sometimes indeed through our own fault, sometimes through another's. For when we plant our foot, wishing to stand firm in the same resolve, the course and incursion of another's instability frequently rushes in and assails the resolve of our stability. So it is, dearest friend, that against the resolve and will of your heart we are forced to remove brother P., the prior of Lapley. We hear, indeed, as many evil rumours about that priory as we receive overseas guests from those parts. Monks and obedientiaries, driven by one impulse, cry out that the house is perishing and that the priory is being reduced to nothing and is already gripped by the greatest poverty. What more? They say there is no monk there, only a half-alive and struggling prior. We are sending then from our presence brother Absalon whose diligence we have experienced in many things and by whose zeal, if the grace of God be with him, we hope those ruins will be repaired and changed for the better. Therefore we commend him to you so that, propped up by your counsel and help, to the honour of God and the salvation of his soul and the benefit of our church, he may have the strength strenuously to carry out those things which are committed to him. Farewell.

no. 106 and the present letter were evidently written while Peter was arranging for the prior's removal, and letter no. 112 seems to indicate that other monks are travelling to Lapley—although it is unclear whether these came before, after or with Absalon. In any case it must be of a similar date to letter no. 106 and the present letter. On Lapley, see also *VCH Staffs.*, iii. 340–3, and *GM* i. 80–1 (but on this affair, both give 1162 × 1181, citing only Peter's letters; see also Haseldine, 'Friendship and rivalry', pp. 404–5). See also *Heads*, p. 105, but none of the priors concerned are closely datable. See also letter no. 144 to Prior Inganus of Lapley. On the heading, see letter no. 84, n. 1.

112

To Ralph of Bedford, prior of Worcester[1]

1162 × *c.*1173

Priori Wigornensi Petrus Sancti Remigii abbas.

Neque subitaneus neque repentinus soleo res magnas disponere sed cum multa maturi consilii deliberatione, finis causarum appensione. Inde est, amice karissime, quod non statim credo omni spiritui,[2] propter illum qui transfigurat se in angelum lucis et sub pallio consultationis offert sepe uenenum deceptionis.[3] Vitium autem est omnibus credere et nulli. Exemplo igitur illius qui omnia nouit antequam fiant et tamen descendit per angelos probare utrum clamor Sodomorum qui ascenderat ad celum opere compleretur an non,[4] diu substiti adquiescere rumoribus cotidianis de fratribus nostris de Lapelee, uel meliores fructus de ficulnea sperans uel iudicium tanquam meridiem[5] expectans. Quia itaque crebrescit, non rarescit, fumus funeste opinionis, securim appono ad radicem arboris,[6] non detruncans sed releuans ramos usque ad terram inclinatos, immo incuruatos, si forte suspensi ferant denuo uuas, non labruscas.[7] Mitto autem a latere nostro fratres integre hactenus apud nos opinionis, quorum conuersationem, si de preteritis futurorum presagia apprehenduntur, bonam in terra uestra credimus futuram et honestam. Sit cum illis manus uestra et consilium quo si quid in eis minus est suppleatur ad bene regendam domum nostram et ad famam dignam reparandam.

112 *Sirmond VII. 9*]

112 [1] Dated as letter no. 111. Evidently a letter of recommendation for other monks being sent to Lapley as part of the revival of the house. It is possible that these include Absalon himself, but he is recommended to Ralph of Bedford separately in letter no. 111. Presumably this letter was written around the same time, i.e. shortly after Absalon's appointment (see letter no. 111, n. 1).

112

To Ralph of Bedford, prior of Worcester[1]

1162 × *c.*1173

To the prior of Worcester, Peter, abbot of Saint-Remi.

I am accustomed to dispose great matters neither abruptly nor hastily but by much consultation with mature counsel and by weighing the outcome of cases. So it is, dearest friend, that I do not believe straight away every spirit,[2] on account of him who transforms himself into an angel of light and under a cloak of consultation offers frequently the poison of deception.[3] It is a fault to believe everyone, but also to believe no one. By the example therefore of Him who knows all things before they are done and yet who still descended through the angels to see whether the cry of the Sodomites which had ascended to heaven was being fulfilled in deed or not,[4] I waited for a long time before I gave assent to the daily rumours about our brothers of Lapley, either hoping for better fruits from the fig-tree or awaiting judgement as the noonday.[5] And so, because the smoke of dismal opinions grows and does not diminish, I lay the axe to the root of the tree,[6] not lopping off but lifting up again the branches which are tending, nay bending, down to the ground, on the chance that having been raised up they should bear grapes again, not wild grapes.[7] I am sending however from our presence brothers of yet-intact reputation among us, whose manner of life, if presentiments of future things can be apprehended from past ones, we believe will be good and honest in your land. May your hand be with them and your counsel, by which any lack they have may be made up so that our house may be well ruled and its worthy reputation restored.

[2] Cf. 1 John 4: 1.
[3] i.e. the devil.
[4] Cf. Gen. 18: 20–1.
[5] Cf. Ps. 36 (37): 6, '[Dominus] . . . educet . . . et iudicium tuum tamquam meridiem.'
[6] Cf. Matt. 3: 10; Luke 3: 9.
[7] Cf. Isa. 5: 2, 4.

113

To Abbot Ranulf of Buildwas[1]

1162 × *c.*1173

Abbati de Beldewas Petrus abbas Sancti Remigii.

In negotiis amicorum gerendis tantumdem bone fidei exigitur quantum et in propriis. Nec ignoro fraternam sollicitudinem uestram operam dedisse quatinus fidei uestre commissum negotium, bono inchoatum principio, fine meliori clauderetur. Fortuna tamen, que non subiacet humano arbitrio, frequenter eludit sollicitudinem nostram et elidit intentionem. Quis enim dominatur potestati maris, immo quis imperat motibus indomiti cordis? Vix quisque potest regere familiam penetralium suorum; alienam uero, quam adire non potest, regere quomodo potest? Iccirco indulgentia Dei nobis non negatur si de commissorum sollicitudine nichil omittatur. In exactione itaque amicali nemo sit durior quam Dominum uult sentire in debita repetendo uel remittendo. His omnibus diligenter inspectis et appensis, ignosco uobis sterilitatem domus nostre de Lapelee quam, ut credo, bonis admonitionibus uestris circumfodistis, sed incrementum, quod solius Dei est, prestare non potuistis.[2] Commendo rursum uobis nouellas istas plantationes que genimine meliori, Deo cooperante, ut speramus, gustabiliorem referent fructum.

113 *Sirmond VII. 11*]

113

To Abbot Ranulf of Buildwas[1]

1162 × c.1173

To the abbot of Buildwas, Peter, abbot of Saint-Remi.

Just as much good faith is required in handling the affairs of one's friends as in handling one's own. I am not unaware that your brotherly concern took pains to ensure that the business committed to your faith, which was started with a good beginning, should be concluded with a better end. Fortune however, which is not subject to human judgement, frequently eludes our concern and excludes our purpose. For who has dominion over the power of the sea, or rather who commands the motions of the ungovernable heart? Scarce anyone can rule the household of his own inner chambers; how then can he rule that of another which he cannot reach? For this reason the indulgence of God is not denied to us so long as nothing is omitted from our concern for those things committed to us. So in exacting something from a friend let no one be harder than he wishes to experience the Lord to be when He demands or remits what is due. Having carefully examined and weighed all these things, I do not blame you for the sterility of our house of Lapley which, so I believe, you have dug about with your good admonitions, but the increase of which, which is for God alone, you were not able to furnish.[2] I commend again to you those new plantings which with God's help will, we hope, with better progeny return tastier fruit.

113 [1] Abbot Ranulf of Buildwas, 1155–87 (*Heads*, p. 129). On Lapley, see letter no. 111, n. 1.

[2] Cf. 1 Cor. 3: 6.

114

To Prior Basil of La Grande Chartreuse and the general chapter of the Carthusian order[1]

*c.*1162 × *c.*1173/4

Dominis et patribus Basilio cum ceteris prioribus Carthusiensis ordinis frater Petrus humilis abbas Sancti Remigii, salutem cum omni deuotione.

Ad glorificandum Christum uos conuenire, quotiescunque conuenitis, non ignoramus. De nullo itaque negotio seculari directionem cordis uestri impedire sine dubio fas est. Commouere autem uos dignum est ut quod facitis usque in finem facere studeatis. Virtus enim boni operis de radice procedit bone intentionis et in perseuerantia dilectionis perficitur, et omnis laus in fine canitur;[2] 'melior' quoque 'est finis orationis quam principium'.[3] Hec ideo premiserim ut, quia manum misistis ad fortia,[4] semper ad ampliora et anteriora caritatis opera extendere contendatis ad eius imitationem qui dum in mundo esset, porrigendo manum, corporum lepras, oculorum cecitates, aurium surditates et labiorum silentia curauit.[5] In fine uero prorsus in cruce manus extendens, celi et terre uniuersaliter plagas et uulnera antidoto sanguinis sui curauit, et contra omnia recidiua ualidissimam medicinam in cornu crucis[6] omnibus posteris 'usque ad consummationem seculi' reposuit ut quicunque crucem suam post eum baiulauerit,[7] uite eterne compos et particeps, contrariam ualetudinem timere non habeat. Frater iste, presentium lator, per nos et per multos alios rogat mitti operarios de uobis in messem Domini. Messis enim multa in Dacia iam alba est ad metendum, sed operarii

114 *Sirmond V. 9*]

114 [1] To Basil, prior of La Grande Chartreuse 1151/5–*c.*1173/4, and the other priors of the Carthusian order on the occasion of the general chapter (on Basil and on the general chapters, see letter no. 35, n. 1). An appeal for more monks to be sent to join the new charterhouse in Denmark. This letter must date from between the foundation of the first Danish charterhouse (not before 1162, see appendix 5) and the resignation of Basil. *DD* puts it in 1162–3, very soon after the foundation, when the community was struggling to establish itself (see *DD* i. II. 265–6, 275–6). According to Le Couteulx, ii. 230–3, the foundation survived only ten or twelve years and Roger, the monk who had gone out initially to establish the settlement (see letter no. 12, n. 9), returned to Mont-Dieu. Under these circumstances, an appeal for help such as this could have been thought necessary at

114

To Prior Basil of La Grande Chartreuse and the general chapter of the Carthusian order[1]

*c.*1162 × *c.*1173/4

To his lords and fathers, Basil and the other priors of the Carthusian order, brother Peter, humble abbot of Saint-Remi, greetings with all devotion.

We are not unaware that you come together, as often as you come together, for the glorification of Christ. And so it is without doubt not right to impede the direction of your heart with any worldly business. It is fitting however to rouse you up so that you be zealous to do what you are doing through to the end. For the virtue of a good work proceeds from the root of a good intention and is perfected in the perseverance of love, and all praise is sung at the end;[2] 'better' also 'is the end of a speech than the beginning'.[3] Let me have set these things down first therefore so that, since you have put out your hand to strong things,[4] you may strive always to reach out to greater and pre-eminent works of love in imitation of Him who, while He was in the world, cured, by stretching out His hand, the leprosies of bodies, the blindnesses of eyes, the deafnesses of ears, and the dumbnesses of lips.[5] But in the end, extending His hands out straight on the cross, He cured the ills and wounds of heaven and earth all together with the antidote of His blood, and put in place, against all relapses, the most powerful medicine in the horn of the cross[6] for all posterity 'even to the consummation of the world' so that whoever, as a sharer and partaker in eternal life, bears his cross[7] after Him may not have to fear for his well-being. This brother, the bearer of this letter, through us and through many others asks for labourers to be sent from among you to the harvest of the Lord. For the great harvest in Denmark is

any time between 1162 and 1173/4, but there is no firm evidence for dating it as closely as *c.*1174, as at Le Couteulx, ii. 399–400.

[2] Possibly a liturgical allusion; (*directionem cordis* above may echo Ps. 118 (119): 7).

[3] Eccles. 7: 9.

[4] Cf. Prov. 31: 19.

[5] Cf. e.g. Matt. 11: 5; Mark 7: 37; Luke 7: 22.

[6] Cf. 'cornu salutis', Ps. 17 (18): 3; Luke 1: 69.

[7] Matt. 28: 20; cf. Luke 14: 27; cf. also John 19: 17; *contrariam ualetudinem* is a metaphor for damnation, continuing the medicinal imagery.

pauci,[8] sed minor numerus qui non potest sufficere ad edendum agnum. Non sit itaque uobis pigrum, non durum, non desperabile, mittere ex uobis qui nomen Dei et sanctum ordinem uestrum in terra illa portent in spe percipiendi fructus centesimi, aut potius millesimi.[9] Corona uestra et gloria, si bono exemplo uestro animas plures Deus lucratus fuerit, et in regno glorie de salute aliorum merces uestra, amplior et gloriosior in conspectu Dei et sanctorum angelorum erit. Valete.

115

To Prior Engelbert of Val-Saint-Pierre[1]

1162 × 1179

Priori de Valle Sancti Petri.

De questione uestra, utrum scilicet salua conscientia uere penitens possit respondere antiqua crimina sibi obicienti, 'Nichil est,' aut, 'Nescio quid dicis,' utinam tempus et licentiam largiorem scribendi obtinerem! Tamen quod in transcursu animo occurrit respondeo. Vera confessio et plena satisfactio omnes Egyptios tanquam plumbum in aquis uehementibus indifferenter submergunt adeo ut solus Israhelita, id est uirtus a Deo concessa, euadat, et Egyptii, id est peccati opprobrium, tollatur a conscientia et ab infamie nota.[2] Sicut enim in baptismo tam originalium quam actualium nulle supernatant reliquie, sic in confessione illustrantur tenebre et nox uertitur in diem ut ueraciter conuerso et confitenti dicatur, 'Fuisti aliquando tenebre, nunc autem lux in Domino'.[3] Et sicut idem Apostolus ait de Christo, 'Etsi noueramus Christum secundum carnem, sed nunc iam non nouimus',[4] sic et de isto dicatur, 'Etsi noueramus peccatorem,

115 *Sirmond VI. 14*]

[8] Combining refs. to Matt. 9: 37–8 and Luke 10: 2 with John 4: 35.
[9] Alluding to Matt. 13: 8, 23; Mark 4: 8, 20; Luke 8: 8.

115 [1] Prior Engelbert of Val-Saint-Pierre, first prior of Val-Saint-Pierre, which was founded in 1140 by Renaud, lord of Rozoy-sur-Serre and Bartholomew, bishop of Laon, (Carthusian, dioc. Laon: see Le Couteulx, i. 469–70, and Aniel, *Maisons de Chartreux*, p. 90). Engelbert became bishop of Châlons-sur-Saône 1173/9 and resigned the see 1181 × 1185 to become prior of Mont-Dieu (see *J. S. Epp.* ii. 209–11, n. 1, where however the foundation of Val-Saint-Pierre is given mistakenly as 1149). On his role in the Becket

white already for harvesting, but the labourers are few[8] and their number is too small to suffice to proclaim the Lamb. And so do not be reluctant, nor find it a hard or hopeless undertaking, to send from among you those who may carry the name of God and your holy order in that land in the hope of gathering harvest a hundred- or rather a thousand-fold.[9] Your crown and glory, if God should gain more souls by your good example, and your reward in the kingdom of glory for the salvation of others, will be greater and more glorious in the sight of God and the holy angels. Farewell.

115

To Prior Engelbert of Val-Saint-Pierre[1]

1162 × 1179

To the prior of Val-Saint-Pierre.

Concerning your question, that is whether the truly penitent can with a sound conscience to one charging him with old sins respond, 'It is nothing,' or, 'I do not know what you are saying,' if only I had more time and freedom for writing! I reply, however, with what comes to mind in passing. True confession and full satisfaction sink without distinction all the Egyptians like lead in the troubled waters so that the Israelite alone, that is the virtue granted by God, may escape, and the Egyptians, that is the burden of sin, be borne away by conscience and by the mark of infamy.[2] For just as in baptism no relics of original, or equally of actual, sins float on the surface, so in confession the darkness is lit up and night is turned into day so that it is said to the one who is truly converted and confessing, 'You were heretofore darkness, but now light in the Lord.'[3] And just as the same Apostle says of Christ, 'Although we knew Christ according to the flesh, yet now we know him so no longer,'[4] so also let it be said of this

dispute, see *J. S. Epp.* ii, pp. xxxiv, xli, 640–3, 646–7, and Barlow, *Thomas Becket*, pp. 167, 179 (he was also the recipient of a number of letters of John of Salisbury and John's pupil). The letter must have been written before 1179, the latest date at which Engelbert can still have been at Val-Saint-Pierre, and the year in which Berneredus of Saint-Crépin, referred to here as abbot, became a cardinal (see letter no. 128, n. 1). On Engelbert's possible earlier links with Albert of Morra, see letter no. 83, n. 1. On the heading, see letter no. 84, n. 1.

[2] Cf. Exod. 14: 22–8; 15: 10. Confession is commonly linked to the Exodus in Patristic writing. The allusion to Peter's denial of Christ above (*Nescio quid dicis*: Matt. 26: 70; Luke 23: 60) may not be intended given the context.

[3] Cf. Eph. 5: 8. [4] Cf. 2 Cor. 5: 16.

mendacem, homicidam, adulterum, iniustum et impium, liquefactis iniquitatibus omnibus in fornace confessionis, reformetur ad sanctitatis imaginem et dicatur bonus, uerax, innocens, castus, iustus et pius'. 'Verte', inquit scriptura, 'impios et non erunt'[5] utique impii. Vt enim tollitur nigredo superueniente albedine, sic malitia superueniente bonitate. Neminem Iesus semiplene curauit, nemini gratiam suam modio iniusto mensurauit ut totum se Deo exponentem non totis ulnis misericordie exciperet. 'Sine penitentia', ait Apostolus, 'sunt dona et uocatio Dei',[6] quia nisi ab ingratis semel a Deo concessa gratia non reuocatur. EST namque in illo est, nec est in illo EST et NON, sed EST tantum in illo est.[7] Cum ergo uere confitens et uere penitens his ditetur priuilegiis, quis nequam oculus audebit dicere iudicia Dei non esse iusta, et opera reprehensibilia? 'An', inquit Dominus in euangelio, 'oculus tuus nequam est quia ego bonus sum? Sic erunt nouissimi', id est grauissimis occupati peccatis, per correptionem 'primi, et primi', qui se iustos arbitrantur, suam iustitiam constituentes, 'nouissimi',[8] id est gratia Dei uacui. His auctoritatibus non improbe asserere possumus ueraciter posse respondere uere penitentem exprobranti sibi antiquas et exterminatas abhominationes, immo per confessionem antiquatas et deletas, 'Nescio ita esse ut dicis,' uel, 'Nichil est quod dicis.' De presenti enim statu unumquemque iudicat Deus, nec alicui ad confusionem priores cicatrices peccatorum a Deo opponuntur, cuius ut aquile iuuentus per innouationem uite renouata est.[9] Quicquid autem iudex ignoscit, aduersarius imputare non potest. Vnde Apostolus: 'Si Deus pro nobis, quis contra nos?'[10] Non enim solum cum penitente immo etiam pro penitente stat Deus, dicens pro ea que in adulterio deprehensa ei dampnanda oblata fuerat, 'Si quis uestrum sine peccato est, prior in illam lapidem mittat.'[11] Qua sententia illa liberata, cum ei diceretur, 'Nemo te condempnauit, mulier?' et illa responderet, 'Nemo, domine', 'Nec ego', inquit, 'te condempnabo'.[12] Nonne recte dicere posset salua conscientia, 'Non sum que fueram, non sum adultera'? Tamen regularius et modestius improperanti et calumpniatori respondendum est taliter: Melius posses dicere uel, 'Deus tibi ignoscat hoc peccatum,' uel, si qua talia sunt, ad exemplum Iesu, cui cum dictum esset, 'Nonne bene dicimus nos quia Samaritanus es

[5] Cf. Prov. 12: 7. [6] Cf. Rom. 11: 29.
[7] Cf. 2 Cor. 1: 17–20.
[8] Matt. 20: 15–16; cf. Matt. 19: 30; Mark 10: 31; Luke 13: 30.
[9] Cf. Ps. 102 (103): 5. [10] Rom. 8: 31.
[11] Cf. John 8: 7. [12] Cf. ibid.: 10–11.

one, 'Although we knew a sinner, a liar, a murderer, an adulterer, an unjust and wicked one, let him, with all his iniquities melted in the furnace of confession, be refashioned in the image of holiness and be called good, true, innocent, chaste, just and devout.' 'Turn the wicked', Scripture says, 'and they shall not be'[5] wicked at all. For as blackness is removed by whiteness laid over it, so is evil by overpowering goodness. Jesus did not half-cure anyone, He did not measure out His grace to anyone with an unfair measure so as not to receive with the complete embrace of mercy one laying himself completely open to God. 'The gifts and the calling of God', says the Apostle, 'are without repentance,'[6] for grace, once conceded by God, is not recalled, except from the ungrateful. For IT IS is in Him, nor in Him is IT IS and IT IS NOT, but only IT IS is in Him.[7] Since, therefore, truly confessing and truly penitent, he is enriched by these privileges, what evil eye will dare to say that the judgements of God are not just, and His works reprehensible? 'Is thy eye', says the Lord in the Gospel, 'evil, because I am good? So shall the last', that is those burdened with the heaviest sins, through reproof 'be first, and the first', who judge themselves just, setting up their own justice, 'last,'[8] that is devoid of the grace of God. With these authorities we are able, not improperly, to assert that the truly penitent can truly reply to the one accusing him of old and extirpated abominations, that is those made old and effaced through confession, 'I do not know that it is as you say,' or, 'That which you say is nothing.' For God judges each one by his present condition, and earlier scars of sins are not brought up against anyone by God to confound one whose youth was renewed like the eagle's by the renewing of his life.[9] But whatever the judge pardons, the adversary cannot impute. Whence the Apostle says: 'If God be for us, who is against us?'[10] For God stands not only with the penitent but even for the penitent, saying on behalf of her who taken in adultery had been presented to Him to be condemned, 'If any of you is without sin, let him first cast a stone at her.'[11] Freed by which judgement, when it was said to her, 'Hath no man condemned thee, woman?', she replied, 'No man, Lord;' 'Neither', said He, 'will I condemn thee'.[12] Could she not have said rightly with a sound conscience, 'I am not what I had been, I am not an adulteress'? However, to one who reproaches and calumniates it is more right and proper to reply as follows: you may with advantage say either, 'May God forgive you this sin,' or, if appropriate, reply after the manner of Jesus who, when it was said to Him, 'Do not we say

tu et demonium habes?', alterum simpliciter negauit dicens, 'Ego demonium non habeo',[13] de alio prorsus tacens. De his hactenus. Abbas Sancti Crispini in presenti nobiscum ad Montem Dei uenturus est et mandat ut nobis ibi occurratis.[14] Si ergo potestis, facite quod amicus rogat, quia de omnibus tunc melius poterimus conferre, et ad inuicem et cum priore. Marcham argenti et dimidiam ad faciendum calicem Ellandus canonicus Sancte Marie Remensis legauit uobis.[15] Orate pro anima eius. Valete.

116

To Abbot Hugh of Bury St Edmunds[1]

1162 × 1180

Abbati Sancti Eadmundi.

Non uilescat uobis nostra littera quam commendat dilectio. Fungitur namque legatione deuoti amici, et paruis expensis supplet impossibilitatem difficillime peregrinationis. Illota forte facie et minus compta uilitate pannorum, sublimes offenderet oculos nisi essent amicabiles. Genus itaque pensandum non decus, quia specimen generationis pluris est quam forma lucratiua adulterii et fornicationis. Nostra ad uos oratio de genere Israhel est, non deprehensa, uel aliquando deprehendenda, macula mendacii, tanquam adulterii. Magnum michi est religiosorum familiaritatem habere, et pretiosum firmiter retinere. Rogo itaque uices mutue orationum nostrarum sepe alterno recursu adinuicem prebeant columbina oscula, et due penne iungantur[2] quarum beneficio celi palatia, Deo annuente, penetrentur. Valete.

116 *Sirmond VI. 10*]

[13] Cf. ibid.: 48–9.

[14] This must be Berneredus of Saint-Crépin (see letter no. 128, n. 1), who was abbot of Saint-Crépin for the whole period in which Engelbert could still have been at Val-Saint-Pierre; the meeting at Mont-Dieu is not datable.

well that thou art a Samaritan and hast a devil?', simply denied the one charge saying, 'I have not a devil,'[13] remaining utterly silent about the other. But enough of these matters. The abbot of Saint-Crépin is about to travel presently to Mont-Dieu together with us and orders you to meet us there.[14] If therefore you are able, do what a friend asks, because we shall then be better able to confer about everything, both with one another and with the prior. Ellandus, canon of Sainte-Marie-de-Reims, has bequeathed to you a mark and a half of silver to make a chalice.[15] Pray for his soul. Farewell.

116

To Abbot Hugh of Bury St Edmunds[1]

1162 × 1180

To the abbot of St Edmunds.

May our letter, which love commends, not be worthless to you, for it discharges the office of a devoted friend and at little expense makes up for the impossibility of a most difficult journey. Perhaps, with its dirty face and the even less elegant meanness of its rags, it would offend sublime eyes if they were not friendly. And so consider the lineage not the adornment, because the sign of its breeding is worth more than the costly beauty of adultery and fornication. Our prayer to you is of the lineage of Israel, no stain of a lie, as of adultery, having been found nor ever to be found in it. It is a great thing to me to have the friendship of those who lead a religious life and a precious thing to hold firmly to it. And so, I ask, let the mutual exchanges of our prayers running back and forth frequently proffer kisses of peace mutually, and let the two wings be joined,[2] by whose favour the palaces of heaven may be penetrated, with God's assent. Farewell.

[15] This must mean a canon of the cathedral (Notre-Dame de Reims). There is no other Sainte-Marie in Reims. For a similar styling, see letter no. 95 and n. 3.

116 [1] Abbot Hugh of Bury St Edmunds, 1157–14/15 Nov. 1180 (*Heads*, p. 32). On the heading, see letter no. 84, n. 1.

[2] Cf. Ezek. 1: 11.

117

To Abbot Hugh of Bury St Edmunds[1]

1171 × May 1172

Karissimo domino et amico suo abbati Sancti Eadmundi Petrus humilis abbas Sancti Remigii, salutem et deuotum obsequium.

Non solum scribere sed nec nuntium mittere a multis temporibus uobis potuimus. Causa non latet nec quidem iacet. Adhuc in pendulo est et magis apud nos dubium quam certum utrum presentes littere salue[a] aliquo modo ad uos peruenire ualeant. Pereant tamen an ueniant, nostra dilectio obire non poterit quia nec hominem timet nec ignem nec aquam nec quamlibet oppressionem ex insidiis fortune. Mediatores illos quorum interuentu familiaritas inter nos oborta est penes uos habetis, de quorum amore tam uester quam noster animus pendet.[2] In ipsis et ex ipsis faciem nostram aspicite, et quam habeamus erga uos affectionem pensate. Plura scriberemus sed digito labellum compescimus[3] quia intutum[b] est ueritatem fines uestros perambulare ubi recenter suffocata et strangulata est nec iam in palam apparere audet.

117 *Sirmond V. 15*]
[a] salua *Sirmond* [b] *corr. Ritchie;* incultum *Sirmond*

117 [1] Abbot Hugh of Bury St Edmunds, 1157–14/15 Nov. 1180 (see letter no. 116, n. 1). This letter seems to be written in the aftermath of the murder of Thomas Becket. The intermediaries referred to are presumably John of Salisbury and possibly also master Geoffrey of St Edmunds, John's kinsman and friend. John wrote to Hugh from exile (see his letters 163, 192 and 283, *J. S. Epp.* ii. 82–5, 262–7, 622–3), and to master Geoffrey both before and during the exile (see his letters 95, 161–2, and 268, *J. S. Epp.* i. 146–8, and ii. 76–83, 540–3). On Geoffrey, see *J. S. Epp.* i. 146, n. 1; he is linked to Hugh in John's letter no. 192 (*J. S. Epp.* ii. 264–7). If John is one of the intermediaries, then this letter must certainly post-date his return to England and the murder of Becket (15 Nov. 1170 and 29

117

To Abbot Hugh of Bury St Edmunds[1]

1171 × May 1172

To his dearest lord and friend the abbot of St Edmunds, Peter, humble abbot of Saint-Remi, greetings and devoted service.

We have been unable for a long time not only to write to you but even to send a messenger. The cause is not hidden, nor indeed in abeyance. It is still undecided and more a matter of doubt than certainty to us whether there is any way that the present letter can get through to you safely. Whether it should perish or arrive, however, our love cannot die because it fears neither man nor fire nor water nor any manner of persecution from the ambushes of fortune. You have with you those intermediaries by whose intervention friendship sprang up between us, on whose love your soul depends as much as mine.[2] Behold in them and from them our face, and consider what affection we have towards you. We would have written more but we check our lip with our finger[3] because it is unsafe for truth to walk across your boundaries where it was recently stifled and strangled and still dare not appear openly.

Dec. 1170 respectively, Barlow, *Thomas Becket*, pp. 220, 247). The reference to the difficulty of communication with England accords with the tone of John of Salisbury's letters written from the end of 1170 on (see esp. his letter no. 310, dated ? 1173, *J. S. Epp.* ii. 754–61; Peter's own letter no. 171 also remarks on this), and also contrasts with the tone of letters from the period of the exile itself, in the 1160s, when references to communication problems are strikingly rare. This suggests a period soon after the death of Becket, and the most likely *terminus ad quem* is Avranches, 19–21 May 1172 (see Barlow, *Thomas Becket*, pp. 260–2), after which things would have been very different.

[2] Presumably John of Salisbury and possibly Geoffrey of St Edmunds; see n. 1 above.

[3] Cf. Juvenal, *Sat.* i. 160.

118

To Abbot Erlembald of Stavelot[1]

1162 × 1181, poss. soon after June 1165

[a]Venerando domino et amico karissimo E⟨rlembaldo⟩ abbati Stabulensis ecclesie Petrus humilis abbas Sancti Remigii, in perpetuum cum Christo gaudere.[a]

Nulla negligentia bona est, non tamen omnis equaliter culpabilis. Cumulat namque aut minuit meritum negligentie amputanda[2] dissimulatio faciendorum aut inconsiderata festinatio non faciendorum. Ea nichilominus que a nobis remota sunt et per procuratores fiunt non consimili[b] a nobis pena exiguntur, si male administrentur, sicut illa que manu nostra[c] et proprio studio peragi solent. Inde est, domine abba et amice karissime, quod aliquantam opponunt pro nobis excusationem si fratres nostri de Marna, non soluendo pecuniam quam debent, molestiam uobis fecerunt, cum factum ab anno preterito estimaremus quod adhuc faciendum modo cognoscimus. Ignoscite itaque culpam quam nec superbia genuit nec contumacia defendit. Dignus namque uenia est qui cito[d] corrigit delictum uel qui pro posse reddit debitum. [e]Domini imperatoris mandatum uestrum et nostrum certe turbauit negotium. Iniungimus preposito nostro ut cito soluat quod iam fecisse debuerat. Vobis gratias agimus de bona patientia uestra et innotescimus quod nunquam utilis nobis fuerit commutatio illa.[e]

118 *Sirmond V. 10*; *Halkin and Roland pp. 509–10* [*Crahay fo. 23*[r]]

[a–a] Amantissimo et reuerentissimo domino et patri E⟨rlebaldo⟩ Dei gratia Stabulensis ecclesie abbati dignissimo frater P⟨etrus⟩ sancti Remigii abbas uocatus salutem et felices successus *Halkin and Roland* [b] simili *Halkin and Roland* [c] propria *Halkin and Roland* [d] *om. Halkin and Roland* [e–e] *om. Halkin and Roland*

118 [1] Abbot Erlembald of Stavelot, occurs from 1159, abdicated 1192, d. 4 March 1193 (*Mon. Belge* ii.1, pp. 85–6, see also *GC* iii. 948 and P. George, 'Erlebald († 1193), gardien des reliques de Stavelot-Malmédy', *Le moyen âge*, xc. (1984), 375–82). The letter concerns a debt owed by the dependent priory of Meerssen to Stavelot (for the full details of which, see Halkin and Roland, p. 509). The reference to an imperial mandate which has affected both Meerssen and Stavelot (and so is not presumably directly connected with those imperial *acta* affecting Meerssen alone, and thus presumably separate from the dispute which is the subject of letters 79, 86, and 94, on which see appendix 10), may be to Frederick Barbarossa's declaration for the anti-pope Paschal III in 1165, after the Council

118

To Abbot Erlembald of Stavelot[1]

1162 × 1181, poss. soon after June 1165

To his venerable lord and dearest friend Erlembald, abbot of the church of Stavelot, Peter, humble abbot of Saint-Remi, to rejoice with Christ for all time.

No negligence is good, yet not all is equally culpable. For the inadmissible[2] neglect of those things which ought to be done, or the heedless rush to do those things which ought not to be done, either builds up or diminishes the reward of negligence. Nevertheless, we are not called to account on pain of a similar penalty for those things which are far removed from us and are conducted through proctors, should they be badly managed, as we are for those things which are normally executed by our hand and through our own effort. Hence it is, lord abbot and dearest friend, that our brethren of Meerssen offer some excuse for us if, by not paying off the money which they owe, they have caused you some trouble, since we were reckoning that that which we now know is still outstanding had been settled last year. Pardon, then, a sin which was neither born out of pride nor is defended with stubbornness. For he is worthy of pardon who puts right a fault quickly or repays a debt as far as possible. The mandate of the lord emperor has certainly thrown your affairs and ours into confusion. We are enjoining our provost to settle quickly that which he ought to have done already. We give thanks to you for your good patience and inform you that we have derived no profit from that exchange.

of Wurzburg. Barbarossa wrote to Erlembald explaining his obedience to the anti-pope (*Die Urkunden Friedrichs I. 1158–1167*, ed. H. Appelt, *MGH*, *Die Urkunden der Deutschen Könige und Kaiser* [*MGH Diplomata*] 10.2 [Hanover, 1979], no. 483, pp. 401–2; *PL* cxc. 1061–2; see also *Mon. Belge*, ii. 1, pp. 85–6). Paschal was anti-pope 22 Apr. 1164–20 Sept. 1168; the declaration of the Council of Pavia, Feb. 1160, is too early for Peter to have been at Saint-Remi. However, the reference here is vague, and the only secure outline dates are those of Peter's abbacy. A confraternity agreement existed between Saint-Remi and Stavelot—see Wibald of Stavelot letter no. 130, P. Jaffé (ed.), *Bibliotheca rerum Germanicarum*, i (Berlin, 1864), p. 207, dated October 1148.

[2] i.e. which you should cut out or banish, and so not admit.

119*

To Abbot Erlembald of Stavelot[1]

1162 × 1181 (poss. after 1175)

Amico suo karissimo E⟨rlembaldo⟩ uenerabili abbati sancti Remacli, P⟨etrus⟩ humilis abbas sancti Remigii, totius dilectionis plenitudinem.

Cum multo gaudio salutationes uestras suscepimus 'et gratiam pro gratia'[2] referimus. De statu quidem uestro quedam contraria et laboriosa audiuimus, sed in ore baiuli litterarum uestrarum 'meliora et uiciniora'[3] gratie et glorie Dei suscepimus. Nam 'secundum multitudinem dolorum' uestrorum[4] et miseriarum que a feris et indomitis hominibus sustinueratis clemens misericordissima manus Dei non solum detersit a facie uestra et sanctissimi patroni uestri Remacli nebulam et caliginem subintroductam, sed etiam more suo Deus supra solitum mirificauit sanctum suum et quod predicabile est in omnibus seculis et terris operatus est. Gratias ergo summo Deo non pro miseria quam sustinuistis sed pro liberatione qua uos et ecclesiam uestram multis miraculis liberare dignatus[a] est. Quod mandastis de iuuene illo a uobis nutrito, libentissime faciemus. De pecunia que a nobis debetur, aure[b] [c]propria audientes ⟨a⟩[c] nuntio uestro, mandauimus et precepimus preposito nostro ut absque molestia per singulos annos uobis redderet.

119 *Halkin and Roland pp. 510–11* [*Crahay fo. 94*]
[a] dignatum *Halkin and Roland* [b] *Halkin and Roland;* [ore *Crahay*] [c] *corr. Hall;* proprio audiente *Halkin and Roland*

119 [1] Erlembald of Stavelot (here styled Saint-Remacle), see letter no. 118, n. 1. The reference to a debt here is not specific enough to place the letter either before or after letter

119*

To Abbot Erlembald of Stavelot[1]

1162 × 1181 (poss. after 1175)

To his dearest friend Erlembald venerable abbot of Saint-Remacle, Peter humble abbot of Saint-Remi, the fullness of all love.

We received your greetings with great joy and we return 'grace for grace'.[2] In the matter of your own condition we have heard of certain misfortunes and burdens, but from the mouth of the bearer of your letter we have received 'better things and nearer to'[3] the grace and glory of God. For, 'according to the multitude of' your 'sorrows'[4] and the miseries which you had endured at the hands of wild and lawless men, the compassionate and most merciful hand of God has not only wiped away from your face and from that of your most holy patron Remaclus the cloud and darkness which had been surreptitiously intruded, but after His fashion God has even magnified His saint above the ordinary and has worked what is worthy to be praised in all ages and in all lands. So thanks be to God on high, not for the misery which you have endured but for that deliverance by which He deigned to deliver you and your church with many miracles. What you have enjoined in the matter of that young man raised under your care, we will most willingly perform. In the matter of the money which we owe, having listened personally to your messenger we have enjoined and ordered our provost to pay it to you without more ado every year.

no. 118, and the reference to the end of misfortunes seems too specific to Stavelot to refer to the end of the papal schism. Halkin and Roland, p. 510, suggest a connection with local events in 1175, but there is nothing conclusive here.

[2] John 1: 16.

[3] Cf. Heb. 6: 9.

[4] Cf. Ps. 93 (94): 19.

120

To the abbot of Lagny-sur-Marne[1]

1162 × 1181

Abbati Latiniacensi abbas Sancti Remigii.

Promissioni nostre et petitioni uestre nec potui nec debui deesse. Cui enim semel animam nostram communicauimus, ualde absurdum esset si ea que infra animam sunt negaremus.[2] Apparens etenim et euidens argumentum est non bene animos coniunctos ubi que possibilia sunt et factu digna, nulla interueniente ratione, ab amicis non prestantur. Et in hoc itaque et in aliis me et mea uobis exhibeo, non diffidens de bonitate uestra, ut si quando simile quid a uobis expostulauero facile michi indulgeatur. Tamen nouerit dilectio uestra, frater, nos opus nostrum incorrectum confidentissime uobis credere, obnixe rogans[a] et supplicans ut limam correctionis adhibeatis, superflua confodiendo, exilia supplendo, male ordinata ad ordinem reuocando, et quicquid inde uobis uisum fuerit tanquam de uestro faciendo.[3] Valete.

121

To Abbot Peter of La Sauve-Majeure[1]

1162 × 1181

Domino Petro abbati de Silua, Petrus abbas Sancti Remigii.

Satis est grata nobis occasio qua uobis scribere compellimur. Cum enim uestram presentiam si a Deo daretur totis semper amplecteremur

120 *Sirmond V. 18*]
[a] rogante *Sirmond*

121 *Sirmond V. 17*]

120 [1] The outline dates are those of Peter's abbacy of Saint-Remi. The abbots of Lagny-sur-Marne in this period, after the deposition of Geoffrey (from 1148, deposed 1162, d. 1162), were, Hugh I (occurs 1162), Hugh II (1163–71), Guarinus (1171–6, d. 1180), and Joscelin (el. 22 Oct. 1176–before 1188, d. before 1190): on all of these, see *GC* vii. 496–9.
[2] A common friendship topos.
[3] It is not apparent which of Peter's works is being referred to here.

120

To the abbot of Lagny-sur-Marne[1]

1162 × 1181

To the abbot of Lagny-sur-Marne, the abbot of Saint-Remi.

I was not able, nor should I have been, to default on our promise and your request. For it would be utterly absurd if we were to deny those things which are less than the soul to him with whom we have once divided our soul.[2] For it is apparent and evident proof that souls are not well united when those things which are possibilities and worth doing, with no reason standing in the way, are not executed by friends. Both in this matter, accordingly, and in others I lay myself and my works before you, trusting fully in your goodness so that if ever I should demand something similar from you it may be granted to me readily. Yet let your love, brother, know that we are most confidently entrusting our uncorrected work to you, earnestly asking and begging that you apply the file of correction, digging out superfluous matter, filling up what is sparse, recalling the disordered to order, and doing to it whatever you think fit as though it were your own.[3] Farewell.

121

To Abbot Peter of La Sauve-Majeure[1]

1162 × 1181

To his lord Peter, abbot of La Sauve-Majeure, Peter, abbot of Saint-Remi.

An occasion on which we are compelled to write to you is very agreeable to us. For since we would always embrace your presence, if God would grant it, with open arms, what wonder is it if even once in

121 [1] Abbot Peter II of La Sauve-Majeure, first occurs 1155 (but his predecessor last occurs 1147), d. 24 Oct. 1183: *GC* ii. 869–70; La Sauve-Majeure or La Grande-Sauve, Benedictine, dioc. Bordeaux, Cott. i. 1324–6; see also M. l'abbé Cirot de la Ville, *Histoire de l'abbaye et congrégation de Notre-Dame de la Grande-Sauve*, 2 vols. (Paris and Bordeaux, 1844–5), ii. 104–9. This and letter no. 122 mention the refusal of the prior of Novy-les-Moines (dep. priory of La Sauve-Majeure, dioc. Reims; Cott. ii. 2105–6) to take up an abbacy (Cirot de la Ville, *Histoire*, ii. 387, records only one prior of Novy in this period: Gausbert, occurs 1180).

brachiis, quid mirum si uel semel in anno absentiam qualicunque stilo alloqui desideramus? Nec tamen que uel quantum uolumus amantissimo amico presentibus litteris insinuamus obstante illa que pene cunctis affectionibus nostris insidioso nouercatur oculo, importunitate congestorum negotiorum que tollit a me animam meam plus sepe nolente quam uolente. Est itaque petitio nostra apud uos pro priore uestro Nouiense, uiro honesto opinionis bone et fame hylaris in partibus nostris. Electus enim in abbatem, excusat se a tanto onere tum propter humilitatem suam tum propter difficultatem laboris quem nondum expertus iam reformidat tanquam expertus. Instillauit enim auribus nostris se potius seculum repetere quam onus istud suscipere. Non quidem approbo tantam hominis in isto negotio constantiam, ne dicam pertinaciam, quia ordinata ecclesie caritas hoc exigit ut gratiam acceptam in inuicem subministremus et iuxta legem Mosaicam maledictionem illam fugiamus qua dicitur maledicta sterilis et que semen non fecerit in Israhel.[2] Quia tamen alias dicitur, 'Quid molesti estis huic mulieri?'[3] et in Canticis, 'Adiuro uos, filie Ierusalem, ne suscitetis, neque euigilare faciatis dilectam donec ipsa uelit',[4] pede postulationis nostre suspenso in ambiguitate spinosa deambulans, uestre discretioni quid potius e duobus eligendum sit relinquo. Officium autem postulantis expleo ut suggerens uobis nullo modo cogendum supra uires hominem discretum definiam.

122

To Abbot Peter of La Sauve-Majeure[1]

1162 × 1181

Abbati de Maiori Silua.

Quod me semel uestris sanctis commendaui orationibus et uice mutua nostras qualescunque orationes repromisi, huic congratulor

122 *Sirmond VI. 17*]

[2] Not Vulgate, but very frequently cited in various similar forms; cf. e.g. Jerome, *Aduersus Heluidium de Marie virginitate perpetua*, 20 (*CSEL* xxv/1. 1891; *PL* xxiii. 213), giving Exod. 23: 26; Augustine, *Contra Faust.* xiv. 13 (*PL* xlii. 302), giving Deut. 25: 7 ('Maledictus omnis qui non suscitauerit semen in Israel').

the year we wish to address your absence in writing of some kind? Yet we are not able to convey to the most loving friend by this present letter what or as much as we want because of an obstacle which with insidious eye plays the stepmother to almost all our feelings—that pressure of the great crush of affairs which takes away my soul from me more often against than with my will. And so our petition is before you for your prior of Novy, an honest man of good reputation and happy renown in our region. For having been elected abbot he is excusing himself from so great a burden both on account of his humility and of the difficulty of the task which, although he has not yet experienced it, he is already dreading as if he had. For he has intimated to us that he would rather seek out the world again than take up this burden. I do not indeed approve of such constancy, not to say contumacy, in the man in this matter because a well-ordered love of the Church demands that having received grace we should supply it in turn and according to the law of Moses should flee that curse by which the barren one is said to be cursed, and the one who has not made seed in Israel.[2] Because, however, it is said elsewhere, 'Why do you trouble this woman?'[3] and in the Song of Songs, 'I adjure you, o ye daughters of Jerusalem, that you stir not up, nor make the beloved to awake till she please,'[4] so, walking with the foot of our request caught up in the thorns of doubt, I am leaving to your discretion which of the two courses it is better to choose. I am, however, discharging the office of a petitioner in suggesting to you that in my judgement a discerning man should in no way be forced beyond what he can stand.

122

To Abbot Peter of La Sauve-Majeure[1]

1162 × 1181

To the abbot of La Sauve-Majeure.

As I once commended myself to your holy prayers and by mutual exchange promised in return our prayers, such as they are, I give thanks for this contract and I desire that it be perpetuated with all

[3] Cf. Matt. 26: 10.

[4] Cf. S. of S. 2: 7; 3: 5; 8: 4.

122 [1] Clearly concerned with the same case as letter no. 121. Presumably this is the later of the two, as negotiations have evidently advanced and the prior is apparently more secure in his refusal, but it cannot be dated more closely. On the heading, see letter no. 84, n. 1.

contractui et perpetuandum totis uiribus exopto.[2] Scintillas in litteris[a] uestris excandentes et recalentes huius nostri mutui amoris cum multa letitia excepi et tanquam de sacro altari igne hausto thuribulum proprie conscientie replens deuotionum nostrarum incensa prout potui adhibui. Scit Deus et Dominus scientiarum[3] quod, de propriis nichil presumens meritis et orationibus, amicorum intercessiones ad illum qui adhuc longe agit legatione fungentes securus mitto, nec aliquatenus uacuas redire spero. Iuxta itaque fidem meam, unus de mediatoribus et reconciliatoribus mee fragilitatis, ad illum qui sedet in throno gratie accedatis et copiosam de plenitudine gratiarum benedictionem infelici et misero peccatori referatis. Ceterum, pro priore de Nouis[4] ualde familiari et amico nostro, uestro autem fidelissimo, paternitatem uestram supplex deprecor quatinus sicut cepistis paterno foueatis gremio nec aliquid aliquando sinistri de illo suspicemini. Quod enim quasi contumaciter onus abbatie recusauit non de proteruitate aut elatione siue inobedientia processit. Venas quidem susurrii de sacratissimo pectoris uestri archano susceperat[5] quod de facili indulgentiam uestram habiturus esset si potius eligeret in potestate uestra et monachus uester remanere quam si emancipationem et abbatiam appeteret. Valete.

123

To Abbot Peter of La Sauve-Majeure[1]

1162 × 1181

Abbati Silue Maioris Petrus abbas S. Remigii.

Iam in itinere posuerant pedem priores uestri[2] ut ad uos uenirent cum ualefacientes nos dixerunt quid humilitas nostra remandaret paternitati uestre. Cepi urgeri utrum in tanta festinatione nudo uerbo an qualicunque scripto salutare uos deberem. Impetrato tamen

[a] libris *Sirmond*

123 *Sirmond VI. 19*]

[2] Possibly a formal prayer association.
[3] Cf. 1 Kgs. (1 Sam.) 2: 3.
[4] See letter no. 121, n. 1.
[5] Cf. Job 4: 12.

123 [1] Peter of La Sauve-Majeure (see letter no. 121, n. 1).

strength.[2] With great joy did I receive the sparks of this love we feel for each other, glowing and growing warm again in your letters, and, as if replenishing the censer of my own conscience with the fire drawn from the sacred altar, I added in the incense of our devotions, as far as I was able. The God and Lord of all knowledge[3] knows that I, presuming nothing about my own merits and prayers, confidently send intercessions of friends which act as ambassadors to Him who is still far away, and do not expect them to return empty at all. And so, in accordance with my trust in you, please, as one of the mediators and restorers of my fragility, approach Him who sits on the throne of grace and bring back a plentiful blessing from that ample store of grace to an unfortunate and wretched sinner. As for other matters, I, a humble suppliant, strongly beseech your fatherly care on behalf of the prior of Novy[4] who is our intimate and friend, but also most faithfully yours, that as you have received him so you may cherish him in the fatherly bosom and never suspect anything perverse about him. For the fact that he has refused the burden of the abbacy almost stubbornly arises not from impudence or pride nor yet from disobedience. Indeed he had received the veins of the whisper[5] from the most sacred sanctuary of your heart that he would easily have your indulgence should he rather elect to remain in your power and as your monk than to strive for emancipation and the abbacy. Farewell.

123

To Abbot Peter of La Sauve-Majeure[1]

1162 × 1181

To the abbot of La Sauve-Majeure, Peter, abbot of Saint-Remi.

Your priors[2] were already on the point of setting out on their journey to you when, as they bade us farewell, they asked what I was sending back to you, from my humility to your authority. I began to be troubled whether I ought to greet you in such a hurry with bare words, or rather with something or other in writing. Having won a very brief pause however, I hastened to the scribe, attempting nothing

[2] i.e. the priors who are travelling and will convey the message, presumably those mentioned at the end of the letter, of Novy-les-Moines, Belval, and Saint-Paul-aux-Bois (see below n. 6). *GC* ii. 870 suggests that this letter was written on the occasion of a general chapter (hence their journey). Cott. i. 1324–6, gives 51 priories of La Sauve-Majeure, so some such meeting is possible.

breuissimo spatio cucurri ad scriptorem nichil excogitatum, nichil premeditatum, nichil emendatum[a] querens, sed sicut in ore nostro et in manu scriptoris accurrebant uerba sic ea incondita litteris mandaui. Nec etenim aliorum thesauros nec nostros pauperes angulos euoluere poteram. Verbum illud quod prope est in ore et in corde non fuit necesse diu querere, hoc est uerbum dilectionis, uerbum salutationis. Semper enim stat in ianuis et omni transeunti occurrit,[3] quod diligo[b] uos et quod uester totus sum et de orationibus uestris apud Deum plurimum confido. Scio sine dubio ad iudicium me properare ubi sola ueritas locum habebit, sed nolo ut sola iustitia sine misericordia portas iudicii preripiat.[4] Ad fugam enim potius me prepararem, si possem, quam ad talem curiam in qua malo suo merito omnis homo condempnaretur et nullus nisi misericordia suas partes interponeret saluaretur. Credo uos aliquid posse apud misericordem et iustum iudicem; siue preire siue sequi uos contingat causam nostram.[5] Dedit enim apud se fideles suos multum posse, qui fideles fecit et ianuam sue amicitie illis aperuit. Sit ergo fiducie mee spes certa non presumptio uana quod de Dei misericordia confido et de intercessione uestra. De his hactenus. Priores uestros, amicos nostros, precipue Nouiensem et de Bella Valle et Sancti Pauli,[6] affectuosius uobis commendo et ut eosdem ad nos remittatis cum bona gratia imploro. Valete.

[a] emendicatum *Sirmond* [b] *corr. Hall;* diligam *Sirmond*

[3] i.e. this is obvious.

[4] Possibly a reference to city gates as judgement seats in the OT, e.g. Deut. 21: 19; 2 Kgs. (2 Sam.) 19: 8; Job 29: 7–10, etc., cf. E. Heaton, *Daily Life in Old Testament Times* (London, 1956), p. 61. Here Peter means the judgement of God (see below and n. 5).

[5] i.e. he is requesting a prayer of intercession.

thought out, nothing premeditated, nothing revised, but, just as the words came flowing into our mouth and to the scribe's hand, so have I committed them unpolished to a letter. For I was not able to draw either on the treasuries of others or on our own poor little nooks. I did not need to seek long to find that word which is at hand, in the mouth and in the heart, that is the word of love, the word of greeting, for this always stands at the door and greets everyone who crosses the threshold:[3] I love you and I am wholly yours and trust above all in your prayers before God. I know without any doubt that I am hastening to the tribunal where truth alone will have a place, but I do not wish that justice alone, without mercy, should be the first to lay hold of the judgement gates.[4] For I would rather prepare myself for flight, if I could, than for a court in which every man is condemned by his own evil worth and no one, unless mercy interpose her good offices, is saved. I believe that you have some power before the merciful and just judge; may it fall to you either to conduct or to follow our case.[5] For He granted that His faithful have much power with Him, who made the faithful and opened the door of His friendship to them. Let therefore the hope of my trust be certain, not a vain presumption, because I have faith in the mercy of God and in your intercession. But enough of these matters. I commend to you most affectionately your priors, our friends, especially the priors of Novy and of Belval and of Saint-Paul,[6] and I beg that you send those same back to us with a good grace. Farewell.

[6] Possibly the same prior of Novy who is the subject of letters 121 and 122 (see letter no. 121, n. 1), but there is nothing to indicate whether this is before or after that dispute. Belval is presumably the priory of La Sauve-Majeure nr. Reims (dioc. Soissons, Cott. i. 338). Saint-Paul is presumably Saint-Paul-aux-Bois, priory of La Sauve-Majeure (dioc. Soissons, Cott. ii. col. 2837); Cirot de la Ville, *Histoire de l'abbaye et congrégation de Notre-Dame de la Grande-Sauve*, ii. 390, records one prior of Saint-Paul-aux-Bois in this period: Seguin, occurs 1174 × 1180.

124

To the abbot of Saint-Riquier[1]

1162 × 1181

Abbati Sancti Richarii.

In precipuis boni pastoris sollicitudinibus non infimum tenent locum deliberatio et moderatio cunctarum suarum actionum. Precipitatio enim et subita animi perturbatio regulam summi arbitri offendit. Qui omnia non mensura et pondere et numero disponit[2] male quoque cuncta ministrat. Vtilius tamen et commodius est corrigere illicita et resecare superflua quam contumaciter semper ad procliuia defluere. Nam Petrus princeps apostolorum, qui est optima forma omnium prelatorum, habenas regni dicitur habere quibus impetum cordis tanquam pullum indomitum refrenet et passibus ordinatis ambulare compellat. Vt ad rem ueniam, sacramentum illud quo monachum uestrum astrinxistis ne ad monasterium cui presidetis quandiu administratio uestra duraret aliquatenus nisi permissione uestra rediret, de sancta penitentia absque ullo pudore et reatu periurii potestis relaxare quod aliquantisper inconsiderate factum est. Si ergo nostro consilio adquiescitis ouem abiectam reuocabitis et potius ad misericordie cornu dextrum quam ad iudicii sinistrum censuram uestram inclinabitis. Misericordia enim superexaltat iudicio. Querit etiam monachus uester utrum tenendum sit tale iuramentum an non. Pro certo respondeo non tenendum nisi urgentissima et exactissima subsit cause necessitas. Valete.

124 *Sirmond VII. 1*]

124 [1] The abbots of Saint-Riquier in this period were Godfrey (occurs 1162 × 1167, predecessor last occurs 1160), Riquier (occurs 1170 × 1172), and Laurent (occurs 1176 × 1181, successor occurs 1184): *GC* x. 1254–5, and L'Abbé Hénocque, 'Histoire de l'abbaye

124

To the abbot of Saint-Riquier[1]

1162 × 1181

To the abbot of Saint-Riquier.

Among the principal concerns of a good pastor, deliberation and moderation in all his actions are by no means the least. For precipitate haste and sudden disturbance of the mind offend the rule of the highest judge. He who does not order all things by measure, weight, and number[2] also administers all things badly. It is more useful, however, and more advantageous, to correct the unlawful and to cut away the superfluous than always obstinately to rush downhill. For Peter, the chief of the apostles, who is the best model for all prelates, is said to hold the reins of the kingdom, with which he may restrain the impulse of the heart as if it were an unbroken foal and force it to walk with ordered steps. To come to the matter in hand, regarding that oath by which you have bound your monk for so long as your administration shall last not to return at all to the monastery over which you rule except with your permission, you can relax it with holy penance without any shame or charge of perjury because it was done in a rash moment. If therefore you acquiesce in our counsel you will recall the sheep which is cast out and will incline your censure to the right horn of mercy rather than to the left of judgement. For mercy rises up above justice. Your monk also asks whether such an oath is to be kept or not. I reply with certainty that it is not to be kept unless the most urgent and demanding necessity of the case supports it. Farewell.

et de la ville de Saint-Riquier', 3 parts, *Mémoires de la Société des Antiquaires de Picardie*, ix–xi (1880–8), i. 442–65. The dates are those of Peter's abbacy of Saint-Remi. An expelled monk had evidently come to Peter for help. On the heading, see letter no. 84, n. 1.

[2] Cf. Wisd. 11: 21.

125

To the abbot of Villers[1]

1162 × 1181

Abbati Villariensi Petrus abbas Sancti Remigii.

Munus amicabile est amico sollicitudinem gerere, pluris etenim est munus animi quam nummi. Sollicitudo autem implet animum non manum, unde nec tam facile tollitur de corde sollicitudo amoris quam cito excutitur de sinu uel manu pignus cuiuslibet materialitatis. Cum igitur a fratre H.[2] diligenter de statu uestro quererem, audiui uos 'in labore hominum'[3] esse, et calicem sororis nostre,[4] que est passio Christi, cum his qui in torculari premunt frequenter bibere. Amara quidem potio bibentibus illam, sed spem salutis optimam in se habet repositam. Nichil enim ad celum euntibus tutius quam sequi stratam sanguine Christi tinctam, quam uestigia clauorum impressa prospicere et ante oculos suos Christum semper perscriptum et prescriptum inspicere.[5] Rectissimum hoc iter ad tribunal gratie. Via hec latronibus uacua et finem suum pertendens ad illum qui peregrinantibus est uia, proficiscentibus ueritas, peruenientibus uita.[6] Duri sunt lapides ad caput Iacob in itinere quiescenti,[7] asperi silices 'cacumina montium'[8] petenti, pungunt spine et tribuli teneros pedes, femori infiguntur sagitte,[9] sed nunquid non erit finis? 'Finem', inquit Apostolus, 'Domini uidistis, patientiam Iob audistis.'[10] Quid igitur post finem, quid in fine? 'Omnis consummationis uidi finem, latum mandatum tuum nimis.'[11] In fine siquidem apprehendemus que sit longitudo, latitudo, sublimitas crucis Christi, et profundum.[12] 'Longitudo

125 *Sirmond VII. 5*]

125 [1] Abbot Ulric of Villers (*c.*1158–84, see letter no. 151, n. 1). The abbot is not named, and the name of the abbey is spelt differently in this letter and letter no. 151 (which is addressed to the whole community and the abbot), but if it is the same Villers, then the abbot must be Ulric.

[2] Unidentified, but evidently a monk of Villers as he is referred to at the end of the letter as the abbot's son (i.e. monk under his charge), and described as returning; but he has been with Peter for some time, and Peter evidently has a need to commend him. There is no monk of the twelfth century with this initial in the lists of the members of the community in É. de Moreau, *L'Abbaye de Villers-en-Brabant aux XIIe et XIIIe siècles*, Recueil de Travaux publiés par les membres des conférences d'histoire et de philologie, xxi (Brussels, 1909), pp. 277–8.

[3] Ps. 72 (73): 5.

[4] Cf. Ezek. 23: 31–4.

125

To the abbot of Villers[1]

1162 × 1181

To the abbot of Villers, Peter, abbot of Saint-Remi.

It is a friendly gift to bring comfort to a friend, for a gift of the soul is worth more than a gift of money. But comfort fills the soul not the hand, and so comfort born of love is not so easily drawn up from the heart as a pledge of any material kind is quickly shaken out of the purse or the hand. When therefore I earnestly asked brother H.[2] about your condition, I heard that you were 'in the labour of men'[3] and frequently drinking the cup of our sister,[4] which is the passion of Christ, with those who tread the press. A bitter draught indeed for those who drink it, but it has laid up in it the best hope of salvation. For nothing is safer for those going to heaven than to follow the way coloured with the blood of Christ, than to look ahead at the impressed marks of the nails and to see Christ before their eyes always writ large as their guide.[5] This is the most direct route to the tribunal of grace. This way is free of robbers and leads on to an end in Him who is the way for pilgrims, the truth for those setting out, and the life for those arriving.[6] The stones beneath Jacob's head are hard to the one who is resting on the journey,[7] the rocks are rough to the one who is seeking the 'tops of the mountains',[8] the thorns and caltrops puncture tender feet, arrows pierce the thigh,[9] but will there be no end? 'You have seen', says the Apostle, 'the end of the Lord, you have heard of the patience of Job.'[10] What then after the end, in the end? 'I have seen an end of all perfection; thy commandment is exceeding broad.'[11] For in the end we shall apprehend what is the length, the breadth, the height of Christ's cross, and the depth.[12] The 'length of days is in her right

[5] '-scriptum' may be an allusion to Christ as the Word, and there may also be an allusion to the superscription on the cross (John 19: 19; Matt. 27: 37; Mark 15: 26; Luke 23: 38–but none say 'Christ'), which is possibly picked up again below (see n. 14).

[6] Cf. John 14: 6: 'dicit ei Iesus "ego sum uia et ueritas et uita"'.

[7] Cf. Gen. 28: 11, 18.

[8] Gen. 8: 5.

[9] Cf. Ecclus. 19: 12: 'As an arrow that sticketh in a man's thigh: so is a word in the heart of a fool,' i.e. slanders which should be ignored.

[10] Cf. Jas. 5: 11.

[11] Cf. Ps. 118 (119): 96.

[12] Cf. Eph. 3: 18.

dierum in dextera eius';[13] latitudo, ut sit tanta cognitio de Deo quanta dilectio, tanta dilectio quanta beatitudo, tanta beatitudo quanta dulcedo Dei, tanta dulcedo quantus ipse Deus; sublimitas in capite Nazarei, Iesus Nazarenus rex angelorum;[14] profundum, cum omnia subiecta erunt ei preter illum qui sibi subiecit omnia.[15] Hec, karissime frater et domine, karissimus filius uester H. a nobis nolens uacuus redire sua instantia extorsit, non a nolente sed ab obsesso multis curis et turbis. Libentissime uidimus nouum hominem factum de ueteri, reuersum de regione dissimilitudinis[16] ad patriam[a] clementissimi pectoris et redundantissime pinguedinis. Hunc uobis affectuosius commendamus tanquam mutue dilectionis pignus et fratrem quem ego aliquantisper enutriui et ualde diligo.

126

To the abbot of Saint-Gilles[1]

1162 × 1181

Abbati Sancti Egidii Petrus abbas Sancti Remigii.

Vagabundas frequenter litteras ad diuersos huc illuc absque emolumento aliquo deuoluimus. Vna uero res seria plura redimit otiosa. Columpna quoque firmiter locata sustinet in se residentia etiam titubantia. Vno lucro plures iacturas compensat sedulus negotiator. Vt ad nostra ueniamus, 'delictum Iudeorum diuitie sunt mundi, et diminutio eorum diuitie gentium'.[2] Hec iccirco prelibauerim ut non sine fructu scribam uobis, fructum dico non qui perit sed qui permanet.[3] Permanet autem quicquid Deo placet. Placet uero Deo uera dilectio, pura oratio, sancta compunctio, mandatorum Dei obseruatio. Suum possessorem nec auarum nec prodigum

[a] *corr. Hall;* patrem *Sirmond*

126 *Sirmond IX. 7*]

[13] Prov. 3: 16, where it is the right hand of wisdom (*sapientia*).

[14] Cf. Gen. 49: 26; Deut. 33: 16, etc. but also possibly an allusion to the superscription on the cross (cf. John 19: 19).

[15] Cf. 1 Cor. 15: 27–8.

[16] Possibly an allusion to Prov. 15: 7; Jer. 23: 10.

126 [1] The dates are those of Peter's abbacy of Saint-Remi; three abbots of Saint-Gilles

hand';[13] the breadth, so that there be as much knowledge of God as there is love, as much love as there is blessedness, as much blessedness as there is sweetness of God, and a sweetness as great as God himself; the height, on the head of the Nazarite, Jesus of Nazareth, king of the angels;[14] the depth, when all will be subject to Him, except Him who has subjected all to Himself.[15] All this, dearest brother and lord, your dearest son H., unwilling to return empty-handed, extorted from us by his insistence, not from one unwilling but from one beset by many cares and tumults. We have seen most gladly the new man made out of the old, turned back from the country of unlikeness[16] to the homeland of the most merciful heart and most abundant richness. I commend him to you most affectionately, a pledge, as it were, of mutual love and a brother whom I nourished for a time and whom I love exceedingly.

126

To the abbot of Saint-Gilles[1]

1162 × 1181

To the abbot of Saint-Gilles, Peter, abbot of Saint-Remi.

We frequently apportion wandering letters to different people here and there without any profit. But one serious matter redeems many unprofitable ones. A column also set up firmly supports even tottering things resting on it. With one profitable transaction the sedulous businessman compensates for many losses. To come to our point, 'the offence of the Jews is the riches of the world, and the diminution of them, the riches of the gentiles'.[2] Let me have given you this foretaste therefore so that I should not write to you without fruit, I mean the fruit which does not perish but which endures.[3] Yet whatever is pleasing to God endures. But pleasing to God is true love, pure prayer, holy remorse, and observance of the commands of God. They make their possessor neither miserly nor prodigal. They would make

occur in this period: Bertrand (occurs 1155 × 1168), Raymond (el. 1169), and Ermengaud (occurs 1179 × 1195; on all of these, see *GC* vi. 487–90). The tone may suggest a letter to a newly elected abbot, which may put the letter in 1169 or ?c.1179.

[2] Cf. Rom. 11: 12, i.e. the crucifixion (cf. Rom. 11: 11, 'I say then, have they [the people of Israel] so stumbled, that they should fall? God forbid. But by their offence, salvation is come to the gentiles . . .').

[3] Cf. John 6: 27.

faciunt. Auarum redderent si dilectionem et orationem amicis non erogaret, prodigum nisi compunctionem et mandatorum Dei obseruationem sibi proprie retineret. Sic monet Sapientia, 'Deriuentur', inquiens, 'fontes tui in plateis',[4] quod ad alios; 'Sit tibi fons proprius et non communicet ex eo alienus',[5] quod ad se ipsum. Bene offert qui sic diuidit.[6] Progrediatur epistola et demissa facie que sequuntur eloquatur. Nobilitas uestra et litteratura, sicut de carne et sanguine sunt sic carnem et sanguinem, nisi condimentum religionis interponatur, sapiunt. Regularia tamen irregularibus ab oppositis sese obiciunt. Claustralis disciplina in habitu et forma regularium deputatur.[a] Carnalia et secularia regulam aut exuunt aut interrumpunt. Operiat itaque[b] uelamen religionis turpitudinem lubrice carnalitatis, et in abbate monacho lateat uentose nobilitatis et superfulgeat uexillum humilitatis. Dicat igitur conscientia 'in uestimentis ouium'[7] sepulta: 'Quoniam non cognoui litteraturam,[c] introibo in potentias Domini.'[8] Item, 'Absit michi gloriari, nisi in cruce Domini mei Iesu Christi'.[9] Vera nobilitas nunquam superbit; litteratura secularis inflat si illam caritas non reprimat. Ecce, super candelabrum preclarum lucerna uestra superposita[10] in abbatia Sancti Egidii, si clare ardet, plurimas aduentantium regiones illuminat,[11] si declinat in obscurum seu uaporem fumi, offendit uidentes. Sic itaque luceat lux uestra ut uidentes glorificent Patrem uestrum qui in celis est.[12]

[a] deputantur *Sirmond* [b] utique *Sirmond* [c] litterarum *Sirmond*

[4] Cf. Prov. 5: 16, 'deriuentur fontes tui foras et in plateis aquas tuas diuide'.

[5] Roughly paraphrasing Prov. 5: 17, 'habeto eas solus nec sint alieni participes tui', continuing from the previous quotation.

[6] Not Vulgate; cf. Gen. 4: 7 sec. LXX (P. Sabatier (ed.), *Bibliorum Sacrorum Latinae versiones antiquae seu vetus Italica* (Reims, 1743), p. 21; also *Vetus Latina, Die Reste der Altlateinischen Bibel*, ed. B. Fischer (Freiburg, 1949–), i. 82: 'Nonne si recte offeras, recte

him miserly if he did not disburse love and prayer to friends, prodigal if he did not keep back specially for himself remorse and observance of the commands of God. Thus Wisdom gives warning in relation to others, saying, 'Let thy fountains be conveyed in the streets',[4] and in relation to oneself, 'You should have your own fountain and let not a stranger share it.'[5] He who divides it so makes a good offering.[6] Let the letter proceed and with a lowered face speak those things which follow. Your nobility and learning, as they are of flesh and blood, so they taste of flesh and blood, unless the flavouring of the religious life be mingled with them. Those things which pertain to the Rule, however, stand against the irregular from opposing positions. Claustral discipline is assigned in the dress and outward show of the regular. Things of the flesh and of the world either despoil or tear asunder the Rule. And so let the veil of the religious life cover the wickedness of wanton carnality, and in a monk who is an abbot let the banner of vain nobility lie hidden and that of humility shine out above. Let conscience therefore, entombed 'in the clothing of sheep',[7] say, 'Because I have not known learning I will enter into the powers of the Lord,'[8] and again, 'Forbid that I should glory, save in the cross of my Lord Jesus Christ'.[9] True nobility is never proud; secular learning puffs up if love does not curb it. Behold, your lamp, set atop the brilliant candlestick[10] in the abbacy of Saint-Gilles, if it burns brightly, lights up the very many regions of those approaching,[11] if it declines into darkness or smoulders it offends those looking on. And so let your light so shine that those looking on may glorify your Father who is in heaven.[12]

autem non diuidas, peccasti?'), but presumably Peter's source was one of the many patristic texts where it is very commonly cited. Cf. letter no. 158 and n. 64.

[7] Matt. 7: 15, but a different meaning is clearly intended.

[8] Cf. Ps. 70 (71): 15–16.

[9] Cf. Gal. 6: 14.

[10] Cf. Num. 8: 3; cf. also Matt. 5: 15; Mark 4: 21; Luke 8: 16; 11: 33.

[11] Saint-Gilles was a great pilgrim centre (note also *J. S. Epp.* ii, p. xxxviii).

[12] Cf. Matt. 5: 16.

127

? To the abbot of Cluny[1]

1162 × 1181

H. abbati Cluniacensi.

Non omissis excubiis Dominice sepulture, uestri habens memoriam sancto Sabbato opus aggredior lege non prohibitum.[2] Nec legere namque nec scribere prohibet lex. Lugeo interim ex lege sua contra legem proscriptum Iesum extra synagogam,[3] extra ciuitatem sanctam tunc profanam, extra uitam. Sed Christus proscriptus meliorem adiit mansionem, populum cariorem, ciuitatem sanctiorem, lectulum gratiorem, mensam suauiorem. Quid plura? Proscriptus a Iudeis ascriptus est rex et Dominus in celis.[4] De exilio migrauit ad regnum, ab his qui odio habuerunt eum gratis ad illos qui obsequuntur semper gratis, a cruce ad celum, a patibulo contumelie ad thronum gratie. O benigna patientia, quousque sustinuisti locum contumeliosum, populum iniuriosum? Certe non una die, non mense, non anno, sed annis multis, quatinus penitentiam de commisso agerent et indulgentiam acciperent.[5] Dormis, Iesu,[a] in monumento, nec ore nec naribus ullos strepitus facis; medium noctis silentium tenent omnia donec surgas, donec euigiles, donec apostolos dispersos

127 *Sirmond IX. 11*]
[a] Iesui *Sirmond*

127 [1] The heading in Sirmond identifies the abbot as 'H' (on the heading, see also letter no. 84, n. 1). The only abbot of Cluny with this initial after Peter left Montier-la-Celle was Hugh IV, de Clermont, 1183–6 Apr. 1199 (*GC* iv. 1143–4). G. Constable, 'The abbots and anti-abbot of Cluny during the papal schism of 1159', *Revue Bénédictine*, xciv (1984), 370–400, notes (at p. 376) that Hugh IV was probably abbot 1183–99, but that the abbots after Peter the Venerable are difficult to date with certainty; see also Pacaut, *Ordre de Cluny*, p. 236 (but Pacaut states wrongly that he was the ex-prior of Lewes, a confusion with his successor Hugh V, d'Anjou, prior of Lewes, occurs 1179 × 1186, abbot of Reading 1186–99, and abbot of Cluny 1199–1207, *GC* iv. 1144; *Heads*, pp. 63, 119). This would make 1183, when Peter was already bishop of Chartres, the only possible date for the letter, but Peter died in Feb. 1183, and the present letter was clearly written at Easter-time (*GC* viii. 1150 states that Peter wrote the letter from Chartres, citing *Bibl. Clun.* 1445–7, which prints the letter under the heading 'Petrus Carnotensis electus Hugoni Abbati Cluniacensi', but as the text here is taken from Sirmond the heading must represent supposition by the editors of the *Bibliotheca Cluniacensis*, ed. M. Marrier and A. Duchesne (Paris, 1614); *GC* suggests 'Petrus episcopus Hugoni electo'). It cannot be a misplaced early letter to Hugh III, de Fraisans (1157–61, Apr. or soon after, see letter no. 31, n. 1, the only other abbot with this initial during Peter's lifetime), because of the reference to a dependent

127

? To the abbot of Cluny[1]

1162 × 1181

To H., abbot of Cluny.

I have not neglected the vigils of our Lord's burial but, remembering you, I am undertaking that work which is not forbidden by law on Holy Saturday.[2] For the law forbids neither reading nor writing. I lament meanwhile for Jesus, proscribed by His own law contrary to the law, without the synagogue,[3] without the holy city, which was at that time profane, without life. But Christ proscribed went to a better house, a dearer people, a holier city, a more gracious bed, a sweeter banquet. What more? Proscribed by the Jews, He was ascribed king and Lord in heaven.[4] He passed from exile to kingship, from these who freely held Him in hatred to those who always freely serve Him, from the cross to heaven, from the gibbet of shame to the throne of grace. O gracious endurance, how long did you bear the place of shame, the unjust people? Certainly not for one day, not a month, not a year, but for many years, until they do penance for the transgression and receive pardon.[5] You are sleeping, Jesus, in the tomb, and you are making no sounds, neither with your mouth nor with your nostrils; all things keep an interval of silence in the night until you rise up, until you awake, until you call back the scattered apostles. Let the cock crow and sing a better song at the resurrection of Christ than at the

house in Provence (presumably Saint-Remi-de-Provence; see letter no. 107, n. 1, and appendix 11): Montier-la-Celle had no dependencies in Provence (see Lalore, *Cartulaires*, vi, pp. xxv–xxvi). The other abbots of Cluny in this period were Stephen of Boulogne (1161–73), Rudolph de Sully (1173–6), Walter de Châtillon (1176–7), William (1177–9) and Theobald de Vermandois (1179–83): Pacaut, *Ordre de Cluny*, p. 236. Stephen and B. of Saint-Remi-de-Provence cannot be identified; there is an apparent reference to a new prior in letter no. 107, but no names are given to identify the character. The priors of Saint-Remi-de-Provence are otherwise unknown for this period. [2] i.e. writing this letter.

[3] Cf. John 9: 22, but the passage clearly refers more generally to Jerusalem and the Passion. Peter is making the link between *proscriptum* and the crucifixion from Gal. 3: 1.

[4] A word play on *proscriptus* and *ascriptus*, possibly alluding to the superscription on the cross, see above n. 3 and cf. Matt. 27: 37; Mark 15: 26; Luke 23: 38; John 19: 19.

[5] This sentence does not seem to fit in with the sequence of events around it—a meditation on Good Friday and Holy Saturday. However, the point is that the risen Christ continues to suffer for the sins of humanity (cf. letter no. 151: 'adhuc manus . . . cruce'). On the silence below, cf. letter 44, n. 15.

reuoces. Mittat gallus uocem et melius cantet in Christi resurrectione quam in Petri negatione.[6] Rauce tunc cantauit dicens, '"rauce facte sunt fauces mee"[7] a conturbatione hominum, a tempestate procellarum.' Vbi enim in terra uox clara quando Verbum suffocabatur, quin immo et uerberabatur, ut Veritas supprimeretur? Sed paruo interuallo factus est terre motus[8] quia surrexit Dominus, et cantauit gallus ⟨quia⟩[b] surrexit Dominus de sepulcro. Non ter sed millies gallus Christianorum singulis noctibus, singulis ciuitatibus, singulis sanctorum congregationibus cantat alleluia, cantat et Christi mortem et resurrectionem, unde 'Gallo canente spes redit etc.'.[9] Alius quidam ineffabilis gallus de celo intonuit dicens, '"Exurge gloria mea, exurge psalterium et cithara".[10] O Fili, gloria mea!'—nam filius sapiens gloria est patris—'exurge, dormisti, sompnum cepisti, satis est, exurge ultra non dormiturus sed mecum in gloria mea uigilaturus ad psallendum, ad citharizandum uicinis et amicis meis qui libenter non impudenter auscultant uocem tuam. Concentum certe celi cantando et psallendo dormire facis.[11] Veni cum psalterio, ueni cum cithara tua. "In psalterio decem chordarum"[12] cantabis quia super nouem ordines angelorum cum homine redempto collocaberis. Citharam quoque passionis tue percute in auribus meis quia illum qui non debuit condempnari condempnaui, et uolo ut senior ille frater qui in agro occidit Abel meam audiat diabolus "symphoniam et chorum",[13] non ut delectetur sed ut confundatur, et sit ei in testimonium sue malignitatis et mee benignitatis, qui dedi Filium ut redimerem seruum.' Hanc portionem[14] michi hodie contulit Dominus de sua passione et resurrectione, antequam ad nostrum capitulum accederemus: Tingite panem uestrum in aquam crassam[15] uituli saginati,[16] et 'sicut adipe et pinguedine repleatur anima' uestra.[17] De his hactenus. Mitto fratrem Stephanum quem diligitis cum fratre suo B.[18] quatinus eo pacto sub fratre suo domus nostre de Prouincia curam habeat ut uos et fratrem eius fideiussores habeam de indemnitate bonorum nostrorum. Est enim in hoc officio nouus et necesse est ut habeat bonos adiutores et consiliarios donec per se ambulare didicerit.

[b] *suppl. Hall*

---

[6] Cf. Matt. 26: 74–5; Mark 14: 71–2; Luke 22: 60–1; John 18: 27.

[7] Ps. 68 (69): 4.

[8] Cf. Matt. 27: 51–4 (but at His death).

[9] Ambrose, *Hymni* i. (J. Fontaine et al. (eds), *Ambroise de Milan, Hymnes* (Paris, 1992), p. 151; *PL* xvi. 1473).

[10] Ps. 56 (57): 9; cf. Ps. 107 (108): 3.

[11] Cf. Job 38: 37.

[12] Ps. 32 (33): 2.

[13] Running together Cain and Abel (cf. Gen. 4: 8) and the prodigal son (cf. Luke 15: 25,

denial of Peter.[6] Then it sang hoarsely, saying, '"My jaws are become hoarse"[7] with the disorder of men, with the storm of strong winds.' For where on the earth was a clear voice when the Word was being stifled, nay even beaten, that Truth be suppressed? But after a short interval there was an earthquake[8] because the Lord arose, and the cock sang because the Lord arose from the tomb. Not three times but a thousand times the cock of the Christians sings alleluia, every night, in every city, in every congregation of the saints, and it sings of the death and resurrection of Christ, whence 'Hope returns with the crowing cock, etc.'.[9] A certain other ineffable cock intoned from heaven, saying, '"Arise, O my glory, arise psaltery and harp".[10] O Son, my glory!'—for the wise son is the glory of the father—'arise, you have slept, you have taken rest, it is enough, arise to sleep no more but to be wakeful with me in my glory, to play the psaltery, to play the harp to my neighbours and friends who listen to your voice gladly not shamelessly. Surely you make the harmony of heaven to sleep[11] by singing and playing the psaltery. Come with the psaltery, come with your harp. You will sing "with the psaltery, the instrument of ten strings,"[12] because you will be set up above the nine orders of angels with man redeemed. Strike also the harp of your passion in my ears, because I have condemned Him who ought not to be condemned, and I wish that elder brother who killed Abel in the field, the devil, to hear my "music and dancing",[13] not so that he should be delighted but so that he should be confounded; and let it be for him a testimony to his wickedness and to my benevolence—I who gave a Son that I might redeem a slave.' Today the Lord conferred this portion[14] on me concerning His passion and resurrection, before we came to our chapter: Moisten your bread in the thick water[15] of the fatted calf[16] and 'let' your 'soul be filled as with marrow and fatness'.[17] But enough of these matters. I am sending brother Stephen, whom you love, with his brother B.,[18] so that he might, under his brother, have the care of our house in Provence on condition that I have you and his brother as guarantors for the indemnity of our goods. For he is new in this office and it is necessary that he have good helpers and counsellors until he learns to walk by himself.

'erat autem filius eius senior in agro et cum ueniret et adpropinquaret domui audiuit symphoniam et chorum').

[14] Possibly a reference to the practice of opening the Bible at random and finding a reading (a 'portion'), but three texts are alluded to in what follows.

[15] 2 Macc. 1: 20.

[16] Cf. Luke 15: 23, 27, 30.

[17] Ps. 62 (63): 6.

[18] See n. 1 above.

128

To Abbot Berneredus of Saint-Crépin[1]

*c.*1162/3 × 1179 before May (or more likely before Mar.)

Karissimo amico suo Berneredo abbati Sancti Crispini frater Petrus humilis abbas S. Remigii, semper bene ualere.

Cariora michi forte et utiliora sunt spatia nocturnalia quam diurna. Siquidem diurna accersitis hinc inde et contra ductis copiosarum occupationum cateruis, animam meam de manibus meis tollunt[2] et me michi tam uiolenter quam fraudulenter assidue subtrahunt. Hiemales autem noctes sua prolixitate non fastidium aut tedium sed interdum duplex beneficium conferunt. Tribuunt etenim corpori requiem et anime renouant uetustatem. Addunt insuper licentiam reuisendi celestia, sua penetralia inquirendi, nec non et amicorum reminiscendi. Dicunt anime cogitationibus siue meditationibus, 'Vacate et uidete quoniam suauis est Dominus.'[3] Ducunt etiam sua quiete et silentio animas 'usque ad tertium celum',[4] dum extra mundum, extra carnem, supra animam, ad regales sedes omnipotentis Verbi sancta desideria prouehunt. Statim Filium hominis ad abyssos humanarum infirmitatum humiliter inclinando pacata consideratione deponunt. Quis autem dum sua reuoluit amici negotia negligit? Plura de hac materia uobis libenter scriberem, sed scriptor noster frater Hugo, abrepta breui cartula, propter finem carte finem fecit scripture nostre. Volui tamen breuiter tangere uerbum illud quod mandastis per fratrem Iohannem[5] et sic respondere ut dicatis illi domine et cognate nostre:[6] 'Terra in conspectu uestro est,[7] potestis bene facere et male. Sed melius est bene facere quam male quia bene facere sequitur gratia et gloria, malefacere uero pena et penitentia.' Dicite ei: 'Melius est modicum iusto super diuitias peccatorum multas.'[8]

128 *Sirmond V. 1*]

---

128 [1] Berneredus, abbot of Saint-Crépin-le-Grand-de-Soissons *c.*1162/3–Mar. × May 1179. His predecessor d. 4 Nov. 1162, or 1163; Berneredus occurs from 1164; became cardinal bishop of Palestrina in 1179 (first occurs as such May 1179, but it is most likely that he was appointed in Mar. 1179, at the Third Lateran Council, which he attended after being nominated by Peter of Pavia for the cardinalate, and after which he evidently never returned to France). There is some confusion over the date of his death: he last occurs as cardinal 11 July 1180, and his successor first occurs 13 Jan. 1181 (*JL* ii. 145); Brixius gives his death as 3 July 1180 (J. M. Brixius, *Die Mitglieder des Kardinalkollegiums von 1130–1181* [Berlin, 1912], p. 60), while *GC* suggests 3 July 1181 (but the wording is imprecise:

128

To Abbot Berneredus of Saint-Crépin[1]

*c.*1162/3 × 1179 before May (or more likely before Mar.)

To his dearest friend Berneredus, abbot of Saint-Crépin, brother Peter, humble abbot of Saint-Remi, to thrive always.

The stretches of the night are perhaps dearer and more profitable to me than those of the day. For the daily ones, having summoned the troops of plentiful affairs here and there and led them back, carry my soul away from my hands[2] and constantly draw me away from myself with as much violence as deceit. But the winter nights confer by their length not aversion or boredom but sometimes a double blessing. For they afford the body rest and renew the time-worn soul. On top of this they add the liberty to look again upon heavenly things, to inquire into one's own inner depths and also to call friends to mind again. They say to the soul in contemplations or meditations, 'Be still and see that the Lord is sweet.'[3] They also conduct souls in their peace and silence 'even to the third heaven,'[4] while they carry holy desires forth beyond the world, beyond the flesh, above the soul, to the regal abodes of the omnipotent Word. At once, by humbly causing the Son of man to incline towards the abysses of human infirmities, they set Him down for peaceful consideration. But who, while turning over his own affairs, neglects those of a friend? I would gladly write more to you on this subject, but our scribe, brother Hugh, having taken a small scrap of parchment, because he has made an end of the leaf has made an end of our writing. I wanted, however, to touch briefly on that message which you sent by way of brother John,[5] and to reply that you should say to that lady and kinswoman of ours:[6] 'The land is before you,[7] you can act well or ill. But it is better to act well than ill because grace and glory follow upon acting well but punishment and repentance follow upon acting ill.' Tell her: 'Better is a little to the just than the great riches of the wicked.'[8] Tell her, I say,

GC ix. 398–9: 'Insequenti'), so while he was evidently alive still on 11 July, a date sometime in the summer of 1180 is probably the most likely for his death.

[2] Possibly implying away from writing.

[3] Cf. Ps. 45 (46): 11; 33 (34): 9.

[4] 2 Cor. 12: 2.

[5] Unidentified.

[6] Possibly Agnes de Baudemont, wife of Robert of Dreux (see letter no. 78, n. 1): she was evidently related to Peter, and this is the right region for her.

[7] Cf. Jer. 40: 4.

[8] Ps. 36 (37): 16.

Dicite, inquam, ei quia nobilius est minora a deuotis gratanter accipere quam ab inuitis insolenter maiora exigere. Valete, et pro nobis orate. Boamundus dicit uias pessimas esse.[9] Seruate nobis litteras istas.

129

To Abbot Berneredus and the community of Saint-Crépin[1]

*c.*1162/3 × 1178 (after 25 Oct.)

Vnicis amicis et fratribus Berneredo uenerabili abbati et sancto conuentui Sanctorum Crispini et Crispiniani frater Petrus humilis abbas S. Remigii, dies solennes et festiuitates preclaras.[2]

Non est michi datum desuper in presenti uobiscum sabbatizare Kalendas precipuas in natalitiis pretiosorum martyrum uestrorum.[3] Vnde quia 'non quod uolo hoc ago sed quod odi illud facio',[4] pene irascor detentionum mearum funiculis qui difficile soluuntur, contorti nec triplici tantum sed multiplici connexione occupationum concatenatarum. Vnum tantum quod uix residuum est michi facio. Scribo itaque amaritudines meas quas cotidie in distractione et distensione spiritus mei experior, dicens Deo, 'Quare posuisti me contrarium tibi, et factus sum michimet ipsi grauis?'[5] Ecce nunc uitulus saginatus immolatur[6] Suessionis apud sanctos martyres Crispinum et Crispinianum, ecce symphonia et chorus,[7] ecce amicorum ibi sanctus conuentus, et ubi ego, et quid ego? Nec saltem hedus compunctionis pro peccatis meis conceditur.[8] Seruate tamen et mittite, amici karissimi, partes nobis de oleo exultationis[9] uestre, de 'adipe et pinguedine'[10] uisitationis superne. Sufficiet enim copiosa gratia de mensa dominorum uestrorum[11] nobis et uobis quia sicut

129 *Sirmond V.* 2]

[9] Unidentified.

129 [1] Dated as letter no. 128, except that it was evidently written soon after 25 Oct., in which case 1179 is ruled out.

[2] A reference to the day of the abbey's two patron saints, Crispin and Crispinian (25 Oct.), as is clear from what follows.

[3] *natalitia*: the anniversary of a saint's death or martyrdom (i.e. birthday into eternal life): see Niermeyer, *natalicius* 1, *natalicium* 1; Latham, *natal/e . . . /icium*.

that it is nobler gratefully to receive less from the devoted than immoderately to extort more from the unwilling. Farewell, and pray for us. Bohemond says that the roads are at their worst.[9] Preserve this letter for us.

129

To Abbot Berneredus and the community of Saint-Crépin[1]

*c.*1162/3 × 1178 (after 25 Oct.)

To his special friends and brothers, Berneredus venerable abbot and the holy community of the saints Crispin and Crispinian, brother Peter, humble abbot of Saint-Remi, holy days and glorious festal occasions.[2]

It has not been granted to me from above to celebrate together with you the Sabbath of the special kalends on the natal day of your precious martyrs.[3] For which reason, because 'I do not that good which I will, but the evil which I hate, that I do,'[4] I am almost angry at the bonds of my detention which, being twisted together not only with a triple but with a multiple intertwining of entwined affairs, are not easily loosed. I am doing the one and only thing which remains to me, albeit scarcely. I am writing then of my sorrows which I experience daily in the pulling asunder and stretching apart of my spirit, saying to God, 'Why hast thou set me opposite to thee, and I am become burdensome to myself?'[5] See now the fatted calf is sacrificed[6] at Soissons before the holy martyrs Crispin and Crispinian, see the music and dancing,[7] see the holy gathering of friends there—and where am I, and what am I? Not even the kid of remorse is given up for my sins.[8] Yet save some portions of the oil of your exultation,[9] of the 'marrow and fatness'[10] of the heavenly visitation, dearest friends, and send them to us. For the plentiful grace from the table of your lords[11] will suffice for us and for you because, as on

[4] Rom. 7: 15, with an allusion to Eccles. 4: 12 in what follows.
[5] Job 7: 20. [6] Cf. Luke 15: 23, 27, 30. [7] Cf. Luke 15: 25.
[8] Cf. Luke 15: 29, likening himself to the prodigal son's elder brother.
[9] Cf. Ps. 44 (45): 8. [10] Ps. 62 (63): 6.
[11] i.e. the two patron saints and martyrs.

animabus suis non pepercerunt propter Christum 'usque ad mortem',[12] sic Deus, gratiam premiorum exequans gratie meritorum, non est quod neget orantibus pro salute animarum. Iam siquidem de se securi, pro suis ueneratoribus adhuc sunt solliciti. Adsunt procul dubio passionum suarum recitatoribus, et precipue imitatoribus. Orate ergo sicut pro uobis sic et pro nobis, quia nullum est detrimentum orationis si pluribus impertiatur, cuius natura est eo magis habundare in effectu quo amplius se dilatauerit in affectu. Valete.

130

To Abbot Berneredus of Saint-Crépin[1]

*c.*1162/3 × 1179, before May (or more likely before Mar.)

Abbati Sancti Crispini Petrus abbas Sancti Remigii.

Mira ueri amoris natura, ignea siquidem est et tamen contra ignis naturam acrius feruet in amicis remotis quam sub oculis constitutis. Queris quare? Quia sollicitudo ministra dilectionis quasi iacet dum quod amat uidet, currit uero cum assiduo impetu mordens animum propter absentem amicum, 'Vbi est', inquiens, 'quem diligit anima mea?[2] Viuitne? Sospesne est? Estne tristis an letus? Estne timens an securus? Estne de me sollicitus an ad se intentus? Estne indigens an copiosus?' Hac fuscinula[3] carbones suos amor mouens et commouens auget flammam, calorem multiplicat, medullam ossium liquefacit, et post dilectum longa reste sollicitum trahit animum. Trahit, inquam, fortius dum longius subtrahit. Sic Tobias pater et senex morantem filium suspirans gemit, accusans se non potius excepisse pecunie dampnum quam pro ipsa misisse uel amisisse filium.[4] Silenter et suauiter dormit dilectio cum nullis euagatur excursibus querens de statu amici amicalis sollicitudo. Experto credendum est.[5] Duros, immo acutos, aculeos uisceribus nostris infigit absentia uestri,

130 *Sirmond VIII. 17*]

[12] Matt. 26: 38; Mark 14: 34; Acts 22: 4; Phil. 2: 8, 27, 30; Rev. 2: 10; 12: 11.

130 [1] Dated as letter no. 128. [2] Cf. S. of S. 3: 3.

[3] Douai-Reims translates 'flesh hook' (cf. Exod. 27: 3; 1 Kgs. (1 Sam.) 2: 13, etc.), but here it must mean poker or fork.

Christ's account they did not spare their souls 'even unto death,'[12] so there is nothing which God, balancing the grace of the rewards with the grace of the merits, would deny them when they pray for the salvation of souls. Now indeed, secure on their own account, they still care for those who revere them. They are present without doubt with those who recite, and especially with those who imitate, their passions. Pray therefore also for us as you do for yourselves, because prayer, whose nature it is to be more abundant in effectiveness the more fully it extends itself in affection, suffers no diminution if it is bestowed on many. Farewell.

130

To Abbot Berneredus of Saint-Crépin[1]

*c.*1162/3 × 1179, before May (or more likely before Mar.)

To the abbot of Saint-Crépin, Peter, abbot of Saint-Remi.

The nature of true love is wonderful; it is indeed like fire and yet, contrary to the nature of fire, it burns more ardently in distant friends than in those who are before the eyes. You ask why? Because concern, the maid-servant of love, lies down as it were while it sees what it loves, but runs with unceasing motion, stinging the mind on account of an absent friend, asking, 'Where is he whom my soul loves?[2] Is he alive? Is he unharmed? Is he sad or happy? Is he afraid or secure? Is he concerned about me or intent on himself? Is he poor or well-off?' Love, moving and stirring its coals with this poker,[3] rouses the flame and multiplies the heat, liquefies the marrow of the bones and draws the caring soul after the beloved with a long cord. It draws, I say, more powerfully the further it withdraws. So Tobias, a father and an old man, sighing, bewails his son who is delaying, blaming himself for not having accepted the loss of money rather than on its account send or lose his son.[4] Love sleeps silently and sweetly when friendly concern is not wandering about with journeyings enquiring after the condition of the friend. You must believe one who has experienced this.[5] Your absence drives into our inwards hard, nay sharp, points, the piercing of which I had not experienced while I had you here,

[4] Cf. Tobias 10: 1–7.
[5] Cf. Virgil, *Aen.* xi. 283.

quorum punctiones non expertus eram dum presentem haberem, dum uiderem, dum frequenter audirem. Pre ceteris, unum habeo non uobiscum sed aduersus uos, quod intemperanter uiuitis non excedendo mensuram iustam uiuendi supra sed infra.[6] Sententia enim que dicit, 'ne quid nimis',[7] plus et minus redarguit. Amplius edere uoracitatis est, minus hypocrisis uel auaritie. Apostolus scit 'habundare et penuriam pati';[8] in omnibus instructus est ad regulam uiuere, qui neque ad ima curuatur neque ad superiora distenditur sed recto cursu bene tenditur.

131

To Abbot Berneredus of Saint-Crépin[1]

*c.*1164 × *c.*1170

Domino et amico karissimo Berneredo abbati Sancti Crispini frater Petrus humilis abbas S. Remigii, suus in omnibus, se ipsum per omnia.

Quotiens in manu sumitur cartula uobis dicanda, totiens mens repletur etsi ante fuerat bonis omnibus uacua. Cum tumultu namque et impetu magno grex innumerabilis diuersarum materiarum egredi accelerantium in ostio exeundi sese impingit, alia dicente, 'Prior ego amicum salutabo,' alia illam transsiliente atque ramum oliue preferente in ore,[2] amici amplexus priores pertinaciter preripiente. Rebecca in utero suo miratur duorum fratrum immo gentium duarum hec intestina et plus quam ciuilia bella.[3] Sed quid mirum si, ubi corpus perfecti et consummati amoris, illuc congregantur aquile[4] alternarum affectionum siue motuum animi ut contendant non 'intrare' sed exire 'per angustam portam'?[5] Forte, quod ait Laban, in terra sua con-

131 *Sirmond V. 3*]

[6] i.e. he is excessively ascetic.
[7] Terence, *Andria*, i. 1. 61 (34); trans. Loeb edn., J. Sargeaunt.
[8] Phil. 4: 12, which is also echoed in what follows.

131 [1] Referring to the trouble at Montier-la-Celle under Peter's successor, Drogo. Peter's immediate successor was Walter, who occurs only for 1163 (*GC* xii. 544—but this may be a confusion with an earlier Walter, see Introduction, p. xxxi). Drogo first occurs 10 Nov. 1163, and last occurs 1165: *GC* xii. 544; Lalore, *Cartulaires*, vi. 6, 216–21, 221–5, nos. 3, 198 and 199 (both documents 198 and 199 here are dated 1164, before 25

while I could see you, while I could hear you frequently. Before all else, I have one point not in your favour but against you, that you are living intemperately, not by exceeding upward the just measure of living, but downward.[6] For the opinion which states, 'moderation in all things',[7] reproves both too much and too little. To eat more is characteristic of greed, to eat less, of hypocrisy or avarice. The Apostle knows how 'to abound and to suffer need';[8] he was instructed in all things to live regularly, he who is neither bent down to lower things nor stretched up to higher, but well directed with a straight course.

131

To Abbot Berneredus of Saint-Crépin[1]

*c.*1164 × *c.*1170

To his dearest lord and friend Berneredus, abbot of Saint-Crépin, brother Peter, humble abbot of Saint-Remi, his own in all things, himself through all things.

Every time I pick up the sheet of parchment to be dedicated to you, my mind is filled up, even if before it was empty of all good things. For with a great tumult and onrush the innumerable flock of diverse subjects hastening to come forth pushes at the exit, one saying, 'I will greet the friend first,' another, leaping over it and carrying an olive branch in its mouth,[2] stubbornly being the first to snatch the friend's earliest embraces. Rebecca wonders at these internal and more than civil wars of the two brothers, nay the two peoples, in her womb.[3] But what wonder is it if, where the body of perfect and consummate love is, there are gathered together the eagles[4] of mutual affections or of impulses of the soul so that they strive not 'to enter' but to exit 'by the narrow gate'?[5] Perhaps, just as Laban said that it was the custom in

March, and in the sixth year of Alexander III, and so presumably fall in 1165 according to modern convention). Drogo's successor, Gerard, first occurs in 1170: *GC* xii. 544; Lalore, *Cartulaires*, vi. 290–1, no. 235. That it was Drogo and not Walter who was the cause for concern is clear from letter no. 155, where he is named. The present letter implies that Drogo's deposition is imminent, but the date of this cannot be inferred from his last occurrence. On Berneredus, see letter no. 128, n. 1.

[2] Cf. Gen. 8: 11.

[3] Combining Lucan, *De bello civili*, i. 1 ('Bella . . . plus quam civilia') and Gen. 25: 22–3.

[4] Cf. Matt. 24: 28; Luke 17: 37.

[5] Cf. Luke 13: 24; cf. also Matt. 7: 13.

suetudinis esse ut priores, licet lippe, filie tradantur ad nuptias, contingat ut Rachel, mire pulchritudinis et amatissimi decoris, non agat choros saltationis immo salutationis ante Liam primogenitam suam, sed in ultimo sequatur cum Ioseph et Beniamin.[6] Semper enim meliora, digniora et saluti uiciniora[7] non tanquam feces in fundo calicis residunt sed tanquam cibi delicatiores, ut fastidium remoueant et appetitum renouent, in extremis apponuntur, quia 'melior est finis orationis quam principium'.[8] Hoc in me ipso, hoc in amico desidero, ut noua semper sint et nunquam ueterascant desideria uestra, et semper sequamur ad palmam superne uocationis, obliti que retro sunt.[9] Non enim tam quatinus perueneris pensare debes quam quo pergendum, et peregrinationis meta figenda atque trahendus funiculus. Sic audio te facere, et ualde congratulor. Ne tamen nimis extendas et protendas funiculum; caue rupturam. Melius est enim tendere quam rumpere. 'Est modus in rebus.'[10] 'Ne quid nimis.'[11] An inuideo quia cito et bene curris? Nequaquam. Amo cursum sed timeo defectum. Virtutes non bene colligit qui matrem uirtutum spernit. A stirpe uirtutum degenerat uirtus que lineam temperantie non seruat. De his hactenus. Ceterum ineptias nostras quia, ut audiui, intemperanter desideras, uolo tibi exponere que sint modo negotia nostra et cui ad presens labori humeros supposuerim. Successor ille noster Cellensis abbas, quia non bene multiplicauit immo non fouit oua que illic reliqueram, sed conculcauit imperfecta, destruxit autem perfecta, ultra dissimulare non possum. Sed aggredior temptare et probare utrum Deus respicere dignetur priores meos labores, illum uel prorsus amouendo ab abbatia uel saltem corrigendo a stultitia sua et in melius commutando. Pene omnes priores[12] mecum sunt et, ut credo, triginta uel amplius de fratribus. Ora ut Deus propitietur michi et domui illi. Frater Hugo ista debuit scribere, et in sero promisit, sed tandiu dormiuit quandiu ista frater Henricus scripsit. Habet enim oculos nullos.[13] Effert tamen bonitatem et pietatem uestram sibi exhibitam usque ad celos et usque ad nubes.[14] Valete, quia deficit pergamenum.

[6] Cf. Gen. 29: 16–30: 24; Jacob preferred Rachel but Leah was married to him, and bore him children, first; Rachel's children, Joseph and Benjamin, though later were better.

[7] Cf. Heb. 6: 9; what follows is possibly alluding to Isa. 51: 17.

[8] Eccles. 7: 9.

[9] Cf. Phil. 3: 13–14; 'palm' here means a prize (Vulgate has *brauium*).

[10] Horace, *Sat.*, i. 1. 106. (Moderation is the mother of virtues referred to below.)

[11] Terence, *Andria*, i. 1. 61 (34); trans. Loeb edn., J. Sargeaunt. What follows seems to echo Gal. 5: 7.

[12] For *priores* in this sense, see Niermeyer, *prior* 9, but he could mean the priors of the dependencies.

his land that the eldest albeit blear-eyed daughters should be given to wed first, it may happen that Rachel of wondrous beauty and most lovable comeliness perform not the movements of the dance, nay of greeting, before Leah her first-born sister, but in the end follow with Joseph and Benjamin.[6] For always things better, worthier, and nearer to salvation[7] do not settle like dregs in the bottom of the cup but, like the finer delicacies, that they might take away cloying and renew the appetite, are laid out at the end, because 'better is the end of a speech than the beginning'.[8] This I desire in myself, this in a friend, that your desires should always be new and never grow old, and that we should always pursue the palm of the heavenly calling, forgetting the things that are behind.[9] For you ought not to consider so much how far you have come as where to proceed, and where the goal of the pilgrimage is to be fixed and the rope drawn in. I hear that you are acting thus, and I rejoice greatly. However, do not stretch the cord too far and over-stretch it: beware a rupture. For it is better to stretch than to rupture. 'There is measure in things.'[10] 'Moderation in all things.'[11] Am I envious because you run quickly and well? By no means. I love the race but I am afraid of failing. He who spurns the mother of virtues does not well understand the virtues. That virtue which does not preserve the line of moderation degenerates from the stock of virtues. But enough of these matters. As for the rest, because, as I have heard, you have an intemperate desire for our absurdities, I want to explain to you what business we have at the moment and to which labour I have at present set my shoulders. I can no longer conceal the fact that our successor, the abbot of Montier-la-Celle, has not well multiplied, or rather not hatched, the eggs which I had left there, but has trampled the imperfect ones and destroyed the perfect. But I am setting out to test and to prove whether God deigns to look again upon my earlier works, by removing him forthwith from the abbacy, or at least by correcting him from his foolishness and changing him for the better. Almost all of the elder monks[12] are with me and so, as I believe, are thirty or more of the brothers. Pray that God have mercy on me and on that house. Brother Hugh ought to have written these words, and promised to do so late at night, but was asleep all the time while brother Henry was writing them. For he has no eyes.[13] Yet he exalts the goodness and kindness which you have shown him unto the heavens and unto the clouds.[14] Farewell, for the parchment is running out.

[13] i.e. presumably that he cannot manage the task, either because his eyes are weak or because he is easily tired.
[14] Cf. Ps. 56 (57): 11.

132

To Abbot Berneredus of Saint-Crépin[1]

prob. 1171/2

Amico suo karissimo Berneredo abbati Sancti Crispini frater Petrus abbas Sancti Remigii, salutem.

Querenti michi materiam unde tibi scribere exordiar, uix una de grege innumerabilium se sequestrans occurrit, arridens quidem prima fronte sed uultum demittens in secessu uel recessu presentie nostre. Queris quenam sit ista materia tam blanda in exordio, tam religiosa seu timida in supremo. Certe fama glorie tue hec est que amicis tuis iocunda et exhilarata facie ciuitates, castella,[2] uicos et plateas discurrit et circuit usque ad palatium regis, usque ad regine thalamum, usque ad comitisse nostre cubiculum.[3] Templa quoque habitu religioso, uultu modesto perambulat, archiepiscopos, episcopos, abbates, clericos et milites sibi concilians et ad uenerationem sui non mediocriter inclinans. Sed timendum ne sol tanti splendoris, tantorum radiorum, uergat ad occasum et dicatur, 'Ad uesperum demorabitur fletus, et ad matutinam letitia.'[4] Quantum enim gaudii de sanctitate et iustitia amici in amicorum amicos profluit, tantum meroris et doloris in euaporatione siue exinanitione earumdem uirtutum circa eosdem residet. Video, uideo cogitationes tuas ad se ipsas tumultuantes et quare amicus tuus talia tibi scribat sollicitissime reuoluere. Timide enim sunt cogitationes tue. Ne sis sollicitus, bone amice, res salua est, signacula clausa sunt. Aquilo durus uentus non congelauit continen-

132 *Sirmond V. 8*]

132 [1] On Berneredus of Saint-Crépin, see letter no. 128, n. 1. The letter refers to trouble between the archbishop (presumably Henry of France, archbishop of Reims, in whose province both Reims and Soissons lay) and his enemies. Berneredus's supposed peacemaking mission at the court of Champagne makes it likely that this refers to the dispute between Henry of France and Count Henry the Liberal of Champagne, during the course of which the archbishop excommunicated the count. Conflict broke out in 1171 and is recorded as still unresolved in March 1172. A detailed account of this dispute and its chronology is in L. Falkenstein, 'Pontificalis maturitas vel modestia sacerdotalis? Alexander III. und Heinrich von Frankreich in den Jahren 1170–1172', *Archivum Historiae Pontificiae*, xxii (1984), 31–88, at pp. 56–69 (see also *RHF* xvi. 194–5, no. clxxiv—excommunication of Henry the Liberal—and ibid. xv. 910, no. cccxii; also T. Gousset, *Les actes de la province ecclésiastique de Reims*, 4 vols. (Reims, 1842–44), ii. 309–10).

132

To Abbot Berneredus of Saint-Crépin[1]

prob. 1171/2

To his dearest friend Berneredus, abbot of Saint-Crépin, brother Peter, abbot of Saint-Remi, greetings.

When I seek a theme for the beginning of my letter to you, only with difficulty does one, setting itself apart from the crowd of innumerable themes, occur to me, smiling indeed at the first encounter but casting down its eyes on its departure or retreat from our presence. You ask what this theme is, so appealing at the outset, so devout, or timid, at the end. It is, to be sure, the reputation of your glory which, with a face delightful to your friends and full of joy, runs around and about cities, towns,[2] villages, and streets, even as far as the royal palace and the queen's chamber and the private chamber of our countess.[3] It makes its way also through churches in religious habit with modest countenance, winning over to itself archbishops, bishops, abbots, clerks, and knights, and inclining them in no small way to veneration of itself. But one should be afraid lest the sun of such splendour, of such great rays, verge towards its setting and it be said, 'In the evening weeping shall have place, and in the morning gladness.'[4] For however much joy pours forth to friends of friends over the sanctity and justice of a friend, just as much sorrow and grief remains among those same ones when those same virtues evaporate or come to naught. I see, I see your thoughts in turmoil about themselves and brooding most anxiously over why your friend is writing such things to you. For your thoughts are fearful. Do not be anxious, good friend; the matter is safe, the seals are unbroken. The harsh north wind has not frozen

[2] Cf. Matt. 9: 35; 10: 11; Luke 8: 1; 13: 22 (in the Vulgate, *castella* are 'towns' not 'castles'; see also letter no. 3, n. 2).

[3] The queen was Adela of Champagne (m. 1160; Arbois de Jubainville, *Comtes de Champagne*, ii. 403 and iii. 45; Diceto, i. 303), the daughter of Theobald II of Champagne and sister of Henry the Liberal (on whom see letter no. 71, n. 1). The countess must be Marie de France, countess of Champagne (Peter calls her 'our countess', and 'of Troyes'), the wife of Henry the Liberal and daughter of Louis VII and Eleanor of Aquitaine (and so sister-in-law and stepdaughter to Queen Adela): on her career see J. F. Benton, 'The court of Champagne as a literary center', *Speculum*, xxxvi (1961), 551–91, now repr. in Benton, *Culture*, pp. 3–43, at 5–6.

[4] Ps. 29 (30): 6.

tiam, caritatem aut opinionem nostram. Qualem te habuimus talem te habemus et semper habituri sumus. Huic quoque presentium latori, si quid ex his imputandum, imputa, qui non solum scribere compulit sed talem materiam prescripsit. Reuocauit enim ad memoriam illa magnifica preconia que auribus nostris instillaueras quando ab illa solennitate Trecensi quantum uacuatus propria et bona conscientia tantum inflatus uana letitia redisti. Dixisti enim te pre aliis exceptum et receptum a Trecensium comitissa, inuitatum ad epulas, glorificatum in mensa, in omni postulatione exauditum, et cum longa cauda glorie reuersum. Caue caudam, cum tam omnis laus quam omne uituperium in cauda, id est in fine, terminetur.[5] Dico autem, quem te ipsum facis? Si hec facis, manifesta te ipsum mundo et nobis. Si enim propheta es in Israhel, ueni ad nos[6] ut ipsis rebus experiamur potentiam, prophetiam et uirtutem tuam. Signis enim que in patria tua facis non credemus[7] nisi te uirum 'cuius spiritus in naribus'[8] ex fructibus cognouerimus. Decurtata tamen est gloria tua quia non fecisti pacem inter archiepiscopum et aduersarios suos. Valete.

133

To Berneredus of Saint-Crépin, cardinal bishop of Palestrina[1]

May (or more likely Mar.) 1179 × summer 1180

Prenestino episcopo Petrus abbas Sancti Remigii.

Plus molesta quam grata et iocunda occurrit materia quotiens ad scribendum unico et quondam collaterali amico abbati sumitur carta. Renouatur namque dolor meus repentina sed et urgenti et urenti corrosione animi dum transmontana remotio intercurrit et amicos diuidit aspectus non tamen affectus. Accedit huic seuerissima

133 *Sirmond VIII. 21*]

[5] There is a sharp critical point to *cauda* here: cf. Isa. 9: 15, ' . . .et propheta docens mendacium ipse cauda est'.

[6] Cf. 4 Kgs. (2 Kgs.) 5: 8.

[7] Cf. John 4: 44, 48; cf. also Matt. 13: 57; Mark 6: 4; Luke 4: 24.

[8] Isa. 2: 22.

our temperateness, our love, or our opinion. We hold you to be, and always will hold you to be, such as we have always held you to be. Give credit also, if there is any credit to be given, to the bearer of this letter, who not only compelled me to write but prescribed such a theme. For he recalled to memory those magnificent praises which you had poured into our ears when you returned from that solemn ceremony in Troyes, as much emptied of your own good conscience as puffed up with vain delight. For you said that you were singled out and received more favourably than the rest by the countess of Troyes, invited to feasts, praised at table, heeded in every request, and sent away with a long tail of glory. Beware the tail, since every insult, as much as every praise, ends in a tail, that is in an end.[5] But whom, I ask, are you making yourself into? If you are doing these things, show yourself clearly to the world and to us. For if you are a prophet in Israel, come to us[6] so that we may experience by these things your power, your prophecy, and your virtue. For we shall not believe in the signs which you perform in your home country[7] unless we know, from the fruits, that you are a man 'whose breath is in his nostrils'.[8] Your glory, however, is curtailed because you have not made peace between the archbishop and his enemies. Farewell.

133

To Berneredus of Saint-Crépin, cardinal bishop of Palestrina[1]

May (or more likely Mar.) 1179 × summer 1180

To the bishop of Palestrina, Peter, abbot of Saint-Remi.

A subject which is more grievous than it is pleasant and joyful presents itself whenever a sheet is taken up to write to a special friend, and one who was once a neighbouring abbot. For my pain is renewed with a sudden, but also a pressing and burning, gnawing of the soul while your removal across the mountains intervenes and divides friendly faces, though not affections. Added to this is that most

133 [1] To Berneredus of Saint-Crépin after he became cardinal bishop of Palestrina (see letter no. 128, n. 1). This may be the first of the three letters (nos. 133–5) written by Peter after Berneredus's elevation, since he stresses his grief at Berneredus's crossing the mountains—although letter no. 135 also falls early in the period, and no sequence can be established with certainty.

desperatio corporalis incorporationis cum forte instet citissima alterutrius solutio anime et corporis.[2] Bone nunc domine, olim amice dulcissime, quem constitues uicarium qui uices tuas suppleat in nostris exequiis, in oculis claudendis extrema salutatione et eterna conclusione? De cuius manibus Saluator suscipiet spiritum meum, cum tuas mundas manus ad hoc delegissem dudum officiosum obsequium? Alius, ut uideo, amicus officiis[a] in his est substituendus. Sed quare conqueror? Quare gemo? Quare uultum obnubilo? Dei enim ordinationi quis resistit? An forte tulit Deus Heliam ut Heliseus duplicem eius reciperet spiritum?[3] Nonne Ioseph asportatio in Egypto fratrum eius et totius successionis fuit saluatio?[4] Nonne Iesus ante apostolos celum ascendit ut Spiritum mitteret et mansiones prepararet?[5] Ecce iuxta latus apostolorum locus a Deo tibi datus est. Quid ergo? Pulsa, excita, 'insta opportune importune'[6] donec et rorem[b] et stillicidia gratie de sanctis oribus[c] immo interpellationibus eorum ⟨in⟩ aridam nostram infundat qui gratiam apostolatus et benedictionem singularem ad nostram eis salutem indulsit. Hoc munus, si per te collatum fuerit, amissis preponderat et una clausula innumera beneficia coagulat. Domino pape de sua gratia ad uos gratias agite. Cancellarium, Tusculanensem, Albanensem, dominum Hyacinthum et Ostiensem sanctum uirum, et si quos habemus alios amicos in curia, salutate.[7]

[a] officii *Sirmond* [b] ros *Sirmond* [c] *corr. Hall;* ossibus *Sirmond*

[2] i.e. their separation is worse because their age makes it more likely that one or other of them will die before they can meet again, as indeed happened. *Desperatio incorporationis* here seems to mean the state of mortality, and so fear of death, but may also refer allusively to their chance of meeting in the flesh.

[3] Cf. 4 Kgs. (2 Kgs.) 2: esp. 9–11.

[4] Cf. Gen. 37 and 42–7.

[5] Cf. John 14: 2–3, 16–17.

[6] 2 Tim. 4: 2.

hopeless despair of bodily embodiment, since it may be that the swiftest loosening of soul and body in either of us draws nigh.[2] Whom will you appoint as your representative, you who are now my good lord yet were once my sweetest friend, to take your place at our funeral rites, closing our eyes in the final farewell and in the eternal conclusion? From whose hands will the Saviour take up my spirit, since I had some time ago chosen your pure hands for this dutiful service? Another friend, so I see, must be substituted in these duties. But why am I complaining? Why am I groaning? Why am I clouding my face? For who resists the ruling of God? Or did God perchance take Elijah up so that Elisha should receive his spirit twofold?[3] Was the carrying away of Joseph into Egypt not the salvation of his brothers and of the whole succession?[4] Did Jesus not ascend to heaven before the apostles so that He might send the Spirit and prepare mansions?[5] See, a place is granted to you by God by the side of the apostles. What then? Knock, rouse up, 'be instant in season, out of season'[6] until He who granted to them the grace of the apostleship and the singular blessing for our salvation pour out upon our aridity both dew and showers of grace from their holy mouths, nay from their intercessions. This gift, should it be conferred through you, outweighs those which are lost and joins innumerable blessings together in a single conclusion. Give thanks to the lord pope for his favour towards you. Convey our greetings to the chancellor, to the cardinal bishops of Tusculum and Albano, to Lord Hyacinth and that holy man the cardinal bishop of Ostia, and to any other friends we have in the Curia.[7]

[7] The chancellor is Albert of Morra (see letter no. 83, n. 1); the cardinal bishop of Tusculum, Peter of Pavia (see letter no. 89, n. 1, and on his role in Berneredus's elevation, see Glorieux, 'Candidats', pp. 21–2); the cardinal bishop of Albano is Henry de Marcy (see letter no. 82, n. 1); 'dominus Hyacinthus' is Cardinal Deacon Giacinto Bobo, later Pope Celestine III (*DP*, pp. 184–6), and the cardinal bishop of Ostia (and Velletri) is Ubaldo Allucingoli, later Pope Lucius III (*DP*, pp. 180–1). The extent or nature of Peter's contact with the latter two is unclear; they occur nowhere else in his letters.

134

To Berneredus of Saint-Crépin, cardinal bishop of Palestrina[1]

May (or more likely Mar.) 1179 × summer 1180

Prenestino episcopo Petrus abbas Sancti Remigii.

Ex multa et pene inconsolabili cordis angustia, ex multorum relatione, perpendo uos usque in conquestionem tedii uite uestre prorumpere. Hoc sine dubio sciatis uiri minus constantis et prudentis esse. Apostolus certe magister non gentium[2] tantum sed omnium Christianorum scit 'habundare et penuriam pati' et in omnibus sufficiens esse.[3] Ad hanc formam utinam componeremus titubantem uitam nostram. Causas tamen pusillanimitatis, immo assidue conquestionis, audire desidero, et tunc uel improbare uel approbare dolorem potero. Triplex siquidem occurrit michi conquerendi ratio siue occasio: aut enim propria temeritas impellit ad aliquid faciendum quod non sit faciendum, aut aliena calliditas, aut, ut uulgo loquar, perplexa diuine predestinationis necessitas. Sed propria temeritas semper culpanda, aliena calliditas cauenda, a Deo ueniens iusta sententia timenda. Freno indiget propria temeritas ut inconsulta, consilio aliena calliditas ut suspecta, superna sententia timore ut fortissima. Non michi ignosco in propria temeritate, accuso me in aliene calliditatis circumuentione, gemo sub manus Dei percussione. Ne iterum precipitet propria temeritas, rationem consulo; ne suffocet laqueus aliene calliditatis, sapientem consulo; ne mucro superne seueritatis usque ad internecionem deseuiat,[4] humiliter imploro. In propria temeritate fragilitatem meam cognosco, in aliena seductione spiritum discretionis aduoco, in flagellis diuinis Deo me totum committo. Quero igitur quam istarum magis suspectam habeas, utrum unam uel duas uel simul tres. Si unam et tuam, propitius tibi esto. Si alienam et meam, indulge michi, potius enim simplicitate quam calliditate usus sum quando, ut tuo episcopo adquiescerem, ire

134 *Sirmond IX. 1*]

134 [1] Dated as letter no. 133. [2] Cf. 2 Tim. 1: 11.
[3] Cf. Phil. 4: 11–12. [4] Cf. 2 Kgs. (2 Sam.) 2: 26.

134

To Berneredus of Saint-Crépin, cardinal bishop of Palestrina[1]

May (or more likely Mar.) 1179 × summer 1180

To the bishop of Palestrina, Peter, abbot of Saint-Remi.

It is from a great and almost inconsolable anguish of the heart, so I judge, from the report of many people, that you are bursting forth even to the point of complaining of the weariness of your life. You should know without doubt that this is characteristic of a man insufficiently constant and wise. The Apostle certainly, a teacher not only of gentiles[2] but of all Christians, knows how 'to abound and to suffer need' and how to be content in all things.[3] If only we could arrange our faltering life according to this model. I wish, however, to hear the causes of your faintheartedness, rather of your incessant complaint, and then I shall be able either to disapprove or approve of the anguish. For a triple reason or occasion for complaint occurs to me: for either one's own rashness drives one to do something which should not be done, or else the cunning of another does so, or else, to put it in common terms, the inscrutable necessity of divine predestination. But one's own rashness is always to be reproached, another's cunning to be avoided, the just judgement coming from God to be feared. One's own rashness needs to be reined in as ill-advised, the cunning of another requires deliberation as suspect, the judgement from on high should be feared as the most mighty. I do not forgive myself in my own rashness, I accuse myself in being tricked by another's cunning, I groan under the smiting of the hand of God. Lest, again, my own rashness cast me down, I consult reason; lest the noose of another's cunning strangle me, I consult the wise; lest the sword of heavenly severity rage even unto utter destruction,[4] I make humble supplication. In my own rashness I recognize my fragility, in the seduction of another I call upon the spirit of discernment, in divine flagellations I commit myself wholly to God. I ask therefore which of these do you suspect the more: is it one or two or all three at once? If it is one, and that your own, be kind to yourself. If it is another's, and that mine, be indulgent to me, for I

cum eo ad concilium ⟨tibi⟩ persuasi.[5] Si te celestis dispensatio illaqueauit, quid tibi irasceris? Quid michi? Quis enim tu? Quis ego qui prohibere possem ne suo cursu curreret quem nulla creatura declinare aut impedire potest? Quid enim Deus cogitet de nobis intra uelum secreti consilii sui, eo usque nos latet donec ad publicum nostrum ipso actu prodeat.[6] Tandiu est nostrum nescire, quandiu suum durauerit celare. Longanimiter quoque expectandum est quod cum uenerit patienter est sustinendum. Non est properandum si differat, non est murmurandum si proferat. 'Iesus Christus heri et hodie':[7] heri, antequam aperiat 'sacramentum uoluntatis sue',[8] hodie, cum manifestauerit secretum prescientie sue. Iccirco sic exclusa sopiatur omnis uestra conquestio ubi nec temeritas apparet reprehensibilis, nec calliditas apprehenditur dampnabilis, nec Dei sententia intolerabilis. Etsi enim priuauit solo paterno, honorauit uos sublimi solio.[9] Miscet namque sapientia in cratere uinum suum ne nimis sit potanti calidum, ne rursus insipidum. Infert exilium presumptori, confert solatium exulanti. Pluris est consolatio quam desolatio uestra. Gregem pusillum dimisistis,[10] egregios cardinales amicos et socios recepistis. Claustralem angulum reliquistis, urbem dominam mundi adquisistis.[11] Abbatis gradum inferiorem episcopali quis nesciat? Si corpora martyrum Crispini et Crispiniani Suessioni sepulta sunt,[12] Petri principis apostolorum et Pauli doctoris gentium[13] sacratiores reliquias in Romana urbe haberi quis ignorat? Si paria in uestra commutatione querantur tam in relictis quam in adeptis, longe imparia omnia inuenientur preter affectum, qui inde torquetur unde alius extolletur. Omnia secundum se affectus moderatur. Nichil apud ipsum magnum nisi in se de se faciat magnum. Si ergo affectus mitigabitur, pacata erunt omnia. Nature quidem mirabilis est animus ex quo gignitur affectus, sed tamen quocunque suus pulsus illum tulerit, omnia ad se trahit[14] et suo nichilominus siue sapore siue colore intingit. Cui turbato nichil quiescit, cui amaro nichil dulcescit,

[5] Berneredus was persuaded to become a cardinal when he attended the Third Lateran Council, having been nominated by Peter of Pavia (see letter no. 128, n. 1). Peter was similarly nominated, but stayed away (Glorieux, 'Candidats', pp. 20–1).

[6] i.e. the final judgement.

[7] Heb. 13: 8.

[8] Eph. 1: 9.

[9] i.e. by taking him from France to the Curia.

[10] Cf. Luke 12: 32 (if this is the allusion intended, then Peter's point is not straightforward; a warning against worldly grandeur could be implied).

[11] i.e. Rome.

[12] The patron saints of Saint-Crépin-le-Grand.

[13] 1 Tim. 2: 7.

[14] Possibly echoing John 12: 32.

employed simplicity rather than cunning when to acquiesce with your bishop I persuaded ⟨you⟩ to go with him to the council.[5] If the dispensation of heaven has ensnared you, why are you angry with yourself? Why with me? For who are you? Who am I, that I could have prevented Him, whom no creature can deflect or impede, from running His own course? For what God thinks about us within the veil of His secret counsel He hides from us until such time as it proceed in very deed at our trial.[6] Our ignorance of this lasts as long as His concealment. Furthermore, that is to be awaited with long-suffering which when it comes must patiently be endured. It is not to be hastened if He delays it; it is not to be murmured at if He advances it. 'Jesus Christ yesterday and today':[7] yesterday, before He open 'the mystery of his will,'[8] today, when He has manifested the secret of his foreknowledge. So let your every complaint be thus shut out and laid to sleep where no reprehensible rashness appears, and where neither damnable cunning nor an unbearable judgement of God is apprehended. For although He has deprived you of the land of your fathers, He has honoured you with a lofty throne.[9] For He mixes His wine in the cup with wisdom so that it should not be too hot for the one drinking it, nor again tasteless. He brings exile upon the presumptuous, He confers solace on the exile. Your consolation is greater than your desolation. You have dismissed the little flock,[10] you have received eminent cardinals as friends and companions. You have abandoned the corner of the cloister, you have acquired the city which is mistress of the world.[11] Who could not know that the rank of abbot is inferior to that of bishop? If the bodies of the martyrs Crispin and Crispinian are buried at Soissons,[12] who does not know that the more sacred relics of Peter, chief of the apostles, and of Paul, doctor of the gentiles,[13] are kept in the city of Rome? If in your translation comparisons are sought between those things which you have left behind and those which you have gained, a great disparity will be found in everything except my affection, which is tortured by the very thing whereby another shall be raised up. Affection moderates all things according to itself. Nothing is great in its sight unless affection makes it great in itself, of itself. If therefore affection is pacified, all things will be at peace. The mind, out of which affection is born, is indeed of a miraculous nature, but still wherever its own impulse takes it, it draws all things unto itself[14] and tinges them no less with its own savour or colour. Nothing is peaceful to it when it is disturbed, nothing is sweet to it when it is bitter, nothing is sufficient

cui auaro nichil sufficit, cui uago nichil consistit. E contra, fixo nulla mobilia flectuntur, pacato tranquilla sunt etiam procellosa, benigno mansuescunt etiam ferocia. Sic Deus adduxit ad Adam cuncta animantia terre et uolatilia celi 'ut uideret quid uocaret ea. Omne enim quod uocauit Adam', 'ipsum est nomen eius.'[15] Procul dubio animi est omnes motus cordis et corporis iudicare et nomina imponere, unde auctoritas dicit, 'Affectus tuus operi tuo nomen imponit.'[16] Preest enim uolatilibus celi cogitando de supernis, preest bestiis terre reprimendo motus carnis, preest etiam piscibus maris moderando uolubiles cogitationes mentis.[17] Omni igitur studio est excolendus, sine quo nullus motus bonus. Laborandum ne sit malus, quia si malus est, non est in ciuitate malum quod ipse non fecerit.[18] Enitendum quoque ut sit bonus quatinus gratia cooperante creet bona, faciat pacem et formet lucem. Diu detinuit epistola amicum occupatum in suis et domini apostolici negotiis. Proinde ueniam peto. Remotissimum namque alloquor quem solebam non cartis ad horam detinere sed horis familiarissimo hinc inde colloquio, diebus plurimis quandoque adiunctis et noctibus, occupare. Valete.

135

To Berneredus of Saint-Crépin, cardinal bishop of Palestrina[1]

1179, after Mar./May (poss. later; × summer 1180)

Prenestino episcopo Petrus abbas Sancti Remigii.

Vix occurro suscipere turbam cogitationum siue materiarum que se ingerunt, insistentes 'opportune importune'[2] uenire ad uos, dicendo, 'Ecce ego, mitte me, ecce ego, mitte me.'[3] Inter ceteras uero adulescentulas medullatarum meditationum famosissima illa et notissima atque nobilissima matrona que ab humero et sursum

135 *Sirmond IX. 2*]

---

[15] Cf. Gen. 2: 19.

[16] Cf. Ambrose, *De officiis min.*, i. 30. 147 (M. Testard, *Saint Ambroise, Les Devoirs* (Paris, 1984), i. 166; *PL* xvi. 71): 'Affectus tuus nomen imponit operi tuo,' but frequently given as here, cf. e.g. Peter Lombard, *Sent.* ii. dist. xl. 1 (Brady, i. 2, p. 557; *PL* cxcii. 747). (English 'affection' is too narrow to convey fully the meaning of *affectus*, a disposition or state of the mind, but not in the sense of *intentio*.)

[17] Cf. Gen. 1: 26, but for *bestiae terrae* (Job 5: 23) and *motus carnis* cf. Gregory, *Moralia in Iob* vi. 33. 52 (*CCSL* cxliii. 321; *PL* lxxv. 757) and *Glossa ad loc.* (*PL* cxiii. 771).

for it when it is greedy, nothing stands still for it when it is restless. On the other hand, when it is set firm no moving things turn, when it is pacified even stormy winds are tranquil, when it is well-disposed even wild things grow tame. Thus God brought to Adam all the beasts of the earth and the fowls of the air 'to see what he would call them. For whatsoever Adam called' every one, 'the same is its name.'[15] Without doubt it pertains to the mind to judge all the impulses of the heart and the body and to give them names, whence authority says, 'Your affection gives a name to your action.'[16] For it has dominion over the fowls of the air by contemplating the highest things, it has dominion over the beasts of the earth by keeping in check the impulses of the flesh, it even has dominion over the fishes of the sea by moderating the whirling thoughts of the mind.[17] That without which there is no good impulse should therefore be cultivated with all eagerness. One must take pains that it be not evil, because if it is evil, there is no evil in the city which it has not done.[18] One must also strive that it be good so that with the aid of grace it may create good things, make peace, and fashion light. This letter has long detained a friend who is occupied in his own affairs and those of the apostolic lord. Accordingly I seek pardon. For I am addressing one who is very far away, whom I was accustomed not to detain for an hour with letters but to occupy for hours with the most friendly exchange of conversation, sometimes for many days and nights together. Farewell.

135

To Berneredus of Saint-Crépin, cardinal bishop of Palestrina[1]

1179, after Mar./May (poss. later; × summer 1180)

To the bishop of Palestrina, Peter, abbot of Saint-Remi.

I can hardly withstand the crowd of thoughts or of subjects which rush up, pressing 'in season, out of season'[2] to come to you, saying, 'See me, send me, see me, send me.'[3] But among the other young

[18] Cf. Amos 3: 6.

135 [1] On letters to Berneredus as cardinal, see letter no. 133, n. 1. Theobald, Berneredus's successor at Saint-Crépin named here, may have been abbot for five months in 1179: it is unclear which five months these were, and his career is difficult to reconstruct (see letter no. 146, n. 1), but the present letter seems to have been written soon after his election. [2] 2 Tim. 4: 2. [3] Cf. Isa. 6: 8.

omnes uirtutes antecedit et precellit, fraterna caritas, de qua ait Apostolus, 'Adhuc excellentiorem uiam uobis demonstro',[4] iure sedem regiam occupat et suo splendore omnes obumbrat, immo illustrat, et suum tenere ordinem post se imperat. Huic obediunt omnia, non solum terrestria sed et ipsa celestia, nam de eius plenitudine omnes accipiunt nomen et uirtutem, gloriam et honorem. Hanc ego licet statura pusillus[5] non attingam, tamen ad unam et minimam uestimenti eius fimbriam[6] totum me superextendo, et de salute nullatenus despero. Hanc cum amicis et inter amicos teneo et cognosco, et prius uolo putrefieri cum uermibus in puluere terre quam fidem semel datam et amicitiam promissam negligentia aut subreptione interrumpere. Matrona hec duas habet claues, unam qua cor claudit et aperit alteram qua atrii exterioris corbonam, id est archam, in necessitatibus familie sue similiter claudit et aperit. Cor est archa federis ubi tabule testamenti, uirga Aaron et manna reponuntur: tabule testamenti ne ignores aut preuarices legem Dei; uirga Aaron, que fronduit et floruit,[7] ut timeas offensam, quia uirga, serues gratiam, quia frondosa et florida; manna ut per 'spiritum adoptionis'[8] degustes et prelibes gloriam absconse dulcedinis Deum timentibus, cuius stillicidium, ad quod letatur germinans,[9] sufficit in presenti uita, et habundantia seruatur in alia. Exclusa itaque omni malitia et iniquitate a corde, sola deambulet in suo pomerio[10] caritas, sola ibi pascat et cubet in meridie.[11] Non uideat illam ingredientem et deambulantem oculus nequam[12] qui fascinauerat Corinthios[13] et iniquos presbyteros.[14] Cum tamen placuerit, aduocet puellas suas de terra Israhel ut afferant ei smegmata suauissimi odoris et oleum letitie[15] de quibus aspergat cubile suum[16] ad aduentum sponsi qui de sua propagine non nisi celestes et mansuros fructus generat. Deinde egreditur ad hortum nucum, ad hortum pomorum suorum, ut uideat poma conuallium et inspiciat si floruerint uinee et germinauerint mala punica;[17] ad hortum utique nucum, eremitarum et reclusorum, hortum pomorum, in seculari habitu religiose uiuentium; poma conuallium, qui elegerunt abiecti esse in domo Dei,[18] uineas, feruentes spiritu,

[4] 1 Cor. 12: 31. [5] Cf. Luke 19: 3.

[6] Cf. Matt. 9: 20; 14: 36; Mark 6: 56; Luke 8: 44.

[7] Cf. Num. 17: 8; *archa federis* is here contrasted with *archa*, above and below. Cf. also Gregory *ep.* viii. 29 (*CCSL* cxlA, 552; *PL* lxxvii. 933 [= *ep.* 30]).

[8] Rom. 8: 15. [9] Cf. Ps. 30 (31): 20; 64 (65): 11.

[10] Cf. Dan. 13: 7. [11] Cf. S. of S. 1: 6.

[12] Cf. Matt. 6: 23; 20: 15; Luke 11: 34.

[13] Cf. Gal. 3: 1 (he has confused Cor. and Gal.). [14] Cf. Dan. 13: 28.

[15] Cf. ibid.: 17. [16] Cf. Prov. 7: 17. [17] Cf. S. of S. 6: 10.

maidens of rich meditations that most celebrated and renowned and noble matron who surpasses and rises head and shoulders above all virtues, namely brotherly love, of whom the Apostle says, 'I show unto you yet a more excellent way,'[4] rightly occupies the royal throne and by her splendour overshadows, nay illuminates, all and commands them to keep to their places behind her. All things obey her, not only the earthly but also the heavenly themselves, for from her abundance all men receive a name and strength, glory and honour. Although being low of stature[5] I may not reach her, yet still I stretch myself out fully to touch just one hem of her garment,[6] and that the least, and I do not at all despair of salvation. I hold on to and recognize her with friends and among friends, and I would rather rot away among the worms in the dust of the earth than, through neglect or deception, break a trust once given and a friendship once promised. This matron has two keys, one with which she closes and opens the heart, the other with which she similarly closes and opens the treasure chest of the outer court, that is the ark, according to the pressing needs of her household. The heart is the ark of the covenant where the tablets of the testament, the rod of Aaron, and the manna are stored: the tablets of the testament lest you be ignorant of or transgress the law of God; the rod of Aaron, which sent forth leaves and flowered,[7] so that you fear displeasure because it is a rod and preserve grace because it is leafy and flowery; manna so that through the 'spirit of adoption'[8] you may taste and have a foretaste of the glory of the sweetness stored up for those who fear God, whose shower, at which it springs up and rejoices,[9] is sufficient in the present life and whose abundance is preserved in the other. So with all malice and iniquity shut out of the heart, let love walk alone in her orchard,[10] let her feed there alone and let her lie in the midday.[11] Let the evil eye[12] which had bewitched the Corinthians[13] and the wicked elders[14] not see her going in and walking about. When it please her, however, let her call her daughters from the land of Israel that they may bring to her washing balls of sweetest odour and oil of joy[15] with which she may perfume her bed[16] ready for the coming of the groom who engenders from his stock only heavenly and lasting fruits. Then she goes out to the garden of nuts, to the garden of her fruits, so that she may see the fruits of the valleys and look to see if the vineyards have flourished and the pomegranates budded;[17] assuredly to the garden of nuts, that is of hermits and of recluses, the garden of fruits, that is of those living a religious life in secular habit, to see the fruits

mala punica, qui crucifigunt carnem suam 'cum uitiis et concupiscentiis'.[19] Ponit namque signa sua, pietatis opera, caritas 'in exitu' actionum 'super summum',[20] id est palam. Ponit namque et proponit quatinus per signa extrinsecus apparentia deprehendatur intus latens ueritas, unde: 'A fructibus eorum cognoscetis eos.'[21] Caritas enim aquas suas in plateis diuidit ut bibant homines et iumenta, quia sapientibus et insipientibus debitrix est.[22] A corde tamen egreditur[a] et ad cor regreditur quia cornua altaris[23] ex ipso sunt procedentia et nullum bonum opus remunerabile quod non surgit de bone uoluntatis radice. Ponit igitur caritas affectum cordis et obsequium operis. Affectus latet, opus patet. Sic habet caritas et secretum suum et publicum. In secreto quiescit, in publico operatur. Imitatur operantem sex diebus et sabbato quiescentem.[24] Duplex uero est officii ratio. Alia enim consideratur inter amicos, alia inter extraneos. Aliud est munus amicale, aliud generale. Amicale de corde exigitur et in corde seruatur. Generale de archa extrahitur nec ibi retinetur. Riuus amoris non siccatur largiendo quod habet, sed archa extenuatur dum euacuatur. Carius itaque est munus quod nec arescit profusione nec deficit largitione. Appetibilius tamen sepe requiritur quod in manu uel sinu refunditur quam illud quod in medullis amicalibus per fidem reconditur. Exteriora siquidem et uisibilia, quia usibus humanis necessaria sunt, ab his amplius diliguntur quorum appetitus tenacius in temporalibus quam in spiritalibus irretitur. Qui uero calcatis grossioribus carnis feculentiis cubilia spiritus ingressi subtiliari[25] in spiritalibus consueuerunt, in amicis querunt gratiam non pecuniam, fidem non extrinsecam possessionem, ueritatem inuiolabilem non utilitatem temporalem. Qui enim cor hominis habet, quid est hominis aut in homine quod non possidet? Hinc est quod in Christo, quem Pater de corde suo eructauit[26] quando uel eternaliter equalem sibi genuit uel temporaliter de Virgine incarnari constituit, omnia nostra sunt, iuxta Apostolum qui ait, 'Siue Cephas, siue Apollo, siue mors, siue uita, omnia uestra, uos autem Christi, Christus autem Dei.'[27] Forte dicitis: 'Vt quid, et ad quid hec?' Quia legi in litteris uestris uos

[a] *sic PL;* regreditur *Sirmond*

[18] Cf. Ps. 83 (84): 11. [19] Cf. Gal. 5: 24. [20] Cf. Ps. 73 (74): 4–5.
[21] Matt. 7: 16, cf. 7: 20. [22] Cf. Prov. 5: 16 and Rom. 1: 14.
[23] Cf. Isa. 46: 8 and Exod. 29: 12; Lev. 4: 7, 34 and many other refs.
[24] Cf. Gen. 1: 1–2: 3. [25] Cf. Latham, *subtil/io*.
[26] Cf. Ps. 44 (45): 2, 'Eructauit cor meum uerbum bonum'; Peter means that Christ as the Word is 'uttered', i.e. sent forth, while at the same time he continues the image of the heart. [27] Cf. 1 Cor. 3: 22–3.

of the valleys, that is those who have chosen to be cast down in the house of God,[18] the vineyards, that is those fervent in spirit, and the pomegranates, that is those who crucify their flesh 'with the vices and concupiscences'.[19] For love places her ensigns, the works of kindness, in the 'going out' of deeds 'and on the highest top,'[20] that is openly. For she places and displays them so that the truth lying hidden within should be understood through visible external signs, whence: 'By their fruits you shall know them.'[21] For love divides her waters in the streets so that men and beasts of burden may drink, because she is a debtor both to the wise and to the unwise.[22] She goes forth, however, from the heart and returns to the heart because the horns of the altar[23] come out from the heart and no good work is worthy of reward which does not arise from the root of goodwill. Therefore love puts in place affection of the heart and service in the deed. Affection lies hidden, a deed is plain to see. Thus love has its secret side and its public. In secret it rests quiet, in public it works. It imitates the One working for six days and resting on the Sabbath.[24] But twofold is the nature of its service. For one side is observed among friends, the other among strangers. One is a friendly gift, the other general. The friendly is demanded of the heart and preserved in the heart. The general is drawn out of the ark and not retained there. The stream of love is not dried up by dispensing what it has, but the ark is diminished as it is emptied. So the gift is dearer which neither dries up by being poured forth nor fails by being disbursed. However what is poured back into the hand or lap is often sought as more desirable than that which is stored up in friendly hearts through faith. Exterior and visible things indeed, because they are necessary to human needs, are more loved by those whose desire is ensnared more firmly in temporal than in spiritual things. But those who, having trodden down the grosser filthiness of the flesh, entering the chamber of the spirit have grown accustomed to be refined[25] in spiritual things, seek in friends grace not wealth, faith not external possessions, inviolable truth not temporal benefit. For he who has a man's heart, what is there of the man or in the man which he does not possess? Hence it is that in Christ, whom the Father uttered forth from His heart[26] when He both eternally begat Him equal to Himself and temporally caused Him to be incarnate of the Virgin, all things are ours, according to the Apostle who says, 'Whether it be Cephas, or Apollos, or death, or life, all are yours, and you are Christ's, and Christ is God's.'[27] Perhaps you are saying: 'What of this, and where is

amisisse ueteres amicos nec comparasse nouos.[28] Concedo amisisse si opinione aut ueritate constat inueteratos esse. Vera certe amicitia puritate uirginea et caloris perpetuitate neque adulteratur neque refrigeratur sed cotidiana renouatione cum sole semper oritur nec moritur. Si unquam ergo habuistis amicos, adhuc habetis non inueteratos, quod esset uitium, sed remotos, quod est opus diuinum. Sic enim Deus homines tanquam grana spargit et seminat. Nonne apostolos seminans ait, 'Euntes in mundum uniuersum predicate euangelium omni creature'?[29] Veniendo euangelica predicatione sparsit, spargendo in uniuersum mundum unitate fidei uniuit. Sic nostre amicitie uinculum neque ruptum neque laxatum erga uos, sed protractum usque ad sedem uestram episcopalem, incorruptum et semper nouum existit. Nescio si fortius, scio tamen quia tenerius absentia me uobis, immo uos michi, inuiscerat quam fecerit presentia. Hoc probabile et necessarium argumentum est perfecte dilectionis quando eo amplius incendit affectus quo remotius separat locus. Presentia siquidem suo uisu solatiatur[30] et satiatur usu, famelica uero absentia pre inopia etiam amaris iuniperi corticibus sustentatur et ad insolitam[b] uisionis dulcedinem uiuacius inflammatur et nutritur tenacius. Duris agitatur stimulis desiderium quod semper querit et nunquam inuenit, unde psalmista, 'Querite Dominum, querite faciem eius semper',[31] et in Canticis anima liquefacta[32] surgit et querit per plateas et uicos ciuitatis quem diligit.[33] Neque igitur stilo inueterato neque animo scribo uobis. De his hactenus. De statu autem nostro significo uobis quod gutte nostre quasdam recenter sentio guttas.[34] Cetera nostra, Deo cooperante, in omni prosperitate sunt. Theobaldum concorditer in abbatem uobis substituimus, et fratrem Iohannem in omnibus ipsi obedientem effecimus, si tamen cum gratia uestra remanere poterit, quod omnino consulimus. Quid enim ualeat ubi est nobiscum certi sumus. Quid uero apud uos facturus sit nescimus. Certa uero pro incertis non sunt relinquenda. Missale nostrum mitto uobis, et breuiarium fratris Luce misimus. Quod uos supra modum in cibo et potu affligitis non approbamus. Si nobiscum uiuere et mori desideratis, non festinetis ad mortem, quia nescitis quid paritura sit

[b] *corr. Hall;* solitam *Sirmond*

---

[28] i.e. because of his move to the Curia.
[29] Mark 16: 15.
[30] Cf. Blaise *Dictionnaire*, *solacior*; Latham, *sol/-acior*.
[31] Cf. Ps. 104 (105): 4.
[32] Cf. S. of S. 5: 6.
[33] Cf. S. of S. 3: 2.
[34] *gutta* has no precise modern equivalent, but *DML*, 2 *gutta* 6 suggests 'arthritis' or 'gout'.

it leading?' The point is that I read in your letter that you have lost old friends and not acquired new ones.[28] I concede that you have lost them if in imagination or in truth it is certain that they are weary of you. But for certain, true friendship, through virginal purity and perpetuity of warmth, is neither defiled nor cooled, but by daily renewal always rises with the sun and suffers no demise. If therefore you have ever had friends, you have them still, not weary of you, which would be a wickedness, but far away, which is God's work. For God thus scatters and sows men like seeds. Does He not say, when sowing the apostles, 'Go ye into the whole world and preach the Gospel to every creature'?[29] Coming, He scattered with evangelical preaching; scattering, He created unity in the unity of the faith in the whole world. Thus the bond of our friendship with you survives neither broken nor loosed but drawn out even unto your episcopal seat, incorrupt and ever new. I do not know if absence roots me in your heart, indeed you in mine, more strongly than presence would have done, but I do know that it does so more tenderly. This is a demonstrable and necessary proof of perfect love, when affection burns the more powerfully the farther apart our homes. Presence indeed gives solace[30] by its sight and is satiated by familiarity, but famished absence is sustained, on account of want, even with the bitter bark of the juniper, and is both more vigorously inflamed at the unaccustomed sweetness of sight and more tenaciously nourished. That desire which always seeks and never finds is roused by harsh goads, whence the Psalmist says, 'Seek ye the Lord, seek his face evermore,'[31] and in the Song of Songs the melted soul[32] arises and seeks whom she loves in the broad ways and the streets of the city.[33] Therefore I am writing to you with neither a pen nor a soul weary of you. But enough of these matters. Concerning our present state, however, I must tell you that lately I am feeling certain twinges of my ailment.[34] As for the rest of our affairs, with God's help they are enjoying every prosperity. We have set up Theobald in your place as abbot without disagreement, and we have made brother John obedient to him in all things, if, that is, he can remain with your blessing, which we advise wholeheartedly. For we are sure what he is capable of when he is with us. But we do not know what he will do when he is with you. But certainties should not be relinquished for uncertainties. I am sending our missal to you, and we have sent brother Luke's breviary. We do not approve that you are afflicting yourself excessively where food and drink are concerned. If you wish

crastina dies.[35] Omnia possibilia sunt apud Deum[36] qui desiderium pauperum frequenter exaudit.[37]

136*

To Abbot Hugh of Saint-Amand[1]

1164 × 1170, prob. early

P⟨etrus⟩ abbas Sancti Remigii abbati Sancti Amandi.

Amicorum fidem articulus necessitatis examinat et qua quisque ad alium moueatur affectione conuincit. Nobis autem, qui iampridem totum animum deuouimus obsequio uestro deuotumque, Deo auctore, immobiliter conseruamus, grauis et onerosa incumbit necessitas quam uestra gratia, de qua plurimum confidimus, speramus et petimus subleuari. Nam (quod fortasse mirabimini) addicti sumus exilio et in eo iugi sollicitamur et torquemur angustia, siquidem clericus quidam nobis longe superamicissimus, cuius omnia tam prospera quam aduersa a multis retro temporibus nostra sunt, litterarum eruditione et morum honestate tanto cunctis probatior quanto notior, ab Anglia exulat apud nos et nos domi nostre exulamus cum illo. Sustinet enim indignationem regis Anglorum non suo quidem merito, ut de nostra et ipsius loquamur conscientia, sed quia domino suo Cantuariensi archiepiscopo, ut oportuit, seruiuit. Is est magister Iohannes de Saresberia, bonum testimonium habens[2] in partibus cismarinis et transmarinis. Vt ergo a nobis ipsis tam proprii quam fraterni exilii amoueatis angustias, dilectioni uestre attentius supplicamus ut eum interuentu comitis Flandr⟨ensis⟩ et uestro reconcilietis regi Angl⟨orum⟩ et, sicut uideritis expedire, ei litteras regis patentes perquiratis quibus secure redeat et suis in pace fruatur bonis. Sciatisque pro certo quia nos in nulla re magis poteritis promereri; nec est quod dissimuletis, quia constat pluribus potestatem uobis esse collatam, si uoluntas affuerit.

136 *Q fo. 5ʳ*]

[35] Cf. Prov. 27: 1; Jas. 4: 14. [36] Cf. Matt. 19: 26.
[37] Cf. Ps. 9 (10): 38 (17).

136 [1] The abbot of Saint-Amand is presumably Hugh, *c.*1150–68 (*GC* iii. 262), but possibly his successor. This letter comes from John of Salisbury's collection, on whose

to live and to die with us, you ought not to hasten towards death, for you know not what tomorrow will bring forth.[35] All things are possible with God[36] who frequently hears the desire of the poor.[37]

136*

To Abbot Hugh of Saint-Amand[1]

1164 × 1170, prob. early

Peter, abbot of Saint-Remi, to the abbot of Saint-Amand.[1]

A moment of critical need tests the faith of our friends and proves what affection one feels for another. A heavy burden of necessity lies on me, of which I hope and trust and ask you to relieve me, who have for long devoted my whole spirit to your service, and kept it (by God's help) immovably fixed in its devotion. You will perhaps be surprised to learn that I have been sentenced to exile and am vexed and tortured by continual distress, since a certain clerk, long one of my closest friends, whose every fortune good or ill has for many years been mine also, whose fame for scholarly learning and honourable character is better appreciated by everyone the better they know him, is in exile from England in our land, and I am in exile with him in my own home. The English king's wrath is on him, not by his own desert (as we can say on our conscience as well as his), but because he has served his master the archbishop of Canterbury as he should. He is master John of Salisbury, having a good report[2] on both sides of the Channel. I earnestly beg you of your affection to take from me the distress of this exile—my own as well as my brother's—and reconcile him to the English king by your own and the count of Flanders's mediation: further (as you will see is needful) ask for royal letters patent to give him a safe return and peaceful enjoyment of his goods. And know for sure that you will never be able to do me any greater service; and there is no ground for you to refuse, since it is well known that you have the power to do it, if you have also the will.

behalf it was written (*J. S. Epp.* ii. 28–31, no. 143); on the date see *J. S. Epp.* ii, pp. xxiii–xxiv. This letter (text and translation) is taken from *The Letters of John of Salisbury, Volume Two. The Later Letters (1163–1180)*, edited by W. J. Miller, S.J., and C. N. L. Brooke (1979) © OUP 1979. Reproduced by permission of Oxford University Press.

[2] Cf. 1 Tim. 5: 10.

137*

To Abbot Gossuin of Anchin[1]

1166, poss. Oct.

Venerabili patri suo Gozuino abbati de Aquiscinio frater Petrus filius eius humilis minister ecclesie beati[a] Remigii, uiam pacis et salutis.[2]

Graui et duro nuntio perculsus de fine et obitu tibi instante, pater dulcissime et amice karissime, in augmentum huius mee calamitatis et hoc accedit quod occupatus preoccupare mortem tuam me despero. Currunt enim ad te simul et meum desiderium et mortis odiose baratrum, istud te retinere secum ambiens illud absorbere festinans. Assistat tamen diuina pietas uoto et desiderio meo ne extinguatur tanta lucerna antequam ueniam et sua sanctissima oratione atque meritorum illustratione illuminet tenebras meas. Quia uero non de insidiis fortune sed de diuina predestinatione hoc incertum pendet, uelocitate cursoris obstacula impedimentorum, prout possum, redimo et sic ista allocutione tanquam presens paternitatem tuam appello et ad solitas miserationes super communem miseriam commoneo.[3] Audi igitur, sancta anima quam Deus 'de presenti seculo nequam'[4] ad diu desideratam societatem angelorum iam euocat, audi, inquam, audi 'gemitum compeditorum',[5] naufragia nauigantium, dolores parturientium, et diuinis hoc instilla auribus quatinus per canales orationum tuarum irrigentur 'areole aromatum',[6] id est suspiria et affectiones Deum desiderantium, Deum amantium, 'dissolvi et cum Christo esse'[7] concupiscentium. Certe quam infelicissime 'terrigene et filii

137 *M fo.* 55^{r-v}, *Do fos.* 24^{r}–25^{v}]
[a] sancti *Do*

137 [1] Addressed to Gossuin, abbot of Anchin 1131–9 Oct. 1166, this letter evidently arrived as he was dying. A reply from his successor Alexander appears in MS M (with a copy in MS Do.), together with this letter (ed. Leclercq, 'Nouvelles', pp. 163–4; see also Introduction, s. II. 2.ii). Gossuin, a former student of dialectic noted for having worsted Abelard in disputation, entered Anchin under Abbot Alvisus and, before becoming abbot, had been sent to assist Abbot Odo of Saint-Crépin, later of Saint-Remi, in reforming the house—he was thus closely linked to houses central to Peter's life and network. Alexander occurs in 1170, but must have been el. fairly soon after Oct. 1166 as he replied to the present letter; he was abbot until 1174. On Gossuin and Alexander, see *GC* iii. 411–12; on Gossuin and the *Vita Gosuini*, see also E. A. Escallier, *L'Abbaye d'Anchin 1079–1792* (Lille, 1852), pp. 61–116 (and on Alexander, pp. 117–24), and C. H. Talbot, 'Odo of

137*

To Abbot Gossuin of Anchin[1]

1166, poss. Oct.

To his venerable father Gossuin, abbot of Anchin, brother Peter, his son, humble minister of the church of the blessed Remigius, the way of peace and salvation.[2]

Struck as I am by the grave and harsh news of your imminent end and passing away, sweetest father and dearest friend, this also is added to the increase of this my calamity, that, being occupied, I despair of arriving before your death. For both my desire and the abyss of hateful death run towards you at the same time, the one striving to keep you with it, the other rushing to devour you. May God's kindness however assist my wish and my desire that such a lamp be not extinguished before I can come, and that it might illuminate my darkness by its most holy prayer and the shining light of its merits. But because this uncertainty depends not on the snares of fortune but on divine predestination, so far as I can I am making up for the obstacles of impediments with the speed of a runner, and thus with this address, as if I were present, I call on your fatherly person and adjure you to the compassion you are wont to have for the common misery.[3] Hear therefore, holy soul, whom God now calls forth 'from this present wicked world'[4] to the long-desired company of the angels, hear, I say, hear 'the groans of them that are in fetters,'[5] the shipwrecks of those at sea, the pains of those giving birth, and pour this into God's ears so that the 'beds of aromatical spices'[6] be irrigated by the channels of your prayers, that is by the sighs and feelings of those desiring God, loving God, longing 'to be dissolved and to be with Christ'.[7] Certainly your eyes have seen

Saint-Remy: a friend of Peter the Venerable', in *Petrus Venerabilis 1156–1956*, *Studia Anselmiana*, xl (1956), 21–37, at pp. 25–6. See also *Dictionnaire de biographie française*, xvi. 668.

[2] Cf. Luke 1: 79; Acts 16: 17

[3] i.e. he is sending a fast messenger with the letter, which will substitute for his presence, and is asking Gossuin to pray for those still on earth when he himself is in heaven.

[4] Gal. 1: 4.

[5] Ps. 101 (102): 21.

[6] S. of S. 5: 13; cf. 6: 1.

[7] Phil. 1: 23.

hominum'[8] se habeant, quam acerrime et durissime fideles Christi principes harum tenebrarum[9] et mundi huius amatores insequantur, tui hactenus uiderunt oculi, tue audierunt aures. Cum itaque deposueris corruptionem non abicias compassionem nec, cum emigraueris a conualle plorationis,[10] cesset in te affectus miserationis. Quanto enim tibi influxerint largius gurgites gratie et glorie celestis tanto profusius communicare orationum suffragia poteris amicis et filiis tuis.[11] Nonne memor esse debes capitis tui[12] in quo semper oculos habuisti, quia 'cum dilexisset suos qui erant in mundo, in finem dilexit eos'?[13] Equidem certa fide teneo quod nouitate celi gaudens anima tua pre admirabili splendore stupebit, pre exultatione illius beatitudinis in nouam affectionem commigrabit. Et quid mirum si priorum non fuerit recordata mestitiarum et omnium que tam fastidiose et coacta diu in mundo sustinuit? Nullatenus tamen, teste Apostolo, 'caritas excidet, siue prophetie euacuabuntur, siue lingue cessabunt'.[14] Per illam igitur caritatem te contestor et adiuro ut cum inueneris dilectum nunties ei quia 'miser factus sum et incuruatus sum'[15] usquequaque, quia 'non quod uolo hoc ago, sed quod odi illud facio',[16] quia 'iniquitates mee' 'multiplicate sunt super capillos capitis mei',[17] et sicut harena maris innumerabilis[18] sic cotidiana offendicula cordis mei. Ora itaque, sanctissime pater, pro me amico tuo et pro sancta congregatione tua atque nostra quatinus immittere [b]nobis dignetur[b] Iesus Christus 'Spiritum qui a Patre procedit',[19] quo consolati ab operibus nostris[20] cessemus a malis et insistamus in bonis, sequentes uestigia tue sancte conuersationis et amplectentes exemplum[c] perfectissime religionis.

[b–b] dignetur nobis *Do*   [c] exempla *Do*

[8] Ps. 48 (49): 3.   [9] Cf. Eph. 6: 12.
[10] Allusions to 1 Cor. 15: 53 and Ps. 83 (84): 7.
[11] i.e. to act as an intercessor.
[12] Possibly also meaning 'life' (cf. *DML*, 2.*caput* 3), or even, here, 'monastery' (cf. Niermeyer, *caput*, 6), i.e. his monks, for whom Peter also asks him to intercede.

already, your ears have heard, how unhappily 'the earthborn and the sons of men'[8] are situated, how bitterly and harshly the chiefs of this darkness[9] and the lovers of this world harry the faithful of Christ. And so when you have put off corruption may you not cast aside compassion, nor, when you have departed the valley of tears,[10] may the feeling of mercy cease in you. For the more plentifully torrents of grace and celestial glory flow into you so the more lavishly will you be able to communicate the support of prayers to your friends and sons.[11] Ought you not to be mindful of your head,[12] in which you always had eyes, because 'having loved His own who were in the world, He loved them unto the end'?[13] Indeed I hold with sure faith that, rejoicing in the novelty of heaven, your soul will be astounded by the wondrous splendour and will migrate to new affection on account of the exultation of its blessedness. And what wonder if it is forgetful of former sorrows and of all things which it long bore in the world so disdainfully and under compulsion? By no means, however, by the witness of the Apostle, will 'charity fall away, whether prophecies shall be made void or tongues shall cease'.[14] I call you to witness therefore and adjure you by that love that when you find the beloved you should announce to Him that 'I am become miserable and am bowed down'[15] everywhere, that 'I do not that good which I will; but the evil which I hate, that I do,'[16] that 'my iniquities' 'are multiplied above the hairs of my head',[17] and as the uncountable sand of the sea,[18] so are the daily stumblings of my heart. Pray then, most holy father, for me your friend and for your holy community and ours that Jesus Christ may deign to dispatch to us 'the Spirit who proceedeth from the Father,'[19] comforted by whom from our works[20] we may cease from evil and pursue the good, following in the footsteps of your holy life and embracing the example of your most perfect religious life.

[13] John 13: 1: Gossuin is exhorted to follow Christ's example.
[14] Cf. 1 Cor. 13: 8. [15] Cf. S. of S. 5: 8; Ps. 37 (38): 7.
[16] Rom. 7: 15 (Vulgate reads 'non enim quod').
[17] Cf. Ps. 39 (40): 13. [18] Cf. Ecclus. 1: 2.
[19] Cf. John 15: 26. [20] Cf. Gen. 5: 29.

138

To Abbot Theobald of Molesme[1]

1166 × Jan. 1171

Venerando, et utinam non uerbo et lingua sed opere et ueritate amico, Theobaldo abbati Molismensi frater Petrus sancti Remigii humilis minister, spiritum ueritatis.

Vox quidem uestra uox Iacob est, et utinam manus non essent manus Esau.[2] Verba uestra uenti sunt, littere 'cymbalum tinniens',[3] promissiones 'nubes sine aqua',[4] sermo sine uoce, flores sine fructu, ignis sine calore, aqua sine humore, corpus sine anima, anima sine uita. Quotiens, dilectissime domine, baculus arundineus[5] michi factus estis dum uobis crederem et nichil acciperem? Quotiens nuntios nostros non primo, non secundo, non tertio fatigastis et uanis atque frustratoriis dilationibus delusistis? Vbi est ergo illud priuilegium amicitie, ut scribitis? Vbi dilectio illa specialis, ubi fides singularis? Communia uestra male estimo cum specialia tam cassa et uana reperio. Homo tante auctoritatis, abbas tante congregationis, monachus et sacerdos ueracissimi Christi, quare non appendit 'in statera iusta'[6] uerba sua ut nunquam exorbitet a regula ueritatis qui regulam professus est beati Benedicti, immo Christiane religionis? Fideliter et ueraciter protestor multa incommoda sequi mendacem dum quisque se et sua illi credere refugit. Si meis adquiescere uolueritis consiliis mutato meliori fundamento diutius et melius cum prosperitate in abbatia uestra durabitis et aduersariis uestris locum aduersum uos malignandi non prestabitis. Debitum nostrum cum Deus uoluerit et uobis placuerit habebo. Verumtamen exinde non promerui laborem et dispendium quia bona fide et cum utilitate ecclesie uestre mutuo centum libras ab Otranno Trecensi accepi. Sufficiunt michi ueteres molestie et pristini labores quos sustinui ne uel una die debitorem[a]

138 *Sirmond VI. 13*]
[a] creditorem *Sirmond*

138 [1] Abbot Theobald, de Châtillon de Bazoches, of Molesme, 1166–25 Jan. 1171: Laurent, *Cartulaires de Molesme*, i. 166–8; *GC* iv. 734 (previously grand prior of Cluny, occurs 1165 and 1166: *GC*, iv. 1167). Theobald owes Peter money, and there is a dispute about how much, and how much has been paid already; meanwhile Peter has covered his obligations by a loan from one Otrannus of Troyes. The salutation echoes 1 John 3: 18.

138

To Abbot Theobald of Molesme[1]

1166 × Jan. 1171

To the venerable Theobald, abbot of Molesme—if only he were a friend not in word and speech but also in deed and truth—brother Peter, humble servant of Saint-Remi, the spirit of truth.

Your voice is indeed the voice of Jacob, and if only your hands were not also the hands of Esau.[2] Your words are blasts of air, your letters are 'a tinkling cymbal',[3] your promises 'clouds without water',[4] speech without voice, flowers without fruit, fire without heat, water without moisture, body without soul, soul without life. How often, dearest lord, have you been made a staff of reed[5] to me, while I believed in you and received nothing? How often did you tire out our messengers—not once or twice or three times—and deceive them with vain and frustrating delays? Where, then, is that privilege of friendship, as you put it in your letter? Where is that special love, where that singular faith? I form a low opinion of your general behaviour when I find that your particular actions are so empty and vain. Why does a man of such authority, an abbot of such a community, a monk and priest of the truest Christ, not weigh his words 'in a just balance'[6] so that, having professed the Rule of St Benedict, indeed of the Christian religion, he never deviates from the rule of truth? I testify faithfully and truthfully that many misfortunes follow the liar, while everyone avoids entrusting themselves and their own to him. If you are willing to acquiesce in my counsels you will last longer and more prosperously in your abbey, on an improved foundation, and not offer your adversaries the opportunity to malign you. I shall have what is due to us when God wishes and it pleases you. Nevertheless I have not incurred trouble and loss on this account because I have received, with good faith and to the benefit of your church, one hundred pounds from Otrannus of Troyes as a loan. The old tribulations and former troubles which I have borne are enough for me without my being made to trouble a debtor for even one day.

[2] Cf. Gen. 27: 22. [3] 1 Cor. 13: 1. [4] Jude 12.
[5] Cf. 4 Kgs. (2 Kgs.) 18: 21; Isa. 36: 6; Ezek. 29: 6: the broken staff of a reed is untrustworthy and dangerous, like Pharaoh. [6] Job 31: 6.

molestarem. Non igitur uadam uobis in occursum pro ista re. Apud nos sunt qui sciunt quid ex debito receperimus et quid non. Si ad nos ueneritis honorifice uos suscipiemus et maxime cum pace si pacem detuleritis. Valete.

139

To Abbot Theobald of Molesme[1]

1166 × Jan. 1171

Theobaldo Molismensi abbati P⟨etrus⟩ abbas Sancti Remigii, salutem.

Statum uestrum cogitans et recogitans pene usque ad nescio quid dicam rapior. Caligine siquidem nimia pressus an hoc aut illud eligam, dicere confundor. Si enim dixero, 'Sta,' casum timeo. Si dixero, 'Susceptum reice onus,' prouidentiam Dei offendere uereor. Proinde uerum est quod ait scriptura: 'Incerta et timida sunt hominum consilia.'[2] Quid ergo? Tacebo et silentio abscondam karissimo amico quid de ipso sentio? Rursus tanquam cecus lapidem iactabo et feriam ubi non uideo? Sed scio quia in ambiguis benignius semper interpretandum est, iuxta Apostolum qui ait, 'Tu quis es, qui iudices alienum seruum? Suo domino stat, aut cadit; stabit autem.'[3] Consulo itaque priores et multos labores in cella Cartusiensis ordinis pro Dei amore perpessos[4] semper te ante oculos habere et tutissimo loco intimi cordis reponere et si datum fuerit desuper nouos cotidie aceruos aggregare. Nunquam enim bono negotiatori questus sufficit hesternus, cotidie namque multa de adquisitis expendimus et forte una iactura plus amittimus quam per annum lucrati fuerimus. Ideo Apostolus que retro oblitus ad anteriora semper tendit,[5] nisi meliora et fortiora agat parum pensans quid egerit. Si ergo lucratiua sunt tibi que facis, fac quod facis. Appende lucrum anime tue, appende tibi

139 *Sirmond VII. 15*]

139 [1] Dated as letter no. 138 above. Theobald had apparently considered resigning his abbacy.

[2] Cf. Wisd. 9: 14. [3] Rom. 14: 4.

[4] Theobald was evidently at one time a Carthusian (Laurent, *Cartulaires de Molesme*, i. 166, n. 11 cites the present letter as the only evidence for this; Theobald does not figure in Le Couteulx).

[5] Cf. Phil. 3: 13; in what follows Peter evidently means that he thinks of the past only to compare it unfavourably with the present.

Therefore I shall not advance to confront you over this matter. There are those around us who know what we have received of the sum owed and what we have not. If you come to us we will receive you honourably and in peace, particularly if you offer peace. Farewell.

139

To Abbot Theobald of Molesme[1]

1166 × Jan. 1171

To Theobald, abbot of Molesme, Peter, abbot of Saint-Remi, greetings.

Thinking your position over again and again, I am drawn almost to the point of not knowing what to say. Oppressed by being too much in the dark as to whether I should choose this or that, I am embarrassed to speak. For if I say, 'Stay,' I fear the outcome. If I say, 'Cast down the burden which you have taken up,' I dread offending the providence of God. Hence it is true what Scripture says: 'The counsels of men are uncertain and fearful.'[2] What then? Shall I keep quiet and conceal in silence from a very dear friend what I feel concerning him? Again, should I throw a stone like a blind man and strike where I do not see? But I know that in doubtful matters the most favourable interpretation should always be drawn, according to the Apostle who says, 'Who art thou that judgest another man's servant? To his own lord he standeth or falleth. And he shall stand.'[3] And so I am reflecting that you have before your eyes always the former and manifold labours undertaken in the cell of the Carthusian order[4] for the love of God, and that you are storing them up in the safest part of the inner heart, and that if more be granted you are accumulating new hoards daily. For yesterday's profit is never enough for a good businessman, for every day we disburse much of our acquired wealth and it may happen that we lose more in one loss than we have gained in profit throughout the year. Therefore the Apostle, forgetful of those things that are behind, always strains to those that are before,[5] thinking little of what he has performed, except in order to perform better and bolder things. If therefore those things which you are doing are profitable to you, do what you are doing. Weigh up the gain to your soul; weigh up the profit of enterprises to

commissorum profectum, appende quid tibi accreuerit in temporalibus, quid iterum in spiritalibus. Pensandum siquidem est quietis pristine dampnum etsi reparat illud nouum emolumentum. Tibi, non michi, crede de bonis tuis, tu enim illa uides et sentis, ego tantum audio et credo. Tibi sunt nota quia uicina interiora tua. Si uentrem doles, nescio nisi dixeris michi: 'Ventrem meum doleo.' Sic nemo 'scit hominum que sunt hominis, nisi spiritus hominis, qui in ipso est'.[6] Itaque cum spiritu tuo, immo cum spiritu Dei,[7] discerne causam tuam et appende 'in statera iusta'[8] ne sis mendax in statera dolosa sanum te asserens cum infirmus sis uel infirmum cum sanus sis. Sed 'omnis homo mendax'[9] non solum in his quorum non penetrat occulta sed etiam in se cuius priuato amore palpat molliter que amputanda essent mordaciter et fortiter. Adhibendum itaque preclarissimum speculum scripturarum ad se cognoscendum et de se iudicandum. Regula ueritatis apponenda que nec modicum tacet fermentum[10] nec dissimulat minimum quoque et ueniale peccatum. Si dormieris inter hos cleros,[11] si accubueris inter hos terminos, si consulueris oraculum inter hos cherubin productiles et aureos,[12] rectos facies gressus tuos,[13] nec erit necesse consilium Achitofel quod aliquando infatuatum est.[14] Infra hos circulos immitte uectes tuos[15] et semper habens archam Dei ante oculos non timebis Philisteos tuos, siue spiritales siue corporales. Ipsa die qua recessistis a nobis uenit frater Henricus.[16] Persuasimus ei de reditu ad uos.

[6] Cf. 1 Cor. 2: 11. [7] Cf. 1 Cor. 2: 11–12.
[8] Job 31: 6. [9] Ps. 115 (116): 11; Rom. 3: 4.
[10] Cf. 1 Cor. 5: 6; Gal. 5: 9, i.e. which corrupts the whole.
[11] Cf. Ps. 67 (68): 14. [12] Cf. Exod. 25: 18.

yourself; weigh up what has accumulated for you in temporalities, and then again in spiritualities. The loss of the former peace must indeed be considered, even if a new benefit restores it. Trust in yourself not in me in the matter of your goods, for you see and perceive them, I only hear and believe. Your inner feelings are known to you because they are close at hand. If you feel a pain in your stomach, I do not know of it unless you say to me: 'I feel a pain in my stomach.' Thus no 'man knoweth the things of a man, but the spirit of a man that is in him'.[6] And so with your spirit, nay with the Spirit of God,[7] look closely at your case and weigh it 'in a just balance'[8] lest, using a deceitful balance, you be a liar, declaring yourself to be healthy when you are sick or sick when you are healthy. But 'every man is a liar'[9] not only in these things, the secret places of which he does not penetrate, but also in himself when with private self-love he softly caresses those things which ought to be cut off ruthlessly and boldly. The brightest mirror of the Scriptures therefore should be used for the purpose of self-knowledge and self-judgement. The rule of truth should be applied which neither keeps quiet about a little leaven[10] nor conceals even the least venial sin. If you sleep among these lots,[11] if you lie down within these bounds, if you consult the oracle between those cherubims of beaten gold,[12] you will make your steps straight[13] and the counsel of Achitophel, which once was made foolish,[14] will not be needed. Insert your bars through these rings[15] and, having the ark of God always before your eyes, you will not fear your Philistines, either spiritual or corporeal. On the very day that you left us brother Henry came.[16] We have persuaded him to return to you.

[13] Cf. Heb. 12: 13.

[14] Cf. 2 Kgs. (2 Sam.) 15: 31.

[15] Cf. Exod. 25: 12–14, and many other refs.: for carrying the ark of the covenant.

[16] Unidentified.

140

To Abbot Elbert (?) of Saint-Hubert[1]

? *c.*1167 × *c.*1170

H. uenerando abbati de Sancto Huberto P⟨etrus⟩ Sancti Remigii dictus abbas, salutem.

⟨Omnes⟩[a] omnia que in tempore fiunt ⟨secundum⟩[b] rationem temporis cum omnibus circumstantiis suis sollicite pensare debent, si finem bonum habere uolunt. Iccirco, bone pater et amice karissime, si susceptam nauigationem ad portum salutis perducere potestis, non deseratis abbatiam uestram, sed in hoc tempore malitie et discordie patiendo et tolerando 'donec transeat iniquitas'[2] resumite uires, et onus diu portatum nolite proicere, cum uestra et multorum lesione, sed paulatim ab humeris deponite. Si enim pax et unitas ecclesie redderetur, nec esset chaos inter nos et uos,[3] fieri possent multa que modo fieri non possunt. Valete.

140 *Sirmond V.* 6]
[a] *suppl. Hall* [b] *suppl. Hall*

---

140 [1] 'H.' in the salutation, but the most likely recipient is Abbot Elbert of Saint-Hubert, ? *c.*1167–*c.*1170, occurs in only one document, and that of doubtful reliability, for *c.*1170, known to have been replaced by 1174, probably ruled *c.*1167–*c.*1170, when he was deposed; d. ? 4 Aug. 1186: see *Mon. Belge*, V. 42–3, with a discussion of the difficulty of establishing his dates and the unreliability of the relevant sources, and refuting *GC*'s

140

To Abbot Elbert (?) of Saint-Hubert[1]

? *c.*1167 × *c.*1170

To the venerable H., abbot of Saint-Hubert, Peter, called abbot of Saint-Remi, greetings.

All men, if they wish to have a good outcome, ought carefully to weigh all things which happen in time according to the exigency of the time, along with all their circumstances. For this reason, good father and dearest friend, if you are able to bring the course undertaken through to the port of salvation, do not desert your abbacy but recover your strength in this time of evil and discord through suffering and enduring 'until iniquity pass away,'[2] and do not be ready, to the harm of yourself and of many others, to cast down the burden which you have carried for a long time, but lower it down from the shoulders little by little. For if peace and unity were restored to the Church, and there were no chaos between us and you,[3] many things could be done which now cannot be done. Farewell.

suggestion that Elbert and Conon claimed the abbacy simultaneously in rivalry for many years (*GC* iii. 972–3). The present letter may be an exhortation not to give up his abbey in the trying times of the schism, to which it refers, or possibly to resist the challenges to his abbacy which resulted in his deposition (the two may be linked). Saint-Hubert, Benedictine, dioc. Liège.

[2] Ps. 56 (57): 2.

[3] Cf. Luke 16: 26, 'et in his omnibus inter nos et uos chasma magnum firmatum est'.

141

? To Prior Odo of Christ Church, Canterbury[1]

1171 × 21 Feb. 1173 (poss. early)

Priori Cantuariensi.

Me debitorem uobis constituit tam obsequium dilectionis quod omnibus ex parte nostra per uos transeuntibus impenditis quam karissimi nostri magistri Iohannis gratia quam plenissime obtinetis.[2] Nouus quoque a Deo uobis collatus martyr ad sue sepulture locum attrahit et allicit.[3] Quem enim pre aliis mortalibus uirum constantem et in fide uera fundatum cognoui, cum sanctis angelis et martyribus iam annumeratum corde credo et ore confiteor. Presumo autem et ipse de orationibus eius utique quia dignum fecit me Deus suis benedictionibus, colloquio, cognitione atque familiaritate. Accedit et hoc ad cumulum totius amicitie quod in turbine illo et tempestate per magistrum Iohannem saluatus et conseruatus est. Noluit Deus stellas omnes cum magno illo sole simul de terra uestra tollere, ideo reliquie salue facte sunt.[4] Plane bene appellauerim stellas, doctrina et uita relucentes, tanti patris filios et tanti doctoris discipulos. Vtinam radios suos libere et absque interpolatione tenebrose noctis exercere ualerent. Ceteris enim terris uestra melior et clarior appareret si doctrinam illorum reciperet.

141 *Sirmond VI. 9*]

141 [1] The prior of Canterbury is presumably Odo, el. probably after 16 May 1168 and probably before Oct./Nov. 1169, el. abbot of Battle 10 July 1175, installed 29 Sept. 1175 (*Fasti*, ii. 10). This letter seems to pre-date the official canonization of Becket (21 Feb. 1173: Barlow, *Thomas Becket*, p. 269); Peter calls Becket a 'new martyr' and asserts his belief in his status as a martyr, but makes no mention of papal confirmation (but cf. letter no. 171 where he declares that Becket's status as martyr is evident without the need for papal confirmation). Even if this is not the case, the present letter must predate John of

141

? To Prior Odo of Christ Church, Canterbury[1]

1171 × 21 Feb. 1173 (poss. early)

To the prior of Canterbury.

The service of love which you extend to all those from our land who pass your way, and equally the support for our dearest master John which you most firmly maintain,[2] has made me your debtor. The new martyr also, conferred on you by God, draws and entices people to the place of his tomb.[3] For him whom I knew to be a man constant above all mortals and grounded in true faith I now believe in my heart and confess with my mouth to be numbered among the holy angels and martyrs. Yet I myself also am confident of his prayers, especially because God made me worthy of his blessings, conversation, acquaintance, and friendship. This too is added to the sum of the entire friendship, that he was saved and preserved in that storm and tempest through master John. God did not wish to remove all the stars at once from your land along with that great sun and so the remnant were made safe.[4] I do well to call the sons of such a father and the disciples of such a teacher stars, shining out as they were with teaching and life. Would that they could put forth their rays freely and without dark night intervening. For your land would appear better and more brilliant than all other lands if it accepted their teaching.

Salisbury's election to Chartres (notified of el. 22 July 1176, consecrated 8 Aug.; see letter no. 102, n. 1). By then the prior would have been Benedict of Peterborough, el. 1175, after July, el. abbot of Peterborough 29 May 1177 (*Fasti*, ii. 10), the recipient of letter no. 142. On the heading, see letter no. 84, n. 1.

[2] John of Salisbury, who is evidently back in favour at Canterbury; (' . . . Iohannis gratia' in this context would seem to mean support accorded to John).

[3] Thomas Becket, martyred 29 Dec. 1170 (Barlow, *Thomas Becket*, p. 247).

[4] i.e. Becket's disciples, whom he is comparing to the remnant of Israel (cf. Isa. 10; Rom. 9: 27, etc.; cf. also letter no. 147 and n. 6).

142

To Benedict of Peterborough, prior of Christ Church, Canterbury[1]

1175, after July × July 1176

Priori Cantuariensi.

Lugdunensem archiepiscopum nobis aliquando scripsisse de reuelatione pretiose mortis sancti et gloriosi martyris Thome non teneo.[2] Audiui quidem, sed a quo audierim mente excidit. Nolui ergo certa pro incertis scribere. Superflua enim sunt impendia lucerne ubi sol meridianus lucet in uirtute sua, et denigrat maiestatem uerorum admixtum modicum fermenti mendacii et falsitatis.[3] Credo enim magis laborandum ut plura demantur miracula que mera ueritate fulciuntur in gloria Dei et prefati martyris quam ut aliqua furtiua et emendicata supponantur. Omni supplicatione et postulatione tam uos quam omnes qui posteris tradituri estis memoriam mirabilium uestri et nostri martyris exoro ut nichil nisi septempliciter examinatum purgatum et colatum fidelissima ueritate scribatur de eo uel de miraculis eius. [a]De monacho Montis Dei nomine Gaufredo refero que ueraciter facta partim ab ipso, plenius a quodam monacho nostro qui tunc temporis ibi scribebat, audiui. Forte ab Anglia carta miraculorum sancti Thome ad nos deuenerat, et a nobis ad fratres

142 *Sirmond VI. 18*]
[a–a] *This section of the letter appears in Benedict of Peterborough* (*see n. 1*) *with slight variations which may represent either the recipient's copy of the letter or Benedict's alterations:* De monacho Montis Dei nomine Gaufrido refero que ueraciter gesta partim ad ipso plenius a monacho nostro [uestro *L*], qui tunc temporis ibi scribebat, audiui. Forte ab Anglia carta miraculorum sancti Thome ad nos deuenerat, et a nobis ad fratres de Monte Dei. Iam dictus frater, turgidus et inflatus toto corpore, ut uere hydropicus, cellam egredi non poterat. Accepta itaque cum fide et inuocatione sancti nominis carta, tetigit pedes suos, et tibias, et totum corpus suum; et in tantum conualuit, ut paruo tempore interposito ad ecclesiam et ad officia sua, non tamen ex toto curatus, rediret.

142 [1] The recipient must be Benedict of Peterborough (prior of Canterbury, 1175, after July–29 May 1177; see letter no. 141, n. 1) who cited this letter in his collection of Becket miracles: 'Scripsit etiam nobis miraculi cuiusdam ueritatem requirentibus uenerabilis abbas Sancti Remigii Petrus inter alia dicens . . .', quoting the passage from this letter 'De monacho Montis Dei . . . ex toto curatus rediret' [with minor differences] (*Materials for the History of Thomas Becket, Archbishop of Canterbury*, ed. J. C. Robertson and J. B. Sheppard,

142

To Benedict of Peterborough, prior of Christ Church, Canterbury[1]

1175, after July × July 1176

To the prior of Canterbury.

I do not recall that the archbishop of Lyons ever wrote to me about a revelation of the precious death of the holy and glorious martyr Thomas.[2] I have heard this indeed, but from whom I heard it has escaped me. I did not wish therefore to set down as certainties things which are uncertain, for the expense of a lamp is superfluous where the midday sun shines in its strength, and a little of the leaven of untruth and falsehood mixed in tarnishes the majesty of those things which are true.[3] For I believe that we should labour more that more miracles which are supported by pure truthfulness in the glory of God and of the aforesaid martyr be taken away than that any which are stolen and begged be slipped in. With all supplication and earnest request, I implore both you and all those of you who will transmit to posterity the memory of the miracles of your and our martyr that nothing be written in most faithful truth about him or his miracles except what has been examined, purified, and sieved seven times. I report concerning a monk of Mont-Dieu called Geoffrey those things which really happened, which I heard partly from him himself and more fully from a certain monk of ours who was engaged in writing there at that time. By chance a record of the miracles of St Thomas had come to us from England, and to the brothers of Mont-Dieu from

Rolls Series, 7 vols. (London, 1875–85), ii. 252). The present letter is clearly a response to a request by Benedict. Master John is presumably John of Salisbury, which puts the letter before his election to Chartres (notified of el. 22 July 1176, consecrated 8 Aug.; see letter no. 102, n. 1). John commuted between Exeter and Canterbury in the years 1170–6 (see letter no. 109, n. 1). On the heading, see letter no. 84, n. 1.

[2] Archbishop Guichard of Lyons, 1165/7–*c*.1180, June or July (*GC* iv. 126–130; he was consecrated 8 Aug. 1165 but did not obtain control of the see until after Aug. 1167–see T. A. Reuter, 'The papal schism, the empire and the west, 1159–1169' (Oxford D.Phil. thesis, 1975), pp. 191–3; see also *J. S. Epp.* ii. 37, n. 12). As abbot of Pontigny (1136–65; *GC* xii. 442), he had been Thomas Becket's host in exile.

[3] Cf. 1 Cor. 5: 6; Gal. 5: 9.

de Monte Dei.[4] Iam dictus frater turgidus et inflatus toto corpore, ut uere hydropicus, cellam egredi non poterat. Accepta itaque cum fide et inuocatione sancti nominis carta, tetigit pedes suos et tibias et totum corpus suum de ipsa, et in tantum conualuit ut paruo tempore interposito ad ecclesiam et ad officia sua, non tamen ex toto curatus, rediret.[a] Addo miraculum plus iocundum quam utile. In capella nostra libellum[b] qui legitur in capitulo de natalitiis sanctorum et de recordatione defunctorum nostrorum nescio quis forte furatus est.[5] Altera die cum flagitarem more solito legi lectionem ex ipso libro, turbatis capellanis non est inuentus libellus. Cum uero de negligentia et de incuria male custodie eosdem capellanos increparem, unus eorum nomine Robertus Anglicus, qui frequenter missam ad altare in quo reliquie sancti Thome continentur celebrabat,[6] in hanc uocem prorupit: 'Certe nunquam credam Thomam esse sanctum nisi reddiderit nostrum libellum.' Fere post mensem redditus est nobis liber. Si hoc miraculum est, istud uerum esse confirmo. Valete. Sanctum conuentum et M. Iohannem salutate.

143

To the prior (most probably Benedict of Peterborough) and community of Canterbury[1]

22 July 1176 × 1181 (prob. early)

Priori Cantuariensi et ceteris fratribus Petrus abbas Sancti Remigii.

Beata occasio qua uobis admoneor scribere. Miserum certe me iudico de inertia que detinet senectutem meam a uisitatione quondam

[b] libellus *Sirmond*

143 *Sirmond VII. 20*]

[4] It is not clear what exact form these writings took (*carta* is a general term—see Niermeyer, *charta*, 'any written document, without regard to material'; cf. *DML*, *charta*), but this does indicate early transmission of written accounts.

[5] This may be the book which is now MS Reims B. M. 346 (see Introduction, p. xxvii), which includes such material.

[6] Robert is unidentified, possibly but not necessarily an Englishman. On the altar consecrated to St Thomas Becket, cf. Prache, *Saint-Remi*, p. 34.

us.[4] The brother just mentioned, being swollen and puffed up throughout his whole body like a true sufferer from dropsy, was not able to leave his cell. And so, having received that record with faith and invoked the holy name, he touched his feet and shins and his whole body with it, and he recovered to such an extent that after a short interval of time, although not completely cured, he returned to the church and to his duties. I append a miracle which is more delightful than profitable. In our chapel a little book containing saints' days and the memorials of our dead which is read out in chapter happened to be stolen by I know not whom.[5] On the next day, when I was urgently demanding that the reading be given in the usual way from that very same book, to the dismay of the chaplains the little book could not be found. But while I was scolding those same chaplains for the negligence and carelessness of their bad guardianship, one of them called Robert Anglicus, who used to celebrate mass frequently at the altar in which the relics of Saint Thomas are kept,[6] blurted out these words: 'I shall certainly never believe that Thomas is a saint unless he returns our little book.' About a month later the book was returned to us. If this is a miracle, I confirm it to be true. Farewell. Greetings to the holy community and to master John.

143

To the prior (most probably Benedict of Peterborough) and the community of Canterbury[1]

22 July 1176 × 1181 (prob. early)

To the prior of Canterbury and the other brothers, Peter, abbot of Saint-Remi.

Happy is the occasion on which I am urged to write to you. Certainly I reckon myself wretched on account of the inactivity which

143 [1] Written between the el. of John of Salisbury to Chartres to which it refers (notified of el. 22 July 1176, consecrated 8 Aug.; see letter no. 102, n. 1) and the end of Peter's abbacy of Saint-Remi. There were three priors of Christ Church during this period: Benedict of Peterborough (1175, after July–29 May 1177), Herlewin (1177–6 Aug. 1179), and Master Alan (6 Aug. 1179–May 1186: on all of these, *Fasti*, ii. 10). This letter reads as if John has recently gone to Chartres, which would give the second half of 1176, when the prior was Benedict of Peterborough. The letter recommends a master G. who has been summoned by the archbishop. This is most likely the same G. as in letter no. 103; even if it is not, this letter is too late for it to concern Gerard Pucelle's introduction to Canterbury (see letter no. 103, n. 1).

amici nunc domini patris et patroni nostri sancti Thome pretiosi martyris Dei.[2] Hinc arguit me conscientia, inde excusat. 'Si uiueret in corpore archiepiscopus Thomas, nonne', inquit conscientia, 'ires et uisitares illum? Nonne et marina pericula postponeres et omnem a te torporem excuteres ut amicum uisitares et mutua conferres colloquia?' Econtra iterum talia refert: 'Sed monachus es, sed abbas, sed senex, sed corpore inualidus. Monachi est non egredi de castris Domini, immo de claustris monasterii; abbatis est procurare cure sue temporalem et regularem sollicitudinem; senis est inniti baculo suo sub oliua et ficu et uite sua et cogitare dies antiquos et annos eternos in mente habere; inualidi est conuerti in erumpna sua dum configitur[a] spina[3] et dicere cotidie, "Quis me liberabit de corpore mortis huius? Gratia Dei per Iesum Christum".'[4] His cogitationibus disputatione sua sic me accusantibus et excusantibus, interponit se statera equitatis mediam, sicque litem resoluit ut neutra de conclusione erubescat sed pace bona alteri cedat altera. Pium namque est ire, pium non ire; bona est peregrinatio quam comitata fuerit sancta deuotio, religiosa nichilominus detentio cui assidue adest pia commemoratio et eo intentio flagrantior quo suo non satiatur desiderio. Vtinam sic me deferret angelus ad sancti sepulcrum sicut Habacuc transtulit ad lacum leonum, non ut deferrem Danieli refectionem[5] sed ut referrem peccatorum remissionem. Constituo autem interim absentie nostre uicarium magistrum G. quem ad se uocauit d⟨ominus⟩ archiepiscopus Cantuariensis.[6] Commendo itaque uobis commendabilem amicum et clericum nostrum eumdem G., qui sentit in se uiscera dilectionis, misericordie et pietatis que ad nos habetis, non pro merito nostro sed pro gratuito beneplacito uestro. Certe si primam familiaritatis uestre portam aperueritis ei gratia nostri, credo quod ex prelibatione auida subsequetur fames, et continuo dicetis, 'Iam non propter tuam loquelam illum diligimus, ipsum enim cognoscimus, et scimus quia dignus est amicitia et contubernio bonorum.' Excipite itaque illum tanquam honestum clericum et bene litteratum ut apud uos possideam hunc ramusculum successione

[a] *corr. Winterbottom;* confringitur *Sirmond*

[2] i.e. visiting Becket's shrine.

[3] Cf. Ps. 31 (32): 4.

[4] Rom. 7: 24–5.

[5] Cf. Dan. 14: 32–8; i.e. whereas Habakkuk benefited Daniel, Peter would benefit from Becket, by attaining remission of sins as a pilgrim to his shrine (there is no evidence that Peter ever did visit England).

[6] Richard of Dover (1173/4–84, see letter no. 103, n. 1); Master G., see n. 1 above. What follows echoes Luke 1: 78; 2 Cor. 7: 15; Col. 3: 12.

prevents me in my old age from visiting a one-time friend, now our master, father, and patron, holy Thomas, precious martyr of God.[2] Conscience accuses me on one side, excuses me on the other. 'If archbishop Thomas were alive in the body', conscience says, 'would you not go and visit him? Would you not disregard the dangers of the sea and shake yourself out of your torpor in order to visit a friend and meet in conversation together?' On the other hand again, it replies with things like: 'But you are a monk, an abbot, an old man sick in the body. It is not for a monk to go out of the Lord's camp, that is the monastic cloister; it is for an abbot to attend to the temporal and spiritual concerns of his cure; it is for an old man to lean on his staff beneath his olive and fig and vine and to contemplate former days and to meditate on the eternal years; it is for a sick man to be turned in his anguish whilst the thorn is fastened,[3] and to say every day, "Who shall deliver me from the body of this death? The grace of God, by Jesus Christ".'[4] With these thoughts in their disputation accusing and excusing me thus, the scales of justice are evenly balanced and resolve the case in such a way that neither is ashamed at the outcome but each concedes to the other in peace. For it is an act of devotion to go, an act of devotion not to go; a pilgrimage attended by holy devotion is good, remaining behind is nevertheless a religious act when it is accompanied assiduously by devout commemoration and intention burning the more because it is not satisfied in its own longing. If only the angel would thus carry me away to the tomb of the holy one just as it carried Habakkuk over to the lions' den, not that I might carry the meal down to Daniel[5] but that I might carry away the remission of sins. In the meantime, however, I appoint as the representative of our absent self master G. whom the lord archbishop of Canterbury[6] has summoned to himself. And so I commend to you that commendable friend and clerk of ours, the same G., who feels in himself the bowels of the love, mercy, and kindness which you bear towards us on account not of our merit but of your freely given good pleasure. Certainly if you open the first portal of your friendship to him as a favour to us, I believe that avid hunger will follow from the foretasting, and you will say forthwith, 'Now we love him not on account of your words, for we know him, and we know that he is worthy of the friendship and the company of the good.' And so receive him as an honourable and well-educated clerk so that I may possess this sapling among you in succession to that great tree which

illius magne arboris que transplantata est in ecclesia Carnotensi. Fuit enim noster alumnus magister Iohannes, et iste, utinam similiter![7]

144

To Prior Inganus of Lapley[1]

+1173 × 1181, prob. late (at or just before Easter)

Petrus humilis abbas Sancti Remigii Ing⟨ano⟩ priori de Lapelee.

Postulas in litteris tuis nostrum stilum recipere non alienum. Sed hebetatus sed retunsus sed denique plenus squalore et rubigine, qua facie transire poterit mare cum potius sua rusticitate cachinnos moueat quam suos letificet hospites? Calamus quoque noster annositate et desuetudine quassatus necnon et terrenorum sollicitudine assidua obstructus et obstrictus rauce sonat, nec iam auditores suos demulcet sed male commouet. Ne tamen filii et amici karissimi petitiunculam excludam uel eludam, emendicatis repressis coloribus rethoricis et leporem sermonis postponens, dies Dominice passionis pre oculis habens,[2] moneo cum Iesu partiri suas contumelias, suas passiones, sua flagella, sua sputa, et totum cursum patientissime dispensationis qua pro nobis usque ad inferna descendit. Reduc Iesum a planta pedis usque ad uerticem uulneratum ante oculos tuos, aut animum deduc ad locum et focum ubi Petrus negauit,[3] et que cordis medulla non liquefacta[4] totum altare tam eneum quam aureum sua aspersione implebit? 'Holocausta', ait psalmista, 'medullata offeram tibi.'[5] Medulla anime non est nisi de infusione gratie. Si anima, licet macra tamen esuriens et sitiens, magno appetitu stillicidia elambuerit gratie 'uespere et mane et meridie'[6]—uespere complantata similitudini mortis Iesu,[7] mane renouata cum resurgente Iesu,

144 *Sirmond IX. 5*]

[7] John of Salisbury's election to Chartres (see n. 1 above). He was not, it seems, ever Peter's pupil ('alumnus') but his clerk. On their early relations and Peter's manner of refering to John (*magistro suo*, *amico suo*, *clerico suo*, *quondam clericus noster* and, here, *noster alumnus*), see *J. S. Epp.* i, pp. xvi–xvii. The force of *alumnus* here seems to be 'nursling' (*LS*), echoing 'sapling' above, and so continuing the metaphor of the tree.

144 [1] Prior Inganus of Lapley, evidently prior after Absalon, who became prior 1162 × *c.*1173 (see letter no. 111, n. 1), but Inganus is not closely datable; he also occurs 1206 × 1207 (*Heads*, p. 105; *VCH Staffs*, iii. 343). Inganus has requested a personal reply from Peter's own hand, i.e. presumably autograph, an indication of the value attached to such letters. On the references here to the building-works at Saint-Remi, see appendix 12.

has been transplanted to the church of Chartres. For master John was our nursling and this one also, may he do likewise.[7]

144

To Prior Inganus of Lapley[1]

+1173 × 1181, prob. late (at or just before Easter)

Peter, humble abbot of Saint-Remi, to Inganus, prior of Lapley.

You ask in your letter to receive a reply from our pen not from that of another. But blunt, but worn down, but lastly full of dust and rust, by what presumption will it be able to cross the sea since it would rouse derisive laughter owing to its rusticity rather than cheer its hosts? Also our pen, being broken down with age and disuse and also blocked and bound up with anxious concern over earthly things, makes a harsh sound, nor does it now soothe its hearers but agitates them. However, so as not to exclude or elude the little petition of a dearest son and friend, suppressing borrowed rhetorical colours and disregarding polished discourse, having the days of the Lord's passion before my eyes,[2] I admonish you to share with Jesus His abuses, His sufferings, His stripes, how He was spat upon, and the whole course of His most patient stewardship by which He descended for us even into hell. Bring back before your eyes Jesus wounded from the sole of the foot even unto the top of the head, or lead the soul down to the place and the hearth where Peter made his denial,[3] and what marrow of the heart, being melted,[4] will not fill up the whole altar, the bronze as much as the gold, by its sprinkling? 'I will offer up to thee', says the Psalmist, 'holocausts full of marrow.'[5] There is no marrow of the soul except by the infusion of grace. If the soul, albeit meagre, yet hungry and thirsty, laps up the droplets of grace with a great appetite in the 'evening and morning and at noon'[6]—in the evening planted together in the likeness of the death of Jesus,[7] in the morning renewed with the rising Jesus, at noon translated to the right hand of the Father with Jesus—it will certainly be drunk with

[2] i.e. it is Lent or Easter.
[3] Cf. Matt. 26: 69–75; Mark 14: 66–72; Luke 22: 55–62; John 18: 25–7.
[4] Possibly alluding to Ps. 21 (22): 15 given the context. Both altars are in Exod. 39: 37–9; many other refs. to each.
[5] Ps. 65 (66): 15. [6] Ps. 54 (55): 18. [7] Cf. Rom. 6: 5.

meridie translata ad dexteram Patris cum Iesu—certe inebriabitur ab ubertate domus Dei, dicens, 'Sicut adipe et pinguedine repleatur anima mea.'[8] Quare non saginaretur de uitulo saginato?[9] Quare non inebriaretur de flumine quod letificat ciuitatem Dei?[10] Habes uinum de uite uera expressum in torculari crucis et attractum aperto ostio lateris. Sicut enim tonellus foratur ut uinum habeatur, sic latus Christi lancea militis apertum est ut exiret aqua baptismatis et sanguis nostre redemptionis.[11] Hunc cotidie sumimus in altari sub specie uini. Altare siquidem est locus pascue de quo dicitur: 'In loco pascue ibi me Dominus collocauit.'[12] Et in Canticis: 'Indica michi quem diligit anima mea, ubi pascas, ubi cubes in meridie.'[13] Quid est 'in meridie'? In luce, in puritate, in ueritate, in caritate. Qui latet ut anguis in herba,[14] abscondens peccata sua, non est in meridie; qui impudice uiuit et templum Dei uiolat immunditia aliqua non est in meridie; qui dolosus et fraudulentus est, speciem pietatis habens et uirtutem abnegans, non est in meridie; qui tepet odio fraterno non est in meridie. Non ergo ipsum uel cum ipso pascit Christus qui dicit, 'Superbo et insatiabili corde cum hoc non edebam.'[15] Non cubat etiam nisi ubi pascit.[16] Sed de his hactenus pro tempore. De me uero si uis scire, onere tam annorum quam peccatorum cotidie more meo solito premor. Tamen benignitate et clementia Dei adhuc excedere ualeo et iniuncta officii negotia utcunque procurare. Pacem etiam bonam cum fratribus nostris et cum archiepiscopo et cum omnibus hominibus habeo. Caput monasterii nostri renouare aggredior,[17] et cum Dei auxilio iam opus inchoatum ridet et sequentis operis auspicia nobilia spondet. Non excidit a memoria quod aliquando michi quasi reprehensorie dixeris, studere alia opera facere et non curare de monasterio. Hoc uerbum etsi perfunctorie fuit dictum non transitorie fuit auditum. Mille enim libras adhuc, simul quingentas postea, pro opere monasterii expendi. Saluto fratrem Dudonem.[18] De bono odore uestre conuersationis gaudeo.

[8] Cf. Ps. 35 (36): 9; 62 (63): 6.
[9] Cf. Luke 15: 23, 27, 30.
[10] Cf. Ps. 45 (46): 5.
[11] Cf. John 19: 34.
[12] Cf. Ps. 22 (23): 2.
[13] S. of S. 1: 6.
[14] Cf. Virgil, *Ecl.* iii. 93.
[15] Cf. Ps. 100 (101): 5.
[16] Referring back to the quotation from S. of S. above. (Douai-Reims: feedest; other translns render: feed . . . flocks.)

the richness of the house of God, saying, 'Let my soul be filled as with marrow and fatness.'[8] Why should it not be fattened on the fatted calf?[9] Why should it not be drunk from the river which gladdens the city of God?[10] You have the wine pressed from the true vine in the press of the cross and drawn through the open door of His side. For just as the cask is pierced that you may have wine, so the side of Christ was opened by the soldier's spear so that the water of baptism and the blood of our redemption should come forth.[11] This we take up every day on the altar in the appearance of wine. For the altar is the place of pasture, of which it is said: 'In a place of pasture, there has the Lord set me.'[12] And in the Song of Songs: 'Show me, o thou whom my soul loveth, where thou feedest, where thou liest in the midday.'[13] What does it mean, 'in the midday'? In light, in purity, in truth, in love. He who lurks like a snake in the grass,[14] concealing his sins, is not in the midday; he who lives unchastely and violates the temple of God with some impurity is not in the midday; he who is deceitful and fraudulent, having the appearance of devotion and denying virtue, is not in the midday; he who burns with hatred of his brother is not in the midday. Therefore Christ, who says, 'With him that had a proud and unsatiable heart I would not eat',[15] does not feed him or feed with him. And moreover he does not lie except where he feeds.[16] But enough of these matters for the time being. But if you wish to know about me, I am daily oppressed in my usual way by the burden both of years and of sins. By the benevolence and clemency of God, however, I am still strong enough to go out and to attend in some measure to the affairs enjoined by my office. I enjoy too a good peace with our brothers and with the archbishop and with all men. I am beginning to renew the chevet of our monastery,[17] and with God's help the work already begun looks well and promises noble auspices of the works to follow. I have not forgotten what you once said to me, as it were in rebuke, that I strove to do other works and not to care for the monastery. This word, even if it was said in passing, was not heard fleetingly. For I have laid out a thousand pounds so far, and at the same time have committed five hundred for a later stage, for the work on the monastery. I send greetings to brother Dudo.[18] I rejoice in the good odour of your manner of life.

[17] *caput*, 'chevet', see appendix 12 (cf. *DML*, 2 *caput* 13. c; Niermeyer, *caput* 4).
[18] Unidentified.

145

To the abbots of Saint-Médard and Saint Crépin-le-Grand, Soissons[1]

1179, after Mar./May × 1181

Sancti Medardi et Sancti Crispini abbatibus Petrus abbas Sancti Remigii.

Nescit uere amicitie naturam qui in amore imitatur 'arundinem uento agitatam'.[2] Sine profunda radice amicitia accidens est non substantia, species non uirtus, fenum de tecto quod antequam euellatur arescit.[3] Tres itaque precipuas ancillas, sine quibus uiuere non potest, comites habet et pedisequas: iustitiam, patientiam et constantiam. Iustitia suum ius unicuique seruat;[4] patientia si forte interuenerit iniuriam salua integritate amicitie tolerat; constantia nec qualitate nec quantitate pacti preuaricati expirat. Quis ergo abduxit, quis seduxit, quis exturbauit funiculum hunc triplicem[5] a sacratissimis uisceribus dominorum et amicorum meorum, abbatis Sancti Medardi et abbatis Sanctorum Crispini et Crispiniani? Moriatur non uiuat tam nefarium et nefandissimum scandalum seruorum Dei quod de radice uetustissimi colubri,[6] id est ineptissime auaritie, prodiit. Subornat se quidem occasio auaritie uestimentis iustitie, sicut Iacob 'uestimentis Esau ualde bonis';[7] et Iacob mentitur se Esau. Pater tamen uniuersorum qui quasi oculos caligantes exhibet dum ipso iudice ipso omnia regente iniustitia iustitiam opprimit nec penam recipit, quasi miratur de tanta hominum fraude qui sub oculis eius non timent mentiri et in inuicem fraudare, dicens: 'Vox quidem, uox Iacob, sed manus, manus sunt Esau.'[8] Prefert quisque altercantium ius authenticum et regulare se habere, 'Nostra', inquiens,

145 *Sirmond V. 21*]

145 [1] An appeal to the abbots of Saint-Médard and Saint-Crépin-le-Grand, Soissons, to resolve their differences and live at peace with one another. It is unlikely that this letter was written during the abbacy of Berneredus of Saint-Crépin (*c.*1162/3–Mar. × May 1179, see letter no. 128, n. 1); the tone of the letter and the lack of any reference to their lifelong friendship make it evident that Peter is not addressing his close friend. The recipients must be Geoffrey of Saint-Médard (1177–85; *GC* ix. 417), and either Theobald of Saint-Crépin (1179, not before Mar./May; *GC* ix. 399, and became abbot of Cluny, see letter no. 146, n. 1) or his successor Leon (occurs 1181 × 1204, but presumably el. earlier; *GC* ix. 399). [2] Matt. 11: 7; cf. Luke 7: 24.

145

To the abbots of Saint-Médard and Saint-Crépin-le-Grand, Soissons[1]

1179, after Mar./May × 1181

To the abbots of Saint-Médard and Saint-Crépin, Peter, abbot of Saint-Remi.

He does not know the nature of true friendship who in love resembles 'a reed shaken with the wind'.[2] Friendship without a deep root is accident not substance, appearance not strength, the grass from the top of the house, which dries up before it be plucked.[3] And so she has three principal maidservants, companions, and attendants without whom she cannot live: justice, patience, and constancy. Justice preserves for each his right;[4] patience bears wrong, if by chance it should arise, preserving the integrity of friendship; constancy does not fail whatever the manner or extent of the pact that is violated. So who has stolen, who has removed, who has dislodged this threefold cord[5] from the most holy hearts of my lords and friends the abbot of Saint-Médard and the abbot of Saint-Crépin? May such a heinous and execrable offence of the servants of God, which arose from the root of the most ancient serpent,[6] that is from the most improper greed, die and not live. The occasion of greed indeed adorns itself with the garments of justice, just as Jacob did with the 'very good garments of Esau';[7] and Jacob pretends to be Esau. The Father of all things, however, who displays, as it seems, failing eyes when with Him as judge, with Him ruling over all, injustice oppresses justice and receives no punishment, is as it were astounded at such deceit of men who are not afraid to cheat before His eyes and to deceive one another, and says, 'The voice indeed is the voice of Jacob, but the hands are the hands of Esau.'[8] Each of the disputants claims that he has an authentic and regular right, saying, 'Our church has had possession in this way for a long time,' and 'Ours in this way.'

[3] Cf. Ps. 128 (129): 6.
[4] Cf. Justinian, *Institutes*, i. 1. 1.
[5] Cf. Eccles. 4: 12, '. . . funiculus triplex difficile rumpitur'.
[6] The devil, but on the language here cf. also Isa. 14: 29.
[7] Gen. 27: 15 (Vulgate has *uestibus*).
[8] Gen. 27: 22. (God can seem, to people, to be deceived, but cannot actually be so.)

'diu sic possedit ecclesia,' et 'Nostra sic.' Ecce Iacob in uoce.[9] Deinde pax cordium concutitur, antiqua familiaritas excutitur, obliquantur oculi, castissimi amplexus soluuntur, de altero alter conqueritur, innexi discipulorum parietes in domus scissuram partiuntur.[10] Ecce manus Esau.[11] Redite, amici karissimi, redite ad cor.[12] Non grandis querela, grandis autem est de hac discordia inter notos et uicinos uestros infamia. Predecessorum uestrorum temporibus, nec in personis nec in rebus monasteriorum uestrorum dicitur fuisse inuenta tanta concordia quantam firmo et fraterno federe hactenus ad inuicem excoluistis. Vnde ergo tam subito ualde odiosa aduenit simultas? Quomodo ausa est sacra penetrare pectora execrabilis et execranda temeritas, qua pacis cubicula inquietarentur et utriusque pacatissima quies intempestiue sollicitata infestaretur? Resarciatur repente amoris uinculum ne caritas in alumnis suis saltem unius diei, ne dicam mensis uel anni, prescriptionis incurrat dispendium.[13] Qui enim ait, 'Sol non occidat super iracundiam uestram',[14] regulam iuris prefixit quam intutum est preuaricari. Grauis enim sumitur uindicta de illo qui euangelii iura uiolat perpetua. 'Quare', inquit Apostolus, 'non magis iniuriam accipitis? Quare non magis fraudem patimini?'[15] Sordet religio ubi preualet ambitio, fama fedatur si res iniuste auferatur uel adquiratur, conscientia molestatur si stimulo elationis quoquo modo pungatur. Oleum quo caput mentis impinguatur[16] extra funditur si pluris pecunia quam iustitia habeatur. Itaque interpono partes nostre amicitie si forte recognita cognatione antique familiaritatis reporrigant sibi hiantia corda reconciliationis mutua brachia. Rogo ut dies per amicos uestros accipiatur in quo de concordia familiariter agatur. Valete.

[9] Cf. Gen. 27: 22.

[10] Possibly alluding to Amos 6: 12, or to Matt. 12: 25; Mark 3: 25; Luke 11: 17.

[11] Cf. Gen. 27: 22.

[12] Cf. Isa. 46: 8.

[13] Possibly meaning a right created by lapse of time (cf. Latham, *prescriptio*, *p. temporis*, *prescribo*).

Behold Jacob in the voice.[9] Then the peace of hearts is shaken up, ancient friendship shaken out, eyes averted, most chaste embraces loosened; one complains about another; the walls which joined disciples together are parted in the house as it is divided.[10] See the hands of Esau.[11] Return, dearest friends, return to the heart.[12] The complaint is not great, but great indeed among your friends and neighbours is the scandal arising from this conflict. It is said that in the time of your predecessors so great a concord was found neither among the persons nor the affairs of your monasteries such as you have heretofore cultivated mutually by a firm and brotherly pact. Whence, then, does this hateful rivalry arise so very suddenly? How did execrable and detestable rashness, by which the chambers of peace are disturbed and by which the most peaceful calm, unseasonably distressed on both sides, is broken, dare to penetrate holy breasts? Let the chain of love be repaired forthwith so that the love between its disciples does not incur the loss of prescriptive right[13] even for one day, not to say a month or a year. For he who says, 'Let not the sun go down upon your anger,'[14] has fixed a rule of law which it is dangerous to transgress. For a great punishment is inflicted on him who violates the eternal law of the Gospel. 'Why', says the Apostle, 'do you not rather take wrong? Why do you not rather suffer yourselves to be defrauded?'[15] The religious life is besmirched where ambition prevails, reputation is defiled if a thing is carried off or acquired unjustly, conscience is troubled if it be pricked in any way by the goad of pride. The oil by which the head of the mind is anointed[16] is poured away outside if money is regarded more highly than justice. And so I am interposing the good offices of my friendship in the hope that, with the connection of ancient intimacy recalled, the sundered hearts may stretch out to each other the mutual arms of reconciliation. I ask that a day be agreed through your friends on which an agreement may be discussed on friendly terms. Farewell.

[14] Eph. 4: 26.

[15] 1 Cor. 6: 7, which begins 'Iam quidem omnino delictum est in uobis quod iudicia habetis inter uos.'

[16] Cf. Ps. 22 (23): 5.

146

To Abbot-elect Theobald of Cluny[1]

1180, poss. early

Theobaldo electo Cluniacensi Petrus abbas Sancti Remigii.

Gemebundas et quasi intestinorum suorum tumultuosa collisione seu conquestione et uelut a fulgure et tempestate percussas a uobis recepi litteras. Hominem siquidem redolebant satis conturbatum et exterritum ac uelut repentino superueniente tonitruo pene iacentem exanimatum. Nec mirum. Res namque noua[2] tam sua nouitate quam magnitudine hominem audacissimum et fortissimum potuit concutere. Qui ad crucem ducitur gemens et lugens, merito conqueritur. Si crux a cruciatu dicitur,[3] nonne in cruce cruciatur cuius humeri importabili oneri supponuntur? Profecto amodo tot molas supportabitis quot monachorum curam recipietis. Quid ergo? Nonne cum Apostolo dicetis, 'Quis infirmatur, et ego non infirmor? Quis scandalizatur, et ego non uror?'[4] Ecce timor, ecce anxietas, ecce cruciatus. Sed quid? Vbi consolatio? Vbi reuelatio? Vbi tanti doloris remedium? Sine dubio in Christo. Nam ipse primus ascensor, mitigator et sanctificator crucis qui suo cruciatu nostros absoluit cruciatus in cruce, et de cruce dixit, 'Mulier ecce filius tuus', et 'discipulo, "Ecce mater tua"'.[5] Sed quid hoc ad rem? Quid ad presentem questionem? Multum per omnem modum. Nam mulier est Cluniacensis ecclesia que est mater omnium nostrum, que de fructu uentris sui[6] plures manipulos sanctarum animarum 'ab oriente

146 *Sirmond IX. 3*]

---

146 [1] Theobald of Cluny's life is difficult to reconstruct. Pacaut, *Ordre de Cluny*, p. 236, gives his family name as 'de Vermandois'; he was one-time prior of Saint-Arnoult-de-Crépy (*GC* ix. 399; ix. 199, correcting *GC* iv. 1142, which gives Saint-Crépin-le-Grand, Soissons; Saint-Arnoul is also known as Crépy-en-Valois); he became abbot of Saint-Crépin-le-Grand in 1179, successor to Bernerederus (on whose dates see letter no. 128, n. 1), which he ruled for only five months (*GC* ix. 399). Although Bernerederus first certainly occurs as cardinal in May 1179, it is most likely that he was appointed in Mar. Theobald is also recorded as abbot of Saint-Basle (dioc. Reims; Cott. ii. 2605–6) later in the same year, before becoming abbot of Cluny, most probably early in 1180. *GC* ix. 199, for Saint-Basle, and *GC* iv. 1142–3, for Cluny, however, give contradictory accounts, and the latter mentions other abbacies. *GC* iv. 1142–3, also gives his el. to Cluny as 1179, and his predecessor's d. as 11 Jan. 1179. However, his predecessor, William Anglicus, d. Jan. 1180 (see *Heads*, p. 62 and refs.). Theobald's five months at Saint-Crépin could have run from as

146

To Abbot-elect Theobald of Cluny[1]

1180, poss. early

To Theobald, abbot-elect of Cluny, Peter, abbot of Saint-Remi.

I have received from you a letter groaning and as it were struck by a tumultuous crashing or complaint of its inwards and by lightning and storm. For it was redolent of a man quite disturbed and terrified and almost lying in a faint at the sudden approach of thunder. Nor is it any wonder. For the recent event[2] could have shaken the boldest and strongest man, as much by its novelty as by its magnitude. He who is led to the cross groaning and wailing has every right to complain. If the cross is so called after crucifixion,[3] is he not crucified on the cross whose shoulders are set under an unbearable load? Assuredly henceforth you will support as many millstones as you will receive monks to care for. What then? Will you not say with the Apostle, 'Who is weak, and I am not weak? Who is scandalized, and I am not on fire?'[4] Behold the fear, behold the anxiety, behold the crucifixion. But what then? Where is the consolation? Where is the revelation? Where is the remedy for such a pain? Without doubt in Christ. For He himself is the first ascender, softener, and sanctifier of the cross who by His own crucifixion freed us from our crucifixion on the cross, and from the cross said, 'Woman, behold thy son,' and 'to the disciple, "Behold thy mother"'.[5] But how is this to the point? What relevance has it to the present question? Much in every way. For the woman is the church of Cluny who is the mother of us all, who from the fruit of her womb[6] has now placed together many companies of holy souls 'from the east and

early as Mar. × Apr. to Aug. × Sept. 1179, leaving a few months for his abbacy of Saint-Basle. However, it is not impossible either that he did not take up residence at Saint-Basle or that he held this and other monasteries with which he is associated in *GC* in plurality. In any case, in the present state of knowledge the identification of Theobald as the abbot of Saint-Crépin, Saint-Basle, and Cluny depends on *GC* alone. Theobald was abbot of Cluny 1180–3, before finally becoming cardinal bishop of Ostia and Velletri, possibly late 1183 (*GC* iv. 1142–3, gives Dec. 1183; in *JL* ii. pp. 431, 492, 528, 535, he occurs as cardinal 15 June 1184 × 29 Oct. 1188; but the last time a predecessor occurs is May 1181–*JL* ii. 145).

[2] Theobald's election.

[3] Cf. Gregory, *Homil. .xl. in Euang.* ii. 37. 5 (*PL* lxxvi. 1277); also Bede, *In Luc.* iv. 19. 27 (*CCSL* cxx. 282; *PL* xcii. 517. (The word play on *cruciatus* meaning crucifixion and torture does not translate.)

[4] Cf. 2 Cor. 11: 29.

[5] Cf. John 19: 26–7.

[6] Cf. Luke 1: 42.

et occidente' in sinu Abrahe, Ysaac et Iacob[7] iam collocauit, et sponso suo poma noua nouitiorum et uetera antiquorum et senum in celesti mensa frequenter obtulit.[8] Quis uero discipulus sit de quo dicitur, 'Mulier ecce filius tuus',[9] iam credo animaduertitis. Tangit enim uos hec sententia, quia eterna predestinatione et moderna uocatione sollicitudinem huius matris uestre decreto inuiolabili gratia Dei iniungit. Temerarium autem est et inhumanum tam diuinam ordinationem respuere quam matri fidele obsequium denegare. Igitur tanquam Ysachar asinus fortis[10] ceruicem et humeros huic electioni supponite et de Dei auxilio fideliter presumite quia spiritus adiuuat infirmitatem uestram. Michi autem amico et fideli uestro gaudium est et exultatio quod tantum amicum in tam excellenti loco merui uidere sublimatum. Nam et ipse seruuus et filius sum Cluniacensis ecclesie.[11] Valete, et per nos, oro, transitum facite.[12]

147

To the general chapter of the Cistercian order[1]

1181

Petrus Carnotensis electus capitulo Cisterciensi.

Sancta sanctorum studia impedire non minoris estimo culpe quam angelica et diuina negotia interrumpere. Tanti uero reatus penam timeo incurrere si uos ad diuina et in diuinis occupatos uanis et superfluis temptauero uerbis retinere. Excusat tamen quandoque urgens necessitas ingerentem se importunitatem quando etsi reprimit ad modicum festinationem non perimit aut deprimit penitus necessariam operationem. 'Vtinam', inquit Apostolus, 'sustineretis modicum quid insipientie mee.'[2] Non arguitur insipientie formica que sibi preparat escam in estate.[3] Non arguitur insipientie uillicus iniquitatis qui fodere non ualens et mendicare erubescens fecit sibi amicos qui

147 *Sirmond IX. 8*]

[7] Cf. Matt. 8: 11; Luke 13: 28–9; 16: 22.
[8] Cf. S. of S. 7: 13; i.e. many Cluniacs have entered heaven (Christ is the bridegroom of the Church).
[9] John 19: 26.
[10] Cf. Gen. 49: 14.
[11] Peter spent some time in his early years at the Cluniac house of Saint-Martin-des-Champs (see Introduction, p. xxx).

the west' in the bosom of Abraham, Isaac, and Jacob,[7] and to her bridegroom has frequently presented the new fruits of novices and the old fruits of the ancient and aged at the heavenly feast.[8] But now I believe you realize who is the disciple of whom it is said, 'Woman, behold thy son.'[9] For this pronouncement applies to you, because by eternal predestination and recent vocation the grace of God enjoins by an inviolable decree concern for this your mother. But it is as rash and inhuman to spurn a divine ordinance as to refuse faithful service to a mother. Like Issachar the strong ass,[10] therefore, submit the neck and shoulders to this election and faithfully trust in God's help because the spirit supports your weakness. To me, however, your friend and confidant, it is a cause for joy and exultation that I have deserved to see so great a friend raised up to such a lofty place. For I myself am a servant and son of the church of Cluny.[11] Farewell, and make your journey, I pray, by way of us.[12]

147

To the general chapter of the Cistercian order[1]

1181

Peter, bishop-elect of Chartres, to the chapter of the Cistercians.

I reckon it no less a fault to impede the holy endeavours of the saints than to interrupt angelic and divine business. Certainly I am afraid to incur the penalty of such guilt if I try to detain you with vain and superfluous words when you are preparing for and occupied in the divine. Sometimes however pressing necessity excuses insistent importunity since, even if it holds it up a little, it does not altogether destroy or suppress necessary business. 'Would', says the Apostle, 'that you could bear with some little of my folly.'[2] The ant which provides food for itself in the summer is not accused of folly.[3] The unjust steward is not accused of folly who, unable to dig and ashamed to beg, made for himself friends to receive him 'into everlasting

[12] Presumably Theobald was not at Cluny when Peter wrote this letter.

147 [1] The chapter was held at Cîteaux. Peter styles himself bishop-elect of Chartres; his predecessor John of Salisbury d. 25 Oct. 1180, but Peter was still at Saint-Remi in Mar. 1181 (see Introduction, p. xxxi).

[2] 2 Cor. 11: 1.

[3] Cf. Prov. 6: 6–8; 30: 25.

reciperent illum 'in eterna tabernacula'.[4] Non ad insipientiam est michi si non de 'mammona iniquitatis'[5] sed de supplicatione humilitatis et debito fraterne caritatis interpello dominos meos et fratres karissimos quatinus me commemorent inter sui gaudii socios et future expectationis amicos. Recolat igitur sanctissimum uestrum collegium unum me esse de alumnis beatissimi Bernardi cuius merito Cisterciensem ordinem Deus usque ad mare et ultra dilatauit et usque ad nubes, ut iste que adhuc supersunt reliquie testantur,[6] magnificauit. Inter cetera sua beneficia contulit michi superna gratia eo uiuente affuisse in his castrorum Dei[7] conuenientibus et commendatum atque receptum tam beneficiis quam orationibus. Translato etiam ipso ad celestem curiam, semel adiui dominos meos et fratres karissimos replicans et inculcans societatem et caritatem antiquitus indultam. Prostratus itaque licet absens pedibus totius sancte huius congregationis, semper expectatum et expetitum nec non etiam expetendum imploro suffragium.[8] Vester fui, uester sum, uester semper ero. Alienos ad sinum suum colligit uestra caritas et me leonibus, lupis, ursis, et malis bestiis indefensum exponitis? Cellensem enutristis, Remensem amastis, Carnotensem proicietis? Vbi maior necessitas, ibi expirabit[a] caritas? Vbi summum periculum, ibi nullum subsidium? Vbi descendens ab Ierusalem in Ihericho semiuiuus relinquitur, post sacerdotis et Leuite negligentiam, Samaritani pectus indurabitur ne oleum et uinum uulneribus sauciati infundantur?[9] Absit ut fons olei arescat, ut lechitus olei in sancto ordine uestro deficiat.[10] Certe si in uobis defecerit sanctus, mundus remanebit immundus. Non esset dolor angelis Dei sicut dolor iste.[11] Pax itaque eterna et gratia sit uobiscum.[12] Amen.

[a] *sic PL;* expriuabit *Sirmond*

[4] Cf. Luke 16: 1–9.

[5] Luke 16: 9.

[6] He could mean relics of St Bernard, but it is more likely that he means the Cistercians, i.e. likened to the remnant of Israel (cf. Isa. 10 and, e.g., Rom. 9: 27; cf. also letter no. 141 and n. 4).

[7] Cf. Gen. 32: 2.

dwellings'.[4] It is not to be put down to folly on my part if I interrupt my lords and dearest brothers not regarding 'the mammon of iniquity'[5] but rather the supplication of humility and the debt of fraternal love so that they might remember me among the companions of their rejoicing and the friends of future hope. May your holiest community therefore recall that I am one of the disciples of the most blessed Bernard by whose merit God has extended the Cistercian order even as far as the sea and beyond and extolled it even unto the clouds, as those remnants who still remain bear witness.[6] Among its other blessings, heavenly grace granted it to me, when Bernard was alive, to be present among those of the camps of God[7] gathering together, when I was both commended and received with blessings and prayers alike. Now that he has been translated to the heavenly court, I have approached my lords and dearest brothers once only, unfolding to them and impressing on them the fellowship and love which was formerly bestowed. Prostrate therefore, although absent, at the feet of the whole of this holy congregation, I beg for your prayers,[8] which are always hoped for and sought, and even now to be sought. I was yours, I am yours and I shall be yours always. Your love gathers others to its bosom, and do you expose me undefended to lions, wolves, bears, and evil beasts? You nourished the man of Celle, you loved the man of Reims, will you cast out the man of Chartres? Where there is greater necessity, will love expire there? Where there is the greatest danger, is there no support there? Where he who was going down from Jerusalem to Jericho is left half alive, neglected by priest and Levite, will the heart of the Samaritan be so hardened that oil and wine will not be poured out on the wounds of the injured man?[9] Far be it that the fount of oil should dry up, that the cruse of oil should waste[10] in your holy order. Certainly if what is holy should waste among you the world will remain unclean. There would be no sorrow for the angels of God like to this sorrow.[11] And so may eternal peace and grace be with you.[12] Amen.

[8] *suffragium*, 'prayer' (cf. Latham, and Blaise, *Dictionnaire*, *suffragium* 3) and specifically also 'a prayer said on the basis of a prayer community' (Niermeyer, *suffragium* 8).

[9] Cf. Luke 10: 30–7.

[10] Cf. 3 Kgs. (1 Kgs.) 17: 14, 16.

[11] Cf. Lam. 1: 12; the point here being that if the Cistercians are not holy then no one is.

[12] An allusion to the conclusion of the Mass ('Pax domini sit semper uobiscum'), but cf. also Rev. 1: 4.

148

To the prior and community of Grandmont[1]

1162 × 1181 (in June)

Priori et fratribus Grandimontis Petrus humilis abbas Sancti Remigii, manus orationis et pretium.[2]

Quanto fragiliores sumus et de nostris minus speramus uiribus tanto si sapimus ardentius ualidiora et ampliora emendicamus suffragia. Ve enim soli quia si ceciderit non habet subleuantem se.[3] Si autem fuerint duo fouebuntur mutuo. Solum estimo qui nec cum Deo in simplicitate et puritate ambulat nec fraternum currum inuincibili societate et inseparabili unitate equitat. Domini et fratres karissimi, 'ego uir uidens' tam 'paupertatem' quam insufficientiam 'meam';[4] ubi audio celestes pauperibus erogari dapes, curro, pulso, quero et de reliquiarum micis offellas quas possum expecto. Vestrum est, uestrum est 'panis oleati'[5] buccellas cum Petro Apostolo, cum conuenitis ad cenam agni,[6] sumere, sed et his qui non preparauerunt sibi partes mittere. Dies enim Domini sanctus est, solennitas Sancti Iohannis Baptiste, quando ad matrem pulli galline reuolant et de singulis locis uestris riuuli ad locum de quo exierunt refluunt ut de paterna instructione et correctione reparato meatu copiosius et fortius iterum fluant.[7] Seruanda et tenenda est hec probabilis et sancta consuetudo quia non tantum ab homine et per hominem sed etiam a lege et Deo hec approbata est institutio. Tribus enim uicibus iubet Dominus in lege ut Hebreus appareat ante Dominum, non tamen uacuis manibus.[8] Nunquam autem uanum aut uacuum est sinus maternos,[a] tanquam sue professionis alumnos, relambere et nouos inde sibi sapores

148 *Sirmond VIII. 7*]
[a] *corr. Ritchie;* paternos *Sirmond*

148 [1] Written on the occasion of the general chapter of the order of Grandmont, which was, on the evidence of this letter and no. 149, on the feast of St John the Baptist, 24 June (see letter no. 149; cf. also letter no. 43, n. 4). (The reference here to *dies . . . Domini* suggests that this fell on a Sunday in the year of writing, giving 1162, 1173, and 1179 as possibilities.)

[2] Here and in letter no. 149 Peter develops the theme of paying a price for their valuable prayers, even though he himself is (spiritually) poor, and the prayers he can offer in return are of little value.

148

To the prior and community of Grandmont[1]

1162 × 1181 (in June)

To the prior and brothers of Grandmont, Peter, humble abbot of Saint-Remi, the hands of prayer and the price.[2]

The weaker we are and the less hope we have in our strength, the more earnestly, if we are wise, do we beg for stronger and greater support. For woe to the one who is alone, because if he should fall he has no one to hold him up.[3] But if there are two they will help each other. I reckon that he is alone who neither walks with God in simplicity and purity nor rides in the fraternal chariot with invincible companionship and inseparable unity. Dearest lords and brothers, 'I am the man that see' both 'my poverty'[4] and my insufficiency; when I hear that heavenly feasts are being disbursed to the poor, I run, I knock, I seek, and I await what morsels of left-over crumbs I can. It is your place, yours, to take up with the Apostle Peter the morsels 'of bread tempered with oil'[5] when you come together at the feast of the Lamb,[6] but also to send down portions to those who have not prepared any for themselves. For it is the holy day of the Lord, the feast of St John the Baptist, when the chicks of the hen fly back to the mother and streams flow back from your separate places to the place whence they came so that they might flow again more abundantly and powerfully along a course repaired by paternal instruction and correction.[7] This commendable and holy custom should be preserved and held on to because this institution is approved not only by man and through man but also by the law and by God. For the Lord commands in the law that the Hebrew should appear before the Lord three times, not however empty-handed.[8] Moreover, it is never vain or empty to be fostered again in the maternal bosom as disciples of its profession and to draw new savours to oneself from there. Therefore I myself, scenting afar

[3] Cf. Eccles. 4: 10.
[4] Lam. 3: 1.
[5] Num. 11: 8.
[6] Cf. Rev. 19: 9.
[7] i.e. possibly indicating that the feast of St John the Baptist fell on a Sunday (see above, n. 1); *locus* can also mean monastic house (cf. Niermeyer, *locus* 5, 6; *DML*, *locus* 7 a); the priors of the houses are the 'streams', flowing back for the general chapter.
[8] Cf. Exod. 23: 14–17; Deut. 16: 16 (although the chapter was annual).

attrahere. Procul igitur odorans[9] ipse ego tam iocundos et festiuos sanctitatis uestre concursus, prompto animo et uultu submisso 'Amen' pauper inclamo et de orationum suffragiis subleuamen expostulo. Hec autem nostra postulatio non usquequaque imbecillis et carens sustentationis baculo claudicans sanctum conuentum uestrum ingreditur quia fratres uestros qui nostris in partibus commorantur diligimus et honoramus, et etiam cellam bonam in nostro habetis patrimonio.[10] Hac ergo securus confidentia, uestrorum rogo societatem bonorum;[11] et cum anima soluto corpore uias ignotas[12] aggressa fuerit, conductum uestrum usque ad meum iudicem deposco. Rescribite si placet et quam misericordiam facere disponitis remandate. Valete.

149

To the community of Grandmont[1]

1162 × 1181 (in June)

Dominis et amicis suis de Grandi Monte Petrus abbas Sancti Remigii, salutem.

Religioso fraternitatis uestre conuentui et sanctissimis orationibus saltem anniuersaria reuolutione nos commendamus. Videtur siquidem michi meatus suos fluuius paradisi quasi ad sinum originalem reuocare cum de singulis partibus orbis ad diem beati Iohannis Baptiste solennem contingit priores uestros in unum conuenire.[2] Refluxus iste pretiosarum gemmarum arena ad utilitatem negotiatorum spiritalium redundat et si quis pretiosas querens margaritas ad littus hoc applicuerit studium sancte negotiationis nequaquam uacuus et inanis exibit. 'Ego', itaque, 'uir uidens paupertatem meam'[3] sed

149 *Sirmond VIII. 22*]

[9] Cf. Job 39: 25.

[10] *cella* (*DML*, 1. *cella*, 4 b; Niermeyer, 1. *cella*, 2, 3): Peter seems to be referring to a Grandmontine house near at hand. If so it must have been short-lived. No house is recorded in the diocese of Reims in Hutchison, *Grandmont*, pp. 351–77 (map and gazeteer), or J. Lusse, 'Le monachisme en Champagne des origines au XIIIème siècle', *La Champagne bénédictine*, Travaux de l'Académie Nationale de Reims, clx (1981), 24–78, pp. 72–3, but Saint-Remi's lands were very widespread.

[11] Presumably a confraternity arrangement or formal prayer agreement (cf. Latham, *soci/us— etas*), possibly also suggested by the term *suffragiis* above (see also letter no. 147, n. 8).

[12] Cf. Virgil, *Aen.* viii. 113 (*soluta* is possible for *soluto*, preceding).

off[9] the gatherings so joyful and festive of your holiness, with a ready soul and a lowered face, being a poor man, call out 'Amen' and beg from the intercessions of your prayers relief. But this our demand, which is not entirely feeble and lacking the staff of support, limps into your holy assembly because we love and honour your brothers who live in our regions—and besides you have a good dependency on our patrimony.[10] Secure therefore in this trust, I ask for the fellowship of your good men;[11] and when the soul, after the body has been dissolved, sets out on unknown paths,[12] I beg you to conduct me even unto my judge. Write back, if it please you, and send back what mercy you are disposed to effect. Farewell.

149

To the community of Grandmont[1]

1162 × 1181 (in June)

To his lords and friends of Grandmont, Peter, abbot of Saint-Remi, greetings.

We commend ourselves to the religious community and holiest prayers of your fraternity at least once a year. Indeed it seems to me that the river of paradise is running backwards, as it were, along its courses to the original source whenever it befalls that your priors assemble together from their own parts of the world on the feast day of the blessed John the Baptist.[2] This flowing back of precious gems over the sand redounds to the profit of spiritual merchants, and if anyone seeking precious pearls brings the zeal of his holy trade to this shore, by no means will he leave empty and needy. And so 'I am the man seeing my poverty'[3] but not neglecting it; I am trying to buy for a

149 [1] As letter no. 148, written on the occasion of the general chapter of the Grandmontine order (24 June, as indicated here); it is unlikely that this was written in the same year as letter no. 148, as both seem to have been sent at the time of the general chapter, and two separate letters in the one year seems unlikely (besides the reference to his commending himself once a year). (Prache, *Saint-Remi*, suggests that this letter post-dates letter no. 168, on the evidence of the reference to building works at Saint-Remi, which would put it after *c.*1171/2, but see appendix 12 on the problems with this dating.)

[2] Cf. Gen. 2: 10; the day is 24 June, i.e. this is the date of the general chapter of Grandmont (see n. 1).

[3] Lam. 3: 1; in this passage Peter means that he is trying to buy their prayers but virtually all that he can offer in return is his devotion.

non negligens, bono et pauco pretio suffragium orationum uestrarum tempto emere. Est autem pretium nostrum rogare, postulare, scribere et tenuissimas orationes rependere. Si pensatis usum estimationis, parum est quod datur, si uotum, immo animum deuotum, multum. Estimabile procul dubio est quod manus legit,[a] impretiabile quod animus. Vt enim ait Gregorius: non quantum sed ex quanto offeratur considerat Deus,[4] id est non quantum pecunie sed ex quanta deuotione. Suggerimus fraternitati uestre supplicatione humili quatinus benefactoribus ecclesie nostre beneficium sancte societatis uestre indulgeatis et precipue illis qui helemosinas suas faciunt nouo operi quod ad honorem et decorem domus Dei et beati Remigii inchoauimus. Nam caput monasterii nostri renouare uolentes, cum Dei adiutorio manum ad fortia mittimus.[5] Rescriptum itaque sigillo uestro roboratum mittite ad excitandos fidelium animos uestra sancta exhortatione et orationum concessione. Valeat sancta congregatio uestra.

150

To the community of Cluny[1]

1162 × 1181

Cluniacensibus Petrus abbas Sancti Remigii, salutem.

In tanta sanctorum congregatione, et persona nostra si adesset uilis et abiecta appareret et uox exigua, timeo ne et littera rusticana. Loquar tamen in medio uestrum ut seruus Abraham,[2] ut puer Daniel,[3] ut senex Iacob,[4] non ut Heliu cuius 'uenter' est ut 'mustum absque spiraculo'.[5] Lego in scripturis Hieremiam lamentantem, Paulum optantem anathema ⟨esse⟩ a Christo pro fratribus suis.[6] Stillicidiis tante caritatis inebriatus, nonne dolere debeo usque ad medullarum ⟨et⟩ compagum discretionem[7] super ruinam matris

[a] legitur *Sirmond*

150 *Sirmond VIII. 23*]

[4] Cf. Gregory *Hom. .xl. in Evang.* ii. 38. 10 (*PL* lxxvi. 1288); cf. also ibid. i. 5. 2 (*PL* lxxvi. 1093).

[5] Cf. Prov. 31: 19; on the building works at Saint-Remi see appendix 12.

150 [1] A complaint against laxity at Cluny, specifically eating and drinking after compline (see also letter no. 24 for another complaint against Cluny).

good and small price the intercession of your prayers. The price we offer is to ask, to beg, to write, and to pay back even fleeting prayers. If you weigh up its utility, that which is given is little; if you weigh up the wish, or rather the devotion of the mind, it is much. Without doubt that which the hand gathers can be estimated, that which the mind gathers is priceless. For as Gregory says, the Lord considers not how much is offered, but out of how much,[4] that is, not how much money, but from how much devotion it is offered. We urge you in brotherhood, with humble supplication, to bestow the blessing of your holy fellowship on the benefactors of our church, and especially those who give their alms to the new work which we have begun to the honour and adornment of the house of God and of the blessed Remigius. For, wishing to renew the chevet of our monastery, with God's help we are putting out our hand to strong things.[5] And so send a reply, confirmed by your seal, to arouse the minds of the faithful by your holy exhortation and by the gift of prayers. May your holy community flourish.

150

To the community of Cluny[1]

1162 × 1181

To the monks of Cluny, Peter, abbot of Saint-Remi, greetings.

In so great a community of the holy our person, if it were present, would appear worthless and low and our voice mean; I am afraid even my written word may seem crude. Let me speak, however, in your midst like the servant of Abraham,[2] like the boy Daniel,[3] like Jacob as an old man,[4] not like Eliu whose 'belly is as new wine which wanteth vent'.[5] I read in the Scriptures Jeremiah lamenting, Paul wishing to be an anathema from Christ for his brethren.[6] Drunk with the showers of such great love, ought I not to grieve even unto the separation of the marrow and of the joints[7] over the ruin of the mother of the daughters of

[2] Cf. Gen. 24.

[3] Cf. Dan. 1; he abstained from the meat and wine of Nebuchadnezzar (but Peter may also have in mind Daniel's speaking before Nebuchadnezzar and interpreting his dreams, in Dan. 2 etc.).

[4] Cf. Gen. 49.

[5] Cf. Job 32: 19.

[6] Cf. Rom. 9: 3.

[7] Cf. Heb. 4: 12.

filiarum Syon, utique cenobii Cluniacensis? Nonne hec est 'urbs fortitudinis nostre'[8] de qua egrediebantur quondam mille per episcopatus, per abbatias, per regum et principum curias, et nunc paucissimi sunt incole eius? Nonne luminare hoc magnum tenebras obscurate religionis per diuersas regiones illuminauit, ordinem reformando, honestatem docendo, caritatem infundendo, et cetera pietatis officia renouando? Vsque ad sedem apostolicam nonne gradibus humilitatis ascendit?[9] O domini! O fratres! O filii Cluniacenses! Ego ipse apud Sanctum Martinum de Campis adolescentulus uerissimis experimentis quod dico gustaui, et uidi ubi erat auro locus in quo conflabatur.[10] Proh dolor! Intepuit et consenuit tantus feruor. 'Quod autem antiquatur et senescit, prope interitum est';[11] quod absit a uobis et ab hereditate Iacob. Melius est certe mori uos in bello uitiorum et uitiosorum, qui more uulpium demoliuntur uineam Domini Sabaoth,[12] quam uidere ultima funera matris uestre et nostre. Repurgate igitur puteos Abrahe, Ysaac et Iacob,[13] et zizania superseminata nocte ab inimico eradicate,[14] precipue illud originarium malum de quo pessima seges ad suffocationem monastice religionis suboritur. Est autem consuetudo comessationum et epotationum que fiunt completorium. Succidite, oro, hanc arborem malam 'in sententia uigilum'.[15] Adsit uobis gratia Spiritus sancti, qua cooperante constituatis quod Deo sit acceptabile, ecclesie Cluniacensi utile, presentibus salubre, posteris remediabile.

[8] Isa. 26: 1.
[9] i.e. Cluny has produced popes; cf. *Regula S. Benedicti* c. v.
[10] Cf. Job 28: 1.
[11] Heb. 8: 13.

Zion, that is to say of the monastery of Cluny? Is not this 'the city of our strength'[8] from which a thousand once went out to bishoprics, abbacies, and the courts of kings and princes, and are not her inhabitants now very few? Did not this great light illumine the shadows of the darkened religious life throughout diverse regions, reforming the order, teaching goodness, pouring in love, and renewing the other duties of piety? Did it not ascend by steps of humility even unto the apostolic see?[9] O my lords, o my brothers, o my sons of Cluny! I myself at Saint-Martin-des-Champs as a young man have tasted what I speak of with the truest proofs, and I have seen where gold had a place wherein it was melted.[10] O sorrow! Such great fervour has cooled and grown old. 'And that which decayeth and groweth old is near its end';[11] forbid that this may apply to you and to the inheritance of Jacob. It is surely better for you to die in the battle against wickedness and the wicked, who like foxes destroy the vineyard of the Lord of Sabaoth,[12] than to see the final death of your mother and ours. Clean out again therefore the wells of Abraham, Isaac, and Jacob,[13] and uproot the cockle oversowed at night by the enemy,[14] especially that original evil from which the worst crop rises up to stifle the religious life of the monastery. Yet there is a custom of feasting and drinking which serves as compline. Cut down, I pray, this tree which is wicked 'by the sentence of the watchers'.[15] May the grace of the Holy Spirit be with you, with whose co-operation you may establish that which is acceptable to God, profitable to the church of Cluny, healthy for the present generation, and healing to posterity.

[12] Cf. S. of S. 2: 15; also Lord of Sabaoth, cf. Jer. 11: 20; Rom. 9: 29; Jas. 5: 4.
[13] Cf. Gen. 26: 15, 18, etc.
[14] Cf. Matt. 13: 24–30.
[15] Cf. Dan. 4, esp. 11, 14, 20.

151

To the abbot and community of Villers[1]

1162 × 1181

Abbati Villarcensi et conuentui Petrus abbas Sancti Remigii.

Cum reo et pro reo, ipse non in uno sed in multis reus, reatus ueniam postulo, causam non iustitie sed misericordie allego, fontem Dauid[2] resignandum et aperiendum sitienti et de uia redeunti imploro. Iudei 'captum a bestia' et 'morticinum' atque carnem porcinam non comedunt,[3] sed Iesus, lilium inter spinas, et captum liberat et morticinum saluat et porci immunditiam sua munditia[4] que 'attingit a fine usque ad finem fortiter et disponit omnia suauiter'[5] emundat et emendat. Fossa iuxta altare[6] que sacrificiorum et holocaustorum reliquias siue superflua solet excipere non nobis oppilata sed aperta reseruetur quia et ipsum altare concauum et 'in modum retis' fieri iussum est[7] quatinus et cineres excipiat et uapores admote flamme intrinsecus usque ad animam foueat. Nostrum altare quod est non huius creationis sed in excelsis paterne tantum generationis et in terris materne nichilominus tantum conceptionis, Iesus Christus, uentrem habet eburneum quidem sed distinctum sapphiris[8] quatinus et ex uirtute Dei nostras deleat ignorantias et peccata et ex susceptione humane nature nostris infirmitatibus ex his que passus est compati nouerit. Noluit autem plagas illas sanctas et uulnera in cruce suscepta ita recludi quod meatus uenie et indulgentie peccatoribus obstruerentur, sed adhuc manus habet expansas in cruce dicens, 'Venite ad me omnes qui laboratis et onerati estis, et ego uos reficiam.'[9] Quia igitur uiris sapientibus scribo, de archa sapientie uestre quantaslibet quisquilias mutuare michi concedat eadem sapientia que nunquam caret

151 *Sirmond VII. 4*]

151 [1] The dates are those of Peter's abbacy of Saint-Remi. The most likely recipients are the Cistercian community of Villers, dioc. Liège (Cott. ii. 3395–7; but for alternative possibilities, see Cott. ii. 3395–9). The abbot would thus have been Ulric, the likely recipient of letter no. 125, who occurs from 1158, abdicated 1184, retired to Vaucelles, d. by 1196: *Mon. Belge* iv. 2, pp. 367–8; see also É. de Moreau, *L'Abbaye de Villers-en-Brabant aux XIIè et XIIIè siècles*, Recueil de Travaux publiés par les membres des conférences d'histoire et de philologie, xxi (Brussels, 1909), pp. 21–4, 271, and *GC* iii. 585–6.

[2] Cf. Zech. 13: 1.

[3] Cf. Lev. 11: 7; 22: 8; Deut. 14: 8, 21.

151

To the abbot and community of Villers[1]

1162 × 1181

To the abbot and community of Villers, Peter, abbot of Saint-Remi.

With the accused and for the accused, accused myself not in one but in many things, I request pardon for the offence, I adduce the cause not of justice but of mercy, I beg that the fountain of David[2] be unsealed and opened up to the one who is thirsting and returning from the road. The Jews do not eat 'that which was taken by a beast' or 'that which dieth of itself', nor the flesh of pigs,[3] but Jesus, the lily among the thorns, both frees that which was taken and saves that which dieth of itself, and cleanses and amends the uncleanness of the pig by His own cleanliness[4] which 'reacheth from end to end mightily and ordereth all things sweetly'.[5] Let the trench next to the altar,[6] which is accustomed to receive the relics or residue of sacrifices and burnt offerings, be kept open for us, not shut up, because the altar itself also was ordered to be made hollow and 'in manner of a net'[7] so that it should both receive ashes and keep warm the vapours of the flame which is applied within even unto the soul. Our altar, which is not of this creation but on high only of the Father's begetting and on earth none the less only of a mother's conceiving, that is Jesus Christ, has indeed a belly as of ivory, but set with sapphires,[8] so that He may both wipe out our ignorance and sins by God's power, and, by taking on human nature, may know from what He suffered how to have compassion for our weaknesses. He did not wish, however, for those holy blows and wounds received on the cross to be closed up again so that the paths of pardon and indulgence would be blocked to sinners, but He still has His hands stretched out on the cross saying, 'Come to me all you that labour and are burdened and I will refresh you.'[9] Because therefore I am writing to wise men, let that same wisdom which never lacks abundant goodness and plentiful generosity permit

[4] A reference to Peter's vision, cf. Acts 10: 11–16.

[5] Wisd. 8: 1 (omitting *enim*).

[6] Cf. 3 Kgs. (1 Kgs.) 18: 35.

[7] Cf. Exod. 27: 4; 38: 4, but the reference is to the grate not the altar.

[8] Cf. S. of S. 5: 14.

[9] Matt. 11: 28, but these words were not spoken on the cross.

affluenti bonitate et copiosa largitate.[10] Pro fratre Ansfredo,[11] immo pro causa eius, qui ad uos reuertitur hec intimare nec michi pigrum est nec uobis onerosum esse debet. Causa equidem sue abscessionis differens fuit ab aliis qui propositum sancte religionis irreuerenter abiciunt et tanquam canis ad uomitum redeunt.[12] Effectus siquidem cause ipsam probat. Non enim abiecto pudore et reuerentia sancti propositi cum meretricibus more aliorum lupanaribus se immiscuit uel aliis enormitatibus secularis conuersationis rupto federe sanctitatis se immersit. Non ergo a uobis uno et indifferenti modo rerum cause pensentur. Quamuis enim in mente diuina causa atque ratio omnium habeatur tamen sicut fluuius qui egreditur de paradiso in quatuor capita diuiditur,[13] sic de illa radice diuine dispositionis rami innumerabilium causarum, et in se eadem manens diuersas propagines exuberat uniuersitate eorum que fuerunt uel sunt uel erunt. Quisque enim euentus siue effectus de propria causa procedit.[14] Inde est, quantum ad presentem causam attinet, quod manus Moysi quam primo de sinu leprosam retraxit secundo remisit et carni relique similis apparuit.[15] Similiter frater Ansfredus cum ad claustrum sancte congregationis uestre, tanquam ad sinum Moysi, conuersus contineretur nulla in eo lepra criminalis peccati apparebat. Cum autem de claustro exiit tanquam leprosus apparuit. Fauente igitur et agente diuina iussione, ad sinum Moysi tanquam ad uirum priorem rediens, dicit, 'Melius michi erat tunc magis quam nunc',[16] nunquam inde postea exiturus nisi ex mandato abbatis uel uocatione celesti in exitu mortis, quando sana et integra, qualis de baptismate exiuit, anima eius ad domum ipso propitio redibit. Non ergo peniteat uos ad horam illum amisisse quem perpetuum fratrem et monachum recipitis. Proderit enim ei sensisse laqueos diaboli quibus Dei adiutorio contritis anima eius liberata est. Tam enim nos quam fratres nostri nec non et clerus de castro nostro testimonium ei perhibemus quod

[10] A complex series of allusions and metaphors: the unclean are now clean, and mercy can prevail over the strict interpretation of the law; this is shown by the image of the trench of leftovers; Christ is then compared to the altar, and this open trench to His open wounds. The open trench/wounds signify mercy, and so are not sealed or closed up, but open to sinners. These relics and residues in the trench are then compared to the other type of leavings (*quisquilias*), of the wisdom of the recipients. The point is that they should be inclined to mercy rather than to a strict and harsh interpretation of the Rule.

[11] Ansfredus is otherwise unknown but was evidently a lay brother of Villers who had been in Reims for almost seven years. No such character appears in Moreau's lists of members of the community, Moreau *L'Abbaye de Villers-en-Brabant*, pp. 272–85. (On the changing use of the term *conuersus* in this period, see G. Constable, *The Reformation of the Twelfth Century* (Cambridge, 1996), pp. 77–9.)

me to borrow from the ark of your wisdom any number of leavings.[10] To impart these things on behalf of brother Ansfredus[11] who is returning to you, or rather on behalf of his cause, is not tiresome to me nor should it be burdensome to you. The cause indeed of his departure was different from that of others who irreverently cast aside the vow of the holy religious life and return like dogs to their vomit.[12] The effect of the cause indeed proves the cause itself. For he did not, like others, with shame and reverence for the holy vow cast aside, betake himself to brothels with harlots, nor did he, with the pact of holiness broken, immerse himself in other irregularities of the worldly life. Do not therefore weigh up the causes of things in one undiscriminating manner. For although the cause and reason of all things is held in the divine mind, yet as the river which goes forth from paradise is divided into four heads,[13] so branches of innumerable causes go forth from that root of divine disposition, and remaining the same in itself, it abundantly brings forth diverse offshoots in the totality of all those things which were, are, or will be. For each event or effect proceeds from its own cause.[14] Hence it is, as far as the present case is concerned, that the hand of Moses which he first brought forth from his bosom leprous he put back a second time, and it appeared similar to the other flesh.[15] Similarly with brother Ansfredus, when he was enclosed as a lay brother in the cloister of your holy community as in the bosom of Moses, no leprosy of criminal sin appeared in him. But when he came out of the cloister he appeared as if leprous. Therefore, with the divine command favouring and impelling him, returning to the bosom of Moses, as if to the first husband, he says, 'It was much better with me then than now,'[16] and he will never go out of there again except on the order of the abbot or at the celestial summons when he departs in death, when, healthy and whole as it went forth from baptism, his soul will return home, if He grant it. Do not therefore let it grieve you that you lost for a time this one whom you are receiving as a brother and monk for ever. For it will profit him to have felt the snares of the devil from which his soul was freed, they having been broken by God's help. For we offer testimony for him, and so do our brethren, and also the clergy of our town, that he conducted himself in a more religious

[12] Cf. Prov. 26: 11; 2 Pet. 2: 22.

[13] Cf. Gen. 2: 10.

[14] i.e. only God knows the true causes of all things, and men should not assume that similar effects have the same cause.

[15] Cf. Exod. 4: 6–7.

[16] Cf. Hos. 2: 7.

religiosius se habuit in seculo quam multi in claustro dum fere septennio nobiscum conuersatus est. Exempla misericordie plurima supponerem nisi uiscera Ioseph iam in uobis mota ad misericordiam[17] presentirem et nisi modum epistolarem excedere timerem. Breuiter tamen et compendiose patrem prodigi filii ad eum reuertentis cum uitulo saginato, stola, anulo et calciamentis occurrentem, immo accurrentem, monstro,[18] et Iesum eque Filium Marie Virginis adhuc Thome Apostolo latus et manus ostendentem[19] ut quasi 'petra refugium erinaciis'[20] in cauernis et foraminibus[21] sue passionis pullos fugientes admittat et ab insecutione milui rapacissimi tutetur. Oleum itaque de capite uestro non deficiat[22] quia postquam Sareptena mulier, id est ecclesia, Heliam pauit, id est Christum recepit, farina misericordie diuine non defecit nec lechitus olei imminutus est.[23] Itaque nec ubera sint uobis arentia nec sterilis uulua.[24] Christus enim non de sterili natus est sed de puella gratia uirginitatis et fecunditatis plena. Valete. Quidam clericus bene litteratus qui in lege Domini die ac nocte meditatur ianuam uestram pulsat, magister Willelmus,[25] ut ad conuiuium siue ad cenam Domini admittatur. Vestem siquidem habet nuptialem,[26] id est pauperem et humilem non uillosam nec pomposam, quo itaque substantia et spiritu pauperior eo societate Christi dignior. Rogo ut illum recipiatis. Orate pro nobis quia ouem uestram detonsam bene uobis conseruauimus et cum multa lana remisimus.[27]

152

To a monk of Saint-Bertin[1]

1162 × 1181

Petrus abbas Sancti Remigii monacho de Sancto Bertino.

Sermones nostros, quos tanquam plumas inutiles et superfluas quatuor uenti celi[2] per diuersa proiecerunt, habere desideras. Si legisti, nonne exangues sensibus sententiarum et eneruës tenuitate

152 *Sirmond VII. 19*]

[17] Cf. Gen. 43: 30. [18] Cf. Luke 15: 22–3, 27, 30. [19] Cf. John 20: 27.
[20] Ps. 103 (104): 18. [21] Cf. S. of S. 2: 14. [22] Cf. Eccles. 9: 8.
[23] Cf. 3 Kgs. (1 Kgs.) 17: 9–16, esp. 14 (cf. *Glossa*, *PL* cxiii, 606–7).
[24] Cf. Hos. 9: 14. [25] Unidentified. [26] Cf. Matt. 22: 11–12.

manner in the world than do many in the cloister while he was dwelling with us for almost seven years. I would supply many examples of mercy did I not foresee that the heart of Joseph had already been moved in you to mercy,[17] and did I not fear to exceed the measure of a letter. Briefly, however, and succinctly I point to the father of the returning prodigal son coming, or rather running, to meet him with the fatted calf, cloak, ring, and boots,[18] and equally to Jesus, Son of the Virgin Mary, still showing His side and hands to Thomas the Apostle[19] so that like 'the rock, a refuge for the irchins,'[20] He may admit the fleeing chicks into the hollow places and clefts[21] of His passion and protect them from the pursuit of the most rapacious kite. And so let not the oil depart from your head,[22] because after the woman of Sareptha, that is the Church, fed Elijah, that is received Christ, the meal of divine mercy did not waste nor was the cruse of oil diminished.[23] And so may you have neither dry breasts nor a barren womb.[24] For Christ was not born of a barren maiden but of one full of the grace of virginity and fecundity. Farewell. A certain well-educated clerk who meditates day and night on the law of the Lord, master William,[25] knocks at your door that he may be admitted to the feast or the supper of the Lord. He has indeed a wedding garment,[26] that is a poor and humble one, not a rich and imposing one; accordingly the poorer he is in substance and spirit the fitter he is for the fellowship of Christ. I ask that you receive him. Pray for us because we have kept your sheep well shorn for you and have sent him back with much wool.[27]

152

To a monk of Saint-Bertin[1]

1162 × 1181

Peter, abbot of Saint-Remi, to a monk of Saint-Bertin.

You wish to have our sermons, which the four winds of heaven[2] have flung out in different directions like useless and superfluous feathers. If you have read them, did you not find them pallid in their perceptions of opinions and enervated in the slightness of their

[27] A reference to the monastic tonsure; i.e. Peter has kept Ansfredus (presumably) obedient to his calling and even spiritually improved.

152 [1] Saint-Bertin, Benedictine, dioc. Saint-Omer (Cott. ii. 2615).
[2] Cf. Dan. 7: 2; 8: 8; 11: 4; Zech. 2: 6; 6:5.

uerborum inuenisti? Si non uidisti, quis persuasit tantopere te querere quos inuentos statim habeas respuere? Curiositas an studii assiduitas te urget[a] uilissimi hominis herbas et cortices[3] insipidos mendicare cum sedeas ad mensas diuitis Augustini, benigni Gregorii, pecuniosi Hieronymi, gloriosi Ambrosii, Bede omnium monetarum nummosi, profundissimi tanquam maris magni Hilarii, suauissimi eloquii Origenis, et aliorum innumerabilium quorum nec micas sub mensa dignus sum colligere?[4] Si noua placent, ecce magistri Hugonis, ecce Sancti Bernardi, ecce magistri Gilleberti et magistri Petri scripta, in quibus nec rose nec lilia desunt.[5] Nostra uero scripta nec de profundo hauriunt nec de alto propinant quia uerba nostra sunt arentia, forte et sterilia. Intentione tamen hac frequenter admoui tabellis stilum quatinus uigiliis solennitatum saltem media hora occuparem me contemplatione[b] sequentium gaudiorum, et subtraherem me a tumultibus me opprimentium iugiter secularium sollicitudinum. Iccirco imperfectos inuenies multos de sermonibus nostris quia post horam, aliquando negligentia mea, aliquando occupatione ingrata, conceptum fetum parturiebam infectum et imperfectum, nec saltem sicut ursa lambendo promouebam postea ad plenum partum. Ecce hoc erit tibi signum, si quando in manus tuas uenerint, qui nostri sunt, si imperfecti, si squalidi, si rusticani, si male amicti prodierint. Tamen da ueniam quia pudibundi non se ingerunt sed compulsi uix publicum ferunt.

[a] urgent *Sirmond* [b] *corr. Hall;* contemplationi *Sirmond*

[3] Cf. Job 30: 4.

[4] Cf. Matt. 15: 27; Mark 7: 28; also Luke 16: 21 (there may be an allusion to Ezek. 47: 10 above).

words? If you have not seen them, who persuaded you to seek out so eagerly those things which, when found, you would have to reject at once? Is it curiosity or an eagerness for study which drives you to beg the tasteless grass and bark[3] of the lowest man when you might sit at the tables of the rich Augustine, the bountiful Gregory, the wealthy Jerome, the glorious Ambrose, Bede well-furnished with all currencies, Hilary most profound like the great sea, Origen of the sweetest eloquence, and innumerable others of whom I am not worthy to gather up even the crumbs under the table?[4] If new works please you, see the writings of master Hugh, see those of St Bernard, of master Gilbert, and master Peter, in which neither roses nor lilies are lacking.[5] But our writings neither draw from the depth nor furnish drink from on high because our words are parched, perhaps also sterile. I have often set my stylus to the tablets, however, with this intention, of occupying myself on the vigils of holy festivals at least for half an hour with contemplation of the joys to follow, and of drawing myself away from the tumults of worldly concerns which oppress me continually. For this reason you will find many of our sermons imperfect because after an hour, sometimes by my neglect, sometimes because of an unpleasant occupation, I used to give birth to the conceived child incomplete and imperfect, nor did I even, like a bear, bring it on later to complete its birth by licking it. See, this will be the sign to you, should they ever come into your hands, which sermons are ours, if they appear imperfect, rough, crude, and badly adorned. Grant pardon, however, because, being ashamed, they do not rush forth but only bear the public gaze reluctantly when forced to do so.

[5] Cf. Ecclus. 39: 17, 19. Master Hugh is probably Hugh of Saint-Victor (whose work figures in the debate between Peter and Nicholas of Clairvaux, see appendix 7); master Gilbert is probably Gilbert de la Porrée, and master Peter, Peter Lombard (who is quoted elsewhere in the letters, see e.g. letter no. 160, nn. 5–6).

153

To a monk of Reading[1]

1162 × 1181

Petrus abbas Sancti Remigii monacho de Reddinges.

Litteras uestre amicitie ad manum non habebam cum nata occasione uobis scribere decreui. Frater enim uester magister Willelmus secum eas asportauerat. Tenorem quoque illarum non bene memorie commendaueram, unde nec recapitulare potui que precipua et digna erant siue responsione siue preconio laudis. Tenuissime siquidem reminiscor quia tanquam in opaca silua tam sensuum quam uerborum grandis in eis preiacebat materia, de qua sapientia excidens columpnas septem, domum Salomonis siue templum Domini posset construere.[2] Itaque factus tanquam uir qui pre inopia racemos colligit in autumno, nec[a] michi occurrit quod uellem prestare amico uenienti de uia,[3] uel anime esurienti magis ex copia quam ex inopia. Equidem non ignoro patere uobis spatiosa illa deambulatoria ubi omnia ligna paradisi,[4] ubi 'uitis habundans in lateribus domus'[5] Dei, ubi 'promptuaria eructantia ex hoc in illud',[6] ubi delicie deliciarum, ubi cantica omnium letantium de sponsi presentia et sponse magnificentia. Puro namque pectore quid iocundius, quid ditius, quid appetibilius? Ibi Deus, ibi angelus, ibi uirtus, ibi 'iuge conuiuium',[7] ibi solennitas solennitatum, ibi mensa refectionis, ibi sompnus quietissime pausationis. Potiora sunt que ibi presentiuntur quam ea que dicuntur. Sic enim in psalmo loquitur talis conscientia: 'Non est sermo in lingua mea',[8] id est que corde sentio, ore non profero. Sic de uobis sentire

153 *Sirmond VI. 22*]
[a] *corr. Hall;* non *Sirmond*

---

153 [1] The monk of Reading here is almost certainly Robert Partes, the author of a poem addressed to Peter in British Library, Egerton 2951, fos. 5[v]-9[r]: see *British Museum. Catalogue of Additions to the Manuscripts 1916–1920* (London, 1933), pp. 297–9. Partes's poems (all of which occur only in this MS) are ed. in W. H. Cornog, 'The poems of Robert Partes', *Speculum*, xii (1937), 215–50. The poem addressed to Peter (pp. 228–33) is a poem of praise for Peter's virtues. Partes was a strong supporter of Becket; we know from the present letter that his own brother (or brother monk) William had been at Saint-Remi (and this may have been connected with the exile of Becket's supporters), and Partes himself acknowledges Peter's generosity to him. Cornog associates the connection between Peter and Reading 'very definitely' with the Becket affair (ibid. p. 219 and n. 2), but this is very insecure: on the evidence of the present letter William may only have visited Saint-Remi. William was

153

To a monk of Reading[1]

1162 × 1181

Peter, abbot of Saint-Remi, to a monk of Reading.

I did not have the letter of your friendship to hand when the opportunity arose and I decided to write to you. For your brother master William had carried it off with him. Furthermore, I had not committed its sense to memory well enough, for which reason I was not able to retrieve the important points that deserved either a reply or a meed of praise. Indeed I remember only dimly, because as in a dark wood there lay in it matter as abundant in perceptions as in words; and wisdom, felling some of this, might construct seven columns, the house of Solomon, or the temple of the Lord.[2] And so I am become like a man who because of poverty gleans the grapes in autumn, and it does not occur to me what I might want to offer to a friend coming from the highway,[3] or to a soul hungry more on account of abundance than want. I know indeed that there lie open to you those spacious promenades where are all the trees of paradise,[4] where is 'the fruitful vine, on the sides of the house'[5] of God, where are 'the storehouses flowing out of this into that,'[6] where are the delights of delights, where are the songs of all those rejoicing in the presence of the bridegroom and in the magnificence of the bride. For what is more joyful than a pure heart, what richer, what more desirable? There is God, there the angel, there virtue, there the 'continual feast',[7] there the festival of festivals, there the table of refreshment, there the sleep of quietest rest. Better are those things which are apprehended there than those which are spoken. For such consciousness speaks thus in the psalm: 'There is no speech in my tongue,'[8] that is, those things which I perceive in the heart I do not

himself the recipient of poems of Robert Partes. Cornog dates the poems to Peter of Celle and William Partes to possibly 1162 × 1170, between Peter's el. to Saint-Remi and Becket's assassination, but notes that they are strictly undatable (ibid. p. 220).

[2] Cf. 3 Kgs. (1 Kgs.) 6–7; Prov. 9: 1.

[3] Cf. Micah 7: 1; Luke 11: 6; what follows contrasts Peter, poor and hungry, with the friend, in his abundance hungry for more rather than starving.

[4] Cf. Gen. 2: 16; 3: 2.

[5] Cf. Ps. 127 (128): 3.

[6] Cf. Ps. 143 (144): 13.

[7] Cf. Prov. 15: 15.

[8] Ps. 138 (139): 4.

michi persuadet fama publica, sic testatur conuersatio sancta et integra atque inuiolabilis propositi obseruatio, quam fortius tenetis proficiendo quam inchoaueritis arripiendo. Contra faciunt qui cum spiritu ceperint carne consummantur. Panes nostros, si tamen nostros, libenter comeditis, et scripta nostra sublimiori honore quam decet excipitis.[9] Nunquam enim de tam immundo uase emanat aqua digna ad sorbendum uel de tam furfureo et cinereo clibano mundus egreditur panis. Dilectio tamen, que cinerem tanquam panem manducat, in uobis habundans, uilia queque amici pretiosa reputat et pallio honestiori ignobilia nostra circumuenustat. Sed utinam lima correctionis uestre omnia scripta nostra explanata essent et emendata.

154

To the prior and community of Saint-Crépin-le-Grand de Soissons[1]

*c.*1162/3 × 1179, before May (or more likely before Mar.)

Priori et conuentui Sanctorum Crispini et Crispiniani Petrus abbas Sancti Remigii.

Si quod consilium, si quod solatium, si denique consolatio ulla in me est, sine inuidia uobis communicare debeo; et tam in uobis nouellas plantationes quam frugiferas arbores qualicunque stillicidio nostrarum exhortationum rigare desidero. Vicarios siquidem affectus erga uos absentis dilecti et karissimi nobis abbatis uestri uiscerali sollicitudine in eius recessu me excepisse reminiscor. Visitare itaque uos affectuosa caritate in uotis[a] habeo, sed concurrentium causarum retardat concatenatio et egra aeris et itineris contemplatio. Suppleat littera quod non ualet presentia. Vniuersitatem igitur uestram, filii

154 *Sirmond VIII. 18*]
[a] *corr. Hall;* uobis *Sirmond*

[9] Presumably a reference to Peter's treatise *De panibus* (see Introduction, p. xxxiv). This does not affect the date of the present letter, as this treatise was evidently already complete by autumn 1157, when John of Salisbury writes of having received it (see *J. S. Epp.* i. 55–8, letter no. 33).

154 [1] To the community of Saint-Crépin-le-Grand, Soissons, written during the absence of the abbot, presumably Berneredus (see letter no. 128, n. 1). Something is known of some

utter from the mouth. Your public reputation persuades me to think thus of you, your holy manner of life so bears witness, as also does your complete and inviolable observance of the vow which you hold to more strongly as you go forward than when you first seized on to it. They do the opposite who, although they start in the spirit, end in the flesh. Our loaves, if indeed they are ours, you freely eat, and our writings you receive with a higher honour than is fitting.[9] For never does water fit for drinking flow from so unclean a vessel or clean bread come out of an oven so soiled with bran and ashes. Love, however, which chews ash like bread, abounding in you, reckons whatsoever worthless things of a friend precious, and with its more honourable cloak surrounds our ignoble things with beauty. But if only all our writings had been made clear and emended by the file of your correction.

154

To the prior and community of Saint-Crépin-le-Grand de Soissons[1]

*c.*1162/3 × 1179, before May (or more likely before Mar.)

To the prior and community of Saint-Crépin, Peter, abbot of Saint-Remi.

If there is in me any counsel, any comfort, lastly any consolation, I ought to share it with you ungrudgingly; and I desire to water the new plantations among you, just as much as the fruit-bearing trees, with the shower, such as it is, of our exhortations. I recall indeed that I have taken it upon myself with deep concern to show towards you in his place, while he is on his retreat, the affections of your absent abbot who is beloved and most dear to us. And so with affectionate love I have it in my prayers to visit you, but a concatenation of concurrent causes is holding me back, as is an anxious contemplation of the weather and the journey. Let a letter make up for what presence cannot manage. I therefore address your whole community, dearest

of Berneredus's movements: as he seems here to be on a retreat, this cannot be his journey to Rome (see letter no. 128, n. 1), or to Troyes (see letter no. 132); he may have been at Mont-Dieu, an evident favourite retreat of Peter's, with which Berneredus is connected in letters 91 and 115 (but no. 115, which mentions a journey of Berneredus to Mont-Dieu, cannot be dated more closely than the present letter). The dates are those of Berneredus's abbacy.

karissimi, alloquor, et in Domino commoneo ne quis de uobis uapor sinistri rumoris erumpat, ne odor suauissime opinionis excidat, ne districtio ordinis aliquatenus tepore aquilonari[2] pereffluens euanescat. Facilius enim potestis seruare quod tenetis quam recuperare quod amiseritis uel adquirere quod nunquam possedistis. Preueniente autem et preoperante Dei gratia, et adiuuante boni patris uestri sancto exemplo atque doctrina, cooperantibusque uestris studiis, triplici, immo multiplici, splendore supernus radius intrinsecus et extrinsecus congregationem uestram illustrauit religione, opinione et temporalium possessione. Hanc Ysaac benedictionem dedit Iacob heredi suo: 'Det', inquit, 'tibi Deus de rore celi et de pinguedine terre habundantiam.'[3] De rore celi pullulat claustralis religio et sanctitatis fragrans optime suauis opinio, de pinguedine terre frumenti, uini et olei exuberans fecunda possessio. Hec gratia gratos non ingratos Deo faciat. Humilia non inflata pectora certe gratia inhabitat, aut fugat aut fugit inflationem, equat inequalia, frangit excelsa, calcata[b] tollit, aspera emollit, fracta consolidat, ficta respuit, dispersa congregat, congregata conseruat, hominem ad Deum eleuat, Deum ad hominem inclinat. Hec decurrit a throno gratie ad thronum sancte conscientie et facit germinare fructus tricenos, sexagenos et centenos.[4] Hanc quamuis erogare uobis non possum, tamen rogare possum. Hec ergo uobiscum et in uobis sit semper. Amen. Orate pro abbate uestro et pro nobis. Fratrem Iohannem cui cura est de omnibus specialiter commendo.[5]

[b] *corr. Ritchie;* elata *Sirmond*

---

[2] *tepore aquilonari* is open to various interpretations (the key may of course lie in another, lost, piece of correspondence), but in this context the most likely image is that of ice melting, as would happen in a northern spring, where there was ice to melt.

brothers, and in the Lord I warn you lest any vapour of evil rumour should break out about you, lest the odour of sweetest reputation should fail, lest the austerity of the order should in any respect vanish, flowing away with northern thawing.[2] For you can more easily preserve what you have than recover what you have lost or acquire what you never possessed. But with the grace of God going on before and working before, and with the holy example and instruction of your good father helping, and with your exertions working together, the heavenly ray has with triple, nay multiple, splendour lit up your congregation inwardly and outwardly in religion, in reputation, and in temporal possessions. Isaac gave this blessing to Jacob his heir: 'God', he said, 'give thee of the dew of heaven, and of the fatness of the earth, abundance.'[3] There springs forth from the dew of heaven the religion of the cloister and a sweet and fragrant reputation for holiness, and from the fatness of the earth the overflowing, abundant possession of fruit, wine, and oil. May this grace make us grateful, not ungrateful, to God. Grace certainly dwells in humble, not puffed up, breasts; it puts to flight or flees from arrogance, it makes the unequal equal, it dashes the lofty in pieces, it lifts up the downtrodden, it softens the harsh, mends the broken, rejects the false, gathers the dispersed, preserves the gathered, raises man up to God, and inclines God to man. This runs down from the throne of grace to the throne of holy conscience and causes the fruit to germinate thirty-fold, sixty-fold, and a hundred-fold.[4] Although I cannot dispense this to you, yet I can ask. So may this be always with you and among you. Amen. Pray for your abbot and for us. I particularly commend brother John who has charge of all things.[5]

[3] Cf. Gen. 27: 28.

[4] Cf. Matt. 13: 8, 23; Mark 4: 8, 20; Luke 8: 8.

[5] Presumably the prior left in charge in Berneredus's absence, and possibly the same John mentioned at the end of letter no. 135.

155

To the community of Montier-la-Celle[1]

*c.*1164 × *c.*1170

Karissimis fratribus, filiis et amicis Cellensis monasterii frater Petrus Sancti Remigii dictus abbas, salutem in Domino.

Presenti epistole delegaui supplere in sancto conuentu uestro, fratres et filii karissimi, si quid negotii est, quod ageret presentia nostra si adesset. Poterit enim tutius proponere sufficienter et insolenter quod nec inutile sit adquiescentibus nec scribenti criminosum. Vndecunque siquidem et de quocunque agere uelim, oculi fascinantes non desunt peruerse interpretantes, maligne arbitrantes ea quorum nec rationem attingunt nec finem apprehendunt.[2] Ipse autem ego Deum constituo arbitrum et iudicem omnium que fiunt ab ipso ⟨ad⟩[a] ueraciter diffiniendum quod est ambiguum, efficaciter executioni mandandum quod fuerit sententia diffinitum, et tenaciter seruandum quod ex labiis eius semel fuerit prolatum. Per ipsum igitur contestor hunc solennem uestre fraternitatis conuentum ne a memoria uestra elabatur difficilis ille congressus sapientie et insipientie, iustitie et iniustitie, in quo grauiter sed fortiter desudastis, quidam fideliter proficientes et constanter perseuerantes, quidam deficientes et retro abeuntes, quorum gloria in confusione ipsorum, qui Deo et michi et uobis mentiti sunt. Iam Drogo eiectus est, ne dicam draco, qui se terram et celum non solum concussurum sed etiam euulsurum armis Iude proditoris, id est pecunia, publice minabatur.[3] Nescio si adhuc 'tertiam partem stellarum' post se trahat;[4] unum scio, quod de predestinatis nullum, Deo iuuante, absorbebit. In causa tamen ista, quia Dei est, nichil usurpet sibi stuppa nostre fragilitatis insultando his qui occupati bello non

155 *Sirmond V. 7*]
[a] *suppl. Hall*

155 [1] Written after the deposition of Abbot Drogo and before the el. of a successor (on the possible dates of Drogo's deposition see letter no. 131, n. 1). There is a possible reference to simony in Drogo's case. The meeting referred to could be that to elect a successor.

[2] Since he cannot be there in person, he needs to express himself in writing so as to avoid malicious misinterpretation of his meaning—as is made clear again in the final

155

To the community of Montier-la-Celle[1]

*c.*1164 × *c.*1170

To his dearest brothers, sons, and friends of the monastery of Montier-la-Celle, brother Peter, called abbot of Saint-Remi, greetings in the Lord.

I have delegated to this present letter, dearest brothers and sons, the completion of any business in your holy community which I would attend to in person were I present. For it will be able more safely to propose, adequately and against custom, what would neither be useless to those acquiescing in it nor a cause for reproach for the one who is writing it. For wherever I might wish to act from, and in whatever cause, there is no lack of bewitching eyes perversely interpreting and wickedly judging those things of which they neither understand the reason nor comprehend the goal.[2] But I myself appoint God as arbiter and judge of all things which are done by Him, to determine truly what is uncertain, to command that whatever should be determined by the judgment be executed effectively, and to preserve tenaciously whatever He has once pronounced on. Through Him therefore I call this solemn assembly of your brotherhood to witness so that you do not forget that difficult confrontation of wisdom and folly, of justice and injustice, in which you have toiled heavily but bravely, some advancing faithfully and persevering with constancy, some, whose glory consists in confounding themselves, failing and turning back, who lied to God and to me and to you. Now Drogo has been expelled, or should I say the dragon, who openly threatened that he would not only shake earth and heaven but also destroy them by the weapons of Judas the traitor, that is by money.[3] I do not know whether he still draws 'the third part of the stars' after him;[4] I know one thing, that, if God help us, he will devour none of the predestined. In this matter, however, because it pertains to God, let the tow of our weakness appropriate nothing to itself by insulting

sentence. It is this which is against custom (*insolenter*—presumably the sense intended here). See n. 8 below.

[3] Cf. Mark 14: 11; Luke 22: 5; also Matt. 26: 15.

[4] Cf. Rev. 12: 4 (the dragon).

interfuerunt uel ex aduerso steterunt.[5] Exultandum quidem cum tremore non insultandum contumeliose in operibus Dei quia semper Dei iudicia suspecta sunt[6] et nunquam caput erigendum dum, in nubibus consignata, sollicitos non securos homines tam in prosperitate quam in aduersitate faciunt. Sit itaque timor Dei in uobis, et apponite cor in his que de Drogone facta sunt ne similia faciatis, quia non similia sed peiora pateremini. Est prouerbium: excaldatus aquam timet. Spiritui igitur paraclito[b] totum negotium et domini archiepiscopi consilio[7] atque uiris religiosis et sapientibus, salua libertate electionis uestre, committite. De mea uero uoluntate nulla sit questio quia nunquam discordabit a gloria uestra, ab honore uestro, et ab utilitate ecclesie uestre. Interim refloreat in uobis ordinis sancta obseruatio, silentii uirtus, lectio claustralis, capituli rigor, psalmodie tenor, unitatis compago, hospitum deuota susceptio; et quicquid de iustitie et honestatis prosapia in exterminium euanuerat, ad propriam conscientie uestre sedem feliciter redeat. Scriptura enim mandatum Domini sui eloquitur succincte, constanter et fideliter, nichil detrahens de iniuncto mandato, nichil addens, non cedens fascinatoribus, non credens adulatoribus. Pro eodem habet si laudetur aut si uituperetur. Quia igitur plures scio solere instanter insidiari ut me capiant in sermone, potius elegi uerba nostra scripto mandare quam inconsiderata elocutione profundere.[8] Valete.

[b] Paracletico *Sirmond*

[5] i.e. against Drogo.

[6] i.e. men cannot know them, but *suspecta* is still an unusual choice of word in respect to God. There could be a corruption from *suscepta*, but the context does strongly suggest something implying uncertainty.

[7] The archbishop of Sens is either Hugh, 1142–68 (see letter no. 8, n. 1), or William aux Blanches Mains (1168–76, see letter no. 4, n. 4).

those who were busy and did not take part in the war or who stood on the opposite side.[5] Indeed where the works of God are concerned one should exult with trembling, not insolently insult, because the judgements of God are always uncertain,[6] and the head should never be held high while they, sealed in the clouds, cause men to be concerned not secure, in prosperity as much as in adversity. And so may the fear of God be among you; and meditate on those things which were done concerning Drogo so that you do not do the like, because you will suffer not like things but worse. There is a proverb: the scalded man fears water. Commit the whole business, then, to the Holy Spirit the Comforter and to the counsel of the lord archbishop[7] and to religious and wise men, saving the freedom of your election. Let there be no question about my will, for it will never be at variance with your glory, your honour, and the true interest of your church. Meanwhile may the holy observance of the order flourish again among you, the virtue of silence, reading in the cloister, rigour in chapter, the tenor of psalmody, the bonding of unity, and the devout reception of guests, and let whatever of the stock of justice and integrity had dwindled to extinction return happily to its own seat in your conscience. For Scripture expresses the order of its Lord succinctly, firmly, and faithfully, taking nothing away from the enjoined order, adding nothing, ceding nothing to bewitchers, trusting not flatterers. It holds it to be the same be it praised or censured. So because I know that many are wont to lay ambush constantly to trap me in my speech, I have chosen rather to commit my words to writing than to pour them out in a hasty delivery.[8] Farewell.

[8] As Scripture is certain because it is written down, so must his own words be written down, to avoid misunderstanding. This letter may thus have been accompanied by a separate document containing specific detailed advice or instruction on the election, or it may originally have been longer, since there is nothing here which would need to be committed to writing for fear of misunderstanding. A trusted verbal messenger was the usual way to ensure confidentiality, but Peter's concern in this affair was clearly for an unambiguous record of his position. The lack of any such content in what survives is an indication of the nature of the material selected for inclusion in the letter collection (see also Haseldine, 'Literary memorial', pp. 360–71, for a discussion of the principles of selection).

156

To the community of Molesme[1]

? 1171/2

Fratribus Molismensibus Petrus abbas Sancti Remigii.

Ad monumentum ordinis nostri cum Ieremia[a] lamentationibus consternatus resideo et quadruplici alphabeto,[2] quia iam quatriduano madet fetore,[3] uehementer afficior. Fuit, fuit quondam de magno genere et nobili progenie ordo iste procreatus, etiam angelicis uirtutibus morum informator prudentissimus, rerum mundanarum contemptor perfectus, et diuine uoluntatis amator idoneus. Hic, hic brachia sua extendit 'a mari usque ad mare',[4] de omni gente que 'sub celo est'[5] portans ⟨filios suos⟩[b] in ulnis suis[6] usque 'ad thronum gratie'[7] et collocans in soliis uacuatis et relictis a Lucifero quando sicut fulgur cecidit in lacum fecis et miserie.[8] O sancti angeli, quot palmites de hac uinea tulistis ad uos! Quot ⟨ex⟩[c] ordine claustrali uobiscum consedere fecistis in celestibus in Christo! Heu, heu! Capite uulpes que demoliuntur uineas,[9] cucullatos[10] qui transferunt terminos patrum et sepem regularis institutionis diripiunt. Hi sunt qui retia Domini rumpunt,[11] qui uestimenta Domini diuidunt,[12] qui lancea lingue sue latus iam pendentis in cruce ordinis effodiunt,[13] intestina religionis in auras exufflant, et si quid uitalis spiritus remanserit,[d] extinguunt. Sic armantur filii contra patrem,[14] sic genimina uiperarum uiscera materna crudeliter concutiunt,[15] sic ab ortu suo 'sepulcrum patens'[16] inordinate uiuendo ordini professo aperiunt. Credo moueri uos contra tante sterilitatis auctores quoties, iuxta uos aspicientes coronam sanctorum spirituum et beatarum animarum,

156 *Sirmond VII. 14*]
[a] *corr. Brooke;* Ieremie *Sirmond* [b] *suppl. Brooke* [c] *suppl. Hall*
[d] remanserat *Sirmond*

---

156 [1] See Laurent, *Cartulaires de Molesme*, i. 167–8, which reasonably places this letter between the death of Abbot Theobald (25 Jan. 1171, see letter no. 138, n. 1) and the el. of his successor, Thomas (1171/2, see letter no. 37, n. 1). It continues the theme of the financial and spiritual decline threatening the monastery which characterizes letters 138 and 139 to Theobald.

[2] Ref. to Lam., which runs four times through the alphabet in its verses.

[3] Cf. John 11: 39 (possibly an allusion to Lazarus, dead for four days before Christ raised him back to life; here, the order).

[4] Ps. 71 (72): 8; Ecclus. 44: 23; Zech. 9: 10. [5] Baruch 5: 3.

156

To the community of Molesme[1]

? 1171/2

To the brothers of Molesme, Peter, abbot of Saint-Remi.

I remain seated at the tomb of our order, overcome, with Jeremiah, by lamentations, and I am violently afflicted by the fourfold alphabet[2] because now it is moist with the stench of four days.[3] Once indeed was this order brought forth from a great stock and noble progeny, once was it also, with angelic powers, the wisest fashioner of conduct, a perfect scorner of worldly things, and a fitting lover of the divine will. This order stretched its arms 'from sea to sea',[4] from every people 'under heaven'[5] bearing its sons in its arms[6] even 'to the throne of grace'[7] and placing them in the seats emptied and abandoned by Lucifer when he fell like lightning into the pit of filth and misery.[8] O holy angels, how many boughs from this vine have you carried up to yourselves! How many from the claustral order have you made to sit with you in the heavens, in Christ! Alas, alas! Catch the foxes that destroy the vines,[9] the cowled[10] who cross the bounds of the fathers and tear asunder the enclosure of the institution of the Rule. These are the ones who tear the nets of the Lord,[11] who divide the garments of the Lord,[12] who with the spear of their tongue pierce the side of the order now hanging on the cross,[13] who blow away the inner parts of religion to the breezes, and if anything of the vital spirit remains, extinguish it. Thus are the sons armed against the father,[14] thus the brood of vipers cruelly distress the maternal womb,[15] thus from their beginning by their unmonastic way of life they expose to the professed order an 'open sepulchre'.[16] I believe that you are roused against the authors of such sterility as often as, looking upon the crown of holy spirits and blessed souls close to you,

[6] Cf. Isa. 49: 22.
[7] Heb. 4: 16.
[8] Cf. Isa. 14: 12–15; Luke 10: 18.
[9] Cf. S. of S. 2: 15.
[10] i.e. monks, cf. *DML*, *cucullare* b.; Niermeyer, *cucullatus*.
[11] Possibly alluding to Matt. 4: 19; Mark 1: 17; Luke 5: 10.
[12] Cf. Matt. 27: 35; Mark 15: 24; Luke 23: 34; John 19: 23.
[13] Cf. John 19: 34.
[14] Cf. Matt. 10: 21; Mark 13: 12.
[15] Cf. Matt. 3: 7; 12: 34; 23: 33; Luke 3: 7.
[16] Cf. Ps. 5 (5): 11; Ps. 13 (14): 3; Rom. 3: 13.

recordamini prioris seculi et magne fertilitatis sinus uestros replentis. Si Finees adesset forte pugione suo hanc iram placaret.[17] Sed ecce quisque ponit 'gladium in uaginam',[18] nec est qui accingatur ad uindicandum sanguinem patris.[19] Inde est quod mundus plenus est cucullatis et pene uacuus monachis.[20] Inde est quod in area Domini palea non uentilatur sed fouetur, non extirpantur spine sed multiplicantur. Ego, ego unus de cucullatis uideo iniquitatem et quid facio? Nequeo resuscitare ordinem mortuum, et qua patientia inter patricidas exequias funeris eius celebrabo? Non ualeo refrenare precipitem cursum ad baratrum;[21] nunquid effici debeo socius furum?[22] Omnes quidem currunt non ad brauium sed ad malum,[23] et ego quid? 'Optabam' cum Apostolo 'anathema esse a Christo pro fratribus meis.'[24] Quis michi det ut ego moriar pro te, ordo sanctissime, in cuius presentia quondam 'principes cessabant loqui et superponebant digitum ori suo'?[25] Iuuenes abscondebantur cum sederet in porta et ⟨senes⟩ assurgebant, nec audebant addere ad uerba eius.[26] Nunc derident illum iuniores tempore quia senuit Ysaac et clare uidere non poterat,[27] senuit Dauid et calefieri uestibus non poterat.[28] At Moyses cxx annorum cum esset nec oculorum caliginem sensit neque dentes ei moti sunt.[29] Etsi regule professores, etsi speciem pietatis habentes, sicut Ysaac et Dauid, senescendo spiritu tepefacti sunt et oculi eorum caligauerunt; tamen Moyses, id est beatus Benedictus, claris obtutibus nunc nostras respicit prauitates et in nouissimo dentibus mordebit accusando apud Dominum suorum decretorum et regularis professionis contemptores. Forte dicitis: 'Quid ad nos parabola ista? Abbas Remensis stilo suo ut quid tam mordaciter ex obliquo tangit nos? Quid de nobis ad ipsum?' Respondeo: Christianitatis societate, ordinis germanitate antiqua, uicinitatis familiaritate noui uos[30] et diligo uos. Doleo itaque quod nimis extenuatur bonus odor Christi[31] in uobis tam apud uicinos quam apud remotos. Doleo quod regionem, immo religionem, uestram coram uobis alieni

[17] Cf. Num. 25: 7–8, 11; Ps. 105 (106): 30.
[18] Cf. John 18: 11.
[19] The father here is the order, as is clear from what follows.
[20] i.e. full of those who wear the habit but do not live like true monks.
[21] Cf. Judg. 5: 15.
[22] Cf. Isa. 1: 23.
[23] Cf. 1 Cor. 9: 24.
[24] Cf. Rom. 9: 3.
[25] Cf. Job 29: 9.
[26] Cf. Job 29: 7–8, 22. Douai-Reims: *abscondebantur*: 'hid themselves'.
[27] Cf. Gen. 27: 1.
[28] Cf. 3 Kgs. (1 Kgs.) 1: 1.
[29] Cf. Deut. 34: 7.
[30] Possibly a reference to Robert of Molesme who had been a monk and prior of Saint-Ayoul, or possibly of Montier-la-Celle itself (see *Lexikon des Mittelalters*, vi. 907; Laurent,

you are reminded of a former age and of a great fertility filling your bosoms. If Phineas were here perhaps he would pacify this anger with his dagger.[17] But see, each one puts up 'the sword into the scabbard,'[18] nor is there any who is girded to avenge the blood of the father.[19] So it is that the world is full of the cowled and almost empty of monks.[20] So it is that on the threshing-floor of the Lord the chaff is not winnowed out but cherished, the thorns are not uprooted but multiplied. I, I myself, one of the cowled, I see the wickedness, and what do I do? I am unable to revive the dead order, and with what suffering shall I celebrate its funeral rites among the parricides? I am not strong enough to rein in the headlong rush to the pit;[21] ought I to become the companion of thieves?[22] All indeed are running not towards the prize but to evil,[23] and what do I do? 'I wished' with the Apostle 'to be an anathema from Christ, for my brethren.'[24] Who would allow me to die for you, holiest order, in whose presence once 'the princes ceased to speak, and laid the finger on their mouth'?[25] The young men hid themselves when he was sitting at the gate and the old men rose up, and they did not dare to add to his words.[26] Now those younger in age mock him because Isaac grew old and could not see clearly,[27] David grew old and could not be warmed with cloaks.[28] But Moses, when he was one hundred and twenty, did not experience dimness of the eyes, nor did his teeth chatter.[29] Although professors of the Rule, although persons having the appearance of piety, just like Isaac and David, they were made indifferent by ageing of the spirit, and their eyes grew dim; Moses, however, that is the blessed Benedict, even now looks upon our wicked deeds with clear vision, and at the last will bite with teeth, accusing before the Lord those who have despised his decrees and the profession of the Rule. Perhaps you are saying: 'What is the meaning of this parable to us? To what end is the abbot of Reims striking obliquely at us so bitingly with his pen? What are we to him?' I reply: I know you through Christian companionship, through the long-standing brotherhood of the order, through neighbourly friendship,[30] and I love you. And so I grieve that the good odour of Christ[31] in you is excessively diminished, among your neighbours as much as among those who are far away. I grieve that strangers are devouring your region, nay your religion, before your eyes, that the moth of usuries and debts is consuming your

Cartulaires de Molesme, i. 168, n. 2, and 145–55, esp. p. 147), but the reference is too general to be a basis for any sure identification.

[31] Cf. 2 Cor. 2: 15.

deuorant, quod tinea usurarum et debitorum substantiam uestram demolitur,[32] quod nobilis puella hactenus duplicibus uestita[33] enormiter expoliatur. Religionis siquidem et possessionis dotibus a fundatoribus suis ecclesia uestra ditata diu floruit, sed nunc iam exaruit. Gallina illa Molismensis plena plumis et bene pennata quot et quales de utero suo fetus produxit dum ex se collegium Cisterciense originario germine pullulauit?[34] Deus meus, de illo uno ouo quam innumerabilis arena monachorum et conuersorum faciem terre operuit, quam lucido splendore cutem mundi denigratam per infectam uiuendi negligentiam reformauit et illustrauit! Respice, respice, Syon, filios tuos, et pelles tuas emarcidas noli contempnere sed resume spiritum adolescentie tue si forte cum Iacob, 'quasi de graui sompno euigilans', audias Ioseph filium tuum in Egypto regnare et de manu eius famem tuam, immo infamiam, possis releuare.[35] Fratres mei, fratres mei, recolligite plumas matris uestre et replantate[e] suis in membris conuersationem uestram emendando, substantiam redimendo, odorem bone opinionis comparando, et ad antiquum statum omnia reuocando. Epistola hec non contristet uos, et si contristauerit utinam ad penitentiam. Valete.

157

To Nicholas of St Albans[1]

*c.*1180/1 (or at least 1171 × 1181)

Nicolao monacho.

Iniqua sorte secularis occupatio et eternorum affectio sollicitudinem nostram diuidunt. Sesquialteram namque et supra anime nostre portionem negotiatio temporalium actionum sibi nullo interueniente bone fidei contractu uindicat et michi de me uel exiguam partem non relinquit. Passam denique iniuriam in alios referre non minus stulti

[e] replantati *Sirmond*

157 *Sirmond VI. 4*]

[32] Cf. Matt. 6: 19.

[33] Cf. Prov. 31: 21. The noble girl is the church of Molesme, but in Prov. the *domestici* of the wise woman are clothed in double garments.

[34] The founders of Cîteaux came from Molesme.

substance,[32] that the noble girl, thus far clothed with double garments,[33] is being despoiled outrageously. Your church flourished indeed for a long time, enriched by its founders with dowries of religious life and properties, but now already she has withered. How often did that well-plumed and feathered hen of Molesme bring forth young from her womb, and of what kind, when she produced from herself as her first seed the Cistercian community?[34] My God, how innumerable were the grains of sand, the monks and lay brethren, who covered the face of the earth from that one egg; with how bright a splendour they refashioned and lit up the surface of the world which was blackened through the corrupt neglect of its way of living. Look, Zion, look upon your sons and do not condemn your withered skins but take up the spirit of your youth again in the hope that with Jacob, 'awaked as it were out of a deep sleep,' you may hear that your son Joseph is ruling in Egypt and may relieve your famine, or rather infamy, from his hand.[35] My brothers, my brothers, gather together again the feathers of your mother and set them back in her wings by mending your manner of life, by redeeming your substance, by procuring the odour of good reputation, and by recalling all things to their ancient state. May this letter not sadden you, and if it does, may it lead you to repentance. Farewell.

157

To Nicholas of St Albans[1]

*c.*1180/1 (or at least 1171 × 1181)

To the monk Nicholas.

The affairs of the world and affection for eternal things divide our concern in unequal measures. For the business of temporal duties claims for itself a portion and a half and more of our soul, with no contract of good faith intervening, and does not leave me even a tiny part of myself. But in the end it is as stupid as it is unjust to blame on others an injustice which one has suffered. Indeed, to make an

[35] Cf. Gen. 45: 25–8, esp. 26.

157 [1] Evidently the first of an exchange of letters with Nicholas of St Albans (monk of St Albans, first occurs 1141), the author of a treatise defending the celebration of the Immaculate Conception of the Virgin Mary, written 1151 × 1162. On this treatise and the dates of letters 157–60, see appendix 13. On the heading, see letter no. 84, n. 1.

quam iniuriosi est. Sumpto siquidem probabili et noto de prope argumento, cauere quisque debet ne de alieno egrotet incommodo. Igitur de quantulacunque relicta michi portione quietis siue furtiui otii subdiuidens indulgeo amico modicum de modico. Gratia quoque tui facio licitum quod de facto non de iure pene redditur illicitum. Sola etenim non licent que sola licere deberent. Ea uero plurima et sine licentia sese ingerunt que salutem magis impediunt quam expediunt. Vnde ergo exordiar? Quam solenne, quam deuotum acturus sum uicinis congratulationis conuiuium[2] qui quasi de morte recepi amicum? Plus falsi quam ueri rumores serere populares in multis expertus, fallaciam eorum[a] equitatis iudicio condempnare soleo. In hoc autem articulo mendacio ramusculose uerbositatis gratias ago, iam namque a multis retro annis te in fata concessisse acceperam, quod ueraciter falsum esse nuper, 'quasi de graui sompno euigilans',[3] gauisus sum, in eo quod adhuc nostre sortis et uite consortem te esse audiui. Equidem de numero amicorum nostrorum ex eo habere te censui ex quo scripta tua legi. Amplius autem nostre amicitie uincula tenacissima intexere debet quod, ex toto corde compassus, Deo animam tuam quam de corpore euolasse ad sinum matris misericordie credebam non semel commendaui. Vicem ergo debes nobis si recte de amicitia iudicaueris, quam iccirco obnixe expostulo quia nescio qua hora quod de te falso opinatus sum michi indubitanter contingat.[4] Et uideo uiscera misericordie Dei nostri fines uestros copiosa benedictione respersisse. Pretiosi namque martyris Thome Cantuariensis archiepiscopi occasus orientalem nobis fenestram aperuit[5] et de fidei atque patientie sue splendore angelicas tenebras illustrauit.[6] Que enim terra tantum de se palmitem protulit, ministeriales celicolas, angelicas utique uirtutes, pro tanto fructu in sinu suo recepto, perpetuo conciliauit. Qua itaque ratione non sepe et frequenter reuisitent terram de qua tantum thesaurum suis gazis intulerunt? Credo manum cultoris siue agricole de quo dicitur, 'Pater meus agricola est',[7] uenas et ualuas nubium suarum nondum

[a] eius *Sirmond*

[2] Possibly alluding to Tobias 8: 22. [3] Gen. 45: 26.

[4] Peter prayed for Nicholas's soul when he thought he was dead, and asks Nicholas to pray for his when he (Peter) dies.

[5] Cf. 4 Kgs. (2 Kgs.) 13: 17.

[6] Cf. Augustine, *De Civ. Dei*, xi. 20 (*CCSL* xlviii. 338–9; *PL* xli. 333); Peter Lombard, *Sent.* ii. dist. xiii. 2.2 (*PL* cxcii. 677; Brady i. 1, p. 390); but Peter is also punning on angels and English (and so presumably has in mind Bede, *Hist.* ii. 1; B. Colgrave and R. Mynors (eds.), *Bede's Ecclesiastical History of the English People* (Oxford, 1969), p. 134).

obvious and familiar point, everyone should take care not to become sick from another's misfortune. Subdividing therefore the portion, however tiny, of calm or of stolen leisure which is left to me, I am bestowing on a friend a little of the little. It is thanks to you also that I am making permissible that which is almost rendered, in fact not in law, impermissible. For those things alone are not permitted which alone ought to be permitted. But those things which more impede than expedite greeting rush on in the greatest numbers even without permission. Where then should I begin? How solemn, how devout a banquet of rejoicing am I going to give to my neighbours[2] when I have as it were received a friend back from the dead? Having experienced in many instances that popular rumours sow more falsehood than truth, I usually with impartial judgement condemn their deceit. On this point, however, I give thanks to the mendacity of many-branched verbosity, since for many years now I had accepted that you had been consigned to the fates, and I was overjoyed recently, 'awaked as it were out of a deep sleep,'[3] to find truly that this was false, that is, when I heard that you were still a sharer in our lot and life. Indeed I reckoned you among the number of our friends from the moment that I read your works. What I have suffered for you with my whole heart, so that I commended your soul to God more than once in the belief that it had flown from the body to the bosom of the mother of mercy, ought to interlock the most tenacious chain of our friendship more completely. You therefore owe us a reciprocation, if you judge rightly in the matter of friendship, which I am demanding strenuously because I do not know at what hour that which I supposed falsely about you may befall me, as it surely will.[4] I see also that the bowels of compassion of our God have showered your country with copious blessing. For the death of the precious martyr Thomas, archbishop of Canterbury, opened the east window for us[5] and lit up the angelic darkness[6] with the splendour of his faith and suffering. For the land which produced from itself such a vine-shoot has procured in perpetuity the favour of those attendants who dwell in heaven, that is the angelic powers, because of the great fruit received in its bosom. Why then should they not often and in large numbers revisit the land from which they took up such a treasure to their treasuries? I believe that the hand of the farmer or the husbandman, of whom it is said, 'My Father is the husbandman,'[7] has not yet closed up the veins and valves of His clouds so as to

[7] John 15: 1, i.e. God.

inclusisse ut abstineat benedicere terre quam compluit sanguine magni sacerdotis Thome. Non immerito igitur undecunque populi aduenientes et tumbam illius uenerantes benedicunt genti, populo et nationi de qua tantus Christi testis ortum habuit. Exora itaque sancta eius merita pro amico tuo et si qua habes noua scripta mitte nobis. Quero a te, memor fauorabilis non odiose altercationis dudum inter nos habite,[8] utrum ficta morte emendatus errorem qui non de odio sed de summo aut plusquam summo fauore Virginis uirginum uenit deleueris aut delinieris. Vellem ergo uidere si quid de uera morte simulata mutauerit, cum absque precipiti ambiguo uexatio inferni, etsi non salubriter tamen penaliter, colonum suum doceat ubi errauerit. Emulanda certe, immo cumulanda imitatione, seria illa non sera preoccupatione anticipat mens cauta et prouida, cotidie aduocans celum et terram cum omni circumlustratione angelorum, hominum et demonum acta singulorum proferentium et debita tormenta allegantium. Felix anima que talibus assueta preludiis fallaces et feroces tempestiue precidit malignorum accusationes, uindictam iudicialem de se ipsa a se ipsa exigens et soluens ut uentilabrum non inueniens quod uexando excutiat[9] sola grana eternis apothecis reponat. Que[b] igitur de imagine ista transsumpseris rogo mandata litteris mittere amico non dedigneris, tuus enim michi placet et stilus et animus. Vale.

[b] Quid *Sirmond* [Quid . . . mandatum *is possible*]

[8] It would seem that Nicholas's earlier treatise (see n. 1 above and appendix 13) had also been the occassion of an earlier epistolary debate with Peter of which nothing survives in Peter's collection, but what follows also seems to allude to writings on death.

refrain from blessing the land on which He rained the blood of the great priest Thomas. It is not without reason then that people, coming whencesoever and venerating his tomb, bless the race, the people, and the nation from which so great a witness of Christ arose. Entreat then his holy intercessions on your friend's behalf and, if you have any new writings, send them to us. I ask of you, mindful of the friendly not hostile dispute which took place between us some time ago,[8] whether, corrected by a false alarm of death, you have either erased or mitigated that error which arose not from hatred but from the highest, or more than highest, favour shown to the Virgin of virgins. I should therefore like to see if the image of death has changed anything concerning real death, since the vexation of hell without the uncertain precipice teaches his husbandman, although not by salvation yet by penance, where he has erred. By imitation, which should certainly be copied, nay repeatedly copied, the prudent and provident mind anticipates those serious things, not attending to them at the last hour but daily calling upon heaven and earth, with all reverence to the angels around as they manifest the deeds of men and demons one by one and adduce the tortures that are due. Happy the soul which, accustomed to such preliminaries, cuts short the false and fearsome accusations of the wicked in good time, exacting and paying the judicial punishment from itself by itself, so that, not encountering the winnowing-fan which would shake it up by agitating it,[9] it may lay up only the grain of the eternal storehouses. I ask you therefore not to disdain to write down and send to a friend what it is that you have derived from this image, for both your style and your mind are pleasing to me. Farewell.

[9] Cf. Matt. 3: 12; Luke 3: 17; i.e. the soul should be as grain, not chaff.

158

To Nicholas of St Albans[1]

*c.*1180/1 (or at least 1174 × 1181)

Petrus Sancti Remigii Nicolao monacho Sancti Albani.

Vacui et uacantis animi esset singulis que in litteris tuis sunt recapitulatis singillatim ad uerbum respondere.[2] Summam itaque responsionum mearum constringens et potioribus epistole tuis dictis astringens, pacis et bone patientie pactum prius hinc inde interpono ne quis nostrum cuiuslibet commotionis scintilla pro quolibet uerbo aduratur uel inflammetur. Sola michi sancti Bernardi iniuria donetur,[3] et quecunque et undecunque uis iacula conglomera siue ut meam rusticitatem confundas siue ut de sensu meo uilissimas sententiarum quisquilias excutias, siue ut thesauros tuos homini pauperi aperias, siue ut nescientem doceas, et sensus tuos fortissimis assertionum repagulis stabilias. Aggredior igitur phantasmata tua, lenocinantia quidem pulchritudinis specie sed titubantia stabilis fundamenti egestate. Quicquid enim Scripture basibus auctoritatum non supportatur nullius roboris stabilitate fulcitur. Nec indignetur Anglica leuitas si ea solidior sit Gallica maturitas; insula enim est circumfusa aqua unde huius elementi propria qualitate eius incole non immerito afficiuntur et nimia mobilitate in tenuissimas et subtiles phantasias frequenter transferuntur, sompnia sua uisionibus comparantes ne dicam preferentes. Et que culpa nature si talis est natura terre? Certe expertus sum sompniatores plus esse Anglicos quam Gallos, cerebrum namque humidius fumositate stomachi citius inuoluitur et quaslibet imagines in se ipso depingit, que ab animali uirtute utcunque spiritali deferuntur, et ex occupatione omnium, tam naturalium quam animalium seu spiritalium, uirtutum infra iudicii ueritatem confinguntur ut phantasmata seu sompnia appellentur. Non sic cauernosa,[4] non sic aquatica Gallia, ubi sunt montes lapidei, ubi ferrum nascitur, ubi terra suo pondere grauatur.

158 *Sirmond VI. 23*]

158 [1] Dated as letter no. 157; on the debate in letters 158–60, see appendix 13.
[2] Evidently a lost letter (see appendix 13).
[3] i.e. only grant that *your* view opposes that of St Bernard (which Peter claims to be defending).

158

To Nicholas of St Albans[1]

*c.*1180/1 (or at least 1174 × 1181)

Peter of Saint-Remi to Nicholas, monk of St Albans.

It would require a free and unoccupied mind to recapitulate and reply individually word by word to each of the individual points in your letter.[2] Drawing together then a summary of my responses, and bringing it together with the more important points of your letter, I first interpose between us a pact of peace and good tolerance so that neither of us should be singed or set alight by the spark of any disagreement on account of any word whatever. Let only the injury of St Bernard be granted me,[3] and amass all the darts you wish from wherever you wish either to confound my crude understanding or to cut out from my perception the most worthless dregs of my opinions, or to open your treasure chests to a poor man, or to teach an ignorant one, and confirm your perceptions with the strongest bolts of demonstrations. I pass therefore to your fantasies, which are indeed alluring, having the appearance of beauty, yet tottering for lack of a stable foundation. For whatever is not supported on the foundations of scriptural authorities is not fortified by the stability of any strength. Nor should English levity be indignant if Gallic maturity be more solid than it, for England is an island surrounded by water, for which reason its inhabitants are, not without cause, influenced by the particular quality of this element and are frequently carried away by excessive movement to the most tenuous and slender fancies, comparing, or should I say preferring, their dreams to visions. And what fault is it of nature if such is the nature of the land? Certainly I know from experience that the English are dreamers, more so than the French, for the moister brain is enveloped more quickly by the vapour of the stomach and it paints in itself any images it likes which are conveyed somehow from the animate faculty to the spiritual and which, taking possession of all the faculties, the natural as much as the animate or the spiritual, are fashioned with less than true judgement so that they are called fantasies or dreams. Not so hollow,[4] not so watery is Gaul, where there are mountains made of rock, where iron is found, where the land

[4] i.e. full of caves.

Quid ergo? Non cito a suo sensu mouentur et ueritatis auctoritatibus tenacius innituntur.[5] 'Meus est', inquit Dominus, 'Galaad',[6] id est aceruus testimonii,[7] et 'in ore duorum aut trium testium stabit omne uerbum'.[8] Leue est ergo omne uerbum quod neque testimonio solidum neque auctoritate uerum est. Nec est alicuius momenti quicquid humani sensus ingeniosa fornax commentata fuerit si examine careat ueritatis. 'Pondus' siquidem 'sanctuarii',[9] quo tam merita quam premia angelorum et hominum appenduntur, clausura dispensabili penes ueritatem in archa iustitie perpetua reconditur custodia. Vagatur itaque uanis euolationibus per aera qui nullius auctoritatis fundamento affixus arundinea uolubilitate et mobilitate[10] circumagitatur, et hospes testamentorum Dei nullis detinetur certis mansionibus. Mira uirtus ueritatis que aduersarios deprehendit nolentes et nescientes in astutia sua, fugitiuos namque suos frequenter urget ad laqueos ineuitabilis conclusionis[11] ut capiantur et illaqueentur sermonibus suis dum inuiti uera loquuntur et quod non sentiunt corde exprimunt ore. Inde est, frater Nicole, quod ridendo uerum dixisti[12] cum me fixum, te mobilem scripsisti. Me petram uocasti, et concedo si pro constantia non pro duritia intellexisti. Sum quidem natura, professione et iam etate ac uoluntate, sicut nomine Petrus, petrinus,[13] radicatus et fundatus[14] in montibus sanctarum auctoritatum et in 'medio petrarum'[15] ubi mater ecclesia nidificat in foraminibus petre et in cauernis macerie.[16] Hinc non exeo nisi ad uocem rotarum que in se habent spiritum uite et stant ac mouentur tanquam uolubiles cum animalibus senas alas habentibus[17] et oculos 'ante et retro'.[18] Securus sequor quia facies leonis precedit ne aliquid noceat, facies hominis ne aliquid decipiat, facies rituli ne uanitatis aliquid interueniat, facies aquile ne aliquid dubietatis remaneat uel tarditatis prepediat.[19] Regula ueritatis

[5] i.e. the moist atmosphere causes dreams to enter English minds, which the English mistake for true visions thus mistaking the effect of their animate (or 'animal') natures, affected by the atmosphere, for spiritual experiences. On English and French attitudes to one another, see e.g. R. W. Southern, *Medieval Humanism and Other Studies* (Oxford, 1970), pp. 135–57.

[6] Ps. 59 (60): 9; 107 (108): 9.

[7] Cf. Gen. 31: 47; standard link: cf. e.g. Jerome, *Lib. interp. heb. nom.* (*CCSL* lxxiii. 67; *PL* xxiii. 788); Augustine *Enarr. in Ps.* lix 9.9 (*CCSL* xxxix. 760; *PL* xxxvi. 719).

[8] Deut. 19: 15; 2 Cor. 13: 1; cf. Matt. 18: 16; 1 Tim. 5: 19.

[9] Num. 7: 13, and many other refs.

[10] Possibly alluding to Matt. 11: 7; Luke 7: 24.

[11] With the double sense of the conclusion of an argument and the shutting of a trap.

[12] Cf. Horace, *Sat.* i. 1. 24.

[13] Word play on Peter (*Petrus*) and stone (cf. Matt. 16: 18, 'tu es Petrus et super hanc

is burdened with its own weight. What then? The French are not moved quickly from their own perceptions, and lean more firmly on the authorities of truth.[5] 'Galaad is mine',[6] says the Lord, that is the hillock of testimony,[7] and 'in the mouth of two or three witnesses every word shall stand'.[8] Therefore every word is light which is neither solid with witness nor true according to authority. Nor is anything which the ingenious furnace of human perception has devised of any weight if it is found wanting in the weighing of truth in the balance. The 'weight of the sanctuary'[9] indeed, by which the merits as well as the rewards of angels and men are weighed, is hidden away under lock and key in the store-room in the presence of truth, in the ark of justice, with a permanent guard. And so he who, attached to no foundation of authority, is driven around with the inconstancy and changeability of a reed,[10] and as a visitor to the testaments of God is kept in no fixed dwellings, floats through the air with feeble flutterings. How wondrous is the power of truth which uncovers enemies against their will, ignorant for all their cunning, for it frequently drives its fugitives into the traps of an unavoidable conclusion[11] so that they are caught and ensnared by their own words while they utter truths unwittingly and express with the mouth what they do not understand in the heart. Hence it is, brother Nicholas, that you spoke the truth in jest[12] when you wrote that I was set firm and you flexible. You called me a rock, and I concede this if you understood it to mean constancy not harshness. I am indeed by nature, by profession, and now by age and will, made of rock just as I am Peter by name,[13] rooted and founded[14] in the mountains of holy authorities and in 'the midst of the rocks'[15] where mother Church builds a nest in the clefts of the rock and in the hollow places of the wall.[16] I do not go out from here except to the noise of the wheels which have in them the spirit of life and stand still and are set in motion as if revolving with the animals which have six wings[17] and 'eyes before and behind'.[18] I follow in safety because the face of the lion goes on before lest anything harm me, the face of the man lest anything ensnare me, the face of the calf lest anything worthless come in the way, and the face of the eagle lest any doubt remain or any tardiness hamper my feet.[19] The rule of truth has

petram aedificabo ecclesiam meam'), also continuing the theme of the relative effects of English vapour and French rock on the temperaments of the two peoples.

[14] Cf. Eph. 3: 17.

[15] Ps. 103 (104): 12.

[16] Cf. S. of S. 2: 14; cf. also Jer. 48: 28.

[17] Cf. Ezek. 1: 20–1; 3: 13, but creatures with *six* wings are in Rev. 4: 8.

[18] Cf. Rev. 4: 6, the animals around the throne of God.

[19] Cf. Rev. 4: 7, here of course the symbols of the Evangelists, his authorities and foundations of truth (cf. also Ezek. 1: 10; 10: 14–all the images in this passage signify truth).

tornauit rotas istas in circino[20] et orbe ueritatis eterne que de mente diuina procedens tante apud Deum maiestatis est ut in summo uertice lucis inhabitabilis resideat, tante auctoritatis ut nullius ditioni subiaceat, tante maturitatis ut nunquam uultum deificum deponat, tante certitudinis ut nulla mutatio aut uicissitudinis obumbratio in ea incurrat, tante seueritatis ut nec Lucifero peccanti in celis locum relinquat, nec homini a Verbo assumpto,[21] petenti, 'Si possibile est transeat a me calix iste',[22] crucem et mortem remittat. Hec eterno tramite stelliferas deambulans regiones, 'imbrem matutinum et serotinum'[23] distillauit et sublunarem regionem arentem, mediante nube uirginea, riuis de sanguine et doctrina illius[a] perpetuis irrorauit. Collactanea eius misericordia, saluo iure priuilegii inuiolabilis, leges mitiores et iura tolerabiliora ab ea impetrauit quatinus peccatorum remissionem et exilii releuationem speraret qui in regno ueritatis correctis erroribus et emendatis moribus uiueret. Neutra tamen sororum istarum adulationum lenocinia admittit, quin potius tanquam fila aranearum uehementissimo turbine corrumpit et tunicam inconsutilem,[24] tam illi quam matri eius, fideli textura componit. Bone amice, quid facit stuppa ubi de auro, hyacintho, purpura, cocco bis tincto et bysso retorta sacerdotalis contexitur uestis,[25] et celo, sole ac luna pretiosior et purior summo sacerdoti aptatur cidaris?[26] Prorsus nichil ad nos, nichil ad angelos, dignius et melius de omnibus thesauris suis protulit eterna trinitas quam templum uirginale et holocaustum quod ad immolandum ex eo traxit et extraxit Verbum Deo Patri coeternum et consubstantiale.[27] Sic corde credo, sic ore confiteor. Nonne et tu? Immo uehementius, ne dicam immoderatius tu. Totum te expendis in laude Virginis, et ego quid? Impendo plane, et expendo, et superimpendo.[28] Tu contendis honorare conceptionem et ego predestinationem ac totam eius retro progeniem, tu rosam ego etiam spinam, tu florem et fructum ego corticem et folium, tu apparentia ego latentia, tu farinam ego furfurem, tu panem ego cinerem, tu solium ego scabellum, tu substantiam ego picturam. Si cursum eius fas esset distinguere et sequestrare in mente diuina a collegio cunctorum creatorum, mitterem animam ab initio predestinationis ut sequeretur

[a] *corr. Ritchie;* illam *Sirmond*

[20] Cf. Isa. 44: 13.

[21] i.e. Christ the Word made flesh, and hence a man taken up by the Word (cf. John 1: 14); the point here being that even Christ was not spared when he prayed before the Passion.

[22] Matt. 26: 39; cf. Mark 14: 36; Luke 22: 42.

[23] Joel 2: 23.

[24] Cf. John 19: 23.

[25] Cf. Exod. 28: 5–6, 15.

[26] Exod. 28: 4, etc.

made these wheels round with the compass[20] and orb of eternal truth which, proceeding from the divine mind, is of such majesty before God that it abides at the highest point of the inhabitable light and is of such authority that it is subject to the dominion of none, of such maturity that it never puts off its divine countenance, of such certainty that no change or shadow of changeableness assails it, and of such severity that it neither leaves room in the heavens for Lucifer the sinner nor remits the cross and death to the man assumed by the Word,[21] pleading, 'If it be possible, let this chalice pass from me.'[22] This truth, crossing the regions of the stars on its eternal course, has dropped down 'the early and the latter rain'[23] and, with the virginal cloud mediating, has watered the dry region beneath the moon with perpetual streams of His blood and teaching. Truth's foster-sister mercy has, saving the right of inviolable privilege, procured from her gentler laws and more tolerable statutes so that he who lives in the kingdom of truth, with his errors corrected and his conduct emended, may hope for remission of sins and alleviation of exile. Neither of these sisters admits the enticements of flatteries but each rather breaks them like spiders' webs in a mighty whirlwind and weaves a seamless coat,[24] both for Him and His mother, with the fabric of faith. Good friend, what use is tow when the priest's vestment is woven of gold, violet, purple, scarlet twice-dyed, and fine twisted linen,[25] and the mitre[26] which is more precious and purer than the sky, sun, and moon is set on the head of the high priest? Absolutely nothing has the eternal Trinity brought forth from all its treasures, for us or for the angels, more worthy and better than the temple of the Virgin and the holocaust which the Word, coeternal and consubstantial with God the Father,[27] drew from it and drew out for sacrifice. So I believe with my heart, so I confess with my mouth. Do not you also? Yes, but more vehemently, or should I say immoderately. You spend your whole self in praise of the Virgin, and what do I spend? Clearly I lay out, I pay out and more than pay out.[28] You strive to honour the conception and I the predestination and her whole ancestry; you the rose, I even the thorn; you the flower and the fruit, I the bark and the leaves; you the manifest, I the hidden; you the flour, I the bran; you the bread, I the husk; you the throne, I the footstool; you the substance, I the image. If it were right to separate off her course and to set her in the divine mind apart from the community of all created things, I would send my soul to follow her footsteps from

[27] Cf. Kelly, *Athanasian Creed*, pp. 17–20, esp. ss. 6, 26, and Burn, *Nicene Creed*, pp. 109, 112–13. Here he means the Virgin birth and Christ's sacrifice on the cross.

[28] Possibly an echo of 2 Cor. 12: 15.

adorando, sancta et suprema ueneratione colendo eius uestigia. Repetenda tibi immo noua et longa expetenda peregrinatio, non ad sanctum Thomam archiepiscopum in Anglia sed ad sanctum Thomam Apostolum in India, quia: semper interero conuenticulis ubi Domine nostre digna celebratur commemoratio,[29] siue nominetur Conceptio, siue Natiuitas, siue Assumptio, siue alia quecunque ueneratio. Cum ergo una gradiamur uia, quid ad rem si diuersa sit semita? Tu sinistram tenes semitam; quare murmuras si ego teneo dexteram? Si tua tibi displicet semita, quia et larga et caritatiua est nostra, cedo et concedo tibi locum iuxta me. Prouerbium est: non sunt dimittende ueteres uie propter nouas. Quis sanctorum, quis antiquorum non ambulauit semitam nostram? Credo et uere fateor si in hoc errassent et hoc eis Deus reuelasset. Quibus enim sua tam familiariter reuelauit consilia ut etiam ad supplementum euangeliorum, epistolarum et prophetarum perpetua stabilitate canones et decreta statuerint pari pene obseruantia tenenda cum euangelio, hoc solum eis tacuisset si periculosum esset?

Sed forte dices michi: 'Audesne tu, qualiscunque abbas, occludere puteos[30] semper continuande deuotionis et profundius cotidie fodiende uenerationis? Nonne eodem spiritu potantur moderni quo et antiqui? Nonne, ut ait Hieronymus, in templo Dei quisque pro uili portione offert, alius aurum, alius argentum, alius lapides pretiosos, alius, ut ad uiliora ueniamus, pilos caprarum et cetera?[31] Non erat ab initio Natiuitas Virginis in ecclesia solennis, sed crescente fidelium deuotione addita est preclaris ecclesie solennitatibus. Quare igitur non similiter et diem Conceptionis obtineat sedulitas Christiane deuotionis?' Ad quod ego: Cataractas celi et fontes abyssi libentius in obsequium Virginis soluerem quam clauderem, et si Filius eius Iesus aliquid omisisset in prerogatiua exaltationis sue matris, ego seruus, ego mancipium, non quidem de effectu sed saltem affectu supplere gestirem. Mallem certe non habere linguam quam aliquid dicere contra Dominam nostram. Ante eligerem non habere animam quam uellem eius extenuare gloriam. Licuit quoque semperque licebit sponsam Christi ecclesiam, que in terris peregrinatur, secundum mutationes rerum, personarum et temporum, uariare rationes decretorum et noua adinuenire medicamina remediorum et statuere sanctis

[29] These words seem to be ascribed to Jesus, but are not Vulgate.

[30] Cf. Gen. 26: 15, 18; on the imagery below, ibid. 7: 11; 8: 2.

[31] Not an exact quotation, but there are many such passages in Jerome. Cf. e.g. Jerome, *Comm. in Ezech.* xiv. 48. 18/20 (*CCSL* lxxv. 737; *PL* xxv. 486), and Jerome, *Apol. adv. libros Rufini*, ii. 26 (*CCSL* lxxix. 63–4; *PL* xxiii. 471).

the beginning of her predestined course, adoring, and worshipping her with holy and supreme veneration. You should seek the pilgrim route again, nay seek out a new and a long one, not to St Thomas the archbishop in England but to St Thomas the Apostle in India, because: I shall always be present among the assemblies where the rightful commemoration of our Lady is celebrated,[29] whether it be called Conception or Nativity or Assumption, or whatever other veneration. Since therefore we are walking by one road, what does it matter if each follows a different track? You keep to the left track; why do you murmur if I keep to the right? If your track displeases you, because ours is the way of bounty and love, I cede and concede to you a place next to me. There is a proverb: old roads should not be deserted for new. Who among the saints, who among the ancients, did not walk our track? I believe and truly confess that, had they erred in this, this too would God have revealed to them. For would He have maintained silence on this point alone if it were dangerous for those to whom He revealed His counsels so familiarly that they established canons and decrees as a supplement to the Gospels, epistles, and prophets with eternal stability to be adhered to with an observance almost equal to that due to the Gospel?

But perhaps you will say to me: 'Do you dare, you a mere abbot, to close up the wells[30] of devotion which should be maintained forever, and of veneration which should be dug deeper every day? Are not new wells drunk from in the same spirit as old? Is it not, as Jerome says, that in the temple of God each makes an offering according to his worthless portion, one gold, another silver, another precious stones, another, to come to more worthless things, goats' hairs etc.?[31] The Nativity of the Virgin was not a festival in the Church from the beginning but, with the growing devotion of the faithful, was added to the distinguished festivals of the Church. Why then should the zeal of Christian devotion not also take up the day of the Conception in the same way?' To which I say: I would more gladly open than close the floodgates of heaven and the fountains of the deep in the service of the Virgin, and if her Son Jesus had omitted anything in exercising His prerogative in the exaltation of His mother, I the slave, I the bondsman, would exult to make it good, if not indeed in effect, at least in affection. I would for sure rather have no tongue than say anything against our Lady. I would choose not to have a soul before I would wish to diminish her glory. It was permitted too and always will be permitted to the Church, the bride of Christ, a pilgrim in the world, to alter the grounds of decrees according to the variations of circumstances, people, and times, and to

adeptione glorie[32] frequentiam solennitatum. 'Est' tamen 'auro locus in quo conflatur' et 'habet argentum uenarum suarum principia',[33] sedem Petri et curiam Romanam que claues celi principaliter tenet[34] et, clausura consiliorum Dei reserata dispensante Deo, unguentum gratie a capite usque in oram uestimenti habet compluere.[35] Hec sedes Petri, id est petra in qua Moyses residet,[36] uidelicet lex Dei immaculata conuertens animas, fragosa queque hereticorum conciliabula elidit et allidit, profanas uocum nouitates resecat et rescindit, superflua confodit et iugulat, hiantia et ecliptica complet et illustrat. Vtinam salua ueritatis auctoritate, lance communis concilii hec domina et moderatrix totius Christianitatis Conceptionem Virginis librasset et approbasset et 'a mari usque ad mare'[37] hanc propagasset. Sole, id est Apostolico, ac luna, id est curia Romana, preeunte, tam secure quam expedite in lumine uultus eorum gressus meos ponerem et disponerem, ex hoc uidens uitare lubricum et sequi solidum et securum. Nichil in ecclesia pessimius presumptione erronea, nichil stultius presumptione temeraria, nichil odibilius presumptione noxia. Vtcunque uero tolerabilis presumptio pia sed non satis probabilis. Abstinere certe ab omni presumptione uolo, gradatim tamen seruatis distinctionibus premissis secundum magis et minus.

Iam destituissem ultra de preiacenti materia scribere—non condempnans errorem tuum, si error dicendus est qui de pietate uenit, nec me opponens gloriosissime Domine nostre cuius non solum terram sed et puluerem lingere summas diuitias reputo,[38] precipue cum in calculo epistole tue asseras nullatenus te posse moueri ab eo quod scripsisti, dicens, 'Quod dixi dixi, quod scripsi scripsi'—nisi lapidem offensionis et petram scandali[39] in eadem epistola tua coniecisses. Dicis Domine nostre animam non solum in passione Filii gladio transfixam sed etiam in Conceptionis sue contradictione. Hic bonus dormitauit Homerus.[40] Bone magister, nunquid non mea et tua Domina super choros angelorum exaltata sic omni plena et

[32] Cf. Ecclus. 44: 7, but here in the sense of ascending to heaven. (The image of the Church as a pilgram is very common, esp. e.g. in Aug. and Bede.)

[33] Cf. Job 28: 1 (but the context does not fit Peter's sense here).

[34] Cf. Matt. 16: 19.

[35] Cf. Ps. 132 (133): 2.

[36] Possibly a ref. to Exod. 33: 21–2.

[37] Ps. 71 (72): 8; Ecclus. 44: 23; Zech. 9: 10. The Conception, here and below, means the feast of the Conception, rather than the conception itself.

[38] Possibly an echo of Ps. 71 (72): 9.

[39] Cf. Isa. 8: 14; Rom. 9: 32–3; 1 Pet. 2: 8; more cuttingly, 'Quod scripsi scripsi' are Pilate's words in John 19: 22.

[40] Cf. Horace, *Ars Poet.* 359: i.e. an otherwise excellent writer commits a fault; despite his

devise new prescriptions for remedies, and to determine for the saints, on attainment of glory,[32] the frequency of festivals. 'Gold', however, 'hath a place wherein it is melted' and 'silver hath beginnings of its veins,'[33] that is the seat of Peter and the Roman Curia which before all others holds the keys of heaven[34] and, with the store-room of the counsels of God opened by God's dispensation, causes the precious ointment of grace to rain down from the head to the skirt of the garment.[35] This seat of Peter, that is the rock on which Moses sits,[36] namely the immaculate law of God which converts souls, strikes down and smites every brittle conventicle of heretics, prunes and cuts away profane novelties of speech, pierces and slits the throat of superfluities, fills up gaps and illuminates those things which are eclipsed. If only, saving the authority of truth, this mistress and moderator of the whole of Christendom had weighed up and approved the Conception of the Virgin in the scales of a general council and had propagated it 'from sea to sea'.[37] With the sun, that is the pope, and the moon, that is the Roman Curia, going on ahead, I would set and order my steps both securely and readily by the light of their countenance, seeing thereby to avoid the slippery way and to follow the solid and safe. There is nothing in the Church worse than erroneous presumption, nothing more stupid than rash presumption, nothing more hateful than harmful presumption. But pious presumption is somehow tolerable but not quite acceptable. I wish to abstain, to be sure, from every presumption, yet at every step maintaining these aforesaid distinctions as to which is greater and which lesser.

At this point I would have abandoned writing further about the above subject—not condemning your error, if that which arises from devotion should be called an error, nor setting myself against our most glorious Lady, the ground, and even the dust, beneath whose feet I reckon it to be highest riches to lick,[38] especially since you assert in the conclusion of your letter that nothing can move you from that which you have written, saying, 'What I have said I have said, what I have written I have written'—had you not thrown down the stone of stumbling and the rock of offence[39] in that same letter of yours. You say that the soul of our Lady is pierced by the sword not only in the passion of her Son but also in the denial of her Conception. Here good Homer nodded.[40] Good master, is it not true that my Lady and yours, who is exalted above choirs of angels, is so full of and

comprehensive refutation of Nicholas's views, Peter maintains the pretence of a few minor disagreements. For Nicholas's response to this choice of words, see letter no. 159 and n. 7.

circumfusa est gloria Patris et Filii et Spiritus sancti et sanctorum angelorum ut nullatenus nostris indigeat obsequiis, nostris neque uioletur aut molestetur negligentiis quantum ad se neque melioretur beneficiis? Esto nostra placent ei obsequia; nunquid passibilis adhuc est eius anima? Fides supplet irrefragabilem conclusionem ut uera impassibilitas et immortalitas nullas admittat molestias ne ad supera transeant feces malorum que inferos exercent pro pena peccatorum. Hic lapis est offensionis, petra uero scandali est,[41] quod beatissimum Bernardum debita exuis ueneratione et uerborum iacula post eum emittis tanquam famam eius possis extenuare uel gloriam euacuare.[42] Bona fide qua te diligo et fidelissima caritate ⟨qua⟩ laudo, consulo et rogo ne amplius in celum ponas os tuum quia nisi caueris tibi in caput tuum recasurus est lapis quo ferreum uis penetrare celum. An excidit a mente tua omni sancto competere: 'Flagellum non appropinquabit tabernaculo tuo'?[43] Super quem certe ceciderit lapis iste incaute missus conteret eum. Subrides et forte nondum correctus labia mordes, 'Que', inquiens, 'huius Bernardi sanctitas, que religio, que meritorum prerogatiua?' Nullus sum ego illius sancta preconia referre. Vita eius, fama eius, opera, scripta, miracula, 'fides, spes, caritas',[44] castitas, abstinentia, mortificatio demum in membris eius, sermo, uultus, habitus et gestus eius, et his similia, ipsa sunt que testimonium perhibent de eo.

Pretermitto ista omnia si nondum emolliri cor tuum potuit. Vnum est in quo clauis in altum defixis arbitror me te apprehensurum et in amorem sancti Bernardi liquefacturum.[45] Alumnus enim familiarissimus fuit Domine nostre cui non unam tantum basilicam sed totius ordinis Cisterciensis basilicas dedicauit, ad cuius laudem politissimos tractatus et facundos composuit. Si ergo potes tangere pupillam oculi Domine nostre, scribe contra Bernardum suum cui loquitur ipsa, 'Qui tangit te, quasi qui tangit pupillam oculi mei.'[46] Cisterciensium[b] quoque nugas nescio quos pre aliis mortalibus seriis et sine fine mansuris intendere uideo. Hi sunt qui monetam nostri iam in agonia positi ordinis reformauerunt. Hi sunt qui regulam beati Benedicti

[b] Cistercienses *Sirmond*

[41] Cf. Isa. 8: 14; Rom. 9: 32–3; 1 Pet. 2: 8.

[42] Bernard famously denounced the feast of the Conception of the Virgin in 1138/9 in a letter to the canons of Lyons (*S. Bernardi Op.* vii. 388–92, letter no. 174, see appendix 13).

[43] Ps. 90 (91): 10.

[44] 1 Cor. 13: 13; the passage also echoes the Gospel accounts of John the Baptist.

[45] Cf. Eccles. 12: 11; S. of S. 5: 6.

[46] Cf. Zech. 2: 8.

surrounded by every glory of the Father and the Son and the Holy Spirit and of the holy angels that she has no need at all of our services, and that she is neither violated nor harmed by our neglect with respect to her nor improved by our observances? It may be that our services please her, yet is her soul still capable of suffering? Faith supplies the indisputable conclusion that a true incapacity for suffering and immortality admit no vexations lest the dregs of evils, which harass those here below for the punishment of sins, cross over to those above. This is the stone of stumbling, this is truly the rock of offence,[41] that you despoil the most blessed Bernard of his due veneration and hurl verbal darts after him as if you could diminish his reputation or wipe out his glory.[42] By the good faith with which I love you and by the most faithful love with which I extol you, I counsel and ask that you raise up your voice to heaven no more because, unless you take care, the stone with which you wish to penetrate the unyielding sky will crash back on to your head. Have you forgotten that this saying is applicable to every holy man: 'The scourge shall not come near thy dwelling'?[43] Certainly this incautiously thrown stone will crush the one on whom it falls. You smile and, perhaps not yet corrected, you bite your lips, saying: 'What is the holiness of this Bernard, what is his religious life, what is his prerogative in merits?' I am not worthy to report the holy praises of that man. His life, his reputation, his works, writings, miracles, 'faith, hope, charity,'[44] chastity, abstinence and then too his mortification of the limbs, his speech, his countenance, bearing and attitude, and such like things—these are the things which bear witness of him.

I say no more about any of these things if your heart is incapable of being softened. But there is one point on which, with nails deeply fastened in, I reckon that I will take hold of you and melt you[45] in the love of St Bernard. For he was the most intimate devotee of our Lady, to whom he dedicated not one church only but the churches of the whole Cistercian order, and in whose praise he composed the most polished and eloquent treatises. If therefore you are powerful enough to touch the apple of our Lady's eye, write against her Bernard to whom she herself says, 'He that touches you, it is as if he touches the apple of my eye.'[46] Furthermore, I do not know of any follies of the Cistercians whom I see intent more than other mortals on serious things and ones that will endure without end. These are they who have refashioned the coinage of our order now arrayed for battle. These are they who have restored the Rule of the blessed Benedict,

pene combustam, sicut Esdras ueterem legem,[47] restaurauerunt. Hi cum Apostolo Corinthiis, id est agricolis et rusticis secularibus, onerosi non sunt sed propriis manibus laborantes se et alios pauperes pro posse exhibent.[48] Claustra illorum castra Dei sunt ubi nocte in psalmis et orationibus 'parati sunt suscitare Leuiathan'[49] qui 'sub umbra dormit, in locis humentibus',[50] et in die in agro Iericho principi militie occurrunt qui tenet gladium bis acutum[51] ut superflua resecet cogitationum et operationum. Querunt ergo cum Iosue dicentes, 'Noster es, an aduersariorum?'[52] Vtilis questio et inefflagitabilis solutio utrum Deus pro nobis an contra nos. Si autem contra nos, quis pro nobis?[53] Ampliorem prouocat amorem si pro nobis, sollicitudinem et timorem si contra nos. Ponamus itaque animam nostram in manibus nostris si contra nos quia etsi 'horrendum incidere in manus Dei'[54] post seculum, melius est tamen incidere in hoc seculo propitiabili quam in manus demonum. Dicamus itaque cum Iob, 'Etiam si occiderit me, in ipso sperabo.'[55] He sunt nuge Cisterciensium.

Statera tua in hoc etiam uidetur mentiri, aut inequalitate ponderis aut iniquitate moderantis, forte plus labiorum non bona distinctione quam sensus falsitate, quod dicis: 'Virgo singularis uicit omne peccatum non omne debellando sed nullum prorsus sentiendo.' Sta hic, frater, tene aciem, infige radiis solis animi intentionem ut discas Virginem nondum matrem et Virginem iam matrem. Attendas domum sapientie inchoatam et iam consummatam, distinguas lanam de prima gratia candidam et purpuram de secunda sanguine conchylii tinctam, diuidas uellus non complutum impregnatione et uellus madefactum incarnatione.[56] Qua enim ratione de ipsa in ecclesia cantaretur: 'Que est ista que' ascendit 'quasi aurora consurgens', utique in natiuitate, 'pulchra ut luna' in sancta conuersatione, 'electa ut sol' diuina conceptione, 'terribilis ut castrorum acies ordinata'[57] celesti exaltatione seu assumptione si nullus ei uirtutum

[47] Cf. 2 Esd. (Neh.) 8.
[48] Cf. 2 Cor. 11: 9; also 1 Cor. 4: 12.
[49] Job 3: 8.
[50] Cf. Job 40: 16.
[51] The angel who appeared to Joshua and to whom the question quoted in the next sentence was put—cf. Josh. 5: 13–14 (two-edged swords occur, but in different contexts, in Ecclus. 21: 4; Prov. 5: 4).
[52] Josh. 5: 13.
[53] Inverting Rom. 8: 31.
[54] Cf. Job 13: 14 and Heb. 10: 31.
[55] Job 13: 15.
[56] i.e. the Immaculate Conception marking the crucial transition, before which she could still earn merit by her own virtues; Bernard had argued that Mary was sanctified in the womb, after her conception, and preserved free from sin throughout her life (*S.*

which was almost burnt out, as Ezra did the old law.[47] These with the Apostle are not a burden to the Corinthians, that is to the farmers and peasants of the world, but working with their own hands provide for themselves and other poor men as far as possible.[48] Their enclosures are camps of God where by night in psalms and prayers they 'are ready to raise up a Leviathan,'[49] 'who sleepeth under the shadow, in moist places,'[50] and in the day, in the field of Jericho, they meet the prince of the host who holds the two-edged sword[51] to cut away the superfluities of thoughts and deeds. Therefore they put the question with Joshua saying, 'Art thou one of ours or of our adversaries?'[52] A useful question, and one to which an answer cannot be exacted, is whether God is for us or against us. But if He is against us, who is for us?[53] He provokes fuller love if He is for us, apprehension and fear if He is against us. Let us then place our soul in our hands if He is against us because, although 'it is a fearful thing to fall into the hands of God'[54] after this world, it is however better to fall into them in this world where propitiation is possible than to fall into the hands of demons. And so let us say with Job, 'Although He should kill me, I will trust in Him.'[55] These are the follies of the Cistercians.

Your scales appear to be deceptive even in this, either through the inequality of the weight or the iniquity of the operator, perhaps more from poor discrimination in speaking than from an error of perception, when you say: 'The singular Virgin conquered every sin, not by vanquishing all but by feeling absolutely none.' Stop here, brother, look closely, fix your attention on the rays of the mind's sun that you may know the Virgin not yet a mother and the Virgin now a mother. Consider the house of wisdom incomplete and now complete; distinguish the pure white wool of the first grace and that of the second which is dyed purple with the blood of the murex; divide the fleece which is not rained upon with impregnation and the fleece moistened by the incarnation.[56] For why in the Church would it be sung of her: 'Who is she that' ascends 'as the morning rising', that is in birth, 'fair as the moon' in her holy manner of life, 'bright as the sun' by the divine conception, 'terrible as an army set in array'[57] by heavenly exaltation or assumption, if she had made no progress or

Bernardi Op. vii. 388–92, letter no. 174, s. 5), and the implication of what Peter goes on to say next is not dissimilar. The imagery echoes common biblical vocabulary; cf. also Jerome, *Ep. supp.* ix. 7 (*PL* xxx. 128).

[57] Cf. S. of S. 6: 3.

fuisset profectus et prouectus? Si ab hora conceptionis nulla cum carne aut cum hoste concertatio superfuisset causa merendi, plurimum dispendium sustinuisset, cum de ea dictum sit quia 'plus est meritis et non natura quam uirgo et homo'.[58] Concedo et credo siquidem quod seua libidinis incentiua Deo preoperante nunquam senserit uel ad modicum; cetera uero impedimenta humane fragilitatis que naturali origine siue scaturigine de natura procedunt, ante diuinam conceptionem sentire potuit sed nullatenus consensit. Et preueniente siquidem gratia et in Virgine sua preludia habente, fomes peccati anhelando extremum spiritum trahebat, solum sepulcrum ei supererat, donec ueniens Spiritus sanctus defunctum perpetue sepulture mandauit et serpentem antiquum[59] suo gladio iugulauit. Dictum namque fuerat: 'Inimicitias ponam inter te et mulierem, et semen tuum et semen illius.'[60] Vnde Hieronymus: 'Etsi cetere uirgines imitantur illam usque ad conceptum partus et Gabrielis noue salutationis obsequium, deinceps totum diuinum est quod operatur in ea teste angelo quia Spiritu sancto et uirtute Altissimi obumbratur. Ante hoc ipsum sane uterus Virginis quamuis mundus, quamuis impollutus et alienus a contagione peccati, quamuis sanctus, tamen adhuc uilitate humanitatis induitur ut ita dicam ac si lana candidissima suique coloris dealbata. Ad quam sane cum accessit Spiritus sanctus, quasi ipsa eademque lana cum inficitur sanguine conchylii uel muricis uertitur in purpuram, uersa est et ipsa sine coitu in matrem ut non sit iam admodum quod fuerat sed purpura ueracissima ad indumentum et gloriam summi regis diuinitus aptissime dedicata ut nulli deinceps ea uti usu femineo licuerit nisi Deo.'[61] Post conceptum itaque suum meruit crystallinam soliditatem que ante gratie plenitudinem non exuerat teneritudinem, sed puram, sed sanctam, sed immaculatam, que consensu[62] uri nullatenus potuit etsi aliquatenus admota temptatione percelli potuit, non ad lesionem sed ad probationem, non ad mortificationem conscientie sed ad confirmationem gratie et ostensionem constantie. Vtquid enim tanta uirtus latitans obdormiret? Vtquid tanta gratia fructum non faciens preter consuetudinem suam uacaret? Vtquid denique tanta gloria

[58] Cf. Jerome, *Ep. supp.* ix. 7 (*PL* xxx. 128): 'Hoc quippe priuilegium non naturae est, sed gratiae beatae uirginis Mariae, de qua natus est ipse Deus et homo. Idcirco et ipsa plus est meritis, et non natura quam uirgo et homo.'

[59] The devil; cf. Rev. 12: 9.

[60] Gen. 3: 15.

[61] Cf. Jerome, *Ep. supp.* ix. 7 (*PL* xxx. 128), which has 'contemptum' for 'conceptum' and lesser variations; for '. . . obumbratur', cf. Luke 1: 35).

[62] Presumably in the sense of consenting to sin, i.e. giving in to temptation (see below, p. 594), but he may simply mean 'common feeling'.

advance in virtues? If from the hour of conception there had been no further struggle with the flesh or with the enemy for the sake of earning merit, she would have suffered a great loss, since it is said of her that she is more than a virgin and a person by merits and not by nature.[58] I concede and I believe indeed that, with God acting beforehand, she never felt the raging incitements of lust even in the smallest degree; but the other impediments of human frailty which proceed from nature by natural origin or by welling up she was able to feel before the divine conception, but in no way consented to them. And indeed, with grace going on ahead and having its preludes in the Virgin, the kindling of sin was gasping and drawing its last breath and only the tomb remained for it until the Holy Spirit arrived and consigned it now dead to a perpetual tomb and slit the throat of the ancient serpent[59] with His sword. For it had been said: 'I will put enmities between thee and the woman, and thy seed and her seed.'[60] Whence Jerome said: 'Although the other virgins imitate that one even unto the conception of a fetus and the performance of a new annunciation by Gabriel, that which is done in her thereafter is wholly divine, by the witness of the angel, because it is overshadowed by the Holy Spirit and the power of the Most High. Before this act, to be sure, the womb of the Virgin, although clean, although unpolluted and a stranger to the contagion of sin, although holy, was however still clothed in the mean dress of humanity, as one might say, just like the whitest wool dressed with its own colour. To be sure, when the Holy Spirit approached her, like that selfsame wool which when dyed with the blood of a conch or murex is turned purple, she herself was also turned into a mother without intercourse, so that she is absolutely not now what she used to be but is deepest purple most fittingly dedicated by divine will to be the garment and glory of the highest king, so that thereafter no one was permitted to use her in the manner of a woman, save only God.'[61] So after she conceived she merited the solidity of crystal, she who before receiving the fullness of grace had not put off softness, but a softness pure, holy, and immaculate, she who could by no means be scorched by consent[62] even if she could by any means be approached and assailed by temptation, not for the sake of hurting but of testing, not for mortification of conscience but for confirmation of grace and to show her constancy. Why then would such great virtue lie hidden and sleep? Why would such great grace not produce fruit but contrary to its own custom lie idle? Why lastly would such great glory of the

matris Domini carnem domando, hostem debellando, peccatum ex omni parte uincendo, toti mundo non se manifestaret? Tolle pugnam, tolles et uictoriam. Tolle uictoriam, tolles et coronam. Tolle coronam, tolles et gloriam. Ne ergo demas gloriam, noli subtrahere pugnam, quia non coronabitur nisi qui legitime pugnauerit.[63] Si recte offeras, et recte diuidas.[64] Quid est igitur Virgo singularis omne peccatum uicit non omne debellando sed nullum prorsus sentiendo? Quam uictricem appellas, debellatricem appellare cur formidas? An times eam debellare in bello quam non potes dicere uincere nisi in prelio aut sine prelio?[65] Segnior est si qua est uictoria sine prelio, fortior que in prelio. Ad ampliorem itaque gloriam assero Dominam nostram peccatum omne uicisse et debellasse. Addis, 'non omne debellando, sed nullum prorsus sentiendo'. Hic si distinxisses non peccasses. Multiformiter enim peccatum sentitur, aliquando cum peccato, aliquando sine peccato. Quod in presenti occurrit, sentio peccatum aliquando tanquam ignem, aliquando tanquam picem, aliquando tanquam lapidem, aliquando tanquam aerem. Ignem generat delectatio, picem consensus uel ipsa perpetratio, lapidem consuetudo uel obstinatio, aerem serpentis sibilatio que Virginis nostre fores potuit pulsare sed non penetrare. 'Hortus' enim erat 'conclusus',[66] annon eadem Domina potuit calcare super serpentes et scorpiones ita quod nichil illam noceret?[67] Re itaque integra potuit hoc modo sentire peccatum non autem consentire peccato. Potuit debellare omne peccatum sine uulnere, sine pudore, sine silentii sui concussione, sine futuri partus uiolatione.

De proposita questione: 'Deus cum omnia possit, non potest de corrupta uirgine facere incorruptam; ualet quidem liberare a pena sed non ualet coronare corruptam,'[68] utinam uim intelligerem uerbi et sensum tenerem Hieronymi; procul dubio neque maligne reconderem neque auare communicarem. Ab eo igitur imploranda solutio qui dignus inuentus est soluere signacula septem libri signati.[69] In epistola tamen Hieronymi aliter dicitur: 'Audenter', inquit, 'loquor: cum omnia possit Deus, uirginem post ruinam suscitare non potest, etc.'[70] Recurrendum proinde est ad materiam locutionis et ad

[63] Cf. 2 Tim. 2: 5.

[64] Not Vulgate: cf. Gen. 4: 7, sec. LXX (cf. letter no. 126, n. 6); commonly cited in patristic authors.

[65] Peter's point is that Nicholas cannot call her a victor without acknowledging that she actually fought sin rather than being immune from temptation.

[66] S. of S. 4: 12.

[67] Cf. Luke 10: 19, the power given to the seventy-two disciples.

[68] Cf. Jerome, *Ep.* xxii. 5 (*CSEL* liv. 150; *PL* xxii. 397); another question raised,

mother of the Lord not show itself to the whole world by subduing the flesh, vanquishing the enemy, and conquering sin in every respect? Take away the fight, and you will take away the victory also. Take away the victory and you will take away the crown also. Take away the crown and you will take away the glory also. Do not take away the fight then, lest you take away the glory, because he will not be crowned except he fight lawfully.[63] If you offer rightly, divide rightly too.[64] How is it then that the singular Virgin conquered every sin not by vanquishing all but by feeling absolutely none? Why do you fear to call her a conqueror when you call her a victor? Or are you afraid that she conquers in a war, whom you cannot call victorious except that you specify in a battle or without a battle?[65] Any victory without a battle is the easier, a victory in battle nobler. And so, to her greater glory, I assert that our Lady conquered and vanquished all sin. You add, 'not by vanquishing all sin but by feeling absolutely none'. If you had made a distinction here you would not have sinned. For sin is felt in many ways, at one time with sin, at another without sin. As it immediately occurs to me, I feel sin now like fire, now like pitch, now like stone, now like air. Delight generates fire, consent or perpetration itself generates pitch, habit or obstinacy generates stone, the whispering of the serpent, which could knock at the door of our Virgin but not enter, generates air. For she was 'a garden enclosed',[66] and was the same Lady not able to tread upon serpents and scorpions so that nothing could hurt her?[67] And so without blemish she could feel sin in this way but not consent to sin. She could vanquish all sin without wound, without shame, without disturbing her silence, without violating her future labour.

Concerning the proposed question: 'God, while He can do all things, cannot make an incorrupt virgin from a corrupt one; He has the power indeed to release from punishment but not to crown the corrupt one,'[68] if only I could understand the force of the argument and grasp the meaning of Jerome, I would without any doubt neither maliciously conceal it nor share it in a miserly way. The solution should therefore be sought from Him who was found worthy to loose the seven seals of the sealed book.[69] In Jerome's letter, however, it is put otherwise: 'I speak', he says, 'boldly: while God can do all things, he cannot raise up again a virgin after her downfall, etc.'[70] One must

presumably, in Nicholas's lost letter (see appendix 13), which may be the source of this paraphrase of this passage from Jerome, which Peter quotes more closely below.

[69] Cf. Rev. 5: 2–9, i.e. Christ the lamb.

[70] Cf. Jerome, *Ep.* xxii. 5 (*CSEL* liv. 150; *PL* xxii. 397).

intentionem loquentis. De obseruanda uirginitate et cauenda corruptione tractabatur. Exaudiuit ergo et ad preconium uirginitatis eloquium suum Hieronymus inflammauit, uenas susurri[71] sui infra Dei potentie et uirginitatis glorie uenas subinferens et uelut munditiam uirginitatis rebus creatis omnibus preferens ut facilius sit Deo celum nouum et terram nouam[71A] et omnem creature defectum reparare quam uirginitatem semel lapsam in priorem statum refigurare. Hoc, inquam, unicum sue imaginis et similitudinis[72] signaculum anime de celo impressit, contestatus in mandatis ut hoc fidele depositum[73] pre aliis omnibus omni diligentia seruaret et tanquam irreparabile dampnum intra medullas suas a latronibus et ab omni casu consignaret. Nil in possessione felicius et Deo similius, in amissione nil miserius et Deo dissimilius. Vt ergo tam egregium et singulare beneficium non negligeretur, durissima conditio apponitur ut quodammodo ad id resarciendum dampnum Deus infirmetur, non de potestate sed de dispensatione. Si enim potentia eius simpliciter attendatur, et a pena ualet liberare et que fuerit aliquando corrupta tanquam incorruptam coronare. Si ad dispensationem et constitutionem eternis legibus fixam et inuariabilem, non ualet quia nichil contra se ipsum ualet, id est uelle potest uel debet. Cum enim simplicissime sit nature Deus de ipso tamen secundum usus nostre locutionis improprie loquimur dicendo eum aliquid posse uel non posse, aliquid nosse uel non nosse, aliquid uelle uel nolle. Quasi igitur in Deo parturiente in misericordia ad redintegrandum fractum uirginitatis signaculum obstetricando immo obstando, iustitia decretorum suorum ostia uentris claudit et, ne de uulua egrediatur aut genibus excipiatur aut uberibus lactetur,[74] aborsum facit ne de corrupta incorrupta iterato pariatur, sicut de baptismo legitur: 'Nunquid', ait Dominus, 'homo cum sit senex potest in uentrem matris sue iterato introire et renasci?'[75] Vicaria denique uicissitudine[76] iustitia in partu suo, refellente misericordia, non dissimiliter periclitatur cum uolens uituli fabricatores delere ait Moysi, 'Dimitte me ut deleam multitudinem hanc, faciamque te in gentem magnam.'[77] At

[71] Cf. Job 4: 12. [71A] Cf. Rev. 21: 1; also Isa. 65: 17; 66: 22; 2 Pet. 3: 13.
[72] Cf. Gen. 1: 26. [73] i.e. virginity. [74] Cf. Job 3: 11–12.
[75] Cf. John 3: 4, words spoken *to* Christ, by Nicodemus. The context seems to give the opposite meaning to Peter's here (i.e. that man can be born again spiritually), but the point here is the position of justice, struggling against mercy. In the rest of the passage mercy opposes justice. The intention is to illustrate the tension between justice and mercy *within* God (whom no external force can restrict).
[76] In the OT *uicissitudo* means 'good turn' or 'recompense'; cf. 1 Kgs. (1 Sam.) 24: 20; 2 Kgs. (2 Sam.) 19: 36, etc.; Prov. 19: 17.

then return to the subject-matter of the discourse and the purpose of the speaker. The guarding of virginity and the avoidance of corruption was being treated. So Jerome heard and kindled his eloquence in the proclamation of virginity, appending the veins of his whisper[71] beneath the veins of the power of God and of the glory of virginity, and as it were putting the purity of virginity before all created things, so that it is easier for God to restore a new heaven and a new earth[71A] and to repair every fault of creation than to restore virginity to its prior state once it has lapsed. This unique seal of his image and likeness,[72] I say, He impressed on the soul from heaven, bearing witness in His commands that the soul should preserve this faithful deposit[73] before all else with all care and seal it in its inmost being away from thieves and from every disaster as something whose loss would be irreparable. Nothing is more fortunate in the possession and more like to God, nothing more wretched in the loss and more unlike God. In order therefore that so excellent and unique a benefit should not be neglected the harshest condition is applied, that in repairing this loss God is somehow weakened, not in power but in dispensation. For if just His power is considered, He can both free from punishment and crown, as if incorrupt, she who was once corrupted. But if we consider the dispensation and constitution which is fixed and invariable by eternal laws, He cannot, because He cannot act against Himself, that is, He neither can nor ought to wish to do so. For although God is of the simplest nature, yet we speak of Him improperly, according to the usage of our speech, by saying that He can or cannot do something, knows or does not know something, wishes or does not wish to do something. So it is as if where God is travailing in mercy to renew the broken seal of virginity by attending at the birth or rather preventing it, the justice of His decrees yet closes the entrance of the belly and, so that it should not come out of the womb or be received upon the knees or be suckled at the breast,[74] it causes a miscarriage so that an incorrupt woman be not born again from a corrupted one, as one reads concerning baptism: 'How', says the Lord, 'can a man when he is old enter a second time into his mother's womb and be reborn?'[75] So then, by a vicarious recompense,[76] justice in her travail, with mercy in opposition, is similarly endangered when, wishing to destroy the makers of the calf, she says to Moses, 'Let me alone that I may destroy that multitude, and I will make of thee a great nation.'[77] But Moses, holding the sword of divine

[77] Cf. Exod. 32: 10.

Moyses gladium diuine animaduersionis tenens et in uaginam mansuetudinis solite refringens respondit, 'Aut dimitte eis hanc noxam aut dele me de libro quem scripsisti.'[78] Sic, quasi quod uoluit Deus non ualuit, propitiabilius se inclinans serui fidelis amicitie quam ingratissimi populi grauissime culpe. Et notandum quia triplex est corruptio, aut corporis tantum aut animi tantum aut simul corporis et animi. De prima dicit Hieronymus: Finge tempore persecutionis aliquam uirginem prostitutam: corrupta est in lege, incorrupta in euangelio.[79] De secunda Apostolus: 'Timeo ne sicut serpens seduxit Euam astutia sua, ita corrumpantur sensus uestri a simplicitate fidei.'[80] De tertia idem Apostolus: 'Templum Dei sanctum est, quod estis uos. Si quis templum Dei uiolauerit, disperdet illum Deus.'[81] A nullo tamen genere corrupta mundatur nisi Deus misereatur et ipsa mereatur. Si autem tanquam uasculi sui fracturam quamcunque manus tornatiles[82] resarcire uoluerint, poteritne plus negligentia uel impotentia quam Dei omnipotentia? Absit. Sane id solum non potest Deus quod se non posse uult.[82A] Quis infinite detrahet potentie etiam uoluntate corruptam mutata uoluntate posse facere, si uoluerit, incorruptam aut coronare tanquam incorruptam? Dictum est ergo non pro diminutione diuine potentie sed pro commendatione sanctissime pudicitie, Deus non ualet, id est non uult, post ruinam coronare corruptam.[83]

Hec spica de agro Booz sorti nostre obuenit saluis messorum grandiusculis aceruis.[84] Extremam apponimus manum ad Samsonis nostri problemata multis sindonibus inuoluta[85] neque paruo pretio resignanda, 'Habeant', inquiens, 'Galli de Anglica questione quod ruminent et Angli de Gallicano haustu quod petissent.' Sicut enim potus est Dagon Anglie sic Baal est cibus Gallie. Malus potus, malus cibus, mala inebriatio, mala ructatio: singulum horum suis cultoribus patrat gehennam. Quam ergo simul inferent penam? Si de refragatione conceptionis agis aut de impossibilitate reparande corruptionis, fornace et sufflatorio utcunque sufficiente capita et membra omnia ydolorum frustatim comminuta atque in puluerem conflata, siue in cibum siue in potum, ab Anglis et Gallis iamiam absumi possunt.[86]

[78] Cf. Exod. 32: 31–2.
[79] Cf. Jerome, *Comm. in Matt.* ii. 11. 30 (*CCSL* lxxvii. 87; *PL* xxvi. 78).
[80] Cf. 2 Cor. 11: 3.
[81] Cf. 1 Cor. 3: 17.
[82] S. of S. 5: 14, the hands of the beloved (and so Christ).
[82A] Cf. Lombard, *Sent.* i. dist. xliii. 7 (Brady, i. 2, p. 301; *PL* cxcii. 639 [= 5]), on Aug. *de Symbolo* i. 1.
[83] Cf. Jerome, *Ep.* xxii. 5 (*CSEL* liv. 150; *PL* xxii. 397).
[84] Cf. Ruth 2.
[85] Cf. Judg. 14: 12–19; the tone shifts markedly here and he may be referring to some earlier exchange of jokes.

reproach and breaking it in the scabbard of accustomed clemency, replied, 'Either forgive them this trespass or strike me out of the book that thou hast written.'[78] Just so, as if God could not do what He wanted, inclining Himself more propitiously to the friendship of the faithful servant than to the most serious fault of the most thankless people. It is to be noted also that corruption is threefold, either of the body alone or of the mind alone or of body and mind together. Concerning the first, Jerome says: Suppose that any virgin is a prostitute in time of persecution: she is corrupted in law, uncorrupted in the Gospel.[79] Concerning the second, the Apostle says: 'I fear lest as the serpent seduced Eve by his subtlety, so your minds should be corrupted from the simplicity of faith.'[80] Concerning the third, the same Apostle says: 'The temple of God is holy, which you are. If any man violate the temple of God, him shall God destroy.'[81] The woman corrupted, however, is cleansed of no kind of corruption unless God has mercy and she herself has merit. But if the turned hands[82] should wish to repair, as it were, some crack in her vessel, will neglect or impotence be able to do more than the omnipotence of God? Never. Clearly the only thing that God cannot do is that which He wants not to be able to do.[82A] Who will deny that the infinite power, if it will, can make even a woman corrupt by her will incorrupt by a change of her will, or crown her as if she were incorrupt? Therefore it is said, not to the diminution of divine power but for the commendation of the holiest modesty, that God cannot, that is, He does not wish to, crown a corrupt woman after her fall.[83]

These ears of corn from the field of Boaz fell to our portion from the undiminished and sizeable heaps of the reapers.[84] We apply our final touch to the riddles of our Samson, wrapped in many shirts[85] and not to be revealed for a small price, saying, 'Let the French take from the English question that which they may ruminate, and let the English take from the French draught that which they had sought.' For just as Dagon is the drink of England, so Baal is the food of France. Evil drink, evil food, evil drunkenness, evil belching: each one of these merits hell for its cultivators. So what punishment will all of them together bring down? If you treat of the rejection of the conception or of the impossibility of repairing corruption, with oven and bellows at all sufficient, all the heads and limbs of the idols broken up into pieces and reduced to dust can be consumed at once in the form either of food or of drink by the English and the French.[86]

[86] Possibly an allusion to Deut. 12: 3; see also Dagon broken, 1 Kgs. (1 Sam.) 5: 2–5, and Baal burnt and broken, 4 Kgs. (2 Kgs.) 10: 26–7 and 2 Chr. 23: 17.

An itaque sitis Anglica et fames Gallica refecte tali cibo et potu conquiescent? Non credo, quia et ⟨uestra⟩ sitis perpetua et nostra fames continua. Furemur autem per disciplinam et conflemus per abstinentiam quod superfluum est in cibo et potu, tanquam ydolum patris nostri Ade quod de ligno scientie boni et mali confictum est;[87] unde ipse et Eua saturati, dimiserunt reliquias paruulis suis, quas sorte missa diuiserunt inter se Angli et Galli ut illi humidioribus resoluerentur, isti solidioribus suffocarentur.[88] Nisi uera scriberem meum 'confiteor' dicerem. Attamen quia 'ueritas odium parit'[89] digito compesco labellum[90] et interim noua tonitrua et fulgurationes Nicolai mei humo absconditus formido. Vale, et ora pro me.

159

From Nicholas of St. Albans[1]

*c.*1180/1 (or at least 1174 × 1181)

Nicolaus monachus Sancti Albani Petro abbati Sancti Remigii.

Inuectionis palliate saturatus opprobrio et ironico crapulatus a uino, uere putabam me missionem accepisse et fedus iam cum silentio pepigisse. Quid senserim sane de priuilegio singularis integritatis in uirginum Virgine scripseram, et metam ibi fixeram. Et ecce meus Petrus de noua materia nouum suscitat ex insperato bellum, et omnes Virginis domesticos prouocat ad indignationem, et doctos in lege Domini ad presumptionis minus Catholice contradictionem. Quandiu tractabatur de articulis qui sic uel aliter poterant intelligi, sana utrinque fide, dissimulabam et animus noster si concepit non peperit dolorem. Nunc autem cum tuba canitur[2] quod Virgo peccatum senserit et sentiendo debellauerit, non dissimulo, non patienter ago, uix manus teneo quin in publicum hostem irruam.[a] Sed priusquam

159 *Sirmond IX. 9*]
[a] irruo *Sirmond*

[87] Presumably a reference to a legend about Adam and Eve.
[88] Possibly also alluding again to the effect of their respective weather and geography on the characters of the English and the French (see above).
[89] Terence, *Andria*, i. 1. 68 (41).
[90] Cf. Juvenal, *Sat.* i. 160.

And will the English thirst and the French hunger abate as a result, restored by such food and drink? I believe not, because your thirst is perpetual and our hunger continuous. But let us steal through discipline and melt down through abstinence that which is superfluous in food and drink, just like the idol of our father Adam which was fashioned from the tree of knowledge of good and evil;[87] when he and Eve were fed full of it they left the remains of it to their children, which the English and French divided between themselves by lot so that the English were made drunk by the more liquid part and the French choked by the more solid.[88] If I were not telling the truth I should make my confession. But since 'truth breeds hatred'[89] I check my lip with my finger[90] and in the meantime, concealed in the ground, I live in dread of new thunderings and lightnings from my Nicholas. Farewell and pray for me.

159

From Nicholas of St Albans[1]

*c.*1180/1 (or at least 1174 × 1181)

Nicholas, monk of St Albans, to Peter, abbot of Saint-Remi.

Sated with the reproach of cloaked invective and drunk with the wine of irony, I truly thought that I had received a discharge and that a treaty had already been agreed with silence. What I felt, to be sure, regarding the privilege of singular integrity in the Virgin of virgins I had written, and there I had set the limit. And see, my Peter provokes a new battle with new material out of the blue and rouses all the household servants of the Virgin to indignation and all those learned in the law of the Lord to contradict this less than Catholic presumption. As long as he was dealing with points which were capable of being interpreted in one way or another, but either way with sound faith, I kept silent and our mind, if it conceived pain, did not beget it. But now that it is announced by the trumpet[2] that the Virgin felt sin and, in feeling, vanquished it, I do not keep silent, I am not acting patiently, I am barely restraining my hand from attacking a public enemy. But before I reply on behalf of the common indignation of all the

159 [1] Dated as letter no. 157 (and see appendix 13). The salutation may have been inverted.

[2] Cf. Joel 2: 1, 15.

pro communi omnium Virginis domesticorum indignatione respondeam, lapidem offensionis et scandali petram[3] contueor, que in nostra epistola inuenit qui nodum in scirpo sepius querit,[4] et 'praua' priuate lesionis 'in directa et aspera' redigam 'in uias planas'.[5] Lapis itaque lapidem offendit[6] in eo quod dixi: 'Virginis ipsius animam pertransiuit gladius, non solum olim in Filii passione sed etiam nuper in Conceptionis sue condempnatione'; et ironico typo subsannans hic bonum dormitasse Homerum,[7] Aristotelico more sic logicat, 'Esto nostra placent ei obsequia; nunquid passibilis est adhuc eius anima? Fides supplet irrefragabilem conclusionem ut uera impassibilitas et immortalitas nullas admittat molestias.'[8] Miror et indignor uirum ecclesiasticum, in diuine scripture figuris exercitatum, has loquendi figuras ignorare uel earum scientiam dissimulare. Nonne legitur Deus zelans, irascens, penitens, dolore cordis intrinsecus tactus,[9] antequam fuerit humanatus? Nunquid ideo eius diuinitas sensit passionum molestias quia nostro more de ipsa loquitur scripture auctoritas? Nunquid ⟨ideo⟩ angelos sollicitudo inquietat quia leguntur securi de sua solliciti de nostra gloria? Tanta est huius tropi copia in diuina pagina quod ipsa habundantia generat inopiam. Pauca igitur de multis sapienti sufficere debent in tam plano articulo. Ad petram uero scandali[10] de corde uestro tollendam plusculum est immorandum quia res exigit ut palam faciam quod celare proposueram. Sanctus ille Bernardus, quem dicis me debita exuere ueneratione et post eum uerborum iacula emittere, quondam sanctorum catalogo ascriptus, nuper est in ecclesia canonizatus et ab humano iudicio exemptus.[11] Exemptus, inquam, est ne de gloria eius dubitemus sed non ut minus de eius dictis disputemus. De gloria beati martyris Cypriani beatus Augustinus non dubitat, tamen in Spiritus sancti datione eum errasse uerissime comprobat. Errorem martyrio deletum scribit, et sic docuit ecclesiam uenerari martyris gloriam ut tamen non imitaretur errorem.[12] Ego autem, etsi dissimili

[3] Cf. Isa. 8: 14 and Rom. 9: 32–3; 1 Pet. 2: 8; i.e. Peter's denunciation of Nicholas's views, see letter no. 158, p. 586.

[4] i.e. to see a difficulty where there is none. Nicholas may have known it from Terence, *Andria*, v. 4. 941 (38).

[5] Isa. 40: 4; Luke 3: 5.

[6] Nicholas had called Peter a rock, and in response Peter elaborated on this (see letter no. 158, p. 580); Peter called Nicholas's point about the condemnation of the feast of the Conception (presumably made in the lost letter to which no. 158 is a reply, but repeated there), the 'stone of stumbling and the rock of offence' (cf. letter no. 158, p. 586). Hence the stone (his argument) has offended the stone/rock (Peter) by making this point.

[7] Cf. Horace, *Ars Poet.* 359 (picking up Peter's reference to the passage in commenting on Nicholas's views in letter no. 158, p. 586).On Conception here, see p. 586, n. 37.

household of the Virgin, I contemplate the stone of stumbling and the rock of offence[3] which he who more often seeks a knot in a bulrush[4] finds in our letter, and I will render 'the crooked' ways of private injury 'straight and the rough ways plain'.[5] And so the stone offends the stone[6] in what I said: 'The sword pierced the soul of the Virgin herself, not only once in the passion of the Son but also recently in the condemnation of her Conception'; and he, offering an insult in an ironic figure of speech that here good Homer nodded,[7] reasons in the manner of Aristotle, 'It may be that our services please her, yet is her soul still capable of suffering? Faith supplies the indisputable conclusion that a true incapacity for suffering and immortality admit no vexations.'[8] I am astonished and indignant that a man of the Church, well-versed in the figures of divine Scripture, is ignorant of these figures of speech or conceals knowledge of them. Do we not read that God was zealous, angry, repentant, touched inwardly with sorrow of heart,[9] before He was made man? Surely His divinity did not therefore feel the vexations of sufferings because the authority of Scripture speaks in our terms about it? Surely worry does not therefore disturb the angels because we read that they are secure about their own glory, worried about ours? So plentiful is this trope in the sacred page that its very abundance generates bewilderment. A few examples from among many, therefore, must be enough to a wise man on so obvious a point. But in order to lift the rock of offence[10] from your heart it is necessary to delay a little longer, because the matter demands that I make plain what I had proposed to conceal. The great St Bernard, whom you say that I deprive of due veneration and against whom you say I hurl barbed words, having previously been entered into the catalogue of the saints was recently canonized in the Church and exempted from human judgement.[11] He was, I say, exempted so that we should not doubt his glory, but not so that we should dispute less about his sayings. The blessed Augustine does not doubt the glory of the blessed martyr Cyprian, yet he most truly proves him to have erred on the subject of the gift of the Holy Spirit. He writes that the error is effaced by the martyrdom, and has taught the Church so to venerate the glory of the martyr without imitating the error.[12] But I, although with inferior knowledge yet with similar

[8] Cf. letter no. 158, p. 588.
[9] Cf. Gen. 6: 6.
[10] Cf. Isa. 8: 14 and Rom. 9: 32–3; 1 Pet. 2: 8.
[11] Peter made the charge in letter no. 158, p. 588; Bernard was canonized in 1174.
[12] Cf. e.g. Augustine, *Contra Cresc.* ii. 38. 49 (*CSEL* lii. 409–10; *PL* xliii. 496).

scientia, simili tamen conscientia, sic ueneror beatum confessorem Bernardum ut laudem et amem eius sanctitatem, qui nec amem nec laudem eius presumptionem in matris Domini conceptione.[b] Et ne putes me magis pertinaci quam bona conscientia dicere que dico, audi quid ab ipsis Cisterciensibus uera religione preditis et Virginem in ueritate diligentibus acceperim de sancto Bernardo, quorum nomina abscondo sub modio[13] ne odiosos faciam fratrum suorum collegio.

In Clareuallensi collegio quidam conuersus bene religiosus in uisu noctis uidit abbatem Bernardum niueis indutum uestibus quasi ad mamillam pectoris furuam habere maculam, quem ex admiratione tristior alloquens, 'Quid est,' inquit, 'pater, quod nigram in te maculam uideo?' Et ille: 'Quia de Domine nostre conceptione scripsi non scribenda, signum purgationis mee maculam in pectore porto.' Frater uisa conuentui innotuit et aliquis fratrum in scriptum redegit. Relatum est in generali Cisterciensi capitulo, et de communi consilio scriptum periit incendio, maluitque abbatum uniuersitas Virginis periclitari gloriam quam sancti Bernardi opinionem. Non sic Paulus, non sic qui se blasphemum et iniuriosum inclamitat ut Redemptoris gloriam amplius extollat.[14] Et certe, ut credo, ea ratione sanctus in propria persona uiro simplici et de talibus nil scienti apparuit et culpam suam innotuit ut totius Cisterciensis capituli discretio deprehenderet eum uelle suum errorem dampnari et Virginee conceptionis gloriam predicari. Igitur si ego publico quod ipse, ut credo, publicari uoluit, hoc non est eius famam extenuare uel gloriam euacuare sed eius uoluntatem super delicti sui penitentia exprimere. Porro facto leui per purgatorium transitu intrauit in gaudium Domini sui qui in diebus suis sanctitate uenerabilis, opinione singularis, eloquentia suauis, et signorum innouatione immutationeque mirabilium extitit mirabilis. Hec ego de beatissimo abbate Bernardo.

Nunc de statera mea que in hoc, ut scribitis, uidetur mentiri quod dixi: 'Virgo singularis uicit omne peccatum non omne debellando sed nullum prorsus sentiendo.'[15] Quod non omne debellauerit, testimonium perhibent homicidium, adulterium, furtum et horum similia

[b] conceptionem *Sirmond*

[13] Cf. Matt. 5: 15; Mark 4: 21; Luke 11: 33.

[14] Cf. 1 Tim. 1: 13.

[15] In letter no. 158, p. 590 (cf. p. 594).

conscience, so venerate the blessed confessor Bernard as to praise and love his sanctity, but neither love nor praise his presumption concerning the conception of the mother of the Lord. And so that you do not think that I am saying what I am saying more out of stubbornness than good conscience, hear what I have heard about St Bernard from Cistercians themselves, endowed with true religion and loving the Virgin in truth, whose names I am hiding under a bushel[13] so that I do not make them hateful to the community of their brothers.

In the community of Clairvaux a certain lay brother of good religious life saw in a vision at night Abbot Bernard clothed in snow-white raiment, having a dark spot almost at the nipple on his chest, and addressing him rather sadly out of amazement he said: 'Father, how is it that I see a black spot on you?' And he said: 'Because I wrote things that should not have been written about the conception of our Lady, I bear the mark on my breast as a sign of my purgation.' The brother made known to the community the things he had seen and one of the brothers wrote it down. It was reported in the Cistercian general chapter, and by common counsel the written account perished in the fire, and the whole body of abbots preferred the glory of the Virgin to be endangered rather than the reputation of St Bernard. Not so Paul, not so he who rebukes himself as a blasphemer and perpetrator of injustice that he may extol more fully the glory of the Redeemer.[14] And certainly, so I believe, for that reason the saint appeared in his own person to a simple man and one knowing nothing of such things, and made known his guilt so that the wisdom of the whole Cistercian chapter might grasp that he wished his error to be condemned and the glory of the conception of the Virgin to be proclaimed. Therefore if I make public what he himself, as I believe, wanted to be made public, this is not to diminish his reputation or to make void his glory, but to express his will concerning his penitence for his offence. Thereafter, with the passage through purgatory lightened, he who appeared in his own days venerable in his sanctity, singular in reputation, sweet in eloquence, and wondrous in the renewal of signs and in miraculous transformations, entered the joy of his Lord. This is what I have to say about the most blessed Abbot Bernard.

Now to turn to my scales which, so you write, appear to be deceptive in what I said: 'The singular Virgin conquered every sin, not by vanquishing all but by feeling absolutely none.'[15] Murder, adultery, theft, and many sins similar to these which never bit into

multa peccata que eius affectum nunquam momorderunt, eius memoriam nunquam contaminarunt, eius denique opinionem nunquam leserunt. Testimonium etiam perhibet conscientia petrina que, etsi cotibus sit durior, hanc tamen abhorret duritiam quam totus mundus abhorret. Os enim aliter sentiens non solum est obstruendum fimo sed lapide conterendum durissimo. Quod nullum prorsus senserit peccatum Virgo peccati destructrix, hoc uidetur sentire beatus Augustinus ubi inhibet Virginis mentionem in peccati mentione.[16] Hoc uidetur sensisse et prophetico spiritu predixisse Dauid ubi Verbum incarnari desiderans dicit: 'Surge in requiem tuam, tu et archa sanctificationis tue.'[17] Surgere enim Verbi fuit ab occulto suo prodire in nostrum publicum, inuisibilem fieri uisibilem, habitu carnis indutum. Incarnatum itaque desiderat surgere in requiem, quam signanter dicit suam ut a communi hominum requie distinguat, quam idem Dauid designat alibi, 'Conuertere', inquiens, 'anima mea in requiem tuam'.[18] Requies anime humane in hac uita est, uel deuicta uel sopita carnis contradictione, sensualitatem rationis imperio de facili obedire. Verbi uero incarnati requies est in carne nullam carnis contradictionem, nullam membrorum legem menti repugnantem sentire.[19] In hanc igitur requiem suam surrexit Verbum incarnatum, et non solum Verbum sed et archa sanctificationis sue,[20] uidelicet mater sua de qua et in qua est Verbum incarnatum. Sicut enim in celo, 'qualis Pater talis Filius,'[21] sic et in terra, qualis Filius talis mater, non dico de Spiritu concepta ut Filius sed de Spiritu repleta et sanctificata ex utero matris ut Filius; quod quidem sensit et scripsit quem laudas auctorem in presenti, abbas Bernardus: inde quippe dies Natiuitatis non Conceptionis Virginee diem haberi solennem, quia que in peccatis concepta est ut uniuersum genus hominum, sine peccato nata est ut pauci hominum.[22] Si igitur sine peccato nata est, consequenter sine peccato conuersata est. Si sine peccato conuersata est, consequenter

[16] A common theme, but he may be thinking of Augustine, *De natura et gratia*, c. 36. 42 (*CSEL* lx. 263–4; *PL* xliv. 267).

[17] Cf. Ps. 131 (132): 8. This and some of the following passages, including the phrase from the Creed below, were discussed in Nicholas's original treatise (Talbot, 'Nicholas of St Albans', cf. e.g. pp. 92, 113), although most of the arguments treated in detail in letters 158–60 are new ones.

[18] Ps. 114 (116): 7.

[19] Cf. Rom. 7: 23.

[20] Cf. Ps. 131 (132): 8.

[21] Cf. Kelly, *Athanasian Creed*, p. 18 (v. 7).

[22] This sentence contradicts Nicholas's own arguments and seems to be a summary or paraphrase of Bernard's position (*S. Bernardi Op.* vii. 388–92, letter no. 174, s. 8)—hence the punctuation given here. Bernard argued that Mary was sanctified in the womb, after her conception and before her birth, and so while not free from original sin (which was

her sensibility, never contaminated her memory, and lastly never harmed her reputation, bear witness to the fact that she did not vanquish all. A conscience of stone also bears witness, which although it is harder than flintstones yet abhors this harshness which the whole world abhors. For the mouth which feels otherwise should not only be blocked up with dung but ground down with the hardest stone. The blessed Augustine seems to perceive that the Virgin, the destroyer of sin, felt absolutely no sin when he prohibits mention of the Virgin in the context of sin.[16] David seems to have perceived this and to have predicted it with the prophetic spirit when, longing for the Word to be made flesh, he says: 'Arise into thy resting place, thou and the ark which thou hast sanctified.'[17] For the rising of the Word was the going forth from its secret place into our public view, the invisible being made visible, clothed in the mantle of the flesh. And so made flesh He longs to rise up into His resting place, which he expressly calls His to distinguish it from the common resting place of men, which the same David indicates elsewhere, saying, 'Turn, o my soul, into thy rest'.[18] The repose of the human soul in this life is the ready obedience of sensuality to the command of reason, the rebellious flesh being conquered or lulled to sleep. But the repose of the Word made flesh is to feel in the flesh no opposition of the flesh, no law of the members fighting against the mind.[19] Into this His resting place therefore the Word made flesh arose, and not only the Word but also the ark of His sanctification,[20] that is to say His mother, of whom and in whom the Word was made flesh. For just as in heaven, 'as is the Father so is the Son,'[21] so also on earth, as is the Son so is the mother, not, I mean, conceived from the Spirit like the Son, but filled with the Spirit and sanctified from the mother's womb like the Son; which indeed the author whom you praise now, Abbot Bernard, perceived and wrote: following from this surely the day of the Nativity, not of the Conception, of the Virgin should be kept as a festival, because she who was conceived in sins like the whole of mankind was born without sin like few men.[22] If therefore she was born without sin, it follows that she lived without sin. If she lived without sin, it follows that she was taken up out of this world to the

contracted with conception), was protected throughout her life from sin. Nicholas's point here (if the text is not corrupt) may be that even if one accepts Bernard's position (which Peter purports to support) it does not follow that the Virgin felt sin. The few men born without sin, or more accurately sanctified within the womb, are Jeremiah, John the Baptist, and, debatably, David (cf. *S. Bernardi Op*. vii. 388–92, letter no. 174, s. 3–4; and discussed in Nicholas's earlier treatise: Talbot, 'Nicholas of St Albans', pp. 96–101).

sine sensu peccati ex hoc mundo ad Patrem assumpta est. Sed dicis eam sine peccato sensisse peccatum. Fateor me nescire quid uelis dicere. Nam exempla sentiendi que proponis nullius sunt auctoritatis et ideo nullius ponderis. De cetero, omnia exempla que ponis solis sensibus corporeis comprehenduntur. Possunt enim uideri, audiri et tangi et forte olfactu et gustu percipi. Et licet quinque sint corporei sensus tamen non dicimus, 'Sentio ignem quia uideo,' nec, 'Sentio aerem quia audio,' nec, 'Sentio lapidem gustu'; forte picem sentio olfactu, sed de sensu olfaciendi nichil ad sensum peccati.[23] Proinde omnia que posuisti sentire te dicis quia tangis. Si igitur Virgo sensit peccatum, cum peccatum tripliciter accipiatur in sacro eloquio, uidelicet pena peccati, culpa peccati, hostia pro peccato, utrum hec omnia an duo an unum tantum senserit, uellem tuo edoceri magisterio. Si enim sic intelligis 'sensit peccatum', id est penam peccati, sic et ego intelligo. More quippe nostro esuriuit, sitiuit, friguit et multis tribulationibus decocta nostris calamitatibus subiacuit, et ex talium in Christo patientia multimoda meritorum prerogatiua effloruit, absque his quibus intrinsecus cotidie proficiebat, noua uidelicet uirginitatis dilectione, singulari Dei contemplatione, incomparabili proximi caritate, tota uirtutum omnium pulchritudine, nulla macule uel leuissime turpitudine. Nam cum meritorum nostrorum summa consistat in patiendo pro Christo et in diligendo Christum, Deum uidelicet et proximum nostrum,[24] in his duobus exercitata[c] est ad plenum agonista nostra ante aduentum Verbi in uterum eius, ut nec ei deesset uel cum carne uel cum hoste certatio nec pacatissimi animi contemplatio. Proinde dispendium merendi non sustinuit que, tot temptationibus exposita, gratia qua ante obumbrationem[25] plena et Dominus cum ea fuit, omnes debellauit et omnes superauit. Dispendium, inquam, merendi non sustinuit que in dies operatione proficiens pariter et amore optimam Marie partem adimpleuit et Marthe sollicitudinem per etatis teneritudinem non exclusit.[26] Quod si intelligis 'sensit peccatum', id est sensit culpam peccati, more nostro legem membrorum[27] sensit, motus pudendos sensit, picem titillationis sensit et inquinata est ab ea, quod absit. Iuo uenerabilis Carnotensium episcopus in Chronicis suis scripsit duodecimo anno etatis sue Virginem ab archangelo Gabriele salutatam et a Spiritu

[c] *corr. Hall;* excitata *Sirmond*

[23] See letter no. 158, p. 594.

[24] Cf. Matt. 19: 19; 22: 37–9; Mark 12: 30–1; Luke 10: 27; Jas. 2: 8; also Lev. 19: 18.

[25] i.e. the Immaculate Conception, cf. Luke 1: 35. (Mary was full of grace and the Lord was with her—Luke 1: 28—before the Immaculate Conception.)

[26] Cf. Luke 10: 38–42.

[27] Cf. Rom. 7: 23.

Father without feeling sin. But you say that she felt sin without sin. I confess that I do not understand what you are trying to say. For the examples of feeling which you propose have no authority, and so no weight. Furthermore, all the examples which you put forward are apprehended only by the bodily senses. For they can be seen, heard, and touched, and possibly perceived by smell and taste. And allowing that the bodily senses are five, we do not, however, say, 'I feel fire because I see,' nor, 'I feel air because I hear,' nor, 'I feel a stone by taste'; perhaps I feel pitch by smell, but nothing of the sense of smell pertains to the sense of sin.[23] Wherefore you say that you feel all the things which you have proposed because you touch them. If therefore the Virgin felt sin, since sin is understood in a threefold way in holy Writ, that is to say, as the punishment of sin, the guilt of sin, and the offering for sin, I would like to be instructed by your teaching as to whether she felt all of these, or two, or only one. For if you thus understand 'she felt sin' to mean that she felt the punishment of sin, I also understand it thus. For she was in our fashion hungry, thirsty, cold and, worn down by many tribulations, was subject to our misfortunes, and out of the endurance of such things in Christ she flourished with a manifold prerogative of merits, apart from those in which she was daily progressing inwardly, namely a new love of virginity, a singular contemplation of God, an incomparable love of neighbour, and the perfect beauty of all virtues with no foulness of even the slightest stain. For since the sum of our merits consists in suffering for Christ and in loving Christ, which is to say God and our neighbour,[24] she our champion was diligent in these two things to the full before the advent of the Word in her womb, so that she was lacking neither combat with the flesh or with the enemy, nor the contemplation proper to a most peaceful soul. Hence she did not suffer a loss of merit who, exposed to so many temptations, vanquished all and overcame them all by the grace with which, before the overshadowing,[25] she was filled, and the Lord was with her. She did not, I say, suffer a loss of merit who, progressing day by day in deed and in love equally, performed the best part of Mary and did not shut out the concern of Martha through the tenderness of age.[26] If you understand 'she felt sin' to mean that she felt the guilt of sin, that she felt the law of the members[27] as we do, that she felt shameful stirrings, that she felt the pitch of titillation and was defiled by this, God forbid. Ivo the venerable bishop of Chartres wrote in his Chronicles that the Virgin was greeted by the archangel Gabriel and

sancto obumbratam, infra quem etatis annum non permittit natura moueri pubescentium genitalia.[28] Terminus igitur pudendi motus in Virgine a Spiritu sancto preuentus, reliquit nos dubios utrum a die conceptionis an a die natiuitatis an certe a die superuentionis Spiritus sancti in Virgine, Virgo liberata sit a contradictione carnis pudenda. Vnde et Augustinus dubitatiue de Christo dixit: 'Quod inde suscepit, aut suscipiendum mundauit aut suscipiendo mundauit.'[29] Sed modis omnibus constare nobis debet quod Virgo singularis nunquam in carne in qua et de qua Christus homo factus est motum illicitum sensit, nunquam legem membrorum[30] sensit, nunquam quod non uoluit egit, nunquam sensit quod sentire non decuit. Cum igitur ante duodennatum ex nature beneficio, post duodennatum ex gratie dono peccatum sentire non potuerit, quando sensit et sentiendo debellauit Virgo peccatum, que aliis temporibus in terris non uixit? Si de Salomone et Achaz das instantiam qui undecimo etatis sue anno genuerunt filios,[31] scias quia singulare priuilegium non facit legem communem,[32] uel certe, quia reprehendit eos scriptura de incontinentia, potuit fieri ut obscenis motibus genitalium infirma irritarent et pudoris claustra rumperent et de animi sui peruersitate iura sue nature inolita peruerterent, non communem hominum naturam exterminarent.

Radicatus et fundatus in montibus sanctarum auctoritatum,[33] da sanctam auctoritatem que perhibeat Dominam nostram sensisse peccatum, que ita distinguat sensum peccati, uidelicet in ignis, in picis, in lapidis, in aeris sensum, et errasse me fatebor. Quod si non occurrit, qua fronte audes fingere noua commenta in tantam Virginem, qua dementia infamare sensum genitalium que Saluatorem saluo pudoris titulo fuderunt? Que prerogatiue distinctio inter singularem Virginem et alias sanctas uirgines si peccatum sensit ut alie sed non consensit peccato sicut nec alie? Quo gratie merito preminuit, ante uirtutis obumbrationem dico, si ipsam cum uniuerso hominum genere exclamare necesse fuit, 'Quis me liberabit de corpore mortis huius?'?[34] Parcius nouas in Virginem adinuentiones de spiritu tuo

[28] A puzzling reference which seems to relate neither to any known work of Ivo of Chartres, nor to any passage in his known works.

[29] Cf. Augustine, *De pecc. meritis*, ii. 24. 38 (*CSEL* lx. 111; *PL* xliv, 174–5).

[30] Cf. Rom. 7: 23.

[31] Cf. Jerome *ep.* lxxii (*CSEL* lv. 8–12; *PL* xxii. 672–6), who also says (s. 3, p. 10/col. 674): 'Simulque consideremus, quod occulte scriptura et Salomonem et Achaz uoluptatis et inpietatis accuset.'

[32] A point made in Nicholas's original treatise (Talbot, 'Nicholas of St Albans', p. 99).

[33] Ironic repetiton of Peter's claim for himself in letter no. 158, p. 580 (echoing Eph. 3: 17).

overshadowed by the Holy Spirit in her twelfth year, under which age nature does not permit the genitals of those approaching puberty to be stirred.[28] With the beginning of shameful stirrings therefore having been forestalled by the Holy Spirit, this has left us in doubt whether the Virgin was freed from the shameful rebellion of the flesh from the day of her conception or from the day of her birth, or to be sure from the day when the Holy Spirit came upon the Virgin. Whence Augustine hesitantly said about Christ: 'What He took up from there he either cleansed for taking up, or cleansed by taking up.'[29] But we ought to be agreed in every way that the singular Virgin never felt an illicit stirring of the flesh in which and out of which Christ was made man, never felt the law of the members,[30] never acted as she did not wish, never felt what it was not proper to feel. Since therefore she was not able to feel sin, by the blessing of nature before she was twelve years old and by the gift of grace after she was twelve, when did the Virgin feel, and by feeling vanquish, sin, she who did not live at other times on earth? If you cite the instance of Solomon and Ahaz, who begat sons when they were eleven,[31] you should know that an individual privilege does not make a general law;[32] or certainly, because Scripture rebukes them for incontinency, it could have happened that they were exciting the weak parts of the genitals with obscene stirrings and breaking the bolt of shame and, from the perversity of their souls, perverting the innate laws of their nature, not driving out the common nature of men.

Rooted and founded in the mountains of holy authorities,[33] cite the holy authority which asserts that our Lady felt sin, which so divides the feeling of sin, that is into the feeling of fire, of pitch, of stone, and of air, and I will confess that I have erred. If you cannot, by what presumption do you dare to fashion new fabrications against so great a Virgin, by what madness to defame the feeling of the genitals which brought forth the Saviour without impairment of her title to modesty? What distinction in prerogative is there between the singular Virgin and other holy virgins if she felt sin like the others but did not consent to sin, as the others did not? By what merit of grace did she stand forth, I mean before the overshadowing of virtue, if it was necessary for her to call out along with the whole human race, 'Who shall deliver me from the body of this death?'?[34] You ought to have been more sparing in forging new inventions from your spirit

[34] Rom. 7: 24.

cudere debuisses quam de Spiritu suo Deus Pater tam gloriose fecundauit. Si ergo aliquid scribo de Virgine quod non legerim in canone, laudem tamen sapit Virginis, laudem et Filii Virginis; et occasione scripture canonice uel uera scribo, licet occulta, uel uerisimilia et ipsa catholica. Presumuntur multa de Virgine que nusquam leguntur, et presumptionibus standum est donec probetur in contrarium. Singularis Virginis priuilegium non habet similitudinis consortium. Non solum singulare est quod Virgo concepit, sed et quod Virgo sola et prima in Israhel uirginitatem adamauit. Non solum inauditum quod uirgo peperit, sed et quod Virgo cito angelo credidit et de facto non dubitans modum conceptionis inquisiuit.[35] Et in hunc modum distingue inter Virginem nondum matrem et Virginem iam matrem ut singulari utrobique ceteris uirginibus prerogetur priuilegio, que singulariter nondum mater angelo testante 'gratia plena' fuit[36] et singulariter iam mater Spiritus sancti sacrarium extitit, que nondum mater, quasi lana candidissima, nullius peccati sensu maculosa fuit et singulariter iam mater, quasi purpura sanguine conchylii tincta, ita Spiritu sancto compluta et madefacta fuit ut nullis de cetero usibus manciparetur nisi diuinis. Multa in hunc modum occurrunt differentiarum genera quibus Virgo nondum mater differt a se Verbi matre, licet nunquam peccatum senserit uel nondum mater uel iam mater. Vellus quippe, cum sit de corpore, ut ait Hieronymus, corporis non sentit passionem;[37] sic et nostre Virginis uirginitas, cum sit in carne, non sensit uitia carnis. Sed dicis: 'Multiformiter peccatum sentitur, aliquando cum peccato, aliquando sine peccato—sine peccato sentitur sicut aer.'[38] Hoc exemplum nullius est auctoritatis, ut dictum est, sed nec intelligentis expressiuum. Aer quippe sentitur aliquando intensius, aliquando remissius, secundum motus sui impetum uel leniorem uel asperiorem; et durior est aeris frigidi sensus asperior quam ignis tepidioris leuior uel lapidis uel picis remotior. Eapropter me non mouent exempla que tam remota sunt a re ad quam explicandam sunt inducta. Recurramus itaque ad sensum ecclesie et secundum quod ipsa sentit de sensu peccati proferamus in medium et uideamus quo sensu Virgo potuerit

[35] Cf. Luke 1: 34.
[36] Cf. Luke 1: 28; he is referring to Peter's distinctions in letter no. 158, pp. 590, 592.
[37] Cf. Jerome, *Ep. supp.* ix. 5 (*PL* xxx. 127; cf. also ibid. 7 and letter no. 158, p. 590).
[38] Cf. letter no. 158, p. 594 (but not the last part).

against the Virgin whom God the Father so gloriously made fruitful from His Spirit. If therefore I write anything about the Virgin which I have not read in the Canon, it still savours of the praise of the Virgin and the praise of the Son of the Virgin; and in the context of canonical Scripture, I either write truths, albeit latent, or verisimilitudes, which are themselves Catholic. Many things are presumed about the Virgin which are nowhere written down, and one must stand by the presumptions until the contrary be proved. The privilege of the singular Virgin has nothing in common with any other. Not only is it unique that the Virgin conceived, but also that the Virgin alone and first in Israel truly loved virginity. It is not only unheard of that a virgin gave birth, but also that the Virgin believed the angel quickly and, not doubting the deed, asked about the mode of conception.[35] And you must distinguish between the Virgin not yet a mother and the Virgin now a mother in such a way that she is set above other virgins in both respects by a unique privilege who uniquely, not yet a mother, by the angel's witness was 'full of grace',[36] and uniquely, now a mother, was the shrine of the Holy Spirit; who, not yet a mother, like purest white wool was stained by no feeling of sin, and uniquely, now a mother, as if dyed purple with the blood of the murex was rained upon and moistened by the Holy Spirit in such a way that thereafter she was delivered up to no uses other than the divine. Many kinds of differences occur in this manner by which the Virgin not yet a mother differs from herself as the mother of the Word, although she never felt sin, either not yet a mother or now a mother. The fleece to be sure, although it is of the body, as Jerome says, does not feel bodily suffering;[37] so also the virginity of our Virgin, although it was in the flesh, did not feel the vices of the flesh. But you say: 'Sin is felt in many ways, at one time with sin, at another without sin—it is felt without sin like air.'[38] This example has no authority, as I have said, but neither is it indicative of one who understands. For air is sometimes felt more intensely, sometimes more slightly, according to the impulse of its motion, either milder or harsher; and the harsher feeling of cold air is harder than the lighter feeling of warmer fire or the more distant feeling of stone or pitch. For that reason examples which are so far distant from the thing which they are adduced to explain do not persuade me. Let us return then to the thinking of the Church and, according to that which she herself perceives concerning the feeling of sin, let us bring it out into the open and see in what sense the Virgin was able to feel sin without

sentire peccatum sine sensu peccati. Cum igitur peccatum ecclesiastico sensu tripliciter dicatur, ut dictum est, uidelicet pena, culpa, hostia, iungamus primo singula singulis, deinde singula omnibus, ut experiamur qua coniunctione uerum sit peccatum sentiri sine peccato, et tandem deprehendamus utrum ueritas equiuoce coniunctionis obuiet clausule uniuoce acceptionis qua dicitur: 'Virgo uicit ex omni parte peccatum, non omne debellando sed nullum prorsus sentiendo.'[39] Attende, rogo, si Virgo penam peccati sensit sine pena peccati, si culpam peccati sensit sine culpa peccati, si hostiam sine hostia sensit, et doce quomodo hec possint fieri. Quod si non occurrit, attende si culpam sine pena uel sine hostia sensit, si hostiam sine pena uel sine culpa sensit, et doce que scriptura hec doceat et quid utilitatis in presenti disquisitione habeant.[d] Perpende denique quod Virgo penam peccati sensit sine culpa peccati, et hoc sensu forte fieri potuit quod peccatum sensit sine peccato, cum peccatum equiuoce pena dicatur et culpa peccati. Sed hic sensus in nullo derogat clausule qua Virgo perhibetur omne uicisse peccatum non omne debellando sed nullum prorsus sentiendo, quia in ea uniuoce ubique peccatum pro culpa peccati accipitur. Ipsa quippe culpam peccati, uidelicet concupiscentiam et cetera que simul sunt et pena et culpa peccati, ex omni parte uicit, quod horum omnium nullum omnino sensit. Nam serpentis sibilatio foris fuit per suggestionem non intus per titillationis pruriginem, nec decuit illam carnem titillari per quam meruit omnis caro a dampnatione titillationis purgari. Non decuit illam carnem inordinate moueri de cuius propagine ordinis disciplina demanauit et omnem mundum sub iustitie moderamine colligens ad uitam eternam reformauit.

[d] habeat *Sirmond*

the sense of sin. Since, then, sin is spoken of in three ways in ecclesiastical thinking, as I have said, that is punishment, guilt, and offering, let us join first each to each, then each to all, that we may test by what combination it is true that sin is felt without sin, and finally let us discover whether the truth of an equivocal combination bars the conclusion of univocal acceptance by which it is stated: 'The Virgin conquered sin in every respect, not by vanquishing all but by feeling absolutely none.'[39] Consider, I ask, whether the Virgin felt the punishment of sin without the punishment of sin, whether she felt the guilt of sin without the guilt of sin, whether she felt the offering without the offering, and teach me how these things may be. If you cannot, consider whether she felt the guilt without the punishment or without the offering, whether she felt the offering without the punishment or without the guilt, and teach me which Scripture teaches these things and of what use they are in the present inquiry. Finally weigh up the proposition that the Virgin felt the punishment of sin without the guilt of sin, and perhaps it could have been in this sense that she felt sin without sin, since sin is referred to equivocally as the punishment and the guilt of sin. But this sense in no way diminishes the conclusion by which the Virgin is asserted to have conquered every sin not by vanquishing all but by feeling absolutely none, because in that conclusion sin is accepted univocally everywhere to mean the guilt of sin. For she herself conquered the guilt of sin in every respect, namely concupiscence and the other things which are at once the punishment and the guilt of sin, because she felt absolutely none of all these things. For the hissing of the serpent was without in the form of suggestion, not within in the form of the itch of titillation; nor was it proper for that flesh to be titillated through which all flesh obtained purgation from the damnation of titillation. It was not proper for that flesh to be moved in a disorderly way from whose progeny the discipline of good order flowed down and, bringing the whole world under the governance of justice, refashioned it for eternal life.

[39] i.e. Nicholas's proposition, presumably in the earlier lost letter, taken up by Peter in letter no. 158, p. 590 ff.; Nicholas now goes on to refine his proof in the light of Peter's objections in letter no. 158.

160

To Nicholas of St. Albans[1]

1181

Petrus Carnotensis electus Nicolao Sancti Albani monacho.

Epistola tua multifarie dentata, dum me acerrime mordere intendit, dentes suos in semet elisos non iniuria collidit. Acutos equidem formido, sed putres contempno. Subtiliter syllogizas uel forte paralogizas sed fallaciter concludis. Nostram irrides simplicitatem, nec mirum, non enim tenes ueritatem. Contra legem fratris tui turpitudinem reuelas,[2] non que est sed quam fingis. In humanis certe mentiri uereor, quanto magis in diuinis? Credo, dico, assero et iuro beatissimam Virginem nostram in eterna predestinatione singulari priuilegio munitam nec a sua conceptione in aliquo uiolatam sed semper mansisse et permansisse illibatam, et sicut beata ultra humanam et ceterorum hominum naturam sic secreta et incognita manet ultra omnium notionem.[3] Quamuis autem more ueruecum adinuicem nostra temptauerimus cornua et uerborum diuersos hinc inde protulerimus sonos, tamen unus et simplex oculus utriusque nostrum in eius obsequio et famulatu nunquam caligauit, sed neque Deo uolente caligabit. Vt autem gustus cibum discernit et alius plus salis alius minus exigit, sic sensus humanus quandoque austeriora quandoque dulciora appetit auidius. Profert alius absque pondere rationis seu auctoritatis quod ei placuerit, recusat alius quicquid sale euangelico aut prophetico conditum non est. Est alius utilior, dulcior alius. Ego utilem dulci prepono. Solas fauces magis demulcet dulcis, omnibus membris utilis plus confert. Tu uerba dulcia, ego utilia quero. Tu lenocinantia, ego salubria et confortantia. Seriis itaque intendamus. Quedam tamen seria iocosa aliquando non respuunt, immo libenter admittunt, quedam uero sic respuunt et expuunt quod etiam anathematizant et

160 *Sirmond IX. 10*]

160 [1] On the date, see appendix 13.
[2] Cf. Lev. 18: 16; 20: 21.
[3] Reflecting Bernard's basic position: *S. Bernardi Op.* vii. 388–92, letter no. 174, s. 5.

160

To Nicholas of St Albans[1]

1181

Peter, bishop-elect of Chartres, to Nicholas, monk of St Albans.

Your many-toothed letter, while it strives to bite me most savagely, harmlessly grinds its worn-down teeth against one another. I am indeed afraid of sharp teeth, but I despise those which are decaying. You reason subtly in syllogisms, or perchance in solecisms, but you conclude fallaciously. You mock our simplicity, and no wonder, for you do not grasp the truth. Contrary to the law, you uncover the nakedness of your brother,[2] not that which exists but that which you make up. In human matters certainly I am afraid to deceive; how much more in divine? I believe, I declare, I assert, and I swear that our most blessed Virgin is in eternal predestination fortified by a unique privilege and that she has not been violated in any way from the moment of her conception, but that she has always remained and abided unharmed, and that just as she is blessed beyond human nature and that of the rest of mankind, so she remains hidden and unknown beyond the recognition of all.[3] But although we have tested our horns against one another like rams, and have brought forth on this side and that the dissonant sounds of words, yet the singular and simple eye of each of us was never blind in duty and servitude to her, nor, God willing, will it be blind. But as the sense of taste discerns food and one man's taste demands more salt, another's less, so human sense strives more eagerly one moment for harsher things and the next for sweeter things. One puts forth without the weight of reason or of authority what pleases him, another rejects whatever is not flavoured with the salt of the Gospel or the prophets. One is more profitable, the other sweeter. I put the profitable before the sweet. The sweet brings delight more to the mouth alone, the profitable confers more on all the limbs. You seek sweet words, I seek profitable ones. You seek flattering words, I seek wholesome and strengthening ones. And so let us turn our attention to serious matters. There are, however, certain serious matters which sometimes do not spurn jokes, indeed which freely admit them, but certain matters so spurn and

suspendunt. Regine Domine nostre beatissime Virginis Marie obsequia uenerationem postulant non adulationem, maturitatem non scurrilitatem, cordis deuotionem non oris uerbositatem, secreti admirationem non publicam discussionem. Vterque nostrum currit post ipsam, et utinam ad ipsam. Vt credo, una intentio animos parificat, sed uarietas sermonum, utpote lingue diuerse, sensus scripture salua fide alternat. An scientiores, an sapientiores sumus Augustino et Hieronymo? Nonne in fide unanimes, in religione concordes, in caritate feruentes, in scientia scripturarum sublimes, in auctoritate pares, in quibusdam sententiis ualde sunt dispares?

In epistola ad Galatas sic legitur: 'Cum uenisset Cephas Antiochiam, in faciem ei restiti quia reprehensibilis erat. Prius enim quam uenirent quidam a Iacobo, cum gentibus edebat. Cum autem uenissent, subtrahebat et segregabat se, timens eos qui ex circumcisione erant' etc.[4] Hieronymus defendit Petrum dicens inuitum fecisse et dispensatorie simulasse ne scilicet Iudeos amitteret, nec in hoc peccabat quia bona intentione id agebat.[5] Augustinus e contra dicit Petrum illa legalia seruasse non dispensatorie sed uere, et eum uere pecasse, non illa seruando sed alios suo exemplo Iudaizare cogendo.[6] Ecce cedri Libani, ecce sublimes abietes, alio et alio impulsu aliter et aliter sentiunt, sed in caritatis radice nunquam dissentiunt. Vnusquisque autem in suo sensu habundat, nequaquam enim in articulis fidei, in iis qui 'sunt due oliue et duo candelabra' ante Deum lucentia,[7] error innascitur pro quo alter periclitetur. Non itaque mirum si nos stipulam siccam uentus rapiat in diuersa.[8] Si tu tendis honorare Virginem, hoc ego collaudo; si contendis defendere incircumcisum sermonem, istud non approbo. Incircumcisus autem sermo est qui originale preputium trahens de uentre sensus humani arbitrii cultro petrino non amputatur ad regulam euangelice auctoritatis.[9] Si omnes sermones superfluos communicarem et huic nostro scripto insererem, nemus iuxta altare complantarem.[10] Saluo nomine et numine sacratissime Virginis, uerbale duellum non

[4] Gal. 2: 11–12 (Vulgate begins *cum autem*, and reads *ab* not *a*).

[5] Peter Lombard, *Collectanea in epistolas Pauli* (*PL* cxcii. 110); cf. also Jerome, *Comm. in iv. ep. Paul*, ad Gal. Prol. and i. c. 2 (*PL* xxvi. 308–9 [332–3], 339–43 [365–7]; and *ep.* 112 (*CSEL* lv. 367–93, esp. 370 ff.; *PL* xxxiii. 251–66 [= no. lxxv]).

[6] Cf. Peter Lombard, ibid.; cf. also Augustine *epp.* 40, 82 (*CSEL* xxxiv. 2 69–81, 351–87; also *CSEL* liv. 666–74, 351–8 [= nos. 67, 116]; *PL* xxxiii. 154–8, 275–92); what follows echoes Isa. 14: 8.

[7] Cf. Rev. 11: 4.

[8] Cf. Ps. 82 (83): 14; Jer. 13: 24.

[9] *petrino* here may also imply 'Petrine', i.e. needing a papally authorized judgement on the matter (cf. below, p. 626). On 'uncircumcised', cf. e.g. Acts 7: 51.

reject them as even to anathematize and suspend them. The services due to the queen, our most blessed Lady the Virgin Mary, require veneration not flattery, maturity not flippancy, devotion of heart not verbosity of mouth, private awe not public debate. Each of us runs after her, would that we each also ran towards her. One purpose, so I believe, makes souls equal, but diversity of words, as for example in a different tongue, changes the senses of Scripture without violation of the faith. Are we more knowledgeable, are we wiser than Augustine and Jerome? Are they not of one accord in faith, united in the religious life, fervent in love, sublime in knowledge of the Scriptures, equal in authority, yet emphatically unequal in certain opinions?

In the letter to the Galatians we thus read: 'When Cephas was come to Antioch, I withstood him to the face because he was to be blamed. For before that some came from James, he did eat with the gentiles, but when they were come, he withdrew and separated himself, fearing them who were of the circumcision' etc.[4] Jerome defends Peter saying that he acted unwillingly and dissembled under special circumstances, that is so that he should not alienate the Jews; nor did he sin in this, because he did that with a good intention.[5] Augustine, on the other hand, says that Peter kept those laws not on account of the special circumstances but truly, and that he truly sinned, not by keeping them but by driving others by his example to judaize.[6] See the cedars of Lebanon, see the lofty fir trees, they feel things in different ways, under different impulses, but they never feel differently in the root of love. Each one, however, is prolific in understanding, for by no means does error by which another might be endangered spring up concerning the articles of the faith in those who 'are two olive-trees and two candlesticks' shining out before the Lord.[7] It is no wonder then if the wind should carry us off like dry straw in different directions.[8] If you are striving to honour the Virgin, this I praise; if you are straining to defend an uncircumcised opinion, I do not approve of this. Now, an opinion is uncircumcised which, having a foreskin from its birth, from the womb of the sense of human judgement, is not curtailed with a stone knife according to the rule of Gospel authority.[9] If I were to communicate every superfluous opinion and to ingraft them into this our letter, I would be planting a grove next to the altar.[10] Saving the name and power of the most sacred Virgin, I would not refuse a verbal duel if there were leisure to read, to write, and to seek out arms among the shield-bearers of

[10] Cf. Judg. 6: 25–8, i.e. the grove around the altar of Baal.

recusarem si uacaret legere, si scribere, si arma querere in scutariis Salomonis.[11] Si aures et oculos suos clauserit Domina nostra et nenias disputatiuncularum nostrarum nichili penderit, in cauernis suis Anglum Francigena conclusum et ligatum usque ad tempus mille annorum consignabit.[12]

O magister doctissime, dormiens an uigilans tubam canentem audisti[13] quod Virgo peccatum senserit, sentiendo debellauerit?[14] Quam sis dolosus interpres in occultis patet in apertis, nam stilum uel calamum nostrum appellas tubam, sed tube officium est uocem exaltare, stili et calami in silentio scribere. Sis ergo Dauus qui interturbat omnia.[15] Quo autem sensu dixerim Virginem peccatum sensisse et debellasse, etsi tu arreptus in tanto furore quod uix manus contines, non potes patienter audire, qui nostra legerit scripta fauore et odio postpositis audiat et in statera equitatis diligenter appendat. Ne uero auctoritate nudus contra[a] Goliath ad bellum congrediar,[16] antepono scutum auctoritatis qua dicitur, 'Inimicitias ponam inter te et mulierem, etc. Ipsa conteret caput tuum et tu insidiaberis calcaneo eius.'[17] Que est hec mulier? Virgo, que pro sexu non pro corruptione mulier appellatur. Quod est eius semen? Iesus, in quo benedicentur omnes gentes. Que sunt ille inimicitie? Lege Apocalypsim Iohannis. 'Postquam', inquit, 'uidit draco quod proiectus est in terram, persecutus est mulierem.'[18] Ecce Virginem Mariam. Euangelium docet quod draco malignus in Herode, sicut aliquando in serpente, querebat occidere Iesum Filium huius sanctissime mulieris. Quare Ioseph cum matre et puero monitus ab angelo secessit in Egyptum tanquam in locum desertum.[19] Luce clarius ad uerbum exponit hoc sermo qui legitur in natiuitate eiusdem Virginis ubi dicitur: 'Inimicitias ponam inter te et mulierem' etc.[20] 'Quid est, fratres,' inquit auctor, 'in hoc loco: "serpentis caput conterere", nisi principalem diaboli suggestionem, id est concupiscentiam, resistendo superare? Si ergo queritur que mulier huiusmodi uictoriam operata sit, profecto non reperitur in linea generationis humane donec perueniatur ad illam de qua nunc agimus sanctarum Sanctam.'[21] Surdus es si non

[a] *corr. Winterbottom;* circa *Sirmond*

[11] Solomon's shields, cf. 3 Kgs. (1 Kgs.) 10: 16; shield-bearers appear only later at 3 Kgs. (1 Kgs.) 14: 27 and 2 Chr. 12: 10.

[12] Like Satan, cf. Rev. 20: 2; on the characters of the French and the English, see letter no. 158, p. 578, and the use of *cauernosa* there. He will continue if Mary looks away from their squabbling.

[13] Cf. Joel 2: 1, 15; see letter no. 159, n. 2.

[14] Cf. letter no. 159, p. 600, 610 etc.

[15] Cf. Terence, *Andria*, iii. 4. 601 (22).

[16] Cf. 1 Kgs. (1 Sam.) 17 (David went without armour to fight Goliath).

Solomon.[11] If, though, our Lady closes her ears and eyes and weighs up the dirges of our little squabbles as nothing, the Frenchman will seal up the Englishman, shut up in his caverns and bound for a thousand years.[12]

O most learned master, was it while sleeping or awake that you heard the trumpet announcing[13] that the Virgin felt sin and in feeling, vanquished it?[14] How treacherous an interpreter you are in obscure matters is revealed in clear ones, for you call our pen or reed-pen a trumpet, but the duty of the trumpet is to exalt the voice, that of the pen and the reed-pen to write in silence. Therefore let you be Davus who confuses everything.[15] Even if you are seized with such fury that you can scarcely control your hands, that you cannot listen patiently, let him who has read our writings hear without favour or hatred and weigh carefully in the scales of equity in what sense I have said that the Virgin felt and vanquished sin. So that I should not go into battle against Goliath[16] without armour of authority, I am holding before me the shield of authority by which it is said, 'I will put enmities between thee and the woman, etc. She shall crush thy head and thou shalt lie in wait for her heel.'[17] Who is this woman? The Virgin, who is called a woman on account of her sex not of corruption. What is her seed? Jesus, in whom all peoples will be blessed. What are those enmities? Read the Apocalypse of John. 'When', he says, 'the dragon saw that he was cast unto the earth, he persecuted the woman.'[18] Lo, the Virgin Mary. The Gospel teaches that the wicked dragon in Herod, as once in the serpent, was seeking to kill Jesus, the Son of this holiest woman. For this reason Joseph with the mother and child, warned by the angel, fled to Egypt as to a deserted place.[19] A sermon which is read on the nativity of the same Virgin expounds this literally, more clearly than light, on the text: 'I will put enmities between thee and the woman' etc.[20] 'What does it mean, brothers,' says the author, 'in this passage: "to crush the head of the serpent", if not to overcome by resistance the principal incitement of the devil, that is concupiscence? If therefore it is asked what woman brought about a victory of this sort, certainly the answer is not found in the line of the human race until one comes to her of whom we are now treating, the holiest of holy women.'[21] You are deaf if you do not hear,

[17] Gen. 3: 15, the missing part of the passage, to which Peter refers below, is: ' . . . et semen tuum et semen illius'; cf. also Gen. 22: 18.

[18] Rev. 12: 13 (the preceding echoes Gal. 3: 8).

[19] Cf. Matt. 2: 13–15 (for *locum desertum* cf. e.g. Matt. 14: 13; Luke 9: 10).

[20] Gen. 3: 15.

[21] Fulbert of Chartres, *Sermones ad populum*, iv. (*PL* cxli. 320).

audis, cecus si non uides, mutus si non clamas, infidelis si non credis, contumax si adhuc contendis. 'Vade ad natatoriam Siloe, et laua' oculos,[22] et uide quomodo uerum sit quia sensit peccatum sine peccato. Sensit equidem non ad lesionem sed ad probationem, sensit non succumbendo sed superando, sensit extrinsecus non intrinsecus, sensit hoste suggestionem iaciendo non carne delectando uel spiritu consentiendo, sensit propulsando non excipiendo uel admittendo. Quis nostrum magis honorat Virginem, qui illam predicat absque certamine felicem an qui in certamine fortem? Nam 'mulierem fortem quis inueniet? Procul et de ultimis finibus pretium eius.'[23] Apostolus ait: 'Non coronabitur nisi qui legitime certauerit.'[24] Spiritus in Apocalypsi dicit: 'Vincenti dabo edere de ligno uite quod est in medio paradisi.'[25] Item: 'Qui uicerit, sic uestietur uestimentis albis.'[26] Item: 'Qui uicerit, faciam illum columpnam in templo Dei mei.'[27] Item: 'Qui uicerit, dabo ei sedere[b] mecum in throno meo.'[28] Virgo nostra sedens iuxta sedentem in throno gratie, Filium suum Iesum, loquitur omnes uictorias quas obtinuit non dormiendo sed uigilando, non otiando sed pugnando, non fugiendo sed resistendo, non cadendo sed cedendo. An mater felicior Filio, an sanctior, an fortior, an gratia plenior? Sed ductus est Iesus in desertum ut temptaretur a diabolo.[29] Sed dicit illum Apostolus 'temptatum per omnia pro similitudine, absque peccato'.[30] Qui temptatur, nonne sentit temptationem? Est autem modus sentiendi secundum uirtutem non temptantis sed temptati; debilis, debilior, debilissimus effectus sentiendi secundum affectum et uirtutem sentientis. Non enim quisquam potest iudicare quid sentias nisi tu qui sentis. Hucusque satis sit de tuba quam fecisti et sonuisti.

Nunc autem ut ad singula epistole tue capitula quibus meam, quam et ego confiteor, arguis insipientiam respondeam, spineta tua sicut hinnulus ceruorum transsilio.[31] Sed me non ignorare tropos diuine locutionis assero,[32] tuos uero in terra conculco. Denique compatior insolentie tue, qui de excellentissimis nostre Virginis montibus ad profundissimam uallem descendisti, ne dicam corruisti. Licet enim in illa nichil sit uerecundum ubi omnia et singula eius membra luna sunt

[b] sedem *Sirmond*

[22] Cf. John 9: 11.
[23] Prov. 31: 10.
[24] Cf. 2 Tim. 2: 5, 'Nam et qui certat in agone non coronatur nisi legitime certauerit.'
[25] Cf. Rev. 2: 7.
[26] Rev. 3: 5.
[27] Rev. 3: 12.
[28] Rev. 3: 21.
[29] Cf. Matt. 4: 1; cf. also Mark 1: 12–13; Luke 4: 1–2.
[30] Heb. 4: 15.
[31] Cf. S. of S. 2: 8–9; 2: 17; 8: 14.

blind if you do not see, dumb if you do not call out, faithless if you do not believe, obstinate if you are still struggling. 'Go to the pool of Siloe and wash' your eyes,[22] and see how it is true that she felt sin without sin. She felt it not to the extent of being harmed but of being tested, she felt it not by succumbing but by overcoming, she felt it externally not internally, she felt it at the enemy's offering of temptation not at the delighting of the flesh nor the consenting of the spirit, she felt it by repelling it not by receiving or admitting it. Which of us honours the Virgin more, he who proclaims her to be fortunate without a struggle or he who proclaims her to be valiant in the struggle? For 'who shall find a valiant woman? Far and from the uttermost coasts is the price of her.'[23] The Apostle says: 'Only he who strives lawfully will be crowned.'[24] The Spirit says in the Apocalypse: 'To him that overcometh I will give to eat of the tree of life which is in the midst of paradise.'[25] Again: 'He that shall overcome shall thus be clothed in white garments.'[26] Again: 'He that shall overcome, I will make him a pillar in the temple of my God.'[27] Again: 'To him that shall overcome, I will give to sit with me in my throne.'[28] Our Virgin sitting next to the One sitting on the throne of grace, her Son Jesus, tells of all the victories which she has won not by sleeping but by being wakeful, not by idling but by fighting, not by fleeing but by resisting, not by falling but by felling. Is the mother more fortunate than the Son, or holier, or stronger, or more full of grace? But Jesus was led into the desert to be tempted by the devil.[29] But the Apostle says that He was 'one tempted in all things like as we are, without sin'.[30] Does not he who is tempted feel temptation? But there is a way of feeling according to the strength not of the tempter but of the tempted; the effect of the feeling is weak, weaker, or weakest according to the attitude and strength of the one who is feeling. For no one can judge what you feel except you who are feeling it. Let this be enough for now about the trumpet which you have fashioned and sounded.

But now, in response to the individual points of your letter by which you prove my folly, which I also confess myself, I skip over your thorns like a young hart.[31] I do, however, assert that I am not ignorant of the tropes of divine discourse,[32] but yours I tread into the ground. In short I pity your insolence, you who have descended, not to say hurtled, from the most exalted mountains of our Virgin to the deepest valley. For although nothing is shameful in her, each and every one of whose limbs is purer than the moon and brighter than

[32] Nicholas's charge in letter no. 159, p. 602.

puriora et sole clariora, tamen nostre fragilitatis teterrima memoria, cum audierit nominari genitalia, uix a sua excutietur palude, uix incipiet non solita cogitare. In Virgine igitur talia sacrosanctis cortinis potius uolo honorando inuoluere quam nudis nominibus, ut[c] manibus, contrectare. Virgo certe uirgineis uerbis et sancto uelamine consecratis delectatur affari. Parco epistole mee tua inserere uerba, que tamen non parco reprehendere. Finem facere festinabam, sed nouum tuum decretum prius uolo discutere, et ex quo consilio promulgatum sit requiro. 'Sicut', inquis, 'in celo, "qualis Pater talis Filius," sic in terra, qualis Filius talis mater.'[33] O Domina, ignosce dicenti quod displicet tibi. Nonne tu Filii tui licet mater tamen ancilla?[34] Nonne 'sicut oculi ancille in manibus domine' sue, ita oculi tui in manibus Domini Filii tui?[35] 'Non adequabitur ei' aurum 'de Ethiopia',[36] nec 'conferetur tinctis Indie coloribus',[37] quia non est inuentus similis ei super terram, qui unus et unicus est et secundum non habet. Sufficit tibi a dextris eius stare, non equalitatis uel qualitatis comparatione sed glorie et beatitudinis stabili et eterna copulatione.

Datis iam dextris pacem habeamus ad Dominam nostram, cuius tu adiutor ego assertor, cuius tu zelator ego amator. Suum in laude Virginis expendere ingenium et studium nec improbabile est nec irremunerabile. Vngulam tamen et in hoc et in omni actione nostra et intentione findere[38] auctoritas iubet et ratio suadet. Discernere autem quid et quomodo debeas laudare, ungulam est findere. Qui alterum postponit, officium laudationis aut peruertit aut prorsus amittit. In modo erras si supra uel infra aut extra metas ueritatis quemlibet laudas, in persona si laude indignum laudare uelis. Vt ad rem ueniam, tu effers nostre Virginis laudes, ego uero offero. Tu in aere euolas, ego interim dum in terra sum pedibus curro. Tu precipitas uerba, ego dispono sermones meos in iudicio et in statera appendo. Tu acerbam et immaturam uindemiam, ego in imbre matutino et serotino iam matura poma noua et uetera[39] ad mensam comporto. Virginem laudas, et ego laudo. Predicas sanctam, et ego. Extollis super choros angelorum, et ego. Dicis immunem ab omni peccato, et ego. Asseris

[c] *corr. Hall;* et *Sirmond*

[33] Cf. letter no. 159, p. 606 (and n. 21), where Nicholas is extrapolating from the Athanasian Creed.

[34] Cf. Luke 1: 38.

[35] Cf. Ps. 122 (123): 2.

[36] Cf. Job 28: 19 (Vulgate has *topazium* for *aurum*).

[37] Job 28: 16.

[38] Cf. Lev. 11: 3 etc.; Deut. 14: 6 etc.

the sun, yet we with our most foul and weak faculties, when we hear genitalia mentioned, will scarcely be roused from the mire, will scarcely begin to think of matters unaccustomed. Therefore in the case of the Virgin I wish to cover up such things with sacrosanct curtains out of respect, rather than to handle them with bare names, as it were with bare hands. The Virgin certainly delights to be addressed with virginal words and words consecrated by a holy veil. I forbear to insert into my letter your words, which however I do not forbear to reproach. I was hurrying to make an end, but first I want to discuss your new decree, and I ask by which council it was promulgated. 'Just as in heaven', you say, '"as is the Father so is the Son," so on earth, as is the Son so is the mother.'[33] O Lady, forgive one saying what displeases you. Were you not, although the mother of your Son, yet His handmaid?[34] 'As the eyes of the handmaid are on the hands of her mistress,' are not your eyes on the hands of the Lord your Son?[35] Gold 'of Ethiopia shall not be equal to' Him,[36] nor will He 'be compared with the dyed colours of India',[37] because there is not found like to Him on the earth, who is one and unique and has no second. It is enough for you to stand at His right hand, not in comparison of equality or quality but in the stable and eternal union of glory and blessedness.

Let us now clasp our right hands and hold our peace before our Lady, of whom you are the helper and I am the advocate, of whom you are the zealot and I am the lover. To expend one's talent and zeal in praise of the Virgin is neither objectionable nor without recompense. Authority however orders, and reason urges, one to divide the hoof[38] both in this and in our every deed and intention. But to discern what and how you ought to praise is to divide the hoof. He who disregards one or the other either perverts or lets fall entirely the service of praise. You err in the measure if you praise anyone above or below or beyond the bounds of truth; you err in the person if you wish to praise one unworthy of praise. To come to the point, you exaggerate praises of our Virgin, whereas I offer them. You fly away in the air, I in the meantime, while I am on earth, run with my feet. You rush into words, I set my statements in order judiciously and weigh them in the scales. You bring to the table the bitter and unripe vintage, I bring the new fruits and the old which are already ripe in the early and the latter rain.[39] You praise the Virgin, and I praise her. You proclaim her to be holy, and so do I. You extol her above the choirs of angels, and so do I. You say she is free from every sin, and so

[39] Combining Joel 2: 23 and S. of S. 7: 13.

Dei genitricem, astruis nostram ad Deum mediatricem, et ego. Versa et reuersa[40] in quolibet statu uenerationis et glorificationis, tecum uado, tecum sentio. Si uero extra communis monete formam uis fabricare aliam quam non approbauerit sedes Petri, cuius est approbare uel improbare ordinem uniuersalis ecclesie, pedem sisto et terminos constitutos non transgredior. Credo et confiteor plura esse apud nos ignota de Virgine sacrosancta quam nota quia confortata est et gratia et gloria et non possumus ad eam.[41] Euangelio non sompniis de illa credo, et si aliter sapio, et hoc ipsum reuelabit Deus[42] quando uoluerit et quomodo uoluerit. Interim autem dum fit uox super firmamentum nec descendit ad nostrum fundamentum, pennas submitto, et mee ignorantie caliginem non a te sed a 'Patre luminum'[43] illustrandam imploro. Si ferrum de manubrio elapsum[44] te in aliquo lesit, da ueniam; eamdem a me recepturus indulgentiam. Ora pro me, amice karissime, et utinam facie ad faciem uiderem te quem scriptorum tuorum bene ornatus habitus non semel prestitit audire.

161

To Guy (or William) and Peter, monks of Pontigny[1]

? 1181 (but poss. much earlier)

[a]P⟨etrus⟩ humilis abbas sancti Remigii, W. et P. fratribus monasterii Pontiniacensis, salutem et omne bonum.[a]

Vt breuiter tumultuosis [b]et scrupulosis cordis uestri[b] questionibus super professione facta tam in ordine Grandimontis quam in Cisterciensi respondeam, id michi uidetur quod fidem promissi non ledit qui soluit quod promiserit; is quoque gratie meritum superaddit qui plus soluerit quam ex uoto debuerit. Non est meum ordines

161 *Di fo.* 5[v], *Sirmond IX.* 12, *d'Achery, p.* 545]
[a–a] *om. Sirmond;* humilis abbas sancti Remigii Vvidoni Petro fratribus monasterii Pontinicensis salutem et omne bonum *d'Achery* [b–b] cordium uestrorum *d'Achery*

[40] Cf. Augustine, *Conf.* vi. 16. 26 (*CCSL* xxvii. 91; *PL* xxxii. 732).
[41] Cf. Ps. 138 (139): 6.
[42] Cf. Nicholas's account of Bernard's appearance to a lay brother in a dream (letter no. 159, p. 604); cf. also Phil. 3: 15.

do I. You assert that she is the mother of God, you argue that she is our mediator before God, and so do I. Turn and turn again[40] in whatever state of veneration and glorification, I advance with you, I feel with you. But if outside the form of the common currency you wish to fashion another which is not approved by the see of Peter, whose place it is to approve or to disapprove the order of the universal Church, I halt and do not cross the established limits. I believe and I confess that more things are unknown among us concerning the sacrosanct Virgin than are known, because she is strengthened both by grace and by glory and we cannot reach to her.[41] I believe in the Gospel not in dreams about her, and if I am otherwise minded, God shall reveal this too[42] when and as He wishes. Meanwhile, however, while the voice is sounded above the firmament and does not descend to our sphere, I put down my pen and beg that the darkness of my ignorance be illuminated not by you but by 'the Father of lights'.[43] If the iron which slipped from the handle[44] hurt you in any way, pardon me; you will receive the same indulgence from me. Pray for me, dearest friend, and I wish that I could see you face to face, you whom the finely fashioned quality of your writings has more than once granted me to hear.

161

To Guy (or William) and Peter, monks of Pontigny[1]

? 1181 (but poss. much earlier)

Peter, humble abbot of Saint-Remi, to W. and P., brothers of the monastery of Pontigny, greetings and every good wish.

To reply briefly to the tumultuous and scrupulous questions of your heart concerning the profession which you have made both in the Grandmontine order and in the Cistercian, it seems to me that he who fulfils what he has promised does no harm thereby to the good faith of his promise; he also adds merit on top of grace who pays more than he owes according to the vow. It is not my place to judge the orders of the holy nor to weigh up their merits on my scales. They

[43] Cf. Ezek. 1: 25; Jas. 1: 17.
[44] Cf. Deut. 19: 5, distinguishing accidental killing from wilful murder.

161 [1] Grandmontine novices who had transferred to Pontigny; see appendix 14.

sanctorum[c] iudicare neque meis stateris merita illorum appendere. Suo domino stant aut cadunt, stant autem.[2] Opinionis tamen mee est plus rigoris, plus iustitie, plus seueritatis, plus etiam discretionis esse in ordine Cisterciensi quam in illo qui michi incognitus est et de quo propter incertitudinem nullam [d]precipitare audeo sententiam.[d] His omissis, [e]ranas et muscas inquietantes[e] penetralia cordis uestri utinam abicere uel potius exterminare breui admonitione possem. Non ignoro apud Aristotelem dubitare de singulis[f] non esse inutile.[3] Teneo autem apud Ippocratem quod mutationes maxime generant morbos. [g]Dicit Gregorius[g] quod plante que sepe transponuntur[h] radices non mittunt.[4] Paulus anathematizat qui aliud euangelium predicauerit [i]quam quod ipse predicauit,[i] [j]etiam angelum de celo.[j] [5] Dominus noster[k] Iesus Christus[l] de Iohanne Baptista dicit: 'Quid existis in desertum[m] uidere? Arundinem uento agitatam?'[6] In parabola quoque euangelii, dum fatue uirgines irent emere oleum clausa est ianua.[7] Harum auctoritatum sensus hic est ne instabiles simus, ne fluctuemus, ne omni uento circumferamur,[8] ne dicamus, 'Ecce hic [n]Christus, ecce illic.'[n] [9] Videte itaque uocationem uestram, et bases et plantas uestras statuite supra petram,[10] et cum Iob dicite, 'In nidulo isto moriar, et sicut[o] palma multiplicabo dies.'[11] Rogo amicitiam et fraternitatem uestram ut parcatis uobismet ipsis et pro certo sciatis quia unum ad salutem sufficiens est et necessarium,[12] Deo se committere, nunquam cum Deo disputare, prelato in omnibus obedire, omnia sua onera humeris eius imponere et sufficientem responsalem[p] in Dei iudicio contra omnes aduersarii allegationes tam ueras quam falsas illum constituere, in simplicitate non in subtilitate Deum querere.[13] Valete.[q]

[c] sanctos *Di* [d–d] audeo sententiam precipitare *d'Achery* [e–e] ranam et muscam perturbantes *d'Achery* [f] omnibus *d'Achery* [g–g] Dicunt *d'Achery* [h] transferuntur *d'Achery* [i–i] *om. Di* [j–j] *om. d'Achery* [k] *om. d'Achery* [l] *om. d'Achery* [m] deserto *Di, Sirmond* (*Vulgate has* desertum) [n–n] ecce illic Christus *d'Achery* [o] tanquam *Di, Sirmond* [p] *om. d'Achery* [q] *om. Sirmond*

[2] Cf. Rom. 14: 4.

[3] Cf. Boethius, *In categorias Aristotelis libri iv*, ii. (*PL* lxiv. 238); pseudo-Bede, *Sententiae . . . ex Aristotele . . . collectae* i (*PL* xc. 990).

stand or fall before their own Lord, or rather stand.[2] In my opinion, however, there is more rigour, more justice, more austerity, more discernment even, in the Cistercian order than in that which is unknown to me and of which, on account of uncertainty, I dare jump to no conclusion. These things aside, I wish that I could cast out the frogs and flies which are upsetting the inner parts of your heart, or rather destroy them with a brief admonition. I am not unaware that, according to Aristotle, it is not unprofitable to have doubts about particular things.[3] But I learn in Hippocrates that changes more than anything else generate diseases. Gregory says that plants which are often transplanted do not send down roots.[4] Paul anathematizes him who preaches a gospel other than that which he himself preached, even an angel from heaven.[5] Our Lord Jesus Christ says of John the Baptist: 'What went you out into the desert to see? A reed shaken with the wind?'[6] Also in the parable in the Gospel, whilst the foolish virgins went out to buy oil the door was shut.[7] The sense of these authorities is that we should not be unstable, that we should not waver, that we should not be carried about with every wind,[8] that we should not say, 'Lo, here is Christ, lo, there He is.'[9] And so see your calling and set your foundations and the soles of your feet on the rock,[10] and say with Job, 'I shall die in that nest, and as a palm tree shall multiply my days.'[11] I beg you as friends and brothers to spare yourselves and to know for certain that one thing is sufficient and necessary for salvation:[12] to commit oneself to God, never to dispute with God, to be obedient to one's superior in all things, to lay all one's burdens on his shoulders and to appoint him as a sufficient respondent in the court of God against all allegations of the enemy both true and false, to seek God in simplicity not in subtlety.[13] Farewell.

[4] Possibly misascribed, or from a florilegium, etc., but cf. Seneca, *Ad Lucil. ep. mor.* ii. 3; Walther, 529; Walther and Schmidt, 561g.

[5] Cf. Gal. 1: 8–9.

[6] Matt. 11: 7; cf. Luke 7: 24.

[7] Cf. Matt. 25: 1–12, esp. 10.

[8] Cf. Eph. 4: 14.

[9] Cf. Matt. 24: 23; Mark 13: 21; cf. also Luke 17: 21.

[10] Cf. Matt. 7: 24–5; Luke 6: 48; Acts 3: 7 (*bases* can mean foundations or feet).

[11] Cf. Job 29: 18.

[12] More than one thing is given, but the ref. is to Luke 10: 42.

[13] Cf. Wisd. 1: 1.

162*

To William, Peter and Guy, monks of Pontigny[1]

? 1181 (but poss. much earlier)

Karissimis in Christo fratribus [a]W., P., Widoni suus P⟨etrus⟩[a] Remensis, 'spiritum consilii et fortitudinis'.[2]

Primum loquar tibi, frater Willelme,[b] quia in te et propter te commota sunt uiscera mea; turbatus sum a facie commotionis, ne[c] dicam commutationis[d] tue. Audieram enim zelum[e] tuum, laudaueram fortitudinem tuam[f], approbaueram discretionem tuam,[g] modo autem nescio quo spiritu exagitatus nutare[h] cepisti qui debueras[i] esse columpna immobilis, qui portaueras iugum ab adolescentia tua, et modo tandem ad frugem melioris uite scilicet ad ordinem Cisterciensem ueniens leuaueras te supra te. Timeo, dilecte, uersutias[j] illius qui 'transfigurat se in angelum lucis',[3] timeo ne in te mutetur color optimus,[4] ne argentum immo aurum uertatur in scoriam,[5] siquidem cum immundus spiritus exierit[k] ab homine, ambulat per loca inaquosa querens requiem [l]et non inueniens, et[l] tunc assumptis septem [m]aliis spiritibus nequioribus se[m] redit in domum suam, et[n] fiunt nouissima [o]hominis illius[o] peiora prioribus.[6] Nec hoc dico[p] quod a te exierit spiritus immundus, qui per gratiam Dei in te non fuit, sed quod a te magis elongatus[q] modo quadam mutabili tua leuitate et leui mutabilitate uicinior tibi fieri conatur, et qui, ut ita dicam, substantiam religionis et sinceritatem zeli tui mundanis istis et manifestis immunditiis non potest corrumpere, quibusdam pessimis accidentibus, locorum scilicet[r] et ordinum mutationibus et occultis illusionibus, [s]nititur te[s] absorbere. Quippe spem habet ut 'influat Iordanis in os eius'.[7] Teste philosopho, 'primum argumentum bene composite mentis existimo posse consistere et secum morari.'[8] Discurrere enim

162 *Di fo. 5*[r–v], *A1 fos. 79*[r]*–81*[r], *A2 fos. 128*[r]*–130*[r] *d'Achery, pp. 544–5*]
[a–a] Willelmo, Petro, Widoni, Petrus *d'Achery* [b] Willerme *Di* [c] *om. d'Achery* [d] commotionis *A1, A2* [e] *om. Di;* propositum *d'Achery* [f] *om. Di, d'Achery* [g] *om. d'Achery* [h] mutari *A1, A2* [i] deberes *A1, A2* [j] mi, versatias *A1, A2* [k] exiit *d'Achery* [l–l] *om. d'Achery;* et non inuenit et *A1, A2* [m–m] nequioribus spiritibus *Di, A1, A2* [n] unde et *d'Achery* [o–o] illius hominis *d'Achery* [p] *om. d'Achery* [q] elongatum *d'Achery* [r] sicut *Di, d'Achery* [s–s] te nititur *A1, A2*

162*

To William, Peter and Guy, monks of Pontigny[1]

? 1181 (but poss. much earlier)

To his dearest brothers in Christ, W⟨illiam⟩, P⟨eter⟩ and Guy, their Peter of Reims, 'the spirit of counsel and of fortitude'.[2]

I shall address you first, brother William, because my heart is doubtful about you and on account of you; I am disturbed by the appearance of your doubts, not to say vacillation. For I had heard of your zeal, I had praised your strength, I had approved your discretion, but now, stirred up by I know not what spirit, you have begun to waver, you who ought to have been an immovable column, who had borne the yoke from your youth and now, coming at last to the fruit of a better life, that is to the Cistercian order, had lifted yourself above yourself. I fear, beloved one, the subtleties of him who 'transformeth himself into an angel of light,'[3] I fear lest the finest colour in you be changed,[4] lest the silver, nay the gold, be turned to dross,[5] since when an unclean spirit is gone out of a man he walks through places without water, seeking rest and not finding, and then, having taken up seven other spirits more wicked than himself, he returns to his house, and the last state of that man is made worse than the first.[6] I am not saying this because an unclean spirit has gone out of you—which by the grace of God was not in you—but rather because, though previously further away, it is now trying to get nearer to you thanks to your changeable levity and light changeableness, and he who, so to say, cannot corrupt the substance of your religious life and the sincerity of your zeal with those worldly and manifest impurities is striving to swallow you up with certain grievous accidentals, that is with changes of places and of orders and with hidden deceits. For he hopes that 'the Jordan may run into his mouth'.[7] By the witness of the philosopher, 'I reckon that the first proof of a well-ordered mind is to be able to be still and to live with oneself.'[8] For to run around and to be worried by changes of

162 [1] Grandmontine novices who had transferred to Pontigny; on this and letter no. 161 see appendix 14.

[2] Cf. Isa. 11: 2.

[3] 2 Cor. 11: 14; i.e. Satan.

[4] Cf. Lam. 4: 1. (*iugum* . . . above, cf. ibid. 3: 27).

[5] Cf. Isa. 1: 22.

[6] Combining Matt. 12: 43–5 and Luke 11: 24–6.

[7] Cf. Job 40: 18 (Behemoth).

[8] Seneca, *Ad Lucil. ep. mor.* ii. 1 (which does not have *bene*).

et locorum mutationibus inquietari, egri [t]et instabilis[t] animi [u]iactatio est,[u] non enim [v]coalescit uel conualescit[v] planta que sepe transfertur.[9] Quod autem de professione prioris uoti moueris, nullum scrupulum habet. Auxisti enim uotum, non fregisti; modo enim imples et plenius adimplebis illud Dauidicum: 'Labores manuum[w] tuarum quia manducabis; beatus es, et bene tibi erit.'[10] [x]Si quidem modo habens manum in manu que non est innocens manus,[11] in labore et sudore uesceris pane tuo.[x] [12] Quid plura? Credo, fateor et obtestor quod de minori ad maius instinctu et inspiratione Spiritus sancti ascendisti, et quanto ascensus altior tanto descensus, ne dicam casus, grauior. Proinde obsecro te, karissime, ego tuus Petrus, iam ex solo auditu pro te usque ad sanguinem[y] anime uulneratus,[13] ne michi dolorem super dolorem adicias, ne [z]clero, populo et diabolo[z] materiam risus prebeas, ne te moueas, ne in [a]felici ascensu[a] ubi non est uoti fractio sed integratio, ubi non[b] est metus timeas. Tibi, frater Petre, incognitus facie, absens corpore presens autem spiritu, et deuoto corde consulo et ad pedes prostratus[c] anxie et obnixe supplico ut non obtentu pristine ad quam suspiras quietis te et alios inquietare incipias. Vera enim quies est in ordine Cisterciensi ubi Martha Marie iungitur, ubi iuxta uerbum sapientis et agenti quiescendum et quiescenti agendum.[14] Sane quod de priore[d] quiete et otio obicis, ut pace tua loquar, ita sine questione [e]omni procul est[e] a ratione ut responsione non indigeat. Vbi enim plus silentii, plus ieiunii, minus sollicitudinis mundane,[f] et ideo plus contemplationis et sancte quietis quam in ordine Cisterciensi? Quiescat ergo[g], quiescat ista tua commotio, et dum paruula est allidatur ad petram, dum uulpecula parua est capiatur et in matutino occidatur ne demoliatur uineam Domini,[15] id est conscientiam tuam, ne sub obtentu cuiusdam[h] uane quietis ad pisces, non dico [i]Egypti, et[i] ad alia, non

[t–t] *om. d'Achery* [u–u] est iactatio *Di, A1, A2* [v–v] conualescit uel coalescit *Di, A1, A2* [w] manum *A1, A2* [x–x] *corr. Brooke; om. d'Achery;* Siquidem modo non habens manum in manu que non est innocens manus, in labore et sudore uesceris pane tuo *Di;* Siquidem modo non habens manum in manu que non est innocens manus in sudore uultus tui uesceris pane tuo *A1, A2* [y] effusionem *D'Achery* [z–z] populo et diabolo clero *Di* [a–a] ascensu felici *A1, A2* [b] nullus *Di* [c] profusus *d'Achery* [d] priori *A2* [e–e] est et procul *A1, A2* [f] humane *A1, A2* [g] igitur *A1, A2* [h] *om. A1, A2* [i–i] Egyptiorum *A1, A2*

[9] Cf. ibid. ii. 3; cf. also letter no. 161, n. 3, where something similar is ascribed to Gregory.

[10] Ps. 127 (128): 2.

[11] Evidently combining or confusing Prov. 11: 21 ('manus in manu non erit innocens

places is the agitation of a sick and unstable soul, since the shoot which is often transplanted neither takes root nor grows strong.[9] But the fact that you are perturbed about the profession of the first vow involves no scruple. For you have supported the vow, not broken it, for now you are fulfilling and will more fulfil that saying of David: 'For thou shalt eat the labours of thy hands; blessed art thou, and it shall be well with thee.'[10] But if now you have your hand in the hand that is not an innocent hand,[11] in toil and sweat shall you eat your bread.[12] What more? I believe, I confess, and I bear witness that you have risen from the lesser to the greater by the impulse and inspiration of the Holy Spirit, and the higher the ascent the heavier the descent, not to say fall. Then, dearest one, I your Peter, by report alone already wounded on your account even unto the blood of my life,[13] beg you not to add pain upon pain for me, not to make yourself a figure of ridicule to the clergy, the people, and the devil, not to perturb yourself, not to be afraid in a fortunate ascent where there is no breaking of a vow but rather a reinforcement, where there is no fear. For you, brother Peter, I a stranger in person, absent in the body yet present in spirit, both feel concern with a devoted heart and, prostrate at your feet, beg you anxiously and earnestly not to begin to disquiet yourself and others by holding out the earlier quiet for which you are sighing. For true quiet is in the Cistercian order where Martha is united with Mary, where, according to the word of the wise man, the active should be quiet and the quiet active.[14] Clearly the objection you make concerning the former quiet and leisure, might I say with your leave, is without any doubt so far from reason that it needs no answer. For where is there more silence, more fasting, less worldly concern and therefore more contemplation and holy quiet than in the Cistercian order? Let therefore that doubt of yours be quiet, let it be quiet and while it is yet very tiny let it be dashed on the rock, while it is yet a little fox let it be caught and killed in the morning lest it destroy the vineyard of the Lord,[15] that is your conscience, and lest you appear by holding out some imaginary quiet to be sighing for the fish, I do not say of Egypt,

malus') and Prov. 16: 5 ('etiam si manus ad manum fuerit non erit innocens'). The extra *non* in MSS Di, A1, A2 makes a nonsense in this context, and the whole sentence may be corrupt.

[12] Cf. Gen. 3: 17, 19, the version in MSS A1 and A2 replaces the combined allusion with a closer quotation of Gen. 3: 19: 'in sudore uultus tui uesceris pane.'

[13] Cf. Gen. 9: 5.

[14] Cf. Luke 10: 38–42; Seneca, *Ad Lucil. ep. mor.* i. 3. 6 (the earlier quiet, above, is Grandmont, the later Pontigny).

[15] Cf. Ps. 136 (137): 9; S. of S. 2: 15.

dico Pharaonis, uidearis suspirare.[16] Inualide sunt[j] ad exprimendum quod super tuis et fratris Willelmi[k] phantasticis[l] illusionibus sentio littere,[m] sed tu cum fratre Willelmo[n] ex paucis multa perpende. Consilium meum est immo, ut paululum audacius loquar, sacre scripture mandatum ut in ordine Cisterciensi sic curratis, sic 'in agone' contendatis,[17] ut brauium superne[o] uocationis feliciter[p] comprehendatis. De te, frater[q] Wido,[r] minus ad presens sollicitus sum; tibi nouissime non tanquam abortiuo[18] sed quasi perfecto, cui non est[s] opus lacte sed solido cibo, soliditati tue congratulans, pauca scribo more matris que magis anxiatur circa paruulum et debilem filium quam circa fortem et perfectum. Tu ergo robustus in Domino alios conforta, uiriliter agens, 'argue, [t]obsecra, increpa',[t] 'opportune, importune'.[19] Arduus quidem est ordo Cisterciensis, 'sed tendit in ardua uirtus,'[20] siquidem iuxta uerbum philosophi, 'Serpens, sitis, ardor arene, dulcia uirtuti; gaudet patientia duris'.[21] Expergiscimini ergo, gloriosi milites Christi, mementote quia [u]transit mundus[u] et figura et [v]gloria et omnis[v] concupiscentia eius.[22] Valete. Magistrum Arraudum,[w] [23] fortem et prudentem Christi athletam, salutat anima mea, et per uos [x]ab eo orationum munus[x] expostulat.

[j] sunt littere *A1, A2* [k] Willermi *Di* [l] *om. A1* [m] *om. A1, A2* [n] Willermo *Di* [o] eterne *d'Achery, A1, A2* [p] *om. A1, A2* [q] nunc *d'Achery* [r] Windo *A1, A2* [s] *om. Di, d'Achery* [t–t] increpa obsecra *Di* [u–u] mundus transit transit *A1, A2* [v–v] omnis gloria est *Di* [w] Arrandum *A1, A2* [x–x] orationem munus ab eo *d'Achery*

and the garlic, I do not say of Pharaoh.[16] Words are too weak to express what I feel about your fantastical illusions and those of brother William, but you along with brother William must weigh out many things from these few words. My advice or, if I may speak a little more boldly, the command of holy Scripture, is that you so run the race in the Cistercian order, you so strive 'for the mastery',[17] as happily to gain the prize of the highest calling. About you, brother Guy, I am less immediately concerned; I am writing a few words to you lastly, like a mother who is more anxious about the tiny and weak son than about the strong and perfect, not as to a child born out of season[18] but as to a perfect one, rejoicing in your solidity who have need not of milk but of solid food. You therefore, being strong in the Lord, support the others, acting manfully, 'reprove, entreat, rebuke', 'in season, out of season'.[19] The Cistercian order is indeed hard, 'but virtue strives for hardships,'[20] for in the words of the philosopher, 'Serpent, thirst, burning sand are sweet to virtue; endurance finds pleasure in tribulations'.[21] Therefore awaken, glorious soldiers of Christ, remember that the world passes away and its fashion and glory and all its concupiscence.[22] Farewell. My soul sends greetings to master Arraudus,[23] a strong and wise contender for Christ, and begs through you the gift of prayers from him.

[16] Cf. Num. 11: 5; the Israelites in the desert ate *manna* without gratitude and longed for the good things of Egypt; Peter means he will *not* go so far as to compare Grandmont to Egypt.

[17] Cf. 1 Cor. 9: 25; 2 Tim. 2: 5.

[18] Cf. 1 Cor. 15: 8.

[19] Cf. 2 Tim. 4: 2.

[20] Ovid, *Ex Ponto*, ii. 2. 111.

[21] Lucan, *De bello civili*, ix. 402–3.

[22] Cf. 1 John 2: 17 and 1 Cor. 7: 31 (*figura*).

[23] Unidentified.

163

To Richard of Salisbury[1]

early 1171 (or 1172, before May) × July 1176

Domino Richardo.

Tanquam de sepulcro Domini species aromaticas quibus Nicodemus et Ioseph Dominicum corpus perunxerunt[2] in monumento litterarum tuarum excepi, et tam ori quam odoratui apponens, spiritum super mel dulcem[3] non semel legendo attraxi. Nichil fetidum, nichil fedum, nichil emortuum uiuus ille sermo tuus nitidus et sale sufficienter respersus continet. Viuit memoria accepti beneficii, relucet narratio compacti amoris, stilus elimatus pondere sententiarum et ornatu uerborum refulget sicut 'sol in clipeos aureos'[4] 'usque ad diuisionem anime et spiritus pertingens'.[5] De intimo et profundo cordis uenas celesti unguento repletas ad medium educit et pulcherrime puelle de terra Israhel speciem spectaculo angelorum et hominum sistit.[6] In uestitu enim deaurato[7] per auctoritates diuini eloquii et colores rethoricos, in lecto eburneo[8] propter uerum et castum sermonem[9] quiescentem hanc inueni, sine macula mendacii et ruga duplicitatis. Spiritus ueritatis talem solet sobolem in mente sancta gignere et spiraculum uite insufflare[10] ne mens amore diuino grauida aliud possit parere quam concepit. Cum adhuc esses, dilectissime, in atrio exteriori et seculari habitu, per foramen nobis

163 *Sirmond VI. 16*]

163 [1] The Richard addressed in letters 163–8 must be the same, i.e. Richard of Salisbury, brother of John of Salisbury. John is named in the present letter, and Richard and John are co-addressees of letters 171, 172, and 175 (on which see also appendix 8). Richard was with John at Reims in exile, as letter no. 171 shows; previously he was in France in 1156–7–his exact whereabouts and the length of his stay are uncertain, but he was back in England by Oct.–Nov. 1157; he is connected with Peter during this time (he is named in John of Salisbury's letter no. 19 of autumn 1156; *J. S. Epp.* i. 32), but does not occur in Peter's early correspondence; he accompanied John of Salisbury to France in 1163/4, returned to Exeter probably in 1165, went to Reims again in summer 1166 where he stayed until the peace of Fréteval (22 July 1170) after which he returned to Exeter (Barlow, 'John of Salisbury', pp. 102–4). Richard's conversion from secular to religious life is mentioned in the present letter and in no. 171; he is addressed as a canon in letters 164 and 167, and as canon of Merton in letters 166 and 168. He evidently became a canon sometime between early 1171 and May 1172 (see letter no. 171, n. 1 and letter no. 175, n. 2; on Richard's life, see Barlow 'John of Salisbury', pp. 100–8, and esp. 104–7). The reference

163

To Richard of Salisbury[1]

early 1171 (or 1172, before May) × July 1176

To master Richard.

I received in the monument of your letter, as if from the sepulchre of the Lord, the aromatic spices with which Nicodemus and Joseph anointed the Lord's body[2] and, applying them equally to the mouth and to the nose, I drew forth the spirit which is sweeter than honey,[3] with more than one reading. That living speech of yours, shining and sufficiently sprinkled with salt, contains nothing fetid, nothing foul, nothing dead. The memory of the gift received lives on, the narration of the compact of love shines out again, the polished style shines brightly with the weight of opinions and the ornament of words like 'the sun upon the shields of gold'[4] 'reaching unto the division of the soul and the spirit'.[5] From the innermost part and the depth of the heart it draws the veins which are filled with heavenly ointment out into the open and sets up the image of the most beautiful girl from the land of Israel as a spectacle for men and angels.[6] For I found her reposing in clothing gilded[7] with the authorities of divine eloquence and rhetorical colours, in a bed of ivory[8] on account of her true and chaste speech,[9] without stain of falsehood or crease of duplicity. The spirit of truth is accustomed to beget such progeny in the holy mind and to breathe in the breath of life[10] so that the mind, pregnant with divine love, cannot bring forth anything other than that which it has conceived. When you, dearest one, were still in the outer court and the secular habit, that invisible lover was sending up His hand,

to Richard's conversion in the present letter may imply that it is soon after; in any case it must also pre-date John of Salisbury's el. to Chartres (notified of el. 22 July 1176, consecrated 8 Aug.; see letter no. 102, n. 1). On the heading, see letter no. 84, n. 1.

[2] Cf. John 19: 38–40; cf. also Luke 23: 50–6.

[3] Cf. Ecclus. 24: 27; cf. also Ps. 18 (19): 11.

[4] 1 Macc. 6: 39.

[5] Cf. Heb. 4: 12.

[6] Cf. 1 Cor. 4: 9; the beautiful girl above represents the letter (possibly also an allusion to Rebecca, 'puella . . . pulcherrima' in Gen. 24: 16—although not from Israel).

[7] Cf. Ps. 44 (45): 10.

[8] Cf. Amos 6: 4, but the context suggests the opposite meaning.

[9] But also echoing Heb. 4: 12 again (see above): 'uiuus est enim Dei sermo'.

[10] Cf. Gen. 2: 7.

incognitum manum submittebat ad anime uentrem inuisibilis ille amator[11] et demulcebat uiscera iamiam sibi legitimo matrimonio copulanda suauitate sibi certe et tibi forte cognita. Quales autem nunc tibi amplexus porrigat, que oscula offerat, cuiusmodi fetus conferat, nemo nouit nisi cum in sermone uel in scriptura partus latentem gratiam prodiderit. Secretum tuum tibi, secretum tuum tibi.[12] Admittendi tamen saluo silentio sunt amici illi cum quibus omnia sunt communia,[13] qui non inuident sed congaudent fortunis prosperis, qui optant et dicunt, 'Crescas in mille millia.'[14] Credo me Petrum cum Iohanne assumendum etiam in transfiguratione, etiam in morte, etiam in resurrectione.[15] Non me prefero Iohanni qui recubuit super pectus,[16] sed presumo post Iohannem et stationem habere et castra nostra ponere.[17] Habeat ut dignum est Iesus cum Patre suo et Spiritu primam in te sessionem, habeat Virgo secundam, habeant sancti in ordine suo tertiam. De incolis autem terre magister Iohannes primam, ego, si placet, secundam; aliis quibuslibet non inuideo tertiam et deinceps. De his hactenus. Si medicus essem et medicinam qua repellerem infirmitatem tuam nossem omnimodam curam adhiberem. Quia uero id non possum facio quod possum. Mitto tibi species qualescunque nostras; utinam in nomine Iesu eis mandare possem effectum salutis et sanitatis.

[11] Cf. S. of S. 5: 4.

[12] Cf. Isa. 24: 16.

[13] Cf. Acts 2: 44; 4: 32. The secret is the spiritual progeny of Richard's impregnation by the spirit of truth, i.e. after his conversion to religious life.

[14] Gen. 24: 60.

through an opening unknown to us, to the womb of the soul,[11] and was caressing the inward parts even then destined to be joined to Him in lawful marriage with a sweetness known certainly to Him and perhaps to you. But no one knows what sort of embraces He is now extending to you, what kisses He is offering, what sort of progeny He is conferring, except when in speech or writing its birth brings forth the hidden grace. Keep your secret to yourself, keep your secret to yourself.[12] But while keeping silence those friends are to be admitted with whom all things are held in common,[13] who do not envy but rejoice in your prosperous fortune, who wish and say, 'Mayest thou increase to thousands of thousands.'[14] I believe that I Peter am to be taken up with John even in transfiguration, even in death, even in resurrection.[15] I am not putting myself before John, who leaned on the breast,[16] but I presume both to have a place and also to pitch my tents[17] after John. Let Jesus have, as is fitting, the first place in you, with His Father and the Spirit, let the Virgin have the second, let the saints in their order have the third. Of the inhabitants of the world, however, let master John have the first place, and me, if it please you, the second; to any others at all I do not begrudge the third place, and the following. But enough of these matters. If I were a doctor and I knew a medicine with which I could drive away your sickness I would apply every manner of cure. But because I cannot do that I am doing what I can. I am sending you some of our medicinal spices, for what they are worth. If only I could order them, in the name of Jesus, to effect well-being and health.

[15] Presumably John of Salisbury (see below) with whom Peter will be taken up in Richard's affections; on the transfiguration, see Matt. 17: 1–9; Mark 9: 1–8; Luke 9: 28–36.

[16] Cf. John 13: 23, 25; 21: 20; likening John of Salisbury to the disciple who leaned on Christ's breast at the last supper.

[17] Possibly another allusion to the transfiguration (i.e. the tabernacles, but the Vulgate does not have *castra*; this is OT vocabulary).

164

To Richard of Salisbury[1]

early 1171 (or 1172, before May) × 1181

Domino Richardo regulari canonico Petrus abbas Sancti Remigii.

Presentium lator bene uobis notus uiua uoce que apud nos geruntur poterit referre, atque ideo parcius uoluimus scribere. Vna enim littera, non atramento sed spiritu Dei scripta, in corde nostro et uestro amplius sufficit quam multa librorum congeries, que est uera et firma caritas. Hec non delebitur 'in diluuio aquarum multarum'[2] quia 'aque multe non poterunt extinguere caritatem'.[3] Hec nullo incisorio[4] sollicitudinum siue occupationum radetur, hec nullo igne tribulationum et malorum conflagrabit. 'Caritas' enim nostra 'nunquam excidit'.[5] Hanc legere potestis sine sole in die, sine lucerna in nocte. Hanc oro ut legatis cum sanctis altaribus assistitis et in conspectu angelorum atque omnium celestium uirtutum. Lectio ista sine 'Tu autem' continuetur. Nullum in auribus Domini Sabaoth strepitum faciet.[6] Non a quiete sua Christus excutitur sonitu huius lectionis, non interrumpitur silentium celi, non excitatur sponsa illa que habens inter ubera sponsum,[7] leuam ipsius sponsi sub capite et dexteram in amplexu habet.[8] Valete.

164 *Sirmond VI. 20*]

164 [1] To Richard of Salisbury after his entry to Merton (see letter no. 163, n. 1).
[2] Ps. 31 (32): 6.
[3] S. of S. 8: 7.
[4] Niermeyer (*incisorium* 2) cites the present letter for this meaning.
[5] 1 Cor. 13: 8.

164

To Richard of Salisbury[1]

early 1171 (or 1172, before May) × 1181

To his lord Richard, canon regular, Peter, abbot of Saint-Remi.

The bearer of this present letter, who is well known to you, will be able to relate by word of mouth what is afoot here, and so we wished to write the more sparingly. For one letter written not in ink but in the Spirit of God furnishes in our heart and yours more than a great heap of books—that is true and secure love. This will not be destroyed 'in a flood of many waters'[2] because 'many waters cannot quench charity'.[3] This will be shorn by no razor[4] of worries or affairs, this will not burn up with any fire of tribulations and evils. For our 'charity never falleth away'.[5] This you can read without the sun in the daytime, without a lamp at night. I pray that you read this when you stand at the holy altars and in the sight of the angels and all the powers of heaven. Let this reading be continued without, 'But thou'. It will make no din in the ears of the Lord of Sabaoth.[6] Christ is not shaken from His rest by the sound of this reading, the silence of heaven is not interrupted, that bride is not awakened who, having the bridegroom between the breasts,[7] has the left hand of the same bridegroom under her head and the right hand embracing her.[8] Farewell

[6] Cf. Jas. 5: 4; also Jer. 11: 20; Rom. 9: 29. 'Tu autem' preceding recalls the concluding words for *lectiones* in the Night Office: 'Tu autem, Domine, miserere nobis,' which in effect demarcated the lessons from one another. Here Peter means that love should continue to be unbroken. The phrase is also a common biblical one, here most closely recalling Jer. 11: 20, 'Tu autem, Domine Sabaoth'.

[7] Cf. S. of S. 1: 12, also alluding to ibid. 2: 7; 3: 5; 8: 4.

[8] Cf. S. of S. 2: 6; 8: 3.

165

To Richard of Salisbury[1]

early 1171 (or 1172, before May) × 1181

Petrus abbas Sancti Remigii Richardo.

Etsi 'non est sermo in lingua mea,'[2] de inopia scientie, tamen in manibus habeo signa de plenitudine amicitie. Fontes qui precedentibus annis rupti sunt et aperti usque ad 'diluuium aquarum multarum'[3] presenti anno siccati sunt et aruerunt usque ad defectum herbarum et uirgultorum. Hec siccitas linguam quidem et fauces tangere potuit sed non uenam dilectionis attigit, nec oleum de capite defecit.[4] Manabit certe cum uita, immo sine dubio et ultra, nam 'caritas nunquam excidit'.[5]

166

To Richard of Salisbury[1]

early 1171 (or 1172, before May) × 1181

Petrus abbas Sancti Remigii R⟨ichardo⟩ canonico Meritone.

'Adipe et pinguedine'[2] spiritali refertas ex parte tua recepi litteras, quibus cibatis et potatis saluo quadragesimali ieiunio[3] 'factum est in ore meo tanquam mel dulce', et medulle replete sunt[4] uberrima exultatione. De uase siquidem bono et optimo eructauit stilus tuus uerba bona, uerba consolatoria que me a 'diluuio aquarum multarum' ad archam Noe, qui interpretatur requies,[5] prouocant et de claustrali

165 *Sirmond VII. 12*]

166 *Sirmond VIII. 13*]

165 [1] Dated as letter no. 164. [2] Ps. 138 (139): 4. [3] Cf. Gen. 7: 11; Ps. 31 (32): 6. [4] Cf. Eccles. 9: 8. [5] 1 Cor. 13: 8.

166 [1] Dated as letter no. 164. Letters 166 and 167 concern Peter's treatise *De disciplina claustrali* (see Introduction, p. xxxiv). This letter is his response to Richard's request that he write on the subject, and no. 167 announces the completion of a part of the work. The treatise cannot be dated any more closely—rather it is these letters which indicate that the

165

To Richard of Salisbury[1]

early 1171 (or 1172, before May) × 1181

Peter, abbot of Saint-Remi, to Richard.

Although 'there is no speech in my tongue,'[2] from lack of knowledge, yet I have in my hands signs of the fullness of friendship. The springs which in previous years have burst and opened causing 'a flood of many waters'[3] have this year failed and run dry, causing a dearth of vegetation and trees. This dryness was able to touch the tongue indeed and the throat but did not touch the vein of love, nor did the oil depart from the head.[4] It will surely flow with life, nay without doubt beyond, for 'charity never falleth away'.[5]

166

To Richard of Salisbury[1]

early 1171 (or 1172, before May) × 1181

Peter, abbot of Saint-Remi, to Richard, canon of Merton.

I have received a letter from you crammed with spiritual 'marrow and fatness'[2] which, when I had eaten and drunk it without breaking my Lenten fast,[3] became 'in my mouth sweet as honey', and my innermost parts were filled[4] with most abundant exultation. Indeed your pen poured good words from a good and excellent vessel, consoling words which call me forth from the 'flood of many waters' to the ark of Noah, which is interpreted as rest,[5] and beg

treatise cannot have been written before 1171 at the earliest. G. de Martel, *Pierre de Celle, L'École du cloître*, Sources Chrétiennes, ccxl (Paris, 1977), pp. 25–7, dates the treatise to 1179 because he takes Peter's professions of illness in the present letter to refer to the same illness (an attack of gout) as in the more closely dated letters 100 and 135 and in the prologue to the treatise, but this cannot be a ground for precise dating.

[2] Cf. Ps. 62 (63): 6.

[3] i.e. he is writing during Lent, and the metaphorical feasting on Richard's letters does not violate the fast.

[4] Cf. Ezek. 3: 3; Rev. 10: 10.

[5] Combining Ps. 44 (45): 2; Ps. 31 (32): 6, and Gen. 6–8; *requies* is the standard interpretation, cf. e.g. *Glossa Ord.* (*PL* cxiii. 103), Ambrose, *De Noe*, i. 2 (*CSEL* xxxii. 1. 413; *PL* xiv. 363); Jerome, *Liber q. heb. in Gen.* v. 29 (*CCSL* lxxii. 9; *PL* xxiii. 947).

disciplina non solum cogitare sed et scribere exorant. Promptum me et facilem nosti in omni obedientia, sed uinctum et occupatum laboriosa sarcina cui noua alluuione accreuit et accessit renum grauissima infirmitas. Non credas quod de solito 'luti et lateris'[6] penso aliquid imminuerit urgentissima principis tenebrarum harum exactio. Componit cotidie strues lignorum, in negotiis addit paleas, et stipulam siccam in nugis et uanis discursionibus.[7] Vexatum[a] denique plagis uariis orationum, psalmodiarum, sanctarum meditationum, helemosinarum, magis ac magis cor eius induratur, negans licentiam in deserto abeundi et immolandi Deo sacrificium iustitie et innocentie.[8] Quomodo itaque in manicis ferreis detentus et supra modum fame lectionis et otii exinanitus, 'speciosa deserti'[9] dinumerare et claustralem disciplinam possum funiculo[10] prophetico dimetiri? Non potuit Iosue filiis Israhel terram promissionis sorte diuidere donec terra quieuit a preliis.[11] Vtinam ueniret Sabbatum delicatum,[12] utinam pax requiesceret in cubili nostro, utinam iubileus annus celebraretur ut sic rediret cor ad possessionem suam et seruus peccati, corpus mortale, ad libertatem suam.[13] Interim tamen claustralis disciplina non atramento sed exercitio compingatur quia is qui sub lege est non Moysi sed Augustini aut beati Benedicti, si precepta seruauerit, premia habebit. Compendiose et succincte claustralem disciplinam uno illo uerbo complector quo Pharao usus est ad Ioseph: 'Ego', inquit, 'sum Pharao, absque tuo imperio non mouebit quisquam manum aut pedem in omni terra Egypti.'[14] Sanctissima et equissima disciplina in claustro ut nichil agatur, nichil dicatur, nichil habeatur nisi cum abbatis licentia, ut nec oculus egrediatur constituta nec manus moueatur ad illicita nec pes currat ad prohibita. His neruis corpus religionis compactum immobile stat; fundamentum habemus preter quod nulla firma est religio.

[a] Vexatus *Sirmond*

---

[6] Cf. Exod. 1: 14; Judith 5: 10, i.e. the hard works with which the Israelites were oppressed in Egypt; also Eph. 6: 12.

[7] References to the process of making bricks, continuing the image of oppression: cf. Exod. 5: 7–19.

[8] i.e. like Pharaoh, cf. Exod. 5:1; cf. also Exod. 4: 21; 7: 3, and the plagues (*plagas*) of Exod. 7–12.

[9] Ps. 64 (65): 13; the phrase occurs in Joel 1: 19–20 in a different context (cf. pp. 280, 406).

me not only to think about claustral discipline but also to write about it. You know me to be prompt and compliant in every manner of obedience, yet chained and occupied by a wearisome burden to which by a new inundation the gravest sickness of the kidneys has been annexed and added. Do not believe that the most pressing exaction of the prince of this darkness has diminished in any way the usual weight of 'clay and brick'.[6] He gathers together every day a heap of wood and adds straw in the form of business affairs and dry stubble in the form of trifles and vain distractions.[7] Troubled finally by various plagues of prayers, psalms, holy meditations, and almsgiving, his heart is hardened more and more, refusing permission to go out into the desert and to offer the sacrifice of justice and innocence to God.[8] And so how can I, detained in iron manacles and exhausted beyond measure by a famine of reading and study, count 'the beautiful places of the wilderness'[9] and measure out claustral discipline with a prophetic measuring line?[10] Joshua could not divide up the promised land by lot among the children of Israel until the land was at peace from battles.[11] If only the delightful Sabbath would come,[12] if only peace would repose in our chamber, if only the jubilee year were to be celebrated, so that in this way the heart might return to its possession and the slave of sin, the mortal body, to its freedom.[13] Meanwhile, however, let claustral discipline be composed not with ink but with exercise, because he who is under the law not of Moses but of Augustine, or of the blessed Benedict, if he keeps the precepts will gain the prizes. I sum up claustral discipline briefly and succinctly in that single speech which Pharaoh used to Joseph: 'I', he said, 'am Pharaoh; without thy commandment no man shall move hand or foot in all the land of Egypt.'[14] The holiest and most equal discipline in the cloister is that nothing be done, nothing be said, nothing be had, except with the abbot's permission, so that the eye should neither go beyond the limits ordained, nor the hand be moved to unlawful things, nor the foot run to things forbidden. The body of the religious life, made firm by these sinews, stands unmoving; we have a foundation without which there is no firm religious life.

[10] Cf. Ps. 77 (78): 54, recalling Joshua (and see below).

[11] Cf. Josh. 1: 6; 11: 23; 13 ff.; 23: 4.

[12] Cf. Isa. 58: 13, '. . . et uocaueris sabbatum delicatum . . .'.

[13] Cf. Lev. 25 on the jubilee year and the freeing of slaves; also v. 10: 'reuertetur homo ad possessionem suam' (cf. v. 13).

[14] Gen. 41: 44. The final passage recalls *Regula S. Benedicti* c. vii.

167

To Richard of Salisbury[1]

early 1171 (or 1172, before May) × 1181

Amico suo karissimo R⟨ichardo⟩[a] canonico Petrus abbas Sancti Remigii.

Vnum quaternum iam impleueram de disciplina claustri et mittere per presentium latorem plurimum festinabam, sed dissuasum est ab amicis ne opus imperfectum amico mitterem, propter rapaces curiosorum manus et oculos. Nam si uiderent, aut abicerent aut retinerent. Si abicerent, forte conculcarent. Si conculcarent, nullum delectum habentes inter utile et inutile, peccarent. Si retinerent, aut legerent aut scriberent aut negligerent. Si legerent aut scriberent, scabrosam forte lectionem et minus compositam offendentes, imperitie et presumptioni non festinationi imputarent, quatinus michi merito illud prouerbium ascribatur quo dicitur, 'Onos lyras', id est 'asinus ad lyram';[2] aut rescriberent et nostra uitia perpetuarent. Si negligerent, quantum ad illos in uanum laborassem et perisset opera et impensa. Quicunque igitur fidelis nuntius post paucissimos dies occurrerit, casibus fortuitis me committens mittam que ad petitionem tuam de disciplina claustri scripsi. Valete.

167 *Sirmond VIII. 6*]
[a] B. *Sirmond*

167

To Richard of Salisbury[1]

early 1171 (or 1172, before May) × 1181

To his dearest friend Richard, canon, Peter, abbot of Saint-Remi.

I had already filled a quire on claustral discipline and was in an exceeding hurry to send it to you by the bearer of this present letter, but I was advised by friends not to send an imperfect work to a friend on account of the grasping hands and eyes of the curious. For if they were to see it, they would either cast it aside or keep it. If they were to cast it aside, perhaps they would tread it underfoot. If they were to tread it underfoot, having no discrimination between the useful and the useless, they would commit a sin. If they were to keep it, they would either read or copy or ignore it. If they were to read it or copy it, perhaps hitting upon a rough reading and one less polished, they would impute this to lack of skill and presumption, not to haste, so that that proverb would deservedly be applied to me which goes, 'Onos lyras', that is, 'an ass at the lyre';[2] or they would copy it again and perpetuate our faults. If they were to ignore it, as far as they are concerned I should have laboured in vain and the work and the outlay have perished. Therefore whichever faithful messenger appears in the next few days, committing myself to the accidents of chance, I shall send what I have written at your petition on claustral discipline. Farewell.

167 [1] Dated as letter no. 164. See also letter no. 166, n. 1, on the references to Peter's *De disciplina claustrali.* (In the present letter he refers to writing on 'disciplina claustri', but the same work must be indicated.)

[2] Cf. Boethius, *De cons. philos.* i. prose iv. 1. (*CCSL* xciv. 6).

168

To Richard of Salisbury[1]

early 1171 (or 1172, before May) × 1181

Petrus abbas Sancti Remigii R⟨ichardo⟩ canonico de Meritonia.

Simul mouetur[a] et manus ad tibi scribendum et nuntius ad iter arripiendum. Non sum immemor antique nostre consuetudinis qua[b] inuicem solebamus quamlibet informes conceptus nostrarum meditationum communicare. Ego ut senex sensu exinanitus, etate fessus, occupatione irretitus, iam parere fetus idoneos ad legendum deficio. Consulens autem naturali erubescentie mee potius abortiuos meos infra latebras suas sepelio quam extra cum pudore profero. Qui enim ramus fronde et fructu formosus de ueternoso et emortuo trunco pullulabit? Fons aridus et cisterna dissipata quas irrigabit areolas cum nec gutta supersit ad proprias consolandas uenas? Vetus itaque homo qui corrumpitur nouitate spiritus renouandus esset nisi et ipse spiritus sua negligentia inueteratus iuxta Apostolum prope interitum esset.[2] Altera istorum uetustas apparet, altera latet. Periculosior autem est latens quam apparens, nullum enim periculum est cubile uitiorum, corpus animale, hospitium de impossibilitate peccati[c] exhibere. Optimum equidem est non peccare, immo[d] nolle, sed et bonum est non posse. Fomes siquidem peccati utitur etate iuuenili uelut fornace in qua tres pueri a rege Babilonio mittuntur,[3] et membra puerilia, tanquam ligna flammis apta, obstinatissime succenduntur. Cum uero senectus euiscerauerit medullas corporis et omnino debilitauerit legem membrorum que repugnat legi mentis,[4] conquiescunt strepitus uitiorum et, quia non habent ubi caput reclinent,[5] exeunt et deserta circumeunt.[6] Potius ergo letandum quam dolendum de ista oppressione que magis operatur uitam quam mortem,

168 *Sirmond IX. 4*]
[a] *corr. Hall;* mouentur *Sirmond* [b] *corr. Hall;* quia *Sirmond* [c] *corr. Hall;* peccatis non *Sirmond* [d] *corr. Hall;* immo et *Sirmond*

168 [1] Dated as letter no. 164. On the references to building work at Saint-Remi, see appendix 12.

[2] Cf. Heb. 8: 13 on the Old and New Testaments, 'dicendo autem nouum ueterauit prius quod autem antiquatur, et senescit prope interitum est'. In what follows Peter contrasts the manifest and harmless, even beneficial, aspect of old age—inability to commit

168

To Richard of Salisbury[1]

early 1171 (or 1172, before May) × 1181

Peter, abbot of Saint-Remi, to Richard, canon of Merton.

At the same time both my hand is moved to write to you and the messenger to hasten on his journey. I am not forgetful of our old custom whereby we were in the habit of sharing with each other the conceptions of our meditations, however unformed. As an old man devoid of sense, worn out with age, ensnared by affairs, I am already failing to bring forth offspring suitable for reading. But deferring to my natural modesty I prefer to bury my abortions within their hiding places than to bring them out with shame. For what branch beautiful with leaf and fruit will sprout forth from an old dead trunk? What gardens will a dry fountain and a drained cistern irrigate when not even a drop remains to refresh its own channels? And so the old man who is broken down would need to be renewed with freshness of the spirit had the spirit itself hardened by its own negligence not also been near to its end, according to the Apostle.[2] One facet of old age in these things is manifest, the other lies hidden. The hidden, however, is more dangerous than the manifest, for on account of the impossibility of committing any sin there is no danger of offering the bed of vices, the living body, as a lodging. It is best indeed not to sin, nay to be unwilling to, but it is also good not to be able to. Indeed the kindling of sin takes advantage of youthful age, like the furnace in which the three boys are put by the king of Babylon,[3] and youthful members, like wood fit for the flames, are set on fire most relentlessly. But when old age has disembowelled the marrows of the body and utterly weakened the law of the members which fights against the law of the mind,[4] the dins of vices are quiet and because they have not where to lay their head[5] they go out and walk about in the desert.[6] One should then rather be gladdened than grieved by this oppression

sins on account of bodily infirmity—with the hidden and dangerous side, spiritual negligence.

[3] Cf. Dan. 3 (who were not burnt).

[4] Cf. Rom. 7: 23.

[5] Cf. Matt. 8: 20; Luke 9: 58.

[6] Cf. Matt. 12: 43; Luke 11: 24.

remedium quam excidium. Hec est apparens et parum nocens uetustas. Latens uero, quia nescitur, minime aut tarde curatur. Vnde Ysaias: 'Vulnus et liuor et plaga tumens non est circumligata, nec curata medicamine, neque fota oleo.'[7] Quis enim medicinam morbo porrigeret quem nec oculus nec manus attingeret? Solus itaque Dei spiritus qui 'omnia scrutatur'[8] spiritum nostrum curat, uiuificat et renouat. In medio istarum uetustatum positus, spiritalem timeo, corporalem iam sperno. In fundo uite mee, ubi sera parsimonia est,[9] de reliquiis prime preuaricationis iamiam feces limosas exhaurio, et lutum uespere indurandum et arescendum presentio. Iesum tamen non minus sapientissimum quam benignissimum figulum expecto qui de uase fictili usque ad minutissimum puluerem effracto potest aliud in resurrectione uas facere in honorem,[10] ut sit clementior, ne dicam cautior, aut potentior in reficiendo quam in faciendo, ut sit maior gloria secunde domus quam prime, et Adam qui primus factus est in animam uiuentem denuo fiat in spiritum uiuificantem.[11] Hec spes in sinu meo reposita excitat uota mea mortem non timere sed amare, non fugere sed patienter expectare. Interim neque dormitare neque dormire uolo, sed iuxta Sapientis consilium quecunque possum instanter operari.[12] Hinc est quod nobilem ecclesiam nostram tam in fronte quam in uentre, cui caput secundum se deerat, fabricandam suscepimus et, ut speramus, cum Dei adiutorio perficiemus.[13]

[7] Isa. 1: 6.

[8] Cf. 1 Cor. 2: 10.

[9] Cf. Seneca, *Ad Lucil. ep. mor.* i. 5: 'sera parsimonia in fundo est', i.e. he is trying too late to salvage some spiritual capital.

[10] Cf. Rom. 9: 21; 2 Tim. 2: 20.

which brings about life more than death, a remedy more than ruination. This is the manifest and harmless facet of old age. But the hidden facet, because it is unknown, is attended to least of all or too late. Whence Isaiah: 'Wounds and bruises and swelling sores, they are not bound up, nor dressed, nor fomented with oil.'[7] For who would proffer medicine for a disease which neither eye nor hand could light upon? And so the spirit of God alone, who 'searcheth all things,'[8] cures, restores, and renews our spirit. Set between these facets of old age, I fear the spiritual and now scorn the bodily. At the bottom of the barrel of my life, where frugality comes too late,[9] I am already emptying out the filthy dregs from the remains of early transgression, and I have a presentiment that the clay will become hard and dry in the evening. Yet I await Jesus, no less the wisest than the kindest potter, who can make from a clay vessel ground even to the finest dust another vessel in resurrection, unto honour,[10] so that He is more merciful, not to say provident, or more powerful in the remaking than in the making, so that the glory of the second house is greater than that of the first, and Adam who first was made into a living soul is made again into a quickening spirit.[11] This hope laid up in my bosom rouses my will not to fear death but to love it, not to flee but patiently to await it. Meanwhile I wish neither to slumber nor to sleep but according to the counsel of the wise man to labour urgently at whatever I can.[12] Hence it is that we have undertaken the construction of our noble church, both its façade and its body which was lacking a chevet in a fitting style, and, so we hope, with God's help we will finish it.[13]

[11] Cf. 1 Cor. 15: 45; Gen. 2: 7; what follows echoes Job 19: 27.

[12] Cf. Matt. 25: 5; Eccles. 9: 10.

[13] Prache suggests that *frons* here refers to the façade, and both *uenter* and *caput* to the chevet, refuting Demaison's suggestion that *uenter* refers to the nave, a part of the building to which Peter is not known to have contributed: see appendix 12.

169

To John of Salisbury[1]

? late 1163 × Nov. 1164

Karissimo amico suo et magistro Iohanni de Saresberia P⟨etrus⟩ suus amicus et discipulus, cum Iesu et in Iesu semper in terra et in celo.

Nouit prudentia tua quod 'granum frumenti cadens in terram nisi mortuum fuerit, ipsum solum manet, si autem mortuum fuerit, multum fructum affert'.[2] Granuli nostri fructum centesimum[3] spero me recepturum, partim roris superni fecunda infusione, partim agri quem benedixit Dominus leta fecunditate. Prouenit namque numerosa proles benedictionum ex accessu dati optimi siue doni perfecti[4] cum libero arbitrio boni hominis. Vbi enim gratia saliendo cum impetu eterne emanationis influit, quid anima nisi uita[a] refluit? Nunquam sterile, nunquam inane est coniugium gratie et anime. Iesus qui saluat populum suum a peccatis eorum fructus benedictus est huius copule. Vbera non habet arentia, non uuluam sine liberis,[5] anima cui adiungitur gratia. Parturit anima quidem sed non gemens, generat gratia sed non corrumpens. Suscipit semen anima cum delectatione sed non delicto; parit fetum de spiritu gratie sed cum salute; uenter non superbia turgescit sed crescit humilitate; lumbi non opprimuntur grauedine sed imprimuntur castitate; mamme non intumescunt lactis recursu sed extumescunt humane fragilitatis decursu. Manus angelice obstetricantur in tam salubri partu; pannis uirtutum inuoluitur fetus donec rapiatur ad Deum et ad thronum eius. Mater autem quid? 'Fugit in solitudinem ubi habet locum paratum a Deo ut ibi pascant illam diebus mille ducentis sexaginta.'[6] Draco namque stat ante

169 *Sirmond IV. 12*]
[a] *corr. Hall;* uitam *Sirmond*

---

169 [1] On letters 169–78 see also appendix 8. The references to a threat to the church (presumably meaning the Becket affair), and the possible implication that John of Salisbury is coming to Saint-Remi, suggest that this may have been written just before or just after the beginning of John's exile. The date of John's move into exile is uncertain; Brooke suggests departure from England between Oct. 1163 and Jan. 1164 (see *J. S. Epp.* ii, pp. xxii–xxiii). John made his way to Paris via a number of other places (see his letter no. 136, *J. S. Epp.* ii. 2–15) and was settled at Reims before Nov. 1164. The present letter does not make it clear whether John was in England contemplating travel or already in Paris (Peter did correspond with John when John was in Paris—see letter no. 170, to which

169

To John of Salisbury[1]

? late 1163 × Nov. 1164

To his dearest friend and master John of Salisbury, Peter, his friend and disciple, always with Jesus and in Jesus on earth and in heaven.

You in your wisdom know that 'unless the grain of wheat falling into the ground die, itself remaineth alone, but if it die, it bringeth forth much fruit'.[2] I hope that I will receive back the hundredfold fruit of our little seed,[3] partly through a fruitful watering of celestial dew, partly through the joyous fecundity of the field which the Lord has blessed. For a numerous progeny of blessings arises from the accession of the best gift, the perfect gift,[4] with the free will of a good man. For where grace flows in by springing with the force of the eternal emanation, what does the soul do except overflow with life? The marriage of grace and the soul is never sterile, never empty. Jesus who saves His people from their sins is the blessed fruit of this union. The soul to which grace is adjoined has not dry breasts nor a womb without children.[5] The soul indeed strives in labour but without groaning, grace engenders but without corrupting. The soul receives the seed with delight but without fault; it brings forth offspring by the spirit of grace but with salvation; the belly does not swell with pride but grows in humility; the loins are not oppressed with heaviness but impressed with chastity; the breasts do not swell with the replenishment of the milk but swell out with the ebbing of human frailty. Angelic hands act the midwife at so healthy a birth; the baby is wrapped in swaddling clothes of virtues until He be taken up to God and His throne. But what of the mother? She 'fled into the wilderness, where she has a place prepared by God, that there they should feed her a thousand two hundred sixty days'.[6] For the dragon stands

this letter may be a companion). Indeed, so much is uncertain here that the letter may belong to a later period altogether. It may also belong to an earlier period: the letter is from Rc, but then so is letter no. 170, which is more clearly from 1164, and so is more securely included among the later letters in this edn. (see Introduction, p. xxxv).

[2] John 12: 24–5, which continues: 'Qui amat animam suam perdet eam et qui odit animam suam in hoc mundo in uitam aeternam custodit eam.'

[3] Cf. Matt. 13: 8, 23; Mark 4: 8, 20; Luke 8: 8.

[4] Cf. Jas. 1: 17.

[5] Cf. Hos. 9: 14.

[6] Rev. 12: 6.

mulierem que est paritura ut deuoret, cum pepererit, filium eius.[7] Non est occultatum a te, magister et amice karissime, qui astutias serpentis antiqui non ignoras, quid esuriat draco, quid sitiat. Quid nisi Filium Virginis? Quid nisi desiderium cordis? Quid nisi prolem uirtutis? Quamobrem rapiatur non tantum a faucibus sed ab aspectibus eius mentis propositum et tota festinatione non delibatum[b] sed illibatum mittatur ad Deum. Certe nisi subuenerit uel preuenerit festinatio in ore draconis, fiet anima nostra delibatio eius.[8] Quam cito autem mater petiuerit[c] deserti solitudinem tam cito Filius conscendet celi celsitudinem. Quo remotius secesserit mater eo altius et remotius rapiet[d] Filium Pater. Nisi fugerit mater, proprii nati uisceribus uiscera draconis implebit. Non est timendum uenire ubi desinis timere.[9] Nil timet, nil odit, nil refugit sic diabolus quomodo solitudinem claustri. Potius deligit porcorum gregem[10] quam sanctorum solitudinem. Sponsus ducit sponsam suam in solitudinem et ibi loquitur ad cor eius.[11] Ysaac 'egressus erat ad meditandum in agro',[12] cum ecce sponsa eius Rebecca 'ascensis camelis'[13] calcando uitia superbie et immunditie sue ueniebat. In solitudine Iesus temptatus 'super aspidem et basiliscum' ambulat et conculcat 'leonem et draconem'.[14] Meritorium animarum est solitudo, castra Domini exercituum est solitudo, sagena ad capiendos pisces est solitudo,[15] paradisus deliciarum est solitudo, gymnasium celestis philosophie est solitudo. Quid amplius? Deambulatorium Dei est solitudo. Solitudo nouit uigilias Iesu; solitudo suscipit lacrimas Iesu; solitudo orationes Iesu audit;[16] solitudo tempus et horam nostre redemptionis cognouit; solitudo nascentem, solitudo predicantem, solitudo turbas pascentem, solitudo in transfiguratione coruscantem faciem Iesu sole clarius attendit; solitudo morientem, solitudo resurgentem, solitudo ascendentem Dominum conspexit. Ecce quare exultant solitudines Iordanis.[17] Si qua asperitas, si qua amaritudo, si qua prius fuerat in solitudine formido, mitigata est sanguinis Iesu effusione, dulcorata est ligni crucis immissione, sublata est Iesu cohabitatione. Socio Iesu quid times? Pascente Iesu quid esuris? Lauante et unguente Iesu quid doloris persentis? Vale.

[b] deliberatum *Sirmond* [c] petit *Sirmond* [d] *corr. Hall;* rapit *Sirmond*

[7] Cf. Rev. 12: 4.
[8] *delibatio*: 'first-fruit', cf. Rom. 11: 16.
[9] Presumably to Saint-Remi; see n. 1.
[10] Cf. Luke 8: 32–3.
[11] Cf. Hos. 2: 14.
[12] Cf. Gen. 24: 63.
[13] Gen. 24: 61 (plural because it refers to Rebecca and her maids).

before the woman who is ready to be delivered so that when she is delivered he might devour her son.[7] It is not hidden from you, master and dearest friend, who are not ignorant of the subtle devices of the ancient serpent, what the dragon hungers and thirsts for. What if not the Son of the Virgin? What if not the desire of the heart? What if not the progeny of virtue? Therefore let the object of his purpose be snatched not only from his jaws but from his sight and be sent to God with all haste, not diminished but unharmed. Certainly, unless haste brings assistance or anticipates the dragon's mouth, our soul will become his first-fruit.[8] But the Son will ascend the height of heaven as quickly as the mother seeks the solitude of the desert. The further the mother withdraws, so much the higher and further will the Father raise up the Son. Unless the mother flees she will fill the inwards of the dragon with the inwards of her own child. You should not fear to come where you cease to fear.[9] The devil fears nothing, hates nothing, flees from nothing so much as the solitude of the cloister. He chooses the herd of swine[10] rather than the solitude of the saints. The bridegroom leads his bride to solitude and there speaks to her heart.[11] Isaac had 'gone forth to meditate in the field'[12] when behold his bride Rebecca was coming, 'being set upon camels,'[13] treading under foot the vices of her pride and impurity. In solitude Jesus when tempted walks 'upon the asp and the basilisk' and tramples under foot 'the lion and the dragon'.[14] The place where souls earn merit is solitude, the camp of the armies of the Lord is solitude, the net for catching fish is solitude,[15] the paradise of delights is solitude, the school of celestial philosophy is solitude. What more? The ambulatory of God is solitude. Solitude knows the vigils of Jesus, solitude receives the tears of Jesus, solitude hears the prayers of Jesus,[16] solitude knows the time and hour of our redemption, solitude attends the face of Jesus being born, preaching, feeding the crowds, shining more brightly than the sun in the transfiguration; solitude saw the Lord dying, rising again, ascending. See why the solitudes of Jordan rejoice.[17] If any harshness, any bitterness, or any fear had been there before in the solitude it was softened by the outpouring of the blood of Jesus, sweetened by the engrafting of the wood of the cross, destroyed by Jesus' cohabitation. With Jesus as companion, what do you fear? With Jesus feeding you, what do you hunger for? With Jesus washing and anointing you, what pain do you feel? Farewell.

[14] Cf. Ps. 90 (91): 13.
[15] Cf. Matt. 13: 47.
[16] i.e. Christ in the garden of Gethsemane.
[17] Cf. Isa. 35: 1.

170

To John of Salisbury[1]

1164, before Nov.

Suo clerico suus abbas.

Satis amenum delegisti, mi karissime, exilium, ubi superhabundant gaudia licet uana, ubi exuberat plus quam in patria panis et uini copia, ubi amicorum frequens affluentia, ubi sociorum non rara contubernia. Quis preter te alius sub celo Parisius non estimauit locum deliciarum, 'hortum plantationum',[2] agrum primitiarum?[3] Ridendo tamen uerum dixisti,[4] quia ubi maior et amplior uoluptas corporum, ibi uerum exilium animarum, et ubi regnat luxuria, ibi miserabiliter ancillatur et affligitur anima. O Parisius, quam idonea es ad capiendas et decipiendas animas! In te retiacula uitiorum, in te malorum decipula, in te sagitta inferni transfigit insipientium corda. Ita Iohannes meus sentit et ideo exilium nominauit. Vtinam scolam[a] istam [b]sicut est exilium uere[b] deputares et ad patriam non uerbo et lingua sed opere et ueritate festinares.[5] Ibi in libro uite[6] non figuras et elementa sed ipsam sicut est diuinitatem et ueritatem oculo ad oculum cerneres, sine labore legendi, sine fastidio uidendi, sine fallacia uel errore intelligendi, sine sollicitudine retinendi, sine timore obliuiscendi. O beata scola, ubi Christus docet corda nostra uerbo uirtutis sue, ubi sine [c]studio et[c] lectione apprehendimus quomodo debeamus eternaliter beate[d] uiuere. Non emitur ibi liber, non redimitur magister

170 *O fo. 106^{r-v}, Sirmond IV. 10*]
[a] *interlinear addn. O; om. Sirmond* [b-b] exilium uere sicut est *Sirmond* [c-c] *om. O* [d] bene *O*

170 [1] The letter refers to John of Salisbury's exile in Paris, in the early stages of the Becket affair. On John's movements, which are uncertain, between his departure from England and arrival at Reims, see letter no. 169, n. 1 and *J. S. Epp.* ii, pp. xxii–xxiii. He was in Paris when he wrote his letter no. 136 (early 1164; *J. S. Epp.* ii. 2–15). While it is conceivable that he reached Paris in late 1163, it is not certain that he left England before Jan. 1164, and he travelled to a number of other places *en route*, as his letter no. 136 describes. Further, Peter's ironic reference to the sweetness of exile in a place like Paris may echo John's letter no. 136 to Becket (early 1164), describing his arrival in Paris, where John quotes Ovid, 'Felix exilium, cui locus iste datur,' (*J. S. Epp.* ii. 6–7; Ovid, *Fasti*, i. 540).

It is possible that this is a preamble to letter no. 169, and may pre-date it, as the present letter is apparently an invitation to Saint-Remi (or at least to leave Paris for the cloister; see

170

To John of Salisbury[1]

1164 before Nov.

To his clerk, his abbot.

You have chosen, my dearest one, a delightful enough exile where pleasures, albeit vain ones, abound in excess, where there is a wealth of bread and wine more plentiful than in your homeland, where there is a constant stream of friends, where the companionship of fellows is no rare thing. Who else under the sky besides you did not reckon Paris to be a place of delights, a 'garden of plants',[2] a field of first-fruits?[3] You however have spoken the truth in jest,[4] because where there is greater and fuller pleasure for bodies, there is the true exile of souls, and where luxury reigns, there the soul is wretchedly enslaved and afflicted. O Paris, how meet you are for seizing and deceiving souls! In you there are nets of vices, in you the snare of evils, in you the arrow of hell transfixes the hearts of the foolish. My John feels it to be so, and so has called it exile. If only you truly regarded this school as it is, as exile, and hastened to your homeland not in word and speech but in deed and truth.[5] There in the book of life[6] you would discern not characters and letters but divinity and truth itself as it is, eye to eye, without the toil of reading, without the tediousness of seeing, without falsehood or error of understanding, without worry about retaining, without fear of forgetting. O blessed school, where Christ instructs our hearts with the word of His virtue, where without study and reading we apprehend how we ought to live happily in eternity. There no book is bought, no master of scribes is employed;

n. 5 below), and letter no. 169 specifically describes the attractions of the cloister, but the references and allusions here are not amenable to precise dating, and as it does not mention Paris, an earlier *terminus a quo* for letter no. 169 remains possible.

[2] Cf. Ecclus. 24: 42.

[3] Cf. 2 Kgs. (2 Sam.) 1: 21; 1 John 3: 18.

[4] Cf. Horace, *Sat.* i. 1. 24.

[5] *patria*, from what follows, evidently means heaven. By wishing John to rush to it Peter is presumably not wishing for his death, but rather urging him to come to the monastery (i.e. given the context, to settle at Saint-Remi while in exile; there is nowhere in the letters any discussion of John contemplating becoming a monk). Presumably the point is that being in the cloister constitutes actively hastening towards heaven, preparing one's soul, which is not the case in Paris, but the shift in sense is rather abrupt and there may be a lost passage.

[6] Cf. Rev. 20: 12.

scriptorum; nulla circumuentio disputationum, nulla sophismatum intricatio; plana omnium questionum determinatio, plena uniuersarum rationum et argumentationum apprehensio.[e] Ibi plus uita confert quam lectio, plus prodest simplicitas quam cauillatio. Ibi nemo concluditur nisi qui excluditur. Vno uerbo omnis ibi soluitur obiectio cum male malam uitam obicienti respondetur, 'Ite, maledicti, in ignem eternum qui paratus est diabolo et angelis eius',[7] cum bene opponenti dicitur, 'Venite, benedicti', etc.[8] Vtinam his melioribus studiis sic intenderent filii hominum quomodo uaniloquiis, quomodo scurrilitatibus uanis et pessimis. Certe fructus exinde uberiores, certe fauores excellentiores, certe honores maiores meterent, et finem ⟨omnis⟩ consummationis,[9] [f]id est[f] Christum, quem in his inuenturi non sunt, sine dubio perciperent. Valete.[g]

171

To John of Salisbury and his brother Richard[1]

early 1171 (poss. after Apr.)

Amicis suis karissimis magistro Iohanni et Richardo fratri suo frater Petrus Sancti Remigii dictus abbas, perpetua pace gaudere.

Stilum scribendi in sepulcro beati martyris Thome Cantuariensis audita eius morte iamiam recluseram arbitrans karissimos meos Iohannem et Richardum ei consepultos nec iterum[a] aura libertatis

[e] conprehensio *O* [f-f] *om. Sirmond* [g] *om. O*

171 *Sirmond V. 14*]
[a] *corr. Hall;* interim *Sirmond*

[7] Cf. Matt. 25: 41.

[8] Cf. Matt. 25: 34: 'Venite benedicti Patris mei, possidete paratum uobis regnum a constitutione mundi' (i.e. the final judgement).

[9] Cf. Ps. 118 (119): 96.

171 [1] This letter is evidently a reply to John of Salisbury's letter no. 305 (*J. S. Epp.* ii. 724–39, early 1171, addressed to John of Canterbury, bishop of Poitiers, but evidently sent to multiple recipients), asking whether Becket should be revered as a martyr before the official canonization (for John's request, see *J. S. Epp.* ii. 736–9; on the canonization, 21 Feb. 1173, see Barlow, *Thomas Becket*, p. 269). John's letter no. 305 was also clearly the source of Peter's news, to which he refers here, that John and Richard were alive (the last direct contact for which there is evidence being John's letter no. 304 to Peter, shortly before the murder of

there is no circumvention of disputations, no entanglement of sophistries; there is a clear conclusion of all questions, a complete understanding of universal reasons and proofs. There life confers more than reading, simplicity is more profitable than sophistry. There no one is shut in except he who is shut out. There, with one word, every objection is removed when to the one wickedly presenting a wicked life the reply is made, 'Go, you cursed, into everlasting fire which was prepared for the devil and his angels';[7] when it is said to the one rightly standing opposite, 'Come, ye blessed,' etc.[8] If only the sons of men would give their attention to these better studies as they do to idle prattle and to vain and base frivolities. From this they would reap certainly more bountiful fruits, certainly more excellent favours, certainly greater honours, and without doubt they would receive the end of all perfection,[9] that is Christ, whom they will not find in these things. Farewell.

171

To John of Salisbury and his brother Richard[1]

early 1171 (poss. after Apr.)

To his dearest friends master John and Richard his brother, brother Peter, called abbot of Saint-Remi, to rejoice in peace everlasting.

I had already locked away the writing pen in the tomb of the blessed martyr Thomas of Canterbury, having heard of his death, reckoning that my dearest John and Richard were buried along with

Becket; *J. S. Epp.* ii. 714–25, Dec. 1170). Barlow, 'John of Salisbury', p. 104, n. 57, suggests a date after Apr. for the present letter, when miracles at Becket's tomb (mentioned in John's letter no. 305) became more commonly reported (see also Barlow, *Thomas Becket*, pp. 264–6 on early miracles at Canterbury). The passage directed to Richard indicates that he had not yet become a canon of Merton. Sirmond interpreted the words to mean that he had (see Sirmond's note, reprinted in *PL* ccii. 569, n. 32), but as Barlow pointed out (Barlow, 'John of Salisbury', pp. 104–5), this does not fit with the tone of the rest of the passage, which laments Richard's escape from the cloister (and for Peter the cloister includes canons; see Haseldine, 'Friendship and rivalry', p. 397; Barlow 'John of Salisbury', p. 105). By the time of the writing of Peter's letter no. 175 Richard evidently was in a cloister. Barlow, 'John of Salisbury', p. 104, concludes that he was at Merton by spring 1172, on the evidence of Peter's letters 171 and 175: thus from these letters, his entry must have been some time between early 1171 and May 1172 at the very latest. Barlow also suggests that Richard may have moved to Merton already when Peter's letter no. 174 was written, because it seems to assume that he is not with John of Salisbury. If so, this might bring the latest date for Richard's conversion forward tentatively to Dec. 1171. However, on John's possible presence at Merton, see Duggan, *Textual History*, pp. 74, 97, 145.

fruituros. Fallax namque rumor et nimium uarius nil nobis de uobis certi afferebat uel asserebat, unde, quod in dubiis semper faciendum censeo, lucem ueritatis patienter sed non gratanter expectabam ne in incertum currerem falsum pro uero retinens, gaudens forsitan cum esset merendum et merens cum esset gaudendum. Resumebam tamen post longam ad me ipsum disputationem, de incommutabili diuinitatis consilio, spiritum et quicquid uobis contigisset post glorificationem sancti martyris in partem uertebam meliorem quia siue contribularemini siue consolaremini[2] in argumentum et augmentum fidei uestre accipiendum non dubitabam. Neque enim tam modice fidei[3] scio uos esse ut timetis calicem Domini bibere in passione quem frequenter bibitis in Christi recordatione.[4] Tandem ex ueraci relatione status uestri, omni absoluta compage omnipotenti et benignissimo Deo medullatas refero grates qui non aufert a uobis solitas suas miserationes sed, ut credo, quia premisistis dilectissimum patronum in celis recipietis sine dubio alium paraclitum uice eius in terris.[5] Ecce, mi dulcissime Richarde, proruo in osculis faciei tue, non sine affectu uiscerali, attendens mutatum habitum, nescio si melioratum animum. Quid enim honestatis, quid maturitatis, quid pietatis, quid caritatis, quid totius religionis deerat cum esses in oculis meis et nostre congregationis speculum bonitatis et forma integra emulande imitationis?[6] Nusquam fuisset illa prepropera sollicitudo regressionis; potuisset tibi sufficere domicilium amice paupertatis et satis care si recolis societatis. Sed o ceca et futurorum nescia mens humana, extra uel ultra diuine moderationis gressum ne porrigas pedem quia labi est a Deo non regi et per se ire perire est. Si nobiscum mansisses solatio contra pene omnem molestiam fuisses, nec a Deo desertum crederem dum huiusmodi pignus sue miserationis mecum tenerem. Sed factum est quod factum est. Sit stimulus maioris desiderii molesta corporis absentia et ubi nulla subest corporalis uisio continuetur oratio. Ne diutius scribam, familiares succedunt interruptiones que animi quietem interrumpere non cessant et laborem perpetuare. De statu autem nostro utrumque amicum certifico, ac de corporali sospitate

[2] i.e. alive or dead.
[3] Cf. Matt. 6: 30; 8: 26; 14: 31; 16: 8.
[4] Cf. Luke 22: 19.
[5] Cf. John 14: 16, on the following passage see above n. 1.
[6] i.e presumably his life was a model of the *imitatio Christi*.

him and were not to enjoy again the air of liberty. For deceitful and excessively diverse rumour was neither bringing to us nor announcing any certain news of you, for which reason, as I think one should always do when in doubt, I was waiting patiently but not joyfully for the light of truth so that I might not run into uncertainty holding false for true, rejoicing perhaps when I ought to have been grieving and grieving when I ought to have been rejoicing. I was however recovering my spirit after a long argument with myself, thanks to the immutable counsel of the divinity, and I was putting whatever might have befallen you after the glorification of the holy martyr in the best light because, whether you were with him in tribulation or consolation,[2] I was in no doubt that this was to be accepted as a demonstration and augmentation of your faith. For I know that you are not of so little faith[3] that you fear to drink in martyrdom the cup of the Lord which you drink frequently in remembrance of Christ.[4] At last, on the basis of a true report of your condition, with every bond loosed, I am offering up heartfelt thanks to the omnipotent and most benign God who does not withdraw His accustomed compassion from you; rather as I believe, because you have sent your dearest patron before you to the heavens, you will without doubt receive another Paraclete in his place on earth.[5] See, my sweetest Richard, I rush forward to kiss your face, not without a stirring of the inwards, contemplating a changed habit, although I do not know about an improved soul. For what was lacking of honour, of maturity, of devotion, of love, of every aspect of the religious life when you were, before my eyes and those of our community, a mirror of goodness and a perfect model of an imitation to be emulated?[6] That anxiety to return would at no point have been over-eager; the dwelling of friendly poverty and of a society dear enough, if you recall, would have sufficed for you. But, o human mind blind and ignorant of the future, do not set your foot outside or beyond the course of divine instruction because not to be ruled by God is to fall and to pursue your own path is to perish. Had you remained with us you would have been a solace in the face of almost every vexation and I would not believe myself deserted by God so long as I kept with me this sort of pledge of His mercy. But what is done is done. Let the grievous absence of the body be a stimulus to greater desire and, where there is no sight of the body close at hand, let prayer be continued. Household interruptions, which never cease to disturb the peace of the soul and to perpetuate toil, are mounting up so that I cannot write any longer.

dico quod qualem dimistis talem adhuc inuenire potestis. Pax in congregatione nostra est et cursu consuetudinario adhuc currimus. Cum omnibus hominibus pacem habemus, maxime cum domino archiepiscopo.[7] Debitis non ualde grauamur. De Marna reditus nostros habemus.[8] Bene est amicis nostris et uestris, Cellensi abbati, Sanctorum Crispini et Crispiniani abbati, Sancti Nicasii ⟨abbati⟩, prioribus de Monte Dei et de Valle Sancti Petri.[9] De questione autem illa quam in fine passionis beati martyris Thome, bone amice, posuisti,[10] credo nullatenus solutionem te latere. Forsitan tamen et meum animum in tuam sententiam translatum non dubitabas sed ut recogitarem quia, quod Deus per se facere disponit hominis auxilium uel auctoritatem non querit, ubi autem ministeria hominum non despicit causa nostre utilitatis uel humilitatis hoc facit. Absque enim omni sacramento, id est uisibilium elementorum uel operum adminiculo, hominem saluare posset nisi exercitia humilitatis uel fidei ad utilitatem saluandorum utilia procurasset. Diffinitiue ergo teneo nulla ratione lucernam accensam in manu Dei posse supprimi uel extingui, nec ibi expectandum hominis iudicium ubi manifesta luce Dei se explanat iudicium.

[7] Archbishop Henry of Reims (1162–75; see letter no. 21, n. 1).

[8] On Meerssen see appendix 10.

[9] In 1171 the abbot of Montier-la-Celle was Gerard (first occurs 1170; occurs 1183, but possibly resigned by 1180 when his successor, Hugh, occurs; *GC* xii. 544); the abbot of Saint-Crépin-le-Grand was Berneredus (*c.*1162/3–1179, Mar. × May; see letter no. 128,

But I can assure both my friends about our state, and say regarding physical health that as you left me so you can find me still. Our community is at peace and we are still running along on the usual course. We enjoy peace with all men, especially with the lord archbishop.[7] We are not seriously burdened with debts. As far as Meerssen is concerned, we are getting our revenues.[8] All is well with our friends and yours the abbot of Montier-la-Celle, the abbot of Saint-Crépin, the abbot of Saint-Nicaise, and the priors of Mont-Dieu and of Val-Saint-Pierre.[9] But concerning that question which, my good friend, you put at the end of your account of the martyrdom of the blessed martyr Thomas,[10] I believe that the solution is not hidden from you at all. Perhaps however you were not in any doubt that my mind also had been persuaded to your opinion, but wished me to reflect that in what God disposes to do through Himself He does not seek the help or authority of man, but when He does not disdain the services of men He does this for the sake of our profit and humility. For He could save man without any sacrament, that is without any support of visible elements or actions, had He not taken care to provide profitable exercises of humility or faith for the benefit of those to be saved. Therefore I assert definitively that by no means can a lamp kindled in the hand of God be suppressed or extinguished; nor should the judgement of man be awaited there where the judgement of God makes itself plain with a clear light.

n. 1); the abbot of Saint-Nicaise was Guy (*c.*1158–79; *GC* ix. 212–13); the prior of Mont-Dieu was Simon (1159–*c.*1184, see letter no. 59, n. 1), and the prior of Val-Saint-Pierre was Engelbert (1140–73/9, see letter no. 115, n. 1).

[10] i.e at the end of John's letter no. 305 (*J. S. Epp.* ii. 736–9), asking whether it was proper to refer to Becket as a martyr before the formal canonization (see n. 1 above).

172

To John of Salisbury and his brother Richard[1]

early 1171 × 1172 (or × 22 July 1176)

Magistro Iohanni Salisberiensi et fratri suo Richardo.

Grande dispendium patitur ardens desiderium si data occasione crassa et supina negligentia negauerit de amico refluere uel ab amico recipere saltem litterale refrigerium. Sit ergo inter nos pactum quod impune preuaricari non liceat quatinus uacua manu uel breuissima salutatione nuntius nullus accedat uel abscedat. Non tamen credo aliquando sic euacuari tempora circumuolitantia ut non alterutrum habeamus unde uel de prosperitate uel de aduersitate aliquatenus conqueramur. Ineptissima plane excusatio quorumdam qui cum moneantur ad confessionem dicunt se nichil habere quod in confessione referant. Reuera tales copia inopes facit, uel solis claritas eos excecauit. Non ergo similes eis efficiamur, dicendo nichil noui nos habere quod referamus, cum nec Francia citra mare perpetuitatem pacis et tranquillitatis adhuc iurauerit nec Anglia uestra ultra et iuxta mare medium silentium post completorium teneat.[2] Solent enim tunc fecundi calices[3] tam apud uos quam apud nos noua et uetera dicere et facere.[4] Sed de his taceamus ne uestrates irascantur qui potu uiliori non minus inebriantur quam nostrates uino meracissimo. Imperator indulsit nobis bona nostra de Marna.[5] Valete.

172 *Sirmond VI. 11*]

172 [1] This letter must post-date no. 171, which was clearly the first letter to John and his brother after the death of Becket; it probably also post-dates Richard's entry to Merton (see letter no. 171, n. 1), as the tone of complaint at his secular life is missing, but this cannot be conclusive. The reference to the lack of peace may indicate that the letter was written before the final settlements of the Becket affair, negotiated between May and Sept. 1172 (Barlow, *Thomas Becket*, pp. 260–1), but there is nothing certain here. In any case, the

172

To John of Salisbury and his brother Richard[1]

early 1171 × 1172 (or × 22 July 1176)

To master John of Salisbury and his brother Richard.

Burning desire suffers a great loss if, given the opportunity, it declines with stupid and indolent negligence to flow back from a friend or to receive from a friend at least the refreshment of letters. Therefore let there be a pact between us which may not be transgressed with impunity, that no messenger should approach or depart empty-handed or with only the briefest greeting. I do not believe, however, that the events swirling about us are ever so empty that we do not have one thing or another, either of prosperity or of adversity, about which we can complain to some degree. Clearly most absurd is the excuse of certain persons who when they are admonished to confess say that they have nothing to confess. Truly abundance makes such persons paupers, or the brightness of the sun has blinded them. Therefore let us not become like them, saying that we have nothing new to report, when France on this side of the sea has not yet sworn to lasting peace and tranquillity and neither does your England beyond and next to the sea hold the great silence after compline.[2] For at that time fruitful cups[3] are accustomed, among you as among us, to cause us to say and do new things and old.[4] But let us be silent about these things lest your countrymen grow angry, who are no less drunk on baser drink than ours are on purest wine. The emperor has granted us our possessions pertaining to Meerssen.[5] Farewell.

present letter pre-dates John of Salisbury's el. to Chartres (notified of el. 22 July 1176, consecrated 8 Aug.; see letter no. 102, n. 1).

[2] i.e. the monastic Great Silence; but cf. also letters 44, n. 15 and 127, n. 5.

[3] Cf. Horace, *Ep.* i. 5. 19.

[4] This is not apparently another critical reference to drinking and gossip after compline (see letter 150 for similar concerns), but simply a metaphor for peace and trouble; *noua et uetera* may be an allusion to Matt. 13: 52 or *Regula S. Benedicti* c. lxiv, or S. of S. 7: 13.

[5] On Meerssen, see appendix 10.

173

To John of Salisbury[1]

1171 × ? 1173 (or × 22 July 1176)

Petrus abbas Sancti Remigii Iohanni de Saresberia.

Nunquam pulsum tuum in litteris a te receptis inequalem aut citatum de superueniente febre regie commotionis deprehendo. Mirarer ⟨te⟩ tam bone et optime animi complexionis nisi antiqua cognitio admirationem compesceret et olim iam notus status tuus maiora et meliora innotuisset. Certe cum illis et de illis te esse non ambigo de quibus dicitur quia 'Vbi erat impetus spiritus, illuc gradiebantur'.[2] Cholerica et celestis complexio tua suis passionibus hilarescit, suis congelationibus frondescit, suis euersionibus excrescit, suis egritudinibus conualescit, suis contrariis infortuniis fortior et audacior enitescit. Quid igitur? Consolabor te? Sed non es desolatus qui desolationem reputas consolationem. Releuabo te? Sed non es deiectus qui dum eiceris eleuaris. Conficiam aliquod emplastrum siue electuarium? Sed neque uulneratus es neque in passione aliqua turbatus. Tamen percusso et non uulnerato, impulso et non deiecto, concusso et non excusso reor congratulandum de constantia, timendum de nondum finita pugna, adhortandum de perseuerantia. Ecce caminus, sed non timet aurum; ecce mare, sed supernatat folium; ecce malleus, sed non confringitur adamas; ecce uentus, sed mons Syon non commouebitur; ecce prelium, sed miles tenet gladium. Superuacuis impendiis laborat qui solem facibus nititur adiuuare.[3] Non ita[a] et scientia et experientia. Si qua tamen tibi ex me potest fieri consolatio, utere ut libet; et presens et absens tuus sum et omnia mea tua sunt. De gente tua et moribus michi satis notum est quia utres immo uentres suos solent implere quin immo superinfundere tam de uino quam de mulso sine reprehensione et, tanquam Hebrei

173 *Sirmond VII. 12*]
[a] *corr. Ritchie;* ista *Sirmond*

173 [1] The reference to trouble in this letter is apparently to a danger of a lesser order than that accompanying the return to England with Becket, and may refer to John's unsettled period between the murder (Dec. 1170) and his establishment as treasurer at Exeter (by May 1173; Barlow, 'John of Salisbury', p. 104), and before Becket's canonization (March 1173), but the only secure *terminus ad quem* is John's el. to Chartres (see letter no. 102, n. 1).

173

To John of Salisbury[1]

1171 × ? 1173 (or × 22 July 1176)

Peter, abbot of Saint-Remi, to John of Salisbury.

I never detect in letters received from you that your pulse is irregular or quickened by the supervening fever of the royal agitation. I would be astonished at such a good and excellent complexion of the mind in you did not old acquaintance restrain my astonishment and had not your state, long ago familiar to me, given me knowledge of greater and better things. Certainly I do not doubt that you are with those and of those of whom it is said: 'Whither the impulse of the spirit was to go, thither they went'.[2] Your choleric and heavenly complexion grows cheerful in its sufferings, puts out leaves in its frozen conditions, burgeons in its uprootings, grows strong in its sicknesses, and shines out stronger and bolder in its adverse fortunes. What then? Shall I console you? But you are not desolate who reckon desolation a consolation. Shall I raise you up? But you are not cast down who while you are cast out are raised up. Shall I confect some plaster or medicine? But you are neither wounded nor troubled by any suffering. However, since you have been struck and not wounded, pushed and not cast down, struck and not beaten, I reckon that I should rejoice with you for your constancy, fear for the fight not yet finished, encourage your perseverance. Behold the furnace, but the gold is not afraid; behold the sea, but the leaf floats on it; behold the hammer, but the diamond is not broken; behold the wind, but mount Zion will not be moved; behold the battle, but the soldier holds the sword. He labours with needless cost who tries to help the sun with torches.[3] Not so knowledge and experience. If however any consolation can be provided for you by me, make use of it as it pleases you; I am yours both present and absent and all that is mine is yours. Regarding your people and their customs, it is well enough known to me that they are accustomed to fill up their wineskins, nay their bellies, even indeed to fill them to overflowing, both with wine and with mead without censure and, as the Hebrews

[2] Ezek. 1: 12.

[3] Cf. Ennodius, *Epp.* ii. 22; ix. 3 (*MGH* auct. ant. vii. pp. 73, 294; *PL* lxiii. 51, 150).

carnem suam circumcidunt in signum quod semen sunt Abrahe, absque opprobrii confusione.[4]

174

To John of Salisbury[1]

1171 × 22 July 1176

Iohanni Salisberiensi.

Si bene recolo iocos prioris seculi dum simul essemus[2] et ad inuicem plura iocando sereremus, occurrit inter cetera quod quasi de magnitudine cassule tunc archiepiscopi Thome, nunc pretiosissimi martyris, conquerebar ubi posset reperiri. Verbum illud fecit Deus, immo risum fecit nobis et toti prouincie uestre et nostre. Inde est quod undecunque non solum Angli sed et Galli quasi ad solennes epulas et ad fertilissimas iubilationes concurrunt ad tumbam predicti sancti; quo et michi miserrimo et indignissimo contingat uenire, uidere mirabilia Dei et adorare Deum in sancto suo antequam moriar. Etsi enim intercipi uoragine maris quod intercurrit possem, non timerem mortem cum uitam quererem. Interim autem corde meo, ore uestro adite presentiam eius, et totis uisceribus atque medullis pro peccatis et miseriis nostris rogate alumnum gratie ne pre ebrietate immensurabilium gaudiorum suorum, qua ab uberibus Christi et gloriose Virginis Marie repletur, nostri obliuiscatur, cum nos comparticipes compassione animi in tribulatione sua aliquando habuerit, et adhuc ⟨habeat⟩ pro posse deuotissimos glorie sue predicatores.[3] De his hactenus. Ceterum de oblatione uestra uniuersitas fratrum

174 *Sirmond VI. 12*]

[4] Apparently a response to a question about drinking; there may be a sarcastic intention here, stating that drunkenness distinguishes the English as circumcision does the Jews (which would fit with the tone of some of his other comments on the English, e.g. in letters 62, 108, 158, and possibly 172), but without the context it is obscure.

174 [1] The recipient must be John of Salisbury (on the heading, see letter no. 84, n. 1): he is English, associated closely with Becket, has spent time in the past with Peter, and has a brother Richard. The letter assumes John to be in contact with both Canterbury and Exeter (and indeed he seems to have travelled regularly between the two in these years; see letter no. 109, n. 1). It must pre-date John's el. to Chartres (see letter no. 102, n. 1). Barlow interprets this and letter no. 109 as letters excusing Peter from attending the reconciliation ceremony at Canterbury Cathedral in Dec. 1171 (Barlow, 'John of Salisbury', p. 106, but

circumcise their flesh as a sign that they are the seed of Abraham, without the disgrace of dishonour.[4]

174

To John of Salisbury[1]

1171 × 22 July 1176

To John of Salisbury.

If I recall rightly the jokes of an earlier time when we were together[2] and we took it in turns to weave many topics in our joking, it happened among other things that I was lamenting, so to speak, as to where a shrine of sufficient magnitude would be found for the then archbishop, now most precious martyr, Thomas. God has realized that word, has indeed brought our jest to pass for us and for the whole of your province and ours. Hence it is that not only English but French folk too flock together from all parts to the tomb of the aforesaid saint as if to solemn feasts and most fruitful jubilations; whither may it fall to me also, most wretched and unworthy, to come, there to see the miracles of God and to adore God in His saint before I die. For even though I might be cut off by the gulf of the sea which runs between, I would not fear death when I was seeking life. In the meantime, however, approach his presence with my heart and with your lips, and with all your inwards and marrow beg the pupil of grace, for the sake of our sins and miseries, not to forget us on account of the drunkenness of his immeasurable joys by which he is filled from the breasts of Christ and the glorious Virgin Mary, since he once had us, through compassion of mind, as co-sharers in his trouble, and still has us as the most devoted possible preachers of his glory.[3] But enough of these matters. As for others, the whole of our brotherhood returns to you such thanks as it is able for your

on this see also letter no. 109, n. 1). However, while letter no. 109 *seems* to assume that John and Richard are together (if not named), this letter is to John alone, and Barlow suggests that it may have been written after Richard's entry to Merton, and so possibly later than letter no. 109. Richard went to Merton some time between early 1171 and May 1172 (see Barlow 'John of Salisbury', pp. 103–4, and letter no. 171, n. 1). All that can be said for certain, however, is that it was written after Becket's death.

[2] On the history of John and Peter's relations, see appendix 8.

[3] i.e. he is asking John to stand in his place at Becket's tomb (there is no evidence to suggest that Peter ever did visit England).

nostrorum grates quas potest uobis rependit, et quem cum fratre uestro Richardo ab annis prioribus in societate bonorum suorum adnumerauit cumulatius amplectitur et iocundius in perpetuam commemorationem astringit. Nondum tamen reditus exinde comparauimus quia nulla opportunitas se obtulit.[4] Instantius autem laborabimus querere quo id maturius efficiatur. De glossis nostris quas retinuistis, utcunque patienter sustineremus si[a] plusquam granum sinapis minutissimam fidem[5] de nobis apud uos deprehenderemus. Tanto tempore nobiscum fuistis, et miror, immo horreo, si tam exiguam de nobis confidentiam ex preteritis actibus et uerbis conceperitis ut libellum paruissimi pretii a nobis gratis retinere formidaretis. Tamen quia ita egressum est de labiis uestris,[6] ne fiant irrita uestra, prorsus sumptus reposcimus grandes et graues ut fiat uobis iuxta fidem uestram. Pretium tamen sine taxatione et sine estimatione est.[7] Dominum episcopum Exoniensem saluto[8] et me sanctissimis suis orationibus commendo. Fratrem uestrum Richardum, quem tenerrime diligo et dulcissime amplector, a Iesu Christo et ab Spiritu sancto, immo a Deo Patre, ubertate gratiarum impleri exopto. Participem enim me totorum bonorum eius non dubito. Valete.

175

To John of Salisbury and his brother Richard[1]

Dec. 1171 × May 1172

Magistro Iohanni et fratri suo Richardo Petrus abbas Sancti Remigii.

Statum nostrum pretermisso proemio uobis notificare studeo, cuius nec satis bonus nec pessimus ad presens occurrit aspectus.

[a] nisi *Sirmond*

175 *Sirmond V.* 20]

[4] It seems that John and Richard may have given some land to Saint-Remi (although there is no other evidence for this), and were in return granted confraternity with the community.

[5] Cf. Matt. 17: 19; Luke 17: 6.

[6] Cf. Deut. 23: 23; Jer. 17: 16.

[7] Heavily ironic: John has not shown trust in his tolerance, so he must be charged accordingly, in proportion to his *fides*; this, however, is beyond price.

[8] Bartholomew, 1161–84 (see letter no. 108, n. 1).

175 [1] The letter refers to the legatine mission of cardinals Albert of S. Lorenzo and

offering, and you whom with your brother Richard it has numbered in the fellowship of its good men from former years it embraces more fully and binds more joyfully in perpetual commemoration. We have not yet, however, procured revenues from it because no opportunity has presented itself.[4] We shall, however, labour more actively to seek how that might be more speedily achieved. As for our glosses which you have retained, we should somehow or other put up with it patiently if only we were able to discern on your part the least bit of faith in us, more than a mustard seed.[5] For so long a time you were with us, and I wonder, nay shudder, if you conceived so meagre a trust in us, on the basis of past actions and words, as to be afraid to retain from us freely a little book of such tiny value. However, because it has come forth from your lips,[6] so that your words be not in vain we do demand at once a great and weighty outlay so as to treat you in proportion to your faith. The value of that, however, is beyond assessment and beyond valuation.[7] I send greetings to the lord bishop of Exeter[8] and commend myself to his most holy prayers. I ardently desire that your brother Richard, whom I love most tenderly and embrace most sweetly, be filled with the richness of grace by Jesus Christ and the Holy Spirit, nay by God the Father. For I do not doubt that I am a sharer in all his blessings. Farewell.

175

To John of Salisbury and his brother Richard[1]

Dec. 1171 × May 1172

To master John and his brother Richard, Peter, abbot of Saint-Remi.

I am eager to inform you without any preamble of our state which looks at present neither good enough nor yet wholly bad. But I am

Theodwin of S. Vitale to Henry II, which reached a conclusion in May 1172 with the settlement of Avranches (*Councils and Synods* i. 2, pp. 942–56). The legates left the Curia in autumn 1171, had reached Henry's lands by Dec. 1171 and met him in the second half of May 1172. Henry himself was in Ireland until Apr., reaching the continent in May. At the time of the writing of the present letter his arrival and replies were still awaited. On these events see Barlow, *Thomas Becket*, pp. 260–1. Peter may have encountered the legates *en route* through France, but their itinerary before Dec. 1171 is not known (see R. Foreville, *L'Église et la royauté en Angleterre sous Henri II Plantagenet (1154–1189)* (Paris, 1942), p. 335, n. 1; but see also Janssen, *Die päpstlichen Legaten*, pp. 86–7, who says that they spent time in the royal demesne, the Loire, Normandy, and Poitou, but their itinerary can only be precisely dated when they were in Le Mans, 5 Dec. 1171). On Albert of S. Lorenzo (Albert of Morra), see letter no. 83, n. 1.

Valde autem sollicitus sum de statu terre uestre, cuius quasi claues et columpnas citra mare, legatos scilicet Romane curie, tenemus. Quid autem statuere, quid deicere, quid aperire quidue claudere debeant, tam ipsis quam nobis incertum est. Tota siquidem clausula negotii pendet ex aduentu et responsis regis Anglie. Tamen modestos presensi nimis animos eorum in executione mandati nisi forte ex contemptu exasperati in duriorem prosilierint sententiam. De proprio ergo statu id enuntio quod, quantum ad personam nostram, cursu consueto ualetudo procedit, quantum autem ad ecclesie communem pacem et prosperitatem, sic se habet quomodo solet. Vnus autem, scilicet frater Herueus, iam nobiscum non ambulat. Iuit uiam suam, utinam non post Satanam. Si ad uos uenerit, equos accipite et si quid aliud honeste ab eo auferri poterit. Super questione autem tua, frater Richarde, amice dilectissime, nolo multiplicare superuacuos circuitus et multorum uerborum anfractus. Queris autem utrum ad singulos de collegio culpa que uidetur respicere economum uel prepositum ipsius deriuatione singulari et certa percurrat et illiciat singulorum conscientias.[2] Ait propheta, 'Anima que peccauerit ipsa morietur, filius non portabit iniquitatem patris, neque pater filii.'[3] Item auctoritas, 'Mala non sunt que nec mentem implicant nec conscientiam ligant.'[4] Item Apostolus, 'Que in macello uenient, edite cum gratiarum actione, nichil interrogantes propter conscientiam.'[5] His omnibus auctoritatibus non michi uidetur singulorum capita percutere si quid a preposito male administratum fuerit, et sufficere claustralibus nescire unde ueniat quod edant uel quod[a] uestiant. Tanta enim simplicitas debet esse columbe que in foraminibus petre et in cauernis macerie nidificat[6] ut remota omni sollicitudine quicquid manus eius inuenerit in lecto siue in refectorio simpliciter accipiat[7] et Deo gratias agat; si quis autem dixerit, 'Hoc ydolothytum est,'[8] id est de rapina uel usura uel alio quolibet modo male adquisitum, abstineat. Valete.

[a] quid *Sirmond*

[2] This is the earliest datable indication that Richard is a member of a religious community (Merton priory, see letter no. 171, n. 1, and on Richard generally letter no. 163, n. 1); *economus* here presumably refers to some sort of steward (Niermeyer, *oeconomus*, 1, 2, suggests 'monastic housekeeper, steward'; Latham, 'steward'); it is not clear what he and the provost have done.

[3] Cf. Ezek. 18: 20.

[4] Cf. Ambrose, *Examreon* i. 8. 31 (*CSEL* xxxii. 1, p. 33; *PL* xiv. 152); Ivo, *Dec.* xiii. cap. 91 (*PL* clxi. 820); Gratian, *Dec.* ii. 15. 1. cap. vi (*PL* clxxxvii. 973).

[5] Cf. 1 Cor. 10: 25, 'omne quod in macello uenit manducate, nihil interrogantes propter conscientiam'.

terribly worried about the state of your land, whose keys as it were and columns, that is the legates of the Roman Curia, remain with us here on this side of the sea. But they are as uncertain as we are as to what they ought to establish, what they ought to cast down, what they ought to open or what to close. The whole outcome of the business, indeed, depends on the arrival and the replies of the king of England. I felt beforehand however that their minds would be too moderate in the execution of their mandate, unless perhaps, provoked by being despised, they might leap to a tougher judgement. So I have this to report concerning our state, that as regards our person, health continues along its accustomed course, and as regards the general peace and prosperity of our church, it is its usual self. One, however, that is brother Hervey, does not now walk with us. He has gone his own way, I hope not following Satan. If he should come to you, take the horses and whatever else can be recovered from him honourably. But on the matter of your question, brother Richard, dearest friend, I do not wish to multiply superfluous circumlocutions and verbose digressions. But you ask whether guilt that seems to affect the *economus* or provost runs through from a single and sure origin in him to the individual members of a community and involves the consciences of individuals.[2] The Prophet says, 'The soul that sinneth, the same shall die; the son shall not bear the iniquity of the father, nor the father that of the son.'[3] Again authority says, 'Those things are not evil which neither implicate the mind nor bind the conscience.'[4] Again the Apostle says, 'Those things which will be sold in the shambles, eat, with performance of thanks, asking no question for conscience's sake.'[5] Considering all these authorities, it does not seem to me that it falls on the heads of individuals if something is badly administered by the prior, and that it is enough for the religious not to know whence comes that which they eat or that which they put on. For so great should be the simplicity of the dove which nests in the clefts of the rock and in the hollow places of the wall[6] that, far removed from all concern, he[7] should receive in all simplicity whatever his hand may find in his bed or in the refectory and give thanks to God, but if anyone should say, 'This is a thing sacrificed to idols,'[8] that is acquired by rapine or usury or whatever other evil means, he should abstain. Farewell.

[6] Cf. S. of S. 2: 14; also Jer. 48: 28.
[7] i.e. the monk, who is the dove here.
[8] *ydolothytum*: cf. e.g. 1 Cor. 8: 7, 10; Rev. 2: 20.

176

To John of Salisbury, bishop of Chartres[1]

mid-1177 × 1179, before May (or more likely before Mar.)

Iohanni episcopo Carnotensi Petrus Sancti Remigii.

In biuio dubietatis positus utrum conquerar de me ipso ad amicum an de amico ad amicum uix discernere possum. Sed si utrumque facio alterum non omitto nam quia utrumque culpabilem inuenio neutrum excuso. Me abbatem, te episcopum quis ignorat? Hactenus unice amicos fuisse quis dubitat? Huius rei testis est aceruus epistolarum marina pericula non timentium cum familiarissimo recursu et brachiali complexu nostra quondam sese reuisitabat amicitia.[2] Vnde autem obstupuit, immo elanguit, communis stilus, non iam quatriduanus stertens immo annuali elapsu deficiens? Certe si episcopalium sollicitudinum allegationes negligentiam istam excipiunt meam eque consimili ratione defendunt. Esto. Nullum fuit tempus uacuum uel ueniendi uel scribendi, nunquid amandi, nunquid recordandi? Procul dubio quamlibet excusationem potest habere omnis actio, nullam dilectio. Si dormis dilectio non dormit. Vnde 'ego dormio et cor meum uigilat'.[3] Quibuscunque tenearis occupationibus et necessitatibus, non impeditur, non compeditur uera dilectio. Vbi es uera dilectio? Certe pallio tuo hyacinthino[4] multi se operiunt sicut falsi prophete qui 'in uestimentis ouium' ueniunt, 'intrinsecus autem sunt lupi rapaces',[5] uel amici rapaces. Nolo, nolo me uel te esse de illis qui 'magnificant fimbrias' ficte amicitie profitentes et promittentes inopinabilia et incredibilia, 'digito autem suo' nec queque modica tangentes.[6] De hoc amicorum genere uel grege nunquam te expertus sum, nec tu me. Tardius enim os in promittendo moueo quam cor in diligendo. Vrget autem me suis stimulis hec de qua loquor dilectio redarguere non superbe neque ficte que de amico audio. Siquidem

176 *Sirmond VII. 22*]

176 [1] John of Salisbury was notified of his el. 22 July 1176, and consecrated 8 Aug. (see letter no. 102, n. 1). Peter accuses John of letting a year go by without writing, which would put this letter around mid-1177; this would also allow time for John to accumulate the complaints against him which are the subject of this letter. (The same sentence includes another puzzling reference to four days—cf. letters 15. n. 4 and 156, n. 3) The reference to Berneredus as abbot of Saint-Crépin gives the *terminus ad quem* (see letter no. 128, n. 1).

176

To John of Salisbury, bishop of Chartres[1]

mid-1177 × 1179, before May (or more likely before Mar.)

To John, bishop of Chartres, Peter of Saint-Remi.

I am poised in a dilemma of doubt and can scarcely tell whether I should complain about myself to a friend or about a friend to a friend. Yet if I do both I am not passing over either, for since I find both blameworthy I excuse neither. Who does not know that I am an abbot and you a bishop? Who is in any doubt that up until now we have been friends to an extraordinary degree? The witness to this is a heap of letters which were not afraid of the dangers of the sea when our friendship used to return visits to itself with a most familiar exchange and locked embrace.[2] But why has the pen we share become paralysed, or rather fainted, not now snoring for four days but rather letting a year slip by without activity? Certainly if excuses of episcopal cares exculpate this neglect they defend mine equally by similar reasoning. Let it be. Was there no spare time either for visiting or for writing, nor for loving, nor for remembering? Every action can doubtless have some excuse, love can have none. If you sleep love does not sleep. Whence: 'I sleep and my heart watcheth'.[3] By whatever occupations and urgent necessities you may be occupied, true love is not impeded, it is not shackled. Where are you, true love? Certainly many conceal themselves with your cloth of violet,[4] like false prophets who come 'in the clothing of sheep, but inwardly they are ravening wolves,'[5] or ravening friends. I do not wish, I do not wish myself or you, to be one of those who 'enlarge the fringes' of feigned friendship, professing and promising things inconceivable and incredible but not touching even minor matters 'with a finger of their own'.[6] I have never known you to be of this kind or flock of friends, nor you me. For I move my mouth to making promises more slowly than I move my heart to loving. But this love of which I speak urges me with its goads to refute not proudly nor falsely what I am hearing about a friend. For on account of our long-standing

[2] i.e. John is again in France, and so has less excuse for not writing.
[3] S. of S. 5: 2.
[4] Cf. Num. 4: 7, 12.
[5] Cf. Matt. 7: 15.
[6] Cf. Matt. 23: 4–5; Luke 11: 46.

propter antiquam nostram amicitiam[7] qui habent aduersus episcopum Carnotensem querelam, abbatem Sancti Remigii conueniunt et quasi magistrum et iudicem proponunt. 'Hec et hec', inquiunt, 'facit episcopus, sic loquitur, sic mouetur, sic mutabilis est in promissis, sic instabilis in uerbis et consiliis suis, sic ingratus beneficiis, sic ad iram facilis, sic improuidus in disponendis iudiciis, sic totus pendet de uoluntate et consilio unius hominis, minus prudentis et multum cupidi.' Ecce capitula que obiciunt episcopo. Quid autem, o amice, respondes ad ea que tibi obiciuntur ab his? Si talis es, in alium uirum mutatus es. Non te talem noueram, non didiceram, non predicaueram. Archiepiscopus noster, uir discretissimus et qui morum scrutator et cognitor est perspicacissimus, discipulum sancti Thome aliter informatum, aliter institutum fide oculata ex diuturna cohabitatione acceperat.[8] Absit, absit a me ista credere, sed rationes uellem habere quibus uanitates istas et insanias falsas possem refellere. Ecce per amantissimum nostrum abbatem Sanctorum Crispini et Crispiniani rescribite[9] et remandate tam de his que ex parte nostra dicturus est uobis quam de his que scribo.

177

To John of Salisbury, bishop of Chartres[1]

mid-1177 × 1179 before May (or more likely before Mar.)

Episcopo Carnotensi Petrus abbas Sancti Remigii.

Facile est amicorum erratibus ignoscere qui contingunt casu non deliberatione. Causales quoque excessus facile corrigit qui occupatione non contemptu delinquit. Amicum nostrum et uestrum, abbatem Sanctorum Crispini et Crispiniani, aliter quam decuit excepistis.[2] In hoc circumspectio uestra oberrauit. Sed hoc debitum cum satisfactione dimittetur cum ad nos ueneritis et culpam recognoueritis.

177 *Sirmond VIII. 5*]

[7] Cf. 2 Macc. 6: 21.

[8] The archbishop of Reims, William aux Blanches Mains, 1175/6–1202: on his dates see letter no. 4, n. 4; on his part in John's el., for which Peter congratulated him, see letter no. 102, n. 1. I.e. John is not living up to what William saw in him, when he knew him as a loyal supporter of Becket (William of course was a significant supporter of Becket and instrumental in his canonization).

friendship[7] those who have a complaint against the bishop of Chartres approach the abbot of Saint-Remi and put him forth as master and judge. 'The bishop', they say, 'does such and such, thus he speaks, thus he is influenced, thus he is changeable in his promises, unstable in his words and counsels, slow to bless, quick to anger, improvident in settling judgements; he depends utterly on the will and counsel of one man, who is unwise and very greedy.' See the charges which they bring against the bishop. But what, o friend, do you reply to those charges which are brought against you by these people? If you are like this, you have changed into another man. I did not know you to be so, I had not learnt, I had not proclaimed you so. Our archbishop, a most discerning man and one who is a most perspicacious examiner and judge of conduct, from the faith apparent by daily association had accepted a disciple of St Thomas otherwise fashioned and otherwise trained.[8] Far, far be it from me to believe these things, but I would like to have grounds by which I could refute these vanities and false insanities. Look, write back through our most loving abbot of Saint-Crépin[9] and send back word regarding those things which he is going to tell you on our behalf, as well as these which I am writing about.

177

To John of Salisbury, bishop of Chartres[1]

mid-1177 × 1179 before May (or more likely before Mar.)

To the bishop of Chartres, Peter, abbot of Saint-Remi.

It is easy to forgive the vagaries of friends which happen by chance not by deliberation. He can easily correct even intentional aberrations who offends through preoccupation, not through disparagement. You have taken otherwise than is fitting our friend and yours, the abbot of Saint-Crépin.[2] In this your circumspection has erred. This debt, however, will be forgiven with satisfaction when you come to us and

[9] Berneredus; see n. 1 above, and letter no. 128, n. 1.

177 [1] Dated as letter no. 176, but perhaps later in the possible period because Peter has now heard better news of John. Although he is not named, John of Salisbury must be the recipient from the references to Berneredus, and to long-standing friendship with Peter, and from the content, which links this to letter no. 176.

[2] Berneredus (see letter no. 128, n. 1); it is not known how he has incurred John's displeasure (Peter recommended him to John in letter no. 176).

Iam quoque nubeculam istam amouit a facie nostra relatio Alexandri amici uestri[3] qua de statu uestro letificauit nos. Solet enim uerum dicere. Prosperum itaque et felicem statum in his que erga uos fiunt asseruit et ambages circumuolantes a corde nostro abegit. Non difficile credo quod multum desidero. Verbis igitur illius credo et ualde congaudeo. Nam a me nichil alienum estimo quicquid de uobis sensero. Radix enim longeua pruina subita non arescit neque marcescit. De his hactenus.

178

To John of Salisbury, bishop of Chartres[1]

mid-1177 × 25 Oct. 1180

Carnotensi episcopo Petrus Sancti Remigii.

Si quando in mente constantis hominis priora mutentur uota seu proposita, considerandum est utrum hoc fiat leuitate aut necessitate aut superueniente affectione. Si leuitate inconstantia, si necessitate fortuna, si affectione ratio pensanda est. Si enim uitiosa est affectio, improbitas est, si iusta, uirtus, et est admittenda. Causa uero unde oritur affectio sorte inter bonam et malam diuidit et nomen imponit.[2] Bona excusat uoti mutabilitatem, mala accusat inconstantiam. Non enim ab inchoatis recedendum est sine ratione, que inchoata sunt cum ratione. Alioquin non est in illo EST, sed EST et NON in illo est,[3] et de illo dicitur quia stultus ut luna mutatur.[4] Ne autem sim oneri occupatissimis auribus Carnotensis episcopi, negotium breuiter et aperte exponam. Postulatio nostra apud uos pro Hugone cognato et amico nostro Remensi canonico[5] ante fores uestras obseratas estatem et hiemem fecit, et ualde lassata et ieiuna ad sinum nostrum reuersa est; et ecce occurrit karissimus amicus et cognatus ampliori affectione suscipiendus in eadem postulatione, G. archidiaconus uester[6] qui

178 *Sirmond VIII. 4*]

[3] Unidentified.

178 [1] Presumably written after letter no. 176 (which was evidently the first letter after John's move to Chartres); the *terminus ad quem* is John's death (*J. S. Epp.* ii, p. xlvii). John is not named, and there is a remote possibility that another could be the addressee.

[2] i.e. the cause determines whether the affection is good or bad, as he goes on to explain.

recognize the fault. Already too the report of your friend Alexander,[3] by which he has cheered us as regards your state, has removed this little cloud from our face. For he is accustomed to speak the truth. And so he affirmed the prosperous and happy state of your affairs and drove from our heart the doubts flying about it. I do not find it difficult to believe what I long for so greatly. I believe his words therefore, and greatly rejoice. For I reckon nothing whatever that I feel concerning you is alien to me, for an ancient root neither dries up nor withers with a sudden frost. But enough of these matters.

178

To John of Salisbury, bishop of Chartres[1]

mid-1177 × 25 Oct. 1180

To the bishop of Chartres, Peter of Saint-Remi.

If ever in the mind of a constant man earlier vows or intentions are changed, one must consider whether this is done out of levity, out of necessity, or out of supervening affection. If it is levity it is to be reckoned inconstancy, if necessity fortune, if affection reason. For if affection is at fault, it is wickedness, if just, it is virtue and to be admitted. But the cause from which the affection arises casts the deciding vote between good and evil and imposes a name.[2] A good cause excuses the change of the vow, a bad one imputes inconstancy. For one must not withdraw without reason from things once begun, which were begun with reason. Otherwise it is not IT IS in him, but IT IS and IT IS NOT in him,[3] and it is said of him that a fool is changed as the moon.[4] But so that I should not be a burden to the most busy ears of the bishop of Chartres, I will set out the business briefly and clearly. Our request before you for Hugh, our relative and friend, canon of Reims,[5] spent a summer and winter before your bolted doors and returned to our bosom exceedingly weary and starved; and behold our dearest friend and relative who should be received with a fuller affection, G., your archdeacon,[6] joins in the

Cf. also Ambrose, *De officiis min.* i. 30. 147 (M. Testard, *Saint Ambroise, les Devoirs* (Paris, 1984), i. 166; *PL* xvi. 71): 'Affectus tuus nomen imponit operi tuo,' which Peter cites elsewhere (see letter no. 59 and n. 36; and no. 134, and n. 16).

[3] Cf. 2 Cor. 1: 17–20. [4] Cf. Ecclus. 27: 12. [5] Unidentified.

[6] Gautier, archdeacon *de Pinserais* (E. de Lépinois and L. Merlot, *Cartulaire de Notre-Dame de Chartres*, 3 vols. (Chartres, 1862–5), i. 207); or possibly Goslenus (ibid.).

uobis de latere et ecclesie uestre magis paratus est seruire. Cedit itaque ille si iste successerit; immo, ut iste succedat, cedo et ego in priori petitione si exauditus fuero in secunda, quin potius ut fiat et citius fiat secunda ne forte steriles anni renuntient michi defectum imbris matutini et serotini,[7] et desperans de messione cessem deinceps arare seu aliquid a uobis petere. Valete.

179

? To Gerard Pucelle[1]

early 1166 × 1168

Petrus abbas Sancti Remigii magistro G. Puell.

Nullum uirtutis dispendium est ubi ab umbraculis eius uitium extrahitur ut reuelata facie quod latebat appareat. Hac etate atque his malignitatis diebus Deus splendescere facit quis sit de gente tenebrarum uel de populo honorificato diei et lucis,[2] dum stricto ense et uniuerso apparatu armorum hinc inde conglobato bonum et malum, uirtus et uitium in castris suis manu conserta cominus acriter dimicant. O quam pompose phalanges Philistinorum multo numero et propriis uiribus confidentes uibrant hastas, intorquent sagittas toxicatas ueneno secularis glorie aduersus Israhel populum humilem, pusillum gregem de se nil presumentem.[3] Ab initio enim, ex quo in ueritate non stetit homicida ille qui tanquam fulgur de celo cecidit,[4] multiplicata sunt mala super terram;[5] et rarescente tam uirtute quam religione super numerum excreuerunt mulieres, Egyptiorum nimirum et Hebreorum, adeo ut vix septem mulieres apprehendant uirum unum,[6] et 'pretiosior sit uir auro, et homo mundo obrizo'.[7]

179 *Sirmond VII. 3*]

---

[7] Cf Joel 2: 23; meaning both of the petitioners mentioned.

179 [1] The most likely recipient is Gerard Pucelle, during his stay at Cologne of early 1166–1168: the letter is evidently addressed to one of Becket's *eruditi*, and it seems to fit Gerard's stay in Cologne. On Gerard, clerk to Thomas Becket, later clerk to Archbishop Richard of Canterbury, and himself bishop of Coventry, May 1183, consecrated 25 Sept. 1183, d. 12 × 13 Jan. 1184, see S. Kuttner and E. Rathbone, 'Anglo-Norman canonists of the twelfth century', *Traditio*, vii (1951), 279–358, at pp. 296–303; and *EEA* xvi, p. 110 and xvii, pp. xxiii–xxv. He went to Germany either at the end of 1165 or early in 1166 (early 1166 is more likely—see *J.S. Epp.* ii. xxviii) and was back in France in 1168, where he took the oath to Henry II which others associated with Becket were still refusing, but was reconciled to Becket later in

same petition, who is the more ready to serve you by your side, and your church. And so the former concedes if the latter has succeeded; indeed, in order that the latter may succeed I too yield in the first request if I am heard in the second, nay rather that the second be settled and be settled more quickly lest perchance the sterile years should bring back word to me of the failure of the early and the latter rain,[7] and despairing for the harvest I should cease thereupon to plough or to seek anything from you. Farewell.

179

? To Gerard Pucelle[1]

early 1166 × 1168

Peter, abbot of Saint-Remi, to master G. Pucelle.

There is no loss of virtue where a vice is drawn out from its shadowy places so that what was hiding should appear with its face uncovered. In this age and in these evil days God makes it brilliantly clear who is of the race of darkness and who of the honoured people of day and light,[2] while with a drawn sword and universal preparation of arms accumulated on this side and that good and evil, virtue and vice, in their camps fight bitterly, joined in hand-to-hand combat. O how vainly the hosts of the Philistines, trusting in their great numbers and their own powers, brandish spears and hurl arrows poisoned with the venom of worldly glory against the humble people of Israel, the little flock which is presuming nothing of itself.[3] For from the beginning, from which time that murderer who fell like lightning from heaven[4] has not stood in truth, evils have been multiplied on the earth;[5] and with virtue growing as scarce as religion women have risen up beyond number, of the Egyptians evidently, and the Hebrews, to such an extent that seven women might scarcely take hold of one man,[6] and 'a man be more precious than gold, yea a man than the finest of gold'.[7]

1168. After another prolonged stay in France, he occurs as principal clerk to Richard of Canterbury *c.*1174 × 1183 (see Kuttner and Rathbone, 'Ango-Norman canonists', pp. 297–8, 302; on his appearance at Canterbury, see also *EEA* ii, with index in *EEA* iii, where he occurs as a witness between 28 Apr. 1174 and Sept. 1183).

[2] Cf. 1 Thess. 5: 5. (The passage may also echo 2 Cor. 3: 18 ff., indicated by *reuelata facie* above.)

[3] Cf. Luke 12: 32, with an echo of Judith 6: 15.

[4] i.e. Satan, cf. Luke 10: 18.

[5] Cf. 1 Macc. 1: 10.

[6] Cf. Isa. 4: 1.

[7] Cf. Isa. 13: 12.

Queris forte quid intendat hoc nostrum prouerbium et quare hanc proposuerimus in exordio litterarum nostrarum querimoniam. Res ipsa sine dubio et ratio temporis nodum questionis soluit, dum in errore schismatico 'qui uidebantur columpne esse'[8] in domo Dei procliuius elabuntur 'pro buccella panis'[9] et pro gloria carnis, que tanquam 'fenum tectorum' euanescit, 'quod priusquam euellatur exaruit'.[10] Vident et agnoscunt homines quod draco tertiam partem stellarum de celo secum deiecerit,[11] nec exterriti tam fedo et crudeli exemplo abhorrent ire post Satanam et detinere ueritatem Dei in mendacium. Vna hec de plagis Egypti que filios Israhel non tangit sed filios huius seculi qui querunt que uidentur et temporalia sunt, non ea que non uidentur et eterna sunt.[12] Secunda autem similis est huic, que maxime debacchatur in partibus uestris transmarinis ubi rex Anglie omnes pene canes sic elingues reddidit ut mutire non ualeant, ne dicam latrare.[13] Superenatauerunt tamen aliqui qui timebant ne simili tinea corroderentur et tabefierent fauces eorum; de quibus est Cantuariensis cum domestica familia sua, ex quibus unum habemus catulum, Iohannem de Saresberia,[14] qui non facit animam suam pretiosiorem se sed domine Egyptiace auferenti tunicam non renuit prius dimittere pallium[15] quam stupro falsitatis corrumpi; et nudus reiecta sindone[16] nudum sequi desiderat Christum. Bone amice, 'et tu de illis es, nam et loquela tua manifestum te facit'.[17] Quamuis enim cum nube umbrosa latites et corporaliter cum illis habites qui de 'lateribus aquilonis'[18] frigescunt, tamen corde bono et optimo tanquam uere philosophie discipulus respicis ad austrum et expectas inde Paraclitum qui nebulas istas aduentus sui illustratione expellat. Faciet autem hoc cum sibi bene placitum erit. Interim offero tibi me et mea, et rogo ut, si opportunum fuerit et necessitas aliqua exegerit, apud archiepiscopum bonum nobis teneas locum.[19]

[8] Gal. 2: 9. [9] Prov. 28: 21. [10] Cf. Ps. 128 (129): 6.

[11] Cf. Rev. 12: 4 (the end of the sentence echoes Rom. 1: 18).

[12] Cf. 2 Cor. 4: 18. (Plagues of Egypt: Exod. 7–12.)

[13] Combining refs to Exod. 11: 7 and oddly Isa. 56: 10. 'Secunda' also reads oddly as this is a ref. to the last plague. Neither allusion seems to fit the context.

[14] John's exile lasted from 1163/4 to Nov. 1170, and he was at Reims by Nov. 1164 (see *J. S. Epp.* ii, pp. xxii–xxiii, and Barlow, *Thomas Becket*, p. 220).

[15] Cf. Matt. 5: 40; Luke 6: 29.

[16] Cf. Mark 14: 51–2. On 'nudus . . . nudum sequi . . . Christum' see e.g. *P. Ven. Epp.* ii. 108–9.

[17] Cf. Matt. 26: 73.

[18] Cf. Isa. 14: 13 (cf. also Ps. 47 (48): 3, where the connotation however is positive).

Perhaps you are asking what this our proverb signifies, and why in the exordium of our letter we have put this complaint. The matter itself without doubt and the circumstance of the time untie the knot of the question, while those 'who seemed to be pillars'[8] in the house of God are sliding away the more steeply in schismatic error 'for a morsel of bread'[9] and for the glory of the flesh, which disappears like 'grass upon the tops of houses, which withereth before it be plucked up'.[10] Men see and know that the dragon has thrown down with him a third part of the stars from the sky,[11] and do not shrink, terrified by so foul and cruel an example, from going after Satan and from holding back the truth of God in falsehood. This is one of the plagues of Egypt which does not touch the sons of Israel but the sons of this world, who seek those things which are seen and are temporal not those which are not seen and are eternal.[12] But like to this is the next which rages greatly in your regions across the channel, where the king of England has rendered almost all the dogs so tongueless that they are not able to make the least noise, let alone bark.[13] Some, however, have swum over who were afraid that they would be gnawed by a similar worm and their throats be rotted away; among them is Canterbury with his private household of whom we have one puppy, John of Salisbury,[14] who does not hold his life more precious than himself but to the Egyptian lady taking away the coat he does not decline to give up the cloak[15] rather than be destroyed by the dishonour of falsehood; and naked, having cast off the linen cloth,[16] he desires to follow the naked Christ. Good friend, 'thou also art one of them, for even thy speech doth discover thee'.[17] For although you lie hidden with an overshadowing cloud and in body live with those who are frozen from 'the sides of the north,'[18] yet with a good and excellent heart like a pupil of true philosophy you look back to the south and await from there the Comforter who can drive away those clouds with the illumination of His approach. But He will do this when it is well pleasing to Him. Meanwhile I offer you myself and my resources and I ask that, if it be opportune and some necessity require it, you keep a good place for us with the archbishop.[19]

[19] Possibly a difficult request to make if Gerard was in Cologne during the schism, but on Saint-Remi's interests and Cologne, see appendix 10. In *c.*mid-Oct. 1166 John of Salisbury wrote to Gerard Pucelle (*J. S. Epp.* ii, no. 185, pp. 222–5) asking him to protect the 'res beati Remigii', presumably through his influence with the archbishop. Reuter interpreted this as a ref. to Meerssen—T. Reuter, 'John of Salisbury and the Germans' in M. Wilks (ed.), *The World of John of Salisbury*, Studies in Church History, Subsidia, iii (Oxford, 1994), pp. 415–25, at p. 425, n. 44.

180*

To King Louis VII of France[1]

1162 × Sept. 1180

Piissimo regi Francorum L⟨udouico⟩ dilecto et illustri domino P⟨etrus⟩ Dei miseratione ecclesie Sancti Remigii humilis minister, temporali felicitate felicitatem promereri sempiternam.

Mandastis michi palefridum qui ad opus uestri faceret. Talem sane nullum habeo, sed habere quam citius potero non differam, nec dissimulabo. Quod si forte non potuero talem inuenire qui uestra dignus gratia uideatur, hoc ipsum uobis remandare et alio genere seruitii recompensare usque ad festum Sancti Andree sollicitus ero. Sciatis enim quod ad seruiendum uobis maior michi semper fuit et adhuc est animus quam facultas. Miror autem quo animo acceperitis seruitia que uobis preterito anno exhibui, quippe cum necdum rescire potuerim nec adhuc michi innotuerit uos scire uel gratum habere quod uobis miserim copiam quatuor marcharum, et domino nostro redam trium equorum occasione uestri seruitii et causa commodauerim, quos nunquam rehabui. Valeat excellentia uestra.

180 *Vat Reg fo. 173*[v]]

180*

To King Louis VII of France[1]

1162 × Sept. 1180

To the most pious king of the Franks, Louis, beloved and illustrious lord, Peter, by the mercy of God humble servant of the church of Saint-Remi, by temporal felicity to merit everlasting felicity.

You have requested from me a palfrey which might meet your needs. I have none such, but I will not delay acquiring one as soon as possible and I will not dissemble. But if perchance I am not able to find such a one as would seem worthy of your grace, I will be concerned to advise you of this very fact and to make recompense with another kind of service by the feast of St Andrew. For you should know that in performing service to you my intent always was and still is greater than my ability. But I am astonished in what spirit you have received those services which I have offered to you in the past year, since I have not yet been able to find out by any means, nor has it yet been made known to me, whether you know or are grateful that I have sent to you the sum of four marks, and that I lent to our lord at the instance and for the sake of your service a three-horse carriage which I have never recovered. May your excellency flourish.

180 [1] King Louis VII, Aug. 1137–Sept. 1180. The feast of St Andrew (below): 30 Nov.

181

To King Knut of Sweden, Archbishop Stephen of Uppsala, the bishops and magnates of Sweden[1]

? early 1171 (or after Sept. 1171, or 1172 × 1173 before Oct.)

Regi Sueorum et ducibus et principibus et eorumdem archiepiscopo et cunctis suffraganeis eius.

Cum animi Deo deuoti principale et summum debeat esse studium ad gloriam et honorem Dei omnia componere, si forte aliquatenus se omnipotenti Deo placere uel leuiter senserit, cumulatis intrinsecus gaudiis totum se effundit tanquam liquefactus post sponsum,[2] acclamans et dicens, 'Exultabimus et letabimur in te memores uberum tuorum'.[3] His nostra paruitas prouocata exemplis, etsi in multis immo pene in omnibus cotidie me sciam peccare et non ut iustum est diuinis mancipari studiis, in hoc uno non usquequaque desperat[a] de misericordia Dei, quia de manu nostra manipulum benigne suscepit, ⟨et⟩ dominum Fulconem episcopum, quondam monachum nostrum et in claustrali religione a nobis enutritum, ad summum prouexit sacerdotium. Recognoscimus in eo uultum nostrum et speramus quod non recedat cor eius a Deo nostro et a mandatis eius.[4] Cum ergo opportunitas grata obtulerit, quod tempus habere possumus adhuc eum instruendi et informandi in ampliorem Dei dilectionem, gratanter et deuote excipimus, quia ulterius non eum uidendum usque 'ad thronum gratie'[5] et ad distributionem eterni stipendii arbitramur. Ad hec ipsa temporis incommoditas cooperatur desiderio nostro. Si enim uterque nostrum uellet, discrimina et pericula que habet

181 *Sirmond VI. 8*]
[a] *corr. Hall;* despero *Sirmond*

---

181 [1] The king of Sweden was Knut Eriksson, 1167–96: P. Holt (ed.), *Historisk Aarstals Liste* (Copenhagen, 1971), p. 26 (I am grateful to Brian Patrick McGuire for supplying this reference). The archbishop was Stephen of Uppsala, 1162–18 Aug. 1185 (Gams, p. 340; Uppsala had archiepiscopal status from Stephen's accession). The letter explains the delay of Fulk, missionary bishop of Estonia, in travelling north (see appendix 9). One of the reasons for this is that he was helping Peter in the administration of the city in the absence of Archbishop Henry of Reims, who has travelled to Rome (on Henry, see letter no. 21, n. 1). This may be connected to Henry's journey to Rome of probably early 1171, to which letter no. 110 is connected. It has been shown that neither the present letter nor letter no. 110 are connected to the events of 1167 (see letter no. 110, n. 1, and the explanation at

181

To King Knut of Sweden, Archbishop Stephen of Uppsala, the bishops and magnates of Sweden[1]

? early 1171 (or after Sept. 1171, or 1172 × 1173 before Oct.)

To the king of the Swedes and the dukes, princes, and archbishop of the same and all of his suffragans.

Since it ought to be the foremost and highest concern of a soul dedicated to God to settle all things to the glory and honour of God, if perhaps it even slightly feels itself to be pleasing in any way to the omnipotent God, with joys inwardly multiplied it pours itself out wholly as if melted in pursuit of the bridegroom,[2] calling out and saying, 'We will be glad and rejoice in thee, remembering thy breasts'.[3] Our smallness, challenged by these examples, although I know that I sin daily in many, nay almost in all, things and am not dedicated to divine studies as much as is proper, in this one matter does not despair utterly of the mercy of God, in that He kindly received from our hand a sheaf, and raised to the highest priesthood the lord bishop Fulk, once our monk and nourished by us in the religious life of the cloister. We recognize in him our likeness and we hope that his heart may not depart from our God and from His commandments.[4] Since therefore a pleasing opportunity has arisen, we joyfully and devotedly take what time we can still have for instructing and fashioning him to fuller love of God, because we reckon we shall not see him again until 'the throne of grace'[5] and the distribution of the eternal reward. In addition the very inclemency of the season conspires with our desire, for if both of us wished it, he could not cross the hazards and dangers which he must. For the

letter no. 93, n. 2), but the proposition that they both refer to the same journey is not so easily established. Fulk's journey north was most likely undertaken after the composition of the papal letters of Sept. 1171 or 1172, which he may have carried with him (see appendix 9 and letter no. 96, n. 1). If he was waiting for these letters before making the journey, then he would not have been ready to go in early 1171, and so the excuses of the present letter would be unnecessary. Alternatively, the original intention could have been to send the letters after him, and he could thus have been anticipating travel before Henry's absence from Reims of early 1171 prevented it. Otherwise, a second journey of Henry to Rome would have to be posited. Fulk probably made the journey north before Oct. 1173 in any case (see letter no. 96, n. 1).

[2] Cf. S. of S. 5: 6.

[3] S. of S. 1: 3.

[4] Cf. Jer. 17:5.

[5] Cf. Heb. 4: 16.

transire non posset. Inundantia enim aquarum, ut audiuimus, tanta est ut uix serenissimis temporibus meabile sit iter quo ad uos peruenitur. Tertia denique causa subest, quia dominus archiepiscopus noster Romam pergens officium suum nos supplere commisit. Nequaquam autem in dedicatione ecclesiarum uel ordinatione clericorum uel confirmatione Christianorum abbatis assurgit dignitas. Per ipsum ergo qui in omnibus noster est implemus quod per nos non possumus. Veniet autem ad uos plenus Dei benedictione cum tempora fuerint meliorata. Valete.

182

To a Nicholas (unidentified)[1]

1162 × 1181

Alii Nicolao.

Iam in desuetudinem pene abierunt reciproce salutationes quas tu bonus sub ouina pelle michi solebas mittere,[2] et ego qualis qualis tibi. Nescio utrum modo sis melior quam tunc, uetustior tamen et pigrior[a] es[3] et terre propinquior. Expecto facetias istas nostras a te cum usura statim solui. Prouolutus ergo pedibus teterrimi ydoli peto indulgentiam de nullo reatu. Mando tamen ut uenias ad festum nostrum quatinus tua pulcherrima et sanctissima facie tota solennitas illustretur et ore illo ueridico anime nostre a plagis et uulneribus suis curentur. Interim mando tibi negotia nostra que tibi frater iste et socius tuus in colore et facie dicet. Vale et ora pro nobis, tua enim oratio penetrat celos.

182 *Sirmond VI. 5*]
[a] *corr. Hall;* nigrior *Sirmond*

---

182 [1] To an unknown recipient, identified only as Nicholas. In Sirmond (and so in the lost Reims MS) this letter follows letter no. 157; on the heading, see letter no. 84, n. 1. It would be attractive to think that this was part of a late attempt at reconciliation with the disgraced and (presumably) estranged Nicholas of Clairvaux (who d. 1175 × 1178—on him see letter no. 49, n. 1), but this note is too brief to give any sure indications.

flooding, so we have heard, is so great that the route to you is scarcely passable at the best of times. Finally there is a third underlying cause, namely that our lord archbishop setting out for Rome has charged us to fulfil his office. But the dignity of an abbot by no means rises to the dedication of churches or to the ordination of clerks or to the confirmation of Christians. Therefore through him who is ours in all things we fulfil that which we cannot do ourselves. But he will come to you filled with the blessing of God when the season improves. Farewell.

182

To a Nicholas (unidentified)[1]

1162 × 1181

To another Nicholas.

There have now almost fallen into desuetude the reciprocal greetings which you, a good man, were accustomed to send to me on sheepskin,[2] and I, such as I am, to you. I do not know whether you are better now than then, yet you are older and slower[3] and nearer to the earth. I am waiting for those jests of ours to be repaid by you with interest forthwith. Grovelling therefore at the feet of the foulest idol, I seek indulgence for no guilt. I order you, however, to come to our feast so that the whole festival may be illuminated by your most beautiful and most holy face and our souls may be cured of their injuries and wounds by that truthful mouth. Meanwhile I commend to you our business which this brother, your companion, will relate to you fully, giving it complexion and features. Farewell and pray for us, for your prayer penetrates the heavens.

[2] i.e. on parchment.

[3] Sirmond's reading *nigrior* could mean 'closer to death', i.e. combining the reference to old age with an allusion to a return to the Benedictine order, and so a black habit, which would fit with Nicholas of Clairvaux (see n. 1, above).

183

Recipient unidentified[1]

1176, in or soon after July

Magistro *** presbytero karissimo amico suo Petrus abbas, salutem.

Memor temporis illius quo feruente non minus studio quam etate in Cellensi monasterio simul commorati sumus, attendo plurimum detraxisse cursum interlabentem a corpore ualetudinis, ab animo lectionis et meditationis. Inexplebili siquidem desiderio nec oculus uisu librorum nec auris satiabatur auditu lectionum. Harum extremitatum Deus erat et medius et primus et ultimus. Saluo namque ordine, salua diuine laudis debiti pensione legebam leges nec amittebam uel omittebam consuetas orationes.[2] Nunc autem, amice bone, cure et solicitudines que me a iuuentute decerpere non destituerunt cotidie accrescunt et, ut michi uidetur, obsidionem perpetuam contra me firmauerunt. Si quid roris gratie, si quid pinguedinis misericordie[3] raptim et quasi furtim de diuinis cellariis interdum attraxit spiritus meus, derepente subitus et intempestiuus totum absorbet nimius estus, unde clamo ad Deum, 'Anima mea sicut terra sine aqua tibi.'[4] Hoc de interiori, de exteriori uero statu gratias ago benignissimo Deo meo quia in omni prosperitate et pace sum, tamen qualem potest dare mundus.[5] Libenter uos uiderem et senectutem meam uel ad tempus sub alis beati Remigii fouerem.[6] Magister Iohannes de Anglia, quondam clericus noster, electus est Carnotensis. Munusculum uestrum accepi et gratias ago. Valete.

183 *Sirmond VII. 7*]

183 [1] The recipient, identified only as 'magister presbyter', evidently knew Peter from Montier-la-Celle. The letter can be dated by the reference to the el. of John of Salisbury to Chartres (notified of el. 22 July, 1176, consecrated 8 Aug.; see letter no. 102, n. 1). (The name Prester may be a possibility, but there is no basis for any sure identification.)

183

Recipient unidentified[1]

1176, in or soon after July

To master * * *, priest, his dearest friend, Abbot Peter, greetings.

Mindful of that time when, with zeal no less fervent than years, we dwelt together in the monastery of Montier-la-Celle, I observe that the intervening passage of time has detracted very much from my body's health and from my mind's capacity for reading and meditation. For because of insatiable desire, neither was the eye then sated with the sight of books nor the ear with listening to readings. God was at once the middle and the beginning and the end of these extremes for, saving the order and saving the payment of the debt of divine praise, I was reading the laws without any loss or omission of the customary prayers.[2] But now, good friend, concerns and worries which have not ceased to tear at me since my youth grow daily and, so it seems to me, have strengthened a perpetual siege against me. If my spirit has in the meantime drawn from the divine store rooms anything of the dew of grace, anything of the fatness of mercy,[3] greedily and as it were by stealth, of a sudden the unexpected and unseasonable excessive heat devours it all, whence I call to God, 'My soul is as earth without water unto thee.'[4] So much for the inner state, but as for the external state I give thanks to my most benign God that I am in all prosperity and peace, but only such as the world can give.[5] I would be glad to see you and to warm my old age, if only for a time, beneath the wings of the blessed Remigius.[6] Master John from England, once our clerk, has been elected to Chartres. I received your little gift and give thanks. Farewell.

[2] i.e. he fitted study in with the monastic offices; laws here may mean God's law (as e.g. in Heb. 8: 10) rather than any form of legal study (i.e. the sense in which it used elsewhere in the letters).

[3] Cf. Gen. 27: 28, 39.

[4] Ps. 142 (143): 6.

[5] Cf. John 14: 27.

[6] i.e. he should visit Peter at Saint-Remi.

APPENDICES

APPENDIX 1

The Disputed Election at Saint-Méen-de-Gaël

Letter no. 1 is written in the name of the community of Saint-Méen-de-Gaël in Brittany (Benedictine, dioc. Saint-Malo; Cott. ii, 2810–11) and concerns a disputed election. For further details of this case, see also *GC* xiv. 1021 and Morice, *Bretagne*, ii. xciv–xcv, both of which cite this letter. Abbot Henry had been deposed by the monks, with the support of Bishop John of Saint-Malo (1144–63, see letter no. 14, n. 1), possibly quite soon after his election—his predecessor Jostho last occurs in 1144, and this letter falls between 1145 and 1147, as explained below. Henry was replaced by the Robert in support of whom letter no. 1 was written, and the new election was approved by Archbishop Hugh II of Tours (1133–47; *GC* xiv. 82–7). Henry subsequently returned, this time with the support of the archbishop (who had changed his mind, as Peter complains in this letter), after which Robert appealed to the pope. The outcome of this appeal is not known, and may not have been known at the time of writing of letter no. 1: Peter accuses Hugh of harassing Robert and seems to fear the case being delegated to the archiepiscopal court. Whatever the immediate outcome, both claimants occur subsequently, Henry styling himself abbot of Saint-Judicäel (another name for Saint-Méen) and Robert, abbot of Saint-Méen—which may indicate that the latter continued to enjoy the support of the monks and was resident. Both appear in a charter of 1163 of a later archbishop of Tours (see *GC* xiv. 1021), but from some point after this date Robert is sole abbot (*GC* assuming it to be the same Robert). The *terminus ad quem* for letter no. 1 must be 1147 since it speaks of the archbishop of Tours changing his mind after a settlement had been reached during the pontificate of Lucius II (12 Mar. 1144–15 Feb. 1145). The only archbishop of Tours during Lucius's pontificate was Hugh II (1133–47, as above); after 1147 Peter would have been dealing with a different archbishop. The recipient of letter no. 1 must thus be Eugenius III (15 Feb. 1145–8 July 1153), and so the salutation preserved in Sirmond is in this case accurate. Peter's involvement in this case is most likely a result of his friendship with John of Saint-Malo. The dispute seems to have some connection to the reform of the house, with Robert being the reformers' candidate.

APPENDIX 2

The Dispute over the Cemetery of La Celle-sous-Chantemerle

Letter no. 3 is an appeal on behalf of the priory of La Celle-sous-Chantemerle (dioc. Troyes, Cott. i. 647), a dependency of Montier-la-Celle which was involved in a dispute over burial rights with the Augustinian house of Saint-Serein-de-Chantemerle (Cott. i. 693; *GC* xii. 592–5—regular canons replaced secular ones in 1135).[1] Lalore, *Cartulaires*, preserves no evidence for a specific grant of a cemetery to the canons (there is no cartulary for the Augustinian house). The earliest specific extant reference to burial rights in Chantemerle is in Lalore, *Cartulaires*, vi. (Montier-la-Celle) 258–60, no. 219, a privilege of Bishop Henry of Troyes, dated before 19 Dec. 1155 on the grounds that it should precede the bull of Hadrian IV noted below (a date for the original grant of 1125 × 1145/6 can be inferred from letter no. 3: see letter no. 3, n. 3). Bishop Henry's privilege includes, among the rights and privileges of Montier-la-Celle, the clause: 'Atrium Sancti Sereni Celle, in quo omnes qui moriuntur in castello Cantumerule, seu in villa Fontis Bethonis, debent tumulari.' For the most part the papal privileges in Lalore, *Cartulaires*, vi. contain general clauses on burial rights, most likely relating to the abbey church of Montier-la-Celle itself, while most of the extant documents detailing possessions of La Celle-sous-Chantemerle make no mention of burial rights at all. However, a bull of Hadrian IV of 19 Dec. 1155 (Lalore, *Cartulaires*, vi. 214–16, no. 197; JL 10099), addressed jointly to Peter of Celle and Prior Thomas of La Celle-sous-Chantemerle, includes among the list of rights and possessions: 'Ecclesiam Sancti Sereni, atrium eiusdem ecclesie.' In letter no. 65, however, addressed to John of Salisbury (which can be dated a little more closely than letter no. 3), Peter refers to an appeal made against him to Rome over this cemetery, contrary to a privilege of Anastasius IV which John himself had evidently had a hand in producing. John's role in this is discussed in *J.S. Epp.* i. 255, n. 5 and R. L. Poole, 'John of Salisbury at the papal court', *English Historical Review*, xxxviii (1923), 321–30, at p. 329,

[1] The dedication of the dependent priory was Notre-Dame, but there is evidently a degree of confusion in the sources and secondary literature, and variants such as Saint-Serein-de-la-Celle-sous-Chantemerle appear. Confusion may have arisen over phrases in the charters such as 'Sancti Sereni Celle' and the references to a church of Saint-Serein pertaining to La Celle-sous-Chantemerle. There may be a confusion between a parochial church and the house of canons, which was dedicated to St Serein.

n. 5. Poole identifies the document alluded to by Peter of Celle with Lalore, *Cartulaires*, vi. 206–11, no. 195, dated 10 Dec. 1153, also JL 9777 and Meinert, *Papsturkunden in Frankreich*, p. 253, no. 61 (where, however, it is dated Dec. 19 1153). However Lalore, *Cartulaires*, vi. no. 195, does not specifically mention burial rights in Chantemerle. In fact three bulls were issued in Montier-la-Celle's favour on 10 Dec. 1153: JL 9775, a general bull confirming the possessions and privileges of Montier-la-Celle; JL 9776, a similar confirmation for the dependency of Saint-Ayoul (or Aigulf) de Provins; and JL 9777, another such confirmation for La Celle-sous-Chantemerle (here identified as Cella S. Sereni) issued at Peter's petition—see also Lalore, *Cartulaires*, vi. xiii, which refers to entries in the eighteenth-century inventory of the two lost cartularies of Montier-la-Celle). It is JL 9775 which is the same document as Lalore, *Cartulaires*, vi. no. 195—as JL notes. Meinert seems to have confused two separate bulls, giving the date of Hadrian IV's bull (19 Dec.) and the year of Anastasius IV's bulls (1153). In fact, three bulls were similarly issued on 19 Dec. 1155, JL nos. 10098, 10099, and 10100, in favour of Saint-Ayoul-de-Provins, La Celle-sous-Chantemerle, and Montier-la-Celle itself respectively (the latter is fragmentary, but evidently a general bull). Meinert, *Papsturkunden in Frankreich*, p. 253, no. 61, names the same prior as JL 10099 but has a different *incipit*, and his source appears to have confused what were probably two very similar bulls: JL 9777 of 10 Dec. 1153 (of which the full text does not survive) and JL 10099 of 19 Dec. 1155 (see Meinert, *Papsturkunden in Frankreich*, pp. 48–9, which records the entries in a later cartulary of Montier-la-Celle, as well as the eighteenth-century inventory which Lalore edited). John of Salisbury may have had a part in drafting all three of the 1153 bulls.

A confirmation of Count Henry the Liberal of Champagne to Peter of Celle of 1154 (Lalore, *Cartulaires*, vi. 14–17, no. 13) makes no mention of burial rights in a detailed list of the possessions of La-Celle-sous-Chantemerle, but as this would fall between the two papal bulls and the dispute would have been ongoing, nothing can be inferred from its silence. Letter no. 3 refers to an inconclusive hearing at the episcopal court in Troyes. The case seems to have gone on beyond the issue of Hadrian IV's bull; it was evidently delegated to Archbishop Hugh of Sens and Bishop Theobald of Paris in *c.*1156, and it may have dragged on for much longer.[2]

[2] Meinert, *Papsturkunden in Frankreich*, p. 49: 'Hadrian IV an Erzbischof Hugo von Sens und Bischoff Theobald von Paris, cr. 1156, wegen eines Streits zwischen den Kanonikers von Chantemerle und den Mönchen aus M-la-Celle ebendort.' Also, John of Salisbury mentions a prior of Chantemerle in a letter to Peter of Celle written within these dates (*J.S. Epp.* i, no. 19, pp. 31–2, dated autumn 1156, after John's return from Rome). John may be referring here to the prior of La-Celle-sous-Chantemerle (and not of Saint-Serein-de-Chantemerle, as suggested in the note in *J.S. Epp.*), but the letter offers no further evidence.

The case seems finally to have gone against Montier-la-Celle. Alexander III issued a confirmation of rights in favour of the canons in 1165 (*PL* cc. 351–2, no. 326; JL 11176; *GC* xii. Instr. 271–2, giving 14 Apr.), referring to a similar confirmation of Hadrian IV, and including, among the list of rights and possessions: 'Totam parochiam castri de cantumerula, atrium cum sepulturis, exceptis his qui manent in mercatu Rainaldi de Puyeio.' This clause seems to contradict Hadrian IV's confirmation to Montier-la-Celle, and may have been added when the bull of Alexander III for the canons was drafted, despite the deliberate reference back to Hadrian IV.

Letter no. 65 clearly falls in the period after the bull of Anastasius IV, to which it refers. As Alexander III's confirmations date from after Peter's departure from Montier-la-Celle it is most likely that no. 65 was written pending an appeal to Hadrian IV, which resulted, presumably, in the bull of 19 Dec. 1155 (but given the evidence for continued disputes, even this cannot be certain). Peter says that the date has been brought forward from the first Sunday in Advent (which was 28 Nov. in 1154, 27 Nov. in 1155) to 18 Oct., which may indicate the letter being written in mid-1155, and definitely before Oct., but this cannot be certain, and does not anyway seriously narrow the range of possible dates. Letter no. 3 could relate to an earlier phase in the dispute, before the issue of Anastasius IV's bull, as it refers back to no act more recent than that of Hato of Troyes. However, this is an argument from silence and so not conclusive. Furthermore, we know from letter no. 65 that the later appeal to the pope (i.e. evidently to Hadrian IV) was initiated by the rival abbot of Saint-Serein. We do not know what action preceded or prompted the issue of Anastasius IV's bull (although it was evidently important or threatening enough to command John of Salisbury's personal attention). In letter no. 3 the rival abbot is said to have appealed, which makes the period before Hadrian IV's bull as likely (giving a possible date for letter no. 3 of late 1153 × 19 Dec. 1155). It is unclear where the inconclusive appeal to the bishop of Troyes mentioned in letter no. 3 fits in, other than that it preceded an/the appeal to the papacy by the rival abbot.

Note: Dr Ludwig Falkenstein has recently kindly sent me a transcript of the *actum* of the delegates noted by Meinert (see n. 2, above). Although incomplete, this document indicates a settlement in favour of Montier-la-Celle in 1156. Letters no. 3 and 65 both apparently refer to a phase of the dispute conducted at the papal Curia (where John of Salisbury was active); however, the precise role of John of Salisbury, and the relation between the bull of 1155 and this settlement, remains unclear. Alexander III's later involvement clearly results from a re-opening of the case, and a separate phrase of the dispute.

APPENDIX 3

Peter of Celle's Appeal on behalf of Matilda of Fontevrault

Letter no. 5 is an appeal on behalf of Fontevrault against the bishop of Poitiers. A dispute arose between the abbey and Gilbert de la Porrée, bishop of Poitiers (1141/2–26 Nov. 1154; *GC* ii. 1175–8) over the election of Matilda of Anjou (abbess of Fontevrault 1149, after Apr.–21 May 1155: *GC* ii. 1318–19, and see J.-M. Bienvenu, 'Aliénor d'Aquitaine et Fontevraud', *Cahiers de civilisation médiévale*, xxix (1986), 15–36, at pp. 18–19 and n. 21, with a brief account of this case and the context). Gilbert had demanded a profession of obedience from Matilda and refused to bless the abbess. Matilda received the support of Eugenius III (see *GC* ii. Instr. 362, no. xlvi, and *RHF* xv. 455, no. lx) and Suger of Saint-Denis (see Bienvenu, 'Aliénor d'Aquitaine et Fontevraud', p. 18 and n. 21), and eventually received a bull from Anastasius IV protecting her rights (Ramackers, *Papsturkunden in Frankreich* 5, pp. 167–71, no. 83, giving 20 Jan. 1154; JL 9806, giving 1153–4; *GC* ii. 1319). However, the case evidently continued later than this (see below) and so these may be the privileges of previous popes to which Peter refers in letter no. 5. Letter no. 5 was presumably written during Matilda's lifetime (as *GC* suggests, and so cannot have been addressed to Alexander III, the address preserved in Sirmond). There is no evidence that the dispute continued into the time of Matilda's successor, Audeburge de Hautes-Bruyères (1155–80), and Matilda is also the only abbess of Fontevrault with whom there is other evidence of Peter having a connection (see letter no. 27). This would suggest that the recipient was either Anastasius IV (12 July 1153–3 Dec. 1154) or Hadrian IV (4 Dec. 1154–1 Sept. 1159), by which time Gilbert was dead and the bishop in question would be Calot (1155–7/8; *GC* ii. 1178). Sirmond notes a *rescriptum* of Hadrian IV in the archives ('in tabulario') of Fontevrault, in which it is stated that the abbess should offer a profession of obedience to the bishop of Poitiers provided that he in turn impose no undue burdens on the house. Thus the most likely date for letter no. 5 would seem to be between the election of Hadrian IV and the death of Matilda, but it could have been addressed to Anastasius IV.[3]

[3] Neither J. de la Mainferme, *Clypeus nascentis Fontebraldensis ordinis*, nov. ed. 3 vols. (Paris, 1684–92), which used subsequently lost material, nor the fragmentary *Grand Cartulaire* (Paris, B.N. nouv. acq. lat. 2414) shed any light on this..

APPENDIX 4

The Disputes at Montier-en-Der

Letter no. 6 is apparently written in the name of Abbot Gautier of Montier-en-Der, who occurs 1161 × 1166, but his predecessor last occurs 1150 (*GC* ix. 919). Two works of doubtful reliability give 1162–6: E. de Barthélemy, *Diocèse ancien de Châlons-sur-Marne*, 2 vols. (Paris, 1861), i. 368, and R. A. Bouillevaux, *Les Moines du Der* [*sic*] (Montier-en-Der, 1845), pp. 163–5, but neither cite their sources. If the abbot in question was Gautier, from the initial G. in letter no. 6, and Peter was still at Montier-la-Celle, neither of which need be the case, then a date of 1161/2 or earlier would be possible. If the address to Alexander III is correct, letter no. 6 must have been written after the end of July 1160, i.e. after his recognition in France (see letter no. 22, n. 1). Also there is no suggestion that the archbishop of Reims mentioned is now dead, so if Peter is still at Montier-la-Celle, a date before 21 Sept. 1161 is also likely (i.e. when Archbishop Samson died: see letter no. 6, n. 8; his successor, Henry of France, was el. in Jan. 1162 and cons. later that year—see letter no. 21, n. 1).

Peter's connection with Montier-en-Der continued when he was abbot of Saint-Remi (see below), and some late letters were preserved among the early collection in the lost Reims manuscript (Rc, see Introduction, II. 1. iv). Gautier is the only abbot of Montier-en-Der with the initial G. recorded during Peter's career, but the problem of his dating leaves a range of dates both before and after 1160/1 possible. This is also the abbot to whom Messiter misattributed Peter's early letters in MS O, where letter no. 6 stands first (see Introduction, II. 1. ii).

No reference to the case which is the subject of letter no. 6, concerning the possession of a church or investiture contested with another, unidentified, G., appears in Lalore, *Cartulaires*, iv. (Montier-en-Der, etc.). Peter seems to have become involved with Montier-en-Der in a more serious and long-running dispute which arose around the same time or slightly later between Abbot Gautier and Bishop Guy of Châlons-sur-Marne. There were two bishops of Châlons-sur-Marne with this name in quick succession: Guy de Dampierre, el. after March 1162, d. 1163, after Aug., with his el. still disputed, and Guy de Joinville, 1164–90. On both see *GC* ix. 882–3; see also Pacaut, *Élections*, pp. 101–3, 106 n. 1, 110, and 141, and L. Falkenstein, 'Alexander III. und der Streit um die Doppelwahl in Châlons-sur-Marne (1162–1164)', *Deutsches Archiv*, xxxii (1976), 444–94. According to Bouillevaux (*Les Moines du Der*, pp. 163–5) the bishop would not

recognize the immunities granted to the abbey by the papacy; the case was delegated to the archbishop of Sens (presumably Hugh, 1142–68, see letter no. 8, n. 1) and Peter of Celle (in which case the bishop of Châlons in question would have been Guy de Dampierre). When the delegates decided in Gautier's favour his enemies accused him of letting discipline lapse and of running down the abbey's finances. In response, Alexander III re-delegated the case to Gerard 'of Cîteaux' and Peter of Celle, and Gautier was exculpated, his excuse being the depredations of 'Brabanters' in the region. This account, however, is riddled with confusions: there was no Abbot Gerard of Cîteaux in this period[4] and so this is presumably either Gerard of Clairvaux (1170–16 Oct. 1175, ref. at letter no. 48, n. 24), or possibly Geoffrey of Auxerre (abbot of Clairvaux 1162–5, see *J.S. Epp.* ii. 178–9, n. 36 and refs.). Furthermore, Bouillevaux treats Peter of Montier-la-Celle and Peter of Saint-Remi as two separate characters. A bull of Alexander III instructed the abbot of Clairvaux and Peter of Celle to deal with Gautier's enemies and oversee the reform of the house, and confirmed the abbey's immunities (presumably this is the bull of 28 May 1171/2 at JL 12074, *PL* cc. 829, no. 943, and *RHF* xv. 919).[5] These events are mentioned more briefly in Barthélemy's account of the abbey (*Diocèse ancien*, i. 135, but again citing no sources) and *GC* ix. 919–20. *GC* refers to a privilege of Alexander III of 1164 addressed to Gautier, and to a visitation of Montier-en-Der ordered by Alexander III and delegated to Gerard 'of Cîteaux' (again presumably Gerard of Clairvaux or Geoffrey of Auxerre) and Peter of Celle which might have taken place under one of three later abbots. These abbots were Jorannus (no dates), Ebalus (no dates), and Rainald (occurs 1174 × 1182; on all three see *GC* ix. 919–20).

These events seem to be unrelated to letter no. 6, especially as the bishop of Châlons-sur-Marne is a judge there and his successor or successors are opponent(s) in this larger dispute. However Peter's request in letter no. 6 that the archbishop of Sens be appointed delegate seems to fit with Bouillevaux's (albeit confused) account, and two cases may have become conflated—i.e. the G. of letter no. 6 could have been acting with the support

[4] On the abbots of Cîteaux in this period see J. Marilier, *Chartes et documents concernant l'abbaye de Cîteaux 1098–1182*, Bibliotheca Cisterciensis, i (Rome, 1961), pp. 26–7: they were Renard de Bar, 1134 (poss. early in year)–16 Dec. 1150; Gossuin, early 1151–31 March 1155; Lambert, April–Aug. 1155–Sept. 1161; Fastrad, Sept. 1161–21 Apr. 1163; Gilbert, end of May 1163–17 Oct. 1168; Alexander of Cologne, Nov. 1168–28 July 1178; William of Toulouse, 1178–27 Nov. 1180; Peter I, end of 1180–March 1184; and Bernard, April–May, and before Sept., 1184–1 Jan. 1196.

[5] Also included in the collection of 56 letters in Sirmond (see Introduction s. II. 1. i), no. 45. Bouillevaux gives the impossible combination of a bull of 1164 addressing Fastrad of Clairvaux (1157–61, see letter no. 48, n. 24); JL 12074 does not name the abbots. Bouillevaux's account throughout, for which he cites no sources, is confused. He may be using Baillet's history (uned.: see ref. in Meinert, *Papsturkunden in Frankreich*, p. 62).

of a bishop or successive bishops of Châlons-sur-Marne, hence Peter's complaint that justice was evaded at the episcopal court of Châlons—but no such mandate survives, and any conclusions about the date and circumstances remain very tentative..

APPENDIX 5

Eskil of Lund and the establishment of the Carthusians in Denmark (and the date of letter no. 12)

Letter no. 12 concerns the establishment of the first Carthusian community in Denmark; it assumes Eskil of Lund (see letter no. 12, n. 1) to be exercising his full authority in the area (as noted in *DD* i. 2, p. 265).[6] It would seem therefore to fall between Eskil's two periods of exile (not before the first, as explained below, and not after Peter had left Montier-la-Celle). The first of these periods of exile ended when Eskil returned to Denmark between Oct. 1157 and 18 Apr. 1158 (after his journey to Rome and subsequent imprisonment at the hands of an ally of Barbarossa). He went into exile again in autumn 1161, returning to Denmark in late 1167. He travelled to France again in 1173, before Oct., and returned to Denmark again in autumn 1176 (but on this date, see letter no. 97, n. 1), before finally resigning his see in spring 1177 and entering Clairvaux (see *SEECO*, vi. 20–8, which gives closer dates for Eskil's movements than *DD* i. 2, p. 340). Eskil certainly visited Saint-Remi during at least one of his periods in France, and was accorded confraternity with the community (see *DD* i. 2, nos. 149–50, pp. 277–8). An earlier date for letter no. 12, before Eskil's first exile, is not likely since the Carthusians were not established in Denmark before 1162 (cf. Le Couteulx, ii. 230–1) and Peter refers in letter no. 12 to a request made by Eskil in the previous year to organize the mission, and to the plea that the monk Roger should be sent to seek a suitable site for a foundation. *DD* i. 2, pp. 265–6 dates the letter 1160 × 1162, with a note that a date after autumn 1161 is unlikely—i.e. just before the establishment of the first Carthusian house in Denmark. However, an earlier date, from late 1157, cannot absolutely be ruled out, even if it is less likely, as there is no evidence as to exactly how much time elapsed between Eskil's original request, Roger's journey north, and the eventual establishment of the house.[7] Eskil evidently visited Mont-Dieu, and possibly first met Peter of Celle, while in France before his capture by Barbarossa's allies, but the mandate of the previous year to which Peter refers here cannot be ascribed to this visit (as Le Couteulx suggests: Le Couteulx, ii. 230–1) with any certainty, and in any

[6] *DD*'s texts of those letters of Peter of Celle which concern Scandinavia are all taken from Sirmond.

[7] However, any date before 1159 makes it more difficult to account for Eskil having made a request the year before, as he was travelling to and from Rome. Furthermore, a letter earlier in the possible period might have made reference to his capture.

case if the identification of the Roger here with the Roger in letter no. 59 is correct, the present letter may be late in the possible period, and so more than a year after Eskil's return to the north (as explained at letter no. 12, n. 9).

It appears that the chapter of La Grande Chartreuse had agreed to support the proposition for a foundation but, as letter no. 114 shows, further requests were needed to realize the support. *DD* prefers the later date for letter no. 12 because letter no. 114, written from Saint-Remi, and therefore after 1162, to Basil of La Grande Chartreuse, reminds the Carthusians that their establishment in Denmark is still insecure. However, the two letters need not be so close in date as the insecurity could have been prolonged, promoting the subsequent request or requests for support, especially as the foundation apparently failed after ten or twelve years (Le Couteulx, ii. 230).

The foundation chronicle of Sorø Abbey, written *c.*1200, records that Absalon (Eskil's successor at Lund, see letter no. 104, n. 1) gave to Sorø land at Asserbo ('Aswardebothe') which he had originally obtained in a deal with Esrom Abbey with the intention of establishing a house for the Carthusians whom he had summoned to the area, but who had abandoned the site at some stage finding it unsuitable, and 'ad propria remearunt' (presumably France). If this is a reference to the Carthusian settlement which Le Couteulx is speaking of, it provides a possible location but no dates. The chronicle may have confused Absalon and Eskil; alternatively Absalon, who was bishop of Roskilde from 1158, may also have had a part in the foundation. A second foundation is unlikely. See J. Langebek, *Scriptores Rerum Danicarum Medii Aevi*, 9 vols. in 8 (Copenhagen, 1772–1878), iv. 469 (I am grateful to Brian Patrick McGuire for bringing this source to my attention).

APPENDIX 6

Simon of Chézy-l'Abbaye, Clairvaux, and the date of letter no. 39

Letter no. 39 may refer to a threatened succession dispute occasioned by the imminent departure of Abbot Simon of Chéy-l'Abbaye for Clairvaux, and if so it affects the traditional date given for his retirement, as explained below (on Simon's dates, see also letter no. 38, n. 1). Simon had long expressed his wish to retire to Clairvaux. St Bernard had forbidden such a move while he himself lived, but promised Simon that he, Simon, would die at Clairvaux (on his wish to transfer, see also *Sancti Bernardi Op.* viii. 210–11, no. 293). After Bernard's death Simon did indeed transfer to Clairvaux where, despite his age and ill-health, he lived for seven years—a feat described as miraculous by the sources: see *Exordium Magnum Ordinis Cisterciensis*, iii. 28 (*PL* clxxxv. 1091), and *Sancti Bernardi Vita Prima, vii, Fragmenta ex Herberti libris de miraculis Cisterciensium monachorum*, iv (*PL* clxxxv. 461–2), which preserve similar texts (these accounts of his age and ill-health fit with the present letter). If Simon died 27 July 1163 (*GC* ix. 431) this would mean that he retired in 1156 (*GC* ix. 431 also connects letter no. 39 with Simon's imminent retirement and calculates its date thus, but confusingly omits the crucial word 'septennium' from its quotation from the *Exordium Magnum*). However, the reference in letter no. 39 to a recent scandal at Cluny must be to the succession dispute of 1157 between Robert le Gros and Hugh de Fraisans (the deposition of Hugh in 1161 is less likely as it would have had less relevance to the present case, and the dates do not fit). On Hugh see letter no. 31, n. 1, and on the dispute at Cluny, G. Constable, 'The abbots and anti-abbot of Cluny during the papal schism of 1159', *Revue Bénédictine*, xciv (1984), 370–400, which however suggests that Peter of Celle is referring in letter no. 39 to Abbot Hugh's support for the anti-pope Victor IV (7 Sept. 1159–20 Apr. 1164). Letter no. 39 could not have been written before Christmas 1156, while Peter the Venerable was still alive (on his death, see *P. Ven. Epp.* ii. 268). However, if the seven years to Simon's death are reckoned inclusively, then the first year is 1157 (whether one reckons from 1 Jan., Lady Day, or Easter). On Peter of Celle's other involvements with Chézy, and with Abbot Simon, see also Haseldine, 'Friendship and rivalry', pp. 406–7, and *Bernard de Clairvaux*, pp. 240–1.

APPENDIX 7

Peter of Celle and Nicholas of Clairvaux's debate on the nature of the body, the soul, and God

Letters 50 and 51 are Peter of Celle's half of an epistolary debate with Nicholas of Clairvaux (on whom see letter no. 49, n. 1). Nicholas's letters themselves, although included by Migne among Peter's letters (in *PL* ccii. along with other letters of Nicholas to Peter on different subjects), form no part of Peter's letter collection and so are not included in the present edn.,[8] but what follows includes a summary of Nicholas's arguments. On the sequence of these letters, see letter no. 50, n. 1, and on the tradition of Nicholas's letters, see Introduction, II. 3.

The debate in this group of letters is primarily about the nature of the body, the soul, and God, and in particular whether unity or simplicity is the definitive characteristic of divinity. The tradition of Neoplatonic thought in the twelfth century, which is the background to these debates and speculations, was far from clear-cut, and gave rise to a confusing variety of interpretations and approaches: 'une indéniable communauté de perceptions laisse à leur jeu des options disparates, dont les constructions révèleront l'incompatibilité dans un syncrétisme indéchiffrable.'[9] Common perceptions in Neoplatonic thought included the opposition between the intelligible and the sense-perceptible worlds, the transcendence of the Deity, and the location of the human soul between the two worlds, bound to the body but capable of spiritual ascent. Rejecting the traditional Neoplatonic theories of the eternity of matter, and of the deity as mere *opifex* or fashioner of formless matter, the Christian tradition sought to redefine the relations between God, souls, and matter so as to accommodate the view of God as the sole eternal entity, Creator of all from nothing, not co-eternal with primal matter. Augustine had stressed the absolute reality of the intelligible, or spiritual, world, dismissing the sense-perceptible as transient and building his system around the notion of divine ideas. The transcendence and purity of God was conveyed by the attribution to Him of simplicity as a defining characteristic. Boethius, attempting to synthesize Plato with Aristotle, maintained the distinction between the two worlds but subjected the relations between entities and states of being to systematic analysis.

[8] In contrast to Peter's exchange of letters with Nicholas of St Albans (see appendix 13). In that case, Nicholas of St Albans's letters exist as an integral part of Peter's collection and survive only as such.

[9] M.-D. Chenu, *La Théologie au douzième siècle* (Paris, 1957), p. 108.

Concerned more with the ontology of the One, he defined the deity not in the more affective language of radical simplicity, but by its composition; hence the definitive characteristic of the absolutely transcendent deity was its unity, contrasted with the degrees of multiplicity, or compound nature, of other entities.

In this debate Nicholas proposes the Boethian view of the primacy of unity as the defining characteristic of God and elaborates his views of the relations between God, souls, and matter. Peter responds with the Augustinian view of the primacy of simplicity. (Here as elsewhere Peter frequently echoes Augustinian views and terms.) The two views are as much a difference of emphasis as radically opposed alternatives. Chenu characterized the two branches of thought as appealing to different audiences, the Boethian more overtly rational, appealing to an interest in the categorization of phenomena ultimately leading to natural science, the Augustinian more affective and spiritual. Peter in these letters is concerned with the transcendence of God but not with the metaphysics of the One. Frequently in this exchange he is as concerned to decry Nicholas's needless sophistries as to enter into detailed debate over the technicalities.[10]

Letter no. 50 is a response to particular arguments raised by Nicholas's letter 'Nuper cum aquilonaris . . .' (*PL* ccii. 491–5, no. 63). In this letter Nicholas begins with a description of a blood-letting at Clairvaux and the time for reflection afforded by the subsequent period of recuperation. He then expounds on the fruits of his reflection, taking as a starting point the text Job 14: 1–2: 'Man, born of a woman, living for a short time, is filled with many miseries. | Who cometh forth like a flower, and is destroyed, and fleeth as a shadow, and never continueth in the same state.' After a lengthy lament on human weakness, he introduces his second text, Ps. 38 (39): 6: 'All things are vanity; every man living.' This is linked directly to the text in Job: '"Brevi", inquit, "uiuens tempore" [Job 14: 1], uere "uniuersa uanitas, omnis homo uiuens" [Ps. 38: 6]' (*PL* ccii. 493). The crucial point is that both texts use the present participle *uiuens* rather than the noun *uita*, and Nicholas derives from this, along with the association in Ps. of *uanitas* and *uiuens*, proof of his chief distinctions (based on Claudianus Mamertus' *De statu anime*, see below): '"Omnis", inquit, "homo uiuens" [Ps. 38: 6], non omnis homo uita. Corpus denique est uiuens, anima est uiua, Deus uita; uiuens ex uanitate, uiua ex simplicitate, uita ex unitate' (*PL* ccii. 493). This is an extension of Claudianus Mamertus's simpler formulation, 'Corpus est uiuens, anima uiua, Deus est uita' (*De statu anime*, iii. 6. 2, *CSEL* xi. 162–

[10] On twelfth-century Neoplatonism, see Chenu, *La Théologie au douzième siècle*, esp. pp. 108–41, and on this exchange, p. 127; for a more detailed account of this exchange, see M.-D. Chenu, 'Platon à Cîteaux', *Archives d'histoire doctrinale et littéraire du moyen âge*, xxi (1954), 99–106, where he compares Nicholas's arguments for the primacy of unity unfavourably with those of Arnaud de Bonneval in *Commentarius in Psalmum CXXXII*, homilia 1 (*PL* clxxxix. 1570–2).

4; *PL* liii, 766), which does not cite Ps. or Job. Nicholas next goes on to offer a more detailed explanation of his distinctions. The body is compound (*compositum*); it is born and dies. The soul is simple (*simplex*); it is created once, and does not die. The distinction is between things born (*orta*), which are transient ('uiuens tempore', Job 14: 1), and things created (*facta*), which are eternal. This corresponds to the distinction between living (*uiuens*) and being alive (*uiua*), the properties, respectively, of bodies and souls. Life itself (*uita*) falls into a different category altogether, being at once 'unum et una', neither simple nor compound, 'quia unius et unice unitatis est hec prerogatiua' (*PL* ccii. 493). Even the simple is created; absolute unity is a defining factor of the uncreated alone, of God. The letter then concludes with a long meditative lament on the text in Job and a valediction complaining of encroaching business and praising Peter.

In letter no. 50, Peter rejects Nicholas's propositions concerning the natures of the body, soul, and God. He begins by attacking the notion that the body can derive its state of living (*uiuens*) from 'vanity' or 'nothingness' (*ex uanitate*) on the grounds that as God is the source of all life then *uanitas* cannot be the source of any form of life. Moving on to the soul and God, he reverses Nicholas's applications of simplicity and unity. Many things can have unity, including certain types of compounds. Only God has both simplicity and unity—an argument developed in greater depth in letter no. 51, in response to Nicholas's reply that simplicity can only apply to the eternal, immutable unity, i.e. God. Peter's chief contention in his reply here is that while unity simply describes the state of existing as a single entity, even one compounded of a variety of elements or qualities, it is simplicity, the state of unmediated elemental purity, which defines the indivisible and uncreated God, and Him alone. Peter adds the important caveat, however, that whatever God's properties or attributes, He does not derive His being from anything, nor can anything properly be said about Him. Finally Peter raises the question of Nicholas's assertion, in a sermon cited here by Peter, that God the Son can somehow be an intermediary between the other two persons of the Trinity.

In response, in the letter 'Anxietatem michi generat' (*PL* ccii. 498–505, no. 65) Nicholas defended his formulation of the distinctions between the states of being of the body, the soul, and God, and their respective derivations, in nothingness, simplicity, and unity, citing Claudianus Mamertus as his authority: 'Corpus est uiuens, anima uiua, Deus est uita,' (Claudianus Mamertus, *De statu anime*, iii. 6. 2; *CSEL* xi. 162–4; *PL* liii. 766). There is a noticeable sharpening in the tone of the exchange as Nicholas charges Peter with making accusations without checking the sources of the views which he is challenging, and goes on to quote Claudianus Mamertus on the origin of things, and specifically the passage which includes the formulation: 'Ac sicut tria sunt, informis materia, formatum exanime, rerum forma: sic itidem tria

sunt, uiuificatum, uiuificans, uita . . . Corpus est uiuens, anima uiua, Deus uita,' (Claudianus Mamertus, *De statu anime*, iii. 6. 2; *CSEL* xi. 162–4; *PL* liii. 766). Nicholas then attempts to defend his own extension of these propositions: 'uiuens ex uanitate, uiua ex simplicitate, uita ex unitate,' (first given in *PL* ccii. 493, no. 63). Beginning with the proposition 'corpus . . . uiuens ex uanitate', Nicholas bases his defence on the distinction between the mortality of the body and the immortality of the soul. Peter had objected, in letter no. 50, that all life comes from God and that no state of being could be described as deriving from nothingness. Nicholas attempts to demonstrate a connection between *uanitas* and *uiuens* through two biblical texts. The first of these is Eccles. 1: 2: 'uanitas uanitatum et omnis uanitas'. If all is nothingness ('vanity' in the Douai-Reims translation) then this must include the body. This is linked to Ps. 38 (39): 6: 'uniuersa uanitas omnis homo uiuens', demonstrating the connection between *uanitas* and *uiuens*. That which is mortal must die. To die is to be deprived of life (*uita*, which Nicholas associates with God alone). Humans are composed of that which must die (the body) and that which is eternal (the soul). The body lives (*uiuit*) but does not possess the quality of life itself (*uita*), hence the choice of words in the text from Psalms: 'Ergo quod moritur in homine, ipsum est quod uiuit in homine; quod ideo uanitas, quia mortalitus est, igitur "uniuersa uanitas, omnis homo uiuens", non omnis homo uita, sed "omnis homo uiuens",' (*PL* ccii. 500). Furthermore, the body and the soul exist in a state of unequal interdependency. The body depends entirely on the soul, which itself is ultimately independent of the body and animated by God and so more than merely 'uiuens'. Nicholas then turns Peter's own citation of Rom. 8: 10 ('corpus . . . mortuum est propter peccatum') back against him, claiming that this is a clear demonstration of the *uanitas* of the body's state.

Moving on to the questions of the soul and of God ('anima . . . uiua ex simplicitate; Deus . . . uita ex unitate'), Nicholas quotes at some length Peter's position on simplicity and on the impossibility of describing God as having any derivation (see also letter no. 50). Then he attacks Peter's proposition: 'omnis res que simpliciter simplex est, et unum et una est', on the grounds that no thing ('nulla res') can fit this definition, other than that which is not a thing but the cause of all things, i.e. God. Peter described unity as a product of simplicity, and applicable to different levels of simplicity, including the simplest form of simplicity, that of God. Nicholas reverses the order of derivation, seeing simplicity as a quality dependent on unity, a unity which is by definition so immutable as only to be applicable to that which is eternal. Everything created is mutable and nothing mutable is simple. The quality of eternal immutability is unity: 'Non est autem uere unam, nisi quod essentialiter et immutabiliter unum est increabile, inuariabile, interminabile, quod nec ad fuit preciditur, nec ab erit expungitur, cui solum et inexpugnabile remanet est,' (*PL* ccii. 502).

Nicholas's next step is to show why numbers are so central to philosophical truth, and so to demonstrate the greater significance of unity, i.e. because it is a concept connected directly to number as opposed to mere simplicity, which is not. In this he combines speculation on the Neoplatonic mystery of the One with Trinitarian doctrine and with extensive quotations from Hugh of Saint-Victor's *Didascalicon*. 'One' is the origin without origins, that upon which all else is founded, and which is indivisible. 'One' is the base number of the Trinity; the three exist in one (and so Nicholas responds to Peter's statements on the Trinity with some of his own). He moves on to Hugh of Saint-Victor's explanation of the use of multiplication to demonstrate the qualities of the soul (a monad) and the body (a dyad), quoting all of *Didascalicon*, ii. 4 and half of ii. 5 (see *Hugonis de Sancto Victore, Didascalicon*, ed. C. H. Buttimer (Washington, DC, 1939), pp. 27–9, cap. 4, line 19–cap. 5, line 13; Nicholas's version has some differences and omissions). The key to this theory is that successive multiplications by 3, beginning with 1, map the states of the soul: thus $3 \times 1 = 3$, $3 \times 3 = 9$, $3 \times 9 = 27$, and $3 \times 27 = 81$. The soul has three powers; it exists in the body, which has nine openings; it pours itself out upon all visible things, symbolized by 27, a cube number; and finally it returns to its own simplicity, when, in the fourth stage, it reappears, as 81, which is also 80 + 1, the natural term of life plus the unity of the soul. Unity similarly reappears at every fourth multiplication to infinity. A similar demonstration is made with the body, symbolized by 2, the number of mutable things: $2 \times 2 = 4$, $2 \times 4 = 8$, $2 \times 8 = 16$, and $2 \times 16 = 32$. Two reappears at each fourth multiplication. Nicholas's aim in all this seems to be to argue for the radical importance of number in philosophical understanding, and thus for the primacy of unity over mere simplicity in determining the nature of God.[11] Finally Nicholas answers the charge (in Peter's letter no. 50) that he has declared the Son to be intermediate between the Father and the Holy Spirit. He does not hold this to be so, he protests, as far as their indivisible substance is concerned, but only as regards their different designations ('uocabulorum differentiam'). Thus, for example, in the Creed they are named in order, with the Son in the middle. He signs off, conscious perhaps of the potentially sensitive nature of speculations about the Trinity and the nature of God, with a plea to Peter to keep his letter secret, showing it only to a Thomas (unidentified), and adds that to avoid unnecessary prying he has written his letter with his own hand.

Peter's response on this occasion (letter no. 51) is less patient. He agrees with Nicholas only so far as the ineffable transcendence of God is concerned. He cites Boethius against Nicholas's purportedly Boethian ideas, accuses

[11] See *The Didascalicon of Hugh of St. Victor*, trans. J. Taylor (Records of Western Civilisation, New York, 1961), pp. 64–6 and notes, for further discussion of the theory outlined here, and of Hugh's own sources.

Nicholas of misrepresenting his arguments, and vehemently denies that he himself differs from Claudianus Mamertus. The new tone of the exchange is characterized by Peter's sarcastic observation that if Nicholas can change from black to white (i.e. from Benedictine to Cistercian; on Nicholas's life, see letter no. 49, n. 1), he thinks he can change anything, including ancient authority. Moving to specific details, Peter firstly divides entities up into simple and compound, rather than according to unity and multiplicity. Then he defines two different types of compound, one made up of units of the same substance, another of units of different substances, one of which is simpler than the other. The soul is the former, the simpler of the two, and so 'naturally simple'. Finally, he argues, there is a third and higher form of simplicity, pertaining to God who is 'simply simple'. Anticipating Nicholas's likely objection that to attribute simplicity to God as well as to souls is to attribute one and the same quality to Creator and creature, Peter distinguishes between being simple and the essence of simplicity itself, the latter being a quality of God alone, who embodies all qualities. There is, in the created world, a progression down from this through different degrees of simplicity. Relating this to unity, Peter counters Nicholas's denial that nothing other than God can be single and simple by defining single as that which is not mixed but conjoined, i.e., once again, those compounds which are made up of elements of the same substance, and so merely conjoined, and not transformed in nature, by being compounded. It was thus that the Word could become flesh without corruption or transformation of His nature. In short, simplicity itself derives from God; unity is a property of many things. Peter repeats his point that God is not derived from anything, including simplicity. Finally, he denies that he has any objection to Claudianus Mamertus' writings, only to Nicholas's additions to them, and asks him to stop writing.

APPENDIX 8

The Sequence of surviving correspondence between Peter of Celle and John of Salisbury

The sequence of surviving letters exchanged between Peter of Celle and John of Salisbury can be established as follows (in this appendix PC = letter of Peter of Celle, and JS = letter of John of Salisbury; the numbers for John's letters given here, and the dates, are taken from *J.S. Epp.*).

There is a vast literature on John of Salisbury which it is beyond the scope of this appendix to address. A good starting-point is D. Luscombe, 'John of Salisbury in recent scholarship', and id., 'John of Salisbury: a bibliography 1953–82', both in M. Wilks (ed.), *The World of John of Salisbury*, Studies in Church History, Subsidia, iii (Oxford, 1994), pp. 21–37, 445–58. Much of John's life is reconstructed in the introductions and notes to *J.S. Epp.* A biography is forthcoming by J. McLoughlin (The Medieval World, Longman).

Longer notes on the dates and sequences of some letters and groups of letters follow the table; otherwise see the notes to the letters themselves.

LETTERS EXCHANGED WHEN PETER WAS AT MONTIER-LA-CELLE

(i) not closely datable or early

PC 63 1147 × 1162
PC 64 1147 × 1162 (or poss. late 1156 × early 1157)
PC 65 5 Dec. 1154 × Oct. 1155

(ii) a late 1156–early 1157 group (see further discussion below)

PC 66 1156, after July and before autumn
JS 19 autumn 1156
a lost PC letter
JS 31 1–8 Apr. 1157
a lost PC letter telling of the fire at Saint-Ayoul: 1157, April × July/Aug.
JS 32 1157, July–Aug.
PC 67 1157, after July/Aug. (and earlier than letter no. 68)
PC 68 1157, after July/Aug.

(iii) a late 1157 group referring to the affairs of a monk Thomas (see further discussion below)

JS 33	autumn 1157, or later
PC 69	prob. late 1157, or later (poss. × April 1161)
JS 34	Oct.- Nov. 1157, or later
JS 35	*c.* Dec. 1157, or later

(iv) later letters of the earlier period

JS 111	autumn 1159
JS 112	? *c.*1159
PC 70	1161 × 1162—see discussion below

LETTERS EXCHANGED WHEN PETER WAS AT SAINT-REMI

(v) letters written during the Becket conflict

PC 169	? late 1163 × Nov. 1164
PC 170	1164, before Nov.
JS 304	Dec. 1170

(vi) letters written between the death of Becket and John's election to Chartres

[JS 305:	early 1171: not addressed to Peter, but evidently widely circulated, and PC 171 contains Peter's response to the question raised—as explained at letter no. 171, n. 1]
PC 171	early 1171 (poss. after Apr.): to John and his brother Richard.
PC 172	early 1171 × 1172 (or × July 1176): to John and his brother Richard
PC 173	1171 × ? 1173 (or × 22 July 1176)
PC 174	1171 × 22 July 1176
PC 175	Dec. 1171 × May 1172: to John and his brother Richard
JS 310	? *c.*1173

(vii) letters written when John was bishop of Chartres

PC 176	mid-1177 × 1179, before May (or more likely before Mar.)
PC 177	mid-1177 × 1179, before May (or more likely before Mar.)
PC 178	mid-1177 × 25 Oct. 1180

ADDITIONAL NOTES ON GROUPS II AND III AND LETTER NO. 70

group (ii) a late 1156–early 1157 group

John of Salisbury's letter no. 32 cannot be a reply to Peter's letter no. 68, as stated in *J.S. Epp.* i. 52, for the reasons given below. The sequence given

here is thus a new one. This new sequence has been established with the help of Christopher Brooke.

Letter no. 67 is a reply to John of Salisbury's letter no. 32 (July–Aug. 1157; *J.S. Epp.* i. 52–4, and see p. 55, n. 3): Peter apologizes for not being able to send the requested relics (of St Aigulf, or Ayoul—but John also requested others). The reason for the delay was that Peter was awaiting the return of a master W. from Rome who would then travel on to England. This messenger did not arrive, and Peter is sending a brother W. instead, who might be identified with the brother William of John of Salisbury's letter no. 35 (*J.S. Epp.* i. 64, and see ibid. i. 55, n. 3), who was sent along with the monks Thomas and Ralph probably on business connected with the appeal for the priory of Saint-Ayoul-de-Provins. Peter was sending around monks with relics to raise funds for the rebuilding of this dependent priory after its destruction in a fire. This is the earliest ref. to the fire in Peter's surviving correspondence and it is likely that he had written to John earlier announcing the news in a now lost letter, prompting John's request for relics in his letter no. 32, which cannot be a reply to Peter's letter no. 68, as stated in *J.S. Epp.* i. 52, as letter no. 68 was clearly accompanied by the relics (but this does not affect the date of John's letter no. 32). The fire is not mentioned in letter no. 66 (1156, after July and before autumn), nor in John of Salisbury's letter no. 31 (1–8 Apr. 1157, *J.S. Epp.* i. 49–51), thus both the fire and Peter's missing letter announcing it must be dated April × July–Aug., 1157, i.e. between John's letters 31 and 32. The priory was rebuilt, and rededicated by Archbishop Hugh of Sens on 30 Aug. 1159 (Godefroy, 'Saint-Ayoul', ii. 34–5). On Saint-Ayoul, see also F. Bourquelot, *Histoire de Provins*, 2 vols. (Provins and Paris, 1839–40), i. 117–21 and 341–9). On the veneration of St Ayoul and other saints associated with Montier-la-Celle, and the tradition of miracles associated with the house, see Godefroy, 'Saint-Ayoul', i.

There is some further supporting, but not in itself decisive, evidence for this sequence. John of Salisbury asks, in his letter no. 31, for copies of letters of Bernard to be sent, and thanks Peter on their receipt in his letter no. 32; Peter, however, in his letter no. 68, makes no mention of sending such letters. While this is an argument from silence, and does not in itself constitute proof of anything, the new sequence, with a missing letter of Peter assumed between John's letters 19 and 32, would also explain this omission.

group (iii) a late 1157 group referring to the affairs of a monk Thomas

The subject of letter no. 69 is one Thomas, evidently a monk of Montier-la-Celle. Such a Thomas occurs in John's letters 33–5. In his no. 33, John's tone regarding Thomas is neutral; he states also that Thomas wants leave (presumably from Peter himself, as John's letter no. 35 indicates) to visit

relatives in England. Thomas had been in England with another monk, Ralph, on some mission, possibly connected with the appeal for the rebuilding of the priory of Saint-Ayoul (see above, note to group ii). In John's letter no. 34 Thomas is praised for his conduct in the mission and distinguished from his companion, Ralph, who has, by his conduct, evidently betrayed both Peter and Thomas, has been excommunicated, and is denounced in both letters 33 and 34. This Ralph, however, does not figure in Peter's surviving correspondence. Thomas is now returning to France with John's commendation. In his letter no. 35, John's tone has changed markedly: a quarrel has broken out between him and Thomas and he is writing to forestall Thomas's complaints against him to Peter. John now accuses Thomas of behaving in a questionable manner (though not nearly so badly as Ralph) from almost the very beginning of his mission in England, which contradicts the tone of John's letter no. 34. John suggests that Thomas is weak and easily led, but essentially not beyond redemption as a monk if kept under close scrutiny. The dispute seems to have arisen when John compelled Thomas to return to France without visiting his relatives (the mention of Thomas's request to visit relatives in both John's letters 33 and 35 thus further corroborating the inference that this is indeed the same Thomas). John acted on his own initiative here because Peter's response to his request about Thomas being allowed to stay was delayed (see *J.S. Epp.* i. 63, where John states that the messenger who had carried his letter no. 33 was also entrusted with the request, but delayed his return).

Letter no. 69 could be Peter's reply to John's letter no. 33, which however arrived only after John had written his letter no. 34 (by which time Thomas was already returning to France), but before he wrote his letter no. 35 (by which time the delayed messenger had returned to John). The problem here is Peter's reference in letter no. 69 to a lapse on Thomas's part, which comes in the same sentence as his request for Thomas's recall: John had had no complaint against Thomas in his letter no. 33, only in his no. 35, by which time Thomas was already on his way back and the messenger bearing Peter's reply had evidently returned. The 'lapse' could refer to the failure of the mission to Earl Hugh (on which see *J.S. Epp.* i. 55 and 58, n. 17), although John is clear in both letters 33 and 34 that this is not Thomas's fault. More likely is that John did communicate some complaint against Thomas by verbal message along with his letter no. 33. This would suggest that letter no. 69 was written in autumn 1157 but not received before *c.* Dec. 1157.

Finally, it is only possible, not certain, that this whole sequence can indeed be dated to 1157 at all. This dating depends on the association of Thomas and Ralph with the mission to raise funds for Saint-Ayoul. In his letter no. 35 John says that Peter had sent brother Thomas of Norwich (i.e. a different Thomas), brother William and others, implying in the subsequent sentence

that the Thomas under discussion is among these others. If this William is the same as the W. in Peter's letter no. 67, then Thomas, and by extension Ralph, could be linked to the Saint-Ayoul appeal—i.e. William would provide the link between Thomas and Ralph in John's letter no. 35 and the mission for Saint-Ayoul in Peter's letter no. 68. This circumstance would also explain Peter's allowing them to travel so freely in England, as it was a peripatetic mission to raise funds. However, this is not certain, and the whole sequence could be later, as indicated in *J.S. Epp.* i. 55, where John's letters in this sequence are discussed. The *terminus ad quem* would then be the death of Archbishop Theobald of Canterbury, who is evidently referred to in Peter's letter no. 69 (see no. 69, n. 3).

Note on Peter's letter no. 70

The dating of this letter depends on the interpretation of what Peter had received from John when he wrote it: a single letter or a copy of John's entire early collection. The tone of Peter's letter suggests more than one letter received, but the argument depends to a greater degree on the analysis of John of Salisbury's collection itself. Christopher Brooke has kindly provided the following reflections on the relation between letter no. 70 and John's early letters,which I quote with his permission:

The early letters of John of Salisbury have been studied by Brooke and Mynors in the Introduction to the edition [*J.S. Epp.* i]; by Sir Richard Southern in his review of it in *English Historical Review*, lxxii (1957), 493–7; and by Alan Piper, 'New evidence for the Becket correspondence and John of Salisbury's Letters', in *The World of John of Salisbury*, ed. M. Wilks (Oxford, 1984), pp. 439–44.

Mynors produced a text based on P (Paris BN Lat. 8625), which I think, after consulting Dr Teresa Webber, can be safely ascribed to the late twelfth century, and C (Cambridge UL Ii. 2. 31) an inferior MS of the fourteenth century, but independent of P; Mynors showed that V (Vatican Lat. 6024) was a copy of P. Southern argued that the state of the texts—evidently from author's drafts, and often without protocols or "Valete"—did not suggest much input by the author; and that C showed two stages of rearrangement, first by John himself, extracting the personal from the business letters with precision, second by an editor with a superficial knowledge of the contents, who rearranged those whose recipient was noted on his copies in order of recipient. Southern thought that Canterbury might have more to do with the formation of the collection than John of Salisbury. Nonetheless, it always seemed to me that the materials, and the basic selection behind C, made John's involvement reasonably certain. I reckoned to have seen the same combination of care in collecting and carelessness in editing behind John's work on the Becket correspondence ([*J.S. Epp.* ii], pp. lviii–lxiii, revised by Anne Duggan [Duggan, *Textual History*], see esp. p. 74).

Our knowledge of the history of John's collections was transformed by Alan Piper's paper of 1984 [*op. cit.*]: he showed by analysis of a fourteenth-century *tabula* in Durham Cathedral Library MS A. IV. 8 traces of a lost MS of John's letters which included (uniquely in surviving MSS) both the early and the late letters, attached to a

copy of the Becket correspondence which could well reflect John's own collecting (Piper, ibid. pp. 439–40; cf. Duggan [*Textual History*], p. 74). The lost MS also included some later letters not in any surviving MS, including at least three likely to have been written after he became bishop of Chartres. The lost MS seems to have been located in Canterbury in the fourteenth century; but the materials it contained must have involved personal activity by John himself near the end of his life. In relation to the early letters, Piper shows reason to think that the lost MS had access both to the material lying behind P and to the material behind C: and this would strongly confirm that John himself was involved in the transmission, and in some sense—however carelessly, however much helped by an incompetent 'editor'—was the creator of the early collection. It is clear that Canterbury was the scene of some of the work; it is likely that Chartres also played a part—and P is likely to be of French provenance.

In 1956 I argued that Peter of Celle's letter no. 70[12] acknowledged the receipt, not of one letter, but of a whole dossier—and very likely a copy of the whole early collection; and if so it could be dated *c.* 1161. Hans Liebeschütz suggested to me years ago that it might refer to the *Policraticus*—and the coincidence of date, 1159, with the dedication of the chapel [of Saint-Ayoul-de-Provins; see also above, notes to group ii], makes the idea attractive. That would fit the references to philosophy, rhetoric and the laws; but 'quod ad amicos attinet' much better fits letters. Furthermore, the repetition 'litterarum . . . litteris' seems to me to make clear that it was a letter or letters that Peter had received. Southern compared the reception of a letter in Peter's letter no. 63 [Southern, *op. cit.*, pp. 494–5, where the letter is cited by its no. in *PL*, LXIX]; but the resemblance is superficial: there is a far greater variety of theme and approach indicated in letter no. 70, philosophy, rhetoric, legal learning, the gospels—'et quod ad amicos attinet, mellito sapore decentissime dulcorantur'.

The early collection as we know it—from P,V,C and the lost MS—contains a coherent gathering of letters written between *c.* 1154 and early 1161—shortly before the death of Archbishop Theobald of Canterbury on 18 April 1161 (*Fasti*, ii. p. 4). Peter's letter no. 70 refers to the translation of the relics of St Aigulf, or Ayoul, which presumably followed the dedication of the chapel on 30 Aug. 1159. One might argue at length this way and that whether the two ceremonies were likely to have coincided—and reach no clear decision. But if the dedication had just occurred, or was to take place with the translation, one would expect Peter to have mentioned it. The letter is likely to be later than 30 Aug. 1159 (though that is not quite certain), and must be before 1162, when Peter left Celle. In theory John might have sent off copies of a batch of letters at any date, say in 1159. But the MS tradition—contrary to that of Gilbert Foliot, for example—does not favour the idea that John released copies of his letters at a variety of dates: all surviving manuscripts of the early letters go back to a collection clearly made *c.* 1161. And it so happens that the outstanding examples of rhetoric and legal learning in the collection—nos. 124 and 131—were both originally written in 1160. Southern thought Peter's response more appropriate to 'the joy experienced in receiving a friend's letter than in perusing . . . a collection of chiefly business correspondence' (Southern, *op. cit.*, p. 495). But there are many gems in it scattered about; and I own that—returning to it after forty years—I feel something of

[12] No. 70 in this edition and also in the *PL* edition, by which number it was cited in 1956 (*J.S. Epp.* i. p. ix, n. 1).

the delight Peter might have felt to have a dossier of his closest friend's letters delivered to him unawares.

In short, I have returned to my original opinion, that Peter's letter is a response to receiving a copy of John's early collection in 1161 or 1162.

APPENDIX 9

Bishop Fulk and the mission to Estonia

Letters 76 and 77 concern Fulk, missionary bishop to Estonia. Letter no. 76 refers to a former monk of Montier-la-Celle who is travelling to the Curia carrying the letter—and so presumably seeking papal authorization for his mission (as indicated in letter no. 77)—before travelling to the lands of 'barbarians'. Letter no. 77 names Fulk, says that he has visited the Curia 'this year', and that he is staying at Saint-Remi before travelling to spread the faith—making the identification of Fulk with the ex-monk of Montier-la-Celle of letter no. 76 very likely. In letter no. 77 Peter supports Fulk's request for privileges, which may be a reference to one of the series of letters which Alexander III directed to Scandinavia. These include the appointment of a native Estonian companion for Fulk, Nicholas, a recommendation of Fulk to the Danish church, a call to crusade in Estonia, and assorted church business concerned with Scandinavia. They are variously dated between 7 and 17 Sept. 1171 or 1172—see JL ii. nos. 12111–12115, 12117–12118, 12120 and 12122; *PL* cc. nos. 973–7, 979–80, and 983–4, cols. 848–52, 854–60, and 862–3, and L. Weibull, 'Påven Alexander III.s septemberbrev till Norden', *Scandia*, xiii (1940), 90–8; see also *DD* i. 3, pp. 28–41, and esp. the discussion at pp. 31–2, which follows Weibull and JL on the dates. Copies of these documents survived among the fifty-six letters of Alexander III in the Saint-Remi collection (see Introduction, II. 1. i), and were presumably sent to Reims prior to Fulk's departure for the north. If so, then both letters 76 and 77 (which fall within the same year as one another on internal evidence), would pre-date these letters of Alexander (as *DD* says, following Weibull: *DD* i. 3, nos. 21–2, pp. 28–31), although it is impossible to say by how long; the implication of letter no. 77 is that Fulk did not bring the letters back from Rome himself—unless it refers to some other, later privileges. On the dates for Fulk's journey north, see letter no. 96, n. 1; see also letter no. 181, and on Fulk's later movements, letter no. 104, n. 3, and no. 105, n. 1. *DD* also notes that the survival of these letters in a Saint-Remi archive further demonstrates Peter's crucial role in Fulk's mission. (Note also JL 12121—also Sept. 1171–2, but not from the Saint-Remi archive—permitting Fulk to dedicate churches and ordain priests, services of which Peter made use in Reims, as indicated in letter no. 181.) Beyond these references, little is known of Fulk's career or his mission: see H. Reuter, *Geschichte Alexanders*

der Dritten und der Kirche seiner Zeit, 3 vols (Leipzig, 1860–4), iii. 615–21; Christiansen says he was consecrated by Eskil in 1164: E. Christiansen, *The Northern Crusades* (London, 1980), p. 58. It is uncertain how successful Fulk's mission was; despite Alexander III's proclamation of a crusade, the Danes did not attempt the conquest and Christianization of Estonia until 1184, and only made headway after 1219 (Christiansen, *Northern Crusades*, pp. 69 and 96–7).

Alexander III's letters will be discussed in L. Falkenstein, 'Die Sirmondsche Sammlung der 56 Litterae Alexanders III.' in *100 Jahre Papsturkundenforschung: Bilanz–Methoden–Ausblick*, ed. R. Hiestand, Abhandlungen der Akademie der Wissenschaften in Göttingen, Philol.-Histor.-Klasse, 3rd. ser. (Göttingen, 2001). I am grateful to Dr Falkenstein for showing me an advance copy of this work.

APPENDIX 10

The Disputes over the priory of Meerssen

Meerssen, a dependency of Saint-Remi in the diocese of Liège, became a source of contention between Saint-Remi and local imperial advocates or others enjoying imperial support during and after the Alexandrine schism. Much of the relevant evidence is referenced in *GM* i. 78–9, notes 148 B–E, although the *Papsturkunden* series occasionally gives closer dating (as noted below; further MS sources for Meerssen are listed in Ramackers, *Papsturkunden in den Niederlanden*, p. 11).

In *c.*1131 Bishop Alexander of Liège confirmed the possession of Meerssen by Saint-Remi (as authorised by the pope and the emperor), and the appropriation of the prebends of the resident provost and canons by the monks on the deaths of the holders (Meinert, *Papsturkunden in Frankreich*, pp. 212–13, no. 30).[13] This was confirmed by Innocent II, 8 June 1135 (Meinert, *Papsturkunden in Frankreich*, pp. 215–16, no. 32; JL i. 7705), and again 23 Nov. 1136 (JL i. 7799; *PL* clxxix. 296). It was undoubtedly the retention of a life interest in the prebends by the canons which gave rise to ambiguities in the settlement and allowed exploitation of the situation by powerful interests and factions during the schism.

Other confirmations followed, by Archdeacon Hermann of Liège (1136), by Bishops Adalberon and Henry of Liège (1136 × 1145 and 1147) and by Pope Eugenius III (as part of a general bull of 14 Dec. 1145, confirming the rights of Saint-Remi; Varin, *Arch. admin.* i. 311–14; JL ii. 8800; *PL* clxxx. 1069). The first imperial *diplomata* are two of Conrad III, of 11 Apr. 1138 and Oct. 1145, of which the later confirmed and ruled on the advocacy.[14]

Frederick Barbarossa issued two *diplomata* in 1152. The first (10 Mar.) confirmed Conrad III's *diplomata*. The second (late April × early Mar.) is a judgement of the imperial court against Goswin of Heinsberg, the advocate.[15]

[13] However, Cott. ii. 1806, in apparent contradiction of this evidence, states that Meerssen was a priory of Saint-Remi from 968. It is possible of course that Saint-Remi did have longer-standing interests here which had subsequently been eclipsed by local powers, giving rise to the dispute in which Peter found himself involved.

[14] *Die Urkunden Konrads III. und seines Sohnes Heinrich*, *MGH Die Urkunden der deutschen Kaiser und Könige*, ix, ed. F. Hausmann (Vienna, 1969), pp. 11–13, 252–4, nos. 6 and 140.

[15] *Die Urkunden Friedrichs I. 1152–1158*, *MGH Die Urkunden der Deutschen Könige und Kaiser*, x.1, ed. H. Appelt (Hanover, 1975), pp. 3–6, 14–16, nos. 2, 8. *GM* lists three for 1152 but the third (MGH, x.1 no. 30) is not relevant to the present case. Note also the letter of Wibald of Stavelot to Arnold II of Cologne, dated summer 1152 (P. Jaffé,

Goswin was the father of Philip, later archbishop of Cologne.[16] Hadrian IV, in a bull dealing with various claims and rights of Saint-Remi, confirmed Barbarossa's settlement and stated that neither Goswin of Heinsberg nor his successors could overstep the powers settled therein (19 Dec. 1154; Meinert, *Papsturkunden in Frankreich*, pp. 258–61, no. 67; JL 9951). Alexander III again confirmed this settlement in *c.*1160 (uned.: *GM*, p. 39, cites B. N. MS lat 12693: Monasticon Benedictinum XXXVI, fo. 147b, and gives *c.*1160, or 1159 × 1162; Varin, *Arch. admin.* i. 324 cites the cartularies A and B of Saint-Remi). It was this settlement which Peter of Celle sought to defend against subsequent attempts of figures in Cologne and Liège enjoying imperial support to alter the balance of power to the detriment of Saint-Remi.

Despite Peter's complaints that unnamed characters enjoying imperial favour took advantage of the schism to extend their powers (letters 79 and 86), the evidence from the years of the schism (Sept./Oct. 1159–24 July 1177) does not present a picture of an embattled priory losing control over its rights. It is doubtful what impact Alexander III's bull of 13 Jan. 1165 stating Saint-Remi's rights, and including Meerssen, meant in this region at that time (Meinert, *Papsturkunden in Frankreich*, p. 96, no. 286; JL 11141), but a case adjudicated in 1165–6 in the name of the anti-pope Victor IV seems to have favoured Saint-Remi: Philip of Heinsberg, dean of Cologne and archdeacon of Liège (the later archbishop of Cologne—see letter no. 94, n. 1) settled a dispute between Peter of Celle and a 'G.' of Meerssen in Peter's favour (Ramackers, *Papsturkunden in den Niederlanden*, pp. 249–50, no. 114, not noted in *GM*). Ramackers identifies this 'G.' as Goswin. This cannot be the Goswin of Heinsberg the advocate named in the bull of Hadrian IV.[17]

Also from the years of the schism come Peter's brief references to

Bibliotheca rerum Germanicarum, i (Berlin, 1864), no. 381, p. 512): 'Monachi sancti Remigii, qui sunt in Marna, multum uexantur calliditate Gozwini; quos nisi pietas uestra protexerit, omnino illudentur.'

[16] On the Heinsberg family see *Lexikon des Mittelalters* iv. 2111, and S. Corsten, 'Erzbischof Philipps Familie', in *Philipps von Heinsberg, Erzbischof und Reichskanzler (1167–1191): Studien und Quellen*, ed. S. Corsten (Heinsberg, 1991), pp. 7–31. Goswin II of Heinsberg (d.1167 or 1168) had seven children including Goswin III (last occurs 1179) and Philip.

[17] Quite apart from the context (this would mean that Philip was acting against his own father or brother—although this is not impossible), the G. of Ramackers's document is described as the brother of Louis and so cannot be a member of the immediate Heinsberg family as reconstructed in Corsten, 'Erzbischof Philipps Familie', p. 31. It is more likely that this is a surviving canon or heir of a canon trying to reclaim some prebend and that this is not directly connected to the central dispute over the rights of the advocate. It seems to illustrate that although the monks had the right to appropriate prebends, the lifetime interests of the canons had left much of the old personnel and apparatus in place and that they were prepared to fight on. However there is little firm evidence here. On John of Salisbury's possible involvement, see T. Reuter, 'John of Salisbury and the Germans', in M. Wilks (ed.), *The World of John of Salisbury*, Studies in Church History, Subsidia, iii (Oxford, 1994), pp. 414–25, at p. 425, n. 44.

Meerssen in two of his letters to John and Richard of Salisbury. In letter no. 171 (written 1171, poss. after April) Peter simply reports: 'De Marna reditus nostros habemus.' In letter no. 172 (written early 1171 × 1172, or poss. × July 1176) he states: 'Imperator indulsit nobis bona nostra de Marna.' Whatever it is that Peter is referring to in these brief notes, and whatever John's or Richard's interest, they seem to indicate a priory which was neither beyond Peter's effective reach owing to the schism, nor subject to the unchecked depredations of enemies.[18]

Interestingly, it was after the schism when troubles seemed to accumulate, and the pictures presented in Peter's letters and in the papal documents begin to diverge. Alexander III issued a bull about a year after the settlement of the schism (7 June 1178, uned.: *GM*, p. 39, cites Arch. dép. de la Marne, H 1377; see also JL 13068, 27 May 1178). Here, according to *GM*, 'Alexandre III à l'instar d'Innocent II, confirme les libertés de l'église de Meerseen, et précise qu'à la mort des chanoines qui y vivent, des moines s'installeront, et auront le droit de présentation. Alexandre III confirme aux religieux le personnat de l'église de Meerseen' (*GM* i. 79). The ref. must be to the bull of Innocent II of 8 June 1135 (Meinert, *Papsturkunden in Frankreich*, no. 32; JL 7705, see above), or 23 Nov. 1136 (JL 7799, see above). Two further confirmations followed in 1181: a bull of 18 Feb. 1181 confirmed the 1152 settlement (Meinert, *Papsturkunden in Frankreich*, p. 336, no. 183; JL 14262), and one of 9 or 15 Mar. 1181 protected Saint-Remi's rights in Meerssen (Meinert, *Papsturkunden in Frankreich*, pp. 338–9, no. 188; JL 14376; Ramackers, *Papsturkunden in den Niederlanden*, pp. 376–7, no. 232, citing Meinert's edn. but giving 9 Mar.).

Peter's letters 79 and 86, however, suggest dissatisfaction. Both were written after the conclusion of the schism (which ended 24 July 1177; both letters refer to it as being over). Both complain that Alexander III has ordered the provost of Meerssen to give a prebend to a clerk of the emperor. Letter no. 86 says that the pope has written a second time, and this in the same year as Alexander III himself granted a privilege which explicitly mentioned canonries or prebends of Meerssen and confirmed them in perpetuity. The reference to the end of the schism and to the pope's unwelcome concession to the emperor make it reasonably certain that the privilege referred to was that of 7 June 1178, by which date the recipient of the letter, Albert of Morra (on whom see letter no. 83, n. 1) was papal chancellor, as he is addressed in letter no. 86. However, letter no. 79 is evidently a response to an earlier, but essentially identical, order from the pope regarding the prebend. Furthermore, it apparently refers to a privilege

[18] These references are far too late for the 1152 settlement to be news, and also too late to refer to the 1165/6 case adjudicated by Philip. The case concerning Meerssen and Stavelot mentioned in letter no. 118, which may date from the years of the schism, is unconnected, and is discussed at letter no. 118, n. 1.

of Alexander III which is not recent, which would then be that of Jan. 1165 (see above). It seems likely then that letter no. 79 preceded the bull of June 1178 (and possibly also JL 13068 of May 1178, see above), and may in part have prompted it. The 1181 confirmations noted above seem too late to fit with the references to the end of the schism, and by this time Peter may already have been on his way to Chartres: 1181 is thus a possible but much less likely alternative date for letters 79 and 86.

Peter's letter no. 94 is harder to date: it refers to prebends in the plural and may refer to a different specific dispute, although still part of the wider ongoing series of disputes over the rights and properties of Meerssen. Philip, the addressee, was archbishop of Cologne from 1167, after 21 Sept., to 13 Aug. 1191 (see also above, on his actions in respect of Meerssen as dean of Cologne and archdeacon of Liège). There is no indication in letter no. 94 as to whether the schism was over or not, and no reference to other privileges, so with the *terminus ad quem* of Peter's departure from Saint-Remi, the letter can only be securely dated Sept. 1167 × 1181. R. Knipping, *Die Regesten der Erzbischöfe von Köln im Mittelater*, ii (Bonn, 1901), p. 226, no. 1179, gives 1170–1181. However, given the direct papal involvement from 1178, a date after the end of the schism for this letter seems unlikely.

APPENDIX 11

Saint-Remi-de-Provence

Letter no. 107 reminds a newly elected bishop of Avignon of his predecessor's defence of the rights of Saint-Remi in his diocese (i.e. the priory of Saint-Remi-de-Provence, as explained at letter no. 107, n. 1). The bishops of Avignon when Peter was abbot of Saint-Remi were Geoffrey I (occurs 1143 × 1166); Peter II (occurs 1167); Geoffrey II (occurs 1173 × ?1174); Pontius (first occurs 1174, d. ?1179); Peter III (occurs 1179); and Rostagnus (occurs ?1182, d. ?30 June 1209—on all of these, see *GC* i. 812–15).

In 1100 Bishop Arbert of Avignon had made a substantial grant of rights and possessions, including the parochial church of Saint-Martin, to the priory of Saint-Remi-de-Provence (*GC* i. Instr. 141–2, no. xiv), which occasioned a long dispute with the monks of Montmajour over rights and possessions in the town. A bull of Calixtus II attempted to settle the division (16 May 1122; JL 6974); Eugenius III confirmed the possessions of Montmajour in 1152; in 1153 Bishop Geoffrey I of Avignon, acting as judge delegate for Eugenius III, decided the issue of parochial rights to Saint-Remi's advantage, and the situation was confirmed by Alexander III sometime between 1160 and 1181. These events are discussed in M. Deloche, 'Saint-Remy de Provence au moyen âge', *Mémoires de l'Institut National de France, Académie des Inscriptions et Belles-lettres*, xxxiv.1 (1892), 53–143, at pp. 70–8, and documents ed. pp. 110–11 and 115–25; see also *GM* i. 78, n. 143; the relevant texts also appear in E. Leroy, *Les Archives communales de Saint-Rémy-de-Provence, des origines au XVIè siècle*, 4 vols. (Saint-Remi-de-Provence, 1949–53), i. 24–6 and 29–31. On Montmajour, dioc. Arles, see Cott. ii. 1962–4.

In letter no. 107 Peter is presumably referring to Geoffrey I's judgement of 1153 rather than Arbert's original privilege (especially given the reference to the protection of existing rights), which would make the addressee either his direct successor Peter II or possibly one of the later bishops. Sirmond's suggestion of Pontius (note repr. in *PL* ccii. 575, n. 37) is presumably based on a confusion between the two Geoffreys—Pontius was successor to Geoffrey II.

APPENDIX 12

Peter of Celle and the building works at Saint-Remi

In letters 144, 149, and 168 Peter mentions building works at Saint-Remi. Peter's abbacy is associated with the construction of the extant façade and chevet of the abbey church—a significant contribution to the development of the Gothic style. Letter no. 144 (+ 1173 × 1181, prob. late), seems to be the latest of the three. In letter no. 168 (early 1171 or 1172, before May × 1181), Peter seems to indicate that work is in the early stages (see no. 168, n. 13). When he wrote letter no. 149 (1162 × 1181, ?poss. 1171/2 × 1181), the work was underway. By the time letter no. 144 was written Peter had already incurred considerable expenditure on the project. The dates of Inganus of Lapley, the recipient of letter no. 144 (see no. 144, n. 1) strengthen the supposition that this letter is later than the others.

A full discussion of these architectural works is in Prache, *Saint-Remi*; on these letters, see pp. 37–8. Prache suggests that letter no. 168 is earlier than no. 149 because only no. 168 mentions the construction of the façade, which is likely to have been completed before the chevet (see also no. 168, n. 13) but the brevity of Peter's references makes this uncertain. On Peter's other experience of building work and his architectural ideas, see Prache, *Saint-Remi*, pp. 37–41; on the architecture of those parts of the building with which Peter was involved—the façade and chevet—see ibid. pp. 45–74. Prache suggests *c.*1165/70–*c.*1175 for the construction of the façade and *c.*1170–*c.*1182/5 for the chevet, but these dates are in part derived from these letters, whose references are vague. See also M. Demaison, 'Les Chevets des églises Notre-Dame de Châlons et Saint-Remi de Reims', *Bulletin archéologique du comité des travaux historiques et scientifiques* (1899), 84–107, at pp. 102–5, and V. Mortet and P. Deschamps, *Recueil de textes relatifs à l'histoire de l'architecture et à la condition des architects en France au Moyen âge XIè–XIIè siècles*, 2 vols. (Paris, 1911–29), ii. 139–40—but note Prache's corrections of both.

APPENDIX 13

Peter of Celle and Nicholas of St Albans's debate on the feast of the Conception of the Blessed Virgin Mary

Letters 157–60 are an exchange between Peter and the English monk Nicholas of St Albans on the subject of the feast of the Conception of the Blessed Virgin Mary (also referred to as the feast of the Immaculate Conception of the Virgin). Uniquely, both sides of the correspondence form part of Peter's collection, and so are included in this edition. On Nicholas, about whom few biographical details are known, see *DS* xi. 296–8 and C. H. Talbot, 'Nicholas of St Albans and St Bernard', *Revue Bénédictine*, lxiv (1954), 83–117 (which includes an edition of Nicholas's earlier treatise on the subject at pp. 92–117). Talbot also disposes of the confusions which have arisen over the years from the identification of this Nicholas with Nicholas of Clairvaux, an identification which, 'since it was exploded long ago by Mabillon, should never have been revived' (Talbot, 'Nicholas of St Albans and St Bernard', pp. 83–7, quotation p. 87).

The feast of the Conception was of English origin. It gave rise to much debate in the years after the Norman Conquest, and spread to the Continent, where it was introduced into the liturgical calendar at Lyons. This prompted an attack on the feast from St Bernard, which in turn gave rise to a number of further writings for and against its celebration. These included Nicholas's earlier treatise (now ed. by Talbot), to which Peter refers back in the much later phase of the debate preserved in the present letters.[19]

The essence of the debate was whether the Virgin's own conception was immaculate—a position which Peter, following St Bernard, denied. The canons of Lyons, defending their celebration of the feast, had argued firstly that as both Jeremiah and John the Baptist had been sanctified in the womb, Mary ought also to be regarded as so sanctified, and secondly that her conception should be honoured by a liturgical feast in the same manner as her nativity. Bernard denied the second of these two propositions, arguing (among other things) that Mary could be sanctified in the womb without the preceding conception itself being immaculate—a position which would lead to the novel doctrine that St Anne was herself a virgin.[20] In response,

[19] See Talbot, 'Nicholas of St Albans and St Bernard', pp. 88–9, for an account of these related controversies and full references to the extant texts.

[20] For a more detailed discussion see ibid., pp. 89–91. Bernard's letter is *S. Bernardi Op.* vii. 388–92, no. 174. Talbot's brief account is overtly partial (e.g. 'How completely he [Bernard] missed the point is seen . . .', at p. 90, and, 'Nicholas' treatise leaves one with a

Nicholas had argued, in his first treatise, that the feast of the Immaculate Conception of the Virgin did not institute anything contrary to the faith, that even if it did not have tradition in its favour it would enrich the liturgy, and that the feast of the Nativity of the Virgin alone (which Bernard felt to be sufficient in honour of Mary's birth) left unresolved the issue of the exact point at which Mary had become sanctified. His solutions to the problems raised concerning the transmission of original sin are summarized by M. O'Carroll in *DS* xi. col. 297:

> . . . il propose deux solutions. Selon la première, la conception de Marie n'est pas venue de la concupiscence de la corruption commune à toute la postérité adamique comme peine du premier péché, mais d'une concupiscence naturelle, innée, et non expérimentée avant la péché. Selon la seconde hypothèse, si 'la chair de la Vierge dans la semence avant l'infusion de l'âme était comme la nôtre, il est permis de croire que l'âme, au moment de cette infusion, fut aussitôt remplie de l'Esprit saint et que la chair fut purifiée de la lèpre de corruption'.[21]

The date of Nicholas's original treatise is not known. Talbot suggests that Peter may have read it while at Montier-la-Celle. It must post-date Bernard's letter to the canons of Lyons (1138/9); *DS* gives 1151 × 1162 (*DS* xi. 296). This treatise presumably occasioned the earlier dispute to which Peter refers in letter no. 157. Peter apparently believed Nicholas to have died in the meantime, and in letter no. 157 is trying to renew the debate on discovering otherwise. The letter was written after the death of Becket (Dec. 1170) to which it refers, but Peter says he has not written for many years. Peter's letter no. 158 appears to be a reply to a lost letter of Nicholas; presumably Nicholas had responded to no. 157 and renewed the debate. The notable change in tone between letters 157 and 158, the request for new writings in letter no. 157, and the fact that few of the specific points debated in letters 158–60 figured in Nicholas's original treatise all point to a lost letter. It is this lost letter, presumably, where Nicholas advanced his proposition, 'Virgo singularis uicit omne peccatum non omne debellando sed nullum prorsus sentiendo'.

In letters 158 and 159 Bernard is referred to as a saint, which suggests a date after his canonization in 1174. Letter no. 159 is Nicholas's reply to no. 158. Although it refers to an invitation (or provocation) to renew the debate after a long silence (which might indicate that it is a reply to letter no. 157), it addresses points raised in, and makes detailed reference to, letter no. 158. It is just possible, but unlikely, that a missing letter of Peter's existed, a sort of

feeling of satisfaction', at pp. 90–1), but provides useful references to the history of this debate; cf. *DS* xi. 296–8.

[21] On all of Nicholas's arguments summarized above, and for a more detailed discussion of the theology involved (including Nicholas's use of Scriptural passages in support of his arguments) and a bibliography on the Immaculate Conception of the Virgin, see M. O'Carroll's art. in *DS* xi. 296–8.

supplement to no. 157 containing the specific points not raised in no. 157, which are addressed in no. 159—but a missing letter of Nicholas, falling between letters 157 and 158, is the more credible option. Letter no. 160 must have been written in 1181 as Peter styles himself bishop-elect of Chartres. We cannot know how much time elapsed between the writing of each of these letters; it is possible that the whole correspondence took place *c.*1181, just before and after Peter's election to Chartres.

APPENDIX 14

The Case of the novices from Grandmont who had transferred to the Cistercians

Letters 161 and 162 concern three Grandmontine novices who had transferred to the Cistercian house of Pontigny and were in doubt as to whether they should return to Grandmont in accordance with their first vows. Two of them are addressed in letter no. 161: 'P.' and 'W.'—and three are named in letter no. 162: William, Peter, and Wido (or Guy). Letter no. 161 is the only letter in Sirmond with neither a salutation nor a preserved rubric; the salutation in MS Di preserves only initials, while d'Achery gives Wido and Peter as the recipients (on these texts, see Introduction, II. 2.i). In letter no. 162 (which does not occur in Sirmond) it is only d'Achery who gives all the names in full in the salutation, but in this case they are also given in full in the text (and it is safe to assume that they refer to the same group as those addressed in letter no. 161). *PL* expands the W. to William in letter no. 161, presumably because he is more prominent than Wido in letter no. 162. The William has been identified as William of Donjon, later archbishop of Bourges.[22]

Both letters occur in MS Di as part of a small collection of four letters all dealing with this case. The others are a copy of Stephen of Tournai's letter no. 71 (also *PL* ccxi. 361–70) and a letter by a G. of Saint-Victor (presumably Abbot Guarinus, 1172–92,[23] who corresponded with Peter of Pavia). The context and date of Stephen of Tournai's involvement are provided by his letter no. 72 (*PL* ccxi. 370–1) which does not occur in MS Di but which was a companion letter to the original version of his no. 71 (addressed to Robert, a monk of Pontigny, named in Stephen's letter no. 72 as Robert 'de Galardon').[24] Stephen's no. 72 is addressed to Peter of Pavia as cardinal bishop of Tusculum and as papal legate, and so during his second legation, and most likely that part of it which was spent in France, that is, from the end of Apr. 1181 to Feb. 1182 (on Peter of Pavia's dates, see letter no. 89, n. 1). It implies that the legate had referred the case to Stephen and effectively commissioned Stephen's letter no. 71: 'Misi uobis epistolam nouitiis Pontiniacensibus nuper scriptam. Quesierat uobis frater Robertus

[22] J. Desilve (ed.), *Lettres d'Étienne de Tournai* (Valenciennes-Paris, 1893), p. 8.

[23] See G. Teske, *Die Briefsammlungen des 12. Jahrhunderts in St. Viktor/Paris* (Bonn, 1993), p. 3.

[24] Stephen's letters are also Desilve (ed), *Lettres d'Étienne de Tournai*, nos. i and lxxxv.

de Galardon, me presente, quid nouitiis illis faciendum erat, qui timore prioris uoti tentabantur ad reditum' (Stephen's letter no. 72, *PL* ccxi. 370–1). This meeting, which clearly preceded Stephen's letter on the case, cannot be dated more precisely than 1181, after the end of April (i.e. during that part of Peter of Pavia's legation which was spent in France, as noted above). Peter of Pavia was in Reims in May 1181 and may have consulted Peter of Celle at this point (if he had already met Robert Galardon by then), but the itinerary of this legation is not certain. It is likely that Peter of Pavia was preparing to return to Rome from Aug. 1181, after Alexander III's death, where he arrived in Feb. 1182 (see Janssen, *Die päpstlichen Legaten*, pp. 119–22). However Peter of Celle's letters, which are addressed to the monks themselves, do not mention Peter of Pavia or Robert Galardon (and nor do Peter's own letters to Peter of Pavia mention this case, but this is inconclusive in itself), and so could have been written at some earlier stage. We do not know when these monks had transferred. In any event a later date is unlikely, as Peter left Saint-Remi in 1181.[25]

For Peter to claim, as he does in letter no. 161, that Grandmont is unknown to him, is an extremely odd statement whenever these letters are dated. Quite apart from letters 148 and 149, also written at Saint-Remi but difficult to date closely, he wrote to the community of Grandmont in very respectful terms when he was still at Montier-la-Celle (letter no. 43). This may be a politic phrasing to avoid a more direct criticism of Grandmont while still supporting the Cistercians. He may have been deliberately stretching the meaning of 'incognitus' to imply simply that he had not visited it in person.

[25] On this dating, even if the well known statute of the Cistercian general chapter banning *transitus* between the order and the Grandmontines had been enacted in 1180 (J. Leclercq, 'Épitres d'Alexandre III sur les Cisterciens', *Revue Bénédictine*, lxiv (1954), 68–82, at pp. 74–6) it cannot have affected this case, either because it had—as is likely—arisen earlier, or simply because statutes did not necessarily have immediate and final effects.

CONCORDANCE OF THIS EDITION WITH OTHER EDITIONS AND MSS[1]

This edition	Sirmond	*PL*	O	Val	R	other
1	I. 6	6	—	—	6	
2	I. 2	2	57	—	2	
3	I. 4	4	—	—	4	
4	I. 5	5	61	—	5	
5	I. 3	3	59	—	3	
6	I. 1	1	60	—	1	
7	I. 7	7	58	—	7	
8	I. 8	8	14	—	8	
9	I. 11	11	15	—	11	
10	I. 9	9	16	—	9	
11	I. 12	12	39	6	12	
12	I. 23	20	38	—	23	
13	I. 21	19	12	—	21	
14	I. 17	15	4	14	17	
15	I. 19	17	5	—	19	
16	I. 20	18	2	—	20	
17	I. 16	14	3	13	16	
18	I. 18	16	6	15	18	
19	I. 15	13	1	—	15	
20	I. 25	23	—	—	25	
21	I. 24	21	28	—	24	
22	I. 26	22	—	—	26	
23	I. 22	10	13	8	22	
24	II. 1	25	7	4	28	
25	II. 11	35	62	—	38	
26	II. 12	36	30	11	39	
27	II. 10	34	11	10	37	various MSS[2]
28	—	—	49	—	—	N 4
29	II. 9	33	53	9	36	
30	II. 7	31	42	16	34	
31	II. 2	26	8	—	29	
32	II. 4	28	10	—	31	

[1] *PL* = *PL* ccii; N = Leclercq, 'Nouvelles'. All MSS and editions recorded here are discussed in the Introduction.

[2] See Introduction, pp. li–lii, for the MSS for this letter.

This edition	Sirmond	*PL*	O	Val	R	other
33	II. 3	27	9	—	30	
34	II. 5	29	—	—	32	
35	V. 12	48	—	—	80	
36	II. 8	32	—	17	35	
37	II. 13	37	43	—	40	
38	II. 14	38	40	—	41	
39	II. 15	39	41	—	42	
40	III. 7	53	46	—	49	
41	—	—	47	—	—	N 2
42	—	—	48	—	—	N 3
43	III. 8	54	37	—	50	
44	IV. 13	76	52	—	68	
45	III. 11	57	27	—	53	
46	III. 12	58	26	—	54	
47	III. 13	59	25	12	55	
48	—	—	24	—	—	N 1
49	IV. 3	61	45	18	58	
50	IV. 2	64	44	—	57	Picard 51
51	IV. 1	66	63	—	56	Picard 53
52	III. 2	41	32	2	44	
53	III. 4[3]	43	34	—	46	
54	III. 4	43	35	—	46	
55	III. 5	44	36	—	47	
56	III. 6	45	—	—	48	
57	III. 3	42	33	3	45	
58	III. 1	40	31	1	43	
59	V. 13	47	—	—	81	
60	V. 11	46	—	—	79	
61	III. 9	55	54	—	51	
62	III. 10	56	—	—	52	
63	IV. 6	69	17	—	61	
64	IV. 8	71	55	19	63	
65	IV. 9	72	18	—	64	
66	IV. 4	67	20	—	59	
67	IV. 11	74	23	—	66	
68	IV. 5	68	22	—	60	
69	—	—	29	—	—	
70	IV. 7	70	21	—	62	
71	II. 6	30	—	—	33	
72	I. 27	24	56	5	27	

[3] Nos. 53 and 54 are run together as one letter in both Sirmond and *PL*.

This edition	Sirmond	*PL*	O	Val	R	other
73	—	—	51	—	—	N 6
74	—	—	50	—	—	N 5
75	—	85	—	—	—	various MSS[4]
76	V. 19	77	—	—	87	
77	VI. 6	78	—	—	95	
78	VIII. 10	81	—	—	144	
79	VIII. 16	84	—	—	150	
80	VIII. 12	83	—	—	146	
81	VIII. 11	82	—	—	145	
82	VIII. 8	80	—	—	142	
83	VI. 1	86	—	—	90	
84	VI. 3	87	—	—	92	
85	VIII. 13	88 bis	—	—	147	
86	VIII. 15	90	—	—	149	
87	VIII. 14	89	—	—	148	
88	VIII. 19	88	—	—	143	
89	VII. 16	91	—	—	128	
90	VII. 18	92	—	—	130	
91	IX. 6	96	—	—	163	
92	I. 10	114	—	7	10	
93	I. 14	111	—	—	14	
94	I. 13	113	—	—	13	
95	V. 5	103	—	—	73	
96	VI. 15	104	—	—	104	
97	VII. 6	105	—	—	118	
98	VII. 13	106	—	—	125	
99	VII. 17	107	—	—	129	
100	VIII. 1	108	—	—	135	
101	VI. 2	116	—	—	91	
102	VII. 8	117	—	—	120	
103	VII. 21	115	—	—	133	
104	VIII. 19	109	—	—	153	
105	VIII. 20	110	—	—	154	
106	VII. 10	129	—	—	122	
107	VIII. 2	126	—	—	136	
108	V. 4	127	—	—	72	
109	V. 16	128	—	—	84	
110	VI. 7	112	—	—	96	
111	VI. 21	152	—	—	110	
112	VII. 9	153	—	—	121	

[4] See Introduction, p. li, for the MSS for this letter.

This edition	Sirmond	*PL*	O	Val	R	other
113	VII. 11	130	—	—	123	
114	V. 9	144 bis	—	—	77	
115	VI. 14	155	—	—	103	
116	VI. 10	134	—	—	99	
117	V. 15	133	—	—	83	
118	V. 10	132	—	—	78	
119[5]	—	—	—	—	—	*
120	V. 18	135	—	—	86	
121	V. 17	136	—	—	85	
122	VI. 17	137	—	—	106	
123	VI. 19	138	—	—	108	
124	VII. 1	141	—	—	113	
125	VII. 5	143	—	—	117	
126	IX. 7	144	—	—	164	
127	IX. 11	146	—	—	168	
128	V. 1	97	—	—	69	
129	V. 2	98	—	—	70	
130	VIII. 17	102	—	—	151	
131	V. 3	99	—	—	71	
132	V. 8	101	—	—	76	
133	VIII. 21	93	—	—	155	
134	IX. 1	94	—	—	158	
135	IX. 2	95	—	—	159	
136	—	147	—	—	—	Q
137	—	—	—	—	—	M, Do, N
138	VI. 13	139	—	—	102	
139	VII. 15	140	—	—	127	
140	V. 6	131	—	—	74	
141	VI. 9	149	—	—	98	
142	VI. 18	150	—	—	107	
143	VII. 20	151	—	—	132	
144	IX. 5	154	—	—	162	
145	V. 21	148	—	—	89	
146	IX. 3	145	—	—	160	
147	IX. 8	174	—	—	165	
148	VIII. 7	157	—	—	141	
149	VIII. 22	158	—	—	156	
150	VIII. 23	159	—	—	157	
151	VII. 4	142	—	—	116	
152	VII. 19	167	—	—	131	

[5] See Introduction, pp. l–li.

This edition	Sirmond	*PL*	O	Val	R	other
153	VI. 22	168	—	—	111	
154	VIII. 18	101 bis	—	—	152	
155	V. 7	100	—	—	75	
156	VII. 14	156	—	—	126	
157	VI. 4	169	—	—	93	
158	VI. 23	171	—	—	112	
159	IX. 9	172	—	—	166	
160	IX. 10	173	—	—	167	
161	IX. 12	175	—	—	169	Di
162	—	176	—	—	—	Di, A1, A2
163	VI. 16	162	—	—	105	
164	VI. 20	162 bis	—	—	109	
165	VII. 12	163	—	—	124	
166	VIII. 3	164	—	—	137	
167	VIII. 6	165	—	—	140	
168	IX. 4	166	—	—	161	
169	IV. 12	75	—	—	67	
170	IV. 10	73	19	—	65	
171	V. 14	121	—	—	82	
172	VI. 11	123	—	—	100	
173	VII. 2	125	—	—	114	
174	VI. 12	124	—	—	101	
175	V. 20	122	—	—	88	
176	VII. 22	118	—	—	134	
177	VIII. 5	120	—	—	139	
178	VIII. 4	119	—	—	138	
179	VII. 3	160	—	—	115	
180	—	177	—	—	—	Vat. Reg.
181	VI. 8	79	—	—	97	
182	VI. 5	170	—	—	94	
183	VII. 7	161	—	—	119	

ADDENDUM

I am grateful to Dr Ludwig Falkenstein for supplying the following identifications (see letter no. 110 n. 2):

The *nepotes* might be Philip of Dreux, archdeacon of Reims (became bishop of Beauvais 1175: Newman, *Seigneurs de Nesle* i. 227, 247), and Henry of Dreux, treasurer (became bishop of Orléans 1186: Newman, *Seigneurs de Nesle* i. 254), the sons of Robert of Dreux and Agnes de Baudement. They first occur in 1168 and 1172 respectively: see Falkenstein, 'Alexandre III et Henri de France', p. 140, n. 120 (where Henry is given as first occurring 1170: the correction is Dr Falkenstein's own) and for 1168 (11 Feb.), *Cartulaire de Saint-Thierry*, Rheims, BM MS 1602, fol. 93^{v}. Both were appointed as minors, and so occur only after reaching their majorities; John de Breteuil acted as *vicearchidiaconus* for Philip for many years. The archdeacon mentioned separately is most likely Boso: for reasons not entirely clear, he is the only archdeacon who occurs in the archiepiscopal sources for some years after Guy de Dampierre's election to the see of Châlons-sur-Marne (see L. Falkenstein, 'Alexander III. und der Streit um die Doppelwahl in Châlons-sur-Marne (1162–1164)', *Deutsches Archiv* xxxii (1976), 444–94, pp. 487–8). Waleran was a canon of Reims who occurs from 1170, and as subdeacon to 1175 (cf. Varin, *Arch. admin.* I. i. 363–4). A Thomas *presbiter* or *sacerdos* occurs 1163 and 1169 × 1171 in the archiepiscopal sources (cf. also JL 11805), and is almost certainly the Thomas cantor who occurs from 1172, d. 1196. Master Ralph is Ralph of Sarre: see L. Falkenstein, 'Zur Entstehungsort und Redaktor der Collectio Brugensis', *Proceedings of the Eighth International Congress of Medieval Canon Law*, ed. S. Chodorow (Vatican, 1992), 117–51, pp. 140–4. This identification confirms the suggestion at *RHF* xvi. 710, note 'f'. On both see also L. Falkenstein, 'Radulf von Sarre als päpstlicher Delegat und seine Mitdelegaten' in R. H. Helmholz, P. Mikat, J. Müller and M. Stolleis eds., *Grundlagen des Rechts: Festschrift für Peter Landau* (Paderborn, 2000), 301–32.

INDEX 1

Dates of the Letters

Dates are given on the left, with the number(s) of corresponding letters on the right.

*c.*1145 × 1156 24
*c.*1145 × ? 1157 38
*c.*1145 × 8 January 1159 13
*c.*1145 × 1162 8, 9, 14, 15, 16, 25, 26, 40, 41, 42, 43, 44, 45, 46, 47, 52, 55, 56, 61, 62, 74
*c.*1145 × 1162 (possibly *c.*1161) 19
15 February 1145 × 1147 1
1146 × 1152 (or × 1149) 50
1146 × 1152 49, 51
1147 × 1162 63
1147 × 1162 (possibly late 1156 × early 1157) 64
1148 × 1162 20
1149, after April × 21 May 1155 27
? March 1151 × January 1162 21
1152 × 1154/5 71
? 30 November 1152 (or earlier) × 1157, probably not later than August 10
30 November 1152 × 1157, probably not later than August 23
*c.*1152 × 1162 29
1152/5 × 1162 28
after 20 August 1153 17
May 1153 × 1154 7
? July 1153 × 1162 (possibly end of July 1160 × 1162) 2
late 1153 × 1155/6 3
? *c.*1154, or earlier 57
? *c.*1154 (or *c.*1145 × 1162) 58
5 December 1154 × October 1155/6 65
1154 × 1156 4
4 December 1154 × 21 May 1155 5
*c.*1155 × 1162 53, 54
January 1155 × May 1162 72, 73
1156, after July and before autumn 66
1156, not before September 30
? 1156 × 1162 48
? 1157 39
1157, not before April (possibly not before July/August) 18
1157, after July/August 11, 67, 68
late 1157 (or 1158, but earlier than letter no. 32) 31
probably late 1157, or later (possibly × April 1161) 69
? late 1157 32
late 1157 × September 1159 33, 34
late 1157 or early 1158 × autumn 1161, (possibly late) 12
1159 × 1162 59
July 1160 (or September 1159 × July 1160) 22
? end of July 1160 × 21 September 1161 (or later) 6
? *c.*1160 or earlier 35
*c.*1160 36
1160, or earlier × 1162 37
Easter 1161 60
1161 × 1162 70
1162 × *c.*1173 106, 111, 112, 113
*c.*1162 × *c.*1173/4 114
1162 × 1179 115
1162 × 1180 116
1162 × September 1180 180
1162 × 1181 84, 120, 121, 122, 123, 124, 125, 126, 127, 148, 149, 150, 151, 152, 153, 182
1162 × 1181, possibly soon after June 1165 118
1162 × 1181 (possibly after 1175) 119
*c.*1162/3 × 1178 (after 25 October) 129
*c.*1162/3 × 1179 before May (or more likely before March) 128, 130, 154
? late 1163 × November 1164 169
1164, before November 170
1164 × 1170, probably early 136
1164 × 1170 (possibly 1169, August–November) 92
*c.*1164 × *c.*1170 131, 155
early 1166 × 1168 179
1166, probably October 137

1166 × January 1171 138, 139
summer 1167 93
mid-November–December 1167 (or possibly *c*.11 December 1167) 75
? *c*.1167 × *c*.1170 140
late 1167 × October 1173, or autumn 1176 × spring 1177 95
September 1167 × 1181 (possibly before July 1177) 94
? *c*.1167 × 1181 107
after 29 September 1169 108
early 1171 (possibly after April) 171
probably early 1171 110
? early 1172 (or after September 1171, or 1172 × 1173 before October) 181
after September 1171, or 1172 × 1173, before October 96
early 1171 × 1172 (or × 22 July 1176) 172
1171 × May 1172 117
December 1171 × May 1172 175
1171 × 21 February 1173 (possibly early) 141
1171 × ? 1173 (or × 22 July 1176) 173
1171 × 22 July 1176 174
early 1171 (or 1172, before May) × July 1176 163
early 1171 (or 1172, before May) × 1181 164, 165, 166, 167, 168
1171/2, before September (or earlier) 76, 77
probably 1171/2 132
? 1171/2 156
1172, possibly May or earlier 83
1172, not before May 101
after February 1173 (or possibly earlier) 109
+1173 × 1181, probably late (at or just before Easter) 144
late 1174 × December 1176 (possibly late 1176) 89, 90
1175, after July × July 1176 142
1176, in or soon after July 183
July × September 1176, probably early 102
1176, possibly autumn or later 97
late 1176 × spring 1177 (probably spring 1177) 98
July 1176 × 1181 103
22 July 1176 × 1181 (probably early) 143
Spring 1177 × 1181 (possibly early) 99
Spring 1177 × 1181 100
mid-1177 × 1179, before May (or more likely before March) 176, 177
mid-1177 × 25 October 1180 178
? *c*.1177 (or 1176 × 1181) 78
early 1178 79
1178, after June 86
1178, summer or later 80
February 1178 × 1181 (most likely early) 85
February 1178 × 1181 104, 105
summer 1178 × early 1179 87
late 1178 × March 1179 82, 88
1179, before March (or possibly as early as summer 1178) 81
1179, after March/May (possibly later; × summer 1180) 135
May (or more likely March) 1179 × summer 1180 133, 134
1179, after Mar./May × 1181 145
1180, possibly early 146
? summer 1180 91
c.1180/1 (or at least 1171 × 1181) 157
c.1180/1 (or at least 1174 × 1181) 158, 159
1181 147, 160
? 1181 (but possibly much earlier) 161, 162

INDEX 2

QUOTATIONS AND ALLUSIONS

Page references are to both Latin and English texts; where quotations run over pages within each text, the reference is to the facing page spread where the relevant footnote appears. References in square brackets are to letter no. 159, written by Nicholas of St Albans. An asterisk (*) in this index indicates that the allusion is not to the Vulgate. Peter of Celle's quotations from or allusions to the Vulgate have not been artificially 'corrected' to coincide with the standard modern edition, as this would risk imposing an anachronisitic notion of the text; 'cf.' in the footnotes indicates variation. (On the nature and scope of the annotation, see also Introduction, III.)

A. BIBLICAL QUOTATIONS AND ALLUSIONS

Genesis (Gen.)
1: 1–2: 3 502–3
1: 2 236–7
1: 11, 21, 24 236–7
1: 11 12–13, 278–9
1: 26 144–5, 208–9, 250–1, 256–7, 258–9, 498–9, 596–7
2: 7 74–5, 224–5, 636–7, 650–1
2: 9 378–9
2: 10–14 306–7
2: 10 544–5, 552–3
2: 11–12 618–19
2: 15 250–1
2: 16 558–9
2: 17 358–9
2: 19 498–9
2: 21–2 198–9
3: 1–6 290–1
3: 1 194–5
3: 2 558–9
3: 3 190–1
3: 7–24 96–7
3: 7 54–5, 144–5, 296–7
3: 15 592–3, 620–1
3: 17, 19 632–3
3: 17 306–7
3: 18 236–7
3: 19 358–9
3: 21 358–9
3: 24 114–15, 188–9, 244–5, 356–7
4: 7* 472–3, 594–5
4: 8 476–7
4: 10 110–11
4: 14 306–7
5: 1 596–7
5: 29 112–13, 376–7, 510–11
6: 6 398–9, [602–3]
6: 8 642–3
6: 14–22 252–3
7: 11 172–3, 584–5, 642–3
8: 2 172–3, 584–5
8: 5 468–9
8: 6–11 188–9
8: 11 484–5
9: 5 632–3
9: 17 276–7
9: 21–5 244–5
15: 11 390–1
16: 12 50–1
16: 14 358–9
17: 12, 27 306–7, 324–5
18 306–7
18: 6–7 268–9
18: 20–21 440–1
18: 27 146–7, 338–9
20: 5 218–9
21: 9–12 20–21
21: 10 144–5
22: 2 198–9
22: 3–5 196–7
22: 6 80–1
22: 7 196–7
22: 13 84–5, 198–9
22: 17–18 198–9
22: 18 620–1
24 418–19, 546–7

Genesis (Gen.) (*cont.*)
24: 16 636–7
24: 46 122–3, 242–3
24: 60 638–9
24: 61 654–5
24: 62 358–9
24: 65 114–15
25: 11 358–9
25: 22–3 484–5
25: 29–34 64–5
26: 14–15, 18 188–9
26: 15–33 244–5
26: 15, 18 548–9, 584–5
26: 19 244–5
27: 1–29, esp. 15 140–1
27: 1 570–1
27: 15 532–3
27: 22 512–13, 532–3, 534–5
27: 28, 39 690–1
27: 28 562–3
27: 37 192–3, 310–11
28: 11, 18 100–1, 468–9
28: 12–15 264–5, 284–5
28: 12 164–5
28: 13 408–9
28: 14 192–3
28: 17 306–7
28: 22 270–1
29: 10 242–3
29: 16—30: 24 486–7
30: 1 198–9
30: 22–4 198–9
30: 32–3, 35, 39 196–7
31 386–7
31: 17–35 408–9
31: 38–41 78–9
31: 45 270–1
31: 47 580–1
32: 2 190–1, 282–3, 540–1
32: 10 28–9, 302–3
32: 24 372–3
35: 14 270–1
35: 18 198–9, 274–5
35: 29 372–3
37 274–5, 492–3
37: 18–28 148–9
37: 20, 33 76–7
37: 31 286–7
38: 29 274–5
39: 6 198–9
41: 42 172–3
41: 44 644–5
42–7 492–3
42 250–1
43: 21–3 94–5
43: 30 554–5
44: 5 308–9
45: 25–8, esp. 26 572–3
45: 26 574–5
49 372–3, 546–7
49: 1–28, esp. 22–6 80–1
49: 1, 18 372–3
49: 4 372–3
49: 5 372–3
49: 14 538–9
49: 26 470–1
Exodus (Exod.)
1: 8 38–9
1: 12 236–7
1: 14 246–7, 380–1, 644–5
2: 3 366–7
2: 16–17 384–5
3: 1–2 218–19
3: 1 92–3, 158–9, 196–7, 244–5, 262–3, 270–1
3: 2–5 114–15
3: 2–3 218–19
3: 18 96–7, 264–5
4: 1–9 344–5
4: 2 302–3
4: 4 196–7
4: 6–7 304–5, 552–3
4: 21 644–5
5: 1 644–5
5: 3 96–7, 264–5
5: 7–19 644–5
7–12 384–5, 644–5, 682–3
7: 3 644–5
7: 9–12 110–11
8: 17, 19–20 110–11
8: 21–4 388–9
8: 27 96–7, 264–5
11: 7 682–3
12 286–7
12: 5 286–7
12: 8–9 140–1
12: 9 286–7
12: 29–32 96–7
12: 44 306–7, 324–5
13: 21–2 302–3
14: 22–8 446–7
14: 23–31 384–5
14: 24 302–3
14: 30 286–7
14: 31 98–9
15: 10 248–9, 446–7

15: 23–5 306–7
15: 23 302–3
16 100–1
16: 12 120–1
17: 8–13 178–9, 158–9
17: 10–12 352–3
18: 14–27 134–5
19: 1 158–9
20: 5 144–5, 178–9
20: 7 122–3
21: 23 168–9
21: 23–4 312–13
23: 14–17 542–3
23: 26* 460–1
25: 4 288–9
25: 7 246–7
25: 10–22 110–11
25: 11 366–7
25: 12–14 516–17
25: 13–15 430–1
25: 17–22 306–7, 366–7
25: 17, 20, 22 276–7
25: 18 114–15, 516–17
25: 23 110–11
25: 30 250–1, 430–1
25: 31 110–11, 390–1
26 114–15
26: 1–6 110–11
26: 1 288–9
26: 7–13 110–11
26: 7 100–1
26: 19, 21, 32 110–11
26: 33 358–9
26: 34 276–7
27: 4 550–1
28 246–7, 416–17
28: 4 582–3
28: 5–6, 15 582–3
29: 5 246–7, 416–17
29: 12 502–3
30: 6 276–7, 358–9
30: 29 100–1
31: 7 276–7
31: 18 110–11
32, esp. 27 374–5
32: 4, 7–8 352–3
32: 10 596–7
32: 15–19 110–11
32: 27 60–1, 178–9, 372–3
32: 31–2 598–9
33: 21–2 586–7
33: 22–3 278–9
34: 7 178–9
34: 28–30, 35 288–9
34: 29–35 34–5
35: 9, 27 246–7
35: 12 276–7
35: 13 250–1
35: 16 100–1
35: 17 110–11
35: 18 252–3
35: 19 352–3
36: 1 390–1
36: 14–18 110–11
36: 19 100–1
36: 24, 25, 30, 36 110–11
37: 6–9 276–7
37: 17 110–11, 390–1
38: 1 100–1
38: 4 550–1
38: 20 252–3
38: 21–2 390–1
39: 2–19 416–17
39: 1–28 246–7
39: 34 276–7
39: 35 250–1
39:37–9 528–9
39: 40 252–3
40: 3 358–9
40: 21 250–1
40: 33 180–1

Leviticus (Lev.)
1: 14 96–7
1: 15 158–9, 284–5
2: 13 54–5, 82–3
3: 17 76–7
4: 6, 17 82–3
4: 7, 34 502–3
5: 7, 11 96–7
5: 8 158–9, 284–5
6: 12–13 384–5
6: 12 430–1
6: 13 30–1
7: 3 324–5
7: 24 290–1
9: 17 196–7
11: 3 188–9, 624–5
11: 7 550–1
11: 44 256–7
12: 6, 8 96–7
14: 22, 30 96–7
15: 14, 29 96–7
16: 2, 14 276–7
16: 2 358–9
17: 5 68–9
17: 14 166–7

Leviticus (Lev.) (*cont.*)
18: 16 616–17
19: 2 256–7
19: 18 156–7, [608–9]
20: 21 616–17
21: 18 250–1
22: 8 550–1
22: 11 306–7, 324–5
22: 22 198–9
23: 10 94–5
23: 17 266–7
23: 42 284–5
24: 4 110–11
24: 5–8 250–1, 430–1
25, esp. 10, 13 644–5
Numbers (Num.)
3: 37 252–3
4: 7, 12 674–5
4: 32 252–3
6: 10 96–7
7: 8 276–7
7: 13 580–1
8: 2 250–1
8: 3 398–9, 472–3
8: 4 110–11, 390–1
11: 5 634–5
11: 8 262–3, 542–3
11: 16–17, 24–5 384–5
11: 25 136–7
13: 14 268–9
14: 14 302–3
14: 18 144–5, 178–9
16: 46 386–7
17: 8 500–1
20: 13 60–1
21: 8–9 302–3
22: 4 352–3
23: 21 34–5
24: 6 238–9
25: 4 78–9
25: 7–8, 11 176–7, 422–3, 570–1
28: 27 196–7
29: 2, 8, 13, 36 196–7
Deuteronomy (Deut.)
1: 33 302–3
5: 9 144–5, 178–9
5: 15 14–15, 72–3
6: 5 192–3, 280–1
7: 19 14–15, 72–3
9: 16 352–3
9: 29 14–15, 72–3
12: 3 598–9
14: 6 188–9, 624–5
14: 8, 21 550–1
16: 16 542–3
19: 5 626–7
19: 15 580–1
19: 21 168–9, 312–13
21: 19 464–5
22: 11 246–7
23: 3 144–5
23: 23 670–1
25: 4 394–5, 400–1
25: 5–10 356–7
25: 7* 460–1
25: 10 54–5
28: 6 394–5
32: 34 46–7, 58–9, 142–3, 324–5
32: 38 244–5
32: 42 76–7, 368–9
33: 14 80–1
33: 16 470–1
33: 19 288–9
34: 7 570–1
Joshua (Josh.)
1: 6 644–5
1: 12 344–5
3: 11 366–7
4: 12 344–5
5: 13 62–3, 590–1
5: 13–14 590–1
6: 26 248–9
11: 23 644–5
13 644–5
23: 4 644–5
Judges (Judg.)
3: 16 236–7, 354–5
5: 15 570–1
6: 25–8 618–19
9: 15 202–3
9: 26–41 70–1
9: 27 18–19
12: 3 342–3, 400–1
14: 12–19 598–9
15: 13–14 124–5
16: 11–12 124–5
20 344–5
20: 16 190–1
Ruth (Ruth)
1: 16 48–9, 384–5
2 598–9
2: 3 408–9
1 Kings (1 Samuel), (1 Kgs. (1 Sam.))
1: 3, 11 236–7
2: 3 462–3
2: 8 170–1, 408–9

2: 12–14 366–7
4: 4 236–7, 382–3
5: 2–5 598–9
5: 2 178–9
5: 4 382–3
6 382–3
6: 7, 10, 12 132–3
8 274–5
14: 25–9 240–1
14: 27, 43 240–1
17 620–1
17: 35 76–7
19: 5 342–3, 400–1
21: 5 268–9
21: 6 418–19
24: 1 266–7
28: 21 342–3, 400–1
29: 6 156–7
2 Kings (2 Samuel), (2 Kgs. (2 Sam.))
1: 10 40–1
1: 20 128–9
1: 21 90–1, 656–7
2: 26 248–9, 494–5
6: 6 366–7
7: 9 420–1
8: 2 236–7
11: 11 366–7
12: 1–14 76–7
15: 31, 34 114–15
15: 31 516–17
16: 23 114–15
17: 7, 14, 21, 23 114–15
22: 11 204–5, 284–5
23: 15 244–5
23: 18–19 316–17
3 Kings (1 Kings), (3 Kgs. (1 Kgs.))
1: 1 570–1
1: 3–4 144–5
1: 3 190–1
1: 33, 38, 44 76–7
2: 17–23 144–5
2: 22 144–5
3: 16–28 124–5, 202–3
3: 18 202–3
4: 33 202–3
5: 6 202–3
6–7 558–9
6: 7 238–9
6: 31 30–1
7: 22 110–11
8: 6 358–9
8: 12 30–1
9: 4 218–19
10: 16 620–1
12: 11, 14 380–1
14: 27 620–1
17: 9–16 554–5
17: 14, 16 52–3, 430–1, 540–1
18: 35 550–1
19: 5 376–7
19: 8 270–1
19: 10, 14 4–5, 60–1, 176–7
19: 12 278–9
22: 39 252–3
4 Kings (2 Kings), (4 Kgs. (2 Kgs.))
2, esp. 9–11 492–3
2: 11 70–1
2: 12 76–7
2: 15 424–5
4 190–1
4: 8–10, 32–5, esp. 9 278–9
4: 13 310–11
4: 31 382–3
4: 38–41 100–1
5: 8 490–1
10: 26–7 598–9
13: 14 76–7
13: 17 96–7, 574–5
14: 9 202–3
18: 21 60–1, 512–13
18: 27 382–3
19: 3 186–7, 246–7
19: 15 382–3
19: 30 318–19, 404–5
24: 13–15 178–9
25: 8, 11, 20 100–1
25: 13–21 76–7
1 Chronicles (1 Chr.)
11: 17 244–5
13: 6 382–3
28: 17 386–7
2 Chronicles (2 Chr.)
5: 7 358–9
10: 11, 14 380–1
12: 10 620–1
19: 7 340–1
23: 17 598–9
35: 13 286–7
1 Esdras (Ezra), (1 Esd.(Ezra))
—— 406–7
9: 5 108–9
2 Esdras, (2. Esd. (Neh.))
—— 406–7
4: 16 266–7
8 590–1

Tobias (Tobias)
8: 2 426–7
8: 22 574–5
10: 1–7 482–3
Judith (Judith)
5: 10 246–7, 380–1, 644–5
6: 15 680–1
7, esp. 11 248–9
Esther (Esther)
9: 22 340–1, 434–5
13: 17 340–1, 434–5
16: 21 340–1, 434–5
Job (Job)
2: 4 432–3
3: 5 14–15
3: 8 590–1
3: 11–12 596–7
4: 12 280–1, 462–3, 596–7
4: 16 198–9
5: 23 498–9
6: 16 24–5
7: 20 480–1
8: 21 300–1
9: 20 280–1
10: 1–2 306–7
10: 22 14–15
11: 14 178–9
13: 12 308–9
13: 14 342–3, 400–1, 590–1
13: 15 590–1
14: 2 426–7
14: 4 164–5
14: 7–8 248–9
19: 17 112–13
19: 27 46–7, 142–3, 650–1
20: 17 280–1
20: 24 24–5
21: 5 386–7
24: 17 14–15
26: 5 98–9, 122–3, 392–3
28: 1 548–9, 586–7
28: 2 238–9
28: 13 192–3
28: 14 192–3
28: 16 624–5
28: 19 624–5
29: 7–8, 22 570–1
29: 9 386–7, 570–1
29: 18 628–9
30: 4 556–7
30: 7 188–9
31: 6 102–3, 512–13, 516–17
31: 20 246–7
31: 24 342–3
32: 19 70–1, 546–7
38: 37 476–7
39: 10 380–1
39: 25 344–5, 392–3, 432–3, 544–5
39: 30 376–7, 434–5
39: 34 302–3
40: 16 590–1
41: 7 262–3
41: 22 286–7
Psalms (Ps.)
1 (1): 2 34–5
3 (3): 2–3 12–13
4 (4): 3 306–7
5 (5): 9 146–7
5 (5): 11 568–9
9 (10): 23 (2) 20–1
9 (10): 38 (17) 174–5, 506–7
10 (11): 2 278–9
11 (12): 3 264–5
12 (13): 4 96–7
13 (14): 3 568–9
16 (17): 8 22–3, 320–1
17 (18): 3 444–5
17 (18): 11 204–5, 284–5
17 (18): 46 114–5
18 (19): 7 40–1
18 (19): 11 384–5, 636–7
19 (20): 4 30–1
22 (23): 2 530–1
22 (23): 5 308–9, 534–5
24 (25): 15 408–9
24 (25): 18 272–3
25 (26): 6 30–1, 176–7
28 (29): 9 408–9
29 (30): 6 488–9
29 (30): 12 296–7
30 (31): 6 168–9
30 (31): 7 208–9
30 (31): 20 100–1, 358–9, 500–1
30 (31): 23 184–5
31 (32): 4 526–7
31 (32): 6 172–3, 252–3, 640–1, 642–3
31 (32): 7 6–7
32 (33): 2 376–7, 476–7
32 (33): 22 84–5
33 (34): 9 318–19, 478–9
35 (36): 8 22–3, 320–1
35 (36): 9 308–9, 530–1
35 (36): 10 330–1
36 (37): 6 440–1
36 (37): 16 478–9
37 (38): 4 382–3

37 (38): 7 510–11
37 (38): 10 266–7
37 (38): 11 268–9
37 (38): 12 146–7
38 (39): 5 90–1
38 (39): 6 142–3, 382–3
39 (40): 6 176–7
39 (40): 13 510–11
40 (41): 9 268–9
41 (42): 2 120–1
41 (42): 8 206–7
42 (43): 1 398–9
43 (44): 25 164–5
44 (45): 2 262–3, 502–3, 642–3
44 (45): 4 60–1, 372–3
44 (45): 8 200–1, 304–5, 480–1
44 (45): 9 252–3
44 (45): 10, 14–15 80–1
44 (45): 10 376–7, 636–7
44 (45): 12 170–1
45 (46): 5 530–1
45 (46): 11 478–9
47 (48): 3 682–3
47 (48): 8 136–7, 208–9, 214–15
47 (48): 11 120–1
48 (49): 3 510–11
48 (49): 15 68–9
50 (51): 4 70–1
50 (51): 8 354–5
50 (51): 10 264–5
50 (51): 12 80–81
50 (51): 19 286–7
51 (52): 10 202–3
54 (55): 7 434–5
54 (55): 18 156–7, 196–7, 528–9
54 (55): 22 264–5
56 (57): 2 22–3, 320–1, 518–19
56 (57): 9 98–9, 476–7
56 (57): 11 486–7
59 (60): 9 580–1
60 (61): 4 266–7
61 (62): 13 380–1
62 (63): 6 262–3, 388–9, 476–7, 480–1, 530–1, 642–3
62 (63): 8 22–3, 320–1
63 (64): 7–8 246–7
64 (65): 2 284–5
64 (65): 9 400–1
64 (65): 11 500–1
64 (65): 13 644–5
65 (66): 12 286–7
65 (66): 15 528–9
67 (68): 14 516–17
67 (68): 16 238–9
67 (68): 18 170–1
67 (68): 28 184–5
67 (68): 31 352–3
68 (69): 2 422–3
68 (69): 4 476–7
68 (69): 5 306–7
68 (69): 28 382–3
68 (69): 33 8–9
70 (71): 15–16 472–3
70 (71): 20 122–3
71 (72): 8 568–9, 586–7
71 (72): 9 586–7
71 (72): 12 340–1
72 (73): 5 468–9
72 (73): 13 30–1, 176–7
73 (74): 4–5 502–3
74 (75): 9 68–9, 138–9, 244–5, 306–7
75 (76): 6 54–5
75 (76): 11 68–9
76 (77): 3 100–1
77 (78): 23 306–7
77 (78): 54 206–7, 644–5
77 (78): 57 190–1
77 (78): 65 168–9
79 (80): 2 382–3
80 (81): 7 240–1, 246–7
80 (81): 9–10 250–1
81 (82): 3–4 338–9
82 (83): 14 618–19
83 (84): 4 304–5
83 (84): 7 170–1, 510–11
83 (84): 11 502–3
87 (88): 10 108–9
89 (90): 6 164–5
89 (90): 13 304–5, 456–7
90 (91): 10 588–9
90 (91): 13 654–5
91 (92): 4 376–7
93 (94): 19 304–5
98 (99): 1 382–3
98 (99): 4 54–5
100 (101): 5 530–1
100 (101): 8 96–7
101 (102): 5 350–1
101 (102): 19 372–3
101 (102): 21 508–9
101 (102): 28 184–5
102 (103): 5 448–9
103 (104): 3 204–5, 284–5
103 (104): 12 580–1
103 (104): 18 202–3, 266–7, 554–5
103 (104): 23 142–3

Psalms (Ps.) (*cont.*)
103 (104): 25 68–9, 406–7
104 (105): 4 504–5
105 (106): 20 70–1
105 (106): 30 570–1
106 (107): 5 188–9
106 (107): 16 166–7
106 (107): 26 122–3
107 (108): 3 98–9, 476–7
107 (108): 9 580–1
108 (109): 15 178–9
109 (110): 3 166–7
110 (111): 1 174–5
112 (113): 8 170–1
113 (114): 13 (5) 98–9
[114 (116): 7] [606–7]
115 (116): 11 516–17
115 (116): 12 58–9, 168–9
118 (119): 7 444–5
118 (119): 49 412–13
118 (119): 54 302–3
118 (119): 80 170–1
118 (119): 96 468–9, 658–9
118 (119): 109 342–3, 400–1
119 (120): 2 314–5
119 (120): 5 158–9
120 (121): 4 412–13
120 (121): 8 156–7
121 (122): 2 96–7
121 (122): 3 410–11
122 (123): 2 624–5
124 (125): 5 76–7
125 (126): 1 26–7
125 (126): 2 300–1
127 (128): 2 632–3
127 (128): 3 558–9
127 (128): 6 76–7
128 (129): 6 350–1, 532–3, 682–3
129 (130): 6 198–9
131 (132): 1 190–1
131 (132): 6 240–1
131 (132): 8 366–7, [606–7]
132 (133): 1 296–7
132 (133): 2 414–15, 424–5, 586–7
136 (137) 366–7
136 (137): 6 166–7
136 (137): 9 632–3
138 (139): 4 558–9, 642–3
138 (139): 6 202–3, 206–7, 626–7
138 (139): 8 184–5, 216–17
138 (139): 11 100–1
141 (142): 6 166–7
142 (143): 6 108–9, 690–1
143 (144): 8, 11 358–9
143 (144): 9 376–7
143 (144): 13 558–9
147 (147): 14 388–9
147 (147): 18 248–9
149 (149): 6 236–7, 354–5

Proverbs (Prov.)
1: 9 172–3
1: 16 358–9
1: 20 368–9
3: 16 470–1
5: 16 472–3, 502–3
5: 17 472–3
6: 6–8 538–9
7: 17 500–1
7: 18 278–9
8: 34 120–1
9: 1 558–9
9: 17 124–5
10: 31 202–3
11: 21 632–3
12: 7 448–9
13: 12 44–5
15: 7 470–1
15: 15 558–9
16: 5 632–3
17: 3 402–3
18: 9 24–5
19: 24 54–5
22: 11 190–1
24: 30–1 236–7
25: 21–2 426–7
26: 8 120–1
26: 11 552–3
26: 15 54–5
27: 1 506–7
27: 17 390–1
28: 21 64–5, 682–3
30: 25 538–9
31: 10 622–3
31: 13 90–1
31: 18 100–1, 246–7, 262–3, 318–19
31: 18–19 32–3
31: 19 92–3, 194–5, 246–7, 444–5, 546–7
31: 21 572–3

Ecclesiastes (Eccles.)
1: 3, 10, 13, 14 162–3
1: 3, 14 142–3
2: 3, 11, 17 etc. 162–3
3: 8 148–9
4: 3 144–5
4: 7 382–3

4: 10 542–3
4: 12 108–9, 144–5, 480–1, 532–3
6: 1–2 30–1
6: 1 144–5
6: 9 294–5
7: 9 32–3, 400–1, 410–11, 444–5, 486–7
7: 29 392–3
9: 8 344–5, 424–5, 554–5, 642–3
9: 10 650–1
10: 1 388–9
10: 5 144–5
12: 11 588–9

Song of Songs, Song of Solomon (S. of S.)
1: 1 218–19, 342–3
1: 2 304–5
1: 3 686–7
1: 4 358–9
1: 6 200–1, 500–1, 530–1
1: 9 202–3
1: 12 46–7, 94–5, 140–1, 170–1, 640–1
1: 13 244–5, 306–7
1: 14 174–5, 288–9
1: 15 322–3
2: 1 202–3, 306–7
2: 4 308–9
2: 6 640–1
2: 7 202–3, 278–9, 460–1, 640–1
2: 8–9 622–3
2: 9, 17 202–3
2: 14 42–3, 204–5, 278–9, 554–5, 580–1, 672–3
2: 15 16–17, 548–9, 568–9, 632–3
2: 17 622–3
3: 1–4 412–13
3: 2 504–5
3: 3 482–3
3: 5 202–3, 278–9, 460–1, 640–1
3: 7–8 110–11, 356–7
3: 10 42–3, 90–1, 302–3, 374–5
4: 1 174–5, 288–9
4: 3 190–1
4: 4 122–3, 192–3, 214–15, 266–7
4: 5 238–9
4: 8 196–7, 284–5
4: 9 140–1
4: 10 342–3
4: 11 300–1
4: 12 132–3, 594–5
4: 13 90–1
4: 14 142–3
4: 15 90–1
4: 16 200–1
5: 1 142–3, 244–5
5: 2 674–5
5: 4 638–9
5: 5 140–1, 400–1
5: 6 504–5, 588–9, 686–7
5: 8 412–13, 510–11
5: 9 72–3, 140–1
5: 13 238–9, 288–9, 300–1, 318–19, 508–9
5: 14 140–1, 288–9, 390–1, 550–1, 598–9
5: 15 110–11
6: 1 300–1, 318–19, 508–9
6: 3 590–1
6: 6 202–3
6: 10 500–1
7: 1 190–1
7: 3 238–9
7: 4 98–9
7: 13 538–9, 624–5, 664–5
8: 2 360–1
8: 3 640–1
8: 4 460–1, 640–1
8: 5 306–7
8: 6 270–1
8: 7 40–1, 268–9, 270–1, 640–1
8: 14 202–3, 204–5, 238–9, 622–3

Wisdom (Wisd.)
1: 1 218–19, 222–3, 628–9
1: 7 354–5
3: 2 202–3
3: 5 46–7
5: 5 356–7
7: 21 92–3
7: 25 104–5
8: 1 40–1, 550–1
9: 14 514–15
9: 15 138–9
10: 17 46–7
11: 21 466–7
15: 1–2 30–1
18: 14 178–9

Ecclesiasticus (Ecclus.)
1: 2 510–11
2: 5 402–3
16: 7 76–7
19: 12 468–9
20: 24 340–1
21: 10 76–7, 246–7
24: 27 384–5, 636–7
24: 29 200–1, 218–19
24: 42 656–7
27: 12 678–9

Ecclesiasticus (Ecclus.) (*cont.*)
28: 22 190–1
35: 26 28–9
36: 12 196–7
36: 14 176–7
39: 17, 19 556–7
44: 7 586–7
44: 23 568–9, 586–7
48: 9 70–1
48: 13 424–5
48: 27 304–5
50: 6 416–17
51: 10 14–15
51: 38 160–1

Isaiah (Isa.)
1: 6 650–1
1: 8 12–13, 366–7
1: 17 338–9
1: 22 630–1
1: 23 570–1
2: 19 310–11
2: 22 490–1
3: 14 368–9
3: 24 358–9
4: 1 680–1
4: 3 244–5
4: 6 12–13, 320–1
5: 2, 4 440–1
5: 13 68–9
5: 14 68–9, 368–9
5: 27 190–1
5: 29 194–5
6: 6–7 66–7, 188–9, 348–9
6: 8 376–7, 498–9
7: 21–2 240–1
8: 14 428–9, 586–7, 588–9, [602–3]
9: 5 82–3
9: 12 18–19
9: 14 12–13
9: 15 490–1
10: 14 178–9
11: 2 630–1
11: 7 400–1
13: 12 680–1
13: 21 406–7
13: 22 406–7
14: 2 68–9
14: 12–15 408–9, 568–9
14: 13 682–3
14: 29 532–3
16: 2 260–1
19: 15 12–13
22: 9–10 406–7
22: 22 240–1
24: 2 352–3
24: 16 638–9
25: 4 12–13, 320–1
25: 6 142–3
26: 1 548–9
26: 8 32–3
26: 12 96–7
28: 15, 18 308–9
28: 20 34–5
33: 14 180–1
34: 5–6 368–9
34: 13 68–9
34: 14 406–7
35: 1 654–5
36: 6 60–1, 512–13
36: 8 120–1
36: 12 382–3
37: 3 186–7, 246–7
37: 16 382–3
38: 6 238–9
38: 17 260–1, 370–1
[40: 4] [602–3]
40: 6–8, esp. 7 306–7
40: 16 198–9
42: 3 426–7
42: 8 14–15
44: 13 582–3
45: 2 166–7, 338–9
45: 9 306–7
46: 8 178–9, 502–3, 534–5
47: 2 136–7
48: 11 14–15
49: 6 132–3
49: 15 112–13
49: 22 568–9
51: 17 486–7
52: 1 366–7
53: 4 168–9, 264–5
53: 8 164–5
54: 2 192–3
56: 7 141–15
56: 10 682–3
57: 17 368–9
58: 7 24–5
58: 9 142–3
58: 13 644–5
59: 6 178–9
59: 7 358–9
59: 11 306–7
60: 8 96–7, 174–5, 284–5
61: 2–3 304–5
61: 3 14–15

61: 10 410–11
65: 7 596–7
65: 25 400–1
66: 22 596–7
Jeremiah (Jer.)
1: 6 376–7
2: 13 352–3
2: 21 318–19
2: 27 146–7
4: 10 422–3
11: 20 412–13, 548–9, 640–1
13: 20 246–7
13: 24 618–19
15: 1 168–9
17: 1 56–7, 404–5, 416–17
17: 5 686–7
17: 13 244–5
17: 16 670–1
22: 3 338–9
23: 1–3 368–9
23: 10 470–1
23: 15 392–3, 434–5
31: 13 340–1, 434–5
32: 33 146–7
39: 13 100–1
40: 4 478–9
41: 10 100–1
43: 6 100–1
46: 10 368–9
48: 28 580–1, 672–3
49: 32 278–9
50: 23 238–9, 390–1
50: 26 72–3
50: 42 266–7
51: 7 132–3
52: 12, 15, 16 100–1
Lamentations (Lam.)
—— 568–9
1: 2 366–7
1: 12 72–3, 306–7, 540–1
2: 19 354–5
3: 1 206–7, 542–3, 544–5
3: 27 380–1
4: 1 178–9, 358–9, 630–1
Baruch (Baruch)
3: 23 192–3
5: 3 568–9
Ezekiel (Ezek.)
1: 4 180–1, 370–1
1: 10 580–1
1: 11 450–1
1: 12 172–3, 666–7
1: 20–1 580–1
1: 25 626–7
3: 3 642–3
3: 13 250–1, 580–1
3: 15 358–9
3: 18, 20 138–9
5: 10, 12 278–9
7: 2 70–1
8: 8–10 406–7
10: 14 580–1
10: 22 172–3
12: 14 278–9
13: 5 388–9
13: 10 54–5
16: 4 264–5
16: 22, 43 366–7
16: 36 210–11
17: 3, 22 188–9
17: 21 278–9
17: 24 98–9
18: 20 672–3
23: 20 382–3
23: 31–2 468–9
23: 35 84–5
24: 16, 21 376–7
27: 24 288–9
28: 13 236–7, 264–5
28: 14 188–9, 358–9
29: 6 60–1, 512–13
33: 6, 8 138–9
34 368–9
40: 23 258–9
44: 17 258–9
45: 19 258–9
46: 1 258–9
Daniel (Dan.)
1, 2 546–7
3 648–9
3: 55 382–3
4 382–3
4, esp. 11, 14, 20 548–9
4: 11, 20 354–5
4: 14 354–5
5: 2–3, 23 76–7, 178–9
6: 22 402–3
7: 2 132–3, 318–19, 554–5
7: 9 248–9
7: 25 260–1
8: 8 132–3, 318–19, 554–5
9: 20 262–3
11: 4 132–3, 318–19, 554–5
12: 7 260–1
13: 7 500–1
13: 17 500–1

Daniel (Dan.) (*cont.*)
13: 28 500–1
13: 55 196–7
14: 32–8 526–7
14: 34 310–11

Hosea (Hos.)
2: 7 366–7, 552–3
2: 14 654–5
4: 16 286–7
6: 1 304–5
6: 4 272–3
8: 9 124–5
9: 14 554–5, 652–3
10: 11 198–9
13: 3 272–3
14: 3 96–7
14: 8 184–5, 278–9

Joel (Joel)
1: 4 178–9, 280–1, 300–1, 406–7
1: 19–20 280–1, 406–7
2: 1, 15 [600–1], 620–1
2: 12 158–9
2: 23 582–3, 624–5, 680–1
2: 25 280–1, 300–1, 406–7
3: 13 390–1

Amos (Amos)
2: 13 350–1
3: 6 498–9
5: 18–19 24–5
6: 4 636–7
6: 12 534–5
6: 14 392–3

Jonah (Jonah)
2 68–9, 404–5
2: 6 422–3
4: 6–10 424–5

Micah (Mic.)
2: 7 52–3
7: 1 558–9

Nahum (Nahum)
3: 14 248–9

Habakkuk (Hab.)
2: 20 180–1
3: 17 426–7

Zechariah (Zech.)
1: 20–1 178–9
2: 6 132–3, 318–19, 554–5
2: 8 588–9
3: 1 4–5
4: 14 96–7
5: 7–8 352–3
6: 5 132–3, 318–19, 554–5
9: 10 568–9, 586–7
11: 15 308–9
12: 10 20–1
13: 1 550–1
13: 7 152–3

Malachi (Mal.)
1: 8 198–9
2: 7 378–9

1 Maccabees (1 Macc.)
1: 10 680–1
2, esp. 26 422–3
6: 34 190–1
6: 39 636–7

2 Maccabees (2 Macc.)
1: 20 386–7, 476–7
6: 21 676–7
8: 7 396–7

Matthew (Matt.)
1: 16 418–19
1: 21 120–1
2: 13–15 620–1
3 80–1, 242–3
3: 4 240–1
3: 7 240–1, 568–9
3: 10 4–5, 354–5, 372–3, 440–1
3: 12 576–7
4: 1 622–3
4: 19 568–9
5: 3 94–5
5: 15 42–3, 324–5, 342–3, 398–9, 472–3, [604–5]
5: 16 472–3
5: 18 26–7, 308–9
5: 29 34–5
5: 39 20–1
5: 40 390–1, 682–3
5: 44 20–1
5: 45 28–9, 30–1
6: 10 54–5
6: 11 254–5
6: 13 304–5
6: 19 46–7, 194–5, 572–3
6: 23 282–3, 500–1
6: 26 302–3
6: 30 350–1, 660–1
6: 34 34–5, 260–1
7: 6 382–3
7: 7–8 120–1, 396–7
7: 13 484–5
7: 15 18–19, 472–3, 674–5
7: 16 502–3
7: 20 502–3
7: 24–5 62–3, 628–9
8: 8 16–17

8: 9 310–11, 374–5
8: 11 538–9
8: 17 264–5
8: 20 26–7, 42–3, 50–1, 168–9, 648–9
8: 24–7 4–5
8: 25 6–7
8: 26 660–1
8: 29 194–5
9: 20–22 124–5
9: 20 158–9, 500–1
9: 35 488–9
9: 37–8 446–7
10: 8 344–5
10: 11 488–9
10: 16 342–3
10: 21 568–9
10: 34 80–1
10: 35 272–3
10: 41 400–1, 414–15
11: 5 444–5
11: 7 532–3, 580–1, 628–9
11: 28 550–1
12: 25 534–5
12: 32 180–1
12: 34 568–9
12: 40 98–9
12: 43–5 630–1
12: 43 648–9
13: 8, 23 28–9, 446–7, 562–3, 652–3
13: 12 102–3
13: 24–30 548–9
13: 31 278–9, 432–3
13: 45 276–7
13: 47 654–5
13: 52 664–5
13: 55 244–5, 308–9
13: 57 490–1
14: 3 242–3
14: 13 620–1
14: 24 300–1
14: 29–30 404–5, 408–9
14: 31 660–1
14: 36 158–9, 500–1
15: 23 48–9
15: 26 370–1
15: 27 556–7
16: 8 660–1
16: 18 62–3, 352–3
16: 19 20–1, 342–3, 356–7, 410–11, 586–7
16: 22 184–5
16: 26 124–5
16: 27 380–1
17: 1–9 638–9
17: 2 376–7
17: 4 184–5, 218–19
17: 19 278–9, 432–3, 670–1
18: 9 34–5
18: 12–13 110–11
18: 16 580–1
19: 12 92–3
19: 19 156–7, [608–9]
19: 21 398–9
19: 26 506–7
19: 30 408–9, 448–9
20: 1–16 72–3, 410–11
20: 2 262–3
20: 2, 12 54–5
20: 15–16 448–9
20: 15 500–1
20: 16 408–9
20: 19 122–3
21: 2–3 382–3
21: 13 414–15
22: 2–10, esp. 5 350–1
22: 11–12 554–5
22: 17–21 252–3, 258–9
[22: 37–9] [608–9]
22: 37 192–3, 280–1
22: 39 156–7
22: 40 364–5
23: 3 324–5
23: 4–5 674–5
23: 4 124–5
23: 5 258–9
23: 33 568–9
23: 37 372–3, 376–7
24: 12 398–9
24: 23 628–9
24: 28 484–5
24: 31 132–3
24: 35 308–9
25: 1–12, esp. 10 628–9
25: 5 650–1
25: 24, 26 318–19
25: 32–3 20–1
25: 34 658–9
25: 35–45 188–9
25: 40 412–13
25: 41 658–9
26: 7 142–3
26: 10 460–1
26: 13 418–19
26: 15 564–5
26: 31 152–3

Matthew (Matt.) (*cont.*)
26: 38 18–19, 168–9, 200–201, 272–3, 482–3
26: 39 20–21, 406–7, 582–3
26: 41 138–9, 350–1
26: 51 186–7
26: 58 202–3
26: 67 288–9
26: 69–75 528–9
26: 70 446–7
26: 73 202–3, 682–3
26: 74–5 476–7
27 290–1
27: 16 34–5
27: 24 202–3
27: 30 356–7
27: 34 406–7
27: 35 568–9
27: 37 474–5
27: 45–50 96–7
27: 48 308–9
27: 51–4 476–7
27: 51 60–1, 82–3
27: 54 202–3
28: 2 242–3
28: 18 62–3
28: 20 444–5
Mark (Mark)
1: 1–11 80–1, 242–3
1: 6 240–1
1: 12–13 622–3
1: 17 568–9
1: 24 194–5
2: 9 248–9
3: 15 344–5
3: 25 534–5
4: 8, 20 28–9, 446–7, 562–3, 652–3
4: 21 42–3, 324–5, 342–3, 398–9, 472–3, [604–5]
4: 25 102–3
4: 31 278–9, 432–3
4: 37–40 4–5
4: 38 6–7
5: 25–34 124–5
5: 27 500–1
5: 41 408–9
6: 3 244–5, 308–9
6: 4 490–1
6: 17 242–3
6: 48 300–1
6: 56 158–9, 500–1
7: 27 370–1
7: 28 556–7
7: 37 444–5
8: 36 124–5
9: 1–8 638–9
9: 2 376–7
9: 4 184–5, 218–19
9: 30 122–3
9: 46 34–5
10: 31 408–9, 448–9
10: 34 122–3
11: 2–3 382–3
11: 17 414–15
12: 14–17 252–3, 258–9
[12: 30–1] [608–9]
12: 30 192–3, 280–1
12: 31, 33 156–7
12: 33 192–3, 280–1
13: 12 568–9
13: 21 628–9
13: 27 132–3
13: 31 308–9
14: 3 142–3
14: 9 418–19
14: 11 564–5
14: 27 152–3
14: 34 18–19, 168–9, 200–1, 272–3, 482–3
14: 35 406–7
14: 36 20–1, 406–7, 582–3
14: 38 138–9, 350–1
14: 47 186–7
14: 51–2 202–3, 682–3
14: 54 202–3
14: 65 288–9
14: 66–72 528–9
14: 71–2 476–7
15 290–1
15: 7 34–5
15: 19 356–7
15: 24 568–9
15: 26 474–5
15: 33–7 96–7
15: 36 308–9
15: 38 60–1, 82–3
15: 39 202–3
16: 4 242–3
16: 15 504–5
Luke (Luke)
1: 11 100–1
1: 15 432–3
[1: 28] [608–9, 612–13]
[1: 34] [612–13]
1: 35 592–3, [608–9]
1: 38 624–5

1: 42 536–7
1: 47 234–5, 316–17
1: 49 116–17
1: 52 116–17
1: 59–63 144–5
1: 69 444–5
1: 78 394–5, 526–7
1: 79 508–9
3: 1–22 80–1, 242–3
[3: 5] [602–3]
3: 7 240–1, 568–9
3: 9 4–5, 354–5, 372–3, 440–1
3: 17 576–7
3: 20 242–3
4: 1–2 622–3
4: 24 490–1
4: 38 194–5
5: 8 186–7
5: 10 568–9
6: 17 242–3
6: 27 20–21
6: 29 20–21, 390–1, 682–3
6: 35 28–9
6: 38 120–1, 380–1, 414–15, 424–5
6: 48 62–3, 628–9
7: 7 16–17
7: 8 310–11, 374–5
7: 14 408–9
7: 22 444–5
7: 24 532–3, 580–1, 628–9
7: 37–8 142–3
8: 1 488–9
8: 8 28–9, 446–7, 562–3, 652–3
8: 16 42–3, 342–3, 398–9, 472–3
8: 23–5 4–5
8: 24 6–7
8: 32–3 654–5
8: 43 124–5
8: 44 158–9, 500–1
8: 54 408–9
9: 10 620–1
9: 22 122–3
9: 25 124–5
9: 28–36 638–9
9: 29 376–7
9: 33 184–5, 218–19
9: 58 26–7, 42–3, 50–1, 168–9, 648–9
9: 62 400–1
10: 2 446–7
10: 7 426–7
10: 9 344–5
10: 18 408–9, 568–9, 680–1
10: 19 594–5
10: 27 156–7, 192–3, 280–1, [608–9]
10: 30–7 540–1
10: 38–42 90–1, [608–9], 632–3
10: 39–40 360–1
10: 42 74–5, 296–7, 628–9
11: 4 304–5
11: 5–8 186–7
11: 6 558–9
11: 9–10 120–1, 396–7
11: 17 534–5
11: 24–6 630–1
11: 24 648–9
11: 33 42–3, 324–5, 342–3, 398–9, 472–3, [604–5]
11: 34–5 116–17
11: 34 282–3, 500–1
11: 46 124–5, 674–5
12: 24 302–3
12: 28 350–1
12: 32 496–7, 680–1
12: 36 396–7
13: 6–9 108–9
13: 19 278–9, 432–3
13: 22 488–9
13: 24 484–5
13: 25 412–13
13: 28–9 538–9
13: 30 408–9, 448–9
14: 16–24, esp. 18–20 350–1
14: 22 32–3
14: 27 444–5
14: 33 390–1
15: 4–6 110–11
15: 8–9 406–7
15: 8 68–9, 90–1
15: 22–3, 27, 30 408–9, 554–5
15: 23, 27, 30 140–1, 476–7, 480–1, 530–1
15: 25 476–7, 480–1
15: 29 480–1
16: 1–9 540–1
16: 3 202–3
16: 9 32–3, 400–1, 414–15, 540–1
16: 17 26–7
16: 19 288–9, 296–7
16: 21 556–7
16: 22 538–9
16: 26 40–1, 518–19
17: 6 278–9, 432–3, 670–1
17: 21 628–9
17: 37 484–5
18: 33 122–3
19: 3 500–1

Luke (Luke) (*cont.*)
19: 12 146–7
19: 20 398–9
19: 21, 22 318–19
19: 26 102–3
19: 30–1 382–3
20: 22–5 252–3, 258–9
21: 33 308–9
22: 5 564–5
22: 19 660–1
22: 32 14–15, 18–19
22: 36 390–1
22: 37 264–5
22: 38 266–7
22: 42 20–1, 406–7, 582–3
22: 50 186–7
22: 54 202–3
22: 55–62 528–9
22: 60–1 476–7
22: 63–4 288–9
23 290–1
23: 18 34–5
23: 34 204–5, 568–9
23: 28 474–5
23: 36 308–9
23: 43 410–11
23: 44–6 96–7
23: 45 60–1, 82–3
23: 46 168–9
23: 50–6 636–7
23: 60 446–7
24: 2 242–3
24: 7, 46 122–3

John (John)
1: 1 308–9
1: 4 208–9
1: 5 100–1
1: 6–36 80–1, 242–3
1: 16 20–1, 70–1, 182–3, 232–3, 272–3, 324–5, 400–1, 456–7
2: 1–11 242–3, 244–5
2: 10 246–7, 290–1
3: 4 596–7
3: 29 418–19
4: 9 376–7
4: 11 242–3
4: 14 236–7, 330–1
4: 35 446–7
4: 36 32–3
4: 44, 48 490–1
5: 8 248–9
5: 35 240–1
6: 27 32–3, 358–9, 470–1
6: 67 146–7
6: 57 200–1
7: 36 222–3
7: 37 42–3
8: 6–8 426–7
8: 7 448–9
8: 10–11 448–9
8: 48–9 450–1
8: 52 36–7
9: 11 622–3
9: 22 474–5
10: 14 368–9
10: 23 412–13
10: 32 386–7
11: 39 248–9, 568–9
11: 43 408–9
12: 3 142–3
12: 7 388–9
12: 24–5 342–3, 652–3
12: 31 248–9, 408–9
12: 32 496–7
13: 1 510–11
13: 14 344–5
13: 23, 25 638–9
14: 2–3, 16–17 492–3
14: 6 468–9
14: 8 188–9, 202–3
14: 9 256–7
14: 16 192–3, 660–1
14: 27 72–3, 690–1
14: 30 248–9, 408–9
15: 1 574–5
15: 13 270–1
15: 15 354–5
15: 16 114–15
15: 26 510–11
16: 11 248–9, 408–9
16: 21 112–13
16: 33 74–5
17: 6 324–5
18: 3 172–3
18: 10 186–7
18: 11 66–7, 570–1
18: 12 76–7
18: 13 172–3
18: 15 202–3
18: 22 288–9
18: 25–9 528–9
18: 27 476–7
18: 40 34–5
19 290–1
19: 1 288–9
19: 17 444–5

19: 19 142–3, 470–1, 474–5
19: 22 586–7
19: 23–4 60–1
19: 23 568–9, 582–3
19: 26 538–9
19: 26–7 536–7
19: 29–30 308–9
19: 34 60–1, 236–7, 530–1, 568–9
19: 38–40 636–7
20: 1 242–3
20: 27 554–5
21: 15–17 18–19
21: 20 638–9
Acts (Acts)
1: 5 80–1
1: 7 126–7
1: 8 96–7
1: 12 98–9
2: 1–5, 15 96–7
2: 3 80–1, 352–3
2: 13 432–3
2: 44 638–9
2: 46 218–19
3: 7 198–9, 628–9
3: 11 412–13
4: 32 638–9
5: 12 412–13
5: 29 432–3
7: 59 100–1
8: 33 164–5
9: 1, 3 408–9
9: 3–7 72–3
9: 15 308–9
9: 40 408–9
10: 10 184–5
10: 11–16 550–1
11: 5 184–5
11: 16 80–1
13: 47 324–5
15: 20, 29 76–7
16: 17 508–9
17: 24 88–9
20: 28 352–3
20: 35 46–7
21: 25 76–7
22: 4 18–19, 200–1, 272–3, 482–3
26: 18 356–7
27 404–5
Romans (Rom.)
1: 11 412–13
1: 14 502–3
1: 18 682–3
2: 6 380–1
2: 11 340–1
2: 24 176–7, 428–9
3: 4 516–17
3: 13 568–9
4: 25 290–1
5: 6 264–5
5: 14 76–7
5: 20 400–1
6: 4 264–5
6: 5 166–7, 528–9
6: 8 324–5
6: 22 238–9
7: 15 480–1, 510–11
7: 23 [606–7, 608–9, 610–11], 648–9
7: 24–5 526–7
7: 24 158–9, 286–7, [610–11]
8: 9 160–1
8: 10 208–9
8: 14 160–1
8: 15 500–1
8: 18 122–3, 238–9
8: 31 302–3, 376–7, 448–9, 590–1
8: 32 290–1
9: 1 156–7
9: 3 546–7, 570–1
9: 12–13 72–3
9: 21 308–9, 650–1
9: 29 412–13, 548–9, 640–1
9: 32–3 428–9, 586–7, 588–9, [602–3]
11: 11 470–1
11: 12 470–1
11: 13 342–3
11: 16 278–9, 654–5
11: 29 448–9
11: 32 386–7
11: 33 242–3
12: 1 342–3, 372–3
12: 3 296–7
12: 17 218–19
12: 20 426–7
13: 12 150–1
14: 4 514–15, 628–9
1 Corinthians (1 Cor.)
1: 12 380–1
2: 10 154–5, 650–1
2: 11–12 516–17
2: 11 516–17
2: 12 88–9, 224–5
3: 6 424–5, 442–3
3: 8 380–1
3: 17 598–9
3: 21–2 290–1
3: 22–3 502–3

1 Corinthians (1 Cor.) (*cont.*)
4: 9 636–7
4: 12 590–1
4: 19 94–5
4: 21 148–9
5: 3 156–7
5: 6 516–17, 522–3
5: 7 284–5
5: 12–13 64–5
6: 3 378–9
6: 7 534–5
6: 10 298–9
7: 31 634–5
7: 39 114–5
8: 7, 10 672–3
8: 10 176–7
9: 9 394–5, 400–1
9: 24 570–1
9: 25 634–5
9: 26 190–1
10: 25 672–3
12: 3 122–3
12: 4–5 376–7
12: 21 200–1
12: 31 500–1
13 184–5
13: 1 512–13
13: 4 52–3
13: 5 190–1
13: 8 272–3, 384–5, 510–11, 640–1, 642–3
13: 10 284–5
13: 13 588–9
14: 33 148–9
15: 3 290–1
15: 4 122–3
15: 8 634–5
15: 10 16–17, 52–3
15: 27–8 470–1
15: 28 240–1
15: 45 650–1
15: 47 268–9
15: 50 62–3, 114–15, 180–1, 292–3
15: 52 158–9, 278–9
15: 53 510–11
15: 56 68–9

2 Corinthians (2 Cor.)
1: 3 274–5, 306–7
1: 3–4 304–5
1: 17–20 448–9, 678–9
2: 15 570–1
3: 7, 13 34–5
3: 18 34–5, 240–1, 246–7, 278–9, 680–1
4: 4 36–7
4: 16 250–1
4: 18 278–9, 682–3
5: 11 154–5
5: 13 184–5
5: 16 446–7
6: 1 368–9
6: 9 302–3
6: 10 302–3
7: 15 526–7
10: 2–3 60–1
11: 1 538–9
11: 3 598–9
11: 9 590–1
11: 14 630–1
11: 23 308–9
11: 25 404–5
11: 27 46–7
11: 28 14–15
11: 29 536–7
12: 2–3 98–9
12: 2 94–5, 184–5, 264–5, 308–9, 478–9
12: 4 94–5
12: 15 582–3
13: 1 580–1

Galatians (Gal.)
1: 4 508–9
1: 8–9 628–9
2: 9 682–3
2: 20 280–1
3: 1 150–1, 178–9, 474–5, 500–1
3: 8 620–1
4: 30 144–5
4: 22–31 20–1
5: 7 150–1, 486–7
5: 9 516–17, 522–3
5: 24 96–7, 276–7, 376–7, 502–3
6: 14 472–3
6: 17 122–3

Ephesians (Eph.)
1: 7–8 400–1
1: 9 496–7
2: 20 274–5
3: 17 36–7, 580–1, [610–11]
3: 18 468–9
4: 14 628–9
4: 20 148–9, 218–19, 260–1
4: 23 250–1
4: 26 534–5
5: 3 170–1

5: 8 446–7
5: 14 408–9
5: 29 24–5, 138–9
6: 5 218–9
6: 9 340–1
6: 12 268–9, 510–11, 644–5
Philippians (Phil.)
1: 6 378–9
1: 8 158–9
1: 23 508–9
2: 7 408–9
2: 8, 27, 30 18–19, 200–1, 272–3, 482–3
2: 9 120–1, 122–3, 216–17
2: 15 198–9
2: 21 200–1
3: 13–14 486–7
3: 13 514–15
3: 15 626–7
4: 7 270–1
4: 11–12 494–5
4: 12 484–5
4: 13 72–3
Colossians (Col.)
1: 15 258–9
1: 24 392–3
2: 3 242–3
2: 5 156–7
2: 14 142–3
3: 12 394–5, 526–7
3: 22 218–19
3: 25 340–1
1 Thessalonians (1 Thess.)
5: 5 150–1, 680–1
5: 19 342–3
2 Thessalonians (2 Thess.)
2: 4 76–7
1 Timothy (1 Tim.)
1: 5 36–7, 200–1
[1: 13] [604–5]
1: 14 28–9, 400–1
1: 15 198–9
2: 2 278–9
2: 5 164–5
2: 7 496–7
3: 1–7 418–19
5: 10 506–7
5: 18 394–5, 400–1, 426–7
5: 19 580–1
6: 7 302–3
6: 18 94–5
2 Timothy (2 Tim.)
1: 11 494–5
2: 3 266–7
2: 5 594–5, 622–3, 634–5
2: 8 264–5
2: 11 324–5
2: 19 368–9
2: 20 650–1
2: 26 194–5
4: 2 492–3, 498–9, 634–5
Philemon (Philem.)
20 164–5
Hebrews (Heb.)
1: 9 200–1, 304–5
4: 12 236–7, 272–3, 354–5, 368–9, 546–7, 636–7
4: 14 352–3
4: 15 622–3
4: 16 218–19, 400–1, 568–9, 686–7
5: 2 170–1
5: 4 114–15
5: 13 238–9
6: 8 236–7
6: 9 344–5, 384–5, 456–7, 486–7
6: 20 352–3
8: 13 548–9, 648–9
9: 1 100–1
9: 3 100–1
9: 4 110–11, 366–7, 386–7
9: 5 114–15, 276–7, 306–7, 366–7
9: 11 264–5
9: 22 82–3
10: 20 190–1
10: 26 268–9
10: 31 590–1
11: 6 424–5
11: 24–6 358–9
11: 33 402–3
12: 13 516–17
12: 20 204–5
13: 8 496–7
13: 12 352–3
13: 14 114–15
James (Jas.)
1: 11 306–7
1: 17 174–5, 626–7, 652–3
2: 1 340–1
2: 8 156–7, 608–9
3: 17 94–5
4: 14 506–7
5: 4 412–13, 548–9, 640–1
5: 11 468–9
1 Peter (1 Pet.)
1: 2 162–3
1: 16 256–7

1 Peter (1 Pet.) (*cont.*)
- 1: 24 — 306–7
- 2: 8 — 428–9, 586–7, 588–9, [602–3]
- 2: 24 — 264–5
- 3: 21 — 140–1
- 5: 8 — 194–5, 402–3

2 Peter (2 Pet.)
- 2: 22 — 552–3
- 3: 13 — 596–7

1 John (1 John)
- 1: 5 — 402–3
- 2: 17 — 634–5
- 3: 2 — 254–5
- 3: 18 — 366–7, 512–13, 656–7
- 4: 1 — 440–1
- 4: 16 — 200–1

3 John (3 John)
- 11 — 160–1

Jude (Jude)
- 12 — 512–13

Revelation (Rev.)
- 1: 4 — 540–1
- 1: 5 — 70–1
- 1: 16 — 372–3
- 2: 7, 11, 17, 29 — 164–5
- 2: 7 — 190–1, 622–3
- 2: 10 — 18–19, 200–1, 272–3, 482–3
- 2: 12 — 372–3
- 2: 17 — 100–1, 358–9
- 2: 20 — 672–3
- 2: 23 — 380–1
- 3: 5 — 622–3
- 3: 6, 13, 22 — 164–5
- 3: 7 — 240–1
- 3: 12 — 622–3
- 3: 15–16 — 244–5
- 3: 18 — 408–9
- 3: 20 — 290–1
- 3: 21 — 622–3
- 4: 6 — 580–1
- 4: 7 — 580–1
- 4: 8 — 580–1
- 4: 9 — 400–1
- 5: 1 — 400–1
- 5: 2–9 — 594–5
- 5: 6, 11 — 32–3
- 5: 13 — 306–7
- 7: 9, 17 — 156–7
- 7: 9 — 158–9
- 7: 14 — 190–1
- 8: 1 — 278–9
- 8: 3 — 386–7
- 10: 10 — 642–3
- 11: 4 — 618–19
- 12: 4 — 564–5, 654–5, 682–3
- 12: 6 — 652–3
- 12: 9 — 592–3
- 12: 11 — 18–19, 200–1, 272–3, 482–3
- 12: 13 — 620–1
- 12: 14 — 260–1
- 13: 9 — 164–5
- 19: 9 — 542–3
- 19: 14 — 190–1
- 19: 15 — 372–3
- 20: 2 — 620–1
- 20: 12 — 656–7
- 21: 1 — 596–7
- 22: 1, 3 — 156–7
- 22: 2 — 378–9
- 22: 5 — 300–1
- 22: 17 — 176–7

B. QUOTATIONS AND ALLUSIONS FROM OTHER SOURCES

Ambrose
- *De Noe* i. 2 — 642–3
- *De officiis ministrorum*, i. 30. 147 — 282–3, 498–9, 678–9
- *Exameron*, i. 8. 31 — 672–3
  - vi. 7. 43 — 36–7
- *Hymni*, i. — 476–7

Augustine
- *Confessiones*, vi. 16. 26 — 626–7
- [*Contra Cresconium*, ii. 38. 49] — 602–3
- *Contra Cresconium*, iii. 47. 51 — 282–3
- *De Civitate Dei*, xi. 20 — 574–5
- *De libero arbitrio*, ii. 16. 41 — 256–7
- [*De natura et gratia*, 36. 42] — 606–7
- [*De peccatorum meritis*, ii. 24. 38] — 610–11
- *De Trinitate*, x. 12. 19 — 254–5
  - v. 1. 2 — 212–13

v. 3–5 256–7
vii. 6 252–3
xv. 23 252–3
Enarrationes in psalmos, xxix. 2. 21 60–1
lix. 9. 9 580–1
lxx. 2. 3 256–7
Epistulae, xl. 618–19
lxxxii. 618–19
clxvi. 2. 4 208–9
cciv. 4 282–3
Sermones de sanctis, cclxxxv. 2 282–3
ccxcvi. 3–4 18–19
cccxxvii.1 282–3
cccxxxi. 2. 2 282–3
Sermones de Scripturis 256–7
cxlvii. 2 18–19
clxxx. 7 208–9
Sermones suppos., cclxxxix. 1 198–9

Bede
De tabernaculo, i. 5. 610–11 366–7
Historia ecclesiastica gentis Anglorum, ii. 1 574–5
Homeliarum euangelii libri ii, i. 6. 210–17 18–19
In Genesim, i. 1. 26 258–9
In Lucae euangelium expositio, ii. 6. 19 352–3
iv. 19. 27 536–7
In Samuelem prophetam allegorica expositio, ii. 10. 17–19 60–1

pseudo-Bede
In Pentateuchum commentarii, Gen. c. iii 600–1
Gen. c. xxiv 114–15
Sententiae . . . ex Aristotele . . . collectae, i 628–9

Benedict, St
Regula Sancti Benedicti, c.ii 6–7, 362–3
c.v 548–9
c.vii 98–9, 644–5
c.xxiii 428–9
c.lxiv 664–5

Bernard, St
De consideratione, i. 5. 6 124–5
Epistola 174 [606–7], 616–17

Boethius
Commentaria in Porph., iv 250–1, 254–5
De consolatio philosophiae, i. prose iv. 1. 646–7
ii. prose v. 16 74–5, 302–3
iii. prose xi. 9 226–7
iv. prose vi. 7 222–3
iv. prose vi. 8 222–3
iv. prose vi. 10 224–5
iv. prose vi. 13 224–5
iv. prose vi. 15 224–5
In categorias Aristotelis libri iv, ii. 628–9
Liber contra Eutychen et Nestorium, vi. 18–72 228–31

Canon of the Mass 372–3, 390–1

Cicero
De amicitia, vi. 20 214–15
xiii. 47 88–9
De officiis, i. 19. 63 10–11, 130–1, 374–5

Claudianus Mamertus
De statu anime, iii. 6. 2 208–9, 234–5, 254–5, 707, 708, 709

Creeds 166–7, 168–9, 210–11, 304–5, 376–7, 582–3, [606–7]

Ennodius
Epistulae, ii. 22 666–7
ix. 3 666–7

Fulbert of Chartres
Sermones ad populum, iv. 620–1

Gerbert of Aurillac
De rationale et ratione uti, vii. 220–1

Gilbert of La Porrée
Commentaria in libros de duabus naturae 220–1

Gratian
Decretum, ii. 2. 6. c.xiv 16–17
ii. 2. 7. c.xxvii 366–7
ii. 15. 1. c.vi 672–3

Gregory the Great
Homiliae .xl. in Euangelia, i. 5. 2 546–7
ii. 35. 1 314–15
ii. 37. 5 536–7
ii. 27. 1 24–5
ii. 33. 8 352–3
ii. 34. 2 426–7
ii. 37. 1 276–7
ii. 37. 5 536–7
ii. 38. 10 546–7
Moralia siue Expositio in Iob, i. 15. 21 114–15
vi. 33. 52 498–9
Registrum epistularum, viii. 29 500–1

Horace
Ars Poetica, 78 44–5
139 374–5
359 586–7, [602–3]
Epistolae, i. 5. 19 664–5
i. 18. 84 152–3
Odes, i. 3 272–3

Horace (*cont.*)
Saturae, i. 1. 24 580–1, 656–7
i. 1. 24–5 162–3
i. 1. 106 486–7
i. 7. 3 162–3, 352–3
Hrabanus Maurus
Commentaria in Ezechielem, vi. c. 13 188–9
Isaac of Stella
Sermo xxi 220–1
Isidore
Etymologiarum siue Originum, vii. 1. 26 208–9
Sententiarum, i. 2. 6 208–9
Ivo of Chartres
Decretum, viii. c.210 198–9
xiii. c.91 672–3
Panormia, vii. c.13 198–9
Jerome
Apologia adversus libros Rufini, ii. 26 584–5
Commentarii in Ezechielem, xiv. 48. 18/20 584–5
Commentarii in Euangelium Matthaei, ii. 11. 30 598–9
Commentarii in iv. epistolas Paulinas, ad Gal., Prol. 618–19
i. c.2 618–19
Epistulae, xxii. 5 594–5, 598–9
lxxii. 610–11
lxxiv. 4 204–5
lxxiv. 5 204–5
cxii. 618–19
cxxxi. 15 36–7
Epistulae supposititiae, [ix. 5] 612–13
ix. 7 590–1, 592–3
In Abacuc, i. 2. 19/20 212–13
Liber interp. Heb. nom. 580–1
Liber quest. Heb. in Gen. 580–1, 642–3
Justinian
Institutes, i. 1. 1. 374–5, 532–3
iv. 1. 1, 6 386–7
Juvenal
Saturae, i. 160 452–3, 600–1
iii. 36 108–9
Lucan
De bello civili i. 1 484–5
ix. 402–3 634–5
Nicholas of Clairvaux
Epistolae, lxiii 206–7, 208–9, 234–5
lxv 226–7, 230–1, 232–3, 234–5
sermo xliii 212–13
Ovid
Epistulae ex Ponto, ii. 2. 111 634–5
ii. 3. 11–12 392–3
Fasti, i. 493 392–3
Metamorphoseon, vii. 518 142–3
Paschasius Radbertus
Liber de corpore et sanguine domini, xi. 3 166–7
Plato (Latinus)
Timaeus 222–3
Peter Cantor
Verbum Abbrev. xii. 282–3
Peter Lombard
Coll. in Ep. ad Rom., v. 13. 14 600–1
Collectanea in epistolas Pauli 618–19
Commentaria in Psalmos, xxix 60–1
Sententiae, i. dist. iii. 7 254–5
i. dist. xliii. 7 598–9
ii. dist. xiii. 2 574–5
ii. dist. xvi. 248–9
ii. dist. xvi. 2 258–9
ii. dist. xvi. 3.1 252–3, 258–9
ii. dist. xvi. 3.2 252–3, 258–9
ii. dist. xvi. 3.6–4.1 252–3
ii. dist. xvi. 4 254–5
ii. dist. xl. 1 498–9
Petrus Alfonsi
Dialogi, tit. i 220–1
Rupert of Deutz
De divinis officiis, xi. 17 254–5
Seneca
Ad Lucilium Epistulae Morales, i. 3. 6 632–3
i. 5 650–1
ii. 1 630–1
ii. 2 106–7
ii. 3 628–9
xi. 1 142–3
lii. 3–4 206–7
lxvi. 11–12 226–7
Smaragdus
Commentaria in Regulam Sancti Benedicti, in Prol. 408–9
Sulpicius Severus
Epistulae, iii. 16 408–9
Vita Sancti Martini Turonensis, preface 1 398–9
Terence
Andria, i. 1. 61 (34) 136–7, 484–5, 486–7
i. 1. 68 (41) 600–1
iii. 3. 565–6 (33–4) 216–17

iii. 4. 601 (22) 620–1
[v. 4. 941 (38)] 602–3
Phormio, i. 2. 72–3 (22–3) 401–2
iii. 3. 541 (8) 62–3, 82–3, 424–5

Virgil
Aeneid, ii. 724 44–5
viii. 113 544–5
xi. 283 482–3
Eclogae, iii. 93 530–1

Note: I have not attempted systematically to annotate allusions to and echoes of glosses, *sententiae* etc., of which there are certainly very many. Some references to the *Glossa Ordinaria* appear in the footnotes, but the nature of such material is too complex, and too little of it edited, to make precise assignations of sources possible.

INDEX 3

Recipients of the Letters

Recipients are given on the left, with the number(s) of corresponding letters on the right.

A., brother, monk of Montier-la-Celle, *see* Montier-la-Celle
A., priest of Provins 61
Absalon, archbishop of Lund 104, 105
Alan, bishop of Auxerre 23
Albert of Morra 83, 84 [?], 85, 86, 87, 88
Alexander III, Pope 2 [?], 6 [?], 75, 76, 77, 78, 79, 80, 81, 82
  see also Roland Bandinelli
Anastasius IV, Pope 3* [?], 4* [?]
Ascelinus, monk of Clairvaux, *see* Clairvaux
Avignon, bishop of 107

Baldwin II, de Boulogne, bishop of Noyon 20
Bartholomew, bishop of Exeter 108, 109
Basil, prior of La Grande Chartreuse with general chapter of Carthusian order 35, 114
Benedict of Peterborough, prior of Christ Church Canterbury 142, 143 [?]
Berneredus, abbot of Saint-Crépin, cardinal bishop of Palestrina 128, 130, 131, 132, 133, 134, 135
  and community of Saint-Crépin 129

Chézy-l'Abbaye, community of 38, 39
Cistercian order, general chapter of 147
Clairvaux:
  prior H., G. cellarer., H., T. infirmarer of 48
  subprior H., Thomas and Ascelinus of 45
  R. of 46, 47
  see also Nicholas of
Cluny, abbot of 127
  community of 150
  see also Hugh de Fraisans; Peter the Venerable

Elbert, abbot of Saint-Hubert 140 [?]
Engelbert, prior of Val-Saint-Pierre 115
Erlembald, abbot of Stavelot 118, 119
Eskil, archbishop of Lund 12, 95, 96, 97, 98, 99, 100
Eugenius III, Pope 1

G., cellarer of Clairvaux, *see* Clairvaux
G., priest of Hastings 62
Geoffrey, abbot of Saint-Médard with the abbot of Saint-Crépin 145
Gerard Pucelle 179 [?]
Gossuin, abbot of Anchin 137
Grandmont, community of 43, 149
  prior and community of 148
  monks of transferred to Pontigny 161, 162

Guy, monk of Pontigny, Grandmontine monk transferred
  to Pontigny, *see* Grandmont, monks of . . .

H., monk of Clairvaux, *see* Clairvaux
H., prior of Clairvaux, *see* Clairvaux
H., subprior of Clairvaux, *see* Clairvaux
Hadrian IV, Pope 3* [?], 4* [?], 5 [?]
Hardouin, abbot of Larrivour 28
Heloise, abbess of Le Paraclet 25 [?]
Henry (of France), bishop of Beauvais, archbishop of Reims 21, 22, 93
Henry I, the Liberal, count of Champagne 71
Hugh, abbot of Bury St Edmunds 116, 117
Hugh abbot of Preuilly 36
Hugh, abbot of Saint-Amand 136
Hugh de Fraisans, abbot of Cluny 31, 32, 33, 34
Hugh de Toucy, archbishop of Sens 8, 9, 10

Inganus, prior of Lapley 144

John, bishop of Saint-Malo 14, 15, 16, 17, 18
  with unidentified other 19

John de Breteuil, chancellor to Henry, archbishop of Reims:
with Rainald, cantor of Compiègne 110
John of Salisbury 63, 64, 65, 66, 67, 68, 69, 70, 169, 170, 173, 174, 176, 177, 178
with Richard of Salisbury 171, 172, 175

Knut Eriksson, king of Sweden, with Stephen, archbishop of Uppsala, bishops and magnates of Sweden 181

Lagny-sur-Marne, abbot of 120
Louis VII, king of France 180

Matilda of Anjou, abbess of Fontevrault 27
Molesme, community of 156
Mont-Dieu, community of 52, 53, 54, 55
prior and community of 56, 57, 58
see also Simon, prior of
Montier-la-Celle, brother A. and community of 42
community of 40, 155
prior of 26
prior and community of 41

Nicholas, unidentified 182
Nicholas of Clairvaux 49, 50, 51
Nicholas of St Albans 157, 158, 160
letter from to Peter of Celle 159

Odo, prior of Christ Church Canterbury 141 [?]

P., monk of Norwich 44
Peter, abbot of La Sauve-Majeure 121, 122, 123
Peter of Pavia 89, 90, 91
Peter, monk of Pontigny, Grandmontine monk transferred to Pontigny, *see* Grandmont, monks of . . .
Peter the Venerable, abbot of Cluny 24
Philip, archbishop of Cologne 94

R. of Clairvaux, *see* Clairvaux
Rainald, cantor of Compiègne, *see* John de Breteuil
Ralph, abbot of Boulancourt 29* [?]
Ralph of Bedford, prior of Worcester 111, 112
Ranulf, abbot of Buildwas 113
Richard of Dover, archbishop of Canterbury 103
Richard Peche, bishop of Coventry 106
Richard of Salisbury 163, 164, 165, 166, 167, 168
see also John of Salisbury, with Richard of Salisbury
Robert, abbot of Boulancourt 29* [?]
Robert Partes, monk of Reading 153
Roland Bandinelli, cardinal:
papal chancellor (later Pope Alexander III) 7

Saint-Bertin, monk of 152
Saint-Crépin, abbot of, *see* Geoffrey, abbot of Saint-Médard
prior and community of 154
see also Berneredus, abbot of
Saint-Gilles, abbot of 126
Saint-Riquier, abbot of 124
Simon, prior of Mont-Dieu, and community 59, 60
Stephen, archbishop of Uppsala, *see* Knut Eriksson, king of Sweden

T., infirmarer of Clairvaux, *see* Clairvaux
Theobald, abbot of Cluny 146
Theobald, archbishop of Canterbury 11
Theobald, bishop of Paris 13
Theobald de Châtillon de Bazoches, abbot of Molesme 138, 139
Thomas, monk of Clairvaux, *see* Clairvaux
Thomas Becket 72, 73, 92
Thomas de Chacenay, prior of Molesme, abbot of Molesme 37

Ulric, abbot of Villers 125
with community 151
unidentified 74, 183

Villain de Choiseul, abbot of Molesme 30

William aux Blanches Mains 101, 102
William of Donjon, monk of Pontigny, Grandmontine monk transferred to Pontigny, *see* Grandmont, monks of . . .

* letter appears twice in this index, under each possible recipient.

INDEX 4

General Index

A., monk of Mont-Dieu 292–3
A., monk of Montier-la-Celle 160 n. 1
  letter to, and community of Montier-la-Celle 160–73
A., priest of Provins, letter to 292–5
Absalon, archbishop of Lund 422 n. 1, 704
  letters to 422–5, 424–7
Absalon, prior of Lapley 438–9, 440 n. 1, 528 n. 1
Adalberon, bishop of Liège 721
Adam Marsh, letters of xlvii
Adela of Champagne, queen of France 488–9
Adrian, *see* Hadrian
Aelred of Rievaulx xx
Agnes de Baudement xxix–xxx, 346–9, 478–9 & n. 6, 737
Agnes de Braine xxix n. 26
Alan, bishop of Auxerre xliv, xlvi n. 109, 22–3 n. 1, 63 n. 1, 93 n. 1, 412–13 & n. 11
  letter to 62–7
Albert, monk of Mont-Dieu 292 n. 36
Albert of Morra, cardinal deacon of S. Adriano, cardinal priest of S. Lorenzo in Lucina, papal chancellor, later Pope Gregory VII 356 n. 1, 360–1 n. 1, 446–7 n. 1, 492–3, 670–3, 723
  letters to 360–3, 366–9, 370–1, 372–5, 374–7
  letter possibly to 364–7
Alexander, unidentified 678–9
Alexander, abbot of Anchin l, 508–9 n. 1
Alexander, bishop of Liège 721
Alexander III, Pope, (Roland Bandinelli) xlvii n. 110, li, 26–7 n. 1, 56–7 n. 1, 62–3, 366–7, 370–1, 386 n. 3, 698, 699, 700–1, 719–20, 723, 725
  collection of 56 letters to Peter of Celle and others xxxvii, liv, lv, 701 n. 5, 719, 722
  letters to 338–41, 340–3, 344–7, 346–9, 348–51, 350–1, 352–5, 356–61
  letter to as Roland Bandinelli, papal chancellor 16–19
  letters possibly to 6–9, 14–17
  schism, Alexandrine xliv, 60 n. 1, 112–3 n. 1, 128–9 n. 1, 342 n. 5, 348–9, 370–1, 372–3, 705, 721–4
  see also Lateran Council, Third
Anastasius IV, Pope 13 n. 1, 312–13, 696–8, 699
  letters possibly to 6–9, 8–11, 10–13, 13 n. 1
Anchin, *see* Alexander, abbot of; Gossuin, abbot of
Andrew de Baudement xxix n. 26
Anselm, St xx, xxxiv n. 56
Ansfredus, lay brother of Villers 552–5
Arnold II, bishop of Cologne 396 n. 5, 721–2 n. 15
Arnulf, monk of Montier-la-Celle 160 n. 1
Arnulf of Lisieux, letters and sermons of xxxix, xl, xlii
Arraudus, master, possibly monk of Pontigny 634–5
Ascelinus, monk of Clairvaux 213 n. 25
  letter to (with others) 182–7
Asserbo 704
Audeburge de Hautes-Bruyères, abbess of Fontevrault 699
Augustine, St 706–7
  see also index of quotations and allusions
Augustinian canons xxi; *see also* Merton; Richard of Salisbury; Saint-Serein-de-Chantemerle
Aunoy-les-Minimes, *see* Peter of Celle, family of
Avignon, bishop of, letter to 428–31, 725
Avranches, compromise of 360–1 n. 1, 452–3 n. 1, 670–1 n. 1

B., of Saint-Remi-de-Provence, 474–5 n. 1, 476–7

Baldwin II, de Boulogne, bishop of Noyon 54 n. 1
letter to 54–5
Barthélemy, bishop of Beauvais 436–7 n. 1
Bartholomew, bishop of Exeter 430–1 n. 1, 670–1
letters to 430–3, 434–5
Bartholomew, bishop of Laon 446–7 n. 1
Basil, prior of La Grande Chartreuse 132–3 n. 1, 704
letters to (with priors of order) 132–5, 444–7
Beaulieu, abbot of 436–7 & n. 3
Beauvais, Council of 60 n. 1
Becket, *see* Thomas Becket
Belval, priory 463 n. 2, 464–5
Benedictine order xxi
see also Cluny; Molesme; Fontevrault
Benedict of Peterborough, prior of Canterbury 520–1 n. 1
letter to 522–5
letter to (possibly), and community 524–9
Bernard, St, abbot of Clairvaux xx, xxiii, xxv, xlv, 10 n. 1, 47 n. 1, 48–9, 56–7 n. 1, 102–3 n. 1, 540–1, 578–9, 588–9, 602–6, 606–7, 616 n. 3, 727–9
works of xlix, li–lii, 36–7 n. 1, 556–7, 705, 714, 727–8
Berneredus, abbot of Saint-Crépin-le-Grand, Soissons, cardinal bishop of Palestrina xxiii, xxvi, 346–7, 385 n. 1, 386–7, 402–3, 404–5, 446–7 n. 1, 450–1, 478 n. 1, 532 n. 1, 536–7 n. 1, 560–1 n. 1, 562–3, 662–3, 674 n. 1, 676–7
letters to 478–81, 480–3, 482–5, 484–7, 488–91, 490–3, 494–9, 498–507
Blois, *see* Henry of, bishop of Winchester
Boethius 706–7, 710
see also index of quotations and allusions
Bohemond, unidentified 480–1
Boso, archdeacon of Reims (possibly) 436–7 & n. 2, 737
Boso, bishop of Châlons-sur-Marne 16–17 & n. 9
Boulancourt (Cistercian), abbots of 102–3 n. 1
Bourgmoyen (Augustinian, Blois) 36 n. 1
Burgensis, *see* John
Calixtus II, Pope 725
Calot, bishop of Poitiers 13 n. 1, 14–15 (possibly), 699
Canterbury, priors of 525 n. 1, *see also* Benedict of Peterborough; Odo
Carthusians xx, xxi, xxiii, xxv–vi & n. 17, 30–3, 93 n. 2, 132–3 n. 1, 276–7 n. 1, 444–5 n. 1, 514–15, 703–4
letters to prior and general chapter of 132–5, 444–7
see also Mont-Dieu
Celestine III, Pope, *see* Giacinto Bobo, cardinal deacon
Celle-sous-Chantemerle, see La Celle-sous-Chantemerle
Châlons-sur-Marne, bishop of, possibly Boson, *see* Boson
Champagne xxiv, xxviii
see also Henry the Liberal, count of; Theobald II, count of
Chantemerle 8–11
see also La Celle-sous-Chantemerle; Saint-Serein-de-Chantemerle
Chartres xxiv, xxix, xxxi, xxxii, xxxiii, 418–19, 539 n. 1
see also John of Salisbury
Chartreuse, see La Grande Chartreuse
Châtillon-sur-Seine (Augustinian) 54 n. 1
Chezy-l'Abbaye (Benedictine) xxi n. 6, xlvi n. 109, 705
abbots of 148–9 n. 1
letters to community of 148–51, 152–5
see also Simon, abbot of; Tes., monk of
Cistercians xxi, xlix–l, 32–3, 102–3 n. 1, 572–3, 589–92, 604–5, 626–35, 730–1
letter to general chapter of 538–41
Cîteaux xxv n. 16, 539 n. 1, 573 & n. 34, 701 n. 4
Clairvaux xxiv–xxv, xxvi–xxvii & n. 19, 56 n. 1, 705, 707
abbots of 200–1 & n. 24
letters to monks of 182–7, 186–93, 194–7; *see also* Nicholas of, letters to
letter to prior and monks of 196–201
monks of xlvii n. 110, 182–3 n. 1, 186–7 n. 1, 192–3 & n. 40, 196–7 n. 1, 213 n. 25, 412–13
priors of xxiv n. 15, 182–3 n. 1, 186–7 n. 1, 213 n. 25, 412–13 & n. 11
see also Ascelinus, monk of; Bernard, St, abbot of; Eskil, archbishop of Lund, later monk of; H., subprior of;

Clairvaux (*cont.*)
Henry de Marcy, abbot of; Nicholas of; R., monk of; Thomas, monk of
Claudianus Mamertus 707–9, 711
see also index of quotations and allusions
Cluny xxi, xxii n. 8, xxvi, xxvii n. 20, 76–7, 112–17 and n. 1, 474–5 n. 1, 536–7 n. 1, 538–9, 705
letter to abbot of 474–7
letter to community of 546–9
see also Hugh de Fraisans, abbot of; Peter the Venerable, abbot of; Theobald abbot of Saint-Crépin-le-Grand, abbot of Cluny, cardinal bishop of Ostia and Velletri; Theobald, grand prior of, abbot of Molesme
community xxii, xxvi, xxvii
Conception of the Virgin Mary, feast of, *see* Immaculate Conception of
Conrad III, king of Germany, emperor 721
Crispin, master, possibly two different characters with the same name [*see also*: Crispin, master, (another)] 378–81, 381 n. 1, 384–5
Crispin, master (another) 402–3, 404 n. 7, 404–5

Darron, priory xxxii n. 41
De disciplina claustrali, treatise, Peter of Celle xxiv, 642–5, 646–7
De panibus, Peter of Celle xxxiv, liv, 560–1
Drogo, abbot of Montier-la-Celle xxxiii, 484–5 n. 1, 486–7, 564–7
Dudo, brother, possibly monk of Lapley 530–1

Ebbo, abbot of Montier-en-Der xxvii n. 20
Elbert, abbot of Saint-Hubert, letter to (possibly) 518–19
Eleanor of Aquitaine, queen of France 326–7 n. 1, 489 n. 3
Ellandus, canon of Reims 450–1
Engelbert, prior of Val-Saint-Pierre xxvi, 132–3 n. 1, 134–5, 360–3, 414–15, 446–7 n. 1, 662–3
letter to 446–51
Erembourg of Maine, 92–3 n. 16
Erlembald, abbot of Stavelot xlviii, l-li, 454–5 n. 1
letters to 454–5, 456–7
Ernulf, master 313 n. 1
Eskil, archbishop of Lund, later monk of Clairvaux xxvi, xxvii n. 20, 28–9 n. 1, 342 n. 5, 398 n. 5, 398–9 n. 1, 402–3 n. 1, 424–5, 703–4
letters to 28–33, 396–9, 398–401, 402–5, 404–7, 406–11, 410–13
Eugenius III, Pope, letter to 4–7, 695, 699, 721, 725
Exordium Magnum Ordinis Cisterciensis 705

Fontevrault xxi, 14–15, 699
see also Matilda of Anjou, abbess of
François de Bar, grand prior of Anchin l
Frederick I Barbarossa, king of Germany, emperor 60 n. 1, 338–9 nn. 1 & 4, 342–3 & n. 5, 348–9, 454–5, 664–5, 703, 721, 722–3
friendship xx, xxi, xxiii, xxiv, xxv, xxvi, xxvii, xliv–xlv
Froger, bishop of Sées 362–3
Fulbert of Chartres, letters of xliii–xliv, xlvii
Fulk, missionary bishop to Estonia 340–7, 398–9 n. 1, 400–1, 422–3, 426–7, 686–9, 719–20
Fulk V, count of Anjou, king of Jerusalem 92–3 & n. 16
Fulk, dean of Reims xxxvii n. 68

G., two figures with the same initial 14–15 & n. 1, 16–17, 700–702
see also Walter, abbot of Montier-en-Der
G., of Meerssen 722
G., archdeacon, possibly of Chartres xxx, 678–9
G., cellarer of Clairvaux, letter to, and others 196–201
G., master 419–21 & nn. 1–2, 525 n. 1, 526–9
G., priest of Hastings, letter to 294–301
Gaucher, 'lord', possibly monk of Clairvaux 412–13
Gautier, *see also* Walter
Gautier, archdeacon *de Pinserais* (Chartres) 679
Gebuin of Troyes, sermons of 330–1, 332–3
Geoffrey, abbot of Saint-Médard, letter to 532–5
Geoffrey, monk of Mont-Dieu 522–5

Geoffrey of Auxerre, abbot of Clairvaux 701
Geoffrey of St Edmunds, master 452–3 nn. 1–2
Gerard, abbot of Clairvaux 701
Gerard, abbot of Montier-la-Celle 484–5 n. 1, 662–3
Gerard Pucelle xx, 419–20 n. 1, 525 n. 1
 letter to 680–3
Gervase, prior of Mont-Dieu 134–5 & n. 8, 260 n. 1, 270–2 n. 1
 letter to, and community 262–9 & n. 1
Giacinto Bobo, cardinal deacon, later Pope Celestine III, 492–3
Gilbert Foliot, letters of xxxiv n. 56, 717
Gilbert de la Porrée, bishop of Poitiers 13 n. 1, 14–15 (possibly), 556–7, 699
Godfrey, bishop of Langres 146–7 & n. 1
Golden Letter, see William of Saint-Thierry
Goslenus, archdeacon of Chartres 679 n. 6
Gossuin, abbot of Anchin xlviii, l
 letter to 508–11
Goswin of Heinsberg 721–2
Grande Chartreuse, La, see La Grande Chartreuse
Grande-Sauve, La, *see* Peter II, abbot of La Sauve-Majeure
Grandmont xxi, 174 n. 1, 175 n. 4, 542 n. 1, 544 n. 10, 545 nn. 1–2, 731
 letters to community of 174–5, 544–7
 letter to prior and community of 542–5
 novices of at Pontigny xxi n. 6, xlix–l; letters to 626–9, 630–5, 730–1
Gratian, papal subdeacon, envoy 388–9 n. 1
Gualterius, *see* Walter
Guarinus, abbot of Saint-Victor xlix, 730
Guichard, archbishop of Lyons, formerly abbot of Pontigny 522–3
Guy III, abbot of Monntiéramy 116–17
Guy, abbot of Saint-Nicaise, Reims xxvii n. 20, 662–3
Guy, Grandmontine novice transferred to Pontigny, *see* Grandmont, novices of at Pontigny
Guy, prior of Southwick, previously canon of Merton xlii, xliii
Guy de Braine xxix n. 26
Guy de Dampierre, bishop of Châlons-sur-Marne xxix n. 26, 700, 737
Guy de Joinville, bishop of Châlons-sur-Marne 700

H., master 10–11
H., monk of Clairvaux, letter to, and others 196–201
H., monk of Villers 468–71
H., prior of Clairvaux, letter to, and others 196–201
H., subprior of Clairvaux:
 letter to, and others 182–7
 possible reference 192–3 & n. 41
 see also Henry, prior or monk of Clairvaux; Hugh, prior of Clairvaux
Hadrian IV, Pope, 26–7 n. 1, 312–13, 696–8, 699, 722
 letters possibly to 6–9, 8–11, 10–13, 12–15
Hadvide, relative of Peter of Celle xxx, xliv, 22–3 n. 1, 64–5 & n. 4, 316–19
 see also Peter of Celle, family of; Pierre de la Tournelle
Hardouin, abbot of Larrivour 93 n. 1
 letter to 92–103
Hastings, *see* G., priest of
Hato, bishop of Troyes 8–9, 200–1 n. 1, 698
Heinsberg, *see* Goswin of; Philip, archbishop of Cologne
Heloise, abbess of Le Paraclet xx, 80 n. 1
 letter possibly to 80–3
Henry, abbot of Saint-Méen-de-Gaël 5 n. 6, 695
Henry, archbishop of Reims, *see* Henry (of France)
Henry, bishop of Autun 146–7
Henry (of France), bishop of Beauvais, archbishop of Reims xx, xxviii, xxxvii n. 68, 36–7 n. 1, 56–7 n. 1, 128–9 n. 1, 213 n. 25, 364–5 n. 1, 386 n. 3, 392–3 nn. 1–2, 416–17 n. 1, 436–7, 488 n. 1, 490–1, 662–3, 686–7 n. 1, 688–9, 700
 letters to 56–9, 60–3, 392–5
Henry, bishop of Beauvais, *see* Henry (of France)
Henry, bishop of Liège 721
Henry, bishop of Troyes xxiv n. 15, 10 n. 5, 17 n. 1, 102–3 n. 1, 696
Henry II, king of England 60 n. 1, 329 n. 3, 360–1 n. 1, 391 n. 16, 430–1 n. 1, 506–7, 670–3, 680–1 n. 1, 682–3

Henry, monk of Molesme (possibly) 516–17
Henry, monk of Saint-Remi 486–7
Henry, ? prior of Clairvaux 213 n. 25
Henry of Blois, bishop of Winchester xx, 118–19 n. 1, 126–7, 128–9 n. 1
Henry of Dreux, treasurer of Reims (possibly) 436–7 & n. 2
Henry I the Liberal, count of Champagne xx, xxviii, xxxiii, 9 n. 3, 11 n. 4, 12–13, 16–17, 33–4 n. 1, 132–3 n. 1, 134–5, 276–7 n. 1, 278–9, 282–3, 326–7 n. 1, 333 n. 5, 364–5 n. 1, 392–3 n. 1, 488 n. 1, 489 n. 3, 697
letter to 326–7
Henry de Marcy, abbot of Clairvaux, cardinal bishop of Albano 356–61, 374–7, 492–3
Henry of Reims, *see* Henry (of France)
Heraclius de Montboissier, archbishop of Lyons 146–7
Herbert I, abbot of Valsery 346–7
Hermann, archdeacon of Liège 721
Hervey, brother, presumably monk of Saint-Remi 672–3
Hilduin, canon of Reims 396–7
Hilduin of Vendeuvre 116–17
Hugh, abbot of Bury St Edmunds, letters to 450–1, 452–3
Hugh, abbot of Preuilly 136–7 n. 1
letter to 136–9
Hugh, abbot of Quincy 146–7
Hugh, abbot of Saint-Amand xliii n. 96, li
letter to 506–7
Hugh, archbishop of Sens, *see* Hugh de Toucy
Hugh II, archbishop of Tours 4–5, 695
Hugh, canon of Reims xxx, 678–9
Hugh, monk of Clairvaux 212–13 & n. 25
Hugh, prior of Clairvaux 182–3 n. 1, 213 n. 25
letter to, and others 196–201
Hugh, scribe, monk of Saint-Remi 478–9, 486–7
Hugh IV, de Clermont, abbot of Cluny 474–5 n. 1
Hugh III, de Fraisans, abbot of Cluny xxvi–xxvii, xlvi n. 109, 112–13 n. 1, 118–19 n. 1, 128–9 n. 1, 474–5 n. 1, 705
letters to 112–17, 118–27, 128–31, 130–3
Hugh of Pierrepont 364–5
Hugh of Saint-Victor 556–7, 710
Hugh de Toucy, archbishop of Sens xlvii n. 110, 16–17 & n. 11, 63 n. 1, 64–5, 566 n. 7, 697, 701, 714
letters to 18–21, 20–3, 22–7
Hyacinth, *see* Giacinto Bobo, cardinal deacon

Immaculate Conception of the Virgin Mary, feast of 573 n. 1, 576 n. 8, 582–626, 727–9
Inganus, prior of Lapley 726
letter to 528–31
Innocent II, Pope 348–9, 370–1, 721, 723
Ivo of Chartres xxxix, xliii–xliv

Jerome, St xxxix
see also index of quotations and allusions
John, brother 478–9
John, bishop of Saint-Malo xliv–xlv, xlvii nn. 110–11, 4–5, 36–7 n. 1, 695
letters to 36–9, 38–43, 44–7, 46–9, 48–51, 52–3
John, monk of Saint-Crépin-le-Grand (possibly references to more than one person) 504–5, 562–3
John de Breteuil, chancellor to Henry (of France), archbishop of Reims, 737; letter to 436–7
John *Burgensis*, son of 402–5
John of Canterbury, bishop of Poitiers 658–9 n. 1
John of Salisbury xx, xxii, xxiii, xxvi, xxviii, xxix–xxx, xxxi, xxxix, xlii, xliv, xlvii, 10 n. 3, 13 n. 10, 22 n. 1, 26–7 n. 1, 48–9 n. 1, 102–3 n. 1, 300–1 n. 1, 304 n. 1, 312–13, 313 n. 1, 316–17 n. 7, 329 n. 2, 330–1 n. 5, 404–5, 416–19, 419–21 & n. 1, 430–1 n. 1, 432 n. 4, 434–5 n. 1, 446–7 n. 1, 452–3 nn. 1–2, 506–7, 520–1 nn. 1–2, 522–3 n. 1, 524–5, 525 n. 1, 528–9, 539 n. 1, 560 n. 9, 636–7 n. 1, 638–9, 652–3 n. 1, 656–7 n. 1, 674 n. 1, 682–3, 690–1, 696, 697 n. 2, 698, 712–18, 722–3
letters of xlvii, li, 300–1 n. 1, 304 n. 1, 310 n. 1, 313 n. 1, 315 n. 1, 316–17 n. 7, 318 nn. 8 & 1, 321 n. 1, 323 n. 1, 338–9 n. 1, 392–3 n. 1, 437 n. 2, 438–9 n. 1, 446–7 n. 1, 452–3 n. 1, 506–7 n. 1, 658–9 n. 1, 662–3, 712–18
and letters of Peter of Celle xlii–xliii

letters to 300–3, 304–9, 310–13, 312–15, 314–19, 318–21, 320–3, 322–7, 652–5, 656–9, 666–9, 668–71, 674–7, 676–9, 678–81
letters to, and Richard of Salisbury 658–63, 664–5, 670–3
see also Richard of Salisbury
John of Verneuil, monk of Saint-Martin-des-Champs xxvii n. 20
Josaphat, abbey (Chartres) xxxii
Joscelin, prior of Saint-Ayoul 82–3 n. 1

Karlsen, Karl and Knud 424 n. 8
Knut Eriksson, king of Sweden, letter to, and others 686–9

La Celle-sous-Chantemerle, priory 8–11 & n. 2, 696–8
Lagny-sur-Marne, abbot of, letter to 458–9
La Grande Chartreuse 32–3, 134 n. 7, 704
see also Basil, prior of
La Grande-Sauve, *see* Peter II, abbot of La Sauve-Majeure
Lanfranc, archbishop of Canterbury, letters of xxxvi n. 61, xlvii
Lapley xxxiii n. 47, 426–9, 438–43, 528–31
see also Absalon, prior of; Inganus, prior of
La Sauve-Majeure, *see* Peter II, abbot of
Lateran Council, Third 350–5, 366 n. 1, 372–5, 386–7, 478 n. 1, 496–7
Leon, abbot of Saint-Crépin-le-Grand, letter to (possibly) 532–5
letter collections xix, xxii, xxxv, xxxvi, 567 n. 8
Liège, bishops of 348–9, 370–1
see also Adalberon, bishop of Liège; Alexander, bishop of Liège; Henry, bishop of Liège
Louis VII, king of France xx, xxviii, xxix, li, 10 n. 1, 22–3, 56–7 n. 1, 60 n. 1, 326–7 n. 1, 338–9 n. 1, 340–1, 346–7, 489 n. 3
letter to 684–5
Lucius II, Pope 4–5, 695
Lucius III, Pope, *see* Ubaldo Allucingoli, cardinal bishop of Ostia and Velletri
Luke, brother 504–5
Lyons, archbishops of, *see* Guichard; Heraclius de Montboissier

M., master 20–1
Mabillon lv–lvi
Mag⟨?nus⟩, unidentified 52–3
Manasses III, count of Rethel 364–5
Marie de France, countess of Champagne 326–7 n. 1, 488–91
Marmery (Champagne) 364–5 n. 1
Marmoutiers 36–7 n. 1
Matilda of Anjou, abbess of Fontevrault li–lii, 13 n. 1, 14–15, 80 n. 1, 92–3 n. 16, 699
letter to 86–93
Matthew, bishop of Troyes 416–17
Meaux, bishops of, 378–9 n. 1, 416–19 & n. 8
see also Peter of Pavia
Meerssen, priory xxxiii n. 47, 348–51, 370–1, 394–7, 454–5, 662–3, 664–5, 683 n. 19, 721–4
Merton, priory xlii, xliii
see also Richard of Salisbury
Milo, count of Bar-sur Seine xxix
see also Agnes de Baudement
Molesme xxi, xxii n. 8
letter to community of 568–73
see also Theobald, prior of Cluny, abbot of Molesme; Thomas de Chacenay, prior of, abbot of; Villain de Choiseul, abbot of
monasticism:
dispute resolution, monastic xxi, xxii, xxv
ideals of xx, xxi n. 6, xxii, xxiv, xxv
order xxi, xxii, xxiii, xxiv, xxv, xxvi
transfer of monks (*transitus*) xxv–vi & n. 17
Mont-Dieu (Carthusian) xx, xxv–vii & nn. 17–20, xxxviii, xlv, xlvi n. 109, xlvii n. 111, 92–3 & n. 2, 94–103, 134 n. 7, 156 n. 1, 158–9, 196–7 nn. 1 & 4, 198–9, 235 n. 1, 280–1, 522–5, 560–1 n. 1, 703
letters to community of 234–45, 246–9, 248–59, 258–61
letters to prior and community of 260–3, 262–9, 270–5; *see also* Simon, prior of, letters to (with community)
monks of 270–1 n. 1, 282–3, 292–3, 444–5 n. 1, 522–5
priors of 132–3 n. 1, 260 n. 1, 262–3 n. 1, 270–1 n. 1
see also Geoffrey, monk of; Gervase, prior of; Robert, monk of Montier-

Mont-Dieu (Carthusian) (*cont.*)
la-Celle transferred to; Roger, monk of; Simon, monk of Montier-la-Celle transferred to; Simon, prior of [possibly same person]; Stephen, monk of Montier-la-Celle transferred to
Montiéramy (Benedictine) xxvii n. 20
see also Guy III, abbot of
Montier-en-Der (Benedictine) 14–17, 700–2
see also Ebbo, abbot of; Walter, abbot of
Montier-la-Celle xxiv, xxix, xxx–xxxi, 17 n. 1, 39 n. 1, 300–1 n. 1, 326–7, 484–5 n. 1, 690–1, 696–8, 714
priors of 82–3 n. 1, 158–9 & n. 18; *see also* Peter, prior of
letters to community of 154–7, 160–73, 564–7
letter to prior of 82–7
letter to prior and community of 156–9
monks of 160 n. 1, 176 n. 1, 262–3 n. 1, 268–9 & n. 38, 270–1 n. 1, 281–2, 292 n. 36, 294–5 & n. 1, 300–1 & n. 12, 316–17, 321 n. 1, 322–3, 713–16, 719
see also Drogo, abbot of; Gerard, abbot of; Ralph, abbot of; Walter, abbot of
Montmajour (dioc. Arles) 725

N. unidentified 34–5
Neoplatonism 204–5 n. 1, 706–11
Nicholas, unidentified, letter to 688–9
Nicholas, monk of Mont-Dieu 282–3
Nicholas of Clairvaux xxv, xxvii n. 20, xxxii–xxxiii, xliv, xlvi n. 109, xlvii, 200–1 n. 1, 688 n. 1, 706–11, 727
letters of lii–liii, liv, 706
letters to 200–205, 204–13, 214–35
Nicholas de Roye, monk of Cluny xxvii n. 20
Nicholas of St Albans 200–1 n. 1, 573 n. 1, 706 n. 8, 727–9
letters to 572–7, 578–601, 616–27
letter of, to Peter of Celle 600–15
Nivelon de Quierzy, bishop of Soissons 346–9
Norwich, *see* P., monk of
Notre-Dame-de-Vertus, *see* William, abbot of
Novy-les-Moines, prior(s) of 459 n. 1, 460–1, 462–3, 463 n. 2, 464–5

Octavian of Monticelli, *see* Victor IV, antipope
Odo, abbot of Saint-Remi 235 n. 1, 508–9 n. 1
Odo, prior of Canterbury, later abbot of Battle, letter to (possibly) 520–1
Otrannus of Troyes 512–13
Otto, cardinal deacon of St Nicholas in Carcere Tulliano 338–9 n. 1, 340–1

P., canon of Saint-Ruf 387 n. 8
P., master, later bishop of Meaux, *see* Meaux, bishops of
P., monk of Norwich, letter to 176–81
P., prior of Lapley 438–9
Paschal III, antipope 454–5 n. 1
Pavia, Council of 60 n. 1, 454–5 n. 1
Peter, *see also* Pierre
Peter II, abbot of La Sauve-Majeure 459 n. 1
letters to 458–61, 460–3, 462–5
Peter, Grandmontine novice transferred to Pontigny, *see* Grandmont, novices of at Pontigny
Peter, prior of Montier-la-Celle, 82–3 n. 1
Peter of Celle:
death of xxxii
family of xxix–xxx, 678–9; *see also* Agnes de Baudement
life of xxviii–xxxiii
nature of letter collection xix–xxviii, xliv–xlv, xlix–l, lvi; other writings of xxv, xxxiii–xxxiv, liv, 458–9; see also *De disciplina claustrali; De panibus*
sermons of 33–5 & n. 1, 554–7
and spirituality xxi, xxii, xxv, xlv
style of letters xix–xxiv
textual tradition of letters xxxiv–lvi
see also, Chartres; friendship; monasticism; Montier-la-Celle; Reims; Saint-Martin-des-Champs; Saint-Remi
Peter Lombard 556–7
see also index of quotations and allusions
Peter of Melun, monk of Saint-Martin-des-Champs xxvii n. 20
Peter of Pavia, cardinal priest of S. Grisogono, cardinal bishop of Tusculum xxvii n. 20, xxxiii, xlix, 356 n. 1, 378–9 n. 1, 386 n. 3, 387 n. 5, 416–19 & n. 8, 478 n. 1, 492–3, 496 n. 5, 730–1
letters to 378–81, 380–5, 384–7

Peter the Venerable, abbot of Cluny xx, xxv, xxvii n. 20, xlvi n. 109, 66–7 n. 1, 116–17, 705
letter to 66–79
Philip (of Heinsberg), archbishop of Cologne 394–5 n. 1, 722–4
letter to 394–7
Philip, bishop elect of Chartres xxxii
Philip, monk of Clairvaux 412–13
Philip of l'Aumône, letters of xliv
Philip of Dreux, archdeacon of Reims (possibly) 436–7 & n. 2, 737
Pierre, *see also* Peter
Pierre de la Tournelle xxx, 22–3 n. 1, 24–5, 64–5 & nn. 4 & 6, 316–19
see also Peter of Celle, family of
Pierre de Viviers 146–7
Pontigny *see* Guichard, archbishop of Lyons, formerly abbot of; Robert Galardon, monk of; Grandmont, novices of at Pontigny
popes, *see* Alexander III; Anastasius IV; Calixtus II; Eugenius III; Hadrian IV; Innocent II; Lucius II
Premonstratensians 32–3
Provins xxxiii
see also A., priest of; Saint-Ayoul-de
Pucelle, *see* Gerard Pucelle

R., archdeacon of Soissons, *see* Ralph, archdeacon of Soissons
R., master 316–17
R., monk of Clairvaux 213 n. 25
letters to 186–93, 194–7
R., monk of Montier-la-Celle 294–5 & n. 1, 300–1 & n. 12
R., prior of Val-Dieu 360–1 n. 1, 414–15
Rainald, cantor of Saint-Corneille de Compiègne, letter to 436–7
Rainier of Thérouanne, prior of Clairvaux 186–7 n. 1
Ralph, abbot of Boulancourt 102–3 n. 1
letter possibly to 102–5
Ralph, abbot of Montier-la-Celle 9 n. 3
Ralph, archdeacon of Soissons, later provost, 10–11 & n. 3
Ralph, presumably monk of Montier-la-Celle 714–16
Ralph, monk of Val-Saint-Pierre, prior of Val-Dieu 360–3 & nn. 1, 6
Ralph of Bedford, prior of Worcester, letters to 438–9, 440–1
Ralph of Sarre 436–7 & n. 2, 737
Ranulf, abbot of Buildwas, letter to 442–3
Reading, *see* Robert Partes, monk of; William, master, monk of
Reginald, bishop of Chartres xxxii
Reims 346–7, 364–5 n. 1, 392–3 n. 1, 436–7, 488 n. 1, 719, 731
archbishop of, possibly Samson, *see* Samson; *see also* Henry (of France); William aux Blanches Mains
Peter of Celle as archiepiscopal vicar in, xxviii, xxxvii n. 68
see also Saint-Remi
Renaud, lord of Rozoy-sur-Serre 446–7 n. 1
Rethel, see Manasses III, count of
Richard, monk of Mont-Dieu 282–3
Richard of Dover, archbishop of Canterbury 419–20 n. 1, 526–7, 680–1 n. 1
letter to 418–21
Richard Peche, bishop of Coventry 426–7 n. 1
letter to 426–9
Richard of Salisbury xxii, xxvii, xlii, 102–3 n. 1, 316–17 n. 7, 434–5 n. 1, 636–7 n. 1, 658–61 & n. 1, 664–5 n. 1, 668–9 n. 1, 670–1, 672 n. 2, 713, 722–3
letters to 636–9, 640–1, 642–3, 642–5, 646–7, 648–51
letters to, and John of Salisbury 658–63, 664–5, 670–3
Robert, son of Pierre de la Tournelle 22–3 n. 1
Robert, abbot of Boulancourt 102–3 n. 1
letter possibly to 102–5
Robert, abbot of Saint-Méen-de-Gaël 5 n. 6, 695
Robert III, bishop of Chartres 50–1
Robert, monk of Clairvaux 186–7 n. 1, 213 n. 25
Robert, monk of Mont-Dieu, *see* Robert, monk of Montier-la-Celle, transferred to Mont-Dieu [possibly same person]
Robert, monk of Montier-la-Celle, transferred to Mont-Dieu 270–1 n. 1, 282–3, 292–3 & n. 36
Robert Anglicus, monk of Saint-Remi 524–5
Robert of Dreux xxix–xxx, 56 n. 1, 346–9, 737

Robert Galardon, monk of Pontigny xlix, 730–1
Robert Guiscard, count of Roucy 364–5
Robert le Gros, of Cluny 705
Robert of Molesme 570 n. 30
Robert Partes, monk of Reading, letter to 558–61
Robin, Dom Guillaume xxxvii
Roger, abbot of Toussaints-en-l'Ile 374–5
Roger, Carthusian monk (possibly the same as Roger, monk of Mont-Dieu) 30–1, 703–4
Roger, monk of Mont-Dieu 282–3, 444–5 n. 1
Roger de Porte Chacre, archdeacon of Soissons, 10–11 n. 3
Rogue, son of Pierre de le Tournelle 22–3 n. 1
Roland Bandinelli, *see* Alexander III, Pope
Rome xxvi, 48 n. 9, 326–7, 392–3 n. 1, 436–7 n. 1, 686–7 n. 1, 696, 703
  see also Lateran Council, Third
Rotrou, count of Perche 360–1 n. 1
Roucy, *see* Robert Guiscard, count of
Rualen, prior of Clairvaux 186–7 n. 1

St, *see* Anselm, Bernard, Jerome, Thomas Becket
St Aigulf, *see* St Ayoul; Saint-Ayoul-de-Provins
Saint-Amand(-les-Eaux, dioc. Tournai) xliii
  see also Hugh of, abbot
Saint-Arnoult-de-Crépy 536–7 n. 1
St Ayoul, relics of 50–1, 316–17, 318–21, 323 n. 1, 326–7, 714
Saint-Ayoul-de-Provins (dep. priory of Montier-la-Celle) xxxiii, 26–7 n. 1, 48–9 n. 1, 50–1, 293 n. 1, 316–21, 324–7, 697, 712, 714–16, 717
  prior(s) of 80 n. 1, 81 n. 8, 82–3; *see also* Joscelin
Saint-Basle (dioc. Reims) 536–7 n. 1
Saint-Bertin (Benedictine, dioc. Saint-Omer), letter to monk of 554–7
Saint-Crépin-le-Grand, Soissons (Benedictine), xxvi, 532 n. 1
  letter to prior and community of 560–3
  see also Berneredus, abbot of; Theobald, abbot of, abbot of Cluny, cardinal bishop of Ostia and Velletri; Leon, abbot of
Sainte-Croix-de-Guingamp (Augustinian, dioc. Tréguier) 36 n. 1
Sainte-Croix-de-Provins (dep. priory of Montier-la-Celle) 293 n. 1
Sainte-Eloi-Fontaine (Augustinian, dioc. Noyon) 54 n. 1
Saint-Flavit-de-Villemaur, priory (dioc. Troyes) 17 n. 1, 18–19, 33 n. 1, 326–7
Saint-Gilles (Benedictine) xxvii n. 20, 473 n. 11
  abbot of, letter to 470–3
Saint-Jean-en-Vallée xxxii
Saint-Jean-des-Vignes, abbot of 346–7
Saint-Judicäel (Benedictine, dioc. Saint-Malo) 695
Saint-Laurence, Liège, see Wautier, abbot of; Wazelin de Fexhe, abbot of
Saint-Malo 36–7 n. 1
  see also John, bishop of
Saint-Martin, Provence, parochial church 725
Saint-Martin-des Champs 33 n. 1
  Peter of Celle at xxx, 33 n. 1, 116–17 & n. 14, 538–9 & n. 11, 458–9
  see also John of Verneuil; Peter of Melun
Saint-Médard, Soissons (Benedictine), *see* Geoffrey, abbot of
Saint-Méen-de-Gaël (Benedictine, dioc. Saint-Malo) 4–7, 695
Saint-Nicaise, Reims (Benedictine), *see* Guy, abbot of
Saint-Paul-aux-Bois, prior of 463 n. 2, 464–5
Saint-Père-en-Vallée xxxii n. 41
Saint-Pierre-aux-Monts, *see* Thomas, abbot of
Saint-Remacle, *see* Stavelot
Saint-Remi xxiv, xxvii, xxviii, xxxi, xxxvii, 364–5 n. 1, 379 n. 3, 386 n. 3, 398 n. 5, 428–9 n. 1, 454–5 n. 1, 524–5, 544 n. 10, 670–1, 703, 719, 721–4
  Peter of Celle as abbot of xxviii, xxix, xxxi
  rebuilding of abbey church xxxiii, 528 n. 1, 530–1, 545 n. 1, 546–7, 648 n. 1, 650–1, 726
  see also Lapley; Meerssen; Saint-Remi-de-Provence
Saint-Remi-de-Provence 428–31 nn. 1, 7, 474–5 n. 1, 476–7, 725

Saint-Riquier, abbot of, letter to 466–7
Saint-Serein-de-Chantemerle (Augustinian, dioc. Troyes) 312–13, 696–8
abbot of 8–11
Saint-Thierry, Reims xxxi n. 36
see also William of
Salisbury, *see* John of; Richard of
Samson, archbishop of Reims 16–17 & n. 9, 700
Sancti Bernardi Vita Prima, see *Vita Prima*
Sauve-Majeure, La, see Peter II, abbot of
schism, papal/ Alexandrine, *see* Alexander III, Pope
Sept-Saulx (Champagne) 364–5 n. 1
sexuality xx n. 4
Simon, abbot of Chézy-l'Abbaye 148–9 n. 1, 152 n. 1, 705
Simon, abbot of Saint-Remi 276–7 n. 1
Simon, archdeacon, later bishop of Meaux, *see* Meaux, bishops of
Simon, bishop of Meaux, *see* Meaux, bishops of
Simon, monk of Montier-la-Celle transferred to Mont-Dieu 262–3 n. 1, 268–9 & n. 38, 270–1 n. 1, 276–7 n. 1
Simon, prior of Mont-Dieu xxvi, 132–3 n. 1, 134–5 & n. 8, 262–3 n. 1, 270–1 n. 1, 276–7 n. 1, 662–3
letters to, and community 276–83, 284–93
Simon, prior of Saint-Ayoul-de-Provins 276–7 n. 1
Soissons, provostship of 10 n. 1
see also Nivelon de Quierzy, bishop of; Ralph, archdeacon of; Roger de Porte Chacre
Sorø, abbey 704
Southwick, priory xxxix, xliii
see also Guy of
Stavelot, *see* Erlembald, abbot of; Wibald, abbot of
Stephen, of Saint-Remi-de-Provence 474–5 n. 1, 476–7
Stephen, abbot of Cluny 112–13 n. 1
Stephen, abbot of Molesme 106–7 n. 1
Stephen, archbishop of Uppsala, letter to, and others 686–9
Stephen, clerk 332–3
Stephen, monk of Montier-la-Celle transferred to Mont-Dieu 270–1 n. 1, 281–2 & n. 40
Stephen of Liciac, prior of Grandmont 174 n. 1
Stephen of Tournai xlix, 730–1
Suger, abbot of Saint-Denis 699

T., canon of Saint-Timothée, Reims 396–7
T., infirmarer of Clairvaux, letter to, and others 196–201
T., monk of Montier-la-Celle, 176–7 & n. 1, 180–1
Tes. (or T.), monk of Chézy-l'Abbaye 148–9 n. 1, 150–1
Theobald, abbot of Molesme, *see* Theobald de Châtillon de Bazoches, grand prior of Cluny, abbot of Molesme
Theobald, abbot of Saint-Crépin-le-Grand, abbot of Cluny, cardinal bishop of Ostia and Velletri 499 n. 1, 504–5, 538–9 n. 12
letter to 536–9
letter to (possibly) 532–5
Theobald, archbishop of Canterbury 26–7 n. 1, 318–19, 322–3, 330–1 n. 5, 420–1, 716, 717
letter to 26–9
Theobald, bishop of Paris xlvi n. 109, 18–19, 33 n. 1, 697
letter to 32–5
Theobald IV, count of Blois, *see* Theobald II, count of Champagne
Theobald V, count of Blois 10 n. 1, 12–13, 326–7 n. 1
Theobald II, count of Champagne, and IV, count of Blois 8–9, 10 n. 1, 33 n. 1, 326–7 n. 1, 489 n. 3
Theobald, grand prior of Cluny, abbot of Molesme, *see* Theobald de Châtillon de Bazoches, grand prior of Cluny, abbot of Molesme
Theobald of Cluny, *see* Theobald abbot of Saint-Crépin-le-Grand, abbot of Cluny, cardinal bishop of Ostia and Velletri
Theobald of Molesme, *see* Theobald de Châtillon de Bazoches, grand prior of Cluny, abbot of Molesme
Theobald de Châtillon de Bazoches, grand prior of Cluny, abbot of Molesme 140 n. 1, 568 n. 1
letters to 512–15, 514–17
Theobald de Vermandois, *see* Theobald, abbot of Saint-Crépin-le-Grand,

Theobald de Vermandois (*cont.*)
abbot of Cluny, cardinal bishop of Ostia and Velletri
Theodwin, cardinal priest of San Vitale 360–1 n. 1, 670–3
Third Lateran Council, *see* Lateran Council, Third
Thomas, abbot of Molesme *see* Thomas de Chacenay
Thomas, abbot of Saint-Pierre-aux-Monts 374–5, 436–7
Thomas, monk of Clairvaux 212–3 & n. 25
letter to, and others 182–7
Thomas, presumably monk of Montier-la-Celle xlii, 322–3, 713, 714–16
Thomas, cantor, of Reims, 426–7 & n. 2, 737
Thomas, prior of La Celle-sous-Chantemerle 696
Thomas Becket xx, xxi, xxvi, xxx, xlvii, 328 n. 1, 338–9 n. 1, 340–1, 360–1 n. 1, 388–9 n. 1, 418–19, 420–1, 430–1 n. 1, 434–5, 446–7 n. 1, 452–3 n. 1, 520–1, 522–5, 526–7, 558–9 n. 1, 574–7, 652–3 n. 1, 658–63, 664–5 n. 1, 666 n. 1, 668–9, 670–1 n. 1, 676–7, 680–1 n. 1, 682–3, 713, 728
letters of li, 338–9 n. 1, 716
letters to 328–31, 330–3, 388–93
Thomas de Chacenay, prior of Molesme, abbot of Molesme 140 n. 1, 568 n. 1
letter to 140–7
Thomas of Molesme, *see* Thomas de Chacenay
Thomas of Norwich 715
Toulouse, episcopal vacancy 356–7
see also Henry de Marcy
Toussaints-en-l'Ile, *see* Roger, abbot of
Tréguier 36 n. 1
Troyes xxiv, xxviii, 132–3 n. 1, 490–1
see also Hato, bishop of; Henry, bishop of; Matthew, bishop of

Ubaldo Allucingoli, cardinal bishop of Ostia and Velletri, later Pope Lucius III 492–3
Ulric, abbot of Villers 550 n. 1
letter to (possibly) 468–71
letter to (possibly), and community 550–5

Val-Dieu (Carthusian, dioc. Sées) 360–3, 414–15
see also R., prior of
Val-Saint-Pierre (Carthusian, dioc. Laon) 360–1 n. 1
see also Engelbert, prior of
Valsery (Premonstratensian, dioc. Soissons), *see* Herbert I, abbot of
Villemaur, *see* Saint-Flavit-de-Villemaur
Victor IV, antipope 60–1 & nn. 1, 5, 705, 722
Villain de Choiseul, abbot of Molesme 106–7 n. 1, 146–7
letter to 106–13
Villers (Cistercian, dioc. Liège), letter to abbot and community of 550–5
see also Ulric, abbot of
Vita Prima, Sancti Bernardi 705
Vivian, master, archdeacon of Orvieto, papal envoy 388–9 n. 1

W., unidentified 316–17
W., master 316–17, 714
W., monk of Montier-la-Celle 316–17, 714, 715–16
Waleran, canon and subdeacon of Reims 436–7 & n. 2, 737
Walter, abbot of Montier-en-Der xli, 15 n. 1, 700–2
Walter, abbot of Montier-la-Celle xxxi, 9 n. 3, 484–5 n. 1
Walter, bishop of Langres 146–7 & n. 1
Wautier, abbot of Saint-Laurence, Liège 130–1 & n. 2
Wazelin de Fexhe, abbot of Saint-Laurence, Liège 130–1 & n. 2
Wibald, abbot of Stavelot 396 n. 5, 454–5 n. 1, 721–2 n. 15
William, abbot of Notre-Dame-de-Vertus 374–5
William, archbishop of Reims, *see* William aux Blanches Mains
William, archbishop of Sens, *see* William aux Blanches Mains
William, bishop of Chartres, *see* William aux Blanches Mains
William (of Donjon), Grandmontine novice transferred to Pontigny, *see* Grandmont, novices of at Pontigny
William, master, clerk 554–5
William, master, monk of Reading 558–9 n. 1
William, monk of Clairvaux 212–3 & n. 25

William Atheling, son of King Henry I of England, 92–3 & n. 16
William aux Blanches Mains, bishop of Chartres, archbishop of Sens, archbishop of Reims, cardinal priest of S. Sabina xxviii, 10–13 & nn. 1, 4, 346–7, 360–1 n. 1, 402–3 n. 1, 404–5, 416–17 nn. 1, 7, 566 n. 7, 676–7
letters to 414–15, 416–19
William of Pavia, cardinal priest of St Peter ad Vincula 338–9 n. 1, 340–1
William of Saint-Thierry, *Golden Letter* of xxxviii–xxxix, 282–3 n. 40
William I, de Toucy, bishop of Auxerre 412–13 n. 11
William Turbe, bishop of Norwich 313 n. 1